AUDUBON'S MAMMALS

THE QUADRUPEDS OF NORTH AMERICA

AUDUBON'S MAMMALS
THE QUADRUPEDS OF NORTH AMERICA

COMPLETE AND UNABRIDGED

WELLFLEET
PRESS

Originally published as *Audubon's Quadrupeds of North America*

Copyright © 1989, 2005

WELLFLEET PRESS
A division of BOOK SALES, INC.
114 Northfield Avenue
Edison, New Jersey 08837
USA

Printed in China

ISBN-13: 978-0-7858-2025-3
ISBN-10: 0-7858-2025-6

CONTENTS

FOREWORD

For over 100 years the works of Audubon have had a universal appeal to the public. His style and technique were a departure from the accepted norm of the period and it is this that has made his works enduring.

His early life was filled with opportunities to hunt, trap and fish; and it was this observance of nature, combined with his artistic explorations, that led to his life long career. His studies of other nature artists led to his new approach of transmitting his visions of the natural world to the general public. His vision would be one of painting from realism, and natural settings; and not the stuffed wired specimens others used. He also added scenic backgrounds, plants and even other animals in order to arrive at a more natural setting.

Following his success with the *Birds of America* he embarked on a study of the quadrupeds, trying to arrive at a definitive work. With the assistance of his two sons, John Woodhouse and Victor Gifford; and Rev. John Bachman, another naturalist and artist, he began on this new major project. Instead of the watercolor originals, used in the *Birds of America*, he used techniques of watercolor combined with pastels, pencil and oils in order to obtain the subtle colors and textures of the animals; and to better give them a character of their own. The final printing was by the new technique of stone lithography.

Stone lithography was a new process that was beginning to be used as a major technique by the time of Audubon's work on the *Quadrupeds*. Here the design is done on a special smooth lithographic stone in pen and grease lithographic crayon or grease ink and transferred to print. The drawing would hold the ink from the rollers and the stone that was not drawn on would repel it. There was an artistic freedom that Audubon felt would give him the naturalness he desired in the finished plates. The resulting prints had no plate marks, as engravings did, and had a subtle quality all there own. They were then hand colored and readied for binding.

J. W. Audubon did the paintings for nearly half of the plates for the *Quadrupeds,* and reduced all the drawings for the quarto edition. The drawings on the stones were done mainly by William E. Hitchcock and R. Trombley. The lithography and printing was done under J. T. Bowen; a Philadelphia firm which was famous for their large size printed works. A few of the prints; including *Common American Wild-cat* and *American Cross Fox* were printed by Nagel and Weingaertner in New York, with coloring by J. Lawrence on some of these.

Viviparous Quadrupeds of North America was printed from 1842-46, the three volume folio coming out in 1846. The folio prints were approximately 22 inches by 28 inches, or 557mm by 713mm. The quarto edition came out in 1854 under John James Audubon and the Rev. John Bachman, and published by V. G. Audubon. The size of this edition was approximately 7 inches by 10 1/4 inches. The folio edition contained 150 hand colored plates, and the quarto edition contained an additional five plates to total 155 hand colored plates. Audubon died in 1851, before the issuance of the quarto volumes, but his sons and the Rev. Bachman saw the work to its final printing.

—William Kammer

INTRODUCTION

In presenting the following pages to the public, the authors desire to say a few words explanatory of the subject on which they have written. The difficulties they have attempted to surmount, and the labour attending their investigations, have far exceeded their first anticipations.

Many of the "Quadrupeds of North America" were long since described by European authors, from stuffed specimens; and in every department of Natural History additions to the knowledge of the old writers have been making for years past; researches and investigations having been undertaken by scientific observers in all parts of the world, and many specimens accumulated in the Museums of Europe. Comparatively little, however, has of late been accomplished toward the proper elucidation of the animals which inhabit the fields, forests, fertile prairies, and mountainous regions of our widely-extended and diversified country.

The works of HARLAN and of GODMAN were confined to the limited number of species known in their day. The valuable "Fauna Boreali Americana" of RICHARDSON was principally devoted to the description of species which exist in the British Provinces, north of the United States; and the more recent work of Dr. DEKAY professes to describe only the Quadrupeds of the State of New York, although giving a catalogue of those noticed by authors as existing in other portions of North America.

Several American and European Zoologists have, however, at different times, given the results of their investigations in various scientific journals, thus making it important for us to examine numberless papers, published in different cities of Europe and America. We have, in all cases, sought to discover and give due credit to every one who has in this manner made known a new species; but as possibly some author may have published discoveries in a journal we have not seen, we must at once announce our conviction, that the task of procuring and reading all the zoological papers scattered through the pages of hundreds of periodicals, in many different languages, is beyond our power, and that no one can reasonably complain when we take the liberty of pronouncing for ourselves on new or doubtful species without hesitation from the sources of knowledge to which we have access, and from our own judgment.

From the observations we have already made, we are induced to believe that a considerable number of species are yet undescribed while others, now imperfectly known, require a closer investigation and a more scientific arrangement, and it will be a part of our task to give an account of the former and define the position of the latter.

The geographical range which we have selected for our investigations is very extensive, comprising the British and Russian possessions to the north, the whole of the United States and their territories, California, and that part of Mexico north of the tropic of Cancer, we having arrived at the conclusion that in undertaking the natural history of a country, our researches should not be confined by the artificial boundaries of States—which may be frequently changed—but by those divisions the limits of which are fixed by nature, and where new *forms* mark the effects of a low latitude and warm climate. In this way America is divided into three parts:—North America, which includes all that country lying north of the tropics; Central or Tropical America, the countries within the tropics; and South America, all that country south of the tropic of Capricorn.

Within the tropical region peculiar forms are presented in every department of nature,—we need only instance the Monkey tribe among the animals, the Parrots among the birds, and the Palms among the plants.

A considerable portion of the country to which our attention has been directed, is at the present period an uncultivated and almost unexplored wild, roamed over by ferocious beasts and warlike tribes of Indians.

The objects of our search, Quadrupeds, are far less numerous than birds at all times, and are, moreover, generally nocturnal in their habits, and consequently obtained with far greater difficulty than the latter.

Although the *Genera* may be easily ascertained, by the forms and dental arrangements peculiar to each, many *species* so nearly approach each other in size, while they are so variable in colour, that it is exceedingly difficult to separate them, especially closely allied squirrels, hares, mice, shrews, &c., with positive certainty.

We are, therefore, far from supposing that our work will be free from errors, or that we shall be able to figure and describe every species that may exist within our range; although we have spared neither time, labour, nor expense, in collecting materials for this undertaking.

We have had our labours lightened, however, by many excellent friends and gentlemen in different portions of the country, who have, at great trouble to themselves, procured and sent us various animals—forwarded to us notes upon the habits of different species, procured works on the subject otherwise beyond our reach, and in many ways excited our warmest feelings of gratitude. Mr. J. K. TOWNSEND, of Philadelphia, allowed us to use the rare and valuable collection of

Quadrupeds which he obtained during his laborious researches on the western prairies, the Rocky Mountains, and in Oregon, and furnished us with his notes on their habits and geographical distribution. SPENCER F. BAIRD, Esq., of Carlisle, Pennsylvania, aided us by carefully searching various libraries for notes and information in regard to species published in different journals, and also by obtaining animals from the wilder portions of his State, &c.; Dr. BARRITT, of Abbeville, S. C., prepared and mounted specimens of *Lepus aquaticus*, and several other species; Dr. THOMAS M. BREWER, of Boston, favoured us with specimens of a new species of shrew-mole (*Scalops Breweri*), and sundry arvicolæ; EDMUND RUFFIN, Esq., of Virginia, sent us several specimens of the rodentia inhabiting that state, and obliged us by communicating much information in regard to their geographical range; the late Dr. JOHN WRIGHT, of Troy, N. Y., furnished us valuable notes on the various species of quadrupeds found in the northern part of the State of New York, and several specimens; Dr. WURDEMAN, of Charleston, supplied us with several specimens of various species of bat from Cuba, thereby enabling us to compare them with genera and species existing in America. To Professor LEWIS R. GIBBES, of the College of Charleston, we express our thanks, for several specimens of rare quadrupeds, and for his kindness in imparting to us much information and scientific knowledge.

Among others to whose zeal and friendship we are most indebted, we are proud to name: Dr. GEO. C. SHATTUCK and Dr. GEO. PARKMAN, of Boston; J. PRESCOTT HALL, Esq., JAMES G. KING, Esq., Major JOHN LECONTE, Mr. J. G. BELL, and our old friend ISSACHAR COZZENS, of New York; Hon. DANIEL WADSWORTH, of Hartford; W. O. AYRES, Esq., of Sag Harbour, Long Island; EDWARD HARRIS, Esq., of Moorestown, New Jersey; Dr. SAMUEL GEORGE MORTON and SAMUEL BISPHAM, Esq., of Philadelphia; WM. CASE, Esq., Cleveland, Ohio; OGDEN HAMMOND, Esq., of South Carolina; GIDEON B. SMITH, Esq., M.D., of Baltimore; Messrs. P. CHOUTEAU, Jr. & Co., St. Louis; Sir GEORGE SIMPSON, of the Hudson's Bay Fur Company; JOHN MARTYN, Jr., Quebec; Mr. FOTHERGILL, of Canada, &c., &c., &c.

In the course of this work we shall not indulge ourselves in the formation of new genera farther than we may find it necessary, and we think the genera at present established will include nearly all our species: we shall change no names of species already given, except in cases where their being retained would lead to error.

We will endeavour to avoid a mischievous habit, into which many naturalists have fallen, who, by the formation of new genera, considered themselves entitled to add their own after the specific name, thus taking credit for discoveries to which they were not entitled; on the contrary, as it appears necessary to give some check to this spirit of innovation, we have resolved to attach to each animal the name of the *first* describer, although it may have been arranged by subsequent authors under other genera.

Conceiving that no author has right to give a name to species which he has neither seen nor described, we have determined to reject the names proposed by closet naturalists who have ventured to name species noticed but not scientifically described by travellers. Hence we do not consider ourselves bound to adopt the names give by RAFINESQUE, HARLAN, and others, to the animals noticed by LEWIS & CLARKE, who neither imposed on them scientific names nor procured specimens. We shall in this respect follow the example of Dr. RICHARDSON, and in illustration of our views, refer our readers to his Fauna Boreali Americana, p. 211.

LEWIS & CLARKE (vol. iii., p. 39) described an animal which they called *Swellel*. No specimens were preserved, and no scientific name was given by them. From the printed account, RAFINESQUE bestowed on it the name of *Anisonyx? Rufa*, which was adopted by DESMAREST; and HARLAN, without any additional information, called it *Arctomys Rufa*. Many years afterwards RICHARDSON obtained a specimen, gave the first scientific description, and named it *Aplodontia Leporina*, very properly rejecting the names of those who had no right to bestow them.

In pursuing our researches we are often compelled to differ from the views of previous writers. In correcting what we conceive to be errors, we will endeavour to be swayed simply by a love of truth, treating all with respect, and adopting such language as can be offensive to none.

For the sake of convenience and uniformity we have written in the plural number, although the facts stated, and the information collected, were obtained at different times by the authors in their individual capacities.

Without entering into details of the labours of each in this undertaking, it will be sufficient to add that the history of the habits of our quadrupeds was obtained by both authors, either from personal observation or through the kindness of friends of science, on whose statements full reliance could be placed.

For the designation of species, and the letter-press of the present volume, the junior author is principally responsible.

In our Illustrations we have endeavoured (we hope not without success,) to place before our patrons a series of plates, which are not only scientifically correct, but interesting to all, from the varied occupations, expressions, and attitudes, we have given to the different species, together with the appropriate accessories, such as trees, plants, landscapes, &c., with which the figures of the animals are relieved; and we have sought to describe those represented in the first fifty plates, so as not only to clear away the obscurity which had gathered over some species, but to make our readers acquainted with their habits, geographical distribution, and all that we could ascertain of interest about them and the mode of hunting or destroying such as are pursued either to gratify the appetite, to furnish a rich fur or skin, or in order to get rid of dangerous or annoying neighbours.

The *twentieth* number of the Illustrations of the Quadrupeds of North America is now nearly ready for our subscribers, and we hope to conclude this portion of the work without much irregularity or delay in the appearance of the remaining plates.

Our sincere thanks are respectfully offered to our patrons for their liberal and generous encouragement of this undertaking, and we beg to assure them we shall ever entertain a lively sense of the interest they have taken in the work, and the substantial support vouchsafed us. A list of subscribers will be found appended to this volume, and farther subscriptions will be acknowledged in our next.

Some of the drawings have been executed by J. W. AUDUBON, under our direction, and he is now engaged in Europe in making figures of those arctic animals, of which accessible specimens exist only in the museums of that quarter of the globe. Many of the backgrounds were painted by V. G. AUDUBON.

Of the manner in which the various artists engaged upon the illustrations, under the direction of Mr. J. T. BOWEN, have done their part, our subscribers are able to judge for themselves: we feel desirous, however, to say, that to our mind the work has been executed in a beautiful style, and we wish publicly to express our thanks to Mr. BOWEN, to Mr. TRIMBLY, Mr. HITCHOCK, and the other artists who transferred the original drawings to the stone, and to Mr. BISBAUGH, whose impressions from their plates merit our praise. To all the other artists employed by us we also owe our acknowledgments for their valuable assistance.

Of the style in which the letter-press is printed, we need only say, it was done at the establishment of Mr. HENRY LUDWIG of this city, and that it has given us satisfaction.

NEW YORK, November, 1846.

Genus Lynx.

Dental Formula.

Incisive $\frac{6}{6}$; *Canine* $\frac{1-1}{1-1}$; *Cheek-Teeth* $\frac{3-3}{3-3}$ = 28.

The teeth in animals of this genus, with the exception of there being one less on each side, in the upper jaw; do not differ from the dental arrangement of the genus FELIS. The canine are very strong, there are but three molars on each side, above: The small false-molar, next to the canine, which exists in the larger species of *long-tailed* cats, such as the lion, tiger, panther, cougar, &c., as well as in the domestic or common cat, is wanting in the lynxes. There is one false-molar, or conical tooth on each side—one carnivorous, with three lobes and a tubercle or blunted heel, on the inner. The third cheek-tooth is rather small, and is placed transversely. In the lower jaw there are on each side, two false, compressed, simple molars, and one canine, which is bicusped.

The head is short, round, and arched; jaws short; tongue aculeated; ears short, erect, more or less tufted.

Fore-feet with five toes, hind-feet with only four; nails retractile. Tail shorter than the head, although nearly as long, in a few instances.

The species heretofore classed in the genus FELIS have been so multiplied by the discoveries of late years in various parts of the world, that they have for some time demanded a careful examination, and the separation of such as present characters essentially different from the types of that genus, into other genera.

Some of the distinctive marks by which the genus LYNX is separated from the old genus FELIS, are the tufted ears and shorter bodies and tails of the Lynxes, as well as the slight difference above mentioned in the dental arrangement of the two genera. In a note in the American Monthly Magazine, vol. i., p. 437, RAFINESQUE, in a few lines, proposed the genus LYNX, but gave no detailed characters, although he states that he had increased the species of this genus from four to fifteen! in which supposition, alas, he was sadly mistaken.

Dr. DEKAY, in the "Natural History of New-York," a work published "By Authority" of the State, has adopted the genus LYNCUS, as established by GRAY.

We have not seen the work in which Mr. GRAY proposed this generic name, and are consequently unable to ascertain on what characters it was founded, and we prefer the more classical name of LYNX. The name Lynx was formerly applied to one of the species of this genus. It is derived from the Greek word λυγξ (*lugx*,) a Lynx. Eight species of Lynx have been described; one being found in Africa, two in Persia, one in Arabia, two in Europe, and two in North America.

Lynx Rufux.—Guldenstaed.

Common American Wild Cat.—Bay Lynx.

Plate I.—Male. $\frac{3}{4}$ Natural Size

L. Cauda capite paullo breviore, ad extremum supra nigra, apice subalbida; auribus pagina posteriore maculo sub albido nigro marginato distinctis; hyeme et auctumno rufo-fuscus; vere et æstate cinereo-fuscus.

Characters.

Tail nearly as long as the head, extremity on the upper surface black, tipped with more or less white; a whitish spot on the hinder part of the ear bordered with black; general colour reddish-brown in autumn and winter, ashy-brown in spring and summer; soles naked.

Synonymes.

BAY LYNX, Pennant, Hist. Quadr., No. 171. Arctic Zool., vol. i., p. 51.
FELIS RUFA, Guld. in Nov. Comm. Petross. xx., p. 499.
FELIS RUFA, Temm., Monog., &c., vol. i., page 141.
LYNX FASCIATUS, Rafin. in Amer. Month. Mag., 1817, p. 46.
LYNX MONTANUS, Idem, Ibid. pp. 46, 2.

COMMON AMERICAN WILD CAT.

LYNX FLORIDANUS, Idem, Ibid. pp. 4, 64.

LYNX AUREUS, Idem, Ibid. p. 46, 6.
FELIS CAROLINENSIS, Desm., Mamm., p. 231.
FELIS RUFA, Godm., Amer. Nat. Hist., vol. iii., p. 239; Fig. in vol. I.

Description.

In size and form, this species bears some resemblance to small specimens of the female Canada Lynx, (*Lynx Canadensis*,) the larger feet and more tufted ears of the latter, however, as well as its grayer colour, will enable even an unpractised observer at a glance to distinguish the difference betwen the two species.

Head of moderate size, rounded; body rather slender; legs long; soles of feet naked; hind-feet webbed to within five-eighths of an inch of the claws; ears large, nearly triangular, erect, tipped with coarse hairs half an inch long, which drop out in summer; the inner surface thinly sprinkled with loose hairs, outer, thickly covered with short fur.

A ruff of elongated hairs surrounding the throat, more prominent in the male than female; tail, short, slender, and slightly turned upwards. mammæ eight; four pectoral and four abdominal.

Colour.

The hind-head and back, yellowish-brown, with a dorsal line more or less distinct, of dark-brown, running from the shoulder to near the insertion of the tail. A few irregular longitudinal stripes on the back, of the same colour. The sides spotted with dark-brown, these spots being more distinct and in closer approximation in some specimens than in others.

Forehead obscurely striped with dark-brown. Over and beneath the eyes, yellowish-white; whiskers nearly all white. Ears, outer surface, a triangular spot of dull white, dilated towards the outer margin, bordered with brownish-black; inner surface yellowish-white. Under surface of body yellowish-white, spotted with black; tail, above, barred with rufous and black, towards the extremity a broad band of black, tipped at the point, and particularly in the centre with white; under surface of tail, light-gray, interspersed with small and irregular patches of black hairs.

Fore-feet, on the upper surface, broadly, and towards the toes minutely, spotted with black on a light yellowish-brown ground; inner surface dull white, with two broad and several narrow bars of black; paws beneath, and hair between the soles, dark-brown. Hind-legs barred and spotted similarly to the fore-legs. Chin and throat dull white, with two black lines, commencing at a point on a line with the articulation of the lower jaw, where they form an acute angle, and thence diverge to the sides of the neck, and unite with the ruff, which is black, mixed with yellowish-brown and gray hairs.

The female is considerably smaller than the male, her body more slender, and her movements have a stronger resemblance, in their lightness and agility, to those of the common house-cat; the markings appear more distinct, and the rounded black spots on the back and sides, smaller and more numerous. There is in this species a considerable diversity in colour, as well as in size. In spring and early summer, before it has shed its winter coat, it is uniformly more rufous, and the black markings are less distinct, than after shedding its hair, and before the new hair is elongated in autumn to form the winter coat.

Our specimens obtained in summer and autumn, are of a light gray colour, with scarcely any mixture of rufous, and all the black markings are brighter and far more distinct than they are in those killed in the winter or spring months.

There are, however, at all seasons of the year, even in the same neighbourhood, strongly-marked varieties, and it is difficult to find two individuals precisely alike.

Some specimens are broadly marked with fulvous under the throat, whilst in others the throat as well as the chin are gray. In some the stripes on the back and spots along the sides are very distinctly seen, whilst in others they are scarcely visible, and the animal is grayish-brown above, with a dark dorsal stripe. A specimen from the mountains of Pennsylvania presents this appearance strikingly, and is withal nearly destitute of the triangular marking under the throat, so that we hesitated for some time in referring it to this species. A specimen from Louisiana is of the same uniform colour above, but with more distinct linear markings on the face, and with coarse hair, not more than half the length of that of individuals from the Northern States. We obtained a specimen in Carolina, which in nearly every particular answers to the description of *Felis Carolinensis* of DEMAREST. If the various supposed new species of Wild Cat, described by RAFINESQUE, HARLAN, DESMAREST, &c., are entitled to a place in our Fauna, on account of some peculiarity of colour, we have it in our power from specimens before us, to increase the number to a considerable extent; but in doing so we think we should only

No. 1. Plate, I.

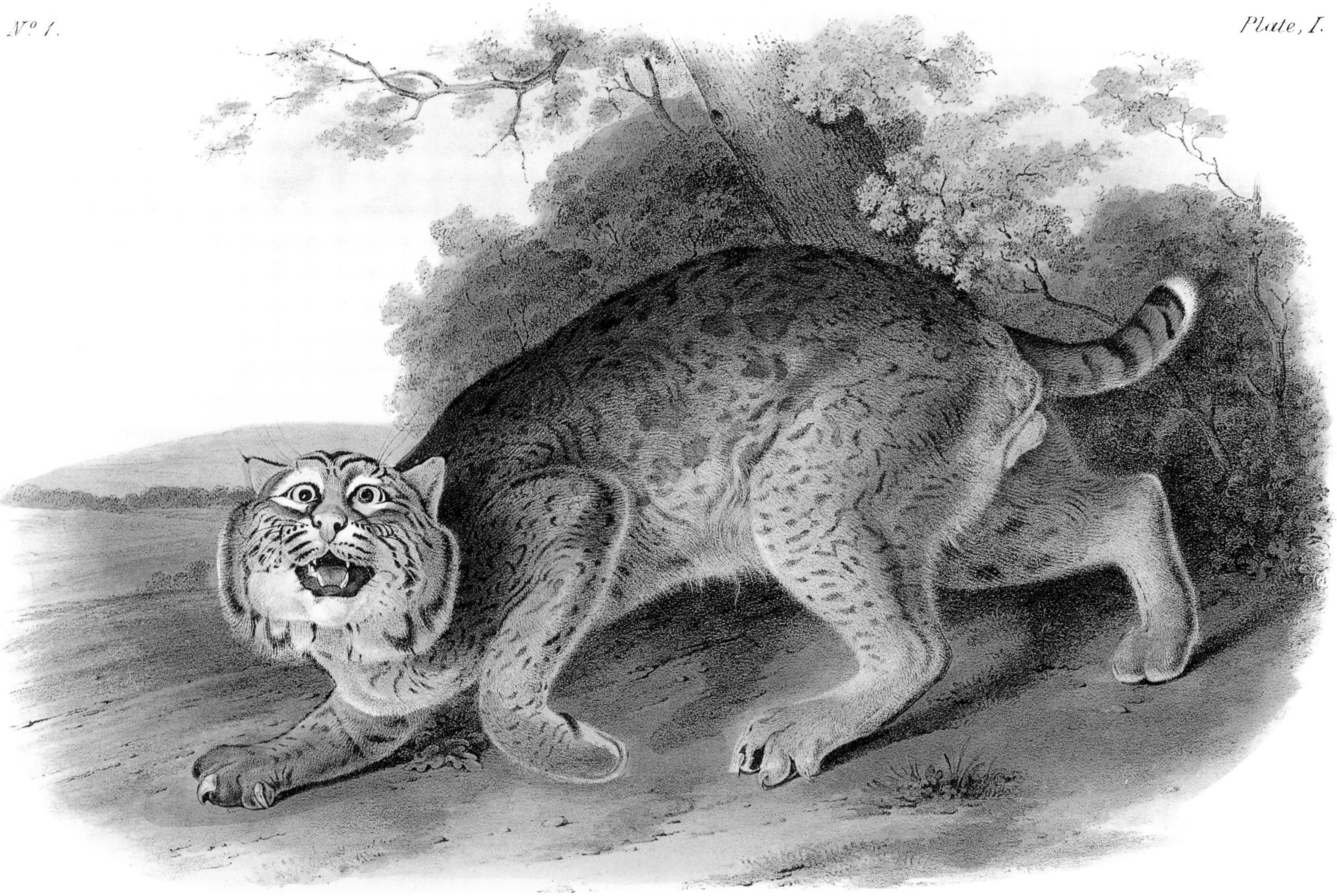

Drawn on Stone by R. Trembly.

Common American Wild-cat.

Drawn from Nature by J. J. Audubon F.R.S.F.L.S. *Male.* Printd. & Cold. by J. T. Bowen. Philada.

swell the list of synonymes, and add to the confusion which already prevails in regard to some of the species belonging to this genus.

Dimensions.

Adult Male.—[Fine Specimen.]

From point of nose to root of tail	30	inches.
Tail (vertebræ)	5	do.
Tail, to end of hair	5½	do.
From nose to end of skull	4½	do.
From nose, following the curvature of the head	6	do.
Tufts on the ears	½	do.
Breadth of ear	1⅝	do.
Anterior length of ear	1¾	do.
Length of neck	4	do.

Weight 17lb.

Habits.

The general appearance of this species conveys the idea of a degree of ferocity, which cannot with propriety be considered as belonging to its character, although it will, when at bay, show its sharp teeth, and with outstretched claws and infuriated despair, repel the attacks of either man or dog, sputtering the while, and rolling its eyes like the common cat.

It is, however, generally cowardly when attacked, and always flies from its pursuers, if it can, and although some anecdotes have been related to us of the strength, daring, and fierceness of this animal; such as its having been known to kill at different times a sheep, a full-grown doe, attack a child in the woods, &c.; yet in all the instances that have come under our own notice, we have found it very timid, and always rather inclined to beat a retreat, than to make an attack on any animal larger than a hare or a young pig. In the American Turf register, there is an interesting extract of a letter from Dr. COLEMAN, U. S. A., written at Fort Armstrong, Prairie du Chien, giving an account of a contest between an eagle and a Wild Cat. After a fierce struggle, in which the eagle was so badly wounded as to be unable to fly, the Cat, scratched and pierced in many places, and having had one eye entirely "gouged out" in the combat, was found lying dead.

In hunting at night for racoons and opossums, in which sport the negroes on the plantations of Carolina take great delight, a Cat is occasionally "treed" by the dogs; and the negroes, who seldom carry a gun, climb up the tree and shake him off as they would do a racoon, and although he fights desperately, he is generally killed by the dogs. During a botanical excursion through the swamps of the Edisto river, our attention was attracted by the barking of a small terrier at the foot of a sapling, (young tree.) On looking up, we observed a Wild Cat, about twenty feet from the ground, of at least three times the size of the dog, which he did not appear to be much afraid of. He seemed to have a greater dread of man, however, than of this diminutive specimen of the canine race, and leaped from the tree as we drew near.

The Wild Cat pursues his prey with both activity and cunning, sometimes bounding suddenly upon the object of his rapacity, sometimes with stealthy pace, approaching it in the darkness of night, seizing it with his strong retractile claws and sharp teeth, and bearing if off to his retreat in the forest.

The individual from which our figure was drawn had been caught in a steel-trap, and was brought to us alive. We kept it for several weeks; it was a fine male, although not the largest we have seen. Like most of the predacious animals, it grew fat in confinement, being regularly fed on the refuse parts of chickens and raw meat, as well as on the common brown rat.

The Bay Lynx, (as this animal is sometimes called,) is fond of swampy, retired situations, as well as the wooded sides of hills, and is still seen occasionally in that portion of the Alleghany mountains, which traverses the States of Pennsylvania and New York. It is abundant in the *Canebrakes*, (patches or thickets of the *Miegia Macrosperma*, of MICHAUX, which often extend for miles, and are almost impassable,) bordering the lakes, rivers, and lagoons of Carolina, Louisiana, and other Southern and South Western States. This species also inhabits the mountains and the undulating or *rolling* country of the Southern States, and frequents the thickets that generally spring up on deserted cotton plantations, some of which are two or three miles long, and perhaps a mile wide, and afford, from the quantity of briars, shrubs, and young trees of various kinds which have overgrown them, excellent cover for many quadrupeds and birds. In these bramble-covered old fields, the "Cats" feed chiefly on the rabbits and rats that make their homes in their almost impenetrable and tangled recesses; and seldom does the cautious Wild Cat voluntarily leave so comfortable and secure a lurking place, except in the breeding season, or to follow in very sultry weather, the dry beds of streams or

brooks, to pick up the cat-fish, &c., or cray-fish and frogs that remain in the deep holes of the creeks, during the drought of summer.

The Wild Cat not only makes great havoc among the chickens, turkeys, and ducks of the planter, but destroys many of the smaller quadrupeds, as well as partridges, and such other birds as he can surprise roosting on the ground. The hunters often run down the Wild Cat with packs of fox-hounds. When hard pressed by fast dogs, and in an open country, he ascends a tree with the agility of a squirrel, but the baying of the dogs calling his pursuers to the spot, the unerring rifle brings him to the ground, when, if not mortally wounded, he fights fiercely with the pack until killed. He will, however, when pursued by hunters with hounds, frequently elude both dogs and huntsmen, by an exercise of instinct, so closely bordering on reason, that we are bewildered in the attempt to separate it from the latter. No sooner does he become aware that the enemy is on his track, than, instead of taking a straight course for the deepest forest, he speeds to one of the largest old-fields overgrown with briary thickets, in the neighbourhood; and having reached this tangled maze, he runs in a variety of circles, crossing and re-crossing his path many times, and when he thinks the scent has been diffused sufficiently in different directions by this manœuvre, to puzzle both men and dogs, he creeps slyly forth, and makes for the woods, or for some well known swamp, and if he should be lucky enough to find a half-dried-up pond, or a part of the swamp, on which the clayey bottom is moist and sticky, he seems to know that the adhesive soil, covering his feet and legs, so far destroys the *scent*, that although the hounds may be in full cry on reaching such a place, and while crossing it, they will lose the track on the opposite side, and perhaps not regain it without some difficulty and delay.

At other times the "Cat," when chased by the dogs, gains some tract of "burnt wood," common especially in the pine lands of Carolina, where fallen and upright trees are alike blackened and scorched, by the fire that has run among them burning before it every blade of grass, every leaf and shrub, and destroying many of the largest trees in its furious course; and here, the charcoal and ashes on the ground, after he has traversed the burnt district a short distance, and made a few leaps along the trunk of a fallen tree, that has been charred in the conflagration, will generally put any hounds at fault. Should no such chance of safety be within his reach, he does not despair, but exerting his powers of flight to the utmost, increases his distance from the pursuing pack, and following as intricate and devious a path as possible, after many a weary mile has been run over, he reaches a long-fallen trunk of a tree, on which he may perchance at some previous time have baffled the hunters as he is now about to do. He leaps on to it, and hastily running to the farther end, doubles and returns to the point from which he gained the tree, and after running backward and forward repeatedly on the fallen trunk, he makes a sudden and vigorous spring, leaping as high up into a tree some feet distant, as he can; he then climbs to its highest forks, (branches,) and closely squatted, watches the movements of his pursuers. The dogs are soon at fault, for he has already led them through many a crooked path; the hunters are dispirited and weary, and perhaps the density of the woods, or the approach of night favours him. The huntsmen call off their dogs from the fruitless search, and give up the chase; and shortly afterwards the escaped marauder, descends leisurely to the earth, and wanders off in search of food, and to begin a new series of adventures.

In some parts of Carolina, Georgia, Mississippi, and Louisiana, the Wild Cat has at times become so great a nuisance as to have aroused the spirit of vengeance in the hearts of the planters, who are constant sufferers from his depredations. They have learned by experience, that one Cat will do as much mischief among the pigs and poultry as a dozen gray foxes. They are now determined to allow their hounds, which they had hitherto kept solely for the favourite amusement of deer hunting, and which had always been whipped-in, from the trail of the Wild-Cat, to pursue him, though thicket, briar patch, marsh, and morass, until he is caught or killed.

Arrangements for the Cat-hunt are made over night. Two or three neighbours form the party, each one bringing with him all the hounds he can muster. We have seen thirty of the latter brought together on such occasions, some of which were not inferior to the best we have examined in England, indeed, great numbers of the finest fox-hounds are annually imported into Carolina.

At the earliest dawn, the party is summoned to the spot previously fixed on as the place of meeting. A horn is sounded, not low and with a single blast, as is usual in hunting the deer, lest the timid animal should be startled from its bed among the broom-grass (*Andropogon dissitiflorus*) and bound away out of the drive, beyond the reach of the hunter's double-barrel loaded with buckshot; but with a loud, long, and oft-repeated blast, wakening the echoes that rise from the rice-fields and marshes, and are reverberated from shore to shore of the winding sluggish river, until lost among the fogs and shadows of the distant forest.

An answering horn is heard half a mile off, and anon comes another response from a different quarter. The party is soon collected, they are mounted, not on the fleetest and best-blooded horses, but on the most sure-footed, (sometimes called "Old field Tackies,") which know how to avoid the stump-holes on the burnt grounds of the pine lands, which stand the fire of the gun, and which can not only go with tolerable speed, but are, to use a common expression, "tough as a pine knot." The hunters greet each other in the open-hearted manner characteristic of the Southern planter. Each pack of dogs is under the guidance of a coloured driver, whose business it is to control the hounds and encourage and aid them in the hunt. The drivers ride in most cases the fleetest horses on the ground, in order to be able, whilst on a deer hunt to stop the dogs. These men, who are so important to the success of the chase, are possessed of a good deal of intelligence and shrewdness, are usually much petted, and regarding themselves as belonging to the aristocracy of the plantation, are apt to look down upon their fellow-servants as inferiors, and consider themselves privileged even to crack a joke with their masters. The drivers are ordered to stop the dogs if a deer should be started, a circumstance which often occurs, and which has saved the life of many a Cat, whose fate five minutes before this unlucky occurrence was believed to be sealed. Orders are given to destroy the Cat fairly, by running him down with the hounds, or if this cannot be done, then by shooting him if he ascends a tree or approaches within gun shot of the stand which the hunter has selected as the most likely place for him to pass near. The day is most auspicious—there is not a breath of wind to rustle the falling leaves, nor a cloud to throw its shadows over the wide joyous landscape. The dew-drops are sparkling on the few remaining leaves of the persimmon tree, and the asters and dog-fennel hang drooping beneath their load of moisture. The dogs are gamboling in circles around, and ever and anon, in spite of all restraint, the joyous note breaks forth—the whole pack is impatient for the chase, and the young dogs are almost frantic with excitement.

But we have not time for a farther description of the scene—whilst we are musing and gazing, the word is given, "Go!" and off start the hounds, each pack following its own driver to different parts of the old fields, or along the borders of the swamps and marshes. Much time, labour and patience are usually required, before the "Cat" can be found by the dogs: sometimes there is a sudden burst from one or other of the packs, awakening expectation in the minds of the huntsmen, but the driver is not to be so easily deceived, as he has some dogs that never open at a rabbit, and the snap of the whip soon silences the riotous young babblers. Again there is a wild burst and an exulting shout, giving assurance that better game than a rabbit is on foot; and now is heard a distant shot, succeeded in a second of time by another, and for an instant all is still: the echoes come roaring up through the woods, and as they gradually subside, the crack of the whip is again heard stopping the dogs. The story is soon told; a deer had been started—the shot was too small—or the distance too great, or any other excuses, (which are always at hand among hunters of fertile imagination,) are made by the unsuccessful sportsman who fired, and the dogs are carried back to the "trail" of the Cat, that has been growing fresher and fresher for the last half hour. At length, "Trimbush," (and a good dog is he,) that has been working on the cold trail for some time, begins to give tongue, in a way that brings the other dogs to his aid. The drivers now advance to each other, encouraging their dogs; the trail becomes a drag; onward it goes through a broad marsh at the head of a rice-field. "He will soon be started now!" "He is up!" What a burst! you might have heard it two miles off—it comes in mingled sounds, roaring like thunder, from the muddy marsh and from the deep swamp. The barred owl, frightened from the monotony of his quiet life among the cypress trees, commences hooting in mockery as it were, of the wide-mouthed hounds. Here they come, sweeping through the resounding swamp like an equinoctial storm—the crackling of a reed, the shaking of a bush, a glimpse of some object that glided past like a shadow, is succeeded by the whole pack, rattling away among the vines and fallen timbers, and leaving a trail in the mud as if a pack of wolves in pursuit of a deer had hurried by. The Cat has gone past. It is now evident that he will not climb a tree. It is almost invariably the case that where he can retreat to low swampy situations, or briar patches, he will not take a tree, but seeks to weary the dogs by making short windings among the almost impassable briar patches. He has now been twisting and turning half a dozen times in a thicket covering only three or four acres—let us go in and take our stand on the very trail where he last passed, and shoot him if we can. A shot is heard on the opposite edge of the thicket, and again all is still; but once more the pack is in full cry. Here he comes, almost brushing our legs as he dashes by and disappears in the bushes, before we can get sight of him and pull trigger. But we see that the dogs are every moment pressing him closer, that the marauder is showing evidences of fatigue and is nearly "done up." He begins to make

narrower circles, there are restless flashes in his eye, his back is now curved upwards, his hair is bristled nervously forward, his tongue hangs out— we raise our gun as he is approaching, and scarcely ten yards off—a loud report—the smoke has hardly blown aside, ere we see him lifeless, almost at our very feet—had we waited three minutes longer, the hounds would have saved us the powder and shot!

One fine morning in autumn, when we had crossed the Ohio river at Henderson, in Kentucky, with the view of shooting some wild turkeys, geese, and perhaps a deer, we chanced to seat ourselves about fifty yards from a prostrate tree, and presently saw a Wild-Cat leap on to it, and go through the manœuvres we have described in a preceding page. He did not see us, and had scarcely reached one of the higher branches of a tall white-oak, after spring into it from the fallen tree, when we heard the dogs, which soon came up, with the hunters following not far behind. They asked, when they perceived us, whether we had seen the "Cat" that had given them the slip. Always willing to assist the hunter who has lost his game, and having no particular liking towards this species, we answered in the affirmative, and showed them the animal, closely squatted on a large branch some distance from the ground. One of the party immediately put his rifle to his shoulder and pulled the trigger: the Cat leaped from the branch into the air, and fell to the earth quite dead. Whilst residing in Louisiana some twenty years since, we chanced one afternoon to surprise one of these depredators. He had secured a hare, (commonly called rabbit,) and was so eagerly engaged in satisfying his hunger as not to observe us, until we were near the spot where he was partially concealed behind a rotten log. At sight of us, he squatted flat on the ground. As we looked at him, we heard a squirrel close by, and turned our head for an instant, but scarce had we glanced at the squirrel, when looking again for the Wild-Cat, he had disappeared, carrying the remains of the hare away with him.

About twenty miles from Charleston, South Carolina, resides a worthy friend of ours, a gentleman well known for his skill in the sports of the field, his hospitality to both friends and strangers, and the excellent manner in which his plantation is managed. The plantation of Dr. DESEL is, in short, the very place for one who likes the sight of several fine bucks hanging on the branches of an old Pecan-nut tree; while turkeys, geese, and poultry of other kinds, are seen in abundance in his well stocked poultry yards, affording certainty of good cheer to his visitors.

The Doctor's geese were nightly lodged near the house, in an enclosure which was rendered apparently safe, by a very high fence. As an additional security, several watch dogs were let loose about the premises; besides an excellent pack of hounds, which by an occasional bark or howl during the night, sounded a note of warning or alarm in case any marauder, whether biped or quadruped approached.

Notwithstanding these precautions, a goose disappeared almost every night, and no trace of the ingress or egress of the robber could be discovered. Slow in attaching suspicion to his servants, the Dr. waited for time and watchfulness to solve the mystery. At length, the feathers, and other remains of his geese, were discovered in a marsh about a quarter of a mile from the house, and strong suspicions were fastened on the Wild-Cat; still, as he came at odd hours of the night, all attempts to catch or shoot him proved for a time unavailing.

One morning, however, he came about day-light, and having captured a good fat goose, was traced by the keen noses of the hounds. The chase was kept up for some time through the devious windings of the thickets, when his career of mischief was brought to a close by a shot from the gun of our friend the Doctor, who, in self-defence, became his executioner. Thus ended his career. In this respect he fared worse than he deserved, compared with those being of a superior nature, who, not understanding that "Honesty is the best policy" outdo our Wild-Cat in his destructive habits, until the laws, so just and useful, when mildly, but always, enforced, put an effectual stop to their criminal proceedings.

The Wild-Cat is a great destroyer of eggs, and never finds a nest of grouse or partridge, wild turkey or other bird, without sucking every egg in it. Indeed, it will if practicable, seize on both young and old birds of these and other species. Its "penchant" for a "poulet au naturel" has suggested the following method of capturing it in Georgia, as related to us by our friend MAJOR LECONTE, late of the United States Army.

A large and strong box-trap is constructed, and a chicken-cock, (rooster,) placed at the farthest end of it from the door, is tied by one leg, so that he cannot move. There is a stout wire partition about half way between the fowl and the door, which prevents the Cat when entering the trap, from seizing the bird. The trap is then set so that when the animal enters, the open door closes behind him by a spring, (commonly the branch of some tree bent down for the purpose, and released by a trigger set at the entrance or just within the trap.)

These traps are placed in different parts of the plantations, or in the woods, and the Wild-Cat is generally attracted by the crowing of the cock at early dawn of day.

MAJOR LECONTE has caught many of them by this artifice, on and about his plantations in the neighbourhood of Savannah, in Georgia; and this method of capturing the Wild-Cat is also quite common in South Carolina. Indeed, this species does not seem to possess the suspicion and cunning inherent in the fox, enabling the latter to avoid a trap of almost any kind. We have seen the Wild-Cat taken from the common log-traps set for racoons. We saw one in a cage, that had been caught in a common box-trap, baited with a dead partridge, and have heard intelligent domestics residing on the banks of the Santee river, state, that after setting their steel traps for otters, they frequently found the Wild-Cat caught in them instead.

When this animal discovers a flock of wild turkeys, he will generally follow them at a little distance for some time, and after having ascertained the direction in which they are proceeding, make a rapid detour, and concealing himself behind a fallen tree, or in the lower branches of some leafy maple, patiently wait in ambush until the birds approach, when he suddenly springs on one of them, if near enough, and with one bound secures it. We once, while resting on a log in the woods, on the banks of the Wabash river, perceived two wild turkey cocks at some distance below us, under the bank near the water, pluming and picking their feathers; on a sudden, one of them flew across the river, and the other we saw struggling in the grasp of a Wild-Cat, which almost instantly dragged it up the bank into the woods, and made off. On another occasion we observed an individual of this species, about nine miles from Charleston, in pursuit of a covey of partridges, (Ortyx Virginiana,)—so intent was the Cat upon its prey, that it passed within ten steps of us, as it was making a circle to get in advance and in the path of the birds,—its eyes were constantly fixed on the covey, and it stealthily concealed itself behind a log it expected the birds to pass. In a second attempt the marauder succeeded in capturing one of the partridges, when the rest in great affright flew and scattered in all directions.

An individual that was kept alive at Charleston, and afterwards for a short time at our house in the City of New-York, showed its affinity to the domestic cat, by purring and mewing at times loud enough to be heard at some distance. At the former place its cry was several times mistaken for that of the common house-cat. In the woods, during the winter season, its loud catter-wauling can be heard at the distance of a mile.

Although this species may perhaps be designated as nocturnal in its habits, it is, by no means, exclusively so, as is shown by the foregoing account. We have, in fact, in several instances seen this Cat engaged in some predatory expedition in full sun-shine, both in winter and summer.

It is not a very active swimmer, but is not averse to taking the water. We witnessed it on one occasion crossing the Santee river when not pursued, and at another time saw one swimming across some ponds to make its escape from the dogs. It has been observed, however, that when it has taken to the water during a hard chase, it soon after either ascends a tree or is caught by the hounds.

The domicile of the Wild-Cat is sometimes under an old log, covered with vines such as the Smilax, Ziziphus volubilus, Rubus, &c., but more commonly in a hollow tree. Sometimes it is found in an opening twenty or thirty feet high, but generally much nearer the ground, frequently in a cavity at the root, and sometimes in the hollow trunk of a fallen tree, where, after collecting a considerable quantity of long moss and dried leaves to make a comfortable lair, it produces from two to four young. These are brough forth in the latter end of March in Carolina; in the Northern States, however, the kittens appear later, as we have heard of an instance in Pennsylvania where two young were found on the 15th day of May, apparently not a week old. Our friend Dr. SAMUEL WILSON, of Charleston, a close observer of nature, has made the following note in our memorandum book. "April 15th, 1839, shot a female Wild-Cat as it started from its bed, out of which four young ones were taken, their eyes were not yet open." Our friend Dr. DESEL, whom we have already mentioned, saw three young ones taken out from the hollow of tree which was thirty feet from the ground. On four occasions, we have had opportunities of counting the young, either in the nest or having been very recently taken from it. In every case there were three young ones. In one instance the nest was composed of long moss, (Tillandsia usneoides,) which seemed to have been part of an old, deserted, squirrel's nest.

We once made an attempt at domesticating one of the young of this species, which we obtained when only two weeks old. It was a most spiteful, growling, snappish little wretch, and showed no disposition to improve its habits and manners under our kind tuition. We placed it in a wooden box, from which it was constantly striving to gnaw its way out. It, one night, escaped into our library, where it made sad work among the books, (which gave us some valuable lessons on the philosophy of patience, we could not have so readily found among our folios,) and left the marks of its teeth on the mutilated window-sashes. Finally we fastened it with a light chain, and had a small kennel built for it in the yard. Here it was constantly indulging its carnivorous propensities, and catching the young poultry, which it enticed within reach of its chain by leaving a portion of its food at the door of its house, into which it retreated until an opportunity offered to pounce on its unsuspecting prey. Thus it continued, growing if possible, more wild and vicious every day, growling and spitting at every servant that approached it, until at last, an unlucky blow, as a punishment for its mischievous tricks, put an end to its life, and with it to one source of annoyance.

The Bay Lynx is generally in fine order, and often very fat. The meat is white, and has somewhat the appearance of veal. Although we omitted to taste it, we have seen it cooked, when it appeared savoury, and the persons who partook of it pronounced it delicious.

The muscular powers of this species are very great, and the fore-feet and legs are rather large in proportion to the body.

Geographical Distribution.

The geographical range of the Bay Lynx is very extensive, it being found to inhabit portions of the Continent from the tropics as far north as 60°. It abounds in Texas, Louisiana, Florida, Georgia, and both the Carolinas, and is found in all the States east of these, and likewise in New Brunswick, and Nova Scotia. We have seen it on the shores of the Upper Missouri more than a thousand miles above St. Louis. We examined one that had been taken a few hours before, by some hunters in Erie county, in the State of New York, and have heard of its existing, although rather sparingly, in Upper Canada, where it has been occasionally captured.

General Remarks.

We are not so fortunate as to possess any specimen from Oregon, or the regions west of the Rocky Mountains, to enable us at this time to institute a close comparison, and therefore cannot be certain that the Cat described by LEWIS and CLARKE, to which naturalists, without having seen it, have attached the name of Felis fasciata, or that the individual described by Dr. RICHARDSON, and referred by him to Felis rufa, are identical with the present species; yet as they do not present greater marks of difference than those observable in many other varieties of it, and as we have carefully examined several hundred specimens in the museums and private collections of Europe and America, and have, at this moment upwards of twenty lying before us, that were obtained in various parts of the country, from Texas to Canada, our present conclusion is, that in the United States, east and north of the Mississippi, there are but two species of Lynx—the well known Canada Lynx, and the Bay Lynx—our present species, and that the varieties in colour, (especially in the latter animal,) have contributed to the formation of many imaginary species. Whatever may be the varieties, however, there are some markings in this species which are permanent, like the white ears and nose of the fox squirrel, (Sc. Capistratus,) and which serve to identify it through all the variations of sex, season, and latitude. All of them have naked soles, and the peculiar markings at the extremity of the slender tail, which terminates as abruptly as if it had been amputated. It may also be distinguished from any variety of the Canada Lynx, (L. Canadensis.) by a white patch behind the ear which does not exist in the latter.

This peculiar mark is to be observed, however, in several species of the genus FELIS. We have noticed it in the jaguar, royal tiger, panther, ocelot, hunting-leopard, and other species.

Genus Arctomys, *Gmel., Cuv.*

Dental Formula.

Incisive $\frac{2}{2}$; *Canine* $\frac{0-0}{0-0}$; *Molar* $\frac{5-5}{4-4}$ = 22.

Incisors strong, narrow, and wedge-shaped, anterior surface rounded; molars, with the upper surface thick and heavy.

Head large, mouth small, and placed below; eyes large, ears short, paws strong; fore-feet with four toes and the rudiment of a thumb; hind-feet with five toes; nails strong, compressed; tail bushy; no cheek pouches.

The name *Arctomys*, is derived from two Greek words αρχτος (*arktos*,) a bear, and μυς, (*mus*,) a mouse.

There are, as far as we are informed, but eight known species of the genus as it is now defined, five on the Eastern Continent and three in North America.

Arctomys Monax—Linn.

Wood-Chuck. Maryland Marmot. Ground-Hog.

Plate II.—Female and Young. Natural Size.

A. Supra fusco cinereus, subtus sub-rufus, capite, cauda, pedibusque fuscis, naso et buccis cinereis.

Characters.

Brownish-gray above; head, tail, and feet, dark-brown; nose and cheeks ashy-brown, under surface reddish.

Synonymes.

MUS MONAX, Linn., 12 ed., p. 81.
MARYLAND MARMOT, Penn., Arct. Zool., vol. I., p. 111.
MONAX, ou MARMOTTE DE CANADA, Buff., Supp. 111.
MARYLAND MARMOT, Godman, Nat. Hist. vol. ii., p. 100, figure.
MARYLAND MARMOT, Griffiths' Cuvier, vol. iii., p. 130, figure.
QUEBEC MARMOT, Pennant, Hist. Quad., 1st ed., No. 259.
MUS EMPETRA, Pallas, Glir., p. 75.
ARCTOMYS EMPETRA, Salt, Linn., Trans., vol. xiii., p. 24.
ARCTOMYS EMPETRA, Godman, Nat. Hist., vol. ii., p. 208.
ARCTOMYS MONAX, et ARCTOMYS EMPETRA, Sabine, Trans. Lin- næan Soc., vol. xiii., pp. 582, 584.
ARCTOMYS EMPETRA, Richardson, Fauna Boreali Americana, p. 147, pl. 9.

Description.

The body is thick, and the legs are short, so that the belly nearly touches the ground. Head short and conical; ears short, rounded, and thinly clothed with hair on both surfaces; eyes moderate; whiskers numerous, extending to the ear; a membrane beneath the ears, on the posterior parts of the cheek, and a few setæ on the eye-brows; legs, short and muscular; fore-feet, with four toes, and the rudiment of a thumb, with a minute nail; hind-feet, with five toes. Toes long and well separated, palms naked, with tubercles at the roots of the toes. The middle toe longest—the first and third, which are nearly equal to each other, not much shorter; the extremity of the nail of the outer, extends only to the base of the nail of the adjoining toe; fore-claws moderately arched, obtuse and compressed; the soles of the hind-feet long, and naked to the heel; hind-feet semi-palmated; nails channelled near the ends. Tail bushy, partly distichous; body clothed with soft woolly fur, which is mixed with coarse long hairs.

Colour.

This species (like the foregoing one) is subject to many variations in the colour of its fur, which may account perhaps for its numerous synonymes. We will, however, describe the animal in its most common colouring.

The finer woolly fur is for two-thirds of its length from the roots upwards, of a dark ashy brown, with the extremities light yellowish-brown. The long hairs are dark brown for two-thirds of their length, tipped sometimes with reddish white, but generally with a silvery white. The general tint of the back is grizzly or hoary; cheeks, and around the mouth, light gray; whiskers black;

head, nose, feet, nails and tail, dark brown; eyes black. The whole under surface, including the throat, breast, belly, and the fore and hind legs, reddish orange.

The specimens before us present several striking varieties of colour; among them is one from Lower Canada, coal-black with the exception of the nose and a patch under the chin, which are light gray; the fur is short, and very soft; and the tail less distichous than in other varieties of this species.

Dimensions.

Adult Male.

From point of nose to root of tail . . . . 18¾ inches.
Tail (vertebræ) . . . . 3⅞ do.
Tail, to end of hair . . . . 5⅞ do.
Ear, posteriorly . . . . ¾ do.
Girth of body . . . . 17 do.
From fore to hind claw, when stretched . . . . 26 do.

We have found some difference in the length of the tail, in different individuals, it being, in some specimens, nearly seven inches long including the hair.

Weight 9 lb. 11 oz.

Habits.

In the Middle States many individuals of this species seem to prefer stony places, and often burrow close to or in a stone wall. When this is the case, it is very difficult to procure them, as they are secure from the attacks of dogs, and much labour would be necessary in removing the large stones, and digging up the earth in order to dislodge them.

From our own observations, we are obliged to contradict the following account given of the habits of this species. It has been said that "When about to make an inroad upon a clover field, all the marmots resident in the vicinity, quietly and cautiously steal towards the spot, being favoured in their march by their gray colour, which is not easily distinguished.

"While the main body are actively engaged in cropping the clover heads, and gorging their '*ample cheek-pouches*,' one or more individuals remain at some distance in the rear as sentinels. These watchmen sit erect, with their fore-paws held close to their breast, and their heads slightly inclined, to catch every sound which may move the air. Their extreme sensibility of ear enables them to distinguish the approach of an enemy long before he is sufficiently near to be dangerous, and the instant the sentinel takes alarm, he gives a clear shrill whistle, which immediately disperses the troop in every direction, and they speedily take refuge in their deepest caves. The time at which such incursions are made is generally about mid-day, when they are less liable to be interrupted than at any other period, either by human or brute enemies," (GODMAN, American Natural History, vol. ii., p. 102.)

We kept two of these animals alive for several weeks, feeding them on different grasses, potatoes, apples, and other fruits and vegetables. We found them to be very active at times, though fond of placing themselves in an erect posture, sitting on their rump, and letting their fore-legs and feet hang loosely down in the manner of our squirrels.

The old female, when approached, opened her mouth, showed her teeth, and made a rattling or clattering noise with the latter, evidently in anger. Neither the female nor the young appeared to become in any degree tame during the period we kept them. The former frequently emitted a shrill whistle-like noise, which is a not of alarm and anger, and may be heard when one is at distance of about fifty yards from the animal. After we had made figures from those specimens, we examined their mouths, but did not find any pouches like those described by Dr. GODMAN, although there appeared to be a cavity, not larger than would admit a common green pea, and which was the only trace of any thing like a pouch in those we procured, and in all that have been observed by us.

When the Wood-Chuck is feeding, it keeps its erect position, inclining the head, and fore-part of its body forward and sideways, so as to reach its food without extending the fore-legs and feet, which are drawn back under it; after getting a mouthful, it draws back its head again and brings its body to an upright posture by the muscular power of the hind-legs and feet. On being surprised or pursued, this species runs very fast for some eight or ten yards, and then frequently stops short and squats down close to the ground, watching to see if it has been observed; and will allow you to approach within a few feet, when it starts suddenly again, and again stops and squats down as before. Not unfrequently, under these circumstances it puts its head under the dry leaves, or amid tufts of grass, to conceal itself from the pursuer. You may then generally capture or kill it with a stick. These animals bite severely, and defend themselves fiercely, and will, when unable to escape, turn and make battle with a dog of more than double their own size. Sometimes whilst they were lying down as if asleep, we have heard them make the clattering noise before spoken of, with their teeth; reminding us of a person's teeth chattering in an ague fit. When walking leisurely, they place their feet flat upon the ground at full length, arching the toes, however, as is the habit of squirrels. These Marmots sleep during the greater part of the day, stealing from their burrows early in the morning and towards evening. They climb trees or bushes awkwardly, and when they have found a comfortable situation in the sunshine, either on the branch of a tree, or on a bush, will remain there for hours. They clean their faces with the fore-feet, whilst sitting up on their hind-legs, like a squirrel, and frequently lick their fur in the manner of a cat, leaving the coat smoothed down by the tongue. The body of the Wood-Chuck is extremely flabby after being killed, its flesh is, however, tolerably good, although a little strong, and is frequently purchased by the humbler classes of people, who cook it like a roasting pig. Occasionally, and especially in autumn, it is exceedingly fat.

This species becomes torpid about the time the leaves have fallen from the trees in the autumn, and the frosty air gives notice of the approach of winter; and remains burrowed in the earth until the grass has sprung up and the genial warmth of spring invites it to come forth.

We once observed one sunning itself at the mouth of its burrow, on the 23d of October, in the State of New-York; and in the same State, saw one killed by a dog on the first of March, when the winter's snow was yet lying in patches on the ground.

Where the nature of the country will admit of it, the Wood-Chucks select a projecting rock, in some fissure under which, they can dig their burrows. In other localities they dig them on the sides of hills, or in places where the surface of the ground is nearly level. These burrows or excavations are sometimes extended to the length of twenty or thirty feet from the opening; for the first three or four feet inclining obliquely downward, and the gallery being continued farther on, about on a level, or with a slight inclination upward to its termination, where there is a large round chamber, to which the occupants retire for rest and security, in which the female gives birth to her young, and where the family spends the winter in torpidity.

Concerning this latter most singular state of existence, we are gratified in being able to communicate the following facts, related to us by the Hon. DANIEL WADSWORTH, of Hartford, Connecticut. "I kept," said he to us, "a fine Wood-Chuck in captivity, in this house, for upwards of two years. It was brought to me by a country lad, and was then large, rather wild, and somewhat cross and mischievous; being placed in the kitchen, it soon found a retreat, in which it remained concealed the greater part of its time every day. During several nights it attempted to escape by gnawing the door and window-sills; gradually it became more quiet, and suffered itself to be approached by the inmates of the kitchen, these being the cook, a fine dog, and a cat; so that ere many months had elapsed, it would lie on the floor near the fire, in company with the dog, and would take food from the hand of the cook. I now began to take a particular interest in its welfare, and had a large box made for its use, and filled with hay, to which it became habituated, and always retired when inclined to repose. Winter coming on, the box was placed in a warm corner, and the Wood-Chuck went into it, arranged its bed with care, and became torpid. Some six weeks having passed without its appearing, or having received any food; I had it taken out of the box, and brought into the parlour;—it was inanimate, and as round as a ball, its nose being buried as it were in the lower part of its abdomen, and covered by its tail—it was rolled over the carpet many times, but without effecting any apparent change in its lethargic condition, and being desirous to push the experiment as far as in my power, I laid it close to the fire, and having ordered my dog to lie down by it, placed the Wood-Chuck in the dog's lap. In about half an hour, my pet slowly unrolled itself, raised its nose from the carpet, looked around for a few minutes, and then slowly crawled away from the dog, moving about the room as if in search of its own bed! I took it up, and had it carried down stairs and placed again in its box, where it went to sleep, as soundly as ever, until spring made its appearance. That season advancing, and the trees showing their leaves, the Wood-Chuck became as brisk and gentle as could be desired, and was frequently brought into the parlour. The succeeding winter this animal evinced the same dispositions, and never appeared to suffer by its long sleep. An accident deprived me of my pet, for having been trodden on, it gradually became poor, refused food, and finally died extremely emaciated."

May we here be allowed to detain you, kind reader, for a few moments, whilst we reflect on this, one among thousands of other instances of the all-wise dispensations of the Creator. Could any of the smaller species of quadrupeds, incapable, as many of them are, of migrating like the swift-winged inhabitants of the air to the sunny climes of the South, and equally unable to find any thing to subsist on among the dreary wastes of snow, or the frost-bound lands of the North during winter, have a greater boon at the hands of Nature than this power of escaping the rigours and cold blasts of that season, and resting securely, in a sleep of insensibility, free from all cravings of hunger and all danger of perishing with cold, till the warm sun of spring, once more calls them into life and activity? Thus this and several other species of quadrupeds, whose organization in this respect differs so widely from general rules, may be said to have no winter in their year, but enjoy the delightful weather of spring, summer, and autumn, without caring for the approach of that season during which other animals often suffer from both cold and hunger.

"Whilst hunting one day, (said a good friend of ours, when we were last in Canada,) I came across a Wood-Chuck, called in Canada by the different names of Siffleur, Ground-Hog, and occasionally Marmot, with a litter of six or seven young ones by her side. I leaped from my horse, feeling confident that I could capture at least one or two of them, but I was mistaken; for the dam, which seemed to anticipate my evil designs, ran round and round the whole of her young 'chucks,' urging them towards a hole beneath a rock, with so much quickness—energy, I may call it—that ere I could lay hands on even one of her progeny, she had them all in the hole, into which she then pitched herself, and left me gazing in front of her well-secured retreat, thus baffling all my exertions!"

We have now and then observed this Marmot in the woods, leaning with its back against a tree, and exposing its under parts to the rays of the hottest sun: on such occasions its head was reclining on its breast, the eyes were closed, the fore-legs hanging down, and it was apparently asleep, and presented a singular and somewhat ludicrous figure.

An intelligent naturalist has in his account of these animals, said that "their burrows, contain large excavations in which they deposit stores of provisions." This assertion contradicts our own observations and experience. We are inclined to doubt whether storing up provisions at any or for any season of the year, can be a habit of this species. In the summer of 1814, in Renssellaer County, in the State of New York, we marked a burrow, which was the resort of a pair of Marmots. In the beginning of November, the ground was slightly covered with snow, and the frost had penetrated to the depth of about half an inch. We now had excavations made, in a line along the burrow or gallery of the Marmots; and at about twenty-five feet from the mouth of the hole, both of them were found lying close to each other in a nest of dried grass, which did not appear to have been any of it eaten or bitten by them. They were each rolled up, and looked somewhat like two misshapen balls of hair, and were perfectly dormant. We removed them to a hay stack, in which we made an excavation to save them from the cold. One of them did not survive the first severe weather of the winter, having, as we thought on examining them, been frozen to death. The other, the male, was now removed to a cellar, where he remained in a perfectly dormant state until the latter part of February, when he escaped before we were aware of his reanimation. We had handled him only two days previously, and could perceive no symptoms of returning vivacity. During the time he was in the cellar, there was certainly no necessity for a "store of provisions" for him, as the animal was perfectly torpid and motionless from the day he was caught, until, as just mentioned, he emerged from that state and made his escape.

In the month of May, or sometimes in June, the female brings forth her young, generally four or five in number. We have however on two occasions, counted seven, and on another eight, young in a litter. In about three weeks, they may be seen playing around the mouth of the burrow, where sitting on their hind-feet in the manner of the Kangaroo, they closely watch every intruder, retreating hastily into the hole at the first notes of alarm sounded by the mother.

The Wood-Chuck, in some portions of our country, exists in considerable numbers, although it is seldom found associating with any of its own species, except while the young are still unable to provide for themselves, until which period they are generally taken care of by both parents.

When the young are a few months old, they prepare for a separation, and dig a number of holes in the vicinity of their early domicile, some of which are only a few feet deep, and are never occupied. These numerous burrows have given rise to the impression that this species lives in communities, which we think is not strictly the case.

Geographical Distribution.

We have found the Wood-Chuck in every state of the Union north-east of South Carolina, and throughout the Canadas, Nova Scotia, and New Brunswick. We have also a specimen from Hudson's Bay; but perhaps it is nowhere more plentiful than on the upper Missouri River, where we found its burrows

Plate II

N°1

Drawn from Nature by J.J. Audubon. F.R.S. F.L.S.

Drawn on Stone by W.E. Hitchcock.

Lith. Printed & Col.d By J.T. Bowen, Philad.a

Maryland Marmot. Woodchuck. Groundhog.

Old & Young

dug in the loamy soil adjoining the shores, as well as in the adjacent woods. It is not found in the maritime districts either of North or South Carolina, but exists very sparingly in the mountainous regions of those states. We have also traced it along the eastern range of the Rocky Mountains as far south as Texas. A Marmot exists in California resembling the present species very nearly, but which will probably prove distinct from the latter, a point which time and a greater number of specimens must determine.

General Remarks.

It will be observed that we have united *A. monax* with *A. empetra*, and have rejected the latter as a species. This must necessarily follow from the fact, that if there is but one species, the name *monax* having been first given, must be retained. SCHREBER appears to have committed the first error in describing from a young specimen of a variety of *A. monax* and erecting it into a new species. The old authors followed, and most of them being mere compilers, have constantly copied his errors. Mr. SABINE (Transactions Linn. Soc., vol. xiii., part 2, p. 584,) described a specimen existing in the British Museum, as *A. empetra*, which we, after a careful examination, consider only a variety of *A. monax*. Mr. SABINE's description of the latter species, is, as he informed us, compiled from various authors. Had he possessed a specimen, we think he would not have fallen into the common error. Dr. RICHARDSON, who appears not to have known the *A. monax*, also described it under the name of *A. empetra*, and gave a figure of it. We have, however, been unable to discover any specific differences between the specimens now before us and the one so accurately described and figured by him in the Fauna-boreali-Americana. We are, therefore, compelled to consider them all as identical.

The great varieties of colour to be observed in different specimens of this Marmot, together with the circumstance that no two of them are of the same size, have tended no doubt to confuse those who have described it. We have seen them of all colours, from black to brown, and from rufous to bluish-gray, although they are most frequently of the colour represented in the plate. We have received a specimen from an eminent British naturalish as *A. empetra*, obtained from Hudson's Bay, which does not differ from the present species, and which instead of being eleven inches in length, the size give to *A. empetra* measures fifteen. As RICHARDSON's species, moreover, was also from seventeen to twenty inches in length, and as we compared his specimen, (now in the museum of the Zoological Society of London,) with several specimens of the Maryland Marmot, without observing the least specific difference between them, we consider it necessary to strike off the Canada Marmot, or *Arctomys empetra*, from the North American Fauna.

From the short and very unsatisfactory description, and the wretched figure of the Bahama Coney, contained in CATESBY, vol. ii., p. 79, plate 79, it is very difficult to decide either on the species or genus which he intended to describe. As however nearly all our writers on natural history have quoted his Bahama Coney as referring to the Maryland Marmot, we have carefully compared his descriptions and figure with this species, and have arrived at the conclusion that CATESBY described and figured one of the species of jutia, (*Capromys Fournieri*, Desm.,) and that his *Cuniculus Bahamiensis* has been therefore erroneously quoted as a synonyme of *A. monax*.

Genus Lepus.—Linn.

Dental Formula.

$$\text{Incisive } \frac{4}{2}; \text{ Canine } \frac{0-0}{0-0}; \text{ Molar } \frac{6-6}{5-5} = 28.$$

Upper incisors in pairs, two in front large and grooved, and two immediately behind, small; lower incisors square; molars, with flat crowns, and transverse laminæ of enamel. Interior of the mouth and soles of the feet furnished with hair; ears and eyes large; fore-feet with five toes; hind-feet with only four; hind-legs very long; tail short; mammæ, from six to ten.

The word Lepus is derived from the Latin, *lepus*, and Greek Eolic, $\lambda\varepsilon\pi o\rho\iota\varsigma$, (*leporis*,) a hare.

There are about thirty known species of this genus, of which rather the largest number, (perhaps sixteen or seventeen species,) exist in North and South America; while the remainder belong to the Eastern continent.

Lepus Townsendii.—Bach.

Townsend's Rocky Mountain Hare.

Plate III.—Male and Female.—Natural size.

L. magnitudine, L. Americano par; auribus, cauda, cruribus tarsisque longissimis; supra diluti cinereus, infra albus.

Characters.

Size of the Northern hare, (L. Americanus:) ears, tails, legs, and tarsus, very long; colour above, light gray; beneath, white.

Synonymes.

LEPUS TOWNSENDII, Bach., Journal Acad. Nat. Sciences, Philadelphia, vol. viii., part 1, p. 90, pl. 2, (1839,) read Aug. 7, 1838.

Description.

Body, long and slender; head, much arched; eyes large; ears, long; tail very long, (compared with others of the genus,) in proportion to the size of the animal; legs long and slender; tarsus very long. The whole conformation of this animal is indicative of great speed.

Colour.

Crown of the head, cheeks, neck, whole upper parts, and the front of the ears and legs, externally, gray; with a faint cream-coloured tinge. Hair, on back and sides, whitish, or silver gray, at the roots, followed by brownish-white, which is succeeded by black, subdued gradually to a faint yellowish-white, and finally tipped with black, interspersed with long silky hairs, some of which are black from their roots. On the chin, throat, under surface, interior of legs, and the tail, (with the exception of a narrow dark line running longitudinally on the top,) the hair is pure white from the roots. Irides light hazel; around the eyes white; back part of the tips of the ears black; external two-thirds of the hinder part of the ears white, running down to the back part of the neck, and then blending with the colour of the upper surface; anterior third of the outer portion of the ear, the same gray colour as the back, fringed on the edge with long hairs, which are reddish fawn colour at the roots and white at the tips; interior of the ear very thinly covered with beautiful fine white hairs, being more thickly clothed near the edge, where it is grizzly-black and yellowish; edge, fringed with pure white, becoming yellowish toward the tip, and at the tip black. Moustaches for the most part white, black at the roots, a few hairs are pure white, others wholly black.

The specimen which was described and first published in the Transactions of the Academy of Natural Sciences of Philadelphia, was a female, procured by J.K. TOWNSEND, Esq., on the Walla-Walla, one of the sources of the Columbia river.

Another specimen now in our possession, the dimensions of which are given below, is in summer pelage, having been obtained on the 9th June. There is scarcely a shade of difference in its general colour, although the points of many of the hairs are yellowish-white, instead of being tipped with black, as in the specimen obtained by Mr. TOWNSEND. There is also a white spot on the forehead. The young is a miniature of the adult; We observe no other differences than that the colour is a little lighter, and the tail pure white.

Dimensions.

Adult Male, (killed on the Upper Missouri river.)

From nose to root of tail . . . . $21\frac{1}{2}$ inches.
Tail (vertebræ) . . . . $3\frac{3}{8}$ do.
Do., to end of hair . . . . $4\frac{3}{4}$ do.
Height of ear, posteriorly . . . . $5\frac{1}{2}$ do.
Length of head in a direct line . . . . $4\frac{5}{8}$ do.
"   "   following the curvature . . . . $5\frac{1}{4}$ do.
"   from heel to end of claw . . . . $5\frac{5}{8}$ do.

Weight, $6\frac{1}{2}$ pounds.

Adult Female, (shot by EDWARD HARRIS, Esq., on the 27th July, 1843.)

From nose to root of tail . . . . 21 inches.
Tail (vertebræ) . . . . 3 do.
Do., to end of hair . . . . $4\frac{1}{2}$ do.
Height of ear, posteriorly . . . . $5\frac{1}{4}$ do.
Between the eyes . . . . 2 do.

Plate III

Drawn from Nature by J J Audubon F.R.S F.L.S

Drawn on Stone by Wᵐ E. Hitchcock

Lith Printed & Colᵈ by J T Bowen Pᵃ.

Townsend's Rocky Mountain Hare

From nose to hind feet (stretched out)	36	do.
Height from foot to shoulder	$13\frac{1}{2}$	do.
Height to rump	14	do.

Young.

From nose to root of tail	12	inches.
Tail (vertebræ)	$1\frac{1}{4}$	do.
Do., to end of hair	$2\frac{1}{8}$	do.
Height of ear, posteriorly	$2\frac{5}{8}$	do.
Height from claw to shoulder	$7\frac{1}{8}$	do.
Length of head in a direct line	$2\frac{3}{4}$	do.
" " following the curve	$3\frac{3}{4}$	do.
" " from heel to end of claw	$3\frac{5}{8}$	do.

Habits.

We subjoin the following note, received from the original discoverer of this Hare, which contains some valuable information in regard to its habits:— "This species is common in the Rocky Mountains. I made particular inquiries both of the Indians and British traders, as to the changes it undergoes at different seasons, and they all agreed that it never was lighter coloured. We first saw it on the plains of the Blackfoot river, east of the mountains, and observed it in all similar situations during our route to the Columbia. When first seen, which was in July, it was lean and unsavory, having, like our common species, the larva of an insect imbedded in its neck; but when we arrived at Walla-Walla, in September, we found the Indians, and the persons attached to the fort, using it as a common article of food. Immediately after we arrived, we were regaled with a dish of hares, and I thought I had never eaten any thing more delicious. They are found in great numbers on the plains covered with wild wormwood, (Artemesia.) They are so exceedingly fleet that no ordinary dog can catch them. I have frequently surprised them in their forms, and shot them as they leaped away, but I found it necessary to be very expeditious and to pull trigger at a particular instant, or the game was off among the wormwood, and I never saw it again. The Indians kill them with arrows, by approaching them stealthily, as they lie concealed under the bushes; and in winter take them with nets. To do this, some one or two hundred Indians, men, women, and children, collect, and enclose a large space with a slight net, about five feet wide, made of hemp; the net is kept in a vertical position by pointed sticks attached to it and driven into the ground. These sticks are placed about five or six feet apart, and at each one an Indian is stationed, with a short club in his hand. After these arrangements are completed, a large number of Indians enter the circle, and beat the bushes in every direction. The frightened hares dart off towards the net, and in attempting to pass are knocked on the head and secured. Mr. PAMBRUN, the superintendent of Fort Walla-Walla, from whom I obtained this account, says that he has often participated in this sport with the Indians, and has known several hundred to be thus taken in a day. When captured alive it does not scream like the common gray rabbit, (L. Sylvaticus.)" "This Hare inhabits the plains exclusively, and seems particularly fond of the vicinity of the aromatic wormwood. Immediately as you leave these bushes, in journeying towards the sea, you lose sight of the Hare."

To the above account, we added some farther information on our last visit to the far West. On the 8th June, 1843, whilst our men were engaged in cutting wood and bringing it on board the steamer Omega, it being necessary in that wild region, to stop and cut wood for fuel for the boat every day, one of the crew started a young Hare, and after a short chase the poor thing squatted, and was killed by a blow with a stick. It proved to be the young of Lepus Townsendii, was large enough to have left its dam, weighed rather more than one pound, and was a beautiful specimen. Its irides were pure amber colour, and the eyes large; its hair was slightly curled. This Hare was captured more than twelve hundred miles east of the Rocky Mountains. On the next day, in the afternoon, one of the negro fire-tenders, being out with a rifle, shot two others, both old individuals; one of them was however cut in two by the ball, and left on the spot. The hair, or fur, of this individual was slightly curled, as in the young one, especially along the back and sides, but shortly after the skins had been prepared this character disappeared. These specimens are now in our collection.

Pursuing our journey up the tortuous and rapid stream, we had not the good fortune to see any more of these beautiful animals until after our arrival at FORT UNION, near the mouth of the Yellow Stone river, where we established ourselves for some time, by the kind permission of the gentlemen connected with the fur trade.

On the 29th of July, on our return from a buffalo-hunt, when we were some forty or fifty miles from the fort, suddenly a fine hare leaped from the grass before us, and stopped within twenty paces. Our friend, EDWARD HARRIS, Esq., was with us, but his gun was loaded with ball, and ours with large buck-shot, intended for killing antelopes; we fired at it, but missed: away it went, and ran around a hill, Mr. HARRIS followed, and its course being seen by Mr. BELL, who observed "Pussy," stealing carefully along, with her ears low down, trying to escape the quick eyes of her pursuers, the former gentleman came up to and shot her.

This species, like all others of the same family, is timid and fearful in the extreme. Its speed, we think, far surpasses that of the European hare, (L. timidus.)

If the form is indicative of character, this animal, from its slender body, long hind legs, and great length of tarsus, must be the fleetest of the hares of the West.

These hares generally place or construct their forms under a thick willow bush, or if at a distance from the water-courses on the banks of which those trees grow, or when they are in the open prairie, they place them under the edge of some rock, or seek the shelter of a stone, or large tuft of grass.

The Rocky Mountain Hare produces from four to six young in the year. As far as we have been able to ascertain, it has but one litter. The young suck and follow the dam for about six weeks, after which she turns them off, and leaves them to provide for themselves. The flesh of this species resembles in flavour that of the European hare, but is white, instead of dark-coloured, as is the case with the latter.

Geographical Distribution.

Although the entire geographical range of this species has not been well defined, yet it must be very considerable. It is found in great numbers, long ere the western traveller has passed the prairies, on the shores of the lower Missouri, and has a range of fifteen hundred miles east of the great Rocky Mountain Chain.

According to Mr. TOWNSEND, it is common on the Rocky Mountains, and exists in considerable numbers on the western side of that great chain; and if travellers have not confounded it with other species, it extends southwardly as far as Upper California.

The period may arrive when civilization shall have drawn wealth, and a large population, into these regions. Then will in all probability this poor hare be hunted by greyhounds, followed by gentlemen on horseback; and whilst the level plains of our vast prairies will afford both dogs and horsemen every opportunity of rapid pursuit, the great swiftness of this species will try their powers and test their speed to the utmost.

General Remarks.

We have, since this species was first described, had some misgivings in regard to its being entitled to the name by which we have designated it.

We had previously (Jour. Acad. Nat. Scien., vol. vii., part 2, p. 349, and vol. viii., part 1, p. 80,) described a species from the West, in its white winter colour, under the name of L. campestris. We had no other knowledge of its summer dress, than that given us by LEWIS and CLARKE. Being however informed by Mr. TOWNSEND, who possessed opportunities of seeing it in winter, that the present species never becomes white, we regarded it as distinct, and bestowed on it the above name. We have however been since assured by the residents of Missouri, that like the Northern hare, Lepus Townsendii assumes a white garb in winter, and it is therefore probable that the name will yet require to be changed to that of L. campestris. As, however, another hare exists on the prairies of the West, the specific characters of which have not yet been determined, we have concluded for the present to leave it as it stands, supposing it possible that the white winter colour may belong to another species. As we hope in a future volume to give a figure of the species in its white dress, we shall have an opportunity of correcting errors, should any on farther investigation be found to exist.

Genus Neotoma.—Say et Ord.

Dental Formala.

$$Incisive\ \frac{2}{2};\ Canine\ \frac{0—0}{0—0};\ Molar\ \frac{3—3}{3—3} = 16.$$

Messrs. SAY and ORD, who established this genus, having given an extended description of its teeth, &c., we shall present a portion of it in their own words.

"Molars, with profound radicles. *Superior jaw*—Incisors even and slightly rounded on their anterior face: first molar with five triangles, one of which is anterior, two exterior, and two interior. Second molar with four triangles; one anterior, two on the exterior side, and a very small one on the interior side: third molar with four triangles; one anterior, two exterior, and a very minute one, interior.

"*Inferior jaw*.—Incisors even, pointed at top: first molar with four divisions or triangles, one anterior, a little irregular, then one exterior, one interior opposite, and one posterior: second molar, with four triangles anterior and posterior, nearly similar in form, an intermediate one opposite to the interior and exterior one: third molar with two triangles, and an additional small angle on the inner side of the anterior one. Tail hairy; fore-feet, four toed, with an armed rudiment of a fifth toe: hind-feet, five toed.

Observations.

"The grinding surface of the molars differs somewhat from that of the molars of the genus ARVICOLA; but the large roots of the grinders constitute a character essentially different. The folds of enamel which make the sides of the crown, do not descend so low as to the edge of the alveolar processes; in consequence of this conformation, the worn down tooth of an old individual must exhibit insulated circles of enamel on the grinding surface."

Neotoma—Gr. νεος, (*neos*,) new; and τεμνω, (*temno*,) I cut or divide.

Two species of this genus have been described, both existing in North America.

Neotoma Floridana.—Say et Ord.

Florida Rat.

Plate iv.—Male, Female, and Young.—Natural size.

N. corpore robusto, plumbeo, quoad lineam dorsalem nigro mixto, facie et lateribus fusco-flavescentibus, infra albo; cauda corpore paullo curtiore, vellere molli

Characters.

Body robust, lead colour, mixed with black, on the dorsal line; face and sides ferruginous-yellow, beneath white, tail a little shorter than the body; fur soft.

Synonymes.

MUS FLORIDANUS, Ord, Nouv. Bull. de la Société Philomatique, 1818.
ARVICOLA FLORIDANUS, Harlan, Fauna Amer., p. 142.
    "   " Godman, Nat. Hist., vol. ii., p. 69.
Mus   " Say, Long's Expedition, vol. i., p. 54.
NEOTOMA FLORIDANA, Say et Ord, Journ. Acad. Nat. Sciences, Philadelphia, vol. iv., part 2, p. 352, figure.
NEOTOMA FLORIDANA, Griffiths, Animal Kingdom, vol. iii., p. 160, figure.

Description.

The form of our very common white-footed or field-mouse, (*Mus leucopus*,) may be regarded as a miniature of that of the present species; its body has an appearance of lightness and agility, bearing some resemblance to that of the squirrel; snout elongated; eyes large, resembling those of the common flying squirrel, (*P. volucella*;) ears large, prominent, thin, sub-ovate, clothed so thinly with fine hair as to appear naked; tail covered with soft hair; whiskers reaching to the ears; legs robust; toes annulate beneath; thumb, minute; in the palms of the fore-feet there are five tubercles, and in the soles of the hind-feet six, of which the three posterior are distant from each other; nails, concealed by hairs, which extend considerably beyond them; mammæ, two before, and four behind.

Colour.

The body and head are lead-colour, intermixed with yellowish and black hair; the black predominating on the ridge of the back and head, forming an indistinct dorsal line of dark brown, gradually fading away into the brownish-yellow colour of the cheeks and sides; border of the abdomen and throat, buff; whiskers, white and black; feet white; under surface of body, white, tinged with cream colour.

In a very young specimen, the colour is dark brown on the upper surface, and plumbeous beneath, differing so much from the adult, that the unpractised observer might easily be led to regard it as a new species.

Dimensions.

Adult Male.

From nose to root of tail	8 inches.
Length of tail	$5\frac{1}{8}$ do.
From fore-claws to hind-claws, when stretched	$13\frac{1}{4}$ do.
From nose to end of ears	$2\frac{1}{2}$ do.

Weight $7\frac{3}{4}$ ounces. Weight of an old Female, 8 ounces.

Young Male.

From nose to root of tail	$5\frac{1}{4}$ inches.
From fore-claws to hind-claws, when stretched	$8\frac{1}{2}$ do.
From nose to end of ear	$2\frac{3}{8}$ do.
Length of tail	$4\frac{1}{4}$ do.

Habits.

The specimens from which we drew the figures we have given on our plate, which represents this species in various ages and attitudes, on the branch of a pine tree, were obtained in South Carolina, and were preserved alive for several weeks, in cages having wire fronts. They made no attempt to gnaw their way out. On a previous occasion we preserved an old female with three young, (which latter were born in the cage, a few days after the mother had been captured,) for nearly a year; by which time the young had attained the size of the adult. We fed them on corn, potatoes, rice, and bread; as well as apples and other fruit. They seemed very fond of corn flour, (Indian meal,) and for several months subsisted on the acorns of the live oak, (*Quercus virens*.)

They became very gentle, especially one of them which was in a separate cage. It was our custom at dark to release it from confinement, upon which it would run around the room in circles, mount the table we were in the habit of writing at, and always make efforts to open a particular drawer, in which we kept some of its choicest food.

There are considerable differences in the habits of this species in various parts of the United States, and we hope the study of these peculiarities may interest our readers. In Florida, they burrow under stones and the ruins of dilapidated buildings. In Georgia and South Carolina they prefer remaining in the woods. In some swampy situation, in the vicinity of sluggish streams, amid tangled vines interspersed with leaves and long moss, they gather a heap of dry sticks, which they pile up into a conical, shape, and which, with grasses, mud, and dead leaves, mixed in by the wind and rain, form, as they proceed, a structure impervious to rain, and inaccessible to the wild-cat, racoon, or fox. At other times, their nest, composed of somewhat lighter materials, is placed in the fork (branch) of a tree.

About fifteen years ago, on a visit to the grave-yard of the Church at Ebenezer, Georgia, we were struck with the appearance of several very large nests near the tops of some tall evergreen oaks, (*Quercus aquaticus*;) on disturbing the nests, we discovered them to be inhabited by a number of Florida rats, of all sizes, some of which descended rapidly to the ground, whilst others escaped to the highest branches, where they were concealed among the leaves. These nests, in certain situations are of enormous size. We have observed some of them on trees, at a height of from ten to twenty feet from the ground, where wild vines had made a tangled mass over head, which appeared to be larger than a cart wheel, and contained a mass of leaves and sticks, that would have more than filled a barrel.

Those specimens, however, which we procured on our journey up the Missouri river, were all caught in the hollows of trees which were cut down by the crew, as we proceeded, for fuel for our steamer. LEWIS and CLARKE, in their memorable journey across the Rocky Mountain, found them nestling among clefts in the rocks, and also in hollow trees. In this region they appeared to be in the habit of feeding on the prickly pear, or Indian fig, (*Cactus opuntia*,) the travellers having found large quantities of seeds, and remnants of those plants, in their nests. In the Floridas, Mr. BARTRAM also found this species. He says, "they are singular, with respect to their ingenuity and great labour in the construction of their habitations, which are conical pyramids about three feet high, constructed with dry branches, which they collect with great labour and perseverance, and pile up without any apparent order; yet they are so interwoven with one another, that it would take a bear or wild cast some time to pull one of these castles to pieces, and allow the animals sufficient time to secure a retreat with their young."

This is a very active rat, and in ascending trees, exhibits much of the agility of the squirrel, although we do not recollect having observed it leaping from branch to branch in the manner of that genus.

The Florida rat is, in Carolina, a very harmless species; the only depredation we have known it to commit, was an occasional inroad on the corn-fields, when the grain was yet juicy and sweet. We have seen several whole ears of Indian corn taken from one of their nests, into which they had been dragged by these animals the previous night. They appear also to be very fond of the Chinquapin, (*Castania pumila,*) and we have sometimes observed around their nests traces of their having fed on frogs and cray-fish.

This species is nocturnal, or at least crepuscular, in its habits. In procuring specimens we were only successful when the traps had been set over night. Those we had in captivity scarcely ever left their dark chambers till after sunset, when they came forth from their dormitories, and continued playful and active during a great part of the night. They were mild in their dispositions, and much less disposed to bite when pursued than the common and more mischievous Norway rat.

Whilst the young are small, they cling to the teats of the mother, who runs about with them occasionally without much apparent inconvenience; and even when older, they still, when she is about to travel quickly, cling to her sides or to her back. Thus on a visit from home, she may be said to carry her little family with her, and is always ready to defend them even at the risk of her life. We once heard a gratifying and affecting anecdote of the attachment to its young, manifested by one of this species, which we will here relate as an evidence that in some cases we may learn a valuable lesson from the instincts of the brute creation.

Our friend, GAILLARD STONEY, Esq., sent us an old and a young Florida rat, obtained under the following circumstances. A terrier was seen in pursuit of a rat of this species, followed by two young, about a third grown. He had already killed one of these, when the mother sprang forward and seized the other in her mouth, although only a few feet from her relentless enemy—hastened through a fence which for a moment protected her, and retreated into her burrow. They were dug out of the ground, and sent to us alive. We observed that for many months the resting place of the young during the day was on the back of its mother.

From three to six are produced at a litter, by this species, which breeds generally twice a year; we have seen the young so frequently in March and August, that we are inclined to the belief that these are periods of their reproduction. We have never heard them making any other noise than a faint squeak, somewhat resembling that of the brown rat. The very playful

character of this species, its cleanly habits, its mild, prominent, and bright eyes; together with its fine form and easy susceptibility of domestication, would render it a far more interesting pet than many others that the caprice of man has from time to time induced him to select.

Geographical Distribution.

This species is very widely scattered through the country. It was brought from East Florida by Mr. ORD, in 1818, but not published until 1825. It was then supposed by him to be peculiar to Florida, and received its specific name from that circumstance. We had, however, obtained a number of specimens, both of this species and the cotton rat, (*Sigmodon hispidum,*) in 1816, in South Carolina, where they are very abundant. In Louisiana, Georgia, Alabama, Mississippi, Missouri, and the former States, it is a common species. Its numbers diminish greatly as we travel eastward. In North Carolina some specimens of it have been obtained. We observed a few nest among the valleys of the Virginia mountains; farther north we have not personally traced it, although we have somewhere heard it stated that one or two had been captured as far to the north as Maryland.

General Remarks.

On a farther examination of BARTRAM's work, which is also referred to by GODMAN, (Nat. Hist., vol. ii., p. 21,) we find his descriptions of the habits of this species very accurate; the first part of that article, however, quoted by Dr. GODMAN, is evidently incorrect. "The wood rat," says BARTRAM, "is a very curious animal; they are not half the size of the domestic rat, of a dark brown or black colour; thin tail, slender and shorter in proportion, and covered thinly with short hair." The error of BARTRAM, in describing one species, and applying to it the habits of another, seems to have escaped the observation of Dr. GODMAN. The cotton rat, or as it is generally called, wood rat, (*Sigmodon hispidum,*) answers this description of BARTRAM, in its size, colour, and tail; but it does not build "conical pyramids;" this is the work of a much larger and very different species—the Florida rat of this article.

The adoption of the genus NEOTOMA, when proposed by SAY and ORD, was met with considerable opposition by naturalists of that day, and some severe strictures were passed upon it by Drs. HARLAN and GODMAN, (See HARLAN, p. 143, GODMAN, vol. ii., p. 72.) They contended that the variations in the teeth that separated this species from *Mus* and *Arvicola*, were not sufficient to establish genuine distinctions.

More recently naturalists have, however, examined the subject calmly and considerately. It is certain that this genus cannot be arranged either under *Arvicola* or *Mus*, without enlarging the characters of one or the other of these genera. Another species, from the Rocky Mountains, has been discovered by Dr. RICHARDSON, (*Neotoma Drummondii,*) and we feel pretty confident that the genus will be generally adopted.

Genus Sciurus.—Linn., Erxleb., Cuv., Geoff., Illiger.

Dental Formula.

Incisive $\frac{2}{2}$; *Canine* $\frac{0-0}{0-0}$; *Molar* $\frac{4-4}{4-4}$ or $\frac{5-5}{4-4}$ = 20 or 22.

Body elongated; tail long and furnished with hairs; head large; ears erect; eyes projecting and brilliant; upper lip divided. Four toes before, with a tubercle covered by a blunt nail; five toes behind. The four grinders, on each side the mouth above and beneath, are variously tuberculated; a very small additional one in front, above, is in some species permanent, but in most cases drops out when the young have attained the age of from six to twelve weeks. Mammæ, eight; two pectoral, the others abdominal.

The squirrel is admirably adapted to a residence on trees, for which nature has designed it. Its fingers are long, slender and deeply cleft, and its nails very acute and greatly compressed; it is enabled to leap from branch to branch, and from tree to tree, clinging to the smallest twigs, and seldom missing its hold. When this happens to be the case, it has an instinctive habit of grasping in its descent at the first object which may present itself, or if about to fall to the earth, it spreads itself out in the manner of the flying squirrel, and thus by presenting a greater resistance to the air, is enabled to reach the ground without injury, and recover itself so instantaneously, that it often escapes the

teeth of the dog that watches its descent, and stands ready to seize upon it at the moment of its fall. It immediately ascends a neighbouring tree, emitting very frequently a querulous bark, which is either a note of fear or of triumph.

Although the squirrel moves with considerable activity on the ground, it rather runs than leaps; on trees, however, its activity and agility are surprising, and it is generally able to escape from its enemies, and conceal itself in a few moments, either among the thick foliage, in its nest, or in a hollow tree. The squirrel usually conveys its food to the mouth by the fore-paws. Nuts, and seeds of all kinds, are held by it between the rudimental thumbs and the inner portions of the palms. When disturbed or alarmed, it either drops the nut and makes a rapid retreat, or seizes it with the incisors, and carries it to its hole or nest.

All our American species of this genus, as far as we have been able to become acquainted with their habits, build their nests either in the fork of a tree, or on some secure portion of its branches. The nest is hemispherical in shape, and is composed of sticks, leaves, the bark of trees, and various kinds of mosses and lichens. In the vicinity of these nests, however, they have a still more secure retreat in some hollow tree, to which they retire in cold or in very wet weather, and where their first litter of young is generally produced.

Several species of squirrels collect and hide away food during the abundant season of autumn, to serve as a winter store. This hoard is composed of various kinds of walnuts and hickory nuts, chesnuts, chinquepins, acorns, corn, &c., which may be found in their vicinity. The species, however, that inhabit the Southern portions of the United States, where the ground is seldom covered

Drawn on Stone by W.ᵐ E. Hitchcock

Florida Rat.

Male, Female & Young of different ages

Drawn from Nature by J. J. Audubon, F.R.S. F.L.S

Lith Printed & Col.ᵈ by J.T. Bowen, Phil

with snow, and where they can always derive a precarious support from the seeds, insects, and worms, which they scratch up among the leaves, &c., are less provident in this respect; and of all our species, the chickaree, or Hudson's Bay squirrel, (*Sc. Hudsonius,*) is by far the most industrious, and lays up the greatest quantity of food.

In the spring, the squirrels shed their hair, which is replaced by a thinner and less furry coat; during summer their tails are narrower and less feathery than in autumn, when they either receive an entirely new coat, or a very great accession of fur; at this season also, the outer surfaces of the ears are more thickly and prominently clothed with fur than in the spring and summer.

Squirrels are notorious depredators on the Indian corn field of the farmer, in some portions of our country, consuming great quantities of this grain, and by tearing off the husks, exposing an immense number of the unripe ears to the mouldering influence of the dew and rain.

The usual note emitted by this genus is a kind of tremulous querulous bark, not very unlike the quacking of a duck. Although all our larger squirrels have shades of difference in their notes, which all enable the practised ear to designate the species even before they are seen, yet this difference cannot easily be described by words. Their bark seems to be the repetition of a syllable five or six times, quack-quack-quack-quack-qua-commencing low, gradually raising to a higher pitch, and ending with a drawl on the last letter in the syllable. The notes, however, of the smaller Hudson's Bay squirrel, and its kindred species existing on the Rocky Mountains, differ considerably from those of the larger squirrels; they are sharper, more rapidly uttered, and of longer continuance; seeming intermediate between the bark of the latter and the chipping calls of the ground-squirrels, (TAMIAS.) The barking of the squirrel may be heard occasionally in the forest during all hours of the day, but is uttered most frequently in the morning and afternoon. Any sudden noise in the woods, or the distant report of a gun, is almost certain, during fine weather, to be succeeded by the barking of the squirrel. This is either a note of playfulness or of love. Whilst barking it seats itself for a few moments on a branch of a tree, elevates its tail over its back towards the head, and bending the point backwards continues to jerk its body, and elevate and depress the tail at the repetition of each successive note. Like the mocking bird and the nightingale, however, the squirrel, very soon after he begins to sing, (for to his own ear, at least, his voice must be musical,) also commences skipping and dancing; he leaps playfully from bough to bough, sometimes pursuing a rival or his mate for a few moments, and then reiterating with renewed vigour his querulous and monotonous notes.

One of the most common habits of the squirrel is that of dodging around the tree when approached, and keeping on the opposite side, so as to completely baffle the hunter who is alone. Hence it is almost essential to the sportsman's success, that he should be accompanied by a second person, who, by walking slowly round the tree on which the squirrel has been seen, and beating the bushes, and making a good deal of noise, causes him to move to the side where the gunner is silently stationed, waiting for a view of him to fire. When a squirrel is seated on a branch, and fancies himself undiscovered, should some one approach, he immediately depresses his tail, and extending it along the branch behind him, presses his body so closely to the bark, that he frequently escapes the most practised eye. Notwithstanding the agility of these animals, man is not their only, nor even their most formidable enemy. The owl makes a frequent meal of those species which continue to seek their food late in the evening and early in the morning. Several species of hawks, especially the red-tailed, (*Buteo borealis,*) and the red-shouldered, (*Buteo lineatus,*) pounce upon them by day. The black snake, rattle snake, and other species of snakes, can secure them; and the ermine, the fox, and the wild cat, are incessantly exerting their sagacity in lessening their numbers.

The generic name Sciurus is derived from the Latin *sciurus,* a squirrel, and from the Greek, σκιουρος, (*skiouros,*) from σκια, (*skia,*) a shade, and ουρα, (*oura,*) a tail.

There are between sixty and seventy species of this genus known to authors; about twenty well determined species exist in North America.

Sciurus Richardsonii.—Bach.

Richardson's Columbian Squirrel.

Plate v.—Male and Female.—Natural size.

S. cauda corpore breviore, apice nigro; supra griseus, subtus sub-albidus, S. Hudsonico minor.

Characters.

Smaller than Sciurus Hudsonius; tail shorter than the body; rusty gray above, whitish beneath; extremity of the tail black.

Synonymes.

BROWN SQUIRREL, Lewis and Clarke, vol. iii., p. 37.
SCIURUS HUDSONIUS, var. B. Richardson, Fauna Boreali Americana, p. 190.
SCIURUS RICHARDSONII, Bachman, Proceedings, Zool. Soc., London, 1838, (read Aug. 14, 1838.)
SCIURUS RICHARDSONII, Bach., Mag. Nat. Hist., London, new series, 1839, p. 113.
         "   "   Bach., Silliman's Journal.

Description.

The upper incisors are small and of a light yellow colour; the lower are very thin and slender, and nearly white. The first or deciduous molar, as in all the smaller species of pine squirrel that we have examined, is wanting.

The body of this diminutive species is short, and does not present that appearance of lightness and agility which distinguishes the *Sciurus Hudsonius.* Head less elongated, forehead more arched, and nose a little more blunt, than in that species. Ears short; feet of moderate size; the third toe on the fore-feet, but slightly longer than the second; claws, compressed, arched, and acute; tail shorter than the body. Thumb nail broad, flat, and blunt.

Colour.

Fur on the back, dark plumbeous from the roots, tipped with rusty brown and black, giving it a rusty gray appearance. It is less rufous than *Sciurus Hudsonius,* and lighter coloured than *Sciurus Douglassii.* Feet, on their upper surface rufous; on the shoulders, forehead, ears, and along the thighs, there is a slight tinge of the same colour. Whiskers, (which are a little longer than the head,) black. The whole of the under surface, as well as a line around the eyes and a small patch above the nostrils, bluish-gray. The tail, for about one-half its length presents on the upper surface a dark rufous appearance, many of the hairs being nearly black, pointed with light rufous. At the extremity of the tail and along it for about an inch and three-quarters, the hairs are black, a few of them slightly tipped with rufous. Hind-feet, from the heel to the palms thickly clothed with short adpressed light-coloured hairs; palms naked. The sides are marked by a line of black, commencing at the shoulder and terminating abruptly on the flanks; this line is about two inches in length, and four lines wide.

Dimensions.

Length of head and body	$6\frac{1}{4}$	inches.
Tail (vertebræ)	$3\frac{3}{4}$	do.
Do., including fur	5	do.
Height of ear posteriorly	$\frac{3}{8}$	do.
Do., including fur	$\frac{5}{8}$	do.
Palm and middle fore-claw	$1\frac{3}{8}$	do.
Sole and middle hind-claw	$1\frac{7}{8}$	do.

Habits.

The only knowledge we have obtained of the habits of this species, is contained in a note from Mr. TOWNSEND, who obtained the specimen from which the above description was taken. He remarks: "It is evidently a distinct species. Its habits are very different from the *Sciurus Hudsonius.* It frequents the pine trees in the high ranges of the Rocky Mountains west of the Great Chain, feeding upon the seeds contained in the cones. These seeds are large and white, and contain a good deal of nutriment. The Indians eat a great quantity of them, and esteem them good.

"The note of this squirrel is a loud jarring chatter, very different from the noise of *Sciurus Hudsonius.* It is not at all shy, frequently coming down to the foot of the tree to reconnoitre the passenger, and scolding at him vociferously. It is, I think, a scarce species."

Geographical Distribution.

LEWIS and CLARKE speak of the "Brown Squirrel", as inhabiting the

Drawn on Stone by Wᵐ E. Hitchcock

Richardson's Columbian Squirrel

Drawn from Nature by J.J.Audubon,F.R.S.F.L.S   Lith. Printed & Colᵈ by J.T.Bowen, Phil

banks of the Columbia river. Our specimen is labelled, Rocky Mountains, Aug. 12, 1834. From Mr. TOWNSEND'S account, it exists on the mountains a little west of the highest ridge. It will be found no doubt to have an extensive range along those elevated regions.

In the Russian possessions to the Northward, it is replaced by the Downy Squirrel (*Sc. lanuginosus*,) and in the South, near the Californian Mountains, within the Territories of the United States, by another small species which we hope to present to our readers hereafter.

General Remarks.

The first account we have of this species is from LEWIS and CLARKE, who deposited a specimen in the Philadelphia Museum, where it still exists. We have compared this specimen with that brought by Mr. TOWNSEND, and find them identical. The description by LEWIS and CLARKE (vol. iii., p. 37) is very creditable to the close observation and accuracy of those early explorers of the untrodden snows of the Rocky Mountains and the valleys beyond, to Oregon.

"The small brown Squirrel," they say, "is a beautiful little animal, about the size and form of the red squirrel (*Sc. Hudsonius*) of the Atlantic States, and Western lakes. The tail is as long as the body and neck, and formed like that of the red squirrel; the eyes are black; the whiskers long and black, but not abundant; the back, sides, head, neck, and outer parts of the legs, are of a reddish brown; the throat, breast, belly, and inner parts of the legs, are of a pale red; the tail is a mixture of black and fox-coloured red, in which the black predominates in the middle, and the red on the edges and extremity. The hair of the body is almost half an inch long, and so fine and soft that it has the appearance of fur. The hair of the tail is coarser and double in length. This animal subsists chiefly on the seeds of various species of pine and is always found in the pine country."

Dr. RICHARDSON, who had not seen a specimen, copied in his excellent work, (*Fauna Boreali Americana*, p. 19,) the description of LEWIS and CLARKE, from which he supposed this species to be a mere variety of the *Sc. Hudsonius*. We had subsequently an opportunity of submitting a specimen to his inspection. When he immediately became convinced it was a different species.

The difference between these two species can indeed be detected at a glance by comparing specimens of each together. The present species, in addition to it's being a fourth smaller,—about the size of our little chipping squirrel (*Tamias Lysteri*)—has less of the reddish brown on the upper surface, and may always be distinguished from the other by the blackness of its tail at the extremity.

Genus Vulpes.—Cuv.

Dental Formula.

Incisive $\frac{6}{6}$; *Canine* $\frac{1-1}{1-1}$; *Molar* $\frac{6-6}{7-7}$ = 42.

Muzzle pointed; pupils of the eyes forming a vertical fissure; upper incisors less curved than in the genus CANIS. Tail, long, bushy, and cylindrical.

Animals of this genus, generally are smaller, and the number of species known, greater, than among the wolves; they diffuse a fœtid odour, dig burrows, and attack none but the weaker quadrupeds, or birds, &c.

The characters of this genus, differ so slightly from those of the genus CANIS, that we were induced to pause before removing it from the subgenus in which it had so long remained. As a general rule, we are obliged to admit that a large fox is a wolf, and a small wolf may be termed a fox. So inconveniently large, however, is the list of species in the old genus CANIS, that it is, we think, advisable to separate into distinct groups, such species as possess any characters different from the true Wolves.

Foxes, although occasionally seen abroad during the day, are noctural in their habits, and their character is marked by timidity, suspicion and cunning. Nearly the whole day is passed by the Fox in concealment, either in his burrow under ground, in the fissures of the rocks, or in the middle of some large fallen-tree-top, or thick pile of brush-wood, where he is well hidden from any passing enemy.

During the obscurity of late twilight, or in the darkness of night, he sallies forth in search of food; the acuteness of his organs of sight, of smell, and of hearing, enabling him in the most murky atmosphere, to trace and follow the footsteps of small quadrupeds or birds, and pounce upon the hare seated in her form, or the partridge, grouse, or turkey on their nests.

Various species of squirrels, field-rats, and moles, afford him a rich repast. He often causes great devastation in the poultry yard; seizes on the goose whilst grazing along the banks of the stream, or carries off the lamb from the side of its mother.

The cautious and wary character of the Fox, renders it exceedingly difficult to take him in a trap of any kind. He eludes the snares laid for him, and generally discovers and avoids the steel-trap, however carefully covered with brush-wood or grasses.

In the Northern States, such as Pennsylvania and New-York, and in New England, the rutting season of the Fox commences in the month of February. During this period he issues a succession of rapid yells, like the quick and sharp barking of a small dog. Gestation continues from 60 to 65 days. The cubs are from 5 to 9 in number, and like young puppies, are born with hair, and are blind at birth. They leave their burrows generally, when three or four months old, and in all predatory expeditions, each individual goes singly, and plunders on his own account, and for his own especial benefit.

The Generic name is derived from the Latin word *vulpes*, a Fox.

There are about twelve well-known species belonging to this Genus—four of which exist in North America.

Vulpes Fulvus.—Desm:
var. Decussalus.—Pennant.

AMERICAN CROSS FOX.

Plate vi.—Male.—$\frac{7}{8}$ Natural size.

V. cruce nigra supra humeros, subtus linea longitudinali nigra, auribus pedibusque nigris.

Characters.

A cross on the neck and shoulders, and a longitudinal stripe on the under surface, black; ears and feet black.

Synonymes.

RENARD BARRÉ, Tsinantontongue, Sagard Theodat., Canada, p. 745.
EUROPEAN CROSS FOX, var. B., Cross Fox, Pennant, Arct., Zool., vol. i., p. 46.
CANIS DECUSSATUS, Geoff., Coll. du Mus.
CANIS FULVUS, Sabine, Franklin's Journal, p. 656.
  "   "   var. B., (decussatus) Rich., Fauna Boreali Americana, p. 93.

Description.

Form, agrees in every particular with that of the common red fox, (*V. fulvus*.) Fur, rather thick and long, but not thicker or more elongated than in many specimens of the red fox that we have examined. Soles of the feet densely clothed with short woolly hair, so that the callous spots at the roots of the nails are scarcely visible. A black longitudinal stripe, more or less distinct, on the under surface.

Colour.

Front of the head, and back, dark gray; the hairs being black at the roots, yellowish white near the ends, and but slightly tipped with black; so that the light colour of the under part of each hair showing through, gives the surface a gray tint; with these hairs a few others are mixed that are black throughout their whole length.

The soft fur beneath these long hairs is of a brownish black. Inner surface of ears, and sides of the neck from the chin to the shoulders, pale reddish yellow; sides, behind the shoulders towards the top of the back, slightly ferruginous; under surface, to the thighs, haunches, and under part of the root of tail, pale ferruginous. Fur underneath the long hair, yellowish. Tail dark brown; fur beneath, reddish yellow; the long hairs, yellowish at base, broadly tipped with black; at the extremity of the tail a small tuft of white hair. Nose, outer surface of ear, chin, throat, and chest, black. A line along the under surface for

No. 2

Plate VI

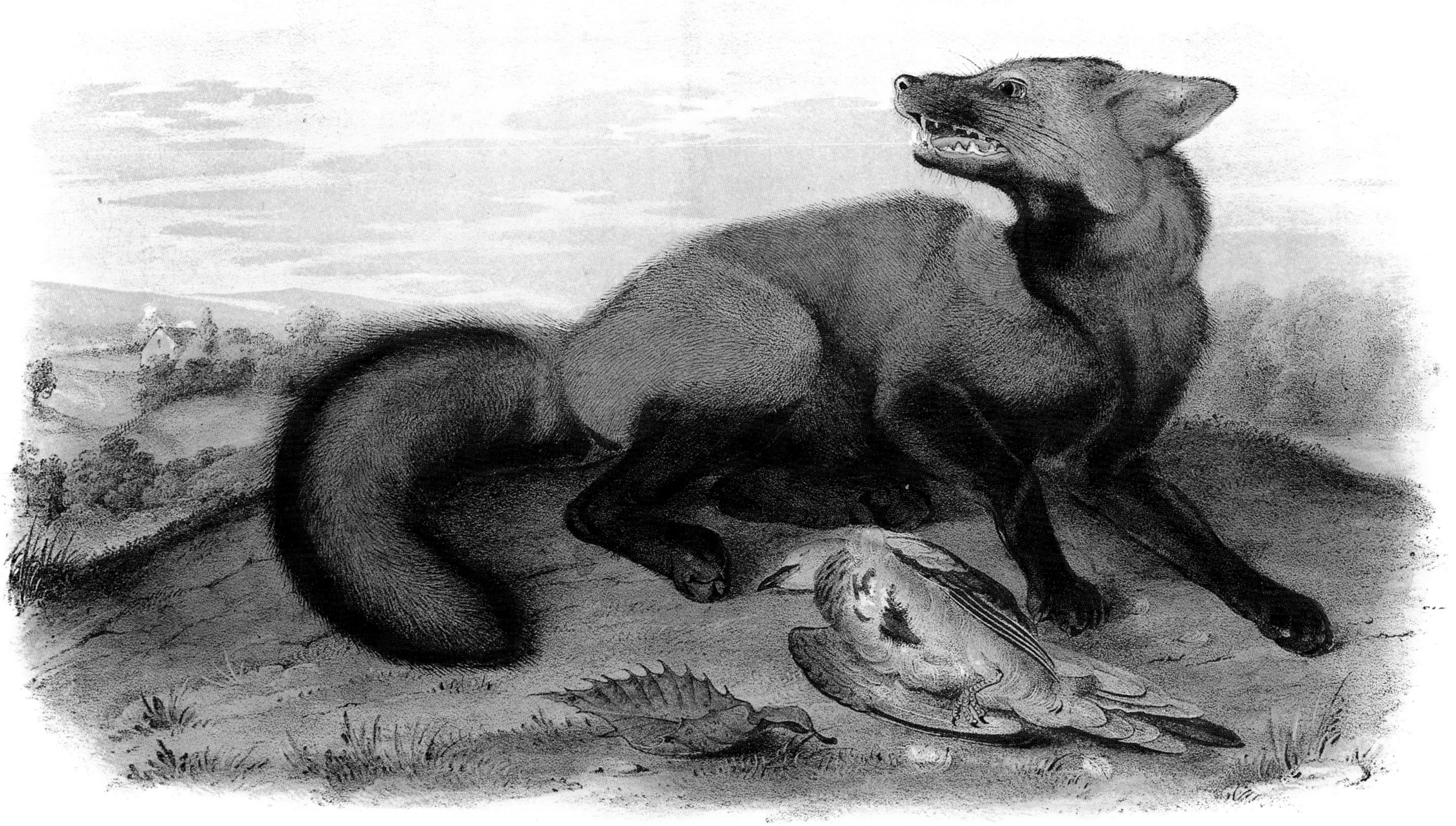

American Cross Fox

Drawn from Nature by J.J. Audubon F.R.S. F.L.S.

Printed by Nagel & Weingaertner N.Y.

half its length, and broadest at its termination, black; a few white hairs intermixed, but not a sufficient number to alter the general colour. The yellowish tint on each side of the neck and behind the shoulders, is divided by a longitudinal dark brown band on the back, crossed at right angles by another running over the shoulders and extending over the fore-legs, forming a cross. There is another cross, yet more distinctly marked, upon the chest; a black stripe, extending downward from the throat towards the belly, being intersected by another black line, which reaches over the chest from the inside of one fore-leg to the other. Hence, the name of this animal does not originate in its ill-nature, or by reason of its having any peculiarly savage propensity, as might be presumed, but from the singular markings we have just described.

Dimensions.

Adult Male.

From nose to root to tail . . . . $24\frac{1}{4}$ inches.
Tail (vertebræ) . . . . $12\frac{1}{2}$ do.
Tail, to end of hair . . . . 16 do.
From nose to end of ear . . . . 8 do.
   "   to eyes . . . . $2\frac{1}{2}$ do.
Weight, 14 pounds.

Habits.

In our youth we had opportunities whilst residing in the northern part of the State of New York, of acquiring some knowledge of the habits of the Fox, and many other animals, which then were abundant around us.

Within a few miles dwelt several neighbours who vied with each other in destroying foxes, and other predacious animals, and who kept a strict account of the number they captured or killed each season. As trappers, most of our neighbours were rather unsuccessful—the wary foxes, especially, seemed very soon, as our western hunters would say, to be "up to trap." Shooting them by star-light, from behind a hay-stack in the fields, when they had for sometime been baited and the snow covered the ground so that food was eagerly sought after by them, answered pretty well at first, but after a few had been shot at, the whole tribe of foxes—red, gray, cross, and black—appeared to be aware that safety was no longer to be expected in the vicinity of hay-stacks, and they all gave the latter a wide berth.

With the assistance of dogs, pick-axes, and spades, our friends were far more successful, and we think might have been considered adepts. We were invited to join them, which we did on a few occasions, but finding that our ideas of sport did not accord precisely with theirs, we gradually withdrew from this club of primitive fox-hunters. Each of these sportsmen was guided by his own "rules and regulations" in the "chase;" the horse was not brought into the field, nor do we remember any scarlet coats. Each hunter proceeded in the direction that to him seemed best—what he killed he kept—and he always took the shortest possible method he could devise, to obtain the fox's skin. He seldom carried a gun, but in lieu of it, on his shoulder was a pick-axe and a spade, and in his pocket a tinder box and steel.

A half-hound, being a stronger and swifter dog than the thorough bred, accompanied him, the true foxhound being too slow, and too noisy for his purpose; we remember one of these half-bred dogs, which was of great size and extraordinary fleetness; it was said to have a cross of the grey-hound.

In the fresh-fallen and deep snows of mid-winter, the hunters were most successful. During these severe snow storms, the ruffed grouse, (*Tetraoumbellus*,) called in our Eastern States the partridge, is often snowed up and covered over; or sometimes plunges from on wing into the soft snow, where it remains concealed for a day or two. The fox occasionally surprises these birds, and as he is usually stimulated at this inclement season by the gnawings of hunger, he is compelled to seek for food by day as well as by night; his fresh tracks may be seen in the fields, along the fences, and on the skirts of the farm-yard, as well as in the deep forest.

Nothing is easier than to track the Fox under these favourable circumstances, and the trail having been discovered, it is followed up, until Reynard is started. Now the chase begins; the half-hound yells out, in tones far removed from the mellow notes of the thorough-bred dog, but equally inspiriting perhaps, through the clear frosty air, as the solitary hunter eagerly follows, as fast as his limited powers of locomotion will admit. At intervals of three or four minutes, the sharp cry of the dog resounds, the Fox has no time to double and shuffle, the dog is at his heels almost, and speed, speed, is his only hope for life. Now the shrill baying of the hound becomes irregular; we may fancy he is at the throat of his victim; the hunter is far in the rear, toiling along the track which marks the course so well contested, but occasionally the voice of his dog softened by the distance, is borne on the wind to his ear. For a mile or two the Fox keeps ahead of his pursuer, but the latter has the longest

legs, and the snow impedes him less than it does poor Reynard; every bound and plunge into the snow, diminishes the distance between the fox and his relentless foe. Onward they rush through field, fence, brushwood, and open forest, the snow flying from bush and briar as they dart through the copse, or speed across the newly-cleared field. But this desperate race cannot last longer. The fox must gain his burrow, or some cavernous rock, or he dies. Alas! he has been lured too far away from his customary haunts and from his secure retreat, in search of prey, he is unable to reach his home; the dog is even now within a foot of his brush. One more desperate leap, and with a sudden snappish growl he turns upon his pursuer, and endeavours to defend himself with his sharp teeth. For a moment he resists the dog, but is almost instantly overcome. He is not killed, however, in the first onset; both dog and fox, are so fatigued that they now sit on their haunches facing each other, resting, panting, their tongues hanging out, and the foam from their lips dropping on the snow. After fiercely eyeing each other for a while, both become impatient—the former to seize his prey, and the latter to escape. At the first leap of the fox, the dog is upon him; with renewed vigour he seizes him by the throat, and does not loose his hold until the snow is stained with his blood, and he lies rumpled, draggled, with blood-shot eye, and frothy open mouth, a mangled carcass on the ground.

The hunter soon comes up: he has made several *short cuts*, guided by the baying of his hound; and striking the deep trail in the snow again, at a point much nearer to the scene of the death-struggle, he hurries toward the place where the last cry was heard, and pushes forward in a half run until he meets his dog, which on hearing his master approach, generally advances towards him, and leads the way to the place where he has achieved his victory.

We will now have another hunt, and pursue a Fox, that is within reach of his burrow when we let loose our dog upon him. We will suppose him "started;" with loud shouts we encourage our half-hound; he dashes away on the Fox's track, whilst the latter, with every muscle strained to the utmost, is shortening the distance between himself and his stronghold; increasing his speed with his renewed hopes of safety, he gains the entrance to his retreat, and throws himself headlong into it, rejoicing at his escape. Whilst yet panting for breath, he hears his foe barking at the entrance of his burrow, and flatters himself he is now beyond a peradventure safe. But perhaps we do injustice to his sagacity; he may have taken refuge in his hole, well aware of the possibility of his being attacked there—yet what better could he do? However this may be, he has escaped one enemy, by means of a swift pair of heels, and has only to dread the skill, perseverance, and invention of the hunter; who in time comes up, rigged out pretty much as we have already described him, with spade, pick-axe, flint and steel.

On arriving at the spot where the Fox has been (in select phrase) "holed," the sportsman surveys the place, and if it is on level ground, where he can use the spade, he throws off his coat, and prepares for his work with a determination to have "that" fox, and no mistake! He now cuts a long slender stick, which he inserts in the hole, to ascertain in what direction he shall dig the first pit. The edge or mouth of the burrow, is generally elevated a little above the adjacent surface of the ground, by the earth which the Fox has brought from within; and this slight embankment, serves to keep out the rain water, that might otherwise flow in from the vicinity in stormy weather.

The burrow at first inclines downward, for four or five feet, at an angle of about twenty-five degrees, it then inclines upward a little, which is an additional security against inundations, and is continued, at a depth of about three or four feet from the surface, until it reaches a point where it is divided into two or three galleries.

This dividing point the hunter discovers after sinking three or four pits—it is generally twenty or thirty feet from the entrance of the burrow. The excavation is now made larger, the earth and rubbish thrown out, the dog is placed in the hole thus laid open, and his aid is sought, to ascertain into which branch of the gallery the Fox has retreated. There are seldom any tortuous windings beyond the spot whence the galleries diverge—the Fox is not far off. The stick is again inserted, and either reaches him, and the hunter is made aware of his whereabouts, by his snapping at it and growling, which calls forth a yelp of fierce anxiety from the dog; or, as frequently happens, the Fox is heard digging for life, and making no contemptible progress through the earth. Should no rocks or large roots interfere, he is easily unearthed, and caught by the dog.

It however very frequently occurs, that the den of the Fox is situated on the mountain side; and that its winding galleries run beneath the enormous roots of some stately pine or oak; or it may be amongst huge masses of broken rock, in some fissure of too great depth to be sounded, and too contracted to be entered by man or dog. What is then to be done? Should a "dead-fall" be set at the mouth of the hole, the Fox will (unless the ground be frozen too hard,) dig another opening, and not go out by the old place of egress; place a steel-trap before it, and he will spring it without being caught. He will remain for days in his retreat, without once exposing himself to the danger of having a dog snapping at his nose, or a load of duck-shot whistling round his ears. Our hunter, however, is not much worried with such reflections as we have just made; he has already gathered an armful or two of dry wood, and perhaps some resinous knots, or bits of the bark of the pine-tree; he cuts up a portion into small pieces, pulls out his tinder-box, flint, and steel, and in a few moments a smart fire is lighted within the burrow; more wood is thrown on, the mass pushed further down the hole, and as soon as it begins to roar and blaze freely, the mouth is stopped with brush-wood covered with a few spadefuls of earth, and the den is speedily exhausted of pure air, and filled with smoke and noxious gases.

There is no escape for the Fox—an enemy worse than the dog or the gun, is destroying him; he dies a protracted, painful death by suffocation! In about an hour the entrance is uncovered, large volumes of smoke issue into the pure air, and when the hunter's eye can pierce through the dense smoky darkness of the interior, he may perhaps discern the poor Fox extended lifeless in the burrow, and may reach him with a stick. If not quite dead, the Fox is at least exhausted and insensible; this is sometimes the case, and the animal is then knocked on the head.

The number of Foxes taken by our neighbours, in the primitive mode of hunting them we have attempted to describe, was, as nearly as we can now recollect, about sixty every winter, or an average of nearly twenty killed by each hunter. After one or two seasons, the number of Foxes in that part of the country was sensibly diminished, although the settlements had not increased materially and the neighbourhood was at that time very wild.

At this time Pennant's marten (*Mustela Canadensis*) was not very scarce in Rensselaer county, and we had three different specimens brought to us to examine.

These, the people called Black Foxes. They were obtained by cutting down hollow trees, in which they were concealed, and to which their tracks on the snow directed the hunters.

We cannot now find any note, in regard to the number of Cross Foxes taken, as compared to the Red, Gray, and Black Foxes; about one-fourth of the whole number captured, however, were Gray Foxes, and we recollect but a single one that was perfectly black with the exception of a white tip at the end of its tail, like the specimen figured in Dr. GODMAN'S work.

On examining several packages of Fox skins at Montreal, we saw about four specimens only of the Cross Fox, and three of the Black Fox, in some three hundred skins. We were informed during our recent visit to the Upper Missouri country, that from fifty to one hundred skins of the Cross Fox were annually procured by the American Fur Company, from the hunters and Indians.

The specimen from which our drawing was made, was caught in a steel-trap, by one of its fore-feet, not far from the falls of Niagara, and was purchased by J. W. AUDUBON copy the proprietor and the "Museum"; kept there to gratify the curiosity of the travellers who visit the great Cataract.

In describing the habits of the Red Fox, (V. *Fulvus*,) which we trust to be able to do hereafter, we conceive that we shall have a further and better opportunity of giving the characteristics of the species of which this is a variety.

Dr. RICHARDSON (Fauna Boreali Americana, p. 93) adheres to the opinion of the Indians, who regard the Cross Fox of the fur traders as a mere variety of the Red Fox. He says, "I found on inquiry that the gradations of colour between characteristic specimens of the Cross and Red Fox, are so small that the hunters are often in doubt with respect to the proper denomination of a skin; and I was frequently told, "This is not a Cross Fox yet, but it is becoming so." It is worthy of remark, moreover, that the European Fox (Vulpes *vulgaris*) is subject to similar varieties, and that the "*Canis crucigera* of GESNER, differs from the latter animal in the same way that the American Cross Fox does from the red one." We have had several opportunities of examining C. *crucigera* in the museums of Europe, and regard it as a variety of the common European Fox, but it differs in many particulars from any variety of the American Red Fox that we have hitherto examined.

The Cross Fox is generally regarded as being more wary and swift of foot, than the Red Fox; with regard to its greater swiftness, we doubt the fact. We witnessed a trial of speed between the mongrel greyhound already referred to in this article, and a Red Fox, in the morning, and another between the same dog and a Cross Fox, about noon, on the same day. The former was taken after an hour's hard run in the snow, and the latter in half that time, which we accounted for from the fact that the Cross Fox was considerably the fattest, and from this circumstance became tired out very soon. We purchased from a country lad a specimen of the Cross Fox, in the flesh, which he told us he had caught with a common cur dog, in the snow, which was then a foot in depth.

In regard to the cunning of this variety, there may be some truth in the general opinion, but this can be accounted for on natural principles: the skin is

considered very valuable, and the animal is always regarded as a curiosity; hence the hunters make every endeavour to obtain one when seen, and it would not be surprising if a constant succession of attempts to capture it, together with the instinctive desire for self-preservation possessed by all animals, should sharpen its wits, and render it more cautious and wild than those species that are less frequently molested. We remember an instance of this kind, which we will here relate.

A Cross Fox, nearly black, was frequently seen in a particular cover. We offered what was in those days considered a high premium, for the animal in the flesh. The fox was accordingly chased, and shot at, by the farmers' boys in the neighbourhood. The autumn and winter passed away, nay, a whole year, and still the fox was going at large. It was at last regarded by some of the more credulous as possessing a charmed life, and it was thought that nothing but a silver ball could kill it. In the spring, we induced one of our servants to dig for the young Foxes that had been seen at the burrow which was known to be frequented by the Cross Fox. With an immense deal of labour and fatigue the young were dug out from the side of a hill; there were seven. Unfortunately we were obliged to leave home and did not return until after they had been given away, and were distributed about the neighbourhood.

Three were said to have been black, the rest were red. The blackest of the young whelps, was retained for us, and we frequently saw at the house of a neighbour, another of the litter, that was red, and differed in no respect from the common Red Fox. The older our little pet became, the less it grew like the Black, and the more like the Cross Fox. It was, very much to our regret, killed by a dog when about six months old, and as far as we can now recollect, was nearly of the colour of the specimen figured in our work.

The following autumn, we determined to try our hand, at procuring the enchanted fox which was the parent of these young varieties, as it could always be started in the same vicinity. We obtained a pair of fine fox-hounds, and gave chase. The dogs were young, and proved no match for the fox, which generally took a straight direction through several cleared fields, for five or six miles, after which it began winding and twisting among the hills, where the hounds on two occasions lost the scent and returned home.

On a third hunt, we took our stand near the corner of an old field, at a spot we had twice observed it to pass. It came at last, swingint its brush from side to side, and running with great rapidity, three-quarters of a mile ahead of the dogs, which were yet out of hearing.—A good aim removed the mysterious charm—We killed it with squirrel-shot, without the aid of a silver bullet. It was nearly jet-black, with the tip of the tail white. This fox was the female which had produced the young of the previous spring that we have just spoken of; and as some of them, as we have already said, were Cross Foxes and others Red Foxes, this has settled the question in our minds, that both the Cross Fox and the Black Fox are mere varieties of the Red.

J. W. AUDUBON brought the specimen he obtained at Niagara, alive to New York, where it was kept for six or seven weeks. If fed on meat of various kinds: it was easily exasperated, having been much teased on its way from the Falls. It usually laid down in the box in which it was confined, with its head toward the front, and its bright eyes constantly looking upward, and forward, at all intruders. Sometimes, during the night, it would bark like a dog, and frequently, during the day, its movements corresponded with those of the latter animal. It could not bear the sun-light shining into its prison, and continued shy and snappish to the last.

The fur of the Cross Fox was formerly in great demand; a single skin sometimes selling for twenty-five dollars; at present, however, it is said not to be worth more than about three times the price of that of the Red Fox.

Geographical Distribution.

This variety seems to originate only in cold climates; hence we have not heard of it in the southern parts of the States of New York and Pennsylvania, nor farther to the South. In the northern portions of the State of New York, in New Hampshire, Maine, and in Canada, it is occasionally met with, in locations where the Red Fox is common. It also exists in Nova Scotia and Labrador. There is a Cross Fox on the Rocky Mountains, but we are not yet satisfied that it will eventually prove to be this variety.

General Remarks.

The animal referred to by SAGARD THEODAT, in his History of Canada, under the name of Renard Barré, Tsinantontongue, was evidently this variety. PENNANT probably also referred to it, (vol. i., p. 46,) although he blended it with the European V. *Crucigera* of GESNER, and the *Korsraef* of the Swedes. GEOFF (Collect. du Mus.) described and named it as a true species. DESMAREST (Mamm., p. 203, 308) and CUVIER (Dict. des Sc. Nat., vol. viii., p. 566) adopted his views. It is given under this name by SABINE

(Franklin's Journ., p. 656.) HARLAN (Fauna, p. 88) published it as a distinct species, on the authority and in the words of DESMAREST. GODMAN, who gave the Black or Silver Fox (*A. argentatus*) as a true species, seemed doubtful whether the Cross Fox might not prove a "mule between the Black and Red Fox." RICHARDSON, under the name of the American Cross Fox finally described it as a mere variety of the Red Fox.

We possess a hunter's skin, which we obtained whilst on the Upper Missouri, that differs greatly from the one we have described, in its size, markings, and the texture of its fur. The body, from point of nose to root of tail, is 33 inches long; tail to end of fur 18½; the skin is probably stretched beyond the natural size of the animal; but the tail, which is very large in circumference, is, we think, of its proper dimensions. The hair is long, being on the neck, sides, and tail, five inches in length; the under fur, which is peculiarly soft, is three inches long. There is scarcely a vestige of the yellowish-brown of our other specimen, on the whole body; but the corresponding parts are gray. The tail is irregularly clouded, and banded, the tip for three inches white. The colour of the remaining portions of the body does not differ very widely from the specimen we have described. The ears, nose, and paws of this specimen (as in most hunters' skins) are wanting. It is not impossible that this may be a variety of a *larger species* of Red Fox, referred to by LEWIS and CLARKE, as existing on both sides of the Rocky Mountains.

Sciurus Carolinensis.—Gmel.

Carolina Gray Squirrel.

Plate VII.—Male and Female.—Natural size.

S. griseus supra, subtus albus, colorem haud mutaris, S. migratorii, minor. Cauda corpore breviore, S. migratorii angustiore.

Characters.

Smaller than the Northern Gray Squirrel, (Sciurus Migratorius,) tail narrower than in that species, and shorter than the body; above, rusty gray; beneath, white; does not vary in colour.

Synonymes.

ECUREUIL GRIS DE LA CAROLINE, Bosc., vol. ii., p. 96, pl. 29.
SCIURUS CAROLINENSIS, Bach., Monog., Proceedings Zool. Soc., London, August, 1838. Mag., Nat. Hist., 1839, p. 113.

Description.

This species, which has been many years known, and frequently described, has been always considered by authors as identical with the Gray Squirrel of the Northern States, (*Sciurus migratorius.*) There are, however, so many marked differences, in size, colour, and habit, that any student of nature can easily perceive the distinction between these two allied species.

Head shorter, and space between the ears proportionately broader than between those of the Northern Gray Squirrel; nose sharper than in that animal. Small, anterior molar, in the upper jaw, permanent, (as we have invariably found it to exist in all the specimens we have examined;) it is considerably larger than in *S. migratorius*, and all our specimens which give indications of the individual having been more than a year old when killed, instead of having a small, thread-like, single tooth, as in the latter species, have a distinct double tooth, with a double crown. The other molars are not much unlike those of *S. migratorius* in form, but are shorter and smaller,—the upper incisors being nearly a third shorter.

Body, shorter and less elegant in shape, and not indicating the quickness and vivacity by which *S. migratorius* is eminently distinguished.

The ears, which are nearly triangular, are so slightly clothed with hair on their interior surfaces, that they may be said to be nearly naked; externally they are sparsely clothed with short woolly hair, which, however does not extend as far beyond the margins as in other species. Nails shorter and less crooked; tail, shorter, and without the broad distichous appearance of that of the Northern Gray Squirrel.

Colour.

Teeth, light orange; nails, brown, lightest at the extremities; whiskers, black; on the nose and cheeks, and around the eyes, a slight tinge of rufous gray.

Fur on the back, for three-fourths of its length, dark plumbeous, succeeded by a slight indication of black, edged with yellowish-brown in some of the hairs, giving it on the surface a dark grayish-yellow tint. In a few specimens there is an obscure shade of light brown along the sides, where the yellowish tint predominates, and a tinge of this colour is observable on the upper surface of the fore-legs, above the knees. Feet, light gray; tail, for three-fourths of its length from the root yellowish-brown; the remainder, black, edged with white; throat, inner surface of the legs, and belly, white.

This species does not run into varieties, as do the Northern Gray Squirrel, and the Black Squirrel; the specimens received from Alabama, Florida, and Louisiana, scarcely present a shade of difference from those existing in South Carolina, which we have just described.

Dimensions.

Length of head and body	9½	inches.
" tail (vertebræ)	7⅓	do.
" " to end of hair	9½	do.
Height of ear	½	do.
Palm to end of middle claw	1¼	do.
Heel to end of middle nail	2½	do.
Length of fur on the back	½	do.
Breadth of tail (with hair extended)	3	do.

Habits.

This species differs as much in its habits from the Northern Gray Squirrel, as it does in form and colour. From an intimate acquaintance with the habits of the latter, we are particularly impressed with the peculiarities of the present species. Its bark has not the depth of tone of that of the Northern species, and is more shrill and querulous. Instead of mounting high on the tree when alarmed, which the latter always does, the *Sc. Carolinensis* generally plays round the trunk, and on the side opposite to the observer, at a height of some twenty or thirty feet, often concealing itself beneath the Spanish moss (*Tillandsia Usneoides*) which hangs about the tree. When a person, who has alarmed one of these Squirrels, remains quiet for a few moments, it descends a few feet, and seats itself on the first convenient branch, in order the better to observe his movements.

It is, however, capable of climbing to the extremity of the branches, and leaping from tree to tree with great agility, but is less wild than the Northern species, and is almost as easily approached as the chickaree, (*Sc. Hudsonius.*) One who is desirous of obtaining a specimen, has only to take a seat for half an hour in any of the swamps of Carolina, and he will be surprised at the immense number of these squirrels that may be seen running along the logs or leaping among the surrounding trees. A great many are killed, and their flesh is both juicy and tender.

The Carolina Gray Squirrel is sometimes seen on high grounds, among the oak and hickory trees, although its usual haunts are low swampy places, or trees overhanging streams, or growing near the margin of some river. In deep cypress swamps, covered in many places with several feet of water during the whole year, it takes up its constant residence, moving among the entwined branches of the dense forest with great facility. Its hole, in such situations may sometimes be found in the trunk of a decayed cypress. On the large tupelo trees, (*Nyssa aquatica*,) which are found in the swamps, many nests of this species, composed principally of Spanish moss and leaves, are every where to be seen. In these nests, or in some woodpecker's hole, they produce their young. These are five or six in number, and are brought forth in March; it is well ascertained also that the female litters a second time in the season,

Drawn on Stone by Wᵐ E Hitchcock

Carolina Grey Squirrel.

Male & Female.

Drawn from Nature by J J Audubon, F R S F L S

Lith Printed & Colᵈ by J T Bowen, Phil

probably about mid-summer.

This species has one peculiarity which we have not observed in any other. It is in some degree, nocturnal, or at least crepuscular, in its habits. In riding along by-paths through the woods, long after sunset, we are often startled by the barking of this little Squirrel, as it scratches among the leaves, or leaps from tree to tree, scattering over the earth the seeds of the maple, &c., which are shaken off from the uppermost branches, as it passes over them.

This species is seldom, if ever, seen in company with the Fox Squirrel, (*Sc. Capistratus*,) or even found in the same neighbourhood; this arises, probably, not so much from any antipathy to each other, as from the fact that very different localities are congenial to the peculiar habits of each.

We have observed the Carolina Gray Squirrel on several occasions by moonlight, as actively engaged as the Flying Squirrel usually is in the evening, and this propensity to prolong its search after food, or its playful gambols, until the light of day is succeeded by the moon's pale gleams, causes it frequently to fall a prey to the Virginian owl, or the barred owl; which last especially, is very abundant in the swamps of Carolina, where, gliding on noiseless pinions between the leafy branches, it seizes the luckless Squirrel ere it is aware of its danger, or can make the slightest attempt to escape. The gray fox and the wild cat often surprise this and other species by stratagem or stealth. We have beheld the prowling lynx, concealed in a heap of brushwood near an old log, or near the foot of a tree frequented by the Squirrel he hopes to capture. For hours together will he lie thus in ambush, and should the unsuspicious creature pass within a few feet of him, he pounces on it with a sudden spring, and rarely fails to secure it.

Several species of snakes, the rattle-snake, (*Crotalus durassus*,) black snake, (*Coluber constrictor*,) and the chicken snake, (*coluber quadrivittatus*,) for instance, have been found, on being killed, to have a Squirrel in their stomach, and the fact that Squirrels, birds, &c., although possessing great activity and agility, constitute a portion of the food of these reptiles, being well established, the manner in which the sluggish serpent catches animals so far exceeding him in speed, and some of them endowed with the power of rising from the earth, and skimming away with a few flaps of their wings, has been the subject of much speculation. Some persons have attributed a mysterious power, more especially to the rattle-snake and black snake—we mean the power of *fascinating*, or as it is commonly called, *charming*.

This supposed faculty of the serpent has, however, not been accounted for. The basilisk of the ancients killed by a look; the eye of the rattle-snake is supposed so to paralyze, and at the same time attract, its intended prey, that the animal slowly approaches, going through an infinite variety of motions, alternately advancing and retreating, until it finally falls powerless into the open jaws of its devourer.

As long as we are able to explain by natural deductions, the very singular manœuvres of birds and squirrels, when "fascinated" by a snake, it would be absurd to imagine that anything mysterious or supernatural is connected with the subject; and we consider that there are many ways of accounting for all the appearances described on these occasions. Fear and surprise cause an instinctive horror, when we find ourselves unexpectedly within a foot or two of a rattle-snake; the shrill, startling, noise proceeding from the rattles of its tail, as it vibrates rapidly, and its hideous aspect, no doubt produce a much greater effect on birds and small quadrupeds. It is said that the distant roar of the African lion causes the oxen to tremble, and stand paralyzed in the fields; and HUMBOLDT relates that in the forests of South America, the mingled cries of monkeys and other animals resound through the whole night, but as soon as the roar of the jaguar, the American tiger, is heard, terror seizes on all the other animals, and their voices are suddenly hushed. Birds and quadrupeds are very curious, also, and this feeling prompts them to draw near to strange objects. "Tolling" wild ducks and loons, as it is called, by waving a red handkerchief or a small flag, or by causing a little dog to bound backward and forward on the beach, has long been successfully practised by sportsmen on the Chesapeake Bay, and elsewhere.

The Indians attract the reindeer, the antelope, and other animals, until they are within bow-shot, by waving a stick to which a piece of red cloth is attached, or by throwing themselves on their backs, and kicking their heels up in the air. If any strange object is thrown into the poultry-yard, such as a stuffed specimen of a quadruped or bird, &c., all the fowls will crowd near it, and scrutinize it for a long time. Every body almost, may have observed at some time or other dozens of birds collected around a common cat in a shrubbery, a tortoise, or particularly a snake. The Squirrel is remarkable for its fondness for "sights," and will sometimes come down from the highest branch of a tree to within three feet of the ground, to take a view of a small scarlet snake, (*Rhinostoma coccinea*,) not much larger than a pipe-stem, and which, having no poisonous fangs, could scarcely master a grasshopper. This might be regarded by believers in the fascinating powers of snakes, as a decided case in

favour of their theories, but they would find it somewhat difficult to explain the following circumstances which happened to ourselves. After observing a Squirrel come down to inspect one of the beautiful little snakes we have just been speaking of, the reptile being a rare species, was captured and secured in our carriage box. After we had driven off, we recollected that in our anxiety to secure the snake, we had left our box of botanical specimens at the place where we had first seen the latter, and on returning for it, we once more saw the Squirrel, darting backward and forward, and skipping round the root of the tree, eyeing with equal curiosity the article we had left behind, and we could not help making the reflection, that if the little snake had "charmed" the Squirrel, the same "fascinating" influence was exercised by our tin box!

Quadrupeds and birds have certain antipathies, they are capable of experiencing many of the feelings that appertain to mankind; they are susceptible of passion, are sometimes spiteful and revengeful, and are wise enough to know their "natural enemies," without a formal introduction. The blue jay, brown thrush, white-eyed fly-catcher, and other little birds are often to be heard scolding, and fluttering about a thicket, in which some animal is concealed; and on going to examine into the cause of their unwonted excitement, you will probably see a wild cat or fox spring forth from the covert. Every one familiar with the habits of our feathered tribes must have seen at times the owl or buzzard chased by the smallest birds, which unite on such occasions for the purpose of driving off a common enemy; in these cases, the birds sometimes approach too near, and are seized by the owl. We once observed some night-hawks (*Chordeiles Virginianus*) darting round a tree upon which an owl was perched. Whilst looking on, we perceived the owl make a sudden movement, and found that he had caught one of them in his sharp claws, and notwithstanding the cries and menaces of the others, he instantly devoured it.

Birds dart in the same manner at snakes, and no doubt are often caught by passing too near—shall we, therefore, conclude that they are fascinated?

One of the most powerful "attractions" which remain to be considered, is the love of offspring. This feeling, which is so deeply rooted in the system of nature, as to be a rule, almost without an exception, is manifested strongly by birds and quadrupeds; and snakes are among the most to be dreaded destroyers of eggs and young birds, and of the young of small species of viviparous animals; is it not likely therefore, that many of the (supposed) cases of fascination that are related, may be referred to the intrepidity of the animals or birds, manifested in trying to defend their young, or drive away their enemy from their vicinity? In our work, the "Birds of America," we represented a mocking-bird's nest attacked by a rattle-snake, and the nest of a red thrush invaded by a black snake; these two plates each exhibit several birds assisting the pair whose nest has been robbed by the snake, and also show the mocking-bird and thrush courageously advancing to the jaws even of their enemy. These pictures were drawn after the actual occurrence before our eyes, of the scenes which we endeavoured to represent in them, and supposing a person but little acquainted with natural history, to have seen the birds, as we did, he might readily have fancied that some of them at least were fascinated, as he could not probably have been near enough to mark the angry expression of their eyes, and see their well-concealed nest.

Our readers will, we trust, excuse us for detaining them yet a little longer on this subject, as we have more to say of the habits of the rattle-snake, in connexion with the subject we are upon.

This snake, the most venomous known in North America, subsists wholly on animal food; it digests its food slowly, and is able to exist without any sustenance for months, or even years, in confinement; during this time it often increases in size, and the number of its rattles is augmented. In its natural state it feeds on rabbits, squirrels, rats, birds, or any other small animals that may come in its way. It captures its prey by lying in wait for it, and we have heard of an instance, in which one of these snakes remained coiled up for two days before the mouth of the burrow of the Florida rat, (*Neotoma Floridana*,) and on its being killed it was found to have swallowed one of these quadrupeds.

As far as we have been able to ascertain, it always strikes its intended prey with its fangs, and thus kills it, before swallowing it. The bite is sudden, and although the victim may run a few yards after it is struck, the serpent easily finds it when dead. Generally the common species of rattle-snake refuses all food when in a cage, but occasionally one is found that does not refuse to eat whilst in captivity. When a rat is turned loose in a cage with one of these snakes, it does not immediately kill it, but often leaves it unmolested for days and weeks together. When, however, the reptile, prompted either by irritation or hunger, designs to kill the animal, it lies in wait for it, cat-like, or gently crawls up to it, and suddenly gives it the mortal blow, after which, it very slowly and deliberately turns it over into a proper position, and finally swallows it.

We have seen a rattle-snake, in a very large cage, using every means within its power, and exerting its cunning, for a whole month, before it could succeed in capturing a brown thrush, that was imprisoned with it. At night the bird roosted beyond the reach of the snake, and during the day-time it was too cautious in its movements, and too agile, snatching up its food at intervals, and flying instantly back to its perch, to be struck by the unwieldy serpent. We now added a mouse to the number of the inmates of the cage; the affrighted animal retreated to a corner, where the snake, slowly crawling up to it, with a sudden blow darted his fangs into and killed it; soon after which he swallowed it. About a week after this adventure, the snake again resumed his attempts to capture the thrush, and pursued it all round the cage.

This experiment offered a fair opportunity for the rattle-snake to exert its powers of fascination, had it possessed any; but as it did not exhibit them, we do not hesitate to say that it was entirely destitute of any faculty of the kind.

After some hours' fruitless manœuvring, the snake coiled itself up, near the cup of water from which the bird drank. For two days the thrush avoided the water; on the third, having become very thirsty, it showed a constant desire to approach the cup; the snake waited for it to come within reach, and in the course of the day struck at it two or three times, the bird darted out of its way, however, and was not killed until the next day.

If, notwithstanding these facts, it is argued, that the mysterious and inexplicable power of *fascination* is possessed by the snake, because birds have been seen to approach it, and with open wings and plaintive voice, seemed to wait upon its appetite, we must be prepared to admit that the same faculty is possessed by other animals. On a certain day, we saw a mocking-bird, exhibiting every appearance, usually, according to descriptions, witnessed when birds are under the influence of fascination. It approached a hog, which was occupied in munching something at the foot of a small cedar. The bird fluttered before the grunter with open wings, uttered a low and plaintive note,

alighted on his back, and finally began to peck at his snout. On examining into the cause of these strange proceedings, we ascertained that the mocking-bird had a nest in the tree, from which several of her younglings had fallen, which the hog was eating! Our friend, the late Dr. WRIGHT, of Troy, informed us that he witnessed a nearly similar scene between a cat-bird and a dog which had disturbed her brood, on which occasion the cat-bird went through many of the movements generally ascribed to the effect of fascination.

Geographical Distribution.

We have received a specimen of this Squirrel, which was procured in the market at New Orleans, where it is said to be exceedingly rare. We have not traced it farther to the South. It is the most abundant species in Florida, Georgia, and South Carolina. We have seen it in the swamps of North Carolina, but have no positive evidence that it extends farther to the northward than that State. We have obtained it in Alabama, and in Mississippi we are told it is found in the swamps. Nothing has been heard of it west of the Mississippi river.

General Remarks.

This species was first described by GMELIN, and afterwards noticed and figured by Bosc. The descriptions in HARLAN, GODMAN, and all other authors who have described this species under the name of *Sciurus Carolinensis*, refer to the *Northern Gray Squirrel*. We believe we were the first to observe and point out the distinctive characters which separate the present species from *S. migratorius*, the Gray Squirrel of the North.

Genus Tamias.—Illiger.

Incisive $\frac{2}{2}$; *Canine* $\frac{0}{0}$; *Molar* $\frac{5-5}{4-4} = 22$.

Upper incisors, smooth; lower ones, compressed and sharp; molars, with short, tuberculous crowns.

Nose, pointed; lip, cloven; ears, round, short, not tufted or fringed; cheek-pouches, ample.

Tail, shorter than the body, hairy, sub-distichous, somewhat tapering. Mammæ exposed; feet, distinct, ambulatory; fore-feet, four toed, with a minute blunt nail in place of a thumb; hind-feet five toed; claws, hooked.

This genus differs from SCIURUS in several important particulars. The various species that have been discovered, have all the same characteristics, and strongly resemble each other in form, in their peculiar markings, and in their habits. In form they differ from the true squirrels, and approach nearer to the spermophiles; they have a sharp, convex, nose, adapted to digging in the earth; they have longer heads, and their ears are placed farther back than those of the former. They have a more slender body and shorter extremities. Their ears are rounded, without any tufts on the borders or behind them. They have cheek-pouches, of which all squirrels are destitute; their tails are roundish, narrow, seldom turned up, and only sub-distichous.

The species belonging to this genus are of small size, and are all longitudinally striped on the back and sides.

Their notes are very peculiar; they emit a chipping clucking sound differing very widely from the quacking chattering cry of the squirrels.

They do not mount trees unless driven to them from necessity, but dig burrows, and spend their nights and the season of winter under ground.

They are, however, more closely related to the squirrels than to the spermophiles. The third toe from the inner side is slightly the longest, as in the former; whilst in the latter, the second is longest, as in the marmots. The genus TAMIAS is therefore nearly allied to the squirrels, whilst the spermophiles approach the marmots.

Authentic species of the genus SCIURUS are already very numerous, and as we have now a number of species, to which constant additions are making by the explorers of our Western regions, which by their cheek-pouches, their markings, and habits, can be advantageously separated from that genus, no doubt naturalists will arrange them in the genus TAMIAS.

When this genus was first established by ILLIGER, but a single species was satisfactorily known, and naturalists were unwilling to separate it from the squirrels, to which it bore so strong an affinity; but we are now, however, acquainted with six species, and doubt not that a few more years of investigation will add considerably to this number. We have consequently adopted the genus TAMIAS of that author.

The word Tamias is derived from the Greek Ταμιας, (*tamias*,) a keeper of stores—in reference to its cheek-pouches.

One species of this genus exists in the Northern portions of the Eastern continent; four in North, and one in South, America. We also possess an undescribed species, the habitat of which is at present unknown to us.

Tamias Lysteri.—Ray.

Chipping Squirrel, Hackee, &c.

Plate VIII.—Male, Female, and Young
(First Autumn.)—Natural size.

T. dorso fusco-cinereo, striis quinque nigris, et duobus luteo-albis longitudinalibus ornato; fronte et natibus fusco-luteis; ventre albo.

Characters.

Brownish gray on the back; forehead and buttocks brownish orange; five longitudinal black stripes, and two yellowish white ones, on the back; under surface, white.

Synonymes.

ECUREUIL SUISSE, Sagard Theodat, Canada, p. 746, A. D. 1636.
GROUND SQUIRREL, Lawson's Carolina, p. 124.
  "   "   Catesby, Carol. vol. ii., p. 75.
EDWARDS, vol. iv., p. 181. Kalm, vol. i., p. 322.
SCIURUS LYSTERI, Ray, Synops. Quad., p. 216, A. D. 1693.
LE SUISSE, Charlevoix, Nouv. Fr., vol. v., p. 196.
STRIPED DORMOUSE, Pennant, Arc. Zool., 4 vols., vol. i., p. 126.
SCIURUS CAROLINENSIS, Brisson, Reg. Anim., p. 155, A. D. 1756.
ECUREUIL SUISSE, (Desm. Enc. Mamm.,) Nota, p. 339, Esp., 547.
SCIURUS STRIATUS, Harlan, Fauna, p. 183.
  "   "   Godman, Nat. Hist., vol. ii., p. 142.
SCIURUS (TAMIAS) LYSTERI, Rich., F. B. A., p. 181, plate 15.
  "   "   "   Doughty's Cabinet Nat. Hist., vol. i., p. 169, pl. 15.
SCIURUS STRIATUS, DeKay, Nat. Hist. of N. Y., part 1, p. 62, pl. 16, fig. 1.

Description.

Body, rather slender; forehead, arched; head, tapering from the ears to the nose, which is covered with short hairs; nostrils, opening downwards, margins and septum naked; whiskers, shorter than the head. A few bristles on the cheeks and above the eye-brows; eyes, of moderate size; ears, ovate, rounded, erect, covered with short hair on both surfaces, not tufted, the hair on those parts simply covering the margins. Cheek-pouches, of tolerable size, extending on the sides of the neck to a little below the ear, opening into the mouth between the incisors and molars. Fore-feet, with four slender, compressed, slightly-curved, claws, and the rudiment of a thumb, covered with a short, blunt, nail; hind-feet, long and slender, with five toes, the middle toe being a little the longest. Tail, rather short and slender, nearly cylindrical above, dilated on the sides, not bushy, sub-distichous. Hair on the whole body short and smooth, but not very fine.

Colour.

A small black spot above the nose; forehead, yellowish-brown; above and beneath the eye-lids, white; whiskers and eye-lashes, black; a dark brown streak running from the sides of the face, through the eye, and reaching the ear; a yellowish-brown stripe extending from near the nose, running under the eye to behind the ear, deepening into chesnut-brown immediately below the eye, where the stripe is considerably dilated.

Anterior portion of the back, hoary gray, this colour being formed by a mixture of gray and black hairs. Colour of the rump, extending to a little beyond the root of the tail, hips, and exterior surface of the thighs, reddish fawn, a few black hairs sprinkled among the rest, not sufficiently numerous to give a darker shade to those parts. A dark dorsal line commencing back of the head is dilated on the middle of the back, and runs to a point within an inch of the root of the tail; this line is brownish on the shoulder, but deepens into black in its progress downwards.

On each flank there is a broad yellowish-white line, running from the shoulder to the thighs, bordered on each side with black. The species may be characterised by its having five black and two white stripes on a gray ground. The flanks, sides, and upper surface of feet and ears, are reddish-gray; whole under surface white, with no line of demarcation between the colours of the back and belly. Tail, brown at its root, afterwards grayish-black, the hair being clouded and in some places banded with black; underneath, reddish-brown, with a border of black, edged with light gray.

There are some varieties observable among specimens procured in different States of the Union. We have noted it, like the Virginian deer, becoming smaller in size as it was found farther to the South. In Maine and New Hampshire, it is larger than in the mountains of Carolina and Louisiana, and the tints of those seen at the North were lighter than the colouring of the Southern specimens we have examined. We possess an albino, sent to us alive, snow-white, with red eyes; and also another specimen jet-black. We have, however, found no intermediate varieties, and in general we may remark that the species of this genus are not as prone to variations in colour as those of the true Squirrels.

Dimensions.

		Inches.	Lines.
Length of head and body		6	3
" head		1	6
" tail (vertebræ)		3	7
" tail, including fur		4	7
Height of ear		0	4
Breadth of ear		0	$3\frac{1}{2}$

Habits.

The Chipping Squirrel, as this little animal is usually called, or Ground Squirrel, as it is named almost as frequently, is probably, with the exception of the common flying squirrel, (*Pteromys volucella*,) one of the most interesting of our small quadrupeds. It is found in most parts of the United States, and being beautifully marked in its colouring, is known to every body. From its lively and busy habits, one might consider it among the quadrupeds as occupying the place of the *wren* among the feathered tribes. Like the latter, the Ground Squirrel, full of vivacity, plays with the utmost grace and agility among the broken rocks or uprooted stumps of trees about the farm or wood pasture; its clucking, resembles the chip, chip, chip, of a young chicken, and although not musical, like the song of the little winter wren, excites agreeable thoughts as it comes on the air. We fancy we see one of these sprightly Chipping Squirrels, as he runs before us with the speed of a bird, skimming along a log or fence, his chops distended by the nuts he has gathered in the

woods; he makes no pause till he reaches the entrance of his subterranean retreat and store-house. Now he stands upright, and his chattering cry is heard, but at the first step we make towards him, he disappears. Stone after stone we remove from the aperture leading to his deep and circuitous burrow; but in vain is all our labour—with our hatchets we cut the tangled roots, and as we follow the animal, patiently digging into his innermost retreat, we hear his angry, querulous tones. We get within a few inches of him now, and can already see his large dark eyes; but at this moment out he rushes, and ere we can "grab" him, has passed us, and finds security in some other hiding place, of which there are always plenty at hand, that he is well accustomed to fly to; and we willingly leave him unmolested, to congratulate himself on his escape.

The Chipping Squirrel makes his burrow generally near the roots of trees, in the centre of a decayed stump, along fences or old walls, or in some bank, near the woods whence he obtains the greater portion of his food.

Some of these retreats have two or three openings, at a little distance from each other. It rarely happens that this animal is caught by digging out its burrow. When hard pressed and closely pursued, it will betake itself to a tree, the trunk of which it ascends for a little distance with considerable rapidity, occasionally concealing itself behind a large branch, but generally stopping within twelve or fifteen feet of the ground, where it often clings, with its body so closely pressed to the trunk, that it is difficult to detect it; and it remains so immoveable that it appears like a piece of bark or some excrescence, till the enemy has retired from the vicinity, when it once more descends, and by its renewed clucking, seems to chuckle over its escape.

We are doubtful whether this species can at any time be perfectly tamed. We have preserved it in cages from time to time, and generally found it wild and sullen. Those we had, however, were not young when captured.

At a subsequent period we obtained in the State of New York, five or six young ones almost half grown. We removed them to Carolina, where they were kept during winter and spring. They were somewhat more gentle than those we had formerly possessed, occasionally took a filbert or a ground-nut from the fingers, but never became tame enough to be handled with safety, as they on more than one occasion were disposed to test the sharpness of their teeth on our hand.

The skin which covered the vertebræ of their tails was so brittle that nearly all of them soon had mutilated them. They appeared to have some aversion to playing in a wheel, which is so favourite an amusement of the true squirrels. During the whole winter they only left their nest to carry into it the rice, nuts, Indian corn, &c., placed in their cage as food.

Late in the following spring, having carried on our experiments as far as we cared to pursue them, we released our pets, which were occasionally seen in the vicinity for several months afterward, when they disappeared.

We were once informed of a strange carnivorous propensity in this species. A lady in the vicinity of Boston said to us, "We had in our garden a nest of young robins, (*Turdus migratorius*,) and one afternoon as I was walking in the garden, I happened to pass very close to the tree on which this nest was placed; my attention was attracted by a noise which I thought proceeded from it, and on looking up I saw a Ground Squirrel tearing at the nest, and actually devouring one of the young ones. I called to the gardener, who came accompanied by a dog, and shook the tree violently, when the animal fell to the earth, and was in an instant secured by the dog." We do not conceive that the unnatural propensity in the individual here referred to, is indicative of the genuine habit of this species, but think that it may be regarded as an exception to a general rule, and referred to a morbid depravity of taste sometimes to be observed in other genera, leading an individual to feed upon that which the rest of the species would loathe and reject. Thus we have known a horse which preferred a string of fish to a mess of oats; and mocking-birds, in confinement, kill and devour jays, black-birds, or sparrows.

We saw and caught a specimen of this beautiful TAMIAS, in Louisiana, that had no less than sixteen chinquapin nuts (*Castanea pumila*) stowed away in its cheek-pouches. We have a specimen now lying before us, sent from Pennsylvania in alcohol, which contains at least one and a half table-spoonfuls of Bush trefoil (*Hedysarum cannabinum*) in its widely-distended sacks. We have represented one of our figures in the plate, with its pouches thus filled out.

This species is to a certain extent gregarious in its habits. We had marked one of its burrows in autumn, which we conceived well adapted to our purpose, which was to dig it out. It was in the woods, on a sandy piece of ground, and the earth was strewed with leaves to the depth of eight inches, which we believed would prevent the frost from penetrating to any considerable depth. We had the place opened in January, when the ground was covered with snow about five inches deep. The entrance of the burrow had been closed from within. We followed the course of the small winding gallery with considerable difficulty. The hole descended at first almost perpendicularly for about three feet. It then continued with one or two windings, rising a

Chipping Squirrel, Hackee.

Drawn from Nature by J.J.Audubon F.R.S F.L.S.

Printed by Nagel & Weingærtner NY

little nearer the surface, until it had advanced about eight feet, when we came to a large nest made of oak leaves and dried grasses. Here lay, snugly covered, three Chipping Squirrels. Another was subsequently dug from one of the small lateral galleries, to which it had evidently retreated to avoid us. They were not dormant, and seemed ready to bite when taken in the hand; but they were not very active, and appeared somewhat sluggish and benumbed, which we conjectured was owing to their being exposed to sudden cold, from our having opened their burrow.

There was about a gill of wheat an.' buckwheat in the nest; but in the galleries we afterwards dug out, we obta..ed about a quart of the beaked hasel nuts, (*Corylus rostrata*,) nearly a peck of acorns, some grains of Indian corn, about two quarts of buckwheat, and a very small quantity of grass seeds. The late Dr. JOHN WRIGHT, of Troy, in an interesting communication on the habits of several of our quadrupeds, informs us, in reference to this species, that "It is a most provident little creature, continuing to add to its winter store, if food is abundant, until driven in by the severity of the frost. Indeed, it seems not to know when it has enough, if we may judge by the surplus left in the spring, being sometimes a peck of corn or nuts for a single Squirrel. Some years ago I watched one of these animals whilst laying up its winter store. As there were no nuts to be found near, I furnished a supply. After scattering some hickory nuts on the ground near the burrow, the work of carrying in was immediately commenced. It soon became aware that I was a friend, and approached almost to my feet for my gifts. It would take a nut from its paws, and dextrously bite off the sharp point from each end, and then pass it to its cheek-pouch, using its paws to shove it in, then one would be placed on the opposite side, then again one along with the first, and finally, having taken one between its front teeth, it would go into the burrow. After remaining there for five or ten minutes it would reappear for another load. This was repeated in my presence a great number of times, the animal always carrying four nuts at a time, and always biting off the asperities."

We perceive from hence, that the Chipping Squirrels retire to winter quarters, in small families, in the early part of November, sooner or later, according to the coldness or mildness of the season, after providing a store of food in their subterranean winter residence. When the snows are melted from the earth in early spring, they leave the retreat to which they had resorted during the first severe frosts in autumn. We have seen them sunning themselves on a stump during warm days about the last of February, when the snows were still on the earth here and there in patches a foot deep; we remarked, however, that they remained only for half an hour, when they again retreated to their burrows.

The young are produced in May, to the number of four or five at a birth, and we have sometimes supposed from the circumstance of seeing a young brood in August, that they breed twice a year.

The Chipping Squirrel does but little injury to the farmer. It seldom disturbs the grain before it is ripe, and is scarcely more than a gleaner of the fields, coming in for a small pittance, when the harvest is nearly gathered. It prefers wheat to rye, seems fond of buckwheat, but gives the preference to nuts, cherry-stones, the seeds of the red gum, or pepperidge, (*Nyssa Multiflora*,) and those of several annual plants and grasses.

This species is easily captured. It enters almost any kind of trap without suspicion. We have seen a beautiful muff and tippet made of a host of little skins of this TAMIAS ingeniously joined together so as to give the appearance fo a regular series of stripes around the muff, and longitudinally along the sides of the tippet. The animals had in most cases been captured in rat-traps.

There is, besides, a simple, rustic, but effectual mode of hunting the Ground Squirrel, to which we are tempted to devote a paragraph.

Man has his hours of recreation, and so has the school-boy; while the former is fond of the chase, and keeps his horses, dogs, and guns, the latter, when released from school, gets up a little hunt, agreeable to his own taste and limited resources. The boys have not yet been allowed to carry fire-arms, and have been obliged to adhere to the command of a careful mother—"don't meddle with that gun, Billy, it may go off and kill you" But the Chip Muck can be hunted without a gun, and Saturday, the glorious weekly return of their freedom and independence from the crabbed schoolmaster and the puzzling spelling-book, is selected for the important event.

There are some very pleasing reminiscences associated with these little sports of boyhood. The lads, full of delightful anticipations, usually meet half an hour before the time appointed. They come with their "shining morning faces," full of glee and talking of their anticipated success. In lieu of fire-arms they each carry a stick, about eight feet long. They go along the old fashioned worm-fences that skirt the woods, a crop of wheat or of buckwheat has just been gathered, and the little Hackee is busily engaged in collecting its winter store.

In every direction its lively chirrup is heard, with answering calls from adjacent parts of the woods, and here and there you may observe one mounted on the top of a fence-stake, and chipping away as it were in exultation at his elevated seat. One of the tiny huntsmen now places his pole on a fence rail, the second or third from the bottom, along which the Ground Squirrel is expected to pass; a few yards behind him is another youngster, ready with his stick on another rail, in case the Chip Muck escapes the first enemy. One of the juveniles now makes a circuit, gets behind the little Hackee, and gives a blow on the fence to drive him toward the others, who are eagerly expecting him. The unsuspecting little creature, with a sweep of his half-erected tail, quickly descends from the top of the fence, along a stake, and betaking himself to some of the lower rails, makes a rapid retreat. If no stone-heaps or burrows are at hand, it runs along the winding fence, and as it is passing the place where the young sportsmen are lying in wait; they brush the stick along the rail with the celerity of thought, hitting the little creature on the nose, and knocking it six yards off. "He is ours," is the exulting shout, and the whole party now hurry to the spot. Perhaps the little animal is not dead, only stunned; and is carried home to be made a pet. It is put into a calabash, a stocking, or a small bag, prepared for the occasion by some fond little sister, who whilst sewing it for her brother, half longed to enjoy the romp and the sport herself. Reader, don't smile at this group of juvenile sportsmen; older and bigger "boys" are often engaged in amusements not more rational, and not half so innocent.

Several species of hawks are successful in capturing the Chipping Squirrel. It furnishes also many a meal for the hungry fox, the wild cat, and the mink; but it possesses an enemy in the common weasel or ermine, (*mustela erminea*) more formidable than all the rest combined. This blood-thirsty little animal pursues it into its dwelling, and following it to the farthest extremity, strikes its teeth into its skull, and like a cruel savage of the wilderness, does not satiate its thirst for blood, until it has destroyed every inhabitant of the burrow, old and young, although it seldom devours one fifth of the animals it so wantonly kills. We once observed one pursue a Chipping Squirrel into its burrow. After an interval of ten minutes it reappeared, licking its mouth, and stroking its fur with its head, by the aid of its long neck. We watched it as it pursued its way through a buckwheat field, in which many roots and stumps were yet remaining, evidently in quest of additional victims. On the following day we were impelled by curiosity to open the burrow we had seen it enter. There we found an old female ground squirrel, and five young, half-grown, lying dead, with the marks of the weasels' teeth in their skulls.

Geographical Distribution.

The Chipping Squirrel has a pretty wide geographical range. It is common on the northern shores of Lakes Huron and Superior; and has been traced as far as the fiftieth degree of north latitude. In the Eastern, Northern, and Middle States, it is quite abundant; it exists along the whole of the Alleghany range, and is found in the mountainous portions of South Carolina, Georgia, and Alabama. In the alluvial districts of Carolina and Georgia, it disappears. We have never found it nearer the seaboard of South Carolina than at Columbia, one hundred and ten miles from Charleston, where it is very rare. It is found in Tennessee and throughout Louisiana.

General Remarks.

We have, at the head of this article, endeavoured to preserve TAMIAS as a valuable genus distinct from SCIURUS. We hope we have offered such reasons as will induce naturalists to separate this interesting and increasing little group, mostly of American species, from the squirrels, to which they bear about the same affinity, as do the marmot squirrels (SPERMOPHILUS) to the true marmots (ARCTOMYS.) We will now inquire whether the present species, (*Tamias Lysteri*,) is a foreigner from Siberia, naturalized in our Western world; or whether it is one of the aborigines of our country, as much entitled to a name as the grisly bear or the cougar.

Two of our American naturalists, HARLAN and GODMAN, supposed that it was the Asiatic species, the *S. striatus* of KLEIN, PALLAS, SCHREBER, and other authors; Dr. RICHARDSON (1829) believed that the descriptions given of *Sciurus striatus*, did not exactly correspond with American specimens, and as he had no opportunity of instituting a comparison, he adopted the specific name of RAY, *Sciurus* (TAMIAS) *Lysteri*, for our species; and quoted what PALLAS had written in regard to the habits of the Asiatic animal, as applying to those of our little Chipping Squirrel. Very recently (1842) Dr. DEKAY, in the work on American quadrupeds, published by order of the State of New York, has again referred it to *S. striatus* of LINNÆUS, and endeavoured to prove the identity of the two species, from European writers. We suspect he had no opportunity of making a comparison from actual specimens.

Reasoning from analogy in regard to the species of birds, or quadrupeds, found to be identical on both continents, we should be compelled to admit that if our species is the *S. striatus* of Asia, it presents a solitary exception to a long-established general rule. That many species of water-birds, such as geese, ducks, gulls, auks, and guillemots, which during the long days of summer, crowd toward the polar regions to engage in the duties and pleasures of reproduction, should be found on both continents, cannot be a matter of surprise; and that the ptarmigan, the white snow-bird, Lapland long-spur, &c., which resort annually to them, should, at that season, take wing and stray to either continent, is so probable a case, that we might think it strange if it were otherwise. Neither need we regard it as singular if a few quadrupeds, with peculiar constitutions and habits suited to the polar regions, should be inhabitants of the northern portions of both continents. Thus, the polar bear which delights in the snow and ice, and which is indifferent as to whether it is on the land or on an iceberg at sea; the reindeer, which exists only in cold regions, and which, by alternately swimming and walking, can make its way over the icy waters in winter, and over rivers and arms of the sea in summer, and which migrates for thousands of miles; the beaver, which is found all over our continent; on the banks of the Mackenzie river, leading into the polar sea, in latitude 68°, and in the Russian settlements near Behring's Straits; the ermine, which riots in the snow-drifts, and has been found as far to the north as man has ever travelled; and the common wolf, which is a cosmopolite, exhibits itself in all colours, and strays from the tropics to the north pole, may be found on both continents, without surprising us: but if this little land animal, the Chipping Squirrel, which is unable to swim, and retires to the earth in cold weather, should be found both in Asia and America, it would oppose all our past experience in regard to American quadrupeds, and be the only exception to a long and universally admitted theory. The highest northern range in which this species has ever been seen is above Lake Huron, as far as latitude 50°; from thence there is a distance of more than 90° of longitude and 18° of latitude, before we reach its Asiatic range, and in its migrations either way it would have to cross Behring's Straits, and traverse regions, which even in summer are covered with snow and ice. From the above facts, and from our knowledge of the adaptation of various animals for extensive migrations, we must conclude that this species cannot possibly exist on both continents, even admitting the correctness of the supposition, that these continents had in some former age been united.

Dr. RICHARDSON says, (p. 181,) "I am not aware that the identity of the species on the two continents has been established by actual comparison." In this he was quite correct. At the period at which his valuable work on American quadrupeds was published, nearly all the figures, and many of the descriptions of *Tamias striatus* of the Eastern continent, were taken from American specimens of *Tamias Lysteri*; and the authors supposing them to be identical, were not sufficiently cautious to note this important fact.

In 1838 we carried to Europe, American specimens of nearly all those species which had their congeners on the Eastern continent. We were surprised at finding no specimen of the *T. striatus* in the museums of either England or France. At Berlin, however, an excellent opportunity was afforded us for instituting a comparison. Through the kindness of Dr. LICHTEN-STEIN, the superintendent of the museum, we were permitted to open the cases, examine several specimens in a fine state of preservation, and compare them with our American species, which we placed beside them. The differences, at first sight were so striking that we could only account for their ever having been considered identical, from the fact that the descriptions of the old authors were so loose and unsatisfactory that many minute but important characteristics had not been noted. The following memorandum was made by us on the occasion:—"The *Tamias striatus* differs so widely from our American Chipping Squirrel or Hackee, that it is unnecessary to be *very* minute in making the comparison. The two species can always be distinguished from each other by one remarkable characteristic, which I have observed running through all the specimens. The stripes on the Asiatic, (*T. striatus*) running over the back, extend to the root of the tail; whilst those on the American, (*T. Lysteri*) do not reach so far by a full inch. There are many other differences which may as well be noticed. *T. striatus* is a little the largest, the stripes on the back are situated nearer each other, and are broader than in the other species; the stripes on each side of the back are nearly black, instead of yellowish-brown; on each side of the black stripe on the centre of the back of *Tamias Lysteri*, there is a broad space of reddish-gray. In *T. striatus* this part of the animal is yellowish; being an alternate stripe of black and yellowish-white. The tail of the latter is black towards the extremity, and tipped with white; its tail and ears also are larger than those of *T. Lysteri*: in short, these two species differ as widely from each other, as *Tamias Lysteri* differs from the four-lined ground squirrel of SAY, (*T. quadrivittatus.*)

Genus Spermophilus. F Cuvier.

Dental Formula.

$$\text{Incisive } \frac{2}{2}; \text{ Canine } \frac{0-0}{0-0}; \text{ Molar } \frac{5-5}{4-4} = 22.$$

The dentition of the Spermophiles differs from that of the true marmots, in the following particulars. The first longitudinal eminence (colline) is nearly obliterated, and the curve (talon) which unites the second to the third, is prolonged much more internally, which makes the molars of the Spermophiles more narrow transversely than longitudinally, as compared with those of the marmots. The teeth of the souslik (*Spermophilus citillus*) were examined by F. CUVIER, and considered as typical of this genus.

Nose, convex; ears, generally short; cheek-pouches.

Body, rather short; mammæ, pectoral and abdominal, from eight to twelve.

Feet, of moderate length, adapted for walking on the ground; nails, less in size than those of the marmots, less hooked than those of the squirrels; on the fore-feet, four toes, with the rudiment of a thumb, protected by a blunt nail; second toe from the thumb longest, as in the marmots, and not the third, as in the squirrels; hind-feet, with five toes.

Tail, generally rather short, and always shorter than the body; in several of the species, capable of a slightly distichous arrangement.

The species belonging to this genus differ from the true marmots, not only in their teeth, as shown above, but also in several other striking particulars. They have cheek-pouches, of which the marmots are destitute. They are by no means clumsy, and in form are rather slender, and possess a degree of lightness and agility, approaching the activity of the squirrels.

With the genus TAMIAS, they assimilate so closely, that some of the species present intermediate characters, and authors may well differ as to which genus they ought to be referred to. Thus *Tamias quadrivittatus*, and *Spermophilus lateralis*, seem to form a connecting link between these two genera. It is to be recollected, however, that analogous cases exist, not only among the mammalia, but in every class of animals, and more especially in birds.

In referring again to the dentition of these allied genera, we may remark that the anterior molar of the upper jaw, which is deciduous and falls out at an early period in most species of true squirrels, remains permanently in all species of the genus TAMIAS and is smaller than in the Spermophiles. These genera differ also in the form and length of their claws. The long nails of the latter, the second claw, moreover, being longest, places them near the marmots; while the shorter, weaker, and more arched nails of the ground squirrels, in which the third claw, besides, is the longest, approximates them more nearly to the true squirrels.

The clucking notes of the chipping squirrels, are replaced in the marmot-squirrels by the shrill whistling or chattering sounds emitted by the marmots.

The generic appellation Spermophilus, is derived from the Greek words οπερμα, (*sperma*,) a seed, and φιλος, (*philos*,) a lover.

There are now twelve species of this genus known as existing in North America, and three in Europe, and a few are set down as belonging to Asia and Africa. Some of the latter may, however, after more careful examination, be found to belong to the genus ARCTOMYS.

Spermophilus Parryi.—Richardson.

Parry's Marmot-Squirrel.—Parry's Spermophile.

Plate ix.—Male. Natural size.

S. flavo-cinereus, supra albo variegatus, genis, lateribus, ventre, pedibusque flavis; fronte aureo, pilis ex flavo et nigro; ad radices flavis, apice nigris.

Characters.

General colour, yellowish-gray; upper parts, mottled with white; cheeks, sides, under parts of the body, and feet, yellow; fore-part of the head, deep rich yellow; the hairs varied with yellow and black; at the roots chiefly deep yellow, and at the points principally black.

Synonymes.

GROUND-SQUIRREL, Hearne's Journey, pp. 141 and 386.
QUEBEC MARMOT, FORSTER, Phil. Trans., vol. lxii., p. 378.
ARCTOMYS ALPINA, Parry, Second Voyage, p. 61, narrative.
ARCTOMYS PARRYI, Richardson, Parry's Second Voyage, App., p. 316.
ARCTOMYS (SPERMOPHILUS) PARRYI, Rich., Fauna Boreali America-
na, p. 158, pl. 10.
SEEK-SEEK, ESQUIMAUX,—THOE-THIAY ROCK-BADGER, CHIPE-
WYANS, Rich.

Description.

This marmot-squirrel, although far from being as thick and heavy as the Maryland marmot, is not nearly so light and graceful as most of the other species of this genus, especially *Sp. Douglassii*; and in form, this animal resembles the marmots more than it does the ground squirrels. The forehead is arched, the nose rather short, thick, and closely covered with short hair; ears, short, triangular, and situated above the auditory opening; eyes, prominent, and of moderate size; a few rather slender hairs over the eye; along the cheeks are whiskers, arranged in five rows. Cheek-pouches, of medium dimensions, and opening into the mouth immediately behind the molars.

Legs and feet rather short and stout; toes well separated; nails long; feet covered with short hairs; palms of the fore-feet naked; soles of hind-feet for half an inch next the heel clothed with hair, the remainder naked. Tail, rather flat, rounded at base, hairs becoming longer towards the extremity; sub-distichous. The under fur on every part of the body, soft, glossy, and of a silky appearance.

Colour.

Hairs of the back, black at the roots, annulated above with black, nearer the tips yellowish-white, or white; extreme tips black.

The longest hairs black; the under, black at the base, then whitish, and shaded into brown at the points. The whole upper surface is irregularly and thickly spotted with white; the spots confluent, especially over the shoulders; on the belly the under-fur is abundant, very soft and silky; grayish-black at the base, and yellowish-white at the tips; the visible portion of the longer hairs, deep yellow on the sides of the body, and paler yellow on the belly. Feet, yellow; hairs on the toes a pale yellow; claws blackish-brown; the hinder half of the tarsus covered beneath with brownish hairs; upper surface of the head, as far back as the eyes, of a deep rich yellow; around the eyes whitish; cheeks yellow; chin, throat, and sides of the muzzle, yellowish-white; tail, at base, coloured like the body; in the middle, the hairs are yellowish, with two rings or bars of black at the tips. The hairs on the under surface of the tail are chiefly of a rusty or brownish-red colour; moustaches black.

Dimensions.

	Inches.	Lines.
From nose to root of tail	11	6
Tail (vertebræ)	4	6
Tail, to end of hair	6	0

	Inches.	Lines.
From heel to end of claw	2	3
From ear to point of nose	2	0
Height of ear	0	2½

Habits.

The only account we have of this handsome spermophile is that given by its talented discoverer, who says of it,—

"It is found generally in stony districts, but seems to delight chiefly in sandy hillocks amongst rocks, where burrows, inhabited by different individuals, may be often observed crowded together. One of the society is generally observed sitting erect on the summit of the hillocks, whilst the others are feeding in the neighbourhood. Upon the approach of danger, he gives the alarm, and they instantly betake themselves to their holes, remaining chattering, however, at the entrance until the advance of the enemy obliges them to retire to the bottom. When their retreat is cut off, they become much terrified, and seeking shelter in the first crevice that offers, they not unfrequently succeed only in hiding the head and fore-part of the body, whilst the projecting tail is, as usual with them when under the influence of terror, spread out flat on the rock. Their cry in this season of distress, strongly resembles the loud alarm of the Hudson's Bay squirrel, and is not very unlike the sound of a watchman's rattle. The Esquimaux name of this animal, *Seek-Seek*, is an attempt to express this sound. According to HEARNE, they are easily tamed, and are very cleanly and playful in a domestic state. They never come abroad during the winter. Their food appears to be entirely vegetable; their pouches being generally observed to be filled, according to the season, and of other trailing shrubs, or the seeds of bents, grasses, and leguminous plants. They produce about seven young at a time."

Captain Ross mentions that some of the dresses of the Esquimaux, at Repulse Bay, were made of the skins of this species; these people also informed him that it was very abundant in that inhospitable region.

Geographical Distribution.

According to Dr. RICHARDSON, "this spermophile inhabits the barren grounds skirting the sea-coast, from Churchill, in Hudson's Bay, round by Melville's Peninsula, and the whole northern extremity of the Continent to Behring's Straits, where specimens precisely similar were procured by Captain BEECHEY. It abounds in the neighbourhood of Fort Enterprise, near the southern verge of the barren grounds in latitude 65°, and is also plentiful on Cape Parry, one of the most northern parts of the continent."

General Remarks.

Our description of this rare animal was drawn up from a specimen deposited by Dr. RICHARDSON in the museum of the Zoological Society of London, which was said to have been the identical skin from which his description was taken.

We possess another specimen, presented to us by Dr. RICHARDSON, which is a little longer in the body, and shorter in the tail, than the one we have just spoken of; the body being 12½ inches in length, and the tail (vertebræ) 3½ inches, including fur 5 inches. The forehead and buttocks of this specimen are reddish-brown.

Genus Scalops.—Cuvier.

Dental Formula.

$$Incisive \ \frac{2}{4}; \ Molar \ \frac{3-3}{3-3}; \ False\text{-}Molar \ \frac{6-6}{3-3} = 36.$$

or

$$Incisive \ \frac{2}{4}; \ Molar \ \frac{6-6}{6-6}; \ False\text{-}Molar \ \frac{4-4}{3-3} = 44.$$

Head, long, terminated by an extended, cartilaginous, flexible, and pointed muzzle; eyes and ears, concealed by the hair, and very minute. Hind-feet, short and slender, with five toes and delicate hooked nails; fore-feet (or hands) broad; claws, long and flat, fitted for excavating the earth.

The name Scalops is derived from the Greek σκαλλω, (*skallo*,) and from the Latin *scalpo*, I scrape.

The various species included in this genus, which approaches very closely to the genus TALPA, of Europe, (European mole,) are, we believe, confined to

North America. There are, so far as we have been informed, only five species known at the present time.

Scalops Aquaticus.—Linn.

Common American Shrew Mole.

Plate x.—Male and Female. Natural size.

S. magnitudine Talpæ Europeæ similis; corpore cylindrato, lanugine sericea, argenteo-cinereo induto.

Characters.

Size of the European mole, (Talpa;) body, cylindrical; fur, velvety; colour, silvery-grayish-brown.

Plate IX

Drawn from Nature by J.J Audubon, F.R. S.F.L S

On Stone by Wᵐ E. Hitchcock

Lith. Printed & Colᵈ by J.T Bowen, Phil

Parry's Marmot Squirrel

Synonymes.

SOREX AQUATICUS, Linn. Syst. Nat., 12th ed. corrected, vol.i., p. 74.
TALPA FUSCA, Pennant, Brit. Zool., Quadrupeds, 314.
SCALOPS CANADENSIS, Desm., Mam., p. 115.
SCALOPE DE CANADA, Cuv., Règne Animal, p. 134.
SHREW MOLE, Godman, Nat. Hist., vol. i., p. 84, pl. 5, fig. 3.
SCALOPS CANADENSIS, Harlan, Fauna, p. 32. Young.
    "   PENNSYLVANICA, Harlan, Fauna, p. 33. Adult.
    "   CANADENSIS, Emmons, Report on Quads. of Mass., p. 15.
    "   AQUATICUS, Bachman, Observations on the Genus Scalops,
                Boston Jour. Nat. Hist., vol. iv., No. 1., p. 28, 1842.
    "   AQUATICUS, Dekay, Nat. Hist. of the State of New York, p. 15.

Description.

Adult:—Teeth 36, corresponding with the first dental formula of this genus, given on the preceding page; incisors of moderate size, rounded on their front surface and flattened posteriorly. Immediately behind the incisors, two minute teeth on each side, crowded together—succeeded by four large false-molars, of a cylindrical shape, and pointed; the fourth, smallest, the fifth a little larger and slightly lobed, and the sixth, which is the largest, more conspicuously lobed; followed by three true molars, each furnished with three sharp tubercles.

In the lower, or inferior jaw, sixteen teeth; the two posterior incisors very small, succeeded on each side by another, much larger, pointed and extending forward; three false-molars which succeed these, are pointed, and the third and largest, slightly lobed; three true molars composed of two parallel prisms, terminated each by three points, and "presenting one of their angles on the outer side, and one of their faces on the internal surface; the two first of equal size, the other somewhat smaller." Part of the above description is in the words of Dr. GODMAN, from his very correct and interesting article on the Shrew Mole, (vol. i., p. 82,) which corresponds exactly with the results of our own investigations of the teeth of this animal, made at various times, during a period of several years.

Young.—We have found in specimens less than a year old, that the two small thread-like teeth inserted behind the incisors in the upper jaw, were entirely wanting, as also the fourth lateral incisor on each side, leaving vacant spaces between them, and presenting the appearance ascribed to them by Baron CUVIER and by DESMAREST; the last mentioned teeth are first developed, the former appearing when the animal is full grown and all the edentate spaces between the molars are filled up.

Body, thick and cylindrical; neck, short, so that the head appears almost as if attached directly to the shoulders; snout, naked, cartilaginous, and very flexible, extending five lines beyond the incisors; the under surface projects a little beyond the nostrils, which are oblong, and open on the upper surface near each other; mouth, large, and when open resembling somewhat (although in miniature) that of the hog; eyes, concealed by the fur, apparently covered by an integument, and so minute, that they can with great difficulty be found. The orifice in the skin in which the eye is placed, is not of larger diameter than would admit a bristle. No external ear; there is, however, a very small circular aperture leading to the ear, about three quarters of an inch behind the eye. The fore-arms are concealed by the skin, and the palms only are visible, they are broad, and might be thought not unlike hands; they are thinly clothed with hair, and bordered with stiff hairs; the fingers are united at the base of the claws; nails, large, slightly curved, nearly convex above, and flattened on the inner surface; hind-feet, small and slender, naked on the under surface, and apparently above, although a close inspection shows the upper surface to be covered with fine short hairs; nails, small, a little arched, and compressed; tail, short, round, appears naked, but is very sparingly clothed with short adpressed hairs. On the inside of the thighs, near the tail, is a gland, about half an inch long, from which a disagreeable musky odour issues, which makes the animal offensive to delicate olfactories. All our other shrew moles, possess similar glands, and we have perceived the musky smell still remaining strong in skins that had been prepared and stuffed several weeks.

Colour.

Snout and palms, in the living animal, pinkish flesh-colour; chin, feet, and tail, dull white; hair on the body, about five lines in length, very soft, smooth, and lustrous; for three-fourths of its length, plumbeous; tips light-brown, giving the surface of the hair, above, a dark-brown colour, which varies in different lights, sometimes exhibiting black, silver-gray, or purple, reflections.

There are many variations in the coloring of different individuals of this species, but none of them permanent: we possess some specimens which are nearly black, and others of a light cream-colour; we also have a specimen, the tail of which, is clothed with short hairs, with a considerable tuft at the extremity. From these, and similar differences in various other animals, it is not surprising that authors have described in their works, many as new, which on being closely examined afterwards prove to be mere accidental varieties of some well-known species.

Dimensions.

	Inches.	Lines.
Adult male.		
From nose to root of tail, ...	5	8
Tail, ...	0	8
Breadth of palm, ...	0	5
A specimen from Carolina.		
From nose to root of tail, ...	4	7
Tail, ...	0	9
Breadth of palm, ...	0	6

Habits.

Whilst almost every farmer or gardener throughout the Northern and Eastern States, is well acquainted with this curious animal, as far as the mere observation of its meandering course through his fields and meadows, his beds of green peas or other vegetables, is concerned, but few have arrived at proper conclusions in regard to the habits of the Shrew Mole; and it is generally caught and killed whenever practicable; the common idea being, that the Mole feeds on the roots of tender plants, grasses, &c.; while the fact that the animal devours great quantities of earth-worms, slugs, and grubs, all hurtful to the fruit trees, to the grasses, and the peas and other vegetables, seems to be unknown, or overlooked.

In justice to the farmer and gardener, however, we must say, that the course taken occasionally, by this species, directly along a row of tender plants, throwing them out of the earth, as it does, or zig-zag across a valuable bed or beautiful lawn, is rather provoking, and we have ourselves caused traps to be set for moles, being greatly annoyed by their digging long galleries under the grass, on our sloping banks, which during a heavy shower, soon filled with water, and presently increased to large gutters, or deep holes, requiring repairs forthwith. At such times also, a Mole-track through loose soil where there is any descent, will be found by the gardener, perchance, to have become a miniature ravine, some twenty or thirty yards in length, and a few (anticipated) bushels of carrots are destroyed. In neglected or sandy soils, one of these gutters becomes deep and wide in a short time, and we may perhaps not err in hazarding the opinion that some of the unsightly ravines which run almost through large estates, occasionally might be traced to no higher origin than the wandering of an unlucky mole!

We kept one of this species alive, for some days; feeding it altogether upon earth-worms, but we soon found it difficult to procure a sufficient supply; forty or fifty worms of moderate size, did not appear too much for its seemingly insatiable appetite. At the expiration of four days, another of this species which we had in confinement, would not touch any vegetable substances, although the cage was filled with clods covered with fine clover, pieces of sweet apples, bread, &c.

We were much interested in observing that no matter how soiled its coat might have become in the cage, it would resume its beauty and glossiness after the mole had passed and re-passed through the earth, eight or ten times, which it always accomplished in a few minutes. We frequently remarked with surprise the great strength of this animal, which enabled it to lift the lid or top of a box in which it was kept although it was large and heavy; the box-top was not however fastened down. Seating ourselves quietly in the room, after putting back the mole into the box, the animal supposing itself no longer watched, very soon raised its body against the side of the box, which was partly filled with earth, and presently its snout was protruded through the small space between the box and the cover; and after a few efforts the creature got his fore-feet on to the edge of the box, raised itself over the latter, and fell upon a table on which we had placed the box. It immediately ran to the edge of the table, and thence tumbled on to the floor; this, however, did not at all incommode it, for it made off to a dark corner of the room at once, and remained there until again replaced in its prison.

When this Mole was fed on earth-worms, (*Lumbricus terrenus*,) as we have just related, we heard the worms crushed in the strong jaws of the animal, with a noise somewhat like the grating of broken glass, which was probably caused by its strong teeth gnashing on the sand or grit contained in the bodies

Drawn on Stone by W.E. Hitchcock.

Lith.d Printed & Col.d by J.T. Bowen, Philad.a

Drawn from Nature by J.J. Audubon F.R.S. F.L.S.

Common American Shrew Mole.
Male & Female.

of the worms. These were placed singly on the ground near the animal, which after smelling around for a moment turned about in every direction with the greatest activity, until he felt a worm, when he seized it between the outer surface of his hands or fore-paws, and pushed it into his mouth with a continually repeated forward movement of the paws, cramming it downward until all was in his jaws.

Small sized earth-worms, were dispatched in a very short time; the animal never failing to begin with the anterior end of the worm, and apparently cutting it as he ate, into small pieces, until the whole was devoured. On the contrary, when the earth-worm was of a large size, the Mole seemed to find some difficulty in managing it, and munched the worm sideways, moving it from one side of its mouth to the other. On these occasions the gritting of its teeth, which we have already spoken of, can be heard at the distance of several feet.

We afterwards put the Mole into a large wire rat-trap, and to our surprise saw him insert his fore-paws or hands, between the wires, and force them apart sufficiently to give him room to pass out through them at once, and this without any great apparent effort. It is this extraordinary muscular power in the fore-paws and arms, that enables the Shrew Moles to traverse the galleries they excavate, with so much rapidity, in doing which they turn the backs of their palms or hands toward each other, push them forward as far as the end of their snout, and then open and bring them round backward, in the manner of a person moving his hands and arms when swimming. When running along on the surface of the ground, they extend the fore-legs as far forward as they will reach, turning the backs of the hands or paws (as just mentioned) towards each other, and placing them edge-wise, instead of flat on the earth as might be supposed, and in this manner they run briskly, and without any awkward movement, crossing beaten-roads, or paved walks, and sometimes running swiftly twenty or thirty feet before they can get into the ground.

The Shrew Mole varies somewhat in its habits, according to our observations, for while a solitary individual will occasionally for some weeks, occupy and root up a large plot of grass, or a considerable portion of a garden, and on his being caught in a trap, the place will remain free from fresh Mole-tracks for a long period, proving that all the mischief was the work of a single Mole, at other times we have caught several out of one gallery on the same day; and while excavating a root-house, the lower part of which was rock, four of these animals came during the night through one gallery and tumbled down into the pit, where, the rock preventing their digging a way out, they were found in the morning. No others ever came through that gallery, while the cellar was in progress, and those thus caught may probably have been one family.

Although generally known to run through the same galleries often, so much so, that the most common method of capturing them, is to set a trap anywhere in one of these tracks, to intercept them when again passing through it, we have known a trap to remain set in a fresh track for eleven days before the animal passed that way, when it was caught; and we are of opinion that many of their tracks are only passed through once, as this animal is known to travel from one field or wood to another, and probably the only galleries they regularly traverse, are those adjacent to the spot they have selected for rearing their young. In relation to this subject, Dr. GODMAN says—

"It is remarkable how unwilling they are to relinquish a long frequented burrow; I have frequently broken down, or torn off the surface of the same burrow for several days in succession, but would always find it repaired at the next visit. This was especially the case with one individual whose nest I discovered, which was always repaired within a short time, as often as destroyed. It was an oval cavity, about five or seven inches in length, by three in breadth, and was placed at about eight inches from the surface in a stiff clay. The entrance to it sloped obliquely downwards from the gallery about two inches from the surface; three times I entirely exposed this cell, by cutting out the whole superincumbent clay with a knife, and three times a similar one was made a little beyond the situation of the former, the excavation having been continued from its back part. I paid a visit to the same spot two months after capturing its occupant, and breaking up the cell, all the injuries were found to be repaired, and another excavated within a few inches of the old one. Most probably numerous individuals, composing a whole family, reside together in these extensive galleries. In the winter they burrow closer to the streams, where the ground is not so deeply frozen."

This species whilst beneath the earth's surface, seems to search for food with the same activity and untiring perseverance that are observable in animals that seek for their provender above ground. It works through the earth, not only in a straight-forward direction, but loosens it to the right and left, beneath and above, so that no worm or insect can escape it. When in contact with any one of the objects of which it has been in search, it seizes it with remarkable quickness both with its fore-feet and its sharp teeth, drawing itself immediately backward with its prize, upon which it begins to prey at once. The Shrew

Mole passes through loose soil, with nearly the same ease and speed that it displays in running, or "scrabbling" along above ground. It moves backward almost as rapidly as it goes forward. The nose is often seen protruded above the surface of the ground.

The snout of this species although apparently delicate, is most powerfully muscular, as well as flexible; the animal can turn it to the right or left, upward or downward, and at times inserts it in its mouth, as if for the purpose of cleansing it, and then suddenly withdraws it with a kind of smack of its lips; this habit we observed three times in the course of a few minutes. The Shrew Mole is exceedingly tenacious of life; it cannot easily be put to death, either by heavy pressure or strangling, and a severe blow on the head seems to be the quickest mode of despatching it.

Although this species, as we have seen, feeds principally on worms, grubs, &c., we have the authority of our friend OGDEN HAMMOND, Esq., for the following example either of a most singular perversity of taste, or of habits hitherto totally unknown as appertaining to animals of this genus, and meriting a farther inquiry. While at his estate near Throg's Neck, on Long Island Sound, his son, who is an intelligent young lad, and fond of Natural History, observed in company with an old servant of the family, a Shrew Mole in tha act of swallowing, or devouring, a common toad—this was accomplished by the Mole, and he was then killed, being unable to escape after such a meal, and was taken to the house, where Mr. HAMMOND saw and examined the animal, with the toad partially protruding from its throat. This gentleman also related to us some time ago, that he once witnessed an engagement between two Moles, that happened to encounter each other, in one of the *noon-day* excursions, this species is so much in the habit of making. The combatants sidled up to one another like two little pigs, and each tried to root the other over, in attempting which, their efforts so much resembled the manner of two boars fighting, that the whole affair was supremely ridiculous to the beholder, although no doubt to either of the bold warriors, the consequences of an overthrow would have been a very serious affair; and the conqueror, would vent his rage upon the fallen hero, and punish him severely with his sharp teeth. We have no doubt these conflicts generally take place in the love season, and are caused by rivalry, and that some "fair Mole" probably rewards the victor. When approached, the Moles attempted to escape, but were both shot on the spot, thus falling victims to their own passions; and if we would read aright, affording us an instructive lesson, either as individuals, or in a national point of view.

The Shrew Moles are able to work their way so rapidly, that in soft or loamy soil, it is almost impossible for the most active man to overtake and turn them out with a spade, unless he can see the spot where they are working, by the movement of the earth, in which case they can be thrown out easily, by sticking the spade in front of them, or at one side of their gallery and with a quick movement tossing them on to the surface.

They have been known to make a fresh track, after rain, during one night, several hundred yards in length—oftentimes they proceed for a considerable distance, in nearly a straight or direct line, then suddenly begin to excavate around and across a small space of not more than a few feet in diameter, until you could hardly place your foot on a spot within this subterranean labyrinth, without sinking through into their track; at this time they are most probably in pursuit of worms, or other food, which may be there imbedded.

Although cold weather appears to us, to put a stop to the movements of the Mole, we do not feel by any means certain that such is the case; and very probably the hardness of the ground when frozen, and the depth at which the Mole is then obliged to seek his food, may be a sufficient reason for our seeing no traces of this busy creature's movements during cold winter weather. We have, however, often perceived their tracks after a day or two of warm weather in January, and have repeatedly observed them about during a thaw, after the first autumnal frosts had occurred. In Carolina there are not many weeks in a winter in which we are not able to find here and there traces of the activity of the Mole. We admit, however, that even in this comparatively mild climate, they appear to be far less active in winter than at other seasons.

From the foregoing facts we are inclined to think the Mole does not become torpid at any time; and in corroboration of this idea, we find that the animal is not at any season found in high Northern latitudes. Dr. RICHARDSON thinks "the absence of the Shrew Mole from these countries is owing to the fact that the earth-worm on which the Scalops, like the common Mole, principally feeds, is unknown in the Hudson's Bay countries."

The idea commonly entertained by uninformed persons, that Moles have no eyes, is an error; although our own experience confirms the opinion of others, that they appear to possess the power of seeing only in a very limited degree. We must not forget, however, that a wise Providence has adapted their organs of vision to the subterranean life they lead. Shut out from the light of the sun by a law of nature requiring them to search for food beneath the earth's surface, these animals would find a large pair of eyes one of the greatest of evils, inasmuch as they would be constantly liable to be filled with sand; thus causing inflammation, blindness, and eventually death.

It is not, however, beyond the reach of possibility, nor contrary to the economy of Nature, to suppose that during the night, when this species is seen occasionally above ground, or when engaged in running or fighting, or for purposes we have not yet discovered, this animal may have the power of expanding its minute orbs, and drawing back the hair that entirely conceals its eyes. This, however, is a mere conjecture, which we have thrown out for the consideration of those who are fond of investigating Nature in her minutest operations.

The inquiry has often been made, if the Shrew Mole does not, feed upon the grains, or roots of the corn, peas, potatoes, &c., planted in rows or in hills, why is it that this pest so ingeniously and so mischievously follows the rows, and as effectually destroys the young plants, as if it had consumed them? We answer, it is not the spirit of mischief by which the Mole is actuated; it is the law of self-preservation. In the rows where these seeds have been sown, or these vegetables planted, the ground has been manured; this, and the consequent moisture around the roots of the plants, attracts worms and other insects, that are invariably found in rich moist earth. To the accusations made against the Shrew Mole as a destroyer of potatoes, and other vegetables, he might often with great truth plead an alibi. LECONTE'S pine mouse, (*Arvicola pinetorum*,) is usually the author of the mischief, whilst all the blame is thrown upon the innocent Shrew Mole. We are, moreover, inclined to think that whilst the earth-worm is the general, it is by no means the only food of the latter, and we had an opportunity of discovering to our cost, that when in captivity, this species relished other fare. We preserved one in a cage in Carolina, during a winter, for the purpose of ascertaining on what kind of food it was sustained, and whether it became dormant. It at no time touched grains or vegetables; the lower part of the cage was filled with a foot of moist earth, in which we occasionally placed a pint of earth-worms. It devoured pieces of beef, and for a week was engaged in demolishing a dead pigeon. Until the middle of January we found it every day actively running through the earth in search of worms. Suddenly however, it seemed to have gone to winter quarters, as we could see no more traces of its customary burrowing. We now carefully searched for it in the box, to ascertain its appearance in a dormant state. But the little creature had forced itself through the wooden bars, and was gone. We examined every part of the room without success, and finally supposed it had escaped through the door. The cage of the Mole had been set on a box, full of earth, in which the chrysolides of some sixty or seventy species of rare butterflies, moths, and sphinges, had been carefully deposited. In this box we a few days afterwards heard a noise, and on looking, discovered our little fugitive. On searching for our choice insects we found not one left; they had all been devoured by the Shrew Mole. He had greatly disappointed us, and had put an end to all our hopes of reading the following spring, a better lesson on entomology than ever could have been taught us—either by FABRICIUS, SPENCE, or KIRBY.

We had an opportunity on two different occasions of examining the nests and young of the Shrew Mole. The nests were about eight inches below the surface, the excavation was rather large and contained a quantity of oak leaves on the outer surface, lined with soft dried leaves of the crab-grass, (*Digitaria sanguinalis*.) There were galleries leading to this nest, in two or three directions. The young numbered in one case, five, and in another, nine.

Our kind friend, J. S. HAINES, Esq., of Germantown, near Philadelphia, informed us that he once kept several Shrew Moles in confinement for the purpose of investigating their habits, and that having been neglected for a few days, the strongest of them killed and ate up the others; they also devoured raw meat, especially beef, with great avidity.

Geographical Distribution.

The Shrew Mole is found inhabiting various parts of the country from Canada to Kentucky, in considerable numbers, and is abundant in Carolina, Georgia, Louisiana, and Florida. It is, according to RICHARDSON, unknown in Labrador, the Hudson's Bay Territories, and probably North of Latitude 50°. We did not see any of them in our trip up the Missouri river, and there are none to be found on the dry prairies of the regions immediately east of the great Rocky Mountain chain. The figures in our plate were drawn from specimens procured near the City of New York. We mention this locality, because the colours differ a little from others that we have seen, and that have been described.

General Remarks.

In restoring to this species the specific name of its first describer we have adhered to a rule, from which, to prevent the repetition of synonymes, we should never depart, unless under very peculiar circumstances. The name "*Aquaticus*," certainly does not apply to the habits of this animal, as, although it is fond of the vicinity of moist ground, where the earth-worm is most abundant, yet it is nowise aquatic. The name of DESMAREST, however, viz., "*Canadensis*," is equally objectionable, as it is far more common in the Southern portion of the United States than in Canada.

Some differences of opinion are observable in the works of authors in regard to the number of teeth which characterize this species.

Although the genus was, until recently, composed of but a single acknowledged species, (*Scalops Canadensis* of DESM.,) its systematic arrangement has caused great perplexity among Naturalists. LINNÆUS placed it among the Shrews, (SOREX,) and PENNANT among the Moles, (TALPA,) Baron CUVIER finally established for it a new genus, (SCALOPS,) in which it now remains. The specimen, however, which he made the type of the genus, contained but thirty teeth. The upper jaw had but three lateral incisors, or false-molars, on each side; leaving considerable intermediate spaces between the incisors and true molars. In this dental arrangement he was followed by DESMAREST, Dr. HARLAN, GRIFFITH, and nearly all the Naturalists of that period. Subsequently, however, FREDERICK CUVIER gave a correct description of the teeth, which he found amounted to thirty-six. Dr. HARLAN finding a skeleton from the vicinity of Philadelphia, which in its dental arrangement corresponded generally with the characters given by FRED. Cuvier, considered it a new species, and described it under the name of *Sc. Pennsylvanica*, (see Fauna Americana, p. 33.)

Dr. RICHARDSON described a specimen which was obtained on the Columbia river, (F. B. A., p. 9,) which contained forty-four teeth, very differently arranged. This animal he referred to our common Shrew Mole, supposing that the difference in the dentition, as observed by different authors, was owing to their having examined and described specimens of different ages.

In 1840, Professor EMMONS (Report on the Quadrupeds of Massachusetts,) characterizes the genus as having 44 teeth. In 1842, Dr. DEKAY, (Nat. History of the State of New York, p. 15,) has very erroneously given as a character, its having from 34 to 46 teeth, and states that he had once seen the skull of one of these species containing 44 teeth.

In an article in the Boston Journal, (vol. iv., No. i., p. 26, 1842.) We endeavoured to explain and correct the contradictory views of former authors, and we feel confident we have it in our power to account for the skull seen by Dr. DEKAY, containing forty-four teeth.

The specimens examined by Baron CUVIER, DESMAREST, and Dr. HARLAN, each containing but 30 teeth, were evidently young animals, with their dentition incomplete. One half of the specimens now lying before us, present the same deficiency in the number of teeth; they also exhibit the edentate spaces between the incisors and grinders remarked by those authors. We have, in deciding this point, compared more than fifty specimens together. Those on the other hand that were examined by F. CUVIER, and Dr. GODMAN, and the skeleton of Dr. HARLAN'S *Scalops Pennsylvanica*, containing 36 teeth, were adults of the same species. Dr. RICHARDSON's specimen was a new species, (*Scalops Townsendii*,) having 44 teeth, (see Journ. Acad. Nat. Sc., Philadelphia, vol. viii., p. 58.) With regard to the skull seen by Dr. DEKAY, we have no doubt of its having belonged to *Scalops Brewerii*, (see Bost. Journ. Nat. Hist., vol. iv., p. 32,) which has 44 teeth, and is not uncommon in the State of New York, as we obtained four specimens from our friend, the late Dr. WRIGHT, who procured them in the vicinity of Troy.

Lepus Americanus.—Erxleben.

Northern Hare.

Plate xi.—Fig. 1, Male; Fig. 2, Young Female. Summer Pelage. Natural Size.
Plate xii.—Winter Pelage. Natural Size.

L. hyeme albus; pilis tricoloribus, apice albis, ad radices cœruleis, medio fulvis; æstate, supra rufo-fuscus, infra albus, auribus capite paullo brevioribus; L. Sylvatica paullo robustior. L. Glacialis minor.

Characters.

Size, larger than the gray rabbit, (Lepus Sylvaticus,) less than the Polar hare; (L. Glacialis.) Colour in summer, reddish-brown above, white beneath; in winter, white; roots of the hairs, blue; nearer the surface, fawn-colour, and the tips, white; ears, a little shorter than the head.

Synonymes.

LIEVRE, (Quenton Malisia,) Sagard Theodat, Canada, p. 747. 1636.
SWEDISH HARE, Kalm's travels in North America, vol. ii., p. 45. 1749.
AMERICAN HARE, Philos. Trans., London, vol. lxii., pp. 11, 376. 1772.
LEPUS AMERICANUS, Erxleben, Syst. regni Animalis, p. 330. 1777.
    "   NANUS, Schreber, vol. ii., p. 881, pl. 234, fig.
    "   HUDSONIUS, Pallas, Glires, pp. 1, 30.
VARYING HARE, Pennant, Arct. Zool., vol. i., p. 95.
LEPUS VIRGINIANUS, Harlan, Fauna, p. 196. 1825.
    "   VARIABILIS, var. Godman, Nat. Hist., vol. ii., p. 164.
AMERICAN VARYING HARE, Doughty, Cabinet Nat. Hist., vol. i., p. 217, pl. 19. Autumn pelage.
THE NORTERN HARE, Audubon, Ornithological Biog., vol. ii., p. 469. Birds of America, pl. 181, (in the talons of the Golden Eagle,) Winter pelage.
LEPUS AMERICANUS, Richardson, Fauna Boreali A., p. 217.
    "   VIRGINIANUS, Bach, Acad. Nat. Sciences, Philadelphia, vol. vii., p. 301.
    "   AMERICANUS, Bach, Ib., p. 403, and Ib., vol. viii., p. 76.
    "   AMERICANUS, Dekay, Nat. Hist. State of New York, p. 95, pl. 26.

Description.

Incisors, pure white, shorter and smaller than in *L. Glacialis;* upper ones moderately grooved; the two posterior upper incisors very small. The margins of the orbits project considerably, having a distinct depression in the frontal bone; this is more conspicuous in the old than in the younger animals. Head rather short; nose blunt; eyes large and prominent; ears placed far back, and near each other; whiskers, long and numerous; body, elongated, thickly clothed with long loose hair, with a soft downy fur beneath; legs, long; hind-legs, nearly twice the length of the fore-legs; feet, thickly clothed with hair, completely concealing the nails, which are long, thin, very sharp, and slightly arched. So thickly are the soles covered with hair, that an impression by the nails, is not generally visible in their tracks made while passing over the snow, unless when running very fast. Tail, very short, covered with fur, but not very bushy. The form of this species is on the whole not very elegant; its long hind legs, although remarkably well adapted for rapid locomotion, and its diminutive tail, would lead the spectator at first sight to pronounce it an awkward animal; which is, nevertheless, far from being the fact. Its fur never lies smooth and compact, either in winter or summer, as does that of many other species, but seems to hang loosely on its back and sides, giving it a somewhat shaggy appearance. The hair on the body, is in summer about an inch and a half long, and in winter, a little longer.

Colour.

In summer, the whole of the upper surface is reddish-brown, formed by hairs that are at their roots and for two-thirds of their length, of a blueish ash colour, then, reddish-yellow, succeeded by a narrow line of dark-brown, the part next the tips or points, reddish-brown, but nearly all the hairs tipped with black—this colour predominating toward the rump. Whiskers, mostly black, a few white, the longest reaching beyond the head; ears, brown, with a narrow black border on the outer margin, and a slight fringe of white hairs on the inner. In some specimens, there is a fawn, and in others a light coloured, edge, around the eyes, and a few white hairs on the forehead. The pupil of the eye is dark, the iris, light silvery-yellow; point of nose, chin, and under the throat, white; neck, yellowish-brown. Inner surface of legs, and under surface of body, white; between the hind-legs, to the insertion of the tail, white; upper surface of the tail, brown, under surface white. The summer dress of this species is assumed in April, and remains without much change till about the beginning of November in the latitude of Quebec, and till the middle of the same month, in the State of New York and the western parts of Pennsylvania; after which season the animal gains its winter pelage. During winter, in high Northern latitudes, it becomes nearly pure white, with the exception of the black edge on the outer borders of the ears. In the latitude of Albany, New York, it has always a tinge of reddish-brown, more conspicuous in some specimens than in others, giving it a wavy appearance, especially when the animal is running, or when the fur is in the least agitated. In the winter season the hair is plumbeous at base, then reddish, and is broadly tipped with white. The parts of the body which are the last to assume the white change, are the forehead and shoulders; we have two winter-killed specimens before us that have the forehead, and a patch on the shoulders, brown. On the under surface, the fur in most specimens is white, even to the roots. A few long black hairs arise above and beneath the eyes, and extend backwards. The soles have a yellowish soiled appearance.

We possess a specimen of the young, about half grown, which in its general aspect resembles the adult; the colour of the back, however, is a shade darker, and the under surface, an ashy white. The black edge is very conspicuous on the outer rim of the ear, and some of the whiskers are of unusual length, reaching beyond the head to the middle of the ear. The tail is very short, black above, and grayish-white beneath. The young become white in the autumn of the first year, but assume their winter colouring a little later in the season than the adults. We have met with some specimens in the New York markets, late in January, in which the change of colour was very partial, the summer pelage still predominating.

Dimensions.

The size and weight of the Northern hare, we have found to vary very much. The measurements hitherto given, were generally taken from stuffed specimens, which afford no very accurate indications of the size of the animal when living, or when recently killed. Dr. GODMAN, on the authority of Prince CHARLES LUCIEN BONAPARTE, gives the measurement of a recent specimen, as thirty-one inches, and Dr. HARLAN's measurement of the same specimen after it had been stuffed, was sixteen inches. We think it probable that the Prince and the Doctor adopted different modes of measuring. All stuffed specimens shrink very much; of a dozen now in our collection, there is not one that measures more than eighteen inches, from point of nose to root of tail, and several white adults measure but fifteen inches.

The following measurements are from the largest specimen we have procured, taken when the animal was recently killed.

Dimensions.

From point of nose to root of tail	$19\frac{1}{4}$ inches.
Tail (vertebræ)	$1\frac{1}{4}$ do.
Do., to end of hair	$2\frac{1}{4}$ do.
From heel to end of middle claw	$5\frac{1}{2}$ do.
Height of ear	$3\frac{1}{2}$ do.

Another specimen of moderate size.

From point of nose to root of tail	16 do.
Tail (vertebræ)	$1\frac{1}{2}$ do.
Do., to end of hair	$2\frac{1}{2}$ do.
From heel to end of middle claw	$5\frac{1}{4}$ do.
Height of ear	$3\frac{1}{2}$ do.

Weight:—This species in the beginning of winter varies from three to six and a half pounds, but we consider $5\frac{1}{2}$ pounds to be the average weight of a full-grown animal in good condition.

Habits.

Our different species of Hares, and more especially the present one and the little gray rabbit, have been so much mixed up in the accounts of authors, that great confusion exists in regard to their habits, and their specific identity. The assertion of WARDEN, that the American Hare retreats into hollow trees when pursued, applies to the gray rabbit, for which it was no doubt intended, but not to the Northern Hare. We are not aware that the latter ever takes

Plate XI

Nº 3.

Drawn from Nature by J.J.Audubon F.R.S.F.L.S.

Drawn on Stone by R. Trembly

Northern Hare. (Old & Young)

Summer pelage.

shelter either in a hole in the earth, or in a hollow tree. We have seen it chased by hounds for whole days, and have witnessed the repetition of these hunts for several successive winters, without ever knowing it to seek concealment or security in such places. It depends on its long legs, and on the thickness of the woods, to aid it in evading the pursuit of its enemies. When hunted, it winds and doubles among thick clusters of young pines and scrub-oaks, or leads the dogs through entangled patches of hemlock and spruce fir, until it sometimes wearies out its pursuers; and unless the hunter should appear, and stop its career with the gun, it is almost certain to escape.

In deep snows, the animal is so light, and is so well supported by its broad furry-feet, that it passes over the surface making only a faint impression, whilst the hounds plunge deep into the snow at every bound, and soon give up the hopeless pursuit. It avoids not only open grounds, but even open woods, and confines itself to the densest and most impenetrable forests. Although it wanders by night in many directions in search of its appropriate food, we have scarcely ever seen its tracks in the open fields; it seems cautiously to avoid the cabbage and turnip fields of the farmer, and seldom even in the most retired places makes an encroachment on his cultivated grounds.

The food of this species, in summer consists of various kinds of juicy and tender grasses, and the bark, leaves, and buds, of several small shrubs; and these Hares seem to be particularly fond of the young twigs of the wild allspice, (*Laurus benzoin*,) but in winter, when the earth is covered with snow, they gain a precarious subsistence from the buds and bark of such trees as are suited to their taste. Sometimes they scratch up the snow to feed on the leaves and berries of the various species of *Pyrola*, found in the Northern States. The bark of the willow, birch, and poplar, and the buds of young pines, are sought after by them with avidity. We have seen persons in the Northern part of the State of New York, who were desirous of shooting these animals by moon-light, watching near American black-poplar trees, (*Populus Hudsonica*,) which they had cut down for the purpose of attracting them to feed on their buds and tender twigs, in which they were often successful. Some of these Hares which we had in a domesticated state, were fed on cabbage leaves, turnips, parsnips, potatoes, and sweet apples. During one very cold winter, when these could not be conveniently obtained, they were frequently supplied with clover-hay, to which, when more agreeable food was not given them, they did not evince any aversion; from time to time also, outer branches of willow, poplar, or apple, trees, were thrown into their enclosure, the bark of which, seemed to be greatly relished by them.

The Northern Hare, like most others of the genus, seeks its food only by night or in the early part of the evening. To this habit it is more exclusively confined during autumn and winter, than in spring and summer. In the latter seasons, especially in spring, these animals are frequently observed in the morning, and as the sun is declining, in the afternoon, cautiously proceeding along some solitary by-path of the forest. Two or three may often be seen associated together, appearing full of activity and playfulness. When disturbed on these occasions, they stamp on the ground, making a noise so loud, that it can be heard at some distance, then hopping a few yards into the thicket, they sit with ears erect, seemingly listening, to ascertain whether they are pursued or not. This habit of thumping on the earth, is common to most hares and rabbits. We have particularly noticed it in the domesticated rabbit, (*L. cuniculus*) and in our common gray rabbit. They are more particularly in the habit of doing it on moonlight nights; it is indicative either of fear or anger, and is a frequent action among the males when they meet in combat. During cold weather, this Hare retires to its form at early dawn, or shelters itself under the thick foliage of fallen tree tops, particularly those of the pine and hemlock. It occasionally retires to the same cover for a number of nights in succession, but this habit is by no means common; and the sportsman who expects on some succeeding day to find this animal in the place from which it was once started, is likely to be disappointed; although we are not aware, that any other of our species of hare are so attached to particular and beaten paths through the woods, as the one now under consideration. It nightly pursues these paths, not only during the deep snows of winter, but for a period of several years, if not killed or taken, wandering through them even during summer. We have seen a dozen caught at one spot, in snares composed of horse-hair or brass wire, in the course of a winter, and when the snow had disappeared, and the spring was advanced, others were still captured in the same way, and in the same paths.

The period of gestation in this species is believed to be, (although we cannot speak with positive certainty,) about six weeks. Two females which we domesticated, and kept in a warren, produced young, one on the tenth, and the other on the fifteenth, of May; one had four, and the other six leverets, which were deposited on a nest of straw, the inside of which was lined with a considerable quantity of hair plucked from their bodies. They succeeded in rearing all their young but one, which was killed by the male of a common European rabbit. They were not again gravid during that season. Ill health, and more important studies, required us to be absent for six months, and when we returned, all our pets had escaped to the woods, therefore we could not satisfactorily finish the observations on their habits in confinement, which had interested and amused us in many a leisure hour.

We, however, think it probable that the females in their wild state, may produce young, twice during the season. Those referred to above, were much harassed by other species which were confined in the same warren, and might therefore have been less prolific than if they had enjoyed their liberty undisturbed, amid the recesses of their native woods. We have frequently observed the young of the Northern Hare in May, and again in July. These last must have been either from a second litter, or the produce of a young female of the previous year. The young, at birth were able to see. They were covered with short hair; and appeared somewhat darker in colour than the adults, at that season. They left their nest in ten or twelve days, and from that time seemed to provide for themselves, and to derive little sustenance or protection from their mothers. The old males at this period seemed to be animated with renewed courage; they had previously suffered themselves to be chased and worried by the common English rabbit, and even retreated from the attacks of the gray rabbit; but they now stood their ground, and engaged in fierce combats with the other prisoners confined with them, and generally came off victorious. They stamped with their feet, used their teeth and claws to a fearful purpose, and in the fight, tore off patches of skin, and mutilated the ears of their former persecutors, till they were left in undisturbed possession of the premises!

The males did not evince the vicious propensity to destroy their young, which is observed in the domesticated English rabbit; on the contrary, they would frequently sit beside their little family, when they were but a day or two old, seeming to enjoy their playfulness and to watch their progress to maturity.

The Northern Hare seems during summer to prefer dry and elevated situations, and to be more fond of grounds covered with pines and firs, than of those that are overgrown with oak or hickory. The swamps and marshes soil their feet, and after having been compelled to pass through them, they are for hours employed in rubbing and drying their paws. In winter, however, when such places are hardened by the frost, they not only have paths through them in every direction, but occasionally seek a fallen tree top as a hiding or resting place, in the centre of a swamp. We have observed them in great numbers in an almost impenetrable thicket of black larch, or hackmatack, (*Larix pendula*,) considerable portions of which were during summer a perfect morass. In what are called the "bark clearings," places where hemlock trees have been cut down to procure tan bark, this species is sometimes so abundant that twenty or thirty of them may be started in a day's walk.

As an article of food, this is the most indifferent of all our species of Hares; its flesh is hard, dry, almost juiceless, possessing none of the flavour of the English hare, and much inferior to that of our gray rabbit. Epicures, however, who often regard as dainties dishes that are scarce, and who, by the skilful application of the culinary art, possess means of rendering things savoury that are of themselves insipid, may dispute this point with us.

The Northern Hare, as is proverbially the case with all the species, has many enemies. It is pursued by men and dogs, by carniverous beasts of the forest, by eagles, by hawks, and by owls. In the northern parts of Maine, in Canada, and in the countries farther north, their most formidable enemies are the Canada lynx, (*Lynx Canadensis*,) the jer falcon, (*Falco Islandicus*,) and the snowy owl, (*Surnea nyctea*.) In the New England States, however, and in New York, the red-tailed hawk, (*Buteo Borealis*,) is occasionally seen with one of these species in its talons. But its most formidable enemy is the great horned owl, (*Bubo Virginianus*.) We have also, on one occasion, observed a common house-cat dragging a full grown Northern Hare from the woods, to feed her young. Lads on their way to school, entrap them with snares attached to a bent twig, placed along the paths they nightly resort to. The hunter finds recreation in pursuing them with hounds, whilst he places himself in some wood-path where they were last seen to pass. The Hare runs from fifty to a hundred yards ahead of the dogs, and in its windings and turnings to escape from them frequently returns to the spot where the hunter is stationed, and falls by a shot from his gun.

The Northern Hare, when rapidly pursued, makes such great efforts to escape, that the poor creature (as we have said already,) is occasionally successful, and fairly outruns the hounds, whilst the hunter is cunningly avoided by it when doubling. After one of these hard chases, however, we have known the animal die from the fatigue it had undergone, or from having been overheated. We once saw one, which had been closely pressed by the dogs nearly all the afternoon, return to a thicket after the hounds had been called off, and the sportsmen had given up the vain pursuit. Next morning we

Plate XII

N°3

Drawn on Stone by W^m E Hitchcock

Northern Hare

Drawn from Nature by J.J.Audubon,F.R.S.F.L.S.

lith. Printed & Col^d by J.T. Bowen,Phil

examined the place it had retired to, and to our surprise, discovered the hare sitting in its form, under a dwarfish, crooked, pine-bush; it was covered with snow, and quite dead. In this instance the hare had no doubt been greatly overheated by the race of the preceding day, as well as exhausted, and terrified; and the poor thing being in that condition very susceptible of cold, was probably chilled by the night air and the falling snow, until its palpitating heart, gradually impelling the vital fluid with fainter and slower pulsations, at length ceased its throbings forever.

Sometimes we have found these Hares dead in the woods after the melting of the snow in the Spring, and on examination we found they were entangled in portions of wire snares, frequently, entwined round their necks; from which they had been unable to extricate themselves.

This species when caught alive cannot be taken into the hand, like the gray rabbit, with impunity; the latter, when seized by the ears or hindlegs, soon becomes quiet, and is harmless; but the Northern Hare struggles to escape, and makes a formidable resistance with its teeth and nails. On one occasion a servant who was expert at catching the gray rabbit in traps, came to us with a rueful countenance, holding a hare in his hands, exhibiting at the same time sundry severe scratches he had received, showing us his torn clothes, and a place on his leg which the animal had bitten, and declaring that he had caught "a rabbit as cross as a cat." We ascertained it to be a Northern Hare, in its summer dress, and although its captor had not been able to distinguish it from the gray rabbit by its colour, he certainly had had a practical lesson in natural history, which he did not soon forget.

A living individual of this species, which we have in Charleston in a partially domesticated state, for the purpose of trying to ascertain the effect of a warm climate on its changes of colour, is particularly cross when approached by a stranger. It raises its fur, and springs at the intruder with almost a growl, and is ready with its claws and teeth to gratify its rage, and inflict a wound on the person who has aroused its ire. When thus excited, it reminded us by its attitudes of an angry racoon.

The skin of the Northern Hare is so tender and easily torn, and the fur is so apt to be spoiled and drop off on being handled, that it is difficult to prepare perfect specimens for the naturalist's cabinet. The pelt is not in much request among the furriers, and is regarded by the hatter as of little value. The hind-feet, however, are used by the latter in a part of the process by which the soft, glossy, surface is imparted to his fabric, and answer the purpose of a soft hat-brush.

Geographical Distribution.

This species is found in portions of the British possessions, as far as the sixty-eighth parallel of North latitude. It is, however, confined to the Eastern portion of our Continent; RICHARDSON, who represents it as "a common animal from one extremity of the Continent to the other," seems to have mistaken for it another species which replaces it on the North West coast. Although it does not range as far to the North as the Polar hare, it is decidedly a Northern species; it is found at Hudson's Bay, in Newfoundland, Canada, all the New-England States, and in the Northern portions of New York, Pennsylvania, and Ohio. Mr. DOUGHTY informed us that he had procured a specimen on the Alleghany Mountains in the Northern part of Virginia, Lat. 40°29′, where it had never before been observed by the inhabitants. On seeking for it afterwards in the locality from which he obtained it, we were unsuccessful, and we are inclined to believe that it is only occasionally that some straggler wanders so far South among these mountains, and that its Southern limit may be set down at about 41°.

General Remarks.

The history of this Hare has been attempted from time to time, by early and recent travellers and naturalists, and most of their accounts of it are only sources of perplexity, and additional difficulties in the way of the naturalist of the present day. Strange mistakes were committed by some of those who wrote on the subject, from PENNANT down to HARLAN, GODMAN, and others still later; and one error appears to have led to another, until even the identity of the species meant to be described by different authors, was finally involved in an almost inextricable web of embarrassment.

As far as we have been able to ascertain, the Northern Hare was first noticed by SAGARD THEODAT, (Hist. de Canada,) in 1636. KALM, (who travelled in America from 1748 to 1751, and whose work was published in the Swedish language, and soon after translated into German and English,) speaks of this species as follows:—"Hares are likewise said to be plentiful even in Hudson's Bay, and they are abundant in Canada, where I have often seen, and found them perfectly corresponding with our Swedish hares. In summer they

have a brownish-gray, and in winter a snowy-white colour, as with us." (KALM'S Travels, &c., vol. ii., p. 45. English translation.)

This judicious and intelligent traveller, undoubtedly here referred to the Northern Hare. He supposed it to be identical with the Alpine, or variable Hare, (Lepus variabilis,) which is found in Sweden and other Northern countries of Europe. That species is a little larger than the Northern Hare, and the tips of its ears are black; but although it is a distinct species, it so nearly resembles the latter, that several authors, GODMAN not excepted, were induced to regard these two species as identical. KALM, (see vol. i., p. 105, Eng. trans.,) whilst he was in the vicinity of Philadelphia, where the Northern Hare never existed, gave a correct account of another species, the American gray rabbit, which we will notice more in detail when we describe that animal. It is very evident that in these two notices of American hares, KALM had reference to two distinct species, and that he pointed out those distinctive marks by which they are separated. If subsequent authors confounded the two species, and created confusion, their errors evidently cannot be owing to any fault of the eminent Swedish traveller.

The first specimens of the Northern Hare that appeared in Europe, were sent by the servants of the Hudson's Bay Company to England, in 1771, (see Phil. Trans., vol. lxii., p. 13.) There were four specimens in the collection, exhibiting the various gradations of colour. In addition to these, a living animal of the same species was received about the same time, probably by the same ship. It was brought to the notice of the Philosophical Society, in a letter from the Hon. DAINES BARRINGTON, read 16th January, 1772. This letter is interesting, since it gives us some idea of the state of natural science in England, at that early day. The animal had for some time remained alive, but had died in the previous November. It had at that time already changed its summer colour, and become nearly white. It was *boiled*, in order to ascertain whether it was a hare or a rabbit, as according to RAY, if the flesh was brown it was a hare, if white a rabbit. It proved to be brown, and was declared to be a hare. The test was strange enough, but the conclusion was correct. In May, of the same year, J. R. FORSTER, Esq., F. R. S., described this, among twenty quadrupeds, that had been sent from Hudson's Bay. After giving an account of the manner in which it was captured by snares made of brass wire and pack thread, he designates its size as "bigger than the rabbit, but less than the Alpine hare." In this he was quite correct. He then goes on to show that its hind-feet are longer in proportion to the body than those of the rabbit, and common hare, &c. He finally speaks of its habits, and here his first error occurs. KALM's accounts of *two* different species were supposed by him to refer to one species only, and whilst the Northern Hare was *described*—some of the *habits* of the American gray rabbit were incorrectly referred to it.

As, however, FORSTER gave it no specific name, and his description on the whole was but a loose one, it was left to another naturalist to give it a scientific appellation.

In 1777, ERXLEBEN gave the first scientific description of it, and named it *Lepus Americanus*. SCHREBER, (as we are prepared to show in our article on *Lepus sylvaticus*,) published an account of it immediately afterwards, under the name of *Lepus nanus*.

This description, as may easily be seen, was principally taken from FORSTER. SCHŒPFF about the same period, and PALLAS in 1778, under the name of *L. Hudsonicus*, and PENNANT in 1780, under that of American hare, followed each other in quick succession.

In GMELIN'S LINNÆUS, (1788,) it is very imperfectly described in one single line. All these authors copied the error of FORSTER in giving to the Northern Hare the habits of the American gray rabbit.

In the work of DESMAREST, (Mammalogie, ou description des espèces de Mammifères, p. 351, Paris, 1820,) a description is given of "Esp. Lièvre d'Amérique, Lepus Americanus." This however, instead of being a description of the true *L. Americanus* of all previous authors, is in most particulars a pretty good description of our gray rabbit. HARLAN, who published his Fauna in 1825, translated and published this description very literally, even to its faults, (see Fauna Americana, p. 196.) Having thus erroneously disposed of the gray rabbit, under the name of *L. Americanus*, the true Lepus Americanus was named by him *L. Virginianus*! The following year, Dr. GODMAN gave a description of the Northern Hare, referring it to the *Lepus variabilis* of Europe!

After Dr. RICHARDSON's return from his perilous journey through the Polar regions, he prepared in England his valuable Fauna Boreali Americana, which was published in 1829. Specimens labelled. *L. Americanus* of ERX-LEBEN, were still in the British Museum, and he published descriptions of his own specimens, under that name. The gray rabbit did not come within the range of his investigations, but having received a hunter's skin, from the vicinity of the Columbia river, he supposed it to be the *L. Virginianus* of HARLAN, and described it under that name. This skin, however, has since proved to belong to a different species; the Northern Hare not being found in the regions bordering that river.

In 1837, having several new species of Hare to describe, we began to look into this subject, and endeavoured to correct the errors in regard to the species, that had crept into the works of various authors.

We had not seen ERXLEBEN's work, and supposing that the species were correctly designated, we published our views of the habits, &c., of the two species, (whose identity and proper cognomen we have, we hope, just established,) under the old names of *L. Virginianus* and *L. Americanus*, (see Jour. of Acad. of Nat. Sciences of Phila., vol. vii., pl. 2 p. 282.) The article had scarcely been printed, before we obtained a copy of ERXLEBEN, and we immediately perceived and corrected the errors that had been committed, giving the Northern Hare its correct name, *L. Americanus*, and bestowing on the gray rabbit, which, through the mistakes we have already described, had been left without any name, that of *Lepus sylvaticus*, (Jour. Acad. Nat. Sciences of Phil. Vol. vii., p. 403.) The reasons for this arrangement were given in our remarks on the genus LEPUS, in a subsequent paper, (Jour. Acad. Sc., vol. viii., pl. 1, p. 75,) where we characterized a number of additional new species. In 1842, Dr. DEKAY, (see Nat. Hist. of New York, p. 95,) acceding to this arrangement of the Northern Hare, under the specific name of *L. Americanus*, remarks, "This Hare was first vaguely indicated by ERXLEBEN in 1777." In a spirit of great fairness, however, that author's original description was published at the foot of the article.

In order to set this matter at rest, remove this species from the false position in which it has so long stood, and give its first describer the credit to which he is entitled, we will here insert the description above alluded to.

"Lepus Americanus, L. cauda abbreviata; pedibus posticis corpore dimidio longioribus; auricularum caudoque apicibus griseis.

"Die Hasen—KALM, Hudson's Bay Quadrup., BARRINGTON, Phil. Trans. vol. lxii., p. 376. Magnitudine medius inter L. cuniculum et timidum Alpinum, (sc. L. timidus, FORSTER, Phil. Trans. vol. lxii., p. 375.) Auriculanum et caudæ apices perpetuo grisei—Pedes postici longiores quam in L. timido et cuniculo, color griseo-fuscus; Hieme in frigidioribus albus.

"Habitat in America boreali ad fretum Hudsoni copiosissimus, nocturnus. Non fœdit, degit sub arborum radicibus, inque cavis arboribus. Parit bis vel semel in anno; pullos quinque ad septem; caro bona, colore L. timidi."

In great deference, we would submit whether the above is not more than a *"vague indication"* of a species. To us it appears a tolerably full description for the era in which the author lived, and considering the few species of Hare then known.

There were at that early period but three Hares with which naturalists were familiar:—*L. timidus*, the common European Hare; *L. variabilis*, the variable Hare; and *L. cuniculus*, the European burrowing rabbit. With these, ERXLEBEN compares this species in size and colour. With the exception of one of the habits he mentions, this description appears to us creditable to him. There have been many occasions, when perplexed in guessing at the species intended to be described by old authors, (the Father of natural history, LINNÆUS himself, not excepted,) we would have hailed a description like this, as a light in darkness. The species ERXLEBEN had in view cannot be mistaken; he describes it very correctly as "*magnitudine medius inter L. cuniculum et timidum Alpinum.*" Our American gray rabbit, instead of being intermediate between *L. cuniculus* and the Alpine hare, is smaller than either. "*Pedes postici longiores quam in L. timido et cuniculo.*" The long hind-feet are distinctive marks of the Northern Hare; but those of our gray rabbit are much shorter than those of *L. timidus*, or common hare of Europe. "*Hieme in frigidioribus albus.*" Our gray rabbit, contrary to the assertion of most authors, does not become white in winter in any latitude. "*Habitat in America boreali ad fretum Hudsoni copiosissimus.*" Dr. RICHARDSON, and every Northern traveller with whom we have conversed, have assured us, that our gray rabbit does not exist at Hudson's Bay, where the Norther Hare is quite abundant, and where that, and the Polar hare, (the last named species existing still further North,) are the only species to be found. We have examined and compared the original specimen described by Dr. RICHARDSON, and also those in the British Museum that have successively replaced the specimens first sent to England, and find that they all belong to this species. In fact our gray rabbit is very little known in England or Scotland; since, after an examination of all the principal Museums in those countries, we met with but two specimens, one of which was not named, and the other was not improperly labelled, "Lepus Americanus Harlan, non Erxleben."

The rigid rule of priority will always preserve for the Northern Hare the name of *L. Americanus*, whilst *L. nanus, L. Hudsonicus*, and *L. Virginianus*, must be set down merely as synonymes.

Genus Fiber.—Illiger.

Dental Formula.

$$\text{Incisive } \frac{2}{2}; \text{ Molar } \frac{3-3}{3-3} = 16.$$

Lower incisors, sharp-pointed, and convex in front; molars, with flat crowns, furnished with scaly transverse zig-zag laminæ. Fore-feet with four toes and the rudiment of a thumb; hind-feet, with five toes, the edges furnished with stiff hairs, which assist the animal in swimming, instead of the feet being palmated or webbed; hind-toes, slightly palmated. Tail, long, compressed, granular, nearly naked, having but a few scattered hairs. Glands, near the origin of the tail, which secrete a white, musky, and somewhat offensive fluid. Mammæ six, abdominal.

This genus differs from the ARVICOLÆ in its dentition; the first inferior molar, has one point more than the corresponding tooth in the latter, and all the molars acquire roots immediately after the animal becomes an adult. We have frequently heard complaints made by students of natural history, of the difficulties they had to encounter at the very outset, from the want of accuracy and uniformity in the works of authors, when stating the characters by which they defined the genera they established. The justness of these complaints may be well illustrated by examining the accounts of the present genus as given by several well-known writers.

ILLIGER says it has four molars on each side, (*Utrinqui quaterni*,) see Prodromus systematis mammaliarum et avum, making in all twenty teeth. WIEGMAN and RUTHE, have given the same dental arrangement, see Handbuch der Zoologie, Berlin, 1832. F. CUVIER, who has been followed by most authors, has given it—Incisive $\frac{2}{2}$; Canine $\frac{3-3}{3-3}$, $=$ sixteen teeth. GRIFFITH, Animal Kingdom, vol. iii., p. 106, describes it as having— Incisive $\frac{2}{2}$, Canine $\frac{4-4}{4-4}$ $=$ twenty teeth; and in his synopsis of the species of mammalia, (sp. 532,) its dental arrangement is thus characterized—Incisive $\frac{2}{2}$, Canine $\frac{3-3}{3-3}$, Cheek-teeth, $\frac{3-3}{3-3}$, giving to it the extravagant number of twenty-eight teeth. This last statement is most probably only a typographical error. A correct examination and description of the teeth of this genus requires a considerable degree of labour, besides great attention and care, as they are placed so close to each other that without a good magnifying glass it is difficult to find the lines of separation, and almost impossible to ascertain their number, without extracting them one by one.

The descriptions and figures of their dental arrangement, by Baron CUVIER, and F. CUVIER are correct: see Ondatras, dents des mammifères, pl. 53, p. 157, and Recherches sur les ossemens fossiles, t. 5, p. 1.

ILLIGER's generic name, Fiber, is derived from the Latin word, *Fiber*, a beaver. There is only one species described as belonging to this genus.

Fiber Zibethicus.—Linn.

Musk-Rat.—Musquash.

Plate xiii.—Old, and Young.—Natural size.

F. supra, rufo-fuscus; subtus cinereus; Leporem sylvaticum magnitudine sub æquans.

Characters.

General colour, reddish-brown above, cinereous beneath; about the size of the American gray rabbit.

Synonymes.

MUSSASCUS, Smith's Virginia, 1626. (Pinkerton's Collection of Voyages and Travels, vol. xiii., p. 31.)
RAT MUSQUÉ, Sagard Theodat, Canada, p. 771.
CASTOR ZIBETHICUS, Linn. Syst. Nat., xii. ed., vol. 1, p. 79.
L'ONDATRA, Buffon, Tom 10, p. 1.
MUSKRAT, Lawson, Carolina, p. 120.
MUSK BEAVER, Pennant, Arc. Zool., vol. i., p. 106.
MUSQUASH, Hearne, Journey, p. 379.
MUS ZIBETHICUS, Linn., Gmel., vol. i., p. 125.
FIBER ZIBETHICUS, Sabine, Franklin's Journey, p. 659.

MUSK RAT, Godman's Nat. Hist., p. 58.
ONDATHRA, Huron Indians.
MUSQUASH, WATSUSS, or WACHUSK; the animal that sits on the ice in
a round form. Cree Indians, (Richardson.)

Description.

Body, of a nearly cylindrical shape, resembling that of the Norway rat.
Head, short; neck, very short, and indistinct; legs, short; thighs, hid in the
body. Tail, two-thirds the length of the body, compressed, convex on the
sides, thickest in the middle, tapering to an acute point at the extremity;
covered with small scales, which are visible through the thinly scattered hairs.
Incisors, large; upper ones, a little rounded anteriorly without grooves,
truncated on the cutting edge; lower ones, a little the longest; nose, thick, and
obtuse; whiskers, moderate in length, seldom reaching beyond the ear; eyes,
small, and lateral, nearly concealed in the fur; ears, short, oblong, covered
with hair, and hidden by the fur.

On the fore-legs, the wrist and fingers only are visible beyond the body,
they are covered with a short shining coat of hair.

The thumb has a conspicuous palm, and is armed with a nail, as long as the
adjoining finger nails. Hind-legs, as short as the fore-legs, so that the body
when the animal is walking touches the ground.

The hind-feet are turned obliquely inwards, and at first sight remind us of
the foot of a duck. The two middle toes may be called semi-palmated, and
there is also a short web between the third and fourth toes. The margins of the
soles, and toes, are furnished with an even row of rigid hairs, curving inwards;
under-surface of feet, naked; claws, conical, and slightly arched.

The whole body is clothed with a short, downy, fur, intermixed with longer
and coarser hairs. In many particulars the skin resembles that of the beaver,
although the fur is far less compact downy and lustrous.

Colour.

Fur, on the upper parts a third longer than beneath; from the roots to near
the extremities, blueish-gray, or lead-colour, tipped with brown; on the under
surface it is a little lighter in colour, and the hairs are tipped with brownish-
gray. This species, when viewed from above, appears of a general dark-brown
colour, with a reddish tint visible on the neck, sides, and legs; chin, throat,
and under-surface, grayish-ash; tail, dark-brown. Incisors, yellow; nails,
white. The colour of this animal, so much resembles that of the muddy banks
on which it is frequently seated, that we have often, when looking at one from
a little distance, mistaken it for a lump or clod of earth, until it moved.

Dimensions.

Length of head and body	. . . .	15 inches.
" of tail	. . . .	10 do.
From heel to longest nail	. . . .	3 do.
Height of ear	. . . .	$\frac{1}{2}$ do.

Habits.

Reader! If you are a native of, or have sojourned in any portion, almost, of
our continent, and have interested yourself in observing the "beasts of the
field" in our woods or along our streams, to the slightest degree, you have
probably often seen the Musk-Rat—or should you have been confined to the
busy marts of commerce, in our large cities; you may even there have seen his
skin, and thought it a beautiful fur. It is, in fact, when the animal is killed in
good season, superior to very many other materials for making beaver (?) hats,
as well as for other purposes, and thousands of Musk-Rat skins are annually
used in the United States, while still greater numbers are shipped to Europe,
principally to Great Britain.

This species is nocturnal, and consequently its manners and customs cannot
be correctly ascertained from the occasional glimpses of it, which we obtain by
day-light, as it may chance to pass rapidly through the water, seeking to
conceal itself under the root of some large tree projecting into the deep pool,
or as it dives suddenly to the mouth of its hole under the shelter of the steep or
over-hanging bank of the stream, into which it hastily retires, when our
appearance has alarmed it.

We have often, in the northern part of the State of New York, or on the
Schuylkill, or near Frankford, in Pennsylvania, gone, during the day, to look
for, and observe these animals, to places where we knew they abounded; but
although we might patiently wait for hours, with book in hand to beguile the
time, we could rarely see one, and should one appear, it was only for an

instant. But at such places, so soon as the last rays of the setting sun have
ceased to play upon the smooth water, and when the last bright sparkling tints
he has thrown as a "farewell till to-morrow," upon rock tree and floweret, are
succeeded by the deep quiet-gray of twilight; the placid surface of the stream
is agitated in every direction, and many a living creature emerges from its
diurnal retreat, and may be observed in full activity above or beneath the
water, and first to appear is the Musk-Rat—which may perchance dart out
from underneath the very old stump, on which we have been so patiently
seated! We are perhaps startled by an unexpected noise and plash—and two
seconds after, up comes the head of the animal to the surface, at least five yards
off—and, if we happen not to be observed, we may look on, and see him
swimming merrily with his companions, or seeking his "breakfast," for his
day has just begun!

When we were about seventeen years of age, we resided on our farm,
"Mill-Grove," situated at the confluence of the Schuylkill river and the
Perkioming creek.

On the latter, above a mill-dam which then existed, there was an island,
divided from the shore on the southerly side by a small channel not more than
twenty-five or thirty feet in width, in which we had occasionally observed
Musk-Rats swimming. Having a friend at our house for a few weeks, we one
evening persuaded him to accompany us to this spot, with the view of
procuring a few of these animals. Accordingly, after due preparation, we made
our way toward the creek. We approached the bank quietly, and seated
ourselves on some moss-covered stones, without disturbing the silence of the
night; the only interruption to which was the gentle ripple of the pure stream,
which, united with the broader Schuylkill, still flows onward, and conveys to
the now great city of Philadelphia, that inestimable treasure, pure water. Here
then, we waited, long and patiently—so long, that our companion became
restless, said that he would like to smoke a cigar, and accordingly lighted a
"fragrant Havana." We remained watching, but saw no Musk-Rats that
evening, as these cunning animals no doubt observed the light at the end of
my friend's cigar. We have since that time known many a sportsman lose a
shot at a fine buck, by indulging in this relaxation, while at a "stand," as it is
generally termed. To return to our Musk-Rats, we went home disappointed,
but on the next evening proceeded to the same spot, and in less than an hour
shot three, which we secured. Next day we made a drawing of one of them,
which was afterwards lost. We have now in our possession only two drawings
of quadrupeds made by us at this early period; one of which represents the
American otter, and the other a mink. They were drawn with coloured chalkes
and crayons, and both are now quite rubbed and soiled, like ourselves having
suffered somewhat from the hand of time, and the jostling we have encountered.

We have sometimes, when examining or describing one of our well-known
animals, allowed ourselves to fall into a train of thought as we turned over the
pages of some early writer, which carried us back to the period of the discovery
of our country, or still earlier explorations of wild and unknown regions. We
have endeavoured to picture to ourselves, the curiosity eagerly indulged, the
gratified hopes, and the various other feelings, that must have filled the minds
of the adventurous voyagers that first landed on AMERICA's forest-margined
coast. What were their impressions, on seeing the strange objects that met
their eyes in all directions? what thought they of the inhabitants they met
with? and what were their ideas on seeing birds and quadrupeds hitherto
unheard of and unknown? The most indifferent or phlegmatic temperament
must have been aroused, and the traveller, whatever his profession—whether
soldier, sailor, trader, or adventurer—at such times, doubtless, would pause
for awhile, conceal himself, and noiselessly observe the strange movements of
the wonderful creature he has just for the first time seen—for all the Creator's
works are wonderful—and it is only because we behold many of them
continually, that we finally cease to marvel at the conformation of the most
common domesticated species.

Something in this way were our reflections directed, while turning over the
pages of Captain JOHN SMITH, whose life was preserved by the fair and
heroic POCAHONTAS. This gallant soldier was, as well as we can learn, the
first person who gave any account of the Musk-Rat. His "General History of
Virginia, New England, and the Summer Isles," was published in London, in
1624, folio; he styles himself, "sometimes Governor in those Countries, and
Admiral of New-England."

SMITH, in this account of Virginia, &c., says of this animal—"A
Mussascus is a beast of the form and nature of our water-rat, but many of them
smell exceedingly strong of musk."

LA HONTAN, in a letter dated Boucherville, May, 1687, (see Trav. in
Canada,) says—"In the same place we killed some Musk-Rats, or a sort of
animals which resemble a rat in their shape, and are as big as a rabbit. The
skins of these rats are very much valued, as differing but little from those of

Plate XIII

Drawn from Nature by J.J.Audubon, F.R.S.F.L.S

Drawn on Stone by W.m E. Hitchcock

Lith Printed & Col.d by J.T Bowen, Phil.

Mush: Rat. — Musquash.

Old & Young.

beavers." He goes on to describe the manner in which the "strong and sweet smell" of musk is produced; in which he so much betrays his ignorance of natural history, that we will not expose the vulgar error by repeating it here. But if one Frenchman of the 17th century, committed some errors, in relating the habits of this species, another, early in the 18th, (1725,) made ample amends, by giving us a scientific description of its form, internal structure, and habits, that would do credit to the most careful investigator of the present day. This accomplished naturalist, was Mons. SARRASIN, King's Physician at Quebec, and correspondent of the French Academy; in honour of whom LINNÆUS named the genus *Sarrasenia*. He dissected a number of Musk-Rats, described the animal, gave an account of the "follicles which contain the perfume," and noted its habits.

To this intelligent physician, BUFFON was principally indebted for the information which enabled him to draw up his article on the Canadian Musk-Rat.

In 1789, KALM, (Beschreibung der Reise nach dem Noerdlichen America,) gives a very correct account of the characteristics and habits of this species.

Musk-Rats are lively playful animals when in their proper element, the water, and many of them may be occasionally seen disporting on a calm night in some mill-pond, or deep sequestered pool, crossing and recrossing in every direction, leaving long ripples in the water behind them, whilst others stand for a few moments on little knolls or tufts of grass, or on stones or logs, on which they can get footing above the water, or on the banks of the pond, and then plunge one after another into the water; at times, one is seen lying perfectly still on the surface of the pond or stream, with its body widely spread out, and as flat as it can be. Suddenly it gives the water a smart flap with its tail, somewhat in the manner of the beaver, and disappears beneath the surface instantaneously—going down head foremost—and reminding one of the quickness and ease with which some species of ducks and grebes dive when shot at. At the distance of ten or twenty yards, the Musk-Rat comes to the surface again, and perhaps, joins its companions in their sports; at the same time, others are feeding on the grassy banks, dragging off the roots of various kinds of plants, or digging underneath the edge of the bank. These animals thus seem to form a little community of social playful creatures, who only require to be unmolested in order to be happy. Should you fire off a fowling-piece, whilst the Musk-Rats are thus occupied, a terrible fright and dispersion ensues—dozens dive at the flash of the gun, or disappear in their holes; and although in the day-time, when they see imperfectly, they may be shot whilst swimming, it is exceedingly difficult to kill one at night. In order to insure success, the gunner must be concealed, so that the animal cannot see the flash when he fires, even with a percussion lock.

The burrows, and houses of this species, are not constructed on such admirable architectural principles as those of the beaver, but are, nevertheless, curious, and well-adapted for the residence of the animal. Having enjoyed opportunities of examining them in several portions of the Northern States, and having been present when hundreds of Musk-Rats were taken, either by digging them out, or catching them in traps, we will endeavour to describe their nests, and the manner in which the hunters generally proceed in order to procure the animals that are in them.

In different localities, the Musk-Rat has very opposite modes of constructing its winter domicil. Where there are overhanging clayey or loamy banks along the stream or pond, they form a winter retreat in the side of the bank, with openings under the water, and their galleries run sometimes to the distance of fifteen or twenty yards from the shore, inclining upward, so as to be above the influence of the high waters, on the breaking up of the ice in spring, or during freshets. There are usually three or four entrances from under the water, which all, however, unite at a point, some distance from the water, and sufficiently high to be secure from inundation, where there is a pretty large excavation. In this "central hall" we have seen nests that would fill a bushel basket. They were composed of decayed plants and grasses, principally sedge, (*Carex*,) the leaves of the arrow-head, (*Sagittaria*,) and the pond-lily, (*Nymphœa*.) They always contained several dried sticks, some of them more than a foot in length; these were sometimes arranged along the sides, but more frequently on the top of the nests. From these nests, there are several, galleries extending still farther from the shore; into the latter the animals retreat, when, after having been prevented from returning to the water, by stopping the entrances, they are disturbed in their chamber. Sometimes we have found their subterranean strongholds leading into others by transverse galleries. These were never so far beneath the surface, as those of the fox, marmot, or skunk. On passing near the burrows of the Musk-Rat, there is always sufficient evidence of their existence in the vicinity; the excrement of the animal, resembling that of the Norway rat, being deposited around, and paths that they have made through the rushes and aquatic plants, that grow in

thick profusion in the immediate neighbourhood, being easily traced; but it is not so easy to discover the entrances. The latter, are always under the water, and usually where it is deepest near the shore. When the Musk-Rat is about to retire to its hole, it swims to within a few feet of the shore, and then dives suddenly and enters it. If you are standing on the bank directly above the mouth of the hole, the rumbling noise under your feet, if you listen attentively, will inform you that it has entered its burrow. It seldom, however, immediately retreats far into its hole, but has small excavations and resting-places on the dry ground a little beyond the reach of the water.

There are, occasionally, very differently constructed nests of the Musk-Rat; we have seen some of them, in the town of Clinton, Dutchess county, and along the margins of swamps in the vicinity of Lake Champlain, in the State of New York; and others, in several localities in Canada. A pond supplied chiefly, if not entirely, by springs, and surrounded by low and marshy ground, is preferred by the Musk-Rats; they seem to be aware that the spring-water it contains, probably will not be solidly frozen, and there they prepare to pass the winter. Such a place, as you may well imagine, cannot without great difficulty be approached, until its boggy and treacherous foundation has been congealed by the hard frosts and the water is frozen over; before this time, the Musk-Rats collect coarse grasses and mud, with which, together with stick, twigs, leaves, and any thing in the vicinity that will serve their purpose, they raise their little houses from two to four feet above the water; the entrance being always from below. We have frequently opened these nests, and found in the centre a dry comfortable bed of grass, sufficiently large to accommodate several of them. When the ponds are frozen over, and a slight fall of snow covers the ground, these edifices resemble small hay-cocks. There is another peculiarity that, it appears to us, indicates a greater degree of intelligence in the Musk-Rat than we are usually disposed to award to it. The animal seems to know that the ice will cover the pond in winter, and that if it has no places to which it can resort to breathe, it will be suffocated. Hence you here and there see what are called breathing places. These are covered over with mud on the sides, with some loose grass in the centre to preserve them from being too easily frozen over. We have occasionally seen these winter-huts of the Musk-Rat, in the vicinity of their snug summer retreats in some neighbouring river's bank, and have sometimes been half inclined to suppose, that for some cause or other, they gave a preference to this kind of residence. We are not, however, aware, that these nests are made use of by the Musk-Rat in spring, for the purpose of rearing its young. We believe these animals always for that purpose resort to holes in the sides of ponds, sluggish streams, or dykes.

In such situations we have frequently observed the young, which when they first make their appearance, are seen emerging from a side gallery leading to the surface, so that they are not of necessity obliged to "take a dive" until they have had a little acquaintance with the liquid element. They are at this time very gentle, and we have on several occasions taken them up with the hand, without their making any violent struggles to escape, or attempts to punish us with their teeth.

The fur of this species was formerly a valuable article of commerce, and is still in some demand. But since so many new inventions are supplying the public with cheap hats, and the Nutria skin has been extensively introduced from South America, the Musk-Rat is less sought after, and in some of our most thickly populated districts has greatly increased in numbers. The country-people, however, continue to destroy it, to prevent its becoming so numerous as to cause loss, by making holes in the mill-dams, embankments, or ditches, that happen to be inhabited by it, and allowing the water to flow through, when frequently much mischief results. The Musk-Rat has little of the cunning of the fox, the beaver, or even the common Norway rat, and may be easily taken in almost any kind of trap, and although it is very prolific, it might by proper attention be so thinned off in a single year as to cease to be a nuisance. A dozen common rat-traps carefully and judiciously attended to, would go far toward reducing, if not exterminating, these pests, in a small neighbourhood, in the course of one or two seasons. The traps should be set in shallow water, near the edge of the stream or pool, or on a log sunk about an inch under the water; with a cord ten or twelve feet long, so as to prevent the animals from running away with the traps when they have been caught; one or two slices of parsnips or sweet apples, may be stuck upon small twigs, so that they will hang about six inches above the traps. The animal, having evidently a good nose, whilst swimming at some little distance from the traps when thus set, suddenly turns as it scents the bait, swims along the shore toward it, and reaching up to seize it, is caught by the foot, and being of course greatly alarmed, jerks the trap off the log or pulls it into deep water, where the weight of the trap soon drowns it. The Musk-Rat also readily enters, and is easily taken in a box-trap, but it ought to be lined with tin or sheet iron, for its formidable incisors otherwise enable the animal to make its escape by gnawing a hole in the box. We have sometimes seen it taken between two boards, in what is called a figure of 4 trap, with a heavy weight on the upper board.

The following mode of hunting the Musk-Rat, frequently affords a considerable degree of amusement. A party is made up to go; a spade, an axe, and a hoe, are carried along, and a spear, or in lieu of it, a pitchfork; in addition to these, a hoop-net is sometimes wanted, but what is most important, and regarded as a *sine quâ non*, is a dog accustomed to hunting these aquatic animals. The season which promises most success in this way of hunting them is the autumn, before the heavy rains have swelled the waters. The party go to some sluggish stream that winds through a meadow, or across a flat country, where the banks are not so high as to render the "digging" that has to be done, too laborious. The little islands, which in such places rise but a few feet above the water, are sometimes perforated by the Musk-Rats, and their holes and excavations undermine them in a great degree, so that it is difficult to find and stop all the mouths of these galleries, and thereby render success tolerably certain. But as these are the very places in which the greatest number of these animals are to be found, it is quite important to "invest" them. It is necessary to be very cautious in digging down along the banks of these islets, in order to reach and stop up the holes, and it usually happens that notwithstanding every precaution is taken, the animals find some way to escape. No sooner is their ancient domicil disturbed, than they issue forth from their holes under the water, to seek some safer retreat along the banks of the main-land; one after another is seen, alternately rising and diving, and making for the shore. If it is ascertained that it is not possible to prevent their escape, the hunters resolve to drive them all from the little islet. A hole is dug in the centre of the place, and the dog encouraged to go in; the few remaining Musk-Rats, at this last and worst alarm, scamper out of the burrows with all haste, and the island is left in possession of the allied forces. All this time, the hunters have been sharply looking out, to observe to what spot the greatest number of Musk-Rats have retired. They have marked the places in front of which they were seen to dive, well knowing that they are closely concealed in some of the holes along the bank. The animals have now retreated far up into their burrows, and are not very apt to make for the water. The ground is struck with a stick, in different places, and where a hollow sound is heard, the hunters know there is an excavation, and at once dig down to it. In this way, several holes are found, and are successively stopped, to prevent the return of the Musk-Rats to the water. The digging is then continued till the hunters reach the nest, which being laid open, is entered by the dog, in order that the sagacious animal may ascertain the gallery into which the Musk-Rats have retired, as a last resort. The digging is seldom fatiguing, as the holes run very near the surface. A net to catch them, is now placed at the hole, or in lieu of it, a man stands with a spear touching the mouth of it, placing his foot immediately behind the spear. As the Rat attempts to rush out the weapon is driven into its neck. Thus, these animals are killed one after another, until the whole colony is destroyed; sometimes they are knocked on the head with a club, instead of being speared. In some places, we have seen more than a dozen killed in one hole, and we have known upwards of fifty to be taken in this manner in a single day.

When the Musk-Rats have gone to their winter huts among the marshes, there is another way of procuring them. The party go to the marshes, when the ice is sufficiently strong to support a man. They proceed cautiously to their nests (the manner of building which, we have already described,) where the Rats are snugly ensconced in their warm beds, within seven or eight inches of the top. A spear with four prongs, about as long as those of a pitch-fork, is used upon the occasion. One of the men strikes the spear into the nest, with all the force he is capable of exerting, and if he understands his business, and knows where to strike, he is almost sure to pin one, if not two or three, of the animals to the earth with one blow. Another hunter stands by with an axe to demolish the little mud habitation, and aid in securing the Musk-Rats, which have been speared by his companion. It often occurs that the water under the ice is shallow, and the ice transparent, in which case the animals may be seen making their way through the water, almost touching the ice, and we have frequently seen them stunned by a blow with the axe on the ice above them, (in the manner in which pike and other fish are sometimes killed in our rivers, when they are frozen over;) a hole is then cut in the ice, and they are secured without difficulty. The houses of the Musk-Rats, which have been broken up by the hunters are soon restored, the repairs commence the following night, and are usually completed by morning!

In regard to the food of the Musk-Rat, our experience induces us to believe, that like its congener, the house rat, it is omnivorous. In 1813, we obtained two of this species, when very young, for the purpose of domesticating them, in order that we might study their habits. They became so perfectly gentle, that they came at our call, and were frequently carried to an artificial fish-pond near the house, and after swimming about for an hour or two, they would go into their cage, which was left for them at the water's edge. A few years

ago, we received from LEE ALLISON, Esq., residing at Aikin, South Carolina, one of this species in a box lined with tin. We have thus had opportunities of ascertaining the kind of food to which they gave a preference. We would, however, remark, that the food taken by an animal in confinement, is no positive evidence of what it would prefer when left to its free choice in the meadows, the brooks, and the fields it inhabits in a state of nature. Their food in summer, consists chiefly of grasses, roots, and vegetables. We have often watched them early in the morning, eating the young grass of the meadows; they seemed very fond, especially of the timothy, (*Phleum pratense*,) and redtop, (*Agrostis*;) indeed, the few bunches of clover, and other kinds of grass remaining in their vicinity, gave evidence that the Musk-Rats had been at work upon them. The injury sustained by the farmer, from these animals, however, is by the destruction of his embankments and the excavations through his meadows, made in constructing their galleries, rather than from the loss of any quantity of grass or vegetables they may destroy; although their depredations are sometimes carried on to the great injury of vegetable gardens.

An acquaintance who had a garden in the neighbourhood of a meadow which contained a large number of Musk-Rats, sent one day, to enquire whether we could aid in discovering the robbers who carried off almost every night a quantity of turnips. We were surprised to find on examining the premises, that the garden had been plundered and nearly ruined by these Rats. There were paths extending from the muddy banks of the stream, winding among the rank weeds and grasses, passing through the old worm fence, and leading to the various beds of vegetables. Many of the turnips had disappeared on the previous night—the duck-like tracks of the Musk-Rats were seen on the beds in every direction. The paths were strewn with turnip leaves, which either had dropped, or were bitten off, to render the transportation more convenient. Their paths after entering the meadow diverged to several burrows, all of which, gave evidence that their tenants had been on a foraging expedition on the previous night. The most convenient burrow was opened, and we discovered in the nest, so many different articles of food, that we were for some time under an impression, that like the chipping squirrel, chickaree, &c., this species laid up in autumn a store of food for winter use. There were carrots, and parsnips, which appeared to have been cut into halves, the lower part of the root having been left in the ground; but what struck us as most singular, was that ears of corn (maize) not yet quite ripe, had been dragged into the burrow, with a considerable portion of the stalk attached.

The corn-stalks then standing in the garden, were so tall, that the ears could not be reached by the Musk-Rats, and on examining the beds from which they had probably some days previously taken the corn we found in the burrow, we ascertained that the stalks had been gnawed off at the roots.

Professor LEE, who resides at Buncomb, North Carolina, lately informed us, that for several summers past, his fields of Indian corn, which are situated near a stream frequented by Musk-Rats, have been greatly injured by their carrying off whole stalks at a time, every night for some weeks together. The above, however, are the only instances, that have come to our knowledge of their doing any injury to the vegetable garden, or to the corn-field, although this may probably be frequently the case, where the fields or gardens skirt the banks of water-courses.

These animals walk so clumsily, that they seem unwilling to trust themselves any distance from the margin of the stream or dam on which they have taken up their residence. We have supposed, that a considerable portion of their food in the Northern States in some localities, was the root of the common arrow-head, (*Sagittaria, sagittifolia*,) as we have often observed it had been gnawed off, and have found bits of it at the mouths of their holes. We have, also, seen stems of the common Indian turnip, (*Arum triphyllum*,) which were cut off, portions of which, near the root, appeared to have been eaten. They also feed on the spice wood, (*Laurus benzoin*.) RICHARDSON says, "they feed in the Northern districts on the roots and tender shoots of the bulrush and reed-mace, and on the leaves of various carices and aquatic grasses." PENNANT says, "they are very fond of the *Acorus verus*, or *Calamus aromaticus*;" and KALM speaks of apples being placed in traps, as a bait for them. Nearly all our writers on natural history, are correct in saying, that fresh water mussels compose a portion of their food. Sometimes several bushels of shells may be found in a small space near their nests. Our young friend, SPENCER F. BAIRD, Esq., assures us that in the neighbourhood of Carlisle, Pennsylvania, on the Conodoguinet creek, he has often observed large quantities of shells, most of which were so adroitly opened by these animals, as not to be at all broken, and would have made very good specimens for the conchologist. He has seen the Musk-Rat eating a mussel occasionally on a log in the water, holding the shell between its fore-paws, as a squirrel holds a nut.

We once placed a quantity of mussels in a cage, to feed some Musk-Rats we had domesticated in the North; they carried them one by one, into an inner compartment, where they were hidden from view. Here we heard them gnawing at the shells; we then removed a slide in the cage, which enabled us to see them at work; they were seated, sometimes, upright like a squirrel, at other times like a rat, with the shell-fish lying on the floor, holding on to it by their fore-paws, and breaking it open with their lower incisors. In Carolina, we obtained for the same purpose, although for a different family of Musk-Rats, a quantity of mussels of the species *Unio angustatus* and *Anodon cataracta;* some of these were too hard to be immediately opened by the animals with their teeth. They were carried by the Musk-Rats, as usual, into a separate and darkened portion of the cage. We heard an occasional gnawing, but three days afterwards, many of the harder species of shell still remained unopened. We did not again examine the cage, till after the expiration of ten days, when the shells were all empty. They had probably opened in consequence of the death of the animal within, when their contents were eaten by the Rats. Oysters were placed in the cage, which on account of their saltness, we believed would not be relished; but a week afterwards the shells only were left. We procured a pint of a small species of imported snail, (*Bulimus decollatus*, GMEL., *mutilatus*, SAY,) that has become very destructive in many of the gardens of Charleston, and the Musk-Rats immediately began to crush them with their teeth, and in a few days nothing but the broken shells remained. We have, therefore, come to the conclusions, that whilst vegetables are the general food of this species, various kinds of shell-fish, form no inconsiderable portion of it. Our Musk-Rats refused fish, but were like most animals in confinement, fond of bread. They were generally fed on sweet potatoes, parsnips, cabbage, and celery; the sweet flag, (*Acorus calamus*,) they rejected altogether.

Although the Musk-Rat walks awkwardly, and proceeds so slowly that it can scarcely be said to run, it swims and dives well. We regard it as a better swimmer than the mink, and from its promptness in diving, at the flash of the gun, it frequently escapes from its pursuers. It may, however, be easily drowned. We once observed several of them which had been driven from their holes, after struggling under the ice for about fifteen minutes rising to the surface; and on taking them out, by cutting holes in the ice, they were found to be quite dead. RICHARDSON speaks of "their being subject at uncertain intervals to a great mortality from some unknown cause." We have no doubt that in very cold winters, when the ice reaches to the bottom of the ponds, and they are confined to their holes, they devour each other, since we have seen many burrows opened in autumn, and except in the instances we have already mentioned, we found no provision laid up for winter use. When a Musk-Rat has been caught by one foot in a trap set on the land, it is frequently found, torn to pieces and partially devoured; and from the tracks around, one might be induced to believe, that, as is the case with porpoises, and many other animals, when one is wounded and cannot escape, its companions turn upon and devour it. When one is shot, and dies in the water, it is very soon carried off by the living ones, if there are any in the vicinity at the time, and is dragged into one of their holes or nests. We have frequently found carcasses of these animals thus concealed, but in these cases the flesh had not been devoured. This singular habit reminds us of the Indians, who always carry their dead off the field of battle when they can, and endeavour to prevent their bodies falling into the hands of their enemies.

After a severe winter on a sudden rise in the water before the breaking up of the ice, hundreds of Musk-Rats are drowned in their holes, especially where there are no high shelving banks to enable them to extend their galleries beyond the reach of the rising waters. During these occasional freshets in early spring, the Musk-Rats that escape drowning, are driven from their holes, and swim about from shore to shore, without shelter and without food, and may be easily destroyed. We remember that two hunters with their guns, coursing up and down opposite sides of a pond on one of these occasions, made such fearful havoc among these animals that for several years afterwards we scarcely observed any traces of them in that locality. Many rapacious birds as well as quadrupeds seize and devour the Musk-Rat. When it makes its appearance on land, the fox and the lynx capture it with great ease. One of our young friends at Dennisville, in the State of Maine, informed us that his greatest difficulty in procuring this species in traps, arose from their being eaten after they were caught, by the snowy owl and other birds of prey, which would frequently sit and watch the traps, as it were keeping guard over them, until the poor Musquash was in the toils, on seeing which, they descended, and made a hearty meal at the trapper's expense, taking good care meanwhile not to expose themselves to his vengeance, by keeping a sharp look out for him in every direction. Our friend, however, got the better of these wary thieves by occasionally baiting his traps with meat instead of apples or vegetables, by which means he often caught an owl or a hawk, instead of a Musk-Rat. Although this species, has such a long list of enemies, it is so prolific, that like the common rat, (*Mus decumanus*,) it continues to increase and multiply in many parts of the country, notwithstanding their activity and voracity.

The Musk-Rat has occasionally been known to leave its haunts along the streams and ponds, and is sometimes found travelling on elevated grounds. We were informed by our friend Mr. BAIRD, that one was caught in a house near Reading, in Pennsylvania, three-quarters of a mile from the water; and the late Dr. WRIGHT of Troy, once discovered one making its way through the snow, on the top of a hill, near that city.

The number of young produced at a litter, varies from three to six. RICHARDSON states that they sometimes have seven, which is by no means improbable. They usually have three litters in a season.

Although the Musk-Rat does not seem to possess any extraordinary instincts by which to avoid or baffle its pursuers, we were witnesses of its sensibility of approaching danger arising from a natural cause, manifested in a way we think deserving of being recorded. It is a well-known fact, that many species of quadrupeds and birds, are endowed by Nature with the faculty of foreseeing or foreknowing, the changes of the seasons, and have premonitions of the coming storm. The swallow commences its long aerial voyage even in summer, in anticipation of the cold. The sea-birds, become excessively restless, some seek the protection of the land, and others, like the loon, (*Colymbus glacialis*,) make the shores re-echo with their hoarse and clamorous screams, previous to excessively cold weather; the swine also, are seen carrying straw in their mouths, and enlarging their beds. After an unusual drought, succeeded by a warm Indian-summer, as we were one day passing near a mill-pond, inhabited by some families of Musk-Rats, we observed numbers of them swimming about in every direction, carrying mouthfuls of withered grasses, and building their huts higher on the land than any we had seen before. We had scarcely ever observed them in this locality in the middle of the day, and then only for a moment as they swam from one side of the pond to the other; but now they seemed bent on preparing for some approaching event, and the successive reports of several guns fired by some hunters, only produced a pause in their operations for five or ten minutes. Although the day was bright and fair, on that very night there fell torrents of rain succeeded by an unusual freshet, and intensely cold weather.

This species has a strong musky smell; to us this has never appeared particularly offensive. It is infinitely less unpleasant than that of the skunk, and we are less annoyed by it than by the smell of the mink, or even the red fox. We have, however, observed in passing some of the haunts of this Rat, at particular periods during summer, that the whole locality was strongly pervaded by this odour.

It is said, notwithstanding this peculiarity, that the Musk-Rat is not an unpalatable article of food, the musky smell not being perceptible when the animal has been properly prepared and cooked; we have, indeed, heard it stated that Musk-Rat suppers are not unfrequent among a certain class of inhabitants on the Eastern shore of Maryland, and that some persons prefer them, when well dressed, to a wild duck. Like the flesh of the bear and some other quadrupeds, their meat somewhat resembles fresh pork, and is too rich to be eaten with much relish for any length of time.

By what we may almost look at as a merciful interposition of Providence, the Musk-Rat is not found on the rice plantations of Carolina; it approaches within a few miles of them, and then ceases to be found. If it existed in the banks and dykes of the rice fields, it would be a terrible annoyance to the planter, and possibly destroy the reservoirs on which his corps depend. Although it reaches much farther South, and even extends to Louisiana, it is never found on the alluvial lands within seventy miles of the sea either in Carolina or Georgia.

The skins of the Musk-Rat are no longer in such high repute, as they enjoyed thirty-five years ago, and they are now, only worth from six and a quarter to twenty-five cents each.

Dr. RICHARDSON states, (in 1824,) that between four and five thousand skins were annually imported into Great Britain from North America.

Geographical Distribution.

The Musk-Rat is found as far North as the mouth of the Mackenzie river, in latitude 69°, on the Rocky mountains, on the Columbia river, and on the Missouri. With the exception of the alluvial lands in Carolina, Georgia, Alabama, and Florida, it abounds in all parts of the United States north of latitude 30°. It exists, although not abundantly, in the mountains of Georgia, and the higher portions of Alabama. In South Carolina, we have obtained it from Aikin, and St. Matthew's parish, on the Congaree river, but have never found traces of it nearer the sea than seventy miles from Charleston.

General Remarks.

The Musk-Rat, although the only species in the genus, was moved about among several genera, before it found a resting place under its present name. SCHREBER placed it under MUS. GMELIN and F. CUVIER described it as a LEMMUS. LINNÆUS and ERXLEBEN, arranged it with the beaver, and referred it to the genus CASTOR. LESSON, LACEPEDE and CUVIER, under ONDATRA. In 1811, ILLIGER proposed changing its specific into a generic name. As LINNÆUS had called it *Castor Fiber*, he then established for it the genus FIBER.

Sciurus Hudsonius. — Pennant.

Hudson's Bay Squirrel. — Chickaree. — Red-Squirrel.

Plate xiv. — Male and Female. — Natural size.

S. cauda corpore breviore, auriculis apice sub-barbatis; corpore supra subrufo, subtus albo; S. migratorii tertia parte minore.

Characters.

A third smaller than the Northern Gray-Squirrel, (Sc. migratorius;) tail shorter than the body; ears, slightly tufted; colour, reddish above, white beneath.

Synonymes.

ECUREUIL COMMUN, OU AROUPEN, Sagard Theodat, Canada, p. 746.
COMMON SQUIRREL, Forster, Phil. Trans., vol. lxii., p. 378, 1772.
SCIURUS VULGARIS, var. E. Erxleben, Syst., An. 1777.
SCIURUS HUDSONICUS, Pallas, Glir., p. 377.
SCIURUS HUDSONICUS, Gmel., Linn.,—1788.
HUDSON'S BAY SQUIRREL, Penn. Arctic Zool., vol. i., p. 116.
"   "   "   Hist. Quadrupeds, vol. ii., p. 147.
COMMON SQUIRREL, Hearnes' Journey, p. 385.
RED SQUIRREL, Warden's Hist. U. S., vol. i., p. 330.
RED BARKING SQUIRREL, Schoolcraft's Journal, p. 273.
SCIURUS HUDSONICUS, Sabine, Franklin's Journey, p. 663.
"   "   "   Godman, vol. ii., p. 138.
"   "   "   Fischer, Mam., p. 349.
ECUREUIL DE LA BAIE D'HUDSON, F. Cuvier, Hist. Nat. des Mammifères.
SCIURUS HUDSONICUS, Bach. Trans. Zool. Soc., London, 1839.
"   "   "   Dekay, Nat. Hist. New York, 1842.

Description.

On examining the teeth of this species, we do not find the small and usually deciduous molar, that exists in all the other species of SCIURUS, with which we are acquainted; it is possible, however, that it may be found in very young animals. It will be perceived, on referring to the dental formula of the genus, (which we have given at p. 38,) that the molars are set down as $\frac{4-4}{4-4}$ or $\frac{5-4}{3-4}$; and we will for the present assign the former arrangement to this species. Forehead, very slightly arched; nose, somewhat obtuse; eyes, of moderate size; ears, broad, rounded, clothed on both sides with short hairs, not distinctly tufted like those of the European Squirrel, (Sc. vulgaris,) although the hairs, when the animal has its winter pelage, project beyond the margins, and resemble tufts; whiskers, a little longer than the head; the body presents the appearance of lightness and agility; the tail is somewhat depressed, and linear, no as bushy as in most other squirrels, but capable of a distichous arrangement; limbs, robust; claws, compressed, sharp, slightly hooked; third toe a little the longest; palms, and under surface of the toes, naked; soles of hind-feet, clothed with hair, except on the tubercles at the roots of the toes.

Colour.

This species exhibits some shades of difference in colour, and we have sometimes, although very rarely, found a specimen that might be regarded as a variety. General colour, deep reddish-brown on the whole of the upper surface; short fur beneath, plumbeous, mixed with so large a quantity of longer hairs, that the colour of the fur, does not show on the surface. These long hairs are dark at the roots, then brown, and are slightly tipped with black. In most specimens, there is an orange hue on the outer surface of the fore-legs, running up to the shoulder; this colour is also frequently visible on the upper surface of the hind-feet, and behind the ears. Whiskers, black; tail, on the upper surface, deep reddish-brown; the hair on the sides may be so arranged, as to present a line of black near the outer borders; on the under side it has two or three annulations of light-brown and black; lips, chin, throat, inside of legs, and belly, white; in some specimens the hairs on these parts of the body are plumbeous at the roots, and white to the tips, giving it a light, grayish-white appearance. There is in a great many specimens a black line, running from near the shoulders along the sides to within an inch of the thighs.

Dimensions.

Recent specimen.

	Inches.	Lines.
Length from nose to root of tail	8	0
Tail (vertebræ)	3	7
Tail to end of hair	6	5

Habits.

The genus SCIURUS is illustrated in North America, by a greater variety of species than any other among the various genera we shall have the pleasure of introducing to our readers:—Permit us to dwell for a moment on the subject, and to relate the following anecdote—

When we began the publication in Great Britain of the "Birds of America," we were encouraged by the approbation of many excellent friends, and by the more essential, although less heartfelt favours, bestowed by those noblemen and gentlemen, who kindly subscribed to the work, and without whose aid, it is frankly acknowledged it could never have been completed. Among those whom we then had the honour of calling patrons, we found as many varieties of character, as among the beautiful feathered inhabitants of our woods, lakes, and sea-shores, themselves; and had we time just now to spare, we might undertake to describe some of them. We published as the first plate of the first number of "The Birds of America," the Wild Turkey Cock, and gave the Turkey Hen and Young, as the first plate of the second number. We need not stop to enumerate the other species of birds that completed those two numbers; but judge of our surprise, on being told gravely, by a certain noble subscriber, that, "as the work was to consist of *Turkeys* only, he begged to be allowed to discontinue his subscription!"

Now, kind reader, we are obliged to follow Nature in the works of infinite wisdom, which we humbly attempt to portray; and although you should find that more Squirrels inhabit our forests than you expected, or desired to be figured in this work, we assure you it would give us pleasure to discover a new species at any time! We are not, however, wanting in a due knowledge of the sympathy and kindness that exist among our patrons toward us, and we hope you will find this really beautiful genus, as interesting as any other among the quadrupeds we desire to place before you.

The Chickaree, or Hudson's Bay Squirrel, is the most common species of this numerous genus, aroung New York and throughout the Eastern States. It is a graceful, lively animal, and were you to walk with us through the woods in the neighbourhood of our great commercial metropolis, where boys and sportsmen(?) for years past, have been hunting in every direction, and killing all the game left in the vicinity; where woodcocks are shot before the first of July, and quails, (Virginian partridges) when they are half-grown, in defiance of the laws for their preservation, you would be glad to find the comparative silence, which now reigns amid the trees, interrupted by the sprightly querulous cry of the Chickaree, and would be glad to find the comparative silence, which now reigns amid the trees, interrupted by the sprightly querulous cry of the Chickaree, and would pause with us to look at him as he runs along the rocky surface of the ground, or nimbly ascends some tree; for in these woods, once no doubt, abounding in both beasts and birds, it is now a hard task to start anything larger than a robin, or a *High-hole*, (*Picus auratus*.) The Hudson's Bay Squirrel is fearless, and heedless, to a great degree, of the presence of man; we have had one occasionally pass through our yard, sometimes ascending an oak or a chesnut, and proceeding leisurely through our small woody lawn. These little animals are generally found singly, although it is not uncommon for many to occupy the same piece of wood-land, if of any extent. In their quick, graceful motions from branch to branch, they almost remind one of a bird, and they are always neat and cleanly in their coats, industrious, and well provided for the cold of winter.

In parts of the country, the Chickaree is fond of approaching the farmer's store-houses of grain, or other products of the fields, and occasionally it ventures even so far as to make a nest for itself in some of his out-buildings, and is not dislodged from such snug quarters without undergoing a good deal of persecution.

One of these Squirrels made its nest between the beams and the rafters of a house of the kind we have just spoken of, and finding the skin of a peacock in the loft, appropriated the feathers to compose its nest, and although it was destroyed several times, to test the perseverance of the animal, it persisted in re-constructing it. The Chickaree, obtained this name from its noisy chattering note, and like most other Squirrels, is fond of repeating its cries at frequent intervals. Many of the inhabitants of our Eastern States refuse to eat Squirrels of any kind, from some prejudice or other; but we can assure our readers that the flesh of this species, and many others, is both tender and well-flavoured, and when nicely broiled, does not require a hunter's appetite to recommend it.

The habits of this little Squirrel are, in several particulars, peculiar; whilst the larger Gray Squirrels derive their sustenance from buds and nuts, chiefly inhabit warm or temperate climates, and are constitutionally fitted to subsist during winter on a small quantity of food, the Chickaree exhibits the greatest sprightliness and activity amidst the snows and frosts of our Northern regions and consequently is obliged, during the winter season, to consume as great a quantity of food as at any other. Nature has, therefore, instructed it to make provision in the season of abundance for the long winter that is approaching; and the quantity of nuts and seeds it often lays up in its store-house, is almost incredible. On one occasion we were present, when a bushel and a half of shell-barks (*Carya alba*), and chesnuts, were taken from a hollow tree occupied by a single pair of these industrious creatures; although generally the quantity of provision laid up by them is considerably less. The Chickaree has too much foresight to trust to a single hoard, and it often has several, in different localities among the neighbouring trees, or in burrows dug deep in the earth. Occasionally these stores are found under leaves, beneath logs, or in brush-heaps, at other times they are deposited in holes in the ground; and they are sometimes only temporarily laid by, in some convenient situation to be removed at leisure. When, for instance, nuts are abundant in the autumn, large quantities in the green state, covered by their thick envelope, are collected in a heap near the tree whence they have fallen; they are then covered up with leaves, until the pericarp, or thick outer covering, either falls off or opens, when the Squirrel is able to carry off the nuts more conveniently. In obtaining shell-barks, butter-nuts, (*Juglans cinerea*) chesnuts, hazel-nuts, &c., this Squirrel adopts the mode of most of the other species. It advances as near to the extremity of the branch as it can with safety, and gnaws off that portion on which the nuts are dependent. This is usually done early in the morning and the noise occasioned by the falling of large bunches of chesnut burrs, or clusters of butter-nuts, hickory, or beech-nuts, thus detached from the parent stem, may be heard more than a hundred yards off. Some of the stems attached to the nuts are ten inches or a foot in length. After having thrown down a considerable quantity, the Squirrel descends and drags them into a heap, as stated above.

Sometimes the hogs find out these stores, and make sad havoc in the temporary depot. But Providence has placed much food of a different kind within reach of the Red-Squirrel during winter. The cones of many of our pines and firs in high northern latitudes, are persistent during winter; and the Chickaree can be supported by the seeds they contain, even should his hoards of nuts fail. This little Squirrel seems also to accommodate itself to its situation in another respect. In Pennsylvania, and the southern part of New York, where the winters are comparatively mild, it is very commonly satisfied with a hollow tree as a winter residence; but in the latitude of Saratoga, N. Y., in the northern part of Massachusetts, in New Hampshire, Maine, Canada, and farther north, it usually seeks for additional protection from the cold, by forming deep burrows in the earth. Nothing is more common than to meet with five or six Squirrel-holes in the ground, near the roots of some white pine or hemlock; and these retreats can be easily found by the vast heaps of scales from the cones of pines and firs, which are in process of time accumulated around them. This species can both swim and dive. We once observed some lads shaking a Red-Squirrel from a sapling that grew on the edge of a mill-pond. It fell into the water, and swam to the opposite shore, performing the operation of swimming moderately well, and reminding us by its movements of the meadow-mouse, when similarly occupied. It was "headed" by its untiring persecutors, on the opposite shore, where on being pelted with sticks, we noticed it diving two or three times, not in the graceful curving manner of the mink, or musk-rat, but with short and ineffectual plunges of a foot or two at a time.

We have kept the Chickaree in cages, but found it less gentle, and more difficult to be tamed, than many other species of the genus.

RICHARDSON informs us that in the fur countries, "the Indian boys kill many with the bow and arrow, and also take them occasionally with snares set round the trunks of the trees which they frequent."We have observed that during winter a steel-trap baited with an ear of corn, (maize,) placed near their burrows at the foot of large pine or spruce trees, will secure them with the greatest ease.

Geographical Distribution.

The limits of the northern range of this species are not precisely determined, but all travellers who have braved the snows of our Polar regions, speak of its existence as far north as their journeys extended. It has been observed in the 68th or 69th parallel of latitude; it also exists in Labrador, Newfoundland and Canada. It is the most common species in New England and New York, and is by no means rare in Pennsylvania and New Jersey, especially in the hilly or mountainous portions of the latter State. It is seen, in diminished numbers, in the mountains of Virginia, although in the alluvial parts of that State, it is scarcely known; as we proceed southwardly, it becomes more rare, but still continues to be met with on the highest mountains. The most southern locality to which we have traced it, is a high peak called the Black mountain, in Buncombe county, N. Carolina. The woods growing in that elevated situation are in some places wholly composed of balsam-fir trees, (*Abies balsamea*,) on the cones of which these Squirrels feed. There this little animal is quite common, and has received a new English name, viz., that of, "Mountain boomer." Toward the west we have traced it to the mountains of Tennessee; beyond the Rocky mountains, it does not exist. In the Russian settlements on the Western coast, it is replaced by the Downy Squirrel, (*Sc. lanuginosus.*) In the vicinity of the Columbia, and for several hundred miles along the mountains South of that river, by RICHARDSON's Columbian Squirrel; and in the mountainous regions bordering on California, by another small species much resembling it, which we hope, hereafter, to present to our readers.

General Remarks.

Although this species from its numbers and familiarity, as well as from its general diffusion, has been longer known than any other of our Squirrels, and has been very frequently described, it has, with few exceptions, retained its name of *Hudsonius*. ERXLEBEN supposed it to be only a variety of the common Squirrel, which in Shaw's General Zoology, vol. ii., p. 141, is given as a variety of *Sciurus Hudsonius*, is our own species, (*Sc. Carolinensis.*) This species was unknown to LINNÆUS. PALLAS appears to have been the first author, who gave the specific name of *Hudsonius*, (see Pall. Glir., p. 377, A. D. 1786,) and GMELIN, in 1788, adopted his name.

In examining the form, and inquiring into the habits of this species; we cannot but observe a slight approach to TAMIAS, and a more distant one to SPERMOPHILUS. Its ears are placed farther back than in the Squirrels generally, its tail is only sub-distichous, and withal it often digs its own burrow, and lives indiscriminately in the ground and on trees. In all these particulars it appears, in connexion with the Downy Squirrel, (*Sc. lanuginosus,*) to form a connecting link between SCIURUS and TAMIAS. It has, however, no cheek pouches, and does not carry its food in it cheeks in the manner of the TAMIÆ and SPERMOPHILI, but between its front teeth, like the rest of the squirrels.

Drawn on Stone by W.ᵐ E. Hitchcock

Hudson's Bay Squirrel - Chickaree - Red Squirrel.

Drawn from Nature by J.J.Audubon, F.R.S.F.L.S.   Lith Printed & Col.ᵈ by J.T.Bowen, Phil

Genus Pteromys.—Illiger.

Dental Formula.

Incisive $\frac{2}{2}$; *Molar* $\frac{5-5}{4-4}$ = 22.

Dentition similar to that of the genus SCIURUS. Head, round; ears, round; upper lip, divided; eyes large; fore-feet, with four elongated toes, furnished with compressed, sharp talons, with the rudiment of a thumb having an obtuse nail; hind-feet, with five long toes, much divided, and fitted for seizing or climbing; tail, long, villose; skin on the sides, extending from the anterior to the posterior extremities, forming a thin membrane, by the aid of which, when extended, the animal sails through the air in a descending curve from a tree or any elevated point, occasionally for some distance.

The generic name *pteromys* is derived from two Greek words, πτερον, (*pteron,*) a wing, and μυς, (*mus,*) a mouse.

There are thirteen well-determined species belonging to this genus. One is found in the north of Europe, four in North America, and the remainder in Asia and other parts of the old world.

Pteromys Oregonensis.—Bachman.

Oregon Flying Squirrel.

Plate xv—Male and Female.—Natural size.

P. magnitudine inter P. volucellam et P. sabrinum medius, supra fuscus, subtus luteo-albus; auribus P. sabrini auriculis longioribus; vellere densiore, membrana volatica largiore, pedibus grandioribus.

Characters.

Intermediate in size between P. volucella, and the Northern species, P. sabrinus; ears, longer than in the latter, and far more compact; lobe of the flying membrane joining the fore-feet, much longer in proportion; making that membrane broader. Foot larger; general colour above, brown; beneath, yellowish-white.

Synonyme.

PTEROMYS OREGONENSIS; Oregon Flying Squirrel, Bach., Jour. Acad. of Nat. Sciences, Phil., vol. viii., pt. i., p. 101.

Description.

This species differs from *P. sabrinus*, in several very striking particulars; the arm which supports the flying membrane is $11\frac{1}{2}$ lines in length, whilst that of the latter in only 9. Thus the smaller of the two has the largest flying membrane.

The fur of *P. sabrinus* is much the longest, and is white, whilst that of *P. Oregonensis* has a yellowish tinge. The hairs on the tail of the former, are only slightly tinged with lead-colour, at the roots, whilst in the latter, that colour extends outwardly, (towards the tips,) for half their length. The different shape of the ear, it being longer and narrower in our present species than in *P. sabrinus*, is a sufficient distinctive character. *P. Oregonensis* differs from the common flying squirrel, (*P. volucella*) so entirely, that it is hardly necessary to give a particular comparison. Besides being much larger than the latter, and not possessing the beautiful downy-white on the belly, it may be distinguished from *P. volucella*, by the hairs on that species being white to the roots, which is not the case with the *Oregonensis*. Whiskers, numerous, and very long.

Colour.

Fur, deep gray at the base, on the back tipped with yellowish-brown; tail, pale-brown above, dusky toward the extremity; beneath, brownish-white; whiskers, chiefly black, grayish at the tips. Hairs covering the flying membrane, mostly black, slightly tipped with pale-brown; feet, dusky; around the eyes, blackish; ears, with minute adpressed brown hairs externally, and brownish-white internally.

Dimensions.

	Inches.	Lines.
Length from point of nose to root of tail	6	8
Tail, to point of fur	6	0
Height of ear posteriorly	0	7
Breadth between the outer edges of the flying membrane	8	0
Longest hind-toe, including nail	0	$5\frac{1}{4}$
" fore-toe, " "	0	$5\frac{1}{2}$
From heel to point of nail	1	$6\frac{1}{2}$
From nose to ear	1	6

Habits.

The habits of this handsome Flying Squirrel, we regret to say, are almost unknown to us, but from its general appearance, it is undoubtedly as active and volatile as our common little species; and much do we regret that we have never seen it launch itself into the air, and sail from the highest branch of one of the enormous pines of the valley of the Columbia river, to some other tall and magnificent tree. Indeed much should we like to know the many works of the Creator, that yet remain to be discovered, examined, figured, and described, in the vast mountain-valleys and forests, beyond the highest peaks of the great Rocky Chain.

We hope, however, to obtain a good deal of information through various sources ere the conclusion of this work, from the remote portions of our Continent that have not yet been well explored by naturalists, and we shall then perhaps be able to say something more in regard to the subject of this article, of which we can now only add, that Mr. TOWNSEND remarks, that it inhabits the pine woods of the Columbia, near the sea, and has the habits of *P. volucella.*

Geographical Distribution.

Dr. RICHARDSON (Fauna Boreali Americana, P. 195,) speaks of a Flying Squirrel, which was "discovered by Mr. DRUMMOND on the Rocky mountains, living in dense pine-forests, and seldom venturing from its retreats, except in the night." This animal he considers, a variety of *P. sabrinus*, (var. *B. Alpinus*.) The locality in which it was found, and parts of his description, however, on the whole incline us to suppose that the specimen procured by Mr. DRUMMOND was one of our present species, although of a very large size. Dr. RICHARDSON says, "I have received specimens of it from the head of Elk river, and also from the south branch of the Mackenzie." So that if this supposition be correct, we may conclude that it inhabits a very extensive tract of country, and is, perhaps, most common on, and to the west, of the Rocky Mountains; in which last locality Mr. TOWNSEND met with it, in the woods on the shores of the Columbia river.

General Remarks.

There are no accounts of this species of Flying Squirrel, or of the larger one, *P. sabrinus*, in LEWIS and CLARKE's Journal. Those travellers not having, as we suppose, heard of either, although they traversed a considerable portion of the country in which both species have since been found.

We hope, when presenting an account of the habits of *P. sabrinus*, to be able to identify the *variety* above-mentioned, (*P. sabrinus*, var. *B. Alpinus* of RICHARDSON,) and if necessary, correct any error in our account of the geographical distribution of the present species (*P. Oregonensis*.)

Drawn on Stone by Wᵐ E. Hitchcock

Oregon Flying Squirrel

Drawn from Nature by J J Audubon, FRSFLS.   Lith Printed & Colᵈ by J.T. Bowen, Phil

Lynx Canadensis. —Geoffroy.

Canada Lynx.

Plate xvi. —Male, $\frac{3}{4}$ Natural size.

L. magnitudine L. rufum superans; auribus triangularibus, apice pilis crassis nigris erectis barbatis; cauda capite breviore, plantis villosis; supra cinereus, maculis obscuris nebulosus, subtus dilutor.

Characters.

Larger than F. rufus; ears, triangular, tipt with an upright slender tuft of coarse black hairs; tail, shorter than the head; soles, hairy; general colour, gray above, a little clouded with irregular darker spots, lighter beneath.

Synonymes.

LOUP-CERVIER, (anaris qua,) Sagard Theodat, Canada, 744, An. 1636.
    "   or LYNX, Dobb's Hudson's Bay, p. 41, An. 1744.
LYNX, Pennant, Arc. Zool., vol. i., p. 50.
    "   or WILD CAT, Hearne's Journey, p. 366.
CANADIAN LXNX, Buff., vol. v., suppl. p. 216, pl. 125.
    "   "   Mackenzie's Journey, p. 106.
FELIS CANADENSIS, Geoffroy, An. du Mus.
    "   CANADENSIS, Sabine, Franklin's Journey, p. 659.
    "   CANADENSIS, Desm. Mam., p. 225.
NORTHERN LYNX, Godman, Nat. Hist., vol. i., p. 302.
FELIS BOREALIS, Temminck, Monographie, t. i., p. 109.
    "   CANADENSIS, Rich., F. B. A. p. 101.
    "   "   Reichenbach, Regnum Animale, sp. 551, p. 46, pl. 551, Lipsiæ, 1836.
LYNCUS BOREALIS, Dekay, Nat. Hist. N. Y., p. 50, pl. 10, fig. 2.

Description.

The species has a rounder, broaders, and proportionably shorter head than (L. rufus,) the Bay Lynx; nose, obtuse; eyes, large; teeth, very strong; whiskers, stiff, horizontal, arranged in three oblique series; ears, acute, thickly clothed with hair on both surfaces, tipped by a long and slender tuft of coarse hairs; beneath the ears commences a broad ruff formed of longer hairs than those on the surrounding parts; this ruff surrounds the throat and reaches the chin, but does not extend around the neck above. The female has the ruff much shorter than the male. Body, robust, thick, and heavy; and from the form, we are inclined to believe that this species is far less fleet than its congener the Bay lynx. The hair has a woolly appearance; under-fur, very dense and soft, mixed with hairs somewhat rigid and two inches in length. On the under surface, the hairs are thinner, and a little longer than those above. Thighs, strong; legs, thick and clumsy, presenting a slight resemblance to those of the bear. Toes, thick, so completely concealed by the fur that the tracks made in the snow by this animal, do not show distinct impressions of them, like those made by the fox, or the Bay lynx. Their tracks are round, leaving no marks of the nails unless the animal is running, when its toes are widely spread, and its nails leave the appearance of slight scratches in the snow. Tail, thickly covered with hair, short, slightly turned upward. Nails, very strong, much larger than those of the Bay lynx, curved, and acuminate.

Colour.

Nose, flesh coloured; pupil of the eye, black, iris amber colour; margin of the lips, and inner surface of the ears, yellowish-brown; face, and around the eyes, light-gray; whiskers, nearly all white, a few black; outer margin of the ear, edged with black, widening as it approaches the extremity, where it is half an inch broad; tuft of ear, black; the ruff under the throat is light-gray, mixed in the centre of the circle with long tufts of black hair. When the hairs on the back are blown aside, they exhibit a dark yellowish-brown colour. The long hairs on the back, black to near the extremity, where there is an annulation of yellowish-brown, finally tipped with black; general colour of the back, gray, with a shade of rufous, and slightly varied with shades of a darker colour; under surface, dull white, with irregular broad spots of dark-brown situated on the inner surface of the fore-legs, and extending along the belly, these spots are partially covered by long whitish hairs in the vicinity. In one of our specimens these dark-coloured spots are altogether wanting. The legs are of the colour of the sides; upper surface of the tail, to within an inch of the tip,

and exterior portion of the thighs, rufous; beneath yellowish-white; extremity of the tail black.

Dimensions.

The Male represented on the Plate:—Recent.

	Inches.
From nose to root of tail	33 inches.
Tail (vertebræ)	5 "
Tail, to end of hair	6 "
Entire length	39 "
From nose to end of skull	6 "
" " root of ears	$4\frac{3}{4}$ "
" " end of ears laid down	$7\frac{1}{2}$ "
Breadth of ears in front	$3\frac{1}{2}$ "
Height of ears	$2\frac{1}{2}$ "
Length of tufts of hair on the ear	2 "
From nose to hind-foot stretched beyond tail	45 "
From do. to end of fore-foot stretched beyond nose	$5\frac{1}{2}$ "
Distance between roots of ears anteriorly	$3\frac{1}{2}$ "
" tips of do.	$7\frac{1}{2}$ "
Spread of fore-foot, between the claws	5 "
Breadth of arm	$2\frac{5}{8}$ "
Height to shoulder from middle of fore-claw	$13\frac{1}{2}$ "

Weight 16 pounds; extremely lean.

A specimen in the flesh from the Petersburg Mountains, east of Troy:—Male.

	Inches.	Lines.
From point of nose to root of tail	37	0
Tail (vertebræ)	4	4
Tail, to end of fur	5	4
Height of ear	2	2
Length of tufts on the ears	1	9
From shoulder to extremity of toes on fore-feet	17	0
From heel to end of hind-claw	7	5

Weight 22 pounds.

Habits.

In some parts of the State of Maine, and in New Brunswick, there are tracts of land, formerly covered with large trees, but over-run by fires not many years since, now presenting a desolate appearance as you look in every direction and see nothing but tall, blackened and charred trunks standing, with only their larger branches occasionally stretching out to the right or left, while many of them are like bare poles, half burnt off near the roots perhaps, and looking as if they might fall to the earth with the slightest breath of air. Into one of these "burnt districts," let us go together. Nature has already begun to replace the stately trees, which the destroying element had consumed, or stripped of all beauty and vitality, and we find the new growth already advanced; instead of the light, brittle, and inflammable pine, the solid and hard, maple, oak, or beech, are thickly and rapidly raising their leafy branches to hide from our view the unsightly trunks that, half-destroyed, charred, and prostrate on the ground, are strewn around in almost every direction. We mush pursue our way slowly and laboriously, sometimes jumping over, and sometimes creeping under, or walking along a fallen tree, our progress impeded by the new growth, by brambles, holes in the ground, and the necessity of cautiously observing the general direction of our crooked and fatiguing march; here and there we come to a small open space, where the wild raspberry tempts us to pause and allay our thirst, and perhaps whilst picking its ripe fruit, a pack of grouse rise with a whirr-whirr, and attract our attention—they are gone ere we can reach our gun: but we are not alone;—and, under cover of yon thicket, crouched behind that fallen pine tree, is the Canada Lynx—stealthily and slowly moving along—it is he that startled the game that has just escaped. Now he ascends to the lower branch of a thick leaved tree, and closely squatted, awaits the approach of some other prey, to dart upon and secure it, ere the unsuspecting object of his appetite can even see whence the devourer comes. We move carefully toward the concealed prowler—but his eyes and ears are full as good as our own—with a bound he is upon the earth, and in an instant is out of sight amid the logs and brush-wood—for savage and voracious as he may be when pursuing the smaller animals, he is equally cowardly when opposed to his great enemy—man; and as his skin is valuable, let us excuse him for desiring to keep it whole.

The Canada Lynx is more retired in its habits than our common wild cat, keeping chiefly far from the habitations of even the settlers who first penetrate into the depths of the wilderness. Its fine long fur enables it to withstand the

Plate XVI

N.º 4

Drawn on Stone by R. Trembly

Printed by Nagel & Weingærtner N.Y.

Canada Lynx

Male

Drawn from Nature by J.J. Audubon F.R.S.F.L.S.

cold of our northern latitudes, and it is found both in the wooded countries north of the great lakes, and as far south as the Middle States, dispersed over a great many degrees of longitude; even occasionally approaching the sea-coast. The specimen from which we drew the figure of this animal, was sent to us from Halifax, Nova Scotia. It had been taken in a wolf-trap, after having, (as was supposed,) destroyed several sheep. We kept it alive for a few weeks, feeding it on fresh raw meat; it ate but a small quantity at a time, and like all predacious animals, appeared able to support a long fast without inconvenience. The precarious life led by beasts of prey, in fact makes this a wise provision of Nature, but for which many would no doubt soon perish, as occasionally several days may pass without their being able to secure a hearty meal.

The Lynx we have just mentioned, when a dog approached the cage in which it was confined, drew back to the farthest part of it, and with open jaws spit forth like a cat at the intruder. We often admired the brilliancy of its large eyes, when it glared at us from a corner of its prison. When killed, it was extremely poor, and we found that one of its legs had been broken, probably by a rifle-ball, some considerable time previous to its having been captured, as the bone was united again pretty firmly; it was in other respects a fine specimen.

When alarmed, or when pursued, the Canada Lynx leaps or bounds rapidly in a straight direction, from the danger; and takes to a tree if hard pressed by the dogs. It is very strong, and possessing remarkably large and powerful fore-legs and claws, is able to climb trees of any size, and can leap from a considerable height to the ground without feeling the jar, alighting on all four feet at the same instant, ready for flight or battle. If dislodged from a tree by the hunter, it is instantly surrounded by the dogs, in which case it strikes with its sharp claws and bites severely.

In crossing the Petersburg mountains east of Albany, more than thirty years ago, we procured from a farmer a male Lynx, the measurement of which was taken at the time, and has just been given by us, (see p. 138.) It had been killed only half an hour before, and was in very fine order. The farmer stated that in hunting for the ruffed grouse, his dog had started this Lynx from a thicket of laurel bushes; it made no doublings, but ran about a quarter of a mile up the side of a hill, pursued by the dog, when it ascended a tree, on which he shot it; it fell to the ground quite dead, after having hung for some time suspended from a branch to which it clung with great tenacity until life was extinct.

It has been stated that the Canada Lynx, "is easily destroyed by a blow on the back, with a slender stick;" this we are inclined to think a mistake, never having witnessed it, and judging merely by the activity and strength manifested by the animal, although we agree with the farther remarks of the same writer, "that it never attacks man." This indeed is a remark applicable to nearly all the beasts of prey in our country, except in extreme cases of hunger or desperation. It is said by Dr. RICHARDSON, that the Canada Lynx "swims well, and will cross the arm of a lake two miles wide"—this is a habit which is also shared by the more southern species. (*Lynx rufus*).

The Canada Lynx, like all other animals of its general habits, breeds but once a year, generally having two young; we have heard of an instance, however, of three whelps being littered at a time.

The skin of this animal is generally used for muffs, collars, &c., and is ranked among the most beautiful materials for these purposes. It varies somewhat in colour, and the best are much lighter, when killed in good season, than the specimen from which our drawing was made.

We have been informed by the northern trappers that the Canada Lynx is usually taken in steel-traps, such as are used for the beaver, and otter, into which he enters very readily.

The Indians we are told, regard its flesh as good eating, which may perhaps, be ascribed to the excellence of their appetites. HEARNE, (see Journey, p. 366,) who ate of it in the neighborhood of York Fort, says, "the flesh is white, and nearly as good as that of the rabbit." We think we would give the preference, however, to a buffalo-hump well roasted, for either dinner or supper.

The stories told of the great cunning of this species, in throwing mosses from the trees in order to entice the deer to feed on them, and then dropping on their backs and tearing their throats, may as well be omitted here, as they fortunately require no refutation at the present day.

Thd food of the Canada Lynx, consists of several species of grouse and other birds, the northern hare, gray rabbit, chipping squirrel, and other quadrupeds. It has been mentioned to us, that in the territories to the north of the Gulf of St. Lawrence, they destroy the Arctic fox, and make great havoc among the lemmings, (GEORYCHUS.) HEARNE informs us, that in Hudson's Bay they "seldom leave a place which is frequented by rabbits, till they have killed nearly all of them." They are said to pounce on the wild goose

at its breeding places, and to destroy many marmots and spermophiles, by lying in wait for them at their burrows. At a public house in Canada, we were shown the skin of one of these Lynxes, the animal having been found quite helpless, and nearly dead in the woods. It appears, that leaping on to a porcupine, it had caught a Tartar, as its head was greatly inflamed, and it was nearly blind. Its mouth was full of the sharp quills of that well-defended animal, which would in a day or two, have occasioned its death. We have heard one or two accounts of the Canada Lynx having killed a deer; we are somewhat sceptical in regard to this being a general habit of the species, although when pressed by hunger, which renders all creatures desperate at times, it may occasionally venture to attack a large animal.

HEARNE states that he "once saw a Lynx that had seized on the carcass of a deer just killed by an Indian, who was forced to shoot it, before it would relinquish the prize," (see HEARNE's Journey, p. 372.) Young fawns, as we have ourselves ascertained, are killed by these animals, and farmers in some of the wilder portions of our Northern States, and of Canada, complain of their carrying off their lambs and pigs. The Canada Lynx is, however, by no means so great a depredator in the vicinity of the farm-yard, as the wild-cat or Bay lynx, as his more retired habits incline him to keep in the deepest recesses of the forests—and besides, for aught we know, he may prefer "game" to "pigs and poultry."

The slow multiplication of this species proves that it is not intended to be abundant, but to exist only in such moderate numbers as are necessary to enable it to play its part with other carnivora in preventing too fast an increase of many of the smaller animals and birds; if the hare, the squirrel, the rat, and all the graminivorous quadrupeds and birds were allowed to increase their species without being preyed upon by the owl, the hawk, the fox, the lynx, and other enemies, the grass would be cut off, and the seeds of plants destroyed, so that the larger animals would find no subsistence, and in time, from the destruction of the seeds by the teeth of the rodentia, the forest itself would become a wide desert.

There is then a meaning in this arrangement of Providence; and the more we investigate the works of Him who hath created nothing in vain, the more we are led to admire the wisdom of His designs.

Geographical Distribution.

The Canada Lynx is a northern species—it is known to exist north of the great Lakes eastward of the Rocky Mountains; it is found on the Mackenzie river as far north as latitude 66°. It exists in Labrador, and in Canada. It still occurs, although very sparingly, in some of the New England States. It is occasionally met with in the northern part of New York. We heard of one having been taken some fifteen years ago in the mountains of Pennsylvania. Farther south, we have not traced it. It is not found in Kentucky or in the valley of the Mississippi. Westward of that river it does not appear to exist. There are Lynxes between the Rocky Mountains and the Pacific Ocean; these seem, however, to be the Bay lynx, or a species so nearly resembling the latter, that they appear to be no more than one of its numerous varieties. There is a specimen in the Museum of the Zoological Society of London, marked *F. borealis*, which is stated to have been brought from California by DOUGLASS, which we did not see, having somehow overlooked it. Its characters and history deserve investigation.

General Remarks

The question whether the Canada Lynx is, or is not, identical with any species of the north of Europe, is by no means settled. PENNANT, considered it the same as the lynx (*Felis lynx*,) of the old world. BUFFON, after pointing out the distinctive marks of each, came to the conclusion that they were mere varieties. These naturalists, however, lived at a period when it was customary to consider the animals of America as mere varieties of those of the Eastern continent. GEOFFROY ST. HILAIRE named our present species, considering it distinct from the Lynxes of Europe; and TEMMINCK described it under the name of *F. borealis*, as existing in the northern parts of both continents, thinking it a species distinct from *Felis lynx* of the north of Europe.

We spent some time with Professor REICHENBACH, in comparing specimens of European and American lynxes, which exist in the museum of Dresden. From the general appearance of these specimens, a great similarity between *L. Canadensis*, and the Lynx (*Felis lynx*,) of the north of Europe, may undoubtedly be remarked, and they might be regarded as mere varieties of one species. The forms of animals, however, approach each other in both continents where there is a similarity of climate. Many of the genera of New York and Pennsylvania plants are largely represented in Germany, and although nearly all the indigenous species are different, they are closely allied. In South

Carolina, there are several birds, quadrupeds, and reptiles, which bear a striking resemblance to those found in Egypt, in nearly the same parallel of latitude. The black-winged hawk (*F. dispar*) resembles the *F. melanopterus* so nearly, that BONAPARTE published them as identical. Our alligator is a near relative of the crocodile, our soft-shelled turtle (*Trionyx ferox*) is much like the *T. Ægypticus*, and our fox squirrel, (*Sc. capistratus*,) has a pretty good representative in *Sc. Madagascariensis*. In a more northern latitude, we may point to the American and European badgers, to *Lepus Americanus*, and *L. variabilis*, and to *Tamias striatus* of Siberia and *T. Lysterii*, as examples of the near approach of distinct species to each other; to which we may add that the wild sheep of the Rocky Mountains (*Ovis montana*) bears so striking a resemblance to the *Ovis Ammon*, another species existing on the mountains of Asia, that the two have been confounded; and our *Spermophilus Townsendii* is in size and colour so like the Souslik, (*Sp. guttatus*,) of the mountains of Hungary, that Dr. RICHARDSON published it as a mere variety. Taking these facts into consideration, after a careful examination of *Lynx Canadensis*, and after having compared it with *Felis lynx*, of Europe, we pronounce them distinct species without hesitation.

Although the *European* lynx varies considerably in colour, especially specimens killed at different seasons of the year, it is, in all the varieties we have seen, of a deeper rufous tint than the Canada Lynx; the spots on the body are more distinct, and the hair, in some specimens from Russia and Siberia, is much shorter than in our animal, while the tail is longer and more tufted. TEMMINCK, a very alose observer, and distinguished naturalist, thinks the Canada Lynx is, found on both continents—in this he may possibly be correct; we, however, saw no specimens in the museums of Europe that corresponded with the description of *L. Canadensis*, that did not come from America. The name, *F. borealis*, which TEMMINCK bestowed on it, can however, only be considered a synonyme, as GEOFFROY described the animal previously, giving it the name of *Felis Canadensis*. We have not been able to find in America, the European species described by TEMMINCK under the name of *Felis cervaria*, which, as he supposes, exists also in the northern part of our continent.

Sciurus Cinereus.—Linn., Gmel.

Cat-Squirrel.

Plate xvii.—Natural size.

S. corpore robusto, S. capistratus minore, S. migratorio majore; cruribus paullum curtis; naso et auribus nunquam albis; cauda corpore paullo longiore.

Characters.

A little smaller than the fox squirrel, (S. capistratus,) larger than the northern gray squirrel, (S. migratorius;) body, stout; legs, rather short; nose and ears, never white; tail, a little shorter than the body.

Synonymes.

SCIURUS CINEREUS, Ray, Quad., p. 215, A.D. 1693.
CAT-SQUIRREL, Catesby, Carolina, vol. ii., p. 74, pl. 74, A.D. 1771.
" " Kalm's Travels, vol. ii., p. 409, English trans.
" " Pennant's Arctic Zoology, vol. i., p. 119, 1784.
SCIURUS CINEREUS, Linn., Gmel.,—1788.
FOX-SQUIRREL, (*S. vulpinus*) Godman, Nat. Hist., vol. ii., p. 128.
CAT-SQUIRREL, " " " " " vol. ii., p. 129.
SCIURUS CINEREUS, Appendix to American Edition of McMurtrie's Translation of Cuvier's Animal Kindgom, vol. i., p. 433.
" " Bach, Monog. Zoological Society, 1838.
Vulgo, FOX-SQUIRREL, of New York, Pennsylvania, and New Jersey, distinct from the Fox-Squirrel (*S. capistratus*,) of the southern States.

Description.

Head, less elongated than that of *S. capistratus*, (the fox-squirrel,) and incisors rather narrower, shorter, and less prominent, than in that species. Ears broad at base and nearly round, thickly clothed on both surfaces with hair; behind the ears the hairs are longer in winter than during summer, and in the former season, extend beyond the margin of the ear. Whiskers, numerous, longer than the head; neck, short; body, stouter than that of *S. capistratus*, or any known species of Squirrel peculiar to our continent. Fur, more woolly, and less rigid than in *S. capistratus*; not as smooth as in *S. migratorius*. Hinder parts heavy, giving it a clumsy appearance. Tail, long, broad, and flat, rather less distichous than in *S. capistratus*, or *S. migratorius*; feet, shorter than in the former. Nails, strong, compressed, moderately arched, and acute.

Colour.

Perhaps none of our squirrels are subject to greater varieties of colour than the present; we have seen specimens in (formerly) PEALE's museum, of every tint, from light-gray almost to black. Two others that came under our observation, were nearly white, and had not red or pink eyes, which last, are a characteristic mark of that variety in any animal which is commonly called an albino.

Between the varieties of our present species, and the almost equally numerous varieties of the fox-squirrel, (*S. capistratus*,) there may be remarked an important difference. In the latter species the varieties are generally permanent, scarcely any specimens being found of intermediate colour, between the well-known shades which exist in different localities or families, whilst in the former, every variety of tint can be observed, and scarcely two can be found exactly alike. The prevailing variety, or colour, however, is gray, and one of this colour we will now describe from a specimen before us.

Teeth, orange; nails, dark-brown near the base, lighter at the extremities. On the cheeks, a slight tinge of yellowish-brown, extending to the junction of the head with the neck; inner surface of the ears, yellowish-brown; outer surface of the ear, fur soft and woolly in appearance, extending a little beyong the margin, light cinereous edged with rusty-brown. Whiskers both black and white, the black ones most numerous; under the throat, inner surface of the legs and thighs, and the whole under-fur, white, producing an iron-gray colour at the surface; tail, less flat and distichous, (being rather more rounded, and narrower,) than in many other species of this genus, composed of hairs which separately examined are of a dull white near the roots, succeeded by a narrow marking of black, then white, followed by a broad line of black, and broadly tipped with white.

Another specimen is dark-gray on the back and head, with a mixture of black and cinereous on the feet, thighs, and under-surface. Whiskers, nearly all white. The markings on the tail, are similar to those of the other specimen. A third specimen, obtained from Pennsylvania, is dark yellowish-brown on the upper-surface; legs and belly, of a bright, orange-colour. A fourth specimen, obtained in the New York market, is grayish-brown above, and black beneath. The bones of this species are invariably of a reddish-colour—this is strikingly perceptible after the flesh is cooked.

We have represented in the plate three of these Squirrels, all of different colours, but the varieties of tint to be observed in different specimens of the Cat-Squirrel, are so great, that among fifty or more perhaps, we never could find two exactly alike; for which reason we selected for our drawing an orange-coloured one, a gray one, and one nearly black.

Dimensions.

	Inches
An old male.—Recent.	
From nose to root of tail	$12\frac{1}{8}$
Length of tail, (vertebræ)	$7\frac{1}{2}$
do. of tail, to end of hair	$11\frac{1}{2}$
do. from fore-claws to hind-claws, stretched out	$18\frac{3}{4}$
Weight, 1 lb. 13 oz.	
Female specimen sent to us, by Mr. BAIRD, of Pennsylvania.	
Length of body	13
do. of tail, from root to end of vertebræ	11
do. of tail, " to end of hair	14
do. to end of hind-legs	19
Extent of fore-legs	$13\frac{3}{4}$
Hind-foot	3
Fore-foot	2
Height of ear, anteriorly	$\frac{10}{12}$
do. of " posteriorly	1
do. of " laterally, (inside,)	$\frac{10}{24}$
Nose of occiput	3

Breadth of ear . . . . $\frac{17}{24}$
do. of tail . . . . $5\frac{3}{12}$

Weight, 2 lb. 5 oz.

Habits.

This Squirrel has many habits in common with other species, residing in the hollows of trees, building in summer its nest of leaves, in some convenient fork of a tree, and subsisting on the same kinds of food. It is, however, the most inactive of all our known species; it climbs a tree, not with the lightness and agility of the northern gray squirrel, but with the slowness and apparent reluctance of the little striped squirrel, (*Tamias Lysteri.*) After ascending, it does not immediately mount to the top, as is the case with other species, but clings to the body of the tree, on the side opposite to you, or tries to conceal itself behind the first convenient branch. We have seldom observed it leaping from bough to bough. When it is induced, in search of food, to proceed to the extremity of a branch, it moves cautiously and heavily, and generally returns the same way. On the ground it runs clumsily, and makes slower progress than the gray squirrel. It is usually fat, especially in autumn, and the flesh is said to be preferable to that of any of our other species of squirrel. The Cat-Squirrel does not appear to be migratory in its habits. The same pair, if undisturbed, may be found in a particular vicinity for a number of years in succession, and the sexes seem paired for life.

WILLIAM BAIRD, Esq., of Carlisle, Pennsylvania, says of this species— "The Fox-Squirrel as this species is called with us, will never, unless almost in the very jaws of a dog, ascend any other tree than that which contains its nest, differing very greatly in this respect from our gray squirrel."

The nest, which we have only seen on two occasions, was constructed of sticks and leaves, in the crotch of a tree about twenty feet from the ground, and in both cases the pair had a safer retreat in a hollow of the same tree above.

This species is said to have young but once a year. We have no positive evidence to the contrary, but suspect that it will hereafter be discovered that it produces a second litter in the summer, or toward autumn.

On taking some of them from the nest, we found on one occasion three, and no another four, young. These nests were placed in the hollows of oak trees.

Geographical Distribution.

The Cat-Squirrel, is rather a rare species, but is not very uncommon in the oak and hickory woods of Pennsylvania, we have seen it near Easton and York; it is found occasionally in Maryland and Virginia, and is met with on Long Island, and in some other portions of the State of New York, but in the northern parts of that State, is exceedingly rare, as we only saw two pair during fifteen years' close observation. At certain seasons, we have found these squirrels tolerably abundant in the markets of the city of New York, and have ascertained that persons who had them for sale were aware of their superior value, as we were frequently charged $37\frac{1}{2}$ cents for one, whilst the common gray squirrel could easily be purchased for $12\frac{1}{2}$ cents. The south-eastern portion of New Jersey seems to be well suited to them. This species is rarely found in Massachusetts, and one we received from the north-western part of that State, was there regarded as a great curiosity.

General Remarks.

This species has been sometimes confounded with the fox-squirrel, (*S. capistratus,*) and at other times with the northern gray squirrel, (*S. migratorius,*) and all three have by some been considered as forming but one species; it is, however, in size, intermediate between the two former, and has some distinctive marks by which it may be known from either.

The northern gray squirrel has (as far as we have been able to ascertain from an examination of many specimens,) permanently five molars on each side in the upper jaw, and the present species has but four. The Cat-Squirrel, however, like the young fox-squirrel, has no doubt, a small deciduous tooth, which drops out in the very young state, and at so early a period that we have not succeeded in detecting it.

Sciurus capistratus is in all its varieties, as far as we have observed, invariably and permanently distinguished by its having white ears and a white nose, which is not the case with *S. cinereus.* The former, is a southern species, the latter, is found in the middle and northern States, but not in the colder portions of New England or in Canada.

S. capistratus, is a longer, thinner and more active species, running with almost the speed of a hare, and ascending the tallest pines to so great a height that nothing but a rifle-ball can bring it down; the present species is heavy, clumsy, and prefers clinging to the body of a tree, not generally ascending to its extreme branches. The hair of *S. capistratus* is more rigid and smoother than that of *S. cinereus,* which is rather soft and woolly.

We have instituted this comparison in order to prove the inaccuracy of a statement contained in one of the last works published in our country, on the American quadrupeds. The author says, "We suspect that GODMAN's fox-squirrel (*S. vulpinus*) as well as his Cat, (*S. cinereus*) are varieties only of the hooded squirrel." Under the above names GODMAN published only one and the same species, but the hooded squirrel, (*S. capistratus*) with white ears and nose, is a very different species, and is not given by GODMAN.

The Cat-Squirrel was the first of the genus described from America. RAY characterizes it as *S. virginianus cinereus major.* CATESBY gives a tolerable description of it, and a figure, which although rather extravagant in the size of its tail, cannot from its short ears, which as well as the nose are destitute of the white marks of *S. capistratus,* be mistaken for the gray variety of the latter species.

He says—"These squirrels are as large as a half-grown rabbit; the whole structure of their bodies and limbs, thicker in proporiton, and of a grosser and more clumsy make than our common squirrels." From this time it became for many years either lost or confounded with other species by naturalists. DESMAREST under the name of *cinereus* entirely mistook the species, and applied it to two others, the Carolina gray, and the northern gray squirrel. HARLAN copied the article, adopting and perpetuating the error. GOD-MAN by the aid of LE CONTE as it appears to us, (see a reference to his letter—Amer. Nat. Hist. vol. ii., p. 129,) was enabled to correct this error, but fell into another, describing one species under two names, and omitting the southern fox-squirrel (*S. capistratus*) altogether, assigning its habits to his *S. vulpinus.* In our monograph of this genus, 1838; we endeavoured to correct the errors into which authors had fallen in regard to this species, time and further experience, have only strengthened us in the views we then expressed.

Lepus Palustris.—Bachman.

Marsh-Hare.

Plate xviii.—Male and Female. Natural size.

L. corpore supra flavo-fuscente, subtus griseo, L. sylvatico minore auribus capite in multum brevioribus, oculis aliquantulum parvis, cauda brevissima, cruribus curtis varipilis.

Characters.

Smaller than the gray rabbit; ears, much shorter than the head; eyes, rather small; tail, very short; legs, short; feet, thinly clothed with hair; upper parts of body, yellowish-brown; beneath, gray.

Synonymes.

LEPUS PALUSTRIS, Bach., Jour. Acad. of Natural Sciences, Philadelphia, vol. vii., pp. 194, 366, read May 10, 1836.

LEPUS DOUGLASSII, Gray, read, Zoological Society, London, Nov. 1837.
LEPUS PALUSTRIS, Audubon—Birds of America, first edition—pounced upon by the common buzzard, (*Buteo vulgaris.*) Ornithological Biography, vol. iv., p. 510.

Description.

Upper incisors, longer and broader than those of the gray rabbit, marked like all the rest of the genus, with a deep longitudinal furrow; the small accessory incisors are smaller and less flattened than those of the gray rabbit, the molars are narrower, and a little shorter. The transverse measurement of the cranium is much smaller, the vertical, about equal. Orbits of the eyes one-third smaller.

This last, is a striking peculiarity, giving this a smaller and less prominent eye than that of any other American hare, of equal size, with which we are acquainted.

The zygomatic processes of the temporal bone, run downwards nearly in a vertical line, whilst those of the gray rabbit, are almost horizontal. Head, rather large; forehead, slightly arched; whiskers, numerous, rigid; nose, blunt; eyes, rather small; ears, short, rounded, broad, clothed on both surfaces

Cat Squirrel.

Drawn from Nature by J.J.Audubon FRS FLS   Printed by Nagel & Weingærtner NY

Drawn on Stone by R.Trembly

with short hairs. Neck, moderately long; body, short, thick, and of rather a clumsy shape; hairs, rather long and much coarser than those of the gray rabbit. Legs, short, and rather small; feet so thinly clothed with hair, that the nails in most of the specimens are not covered, but project beyond the hair; the feet leave a distinct impression of the toes and claws, on the mud, or in moist places where their tracks can be seen. Heel, short, thinly covered with hair; nails, long, stout, and very acute; tail, short; scarcely visible whilst the animal is running.

Colour.

Teeth, yellowish-white; eyes, dark-brown, appearing in certain lights, quite black. Upper part of the head, brown, and grayish-ash. Around the orbits of the eyes, slightly fawn-coloured; whiskers, black; ears, dark grayish-brown. Back, whole upper-parts, and upper-surface of the tail, yellowish-brown intermixed with many strong black hairs. The hairs, when examined singly, are bluish-gray at the roots, then light-brown, and are tipped with black. Throat, brownish-gray. Outer-surface of fore-legs, and upper-surface of thighs, reddish-yellow. The fur beneath, is light plumbeous; under the chin, gray; belly, and under-surface of tail, light-gray; the fur beneath, bluish, giving it a dark yellowish-brown appearance. Under-surface of the tail, ash-colour, edged with brown. During winter the upper surface becomes considerably darker than in summer, and the under-parts of the tail in a few specimens become nearly white.

Dimensions.

A specimen in the flesh.

Length from point of nose to insertion of tail	13	inches.
do. of tail, (vertebræ)	1	"
do. do. do. including fur	$1\frac{1}{2}$	"
Height from end of middle claw to top of shoulder	7	"
Length of head	$3\frac{1}{2}$	"
do. ears	$2\frac{1}{2}$	"
do. hind-foot	3	"

Weight, $2\frac{1}{2}$ lb.

Habits.

The Marsh-Hare, chiefly confines itself to the maritime districts of the southern States, and is generally found in low marshy grounds that are sometimes partially inundated, near rivers subject to freshets that occasionally overflow their banks, or near the large ponds called in Carolina, "reserves," which are dammed up or otherwise made to retain the water intended to flood the rice-fields at the proper season.

In these situations—to which few persons like to resort, on account of the muddy nature of the ground, and the many thorny and entangling vines and other obstructions that abound near them; and which, besides, continually exhale from their stagnant waters a noxious vapour, which rapidly generates disease—surrounded by frogs, water-snakes and alligators, this species resides throughout the year, rarely molested by man, and enabled by its aquatic habits, to make up for any want of speed when eluding the pursuit of its enemies.

It winds with great facility through miry pools, and marshes overgrown with rank weeds and willow bushes, and is quite at its ease and at home in the most boggy and unsafe parts of the swamps.

We have met with this animal a few miles from Columbia, South Carolina, one hundred and twenty miles north of Charleston, along the muddy shores of the sluggish rivers and marshes, but on arriving at the high grounds beyond the middle country, where the marshes disappear, it is no longer to be found.

In its movements it is unlike most of our other hares; it runs low on the ground, and cannot leap with the same ease strength and agility they display. From the shortness of its legs and ears, and its general clumsy appearance as we see it splashing through the mud and mire, or plunging into creeks or ponds, it somewhat reminds us of an over-grown Norway rat endeavouring to escape from its pursuers.

The Marsh-Hare is so slow of foot, that but for the protection afforded it by the miry tangled and thorny character of its usual haunts, it would soon be overtaken and caught by any dog of moderate speed. We have observed the negroes of a plantation on a holiday, killing a good many of them by first setting fire to the half-dried grasses and weeds in a marshy piece of ground during a continued drought, when the earth had absorbed nearly all the moisture from it, and then surrounding the place, with sticks in their hands, and waiting until the flames drove the hares from their retreats, when they

were knocked down and secured as they attempted to pass. Several gray-rabbits ran out of this place, but the men did not attempt to stop them, knowing their superior speed, but every Marsh-Hare that appeared, was headed, and with a loud whoop set upon on all sides and soon captured.

The feet of the Marsh-Hare are admirably adapted to its aquatic habits. A thick covering of hair on its feet, like that on the soles of other species, would be inconvenient; they would not only be kept wet for a considerable length of time, but would retard the animal in swimming. Quadrupeds that frequent the water, such as the beaver, otter, musk-rat, mink &c., and aquatic birds, have nearly naked palms; and it is this peculiar structure, together with the power of spreading out its feet, and thus increasing the space between each of its toes, that enables this quadruped to swim with great ease and rapidity. Its track when observed in moist or muddy situations differs very much from that of other species. Its toes are spread out, each leaving a distinct impression like those of the rat. Some of the habits of this Hare, differ greatly from those of others of the genus; it seeks the water, not only in order the easier to escape from its pursuers, but when in sportive mood; and a stranger in Carolina should he accidentally see one amusing itself by swimming about, if unacquainted with the habits of the animal, would be puzzled by its manœuvres.

When the Marsh-Hare is startled by the approach of danger, instead of directing its flight toward high grounds like the gray rabbit, it hastens to the thickest part of the marsh, or plunges into some stream, mill-pond, or "reserve," and very often stops and conceals itself where the water is many feet deep, among the leaves of lilies or other aquatic plants.

After a heavy rain had produced a flood, which inundated some swamps and rice-fields near us, we sallied forth to see what had become of the Marsh-Hares, and on beating the bushes, we started many of them which ran from their hiding places, plunged into the water, and swam off with such rapidity that some escaped from an active Newfoundland dog that we had with us. Several of them, supposing they were unobserved, hid themselves in the water, about fifteen yards from the shore, protruding only their eyes and the point of their nose above the surface; when thus almost entirely under the muddy water, with their ears pressed back and flat against their neck, they could scarcely be discovered. On touching them with a stick they seemed unwilling to move until they perceived that they were observed, when they swam off with great celerity.

A few evenings afterwards when the waters had subsided and returned to their ordinary channels, we saw a good many of these Hares swimming in places where the water was seven or eight feet deep, meeting, or pursuing each other, as if in sport, and evidently enjoying themselves.

When the gray-rabbit approaches the water, it generally goes around or leaps over it, but the Marsh-Hare enters it readily and swims across.

We have on a few occasions seen this Hare, take to a hollow tree when hard pressed by dogs, but (as we have just remarked) it usually depends more for its safety, on reaching marshy places, ponds, or impenetrable thickets.

This species possesses a strong marshy smell at all times, even when kept in confinement, and fed on the choicest food. Its flesh, however, although dark, is fully equal, if not superior, to that of the gray rabbit.

The Marsh-Hare never, that we are aware of, visits gardens or cultivated fields, but confines itself throughout the year to the marshes. It is occasionally found in places overflowed by salt, or brackish, water, but seems to prefer fresh-water marshes, where its food can be most conveniently obtained. It feeds on various grasses, and gnaws off the twigs of the young sassafras, and of the pond-spice (*Laurus geniculata*.) We have seen many places in the low grounds dug up, the foot-prints indicating that it was the work of this species in search of roots. It frequently is found digging for the bulbs of the wild potatoe, (*Apios tuberosa*,) as also for those of a small species of amaryllis, (*Amaryllis atamasco*.)

We kept an individual of this species in confinement, which had been captured when full-grown. It became so gentle in a few days that it freely took its food from the hand. It was fed on turnips and cabbage-leaves, but preferred bread to any other food that was offered to it. In warm weather it was fond of lying for hours in a trough of water, and seemed restless and uneasy when it was removed; scratching at the sides of its cage, until the trough was replaced, when it immediately plunged in, burying the greater part of its body in the water.

This species, like all others of the genus existing in this country, as well as the deer and squirrels, is infested with a troublesome larva of an œstrus in the summer and autumn; which penetrating into the flesh and continually enlarging, causes pain to the animal and renders it lean.

The Marsh-Hare deposits its young in a pretty large nest, frequently composed of a species of rush, (*Juncus effusus*) growing in convenient situations. The rushes appear to be cut by it into pieces of about a foot in length. We have seen these nests nearly surrounded by, and almost floating on the

Plate XVIII

N° 4

Drawn on Stone by R Trembly

Marsh Hare

Printed by Nagel & Weingärtner N.Y.

Drawn from Nature by J.J.Audubon F.R.S. F.L.S.

water. They were generally arched by carefully bending the rushes or grasses over them, admitting the mother by a pretty large hole in the side. A considerable quantity of hair was found lining them, but whether plucked out by the parent, or the result of the natural shedding of their coat, (it being late in the spring, when these animals shed their hair,) we were unable to ascertain.

The young number from five to seven. They evidently breed several times in the season, but we have observed that the females usually produce their young at least a month later than the gray rabbit. Twenty-one specimens were obtained from the 9th to the 14th day of April; none of the females had produced young that season, although some of them would have done so in a very few days. On one occasion only, have we seen the young in March. They bear a strong resemblance to the adult, and may almost at a glance be distinguished from those of the gray rabbit.

Geographical Distribution.

The Marsh-Hare has been seen as far north as the swamps of the southern parts of North Carolina. In South Carolina, it is in some localities quite numerous. Nearly all the muddy swamps and marshes abound with it. We have known two persons to kill twenty in the course of a few hours.

In high grounds it is never seen; it continues to increase in numbers as we proceed southwardly. It is abundant in the swamps of Georgia, Alabama, and Louisiana. We received a living specimen from Key West, the southern point of Florida. We have seen it in Texas, from whence the specimen described by GRAY was brought, and we are inclined to believe that it will be found to extend into the northern part of Mexico.

General Remarks.

As a remarkable instance of a species continuing to exist in a thickly settled country without having found its way into scientific works, we may refer to this very common species. We obtained specimens in Carolina in the spring of 1815. It was called by the inhabitants by the names of Swamp, and Marsh, Hare, and generally supposed to be only a variety of the gray rabbit. We did not publish a description of the species until 1836. In the following year, GRAY, who had not then seen the Transactions of the Acad. of Natural Sciences of Philadelphia, in which our description was contained, described it under the name of *Lepus Douglassii*.

This species may always be distinguished from our other hares, by its colour, its rather short and broad ears, its short tail, which is never pure white beneath, by its narrow hind-feet, and by its aquatic habits.

Sciurus Mollipilosus.—Aud. and Bach.

Soft-Haired Squirrel.

Plate xix.—Natural Size.

S. cauda corpore curtiore; dorso fusco; iliis partibusque colli lateralibus rufis; abdomine cinereo.

Characters.

Tail, shorter than the body; back, dark brown; sides of the neck, and flanks, rufous; under surface, cinereous.

Synonyme.

SCIURUS MOLLIPILOSUS, Aud. and Bach., Journal Acad. of Nat. Sciences, Philadelphia, Oct. 1841, p. 102.

Description.

A little larger than the chickaree, (S. *Hudsonius*;) head, rather large, slightly arched: ears, round, broad, but not high, clothed on the outer and inner surfaces with short, smooth hairs; whiskers, longer than the head.

In form this species does not approach the TAMIÆ, as S. *Hudsonius* does in some degree: it, on the contrary, very much resembles the Carolina gray-squirrel, S. *Carolinensis*, which is only an inch longer.

Legs, robust; toes, rather long; nails, compressed, arched; tail bushy, but apparently not distichous, as far as can be judged from the dried specimen; hairs of the tail about as long as those of the Carolina gray-squirrel. The hairs on the whole of the body are soft and very smooth.

Colour.

Teeth, light yellow; upper parts, including the nose, ears, and outer surface of the tail, dark-brown; this colour is produced by the hairs being plumbeous at the roots, tipped with light-brown and black. On the sides of the neck, the

shoulder, and near the thighs, it is of a reddish-brown colour. The tail is brown, twice annulated with black; a few of the hairs are tipped with gray. On the under surface, the lips and chin are grayish-brown; inner surface of the fore-legs, throat, and abdomen, cinereous, lightly tinged in some places with rufous.

Dimensions.

	Inches.	Lines.
Length of head and body	8	6
" of tail (vertebræ)	5	6
" " to end of hair	7	0
Height of ear	0	5
From heel to end of nail	2	1

Habits.

This species was procured in Upper California, near the Pacific ocean, and we are obliged to confess ourselves entirely unacquainted with its habits. From its form, however, we have no doubt of its having more the manners of the Carolina gray-squirrel, than those of the chickaree. We may suppose that it lives on trees, and never burrows in the ground, as the chickaree sometimes does.

Geographical Distribution.

Our specimens were obtained in the northern part of California, near the Pacific ocean.

General Remarks.

This species differs so widely in all its details from S. *Hudsonius*, that it is scarcely necessary to point out the distinctive marks by which it is separated from the latter. The space occupied by the lighter colours on the under surface, is much narrower than in S. *Hudsonius*, and there is not, as in that species, any black line of separation between the colours of the back and under surface.

Tamias Townsendii.—Bach.

Townsend's Ground-Squirrel.

Plate xx.—Natural size.

T. obscurus, supra flavo-fuscescens, striis quinque nigris longitudinalibus subequaliter distantibus dorsali usque ad caudam porrecta; subtus cinereus. T. Lysteri magnitudine superans.

Characters.

A little larger than Tamias Lysteri; tail much longer; upper surface, dusky yellowish-brown, with five nearly equidistant parallel black stripes on the back, the dorsal one extending to the root of the tail; under surface cinereous.

Synonyme.

TAMIAS TOWNSENDII, Townsend's Ground Squirrel, Journal Acad. of Natural Sciences, Philadelphia, vol. viii., part 1, 1839.

Soft haired Squirrel.

Drawn from Nature by J.J. Audubon F.R.S.F.L.S.

Drawn on Stone by R.Trembly.

Description.

Head, of moderate size; forehead, convex; nose, rather obtuse, clothed with very short hairs; nostrils, opening downward, their margins and spetum naked; whiskers, as long as the head; eyes, large; ears, long, erect, obovate, clothed with short hair on the outer, and nearly naked on the inner surface; cheek-pouches, tolerably large. In form this species resembles *T. Lysteri*; it is, however, longer and stouter. Legs, of moderate size; toes, long; the fore-feet have four toes, with the rudiment of a thumb, protected by a short convex nail; the palms are naked, with five tubercles. Claws, curved, compressed, and sharp-pointed. On the hind-feet, five toes, the third and fourth nearly of equal length, the second a little shorter, and the first, or inner toe, shortest. Tail, long and subdistichous.

Colour.

Teeth, dark orange; whiskers, black; a line of fawn-colour, commencing at the nostrils, run over the eye-brows, and terminates a little beyond them in a point of lighter colour; a patch of a similar colour commences under the eye-lids, and running along the cheeks terminates at the ear.

A line of dark brown, commencing at the termination of the nose, where it forms a point, and bordering the fawn-colour above, is gradually blended with the colours of the head; fur on the outer surface of the ear, brown on the anterior parts, with a patch of white covering about one-fourth of the ear. On the posterior part of the ear there is a slight cinereous tint about six lines in length, terminating near the shoulder. A black stripe commences on the hind part of the head and runs over the centre of the back, where it spreads out to the width of four lines, terminating in a point at the insertion of the tail; a line of the same colour commences at the shoulders, and running parallel to the first terminates a little beyond the hips; another, but narrower and shorter, line of black runs parallel with this, low down on the sides, giving it five black stripes about equi-distant from each other. On the throat, belly, and inner parts of the legs and thighs, the colour is light cinereous; there is no line of separation between the colours of the back and belly. The tail is, on the upper surface, grayish-black, having a hoary appearance. Underneath, it is reddish-brown for two-thirds of its breadth, then a narrow line of black, tipped with light ash. Nails, brown.

Dimensions.

	Inches.	Lines.
Length of head and body	6	9
" tail (vertebræ)	4	0

" " including fur	5	0
" head	2	0
Height of ear	0	6
Length from heel to end of nail	1	6

Habits.

No doubt the different species of this genus are as uniform in their habits as the true squirrels. They are usually found seated low, on stumps or rocks, at the roots of or near which, they have their burrows. Their cheek-pouches enable them to carry to these hiding-places, nuts, grains, &c., to serve them for food in winter. Mr. TOWNSEND, who procured the specimens from which we have drawn up our description, observes, "This pretty little fellow, so much resembling our common *T. striatus*, (*Lysteri*,) is quite common; it lives in holes in the ground; running over your foot as you traverse the woods. If frequently perches itself upon a log or stump, and keeps up a continual clucking, which is usually answered by another at some distance, for a considerable time. Their note so much resembles that of the dusky grouse, (*Tetrao obscurus*,) that I have more than once been deceived by it."

Geographical Distribution.

We have heard of this species as existing from the 37th to the 45th degree of latitude, on the Rocky Mountains. It probably does not extend to the eastward of that chain, as we saw nothing of it on our late expedition up the Missouri river, to the mouth of the Yellow-Stone, &c.

General Remarks.

The markings of this Ground-Squirrel differ widely from those of any other known species. From *Tamias Lysteri* it differs considerably, being larger and having a much longer tail; it has a white patch behind the ear, and cinereous markings on the neck, of which the latter is destitute; the ears are a third longer than in *T. Lysteri*. The stripes on the back are also very differently arranged. In *Tamias Lysteri* there is first a black dorsal stripe, then a space of grayish-brown, half an inch wide, then two shorter stripes, within two lines of each other; which narrow intervening portion is yellowish-white. The stripes in the present species are at a uniform distance from each other, the dorsal one running to the tail; whereas, in the other it does not reach within an inch of it, and the intervening spaces are filled up by a uniform colour. This species has not the whitish stripes on the sides, nor the rufous colour on the hips, which are so conspicuous in *T. Lysteri*.

Vulpes Virginianus. —Schreber.

Gray Fox.

Plate xxi. —Male. 5-7ths Natural size.

V. griseo nigroque variegatus, lateribus et partibus colli lateralibus fulvis, genis nigris.

Characters.

Gray, varied with black, sides of neck and flank, fulvous; black on the sides of the face between the eye and nose.

Synonymes.

FOX OF CAROLINA, Lawson, Car., p. 125.
GRAY FOX, Catesby, Car., vol. ii., p. 78, fig. C.
"   "   Pennant, Synop., p. 157, 114.
CANIS VIRGINIANUS, Schreber, Säugethiere, p. 361, 10 to 92 B, 1775.
"   "   Erxleben, Syst., p. 567, 10, 1777.
"   "   Linn., Syst. Nat., ed. Gmel., vol. i., p. 74, 16, 1788.
"   CINEREO-ARGENTEUS, Erxleben, Syst., p. 576, 9.
"   CINEREO-ARGENTATUS, Say, Long's Expedition, vol. ii., p. 340.
"   VIRGINIANUS, Desm., Mamm., p. 204.
"   CINEREO-ARGENTATUS, Godman, Nat. Hist., vol. i., p. 280, fig. 2.

"   (VULPES) VIRGINIANUS, Rich., F. Boreali A., p. 96.
VULPES VIRGINIANUS, Dekay, Nat. Hist. of New York, p. 45.

Description.

Head, considerably broader and shorter than that of the red fox, (*Vulpes fulvus*;) nose, also shorter, and a little more pointed; teeth, not so stout; ears, a little longer than in the latter animal, of an oval shape, and thickly clothed with hair on both surfaces; whiskers, half the length of the head. Body, rather thicker and more clumsy in appearance than that of either the swift fox, (*V. velox*,) or the red fox; fur, much coarser than that of the other species. Legs, rather long; nails, strong, slightly arched, visible beyond the fur; soles, with five stout tubercles, not clothed with hair; tail, large, bushy, clothed like the body with two kinds of hair; the fur, or inner hair, being soft and woolly, the outer hairs longer and coarser.

Colour.

There are slight differences in the colour of different specimens; we will, however, give a description of one which is of the colour most common to this species in every part of the United States. Head, brownish-gray; muzzle, black; a broad patch of dark brown runs from the eye to the nose, on each side of the face; whiskers, black; inner surface of ears, dull white; outer surface of ears, sides of neck, outer surface of fore-legs and thighs, tawny; a yellowish wash under the throat, and along the sides; chin, and around the mouth, dark-brown; cheeks, throat, and under surface of body, dull white, occasionally tinged with a yellowish shade; under surface of hind and fore-feet, yellowish-brown: upper surface of feet and legs, grizzly black and white; nails,

Plate XX

Drawn from Nature by J.J.Audubon FRS FLS

Drawn on Stone by R Trembly

Townsend's Ground Squirrel.

Printed by Nagel & Weingærtner N.Y.

Colored by J.Lawrence

dark-brown. The soft inner fur on the back, which is about an inch and a half long, is for half its length from the roots, plumbeous, and pale yellowish-white at the tips. The long hairs which give the general colour to the body above, are white at their roots, then for more than a third of their length black, then white, and are broadly tipped with black, giving the animal a hoary or silver-gray appearance. It is darkest on the shoulder, along the back and posterior parts. The fur on the tail, has a little more fulvous tinge than that of the back; the longer hairs are much more broadly tipped with black. When the fur lies smooth, there is a black line along the upper surface of the tail from the root to the extremity; end of brush, black. Some specimens are a little lighter coloured, having a silver-gray appearance. Specimens from the State of New York are rather more fulvous on the neck, and darker on the back, than those of Carolina. In some specimens there is a dark spot on the sides of the throat about an inch from the ear.

We possessed for many years a beautiful specimen of a variety of the Gray Fox, which was barred on the tail like the racoon, and had a dark cross on the back like that of *Canis crucigera* of GESNER, which latter is regarded by Baron CUVIER as a mere variety of the European fox.

Dimensions.

Length of head and body	28	inches.
" of tail (vertebræ)	12½	do.
" to end of hair	14	do.
Height of ear	2½	do.
From heel to end of nail	5	do.

Habits.

Throughout the whole of our Atlantic States, from Maine to Florida, and westwardly to Louisiana and Texas, there are but two *species* of fox known, viz., the red fox, (*V. fulvus*,) and the present species, (*V. Virginianus*,) although there are several permanent *varieties*. The former may be regarded as a Northern, the latter as a Southern species. Whilst the Northern farmer looks upon the red fox as a great annoyance, and detests him as a robber, who is lying in wait for his lambs, his turkeys, and his geese, the Gray Fox, in the eyes of the Southern planter, is the object of equal aversion. To ourselves, however, who have witnessed the predatory dispositions of each, in different portions of our country, it appears that the red fox is far more to be dreaded than the gray; the latter is a pilfering thief, the former a more daring and cunning plunderer. When they have whelps, the females of both species, urged by the powerful pleadings of their young, become more bold and destructive than at any other time; the red fox produces its young very early in the season, sometimes indeed whilst the snow is still remaining here and there in large banks unthawed on the ground, and becomes more daring in consequence of being stinted for food; whilst the present species, having its young later when breeding in the Northern States, and finding a more abundant supply of food when inhabiting the Middle or Southern States, is less urged by necessity to depredate on the poultry of the planter.

We have never, indeed, heard any well authenticated account of this species having entered the poultry-yard of the farmer; it is true, it will seize on a goose, or a turkey hen, that happens to stray into the woods or fields and make its nest at some distance from the house; but we have not heard of its having attempted to kill pigs, or like the red fox, visited the sheep pasture in spring, and laid a contribution, from day to day, on the young lambs of the flock.

The Gray Fox is shy and cowardly, and the snap of a stick or the barking of a dog will set him off on a full run. Although timid and suspicious to this degree, his cunning and voracity place him in a conspicuous rank among the animals that prey upon other species weaker than themselves. The wild turkey hen often makes an excavation in which she deposits her eggs, at a consider-able distance from the low grounds, or makes her nest on some elevated ridge, or under a pile of fallen logs covered over with scrub oaks, ferns, tall weeds and grasses; we have often seen traces of a violent struggle at such places; bunches of feathers scattered about, and broken egg-shells giving sufficient evidence that the Fox has been there, and that there will be one brood of wild turkeys less that season. Coveys of partridges, which generally at the dusk of the evening, fly into some sheltered place, and hide in the tall grass, arrange themselves for the night in a circle, with their tails touching each other, and their heads turned outward; the Gray Fox possessing a considerable power of scent, winds them like a pointer dog, and often discovers where they are thus snugly nestled, and pounces on them, invariably carrying off at least one of the covey.

On a cold, drizzly, sleety, rainy day, while travelling in Carolina, we observed a Gray Fox in a field of broom-grass, coursing against the wind, and hunting in the manner of the pointer dog. We stopped to witness his manœuvres: suddenly he stood still, and squatted low on his haunches; a moment after, he proceeded on once more, but with slow and cautious steps; at times his nose was raised high in the air, moving about from side to side. At length he seemed to be sure of his game, and went straight forward, although very slowly, at times crawling on the earth; he was occasionally hidden by the grass, so that we could not see him very distinctly; however, at length we observed him make a dead halt. There was no twisting or horizontal movement of the tail, like that made by the common house-cat when ready to make a spring, but his tail seemed resting on the side, whilst his ears were drawn back and his head raised only a few inches from the earth; he remained in this attitude nearly half a minute, and then made a sudden pounce upon this prey; at the same instant the whirring of the distracted covey was heard, as the affrighted birds took wing; two or three sharp screams succeeded, and the successful prowler immediately passed out of the field with an unfortunate partridge in his mouth, evidently with the intention of seeking a more retired spot to make a dainty meal. We had a gun with us, and he passed within long gun-shot of us. But why wound or destroy him? He has enabled us for the first time to bear witness that he is not only a dog, but a good pointer in the bargain; he has obeyed an impulse of nature, and obtained a meal in the manner in which it was intended by the wise Creator that he should be supplied. He seized only a single bird, whilst man, who would wreak his vengeance on this poacher among the game, is not satisfied till he has killed half the covey with the murderous gun, or caught the whole brood in a trap, and wrung off their necks in triumph. Condemn not the Fox too hastily; he has a more strikingly carnivorous tooth than yourself, indicating the kind of food he is required to seek; he takes no wanton pleasure in destroying the bird, he exhibits to his companions no trophies of his skill, and is contented with a meal; whilst you are perhaps not satisfied when your capacious bird-bag is filled.

That this Fox occasionally gives chase to the gray rabbit, pursuing him in the manner of the dog, we have strong reason to suspect. We on one occasion observed a half-grown rabbit dashing by us with great rapidity, and running as if under the influence of fear; an instant afterwards a Fox followed, seeming to keep the object of his pursuit fairly in sight; scarcely had they entered the woods, when we heard the repeated cry of the rabbit, resembling somewhat that of a young child in pain, and although we were not eye witnesses of his having captured it by sheer speed, we have no doubt of the fact. We do not believe, however, that the Fox is an enemy half as much to be dreaded by the family of hares as either the Bay lynx, or the great horned owl, (*Strix Virginianus*.)

In the Southern States this species is able to supply itself with a great variety and abundance of food, and is consequently generally in good condition and often quite fat. We have followed the track of the Gray Fox in moist ground until it led us to the scattered remains of a marsh hare, which no doubt the Fox had killed; many nests of the fresh water marsh hen (*Rallus elegans*) are torn to pieces and the eggs devoured by this prowler. In Pennsylvania and New-Jersey, the meadow-mouse (*Arvicola Pennsylvanica*,) is often eaten by this species, and in the Southern States, the cotton-rat, and Florida rat, constitute no inconsiderable portion of its food. We have seen places where the Gray Fox had been scratching the decayed logs and the bark of trees in order to obtain insects.

This species is not confined exclusively to animal food; a farmer of the State of New York called our attention to a field of corn, (maize,) which had sustained no inconsiderable injury from some unknown animals that had been feeding on the unripe ears. The tracks in the field convinced us that the depredation had been committed by Foxes, which was found to be the case, and they were afterwards chased several successive mornings, and three of them, apparently a brood of the previous spring, were captured.

Although this Fox is nocturnal in his habits, we have frequently observed him in search of food at all hours of the day; in general, however, he lies concealed in some thicket, or in a large tuft of tall broom-grass, till twilight invites him to renew his travels and adventures.

On a cold starlight night in winter, we have frequently heard the hoarse querulous bark of this species; sometimes two of them some distance apart were answering each other in the manner of the dog.

Although we have often seen this Fox fairly run down and killed by hounds, without his having attempted to climb a tree, yet it not unfrequently occurs that when his strength begins to fail he ascends one that is small or sloping, and standing on some horizontal branch 20 or 30 feet from the ground, looks down on the fierce and clamorous pack which soon comes up and surrounds the foot of the tree. We were on one occasion, in company with a friend, seeking for partridges in an old field partially overgrown with high grass and bushes, when his large and active pointer dog suddenly started a Gray Fox, which

Plate XXI

N° 5

Lith. Printed & Col.d by J.T. Bowen, Phil.

On Stone by Wm E. Hitchcock

Grey Fox

Drawn from Nature by J.J.Audubon, F.R.S.F.L.S.

instantly took to its heels, pursued by the dog: after a race of minute, the latter was so close upon the Fox that it ascended a small tree, and our friend soon came up, and shot it. We were unable to obtain any information in regard to the manner in which the Fox trees, as he does not possess the retractile nails of the cat, or the sharp claws of the squirrel, until we saw the animal in the act. At one time when we thus observed the Fox, he first leaped on to a low branch, four or five feet from the ground, from whence he made his way upwards by leaping cautiously and rather awkwardly from branch to branch, till he attained a secure position in the largest fork of the tree, where he stopped. On another occasion, he ascended in the manner of a bear, but with far greater celerity, by clasping the stem of a small pine. We have since been informed that the Fox also climbs trees occasionally by the aid of his claws, in the manner of a racoon or a cat. During winter only about one-fifth of the Foxes chased by hounds, will take a tree before they suffer themselves to be run down; but in summer, either from the warmth of the weather causing them to be soon fatigued, or from the greater number being young animals, they seldom continue on foot beyond thirty or forty minutes before they fly for protection to a tree. It may here be observed that as long as the Fox can wind through the thick underbrush, he will seldom resort to a tree, a retreat to which he is forced by open woods and a hard chase.

In general, it may be said that the Gray Fox digs no burrow, and does not seek concealment in the earth; we have, however, seen one instance to the contrary, in a high, sandy, pine-ridge west of Albany, in the State of New-York. We there observed a burrow from which a female Gray Fox and four young were taken. It differed widely from the burrows of the red fox, having only a single entrance. At about eight feet from the mouth of the burrow there was an excavation containing a nest composed of leaves, in which the young had been deposited. We have, on several occasions, seen the kennel of the Gray Fox—it is usually in a prostrate hollow log; we once, however, discovered one under the the roots of a tree. In the State of New-York we were shown a hollow tree, leaning on another at an angle of about forty-five degrees from a large hole in which two Gray Foxes had been taken; they were traced to this retreat by their footsteps in the deep snow, and from the appearance of the nest it seemed to have been their resort for a long time.

This species, in many parts of the country where caves, fissures, or holes in the rocks, offer it a safe retreat from danger, makes its home in such places. Some little distance above the city of New-York, in the wild and rocky woods on the Jersey side of the Hudson river, a good many Gray Foxes abide, the number of large fissures and holes in the rocks thereabouts furnishing them secure dwelling places, or safe resorts in case they are pursued. In this neighbourhood they are most easily killed by finding the paths to their hole, and, after starting the animal, making the best of your way to near the entrance of it, while he doubles about a little before the dogs; you can thus generally secure a shot at him as he approaches his home, which if the dogs are near he will do without looking to see if he be watched. The Gray Fox is frequently caught in steel-traps, and seems to possess far less cunning than the red species; we have never, however, seen it taken in box-traps, into which the Bay lynx readily enters; and it is not often caught in dead-falls, which are very successful in capturing the racoon and opossum.

The Gray Fox does not possess the rank smell of the red fox, or the European fox; as a pet, however, we have not found him particularly interesting. It is difficult to subdue the snappish disposition of this species, and we have never seen one that was more than half tamed. It does not at any time become as playful as the red fox, and continually attempts to escape.

This species affords good sport when chased, winding and doubling when in favourable ground, so that when the hunter is on foot even, he can occasionally obtain a "view," and can hear the cry of the pack almost all the while. When started in an open part of the country the Gray Fox, however, generally speeds toward some thickly grown and tangled retreat, and prefers the shelter and concealment of a heavy growth of young pines along some elevated sandy ridge; having gained which, he threads along the by-paths and dashes through the thickets, some of which are so dense that the dogs can hardly follow him. He does not, like the red fox, run far ahead of the pack, but generally courses along from seventy to a hundred yards in advance of his pursuers.

We have been told that the Gray Fox has been run down and caught in the winter season, by a remarkably fleet pack of hounds, in forty minutes, but a two hours' chase is generally necessary, with tolerably good dogs, to tire out and capture him. As many as two or three Foxes have been occasionally caught on the same day by one pack of hounds; but in most cases both hunters and dogs are quite willing to give over for the day, after they have captured one.

From Maryland to Florida, and farther west, through Alabama to Mississippi and Louisiana, fox-hunting, next to deer-hunting, is the favourite amusement of sportsmen, and the *chase* of that animal may in fact be regarded exclusively as a Southern sport in the United States, as we believe the fox is never followed on horseback in the Northern portion of our country, where the rocky and precipitous character of the surface in many districts prevents the best riders from attempting it; whilst in others, our sturdy independent farmers would not much like to see a dozen or more horsemen leaping their fences, and with break-neck speed galloping through the wheat-fields or other "fall" crops. Besides, the red fox, which is more generally found in the Northern States than the Gray species, runs so far before the dogs that he is seldom seen, although the huntsmen keep up with the pack, and after a chase of ten miles, during which he may not have been once seen, he perhaps takes refuge in some deep fissure of a rock, or in an impenetrable burrow, which of course ends the sport very much to the satisfaction of—the Fox!

In the Southern States, on the contrary, the ground is in many cases favorable for this amusement, and the planter sustains but little injury from the passing hunt, as the Gray Fox usually courses through woods, or worn-out fields, keeping on high dry grounds, and seldom during the chase running across a cultivated plantation.

Fox-hunting, as generally practised in our Southern States, is regarded as a healthful, manly exercise, as well as an exhilarating sport, which in many instances would be likely to preserve young men from habits of idleness and dissipation. The *music* of the hounds, whilst you breathe the fresh sweet morning air, seated on a high-mettled steed, your friends and neighbours at hand with light hearts and joyous expectations, awaiting the first break from cover, is, if you delight in nature and the recreation we are speaking of, most enlivening; and although we ourselves have not been fox-hunters, we cannot wholly condemn the young man of leisure who occasionally joins in this sport; at the same time let him not forget that whilst exercise and amusement are essential to health and cheerfulness of mind; the latter especially was not intended to interfere with the duties of an active and useful life, and should never be more than a relaxation, to enable him to return the more energetically to the higher and nobler pursuits which are fitted for an intelligent and immortal mind.

In fox-hunting, the horse sometimes becomes as much excited as his rider, and at the cry of the hounds we have known an old steed which had been turned loose in the woods to pick up a subsistence, prick up his ears, and in an instant start off full gallop until he overtook the pack, keeping in the van until the chase was ended. Although exercise and amusement are the principal inducements to hunt the Fox, we may mention that it is also a desirable object in many parts of our country, to get rid of this thievish animal, which exists in considerable numbers in some neighbourhoods.

We will now return to our subject, and try to make you familiar with the mode of hunting the Gray Fox generally adopted in Carolina and Louisiana. The hounds are taken to some spot where the animal is likely to be found, and are kept as much as possible out of the "drives" frequented by deer. Thickets on the edges of old plantations, briar patches, and deserted fields covered with broom-grass, are places in which the Fox is most likely to lie down to rest. The trail he has left behind him during his nocturnal rambles is struck, the hounds are encouraged by the voices of their masters, and follow it as fast as the devious course it leads them will permit. Now they scent the Fox along the field, probably when in search of partridges, meadow-larks, rabbits, or field-mice; presently they trace his footsteps to a large log, from whence he has jumped on to a worm-fence, and after walking a little way on it, has leaped a ditch and skulked toward the borders of a marsh. Through all his crooked ways the sagacious hounds follow his path, until he is suddenly aroused, perchance from a sweet, dreamy vision of fat hens, geese, or turkeys, and with a general cry the whole pack, led on by the staunchest and best dogs, open-mouthed and eager, join in the clase. The startled Fox makes two or three rapid doublings, and then suddenly flies to a cover perhaps a quarter of a mile off, and sometimes thus puts the hounds off the scent for a few minutes, as when cool and at first starting, his scent is not so strong as that of the red fox; after the chase has continued for a quarter of an hour or so, however, and the animal is somewhat heated, his track is followed with greater ease and quickness and the scene becomes animating ane exciting. Where the woods are free from under-brush, which is often the case in Carolina, the grass and bushes being burnt almost annually, many of the sportsmen keep up with the dogs, and the Fox is very frequently in sight and is dashed after at the horses' greatest speed. He now resorts to some of the manœurvres for which he is famous; he plunges into a thicket, doubles, runs into the water, if any be at hand, leaps on to a log, or perhaps gets upon a worm-fence and runs along the top of it for a hundred yards, leaping from it with a desperate bound and continuing his flight instantly, with the hope of escape from the relentless pack. At length he becomes fatigued, he is once more concealed in a thicket where he doubles hurriedly; uncertain in what direction to retreat, he hears, and perhaps sees, the dogs almost upon him, and as a last resort climbs a small tree. The hounds and hunters are almost instantly at the foot of it, and whilst the former are barking fiercely at the terrified animal, the latter determine to give him another chance for his life. The dogs are taken off to a little distance, and the Fox is then forced to leap to the ground by reaching with a long pole, or throwing a billet of wood at him. He is allowed a quarter of an hour before the hounds are permitted to pursue him, but he is now less able to escape than before; he has become stiff and chill, is soon overtaken, and falls and easy prey, turning however upon his pursuers with a growl of despair, and snapping at his foes until he bites the dust, and the chase is ended.

The following anecdotes of the sagacity of this animal, we hope, may interest our readers. Shortly after the railroad from Charleston to Hamburgh, South Carolina, had been constructed, the rails for a portion of the distance having been laid upon timbers at a considerable height from the ground, supported by strong posts, we observed a Fox which was hard pressed by a pack of hounds, mounting the rails, upon which he ran several hundred yards; the dogs were unable to pursue him, and he thus crossed a deep cypress swamp over which the railroad was in this singular manner carried, and made his escape on the opposite side. The late BENJAMIN C. YANCEY, ESQ., an eminent lawyer, who in his youth was very fond of fox-hunting, related the following. A Fox had been pursued, near his residence at Edgefield several times, but the hounds always lost the track at a place where there was a foot-path leading down a steep hill. He, therefore, determined to conceal himself near this declivity the next time the Fox was started, in order to discover his mode of baffling the dogs at this place. The animal was accordingly put up and chased, and at first led the hounds through many bayous and ponds in the woods, but at length came running over the brow of the hill along the path, stopped suddenly and spread himself out flat and motionless on the ground; the hounds came down the hill in pursuit at a dashing pace, and the whole pack passed and did not stop until they were at the bottom of the hill. As soon as the immediate danger was over, the Fox casting a furtive glance around him, stared up, and ran off at his greatest speed on his "back track."

The Gray Fox produces from three to five young at a time. In Carolina this occurs from the middle of March to the middle of April; in the State of New York they bring forth somewhat later. Gestation continues for about three months.

Geographical Distribution.

The Gray Fox is scarce in New England, and we have not heard of it to the north of the State of Maine; in Canada we have heard of its occasional, but rare appearance. In the vicinity of Albany, N. Y., it is not an uncommon species; south of this, through Pennsylvania and New Jersey, it is about as abundant as the red fox. In the Southern States, except in the mountains of Virginia, it is the only species, and is abundant. It exists plentifully in Florida, Mississippi, and Louisiana; it is found on the prairies of the West, and we have received a specimen from California, scarcely differing in any of its marking from those of Carolina.

General Remarks.

This species was noticed by LAWSON, CATESBY, and PENNANT. SCHREBER, in 1775, gave it a specific name; he was followed two years afterwards by ERXLEBEN, and in 1788 by GMELIN. In the meantime ERXLEBEN, SCHREBER, and GMELIN published a variety of the Gray Fox, which was a little more cinereous in colour, as a new species, under the name of *Canis cinereo-argenteus*: RICHARDSON was correct in having applied the specific name of *Virginianus* to the Gray Fox, but he erred in referring the Western kit-fox or swift-fox, (*V. velox*,) to *C. cinereo-argentatus*. To us, the short description of these authors, of *C. cinereo-argentatus*, appears to apply more strictly to the Gray Fox than to their accounts of *C. Virginianus*; the latter, we know, is intended for the present species, as it is the only fox in Virginia, with the exception of the red fox, which exists sparingly in the mountains. The views of DESMAREST in regard to our American foxes are very confused, and the translation by HARLAN partakes of all the errors of the original. RICHARDSON did not meet with this species in the Northern regions he visited, and on the whole very little has been said of its habits by any author.

Lepus Sylvaticus. — Bachman.

Gray Rabbit.

Plate xxii. Old Male, Female, and Young. Natural size.

L. auribus capite curtioribus, aurium apice et margine aut nigro; corpore L. Americano minore, supra cinereo-fulva, fusco, mixto, subtus subalbido.

Characters.

Smaller than the Northern hare; ears, shorter than the head, not tipped or margined with black; colour, grayish-fawn, varied with brown above; whitish beneath.

Synonymes.

CONY, Third Voyage of the English to Virginia, 1586, by Thomas Herriott. From Pinkerton's Voy., vol. xii., p. 600.
HARE, HEDGE CONEY, Lawson, p. 122, Catesby, Appendix 28.
AMERICAN HARE, Kalm's Travels, vol. i., p. 105.
LEPUS AMERICANUS, Desmarest, Mam., p. 351.
    "   "   Harlan, Fauna, p. 193.
    "   "   Godman, Nat. Hist., vol. ii., p. 157.
    "   "   Audubon, Birds of America, vol. ii., p. 51, in the talons of Falco Borealis; Ornithological Biography, vol. i., p. 272.
LEPUS AMERICANUS, Bach., Jour. Ac. Sc. Phil., vol. vii., p. 326.
    "   SYLVATICUS, Bach., Jour. Ac. Sc. Phil., vol. vii., p. 403, & vol. viii., p. 78 & 326.
    "   AMERICANUS, Emmons, Mass. Report, 1840, p. 56.
    "   NANUS, Dekay, Nat. Hist. of New York, 1842.

Description.

This species bears some resemblance to the European burrowing rabbit, (*L. cuniculus*,) in the gray colour which is natural to the latter in a wild state, but does not change to the different colours the European rabbit present in a state of domestication. It is a little smaller, and is of a more slender form than *L. cuniculus*. Head, short; eyes, large; ears, well clothed with short hairs on the outer surface; within, the hairs are a little longer, but less dense, the outer border for the fourth of an inch pretty well covered, but nearer the orifice the skin visible through the thinly scattered hairs; legs, of moderate size; claws, strong, sharp, and nearly straight, concealed by the hair; tail, longer in proportion than that of the Northern hare. Fur, compact and soft, about an inch and a quarter in length in winter.

Colour.

Summer dress. — Fur on the back, yellowish-brown; soft fur, from the roots to the surface, plumbeous; the long hairs which extend beyond the fur, and give the general colour to the animal, are for three-fourths of their length lead coloured, then yellowish, and are tipped with black. Ears, dark-brown on the outer surface, destitute of the distinct black border seen in the Northern hare, and not tipped with black like those of the Polar and the variable hare; whiskers, nearly all black; iris, light brownish-yellow; a circle of fawn colour around the eye, more conspicuous nearest the forehead. Cheeks, grayish; chin, under surface of body, and inner surface of legs, light grayish-white; tail, upper surface grayish-brown, beneath, white. Breast, light yellowish-gray; behind the ears, a broad patch of fawn colour; outer surface of fore-legs and thighs, yellowish-brown.

Winter colour. — Very similar to the above; in a few specimens, the hairs are whitest at the tips; in others, black tips prevail. This Hare never becomes white in any part of our country, and so far as our researches have extended, we have scarcely found any variety in its colouring.

Dimensions.

Adult Male.	Inches.	Lines.
Length of head and body	15	0
" head	3	5
" ears	3	0
" tail (vertebræ)	1	2
" tail, including fur	2	2
From heel to end of middle claw	3	7

Weight, 2 lb. 7 oz.

Habits.

This species abounds in our woods and forests, even in their densest coverts; it is fond of places overgrown with young pines thickly crowded together, or thickets of the high bush-blackberry, (*Rubus villosus*;) and is also fond of frequenting farms and plantations, and occupying the coppices and grassy spots in the neighbourhood of cultivation, remaining in its form by day, concealed by a brush-heap, a tuft of grass, or some hedge-row on the side of an old fence; from which retreat it issues at night, to regale itself on the clover, turnip, or corn-fields of the farmer. It not unfrequently divests the young trees in the nursery of their bark; it makes frequent inroads upon the kitchen-garden, feasting on the young green peas, lettuces, cabbages, &c., and doing a great deal of mischief; and when it has once had an opportunity of tasting these dainties, it becomes difficult to prevent its making a nightly visit to them; although the place it enters at may be carefully closed, the Rabbit is sure to dig a fresh hole every night in its immediate vicinity; and snares, traps, or guns, are the best auxiliaries in such cases, soon putting an end to farther depredations.

This animal, when first started, runs with greater swiftness, and makes fewer doublings than the Northern hare, (*L. Americanus*,) having advanced a hundred yards or more it stops to listen; finding itself pursued by dogs, should the woods be open and free from swamps or thickets, it runs directly toward some hole in the root of a tree or hollow log. In the lower parts of Carolina, where it finds protection in briar patches, and places thickly overgrown with smilax and other vines, it continues much longer on foot, and by winding and turning in places inaccessible to larger animals, frequently makes its escape from its pursuers, without the necessity of resorting for shelter to a hollow tree.

The Gray Rabbit possesses the habit of all the other species of this genus, with which we are acquainted, of stamping with its hind feet on the earth when alarmed at night, and when the males are engaged in combat. It is also seen during the spring season, in wood-paths and along the edges of fields, seeking food late in the mornings and early in the afternoons, and during the breeding season even at mid-day: on such occasions, it may be approached and shot with great ease. This species, like all the true hares, has no note of recognition, and its voice is never heard, except when wounded or at the moment of its capture, when it utters a shrill, plaintive cry, like that of a young child in pain; in the Northern hare this cry is louder, shriller, and of longer continuance. The common domesticated European rabbit seems more easily made to cry out in this way than any other of the genus.

Dr. RICHARDSON, in his work on the American quadrupeds, expresses an opinion from a careful examination of many specimens in different States that the change to the winter dress in the Northern hare, is effected not by a shedding of its hair, but by a lengthening and blanching of the summer fur. Having watched the progress of this change, in the present species in a state of confinement, and having also examined many speciments at all seasons of the year, we have arrived at the opposite conclusion as far as regards the Gray Rabbit. In autumn, the greater portion, if not all, the summer fur drops off in spots, and is gradually replaced by the winter coat. In this state, as there are shades of difference between the summer and winter colours, the animal presents a somewhat singular appearance, exhibiting at the same time, (as in the Northern hare, although far less conspicuously,) patches of different colours. The Gray Rabbit, although it breeds freely in enclosed warrens, seldom becomes tame, and will probably never be domesticated. When captive, it seems to be constantly engaged in trying to find some means of escape, and though it digs no burrows in a state of nature, yet, when confined, it is capable of digging to the depth of a foot or more under a wall, in order to effect its object. We, however, at the house of Dr. DE BENNEVILLE at Milestown, near Philadelphia, saw five or six that were taken from the nest when very young and brought up by hand, so completely tamed that they came at the call and leapt on to the lap of their feeder; they lived sociably and without restraint in the yard, among the dogs and poultry. The former, although accustomed to chase the wild rabbit, never molesting those which had, in this manner, grown up with them, and now made a part of the motley tenants of the poultry-yard. We have not only observed dogs peacefully associating with the hare when thus tamed; but have seen hounds, accustomed to the chase of the deer, eating from the same platter with one of those animals that was domesticated and loose in the yard, refraining from molesting it, and even defending it from the attacks of strangers of their own species, that happened to come into the premises; and when this tame deer, which occasionally visited the woods, was started by the pack of hounds here referred to, they refused to pursue it.

The Gray Rabbit is one of the most prolific of all our species of this genus; in the Northern States it produces young about three times in the season, from five to seven at a litter, whilst in Carolina, its young are frequently brought forth as early as the twentieth of February, and as late as the middle of October, and in all the intermediate months. Nature seems thus to have made a wise provision for the preservation of the species, since no animal is more defenceless or possesses more numerous enemies. Although it can run with considerable swiftness for some distance, its strength in a short time is exhausted, and an active dog would soon overtake it if it did not take shelter in some hole in the earth, heap of logs, or stones, or in a tree with a hollow near its root; in these retreats it is often captured by young hunters.

In the Northern and Middle States, where the burrows of the Maryland marmot (*Arctomys monax*) and the holes resorted to by the common skunk, (*Mephitis chinga*,) are numerous, the Gray Rabbit, in order to effect its escape when pursued, betakes itself to them, and as they are generally deep, or placed among rocks or roots, it would require more labour to unearth it when it has taken possession of either of these animals' retreats than it is worth, and it is generally left unmolested. It is not always safe in these cases, however, for the skunk occasionally is "at home" when the Rabbit runs into his hole, and often catches and devours the astonished fugitive before it can retrace its steps and reach the mouth of the burrow.

This species is also captured occasionally by the skunk and other carnivorous animals when in its form. Its most formidable enemy, however, is the ermine, which follows its tracks until it retires to a hole in the earth or to a hollow tree, which the little but ferocious creature, although not one-fourth as large as the timid Rabbit, quickly enters and kills it—eating off the head, and leaving the body until a want of food compels it to return for more.

Whilst residing in the State of New-York many years ago, we were desirous of preserving a number of Rabbits during the winter from the excessive cold and from the hands of the hunters, who killed so many that we feared the race would be nearly extirpated in our neighbourhood; our design being to set them at liberty in the spring. At this period we had in confinement several weasels of two species existing in that part of the country, (*Putorious erminea* and *P. fusca*,) in order to ascertain in what manner their change of colour from brown in summer to white in winter, and *vice versâ*, was effected.

We bethought ourselves of using one of each species of these weasels instead of a ferret, to aid in taking the Rabbits we wanted, and having provided ourselves with a man and a dog to hunt the Rabbits to their holes, we took the weasels in a small tin box with us, having first tied a small cord around their necks in such a manner as to prevent them from escaping, or remaining in the holes to eat the Rabbits, whilst it could not slip and choke them.

We soon raced a Rabbit to its hole, and our first experiment was made with the little brown weasel, (*P. fusca*;) it appeared to be frightened, and refused to enter the hole; the common species, (*P. erminea*,) although we had captured the individual but a few days before, entered readily; but having its jaws at liberty, it killed the Rabbit. Relinquishing the weasel to our man, he afterwards filed its teeth down to prevent it from destroying the Rabbits; and when thus rendered harmless, the ermine pursued the Rabbits to the bottom of their holes, and terrified them so that they instantly fled to the entrance and were taken alive in the hand; and although they sometimes scrambled up some distance in a hollow tree, their active and persevering little foe followed them, and in-instantly forced them down. In this manner the man procured twelve Rabbits alive in the course of one morning, and more than fifty in about three weeks, when we requested him to desist.

On more than one occasion we have seen the tracks of this species on the snow, giving evidence, by their distance from each other, that the animal had passed rapidly, running under the influence of fear. Examining the surface of the snow carefully, we observed the foot-prints of the weasel, as if in pursuit, and following up the double trail, we found, at the mouth of a hole a short distance beyond, the mutilated remains of the luckless Rabbit.

The Canada lynx, the Bay lynx, (wild cat,) the red and the gray fox, &c., capture this species by stratagem or stealth; various species of hawks and owls prey upon them, and the rattle-snake, chicken-snake, and other serpents have been killed with the Gray Rabbit in their stomach. These reptiles probably caught their victims by stratagem, or by stealing upon them when in their form, and enclosing them in their twining folds, as the boa constrictor captures larger animals.

In order to catch or kill the Gray Rabbit, different means are resorted to according to the fancy of the hunter or the nature of the locality in which the animal may be. In the northern parts of the United States it is pursued with dogs, and either shot or taken from the hole or other retreat to which it may have been driven. It is also frequently captured in box-traps, or snares placed in the gaps of some brush-fence made in the woods for the purpose. In the Southern States it is generally hunted with pointer dogs and shot at the moment when it leaps from its form.

Plate XXII

Nº 5.

Drawn on Stone by R. Trembly.

Printed by Nagel & Weingærtner N.Y.

Grey Rabbit.
Old & Young.

Drawn from Nature by J J Audubon, F.R.S., F.L.S.

Geographical Distribution.

We have not heard of the existence of this species farther north than the southern counties of the State of New Hampshire, beyond which it is replaced by other and larger species. It cannot be said to be abundant in the New England States, except in a few localities, and it does not seem to prefer high mountainous regions. In occasional botanical excursions among the Catskill mountains, and those of Vermont and New Hampshire, where we saw considerable numbers of the Northern hare we found scarcely any traces of the present species, especially in the mountains east of the Hudson river. It exists in the chain of the Alleganies running through Virginia to the upper parts of Carolina, but is there far from being abundant. It was exceedingly scarce north-east of Albany thirty-five years ago, where it has now become far more numerous than the Northern hare, which was then the only species usually met with. It abounds in the sandy regions covered with pine trees west of that city. From Dutchess county to the southern limits of New-York it is found in considerable numbers. In Pennsylvania, New-Jersey, Maryland, and all the Southern States, hunting the Gray Rabbit affords more amusement to young sportsmen than the pursuit of any other quadruped in the country. We have traced this species through all the higher portions of Florida. To the west we have seen it in all the Southern States, and it is very abundant on the upper Missouri River to nearly 1000 miles above Saint Louis.

General Remarks.

This being the most common of our hares in the Atlantic States of America, it has been longest and most familiarly known. HERRIOTT, who gave an account of the third voyage of the English to Virginia in 1586, in enumerating the natural productions of that country, under the head of Conies, says, "Those that we have seen, and all that we can hear of, are of a gray colour like unto hares; in some places there are such plenty that all the people, of some towns, make them mantles of the fur, or fleece of the skins of those which they usually take." It is subsequently mentioned by the intrepid Governor SMITH of Virginia, by LAWSON and by CATESBY. KALM, in the 1st vol. of his Travels in America, gave a correct description, not only of the animal, but of its habits. The following is an extract from his Journal, the entry was made either at Philadelphia or his favourite retreat "Racoon," in the vicinity of that city, on the 6th Jan. 1749. "There are a great number of hares in this country, but they differ from our Swedish ones in their size, which is very small, and but little bigger than that of a rabbit; they keep almost the same gray colour both in summer and winter, which our Northern hares have in summer only; the tip of their ears is always gray,and not black; the tail is likewise gray on the upper side, at all seasons; they breed several times a year. In spring they lodge their young ones in hollow trees, and in summer, in the months of June and July, they breed in the grass. When they are surprised they commonly take refuge in hollow trees, out of which they are taken by means of a crooked stick, or by cutting a hole into the tree, opposite to the place where they lie; or by smoke which is occasioned by making a fire on the outside of the tree. On all these occasions the greyhounds must be at hand. These hares never bite, and can be touched without any danger. In the day-time they usually lie in hollow trees, and hardly ever stir from thence, unless they be disturbed by men or dogs; but in the night they come out and seek their food. In bad weather, or when it snows, they lie close for a day or two, and do not venture to leave their retreats. They do a great deal of mischief in the cabbage-fields, but apple-trees suffer infinitely more from them, for they peel off all the bark next to the ground. The people here are agreed that the hares are fatter in a cold and severe winter, than in a mild and wet one, for which they could give me several reasons from their own conjectures. The skin is useless because it is so loose that it can be drawn off; for when you would separate it from the flesh, you need only pull at the fur and the skin follows. These hares cannot be tamed. They were at all times, even in the midst of winter, plagued with a number of common fleas."

In 1820 (as we have observed in our article on *L. Americanus*) DESMAREST mistaking the species, gave a pretty good description of the Gray Rabbit, and unfortunately referred it to *L. Americanus*. He had evidently been misled by FORSTER, SCHŒPFF, PENNANT, ERXLEBEN and BODD, who having confounded these two species, induced him to believe that as he was describing an American hare, only one American species at that time being known, it must be the one referred to by previous authors. Hence he quoted GMELIN, SCHŒPFF, ERXLEBEN, PALLAS and BODD, and gave to the species the extravagant geographical range, from Churchill, Hudson's Bay, to California, and assigned it a habitation in New-Albion, Louisiana, Florida, the two Carolinas, &c., HARLAN, in giving an account of the American quadrupeds in 1825, finding the Gray Rabbit described by DESMAREST,

translated the article very literally, even to its faults, from the French of that author, (See Encyclopédie de Mammalogie, p. 351.) HARLAN's translation represents the fur as "becoming whiter during winter, but the ears and tail remaining always of the same gray." In the following year GODMAN (Amer. Nat. Hist., vol. ii., p. 157) once more described this species under the (wrong) name of *Lepus Americanus*. In speaking of its colour, he says, "in winter the pelage is nearly or altogether white," and he gives it the extraordinary weight of seven pounds. This is rather surprising, as we know no city in the union where the market in winter is better supplied with this species of hare than Philadelphia.

In this singular manner the Gray Rabbit, the most common and best known of all the species of quadrupeds in America, had never received a specific name that was not pre-occupied. In 1827, we proposed the name of *Lepus sylvaticus*, and assigned our reasons for so doing in a subsequent paper, (See Journ. Acad. Nat. Sc., vol. viii., part 1, p. 75.) In 1840, Dr. EMMONS also, (Report on Quadrupeds of Massachusetts,) described it under the (wrong) name of *L. Americanus*, giving as synonymous, *L. Hudsonius*, PALLAS; American hare, FORSTER, PENNANT, Arct. Zool. HEARNE's Journey, SABINE, PARRY and RICHARDSON; who each described the Northern hare, and not this species. He, however, quoted HARLAN and GODMAN correctly, with the exception of the name which they had misapplied.

In 1842 Dr. DEKAY (See Nat. Hist. N. York, part 1st, p. 93,) refers this species to *Lepus nanus* of SCHREBER, supposing the description of that author, (which is contained in an old work that is so scarce in America that our naturalists have seldom had an opportunity of referring to it,) to have escaped the notice of modern authors. After giving a translation from SCHREBER, he remarks, "The whole history of the habits of this species, and its abundance, sufficiently confirm the fact, that SCHREBER had our Rabbit in view, although he was misled by SCHŒPFF and PENNANT, and confounded two species."

We regret that we are obliged to differ from an author who is generally accurate, and who is always courteous in his language towards other naturalists, but in this case we must do so.

In order to save the student of natural history the labour of searching for SCHREBER's work, to refer to his description, we have concluded to insert it here, together with our translation of the article, adding the references to authors, &c., which were omitted by DEKAY, and which we conceive very important in pursuing our inquiries.

Extract From Schreber.

"Der Wabus, Oder Amerikanische Hase.

Tab. ccxxxiv. B.

Lepus nanus. Lepus auribus extrorsum nigro marginatis, cauda supra nigricante.

Synonymes.

LEPUS HUDSONIUS.
LEPUS APICE AURIUM CAUDÆQUE CINEREO, Pall., Nov. Spec. Glis., p. 30, 15, Zimmerm., E. E. z. 336.
LEPUS AMERICANUS, Lepus cauda abbreviata pedibus postici corpore dimidio longioribus auricularum caudæque apicibus griseis, Erxleben, Mamm., p. 330.
AMERICAN HARE, Forster, Phil. Tr., lxxii., p. 376, Pennant, Hist., p. 372 u. 243.
HARE, HEDGE CONEY, Lawson, Car., p. 122, Catesby's App., p. xxviii.
HARAR, en art som är midt emellan hare ach canin, Kalm, Rese, vol. ii., p. 236, vol. iii, p. 8, 285.
DER AMERIKANISCHE HASE, Forster, von den Thieren in Hudson's Bay, in Sprenge's Beyt.
DER NORDAMERIKANISCHE HASE, Schœpff.
WABUS, (ALGONQUINISCH,) Jefferson's Notes, (Phil. 1788,) p. 51, 57.

Beschreibung.

Der Kopf hat nichts Unterscheidendes. Die Backen sind dickhärig. Die Ohren dünne, auswendig dünne behaart, inwendig kahl, und reichen, vorwärts gebogen, noch nicht bis an die Nasenspitze; nach hinten gelegt, bis an die Schulterblätter. Ueber den grossen schwarzen Augen vier bis fünf Börsten. Die Bartbörsten grossentheils schwarz; einige weiss; dielängsten scheinen länger als der Kopf zu sein.

Die Sommerfarbe ist folgende. Die Ohren bräunlich, mit einer sehr schmalen schwarzen Einfassung am äussern Rande, die an der Spitze eben die Breite behält, oder gegen die Spitze hin gar verschwindet. Stirne, Backen, Rücken und Seiten, Aerme und Schenkel auswendig leicht braun, mit Schwarz überlaufen.

Der Umfang des Afters weiss. Die Füsse dicht und kurz behaart, von einem hellern leicht Braun, ohne alles Schwarz, an der innern Seite stärker in grau-weiss abfallend. Der Schwanz oben auf von der Farbe des Rückens, (vermuthlich stärker mit Schwarz überlaufen denn Herr PENNANT beschreibt ihn oben schwarz,) unten weiss. Die Kehle weiss; der Untertheil des Halses leicht braun, mit Weiss überlaufen.

Brust, Bauch, innere Aerme und Schenkel, einem weichen Weiss. Die Winterfarbe, wo sie verschieden, ist weiss. Backenzähne oben und unten auf jeder Seite fünf. Die Länge des Körpers höchstens anderthalb englische Fuss; des Schwanzes nicht viel über zwei Zoll. Das Gewicht $2\frac{1}{4}$ bis 3 Pfund; nach Herrn Pennant 3 bis $4\frac{1}{2}$ Pfund.

Die unterscheidenden Merkmale dieser Art sind nach den Herren FORSTER, PENNANT und SCHŒPFF, 1. die Grösse, er kommt dem gemeinen und veränderlichen Hasen lange nicht bei, und ist kaum grösser als ein Kaninchen, daher er auch in Nord-Amerika nicht selten den Namen Rabbit oder Kaninchen bekommt. 2. Das Verhältniss der Füsse; die Vorterfüsse sind kürzer und die Hinterfüsse länger als an allen Dreien. 3. Die Farbe der Ohren; sie haben eine schwarze Einfassung auswendig, aberkeinen schwarzen Fleck an der Spitze. Ihre geringere Länge unterscheidet von den Ohren des gemeinen Hasen. 4. Die Farbe des Schwanzes; diese ist oben auf nicht schwarz, oder doch nicht so sattschwarz als am Hasen. 5. Die Farbe des Körpers. 6. Die Lebensart und Eigenschaften. Er kann also unmöglich etwas anders als eine für sich bestehende Art sein. Sein Vaterland is ganz Nord-Amerika, von Hudson's Bay an bis nach Florida hinab. Er schweift nicht herum, sondern schränkt sich auf kleine Räume ein.

In Hudson's Bay, Canada und Neu-England vertauscht er sein kurzes Sommerhaar im Herbste gegen ein langes seitenartiges und bis an die Wurzel silberweisses Haar, und nur der Rand der Ohren und der Schwanz behalten ihre Farbe, (PENNANT, KALM.) In den südlichen Ländern bleibt die Farbe, auch in den härtesten Wintern, unverändert, (KALM.)

Dahar könnte man diesen Hasen füglich den *halb*-veränderlichen nennen."

In carefully reading the above description, the attentive reader can scarcely have failed to remark that if *Lepus Americanus* of ERXLEBEN, and *Lepus Hudsonius* of PALLAS, are the Northern hare, *Lepus nanus* must be the same species, as the descriptions agree in every particular; and where SCHREBER enters more into detail, he describes the Northern hare still more minutely, and only confirms us still farther in the conviction that he had never seen the Gray Rabbit, and was describing the very species he professed to describe, viz., the Hudson's Bay quadruped of DAINES BARRINGTON, (See vol. lxii. Phil. Trans., p. 11,) and the "American hare, called rabbit at Hudson's Bay," of FORSTER, (See the above vol., p. 376,) which, however, had already received form two of his countrymen, PALLAS and ERXLEBEN, the names of *L. Americanus* and *L. Hudsonius*.

The time when this description was made must not be overlooked. At the close of the year 1772, the Philosophical Transactions, containing the two accounts of this new American hare, were published. No specific *Latin name*, such as would according to the binary system which was then coming into use, entitle the first describer to the species, had as yet been given to it; and whilst the English naturalists were looking for decided characters, by which it could be distinguished, (and we know from experience with how much difficulty these characteristics are found in the hares,) the German naturalists, with the example of LINNÆUS, their next door neighbour, before their eyes, went forward in hot haste to describe the species. Leaving the English philosophers to *cook* their animal, to ascertain by the colour of its flesh whether it was a hare or a rabbit, they sought for a Latin cognomen, desirous that their own names should be handed down to posterity along with it. Hence ERXLEBEN, PALLAS and SCHREBER, (the two former evidently without the knowledge of the latter,) named the species, very likely, as we are inclined to think, without having had any specimen before them, and simply attaching a name to the descriptions of the English naturalists. Be this as it may, in less than three years it had already received, in Germany alone, the several names of *L. Americanus, nanus*, and *Hudsonius*. If SCHREBER, who had the Philosophical Transactions lying before him when he drew up his description, (for he quotes both the accounts,) and who also possessed the accounts of ERXLEBEN and PALLAS, had examined a different species, surely *he* would have made the discovery; but after a careful examination, and not a bad description, he gives the size, colour, and measurements of the Northern hare, and finally quotes FORSTER, PENNANT, SCHŒPFF, &c., as his authorities for the species.

The name *Lepus nanus*, given to it by SCHREBER, might at first lead us to conjecture that as he meant to designate his species as a small hare, and as the Northern hare is rather large, he could not have intended it for the latter, but had in view the Gray Rabbit—hence the name, *nanus*, dwarf. There can, however, be no difficulty in accounting for the choice of that name. On turning to the eleventh page of the Philosophical Transactions, vol. xlii., where the species was first announced, it will be perceived that BARRINGTON had been closely investigating the several species of hare with which the naturalists of Europe were acquainted at that early day; and he gives the following measurements:—

	Fore-leg.*	Hind-leg.*	Back and Head.
Rabit	$4\frac{1}{2}$ inches	$6\frac{1}{4}$ inches	$16\frac{1}{2}$ inches
Hare	$7\frac{3}{4}$ "	11 "	22 "
Hudson's Bay quadruped	$6\frac{1}{4}$ "	$10\frac{3}{4}$ "	18 "
Alpine hare	$6\frac{1}{2}$ "	$16\frac{3}{4}$ "	22 "

*From uppermost joint to toe.

Here then we have the relative sizes of the several species. The first is the common wild rabbit of England, (*L. cuniculus*,) which is a little larger than our Gray Rabbit. The second is the common English hare, (*L. timidus*.) The third, the American hare from Hudson's Bay; and the fourth, the Alpine or variable hare, (*L. variabilis*.) The rabbit being a *burrowing* animal with *white* flesh, was not considered a *hare*, and the American animal was smaller than either the European or the Alpine hare, measuring only eighteen inches in length, whilst these last measured twenty-two inches each. We, perceive, therefore, that it was called *Lepus nanus*, because it was the smallest of the species then known. For the same reason our American woodcock was called *scolopax minor*, because it was smaller than the English woodcock, although it finally proved to be the largest snipe in America.

Let us compare the description of SCHREBER's *L. nanus*, with the Northern hare, of which we have a number of specimens, (including all its various changes of colour,) before us, to refer to as we proceed.

Translation.	Remarks.
Lepus nanus.	*Lepus Americanus.*
The head has nothing peculiar; cheeks, thickly haired; ears, thin, externally with few hairs, naked within, and when bent forward do not reach the point of the nose, when bent backward they reach the shoulder blades.	This description agrees with *L. Americanus*; the ears in our dried specimens are none of them more than $3\frac{1}{2}$ inches long, whilst from nose to ear they measure 4 inches; the ears therefore could not reach the nose.
Eyes, large and black, with four or five bristles above them; whiskers, mostly black; some are white, the longest appear to be longest appear to be longer than the head.	Applies perfectly to our specimens of *L. Americanus*, except the colour of the eyes, which applies to neither the Northern hare nor the Gray Rabbit, and which he must have obtained from some other source than a dried skin.
The following is the colour in summer; ears, brownish, with a very narrow black border on the outer margin, being at the tips the same breadth, or it even disappears towards the tips.	The very narrow black border on the outer margin betrays the species; it belongs to the Northern hare, but not to the Gray Rabbit. They only become effaced when covered with white hair in winter; and it is evident this last expression was taken from KALM, who say of the Rabbit, "the tip of their ears is always gray, and not black, as is the case in the European, common, and Alpine hares."
Forehead, cheeks, back and sides, fore and hind-legs externally, light brown, mixed with black; around the breech, white.	All agreeing with the description of the Norther hare.
Feet, thickly covered with short hairs of a light brown, unmixed with black, changing on the inside to a grayish white.	Such is the colour of the feet of several of our specimens of the Northern hare in summer pelage.

Upper part of the tail the colour of the back, (perhaps mixed with black, as PENNANT describes it black above,) beneath white.

Throat, white; lower part of the neck, bright brown, mixed with white; chest and belly, inside of fore and hind-legs, a dull white.

Colour in winter, when it does change, white.

Molars above and beneath, on each side, five. The length of the body at farthest eighteen inches, the tail not over two inches.

The weight is from $2\frac{1}{4}$ to 3 lbs.; according to PENNANT, from 3 to $4\frac{1}{2}$ lbs.

Translation.

The most striking distinctions in this species, according to FORSTER, PENNANT, and SCHŒPFF, are, 1st, its size; it is not near as large as the common hare or the changeable hare, and scarcely larger than a rabbit; hence in North America he is frequently called rabbit.

2d, The proportion of the legs. The hind-feet being longer and the fore-feet shorter than either of the three.

3d, The colour of the ears; they have a black margin outside, but no black spot at the tip.

The ear being less in length separates it from the common hare.

4th, The colour of the tail; this is

The upper part of the tail is like the back in most specimens, but it is seen how anxious he was not to depart from the views of PENNANT, who describes it as black, which is the case in some specimens.

These distinctive marks all belong to the Northern hare.

The Gray Rabbit does not become white in winter.

This size applies to the Northern hare, and not to the Gray Rabbit. None of our dried specimens of the former reach quite eighteen inches, and none of the Gray Rabbit beyond fifteen. Tail of the Northern hare, including fur, two inches; that of the Gray Rabbit is longer.

These weights were compiled from authors. CARVER, who had reference to the Gray Rabbit, gave the lesser weight; and PENNANT, who referred to the Northern hare, gave the greater.

Remarks.

FORSTER says in regard to the Northern hare—"The proper characteristics of this species seem to be, 1st, its size, which is somewhat bigger than a rabbit, but less than that of the Alpine or lesser hare."

2d, FORSTER says, "The proportion of its limbs. Its hind-feet being longer in proportion to the body than those of the rabbit and the common hare.

3d, "The tip of the ears and tail, which are constantly gray, not black," KALM's Travels, vol. ii., p. 45.

The ears of the Northern hare, the species here referred to, are considerably less in length than those of the common European hare.

The upper side of the tail of the

on the upper surface not black, or as intensely black as that of the hare.

5th, The colour of the body.

6th, Its mode of living and habits.

It can therefore only be a distinct species.

It is a native of all North America, from Hudson's Bay to Florida. It does not migrate far, but confines itself to a narrow compass.

In Hudson's Bay, Canada, and New England, it changes in autumn this short summer hair into a long silky fur, white from the roots, and only the border of the ears and the tail preserve their colour, (PENNANT, KALM.)

In the Southern parts, his colour, even in the coldest winters, remains unchanged, (KALM.) He might, therefore, be properly called the half changing hare.

European hare, (L. timidus,) is black, that of the Northern hare generally dark brown.

That of the European hare is not as dark.

In the description of these habits by FORSTER, two species had been blended.

He meant distinct from those of Europe.

The Gray Rabbit is not found at Hudson's Bay, where the other abounds. In his view of the Southern range of the Northern hare, he was misled by FORSTER, and supposing KALM's rabbit referred to the same species, he quoted KALM as authority for its existence as far south as Florida.

The Gray Rabbit does not change in this manner. He meant by this to show that whilst this species became white in winter, the border of the ear and upper part of the tail underwent no change.

SCHREBER, never having been in America, had to compile his account of its habits from others. It is easily seen that in this he was misled by FORSTER, who misunderstood KALM; the latter having here referred to the Gray Rabbit, which never changes its colour.

DEKAY conceives SCHREBER to have described the Gray Rabbit, from the abundance of the species; but the Northern hare, where it does exist, is not less abundant. In particular localities in the Northern States, it is more frequently met with than the Gray Rabbit in the Middle or Southern States.

HEARNE says that on the south side of Anawed Lake they were so plentiful, that several of the Indians caught twenty or thirty of a night with snares; and at Hudson's Bay, where all the specimens first brought to Europe were procured, it is represented as very abundant.

We think we have now shown that SCHREBER's account of L. nanus—its size, length of legs, the black margin around the ear, its change of colour, and his references to authors all prove explicitly that he had no reference to the Gray Rabbit, but described the Northern hare.

His name must therefore stand as a synonyme of L. Americanus, which is to be somewhat regretted, as although the name itself is very objectionable, his description of that species appears to us the best that was given, from its first describer, FORSTER, down to the time of RICHARDSON, whose description is so accurate that nothing need be added to it.

Genus Mus.—Linn.

$$\text{Incisive } \tfrac{2}{2}; \text{ Canine } \tfrac{0-0}{0-0}; \text{ Molar } \tfrac{3-3}{3-3} = 16.$$

Cheek-teeth, furnished wth tubercles; ears, oblong or round, nearly naked; without cheek-pouches; fore-feet, with four toes and a wart, covered with an obtuse nail, in place of a thumb; hind-feet, pendactylous; tail, long, usually naked and scaly; fur, with a few long, scattered hairs, extending beyond the rest.

The generic name MUS is derived from the Latin mus, a mouse, from the Greek μυς, (mus,) a mouse.

There are upwards of two hundred species of this genus described as existing in various quarters of the globe, of which about nine well-determined species are found in North America, three of which have been introduced.

Mus Rattus.—Linn.

Black Rat.

Plate xxiii.—Old and Young, Of Various Colours. Natural size.

M. cauda corpore longiore; pedibus anterioribus ungue pro pollice instructis; corpore atro, subtus cinereo.

No. 5

Plate XXIII

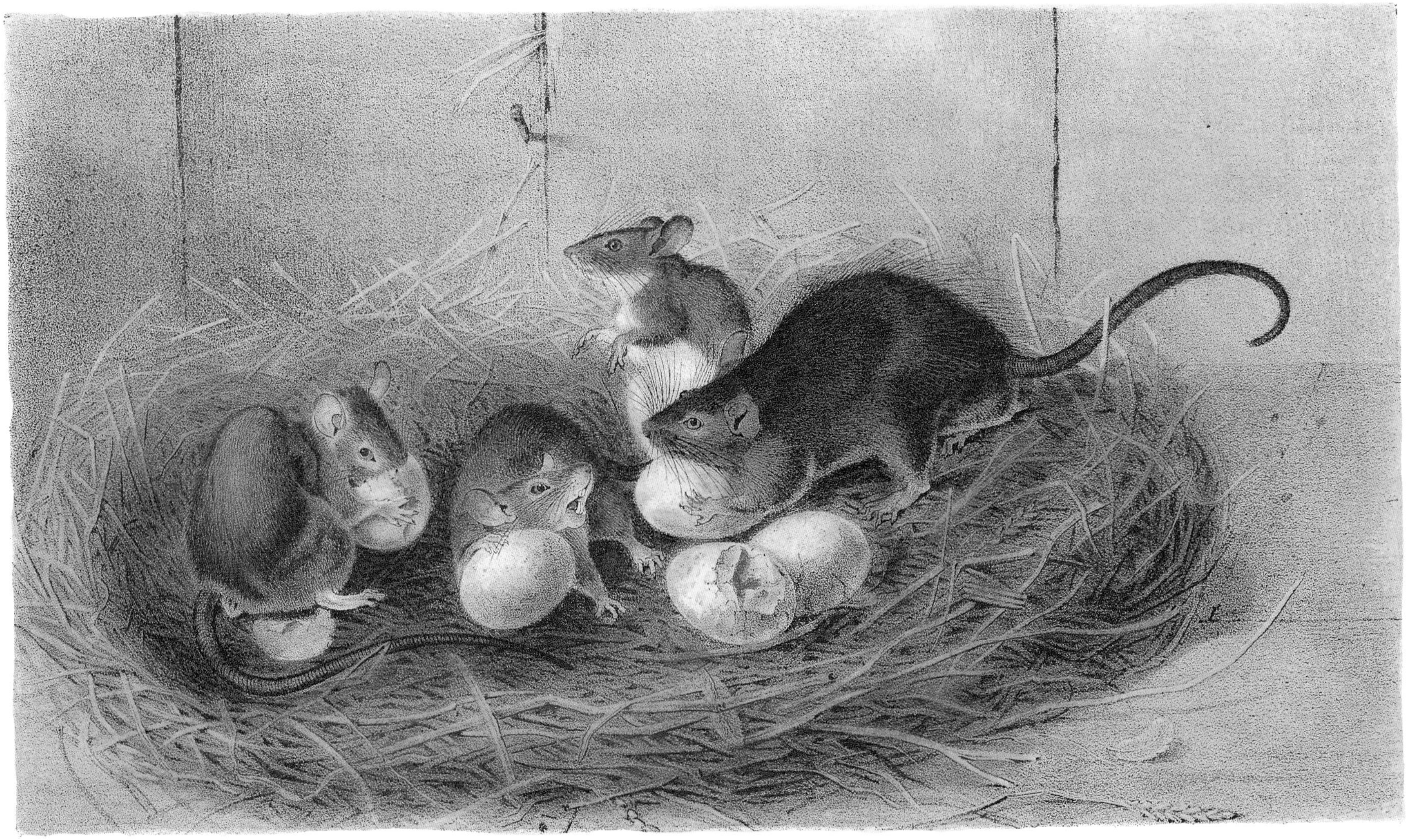

Drawn on Stone by R Trembly.

Black Rat

Old & Young.

Drawn from Nature by J.J. Audubon, F.R.S. F.L.S.

Printed by Nagel & Weingærtner, N.Y.

Characters.

Tail, longer than the body; fore-feet, with a claw in place of a thumb, bluish-black above, dark ash-coloured beneath.

Synonymes.

MUS RATTUS, Linn., 12th ed., p. 83.
"   "   Schreber, Säugethiere, p. 647.
"   "   Desmar., in Nouv. Dict., 29, p. 48.
RAT, Buffon, Hist. Nat., vol. vii., p. 278, t. 36.
RAT ORDINAIRE, Cuv., Règne Anim., p. 197.
BLACK RAT, Penn., Arc. Zool., vol. i., p. 129.
ROLLER PONTOPP., Dan. i., p. 611.
MUS RATTUS, Griffith's Animal Kingdom, vol. v., 578, 5.
"   "   Harlan, p. 148.
"   "   Godman, vol. ii., p. 83.
"   "   Richardson, p. 140.
"   "   Emmons, Report on Quadrupeds of Massachusetts, p. 63.
"   "   Dekay, Natural History of New York, vol. i., p. 80.

Description.

Head, long; nose, sharp pointed; lower jaw, short; ears, large, oval, broad and naked. Whiskers, reaching beyond the ear.

Body, smaller and more delicately formed than that of the brown rat; thickly clothed with rigid, smooth, adpressed hairs.

Fore-feet, with four toes, and a claw in place of a thumb. Feet, plantigrade, covered on the outer surface with short hairs. Tail, scaly, slightly and very imperfectly clothed with short coarse hairs. The tail becomes square when dried, but in its natural state is nearly round. Mammæ, 12.

Colour.

Whiskers, head, and all the upper surface, deep bluish-black; a few white hairs interspersed along the back, giving it in some lights a shade of cinereous; on the under surface it is a shade lighter, usually cinereous. Tail, dusky; a few light-coloured hairs reaching beyond the toes, and covering the nails.

Dimensions.

Length of head and body 8   inches.
"   tail . . . . $8\frac{1}{4}$ do.

Habits.

The character of this species is so notoriously bad, that were we to write a volume in its defence we would fail to remove those prejudices which are every where entertained against this thieving cosmopolite. Possessing scarcely one redeeming quality, it had by its mischievous propensities caused the world to unite in a wish for its extermination.

The Black Rat is omnivorous, nothing seeming to come amiss to its voracious jaws—flesh, fowl or fish, and grain, fruit, nuts, vegetables, &c., whether raw or cooked, being indiscriminately devoured by it. It is very fond of plants that contain much saccharine or oleaginous matter.

The favourite abodes of this species are barns or granaries, holes under out-houses or cellars, and suck like places; but it does not confine itself to any particular locality. We have seen its burrows under cellars used for keeping the winter's supply of sweet potatoes in Carolina, in dykes surrounding rice-fields sometimes more than a mile from any dwelling, and it makes a home in clefts of the rocks on parts of the Alleghany mountains, where it is very abundant.

In the neighbourhood of the small streams which are the sources of the Edisto river, we found a light-coloured variety, in far greater numbers than the Black, and we have given three figures of them in our Plate. They were sent to us alive, having been caught in the woods, not far from a mill-pond. We have also observed the same variety in Charleston, and received specimens from Major LECONTE, who obtained them in Georgia.

During the summer season, and in the autumn, many of these rats, as well as the common or Norway rat, (*Mus decumansu,*) and the common mouse, (*Mus musculus,*) leave their hiding places near or in the farmer's barns or hen-houses, and retire to the woods and fields, to feed on various wild grasses, seeds, and plants. We have observed Norway rats burrowing in banks and on the borders of fields, far from any inhabited building; but when the winter season approaches they again resort to their former haunts, and possibly invite an additional party to join them. The Black Rat, however, lives in certain parts of the country permanently in localities where there are no human habitations, keeping in crevices and fissures in the rocks, under stones, or in hollow logs.

This species is by no means so great a pest, or so destructive, as the brown or Norway rat, which has in many parts of the country either driven off or exterminated it. The Black Rat, in consequence, has become quite rare, not only in America but in Europe.

Like the Norway rat this species is fond of eggs, young chickens, ducks, &c., although its exploits in the poultry house are surpassed by the audacity and voraciousness of the other.

We have occasionally observed barns and hen-houses that were infested by the Black Rat, in which the eggs or young chickens remained unmolested for months together; when, however, the Rats once had a taste of these delicacies, they became as destructive as usual, and nothing could save the eggs or young fowls but making the buildings rat-proof, or killing the plunderers.

The following information respecting this species, has been politely communicated to us by S. W. ROBERETS, ESQ., civil engineer:—

"In April, 1831, when leading the exploring party which located the portage railroad over the Alleghany mountains, in Pennsylvania, I found a multitude of these animals living in the crevices of the silicious limestone rocks on the Upper Conemaugh river, in Cambria county, where the large viaduct over that stream now stands. The county was then a wilderness, and as soon as buildings were put up the rats deserted the rocks, and established themselves in the shanties, to our great annoyance; so that one of our assistants amused himself shooting at them as he lay in bed early in the morning. They ate all our shoes, whip-lashes, &c., &c., and we never got rid of them until we left the place."

We presume that in this locality there is some favourite food, the seeds of wild plants and grasses, as well as insects, lizards, (*Salamandra,*) &c., on which these Rats generally feed. We are induced to believe that their range on the Alleghanies is somewhat limited, as we have on various botanical excursions, explored these mountains at different points, to an extent of seven hundred miles, and although we saw them in the houses of the settlers, we never observed any locality where they existed permanently in the woods, as they did according to the above account.

The habits of this species do not differ very widely from those of the brown or Norway rat. When it obtains possession of premises that remain unoccupied for a new years, it becomes a nuisance by its rapid multiplication and its voracious habits. We many years ago spent a few days with a Carolina planter, who had not resided at his country seat for nearly a year. On our arrival, we found the house infested by several hundreds of this species; they kept up a constant squeaking during the whole night, and the smell from their urine was exceedingly offensive.

The Black Rat, although capable of swimming, seems less fond of frequenting the water than the brown rat. It is a more lively, and we think a more active, species than the other; it runs with rapidity, and makes longer leaps; when attacked, it shrieks and defends itself with its teeth, but we consider it more helpless and less courageous than the brown or Norway rat.

It is generally believed that the Black Rat has to a considerable extent been supplanted both in Europe and America by the Norway rat, which it is asserted kills or devours it. We possess no positive facts to prove that this is the case, but it is very probably true.

We have occasionally found both species existing on the same premises, and have caught them on successive nights in the same traps; but we have invariably found that where the Norway rat exists in any considerable numbers the present species does not long remain. The Norway rat is not only a gross feeder, but is bold and successful in its attacks on other animals and birds. We have known it to destroy the domesticated rabbit by dozens; we have seen it dragging a living frog from the banks of a pond; we were once witnesses to its devouring the young of its own species, and we see no reason why it should not pursue the Black Rat to the extremity of its burrow, and there seize and devour it. Be this as it may, the latter is diminishing in number in proportion to the multiplication of the other species, and as they are equally prolific and equally cunning, we cannot account for its decrease on any other supposition than that it becomes the prey of the more powerful and more voracious Norway rat.

The Black Rat brings forth young four or five times in a year; we have seen from six to nine young in a nest, which was large and composed of leaves, hay, decayed grasses, loose cotton, and rags of various kinds, picked up in the vicinity.

Geographical Distribution.

This species is constantly carried about in ships, and is found, although very sparingly, in all our maritime cities. We have met with it occasionally in nearly all the States of the Union. On some plantations in Carolina, particularly in the upper country, it is the only species, and is very abundant. We have, however, observed that in some places where it was very common a few years ago, it has altogether disappeared, and has been succeeded by the Norway rat. The Black Rat has been transported to every part of the world where men carry on commerce by means of ships, as just mentioned.

General Remarks.

PENNANT, KALM, LINNÆUS, PALLAS, DESMAREST, and other European writers, seen disposed to consider America the Fatherland of this pest of the civilized world. HARLAN adopted the same opinion, but BARTRAM, (if he was not misunderstood by KALM,) did more than any other to perpetuate the error.

In the course of a mutual interchange of commodities, the inhabitants of the Eastern and Western Continents have presented each other with several unpleasant additions to their respective productions, especially among the insect tribe.

We are willing to admit that the Hessian fly was not brought to America in straw from Hanover, as we sought in vain for the insect in Germany; but we contend that the Black Rat and the Norway rat, which are in the aggregate, greater nuisances, perhaps, than any other animals now found in our country, were brought to America from the old world. There are strong evidences of the existence of the Black Rat in Persia, long before the discovery of America, and we have no proof that it was known in this country till many years after its colonization. It is true, there were rats in our country, which by the common people might have been regarded as similar to those of Europe, but these have now been proved to be of very different species. Besides, if the species existed in the East from time immemorial, is it not more probable that it should have been carried to Europe, and from thence to America, than that it should have been originally indigenous to both continents? As an evidence of the facility with which rats are transported from one country to another, we will relate the following occurrence. A vessel had arrived in Charleston from some English port, we believe Liverpool. She was freighted with a choice cargo of the finest breeds of horses, horned cattle, sheep, &c., imported by several planters of Carolina. A few pheasants (*Phasianus colchicus*) were also left on board, and we were informed that several of the latter had been killed by a singular looking set of rats, that had become numerous on board of the ship. One of them was caught and presented to us, and proved to be the Black Rat. Months after the ship had left, we saw several of this species at the wharf where the vessel had discharged her cargo, proving that after a long sea voyage they had given the preference to terra firma, and like many other sailors, at the clearing out of the ship had preferred remaining on shore.

We have seen several descriptions of rats, that we think will eventually be referred to some of the varieties of this species. The *Mus Americanus* of GMELIN, *Mus nigricans* of RAFINESQUE, and several others, do not even appear to be varieties; and we have little doubt that our light-coloured variety, if it has not already a name, will soon be described by some naturalist, who will consider it *new*. To prevent any one from taking this unnecessary trouble, we subjoin a short description of this variety, as observed in Carolina and Georgia.

Whole upper surface, grayish-brown, tinged with yellow; light ash beneath; bearing so strong a resemblance to the Norway rat, that without a close examination it might be mistaken for it.

In sharp, size, and character of the pelage, it does not differ from the ordinary black specimens.

Tamias Quadrivittatus. —Say.

Four Striped Ground-Squirrel.

Plate xxv.—Male, Female, and Young. Natural size.

T. striis quinque sub nigris longitudinalibus, cum, quatuor sub albidis dorso alternatum distributis; corpore magnitudine T. Lysteri minore; lateribus rufo fuscis, ventre albo.

Characters.

Smaller than Tamias Lysteri; five dark brown stripes, and four light-coloured stripes occupying the whole back; sides, reddish-brown; underneath, white.

Synonymes.

SCIURUS QUADRIVITTATUS, Say, Long's Expedition, vol. ii., p. 349.
    "   "   Griffith, Animal Kingdom, vol. v., No. 665.
    "   "   Harlan, Fauna, p. 180.
    "   "   Godman, vol. ii., p. 137.
SCIURUS (TAMIAS) QUADRIVITTATUS, Rich., Zool. Jour., No. 12, p. 519, April, 1828; Fauna Boreali Americana, p. 184, pl. 16.
TAMIAS MINIMUS, Bach., Journ. Acad. Nat. Sc. Phila., vol. viii., part 1, Young.

Description.

Head, of moderate size; nose, tapering, but not very sharp. The mouth recedes very much, (as in all the other species of Tamias;) cheek-pouches, of moderate size; whiskers, about the length of the head; eye, small; ears, erect, of moderate length, clothed on both surfaces with very short hairs; body, rather slender; fore-feet, with four toes and a small thumb, armed with an obtuse nail; palms, naked; claws, compressed, and curved like those of *Tamias Lysteri*. Hind-feet, with five slender toes; soles, covered with short hairs for three-fourths of their length; tail, long, narrow and sub-distichous.

Colour.

Forehead, dark-brown, with a few whitish hairs interspersed; a narrow black line from the nostril to the corner of the eye; above and beneath the eye, a line of white, which continues downward to the point of the nose.

A dark-brown dorsal line, commencing behind the ears, continues along the back to the insertion of the tail; another line, which is not quite so dark, begins at each shoulder and ends on the buttocks, near the tail; on each flank there is another shorter and broader line, which runs along the sides to near the haunches; on each side of the dorsal line there is a light-coloured stripe running down to near the insertion of the tail. The outer brown stripes are also separated by a line of yellowish-white; thus the whole back is covered by five dark and four pale lines. From the neck a broad line of reddish-brown extends along the sides, terminating at the hips; feet, light yellowish-brown; under surface of the body, and inner surface of the legs, grayish-white.

The tail, which is slightly distichous, is composed of hairs yellowish-brown at the roots, then dark-brown, and tipped with reddish-brown; on its under surface they are reddish-brown, then black for a narrow space, and reddish-brown at the tips.

Dimensions.

A fine Male (killed Aug. 19th, 1843, on the Upper Missouri river.)

Nose to anterior canthus	$\frac{1}{2}$	inch
Nose to opening of ear	$1\frac{1}{8}$	do.
Height of ear	$\frac{1}{4}$	do.
Width of ear	$\frac{7}{16}$	do.
Between centre of eyes	$\frac{5}{8}$	do.
Length of head and body	$4\frac{1}{3}$	do.
Tail (vertebræ)	$3\frac{1}{4}$	do.
Tail to end of hair	$4\frac{1}{4}$	do.
Heel to end of hind-claws	$1\frac{1}{16}$	do.
Palm and fore-feet to claws	$1\frac{1}{16}$	do.

Weight 4 oz.

Habits.

This pretty little species was discovered by Mr. SAY, during Colonel LONG's expedition. Mr. SAY doe not however appear to have seen much of its habits, and gives us but the following short account of them:—

"It does not seem to ascend trees by choice, but nestles in holes, and on the edges of rocks. We did not observe it to have cheek-pouches. Its nest is composed of a most extraordinary quantity of the burrs of the cactus, and their branches, and other portions of the large upright cactus, and small branches of pine trees and other vegetable productions, sufficient in some instances, to fill an ordinary cart. What the object of so great and apparently so superfluous an assemblage of rubbish may be we are at a loss to conjecture; we do not know what peculiarly dangerous enemy it may be intended to exclude by so much labour. Their principal food, at least at this season, is the seeds of the pine, which they readily extract from the cones."

We met with this species as we were descending the Upper Missouri river in 1843; we saw it first on a tree; afterwards we procured both old and young, among the sandy gulleys and clay cliffs, on the sides of the ravines near one of our encampments.

These Ground Squirrels ascend trees when at hand and offering them either shelter or food, and seem to be quite as agile as the common species *Tamias Lysteri.*

Dr. RICHARDSON, who found this Ground Squirrel, during his long and laborious journeyings across our great continent, says of it—"it is an exceedingly active little animal, and very industrious in storing up provisions, being very generally observed with its pouches full of the seeds of leguminous plants, bents and grasses. It is most common in dry sandy spots, where there is much underwood, and is often seen in the summer, among the branches of willows and low bushes. It is a lively restless animal, troublesome to the hunter, and often provoking him to destroy it, by the angry chirruping noise that it makes on his approach, and which is a signal of alarm to the other inhabitants of the forest. During winter it resides in a burrow with several openings, made at the roots of a tree; and is even seen on the surface of the snow. At this season, when the snow disappears, many small collections of hazel-nut shells, from which the kernel has been extracted by a minute hole gnawed in the side, are to be seen on the ground near its holes."

Dr. RICHARDSON further informs us that on the banks of the Saskatchawan, the mouths of the burrows of this species are not protected with heaps of vegetable substances, as described by Mr. SAY, and we have no doubt the animal adapts its nest (as many of our birds do) to the locality and circumstances that surround it.

These animals bite severely when captured, and probably resemble *Tamias Lysteri* in their general habits and mode of living.

Geographical Distribution.

This species was originally discovered by SAY, who procured it to the rocky Mountains, near the sources of the Arkansas and Platte rivers. We obtained it on the Upper Missouri, and Mr. DRUMMOND brought specimens from the sources of the Pearl river. It is found as far north as Lake Winnipeg, in lat. 50°.

General Remarks.

When we published *Tamias minimus,* we had some misgivings lest it might prove the young of the present species. The discoverer however assured us that the two species did not exist within many hundred miles of each other, and that the specimens he sent us were those of full grown animals; we consequently ventured on their publication. Having, however, since procured young specimens of *T. quadrivittatus,* we are satisfied of the error we committed, and hasten to correct it. In the investigation of species existing in distant and little known portions of country, it always requires a length of time to settle them beyond the danger of error. The traveller who makes these investigations very hastily, and seizes on a specimen wherever there is a moment's pause in the journey, is often himself deceived, and the describer, having perhaps only a single specimen, is very apt to fall into some mistake. The investigation of described species in every branch of natural history, both in Europe and America, occupied much of the time of the naturalists of our generation, who corrected many of the errors of a former age; most fortunate are they who are permitted to live to correct their own.

Sciurus Lanuginosus.—Bachman.

Downy Squirrel.

Plate xxv. Natural size.

S. auribus brevibus, cauda subdisticha; S. Hudsonico paullo robustior, supra castaneo-fuscus, subtus albus, naso concolori; lateribus argenteis; occipite maculo distincto.

Characters.

Ears, short; tail, sub-distichous; light chesnut-brown on the upper surface; sides, silver-gray. A spot on the hind part of the head, nose, and under surface of body, pure white. A little stouter than S. Hudsonius.

Synonyme.

SCIURUS LANUGINOSUS, Bach., Jour. Acad. Nat. Sc. of Phila., vol. viii., pt. 1, p. 67, 1838.

Description.

Head, broader than in *S. Hudsonius;* forehead, much arched; ears, short and oval; whiskers, longer than the head; feet and toes, short; thumb, armed with a broad flat nail. Nails, compressed and acute; the third, on the fore-feet, longest.

The tail, (which bears some resemblance to that of the flying squirrel, *P. volucella,*) is clothed with hairs a little coarser than those on the back, and is much shorter than the body. On the fore-feet the palms are nearly naked, the under surface of the toes being only partially covered with hair; but on the hind-feet, the under surface from the heel to the extremity of the nails is thickly covered with soft short hairs. Fur, softer and more downy than that of any other of our species. The fur indicates that the animal is an inhabitant of a cold region.

Colour.

Teeth, dark orange; whiskers, brown; fur on the back from the roots to near the tip of the hair, light plumbeous, tipped with light chesnutbrown; on the sides tipped with silver-gray. A broad line of white around the eyes, a spot of white on the hind part of the head, a little in advance of the anterior portion of the ears; nose, white, which colour extends along the forehead over the eyes, where it is gradually blended with the colour of the back; the whole under surface, feet, and inner surface of the legs, pure white. Tail, irregularly covered with markings of black, light brown, and white, scarcely two hairs being uniform in colour.

In general it may be said that the tail, when examined without reference to its separate hairs, is light-ash at the roots of the hairs, a broad but not well defined line of light rufous succeeding, then a dark brown space in the hairs, which are tipped with rufous and gray.

Dimensions.

	Inches.	Lines.
Length of head and body	7	11
" tail (vertebræ)	4	8
" tail, including fur	6	0
Palm, and middle fore-claw	1	0
Sole and middle hind-claw	1	9
Length of fur on the back	0	7
Height of ear, measured posteriorly	0	5
Distance between the orbits	0	6

Habits.

This downy and beautifully furred squirrel exists in the north-western portions of our continent. The specimen from which our drawing was made, is the only one which we have seen, and was brought from near Sitka, by Mr. J. K. TOWNSEND, who kindly placed it in our hands, in order that we might describe it. As the animal was presented to Mr. TOWNSEND by an officer attached to the Hudson's Bay Company, and was not observed by him, he could give us no account of its habits. We think, however, that from its close approximation to that group of squirrels, of which the Hudson's Bay, or chickaree squirrel, is the type, and with which we are familiar, we can form a pretty correct judgment in regard to its general characteristics, and we will venture to say that it is less agile, and less expert in climbing than the chickaree; it no doubt burrows in the earth in winter like the latter species, and as its tail is more like that of a spermophile than the tail of a squirrel, although the rest of its specific characters are those of the true squirrels, we are disposed to consider it a closely connecting link between these two genera, and it very probably, according to circumstances, adopts the mode of life commonly observed in each.

Plate XXIV

Drawn on Stone by R.ª Trembly

Printed by Nagel & Weingærtner NY

Drawn from Nature by J. J. Audubon F.R.S. F.L.S.

Four striped Ground Squirrel.
1 Male, 2 Female, 3 & 4 Young.

Geographical Distribution.

This species is found several degrees to the north of the Columbia river, and is said to extend through the country adjoining the sea-coast as far as into the Russian settlements. Mr. TOWNSEND says, "It was killed on the coast near Sitka, and given me by my friend, W. F. TOLMIE, ESQ., Surgeon of the Honourable Hudson's Bay Company."

Genus Gulo.—Storr.

Dental Formula.

Incisive $\frac{6}{6}$; *Canine* $\frac{1-1}{1-1}$; *Molar* $\frac{5-5}{6-6}$ = 38.

The three first molars in the upper, and the four first in the lower jaw, small; succeeded by a larger carnivorous or trenchant tooth, and a small tuberculous tooth at the back.

In the upper jaw the three first molars are uni-cuspidateous, and may be called false-carnivorous teeth, increasing successively in size; the following or carnivorous tooth is large and strong, furnished with two points on the inner side, and a trenchant edge in front; the last tooth is small, and tuberculous or flattish.

In the lower jaw the first four molars are false, each presenting only one point or edge; the fifth is long and large, with two trenchant points; the last molar is nearly flat. All the teeth touch each other successively, (CUV.)

Head, of moderate length; body, long; legs, short; tail, bushy; feet, with five deeply divided toes, terminated by long curved nails.

No glandular pouch in some of the species, but a simple fold beneath the tail.

Habits, carnivorous and nocturnal.

The generic name is derived from the Latin *gulo*, a glutton.

Four species of this genus have been described; one existing in the Arctic regions of both continents, two in South America, and one in Africa.

Gulo Luscus.—Linn.

The Wolverene, or Glutton.

Plate xxvi. Three quarters natural size.

G. subniger; fasciâ subalbida utrinque humero per ilia producta, fasciis supra coxas se jungentibus; caudâ pilis longis hirsutâ.

Characters.

Dark-brown, passing into black, above; a pale band on each side, running from the shoulders aroung the flanks, and uniting on the hips; tail, with long bushy hairs.

Synonymes.

MUSTELA GULO, Linn., Syst. Nat., 12th edit.
URSUS LUSCUS, Linn., Syst. Nat., 12th edit.
URSUS GULO, Pallas, do., Schreber, Säugeth., p. 525.
" " F. Cuv., in Dict. des Sc. Nat., 19th edit, p. 79, c. fig.
QUICKHATCH or WOLVERINE, Ellis, Voy. Hudson's Bay, p. 42.
URSUS FRETI HUDSONIS, Briss, Quad., p. 188.
WOLVERINE, Cartwright's Journal, vol. ii., p. 407.
WOLVERINE, Pennant's Hist. Quad., vol. ii., p. 8, t. 8, Hearne's Journery, p. 372.
GULO ARCTICUS, var. A GLOUTON WOLVERINE, Desm., Mamm., p. 174.
GULO LUSCUS, (Capt.) Sabine, supp. Parry's 1st Voyage, p. 184.
" " Sabine, (Mr.) Franklin's 1st Journey, p. 650.
" " Richardson's Appendix Parry's 2d Voyage, p. 292.
" " Fischer's Mammalium, p. 154.
THE GLUTTON, Buffon, vol. vii., p. 274, pl. 243.
URSUS GULO, Shaw's Gen. Zool., vol. i., p. 46.
GULO VULGARIS, Griffith's Animal Kingdom, sp. 332.
GULO LUSCUS, Rich., F. B. A., p. 41.
" " Capt. Ross, Expedition, p. 8.
CARCAJOU, French Canadians; QUICKHATCH, English residents.

Description.

Head, of moderate size, broad on the hinder part, much arched, rounded on all sides; nose, obtuse, naked; eyes, small; ears, short, broad, rounded, and partially hidden by the surrounding fur. The whole head bears a strong resemblance to that of some of the varieties of the dog.

Body, very long, stout, and compactly made; back, arched; the whole form indicating strength without much activity. The Wolverene is covered with a very thick coat of two distinct kinds of hair. The inner fur, soft and short, scarcely an inch long; the intermixed hairs, numerous, rigid, smooth, and four inches long; giving the animal the appearance of some shaggy dog.

Legs, short and stout; feet, broad, clothed on the under surface with a compact mass of woolly hair. Toes, distinct, and armed with five stong, rounded, and pretty sharp claws. The tracks made in the snow by this species are large, and not very unlike those of the bear. There are five tubercles on the soles of the fore-feet, and four on the hind-feet; no tubercle on the heel.

The tail is rather short, hangs low, and is covered with pendulous hairs. "There are two secretory organs about the size of a walnut, from which it discharges a fluid of a yellowish-brown colour and of the consistence of honey, by the rectum, when hard pressed by its enemies."—Ross.

Colour.

Under fur, deep chesnut-brown, a shade lighter near the roots; the longer hairs are blackish-brown throughout thier whole length, the hair having very much the appearance of that of the bear. Eyes, nose, and whiskers, black; a pale reddish-brown band commences behind the shoulder, and running along the flanks, turns up on the hip, and unites on the rump with similar markings on the opposite side. There is a brownish-white band across the forehead running from ear to ear. On the sides of the neck there are tufts of white hair extending nearly in a circle from the inside of the legs around the chest. Legs and tail, brownish-black; claws, dark-brown. The colour varies greatly in different specimens, and although there is a strong general resemblance among all we have examined, we are not surprised that attempts have been made from these varieties to multiply the species. There are however no permanent varieties among the many specimens we have examined. The peculiar lateral band, although it is of a chesnut colour, in others light ferruginous, and in a few cases ash-coloured. We find these differences of colour existing on both continents, and not confined to either. We have never seen a specimen of a Wolverene as light in colour as that to which LINNÆUS gave the specific name of *luscus*, and we regard it as a mere accidental variety. We have found American specimens obtained in the Polar regions fully as black as those from Russia.

Dimensions.

Recent specimen, obtained in Rensselaer county, N. Y.

	Feet.	Inches.	Lines.
From point of nose to root of tail	2	9	0
Tail (vertebræ)	0	8	0
Height to shoulder	1	0	0
" of ear, posteriorly	0	1	6
Length of hair on body	0	4	0
From heels to point of nails	0	5	0
Breadth of hind-foot	0	4	7

Specimen from which our figure was made.

	Feet.	Inches.	Lines.
From point of nose to root of tail	2	6	0
Tail (vertebræ)	0	6	0
Tail, including fur	0	10	0
Height of ear	0	1	4

Habits.

The Wolverene, or Glutton as he is generally called, is one of the animals whose history comes down to us blended with the superstitions of the old writers. Errors when once received and published, especially if they possess the charm of great singularity or are connected with tables of wonder, become fastened on the mind by early reading and the impressions formed in youth,

Downy Squirrel.

Drawn from Nature by J.J.Audubon F R S F L S.

Printed by Nagel & Weingartner

until we are familiarized with their extravagance, and we at length regret to find ides (however incorrect) adopted in early life, not realized by the sober inquiries and investigations of maturer years.

The Wolverene, confined almost exclusively to Polar regions, where men have enjoyed few advantages of education, and hence have imbibed without much reflection the errors, extravagances, and inventions of hunters and trappers, has been represented as an animal possessing extraordinary strength, agility, and cunning, and as being proverbially one of the greatest gormandizers among the "brutes." OLAUS MAGNUS tells us that "it is wont when it has found the carcass of some large beast to eat until its belly is distended like a drum, when it rids itself of its load by squeezing its body betwixt two trees growing near together, and again returning to its repast, soon requires to have recourse to the same means of relief." It is even said to throw down the moss which the reindeer is fond of, and that the Arctic fox is its jackal or provider. BUFFON, in his first description of this animal, seems to have adopted the errors and superstitions of OLAUS MAGNUS, SCHOEFFER, GESNER, and the early travellers into Sweden and Lapland. He says of this animal, (vol. vii., p. 277,) "the defect of nimbleness he supplies with cunning, he lies in wait for animals as they pass, he climbs upon trees in order to dart upon his prey and seize it with advantage; he throws himself down upon elks and reindeer, and fixes so firmly on their bodies with his claws and teeth that nothing can remove him. In vain do the poor victims fly and rub themselves against trees; the enemy attached to the crupper or neck, continues to suck their blood, to enlarge the wound, and to devour them gradually and with equal voracity, till they fall down."

"More insatiable and rapacious than the wolf, if endowed with equal agility the Glutton would destroy all the other animals; but he moves so heavily that the only animal he is able to overtake in the course is the beaver, whose cabins he sometimes attacks, and devours the whole unless they quickly take to the water, for the beaver outstrips him in swimming. When he perceives that his prey has escaped, he seizes the fishes; and when he can find no living creature to destroy, he goes in quest of the dead, whom he digs up from their graves and devours with avidity."

Even the intelligent GMELIN, who revised and made considerable additions to the great work of LINNÆUS, on a visit to the North of Europe imbibed many of the notions of the Siberian hunters, and informs us, without however giving full credence to the account, that the Wolverene "watches large animals like a robber, or surprises them when asleep," that "he prefers the reindeer," and that "after having darted down from a tree like an arrow upon the animal, he sinks his teeth into its body and gnaws the flesh till it expires; after which he devours it at his ease, and swallows both the hair and skin."

However, although BUFFON in his earlier history of the species, adopted and published the errors of previous writers, he subsequently corrected them and gave in a supplementary chapter not only a tolerable figure but a true history. He received a Wolverene alive from the northern part of Russia, and preserved it for more than eighteen months at Paris. And when the Count was thus enabled to examine into its habits, as they were developed from day to day, he found them of a very ordinary character, and it was discovered to be an animal possessing no very striking peculiarities. He informs us, "He was so tame that he discovered no ferocity and did not injure any person. His voracity has been as much exaggerated as his cruelty; he indeed ate a great deal, but when deprived of food he was not importunate."

"The animal is pretty mild; he avoids water, and dreads horses, and men dressed in black. He moves by a kind of leap, and eats pretty voraciously. After taking a full meal he covers himself in the cage with straw. When drinking he laps like a dog. He utters no cry. After drinking, he throws the remainder of the water on his belly with his paws. He is almost perpetually in motion. If allowed he would devour more than four pounds of flesh in a day; he eats no bread, and devours his food so voraciously, and almost without chewing, that he is apt to choke himself."

We have seen this species in a state of confinement in Europe; the specimens came, we were informed, from the north of that continent. In Denmark, a keeper of a small caravan of animals allowed us the privilege of examining a Wolverene which he had exhibited for two years. We took him out of his cage; he was very gentle, opened his mouth to enable us to examine his teeth, and buried his head in our lap whilst we admired his long claws, and felt his woolly feet; he seemed pleased to escape from the confinement of the cage, ran round us in short circles, and made awkward attempts to play with and caress us, which reminded us very much of the habit of the American black bear. He had been taught to sit on his haunches, and hold in his mouth a German pipe. We observed he was somewhat averse to the light of the sun, keeping his eyes half closed when exposed to its rays. The keeper informed us that he suffered a good deal from the heat in warm weather, that he drank water freely, and ate

meat voraciously, but consumed more in winter than in summer. There was in the same cage a marmot from the Alps, (Arctomys marmota,) to which the Wolverene seemed much attached. When returned to his cage he rolled himself up like a ball, his long shaggy hairs so completely covering his limbs that he presented the appearance of a bear-skin rolled up into a bundle.

In the United States the Wolverene has always existed very sparingly, and only in the northern districts. About thirty-five years ago, we saw in the possession of a country merchant in Lansingburg, New York, three skins of this species, that had as we were informed been obtained on the Green Mountains of Vermont; about the same time we obtained a specimen in Rensselaer county, near the banks of the Hoosack river. While hunting the Northern hare, immediately after a heavy fall of snow, we unexpectedly came upon the track of an animal which at the time we supposed to be that of a bear, a species which even then was scarcely known in that portion of the country, (which was already pretty thickly settled.) We followed the broad trail over the hills and through the devious windings of the forest for about five miles, till within sight of a ledge of rocks on the banks of the Hoosack river, when, as we found the night approaching, we were reluctantly compelled to give up the pursuit for that day, intending to resume it on the following morning. It snowed incessantly for two days afterwards, and believing that the bear had retired to his winter retreat, we concluded that the chance of adding it to our collection had passed by. Some weeks afterwards a favourite servant, who was always anxious to aid us in our pursuits, and who not only knew many quadrupeds and birds, but was acquainted with many of their habits, informed us that he had on a previous day seen several tracks similar to those we had described, crossing a new road cut through the forest. As early on the following morning as we could see a track in the snow, we were fully accoutred, and with a gun and a pair of choice hounds, started on what we conceived our second bear-hunt. Before reaching the spot where the tracks had been observed, however, we met a fresh trail of the previous night, and pursued it without loss of time. The animal had joined some foxes which were feeding on a dead horse not a hundred yards from a log cabin in the forest, and after having satiated itself with this delicate food, made directly for the Hoosack river, pursuing the same course along which we had formerly traced it. To our surprise it did not cross the river, now firmly bound with ice, but retired to its burrow, which was not far from the place where we had a few weeks before abandoned the pursuit of it. The hounds had not once broke into full cry upon the track, but no sooner had they arrived at the mouth of the burrow than they rushed into the large opening between the rocks, and commenced a furious attack on the animal within. This lasted but for a few moments, and they came out as quickly as they had entered. They showed some evidence of having been exposed to sharp claws and teeth, and although they had been only a moment engaged in battle, had no disposition to renew it. No effort of ours could induce them to re-enter the cavern whilst their furious barking at the mouth of the hole was answered by a growl from within. The animal, although not ten feet from the entrance, could not be easily reached with a stick on account of his having retreated behind an angle in the chasm. As we felt no particular disposition to imitate the exploits of Colonel PUTNAM in his rencontre with the wolf, we reluctantly concluded to trudge homeward through the snow, distance of five miles, to obtain assistance. On taking another survey of the place, however, we conceived it possible to effect an opening on one of its sides. This was after great labour accomplished by prying away some heavy fragments of the rock. The animal could now be reached with a pole, and seemed very much irritated, growling and snapping at the stick, which he once succeeded in tearing from our hand, all the while emitting a strong and very offensive musky smell. He was finally shot. What was our surprise and pleasure on discovering that we had, not a bear, but what was more valuable to us, a new species of quadruped, as we believed it to be. It was six months before we were enabled, by consulting a copy of BUFFON, to discover our mistake and ascertain that our highly prized specimen was the Glutton, of which we had read such marvellous tales in the school-books.

In some of the figures that we have seen of the Wolverene, or Glutton, he is represented as touching the ground to the full extent of his heel, and several of the descriptions this habit is also assigned to him. Our notes, in reference to this point were made in early life, and it is possible that we may have laboured under a mistake; but we are confident, from our own observation, that the animal treads upon its hind-feet in the manner of the dog, that the impression of the tarsus or heel can only be observed in deep snow, and that in its ordinary walk on the ground the heel seldom touches the earth. We made no note in regard to the living Wolverene we saw in Europe, but are under an impression that its method of walking was similar to that stated above. There is another peculiarity in the tracks of the animal: in walking, the feet do not cross or approach each other in the manner of the feet of a fox or wolf, but make a double track in the snow, similar in this respect, to that of the skunk.

Plate XXVI.

Nº 6

Drawn on stone by R. Trembly

Drawn from Nature by J. J. Audubon. F.R.S.L.S

Wolverene.

Printed & Colᵈ by J T Bowen, Philadᵃ

There was a large nest of dried leaves in the cavern, which had evidently been a place of resort for the Wolverene we have been speaking of, during the whole winter, as its tracks from every direction led to the spot. It had laid up no winter store, and evidently depended on its nightly excursions for a supply of food. It had however fared well, for it was very fat.

It has been asserted that the Wolverene is a great destroyer of beavers, but we are inclined to think that this can scarcely be the case, unless it be in summer, when the beaver is often found some distance from the water. In such cases we presume that the Wolverene, although not swift of foot, could easily overtake that aquatic animal. But, should he in winter attempt to break open the frozen mud-walls of the beaver-huts, which would be a very difficult task, this would only have the effect of driving the occupants into their natural element, the water, where their hungry pursuer could not follow them. The statement of his expertness in swimming, diving, and catching fish, we believe to be apocryphal.

We are inclined to adopt the views of RICHARDSON in regard to the Wolverene, that it feeds chiefly on the carcasses of beasts that have been killed by accident. "It also devours meadow-mice, marmots, and other rodentia, and occasionally destroys disabled quadrupeds of a larger size."

That it seizes on deer or large game by pouncing on them is incredible; it neither possesses the agility nor the strength to accomplish this feat. This habit has also been ascribed to the Canada lynx as well as to the Bay lynx; we do not think it applies to either. That the Wolverene occasionally captures the grouse that have plunged into the fresh snow as a protection from the cold is probable.

RICHARDSON observes that he saw one chasing an American hare, which was at the same time harassed by a snowy owl. The speed of the hare however is such that it has not much to fear from the persevering but slow progress of the Wolverene; and the one seen by RICHARDSON, in his efforts to catch the tempting game must have been prompted by a longing desire after hare's flesh, rather than by any confidence in his ability to overtake the animal.

All Northern travellers and writers on the natural history of the Arctic regions, ELLIS, PENNANT, HEARNE, PARRY, FRANKLIN, RICHARDSON, &c., speak of the indomitable perseverance of the Wolverene in following the foot-steps of the trappers, in order to obtain the bait, or take from the traps the Arctic fox, the marten, beaver, or any other animal that may be caught in them. They demolish the houses built around the dead-falls, in order to obtain the bait, and tear up the captured animals apparently from a spirit of wanton destructiveness. HEARNE (p. 373) gives an account of their amazing strength, one of them having overset the greatest part of a large pile of wood, measuring upwards of seventy yards round, to get at some provisions that had been hid there. He saw another take possession of a deer that an Indian had killed, and though the Indian advanced within twenty yards he would not relinquish his claims to it, but suffered himself to be shot, standing on the deer. HEARNE farther states, "they commit vast depredations on the foxes during the summer, while the young ones are small; their quick scent directs them to their den, and if the entrance be too small, their strength enables them to widen it, and go in and kill the mother and all her cubs; in fact they are the most destructive animals in this country."

Capt. J. C. Ross, R.N., F.R.S., who gave an interesting account of the animals seen in the memorable expedition of Sir JOHN ROSS, relates the following anecdote of this species:—"In the middle of winter, two or three months before we abandoned the ship, we were one day surprised by a visit from a Wolverene, which, hard pressed by hunger, had climbed the snow wall that surrounded our vessel, and came boldly on deck where our crew were walking for exercise. Undismayed at the presence of twelve or fourteen men he seized upon a canister that had some meat in it, and was in so ravenous a state that whilst busily engaged at his feast he suffered me to pass a noose over his head, by which he was immediately secured and strangled."

The Wolverene is at all times very suspicious of traps, and is seldom taken in the log-traps set for the marten and Arctic fox; the usual mode in which it is obtained is by steel-traps, which must be set with great caution and concealed with much art.

Captain CARTWRIGHT in his journal speaks of having caught all he obtained at Labrador in this manner, and we have seen several skins giving evidence that the animals had been taken by the foot.

Captain CARTWRIGHT (see Journal, vol. ii., p. 407) records an instance of strength and cunning in this species that we cannot pass by in giving its history; we will use his own words. "In coming to the foot of Table Hill I crossed the track of a Wolverine with one of Mr. CALLINGHAM's traps on his foot; the foxes had followed his bleeding track. As this beast went through the thick of the woods, under the north side of the hill, where the snow was so deep and light that it was with the greatest difficulty I could follow him even in Indian rackets, I was quite puzzled to know how he had contrived to prevent the trap from catching hold of the branches of the trees or sinking in the snow. But on coming up with him I discovered how he had managed; for after making an attempt to fly at me, he took the trap in his mouth and ran upon three legs. These creatures are surprisingly strong in propotion to their size; this weighed only twenty-six pounds and the trap eight; yet including all the turns he had taken he had carried it six miles."

The Wolverene produces young but once a year, from two to four at a litter. RICHARDSON says the cubs are covered with a downy fur of a pale or cream colour. The fur of the Wolverene resembling that of the bear, is much used for muffs, and when several skins are sewed together makes a beautiful sleigh-robe.

Geographical Distribution.

The Wolverene exists in the north of both continents. On the Eastern continent it inhabits the most northern parts of Europe and Asia, occurring in Sweden, Norways, Lapland, and Siberia, as well as in some of the Alpine regions, and in the forests of Poland and Courland. In North America it is found throughout the whole of the Arctic circle. They were caught to the number of ten or twelve every winter by Capt. CARTWRIGHT in Labrador. It exists at Davis' Straits, and has been traced across the continent to the shores of the Pacific. If is found on the Russian islands of Alaska. RICHARDSON remarks, "It even visits the islands of the Polar sea, its bones having been found in Melville Island, nearly in latitude 75°. It occurs in Canada, although diminishing in numbers the farther we proceed southerly. We have seen specimens procured at Newfoundland, and have heard of its existence, although very sparingly, in Maine. Professor EMMONS, (DEKAY, Nat. Hist. of New York) states that it still exists in the Hoosack Mountains of Massachusetts. We examined a specimen obtained in Jefferson county, near Sackett's Harbour, N. Y., in 1827, and in 1810 we obtained a specimen in Rensselaer county, latitude 42° 46'; we have never heard of its existence farther south.

General Remarks.

This species has been arranged by different authors under several genera. LINNÆUS placed it under both MUSTELA and URSUS. STORR established for it the genus GULO, which was formed from the specific name, as it had been called *Ursus Gulo*, by LINNÆUS. STORR's generic name has been since adopted by CUVIER and other modern naturalists. GRAY named it GRISONIA. LINNÆUS is notwithstanding entitled to the specific name, although this is the result of an error into which he was led in this manner: EDWARDS had made a figure from a living specimen imported from America. It was a strongly marked variety, with much white on its forehead, sides, and neck. LINNÆUS regarding it as a new species described it as such. In seeking for some name by which to designate it, he observed that it had lost one eye, and it is supposed applied the trivial name "luscus," one-eyed, to the animal, merely on account of the above accidental blemish.

The vulgar names Glutton, Carcajou, &c., have given rise to much confusion in regard to the habits of the species.

The name Glutton induced many ancient authors to ascribe to it an appetite of extravagant voraciousness.

Carcajou appears to be some Indian name adopted by the French, and this name has evidently been applied to different species of animals. CHARLEVOIX, in his Voyage to America, vol. i., p. 201, speaks of the "carcajou or quincajou, a kind of cat, with a tail so long that he twists is several times round his body, and with a skin of a brownish red." He then refers to his climbing a tree, where after two foxes have driven the elk under the tree, the cat being on the watch pounces on it in the manner ascribed to the Wolverene. Here he evidently alludes to the cougar, as his long tail and colour apply to no other animal in our country. LAWSON refers the same singular habit to the wild cat of Carolina; he says, (p. 118,) "the wild cat takes most of his prey by surprise, getting up the trees which they pass by or under, and thence leaping directly upon them. Thus he takes deer, which he cannot catch by running, and fastens his teeth into their shoulders. They run with him till they fall down for want of strength and become a prey to the enemy."

In the last work published on American Quadrupeds, LAWSON is quoted as authority for the former existence of the Wolverene in Carolina, and a reference is also made to a plate of that species. On looking over the work of LAWSON, (London, 1709,) we find that no mention is made of the Wolverene, and no plate of the animal is given. We have supposed it possible that the author of the "Natural History of New York" might have intended refer to CATESBY; but the latter gave no plate of the species, and only noticed it as existing in the very northern parts of America. We feel confident that the geographical range of the Wolverene has never extended to Carolina, that it existed only as a straggler in the northern portion of the Middle States, and that it is now, and ever has been, almost entirely confined to the Northern regions.

Sciurus Lanigerus.—Aud. & Bach.

Woolly Squirrel.

Plate xxvii. Natural size.

Sc. migratorii magnitudine; pilis longis et lanosis; cauda ampla, villosa vixque disticha; naso, auriculis, pedibusque pene nigris; vellere supra ex-cinereo fusco; subtus dilute fusco.

Characters.

Size of Sciurus migratorius; hair, long and woolly; tail, large and bushy; nose, ears, and feet, nearly black; upper surface, grizzly dark gray, and brown; under parts, pale brown.

Synonyme.

SCIURUS LANIGERUS, Aud. and Bach., Journal of the Acad. Nat. Sc., Philad., 1841, p. 100.

Description.

Head, short; forehead, arched; nose, blunt; clothed with soft hair; whiskers, longer than the head; eyes, large; ears, large, broad at base, ovate.

Body, stout, covered with long and woolly hairs, which are much longer and a little coarser than those of the Northern gray squirrel.

Legs, stout; feet, of moderate size; claws, strong, compressed, arched and sharp. The third toe, longest; a blunt nail in place of a thumb. Palms, naked; toes, hairy to the extremity of the nails.

Tail, long and bushy, and the hairs long and coarse.

Colour.

Incisors, dark orange on the outer surface; the head, both on the upper and lower surface, as far as the neck, the ears, whiskers, fore-legs to the shoulder, feet, and inner surface of hind-legs, black; with a few yellowish-brown hairs intermixed. The long fur on the back is for half its length from the roots, light plumbeous, then has a line of light-brown, and is tipped with reddish-brown and black.

The hairs on the tail, in which the annulations are very obscure, are for one third of their length brownish-black, then light-brown, then brownish-black, and are tipped with ashy-white. One the under surface the hairs, which are short, are at the base light-plumbeous, tipped with light-brown and black; the throat is light grayish-brown.

Of two specimens received from the same locality, the head of one is lighter-coloured than that of the other, having a shade of yellowish-brown; in other respects they are precisely similar; a figure of each is given on the plate.

Dimensions.

Length of head and body . . . . $11\frac{7}{8}$ inches.
Tail (vertebræ) . . . . 10 do.
Tail, to end of fur . . . . 12 do.
Height of ear posteriorly . . . . $0\frac{5}{4}$ do.
Breadth of ear . . . . $0\frac{1}{4}$ do.
From heel to end of middle claw . . . . $2\frac{1}{3}$ do.
Hairs on the back . . . . $1\frac{1}{8}$ do.

Habits.

We have been unable to obtain any information in regard to the habits of this species. Its form, however, indicates that it is a climber, like all the species of the genus, living in forests, feeding on nuts and seeds. Its long woolly coat proves its adaptation to cold regions.

Geographical Distribution.

Our specimens were procured from the northern and mountainous portions of California.

General Remarks.

The difficulty in finding characters by which the various species of this genus can be distinguished, a very great. There is, however, no variety of any other species of squirrel that can be compared with that here described. Its black head and legs, brown back and belly, its broad ears and long woolly hair, are markings by which it may be easily distinguished from all others.

Owing to an error in the lettering of our plate of this species, the name attached to the figures was improperly given as *S. longipilis*.

Pteromys Volucella.—Gmel.

Common Flying-Squirrel.

Plate xxviii.—Males, Females, and Young. Natural size.

Pt. Tamias Lysteri magnitudine, supra ex fusco-cinereo et albido, infra ex albo.

Characters.

Size of Tamias Lysteri; above, brownish-ash tinged with cream colour; beneath, white.

Synonymes.

ASSAPANICK, Smith's Virginia, p. 27, 1624.
SCIURUS AMERICANUS VOLANS, Ray, Syn. Quad.
FLYING SQUIRREL, Lawson's Carolina, p. 124.
LA PALATOUCHE, Buff., X., pl. 21.
SCIURUS VOLUCELLA, Pallas, Glires, p. 353, 359.
  "   "   Schreber, Säugethiere, p. 808, 23, t. 222.
  "   "   Gmelin, Linn., Syst. Nat., p. 155, 26.
SCIURUS VIRGINIANUS, Gmelin, Syst. Nat.
  "   "   Shaw's Gen. Zool., vol. ii., p. 155, t. 150.
FLYING SQUIRREL, Catesby's Carolina, vol. ii., p. 76.
  "   "   Pennant's Quadrupeds, p. 418, 283.
PTEROMYS VOLUCELLA, Desm., Mamm., p. 345, 554.
  "   "   Harlan, p. 187.
  "   "   Godman, vol. ii., p. 146.
  "   "   Emmons, Report, p. 69.
  "   "   Dekay, p. 65.

Description.

Head, short and rounded; nose, blunt; eyes, large and prominent; ears, broad and nearly naked; whiskers, numerous, longer than the head; neck, short; body, rather thicker than that of the chipping squirrel. The flying membrane is distended by an additional small bone of about half an inch in length, articulated with the wrist. The fur on the whole body is very fine, soft and silky; legs, rather slender; claws, feeble, compressed, acute, and covered with hair; tail, flat, distichous, rounded at the tip, and very thickly clothed with fine soft fur. Ten mammæ.

Colour.

A line of black around the orbits of the eye; whiskers, nearly all black, a few are whitish toward their extremities. Ears, light-brown. In most specimens there is a light-coloured spot above the eyes; sides of the face and neck, light cream-colour; fur on the back, dark slate-colour, tipped with yellowish-brown. On the upper side of the flying membrane the colour gradually becomes browner till it reaches the lower edge, where it is of a light cream-colour; throat, neck, inner surface of legs, and all beneath, white; with occasionally a tint of cream-colour. The upper surface of the tail is of the colour of the back; tail, beneath, light fawn.

Dimensions.

Length of head of body . . . . $5\frac{1}{4}$ inches.
"   head 1   do.
"   tail (vertebræ) 4   do.
"   tail, including fur 5   do.

Of a specimen from which one of our figures was drawn.
From nose to eye . . . . $\frac{5}{8}$ inches.
"   "   opening of ear . . . . $1\frac{3}{4}$ do.
"   "   root of tail . . . . $5\frac{1}{4}$ do.
Tail (vertebræ) . . . . $3\frac{3}{4}$ do.
Tail, to end of hair . . . . $4\frac{1}{2}$ do.
Breadth of tail, hair extended . . . . $1\frac{5}{8}$ do.
Spread of fore-legs to extremity of claws . . . . $6\frac{7}{8}$ do.
Spread of hind-legs 7   do.

Habits.

It has sometimes been questioned whether the investigation of objects of natural history was calculated to improve the moral nature of man, and whether by an examination into the peculiar habits of the inferior animals he would derive information adapted to the wants of an immortal being, leading him from the contemplation of nature up to nature's God.

Leaving others to their own judgment on this subject, we can say for ourselves that on many occasions when studying the varied characters of the inferior creatures, we have felt that we were reading lessons taught us by nature, that were calculated to make us wiser and better. Often, whilst straying in the fields and woods with a book under our arm, have we been tempted to leave HOMER or ARISTOTLE unopened, and attend to the teachings of the quadrupeds and birds that people the solitudes of the wilderness. Even the gentle little Flying-Squirrel has more than once diverted our attention from the pages of GRIESBACH and MICHAELIS, and taught us lessons of contentment, of innocence, and of parental and filial affection, more impressive than the theological disquisitions of learned commentators.

We recollect a locality not many miles from Philadelphia, where, in order to study the habits of this interesting species, we occasionally strayed into a meadow containing here and there immense oak and beech trees. One afternoon we took our seat on a log in the vicinity to watch their lively motions. It was during the calm warm weather peculiar to the beginning of autumn. During the half hour before sunset nature seemed to be in a state of silence and repose. The birds had retired to the shelter of the forest. The night-hawk had already commenced his low evening flight, and here and there the common red bat was on the wing; still for some time not a Flying-Squirrel made its appearance. Suddenly, however, one emerged from its hole and ran up to the top of a tree; another soon followed, and ere long dozens came forth, and commenced their graceful flights from some upper branch to a lower bough. At times one would be seen darting from the topmost branches of a tall oak, and with wide-extended membranes and outspread tail gliding diagonally through the air, till it reached the foot of a tree about fifty yards off, when at the moment we expected to see it strike the earth, it suddenly turned upwards and alighted on the body of the tree. It would then run to the top and once more precipitate itself from the upper branches, and sail back again to the tree it had just left. Crowds of these little creatures joined in these sportive gambols; there could not have been less than two hundred. Scores of them would leave each tree at the same moment, and cross each other, gliding like spirits through the air, seeming to have no other object in view than to indulge a playful propensity. We watched and mused till the last shadows of day had disappeared, and darkness admonished us to leave the little triflers to their nocturnal enjoyments.

During the day this species avoids the light, its large eyes like those of the owl cannot encounter the glare of the sun; hence it appears to be a dull and uninteresting pet, crawling into your sleeve or pocket, and seeking any dark place of concealment. But twilight and darkness are its season for activity and pleasure. At such times, in walking through the woods you hear a rattling among the leaves and branches, and the falling acorns, chesnuts, and beech-nuts, give evidence that this little creature is supplying itself with its food above you.

This is a harmless and very gentle species, becoming tolerably tame in a few

hours. After a few days it will take up its residence in some crevice in the chamber, or under the eaves of the house, and it or its progeny may be seen in the vicinity years afterwards. On one occasion we took from a hollow tree four young with their dam; she seemed quite willing to remain with them, and was conveyed home in the crown of a hat. We had no cage immediately at hand, and placed them in a drawer in our library, leaving a narrow space open to enable them to breathe; next morning we ascertained that the parent had escaped through the crevice, and as the window was open, we presumed that she had abandoned her young rather than be subject to confinement in such a narrow and uncomfortable prison. We made efforts for several days to preserve the young alive by feeding them on milk; they appeared indifferent about eating, and yet seemed to thrive and were in good order. A few evenings afterwards we were surprised and delighted to see the mother glide through the window and enter the still open drawer; in a moment she was nestled with her young. She had not forsaken them, but visited them nightly and preserved them alive by her attentions. We now placed the young in a box near the window, which was left partly open. In a short time she had gained more confidence and remained with them during the whole day. They became very gentle, and they and their descendants continued to reside on the premises for several years.

During the first winter they were confined to the room, boxes were placed in different parts of it containing Indian meal, acorns, nuts, &c. As soon as it was dark they were in the habit of hurrying from one part of the room to the other, and continued to be full of activity during the whole night. We had in the room a wheel that had formerly been attached to the cage of a Northern gray squirrel. To this they found an entrance, and they often continued during half the night turning the wheel; at times we saw the whole group in it at once. This squirrel, we may conclude, resorts to the wheel not from compulsion but for pleasure.

In an interesting communication which we have received from GIDEON B. SMITH, ESQ., M.D., of Baltimore, he has given us the following details of the singular habits of this species:—

"After having arrived at the top of a tree from which they intend to make their airy leap, they spring or jump, stretch their fore-legs forward and outward and their hind-legs backward and outward, by this means expanding the loose skin with which they are clothed, and which forms a sort of gliding elevator. In this way they pass from tree to tree, or to any other object, not by flying as their name imports, but by descending from a high position by a gliding course; as they reach the vicinity of the earth, their impetus, aided by their expanded skin, enables them to ascend in a curved line and alight upon the tree aimed at, about one-third as high from the ground as they were on the tree they left. On reaching a tree in this manner they run briskly up its trunk as high as they wish to give them a start for another; in this way they will travel in a few minutes, from tree to tree or object to object a quarter of a mile or more. There is nothing resembling flying in their movements.

"They are gregarious, living together in considerable communities, and do not object to the company of other and even quite different animals. For example, I once assisted in taking down an old martin-box, which had been for a great number of years on the top of a venerable locust tree near my house, and which had some eight or ten apartments. As the box fell to the ground we were surprised to see great numbers of Flying-Squirrels, screech-owls, and leather-winged bats running from it. We caught several of each, and one of the Flying-Squirrels was kept as a pet in a cage for six months. The various apartments of the box were stored with hickory-nuts, chesnuts, acorns, corn, &c., intended for the winter supply of food. There must have been as many as twenty Flying-Squirrels in the box, as many bats, and we know there were six screech owls. The crevices of the house were always inhabited by the Squirrels. The docility of the one we kept as a pet was remarkable; although he was never lively and playful in the day-time, he would permit himself to be handled and spread out at the pleasure of any one. We frequently took him from the cage, laid him on the table or on one hand, and exposed the extension of his skin, smoothed his fur, put him in our pocket or bosom, &c., he pretending all the time to be asleep.

"It was a common occurrence that these Squirrels flew into the house on a summer's evening when the windows were open, and at such times we caught them. They were always perfectly harmless. Although I frequently seized them in my hand I was never bitten. We caught so many of them one season that the young girls bordered their winter capes with their tails which are very pretty. It was a curious circumstance that the Flying-Squirrels never descended to the lower parts of the house, and we never knew of any rats in the upper rooms. Whether the Squirrels or the rats were the repulsive agents I do not know; certain it is they never inhabited the lower location in common."

The Flying-Squirrel, as is shown above, is gregarious. In Carolina, we have generally found six or seven in one nest; it is difficult, however, to count

Drawn on stone by R. Trembly

Long Haired Squirrel.

Drawn from Nature by J.J. Audubon, FRS FLS   Printed & Col.d by J.T. Bowen, Philad.

them, as on cutting down a tree which they inhabit, several escape without being noticed. In New Jersey, Pennsylvania, and Virginia, they appear to be more numerous, and the families are larger.

The Flying-Squirrels never build their nest of leaves on the trees during summer like the true squirrels, but confine themselves to a hollow, or some natural cavity in the branches or trunk. We have very frequently found them inhabiting the eaves and roofs of houses, and we discovered a considerable number of them in the crevices of a rock in the vicinity of the Red Sulphur Springs in Virginia.

Although the food of this species generally consists of nuts and seeds of various kinds, together with the buds of trees in winter, yet we have known many instances in which it manifested a strong desire for animal food. On several occasions we found it caught in box-traps set for the ermine, which had been baited only with meat. The bait, (usually a blue jay,) was frequently wholly consumed by the little prisoner. In a room in which several Flying-Squirrels had been suffered to go at large, we one evening left a pine grosbeak, (*Corythus enucleator,*) a rare specimen, which we intended to preserve on the following morning. On searching for it however next day it was missing; we discovered its feet and feathers at last in the box of the Flying-Squirrels, they having consumed the whole body.

This species has from three to six young at a time. We have been assured by several persons that they produce young but once a year in the Northern and Middle States. In Carolina, however, we think they have two litters in a season, as we have on several occasions seen young in May and in September.

A writer in LOUDON's Magazine, under the signature of D. W. C., says at p. 571, vol. ix., in speaking of the habits of this animal in confinement in England, "I found that as soon as the female was pregnant she would not allow any one to approach her; and as the time went on, she became more savage and more tenacious of the part of the cage which she had fixed upon for her nest, which she made of leaves put in for that purpose. Two of the females produced young last spring. I think the period of their gestation is a month; but of this fact I am not certain. The young are blind for three weeks after their birth, and do not reach puberty till the next spring. I never obtained more than two young ones at a time, nor more than one kindle in a year from the same female. The young were generally born in March or April. The teats of the female appear through the fur some time before she brings forth. One of them produced two young ones without making a distinct nest, or separating herself from the rest, but the consequence was that they disappeared on the third day."

"If on any occasion we disturbed the young in their nest, the mother removed them to another part of the cage. The common squirrel of this country, (England,) is said to remove her young in the same manner, if disturbed. Finding this the case we often took the young Squirrels out of their nest, for the purpose of watching the mother carry them away, which she did by doubling the little one up under her body with her fore-feet and mouth till she could take hold of the thigh and the neck, when she would jump away so fast that it was difficult to see whether she was carrying her young one or not.

"As the young increased in size (which they soon do) and in weight, the undertaking became more difficult. We then saw the mother turn the young one on its back, and while she held the thigh in her mouth, the fore-legs of the young one were clasped round her neck. Sometimes when she was attempting to jump upon some earthen pots which I had placed in the cage, she was overbalanced and fell with her young to the ground, she would drop the young Squirrel, so as to prevent her own weight from crushing it, which would have been the case if they had fallen together. I have seen the young ones carried in this manner till they were half-grown."

Geographical Distribution.

This species is far more numerous than it is generally supposed to be; in traps set for the smaller rodentia in localities where we had never seen the Flying Squirrel, we frequently caught it. We have met with it in all the Atlantic States, and obtained specimens in Upper Canada, within a mile of the falls of Niagara. In Lower Canada it is replaced by a larger species, (*P. sabrinus,*) and we have reason to believe that it does not exist much to the north of the great lakes; we obtained specimens in Florida and in Texas, and have seen it in Missouri, and according to LICHTENSTEIN it is found in Mexico.

General Remarks.

This species was among the earliest of all our American quadrupeds noticed by travellers. Governor SMITH of Virginia, in 1624, speaks of it as "a small beaste they call Assapanick, but we call them Flying Squirrels, because spreading their legs, and so stretching the largeness of their skins, that they have been seen to fly thirty or forty yards." RAY and LINNÆUS supposed it to be only a variety of the European *P. volans*, from which it differs very widely. LINNÆUS arranged it under MUS; GMELIN, PALLAS, CUVIER, RAY, and BRISSON under SCIURUS; F. CUVIER and DESMAREST under SCIUROPTERUS; FISCHER under PETAURISTUS; and GEOFFROY and more recent naturalists, under PTEROMYS.

Neotoma Drummondii. — Richardson.

Rocky Mountain Neotoma.

Plate xxix. Winter and Summer colours. Natural Size.

N. subtus albida; supra hyeme flavo-fuscescens, æstate saturate cinereus; cauda crassa, corpore longiore muse decumano robustior.

Characters.

Colour. above. yellowish-brown in winter and dark-ash in summer; whitish beneath; tail. bushy and longer than the body; larger than the Norway rat.

Synonymes.

RAT OF THE ROCKY MOUNTAINS, Lewis and Clarke, vol. iii., p. 41.
MYOXUS DRUMMONDII, Rich., Zool. Jour., 1828, p. 5, 7.
NEOTOMA DRUMMONDII, Rich., Fauna Boreali Americana, p. 137, pl. 7.

Description.

This species bears a striking resemblance to the Florida rat. It differs from the Norway rat by its longer and broader ears, and by its bushy tail and light active form. Fur, long and loose, bearing a considerable resemblance to that of the gray rabbit; nose, rather obtuse; the nostrils have a very narrow naked margin; the tip of the nose is covered with short hairs; ears, large, oval, and rounded, nearly naked within, except near the margins, where they are slightly clothed with short hairs. On the outer surface there are a few more hairs, but not enough to conceal the skin beneath; eyes, small, much concealed by the fur; whiskers, like hogs' bristles, very strong, the longest reaching to the shoulders; neck, short, and fully as thick as the head.

Fore-legs, short; feet, of moderate size, with four toes; claws, small, compressed, and pointed. The third toe nearly equals the middle one, which is the longest, the first is a little shorter, and the outer one not more than half the length of the other two; there is also the rudiment of a thumb, which is armed with a minute nail. The toes of the hind-feet are longer than those of the fore-feet, and the claws less hooked; the middle toe is the longest, those on each side of it of nearly an equal length; the outer one a little shorter, and the inner shortest of all. The palms on the fore and hind-feet are naked, but the toes, even beyond the nails, are covered with short, adpressed hairs. The hairs of the tail (which are not capable of a distichous arrangement) are short near the root, and gradually lengthen toward the end, where it is large and bushy, the hairs being one inch in length.

Colour.

Incisors, yellow; on the whole of the back, the head, shoulders, and outsides of the thighs, a dusky darkish-brown, proceeding from a mixture of yellowish-brown and black hairs. From the roots to near the tips, the fur is of a dark lead-colour, tipped with light-brown and black. The sides of the face and the ventral aspect, are bluish-gray. Margin of the upper lip, chin, feet, and under surface, dull white; whiskers, black and white, the former colour predominating; tail; grayish-brown above, dull yellowish-white beneath.

The above is the colour of this species from the end of summer through the following winter to the time of shedding the hair in May; when in its new coat it has far less of yellowish-brown, and puts on a gray appearance on the back, this colour gradually assuming more of the yellowish hue as the autumn advances and the fur lengthens and thickens toward winter.

Dimensions.

From point of nose to root of tail . . . . .9 inches.

Common Flying Squirrel.

1.2 Males, 3, 4 Females, 5 Young

Drawn from Nature by J.J.Audubon, F.R.S.F.L.S. Printed & Colᵈ by J.T. Bowen, Phil

Tail (vertebræ)	7½ do.
Tail, including fur	8½ do.
Height of ear, posteriorly	1 do.
Length of whiskers	4 do.

Habits.

We regret that from personal observation, we have no information to give in regard to the habits of this species, having never seen it in a living state. It was, however, seen by LEWIS and CLARKE, by DRUMMOND, DOUGLASS, NUTTALL, and TOWNSEND. According to the accounts given by these travellers, this Neotoma appears to have nearly the same general habits as the smaller species, (*N. Floridana*,) the Florida rat, but is much more destructive than the latter. It has a strong propensity to gnaw, cut to pieces, and carry to its nest every thing left in its way. The trappers dread its attacks on their furs more than they would the approach of a grisly bear. These rats have been known to gnaw through whole packs of furs in a single night. The blankets of the sleeping travellers are sometimes cut to pieces by them, and they carry off small articles from the camp of the hunter.

"Mr. DRUMMOND," says RICHARDSON, "placed a pair of stout English shoes on the shelf of a rock, and as he thought, in perfect security; but on his return, after an absence of a few days, he found them gnawed into fragments as fine as saw-dust."

Mr. DOUGLASS, who unfortunately lost his life in ascending Mouna Roa, in the Sandwich Islands, by falling into a pit for catching wild bulls, where he was gored by one of those animals, was one of the most indefatigable explorers of the Western portions of our continent, and kept a journal of his travels and discoveries in natural history. It was never published, but a few copies were printed some time after his death, by his friend and patron, Sir WILLIAM HOOKER, who presented one of them to us. In it we found the following account of this animal:—

"During the night I was annoyed by the visit of a herd of rats, which devoured every particle of seed I had collected, ate clean through a bundle of dried plants and carried off my soap, brush, and razor. As one was taking away my inkstand, which I had been using shortly before, and which lay close to my pillow, I raised my gun, which, with my faithful dog, always is placed under my blanket by my side with the muzzle to my feet, and hastily gave him the contents. When I saw how large and strong a creature this rat was, I ceased to wonder at the exploits of the herd in depriving me of my property. The body and tail together measured a foot and a half; the hair was brown, the belly white; it had enormous ears three quarters of an inch long, and whiskers three inches in length. Unfortunately the specimen was spoiled by the shot which in my haste to secure the animal and recover my inkstand, I did not take time to change; but a female of the same sort venturing to return some hours after, I handed it a smaller shot, which did not destroy the skin. It was in all respects like the former, except being a little smaller." This identical specimen is in the museum of the Zoological Society of London, where we examined it.

Mr. TOWNSEND has kindly furnished us with some remarks on this species, from which we make the following extracts:—"I never saw it in the Rocky Mountains, but it is very common near the Columbia river. It is found in the store-houses of the inhabitants, where it supplies the place of the common rat, which is not found here. It is a remarkably mischievous animal, destroying every thing which comes in its way—papers, books, goods, &c. It has been known not unfrequently to eat entirely through the middle of a bale of blankets, rendering the whole utterly useless; and like a pet crow carries away every thing it can lay its *hands* on. Even candle-sticks, porter-bottles, and large iron axes, being sometimes found in its burrows."

The food of this species consists of seeds and herbage of various kinds; it devours also the small twigs and leaves of pine trees, and generally has a considerable store of these laid up in the vicinity of its residence.

It is said by DRUMMOND to make its nest in the crevices of high rocks. The nest is large, and is composed of sticks, leaves, and grasses. The abode of this Rat may be discovered by the excrement of the animal, which has the colour and consistence of tar, and is always deposited in the vicinity. It is stated by those who have had had the opportunity of observing, that this species produces from three to five young at a time.

Geographical Distribution.

We were informed by a gentleman who was formerly engaged as a clerk in the service of the Missouri fur company, that this Rat exists in the valleys, and along the sides, of the Rocky Mountains, through an extent of thirty degrees of latitude. DOUGLASS states that it is very numerous near the Mackenzie and Peace rivers, latitude 69°. TOWNSEND found it in Oregon. We have seen a specimen that was said to have been obtained in the Northern mountains of Texas, and have heard of its existence in North California.

Genus Sigmodon.—Say and Ord.

Dental Formula.

$$\text{Incisive } \tfrac{2}{2}; \text{ Canine } \tfrac{0-0}{0-0}; \text{ Molar } \tfrac{3-3}{3-3} = 16.$$

As the present genus was instituted after a careful examination of the teeth of *Sigmodon hispidum*, by Messrs. SAY and ORD, who first described that species; we think it due to those distinguished naturalists, to give the dental formula in their own words, more especially as this species was named by us, in our illustrations, *Arvicola hispidus*, we having had some doubts whether it was sufficiently distinct from the arvicolæ in its generic characters, to warrant us in adopting the genus SIGMODON, to which we now cheerfully transfer it.

"Superior Jaw.—Incisor, slightly rounded on its anterior face, truncated at tip; first molar, equal to the second, composed of four very profound, alternate folds, two on each side, extending at least to the middle of the tooth; second molar, quadrate, somewhat wider, and a little shorter than the preceding, with three profound folds extending at least to the middle, two of which are on the exterior side; posterior molar, a little narrower, but not shorter than the preceding, with three profound folds, two of which are on the exterior side, extending at least to the middle; the inner fold, opposite to the anterior exterior fold, and not extending to the middle.

"Inferior Jaw.—Incisor obliquely truncate at tip, the acute angle being on the inner side; it originates in the ascending branch of the maxillary bone, passing beneath the molars; molars, subequal in breadth, inclining slightly forwards; first molar, a little narrower than the second, with five profound alternate folds, three of which are on the inner side; second molar, subquadrate, with two alternate profound folds, the inner one anterior; third molar, about equal in length and breadth to the anterior one, but rather larger and somewhat narrower than the second, with which it corresponds in the disposition of its folds, excepting that they are less compressed."

Observations.

"The enamel of the molars is thick, but on the anterior face of each fold excepting the first is obsolete. From the arrangement of the folds, as above described, it is obvious that the configuration of the triturating surface, (occasioned by the folds of enamel dipping deeply into the body of the tooth, in the second and third molar of the lower jaw,) accurately represents the letter S, which is reversed on the right side; that bearing considerable resemblance to the posterior tooth of the genus SPALAX, and to which also it has a slight affinity in the truncature of the inferior incisors. The configuration of the intermediate molar of the upper jaw may be compared to the form of the Greek letter Σ, whence our generic name."

"In respect to its generic affinities, it is very obvious that its system of dentition indicates a proximity to ARVICOLA, but the different arrangement of the folds, and the circumstance of the molars being divided into radicles, certainly exclude it from that genus. With respect to the radicles, it resembles the genus FIBER; but is allied to this genus in no other respect."

"We may further remark that the teeth of our specimen are considerably worn, a condition that materially affects the depths of the folds."

Although the animal described below is the only species of SIGMODON at present admitted into this genus, there are several well known, and one undescribed, species, that we apprehend will yet be arranged under it.

Sigmodon Hispidum.—Say and Ord.

Cotton-Rat.

Plate xxx.—Natural size.

S. flavo fuscescens, infra cinereum; cauda corpore breviore; auribus amplis rotundatisque; Tamiæ Lysteri magnitudine.

Plate XXIX

N.º 6

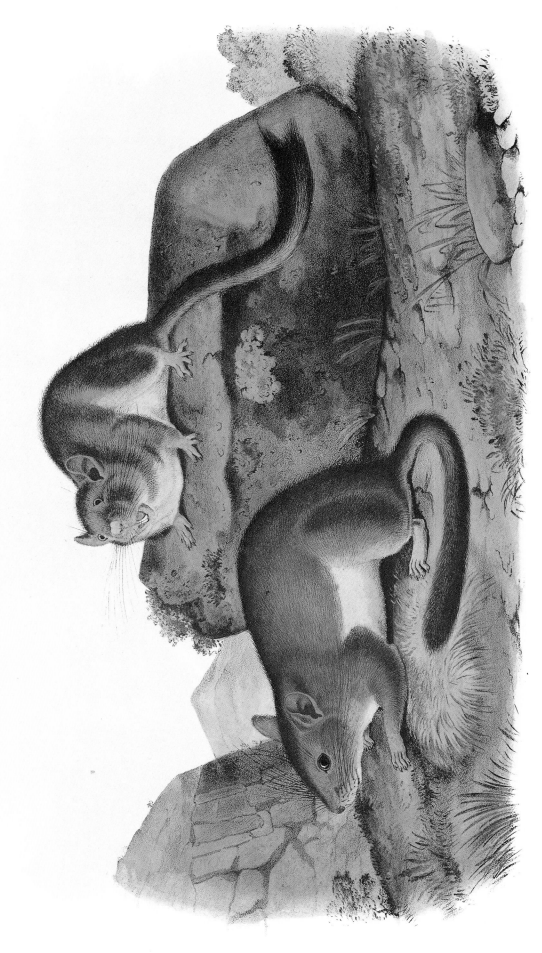

Drawn from Nature by J.J.Audubon, F.R.S.F.L.S.

Drawn on Stone by Wᵐ. E. Hitchcock

Rocky Mountain Neotoma

Printed & Colᵈ by J.T. Bowen, Phil.

Characters.

Size of the chipping squirrel, (T. Lysteri;) tail, shorter than the body; ears, broad and rounded; above, dark yellowish-brown; cinereous beneath.

Synonymes.

MARSH-RAT, Lawson's Carolina, 1709, p. 125.
THE WOOD-RAT, Bartram's Travels in East Florida, 1791, p. 124.
SIGMODON HISPIDUM, Say and Ord, Journ. Ac. Nat. Sc., Phila., vol. iv., pt. 2, p. 354, read March 22d, 1825.
ARVICOLA HORTENSIS, Harlan, Fauna, 1825, p. 138.
    "   HISPIDUS, Godman, vol. ii., p. 68, 1826.
    "   HORTENSIS, Griffith, Cuvier, vol. v., sp. 547.

Description.

In its general external appearance this species approaches nearer to the genus ARVICOLA than to MUS. It has the thick short form of the former, and the broad and rather long ears of many species of the latter. The fur is long and coarse.

Head, of moderate size, rather long; nose, pointed; whiskers, few, weak, and shorter than the head; eyes, of moderate size and rather prominent; ears, broad, rounded, and slightly covered with hair.

Fore-legs, rather short and slender; four toes on each foot, the middle ones nearly of equal length, the inner one a size shorter, and the outer shortest; there is also a rudimentary thumb, protected by a strong conical nail. Hind-legs, stouter; five toes on each foot, much longer than those on the fore-feet; middle claw longest, the two on each side nearly equal, the outer, not one-third the length of the others, and the inner, which rises far back, shortest of all; nails, rather small, sharp, and slightly arched; toes, covered with hair extending to the roots of the nails; tail, clothed with short hairs.

Colour.

Hairs, on the whole upper surface of the body of a dark plumbeous colour from the roots to near the extremities, edged with brown, and irregularly tipped with black; giving it a rusty reddish-brown appearance. The ears, head, and tail, are of the colour of the back; chin, throat, and under surface of body, dull-white, the hairs being ashy-gray at the roots, and whitish at the points.

Dimensions.

From point of nose to root of tail	6 inches.
Tail	4 do.
Length of ear	$\frac{1}{2}$ do.
Breadth of ear	$\frac{1}{2}$ do.
From eye to point of nose	$\frac{5}{8}$ do.
From point of nose to ear	$1\frac{1}{2}$ do.
From heel to point of longest nail	$1\frac{1}{2}$ do.

Habits.

This is the most common wood-rat existing in the Southern States, being even more abundant than any of the species of meadow-mice in the Northern and Eastern States. It is however a resident rather of hedges, ditches, and deserted old fields, than of gardens or cultivated grounds; it occasions very little injury to the planter. Although its paths are everywhere seen through the fields, it does not seem to destroy many plants or vegetables. It feeds on the seeds of coarse grasses and leguminous plants, and devours a considerable quantity of animal food. In its habits it is gregarious. We have seen spots of half an acre covered over with tall weeds, (*Solidago* and *Eupatorium*,) which were traversed in every direction by the Cotton-Rat, and which must have contained several hundred individuals.

Although this species does not reject grains and grasses, it gives the preference in all cases to animal food, and we have never found any species of rat more decidedly carnivorous. Robins, partridges, or other birds that are wounded and drop among the long grass or weeds in the neighbourhood of their burrows are speedily devoured by them. They may sometimes be seen running about the ditches with crayfish, (*Astacus Bartoni*) in their mouths, and have been known to subsist on Crustacea, especially the little crabs called fiddlers, (*Gelasimus vocans*.)

We have frequently kept Cotton-Rats in cages; they killed and devoured every other species placed with them, and afterwards attacked each other; the weakest were killed and eaten by the strongest. They fight fiercely, and one of them will overpower a Florida rat twice its own size.

The old males when in confinement almost invariably destroy their young.

This species delights in sucking eggs, and we have known a Virginian partridge nest as completely demolished by these animals, as if it had been visited by the Norway rat. They will sometimes leave Indian-corn and other grain untouched, when placed as a bait for them in traps, but they are easily caught when the traps are baited with meat of any kind.

Although the Cotton-Rat is nocturnal in its habits, it may frequently be seen by day, and in places where it is seldom disturbed, it can generally be found at all hours.

The galleries of this species often run twenty or thirty yards under ground, but not far beneath the surface; and the ridges thrown up as the animals excavate their galleries, can often be traced along the surface of the earth for a considerable distance, like those formed by the common shrew-mole.

Each burrow or hole contains apparently only one family, a pair of old ones with their young; but their various galleries often intersect each other, and many nests may be found within the compass of a few yards; they are composed of withered grasses, are not very large, and may usually be found within a foot of the surface. In summer the nests are often seen in a cavity of the earth, on the surface in some meadow, or among rank weeds.

This is a very prolific species, producing young early in spring, and through all the summer months, till late in autumn. We have on several occasions known their young born and reared in cages. They produce from four to eight at a litter. The young are of a bright chesnut-brown colour, and at the age of five or six days begin to leave the nest, are very active and sprightly, and attain their full growth in about five months.

This species has no other note than a low squeak, a little hoarser than that of the common mouse; when captured it is far more savage than the Florida rat. On one occasion, while seizing one of them, we were bitten completely through a finger covered by a buckskin glove.

The Cotton-Rat is fond of burrowing in the old banks of abandoned rice-fields. In such situations we have, during freshets, observed that it could both swim and dive like the water-rat of Europe, and WILSON'S meadow-mouse of the Middle States.

This species supplies a considerable number of animals and birds with food. Foxes and wild-cats especially, destroy thousands; we have observed minks coursing along the marshes in pursuit of them, and have frequently seen them with one of these Rats in their mouth. Marsh-hawks, and several other species, may be constantly seen in the autumn and winter months sailing over the marsh, looking out for the Cotton-Rat. No animal in the Southern States becomes more regularly the food of several species of owls than this. The barred owl (*Syrnium nebulosum*) is seen as early as the setting of the sun, flitting along the edges of old fields, seeking to make its usual evening meal on it or carry it off as food for its young. We were invited some years since to examine the nest of the American barn-owl (*Strix Americana*) in the loft of a sugar refinery in Charleston. There were several young of different sizes, and we ascertained that the only food on which they were fed was this Rat, to obtain which the old birds must have gone several miles.

The Cotton-Rat has obtained its name from its supposed habit of making its nest with cotton, which it is said to collect for the purpose in large quantities. We have occasionally, although very seldom, seen cotton in its nest, but we have more frequently found it composed of leaves and withered grasses. Indeed, this species does not appear to be very choice in selecting materials for building its nest, using indiscriminately any suitable substance in the vicinity. We should have preferred a more characteristic English name for this Rat, but as it already has three names, Cotton-Rat, Hairy Campagnol, and Wood-Rat, the latter being in Carolina applied both to this and the Florida rat, we have concluded not to add another, although one more appropriate might be found.

Geographical Distribution.

We have traced the Cotton-Rat as far north as Virginia, and have seen it in North Carolina, near Weldon and Wilmington. It is exceedingly abundant in South Carolina, Georgia, and Florida; in Alabama, Mississippi, and Louisiana, traces of it are every where seen. We have received a specimen from Galveston, Texas, but have had no opportunity of ascertaining whether it exists farther south.

General Remarks.

Although this species was noticed by LAWSON a century and a half ago, it was not described until a comparatively recent period. ORD obtained speci-

Plate XXX

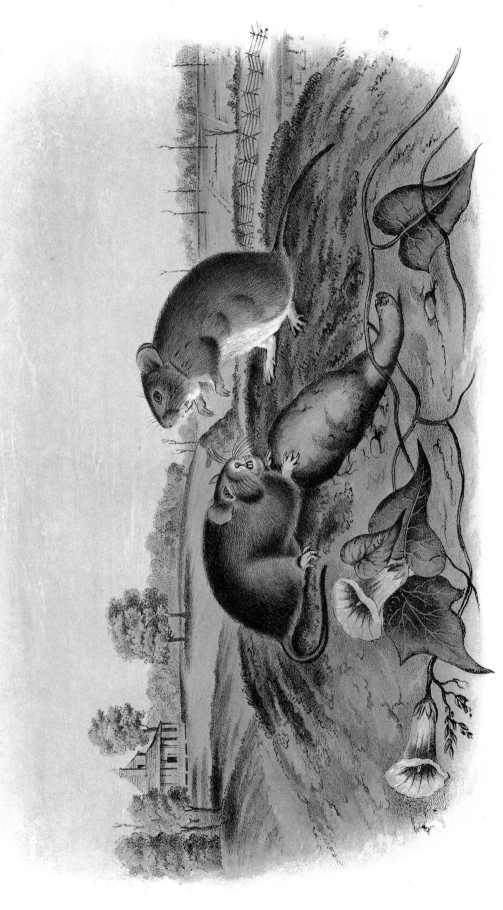

Drawn from Nature by J J Audubon, F R S F L S

Drawn on Stone by Wᵐ E Hitchcock

Lith Printed & Colᵈ by J T Bowen Phil

Cotton Rat

mens in Florida in 1818, and it was generally supposed that it was not found further to the north. In the spring of 1815, three years earlier than Mr. ORD, we procured a dozen specimens in Carolina, which we neglected to describe. SAY and ORD, and HARLAN, described it about the same time, (in 1825,) and GODMAN a year afterwards. We prefer adopting the name given to it by the individual who first brought it to the notice of naturalists. In its teeth it differs in a few particulars from ARVICOLA, and approaches nearer to MUS. The genus SIGMODON, at the time it was proposed, was strongly objected to by HARLAN and GODMAN; we have, however, after a good deal of investigation, concluded to adopt it, although our plate of the Cotton-Rat was lettered *Arvicola hispidus*.

Genus Dycotyles.—F. Cuvier.

Dental Formula.

Incisive $\frac{4}{6}$; *Canine* $\frac{1-1}{1-1}$; *Molar* $\frac{6-6}{6-6}$ = 38.

Tusks or canine teeth, projecting slightly, not curved near the points as in the common hog, (SUS,) small, triangular, and very sharp; molars, with tubercular crowns; tubercles, rounded and irregularly disposed. Head, broad and long; snout, straight, terminated by a cartilage; ears, of moderate size and pointed; eyes, rather small, pupil round. Fore-feet, with four toes, the two middle toes largest, the lateral toes quite short, not reaching to the ground; hind-feet, with three toes, the external little toe of the hog wanting in this genus.

The metatarsal and metacarpal bones of the two largest toes on all the feet are united together like those of the ruminantia; all the toes are protected by hoofs. A gland situated on the back a few inches from the root of the tail, concealed by the hair, discharges an oily fœtid secretion. Body, covered with strong, stiff, bristles; tail, a mere tubercle.

Only two species are known, both inhabiting the warmer climates of America; the generic name Dycotyles, is derived from the Greek words, δις, (*dis*,) *double*, and κοτυλη, (*kotule*,) a *cavity*; or double navel, from the opening on the back.

Dycotyles Torquatus.—F. Cuvier.

Collared Peccary.

Plate xxxi. Four-sevenths natural size.

D. pilis nigro alboque annulatis; vitta albida ab humeris in latere colli utroque decurrente.

Characters.

Hair, annulated with black and white; a light-coloured band extending from the sides of the neck around the shoulders, and meeting on the back.

Synonymes.

TAYTETOU, D'Azara, Quad. du Paraguay, vol. i., p. 31.
TAJACU, Buffon, vol. v., p. 272, pl. 135.
SUS TAJACU, Linn., 12th ed. vol. i., p. 103.
QUAVHTLA COYMATL, QUAHEROTL, Hern., Mex., 637.
TAJACU, Ray, Quad., p. 97.
SUS TAGASSA, Erxleben, Syst., p. 185.
SUS TAGASSA, Schreber, Säugethier, t. 325.
APER AMERICANUS, Briss., Règne An., p. 3
TAJACU CAAIGOANA MARCGR, Bras., p. 229.
MEXICAN HOG, Pennant, Quadr., p. 147.
PORCUS MOSCHIFERUS, Klein, Quadr., p, 25.
PECCARI, Shaw, Gen. Zool., vol. ii., p. 469, 224.
DYCOTYLES TORQUATUS, F. Cuvier, Dict. des Sciences Naturelles,
       tom. ix., p. 518.
    "   "   Desm., Mamm., p. 393.
    "   "   Cuv., Règne An., vol. i., p. 237.
    "   "   Pr. Maxim. Beitr., vol. ii., p. 557.
    "   "   Harlan, Fauna, p. 220.
    "   "   Griffith's Animal Kingdom, sp. 740.

Description.

The form of the Collared Peccary bears a very striking resemblance to that of the common domesticated hog, it is however smaller in size, shorter, and more compact.

Head, rather large; snout, long; ears, upright, and of moderate size; eyes, rather small. The cartilage on the extremity of the nose is naked, with the exception of a few bristles on the upper lip. On the upper surface of the nose, near the cartilage, there is a spot half an inch in length that is naked; nostrils, large; the upper tusks, in the living animal, protrude downward below the lower lips half an inch; the ears are on both surfaces thinly clothed with hair that is softer than that on the remainder of the body. The hairs on the head are short. From the hind part of the head along the dorsal line on the back, there are long strong bristles, which are erected when the animal is irritated. Many of these bristles are five inches in length, whilst the hairs on the other parts of the body are generally about three.

On the lower part of the back, a slight distance from the rump, there is a naked glandular orifice surrounded by a few bristles in a somewhat radiated direction. From this orifice there exudes a strong scented fluid. This part of the animal has been vulgarly supposed to be its navel.

The legs, which strongly resemble those of the common hog, are rather short. There is not even a vestige of the small upper external hind-toe, which is always present in the common hog. There is a ruff under the throat, protruding about three inches beyond the surrounding hairs. The under surface of the body is rather thinly clothed with hair.

In place of a tail there is a mere protuberance about half an inch in length, which is rounded and like a knob.

Colour.

Eyes, dark-brown; nostrils, flesh-colour. The hairs are at their roots yellowish-white, are thrice annulated with dark-brown and yellowish-white, and are tipped with black. Head, cheeks, and sides of the neck, grayish; legs, dark-brown; a whitish band two inches broad runs from the top of the shoulder on each side toward the lower part of the neck. The long hairs on the dorsal line are so broadly tipped with black that the animal in those parts appears of a black colour; along the sides however the alternate annulations are so conspicuous that it has a deep gray or grizzled appearance. On the chest, outer surface of shoulders and thighs, it is of a darker colour than on the sides. Immediately behind the lightish collar on the shoulders the hairs are dark, rendering this collar or band more conspicuous.

The young have a uniform shade of red.

Dimensions.

		Feet.	Inches.
Living female.			
Length of head and body		2	10
" head		0	11
" ear		0	3
Height to shoulder		1	8
Length of tail		0	$0\frac{1}{2}$
Adult male (recent) obtained in Texas.			
From nose to anterior canthus		0	$5\frac{1}{2}$
From nose to beginning of ear		0	$9\frac{1}{4}$
Length of ear		0	$3\frac{1}{2}$
Breadth of ear		0	$2\frac{7}{8}$
Length from snout to root of tail		3	4
Tail		0	$0\frac{3}{4}$
From knee to end of hoof		0	$5\frac{3}{4}$
Hind-knee to end of hoof		0	$7\frac{1}{4}$
Spread of fore-feet		0	$1\frac{1}{2}$
Girth across the centre of body		2	5
Spread of mouth when fully extended		0	$5\frac{1}{2}$
Breadth between the eyes		0	$2\frac{3}{4}$

Habits.

The accounts that have been handed down to us of the habits of this species by old travellers, ALDROVANDA, FERNANDEZ, Mons. DE LA BORDE,

Plate XXXI

N°7

Drawn from Nature by J.J.Audubon F.R.S.F.L.S.

Drawn on Stone by R Trembly.

Collared Peccary.

Printed by Nagel & Weingærtner N.Y.

MARCGRAVE, ACOSTA, and others, who furnished the information from which BUFFON, BRISSON, RAY, and LINNÆIUS, drew up their descriptions of the Mexican hog, are not to be fully relied on, inasmuch as their descriptions referred to two very distinct species, the white-lipped peccary, (D. *labiatus*,) and the subject of the present article. Neither LINNÆUS nor his contemporaries seem to have been aware of the difference which exists between the species, and although BUFFON was informed by M. DE LA BORDE that another and larger species existed at Cayenne, he does not appear to have drawn any line of distinction between it and our animal.

D'AZARA, who visited South America in 1783, (Essais sur l'Histoire Naturelle des Quadrupedes de la Province du Paraguay, Paris, 1801,) endeavoured to correct the errors into which previous writers had fallen, and gave an account of the present species, which, although somewhat unmethodical, is nevertheless of such a character that it may on the whole be relied on. He commences his article on the "taytetou," as he designates this species, by first giving correct measurements; afterwards he describes the colour of the adult and young, points out the distinctive marks which separate this species from the white-lipped peccary, which he calls "tagnicate," and then gives a tolerable account of the habits of the species now under consideration. From the accounts which travellers have given us of the Collared Peccary it appears that this species is gregarious, and associates for mutual protection in pretty large families; it is however stated by D'AZARA that the white-lipped peccary is more disposed to congregate in very large herds than our animal.

Although they are usually found in the forests and prefer low and marshy grounds, like common hogs, Peccaries wander wherever they can find an abundance of food, often enter the enclosures of the planters, and commit great depredations on the products of their fields.

When attacked by the jaguar, the puma, the wolf, the dog, or the hunter, they form themselves into a circle, surrounding and protecting their young, repelling their opponents with their sharp teeth, and in this manner sometimes routing the larger predatory animals, or severely wounding the dogs and the hunters.

When angry they gnash their teeth, raise their bristles, (which at such time resemble the quills of the porcupine,) and their sharp, shrill grunt can be heard at a great distance.

This species feeds on fruits, seeds, and roots; and like the domesticated hog is constantly rooting in the earth in quest of worms, insects, reptiles, or bulbous roots. It is said also to devour the eggs of alligators, turtles, and birds; and to be destructive to lizards, toads, and snakes. In fact, like the common hog it is omnivorous, feeds upon every thing that comes in its way, and is not particularly choice in the selection of its food.

Mons. DE LA BORDE (D'AZARA, Quad. du Paraguay, vol. i., p. 31,) relates that "they are easily shot; for instead of flying, they assemble together, and often give the hunters an opportunity of charging and discharging several times." He mentions "that he was one day employed, along with several others, in hunting these animals, accompanied by a single dog, which as soon as they appeared, took refuge between his master's legs. For greater safety he with the other hunters stood on a rock. They were nevertheless surrounded by the herd of hogs. A constant fire was kept up, but the creatures did not retire till a great number of them were slain." "These animals, however," he remarks, "fly after they have been several times hunted. The young, when taken in the chase, are easily tamed, but they will not associate or mix with the domestic species. In their natural state of liberty they frequent the marshes, and swim across large rivers. Their flesh," says he, "has an excellent taste, but is not so tender as that of the domestic hog; it resembles the flesh of the hare, and has neither lard nor grease."

The same author also states that "when pursued they take refuge in hollow trees, or in holes in the earth dug by the armadilloes. These holes they enter backwards and remain in as long as they can. But when highly irritated they instantly issue out in a body. In order to seize them as they come out, the hole is inclosed with branches of trees; one of the hunters, armed with a pitchfork, stands above the hole to fix them by the neck, while another forces them out, and kills them with a sabre."

"When there is but one in a hole, and the hunter has not leisure to seize it, he shuts up the entrance, and is sure of his game next day."

All authors agree in stating that the dorsal glands of either the male or female should be cut off instantly after the animal is killed, for their retention for only a single hour gives the meat so strong an odour that it can scarcely be eaten.

The only recent account we have thus far received, that contains original and authentic information about this singular wild hog, was furnished us by Mr. WILLIAM P. SMITH. He had been sent to this country by our ever kind friend, the Right Honourable the EARL OF DERBY, for the purpose of procuring living animals to enrich his collection at Knowsley, near Liverpool.

We engaged him also to obtain for us any rare species he could meet with in Texas, and to send descriptions of their habits, and any other information likely to be of interest to the readers of this work. Mr. SMITH went to Texas in 1841, and shortly afterwards sent us the following account of the Peccary. He says,—

"The Mexican hogs previous to the overflowing of the bottom lands in 1833, struck terror into the hearts of the settlers in their vicinity, oftentimes pursuing the planter whilst hunting or in search of the lost track of his wandering cattle—at which time they frequently killed his dogs, or even at times forced him to ascend a tree for safety, where he would sometimes be obliged to wait until the hogs got tired of dancing attendance at the foot of his place of security, or left him to go and feed. These animals appeared quite savage, and would, after coming to the tree in which the planter had ensconced himself, snap their teeth and run about and then lie down at the root of the tree of wait for their enemy to come down. At this early period of the settlement of Texas, (this refers to 1833,) they used to hunt this animal in company. From five to fifteen planters together, and occasionally a larger number of hunters, would join in the pursuit of these ravagers of their corn-fields, in order to diminish their number and prevent their farther depredations, as at times they would nearly destroy a farmer's crop. Since this time, however, their number has greatly decreased, and it is now a difficult matter to find them."

"On some parts of the Brazos they still exist, and in others are quite abundant."

Mr. SMITH further says, "The two I send you are the only ones I have heard of since my arrival in this country. I happened with the assistance of a person, to find out their lair, which is always in some hollow tree, although they have many sleeping places. Being late in the day I was determined not to disturb them until a more favourable time would present itself, as I was anxious, if possible, to procure them alive. Some time passed, and everything being ready, the dogs soon compelled them to make for home, when they having entered, we secured the entrance of their hole, and cut a large opening up the body of the tree, a few feet above them, from which "point of vantage" we were enabled easily to drop a noose round their necks, which we tightened until we thought they were nearly suffocated; we then drew them out, tied their legs and feet securely, and fastened their mouths by binding their jaws together with cords, and then left them lying on the ground for a time. On our return we found that they had got over the effect of the 'experimental hanging' they had gone through. We put them across a horse, and in trying to get loose they so tightened the ropes and entangled them about their necks, that they died before we observed this on our way home with them. This is the usual mode of taking these animals alive, although some are caught in pits. They have a large musk-bag upon the back, from which a very disagreeable odour is emitted whilst the animal is excited; but this is not observable after they are killed. The flesh of the female is good at some seasons of the year, but that of the male is strong, coarse and disagreeable at all times. Their principal food consists of nuts of every description (mast) during winter; but in summer they feed on succulent plants, with which the bottom lands in the Brazos abound. The male measured forty inches from the tip of its nose to that of its tail; the female is shorter by two inches. The eyes are very dark hazel colour."

"As soon as they get within their den, one of them, probably the oldest male, stands sentinel at the entrance. Should the hunter kill it, another immediately takes its place, and so in succession until all are killed. This animal, which in Texas is always called the wild hog, is considered the bravest animal of these forests, for it dreads neither man nor beast."

The Collared Peccary is easily domesticated, and breeds readily in confinement. We saw a pair on board of a ship that arrived in Charleston from South America, the female of which had produced two young whilst on the passage; they were then several weeks old, and seemed to be in a thriving condition.

Mons. M. L. E. MOREAU SAINT MERY, the translator of the work of D'AZARA, from the Spanish into the French language, states that in 1787 he saw at the residence of the Governor General LA LUZERNE, a tame Collard Peccary, which he had procured from Carthagena, with the intention of multiplying the species in San Domingo, (Note du Traducteur D'AZARA, tom. i., p. 42.) We observed at the Zoological Gardens in London, young Peccaries that had been born in the menagerie. This animal, however, is less prolific than the common domesticated hog, and its odorous glands being moreover offensive, the extensive domestication of it would not be attended with any profit to the agriculturist.

We have frequently seen the Collard Peccary in confinement. One that is at present (1846) in a menagerie in Charleston, is exceedingly gentle, taking its food from the hand, and allowing itself to be caressed even by strangers. It lies down in the manner of a pig, and next to giving it food, the greatest favour you can bestow on it is to scratch it either with the hand or a stick. It however is easily irritated. We noticed that it has a particular antipathy to the dog, and when approached by that animal immediately places itself in a defensive attitude, raising its bristles, showing its tusks, stamping its feet, and uttering a sharp cry which might be heard at the distance of seventy yards; when in a good humour, however, it occasionally utters a low grunt like a pig. It seems to suffer much from cold, and is always most lively and playful on warm days. It appears to prefer Indian-corn, potatoes, bread and fruits, but like the domestic hog evinces no unwillingness to take any kind of food that is presented to it. We remarked, however, that it is decidedly less carnivorous than the common hog.

It is stated by authors that this species produces but once a year, and brings forth only two at a litter.

Geographical Distribution.

The Collard Peccary has a most extensive geographical range. It was seen by NUTTAL at the Red River in Arkansas, north latitude 31°. Our specimens were obtained in Texas. It exists in all the lower portions of Mexico and Yucatan, and is found every where within the tropics. It is said by D'AZARA to be abundant at Paraguay, south latitude 37°, thus spreading itself through an extent of sixty-eight degrees of latitude.

General Remarks.

This species has been noticed by all the early travellers in South America and Mexico. They however almost invariably confounded the habits of two species. D'AZARA pointed out the distinctive marks which separate these species. They differ so much from each other that they ought never to have been mistaken. LINNÆUS applied the name *Sus tajacu*, but as it is impossible to ascertain which species he had in view we cannot use his name for either. RAY, ERXLEBEN, and SCHREBER applied the same name, and committd the same error. BRISSON gave the name *Aper Americanus*, and KLEIN that of *Porcus muschiferus* in the same manner, without discriminating the species. Baron CUVIER established the genus DYCOTYLES, and F. CUVIER applied the specific name of *torquatus*. BUFFON, who had heard from M. DE LA BORDE that there were two distinct species in Cayenne, considered them as mere varieties produced by age, but gave as he supposed a figure of each; his figures, however, which are of no value, both refer to the present species, and bear no resemblance to the white-lipped Peccary, (*D. labiatus.*)

It is somewhat strange that GRIFFITH, in his "Animal Kingdom," which he states was arranged by Baron CUVIER, should have completely misunderstood D'AZARA, (Histoire Naturelle, tom. i., p. 31,) and reversed the habits of the two species, (CUVIER, Animal Kingdom, by GRIFFITH, vol. iii., p. 411,) giving D'AZARA as authority for applying the habits of the present species, Tajassu, (*Dycotyles torquatus*,) to those of his Tagnicati, (*D. labiatus*,) giving at the same time a pretty good figure of the latter. It may however be easily seen that the whole object of D'AZARA's article on these species was to correct the very error into which GRIFFITH has fallen.

Lepus Glacialis.—Leach.

Polar Hare.

Plate xxxii.—Male. In summer pelage. Natural size.

L. æstate dilute cinereus, hyeme niveus, pilis apice ad radicem albis; aurium apicibus nigris; vulpes magnitudine.

Characters.

As large as a fox; colour, in summer, light gray above; in winter, white, the hairs at that season being white from the roots. Tips of ears, black.

Synonymes.

WHITE HARES, Discoveries and Settlements of the English in America, from the reign of Henry II. to the close of that of Queen Elizabeth, quoted from Pinkerton's Voyages, vol. xii., p. 276.
ALPINE HARE, Philosophical Transactions, London, vol. lxvi., p. 375, An. 1777.
LEPUS TIMIDUS, Fabri., Fauna Grœnlandica, p. 25.
VARYING HARE, Pennant, Arc. Zool., vol. i., p. 94.
WHITE HARE, Hearne's Journey, p. 382.
    "   "   Cartwright's Journal, vol. ii., p. 75.
LEPUS GLACIALIS, Leach, Zool. Miscellany, 1814.
    "   "   Ross's Voyage.
    "   "   Captain Sabine's Suppl. Parry's 1st Voyage, p. 188.
    "   "   Franklin's Journal, p. 664.
    "   "   Richardson, Appendix to Parry's 2d Voyage, p. 321.
POLAR HARE, Harlan, Fauna, p. 194.
    "   "   Godman, Nat. Hist., vol. ii., p. 162.
LEPUS GLACIALIS, Richardson, Fauna Boreali Americana, p. 221.
    "   "   Bachman, Acad. Nat. Sciences, Phila., vol. vii., part 2.

Description.

This fine species is considerably larger than the English hare, (*L. timidus.*) Head, larger and longer than that of the European hare; forehead, more arched; body, long; nose, blunt; eyes, large; ears, long; whiskers, composed of a few stiff long hairs; legs, long; soles of feet, broad, thickly covered with hair concealing the nails, which are long, moderately broad, and somewhat arched. Tail, of moderate length, woolly at the roots, intermixed with longer hairs. The fur on the back is remarkably close and fine; that on the under surface is longer, and not quite so close.

Colour.

In winter, the Polar Hare is entirely white on every part of the body except the tips of the ears; the hairs are of the same colour to the roots. The ears are tipped with hairs of a brownish-black colour. In its summer dress, this species is of a grayish-brown colour on the whole of the head extending to the ears; ears, black, bordered with white on their outer margins; under parts of the neck, and the breast, dark bluish-gray; the whole of the back, light brownish-gray. The fur under the long hairs of the back is soft and woolly, and of a grayish-ash; the hairs interspersed among the fur are dark blue near the roots, then black, tipped with grayish-fawn colour; a few black and white hairs are interspersed throughout. The wool on the under surface is bluish-white, interspersed with long hairs of a slate colour; the hairs forming the whiskers are white and black, the former predominating. The inner sides of the forelegs, thighs, and under surface of the tail, pure white, the hairs on the soles are yellowish-brown; nails, nearly black. According to RICHARDSON, "the irides are of a honey-yellow colour." The skin of this species appears to be nearly as tender as that of the Northern hare.

Dimensions.

Specimen, obtained at Labrador.

Length of head and body	26	inches.
" from point of nose to ear	4½	do.
" of ear, measured posteriorly	4¾	do.
" tail (vertebræ)	1½	do.
" tail, including fur	3½	do.
" whiskers	3	do.
" from wrist-joint to point of middle claw	3¾	do.
" " heel to middle claw	6½	do.

Weight, from 7 to 11 lbs.

These measurements were taken from the specimen after it had been stuffed. We are under the impression that it was a little longer in its recent state.

Habits.

It is to the cold and inhospitable regions of the North, the rugged valleys of Labrador, and the wild mountain-sides of that desolate land, or to the yet wilder and more sterile countries that extend from thence toward the west, that we must resort, to find the large and beautiful Hare we have now to describe; and if we advance even to the highest latitude man has ever reached, we shall still find the Polar Hare, though the mercury fall below zero, and huge snow drifts impede our progress through the trackless waste.

Both Indians and trappers are occasionally relieved from almost certain starvation by the existence of this Hare, which is found throughout the whole range of country extending from the Eastern to the Western shores of Northern America, and includes nearly thirty-five degrees of latitude, from the extreme North to Newfoundland.

In various parts of this thinly inhabited and unproductive region, the Polar Hare, perhaps the finest of all the American hares, takes up its residence. It is covered in the long dark winter with a coat of warm fur, so dense, that it cannot be penetrated by the rain and is an effectual protection from the intense cold of the rigorous climate.

Its changes of colour help to conceal it from the observation of its enemies; in summer it is nearly of the colour of the earth and the surrounding rocks, and in winter it assumes a snow-white coat. The changes it thus undergoes, correspond with the shortness of the summers and the length of the Arctic winters. In the New England States the *Northern* hare continues white for above five months, that being the usual duration of the winters there; but in the Arctic regions, where the summer lasts for about three months only, whilst the earth during the remainder of the year is covered with snow, were the Polar Hare not to become white till November, (the time when the Northern hare changes,) it would for two months be exposed to the keen eyes of its greatest destroyers, the golden eagle and the snowy owl, as its dark fur would be conspicuous on the snow; or were it to become brown in April, it would wear its summer dress long before the earth had thrown off its mantle of white, or a single bud had peeped through the snow.

The eye of the Polar Hare is adapted to the twilight that reigns during a considerable part of the year within the Arctic circle; in summer it avoids the glare of the almost continual day-light, seeking the shade of the little thickets of dwarfish trees that are scattered over the barren grounds, the woods that skirt the streams, or the shelter of some overhanging rock.

In addition to the circumstance that the eye of this Hare is well fitted for seeing with a very moderate light, it may be remarked that in winter the frequent and long continued luminous appearance of the heavens caused by the aurora borealis, together with the brightness of the unsullied snow, afford a sufficient degree of light for it to proceed with its customary occupations.

During the summer this species is found on the borders of thickets, or in stony or rocky places. In winter it is ofter seen in the barren and open country, where only a few stunted shrubs and clumps of spruce fir, (*Abies rubra*,) afford it shelter, differing in this habit from the Northern hare, which confines itself to thick woods throughout the year, avoiding cleared fields and open ground.

Captain Ross says of the Polar Hare, "There is scarcely a spot in the Arctic regions, the most desolate and sterile that can be conceived, where this animal is not to be found, and that too, throughout the winter; nor does it seek to shelter itself from the inclemency of the weather by burrowing in the snow, but is found generally sitting solitarily under the lee of a large stone, where the snow drift as it passes along, seems in some measure to afford a protection from the bitterness of the blast that impels it, by collecting around and half burying the animal beneath it."

The food of this species varies with the season. HEARNE tells us that "in winter it feeds on long rye-grass and the tops of dwarf willows, but in summer it eats berries and different sorts of small herbage."

According to RICHARDSON, "it seeks the sides of the hills, where the wind prevents the snow from lodging deeply, and where even in the winter it can procure the berries of the Alpine arbutus, the bark of some dwarf willows, (*Salix*,) or the evergreen leaves of the Labrador tea-plant," (*Ledum latifolium*.) Captain LYON, in his private journal has noted that on the barren coast of Winter Island, the Hares went out on the ice to the ships, to feed on the tea-leaves thrown overboard by the sailors."

The Polar Hare is not a very shy or timid animal, but has on being approached much the same habits as the Northern hare. "It merely runs to a little distance, (says RICHARDSON,) and sits down, repeating this man-œuvre as often as its pursuer comes nearly within gun-shot, until it is thoroughly scared by his perseverance, when it makes off. It is not difficult to get within bow-shot of it by walking round it and gradually contracting the circle—a method much practised by the Indians." HEARNE had previously made the same observations; he says also, "the middle of the day, if it be clear weather, is the best time to kill them in this manner, for before and after noon the sun's altitude being so small, makes a man's shadow so long on the snow as to frighten the Hare before he can approach near enough to kill it. The same may be said of deer when on open plains, which are frequently more frightened at the long shadow than at the man himself."

All travellers concur in stating the flesh of this animal to be of a finer flavour than that of any of our other hares. We obtained one while at St. George's Bay, in Newfoundland, and all our party made a meal of it; we pronounced it delicious food.

A lady residing at that place informed us that she had domesticated the Polar Hare, and had reared some of them for food. She said that the flesh was

fine-flavoured, and the animals easily tamed, and that she had only been induced to discontinue keeping them in consequence of their becoming troublesome, and destructive in her garden.

The Polar Hare is stated by RICHARDSON, on the authority of Indian hunters, to bring forth once in a year, and only three young at a litter: That, owing to the short summer of the Arctic regions, it does not produce more than once annually, is no doubt true, but the number of young brought forth at a time, we are inclined to believe was nor correctly given by the Indian hunters.

CARTWRIGHT (see Jour., vol. ii., p. 76) killed a female of this species at Labrador on the 11th June, from which he took five young.

Capt. Ross says, "a female killed by one of our party at Sheriff Harbour on the 7th of June, had four young in utero, perfectly mature, $5\frac{1}{2}$ inches long, and of a dark gray colour. In one shot at Igloolik, on the 2d June, six young were found, not quite so far advanced."

An intelligent farmer who had resided some years in Newfoundland, informed us that he had on several occasions counted the young of the Polar Hare, and had never found less than five, and often had taken seven from one nest. He considered the average number of young to each litter as six. FABRICIUS, alluding to the habits of this species as existing in Greenland, says, "They pair in April, and in the month of June produce eight young at a birth."

Some idea may be formed of the very short period this species continues in its summer colours, from the following remarks of different observers. In BEACHY'S Narrative, (p. 447,) is the following notice:—"*May 5th.* The party killed a white Hare, it was getting its summer coat."CARTWRIGHT killed one on the 11th June, and remarks that it was yet white. We obtained a specimen on the 15th August, 1833, and ascertained that the change from summer to winter colours had already commenced. There was a large spot, nearly a hand's breadth, of pure white on the back, extending nearly to the insertion of the tail; three or four white spots about an inch in diameter were also found on the sides.

Captain Ross states—"One taken by us on the 28th of June, a few days after its birth, soon became sufficiently tame to eat from our hands, and was allowed to run loose about the cabin. During the summer we fed it on such plants as the country produced, and stored up a quantity of grass and astragali for its winter consumption; but it preferred to share with us whatever our table could afford, and would enjoy peas-soup, plum-pudding, bread, barley-soup, sugar, rice, and even cheese, with us. It could not endure to be caressed, but was exceedingly fond of company, and would sit for hours listening to a conversation, which was no sooner ended than he would retire to his cabin; he was a continual source of amusement by his sagacity and playful-ness." *** "The fur of the Polar Hare is so exceedingly soft, that an Esquimaux woman spun some of its wool into a thread, and knitted several pairs of gloves, one pair of which, beautifully white, came into my possession. It resembled the Angola wool, but was still softer."

The specimen we procured in Newfoundland weighed seven and a half pounds; it was obtained on the 15th August, in the midst of summer, when all hares are lean. It was at a period of the year also, when in that island they are incessantly harassed by the troublesome moose-fly. Deer, hares, &c., and even men, suffer very much in consequence of their attacks. The Indians we saw there, although tempted by a high reward, refused to go in search of these Hares, from a dread of this persecuting insect, and our party, who had gone on a moose-hunt, were obliged by the inflammation succeeding the bites inflicted on them to return on the same day they started.

Dr. RICHARDSON sets down the weight of a full grown Polar Hare as varying according to its condition from seven to fourteen pounds.

In BEACHY'S Narrative there is an account of a Polar Hare, killed on the 15th May, that weighed nearly twelve pounds; and HEARNE (see Journey, p. 383) says that, "in good condition many of them weigh from fourteen to fifteen pounds."

Geographical Distribution.

This species occupies a wide range in the northern portions of our continent; it extends from the shores of Baffin's Bay across the continent to Behring's Straits. It has been seen as far north as the North Georgian Islands, in latitude 75°. On the western portion of the American continent it has not been found further to the south than latitude 64°, but on the eastern coast it reaches much farther south. RICHARDSON has stated that its most southerly known habitat is in the neighbourhood of Fort Churchill, on Hudson's Bay, which is in the 58th parallel of latitude, but remarks, that it may perhaps extend farther to the southward on the elevated ridges of the Rocky Mountains, or on the Eastern coast, in Labrador. We have ascertained that on the eastern coast of

Plate XXVII.

Drawn from Nature by J J Audubon. F.R.S.F.L.S.

Drawn on stone by R. Trembly

Polar Hare.

Printed & Col.ᵈ by J T Bowen. Philadᵃ

America it exists at least ten and a half degrees south of the latitude assigned to it above; as we procured our specimen at Newfoundland, in latitude $47\frac{1}{2}°$, where it was quite common; and we have been informed that it also exists in the northern portions of Nova Scotia. To the north-east, it has found its way across Baffin's Bay, and exists in Greenland.

General Remarks.

Although the Polar Hare was noticed at a very early period in the history of America, until recently it was considered identical with other species that have since been ascertained to differ from it. The writer of the History of Discoveries and Settlements of the English in America, from the reign of Henry VII. to the close of that of Queen Elizabeth, speaking of the animals at Churchill and Hudson's Bay (see PINKERTON, Voy., vol. vii., p. 276) says "the hares grow white in winter, and recover their colour in spring; they have very large ears which are always black; their skins in winter are very pretty, of fine long hair which does not fall; so that they make very fine muffs."

There can be no doubt that the Polar Hare was here alluded to. PENNANT remarked that its size was greater than that of the varying hare, with which it had so long been considered identical. HEARNE, who observed it on our continent, and FABRICIUS, who obtained it in Greenland, regarded it as the varying hare. LEACH, in 1814 (Zoological Miscellany) characterized it as a new species. It was subsequently noticed by SABINE, FRANKLIN, and RICHARDSON. As an evidence of how little was known of our American hares until very recently, we would refer to the fact that in the last *general* work on American quadrupeds, published by an American author, published by Dr. GODMAN in 1826, only two hares were admitted into our Fauna—*Lepus Americanus*, by which he referred to our gray rabbit, and *Lepus glacialis*, which together with *Lepus Virginianus* of HARLAN, he felt disposed to refer to *Lepus variabilis* of Europe, leaving us but one native species, and even to that applying a wrong name. We hope in this work to be able to present our readers with at least fourteen species of true hares, that exist in America north of the tropic of Cancer, all peculiar to this country.

In 1829 Dr. RICHARDSON gave an excellent description, (Fauna Boreali Americana, p. 221,) removing every doubt as to *Lepus glacialis* being a true species. In 1838, having obtained a specimen in summer pelage, the only one that as far as we have learned existed in any collection in our country, we were induced to describe it, (Journal Acad. Nat. Sciences, Phildadelphia, vol. vii., p. 285.)

Genus Putorius.—Cuv.

Dental Formula.

Incisive $\frac{6}{6}$; *Canine* $\frac{1-1}{1-1}$; *Molar* $\frac{4-4}{5-5}$ = 34.

There are two false molars above, and three below; the great carnivorous tooth below, without an internal tubercle; the tuberculous tooth in the upper jaw, very long.

Head, small and oval; muzzle, short and blunt; ears, short and round; body, long and vermiform; neck, long; legs, short; five toes on each foot, armed with sharp crooked claws; tail, long and cylindrical. Animals of this genus emit a fetid odour, and are nocturnal in habit; they are separated from the martens in consequence of having one tooth less on each side of the upper jaw; their muzzle is also shorter and thicker than that of the marten. The species are generally small in size, and seldom climb trees like the true martens.

There are about fifteen well determined species of this genus, six of which belong to America, and the remainder to the Eastern continent.

The generic name *putorius* is derived from the Latin word *putor*—a fetid smell.

Putorius Vison.—Linn.

Mink.

Plate xxxiii. Male and Female. Natural size.

P. fulvus, mente albo; auribus curtis; pedibus semi-palmatis; cauda corporis dimidiam longa. Mustela marte minor.

Characters.

Less than the pine marten; general colour, brown; chin white; ears short; feet semi-palmate; tail, half the length of the body.

Synonymes.

THE MINK, Smith's Virginia, 1624. Quoted from Pinkerton's Voyages, vol. xiii., p. 31.
OTAY, Sagard Theodat, Hist. du Can., p. 749, A.D. 1636.
FOUTEREAU, La Hontan, Voy. 1., p. 81, A.D. 1703.
MINK, Kalm's Travels, Pinkerton's Voy., vol. xiii., p. 522.
LE VISON, Buffon, xiii., p. 308, t. 43.
MUSTELA VISON, Linn., Gmel., i., p. 94.
MINX, Lawson's Carolina, p. 121.
MUSTELA LUTREOLA, Forster, Phil. Trans., lxii., p. 371.
MINX OTTER, Pennant, Arct. Zool., i., p. 87.
VISON WEASEL, Ibid., i., p. 78.
JACKASH, Hearne's Journey, p. 376.
MUSTELA VISON, CUV., Règne Anim., vol. i., p. 150, t. 1, fig. 2.
MUSTELA LUTREOLA, Sabine, Frank Journ., p. 652.

MUSTELA VISON and M. LUTREOCEPHALA, Harlan, Fauna, p. 63, 65.
MINK, Godman, Nat. Hist., vol. i., p. 206.
PUTORIUS VISON, Dekay, Nat. Hist. New-York, p. 37, fig. 3, a. b. skull.

Description.

Body, long and slender; head, small and depressed; nose, short, flat, and thick; eyes, small, and placed far forward; whiskers, few, and reaching to the ears; ears, broad, short, rounded, and covered with hair; neck, very long; legs, short and stout. The toes are connected by short hairy webs, and may be described as semi-palmated. There are short hairs on the webs above and below. Claws, very slightly arched, and acute. On the fore-feet, the third and fourth toes, counting from the inner side, are about of equal length; the second a line shorter, the fifth a little less, and the first, shortest. On the hind-feet, the third and fourth toes are equal, the second and fifth shorter and nearly equal, and the first very short. There are callosities on the toes resembling in miniature those on the toes of the Bay lynx. The feet and palms are covered with hair even to the extremity of the nails; tail, round, and thick at the roots, tapering gradually to the end; the longer hairs of the tail are inclined to stand out horizontally, giving it a bushy appearance. There are two brown-coloured glands situated on each side of the under surface of the tail, which have a small cavity lined by a thin white wrinkled membrane; they contain a strong musky fluid, the smell of which is rather disagreeable. Mammæ, six, ventral.

The coat is composed of two kinds of hair: a very downy fur beneath, with hairs of a longer and stronger kind interspersed. The hairs on the upper surface are longer than those on the lower. They are smooth and glossy both on the body and the tail, and to a considerable extent conceal the downy fur beneath.

Colour.

Under fur light brownish-yellow; the longer hairs, and the surface of the fur, are of a uniform brown or tawny colour, except the ears which are a little lighter, and the sides of the face, under surface, tail, and posterior part of the back, which are a little darker than the general tint, lower jaw white. In most specimens there is a white spot under the throat, and in all that we have seen, a longitudinal white stripe on the breast between the fore-legs, much wider in some specimens than in others; tail, darkest toward the end; for an inch or two from the tip it is often very dark-brown or black.

There are some striking and permanent varieties of the Mink, both in size and colour. We possess a specimen from Canada, which is considerably darker than those of the United States. Its tail is an inch longer than usual, and the white markings on its throat and chest are much narrower and less conspicuous than in most individuals of this species. In other respects we can see no difference.

In the Southern salt-water marshes this species is considerably larger in size, the white markings on the chin and under surface are broader, the hair is much coarser, the colour lighter, and the tail less bushy, than in Northern specimens. Those, however, which we obtained on the head waters of the Edisto river are as dark as specimens from Pennsylvania and New-York.

Along the mountain streams of the Northern and Middle States, we have

No. 7.

Plate XXXIII.

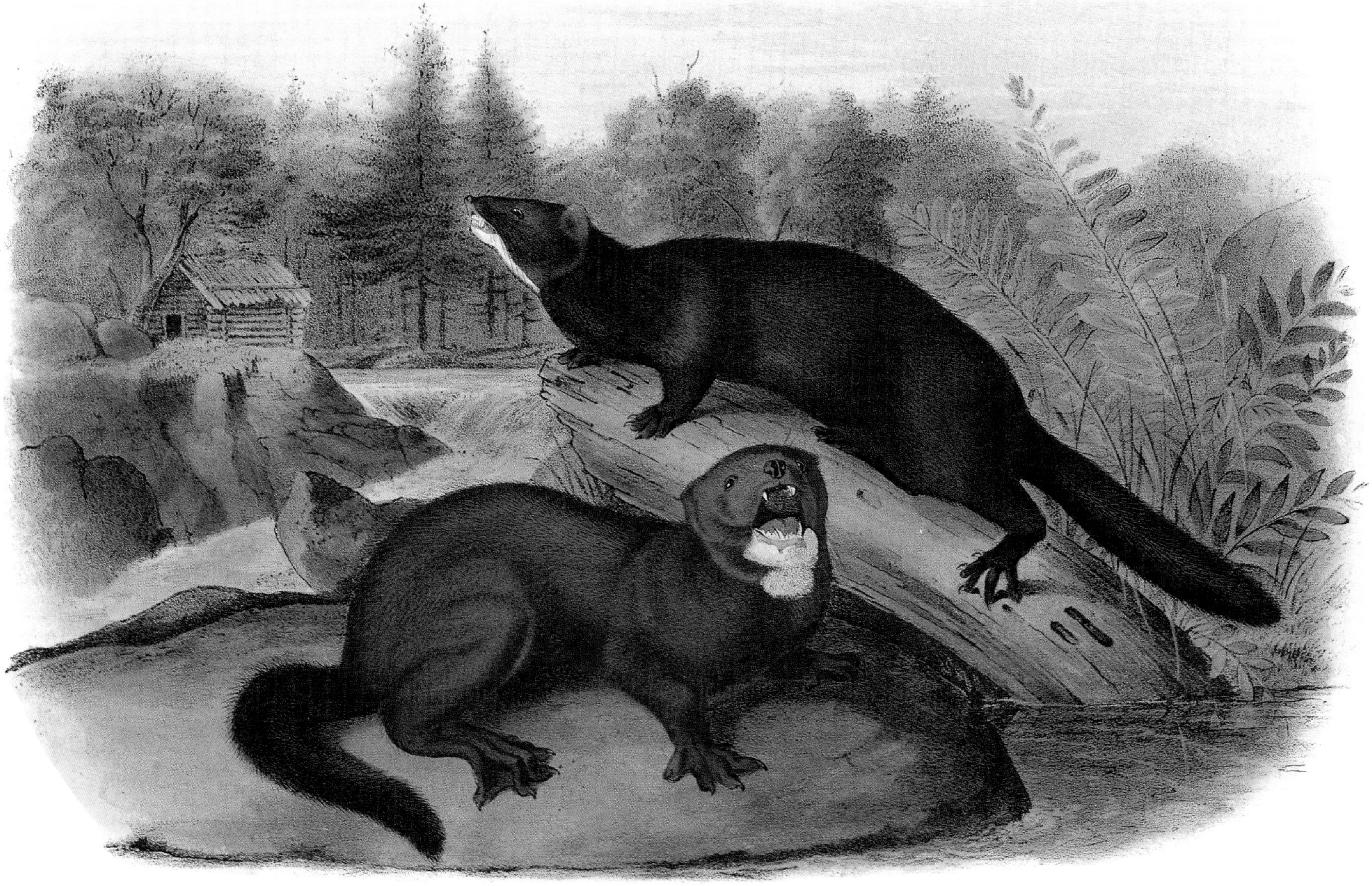

Drawn on stone by R. Trembly

Mink.

Male & Female

Drawn from Nature by J. J. Audubon, F.R.S. F.L.S.

Printed & Cold. by J. T. Bowen, Philada.

often met with Minks which were considerably smaller and darker than those found on large water-courses or around mill-ponds. The size, however, (and in this there was no uniformity,) and the colour, constituted the only differences between the small and the large ones, that we could perceive, and there were no specific characters that would warrant us in designating the former as a new species.

The upper figure on the plate represents this variety.

Dimensions.

Length of head and body . . . . 13 inches.
" tail (vertebræ) . . . . 7 do.
" tail, to end of fur . . . . 8 do.

Another specimen.
Length from point of nose to root of tail . . . . 14 do.
Length of tail (vertebræ) . . . . 7½ do.
" tail, to end of hair . . . . 8 do.

A small specimen, of a black colour, from the Catskill mountains.
Length of head and body . . . . 11 inches.
" tail (vertebræ) . . . . 6 do.
" tail, to end of hair . . . . 7 do.

Habits.

Next to the ermine, the Mink is the most active and destructive little depredator that prowls around the farm-yard, or the farmer's duck-pond; where the presence of one or two of these animals will soon be made known by the sudden disappearance of sundry young ducks and chickens. The vigilant farmer may perhaps see a fine fowl moving in a singular and most involuntary manner, in the clutches of a Mink, towards a fissure in a rock or a hole in some pile of stones, in the gray of the morning, and should he rush to the spot to ascertain the fate of the unfortunate bird, he will see it suddenly twitched into a hole too deep for him to fathom and wish he had carried with him his double-barreled gun, to have ended at once the life of the voracious destroyer of his carefully tended poultry. Our friend, the farmer, is not, however, disposed to allow the Mink to carry on the sport long, and therefore straitway repairs to the house for his gun, and if it be loaded and ready for use, (as it always should be in every well-regulated farm-house,) he speedily returns with it to watch for the re-appearance of the Mink and shoot him ere he has the opportunity to depopulate his poultry-yard. The farmer now takes a stand facing the retreat into which the Mink has carried his property, and waits patiently until it may please him to show his head again. This, however, the cunning rogue will not always accommodate him by doing, and he may lose much time to no purpose. Let us introduce you to a scene on our own little place near New-York.

There is a small brook, fed by several springs of pure water, which we have caused to be stopped by a stone dam to make a pond for ducks in the summer and ice in the winter; above the pond is a rough bank of stones through which the water filters into the pond. There is a little space near this where the sand and gravel have formed a diminutive beach. The ducks descending to the water are compelled to pass near this stony bank. Here a Mink had fixed his quarters with certainly a degree of judgment and audacity worthy of high praise, for no settlement could promise to be more to his mind. At early dawn the crowing of several fine cocks, the cackling of many hens and chickens, and the paddling, splashing, and quacking of a hundred old and young ducks would please his ears; and by stealing to the edge of the bank of stones, with his body nearly concealed between two large pieces of broken granite, he could look around and see the unsuspecting ducks within a yard or two of his lurking place. When thus on the look out, dodging his head backward and forward he waits until one of them has approached close to him, and then with a rush seizes the bird by the neck, and in a moment disappears with it between the rocks. He has not, however, escaped unobserved, and like other rogues deserves to be punished for having taken what did not belong to him. We draw near the spot, gun in hand, and after waiting some time in vain for the appearance of the Mink, we cause some young ducks to be gently driven down to the pond—diving for worms or food of various kinds while danger so imminent is near them—intent only on the objects they are pursuing, they turn not a glance toward the dark crevice where we can now see the bright eyes of the Mink as he lies concealed. The unsuspecting birds remind us of some of the young folks in that large pond we call the world, where, alas! they may be in greater danger than our poor ducks or chickens. Now we see a fine hen descend to the water; cautiously she steps on the sandy margin and dipping her bill in the clear stream, sips a few drops and raises her head as if in gratitude to the Giver of all good; she continues sipping and advancing gradually; she has now approached the fatal rocks, when with a sudden rush the Mink has seized her; ere he can regain his hole, however, our gun's sharp crack is heard and the marauder lies dead before us.

We acknowledge that we have little inclination to say anything in defence of the Mink. We must admit, however, that although he is a cunning and destructive rogue, his next door neighbour, the ermine or common weasel, goes infinitely beyond him in his mischievous propensities. Whilst the Mink is satisfied with destroying one or two fowls at a time, on which he makes a hearty meal; the weasel, in the very spirit of wanton destructiveness, sometimes in a single night puts to death every tenant of the poultry-house!

Whilst residing at Henderson, on the banks of the Ohio river, we observed that Minks were quite abundant, and often saw them carrying off rats which they caught like the weasel or ferret, and conveyed away in their mouths, holding them by the neck in the manner of a cat.

Along the trout streams of our Eastern and Northern States, the Mink has been known to steal fish that having been caught by some angler, had been left tied together with a string while the fisherman proceeded farther in quest of more. An angler informed us that he had lost in this way thirty or forty fine trout, which a Mink dragged off the bank into the stream and devoured, and we have been told that by looking carefully after them, the Minks could be seen watching the fisherman and in readiness to take his fish, should he leave it at any distance behind him. Mr. HUTSON of Halifax informed us that he had a salmon weighing four pounds carried off by one of them.

We have observed that the Mink is a tolerably expert fisher. On one occasion, whilst seated near a trout-brook in the northern part of the State of New York, we heard a sudden splashing in the stream and saw a large trout gliding through the shallow water and making for some long overhanging roots on the side of the bank. A Mink was in close pursuit, and dived after it; in a moment afterwards it re-appeared with the fish in its mouth. By a sudden rush we induced it to drop the trout, which was upwards of a foot in length.

We are disposed to believe, however, that fishes are not the principal food on which the Mink subsists. We have sometimes seen it feeding on frogs and cray-fish. In the Northern States we have often observed it with a WILSON's meadow-mouse in its mouth, and in Carolina the very common cotton-rat furnishes no small proportion of its food. We have frequently remarked it coursing along the edges of the marshes, and found that it was in search of this rat, which frequents such localities, and we discovered that it was not an unsuccessful mouser. We once saw a Mink issuing from a hole in the earth, dragging by the neck a large Florida rat.

This species has a good nose, and is able to pursue its prey like a hound following a deer. A friend of ours informed us that once while standing on the border of a swamp near the Ashley river, he perceived a marsh-hare dashing by him; a moment after came a Mink with its nose near the ground, following the frightened animal, apparently by the scent, through the marsh.

In the vicinity of Charleston, South Carolina, a hen-house was one season robbed several nights in succession, the owner counting a chicken less every morning. No idea could be formed, however, of the manner in which it was carried off. The building was erected on posts, and was securely locked, in addition to which precaution a very vigilant watch-dog was now put on guard, being chained underneath the chicken-house. Still, the number of fowls in it diminished nightly, and one was as before missed every morning.

We were at last requested to endeavour to ascertain the cause of the vexatious and singular abstraction of our friends' chickens, and on a careful examination we discovered a small hole in a corner of the building, leading to a cavity between the weather-boarding and the sill. On gently forcing outward a plank, we perceived the bright eyes of a Mink peering at us and shining like a pair of diamonds. He had long been thus snugly ensconced, and was enabled to supply himself with a regular feast without leaving the house, as the hole opened toward the inside on the floor. Summary justice was inflicted of course on the concealed robber, and peace and security once more were restored in the precincts of the chicken-yard.

This species is very numerous in the salt-marshes of the Southern States, where it subsists principally on the marsh-hen, (*Rallus crepitans,*) the sea-side finch, (*Ammodramus maritimus,*) and the sharp-tailed finch, (*A. caudacutus,*) which, during a considerable portion of the year, feed on the minute shell-fish and aquatic insects left on the mud and oysterbanks, on the subsiding of the waters. We have seen a Mink winding stealthily through the tall marsh-grass, pausing occasionally to take an observation, and sometimes lying for the space of a minute flat upon the mud: at length it draws its hind-feet far forwards under its body in the manner of a cat, its back is arched, its tail curled, and it makes a sudden spring. The screams of a captured marsh-hen succeed, and its upraised fluttering wing gives sufficient evidence that it is about to be transferred from its pleasant haunts in the marshes to the capacious maw of the hungry Mink.

It is at low tide that this animal usually captures the marsh-hen. We have often at high spring tide observed a dozen of those birds standing on a small field of floating sticks and matted grasses, gazing stupidly at a Mink seated not five feet from them. No attempt was made by the latter to capture the birds that were now within his reach. At first we supposed that he might have already been satiated with food and was disposed to leave the tempting marsh-hens till his appetite called for more; but we were after more mature reflection inclined to think that the high spring tides which occur, exposing the whole marsh to view and leaving no place of concealment, frighten the Mink as well as the marsh-hen; and as misery sometimes makes us familiar with strange associates, so the Mink and the marsh-hen like neighbour and brother hold on to their little floating islands till the waters subside, when each again follows the instincts of nature. An instance of a similar effect of fear on other animals was related to us by an old resident of Carolina: some forty years ago, during a tremendous flood in the Santee river, he saw two or three deer on a small mound not twenty feet in diameter, surrounded by a wide sea of waters, with a cougar seated in the midst of them; both parties, having seemingly entered into a truce at a time when their lives seemed equally in jeopardy, were apparently disposed peaceably to await the falling of the waters that surrounded them.

The Minks which resort to the Southern marshes, being there furnished with an abundant supply of food are always fat, and appear to us considerably larger than the same species in those localities where food is less abundant.

This species prefers taking up its residence on the borders of ponds and along the banks of small streams, rather than along large and broad rivers. It delights in frequenting the foot of rapids and waterfalls. When pursued it flies for shelter to the water, an element suited to its amphibious habits, or to some retreat beneath the banks of the stream. It runs tolerably well on high ground and we have found it on several occasions no easy matter to overtake it, and when overtaken, we have learned to our cost that it was rather a troublesome customer about our feet and legs, where its sharp canine teeth made some uncomfortable indentations; neither was its odour as pleasant as we could have desired. It is generally supposed that the Mink never resorts to a tree to avoid pursuit; we have, however, witnessed one instance to the contrary. In hunting for the ruffed-grouse, (*T. umbellus*,) we observed a little dog that accompanied us, barking at the stem of a young tree, and on looking up, perceived a Mink seated in the first fork, about twelve feet from the ground. Our friend, the late Dr. WRIGHT, of Troy, informed us that whilst he was walking on the border of a wood, near a stream, a small animal which he supposed to be a black squirrel, rushed from a tuft of grass, and ascended a tree. After gaining a seat on a projecting branch, it peeped down at the intruder on its haunts, when he shot it, and picking it up, ascertained that it was a Mink.

We think, however, that this animal is not often seen to ascend a tree, and these are the only instances of its doing so which are known to us.

This species is a good swimmer, and like the musk-rat dives at the flash of a gun; we have observed, however, that the percussion-cap now in general use is too quick for its motions, and that this invention bids fair greatly to lessen its numbers. When shot in the water the body of the Mink, as well as that of the otter, has so little buoyancy, and its bones are so heavy, that it almost invariably sinks.

The Mink, like the musk-rat and ermine, does not possess much cunning, and is easily captured in any kind of trap; it is taken in steel-traps and box-traps, but more generally in what are called dead-falls. It is attracted by any kind of flesh, but we have usually seen the traps baited with the head of a ruffed grouse, wild duck, chicken, jay, or other bird. The Mink is exceedingly tenacious of life, and we have found it still alive under a dead-fall, with a pole lying across its body pressed down by a weight by 150 lbs., beneath which it had been struggling for nearly twenty-four hours.

This species, as well as the skunk and the ermine, emits an offensive odour when provoked by men or dogs, and this habit is exercised likewise in a moderate degree whenever it is engaged in any severe struggle with an animal or bird on which it has seized. We were once attracted by the peculiar and well known plaintive cry of a hare, in a marsh on the side of one of our Southern rice-fields, and our olfactories were at the same time regaled with the strong fetid odour of the Mink; we found it in possession of a large marsh-hare, with which, from the appearance of the trampled grass and mud, it had been engaged in a fierce struggle for some time.

The latter end of February or the beginning of March, in the latitude of Albany, N. Y., is the rutting season of the Mink. At this period the ground is usually still covered with snow, but the male is notwithstanding very restless, and his tracks may every where be traced, along ponds, among the slabs around saw-mills, and along nearly every stream of water. He seems to keep on

foot all day as well as through the whole night. Having for several days in succession observed a number of Minks on the ice hurrying up and down a mill-pond, where we had not observed any during a whole winter, we took a position near a place which we had seen them pass, in order to procure some of them.

We shot six in the course of the morning, and ascertained that they were all large and old males. As we did not find a single female in a week, whilst we obtained a great number of males, we came to the conclusion that the females, during this period, remain in their burrows. About the latter end of April the young are produced. We saw six young dug from a hole in the bank of a Carolina rice-field; on another occasion we found five enclosed in a large nest situated in the marshes of Ashley river. In the State of New York, we saw five taken from a hollow log, and we are inclined to set down that as the average number of young this species brings forth at a time.

The Mink, when taken young, becomes very gentle and forms a strong attachment to those who fondle it in a state of domestication. RICHARDSON saw one in the "possession of a Canadian woman, that passed the day in her pocket, looking out occasionally when its attention was roused by any unusual noise." We had in our possession a pet of this kind for eighteen months; it regularly made a visit to an adjoining fish-pond both morning and evening, and returned to the house of its own accord, where it continued during the remainder of the day. It waged war against the Norway rats which had their domicile in the dam that formed the fish-pond, and it caught the frogs which had taken possession of its banks. We did not perceive that it captured many fish, and it never attacked the poultry. It was on good terms with the dogs and cats, and molested no one unless its tail or foot was accidentally trod upon, when it invariably revenged itself by snapping at the foot of the offender.

It was rather dull at mid-day, but very active and playful in the morning and evening and at night. It never emitted its disagreeable odour except when it had received a sudden and severe hurt. It was fond of squatting in the chimney-corner, and formed a particular attachment to an arm-chair in our study.

The skins of the Mink were formerly an article of commerce, and were used for making muffs, tippets, &c.; they sold for about fifty cents each. RICHARDSON states that at present they are only taken by the traders of the fur company to accommodate the Indians, and that they are afterwards burnt, as they will not repay the expense of carriage. The fur, however, although short, is even finer than that of the marten.

A short time since, we were kindly presented by CHARLES P. CHOUTEAU, Esq., with a Mink skin of a beautiful silver-gray colour, the fur of which is quite different from the ordinary coat of the animal. These beautiful skins are exceedingly rare, and six of them, when they are united, will make a muff, worth at least a hundred dollars. A skin, slightly approaching the fine quality and colour of the one just mentioned, exists in the Academy of Natural Sciences at Philadelphia, but it is brownish, and the fur is not very good.

Geographical Distribution.

The Mink is a constant resident of nearly every part of the continent of North America. RICHARDSON saw it as far north as latitude 66°, on the banks of the Mackenzie river, and supposed that it ranged to the mouth of that river in latitude 69°; it exists in Canada, and we have seen it in every State of the Union. We observed it on the Upper Missouri and on the Yellow Stone river; it is said to exist also to the West of the Rocky Mountains and along the shores of the Pacific ocean.

General Remarks.

This species appears, as far as we have been able to ascertain, to have been first noticed by Governor SMITH of Virginia, in 1624, and subsequently by SAGARD THEODAT and LA HONTAN. The latter calls it an amphibious sort of little pole-cat,—"Les fouteriaux, qui sont de petites fouines amphibies." KALM and LAWSON refer to it; the former stating that the English and the Swedes gave it the name of Mink, Moenk being the name applied to a closely allied species existing in Sweden.

The doubts respecting the identity of the American Mink (*P. vison*) and the *Mustela lutreola* of the north of Europe, have not as yet been satisfactorily solved. PENNANT in one place admits the American *vison* as a true species, and in another supposes the *M. lutreola* to exist on both continents. Baron CUVIER at one time regarded them as so distinct that he placed them under different genera; but subsequently in a note stated his opinion that they are both one species. Dr. GODMAN supposed that both the *Pekan* (*Mustela Canadensis*) and *vison* (*P. vison*) are nothing more than mere varieties of *Mustela lutreola*; in regard to the Pekan he was palpably in error. RICHARDSON considers them distinct species, although he does not seem to have had an opportunity of instituting a comparison. We have on two or three occasions compared specimens from both continents. The specimens, however, from either country differ so considerably among themselves that it is somewhat difficult without a larger number than can generally be brought together, to institute a satisfactory comparison.

The fact that both species exist far to the northward, and consequently approach each other toward the Arctic circle, presents an argument favourable to their identity. In their semi-palmated feet, as well as in their general form and habits, they resemble each other.

The following reasons, however, have induced us, after some hesitation, and not without a strong desire for farther opportunities of comparison, especially of the skulls, to regard the American *P. vison* as distinct from the *lutreola* of the north of Europe.

P. lutreola, in the few specimens we have examined, is smaller than *P. vison*, the body of the latter frequently exceeding eighteen inches, (we have a large specimen that measures twenty-one inches,) but we have never found any specimen of the *lutreola* exceeding thirteen inches from nose to root of tail, and have generally found that specimens, even when their teeth were considerably worn, thereby indicating that the animals were adults, measured less than twelve inches.

P. lutreola is considerably darker in colour, resembling in this respect the small black variety mentioned by us as existing along our mountain streams. The tail is less bushy, and might be termed sub-cylindrical. *P. lutreola* is, besides, more deficient in white markings on the under surface than the other species; the chin is generally, but not always, white; but there is seldom any white either on the throat or chest.

Sciurus Niger.—Linn.

Black Squirrel.

Plate xxxiv.—Male and Female. Natural size.

S. corpore S. migratorio longiore; vellere molli nitidoque, auribus, naso et omni corporis parte nigerrimis, cirris albis dispersis.

Characters.

A little larger than the Northern gray squirrel; fur, soft and glossy; ears, nose, and all the body, black; a few white tufts of hair interspersed.

Synonymes.

SCIURUS NIGER, Godman, Nat. Hist., vol. ii., p. 133.
"   "   Bachman, Proceedings Zool. Society, 1838, p. 96.
"   "   Dekay, Nat. Hist. of New York, part i., p. 60.

Description.

Head, a little shorter and more arched than that of the Northern gray squirrel, (in the latter species, however, it is often found that differences exist, in the shape of the head, in different individuals.) Incisors, compressed, strong, and of a deep orange colour anteriorly; ears, elliptical, and slightly rounded at the tip, thickly clothed with fur on both surfaces, the fur on the outer surface extending three lines beyond the margin; there are however no distinct tufts; whiskers, a little longer than the head; tail, long, not very distichous, thickly clothed with moderately coarse hair; the fur is softer than that of the Northern gray squirrel.

Colour.

The whole of the upper and lower surfaces, and the tail, glossy jet black; at the roots the hairs are a little lighter. Specimens procured in summer do not differ materially in colour from those obtained in winter, except that before the hairs drop out late in spring, they are not so intensely black. In all we have had an opportunity of examining, there are small tufts of white hairs irregularly disposed on the under surface, resembling those on the body of the mink. There are also a few scattered white hairs on the back and tail.

Dimensions.

	Inches.	Lines.
Length of head and body	13	0
" tail (vertebræ)	9	1
" tail, including fur	13	0
Palm, to end of middle fore-claw	1	7
Length of heel to the point of middle claw	2	7
" fur on the back	0	7
Breadth of tail with hair extended	5	0

Habits.

An opportunity was afforded us, many year since, of observing the habits of this species, in the northern part of the State of New York. A seat under the shadow of a rock near a stream of water, was for several successive summers our favourite resort for retirement and reading. In the immediate vicinity were several large trees, in which were a number of holes, from which at almost every hour of the day were seen issuing this species of Black Squirrel. There seemed to be a dozen of them; they were all of the same glossy black colour, and although the Northern gray squirrel and its black variety were not rare in that neighbourhood, during a period of five or six years we never discovered any other than the present species in that locality; and after the lapse of twenty years, a specimen (from which our description was in part drawn up,) was procured in that identical spot, and sent to us.

This species possesses all the sprightliness of the Northern gray squirrel, evidently preferring valleys and swamps to drier and more elevated situations. We observed that one of their favourite trees, to which they retreated on hearing the slightest noise, was a large white-pine (*Pinus strobus*) in the immediate vicinity. We were surprised at sometimes seeing a red squirrel, (*Sciurus Hudsonius*,) which had also given a preference to this tree, pursuing a Black Squirrel, threatening and scolding it vociferously, till the latter was obliged to make its retreat. When the Squirrels approached the stream, which ·ran within a few feet of our seat, they often stopped to drink, when, instead of lapping the water like the dog and cat, they protruded their mouths a considerable distance into the stream, and drank greedily; they would afterwards sit upright, supported by the tarsus, and with tail erect, busy themselves for a quarter of an hour in wiping their faces with their paws, the latter being also occasionally dipped in the water. Their barking and other habits did not seem to differ from those of the Northern gray squirrel.

Geographical Distribution.

Many of our specimens of the Black Squirrel, were procured through the kindness of friends, in the counties of Rensselaer and Queens, New York. We have seen this species on the borders of Lake Champlain, at Ogdensburg, and on the eastern shores of Lake Erie; also near Niagara, on the Canada side. The individual described by Dr. RICHARDSON, and which may be clearly referred to this species, was obtained by Captain BAYFIELD, at Fort William on Lake Superior. Black Squirrels exist through all our western forests, and to the northward of our great lakes; but whether they are of this species, or the black variety of the gray squirrel, we have not had the means of deciding. It is a well ascertained fact that the Black Squirrel disappears before the Northern gray squirrel. Whether the colour renders it a more conspicuous mark for the sportsman, or whether the two species are naturally hostile, we are unable to decide. It is stated by close observers that in some neighbourhoods where the Black Squirrel formerly abounded, the Northern gray squirrel now exclusively occupies its place.

General Remarks.

We have admitted this as a true species, not so much in accordance with our own positive convictions, as in deference to the opinions of our naturalists, and from the consideration that if it be no more than a variety, it has by time and succession been rendered a permanent race. The only certain mode of deciding whether this is a true species or merely a variety, would be to ascertain whether male and female Black Squirrels and gray squirrels associate and breed together in a state of nature. When a male and a female, however different in size and colour, unite in a wild state and their progeny is prolific, we are warranted in pronouncing them of the same species. When, on the contrary, there is no such result, we are compelled to come to an opposite conclusion.

We had great doubts for many years whether this species might not

On Stone by W.ᵐ E. Hitchcock

Black Squirrel

Drawn from Nature by J.J.Audubon F.R.S.F.L.S   Lith. Printed & Col.ᵈ by J.T.Bowen, Phil

eventually prove another of the many varieties of the Northern gray squirrel, (*S. migratorius.*) Although these doubts have not been altogether removed by our recent investigations, they were considerably lessened on ascertaining the uniformity in size, shape, colour, and habits of all the individuals we have seen in a living state, as well as all the prepared specimens we have examined.

Much difficulty has existed among authors in deciding on the species to which the name of *S. niger* should be appropriated. The original description by LINNÆUS was contained in the single word *"niger."* If he had made no reference to any author, his description would have served quite well, as this was the only species of squirrel purely black, that was known at that day. He however made a reference to CATESBY, who figured the black variety of the Southern fox-squirrel, (*S. capistratus,*) and BRISSON, PENNANT, ERX-LEBEN, and SCHREBER referred the species in the same manner to the description and figure of CATESBY. Our American writers on natural history, as well as Dr. RICHARDSON, have however adopted the name given by LINNÆUS, and applied it to this species. We consider it advisable to retain the name, omitting the reference to CATESBY.

It is difficult to decide, from the descriptions of Drs. HARLAND and GODMAN, whether they described from specimens of the black variety of the Northern gray squirrel or from the present species.

Dr. RICHARDSON has, under the head of *Sciurus niger,* (see Fauna Boreali Americana, p. 191,) described a specimen from Lake Superior, which we conceive to be the black variety of the gray squirrel; but at the close of the same article (p. 192) he described another specimen from Fort William, which answers to the description of this species.

Sciurus Migratorius.—Aud. and Bach.

Migratory Gray Squirrel.—Northern Gray Squirrel.

Plate xxxv. Male, Female, and Young. Natural size.

S. S. Carolinense robustior, S. cinereo minor; cauda corpore multo longiore; variis coloribus.

Character.

Larger than the Carolina gray squirrel; smaller than the cat-squirrel; tail, much longer than the body; subject to many varieties of colour.

Synonymes.

GRAY SQUIRREL, Pennant, Arct. Zool., vol. i., p. 185, Hist Quad., No. 272.
SCIURUS CINEREUS, Harlan, Fauna, p. 173.
" CAROLINENSIS, Godman, non Gmel.
SCIURUS LEUCOTIS, Gapper, Zool. Journ., London, vol. v., p. 206, (published about 1830.)
SCIURUS LEUCOTIS, Bach., Proceedings of the Zoological Society, p. 91, London, 1838.
COMMON, or LITTLE GRAY SQUIRREL, Emmons, Report, 1842, p. 66.
SCIURUS LEUCOTIS, Dekay, Nat. Hist. N. Y., p. 57.
" VULPINUS, do. do. do. p. 59.

Description.

This Squirrel seems to have permanently twenty-two teeth. A large number of specimens procured at different seasons of the year, some of which from the manner in which their teeth were worn appeared to be old animals, presented the small front molars in the upper jaw. Even in an old male, obtained in December, with tufted ears, (the measurements of which will be given in this article,) the small molar existed. This permanency in teeth that have been usually regarded as deciduous, would seem to require an enlargement of the characters given to this genus; it will moreover be seen that several of our species are similar to this in their dental arrangement.

Incisors, strong, and compressed, a little smaller than those of the cat-squirrel, convex, and of a deep orange colour anteriorly. The upper ones have a sharp cutting edge, and are chisel-shaped; the lower are much longer and thinner. The anterior grinder, although round and small, is as long as the second; the remaining four grinders are considerably more excavated than those of the cat-squirrel, presenting two transverse ridges of enamel. The lower grinders corresponding to those above have also elevated crowns.

The hair is a little softer than that of the cat-squirrel, being coarsest on the forehead.

Nose, rather obtuse; forehead, arched; whiskers, as long as the head; ears, sharply rounded, concave on both sides, covered with hair; on the outside the hairs are longest. In winter the fur projects upward, about three lines beyond the margin; in summer, however, the hairs covering the ears are very short, and do not extend beyond the margin.

Colour.

This species appears under many varieties; there are, however, two very permanent ones, which we shall attempt to describe.

1st, Gray variety.—The nose, cheeks, a space around the eyes extending to the insertion of the neck, the upper surface of the fore and hind-feet, and a stripe along the sides, yellowish-brown; the ears on their posterior surface, are in most specimens brownish-yellow; in about one in ten they are dull white, edged with brown. On the back, from the shoulders there is an obscure stripe of brown, broadest at its commencement, running down to a point at the insertion of the tail. In some specimens this stripe is wanting. On the neck, sides, and hips, the colour is light gray; the hairs separately are for one half their length dark cinereous, then light umber, then a narrow mark of black, and are tipped with white; a considerable number of black hairs are inter-spersed, giving it a yellowish-brown colour on the dorsal aspect, and a light gray tint on the sides; the hairs in the tail are light yellowish-brown from the roots, with three stripes of black, the outer one being widest, and broadly tipped with white; the whole under surface is white. The above is the most common variety.

There are specimens in which the yellowish markings on the sides and feet are altogether wanting. Dr. GODMAN, (vol. ii., p. 133,) supposed that the golden colour of the hind-feet is a very permanent mark. The specimens from Pennsylvania in our possession, and a few from the Upper Missouri, have generally this peculiarity, but many of those from New York and New England have gray feet, without the slightest mixture of yellow.

2d, Black variety.—This we have on several occasions seen taken with the gray variety from the same nest. Both varieties breed and rear their young together.

The black ones are of the same size and form as the gray; they are dark brownish-black on the whole upper surface, a little lighter beneath. In summer their colour is less black than in winter. The hairs of the back and sides of the body, and of the tail are obscurely annulated with yellow. There is here and there a white hair interspersed among the fur of the body, but no tuft of white as in *Sciurus niger.*

Dimensions.

A Female in summer.	Inches.	Lines.
Length of head and body	11	9
" tail (vertebræ)	10	0
" tail, to the tip	13	0
Height of ear	0	7
Palm to the end of middle claw	1	10
Heel to the end of middle nail	2	6
Length of fur on the back	0	5
Breadth of tail with hairs extended	4	2

An old Male in winter pelage, obtained Dec. 16th.	Inches.	Lines.
Length of head and body	12	6
" tail (vertebræ)	11	0
" tail, to end of hair	14	0
Height of ear	0	7
" ear, to end of fur	0	9
Heel to end of longest nail	2	6
Length of fur on the back	0	8

Weight 1 lb. 6 oz.

Habits.

This appears to be the most active and sprightly species of squirrel existing in our Atlantic States. It sallies forth with the sun, and is industriously engaged in search of food for four or five hours in the morning, scratching

Migratory Squirrel

Drawn from Nature by J.J.Audubon,FRSFLS.   Lith.Printed & Col.d by J.T Bowen,Phil

among leaves, running over fallen logs, ascending trees, or playfully skipping from bough to bough, often making almost incredible leaps from the higher branches of one tree to another. In the middle of the day it retires for a few hours to its nest, resuming its active labours and amusements in the afternoon, and continuing them without intermission till long after the setting of the sun. During the warm weather of spring and summer it prepares itself a nest on a tree, but not often at its summit. When constructing this summer-house it does not descend to the earth in search of materials, finding them ready at hand on the tree it intends to make its temporary residence. It first breaks off some dry sticks, if they can be procured; if however, such materials are not within reach, it gnaws off green branches as large as a man's thumb, and lays them in a fork of the stem, or of some large branch. It then proceeds to the extremities of the branches, and breaks off twigs and bunches of leaves, with which a compact nest is constructed, which, on the inner side is sometimes lined with moss found on the bark of the tree. In the preparation of this nest both male and female are usually engaged for an hour in the morning during several successive days; and the noise they make in cutting the branches and dragging them with their leaves to the nest can be heard at a great distance. In winter they reside altogether in holes in trees, where their young in most instances are brought forth.

Although a family, to the number of five or six, probably the offspring of a single pair the preceding season, may occupy the same nest during winter, they all pair off in spring, when each couple occupies a separate nest, in order to engage in the duties of reproduction. The young, in number from four to six, are brought forth in May or June; they increase in size rapidly, and are sufficiently grown in a few weeks to leave the nest; at this time they may be seen clinging around the tree which contains their domicile; as soon as alarmed they run into the hole, but one of them usually returns to the entrance of it, and protruding its head out of the hollow, watches the movements of the intruder. In this stage of their growth they are easily captured by stopping up the entrance of the nest, and making an opening beneath; they can then be taken out by the hand protected by a glove. They soon become tolerably gentle, and are frequently kept in cages, with a wheel attached, which revolves as they bound forward, in which as if on a treadmill they exercise themselves for hours together.

Sometimes two are placed within a wheel, when they soon learn to accommodate themselves to it, and move together with great regularity. Notwithstanding the fact that they become very gentle in confinement, no instance has come to our knowledge of their having produced young while in a state of domestication, although in a suitable cage such a result would in all probability be attained. This species is a troublesome pet; it is sometimes inclined to close its teeth on the fingers of the intruder on its cage, and does not always spare even its feeder. When permitted to have the freedom of the house, it soon excites the displeasure of the notable housewife by its habit of gnawing chairs, tables, and books.

During the rutting season the males (like deer and some other species) engage in frequent contests, and often bite and wound each other severely. The story of the conqueror emasculating the vanquished on these occasions, has been so often repeated, that it perhaps is somewhat presumptuous to set it down as a vulgar error. It may, however, be advanced, that the admission of such skill and refinedment in inflicting revenge would be ascribing to the squirrel a higher degree of physiological. and anatomical knowledge than is possessed by any other quadruped. From the observations we have been enabled to make, we are led to believe that the error originated from the fact that those parts in the male, which in the rutting season are greatly enlarged, are at other periods of the year diminished to a very small size; and that, in young males especially, they are drawn into the pelvis by the contraction of the muscles. A friend, who was a strenuous believer in this spiteful propensity ascribed to the squirrel, was induced to test the truth of the theory by examining a suitable number of squirrels of this species. He obtained in a few weeks upwards of thirty males; in none of these had any mutilation taken place. Two however out of this number were triumphantly brought forward as evidences of the correctness of the general belief. On examination it appeared that these were young animals of the previous autumn, with the organs perfect, but concealed in the manner above stated.

It is generally believed that this species lays up a great hoard of food as a winter supply; it may however be reasonably doubted whether it is very provident in this respect. The hollow trees in which these Squirrels shelter themselves in winter are frequently cut down, and but a very small supply of provisions has ever been found in their nests. On following their tracks in the snow, they cannot be traced to any hoards buried in the ground. We have sometimes observed them during a warm day in winter coming from great distances into the open fields, in search of a few dry hickory nuts which were still left suspended on the trees. If provisions had been laid up nearer home,

they would hardly have undertaken these long journeys, or exposed themselves to so much danger in seeking a precarious supply. In fact, this species, in cold climates, seldom leaves its nest in winter, except on a warm sunny day, and in a state of inactivity and partial torpidity, it requires but little food.

Although this Squirrel is at particular seasons of the year known to search for the larvæ of different insects, which it greedily devours, it feeds principally on nuts, seeds, and grain, which are periodically sought for by all the species of this genus; among these it seems to prefer the shellbark, (*Carya alba*,) and several species of hickory nuts, to any other kind of food. Even when the nuts are so green as to afford scarcely any nourishment, it may be seen gnawing off the thick pericarp or outer shell which drops in small particles to the ground like rain, and then with its lower incisors it makes a small linear opening in the thinnest part of the shell immediately over the kernel. When this part has been extracted, it proceeds to another, till in an incredibly short space of time, the nut is cut longitudinally on its four sides, and the whole kernel picked out, leaving the dividing portions of the hard shell untouched.

At the season of the year when it feeds on unripe nuts, its paws and legs are tinged by the juices of the shells, which stain them an ochrey-red colour, that wears off, however, towards spring.

Were this species to confine its depredations to the fruit of the hickory, chestnut, beech, oak and maple, it would be less obnoxious to the farmer; but unfortunately for the peace of both, it is fond of the green Indian-corn and young wheat, to which the rightful owner imagines himself to have a prior claim. A war of extermination consequently ensues, and various inducements have been held out at different times to tempt the gunner to destroy it. In Pennsylvania an ancient law existed offering three pence a head for every squirrel destroyed, and in one year (1749) the sum of eight thousand pounds was paid out of the treasury in premiums for the destruction of these depredators. This was equal to 640,000 individuals killed. In several of the Northern and Western States the inhabitants, on an appointed day, are in the habit of turning out on what is called a squirrel hunt. They arrange themselves under opposite leaders, each party being stimulated by the ambition of killing the greatest number, and fastening on the other the expense of a plentiful supper. The hunters range the forest in every direction, and the accounts given us of the number of squirrels brought together at the evening rendezvous are almost incredible.

In addition to the usual enemies of this species in the Northern States, such as the weasel, fox, lynx, &c., the red-tailed hawk seems to regard it as his natural and lawful prey. It is amusing to see the skill and dexterity exercised by the hawk in the attack, and by the squirrel in attempting to escape. When the hawk is unaccompanied by his mate, he finds it no easy matter to secure the little animal; unless the latter be pounced upon whilst upon the ground, he is enabled by dodging and twisting round a branch to evade the attacks of the hawk for an hour or more, and frequently worries him into a reluctant retreat.

But the red-tails learn by experience that they are most certain of this prey when hunting in couples. The male is frequently accompanied by his mate, especially in the breeding season, and in this case the Squirrel is soon captured. The hawks course rapidly in opposite directions, above and below the branch; the attention of the Squirrel is thus divided and distracted, and before he is aware of it the talons of one of the hawks are in his back, and with a shriek of triumph the rapacious birds bear him off, either to the aerie in which their young are deposited, to some low branch of a tree, or to a sheltered situation on the ground, where with a suspicious glance towards each other, occasionally hissing and grumbling for the choice parts, the hawks devour their prey.

This species of squirrel has occasionally excited the wonder of the populace by its wandering habits and its singular and long migrations. Like the lemming (*Lemmus Norvegicus*) of the Eastern continent, it is stimulated either by a scarcity of food, or by some other inexplicable instinct, to leave its native haunts, and seek for adventures or for food in some (to it) unexplored portion of our land.

The newspapers from the West contain many interesting details of these migrations; they appear to have been more frequent in former years than at the present time. The farmers in the Western wilds regard them with sensations which may be compared to the anxious apprehensions of the Eastern nations at the flight of the devouring locust. At such periods, which usually occur in autumn, the Squirrels congregate in different districts of the far North-west; and in irregular troops bend their way instinctively in an eastern direction. Mountains, cleared fields, the narrow bays of some of our lakes, or our broad rivers, present no unconquerable impediments. Onward they come, devouring on their way every thing that is suited to their taste, laying waste the corn and wheat-fields of the farmer; and as their numbers are thinned by the gun, the dog, and the club, others fall in and fill up the ranks, till they occasion infinite mischief, and call forth more than empty threats of vengeance. It is often inquired, how these little creatures, that on common occasions have such an instinctive dread of water, are enabled to cross broad and rapid rivers, like the Ohio and Hudson for instance. It has been asserted by authors, and is believed by many, that they carry to the shore a suitable piece of bark, and seizing the opportunity of a favourable breeze, seat themselves upon this substitute for a boat, hoist their broad tails as a sail, and float safely to the opposite shore. This, together with many other traits of intelligence ascribed to this species, we suspect to be apocryphal. That they do migrate at irregular, and occasionally at distant periods, is a fact sufficiently established; but in the only two instances in which we had opportunities of witnessing the migrations of these Squirrels, it appeared to us, that they were not only unskilful sailors but clumsy swimmers. One of these occasions, (as far as our recollection serves us) was in the autumn of 1808 or 1809; troops of Squirrels suddenly and unexpectedly made their appearance in the neighbourhood; among them were varieties not previously seen in those parts; some were broadly striped with yellow on the sides, and a few had a black stripe on each side, bordered with yellow or brown, resembling the stripes on the sides of the Hudson's Bay squirrel, (S. Hudsonius.) They swam the Hudson in various places between Waterford and Saratoga; those which we observed crossing the river were swimming deep and awkwardly, their bodies and tails wholly submerged; several that had been drowned were carried downwards by the stream, and those which were so fortunate as to reach the opposite bank were so wet and fatigued, that the boys stationed there with clubs found no difficulty in securing them alive or in killing them. Their migrations on that occasion did not, as far as we could learn, extend farther eastward than the mountains of Vermont; many remained in the county of Rensselaer, and it was remarked that for several years afterwards squirrels were far more numerous there than before. It is doubtful whether any ever return to the west, as finding forests and food suited to their taste and habits, they take up their permanent residence in their newly explored country, where they remain and propagate their species, until they are gradually thinned off by the increase of inhabitants, new clearings, and the dexterity of the sportsmen around them. The other instance occurred in 1819, when we were descending the Ohio river in a flat-boat, or ark, chiefly with the intention of seeking for birds then unknown to us. About one hundred miles below Cincinnati, as we were floating down the stream, we observed a large number of Squirrels swimming across the river, and we continued to see them at various places, until we had nearly reached Smithland, a town not more than about one hundred miles above the mouth of the Ohio.

At times they were strewed, as it were, over the surface of the water, and some of them being fatigued sought a few moments' rest on our long "steering oar," which hung into the water in a slanting direction over the stern of our boat. The boys, along the shores and in boats were killing the Squirrels with clubs in great numbers, although most of them got safe across. After they had reached the shore we saw some of them trimming their fur on the fences or on logs of drift-wood.

We kept some of these Squirrels alive; they were fed with hickory nuts, pecans, and ground or pea-nuts, (Arachis hypogæa.) Immediately after eating as much as sufficed for a meal, they hid away the remainder beneath the straw and cotton at the bottom of their cage in a little heap. A very tame and gentle one we had in a room at Shippingport, near Louisville, Kentucky, one night ate its way into a bureau, in which we had a quantity of arsenic in powder, and died next morning a victim to curiosity or appetite, probably the latter, for the bureau also contained some wheat.

Geographical Distribution.

This species exists as far to the north as Hudson's Bay. It was formerly very common in the New England States, and in their least cultivated districts is still frequently met with. It is abundant in New York and in the mountainous portions of Pennsylvania. We have observed it on the northern mountains of Virginia, and we obtained several specimens on the Upper Missouri. The black variety is more abundant in Upper Canada, in the western part of New York, and in the States of Ohio and Indiana, than elsewhere. The Northern Gray Squirrel does not exist in any of its varieties in South Caroliana, Georgia, Florida, or Alabama; and among specimens sent to us from Louisiana, stated to include all the squirrels existing in that State, we did not discover this species.

General Remarks.

There exists a strong general resemblance among all our species of this genus, and it is therefore not surprising that there should have been great difficulty in finding characters to designate the various species. In the

museums we examined in Europe, we observed that several species had been confounded, and we were every where told by the eminent naturalists with whom we conversed on the subject, that they could find no characters by which the different species could be distinguished. The little Carolina gray squirrel was first described by GMELIN. DESMAREST, who created a confusion among the various species of this genus, which is almost inextricable, confounded three species—the Northern Gray Squirrel, the Southern Carolina squirrel, and the cat-squirrel—under the name of Sc. cinereus, and gave them the diminutive size of ten inches six lines. His article was literally translated by HARLAN, including the measurements, (DESM., Mamm., p. 332; HARLAN's Fauna, p. 173,) and he also apparently blended the three species—S. cinereus, S. migratorius, and S. Carolinensis. GODMAN called the Northern species S. Carolinensis, and LECONTE, who appears to have had a more correct view of the species generally than all previous authors, (see Appendix to McMURTRIE's translation of CUVIER, vol. i., p. 433,) regarded the Carolina and the Northern Gray Squirrel as identical.

In 1833 and 1834 GAPPER, (Zoological Journal, vol. v., p. 201,) found in Upper Canada an individual, of what we suppose to be a variety of the Northern Gray Squirrel, with white ears, with the upper parts varied with a mixture of white, black, and ochre, and with a stripe of similar colour along the sides. Supposing it to be a species different from the common gray squirrel, he bestowed on it the characteristic name of Sciurus Leucotis (white eared). In our monograph of the genus SCIURUS, read before the Zoological Society, (Proceedings Zool. Soc., 1838, Op. Sup., cit., p. 91,) we adopted the name of GAPPER, without having seen his description, having been informed by competent naturalists that he had described this species.

Having, however, afterwards obtained a copy of the articles of GAPPER, and ascertained that he had described a variety that is very seldom met with, we were anxious to rid our nomenclature of a name which is very inappropriate to this species, and which is calculated constantly to mislead the student of nature.

GAPPER compared his specimen with the Northern Gray Squirrel, and finding that the latter species was gray, and not of an ochreous colour like the one he described, with ears not white but of the colour of the back, he regarded his variety as a different species. He designated the Northern Gray Squirrel as the Carolina squirrel, the difference between the Northern and Southern Gray Squirrels not having been pointed out till it was done in our monograph four years afterwards.

As a general rule we adhere to the views entertained by naturalists, that it is best to retain a name once imposed, however inappropriate, unless likely to propagate important errors; in the present instance, however, we propose the name of S. migratorius, as applicable to the wide-ranging habits of this Squirrel, it being the only one in our country that appears to possess this peculiarity.

The name leucotis is appropriate only to the Southern fox-squirrel, which has permanently, and in all its varieties, white ears.

We have been somewhat at a loss where to place the species given as the fox-squirrel, S. vulpinus of DEKAY, (see Nat. Hist. New York, p. 59,) and have marked our quotation with a doubt. His description does not apply very well to the Pennsylvania fox-squirrel, (S. cinereus,) of which GMELIN's S. vulpinus is only a synonyme. He states indeed, "We suspect that GODMAN's fox-squirrel as well as his cat-squirrel, are varieties only of the hooded squirrel, and not to be referred to our Northern animal." We have, in our article on S. cinereus, noticed the errors contained in the above quotation, and only allude to it here as a possible clue to the species he had in view, viz., "not the species" given by GODMAN as S. cinereus, but another that agrees with the Northern Gray Squirrel "in every particular except the size." He further adds, that "its habits and geographical distribution are the same as in the preceding," meaning the Northern Gray Squirrel.

He evidently has reference to a larger species of the Gray Squirrel as existing in the same localities, with "the hair on the posterior surface of the ears projecting two lines beyond the margins," differing from the species he had just described as the Northern Gray Squirrel, which he characterized as having ears "covered with short hairs; no pencil of hairs at the tips." Although his figure resembles in several particulars that of the cat-squirrel, (S. cinereus,) parts of his description and his account of the habits seem more appropriate to the tufted winter specimens of the present species. The appearance of the ears in specimens obtained in winter and summer pelage differs so widely that we ourselves were for many years misled by the tufts and larger size of the old in winter. We recollect that in our school-boy days we were in the habit of obtaining many specimens of the Gray Squirrel during summer and autumn, which answered to the description of S. migratorius, having their ears clothed with short hairs which did not project beyond the margins on the posterior surface. During the following winter, however, we occasionally caught in a steel-trap a specimen much larger, very fat, and with ears tufted like that described as *S. vulpinus*; and we prepared the specimens under an impression that a new species had made its appearance in the neighbourhood. The following summer, however, we procured in that locality no other than the common Gray Squirrel, destitute of the fringes on the ears. We now resorted to a different mode of solving the problem. We obtained several young Northern Gray Squirrels, which we kept in cages; during the first winter their ears underwent no particular change. But in the month of December of the second year, when they had become very fat and had grown considerably larger, their ears on the posterior surface became fringed and exactly corresponded with the winter specimens we had previously obtained. As we could not feel a perfect confidence in our own notes made more than thirty years ago, we recently made inquiries from Dr. LEONARD, of Lansingburg, New York, an accurate and intelligent naturalist, whose answer we subjoin:—"It is considered established by naturalists and observing sportsmen, that the Gray Squirrel, after the first year, has fringed ears in its winter pelage, and that of course there is but one speccies. Of ten prepared specimens, which I have recently examined, eight have bare ears, and two (one of them being of the black variety) have the ears fringed; differing in no other respect, except the general fuller development of the hair, from the other specimens of their respective varieties."

We are moreover under an impression that the specimen of the Northern Gray Squirrel, from which DEKAY took his measurement, must have been a young animal. He gives head and body, eight inches; tail, eight inches five lines. Out of more than fifty specimens that we have measured in the flesh, there was not one that measured less than ten inches in body and eleven inches in tail.

The true *S. cinereus* or *S. vulpinus* has moreover not the same geographical range as the Northern Gray Squirrel. It is not found in Canada, where the present species is common, nor in the most northerly parts of either New York or the New England States. We obtained several specimens from the New York market, and as we have shown in our article on *S. cinereus*, it is occasionally found in the southern counties of the State; but it is a very rare species north and east of Pennsylvania, and is principally confined to the Middle and some of the South-western States.

The Northern Gray Squirrel (*S. migratorius*) may be easily distinguished from the Carolina Gray Squirrel (*S. Carolinensis*) by its larger size, broader tail, and lighter gray colours on the sides, and by its smaller persistent tooth.

S. cincereus or *S. vulpinus* differs from this species in being a little longer, having a much stouter body and legs, and a longer tail. It has, in proportion to its size, shorter ears, which are more rounded, and have the tufts or fringes in winter much shorter. The fur is also coarser, and it has in each upper jaw but four teeth, dropping its milktooth when very young, whilst the Northern Gray Squirrel (*S. migratorius*) has five on each side, which appear to be permanent.

Genus Hystrix.—Linn.

Dental Formula.

Incisive $\frac{2}{2}$; *Canine* $\frac{0-0}{0-0}$; *Molar* $\frac{4-4}{4-4}$ = 20.

Superior incisors, on the anterior portion, smooth, cuneiform at their extremity; inferior incisors, strong and compressed.

Molars, compound, with flat crowns, variously modified by plates of enamel, between which are depressed intervals.

Head, strong; snout, thick and tumid; ears, short and round; tongue, bristled with spiny scales; fore-feet, four-toed; hind-feet, five-toed; all the toes armed with powerful nails.

Spines on the body, sometimes intermixed with hair: tail, moderately long, in some species of the genus, prehensile.

Herbivorous, feeding principally on grain, fruits, roots, and the bark of trees—dig holes in the earth, or nestle in the hollows of trees.

The generic name is derived from the Greek word, δστβιξ (*hustrix,*) a porcupine—υς, (*hus,*) a hog, and θριξ, (*thrix,*) a bristle.

There are two species in North, and three in South America, one in Southern Europe, one in Africa, and one in India.

Hystrix Dorsata.—Linn.

Canada Porcupine.

Plate xxxvi.—Male. 4-5ths Natural size.

H. spinus brevibus, vellere sublatentibus; sine jubea; capite et collo setis longis vestitis; colore inter fulvum et nigrum variante.

Characters.

Spines, short, partially concealed by long hair; no mane; long bristles on the head and neck; colour, varying between light-brown and black.

Synonymes.

HYSTRIX PILOSUS AMERICANUS, Catesby, Cuv., App., p. 30, 1740.
THE PORCUPINE FROM HUDSON'S BAY, Edwards' Birds, p. 52.
HYSTRIX HUDSONIUS, Brisson, Régne Animal, p. 128.
HYSTRIX DORSATA, Linn., Syst., Edwards, xii., p. 57.
    "   "   Erxleben, p. 345.
    "   "   Schreber, Säugethiere, p. 605.
L'URSON, Buffon, vol. xii., p. 426.
CANADA PORCUPINE, Forst., Phil. Trans., vol. lxii., p. 374.
    "   "   Penn., Quadrupeds, vol. ii., p. 126.
    "   "   Arctic Zoology, vol. i., p. 109.

THE PORCUPINE, Hearne's Journal, p. 381.
ERETHIZON DORSATUM, F. Cuv., in Mém. du Mus., ix., t. 20.
PORC-EPIC VELU, Cuv., Règne Animal, i., p. 209.
HYSTRIX DORSATA, Sabine, Franklin's Journ., p. 664.
    "   "   Harlan, Fauna, p. 109.
    "   "   Godman, Nat. Hist., vol. ii., p. 160.
    "   PILOSUS, Rich., Fauna Boreali Americana, p. 214.
    "   HUDSONIUS, Dekay, Nat. Hist. New York, p. 77.

Description.

The body of this species is thick, very broad, cylindrical, and to a high degree clumsy. The back is much arched in a curve from the nose to the buttocks, when it declines in an angle to the tail.

The whole upper surface of the body from the nose to the extremity of the tail is covered by long and rather coarse hair, intermixed with a dense mass of spines or quills. These are of cylindrical shape, very sharp at the extremity and pointed at the roots. The animal is capable of erecting them at pleasure, and they are detached by the slightest touch; they are barbed with numerous small reversed points or prickles, which, when once inserted in the flesh, will by the mere movement of the limbs work themselves deeper into the body. There seems to be in certain parts of the body of this species a regular gradation from hair to spines; on the nose for instance, the hair is rather soft, a little higher up it is succeeded by bristles intermixed with small spines. These spines continue to lengthen on the hinder parts of the head, to increase in size on the shoulders, and are longer and more rigid on the buttocks and thighs. In specimens of old animals, the whole upper surface of the body is covered by a mass of quills, with thin tufts of long hairs, six inches in length, on the forehead, shoulders, and along the sides.

Head, rather small for the size of the animal, and very short; nose, truncated, broad, flattish above, and terminating abruptly. The eyes are lateral and small; ears, small, rounded, covered by short fur, and concealed by the adjoining long hair; incisors, large and strong.

Legs, very short, and rather stout; claws, tolerably long, compressed, moderately arched, and channeled beneath.

There are tufts of hair situated between the toes; palms, naked, and nearly oval, hard and tuberculous; on the fore-feet there are four short toes, the second, counting from the inside, longest, the third a little smaller, the first a size less, and the fourth smallest. On the hind-foot there are five toes, with claws corresponding to those on the fore-foot. The hairs are so thickly and broadly arranged along the sides of the soles that they give a great apparent breadth to the foot, enabling this clumsy animal to walk with greater ease in the snow. It is plantigrade, and like the bear, presses on the earth throughout the whole length of the soles. Tail, short and thick, covered above with spines, beneath with long rigid hairs; when walking or climbing, it is turned a little upwards. Four mammæ, all pectoral.

Whilst the whole upper surface of the body is covered with spines, the under surface is clothed with hair intermixed with fur of a softer kind. The

Canada Porcupine.

Drawn from Nature by J.J.Audubon,F.R.S.F.L.S.

Lith.ᵈ, Printed & Col.ᵈ by J.T. Bowen, Philad.ᵃ

hair on the throat, and under the belly is rather soft; along the sides it is longer and coarser, and under the tail appears like strong bristles.

Colour.

Incisors, deep orange; whole upper surface, blackish-brown, interspersed with long hairs, many of them being eight inches in length; these hairs are for four-fifths of their length dark-brown, with the points from one to two inches white. There are also long white hairs interspersed under the fore-legs, on the chest, and along the sides of the tail.

The spines, or quills, which vary in length from one to four inches, are white from the roots to near their points, which are generally dark brown or black; frequently brown, and occasionally white. On some specimens the spines are so abundant and protrude so far beyond the hair that portions of the body, especially the hips, present a speckled appearance, owing to the preponderance of the long white quills tipped with black. The nails and whole under surface are dark brown.

There is in this species a considerable difference both in the size and colour of different specimens.

There are three specimens before us, that with slight variations answer to the above description and to the figure on our plate. Another, which we obtained at Fort Union on the Missouri, is of enormous size, measuring thirteen inches across the back; the long hairs on the shoulders, forehead, and sides of which, are light yellowish-brown, whilst another specimen from the same locality, which appears to be that of a young animal, is dull white, with brown nose ears and rump. In every specimen, however, the hair on the hips, upper surface of tail, and under surface of body, are dark blackish-brown. In all these cases, it is the long, overhanging, light-coloured hairs, that give the general whitish appearance.

The difference between these specimens is so striking, that whilst those from Lower Canada may be described as black, the others from the far West, may be designated as light-gray. Except in size and colour, there are no especial marks of difference.

Dimensions.

Length of head and body	29	inches.
Tail (vertebræ)	7	do.
Tail, to end of fur	$8\frac{1}{2}$	do.
Breadth of nose	$1\frac{1}{8}$	do.
From heel to longest nail	$3\frac{1}{2}$	do.

We possess one specimen a little larger than the above, and several that are considerably smaller.

Habits.

The Canada Porcupine, of all North American quadrupeds, possesses the strangest peculiarities in its organization and habits. In its movements it is the most sluggish of all our species. Although the skunk is slow of foot, he would prove no contemptible competitor with it in a trial of speed. Under such circumstances the inquiry arises, what protection has this animal against the attacks of the wolverene, the lynx, the wolf, and the cougar? and how long will it be before it becomes totally exterminated? But a wise Creator has endowed it with powers by which it can bid defiance to the whole ferine race, the grisly bear not excepted. If the skunk presents to its enemies a formidable battery, that stifles and burns at the same time, the Porcupine is clothed in an impervious coat of mail bristling with bayonets.

We kept a living animal of this kind in a cage in Charleston for six months, and on many occasions witnessed the manner in which it arranged its formidable spines, in order to prove invulnerable to the attacks of its enemies.

It was occasionally let out of its cage to enjoy the benefit of a promenade in the garden. It had become very gentle, and evinced no spiteful propensities; when we called to it, holding in our hand a tempting sweet-potatoe or an apple, it would turn its head slowly toward us, and give us a mild and wistful look, and then with stately steps advance and take the fruit from our hand. It then assumed an upright position, and conveyed the potatoe or apple to its mouth with its paws. If it found the door of our study open it would march in, and gently approach us, rubbing its sides against our legs, and looking up at us as if supplicating for additional delicacies. We frequently plagued it in order to try its temper, but it never evinced any spirit of resentment by raising its bristles at us; but no sooner did a dog make his appearance than in a moment it was armed at all points in defence. It would bend its nose downward, erect its bristles, and by a threatening sideway movement of the tail, give evidence that it was ready for the attack.

A large, ferocious, and exceedingly troublesome mastiff, belonging to the neighbourhood, had been in the habit of digging a hole under the fence, and entering our garden. Early one morning we saw him making a dash at some object in the corner of the fence, which proved to be our Porcupine, which had during the night made its escape from the cage. The dog seemed regardless of all its threats, and probably supposing it to be an animal not more formidable than a cat, sprang upon it with open mouth. The Porcupine seemed to swell up in an instant to nearly double its size, and as the dog pounced upon it, it dealt him such a sidewise lateral blow with its tail, as caused the mastiff to relinquish his hold instantly, and set up a loud howl in an agony of pain. His mouth, tongue, and nose, were full of porcupine quills. He could not close his jaws, but hurried open-mouthed out of the premises. It proved to him a lesson for life, as nothing could ever afterwards induce him to revisit a place where he had met with such an unneighbourly reception. Although the servants immediately extracted the spines from the mouth of the dog, we observed that his head was terribly swelled for several weeks afterwards, and it was two months before he finally recovered.

CARTWRIGHT, (Journal, vol. ii., p. 59,) gives a description of the destructive habits of the Porcupine, which in many particulars is so much in accordance with our own observations, that we will present it to our readers.

"The Porcupine readily climbs trees; for which purpose he is furnished with very long claws; and in the winter, when he mounts into a tree, I believe he does not come down until he has eaten the bark from the top to the bottom. He generally makes his course through the wood in a straight direction, seldom missing a tree, unless such as are old. He loves young ones best, and devours so much, (only eating the inner part of the rind,) that I have frequently known one Porcupine to ruin nearly a hundred trees in a winter.

"A man who is acquainted with the nature of these animals will seldom miss finding them when the snow is on the ground. If he can but hit upon the rinding of that winter, by making a circuit around the barked trees, he will soon come on his track unless a very deep snow should have chanced to fall after his last ascent. Having discovered that, he will not be long ere he find the animal."

In reference to the manner in which the Porcupine defends itself with its quills, he makes the following observations: "It is a received opinion that a Porcupine can dart his quills at pleasure into a distant object, but I venture to affirm that this species cannot, (whatever any other may do,) for I have taken much pains to discover this fact. On the approach of danger he retreats into a hole, if possible, but where he cannot find one he seizes upon the best shelter that offers, sinks his nose between his fore-legs, and defends himself by a sharp stroke of his tail, or a sudden jerk of his back. As the quills are bearded at their points and not deeply rooted in the skin, they stick firmly into whatever they penetrate; great care should be taken to extract them immediately, otherwise by the muscular motion of the animal into which they are stuck, enforced by the beards of the quills, they soon work themselves quite through the part, but I never perceived the puncture to be attended with any worse symptoms than that of a chirurgical instrument."

We had on three occasions in the northern and western parts of New York opportunities of witnessing the effects produced by the persevering efforts of this species in search after its simple food. In travelling through the forest from Niagara to Louisville a few years ago, we passed through two or three acres of ground where nearly all the young trees, had on the previous winter been deprived of their bark, and were as perfectly killed as if a fire had passed through them. We were informed by our coachman that in driving through this place during the winter he had on several occasions seen the Porcupine on one of these trees, and that he believed all the mischief had been done by a single animal. We perceived that it had stripped every slippery elm (Ulmus fulva) in the neighbourhood, left not a tree of the bass wood (Tilia glabra) alive, but had principally feasted on the hemlock, (Abies Canadensis.)

Mr. J. G. BELL, one of our companions in our recent journey to the West, met with some Porcupines that resorted to a ravine, in which about a hundred cotton-wood trees (Populus angulatus) were standing, that had been denuded of both the bark and leaves. They had remained in this locality until they had eaten not only the tender branches, but had devoured the bark of some of the largest trees, by which they killed nearly every one. They then were forced in their own defence to remove to new quarters. We were informed that in a similar ravine to the one just spoken of, no less than thirteen Porcupines were killed in a single season by a young hunter.

On a visit to the western portion of the county of Saratoga, New York, in the winter of 1813, a farmer residing in the vicinity carried us in his sleigh to show us a Porcupine which he had frequently seen during the winter, assuring us that he could find it on the very tree where he had observed it the previous day. We were disappointed, finding that it had deserted the tree; we however traced it in the snow by a well beaten path, which it seemed to have used daily, to a beech tree not far distant, which we cut down, and at the distance of twenty feet from the root we found the object of our search in a hollow part. It growled at us, and was particularly spiteful towards a small dog that was with us. Our friend killed it by a blow on the nose, the only vulnerable part as he informed us. It seemed to have been confined to a space of about two acres of ground through the winter. It had fed principally on hemlock bark, and had destroyed upwards of a hundred trees. The observations made on this occasion incline us to doubt the correctness of the statement that the Canada Porcupine does not leave a tree until it has eaten off all the bark, and that it remains for a week or more on the same tree; we were on the contrary led to suppose that the individual we have just spoken of, retired nightly to its comfortable domicile and warm bed in the hollow beach, in which we discovered it.

The Porcupine we kept in Charleston did not appear very choice in regard to its food. It ate almost any kind of vegetable we presented to it. We gave it cabbages, turnips, potatoes, apples, and even bread, and it usually cut to pieces every thing we placed in the cage that it could not consume. We had a tolerably large sweet bay tree (*Laurus nobilis*) in the garden: the instant that we opened the door of the cage the Porcupine would make its way to this tree, and not only feed greedily on its bark, but on its leaves also. When it had once fixed itself on a tree it was exceedingly difficult to induce it to come down, and our efforts to force it from the tree were the only provocatives by which it could be made to growl at us. We occasionally heard it during the night, uttering a shrill note, that might be called a low querulous shriek.

As the spring advanced, we ascertained that the constitution of our poor Porcupine was not intended for a warm climate; when the hot weathewr came on it suffered so much that we wished it back again in its Canadian wilds. It would lie panting in its cage the whole day, seemed restless and miserable, lost its appetite and refused food. We one evening placed it on its favourite bay tree; it immediately commenced gnawing the bark, which we supposed a favourable symptom, but it fell off during the night, and was dead before morning.

Whilst on the Upper Missouri river, in the year 1843, as our companion, Mr. J. G. BELL, was cautiously making his way through a close thicket of willows and brush-wood in search of a fine buck elk, that he with one of our men had seen enter into this cover when they were at least a mile distant, he could not avoid cracking now and then a dry stick or fallen branch. He could not see more than ten paces in any direction, from the denseness of the thicket, and, as he unfortunately trod upon a thicker branch than usual which broke with a crash, the elk brushed furiously out of the thicket, and was gone in a moment, making the twigs and branches rattle as he dashed them aside with (shall we say) "telegraphic" rapidity. Mr. BELL stood motionless for a minute, when as he was about to retreat into the open prairie, and join his companion after this unsuccessful termination of the elk hunt, his eyes were fixed by an uncouth mass on the ground, almost at his feet; it was a Porcupine; it remained perfectly still, and when he approached did not attempt to retreat. Our friend was rather perplexed to know how to treat an enemy that would neither "fight nor fly," and seizing a large stick, he commenced operations by giving the Porcupine (which must have been by this time displeased at least, if not "fretful,") a severe blow with it on the nose. The animal immediately concealed the injured organ, and his whole head also, under his belly; rolling himself up into a ball, with the exception of his tail, which he occasionally jerked about and flirted upwards over his back. He now remained still again, and Mr. BELL drew a good sized knife, with which he tried to kill him by striking at his side so as to avoid the points of the quills as much as he could. This fresh attack caused the Porcupine to make violent efforts to escape, he seized hold of the branches or roots within reach of his forefeet, and pulled forwards with great force; Mr. BELL then placed his gun before him, which stopped him; then finding he could not lay hold of him nor capture him in any other way, he drew his ramrod, which had a large screw at the end, for wiping out his gun, and commenced screwing it into the Porcupine's back. This induced the poor animal again to make violent efforts to escape, but by the aid of the screw and repeated thrusts with the knife, he soon killed the creature.

He was now anxious to rejoin his companion, but did not like to relinquish his game; he therefore, not thinking it advisable to stop and skin it on the spot, managed to tie it by the fore-legs, and then dragged it on the ground after him until he arrived at the spot where the hunter was impatiently waiting for him. Here he skinned the Porcupine, and turned the skin entirely inside out, so that the quills were all within, and then no longer fearing to handle the skin, it was secured to the saddle of his horse, and the carcass

thrown away.

A Porcupine that was confined for some time in the garret of a building in Broadway, New York, in which PEALE's Museum was formerly kept, made its escape by gnawing a hole in a corner of the garret, and, (as was supposed,) got on to the roof, from whence it tumbled into the street, either by a direct fall from this elevation, or by pitching on to some roof in the rear of the main building, and thence into Murray-street. It was brought the next day to the museum for sale, as a great curiosity. The man who brought it, of course not knowing from whence it came, said that early in the morning, he (being a watchman) was attracted by a crowd in the Park, and on approaching discovered a strange animal which no one could catch; he got a basket, however, and captured the beast, which he very naturally carried off to the *watch-house*, thinking of course no place of greater security for any vagrant existed in the neighbourhood.

On an explanation before the keeper of the museum, instead of the police justices, and on payment of half a dollar, the Porcupine was again restored to his friends. He was now, however, watched more closely, and bits of sheet tin were frequently nailed in different parts of the room on which he had a predilection for trying his large teeth.

We have mentioned in our article on the Canada lynx, that one of those animals was taken in the woods in a dying state, owing to its mouth being filled with Porcupine quills. We have heard of many dogs, some wolves, and at least one panther, that were found dead, in consequence of inflammation produced by seizing on the Porcupine.

Its nest is found in hollow trees or in caves under rocks. It produces its young in April or May, generally two at a litter; we have however heard that three, and on one occasion four, had been found in a nest.

The Indians residing in the North, make considerable use of the quills of the porcupine; mocassins, shot-pouches, baskets made of birch bark, &c., are ingeniously ornamented with them, for which purpose they are dyed of various bright colours.

The flesh of this species is sometimes eaten, and is said to have the taste of flabby pork.

The following information respecting the Porcupine was received by us from our kind frined WILLIAM CASE, Esq., of Cleveland, Ohio. "This animal was several years since (before my shooting days) very abundant in this region, the Connecticut Western Reserve, and no more than ten years ago one person killed seven or eight in the course of an afternoon's hunt for squirrels, within three or four miles of this city, while now probably one could not be found in a month. They are rapidly becoming extinct: the chief reason is probably the extreme hatred all hunters bear them on account of the injuries their quills inflict on their dogs. They do not hibernate neither do I think they are particularly confined to their hollow trees during the coldest days in winter. Their movements from tree to tree in search of food (browse and bark) are rather slow and awkward, their track in the snow very much resembles that of a child (with the aid of imagination.)

"They most delight in browsing and barking young and thrifty Elms, and are generally plenty in Elm, or Bass-wood Swail."

Geographical Distribution.

This species, according to RICHARDSON, has been met with as far north as the Mackenzie river, in latitude 67°. It is found across the continent from Labrador to the Rocky Mountains, and is tolerably abundant in the woody portions of the western part of Missouri. To us this has been rather a rare species in the Atlantic districts; we having seldom met with it in the Northern and Eastern States. It is found, however, in the northern and western parts of New York, and is said to be increasing in some of the western counties of that State. Dr. LEONARD, of Lansingburg, recently obtained specimens from the mountains of Vermont. It exists sparingly in the mountains of the northern portion of Pennsylvania, and in a few localities in Ohio; we obtained it on the Upper Missouri. LEWIS and CLARKE have not enumerated it as one of the species inhabiting the west of the Rocky Mountains.

It does not exist in the southern parts of New York or Pennsylvania. DEKAY (Nat. Hist. of New York, p. 79) states, that it is found in the northern parts of Virginia and Kentucky. We however sought for it without success in the mountains of Virginia, and could never hear of its existence in Kentucky.

Lepus Aquaticus.—Bach.

Swamp-Hare.

Plate xxxvii.—Male. Natural size.

L. L. Americani magnitudine; capite, auribus, caudaque longis; pedibus longis minus pilosis quam in L. sylvatico; supra fuscus; subtus albus.

Characters.

Size of the Northern hare; head, ears, and tail, long; feet, long, less covered with hair than those of the gray rabbit; general colour, dark grayish-brown above, white beneath.

Synonymes.

LEPUS AQUATICUS, Bach., Journal Acad. Nat. Sc., Philad., vol. vii., p. 2, p. 319, read March 21, 1837.
LEPUS DOUGLASSII, var. 1, Gray, Magazine Nat. Hist., London, November, 1837.

Description.

The body of this species is large, and formed both for strength and speed; the hairs do not hang as loosely on the surface as those of the Northern hare, but lie smooth and compact; the fur is coarser and more glossy than that of the gray rabbit.

Head, long, and moderately arched; skull, considerably larger than that of the Northern hare, (*L. Americanus,*) with a larger orbital cavity. The margins of the orbits project so as to produce a visible depression in the anterior part of the frontal bone; whiskers, half the length of the head; ears, long, shaped like those of the marsh-hare, clothed externally with a dense coat of very short hairs; internally, they are partially covered along the margins, but nearer the orifice are nearly naked.

The feet bear no resemblance to those of the Northern hare or those of the gray rabbit. Instead of bieng clothed, as in those species, with a compact mass of hair, they are formed like those of the marsh-hare; the toes, when spread, leaving distinct impressions on the earth. The fore-toes are long, and their claws large and considerably curved; on the hind-feet, the claws are very stout and broad, nearly double the size of those of the Northern hare.

The tail is rather long for the genus, upturned, and thickly clothed on both surfaces with long fur.

Colour.

Teeth, yellowish-white; the whole of the upper part of the body light brownish-yellow, blotched on the surface with black; in the winter, the whole of the back and the sides of the head, become brownish-black, with here and there a mixture of reddish-brown visible on the surface; the fur beneath the long hairs is dark plumbeous, tipped with black. The long hairs when examined singly, are dark-blue at the roots, then light buff, and are pointed with black. Behind the ears, rufous, with a stripe of a similar colour extending to the shoulders. A line around the eyes, light reddish-buff. Upper lip, chin, and belly, white, tinged with blue. Nails, in a winter specimen of a young male, dark-brown; in an old female procured in summer, yellowish; whiskers, black; inner surface of the ears, light grayish-white; outer surface, above, edged with black; under surface of the tail, pure white.

Dimensions.

(The following measurements were taken by Dr. LEE, of Alabama, from a specimen in the flesh.)

Length from point of nose to insertion of tail	20	inches.
" of head	$4\frac{1}{2}$	do.
" of ears, posteriorly	$3\frac{7}{8}$	do.
Height to shoulder	11	do.
Length of the hind-foot	$4\frac{1}{2}$	do.
" of tail (vertebræ)	$5\frac{7}{8}$	do.
" tail, including fur	$2\frac{1}{8}$	do.
" of the middle hind-claw	3	do.

Weight of a female killed in the spring, (when suckling its young, and not in good condition,) 6 lbs.

Habits.

The habits of this animal are very singular, differing in one remarkable peculiarity from those of any other species of hare yet known, with the exception of the marsh-hare. Although the Swamp-Hare is occasionally seen on high grounds in the dense forest, it prefers low and marshy places, or the neighbourhood of streams and ponds of water, to which it is fond of resorting. It swims with great facility from one little islet to another, and is generally found seeking its food in wet places, or near the water, as it subsists on the roots of various kinds of aquatic plants, especially on species of iris growing in the water.

Persons who have given us information on the subject of this hare, inform us, that when first started, and whilst running, its trampings are louder, and can be heard at a greater distance, than those of any other hare.

As it suddenly leaps or bounds from its hiding place ere it is seen, it is apt to startle the rambler who has intruded upon its solitary retreat, and he may be impressed with the belief that he has started a young deer. When chased by dogs, the Swamp-Hare runs with great swiftness, and is able to escape from them without difficulty; but it almost invariably directs its flight towards the nearest pond, as if led by instinct to seek an element in which all traces of its scent are soon lost to its eager pursuers. There is a specimen of the Swamp-Hare, which we added to the collection of the Academy of Natural Sciences, Philadelphia, considerably larger than the Northern hare; this individual, on being pursued by hounds, swam twice across the Alabama river, and was not captured till it had finally retreated to a hollow tree.

We have been informed that it is a very common habit of this species when pursued, to swim to the edge of some stream or pond, retreat beneath the overhanging roots of the trees that may be growing on its border, or seek for a secure shelter under the hollows made by the washing of the banks. The swiftness of foot possessed by this Hare, and the stratagems to which it is capable of resorting might easily enable it to elude pursuit but for this habit of seeking for shelter as soon as it is chased, which is the cause of its being frequently captured.

When the waters in the swamps are low, it seeks the first hollow tree, where it is easily secured. In this manner, Major LEE informed us, that in his vicinity the boys and the domestics caught thirty or forty in three days.

The young of this Hare are frequently found in nests formed of leaves and grasses, placed on hillocks in the swamps, or in the hollow of some fallen tree. We have been informed that it produces young at least twice in a season, and from four to six at a litter.

Geographical Distribution.

We have not heard of the existence of this animal to the east or north of the State of Alabama, but it is numerous in all the swamps of the western part of that State, is still more abundant in the State of Mississippi, and in the lower part of Louisiana, and is frequently brought by the Indians to the market of New Orleans. It was also obtained in Texas by DOUGLASS and by J.W. AUDUBON. GRAY states that it exists in California; we have however carefully inquired into the history of the specimen in the British Museum, which was received after the melancholy death of DOUGLASS, and have reason to believe that the label was accidentally misplaced, and that it came from the eastern portion of Texas.

General Remarks.

Although all our hares bear a strong resemblance to each other, particularly in their summer colours, yet all have different marks, by which they can, with a little attention be distinguished. The present species, in its colour on the upper surface and in its aquatic habits, is closely assimilated to the marsh-hare; it differs, however, very widely in other respects.

The Swamp-Hare is a third larger than the marsh-hare; the largest specimen of the latter in more than fifty that we measured, was only fourteen inches long, whilst the largest Swamp-Hare was twenty-two inches, and we are informed that it is often much larger. The tail of the marsh-hare is exceedingly short, its vertebræ being not more than an inch long, whilst that of the present species is two inches and an eighth, being more than double the length. The ears differ in the same proportion. The under surface of the tail of the marsh-hare is ash-coloured, mixed with brown, whilst that of the present species is pure white. Its feet are thinly covered with hair, and its toes, (which are capable of being widely spread,) are well adapted to enable it to swim, and to pass over marshy and muddy places.

The tracks of this species, and of the marsh-hare, in the mud, leave a distinct impression of the toes, whilst on the contrary the tracks of the gray

Plate XXXVII

N.º 8.

Drawn on Stone by Wᵐ E Hitchcock

Lith Printed & Colᵈ by J T Bowen, Phil

Swamp Hare.

Male.

Drawn from Nature by J J Audubon, F R S F L S

rabbit, the Northern hare, and the Polar hare, exhibit no such traces, their feet being so thickly clothed with long hair that even the points of the nails are scarcely perceptible. The present species is larger than the gray rabbit, being very nearly the size of the Northern hare, which it probably exceeds in weight. Indeed the Northern hare and this species, when divested of their hides, are very nearly equal in size; but the fur of the former being loose and long, whilst that of the present species lies compact and smooth, the Northern hare appears to be the larger of the two. This species differs from the gray rabbit in other particulars; whilst the points of the hair in the latter animal become whiter in winter, those of the Swamp-Hare become jet-black; whilst the gray rabbit strenuously avoids water, the present species plunges fearlessly into it, and finds it a congenial element.

Sciurus Ferruginiventris. —Aud. and Bach.

Red-Bellied Squirrel.

Plate xxxviii. —Male, Female, and Young. Natural size.

Sc. Caroliniano paullulum minor; cauda corpore longiore; vellere, supra albo-cinereo, infra rufo, armis fuscis.

Characters.

A size smaller than the Carolina gray squirrel; tail, longer than the body; light gray above, reddish-brown on the shoulders, beneath, bright rufous.

Synonyme.

SCIURUS FERRUGINIVENTRIS, Aud. and Bach., Jour. Acad. of Nat. Sc., Philadelphia, read October 5, 1841.

Description.

This species in form bears some resemblance to the Carolina gray squirrel, but differs widely from it in colour. The forehead is arched; nose, rather sharp, clothed with short fur; eyes, of moderate size; whiskers, as long as the head; ears, rather long, broad at base, ovate in shape.

The body is slender, seemingly formed for an agility equalling that of *Sciurus Hudsonius*. It is covered with a soft thick coat of fur, intermixed with longer hairs.

The feet are rather robust. Like all the squirrels, it has a blunt nail in place of a thumb, and the third toe, counting from the inner side, is longest; palms, nearly naked.

The tail is long, and capable of a distichous arrangement, but the hairs are not very thick or bushy.

Colour.

Teeth, yellow; nails, brown; point of nose and whiskers, black; ears, on the outer edges, tinged with brown, within gray; behind the ears on the neck a line of dull white. On the upper surface, the head, neck, back, and tail, are light gray, formed by hairs, which are light plumbeous from the roots to near the tips, where they have white and black annulations; most of the hairs are tipped with white. From the outer surface of the fore-legs there is a reddish-brown tinge, which extends over the shoulders and nearly meets on the back, gradually fading into the colours of the back and neck. The hairs on the tail are black at the roots, then yellowish, succeeded by a broad line of black tipped with white. The feet on the upper surface are grizzled with white and black. Sides of the face, chin, and throat, light-gray. All the rest of the under surface of the body, a line around the eyes, the neck, and the inner surface of the legs, are of a uniform bright rufous colour.

Dimensions.

	Inches.	Lines.
Length of head and body	8	9
" tail	10	0
Height of ear, posteriorly	5	0
Length of tarsus	2	5

Habits.

We are unfortunately without any information or account of the habits of this singularly marked and bright coloured Squirrel. We have represented three of them in our plate in different attitudes on a branch of mulberry.

Geographical Distribution.

Several specimens, differing a little in colour, which differences we have represented in our plate, were received from California; the precise locality was not given.

General Remarks.

This species should perhaps be compared with the dusky squirrel (*S. nigrescens*) of BENNET, to which it bears some resemblance. From the description, however, which we made of the original specimen of *S. nigrescens*, deposited in the museum of the London Zoological Society, we have little hesitation in pronouncing this a distinct species.

To *Sciurus socialis* of WAGNER, (Beitrage zur Kentniss der warmblutigen Wirbelthiere Amerikas, p. 88, Dresden,) the present species also bears some distant resemblance, but in some of its markings differs widely from WAGNER's animal.

Spermophilus Tridecem Lineatus. —Mitchill.

Leopard-Spermophile.

Plate xxxix. —Male and Female. Natural size.

Magnitudine Tamiæ Lysteri; supra striis octo longitudinalibus dilute fulvis cum striis novem fulvis alternatum distributis; harum quinque, stria media et duabus utrinque proximis guttis subalbidis *subquadratus* distinctis.

Characters.

Size of the chipping-squirrel (Tamias Lysteri); eight pale yellowish-brown stripes on the back, which alternate with nine broader yellowish-brown ones; the five uppermost being marked with a row of pale spots.

Synonymes.

LEOPARD GROUND-SQUIRREL, Schoolcraft's Travels, p. 313, and Index, anno 1821.
SCIURUS TRIDECEM LINEATUS, Mitchill, Med. Repository, 1821.
ARCTOMYS HOODII, Sabine, Linn. Trans., vol. xiii., p. 590, 1822.
    "   "   Franklin's Journey, p. 663.
STRIPED AND SPOTTED GROUND-SQUIRREL, Say, Long's Expedition.
SPERMOPHILE, F. Cuvier, Hist. Nat. des Mamm.
ARCTOMYS TRIDECEM LINEATA, Harlan, Fauna, p. 164.
HOOD'S MARMOT, Godman, vol. ii., p. 112.
ARCTOMYS HOODII, Fischer's Synopsis, p. 544.
SPERMOPHILUS HOODII, Less., Mamm., p. 243, 654.
    "   "   Desmarest, in Dict. des Sc. Nat., L. p. 139.
    "   "   F. Cuv. et Geoff., Mamm., fasc. 46.
ARCTOMYS TRIDECEM LINEATA, Griffith, sp. 641.
ARCTOMYS (SPERMOPHILUS) HOODII, Rich., Fauna Boreali America-
    na, p. 177, pl. 14.

Description.

In form this species bears a considerable resemblance to the very common chipping squirrel of the Atlantic States; by its shorter ears, however, and by its longer nails, which are intended more for digging than climbing, it approaches the marmots. The head has a convex shape and is very much curved, especially from the forehead to the nose; the nose is obtuse, and with

Red-Bellied Squirrel

Drawn from Nature by J.J. Audubon, F.R.S. F.L.S.   Lith.ᵈ Printed & Col.ᵈ by J.T. Bowen, Philad.ᵗ

the exception of the nostrils and septum is completely covered with very short hairs. The mouth is far back; the cheek-pouches of moderate size. Whiskers, a little shorter than the head; eyes, large; ears, very short, consisting merely of a low short lobe behind and above the auditory opening; they are covered with very short hairs. The hair on the whole body is short, adpressed, and glossy.

Legs and feet, rather slender; nails, long, slightly arched, and channeled beneath toward their extremities. On the fore-feet the thumb has one joint, with an obtuse nail; the second toe is longest, (as in the spermophiles, and not the third, as in the squirrels;) the first and third are of equal length; the fourth shortest, and removed far back. The tail is linear; for an inch from the root the fur lies so close that it appears rounded, it then gradually widens, becomes flattened, and seems capable of a slight distichous arrangement. Mammæ, twelve, situated along the sides of the abdomen.

Colour.

A line around the eye and a spot beneath, inner and outer surfaces of the legs, and the whole under part of the body, of a pale yellowish colour; on the sides of the neck, the fore-legs near the shoulders, and on the hips, there are tinges of reddish-brown; the feet near the nails, and the under-jaw, are dull white. On the head, there are irregular and somewhat indistinct alternate stripes of brown and yellowish-white, being an extension of the stripes on the back, which, from the irregular blending of the colours, give it a spotted appearance.

On the back there are five longitudinal brown stripes, each having regular rows of square spots of yellowish-white; the dorsal stripe, which runs from the back part of the head, and extends for half an inch beyond the root of the tail, is a little the broadest. These dark-coloured stripes are separated from each other by straight and uniform lines of yellowish-white. There are also on each side, two less distinct brown stripes, that are not spotted. Thus the animal has five brown stripes that are spotted, and four that are plain and without spots, together with eight yellowish-white stripes.

The hairs in the tail are yellowish-white at the roots, then broadly barred with black, and at the tips yellowish-white, giving it when distichally arranged a bar of black on each side of the vertebræ.

Dimensions.

Head and body	$6\frac{1}{8}$	inches.
Tail (vertebræ)	$3\frac{1}{2}$	do.
Tail, to end of hair	$4\frac{1}{2}$	inches.
From heel to end of nail	$1\frac{1}{2}$	do.
Longest claw on the fore-foot	$0\frac{3}{8}$	do.

Measurement of an old female.

Nose to root of tail	$6\frac{3}{4}$	do.
Tail (vertebræ)	$3\frac{1}{2}$	do.
Tail, to end of hair	$4\frac{3}{8}$	do.
Fore-feet to end of claws	$0\frac{7}{8}$	do.
Heel to end of longest claw	$1\frac{3}{8}$	do.
Nose to opening of ear	$1\frac{1}{2}$	do.
Length of pouch, to angle of mouth	$1\frac{7}{16}$	do.

Dr. RICHARDSON measured a male that was nine inches to the insertion of the tail. He remarks that the females are smaller than the males.

Habits.

We believe it is generally supposed that "birds," with their varied and pleasing forms, their gay and beautiful plumage, their tuneful throats, and their graceful movements through the air, present greater attractions to the student of nature than "quadrupeds," and awaken in him a stronger desire to acquire a knowledge of their natures and characters than he may entertain to study the habits of the mammalia.

In addition, however, to the fact that the latter are like ourselves viviparous, and approach our own organization, it should be remembered that all the productions of nature are the work of so infinite a wisdom, that they must, in every department of the physical world, excite our greatest interest and our admiration, even when examined superficially.

Among the quadrupeds, there are innumerable varieties of form and character, and although most animals are nocturnal, and therefore their habits cannot be studied with the same facility with which the manners and customs of the lively diurnal species of birds may be observed; yet when we follow them in their nightly wanderings, penetrate into their retreats, and observe the sagacity and extraordinary instincts with which they are endowed, we find in them matter to interest us greatly, and arouse our curiosity and astonishment.

Owls seem to us a dull and stupid race, principally because we only notice them during the day, which nature requires them to spend in sleep, the structure of their eyes compelling them to avoid the light, and seek concealment in hollow trees, in caves, and obscure retreats. But we should recollect that the diurnal birds are, during night, the time for their repose, as dull and stupid as owls are during the day. We should therefore not judge the habits of quadrupeds by the same standard. In regard to their fur, and external markings, there are many that will strike even the most careless observer as eminently beautiful. The little animal which is here presented to you is one of this description. In the distribution of the tints that compose its gaudy dress, in the regularity of its lines and spots, and in the soft blendings of its various shades of colour, we have evidence that even species whose habitations are under ground, may present to the eye as rich and beautiful a vesture as is found in the garb of a majority of the lively songsters of the woods.

In the warm days of spring the traveller on our Western prairies is often diverted from the contemplation of larger animals, to watch the movements of this lively little species. He withdraws his attention for a moment from the bellowing buffalo herd that is scampering over the prairies, to fix his eyes on a lively little creature of exquisite beauty seated on a diminutive mound at the mouth of its burrow, which seems by its chirrupings and scoldings to warn away the intruder on its peaceful domains. On a nearer approach it darts into its hole; but although concealed from view, and out of the reach of danger, its tongue, like that of other scolds of a more intelligent race, is not idle; it still continues to vent its threats of resentment against its unwelcome visitor by a shrill and harsh repetition of the word "seek—seek."

There is a great similarity in the habits of the various spermophili that compose the interesting group to which the present species belongs.

They live principally on the open prairies, make their burrows in the earth, and feed on roots and seeds of various kinds, which they carry in their pouches to their dark retreats under ground.

The holes of this species, according to RICHARDSON, run nearly perpendicularly, and are so straight, that they will admit a stick to be inserted to the depth of four or five feet. He supposes that owing to the depth of their burrows, which the sun does not penetrate very early in spring, they do not make their appearance as early as some others, especially *S. Richardsonii.*

As soon as they feel the warmth of spring they come forth and go in quest of their mates; at this period they seem fearless of danger, and are easily captured by the beasts and birds of prey that frequent the plains. The males are said to be very pugnacious at this season.

This is believed to be the most active and lively of all our known species of marmot-squirrels; we recently observed one in New York that played in a wheel in the manner of the squirrel. We saw in Charleston a pair in a cage, that were brought from Missouri by an officer of the army. They were adults, had but recently been captured, and were rather wild. They seemed to keep up a constant angry querulous chattering; they were fed on various kinds of nuts and grains, but principally on corn-meal and pea or ground-nuts, (*Arachis hypogœa.*) They would come to the bars of the cage and take a nut from the hand, but would then make a hasty retreat to a little box in the corner of their domicile. On our placing a handful of filberts in front of the cage, they at first came out and carried off one by one to their store-house, but after we had retired so as not to be observed, they filled their pouches by the aid of their paws, and seemed to prefer this mode of transporting their provisions. As we were desirous of taking measurements and descriptions, we endeavoured to hold one in the hand by the aid of a glove, but it struggled so lustily and used it teeth so savagely that we were compelled to let it go.

This species frequently takes up its residence near the fields and gardens of the settlers, and in the neighbourhood of Fort Union and other places, was represented as particularly destructive to the gardens.

We found the Leopard-Spermophile quite abundant near Fort Union, on the Upper Missouri. Their burrows were made in a sandy gravelly soil, they were never deep or inclined downwards, but ran horizontally within about a foot of the surface of the earth. This difference in habit from those observed by RICHARDSON may be owing to the nature of the different soils. We dug some of their burrows and discovered that the holes ran in all directions, containing many furcations.

RICHARDSON states that "the males fight when they meet, and in their contests their tails are often mutilated." All the specimens, however, that we obtained were perfect and in good order.

The Leopard-Spermophile has two more teats than are found in the majority of the species of this genus, and hence it may be expected to produce and additional number of young. RICHARDSON informs us that ten young were taken from a female killed at Carlton House. This was on the 17th May, and

Drawn from Nature by J. J. Audubon, FRS.F.L.S.

Drawn on Stone by W.ᵐ E. Hitchcock.

Lith Printed & Col.ᵈ by J.T.Bowen,Phil

Leopard Spermophile.

we from hence presume that they produce their young soon after this period.

Geographical Distribution.

We have not heard of the existence of this species farther to the north than latitude 55°. It was found by SAY at Engineer Encampment on the Missouri; we found it at Fort Union, latitude 40° 40′; and it is said to extend along the prairies on the Eastern side of the Rocky Mountains into Mexico.

General Remarks

The name *tridecem lineatus* (thirteen lined) is not particularly euphonious, nor very characteristic, yet as it has in conformity with long established usages existing among naturalists, been admitted into our standard works, we have concluded to adopt it.

The figures given by SABINE and F. CUVIER of this species, are defective, each having been taken from a specimen in which the tail had been mutilated. That given by RICHARDSON, Fauna boreali Americana, drawn by LAND-SEER, is more characteristic.

Mus Leucopus. — Rafinesque.

American White-Footed Mouse.

Plate xl. Male, Female and Young. Natural size.

Cauda elongata, villosa; auribus magnis; supra fulvo-fuscescens, subtus albus; pedibus albis.

Characters.

Tail, long and hairy; ears, large; yellowish brown above; feet and lower parts of the body, white.

Synonymes.

MUS SYLVATICUS, Forster, Phil. Trans., vol. lxii., p. 380.
FIELD-RAT, Penn., Hist. Quad., vol. ii., p. 185.
      "   Arctic Zool. i., p. 131.
MUSCULUS LEUCOPUS, Rafinesque, Amer. Month. Review, Oct. 1818, p. 444.
MUS LEUCOPUS, Desmar. Mamm., esp. 493.
MUS SYLVATICUS, Harlan, Fauna, p. 151.
MUS AGRARIUS, Godm., Nat. Hist., vol. ii., p. 88.
MUS LEUCOPUS, Richardson, F. B. A., p. 142.
ARVICOLA NUTTALLII, Harlan, variety.
ARVICOLA EMMONSII, Emm., Mass. Report, p. 61.
MUS LEUCOPUS, Dekay, Nat. Hist. N. Y., pl. 1, p. 82.

Description.

Head, of moderate size; muzzle, sharp pointed; eyes, large; ears, large, membranous, rounded above, nearly naked. There are a few short hairs on the margins, on both surfaces, not sufficient to conceal the integument. Whiskers, longer than the head.

The form of this species is delicate and of fine proportions; the fur (which is not very long) is soft and fine, but not lustrous.

Feet, slender, and clothed with short adpressed hairs, covering the toes and nails; there are four toes on the fore-feet, with six tubercles on each palm; the thumb is rudimentary, and covered by a very small blunt nail. The nails are small, sharp, and hooked; the hind-feet are long, especially the tarsal bones; the toes are longer than on the fore-feet. The tail is round, slender, tapering, and thickly clothed with short hairs; no scales being visible like those on the common mouse, (*Mus musculus.*)

Colour.

Fur, from the roots to near the extremity, dark bluish-gray; on the upper parts, brownish yellow; being a little darker on the crown and back, and lighter on the sides; the colour of the cheeks and hips approaches reddish-brown. This above is the colour of this species through the winter and until it sheds its hair late in spring, when it assumes a bluish-gray tint, a little lighter than that of the common mouse. Whiskers, white and black; upper surface of the tail, the colour of the back. The lips, chin, throat, feet, legs, and the whole under surface of the body and tail, are pure white. On the sides, this colour extends high up along the flanks; there is a very distinct line of demarcation between the colours of the back and sides.

There are some varieties in this species; specimens which we examined, from Labrador, Hudson's Bay, and Oregon, were lighter in colour, and the white on the under surface extended farther toward the back, than on those from the Atlantic States; we also observed a striking difference in the length of their tails, some being longer than the body, whilst others were not much more than half the length. In size they also differ widely; we have seen some that are scarcely larger than the common mouse, whilst others are nearly double that size; they are considerably larger in Carolina than in the Eastern States.

Dimensions.

Length of head and body . . . .$2\frac{1}{4}$ inches.
   "   " tail . . . .$2\frac{1}{2}$ do.

Another specimen.
Length of head and body . . . .$3\frac{1}{2}$ do.
   "   " tail . . . .$2\frac{1}{4}$ do.

Habits.

Next to the common mouse, this is the most abundant and widely diffused species of mouse in North America. We have received it (under various names) from every State in the Union, and from Labrador, Hudson's Bay, and the Columbia River. Being nocturnal in its habits it is far more common than is generally supposed. In familiar localities, where we had never knwon of its existence, we found it almost the only species taken in traps at night.

The White-footed Mouse is an exceedingly active species. It runs, leaps, and climbs, with great facility. We have observed it taking up its abode in a deserted squirrel's nest, thirty feet from the earth; we have seen a family of five or six scamper from a hollow in an oak that had just been cut down; we have frequently found them in the loft of a corn-house or stable in Carolina; and at times have discovered their nests under stone-heaps or old logs, or in the ground.

In New Jersey their favourite resorts are isolated cedars growing on the margins of damp places, where green briars (*Smilax rotundifolio*, and *S. herbacea*) connect the branches with the ground, and along the stems of which they climb expertly.

When started from their nest in these trees, they descend along the vines in safety to the earth. When thus disturbed, however, if the nest is at some distance from the ground, they hesitate before they come down, and go out on a branch perhaps, to scrutinize the vicinty, and, if not farther molested, appear satisfied, and again retreat to their nests. They have been known to take possession of deserted birds' nests—such as those of the cat-bird, red-winged starling, song thrush, or red-eyed fly-catcher.

In the northern part of New York we could always obtain specimens from under the sheaves of wheat that were usually stacked in the harvest fields for a few days before they were carried into the barn. We have also occasionally found their nests on bushes, from five to fifteen feet from the ground. They are in these cases constructed with nearly as much art and ingenuity as the nests of the Baltimore Oriole. There are several nests now lying before us, that were found near Fort Lee, New Jersey. They are seven inches in length and four in breadth, the circumference measuring thirteen inches; they are of an oval shape and are outwardly composed of dried moss and a few slips of the inner bark of some wild grape-vine; other nests are more rounded, and are composed of dried leaves and moss. We have sometimes thought that two pair of these Mice might occupy the same nest, as we possess one, nine inches in length and eight inches in diameter, which has two entrances, six inches apart, so that in such a case the little tenants need not have interfered with each other. The entrance in all the nests is from below, and about the size of the animal.

When we first discovered this kind of nest we were at a loss to decide whether it belonged to a bird or a quadruped; on touching the bush, however, we saw the little tenant of this airy domicile escape. At our next visit she left the nest so clumsily, and made her way along the ground so slowly, that we took her up in our hand, when we discovered that she had four young about a

Plate XL

Drawn from Nature by J.J. Audubon, F.R.S. F.L.S.

White Footed Mouse.

Lith Printed & Col⁴ by J.T. Bowen, Philada

fourth grown, adhering so firmly to the teats that she dragged them along in the manner of the jumping mouse (*Meriones Americanus*), or of the Florida rat. We preserved this little family alive for eighteen months, during which time the female produced several broods of young. During the day they usually concealed themselves in their nests, but as soon as it was dark they became very active and playful, running up and down the wires of their cages, robbing each other's little store-houses, of various grains that had been carried to them, and occasionally emitting the only sound we ever heard them utter,—a low squeak resembling that of the common mouse. We have been informed by WILLIAM COOPER, Esq., of Weehawken, New Jersey, an intelligent and close observer, to whom science is indebted for many excellent papers on various branches of natural history, that this species when running off with its young to a place of safety, presses its tail closely under its abdomen to assist in holding them on to the teats—a remarkable instance of the love of offspring.

The White-footed Mouse seems less carnivorous than most of its kindred species. We found it when in confinement always dragging to its nest any kind of meat we placed in the cage, but it was generally left there unconsumed. We have often caught it in traps, set for larger animals, and baited with meat. Its first object is to drag the meat to its little store-house of provisions; the bait, however, being tied with a string to the pan of the steel-trap, is not so easily carried off; but, without much loss of time the mouse gnaws the string in two, and, if not caught in the attempt, drags off the meat. Our friend, the late Dr. JOHN WRIGHT, of Troy, furnished us with information confirming the above; he says, "In trapping for a weasel last summer I tied bits of beef above each trap with twine. On my first visit to the traps I found the twine at one, cut, and the meat in the jaws of the trap. The next day the same thing was observed at one of the traps, but another held fast a specimen of the *Mus leucopus*. I am informed that the trapper is not unfrequently troubled in this manner."

We have known this Mouse to cut into pieces snares set for the ruffed grouse, placed in gaps left for the purpose in fences of brushwood.

In its wild state it is continually laying up little stores of grain and grass seeds. We have seen it carrying in its mouth acorns and chinquepins. In the Northern States, these little hoards are often composed wholly of wheat; in the South, of rice. This species, like all rats and mice, is fond of Indian-corn, from which it only extracts the choicest, sweetest portions, eating the heart and leaving the rest untouched.

In the thickly settled portions of the United States this Mouse avoids dwellings, and even outhouses, and either confines itself to the woods, or keeps near fences, stone-heaps, &c., but in partially deserted houses, or in newly formed settlements, it seems to take the place of the common mouse. RICHARDSON states that in the fur countries it becomes an inmate of the dwelling houses. Dr. LEITNER, and eminent botanist, who, whilst acting as surgeon in the army, was unfortunately killed in the Florida war, informed us that whilst on a botanizing tour through Florida a few years ago, he was frequently kept awake during a portion of the night by the White-footed Mice which had taken possession of the huts of the Indians and the log cabins of the early white settlers. We are under an impression that in these localities the common cat, and the Norway rat, were both absent; as we have reason to believe that this species deserts premises whenever they are frequented by either of the above animals. We kept a pair of white Norway rats (Albino variety) separated by a partition from an interesting family of white-footed mice, but before we were aware of it, the rats gnawed through the partition and devoured all our little pets.

This is a timid and very gentle species; we have seldom known it to bite when taken into the hand, and have observed that in a state of confinement it suffered itself to be killed by the very carnivorous cotton-rat (*Sigmodon hispidum*) without making any resistance.

We are disposed to believe that this species produces at least two litters of young in a season, in the Northern States, and three, in the Southern. In the State of New York we have seen the young every month from May to September, and in Carolina a female that was kept in confinement had young three times, first having three, at a second litter five, and having six at a third.

The White-footed Mouse has many enemies. Foxes, wild-cats, and owls, destroy it frequently; the house-cat strays into the fields and along fences in search of it. In Carolina some domesticated cats live in the fields and woods in a partially wild state, avoiding houses altogether; these subsist on birds and the smaller rodentia, and this species furnishes a considerable portion of their food; but we are disposed to regard the ermine (common weasel) as its most formidable and voracious persecutor. We believe that the White-footed Mouse does not always dig a burrow of its own, but that it takes possession of one dug by some other small species; in the Northern States, generally that of the chipping squirrel. Be this as it may, it is certain that wherever the White-footed Mouse can enter, the ermine can follow, and he not only feeds up-on it,

but destroys whole families. An ermine at one time made its escape from us, carrying with it a small portion of a chain fastened around its neck: it was traced by a servant over the snow a mile into the woods, to a spot where it entered a very small hole. It was dug out, and the man brought us five or six Mice, of this species, that he found dead in the hole, having been killed, doubtless, by the ermine. From appearances, two only had been devoured, the remainder we observed had not been seized by the throat in the manner of the cat, but had the marks of the ermine's teeth in their skulls.

We do not regard this species as doing very extensive injury either to the garden or farm, in any of the Atlantic States of America. We suspect that its reputation in this respect, as well as that of the shrew-mole, has been made to suffer very unjustly, when in reality the author of the mischief is the little pine-mouse (*Arvicola pinetorum*, LE CONTE), or perhaps WILSON's meadow-mouse, (*Arvicola Pennsylvanica*, ORD, *A. hirsutus*, EMMONS, and DEKAY). The farmers and gardeners, of the Northern and Eastern States, however, complain that this Mouse, which they generally call the "Deer-mouse," destroys many of their cabbage-plants and other young and tender vegetables, and gnaws the bark from young fruit trees, and if they have made no mistake in regard to the species, it must be much more destructive than we have heretofore considered it.

Geographical Distribution.

According to RICHARDSON this species is found as far north as Great Bear Lake. We saw in the London museums several specimens from Hudson's Bay; it extends across the continent to the Columbia River on the Pacific, from whence Mr. TOWNSEND brought us several skins. We received specimens from Florida by Dr. LEITNER, we found it west of the Mississippi at Fort Union, where it commits depredations in the garden attached to the Fort, and we have received specimens from Arkansas and Texas.

General Remarks.

That a species so widely distributed, and subject to so many varieties in size, length of tail, and colour, should have been often described under different names is not surprising. We have ourselves often been in a state of doubt on obtaining some striking variety. The name *Hypudæus gossipinus* of our friend, Major LE CONTE, (see Appendix to McMURTRIE's translation of CUV. An. Kingd., vol i., p. 434,) was intended for this species, as it is found in the Southern States. We were for several years disposed to regard it as distinct, and have, not without much hesitation, and after an examination of many hundred specimens, been induced to set it down as a variety only.

We have adopted the name given to it by RAFINESQUE, in deference to the opinions of RICHARDSON who supposed that it applied to this species, RICHARDSON himself, however,—not RAFINESQUE, gave a true description of it.

GODMAN, in describing *Mus agrarius*, we feel confident, had reference to this species. He had, however, never seen the European *Mus agrarius* of PALLAS, else he would not have made so great a mistake; we have on several occasions in Denmark and Germany compared them, and found that they scarcely bear any resemblance to each other. *Mus agrarius* has a short tail and short hairy ears. FORSTER, and HARLAN, refer this species to *Mus sylvaticus* of Europe. FORSTER's specimens came from Hudson's Bay at an early period, when it was customary to consider American species of Quadrupeds and Birds as mere vaieties of those of Europe. HARLAN instead of describing from an American specimen, literally translated DESMAREST's description of the European *Mus sylvaticus* and applied it to our species, (see Mam. p. 301,) in doing which by neglecting to institute a comparison he committed a great error.

We were favoured with the privilege of comparing specimens of *Mus sylvaticus* and *M. leucopus*, through the kindness of Prof. LICHTENSTEIN at the Berlin museum. Although there is a general resemblance, a moment's examination will enable the naturalist to discover sufficient marks of difference to induce him to separate the species. *Mus leucopus* has a little longer tail. Its ears are longer, but not so broad. The under surface of the tail of *Mus sylvaticus* is less white, and the white on the under surface of the body does not extend as high on the sides, nor is there any distinct line of separation between the colours of the back and under surface, which is a striking characteristic in the American species. But they may always be distinguished from each other at a glance by the following mark: in more than twenty specimens we examined of *Mus sylvaticus* we have always found a yellowish line edged with dark-brown, on the breast. In many hundred specimens of *Mus leucopus* we have without a single exception found this yellow line entirely wanting, all of them being pure white on the breast, as well as on the whole under surface. We have no hesitation in pronouncing the species distinct.

Genus Mustela.—Cuv.

Dental Formula.

Incisive $\frac{6}{6}$; *Canine* $\frac{1-1}{1-1}$; *Molar* $\frac{5-5}{6-6}$ = 38.

Head, small and oval; muzzle, rather large; ears, short and round; body, long, vermiform; tail, usually long and cylindrical; legs, short; five toes on each foot, armed with sharp, crooked, slightly retractile claws. No anal pouch, but a small gland which secretes a thickish offensive fluid. Fur, very fine.

This genus differs from the genus PUTORIUS, having four carnivorous teeth on each side, in the upper jaw, instead of three, the number the true weasels exhibit, and, the last carnivorous tooth on the lower jaw, has a rounded lobe on the inner side, which renders this genus somewhat less carnivorous in its habit than PUTORIUS, and consequently a slight diminution of the cruelty and ferocity displayed by animals of the latter genus, may be observed in those forming the present.

There are about twelve species of true Martens known, four of which inhabit North America.

The generic name MUSTELA, is derived from the Latin word *mustela*, a weasel.

Mustela Canadensis.—Schreber.

Pennant's Marten or Fisher.

Black Fox or Black Cat of the Northern Hunters.

Plate xli.—Male. Natural size.

Capite et humeris cano fuscoque mixtis; naso, labiis, cruribus, et cauda, fusco-nigris.

Characters.

Head and shoulders, mixed with gray and brown; nose, lips, legs, and tail, dark brown.

Synonymes.

LE PEKAN, Buffon, vol. xiii., p. 304, A.D. 1749.
MUSTELA CANADENSIS, Schreber, Säugeth. p. 492, 1775.
MUSTELA PENNANTI, Erxleben Syst., p. 470, A.D. 1777.
FISHER, Penn., Arct. Zool., 4 vol. i., p. 82, A.D. 1784.
MUSTELA CANADENSIS, Gmel., Lin., vol. i., p. 95, 1788.
WEJACK, Hearne's Journey.
FISHER, or BLACK FOX, Lewis and Clarke, vol. iii., p. 25.
FISHER, WEASEL, or PEKAN, Warden's United States.
MUSTELA PENNANTI, Sabine, Frank. First Journey, p. 651.
MUSTELA CANADENSIS, Harlan, F., p. 65.
      "   " Godman, vol., p. 203.
MUSTELA GODMANI, Less., Mamm., p. 150.
MUSTELA CANADENSIS, Rich., F. B. A., p. 52.
PEKAN, or FISHER, Dekay, Nat. His. N. Y., p. 31.

Description.

The head of this species bears a stronger resemblance to that of a dog than to the head of a cat. Its canine teeth, in the upper jaw, are so long that with the slightest movement of the lip they are exposed. Head, broad and round, contracting rather suddenly toward the nose, which is acute. Eyes, rather small and oblique; ears, low, broad, semicircular, and far apart, covered on both surfaces with short soft fur; whiskers, half the length of the head; body, long, and formed for agility and strength.

The pelage is formed of a short fine down next to the skin, intermixed with longer and coarser hairs about an inch and a half in length; these hairs are longer on the posterior parts of the animal than on the shoulders.

The feet are robust. Fore-feet, shorter than the hind-feet, thickly clothed with rather fine and short hairs; nails, long, strong, curved, and sharp; soles, hairy; the toes on all the feet are connected at the base by a short hairy web; the callosities consequently make only a slight impression when the animal is walking or running on the snow.

Tail, long, bushy, and gradually diminishing to a point toward the extremity.

This species has so strong a smell of musk, (like the pine marten,) that we have found the skin somewhat unpleasant to our olfactories, several years after it had been prepared as a specimen.

Colour.

Fur on the back, from the roots to near the extremity, chesnut-brown, tipped with reddish-brown and light gray. On the head, shoulders, and fore part of the back, there are so many long whitish hairs interspersed, that they produce a somewhat hoary appearance. Whiskers, nose, chin, ears, legs, feet, and tail, dark-brown; margins of the ears, light-brown; hips and posterior part of the back, darker than the shoulders; eyes, yellowish-brown; nails, light horn-colour.

In some specimens, we have seen a white spot on the throat, and a line of the same colour on the belly; others, (as was the case with the one from which our drawing was made,) have no white markings on the body. We have seen a specimen, nearly white, with a brown head. Another obtained in Buncombe county, North Carolina, was slightly hoary on the whole upper surface.

Dimensions.

From point of nose to root of tail	23	inches.
Tail (vertebræ)	12	do.
" to end of hair	14½	do.
Breadth of head	3½	do.
Height of ear	1	do.
Breadth of ear	2	do.
From point of nose to eye	2	do.
" heel to point of longest nail	4¼	do.

Weight, 8½ lbs.

Habits.

Although this species is represented as having been rather common in every part of the Northern and Middle States, in the early periods of our history, and is still met with in diminished numbers, in the thinly settled portions of our country; very little of its history or habits has been written, and much is still unknown. We have occasionally met with it, but it has been to us far from a common species. Even in the mountainous portions of the Northern and Eastern States, the Fisher, thirty years ago, was as difficult to procure as the Bay lynx. It has since become still more rare, and in places where it was then known, scarcely andy vestige of the knowledge of its former existence can now be traced.

Dr. DEKAY (Nat. Hist. N. Y., p. 32, 1843,) states that, "in Hamilton county, (N. Y.,) it is still numerous and troublesome." On an excursion we made in the State of New York, in 1827, we heard of it occasionally near the head waters of Lake Champlain, along the St. Lawrence, and to the west as far as Lake Erie, but it was every where represented as a species that was disappearing.

Whilst residing in the northern part of our native State, (New York,) thirty-five years ago, the hunters were in the habit of bringing us two or three specimens of this Marten in the course of a winter. They obtained them by following their tracks in the snow, when the animals had been out in quest of food on the previous night, thus tracing them to the hollow trees in which they were concealed, which they chopped down. They informed us that as a tree was falling, the Fisher would dart from the hallow, which was often fifty feet from the ground, and leap into the snow, when the dogs usually seized and killed him, although not without a hard struggle, as the Fisher was infinitely more dangerous to their hounds than either the gray or the red fox. They usually called this species the Black Fox.

A servant, on one occasion, came to us before daylight, asking us to shoot a raccoon for him, which, after having been chased by his dogs the previous night, had taken to so large a tree that he neither felt disposed to climb it nor to cut it down. On our arrival at the place, it was already light, and the dogs were barking furiously at the foot of the tree. We soon perceived that instead of being a raccoon, the animal was a far more rare and interesting species, a Fisher. As we were anxious to study its habits we did not immediately shoot, but teased it by shaking some grape vines that had crept up nearly to the top of the tree. The animal not only became thoroughly frightened but seemed furious; he leaped from branch to branch, showing his teeth and growling at the same time; now and then he ran half way down the trunk of the tree, elevating his back in the manner of an angry cat, and we every moment expected to see him leap off and fall among the dogs. He was brought down after several discharges from the gun. He seemed extremely tenacious of life, and was game to the last, holding on to the nose of a dog with dying grasp. This animal proved to be a male, the body measured twenty-five inches, and the tail, including the fur, fifteen. The servant who had traced him, informed us that he appeared to have far less speed than a fox, that he ran for ten minutes through a swamp in a straight direction, and then took to a tree.

The only opportunity that was ever afforded us of judging of the speed of the Fisher occurred near the Virginia Gray-Sulphur Springs, in 1839. We had ascended Peter's Mountain in search of rare plants for our herbarium; out of health and fatigued, we had for some time been seated on a rock to rest, when we observed a gray squirrel pass within ten feet of us, seemingly in a great fright, and with all the speed it could command, with a Fisher in full pursuit. They were both too much occupied with their own affairs to take any notice of us. The Fisher seemed to make more rapid progress than the squirrel, and we feel confident that if the latter had not mounted a tree it would have been overtaken before it could have advanced many feet farther; it ran rapidly up the sides of a cucumber tree, (*Magnolia acuminati,*) still pursued by its hungry foe. The squirrel leaped lightly among the smaller branches, on which its heavier pursuer seemed unwilling to trust himself. At length the affrighted animal pitched from one of the topmost boughs and landed on its feet unhurt among the rocks beneath. We expected every moment to see the Fisher give us a specimen also of his talent at lofty tumbling, but he seemed to think that the "better part of valour was discretion," and began to run down the stem of the tree. At this point we interfered. Had he imitated the squirrel in its flying leap, he might have been entitled to the prey, provided he could overtake it, but as he chose to exercise some stratagy and jockeying in the race, when the chances were so much in his favour, we resolved to end the chase by running to the foot of the tree which the Fisher was descending. He paused on the opposite side as if trying to ascertain whether he had been observed; we were without a gun, but rattled away with a knife on our botanizing box, which seemed to frighten the Marten in his turn, most effectually;—the more noise we created the greater appeared to be his terror; after ascending to the top of the tree he sprang to another, which he rapidly descended, till within twenty feet of the earth, when he jumped to the ground, and with long leaps ran rapidly down the side of the mountain, and was out of sight in a few moments.

This scene occurred in the morning of a warm day in the month of July, a proof that this species is not altogether nocturnal in its habits. We are, however, inclined to believe that the above was only an exception to the general character of the animal.

Species that are decidedly nocturnal in their habits, frequently may be seen moving about by day during the period when they are engaged in providing for their young. Thus the raccoon, the opossum, and all our hares, are constantly met with in spring, and early summer, in the morning and afternoon, whilst in the autumn and winter they only move about by night.

In the many fox-hunts, in which our neighbours were from time to time engaged, not far from our residence at the north, during the period when we obtained the information concerning their primitive mode of enjoying that amusement, which we have laid before our readers, in pages 49 and 50, (where we also spoke of Pennant's Marten as not being very scarce at that time in Rensselaer county, N. Y.,) we never heard of their having encountered a single Fisher in the day-time; but whey they traversed the same grounds at night, in search of raccoons, it was not unusual for them to discover and capture this species. We were informed by the trappers that they caught the Fisher in their traps only by night.

The specimen, from which the figure in our plate was drawn, was taken alive in some part of the Alleghany Mountains, in the State of Pennsylvania, and we soon afterwards received a letter from our esteemed friend, SPENCER F. BAIRD, Esq., of Carlisle, in that State, informing us of its having been captured, which enabled us, through that gentleman, to purchase it. We received it at New-York, in good condition, in a case tinned inside, with iron bars in front, to prevent the animal from making its escape, as it was so strong and so well supplied with sharp teeth that it could easily have eaten its way out of a common wooden box. In Mr. BAIRD's note he says, "all the account I was able to procure respecting this species was the following:—It was found in company with an older one, in Peter's Mountain, six miles above Harrisburgh, about five weeks ago. (His letter is dated Carlisle, March 16th, 1844.) After a most desperate resistance the old one was killed, after having beaten off the dogs, to whose assistance the hunters were obliged to come. This individual ran up a tree, and being stoned by the hunters, jumped off from a height of about forty feet! when being a little stunned by the leap, the men ran up quickly, threw their coats over it, and thus secured it. The old one was said to have been about the size of a pointer dog. The young one is very savage, and

emits a rather strong musky odour."

We kept this individual alive for some days, feeding it on raw meat, pieces of chicken, and now and then a bird. It was voracious, and very spiteful, growling snarling and spitting when approached, but it did not appear to suffer much uneasiness from being held in captivity, as, like many other predacious quadrupeds it grew fat, being better supplied with food than when it had been obliged to cater for itself in the woods.

The older one, which, as Mr. BAIRD mentions, was killed by the dogs and the hunters, was a female, and no doubt was the mother of the one that was captured, and probably died in the hope of saving her young.

On several occasions we have seen the tracks of the Fisher in the snow; they resemble those of the pine marten, but are double their size. To judge by them, the animal advances by short leaps in the manner of a mink. Pennant's Marten appears to prefer low swampy grounds. We traced one which had followed a trout stream for some distance, and ascertained that it had not gone into the water. Marks were quite visible in different places where it had scratched up the snow by the side of logs and piles of timber, to seek for mice, or other small quadrupeds, and we have no doubt it preys upon the Northern hare, gray rabbit, and ruffed grouse, as we observed a great many tracks of those species in the vicinity. In further appears, that this animal makes an occasional meal on species which are much more closely allied to it than those just mentioned.

In a letter we received from Mr. FOTHERGILL, in which he furnished us with notes on the habits of some of the animals existing near Lake Ontario, he informs us that "a Fisher was shot by a hunter named MARSH, near Port Hope, who said it was up in a tree, in close pursuit of a pine marten, which he also brought with it." Mr. FOTHERGILL stuffed them both at the time.

LEWIS and CLARKE state that in Oregon the Fisher captures not only the squirrel, but the raccoon, and that in pursuing them it leaps from tree to tree.

RICHARDSON remarks that, "the Fisher is said to prey much on frogs in the summer season; but I have been informed that its favourite food is the Canada porcupine, which it kills by biting in the belly." He says also, "it will feed on the hoards of frozen fish laid up by the residents."

We can scarcely conceive in what manner it is able to overturn the porcupine, so as a bite it on the belly, as it is large and heavy, and is armed with bristles at all points.

It is stated by Dr. DEKAY, on the authority of a person who resided many years near Lake Oneida, New York, that the name (Fisher) "was derived from its singular fondness for the fish used to bait traps."

An individual of this species, which had been caught in a steel-trap, was brought to Charleston and exhibited in a menagerie. It had been taken only a few months, and was sullen and spiteful; when fed, it gulped down a moderate quantity of meat in great haste, swallowing it nearly whole, and then retired in a growling humour to a dark corner of its cage.

The Fisher is represented as following the line of traps set by the trappers, and in the manner of the wolverene, robbing them of their bait. The season for hunting this species is stated, by Dr. DEKAY, to commence in the western part of New York, about the 10th of October, and to last till the middle of May; and he says the ordinary price paid for each skin is a dollar and a half.

This species brings forth once a year, depositing its young in the trunk of a large tree, usually some thirty or forty feet from the ground. Dr. RICHARDSON observes that it produces from two to four young at a litter; DEKAY confines the number to two. We once saw three extracted from the body of a female on the 20th of April, in the northern part of New York.

Geographical Distribution.

This species inhabits a wide extent of country. To the north it exists, according to RICHARDSON, as far as Great Slave Lake, latitude 63°. It is found at Labrador, and extends across the continent to the Pacific. It is stated by all our authors that it does not exist further south than Pennsylvania. This is an error, as we saw it on the mountains of Virginia. We had an opportunity of examining a specimen obtained by Dr. GIBBES, of Columbia, South Carolina, from the neighbourhood of Ashville, Buncombe county, North Carolina. We have seen several skins procured in East Tennessee, and we have heard of at least one individual that was captured near Flat-Rock, in that State, latitude 35°.

We have also seen many skins from the Upper Missouri, and the Fisher is enumerated, by LEWIS and CLARKE, as one of the species existing on the Pacific Ocean, in the vicinity of the Columbia River.

General Remarks.

Notwithstanding the fact that on our plate we gave to LINNÆUS the

Drawn on Stone by W. E. Hitchcock.

Pennant's Marten or Fisher.

Drawn from Nature by J. J. Audubon, F.R.S. F.L.S.   lith.ᵈ Printed & Col.ᵈ by J. T. Bowen, Philad.ª

credit of having first applied a scientific name to this species, we must now transfer it to SCHREBER, by whom, LINNÆUS having been unacquainted with it, it was described in 1775. It was described two years afterwards by ERXLEBEN, and in 1788, by GMELIN, &c. It is probable that, by some mistake, the habits of the mink have been ascribed to the Fisher; hence its English name seems to be inappropriate, but as it appears to be entitled to it, by right of long possession, we do not feel disposed to change it. We are, however, not quite sure of its having no claim to the name by its mode of living. Its partially webbed feet seem indicative of aquatic habits; it is fond of low swampy places, follows streams, and eats fish when in captivity. We feel

pretty confident that it does not dive after the finny tribes, but it is not improbable that it surprises them in shallow water, and we are well informed that, like the raccoon, it searches under the banks of water-courses for frogs, &c.

By the Canadian hunters and trappers, it is universally called the Pekan. In New England and the Northern counties of New york it is sometimes named the Black Fox, but more frequently is known as the Fisher. According to DEKAY, it is called the Black Cat by the inhabitants of the western portion of New York.

Genus Mephitis.—Cuv.

Dental Formula.

Incisive $\frac{6}{6}$; *Canine* $\frac{1-1}{1-1}$; *Molar* $\frac{4-4}{5-5}$ = 34.

Canine teeth, very strong, conical; two small anterior cheek-teeth, or false molars, above, and three below, on each side. The superior tuberculous teeth, very largy, as broad as they are long; inferior molars having two tubercles on the inner side.

Head, short; nose, somewhat projecting; snout, in most of the species blunt.

Feet, with five toes; toes of the fore-feet, armed with long, curved nails, indicating the habit of burrowing in the earth; heel very little raised in walking.

Hairs on the body, usually long, and on the tail, very long.

The anal glands secrete a liquor which is excessively fetid. The various species of this genus burrow in the ground, or dwell in fissures of rocks, living on poultry, bird's eggs, small quadrupeds, and insects. They move slowly, and seldom attempt to run from man, unless they chance to be near their burrows. They are to a considerable extent, gregarious; large families being occasionally found in the same hole.

In the recent work of Dr. LICHTENSTEIN, (Ueber die Gattung Mephitis, Berlin, 1838,) seventeen species of this genus are enumerated, one of which is found at the Cape of Good Hope, two in the United States of America, and the remainder in Mexico and South America.

The generic name Mephitis, is derived from the latin word *Mephitis*, a strong odour.

Mephitis Chinga.—Tiedimann.

Common American Skunk.

Plate xlii.—Female. Natural size.

Magnitudine F. cati; supra nigricans, stries albis longitudinalibus insigneta; cauda longa villosissima.

Characters.

Size of a cat; general colour, blackish-brown, with white longitudinal stripes on the back; many varieties in its white markings; tail, long and bushy.

Synonymes.

OUINESQUE, Sagard Theodat, Canada, p. 748.
ENFANT DU DIABLE, Charlevoix, Nouv. France, iii., p. 133.
SKUNK-WEASEL, Pennant's Arctic Zool., vol. i., p. 85.
SKUNK, Hearne's Journey, p. 377.
MEPHITIS CHINGA, Tiedimann, Zool. i., p. 361, (Anh. 37,) 1808.
POLE-CAT SKUNK, Kalm's Travels, vol. ii. p. 378.
VIVERA MEPHITIS, Gmel. (L.) Syst. Nat., p. 88.
MUSTELA AMERICANA, Desm. Mam., p. 186, A. D. 1820.
MEPHITIS AMERICANA, Sab., Frank. Journal, p. 653.
       "   "   Harlan, Fauna, p. 70.
THE SKUNK, Godm., Nat. Hist., vol. i., p. 213.
MEPHITIS AMERICANA, Var. HUDSONICA, Rich., F. B. A., p. 55.
       "   CHINGA, Lichtenstein, Darstellung neuer order weing bekannter Säugethiere, Berlin, 1827–34, xlv. Tafel, 1st figure.
       "   CHINQUE, LICHT., Ueber die Guattung Mephitis, p. 32,

Berlin, 1838.
   "   AMERICANA, Dekay, Nat. Hist. N. Y., pt. 1, p. 29.

Description.

This species in all its varieties has a broad fleshy body, resembling that of the wolverene; it stands low on its legs, and is much wider at the hips than at the shoulders. Fur, rather long and coarse, with much longer, smooth and glossy hairs, interspersed.

The head is small compared with the size of the body; forehead, somewhat rounded; nose, obtuse, covered with short hair to the snout which is naked; eyes, small; ears, short, broad and rounded, clothed with hair on both surfaces; whiskers, few and weak, extending a little beyond the eyes; feet, rather broad, and covered with hair concealing the nails, which on the fore-feet, are robust, curved, compressed, and acute; palms, naked. The trunk of the tail is nearly half as long as the body. Hair on the tail, very long and bushy, containing from within an inch of the root to the extremity, no mixture of the finer fur. The glands are situated on either side of the rectum: the ducts are about an inch in length, and are of a somewhat pyriform shape. The inner membrane is corrugated; the principal portion of the glands is a muscular tendinous substance. The sac is capable of containing about three drachms. When the tail is erected for the purpose of ejecting the nauseous fluid, the open orifices of the ducts are perceptible on a black disk surrounding the anus. The exit from the duct at the anus when distended will admit a crow-quill.

Colour.

This species varies so much in colour that there is some difficulty in finding two specimens alike; we have given a representation on our plate of the colour which is most common in the Middle States, and which Dr. HARLAN described as *Mephitis Americana*, our specimen only differing from his in having a longitudinal stripe on the forehead.

The under fur on all those portions of the body which are dark coloured, is dark brown; in those parts which are light coloured, it is white from the roots. These under colours, however, are concealed by a thick coat of longer, coarser hairs, which are smooth and glossy.

There is a narrow white stripe commencing on the nose and running to a point on the top of the head; a patch of white, of about two inches in length, and of the same breadth, commences on the occiput and covers the upper parts of the neck; on each side of the vertebræ of the tail there is a broad longitudinal stripe for three fourths of its length; the tail is finally broadly tipped with white, interspersed with a few black hairs. The colour on every other part of the body is blackish-brown.

Another specimen from the same locality has a white stripe on the forehead; a large white spot on the occiput, extending downwards, diverging on the back, and continuing down the sides to within two inches of the extremity of the tail, leaving the back, the end of the tail, and the whole of the under surface blackish-brown.

The young on the plate are from the same nest; one has white stripes on the back, with a black tail; the other has no stripes on the back, but the end of its tail is white.

In general we have found the varieties in a particular locality marked with tolerable uniformity. To this rule, however, there are many exceptions.

In the winter of 1814 we caused a burrow to be opened in Renssellaer county, N. Y., which we knew contained a large family of this species. We found eleven: they were all full grown, but on examining their teeth and claws, we concluded that the family was composed of a pair of old ones, with their large brood of young of the previous season. The male had a white stripe on the forehead; and from the occiput down the whole of the back had another white stripe four inches in breadth; its tail was also white. The female had no

Common American Skunk.

Drawn from Nature by J.J.Audubon F.R.S.F.L.S.

white stripe on the forehead, but had a longitudinal stripe on each side of the back, and a very narrow one on the dorsal line; the tail was wholly black. The young differed very widely in colour; we could not find two exactly alike; some were in part, of the colour of the male, others were more like the female, whilst the largest proportion were intermediate in their markings, and some seemed to resemble neither parent. We recollect one that had not a white hair, except the tip of the tail and a minute dorsal line.

On the other hand, we had in February (the same winter) another family of Skunks, captured with a steel-trap placed at the mouth of their burrow; they were taken in the course of ten days, and we have reason to believe none escaped. In this family there was a very strong resemblance. The animals which we considered the old pair, had two longitudinal stripes on the back, with a spot on the forehead; in the young, the only difference was, that in some of the specimens the white line united on the back above the root of the tail, whilst in others it extended down along the sides of the tail till it nearly reached the extremity; and in some of the specimens the tail was tipped with white, in others, black. We had an opportunity near Easton, Pennsylvania, of seeing an old female Skunk with six young. We had no knowledge of the colour of the male. The female, however, had two broad stripes, with a very narrow black dorsal line; they young differed considerably in their markings, some having black, and others white, tails.

In the sand-hills near Columbia, South Carolina, we met along the sides of the highway four half-grown animals of this species; they all had a narrow white line on each side of the back, and a small white spot on the forehead; the tails of two of them were tipped with white; the others had the whole of their tails black.

From all the observations we have been able to make in regard to the colours of the different varieties of this species, we have arrived at the conclusion that when a pair are alike in colour the young will bear a strong resemblance in their markings to the old. When on the contrary the parents differ, the young assume a variety of intermediate colours.

Dimensions.

From point of nose to root of tail 17	inches.
Tail (vertebræ) . . . . 8$\frac{3}{4}$	do.
Tail, to end of hair . . . . 12$\frac{3}{4}$	do.
Distance between eyes . . . . 1$\frac{1}{8}$	do.
From point of nose to corner of mouth . . . . 1$\frac{3}{8}$	do.

Weight, 6$\frac{1}{2}$ pounds.

Habits.

There is no quadruped on the continent of North America the approach of which is more generally detested than that of the Skunk: from which we may learn that, although from the great and the strong we have to apprehend danger, the feeble and apparently insignificant may have it in their power to annoy us almost beyond endurance.

In the human species we sometimes perceive that a particular faculty has received an extraordinary development, the result of constant devotion to one subject; whilst in other respects the mind of the individual is of a very ordinary character. The same remark will hold good applied to any particular organ or member of the body, which, by constant use, (like the organs of touch in the blind man,) becomes so improved as to serve as a substitute for others: but in the lower orders of animals this prominence in a particular organ is the result of its peculiar conformation, or of instinct. Thus the power of the rhinoceros is exerted chiefly by his nasal horn, the wild boar relies for defence on his tusks, the safety of the kangaroo depends on his hind-feet, which not only enable him to make extraordinary leaps, but with which he deals vigorous blows, the bull attacks his foes with his horns, the rattlesnake's deadly venom is conveyed through its fangs, and the bee has the means of destroying some of its enemies by its sting, whilst in every other power for attack or self-defence thes various creatures are comparatively feeble.

The Skunk, although armed with claws and teeth strong and sharp enough to capture his prey, is slow on foot, apparently timid, and would be unable to escape from many of his enemies, if he were not possessed of a power by which he often causes the most ferocious to make a rapid retreat, run their noses into the earth, and roll or tumble on the ground as if in convulsions; and, not unfrequently, even the bravest of our boasting race is by this little animal compelled suddenly to break off his train of thought, *hold his nose*, and run, as if a lion were at his heels!

Among the first specimens of natural history we attempted to procure was the Skunk, and the sage advice to "look before you leap," was impressed on our mind, through several of our senses, by this species.

It happened in our early school-boy days, that once, when the sun had just set, as we were slowly wending our way home from the house of a neighbour, we observed in the path before us a pretty little animal, playful as a kitten, moving quietly along: soon it stopped, as if waiting for us to come near, throwing up its long bushy tail, turning round and looking at us like some old acquaintance: we pause and gaze; what is it? It is not a young puppy or a cat; it is more gentle than either; it seems desirous to keep company with us, and like a pet poodle, appears most happy when only a few paces in advance, preceding us, as if to show the path: what a pretty creature to carry home in our arms! it seems too gentle to bite; let us catch it. We run towards it; it makes no effort to escape, but waits for us; it raises its tail as if to invite us to take hold of its brush. We seize it instanter, and grasp it with the energy of a miser clutching a box of diamonds; a short struggle ensues, when—faugh! we are suffocated; our eyes, nose, and face, are suddenly bespattered with the most horrible fetid fluid. Imagine to yourself, reader, our surprise, our disgust, the sickening feelings that almost overcome us. We drop our prize and take to our heels, too stubborn to cry, but too much alarmed and discomfitted just now, to take another look at the cause of our misfortune, and effectually undeceived as to the real character of this seemingly mild and playful little fellow.

We have never felt that aversion to the musky odour imparted by many species of the ferine tribe of animals, that others evince; but we are obliged to admit that a close proximity to a recently killed Skunk, has ever proved too powerful for our olfactories. We recollect an instance when sickness of the stomach and vomiting were occasioned, in several persons residing in Saratoga county, N. Y., in consequence of one of this species having been killed under the floor of their residence during the night. We have seen efforts made to rid clothes which have been sprinkled by a Skunk, of the offensive odour: resort was had to burying them in the earth, washing, and using perfumes; but after being buried a month they came forth almost as offensive as when they had first been placed in the ground, and as for the application of odoriferous preparations, it seemed as if all the spices of Araby could neither weaken or change the character of this overpowering and nauseating fluid. Washing and exposure to the atmosphere certainly weaken the scent, but the wearer of clothes that have been thus infected, should he accidently stand near the fire in a close room, may chance to be mortified by being reminded that he is not altogether free from the consequences of an "unpleasant" hunting excursion. We have, however, found chloride of lime a most effectual disinfector when applied to our recent specimens. That there is something very acrid in the fluid ejected by the Skunk, cannot be doubted, when we consider its effects. Dr. RICHARDSON states that he knew several Indians who lost their eyesight in consequence of inflammation produced by its having been thrown into them by the animal. The instant a dog has received a discharge of this kind on his nose and eyes, he appears half distracted, plunging his nose into the earth, rubbing the sides of his face on the leaves and grass, and rolling in every direction. We have known several dogs, from the eyes of which the swelling and inflammation caused by it did not disappear for a week; still we have seen others, which, when on a raccoon hunt, did not hesitate in despite of the consequences, to kill every Skunk they started, and although severely punished at the time, they showed no reluctance to repeat the attack the same evening, if a fresh subject presented itself.

This offensive fluid is contained in two small sacs situated on each side of the root of the tail, and is ejected through small ducts near the anus. We have on several occasions witnessed the manner in which this secretion is discharged. When the Skunk is irritated, or finds it necessary to defend himself, he elevates his tail over his back, and by a strong muscular exertion ejects it in two thread-like streams in the direction in which the enemy is observed. He appears to take an almost unerring aim, and almost invariably salutes a dog in his face and eyes. Dr. RICHARDSON states that he ejects this noisome fluid for upwards of four feet; in this he has considerably underrated the powers of this natural syringe of the Skunk, as we measured the distance on one occasion, when it extended upwards of fourteen feet. The notion of the old authors that this fluid is the secretion of the kidneys, thrown to a distance by the aid of his long tail, must be set down among the vulgar errors, for in that case whole neighbourhoods would be compelled to breathe a tainted gale, as Skunks are quite common in many parts of the country.

The Skunk, in fact, is a very cleanly animal, and never suffers a drop of this fluid to touch his fur; we have frequently been at the mouth of his burrow, and although a dozen Skunks might be snugly sheltered within, we could not detect the slightest unpleasant smell. He is as careful to avoid soiling himself with this fluid, as the rattlesnake is, not to suffer his body to come in contact with his poisonous fangs.

Should the Skunk make a discharge from this all-conquering battery during the day, the fluid is so thin and transparent that it is scarcely perceptible, but at night it has a yellowish luminous appearance; we have noticed it on several occasions, and can find no more apt comparison than an attenuated stream of phosphoric light. That the spot where a Skunk has been killed will be tainted for a considerable time, is well known. At a place where one had been killed in autumn, we remarked that the scent was still tolerably strong after the snows had thawed away the following spring. Generally, however, the spot thus scented by the Skunk is not particularly offensive after the expiration of a week or ten days. The smell is more perceptible at night and in damp weather, than during the day or in a drought.

The properties of the peculiarly offensive liquor contained in the sacs of the Skunk, have not, so far as we are advised, been fully ascertained. It has, however, been sometimes applied to medical purposes. Professor IVES, of New Haven, administered to an asthmatic patient a drop of this fluid three times a day. The invalid was greatly benefitted: all his secretions, however, were soon affected to such a degree, that he became highly offensive both to himself and to those near him. He then discontinued the medicine, but after having been apparently well for some time the disease returned. He again called on the doctor for advice,—the old and tried recipe was once more recommended, but the patient declined taking it, declaring that the remedy was worse than the disease!

We were once requested by a venerable clergyman, an esteemed friend, who had for many years been a martyr to violent paroxysms of asthma, to procure for him the glands of a Skunk; which, according to the prescription of his medical adviser, were kept tightly corked in a smelling bottle, which was applied to his nose when the symptoms of his disease appeared.

For some time he believed that he had found a specific for his distressing complaint; we were however subsequently informed, that having uncorked the bottle on one occasion while in the pulpit during service, his congregation finding the smell too powerful for their olfactories, made a hasty retreat, leaving him nearly alone in the church.

We are under an impression, that the difficulty of preparing specimens of this animal may be to a considerable extent obviated, by a proper care in capturing it. If it has been worried and killed by a dog, skinning a recent specimen is almost insupportable; but if killed by a sudden blow, or shot in a vital part, so as to produce instant death, the Skunk emits no unpleasant odour, and the preparation of a specimen is even less unpleasant than stuffing a mink. We have seen several that were crushed in deadfalls, that were in nowise offensive. We had one of their burrows opened to within a foot of the extremity, were the animals were huddled together. Placing ourselves a few yards off, we suffered them successively to come out. As they slowly emerged and were walking off, they were killed with coarse shot aimed at the shoulders. In the course of half an hour, seven, (the number contained in the burrow,) were obtained; one only was offensive, and we were enabled without inconvenience to prepare six of them for specimens.

The Skunk does not support a good character among the farmers. He will sometimes find his way into the poultry-house, and make some havoc with the setting hens; he seems to have a peculiar penchant for eggs, and is not very particular whether they have been newly laid, or contain pretty large rudiments of the young chicken; yet he is so slow and clumsy in his movements, and creates such a commotion in the poultry-house, that he usually sets the watch-dog in motion, and is generally detected in the midst of his depredations; when, retiring to some corner, he is either seized by the dog, or is made to feel the contents of the farmer's fowling piece. In fact the poultry have far more formidable enemies than the Skunk. The ermine and brown weasel are in this respect rivals with which his awkward powers cannot compare; and the mink is a more successful prowler.

The Skunk is so slow in his actions, that it is difficult to discover in what manner he obtains food to enable him always to appear in good condition. In the northern part of New York the gray rabbit frequently retires to the burrow of the fox, Maryland marmot, or Skunk. Many of them remain in these retreats during the day. We have seen the tracks of the Skunk in the snow, on the trail of the gray rabbit, leading to these holes, and have observed tufts of hair and patches of skin scattered in the vicinity, betokening that the timid animal had been destroyed. We on one occasion marked a nest of the ruffed grouse, (*T. umbellus*,) with the intention of placing the eggs under a common hen a few days before they should hatch, but upon going after them we found they had been eaten, and the feathers of the grouse were lying about the nest. Believing the depredator to have been an ermine, we placed a box-trap near the spot baited with a bird; and on the succeeding night caught a Skunk, which we doubt not was the robber. This species also feeds on mice, frogs, and lizards; and during summer no inconsiderable portion of its food consists of insects, as its excrements usually exhibit the legs and backs of a considerable number of beetles.

On dissecting a specimen which we obtained from the middle districts of Carolina, we ascertained that the animal had been a more successful collector of entomological specimens than ourselves, as he had evidently devoured on the night previous a greater number (about a dozen) of a very rare and large beetle, (*Scarabæus tityus*,) than we had been able to find in a search of ten years.

The Skunk being very prolific, would, if allowed to multiply around the farm-yard, prove a great and growing annoyance. Fortunately there are nocturnal animals that are prowling about as well as he. The dog, although he does not eat this species, scarcely ever fails to destroy a Skunk whenever he can lay hold of him. A wolf that had been sent from the interior of Carolina to Charleston, to be prepared as a specimen, we observed was strongly tainted with the smell of this animal, and we concluded from hence, that as a hungry wolf is not likely to be very choice in selecting his food, he will, if nothing better offers, make a meal on it. Whilst riding along the border of a field one evening, we observed a large bird of some species darting to the ground, and immediately heard a struggle, and were saluted by the odour from the "Enfant du diable," as old CHARLEVOIX has designated the Skunk. We visited the spot on the following day, and found a very large animal of this species partly devoured. We placed a fox-trap in the vicinity, and on the following morning found our trap had captured a large horned owl, which had evidently caused the death of the Skunk, as in point of offensive effluvia there was no choice between them; this species is generally very easily taken in traps. It will not avoid any kind of snare—is willing to take the bait, whether it be flesh, fish, or fowl, and proves a great annoyance to the hunters whose traps are set for the fisher and marten. The burrows of the Skunk are far less difficult to dig out than those of the fox. They are generally found on a flat surface, whilst the dens of the fox are more frequently dug on the side of a hill. They have seldom more than one entrance, whilst those of the fox have two, and often three. The gallery of the burrow dug by the Skunk runs much nearer the surface than that excavated by the fox. After extending seven or eight feet in a straight line, about two feet beneath the surface, there is a large excavation containing an immense nest of leaves. Here during winter may be found lying, from five to fifteen individuals of this species. There are sometimes one or two galleries diverging from this bed, running five or six feet further; in which, if the burrow has been disturbed, the whole family may generally be found, ready to employ the only means of defence with which Nature has provided them.

This animal generally retires to his burrow about December, in the Northern States, and his tracks are not again visible until near the tenth of February. He lays up no winter store; and like the bear, raccoon, and Maryland marmot, is very fat on retiring to his winter quarters, and does not seem to be much reduced in flesh at his first appearance toward spring, but is observed to fall off soon afterwards. He is not a sound sleeper on these occasions; on opening his burrow we found him, although dull and inactive, certainly not asleep, as his black eyes were peering at us from the hole, into which we had made an opening, seeming to warn us not to place too much reliance on the hope of finding this striped "weasel asleep."

In the upper districts of Carolina and Georgia, where the Skunk is occasionally found, he, like the raccoon in the Southern States, does not retire to winter quarters, but continues actively prowling about during the night through the winter months.

A large Skunk, which had been in the vicinity of our place, near New York, for two or three days, was one morning observed by our gardener in an old barrel with only one head in, which stood upright near our stable. The animal had probably jumped into it from an adjoining pile of logs to devour an egg, as our hens were in the habit of laying about the yard. On being discovered, the Skunk remained quietly at the bottom of the barrel, apparently unable to get out, either by climbing or by leaping from the bottom. We killed him by throwing a large stone into the open barrel;—he did not make the least effort to eject the nauseous fluid with which he was provided. Had he not been discovered, he would no doubt have died of starvation, as he had no means of escaping. At times, especially during the summer season, the Skunk smells so strongly of the fetid fluid contained in his glands, that when one or two hundred yards distant it is easily known that he is in the neighbourhood.

We doubt not the flesh of the Skunk is well tasted and savoury. We observed it cooked and eaten by the Indians. The meat was white and fat, and they pronounced it better than the opossum,—infinitely superior to the raccoon, (which they called rank meat,) and fully equal to roast pig. We now regret that our squeamishness prevented us from trying it.

We have seen the young early in May; there were from five to nine in a litter.

The fur is rather coarse. It is seldom used by the hatters, and never we think by the furriers; and from the disagreeable task of preparing the skin, it is not considered an article of commerce.

Geographical Distribution.

This species has a tolerably wide range, being found as far to the north as lat. 56° or 57°. We have met with it both in Upper and Lower Canada, where it however appeared less abundant than in the Atlantic States. It is exceedingly abundant in every part of the Northern States. In New England, New York, and Pennsylvania, it is more frequently met with than in Maryland, Virginia, and the more Southern States. It is not uncommon on both sides of the Virginia Mountains, and is well known in Kentucky, Indiana, and Illinois. It is not unfrequently met with in the higher portions of South Carolina, Georgia, and Alabama. In the alluvial lands of these three States, however, it is exceedingly rare. We possess in the Charleston Museum two specimens procured in Christ Church Parish, by Professor EDMUND RAVENEL, that were regarded as a great curiosity by the inhabitants. It becomes more common a hundred miles from the seaboard, and is not unfrequently met with in the sand-hills near Columbia. To the south we have traced it to the northern parts of Florida, and have seen it in Louisiana. To the west it has been seen as far as the banks of the Mississippi. LEWIS and CLARKE, and others, frequently saw Skunks west of the Rocky Mountains, near their winter encampments, but we have as yet had no means of ascertaining that they were of this species.

General Remarks.

Although we do not regard the distribution of colours in the American Skunk, as of much importance in deciding on the species, and hence, have rejected as mere varieties, all those that can only be distinguished from each other by their markings, we nevertheless differ very widely from Baron CUVIER (Ossemens Fossiles, iv.) and others, who treat all the American Mephites as mere varieties. We have examined and compared many specimens in the museums of Europe and America, and possess others from Texas and other portions of the United States, and we feel confident that both in North and South America several very distinct species exist. We will endeavour, as we proceed in the present work, to investigate their characters, and describe those species that are found within the range to which we have restricted our inquiries. We have in the museums of London examined and compared the species described by BENNET, (Proceeds. Zool. Soc., 1833, p. 39,) as *M. nasuta*, which appears to have been previously described by Dr. LICHTEN-STEIN, of Berlin, under the name of *M. mesoleuca*, (Darst. der Säugeth. tab. 44, fig. 2,) as also several species characterized by GRAY, (Magazine of Nat. Hist., 1837, p. 581,) that are very distinct from the present. In the immense collection existing in the museum at Berlin, one of the best regulated museums in Europe, and which is particularly rich in the natural productions of Mexico, Texas, California, and South America, several species are exhibited that cannot be referred to our Skunk. We are under obligations to Dr. LICHTENSTEIN for a valuable work, (Darstellung neuer oderwenig bekannter Säugethiere, Berlin, 1827–1834,) which contains figures and descriptions of a number of new species of Skunks. Also a monograph, (Ueber die Gattung Mephitis, Berlin, 1838,) in sixty-five pages, quarto, with plates, which contains much learned research, and has greatly extended our previous knowledge of the species. He describes seventeen species, all, with one African exception, belonging to North and South America. North of Texas, however, he recognizes only two species, the present, and *Mephitis interrupta*, of RAFINESQUE; the latter, however, still requires a more careful comparison. All our American authors have applied the name *Mephitis Americana*, of DESMAREST, to our present species. It is now ascertained, however, that TIEDIMANN described it twelve years earlier under the name of *M. chinga*, which, according to the rigid rules to which natruralists feel bound to adhere, must be retained, and we therefore have adopted it in our text although our plate was lettered *M. Americana*, DESMAREST.

Sciurus Leporinus.—Aud. & Bach.

Hare Squirrel.

Plate xliii.—Natural size.

S. magnitudine S. cinereum inter et S. migratorium intermedius; cauda corpore longiore, crassa maximeque disticha; vellere supra ex cinereo fusco; subtus albo.

Characters.

Intermediate in size between the Northern gray squirrel and the cat squirrel. Tail, longer than the body, large and distichous; colour, grayish-brown above, white beneath.

Synonymes.

SCIURUS LEPORINUS, Aud. & Bach., Proceedings of the Acad. of Nat. Sci., Philadelphia, 1841, p. 101.

Descriptions.

Head, of moderate size; nose, blunt, covered with short hairs; fore-head, arched; eyes, large; whiskers, numerous, extending to the ears; ears, broad at base, rounded at the edges, and forming an obtuse angle at the extremity, clothed with sharp hairs on both surfaces. Body, stout, covered by a coat of thick but rather short hair, coarser than that of the Northern gray squirrel; limbs, large, and rather long; tail, distichous, but not very bushy.

Colour.

Teeth, orange; whiskers, black; nose, dark brown; ears, light brown; behind the ears, a tuft of soft cotton-like, whitish fur. The hairs of the back are cinerous at the roots, then light brown, and are tipped with brown and black, giving it so much the colour of the English hare that we determined to borrow from it our specific name. On the sides, the colour is a shade lighter than on the back; the tail, which from the broad white tips of the hair, has a white appearance, is brown at the roots, and three times annulated with black. The upper lips, chin, neck, and whole under surface, including the inner surface of the legs, white; the hair being of this colour from the roots. Feet, dull yellowish-white. On the outer surface of the hind-leg, above the heel, a small portion of the fur is brown; there is also a spot of the same colour on the upper surface of the hind-foot.

Dimensions.

	Inches.	Lines.
Length of head and body	11	9
" " tail	12	6
Height of ear,	0	8
Heel to end of middle claw	2	9
Breadth of tail with hairs extended	5	6

Habits.

This species, which is one of our most beautifully furred Squirrels, is especially remarkable for its splendid tail, with its broad white border. We know nothing of its habits, as it was brought from California, without any other information than that of its locality.

We have represented two of these Squirrels in our plate, on a branch of hickory, with a bunch of nearly ripe nuts attached.

Geographical Distribution.

The range of this Squirrel through California, is, as well as habits, totally unknown to us. It will not be very long, however, we think, before a great deal of information respecting that portion of our continent, so rich in rare and new species, may be expected, and we should not be surprised to find it extending toward the south-western portions of Texas, where several species of Squirrels that we have not obtained, are said to exist.

General Remarks.

This species, in its general appearance, so much resembles some varieties of *Sciurus migratorius* and *S. cinereus*, that had it not been for its distant western locality, we should at first have been tempted to set it down, without further examination, as one or other of those species. There can, however, be no doubt, from its differing in size and in so many details of colour from all other species, that it must be regarded as distinct, It should be further observed that *S. migratorius* has never been found south of Missouri, and that *S. cinereus* is not found west of the Mississippi. Indeed the geographical range of the latter terminates several hundred miles to the eastward of that river, and it would be contrary to all our past experience, that a species existing in one part of our continent should be found in another, separated by an extent of several thousand miles of intermediate country, in no portion of which is it known to exist.

Drawn on Stone by W.E. Hitchcock.

Hare Squirrel.

Drawn from Nature by J.J. Audubon, F.R.S F.L.S.

Lith.ᵈ Printed & Col.ᵈ by J.T. Bowen Philad.ᵃ

Genus Pseudostoma.—Say.

Dental Formula.

Incisive $\frac{2}{2}$; *Canine* $\frac{0-0}{0-0}$; *Molar* $\frac{4-4}{4-4}$ = 20.

Incisors, naked, truncated; molars, destitute of radicles; crowns, simple, oval; anterior ones, double.

Head, large and depressed; nose, short; mouth, small.

The cheek-pouches are large, and open exterior to the mouth.

The eyes are small and far apart. The external ear is very short; auditory openings, large. Body, sub-cylindrical; tail, rather short, round tapering slightly, clothed with short hairs.

Legs, short, with five toes to each foot.

Burrowing in sandy soils, feeding on grasses, roots, nuts, &c., which they convey to their burrows in their capacious cheek-pouches, are habits common to this genus.

There are about six well determined species of Pouched Rats, all existing in North America.

The generic name is derived from $\psi\varepsilon o\delta\vartheta$, (*pseudo*,) false, and $\sigma\tau o\mu a$, (*stoma*,) a mouth, in illusion to the false mouths or cheek-pouches of the genus.

Pseudostoma Bursarius.—Shaw.

Canada Pouched Rat.

Plate xliv.—Males, Female and Young. Natural size.

P. supra, rufo-fuscus; subtus, cinereo-fuscus; pedibus, albis.

Characters.

Reddish-brown above, ashy-brown beneath; feet, white.

Synonymes.

MUS BURSARIUS, Shaw, Descript. of the M. Bursarius in Linn. Transact., vol. v., p. 227 to 228.
MUS BURSARIUS, Shaw's Gen. Zool., vol. ii., p. 100, pl. 138, (figures with cheek-pouches unnaturally inverted.)
MUS BURSARIUS, Mitchill, Silliman's Journal, vol. iv., p. 183.
MUS SACCATUS, Mitchill, N. Y. Medical Repository, Jan. 1821.
SACCOPHORUS BURSARIUS, Kuhl, Beit., p. 66.
CRICETUS BURSARIUS, Desm. in Nouv. Dict., 14, p. 177.
"   "   F. Cuv. in Dict. des Sc. Nat., t. xx, p. 257.
PSEUDOSTOMA BURSARIUS, Say, in Long's Expedi., vol. i., p. 406.
"   "   Godm., vol. ii., p. 90, fig. 2.
"   "   Harlan, p. 133.
GEOMYS? BURSARIUS, Rich., F. B. A., p. 203.

Description.

Head, large; nose, broad and obtuse, covered with hair, with the exception of the margins of the nostrils, which are naked; the nostrils are small oblong openings a line apart, and are on their superior margins considerably vaulted.

The incisors protrude beyond the lips; they are very large and truncated; in the superior jaw they are each marked by a deep longitudinal groove near the middle, and by a smaller one at the inner margin: in the young, they exhibit only a single groove. The molars penetrate to the base of their respective alveoles without any division into roots, their crowns are simply discoidal, transversely oblong-oval, margined by the enamel; the posterior tooth is rather more rounded than the others, and that of the upper-jaw has a small prominent angle on its posterior face; the anterior tooth is double, in consequence of a profound duplicature in its side, so that its crown presents two oval disks, of which the anterior one is smallest, and in the lower-jaw somewhat angulated. (SAY.)

Eyes, small; ears, very short, and scarcely visible; whiskers, not numerous, shorter than the head.

The cheek-pouches are very large, extending from the sides of the mouth to the shoulders, and are internally lined with short soft hairs; the body is broad and stout, sub-cylindrical, and has a clumsy appearance, not unlike that of the shrew-mole. It is thickly clothed on both the upper and lower surfaces with soft hair, that on the back being in some parts half an inch long, whilst on the under surface it is much shorter, and more compact.

The feet have five toes each; the fore-feet are robust, with large, elongated, compressed, and hooked nails; the middle nail is much the longest, the fourth is next in length, the second shorter, the fifth still shorter, and the first very short: there is a large callous protuberance on the hinder-part of the palms. On the hind-feet the toes are short, and the nails are very short, concave beneath, and rounded at tip; the middle nail is longest, the second almost as long, the fourth a little shorter, the first still shorter, the fifth very short. This Rat is plantigrade, and presses on the earth from the heel to the toes.

The tail is for one third of its length from the root clothed with hair, but toward the extremity is naked.

Colour.

Incisors, yellow; nostrils, light pink; eyes, black. The fur is plumbeous from the roots near the extremity, where it is broadly tipped with reddish-brown; on the under surface it is a little paler, owing to the ends of the hairs being but slightly tipped with brown.

The head and the dorsal line are a shade darker than the surrounding parts.

Moustaches, white and black; nails, and all the feet, white.

The colours here described are those which this species exhibits during winter and the early part of summer. Immediately after shedding its hair it takes the colour of the young, light-pulmbeous, which gradually deepens at the approach of winter.

Dimensions.

From nose to root of tail	$9\frac{3}{4}$	inches.
" " to ear	2	do.
" " to end of pouch	$4\frac{1}{4}$	do.
Tail	$2\frac{1}{4}$	do.
Depth of pouch	3	do.
Fore-foot with longest claw	$1\frac{5}{8}$	do.
Distance between the eyes	$\frac{7}{8}$	do.

Weight of largest specimen, 14 oz.

Habits.

During a visit which we made to the Upper Missouri in the spring and summer of 1843, we had many opportunities of studying the habits of this species. In the neighbourhood of St; Louis, at the hospitable residence of PIERRE CHOUTEAU, Esq., we procured several of them alive. In that section of country they are called "Muloes."

They are considered by the gardeners in that vicinity as great plagues, devouring every tap-root vegetable, or grass, within their reach, and perforating the earth in every direction, not only at night, but often-times during the day.

Having observed some freshly thrown up mounds in Mr. CHOUTEAU's garden, several servants were called, and set to work to dig out the animals, if practible, alive; and we soon dug up several galleries worked by the Muloes, in different directions. One of the main galleries was about a foot beneath the surface of the ground, except where it passed under the walks, in which places it was sunk rather lower. We turned up this entire gallery, which led across a large garden-bed and two walks, into another bed, where we discovered that several fine plants had been killed by these animals eating off their roots just beneath the surface of the ground. The burrow ended near these plants under a large rose-bush. We then dug out another principal burrow, but its terminus was amongst the roots of a large peach-tree, some of the bark of which had been eaten off by these animals. We could not capture any of them at this time, owing to the ramifications of their galleries having escaped our notice whilst following the main burrows. On carefully examining the ground we discovered that several galleries existed, that appeared to run entirely out of the garden into the open fields and woods beyond, so that we were obliged to give up the chase. This species throws up the earth in little mounds about twelve or fifteen inches in height, at irregular distances, sometimes near each other, and occasionally ten, twenty, even thirty, paces asunder, generally opening near a surface well covered with grass or vegetables of different kinds.

The Pouched Rat remians under ground during cold weather in an inactive state, most probably dormant, as it is not seen to disturb the surface of the earth until the return of spring, when the grass is well grown.

The earth when thrown up is broken or pulverized, and as soon as the animal has completed his galleries and chambers, he closes the aperture on the side towards the sun, or on the top, although more usually on the side, leaving

Plate XLIV

Drawn from Nature by J.J. Audubon. F.R.S. F.L.S.

Canada Pouched Rat.

Lith. Printed & Col.d by J.T. Bowen, Philada.

a sort of ring or opening about the size of his body.

Possessed of an exquisite sense of hearing, and an acute nose, at the approach of any one travelling on the ground the "Muloes" stop their labours instantaneously, being easily alarmed; but if you retire some twenty or thirty paces to *leeward* of the hole, and wait there for a quarter of an hour or so, you will see the "Gopher" (another name given to these animals by the inhabitants of the State of Missouri), raising the earth with his back and shoulders, and forcing it out before and around him, leaving an aperture open during the process. He now runs a few steps from the hole and cuts the grass, with which he fills a his cheek-pouches, and then retires into his burrow to eat it undisturbed.

You may see the Pseudostoma now and then sitting on its rump and basking in the rays of the sun, on which occasions it may easily be shot if you are prompt, but if missed it disappears at once, is seen no more, and will even dig a burrow to a considerable distance, in order to get out of the ground at some other place where it may not be observed.

This species may be caught in steel-traps, or common box-traps, with which we procured two of them. When caught in a steel-trap, they frequently lacerate the leg by which they are held, which is generally the hind one, by their struggles to get free. They are now and then turned up by the plough, and we have known one caught in this manner. They sometimes destroy the roots of young fruit-trees to the number of one or two hundred in the course of a few days and nights; and they will cut those of full grown trees of the most valuable kinds, such as the apple, pear, peach and pulm. This species is found to vary in size very greatly on comparing different individuals, and they also vary in their colour according to age, although we found no difference caused by sex.

The commonly received opinion is, that these rats fill their pouches with the earth from their burrows, and empty them at the entrance. This is, however, quite an erroneous idea. Of about a dozen, which were shot dead in the very act of rising out of their mounds and burrows, none had any earth in their sacs; but the fore-feet, teeth, nose, and the anterior and upper portion of their heads, were found covered with adherent earth. On the contrary, most of them had their pouches filled with either blades of grass or roots of different trees; and we think of these pouches, that their being hairy within, rather corroborates the idea that they are only used to convey food to their burrows. This species appears to raise up the earth very much in the manner of the common shrew-mole.

When running, the tails of these animals drag on the ground, and they hobble along at times with their long front claws bent underneath their feet as it were, backwards, and never by leaps. They can travel almost as fast backwards as forwards. When turned on their backs they have great difficulty in regaining their natural position, and kick about in the air for a minute or two with their legs and claws extended, before they can turn over. They can bite severly; as their incisors by their size and sharpness plainly indicate; and they do not hesitate to attack their enemies or assailants with open mouth, squealing when in a rage like the common Norway or wharf rat, (*Mus decumanus.*) When they fight among themselves they make great use of their snouts, somewhat in the manner of hogs. They cannot travel faster when above ground than a man walks; they feed frequently whilst seated on their rump, using their fore-feet and long claws somewhat in the manner of squirrels. When sleeping they place their heads beneath the shoulder on the breast, and look like a round ball or a lump of earth. They clean their hair, whiskers, and body, in the same manner as rats, squirrels, &c.

We kept four of these animals alive for several weeks, and they never during that time drank any thing, although we offered them both water and milk. We fed them on cabbages, potatoes, carrots, &c., of which they ate a larger quantity than we supposed them capable of consuming. They tried constantly to make their escape, by gnawing at the floor of the apartment. They slept on any of the clothing about the room which would keept them warm; and these mischievous pets cut the lining of our hunting coat, so that we were obliged to have it repaired and patched. We had left a handkerchief containing sundry articles, tied as we thought securely, but they discovered it, and on opening it one of them caught hold of our thumb, with (luckily) only one of his incisors, and hung on until we shook it off violently. While confined thus in our room, these animals gnawed the leather straps of our trunks, and although we rose frequently from our bed at night to stop their career of destruction, they began to gnaw again as soon as we were once more snugly ensconced beneath the counterpane. Two of them entered one of our boots, and probably not liking the idea of returning by the same way, ate a hole at the toes, by which they made their exit. We have given in our plate four figures of this singular species.

The nest of the Canada Pouched Rat is usually rounded, and is about eight inches in diameter. It is well lined with soft substances as well as with the hair

of the female. It is not placed at the end of a burrow, nor in a short gallery, but generally in one that is in the centre of sundry others diverging to various points, at which the animal can escape if pursued, and most of which lead to the vicinity of grounds where their favourite food is abundant.

The female brings forth from five to seven young at a litter, about the end of March or early in April. They are at a very early period able to run about, dig burrows, and provide for themselves.

Geographical Distribution.

The *Pesudostoma bursarius* has a wide geographical range. We found it in all those places we visited, east of the Rocky Mountains and west of the Mississippi, where the soil and food suited its habits. It has been observed as far to the north as lat. 52°. It abounds in Michigan and Illinois. Farther to the south it extends along the western prairies, and it was observed near the shores of the Platte, Arkansas, Canadian, and Red Rivers, to lat. 34°, and probably ranges still further to the south.

There are pouched rats in Texas and Mexico, but we are at present unable to determine whether they are of this species.

General Remarks.

The first naturalist who gave a specific name to this Pouched Rat was Dr. SHAW, in the Linnæan Transactions, accompanied by a figure representing it as having only three toes. The drawing had been made by Major DAVIES. Subsequently (in 1801) he again described and figured it in his General Zoology, vol. ii., p. 100, pl. 138. The pouches in both cases are inverted, and hanging down like long sacks on each side. These would be very inconvenient, as the animal could not place its nose on the earth or fill its sacks, with such an unnatural appendage dangling at its mouth. The error seems to have originated from the whim or ignorance of an Indian. It is recorded, that in 1798 one of this species was presented by a Canadian Indian to the Lady of Governor PRESCOTT. Its pouches had been inverted, filled, and greatly distended with earth; and from this trivial circumstance an error originated which has been perpetuated even to the present day.

RAFINESQUE, who was either careless or unscrupulous in forming new genera and species, and whose writings are so erroneous that we have seldom referred to him, contributed to create still farther confusion among the species of this genus. He arranged them under two genera. GEOMYS, with cheek-pouches opening into the mouth, and DIPLOSTOMA, with cheek-pouches opening exterior to the mouth. This last genus he characterizes by its having no tail, and only four toes on each foot, (Am. Monthly Magazine, 1817.)

We consider it unfortunate that our friend Dr. RICHARDSON should have adopted both these genera, and given several species under each. We have examined nearly all the original specimens from which his descriptions were taken, and feel confident that they all belong to the genus PSEUDOSTOMA, of SAY.

In regard to the present species, Dr. RICHARDSON was undecided under what genus it should be placed. The opportunities afforded us for making a careful examination, leave no room for any doubt on that subject.

That there are several species of pouched rats on both sides of the Rocky Mountains from Mexico to Canada, cannot be doubted, but the difficulty of distinguishing the species is greater than is usually supposed.

They possess similar habits, specimens belonging to the same species are found of different sizes and of different colours; all the species have short ears and tails. They live under the earth; and many persons who have for years resided in their immediate vicinity, although they daily observe traces of their existence, have never seen the animals.

American naturalists have sometimes been reminded by their European brethren, of the duty devolving on them of investigating the habits and describing the species of animals existing in their country. The charge of our having hitherto depended too much on Europeans to effect this laudable object, is true to a considerable extent. It should, however, be borne in mind, that this vast country belongs to many nations, that large portions of it are either unpeopled deserts or are roamed over by fierce savage tribes, that the Northern regions visited by RICHARDSON are exclusively under the control of Great Britain, and that the vast chain of the Rocky Mountains presents more formidable barriers than the oceans which separate Europe from the Western shores of America.

It is not, therefore, surprising, that in order to become acquainted with some rare species, American naturalists are obliged to seek access to European museums, instead of the imperfect private collections of their own country.

In the United States, east of the Rocky Mountains, we are not aware of the existence of more than two species of Pouched Rat,—the present species and another existing in Georgia and Florida. It is, however, not improbable that *Pseudostoma Mexicanus* may yet be found in Texas.

Genus Arvicola.—Lacépède.

Dental Formula.

Incisive $\frac{2}{2}$; *Canine* $\frac{0—0}{0—0}$; *Molar* $\frac{3—3}{3—3}$ = 16.

Incisors, in the upper jaw, large and cuneiform; in the inferior jaw, sharp.

Molars, compound, flat on their crowns, the enamel forming angular ridges on the surface.

Fore-feet, having the rudiments of a thumb, and four toes, furnished with weak nails.

Hind-feet, with five toes, hairy on their borders, armed with claws.

Ears, clothed with hair; tail, cylindrical and hairy, shorter than the body. From eight to twelve pectoral and ventral mammæ.

The old family of MUS has undergone many subdivisions. It formerly included many of our present genera. The Arvicolæ, by the structure of their teeth, and the hairy covering of their ears and tail, the latter being besides short, may advantageously be separated from the rest.

They burrow in the earth, and feed on grain, bulbous roots and grasses; some are omnivorous, they do not climb, are not dormant in winter, but seek their food during cold weather, eating roots, grasses, and the bark of trees.

There have been about forty species of Arvicola described; some of these, however, are now arranged under other genera. Some of the species are found in each quarter of the world, about seven species inhabit North America.

The generic name is derived from two Latin words, *arvus*, a field, and *colo*, I inhabit.

Arvicola Pennsylvanica.—Ord.

Wilson's Meadow-Mouse.

Plate xlv.—Two figures. Natural size.

A. supra, cervinus; subtus, subalbicans; auriculis abreviatis rotundatisque.

Characters.

Browish fawn-colour above; beneath, grayish-white; Eyes, small; ears, short and round.

Synonymes.

SHORT-TAILED MOUSE, Forster, Phil. Trans., vol. lxii., p. 380, No. 18.
MEADOW MOUSE, Pennant's Arctic Zoology, vol. i., p. 133.
THE CAMPAGNOL or MEADOW MOUSE of PENNSYLVANIA, Warden's Description of the U. S., vol. v., p. 625.
ARVICOLA PENNSYLVANICUS, Ord, Guthrie's Geography.
    "   "   " in Wilson's Ornithology, vol. vi., pl. 50, fig. 3.
    "   PENNSYLVANICA, Harlan, F. A., p. 144.
ARVICOLA ALBO-RUFESCENS, Emmons, Mass. Reports, p. 60, variety.
ARVICOLA HIRSUTUS, Emmons, Mass. Report.
    "   "   Dekay, Nat. Hist. N. Y., p. 86.

Description.

Body, robust, cylindrical, broadest across the shoulders; diminishing towards the loins; fur, on the whole body, long and fine, but not lustrous; on the upper surface (in winter specimens) half an inch long, but not more than half that length beneath.

Head, large and conical; forehead, arched; nose, rather blunt; incisors, projecting; eyes small, situated equidistant from the auditory opening and the point of the nose; the longest whiskers, about the length of the head; nostrils, lateral; nose, bilobate, clothed with short hairs; lips, fringed with longer hairs; mouth, beneath, not terminal; ears, large, rounded, membranous, concealed by the fur, naked within, except along the margins where they have a few long soft hairs; auricular opening, large. The neck is so short that the head and shoulders seem united, like those of the shrew-mole.

Fore-feet, slender, having four toes and a thumb, which is furnished with a sharp nail; nails, small, compressed, slightly hooked and sharp. The toes have five tubercles; the second toe from the thumb is longest, the third a little shorter, the first still shorter, and the outer one shortest.

The hind-feet are a little longer than the fore-feet; the third and fourth toes from the inner side are nearly of equal length, the second toe is a little shorter, the fifth still shorter, and the first is shortest. The soles of the hind-feet have five distinct tubercles; all the feet are clothed with short, adpressed, hairs. The tail is short, scaly, cylindrical, slightly clothed with rigid hair extending beyond the vertebræ.

Colour.

Teeth, dark orange; fur, from the roots to near the tips, on every part of the body, dark plumbeous. The colour differs a shade or two between winter and summer. It may be characterized as brownish-gray above, a little darker on the back. The lips, chin, throat, and abdomen, are light bluish-gray. Feet, dark-brown; tail, brown above, and a shade lighter beneath: eyes, black; whiskers, white and black.

Dimensions.

Length of head and body	5	inches.
" " tail	$1\frac{3}{4}$	do.

Another specimen.

Length of head and body	$5\frac{1}{2}$	do.
" " tail (vertebræ)	$1\frac{1}{2}$	do.
" " " including fur	$1\frac{3}{4}$	do.

Habits.

We have had opportunities in New-York, Pennsylvania, and the New England States, of learning some of the habits of this species. It is, in fact, the common Meadow-Mouse of the Northern and Eastern States.

Wherever there is a meadow in any of these States, you may find small tortuous paths cut through the grass, appearing as if they had been partially dug into the earth, leading to the roots of a stump, or the borders of some bank or ditch. These are the work of this little animal. Should you dig around the roots, or upturn the stump, you may find a family of from five to ten of this species, and will see them scampering off in all directions, and although they do not run fast, they have so many hiding places, that unless you are prompt in your attack, they are likely to escape you. Their galleries do not run under-ground like those of the shrew-mole, or the mischievous pine-mouse (of LECONTE,) but extend along the surface sometimes for fifty yards.

The food of this species consists principally of roots and grasses. During summer it obtains an abundant supply of herds-grass, (*Phleum pratense,*) red-top, (*Agrostis vulgaris,*) and other plants found in the meadows; and when the fields are covered with snow it still pursues its summer paths, and is able to feed on the roots of these grasses, of which there is always a supply so abundant that it is generally in good condition. It is also fond of bulbs, and feeds on the meadow-garlic, (*Allium Canadense,*) and red lily, (*Lilium Philadelphicum.*)

We doubt whether this active little arvicola ever does much injury to the meadows, and in the wheat-fields it is not often a depredator, as it is seldom seen on high ground. Still, we have to relate some of its habits that are not calculated to win the affections of the farmer. In very severe winters, when the ground is frozen, and there is no covering of snow to protect the roots of its favourite grasses, it resorts for a subsistance to the stems of various shrubs and fruit trees, from which it peals off the bark, and thus destroys them. We possessed a small but choice nursey of fruit trees, which we had grafted ourselves, that was completely destroyed duing a severe winter by this Meadow-Mouse, the bark having been gnawed from the wood for several inches from the ground upwards. Very recently our friend, the late Dr. WRIGHT, of Troy, sent us the following observations on this species:—

"Two or three winters ago several thousand young fruit trees were destroyed in two adjoining nurseries near our city; the bark was gnawed from them by some small animal, for the space of several inches, the lowest part of the denuded surface being about ten inches from the ground. I examined the premises the following spring. The ground had been frozen very hard all winter, owing to the small quantity of snow that had fallen. I supposed that some little animal that subsists on the roots of grasses, had been cut off from its ordinary food by the stony hardness of the ground, and had attacked the trees from the top of the snow. I looked around for the destroyer, and found a number of the present species and no other. I strongly suspect that this animal caused the mischief, as it is very abundant and annoys the farmer not a little.

"A few years ago a farmer gave me permission to upset some stacks of corn on a piece of low land, I found an abundance of this species in shallow holes under them, and discovered some distance up between the stalks, the remains of cobs and kernels, showing that they had been doing no friendly work for the farmer."

We suspect, however, that the mischief occasioned to the nursery by this species is infinitely greater than that arising from any depredations it commits on wheat or corn-fields.

The nests of this arvicola are always near the surface; sometimes two or three are found under the same stump. We have frequently during summer, observed them on the surface in the meadows, where they were concealed by the over-shadowing grasses. They are composed of about a double handful of leaves of soft grasses, and are of an oval shape, with an entrance on the side.

WILSON's Meadow-Mouse, swims and dives well. During a freshet which covered some neighbouring meadows, we observed several of them on floating bunches of grass, sticks, and marsh weeds, sitting in an upright posture as if enjoying the sunshine, and we saw them leaving these temporary resting places and swimming to the neighbouring high grounds with great facility; a stick thrown at them on such occasions will causes them to dive like a musk-rat.

This species does not, in any part of the United States, visit dwellings or outhouses, although RICHARDSON states that it possesses this habit in Canada. We have scarcely ever met with it on high grounds, and it seems to avoid thick woods.

It produces young three or four times during the summer, from two to five at a birth. As is the case with the Florida rat and the white-footed mouse, the young of this species adhere to the teats, and are in this way occasionally dragged along by the mother. We would, however, here remark that this habit, which is seen in the young of several animals, is by no means constant. It is only when the female is suddenly surprised and driven from her nest whilst suckling her young, that they are carried off in this manner. The young of this species that we had in confinement, after satisfying themselves, relinquished their hold, and permitted the mother to run about without this incumbrance.

This species is easily caught in wire-traps baited with a piece of apple, or even meat; we have occasionally found two in a trap at the same time. When they have become accustomed to the confinement of a cage they are somewhat familiar, feed on grass and seeds of different kinds, and often come to the bars of the cage to receive their food.

They frequently sit erect in the manner of marmots or squirrels, and while in this position clean their faces with their paws, continuing thus engaged for a quarter of an hour at a time. They drank a good deal of water, and were nocturnal in their habits. During the day-time they constantly nestled under some loose cotton, where they lay, unless disturbed, until dusk, when they ran about their place of confinement with great liveliness and activity, clinging to the wires and running up and down in various directions upon them, as if intent on making their escape.

Geographical Distribution.

We have found this species in all the New England States, where it is very common. It is abundant in all the meadows of the State of New York. It is the most common species in the neighbourhood of Philadelphia. We have found it in Maryland and Delaware. It exists in the valleys of the Virginia Mountains; and we obtained a number of specimens from our friend, EDMUND RUF-FIN, Esq., who procured them on the Pamunkey River, in Hanover county, in that State, where it is quite abundant. We have traced it as far south as the northern boundary of North Carolina; and to the north have met with it in Upper and Lower Canada. FORSTER obtained it from Hudson's Bay, and RICHARDSON speaks of it as very abundant from Canada to Great Bear Lake, latitude 65°.

To the west it exists along the banks of the Ohio, but we were unable to find it in any part of the region lying between the Mississippi and the Rocky Mountains.

General Remarks.

We are fully aware of the difficulty of finding characters by which the various species of this genus may be distinguished. We cannot speak positively of WILSON's diminutive figure of the Meadow-Mouse, (American Ornithology, vol. vi., plate 50, fig. 3; description given, p. 59, in the article on the barn-owl,) but the accurate description of it by ORD, which is creditable to him as a naturalist, cannot possibly apply to any other species than this. It is the most common arvicola near Philadelphia, and no part of the description will apply to either of the only two other species of this genus existing in that vicinity.

We had an opportunity, at the museum of Zurich, to compare specimens of this species with the compagnol or meadow-mouse of Europe, *Mus agrestis* of LINNÆUS, and *Arvicola vulgaris* of DESMAREST, to which GODMAN, (Nat. Hist., vol. ii., p. 88,) referred it. There is a strong general resemblance, but the species are distinct. The European animal has longer and narrower ears, protruding beyond the fur; its tail is shorter, and the body is more ferruginous on the upper surface than in our species.

In the last work published on American quadrupeds, the writer endeavours to show that this species, (which he has named *A. hirsutus*,) differs from *A. Pennsylvanica*. The following remarks are made at p. 87:—"Upon the suggestion that it might possibly be the *Pennsylvanicus* of ORD and HARLAN, it was shown to both those gentlemen, who pronounced it to be totally distinct." To this we would observe, without the slightest design of undervaluing the scientific attainments of the respectable naturalists here referred to, that it was taxing their memories rather too much, to expect them, after the lapse of fifteen or twenty years, during which time their minds had been directed to other pursuits, to be as well qualified to decide on a species as they were when they first described it, (with all the specimens before them,) and when the whole subject was fresh in their minds. In regard to Dr. HARLAN, he candidly wrote in answer to our inquiries respecting this and several other species, that having been long engaged in other investigations, and never having preserved specimens, he could not rely on his present judgment with any degree of accuracy. His description, moreover, being contained in two and a half lines, cannot be depended on, and is equally applicable to a considerable number of species. In regard to referring subjects, requiring such minute investigation, to the memory, when the period at which the specimens were examined has long passed, we have in mind the reply of JOHNSON, the great philologist, to an inquiry for information in regard to the derivation of a word, and of NEWTON, when asked for a soloution of some knotty point in the higher branches of science: the former referred the inquirer to his "Dictionary,"—the latter, to his "Principia." The description of Mr. ORD is full and accurate, and by this we are quite willing to abide. We, moreover, are perfectly satisfied that when that gentleman has an opportunity of comparing specimens of the several species found in the vicinity of Philadelphia with his own descriptions, he will refer the species described and figured as *A. hirsutus* to his *A. Pennsylvanica.*

The arvicola *Albo-rufescens* of EMMONS is evidently a variety of this species. We obtained a specimen from a nest in the northern part of New York, which answered in every particular to his description. From the same nest two others were taken, with white rings round their necks, and three marked like the common *Arvicola Pennsylvanica*, differing in no respect from *Arvicola hirsutus*.

Genus Castor.—Linn.

Dental Formula.

Incisive $\frac{2}{2}$; *Canine* $\frac{0-0}{0-0}$; *Molar* $\frac{4-4}{4-4}$ = 20.

Incisors very strong. In the upper jaw their anterior surface is flat and their posterior surface angular. The molars differ slightly from each other in size, and have one internal and three external grooves. In the lower jaw the incisors present the same appearance as those of the upper; but are smaller. In the molars there are three grooves on the inner side, with one on the external.

Eyes small; ears short and round; five toes on each foot. On the fore-feet the toes are short and close; on the hind-feet long and palmated. Tail, large, flat, and scaly. Mammæ, four, pectoral: a pouch near the root of the tail, in which an unctuous matter is secreted.

There is but one well established species known to belong to this genus. The generic name is derived from the Latin word *Castor*, a beaver.

Castor Fiber.—Linn.
(Var. Americanus.)

American Beaver.

Plate xlvi. Two-thirds natural size.

Plate XLV

Drawn from Nature by J. J. Audubon, F.R.S. F.L.S.

Wilson's Meadow Mouse

Lith. Printed & Col.d by J. T. Bowen, Philad.ª

C. Arct. monace major, supra badius, infra dilutior; cauda plana, ovata, squamosa.

Characters.

Larger than the ground-hog, (Arctomys monax;) of a reddish-brown colour, with a short downy grayish fur beneath; tail, flat, scaly, and oval.

Synonymes.

CASTOR FIBER, Linn., 12th ed., p. 78.
CASTOR, Sagard Theodat, Canada, p. 767.
BEAVER, CASTOR, Pennant, Arc. Zool., vol. i., p. 98.
CASTOR ORDINAIRE, Desm., Mamm.
CASTOR AMERICANUS, F. Cuvier.
CASTOR FIBER. Lewis and Clarke's Expedition, vol. i.
THE BEAVER, Hearne's Journal, vol. viii., p. 245.
BEAVER, Cartwright's Journal, vol. i., p. 62.
   "   Catesby, App., p. 29.
CASTOR FIBER, Harlan, Fauna, p. 122.
   "   "   Godman, vol. ii., p. 21.
   "   "   AMERICANUS, Richardson, F. B. A., p. 105.
   "   "   Emmons, Mass. Reports, p. 51.
   "   "   Dekay, pl. 1, p. 72.

Description.

The shape of the body bears a considerable resemblance to that of the musk-rat; it is, however, much larger, and the head is proportionally thicker and broader. It is thick and clumsy, gradually enlarging from the head to the hips, and then is somewhat abruptly rounded off to the root of the tail.

Nose, obtuse and divided; eyes, small; ears, short, rounded, well clothed with fur, and partially concealed by the longer surrounding hairs; moustaches, not numerous, but very rigid like hogs' bristles, reaching to the ears; neck, rather short. The fur is of two kinds. The upper and longer hair is coarse, smooth, and glossy; the under coat is dense, soft, and silky. Fore-feet, short and rather slender; toes, well separated and very flexible. The fore-feet are used like hands to convey food to the mouth. The fore-claws are strong, compressed, and channelled beneath. The middle toe is the longest, those on each side a little shorter, and the outer and inner ones shortest.

The hind-feet bear some resemblance to those of the goose. They are webbed beyond the roots of the nails, and have hard and callous soles. In most of the specimens we have seen, there is a double nail on the second inner toe. The palms and soles are naked. When walking, the whole heel touches the ground. The Beaver is accustomed to rest itself on its hind-feet and tail; and when in this sitting position contracts its fore-claws in the manner of the left hand figure represented in the plate. The upper surface of all the feet, with the exception of the nails, which are naked, is thickly covered with short adpressed hairs.

The tail is very broad and flat, tongue-shaped, and covered with angular scales. The root of the tail is for an inch covered with fine fur. The glandular sacs containing the castoreum, a musky unctuous substance, are situated near the anus.

Colour.

Incisors, on their outer surface, orange; moustaches, black; eyes, light-brown. The soft under down is light grayish-brown. The upper fur on the back is of a shining chestnut colour; on the under surface, and around the mouth and throat, a shade lighter. Nails, brown; webs between the toes, and tail, grayish-brown. We have seen an occasional variety. Some are black; and we examined several skins that were nearly white.

Dimensions.

Male, represented in the plate.—Rather a small specimen.

From nose to root of tail,	23	inches.
Tail,	10	do.
From heel to end of middle claw,	$5\frac{1}{2}$	do.
Greatest breadth of tail,	$3\frac{1}{4}$	do.
Thickness of tail,	$\frac{7}{8}$	do.

Weight, $11\frac{1}{4}$ lbs.

Habits.

The sagacity and instinct of the Beaver have from time immemorial been the subject of admiration and wonder. The early writers on both continents have represented it as a rational, intelligent, and moral being, requiring but the faculty of speech to raise it almost to an equality, in some respects, with our own species. There is in the composition of every man, whatever may be his pride in his philosophy, a proneness in a greater or less degree to superstition, or at least credulity. The world is at best but slow to be enlightened, and the trammels thrown around us by the tales of the nursery are not easily shaken off. Such travellers into the northern parts of Sweden, Russia, Norway, and Lapland, as OLAUS MAGNUS, JEAN MARIUS, RZACZYNSKY, LEEMS, &c., whose extravagant and imaginary notions were recorded by the credulous GESNER, who wrote marvellous accounts of the habits of the Beavers in Northern Europe, seem to have worked on the imaginations and confused the intellects of the early explorers of our Northern regions—LA HONTAN, CHARLEVOIX, THEODAT, ELLIS, BELTRAMI, and CARTWRIGHT. These last, excited the enthusiasm of BUFFON, whose romantic stories have so fastened themselves on the mind of childhood, and have been so generally made a part of our education, that we now are almost led to regret that three-fourths of the old accounts of this extraordinary animal are fabulous; and that with the exception of its very peculiar mode of constructing its domicile, the Beaver is in point of intelligence and cunning greatly exceeded by the fox, and is but a few grades higher in the scale of sagacity than the common musk-rat.

The following account was noted down by us as related by a trapper named PREVOST, who had been in the service of the American Fur Company for upwards of twenty years, in the region adjoining the spurs of the Rocky Mountains, and who was the "Patroon" that conveyed us down the Missouri river in the summer and autumn of 1843. As it confirms the statements of HEARNE, RICHARDSON, and other close observers of the habits of the Beaver, we trust that although it may present little that is novel, it will from its truth be acceptable and interesting to our readers. Mr. PREVOST states in substance as follows.

Beavers prefer small clear-water rivers, and creeks, and likewise resort to large springs. They, however, at times, frequent great rivers and lakes. The trappers believe that they can have notice of the approach of winter weather, and of its probable severity, by observing the preparations made by the Beavers to meet its rigours; as these animals always cut their wood in good season, and if this be done early, winter is at hand.

The Beaver dams, where the animal is at all abundant, are built across the streams to their very head waters. Usually these dams are formed of mud, mosses, small stones, and branches of trees cut about three feet in length and from seven to twelve inches round. The bark of the trees in all cases being taken off for winter provender, before the sticks are carried away to make up the dam. The largest tree cut by the Beaver, seen by PREVOST, measured eighteen inches in diameter; but so large a trunk is very rarely cut down by this animal. In the instance just mentioned, the branches only were used, the trunk not having been appropriated to the repairs of the dam or aught else by the Beavers.

In constructing the dams, the sticks, mud and moss are matted and interlaced together in the firmest and most compact manner; so much so that even men cannot destroy them without a great deal of labour. The mud and moss at the bottom are rooted up with the animal's snout, somewhat in the manner hogs work in the earth, and clay and grasses are stuffed and plastered in between the sticks, roots, and branches, in so workmanlike a way as to render the structure quite water-tight. The dams are sometimes seven or eight feet high, and are from ten to twelve feet wide at the bottom, but are built up with the sides inclining towards each other, so as to form a narrow surface on the top. They are occasionally as much as three hundred yards in length, and often extend beyond the bed of the stream in a circular form, so as to overflow all the timber near the margin, which the Beavers cut down for food during winter, heap together in large quantities, and so fasten to the shore under the surface of the water, that even a strong current cannot tear it away; although they generally place it in such a position that the current does not pass over it. These piles or heaps of wood are placed in front of the lodges, and when the animal wishes to feed he proceeds to them, takes a piece of wood, and drags it to one of the small holes near the principal entrance running above the water, although beneath the surface of the ground. Here the bark is devoured at leisure, and the wood is afterwards thrust out, or used in repairing the dam. These small galleries are more or less abundant according to the number of animals in the lodges. The larger lodges are, in the interior, about seven feet in diameter, and between two and three feet high, resembling a great oven. They are placed near the edge of the water, although actually built on or in the

Plate XLVI

Drawn from Nature by J. J. Audubon, F.R.S.F.L.S

On Stone by Wm E. Hitchcock

Lith. Printed & Col.^d by J.T. Bowen, Phil.

American Beaver

ground. In front, the Beavers scratch away the mud to secure a depth of water that will enable them to sink their wood deep enough to prevent its being impacted in the ice when the dam is frozen over, and also to allow them always free egress from their lodges, so that they may go to the dam and repair it if necessary. The top of the lodge is formed by placing branches of trees matted with mud, grasses, moss, &c., together, until the whole fabric measures on the outside from twelve to twenty feet in diameter, and is six or eight feet high, the size depending on the number of inhabitants. The outward coating is entirely of mud or earth, and smoothed off as if plastered with a trowel. As Beavers, however, never work in the day-time, no person we believe has yet seen how they perform their task, or give this hard-finish to their houses. This species does not use its fore-feet in swimming, but for carrying burthens: this can be observed by watching the young ones, which suffer their fore-feet to drag by the side of the body, using only the hind-feet to propel themselves through the water. Before diving, the Beaver gives a smart slap with its tail on the water, making a noise that may be heard a considerable distance, but in swimming, the tail is not seen to work, the animal being entirely submerged except the nose and part of the head; it swims fast and well, but with nothing like the speed of the otter, (*Lutra Canadensis.*)

The Beavers cut a broad ditch all around their lodge, so deep that it cannot freeze to the bottom, and into this ditch they make the holes already spoken of, through which they go in and out and bring their food. The beds of these singular animals are separated slightly from each other, and are placed around the wall, or circumference of the interior of the lodge; they are formed merely of a few grasses, or the tender bark of trees: the space in the centre of the lodge being left unoccupied. The Beavers usually go to the dam every evening to see if repairs are needed, and to deposit their ordure in the water near the dam, or at least at some distance from their lodge.

They rarely travel by land, unless their dams have been carried away by the ice, and even then they take the beds of the rivers or streams for their roadway. In cutting down trees they are not always so fortunate as to have them fall into the water, or even towards it, as the trunks of trees cut down by these animals are observed lying in various positions; although as most trees on the margin of a stream or river lean somewhat towards the water, or have their largest branches extended over it, many of those cut down by the Beavers naturally fall in that direction.

It is a curious fact, says our trapper, that among the Beavers there are some that are lazy and will not work at all, either to assist in building lodges or dams, or to cut down wood for their winter stock. The industrious ones beat these idle fellows, and drive them away; sometimes cutting off a part of their tail, and otherwise injuring them. These "Paresseux" are more easily caught in traps than the others, and the trapper rarely misses one of them. They only dig a hole from the water running obliquely towards the surface of the ground twenty-five or thirty feet, from which they emerge when hungry, to obtain food, returning to the same hole with the wood they procure, to eat the bark.

They never form dams, and are sometimes to the number of five or seven together; all are males. It is not at all improbable, that these unfortunate fellows have, as is the case with the males of many species of animals, been engaged in fighting with others of their sex, and after having been conquered and driven away from the lodge, have become idlers from a kind of necessity. The working Beavers, on the contrary, associate, males, females, and young together.

Beavers are caught, and found in good order at all seasons of the year in the Rocky Mountains; for in those regions the atmosphere is never warm enough to injure the fur; in the low-lands, however, the trappers rarely begin to capture them before the first of September, and they relinquish the pursuit about the last of May. This is understood to be along the Missouri, and the (so called) Spanish country.

CARTWRIGHT, (vol. i., p. 62,) found a Beaver that weighed forty-five pounds; and we were assured that they have been caught weighing sixty-one pounds before being cleaned. The only portions of their flesh that are considered fine eating, are the sides of the belly, the rump, the tail, and the liver. The tail, so much spoken of by travellers and by various authors, as being very delicious eating, we did not think equalled their descriptions. It has nearly the taste of beef marrow, but is rather oily, and cannot be partaken of unless in a very moderate quantity, except by one whose stomach is strong enough to digest the most greasy substances.

Beavers become very fat at the approach of autumn; but during winter they fall off in flesh, so that they are generally quite poor by spring, when they feed upon the bark of roots, and the roots of various aquatic plants, some of which are at that season white, tender, and juicy. During winter, when the ice is thick and strong, the trappers hunt the Beaver in the following manner. A hole is cut in the ice as near as possible to the aperture leading to the dwelling of the animal, the situation of which is first ascertained; a green stick is placed

firmly in front of it, and a smaller stick on each side, about a foot from the stick of green wood; the bottom is then patted or beaten smooth and even, and a strong stake is set into the ground to hold the chain of the trap, which is placed within a few inches of the stick of green wood, well baited, and the Beaver, attracted either by the fresh bark or the bait, is almost always caught. Although when captured in this manner, the animal struggles, diving and swimming about in its efforts to escape, it never cuts off a foot in order to obtain its liberty; probably because it is drowned before it has had time to think of this method of saving itself from the hunter. When trapping under other circumstances, the trap is placed within five or six inches of the shore, and about the same distance below the surface of the water, secured and baited as usual. If caught, the Beavers now and then cut off the foot by which they are held, in order to make their escape.

A singular habit of the Beaver was mentioned to us by the trapper, PREVOST, of which we do not recollect having before heard. He said that when two Beaver lodges are in the vicinity of each other, the animals proceed from one of them at night to a certain spot, deposit their castoreum, and then return to their lodge. The Beavers in the other lodge, scenting this, repair to the same spot, cover it over with earth, and then make a similar deposit on the top. This operation is repeated by each party alternately, until quite a mound is raised, sometimes to the height of four or five feet.

The strong musky substance contained in the glands of the Beaver, is called castoreum; by trappers, bark-stone; with this the traps are baited. A small stick, four or five inches long, is chewed at one end, and that part dipped in the castoreum, which is generally kept in a small horn. The stick is then placed with the anointed end above water, and the other end downwards. The Beaver can smell the castoreum at least one hundred yards, makes towards it at once, and is generally caught.

Where Beavers have not been disturbed or hunted, and are abundant, they rise nearly half out of water at the first smell of the castoreum, and become so excited that they are heard to cry aloud, and breathe hard to catch the odour as it floats on the air. A good trapper used to catch about eighty Beavers in the autumn, sixty or seventy in the spring, and upwards of three hundred in the summer, in the mountains; taking occasionally as many as five hundred in one year. Sixty or seventy Beaver skins are required to make a pack weighing one hundred pounds; which, when sent to a good market, is worth, even now, from three to four hundred dollars.

The Indians occasionally destroy Beaver-dams in order to capture these animals, and have good dogs to aid them in this purpose. The Mountain Indians, however, are not trappers.

Sometimes the Indians of the Prairies break open Beaver lodges in the summer-time, as, during winter they are usually frozen hard. The Beaver is becoming very scarce in the Rocky Mountains, so much so, that if a trapper now secures one hundred in the winter and spring hunt, he is considered fortunate.

Formerly, when the fur was high in price, and the animals abundant, the trading companies were wont to send as many as thirty or forty men, each with from six to twelve traps and two good horses: when arrived at a favourable spot to begin their work, these men erected a camp; and each one sought alone for his game, the skins of which he brought to camp, where a certain number of men always remained to stretch and dry them.

The Trappers subsist principally upon the animals they kill, having a rifle and a pair of pistols with them. After a successful hunt, on meeting each other at the camp, they have a "frolic" as they term it.

Some old and wary Beavers are so cunning, that on finding the bait they cover it over, as if it were on the ground, with sticks, &c., deposit their own castoreum on the top, and manage to remove the trap. This is often the case when the Beaver has been hunted previously. In places where they have remained undisturbed, but few escape the experienced trapper. The trappers are not very unfrequently killed by the Indians, and their occupation is one involving toil and hazard. They rarely gain a competence for their old age, to say nothing of a fortune, and in fact all the articles they are of necessity obliged to purchase in the "Indian country," cost them large sums, as their price is greatly increased by the necessary charges for transportation to the remote regions of the West.

When at Fort Union, we saw a trapper who had just returned from an unfortunate expedition to the mountains; his two horses had been stolen, and he lost his gun and rifle in coming down the river in a slender canoe, and was obliged to make for the shore, dig a hole wherein to deposit the few furs he had left, and travel several hundred miles on foot with only berries and roots for his food. He was quite naked when he reached the Fort.

The Beaver which we brought from Boston to New York was fed principally on potatoes and apples, which he contrived to peel as if assisted with a knife, although his lower incisors were his only substitute for that useful implement.

While at this occupation the animal was seated on his rump, in the manner of a ground-hog, marmot, or squirrel, and looked like a very large wood-chuck, using his fore-feet, as squirrels and marmots are wont to do.

This Beaver was supplied every day with a large basin filled with water, and every morning his ordure was found to have been deposited therein. He generally slept on a good bed of straw in his cage, but one night having been taken out and placed at the back of the yard in a place where we thought he would be secure, we found next morning to our surprise that he had gnawed a large hole throught a stout pine door which separated him from that part of the yard nearest the house, and had wandered about until he fell into the space excavated and walled up outside the kitchen window. Here he was quite entrapped, and having no other chance of escape from this pit, into which he had unluckily fallen, he gnawed away at the window-sill and the sash, on which his teeth took such effect that on an examination of the premises we found that a carpenter and several dollars' worth of work were needed, to repair damages. When turned loose in the yard in the day-time he would at times slap his tail twice or thrice on the brick pavement, after which he elevated this member from the ground, and walked about in an extremely awkward manner. He fell ill soon after we had received him, and when killed, was examined by Dr. JAMES TRUDEAU, who found that he would shortly have died of an organic disease.

It is stated by some authors that the Beaver feeds on fish. We doubt whether he possesses this habit, as we on several occasions placed fish before those we saw in captivity, and although they were not very choice in their food, and devoured any kind of vegetable, and even bread, they in every case suffered fish to remain untouched in their cages.

The food of this species, in state of nature, consists of the bark of several kinds of trees and shrubs, and of bulbous and other roots. It is particularly fond of the bark of the birch, (*Betula*,) the cotton-wood, (*Populus*,) and of several species of willow, (*Salix*;) it feeds also with avidity on the roots of some aquatic plants, especially on those of the *Nuphair luteum*. In summer, when it sometimes wanders to a distance from the water, it eats berries, leaves, and various kinds of herbage.

The young are born in the months of April and May; those produced in the latter month are the most valuable, as they grow rapidly and become strong and large, not being checked in their growth, which is often the case with those that are born earlier in the season. Some females have been taken in July, with young, but such an event is of rare occurrence. The eyes of the young Beaver are open at birth. The dam at times brings forth as many as seven at a litter, but from two to five is the more usual number. The young remain with the mother for at least a year, and not unfrequently two years, and when they are in a place of security, where an abundance of food is to be procured, ten or twelve Beavers dwell together.

About a month after their birth, the young first follow the mother, and accompany her in the water; they continue to suckle some time longer, although if caught at that tender age, they can be raised without any difficulty, by feeding them with tender branches of willows and other trees. Many Beavers from one to two months old are caught in traps set for old ones. The gravid female keeps aloof from the male until after the young have begun to follow her about. She resides in a separate lodge till the month of August, when the whole family once more dwell together.

Geographical Distribution.

According to RICHARDSON the Beaver exists on the banks of the Mackensie, which is the largest river that discharges itself into the Polar Sea: he speaks of its occurring as high as $67\frac{1}{2}$ or 68° north latitude, and states that its range from east to west extends from one side of the continent to the other. It is found in Labrador, Newfoundland, and Canada, and also in some parts of Maine and Massachusetts. There can be no doubt that the Beaver formerly existed in every portion of the United States. CATESBY noticed it as found in Carolina, and the local names of Beaver Creek, Beaver Dam, &c., now existing, are evidences that the animal was once known to occupy the places designated by these compounds of its name. We have indeed, examined several localities, some of which are not seventy miles from Charleston, where we were assured the remains of old Beaver dams existed thirty-five years ago. BARTRAM, in his visit to Florida in 1778, (Travels, p. 281,) speaks of it as that time existing in Georgia and East Florida. It has, however, become a scarce species in all the Atlantic States, and in some of them has been entirely extirpated. It, however, may still be found in several of the less cultivated portions of many of our States. Dr. DEKAY was informed that in 1815 a party of St. Regis Indians obtained three hundred Beavers in a few weeks, in St. Lawrence county, N. Y. In 1827 we were shown several Beaver-houses in the north-western part of New York, where, although we did not see the animals,

we observed signs of their recent labours. DEKAY supposes, (N. Y. Fauna, p. 78,) that the Beaver does not at present exist south of certain localities in the State of New York. This is an error. Only two years ago we received a foot of one, the animal having been caught not twenty miles from Ashville in North Carolina. We saw in 1839 several Beaver-lodges a few miles west of Peter's Mountain in Virginia, on the head waters of the Tennessee River, and observed a Beaver swimming across the stream. There is a locality within twenty miles of Milledgeville, Georgia, where Beavers are still found. Our friend, Major LOGAN, residing in Dallas county, Alabama, informed us that they exist on his plantation, and that within the last few years a storekeeper in the immediate vicinity purchased twenty or thirty skins annually, from persons residing in his neighbourhood.

We were invited to visit this portion of Alabama to study the habits of the Beaver, and to obtain specimens. Some years ago we shot one near Henderson, Kentucky, in Canoe Creek; it was regarded as a curiosity, and probably none have been seen in that section of the country since. We have heard that the Beaver was formerly found near New Orleans, but we never saw one in Louisiana. This species exists on the Arkansas River, in the streams running from the Rocky Mountains, and along their whole range on both sides; we have traced it as far as the northern boundaries of Mexico, and it is no doubt found much farther south along the mountain range. Thus it appears that the Beaver once existed on the whole continent of North America, north of the Tropic of Cancer, and may still occur, although in greatly diminished numbers, in many localitie in the wild and uncultivated portions of our country; we are nevertheless under the impression, that in the Southern States the Beaver was seldom found in those ranges of country where the musk-rat does not exist, hence we think it could never have been abundant in the alluvial lands of Carolina and Georgia, as the localities where its dams formerly existed are on pure running streams, and not on the sluggish rivers near the sea-coast.

General Remarks.

It is doubted by some authors whether the American Beaver is identical with the Beaver which exists in the north of Europe; F. CUVIER, KUHL, and others, described it under the names of *C. Americanus, C. Canadensis*, &c. From the amphibious habits of this animal, and its northern range on both continents, strong arguments in favour of the identity of the American and European species, might be maintained, even without adopting the theory of the former connexion of the two adjacent continents. We carefully compared many specimens (American and European,) in the museums of Europe, and did not perceive any difference between them, except that the American specimens were a very little larger than the European. We saw a living Beaver in Denmark that had been obtained in the north of Sweden; in its general appearance and actions it did not differ from those we have seen in confinement in America. It has been argued, however, that the European animal differs in its habits from the American, and that along the banks of the Weser, the Rhone, and the Danube, the Beavers are not gregarious, and that they burrow in the banks like the musk-rat. But change of habit may be the result of altered circumstances, and is not in itself sufficient to constitute a species. Our wild pigeon (*Columba migratoria*,) formerly bred in communities in the Northern States; we once saw one of their breeding places near Lake Champlain, where there were more than a hundren nests on a single tree. They still breed in that portion of the country, but the persecutions of man have compelled them to adopt a different habit, and two nests are now seldom found on a tree.

The banks of the European rivers, (on which the Beaver still remains although scarcely more than a straggler can be found along them now,) have been cultivated to the water's edge, and necessity, not choice, has driven the remnant of the Beaver tribe to the change of habit we have referred to. But if the accounts of travellers in the north of Europe are to be relied on, the habits of the Beaver are in the uncultivated portions of that country precisely similar to those exhibited by the animal in Canada. We consider the account of these animals given us by HEARNE, (p. 234,) as very accurate. He speaks of their peculiarly constructed huts, their living in communities, and their general habits. In the account of Swedish Lapland, by Professor LEEMS, published in Danish and Latin, Copenhagen, 1767, we have the following notice of the European species: (we quote from the English translation in PINKERTON's Voyages, vol. i., p. 419.) "The Beaver is instinctively led to build his house near the banks of lakes and rivers. He saws with his teeth birch trees, with which the building is constructed; with his teeth he drags the wood along to the place destined for building his habitations; in this manner one piece of timber is carried after another, where they choose. At the lake or river where their house is to be built, they lay birch stocks or trunks, covered with their bark, in the bottom itself, and forming a foundation, they complete the rest of the building, with so much art and ingenuity as to excite the admiration of the beholders. The house itself is of a round and arched figure, equalling in its circumference the ordinary hut of a Laplander. In this house the floor is for a bed, covered with branches of trees, not in the very bottom, but a little above, near the edge of a river or lake; so that between the foundation and flooring on which the dwelling is supported, there is formed as it were a cell, filled with water, in which the stalks of the birch tree are put up; on the bark of this, the Beaver family who inhabit this mansion feed. If there are more families under one roof, besides the laid flooring, another resembling the former is built a little above, which you may not improperly name a second story in the building. The roof of the dwelling consists of branches very closely com-

pacted, and projects out far over the water. You have now, reader, a house consisting and laid out in a cellar, a flooring, a hypocaust, a ceiling, and a roof, raised by a brute animal, altogether destitute of reason, and also of the builder's art, with ono less ingenuity than commodiousness."

It should be observed that LEEMS, who was a missionary in that country, gave this statement as related to him by the Laplanders who reside in the vicinity of the Beavers, and not from his own personal observations. This account, though mixed up with some extravagancies and the usual vulgar errors, (which we have omitted,) certainly proves that the habits of the Beaver in the northern part of Europe are precisely similar to those of that animal on the northern continent of America.

Genus Meles. — Brisson.

Dental Formula.

$Incisive \frac{6}{6}$; $Canine \frac{1-1}{1-1}$; $Molar \frac{4-4}{5-5}$ = 34.

or,

$Incisive \frac{6}{6}$; $Canine \frac{1-1}{1-1}$; $Molar \frac{4-4}{3-3}$ = 32.

The canine teeth in this genus are rather large and strong. In addition to the four persistent molars on each side in the upper jaw, there is an additional small molar which is deciduous, dropping out when the animal is quite young.

Nose, somewhat elongated, obtuse at the point; tongue, smooth; ears, short and round; eyes, small; body, thick-set; legs, short. Mammæ, six , two on the lower part of the chest and four on the abdomen. There are transverse glandular follicles between the anus and the root of the tail, which discharge a fetid matter.

The feet are five-toed, and are armed with strong nails. The fore-feet are longer than the hind-feet.

Three species of this genus have been described; one inhabits Europe, one India, and one America.

The generic name is derived from the Latin word *Meles*, a badger.

Meles Labradoria. — Sabine.

American Badger.

Plate xlvii. — Male. Natural size.

Supra, fusco-ferruginea; infra, subalbida; capite, fascia longitudinale alba; cruribus et pedibus nigris.

Characters.

Colour above, hoary-yellowish-brown; a broad white longitudinal line dividing the head above into two equal parts; dull white, beneath; legs and feet, black.

Synonymes.

CARCAJOU, Buffon, tom. vi., p. 117, pl. 23.
COMMON BADGER, Pennant's Arctic Zool., vol. i., p. 71.
BADGER, Var. B. AMERICAN, Penn. Hist. Quad., vol. ii., p. 15.
URSUS TAXUS, Schreber, Säugeth, p. 520.
    "   LABRADORIUS, Gmel., vol. i., p. 102.
PRAROW, Gass, Journal, p. 34.
BLAIREAU, Lewis and Clarke's Voyage, vol. i., pp. 50, 137, 213.
TAXUS LABRADORICUS, Long's Expedition, vol. i., p. 261.
MELES LABRADORIA, Sabine, Franklin's First Journey, p. 649.
AMERICAN BADGER, Harlan, F., p. 57.
    "   "   Godm., vol. i., p. 179.
BLAIREAU D'AMERIQUE, F. Cuvier, Hist. Nat. des Mamm.
MELES LABRADORIA, Richardson, F. B. A., pl. 2.
    "   "   Waterhouse, Trans. Zool. Soc., London, vol. ii., p. 1, p. 343.

Description.

There is a very very striking difference between the teeth of thi species and those of the European Badger, (*Meles vulgaris;*) besides which the present species has one tooth less than the latter on each side in the lower jaw. We have ascertained, by referring to three skulls in our possession, that the dentition of the American Badger corresponds so minutely with the scientific and accurate account given of it by WATERHOUSE, in the Transactions of Zool. Society of London, vol. ii., part 5, p. 343, that we are willing to adopt his conclusions.

He says: "The subgeneric name, TAXIDEA, may be applied to the American Badger, and such species as may hereafter be discovered with incisors $\frac{6}{6}$; canines $\frac{1-1}{1-1}$; false molars $\frac{2-2}{2-2}$, the posterior false molar of the lower jaw, with an anterior large tubercle, and a posterior smaller one; molars $\frac{2-2}{2-2}$; the carnassière and the grinding molars of the upper jaw each of a triangular form, or nearly so, and about equal in size. The modification observable in the form of the molars of the upper jaw of TAXIDEA, furnishes us with an interesting link between MEPHITIS and MELES, whilst the former of these genera links the Badger with MUSTELA and its subgenera."

The body of this species is thick, heavy, flat, very broad and fleshy, and its whole structure indicates that it is formed more for strength than speed.

Head, of moderate size, and conical; the skull, between the ears, broad, giving it somewhat the appearance of a pug-faced dog. Tip of the nose, hairy above; ears, short, and of an oval shape, clothed on both surfaces with short hairs; whiskers, few, not reaching beyond the eyes. The fur on the back is (in winter) three inches long, covering the body very densely; on the under surface it is short, and so thin that it does not conceal the colour of the skin. There is, immediately below the tail, a large aperture leading into a kind of sac. Although there seems to be no true glandular apparatus, this cavity is covered on its sides by an unctuous matter; there is a second and smaller underneath, in the midst of which the anus opens, and on each side of the anus is a pore from which an unctuous matter escapes, which is of a yellow colour and offensive smell. Legs, short; feet, robust, palmated to the outer joint; nails, long and strong, slightly arched, and channelled underneath toward their extremities; palms, naked. The heel is well clothed with hair; the tail is short, and is covered with long bushy hairs.

Colour.

Hair on the back, at the roots dark-gray, then light-yellow for two-thirds of its length, then black, and broadly tipped with white; giving it in winter a hoary-gray appearance; but in summer it makes a near approach to yellowish-brown. The eyes are bright piercing black. Whiskers, upper lips, nose, forehead, around the eyes, and to the back of the head, dark yellow-brown. There is a white stripe running from the nose over the forehead and along the middle of the neck to the shoulder. Upper surface of ear, dark-brown; inner surface and outer edge of ear, white; legs, blackish-brown; nails, pale horn-colour; sides of face, white, which gradually darkens and unites with the brown colour above; chin and throat, dull white; the remainder of the under surface is yellowish-white; tail, yellowish-brown.

We have noticed some varieties in this species. In one of the specimens before us the longitudinal white line does not reach below the eyes, leaving the nose and forehead dark yellowish-brown. In two of them the under surface of the body is yellowish-white, with a broad and irregular longitudinal line of white in the centre; whilst another and smaller specimen has the whole of the under surface pure white, shaded on the sides by a line of light yellow.

No. 10

Plate XLVII

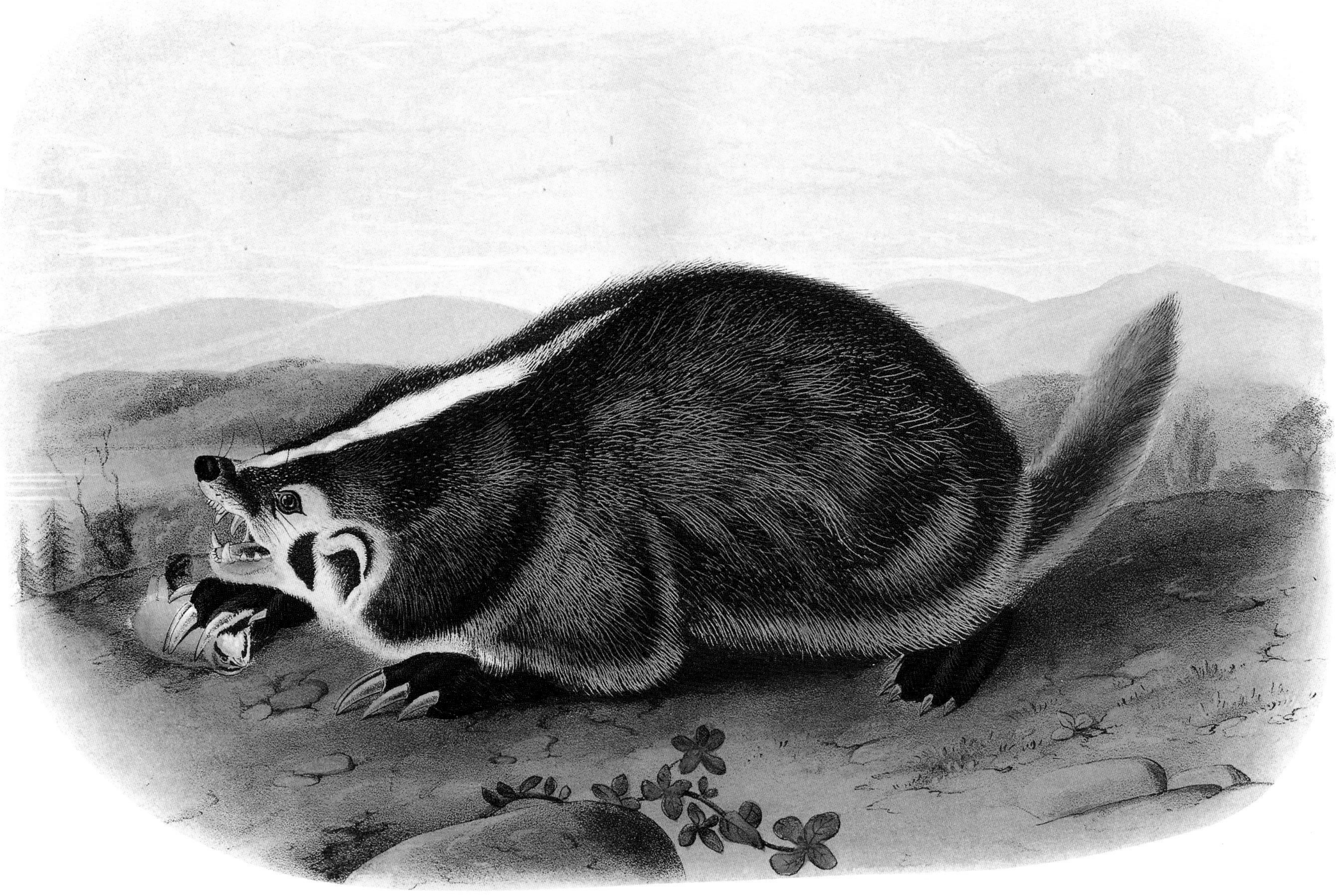

On Stone by Wm. E. Hitchcock

Drawn from Nature by J. J. Audubon F.R.S. F.L.S.

American Badger.

Lith. Printed & Col'd by J. T. Bowen, Phil.

Dimensions.

A male in winter pelage.

From point of nose to root of tail,	....	21	inches.
Tail, (vertebræ,)	....	4	do.
" to end of hair,	....	$6\frac{1}{2}$	do.
Nose to root of ear,	....	$3\frac{5}{8}$	do.
Between the ears,	....	4	do.
Height of "	....	$1\frac{1}{4}$	do.
Breadth of "	....	$1\frac{3}{8}$	do.
Length of head,	....	$4\frac{5}{8}$	do.
Breadth of body,	....	$10\frac{1}{8}$	do.
Length of fore-leg to end of claw,	....	$7\frac{3}{4}$	do.

Weight, $16\frac{1}{2}$ lbs.

A living specimen, (examined in a menagerie at Charleston, S. Carolina.)

Length of head and body	....	30	inches.
" tail, (vertebræ,)	....	5	do.
" " to end of hair,	....	$7\frac{1}{2}$	do.
Breadth of body,	....	12	do.
Heel to end of nail,	....	4	do.

Weight, 23 lbs.

A stuffed specimen in our collection.

Length of head and body,	....	31	inches.
" tail, (vertebræ,)	....	$5\frac{1}{2}$	do.
" " to end of hair,	....	$7\frac{1}{2}$	do.
" heel to end of nail,	....	$4\frac{1}{2}$	do.

HABITS.

During our stay at Fort Union, on the Upper Missouri River, in the summer of 1843, we purchased a living Badger from a squaw, who had brought it from some distance to the Fort for sale; it having been caught by another squaw at a place nearly two hundred and fifty miles distant, among the Crow Indians. It was first placed in our common room, but was found to be so very mischievous, pulling about and tearing to pieces every article within its reach, trying to dig up the stones of the hearth, &c., that we had it removed into an adjoining apartment. It was regularly fed morning and evening on raw meat, either the flesh of animals procured during the day, or small birds shot during our researches through the adjacent country. It drank a good deal of water, and was rather cleanly in its habits. In the course of a few days it managed to dig a hole under the hearth and fire-place nearly large and deep enough to conceal its body, and we were obliged to drag it out by main force whenever we wished to examine it. It was provoked at the near approach of any one, and growled continuously at all intruders. It was not, however, very vicious, and would suffer one or two of our companions to handle and play with it at times.

At that period this Badger was about five months old, and was nearly as large as a full grown wood-chuck or ground-hog, (Arctomys monax.) Its fur was of the usual colour of summer pelage, and it was quite a pretty looking animal. We concluded to bring it to New York alive, if possible, and succeeded in doing so after much trouble, it having nearly made its escape more than once. On one occasion when our boat was made fast to the shore for the night, and we were about to make our "camp," the Badger gnawed his way out of the box in which he was confined, and began to range over the batteau; we rose as speedily as possible, and striking a light, commenced a chase after it with the aid of one of the hands, and caught it by casting a buffalo robe over it. The cage next day was wired, and bits of tin put in places where the wooden bars had been gnawed through, so that the animal could not again easily get out of its prison. After having become accustomed to the box, the Badger became quite playful and took exercise by rolling himself rapidly from one end to the other, and then back again with a reversed movement, continuing this amusement sometimes for an hour or two.

On arriving at our residence near New York we had a large box, tinned on the inside, let into the ground about two feet and a half, and filled to the same depth with earth. The Badger was put into it, and in a few minutes made a hole, in which he seemed quite at home, and where he passed most of his time during the winter, although he always came out to take his food and water, and did not appear at all sluggish or inclined to hibernate even when the weather was so cold as to make it necessary to pour hot water into the pan that was placed within his cage, to enable him to drink, as cold water would have frozen immediately, and in fact the pan generally had a stratum of ice on the bottom which the hot water dissolved when poured in at feeding-time.

Our Badger was fed regularly, and soon grew very fat; its coat changed completely, became woolly and of a buff-brown colour, and the fur by the month of February had become indeed the most effectual protection against cold that can well be imagined.

We saw none of these animals in our hunting expeditions while on our journey up the Missouri River, and observed only a few burrowing places which we supposed were the remains of their holes, but which were at that time abandoned. We were informed that these animals had burrows six or seven feet deep running beneath the ground at that depth to the distance of more than thirty feet. The Indians speak of their flesh as being good; that of the one of which we have been speaking, when the animal was killed, looked very white and fat, but we omitted to taste it.

Before taking leave of this individual we may remark that the change of coat during winter from a *hairy* or furry texture to a woolly covering, is to be observed in the Rocky-mountain sheep, (*Ovis montana,*) and in other animals exposed in that season to intense cold. Thus the skin of *Ovis montana,* when obtained pending the change from winter to summer pelage, will have the outside hairs grown out beyond the wool that has retained the necessary warmth in the animal during the cold weather. The *wool* begins to drop out in early spring, leaving in its place a coat of hair resembling that of the elk or common deer, thus giving as a peculiarity of certain species, a *change* of pelage, quite different in character from the ordinary thickening of the coat or hair, common to all furred animals in winter, and observed by every one,—for instance, in the horse, the cow, &c., which shed their winter coats in the spring.

We had an opportunity in Charleston of observing almost daily for a fortnight, the habits of a Badger in a menagerie; he was rather gentle, and would suffer himself to be played with and fondled with impunity by his keeper, but did not appear as well pleased with strangers; he occasionally growled at us, and would not suffer us to examine him without the presence and aid of his keeper.

In running, his fore-feet crossed each other, and his body nearly touched the ground. The heel did not press on the earth like that of the bear, but was only slightly elevated above it. He resembled the Maryland marmot in running, and progressed with about the same speed. We have never seen any animal that could exceed him in digging. He would fall to work with his strong feet and long nails, and in a minute bury himself in the earth, and would very soon advance to the end of a chain ten feet in length. In digging, the hind, as well as the fore-feet, were at work, the latter for the purpose of excavating, and the former, (like paddles,) for expelling the earth out of the hole, and nothing seemed to delight him more than burrowing in the ground; he seemed never to become weary of this kind of amusement; when he had advanced to the length of his chain he would return and commence a fresh gallery near the mouth of the first hole, thus he would be occupied for hours, and it was necessary to drag him away by main force. He lived on good terms with the raccoon, gray fox, prairie wolf, and a dozen other species of animals. He was said to be active and playful at night, but he seemed rather dull during the day, usually lying rolled up like a ball, with his head under his body for hours at a time.

This Badger did not refuse bread, but preferred meat, making two meals during the day, and eating about half a pound at each.

We occasionally saw him assuming rather an interesting attitude, raising the fore-part of his body from the earth, drawing his feet along his sides, sitting up in the manner of the marmot, and turning his head in all directions to make observations.

The Badger delights in taking up his residence in sandy prairies where he can indulge his extravagant propensity for digging. As he lives upon the animals he captures, he usually seeks out the burrows of the various species of marmots, spermophiles, ground-squirrels, &c., with which the prairies abound; into these he penetrates, enlarging them to admit his own larger body, and soon overtaking and devouring the terrified inmates. In this manner the prairies become so filled with innumerable Badger-holes that when the ground is covered with snow they prove a great annoyance to horsemen.

RICHARDSON informs us that early in the spring when they first begin to stir abroad they may be easily caught by pouring water into the holes, the ground at that time being so frozen that the water cannot escape through the sand, but soon fills the hole and its tenant is obliged to come out.

The Badger, like the Maryland marmot, is a rather slow and timid animal, retreating to its burrow as soon as it finds itself pursued. When once in its snug retreat no dexterity in digging can unearth it. RICHARDSON states that "the strength of its fore-feet and claws is so great that one which had insinuated only its head and shoulders into a hole, resisted the utmost efforts of two stout young men, who endeavoured to drag it out by the hind-legs and tail, until one of them fired the contents of his fowling-piece into its body."

This species is believed to be more carnivorous than that of Europe, (*Meles taxus.*) RICHARDSON states that a female which he had killed had a small marmot nearly entire, together with some field-mice, in its stomach, and that it had at the same time been eating some vegetables. As in its dentition it approaches the skunk, which is very decidedly carnivorous in habit, we should suppose that its principal food in its wild state is meat.

From November to April the American Badger remains in its burrow, scarcely ever showing itself above ground; here it passes its time in a state of semi-torpidity. It cannot, however, be a very sound sleeper in winter, as not only the individual which we examined in Charleston, but even that which we kept in New York, continued tolerably active through the winter. During the time of their long seclusion they do not lose much flesh, as they are represented to be very fat on coming abroad in spring. As this, however, is the pairing season, they, like other animals of similar habits, soon become lean.

The American Badger is said to produce from three to five young at a litter.

Several European writers, and among the more recent, GRIFFIFTH, in his Animal Kingdom, have respresented the Badger as leading a most gloomy and solitary life, but we are not to suppose from the subterranean habits of this species that it is necessarily a dull and unhappy creature. Its fat sides are certainly no evidence of suffering or misery, and its form is well adapted to the life it is destined to lead. It is, like nearly all our quadrupeds, nocturnal in its habits, hence it appears dull during the day, and cannot endure a bright light. To a being constituted like man, it would be a melancholy lot to live by digging under ground, shunning the light of day and only coming forth under the shadow of night; but for this life the Badger was formed, and he could not be happy in any other. We believe that a wise Providence has created no species which, from the nature of its organization, must necessarily be miserable; and we should, under all circumstances, rather distrust our short-sighted views than doubt the wisdom and infinite benevolence of the Creator.

Geographical Distribution.

The American Badger has a very extensive range. It has been traced as far north as the banks of Peace River, and the sources of the River of the Mountains, in latitude 58°. It abounds in the neighbourhood of Carlton-House, and on the waters that flow into Lake Winnepeg.

LEWIS and CLARKE, and TOWNSEND, found it on the open plains of the Columbia, and also on the prairies east of the Rocky Mountains.

We have not been able to trace it within a less distance from the Atlantic than the neighbourhood of Fort Union. To the south we have seen specimens which were said to have come from the eastern side of the Rocky Mountains, in latitude 36°. There is a specimen in the collection of the London Zoological Society, the skull of which was described and figured by WATERHOUSE, that was stated to have been received from Mexico. It is probable that the Flacoyole of FERNANDEZ, which was described as existing in Mexico, is the same species. There is also another specimen in the museum of the Zoological Society of London, that was brought by DOUGLASS, which is believed to have come from California.

It is very doubtful whether it exists on the eastern side of the American continent.

We are not aware that it has ever been found either in Upper or Lower Canada, and we could obtain no knowledge of it in our researches at Labrador.

General Remarks.

The difference between the European and American species of Badger is so great that it is unnecessary to institute a very particular comparison. Our species may be distinguished from that of Europe by its muzzle being hairy above, whilst it is naked in the other; the forelimbs are stouter, and the claws stronger; its head is also more conical in form. The European species has more conspicuous ears; it has three broad white marks, one on the top of the head, and one on each side, and between them are two broad black lines, which include the eyes and ears; and the whole of the throat and under-jaw are black; whilst the throat and lower-jaw of the American species are white; there is also a broad white patch separating the black colours between the sides of the forehead and ear. There are several other marks of difference which it is unnecessary to particularize, as the species are now universally admitted to be distinct.

SABINE supposed the American Badger to be a little the smallest. There is a considerable difference among different individuals of both species, but we have on an average found the two species nearly equal in size. Mr. SABINE's American specimen was a small one, measuring two feet two inches in body. BUFFON'S specimen was two feet four inches. One of ours was two feet seven. On the other hand, SHAW gives the length of head and body of the European species as about two feet. FISCHER in his synopsis gives it as two and one third, and CUVIER as two and a half. We have not found any European specimen measuring more than two feet six inches.

It was for a long time supposed, and was so stated, by BUFFON, that there was no true species of Badger in America; that author, however, afterwards received a specimen that was said to have come from Labrador, which was named by GMELIN after the country where it was supposed to be common. The name "*Labradoria*" will be very inappropriate should our conjectures prove correct, that it is unknown in that country. BUFFON's specimen had lost one of its toes; hence he described it as four toed. GMELIN who gave it a scientific name, made "*Palmis tetradactylis*" one of its specific characters.

SCHREBER first considered the American, as a distinct species from the European, Badger; CUVIER seems to have arrived at a different conclusion; SHAW gave tolerably good figures of both species on the same plate, pointing out their specific differences; and SABINE entered into a minute comparison. RICHARDSON (F. B. A.,) added considerably to our knowledge of the history and habits of the American Badger; and our esteemed friend, G. R. WATERHOUSE, Esq., has given descriptions and excellent figures of the skull and teeth, in which the distinctive marks in the dentition of the two species are so clearly pointed out, that nothing farther remains to be added in that department.

We have compared specimens of the *Blaireux* of LEWIS and CLARKE, found on the plains of Missouri, with those obtained by TOWNSEND near the Columbia, and also with specimens from the plains of the Saskatchewan in the Zoological museum, and found them all belonging to the same species.

Sciurus Douglassii.—Bach.

Douglass' Squirrel.

Plate xlviii.—Male and Female. Natural size.

S. Hudsonio quarta parte major; cauda corpore curtiore; supra subniger, infra flavus.

Characters.

About one-fourth larger than the chickaree (S. Hudsonius); tail, shorter than the body; colour, dark-brown above, and bright-buff beneath.

Synonymes.

SCIURUS DOUGLASSII, Gray, Proceedings Zool. Society, London, 1836, p. 88, named, but apparently not described.
  " " Bachman, monograph of the Genus Sciurus, Proceedings Zool. Soc., London, 1838.

Description.

Incisors, a little smaller than those of *Sciurus Hudsonius*; in the upper jaw the anterior molar, which is the smallest, has a single rounded eminence on the inner side; on the outer edge of the tooth there are two acute points, and there is one in front; the next two grinders, which are of equal size, have each a similar eminence on the inner side, with a pair of points externally; the posterior grinder, although larger, is not unlike the anterior one. In the lower jaw the bounding ridge of enamel in each tooth forms an anterior and posterior pair of points. The molars increase gradually in size from the first, which is the smallest, to the posterior one, which is the largest.

This species, in the form of its body, is not very unlike *Sciurus Hudsonius*; its ears and tail, however, are much shorter in proportion, and in other respects, as well as in size, it differs widely from *Hudsonius*.

Head, considerably broader; and nose, less elongated and blunter than in the latter; body, long and slender; ears, rather small, nearly rounded, slightly tufted posteriorly. As usual in this genus, the third inner toe is the longest, and not the second, as in the spermophiles.

Colour.

The whiskers, which are longer than the head, are black; hair, from the roots to near the points, plumbeous, tipped with brownish-gray, a few lighter coloured hairs interspersed, giving it a dark-brown appearance. When closely examined it has the appearance of being thickly sprinkled with minute points of rust colour on a black ground. The tail, which is distichous but not broad, is for three-fourths of its length the colour of the back; in the middle the fur is plumbeous at the roots, then irregularly marked with brown and black, and is tipped with dull white, giving it a hoary appearance; on the extremity of the tail the hairs are black from the roots, and are tipped with light brown; the belly, the inner sides of the extremities and the outer surfaces of the feet, together with the throat and mouth and a line above and under the eyes, are bright-buff. The colours on the upper and under parts are separated by a line of black, commencing at the shoulders, and running along the flanks to the thighs; this line is broadest in the middle of the body and is there about three lines wide, narrowing from thence to a point. The hairs, which project beyond the outer margins of the ears and form a slight tuft, are dark-brown, and in some specimens black.

Dimensions.

	Inches.	Lines.
Length from point of nose to insertion of tail	8	4
Tail (vertebræ)	4	6
Tail, including fur	6	4
Height of ear posteriorly	0	6
Palm to end of middle fore-claw	1	4
Heel and middle hind-claw	1	10

Habits.

Our specimens of Douglass' Squirrel were procured by Mr. TOWNSEND. He remarks in his notes:—"This is a very plentiful species, inhabits the pine trees along the shores of the Columbia River, and like our common Carolina squirrel lays in a great quantity of food for consumption during the winter months. This food consists of the cones of the pine, with a few acorns. Late in autumn it may be seen very busy in the tops of the trees, throwing down its winter-stock; after which, assisted by its mate, it gathers in and stows away its store, in readiness for its long incarceration."

Geographical Distribution.

DOUGLASS obtained his specimens of this Squirrel on the Rocky Mountains, and TOWNSEND found it on the Columbia River.

General Remarks.

This species was found by DOUGLASS and by TOWNSEND about the same time. These gentlemen, if we have been rightly informed, met together in the Far West. We drew up a description from specimens sent us by Mr. TOWNSEND, and used the grateful privilege of a describer, in naming it (*S. Townsendii*) after the individual who we supposed had been the first discoverer. Under this name we sent out description to the Acad. of Nat. Sciences of Philadelphia, which was read Aug. 7th, 1838. After arriving in England, however, the same year, we saw a similar specimen in the Museum of the Zool. Society, and heard that it had been named by GRAY, on the 11th October, 1836, who had called it after DOUGLASS, (*S. Douglassii*.) He had not, as far as we have been able to ascertain, published any description of it. All that we can find in reference to this species is the following: "Mr. GRAY gave a description of two foxes, a squirrel (*Sciurus Douglassii*), and three hares." The foxes and hares were described by him in the Magazine of Nat. Hist., (new series,) Nov., 1837, vol. i., p. 578, but for some reason he appears never to have published a description of this species.

We, however, supposing that he had described it, immediately changed our name to that proposed by GRAY, and in our monograph of the genus assigned to him the credit of having been the first describer, although he had, it appears, only named the animal.

Spermophilus Douglassii.—Richardson.

Douglass' Spermophile.

Plate xlix. Natural size.

Auribus insignibus; versus humeros canescens; corpore dilute fusco, striis multis indistinctis transversis fuscis et albis, linea nigra inter humeros; cauda, longa, cylindrica, pilis albo nigroque annulatis.

Characters.

Ears, conspicuous; hoary on the shoulders, with a black stripe between them; general colour of the body, pale-brown, with many indistinct transverse marks of dark-brown and white. Tail, long and cylindrical, hairs annulated with white and black.

Synonymes.

ARCTOMYS (SPERMOPHILUS?) DOUGLASSII, Richardson, F. B. A., p. 172.
ARCTOMYS (SPERMOPHILUS) BEECHEYI, Richardson, F. B. A., p. 170.?

Description.

In the general form of the body Douglass' Spermophile bears a strong resemblance to several species of Squirrel. Its rather slender shape, its long ears and tail, together with its large eyes and the form of its head, assimilate it to the Northern gray Squirrel, (*S. migratorius.*) Its coarser fur, however, its cheek-pouches, rounder tail, and the shape of its claws, clearly designate the genus to which it belongs.

Head, rather short, broad and depressed; nose, obtuse; ears, long, semi-oval, covered on both surfaces with short hairs, which in winter specimens extend a line beyond the margins at their extremities; cheek-pouches of moderate size.

The longer hairs of the body are rather coarse, they are slender at their roots, gradually enlarge as they ascend, and suddenly taper off to a point at the tips.

The fur beneath is on the back and sides soft and dense; on the under surface, however, the longer hairs predominate, and the animal is in those parts but thinly clothed.

There are on the four-feet four toes with a blunt nail in place of a thumb. The second toe is longest; the nails are of moderate size, and slightly hooked. The feet are covered with short adpressed hairs, to the roots of the nails; the tail is long and cylindrical, the longest hairs two inches in length. Mammæ ten, four pectoral and six abdominal.

Colour.

Incisors, dark orange; moustaches, black; on the nose and forehead, a tinge of reddish-brown; around the eyes, white; inner surface of ear, dull yellowish-brown; outer surface, dark-brown becoming nearly black at the tips; sides of the face, yellowish white. The sides of the neck and shoulders have a hoary appearance. There is a broad, dark-brown stripe commencing on the neck, widening in its descent, and continuing along the centre of the back for about half the length of the body, when it gradually blends with the colours on the sides and hips, which are irregularly speckled with white and black on a yellowish-brown ground. Nails, black; inner surface of legs, and whole under surface of body, dull yellowish-white. All the feet are grayish-brown.

The under-fur on every part of the back is dark-brown; the longer hairs are brown at their roots, then yellowish; those on the dorsal line are broadly tipped with black, whilst on the shoulders the tips are white. The spots on the back and hips are formed by some of the hairs being tipped with white, others with black. The hairs on the tail are at their roots white, then three times annulated with black and white, and are tipped with white; thus when distichously arranged (which, however, does not seem natural to the animal,) the tail presents three narrow longitudinal black stripes, and four white ones. Under-surface of tail, dull yellowish-gray.

There are some variations in the colour of different specimens. An old female that was suckling her young at the time she was caught had the dark dorsal line on the shoulders very indistinctly visible, and her feet were much lighter coloured than in younger specimens.

On Stone by Wm H. Hitchcock

Douglass Squirrel

Drawn from Nature by J.J.Audubon F.R.S.F.L.S   Lith Printed & Col.^d by J.T.Bowen, Phil.^a

Dimensions.

An old female.

Length of head and body	$13\frac{1}{2}$	inches.
Tail (vertebræ)	$7\frac{1}{2}$	do.
Tail, to end of fur	9	do.
Height of ear	$\frac{1}{2}$	do.
From heel to longest nail	$2\frac{1}{4}$	do.
From eye to point of nose	$1\frac{1}{4}$	do.

An old male.

Length of head and body	$13\frac{3}{4}$	inches.
Tail (vertebræ)	8	do.
Tail, to end of fur	$9\frac{1}{3}$	do.
Height of ear	$\frac{1}{2}$	do.
From heel to point of nail	$2\frac{1}{4}$	do.

Young.

Length of head and body	9	do.
Tail (vertebræ)	$5\frac{1}{2}$	do.
Tail, to end of fur	$6\frac{1}{3}$	do.
Height of ear	$\frac{1}{2}$	do.
Tarsus	2	do.

Habits.

We regret to state, that with the habits of this species we are wholly unacquainted. Mr. TOWNSEND, who kindly loaned us four specimens, from which we made our drawing and prepared our description, did not furnish us with any account of them.

Of *Spermophilus Beecheyi*, which we have supposed might be found identical with this species, Dr. RICHARDSON states that, "Mr. COLLIE, surgeon of his majesty's ship Blossom, informs me that this kind of Spermophile burrows in great numbers in the sandy declivities and dry plains in the neighbourhood of San Francisco and Monterey, in California, close to the houses. They frequently stand upon their hind-legs when looking round about them. In running they carry the tail generally straight out, but when passing over any little inequality, it is raised as if to prevent its being soiled. In rainy weather, and when the fields are wet and dirty, they come but little above ground. They take the alarm when any one passes within twenty or thirty yards of them, and run off at full speed till they can reach the mouth of their hole, where they stop a little and then enter it; they soon come out again, but with caution, and if not molested, will proceed to their usual occupation of playing or feeding. *Artemesias* and other vegetable matters were found in their stomachs."

Geographical Distribution.

One of the specimens obtained by Mr. TOWNSEND is marked "Falls of the Columbia River," another "Walla-walla;" the specimen procured by DOUGLASS was obtained on the banks of the Columbia River, and if our conjectures are correct, that *S. Beecheyi* is the same as the present species, it exists also in considerable numbers in California.

General Remarks.

The first description of this species was given by Dr. RICHARDSON, who received from DOUGLASS a hunter's skin, which, containing no skull, he was prevented from deciding on the genus. We have ascertained that in its dentition it is a true spermophile, and in all other respects possesses the characteristics of that genus.

In the valuable collection of the London Zoological Society we examined a specimen of *S. Beecheyi*, brought by Mr. COLLIE, which so strikingly resembles this species, that we are greatly inclined to think they will yet be found identical; we have, therefore, quoted it for the present as a synonyme, but marked it with a doubt, as an examination of a greater number of specimens might probably change our views.

Spermophilus Richardsonii. —Sab.

Richardson's Spermophile.

Plate 1.—Natural size.

Sciuro Hudsonio aliquantulum major; dorso fulvescente, pilis nigris mixtis; ventre fusco-rufescens; cauda mediocri, ad extremum nigra, apice fulva; auriculis brevissimis.

Characters.

A little larger than the Hudson's Bay squirrel; back, yellowish-gray, interspersed with black hair; belly, pale grayish-orange; tail, rather short, black at the extremity, tipped with fawn colour; ears, very short.

Synonymes.

ARCTOMYS RICHARDSONII, Sabine, Linn. Trans., vol. xiii., p. 589, t. 28.
    "   "   Idem, Franklin's Jour., p. 662.
    "   "   Griffith's An. Kingd., vol. v., p. 246.
TAWNEY AMERICAN MARMOT, Godm., Nat. Hist., vol. ii., p. 111.
ARCTOMYS (SPERMOPHILUS) RICHARDSONII, Rich., F. B. A., p. 164, pl. 11.

Description.

Body, rather short and thick; forehead, arched. nose, blunt, covered with short hairs; margins of the nostrils, and septum, naked; whiskers, few, and shorter than the head; eyes, large; ears, small, rounded, clothed with short hairs on both surfaces; cheek-pouches, of moderate size. The fur on the whole body is short and fine.

Legs, rather short; nails, long, weak, compressed, and slightly arched. On the fore-feet there are four toes and a minute thumb; the toes are covered on the upper surface with short hairs which reach the root of the nails. Palms, naked, containing five callosities. The thumb has a very short joint and is covered by a convex nail. Middle toe longest; the first and third are of equal length, and the outer one is shortest and farthest back.

On the hind-feet there are five toes. The three middle ones are nearly of equal length, the other two are smaller, and are situated farther back; the claws are shorter than those of the fore-feet; the soles are naked, but the heel is covered with hairs along the edges which curve over it. The tail is not very bushy and is about the size of that of the chipping-squirrel, (*Tamias Lysteri.*)

Colour.

Teeth, light orange; whiskers, black; nails, dark-brown; the back is yellowish-brown, intermixed with a few blackish hairs; on the sides, this colour is a shade lighter; on the nose, there is a slight tinge of chesnut-brown. The cheeks, throat, and inside of the thighs, are dull white; belly, brownish-gray. The tail is of the colour of the back; the hairs on the margins, near the end, are dark-brown tipped with yellowish-white.

Dimensions.

Adult female.

From point of nose to root of tail	$9\frac{1}{4}$	inches.
Head	2	do.
Tail (vertebræ)	$2\frac{1}{2}$	do.
Tail, to end of hair	$3\frac{1}{2}$	do.
From heel to end of middle claw	$1\frac{1}{2}$	do.
Height of ear	$0\frac{1}{4}$	do.

Habits.

We possess no personal knowledge of this species, never having met with it in a living state. The specimens from which our figures and descriptions were made, were obtained by Mr. TOWNSEND, and we are indebted to the excellent work of RICHARDSON for the following account of its habits: "This animal inhabits sandy prairies, and is not found in thickly wooded parts. It is one of the animals known to the residents of the fur countries by the name of Ground-squirrel, and to Canadian voyagers by that of Siffleur. It has considerable resemblance to the squirrels, but is less active, and has less sprightliness and elegance in its attitudes.

"It can scarcely be said to live in villages, though there are sometimes three

Plate XLIX

Drawn from Nature by J J Audubon. F.R.S.F.L.S

Douglasses Spermophile.

Lithd Printed & Cold by J T Bowen. Philada.

and four of its burrows on a sandy hummock or other favourable spot. The burrows generally fork or branch off near the surface, and descend obliquely downwards to a considerable depth; some few of them have more than one entrance. The earth scraped out, in forming them, is thrown up in a small mound at the mouth of the hole, and on it the animal seats itself on its hind-legs, to overlook the short grass, and reconnoitre before it ventures to make an excursion. In the spring, there are seldom more than two, and most frequently only one individual seen at a time at the mouth of a hole; and, although I have captured many of them at that season, by pouring water into their burrows, and compelling them to come out, I have never obtained more than one from the same hole, unless when a stranger has been chased into a burrow already occupied by another. There are many little well-worn pathways diverging from each burrow, and some of these roads are observed, in the spring, to lead directly to the neighbouring holes, being most probably formed by the males going in quest of a mate. They place no sentinels, and there appears to be no concert between the Tawny Marmots residing in the neighbourhood, every individual looking out for himself. They never quit their holes in the winter; and I believe they pass the greater part of that season in a torpid state. The ground not being thawed when I was at Carlton House, I had not an opportunity of ascertaining how their sleeping apartments were constructed, nor whether they lay up stores of food or not. About the end of the first week of April, or as soon as a considerable portion of the ground is bare of snow, they come forth, and when caught on their little excursions, their cheek-pouches generally contain the tender buds of the *Anemone Nuttalliana*, which is very abundant, and the earliest plant on the plains. They are fat when they first appear, and their fur is in good condition; but the males immediately go in quest of the females, and in the course of a fortnight they become lean and the hair begins to fall off. They run pretty quick, but clumsily, and their tails at the same time move up and down with a jerking motion. They dive into their burrows on the approach of danger, but soon venture out again if they hear no noise, and may be easily shot with bow and arrow, or even knocked down with a stick, by any one who will take the trouble to lie quietly on the grass near their burrow for a few minutes. Their curiosity is so great that they are sure to come out to look around.

"As far as I could ascertain, they feed entirely on vegetable matter, eating in the spring the young buds and tender sprouts of herbaceous plants, and in the autumn the seeds of grasses and leguminous plants.

"Their cry when in danger, or when angry, so nearly resembles that of *Arctomys Parryi*, that I am unable to express the difference in letters.

"Several species of falcon that frequent the plains of the Saskatchewan, prey much on these Marmots; but their principal enemy is the American badger, which, by enlarging their burrows, pursues them to their inmost retreats. Considerable parties of Indians have also been known to subsist for a time on them when large game is scarce, and their flesh is palatable when they are fat."

Geographical Distribution.

This species has not been observed further north than latitude 55°. In the appendix to FRANKLIN's Journey, it was said to inhabit the shores of the Arctic Sea, but it appears that another species had been mistaken for it. It is found in the grassy plains that lie between the north and south branches of the Saskatchewan River. It is very common in the neighbourhood of Carlton House, its burrows being scattered at short distances over the whole plain. TOWNSEND obtained his specimens in the Rocky Mountains, (about latitude 45°,) and we have traced it as far south as latitude 38°.

General Remarks.

"The Tawny Marmot Squirrel is most readily distinguished from the true squirrels by the smallness of its ears, the shape of its incisors, which are larger but not so strong and much less compressed; the second and not the third toe being the largest, and its comparatively long claws and less bushy tail. It seems to be the American representative of *A. concolor* or the *Jevraska* of Siberia."—(RICHARDSON.) The males of this species are represented as very pugnacious in their habits, and we have represented one in our plate that has lost the end of its tail, the figure being taken from one of the specimens sent to us.

Genus Lutra.—Ray., Cuv., Mustela Spec., Linn., Aonyx, Lesson.

Dental Formula.

Incisive $\frac{6}{6}$; *Canine* $\frac{1-1}{1-1}$; *Molar* $\frac{5-5}{5-5}$ = 36.

THE second inferior incisor on each side, a little receding in most of the species; the canine much dilated, hooked; first superior molar, small, blunt, and sometimes deciduous; the second, cutting; the third, of similar form, but larger; the fourth, with two external points, but furnished with a strong spur on the inner side; the fifth has externally three small points, with a broad spur internally. The inferior molars in this genus vary from five to six, the first being wanting in some of the species.

Head large and flattish, terminating in a blunt muzzle; ears short and round; tongue slightly papillous. Body long and slender; legs short; toes five on each foot. In some of the species the fifth toe on the hind foot is rudimental. Toes webbed, armed with short claws which are not retractile. Tail, not as long as the body, thick, and flattened horizontally.

Body covered externally with long, rigid and glossy hair, with a softer, shorter, downy fur intermixed.

On each side of the anus, there is a small gland secreting fetid matter.

All the species are good swimmers, live along the banks of rivers and ponds, and feed on fish.

The generic appellation is derived from Lutra—an Otter: from the Greek λοvω (lous), wash.

There are eleven species enumerated by authors, inhabiting the following countries: Europe 1, Island of Trinidad 1, Guyana 1, Brazil 1, Kamtschatka 1, Java 1, Malay 1, Pondicherry 1, The Cape of Good Hope 1, and North America 2.

Lutra Canadensis.—Sabine.

Canada Otter.

Plate li.—Male. Natural Size.

L. vellere nitido, saturate fusco; mento gulâque fusco albis; L. vulgare major.

Characters.

Larger than the European Otter, L. Vulgaris. Dark glossy brown; chin and throat dusky white; five feet in length.

Synonymes.

LOUTRE DE CANADA, Buffon, vol. xiii., p. 326, t. 44.
COMMON OTTER, Pennant, Arctic Zoolog., vol. i., p. 653.
LAND OTTER, Warden's Hist. U. S., p. 206.
LUTRA CANADENSIS, Sabine, Franklin's Journ., p. 653.
    "   BRASILIENSIS, Harlan, Fauna, p. 72.
    "   "   Godman, Nat. Hist., vol. i., p. 222.
    "   CANADENSIS, Dekay, Zool., p. 1., p. 39.

Description.

Head, large and nearly of a globular form; nose, blunt and naked; lips, thick; ears, round, slightly ovate, and closer together than in *L. Vulgaris*, clothed densely with short hair on both surfaces; body, long, cylindrical; neck, long; legs, short and stout; moustaches, very rigid, like bristles; soles of the feet, thinly clothed with hair between the toes, tubercles at the roots of the claws, naked; feet, webbed to the nails; Tail, stout, gradually tapering toward the extremity, depressed at the base, continuing flattened through half its length; at the base there are two oval glands. The longer hairs covering the fur, are glossy and rigid; fur, soft, dense, and nearly as fine as that of the Beaver, continuing through the whole extent of the body, even to the extremity of the tail, but shorter on the forehead and extremities.

We overlooked the opportunity of instituting a careful comparison between the skulls and teeth of the European and American Otters, and have no access to specimens of the former. We therefore quote the language of Dr. DEKAY, whose observations in this respect correspond with our recollections

Plate L.

Drawn from Nature by J.J.Audubon.F.R.S.F.L.S.

Richardsons Spermophile?

Lith⁴ Printed & Col⁴ by J.T.Bowen, Philad⁴

of a general comparison made at the Berlin Museum, eleven years ago. "In their dentition the Otters are eminently characterized by the enormous dilation of the two posterior cheek teeth in the upper jaw. Our species, in this particular, offers some variations from the European Otter. The penultimate jaw tooth, in our species, has a broad internal heel directed obliquely forward, with a deep fissure dividing the surface into two rounded and elevated portions; and the pointed tubercle is broad, with a high shoulder posteriorly, and comparatively little elevated. The last tubercular tooth subquadrate, nearly as large as the preceding, and its greater axis directed obliquely backwards with four or rather six distinct elevated points; but the outer raised margin, which is so conspicuous in the European Otter, appears to be indistinct or simply elevated into two pointed tubercles, or wanting entirely, in the American."

In age, the canine as well as the anterior molars become much worn. In a specimen from Carolina, the incisors are worn down to the upper surface of the jaw teeth; in another from Georgia, all the teeth are worn down to the gums. A specimen from Canada and another from Texas have the teeth very pointed, and the canine projecting beyond the lips. These were evidently younger animals. In older specimens we have on several occasions found the two anterior jaw teeth entirely wanting, as well as some of the incisors, the former appearing to have dropped out at about the fourth year.

Colour.

A specimen from Lower Canada. Moustaches very light brown, many being white, those on the sides of the face dingy white; upper lip and chin light grayish brown, a shade darker under the throat; the long hairs covering the fur are in one half of their length from their roots dingy white, gradually deepening into brown. The general colour on the upper surface is that of a rich dark chesnut brown, a shade lighter on the whole of the under surface. RICHARDSON states: "The Canada Otter may be distinguished from the European species by the fur of its belly being of the same shining brown colour with that of the back." In this particular our observations do not correspond with those of our distinguished friend. Out of more than a hundred specimens of American Otters which we have examined, many of which came from Canada and the Rocky Mountains, we have but with one or two exceptions found the colour on the under surface lighter than on the back.

A specimen from Carolina, an old male, teeth much worn.

Upper lip from the nostrils, chin and throat to near the chest, grayish white; the fur on the back, although not quite so long as that of specimens from Canada, is quite dense and silky, and very nearly equal in fineness. It is whitish at the roots, with a bluish tinge towards the extremities. The longer hairs which conceal the fur and present the external colouring are very nearly of the same tint as in those procured in Canada, so that the specimens from these widely separated localities can scarcely be regarded even as varieties.

A specimen from Colorado, Texas.

(The form is precisely similar to the Otters of Canada and those existing in various intermediate States. The palms are naked, with a little less hair between the toes on the upper and under surfaces.) The colour is throughout two shades lighter than that of specimens from Canada, but the markings are similarly distributed. Fur on the back from the roots soiled white, inclining to brown at the tips. The long and rigid hairs on the upper surface lightish brown at the roots, then dark brown, tipped with lightish brown.

Dimensions.

Specimen from Canada.—Adult male.

	Feet.	Inches.
From point of nose to root of tail,	2	5
Tail,	1	7
From point of nose to eye,	0	$1\frac{3}{4}$
From point of nose to ear,	0	4
Height of ear,	0	$0\frac{3}{4}$
Breadth of ear at base,	0	$0\frac{3}{4}$

Specimen from Carolina.

From point of nose to root of tail,	2	7
Tail,	1	5
Point of nose to eye,	0	$1\frac{3}{4}$
" " to ear,	0	$3\frac{3}{4}$
Height of ear,	0	$0\frac{3}{4}$
Breadth at base,	0	$0\frac{3}{4}$

Weight, 23 lbs.

Specimen from the Colorado, in Texas.

From nose to root of tail,	2	7
Length of tail,	1	6
From point of nose to eye,	0	$1\frac{3}{4}$
" to ear,	0	$3\frac{3}{4}$
Between the ears,	0	10
Height,	0	$5\frac{3}{8}$
Around the body behind the shoulder,	1	$7\frac{1}{8}$
Around the body, (middle,)	1	

Weight 20 lbs.

Habits.

We concluded our first volume with a brief account of *Spermophilus Richardsonii*, the last animal figured in plates 1 to 50 inclusive, of our illustrations of the Quadrupeds of North America. Having, since that volume was written, published about 60 more plates, we now take up our pen to portray the habits and describe the forms and colours of the species figured in plates 51 to 100 inclusive, and shall, we hope, be able to give of our readers tolerably good accounts of them; although, alas! the days of our youth are gone, when, full of enthusiasm, and anxious to examine every object in nature within our reach, the rising sun never found us slumbering away the fresh hours of the morning, but beamed upon our path through the deep forest, or lighted up to joy and gladness the hill side or mountain top, which we had already gained in quest of the birds or the beasts that were to be met with; and where we often prolonged our rambles until the shades of evening found us yet at a distance from our camp, loaded with wild turkeys, ducks, geese, and perchance an Otter.

Fresh and pleasant in our mind is the recollection of our early expeditions among the wild woods, and along the unvisited shores of our new country; and although more than forty years of varied and busy life have passed since the Otter was shot and drawn, whose figure we have given, we will try to take you with us to a spot on the eastern banks of the fair Ohio. It is a cold wintry morning: the earth concealed by a slight covering of snow, and the landscape in all its original wildness. Here let us proceed cautiously, followed by that constant companion, our faithful dog. Whilst we are surveying the quiet waters as they roll onward toward the great Mississippi, in whose muddy current they will lose their clear and limpid character, and become as opaque and impetuous as the waves of that mighty river of the West, we see a dark object making its way towards the spot on which we stand, through the swiftly dividing element. It has not observed us: we remain perfectly still, and presently it is distinctly visible; it is an Otter, and now within the range of our old gun "Tear Jacket," we take but one moment to raise our piece and fire; the water is agitated by a violent convulsive movement of the animal, our dog plunges into the river, and swimming eagerly to the Otter, seizes it, but the latter dives, dragging the dog with it beneath the surface, and when they reappear, the Otter has caught the dog by the nose and is struggling violently. The brave dog, however, does not give up, but in a few moments drags the wounded Otter to the shore, and we immediately despatch it. Being anxious to figure the animal, we smooth its disordered fur and proceed homewards with it, where, although at that time we had not drawn many quadrupeds, we soon select a position in which to figure the Otter, and accordingly draw it with one foot in a steel-trap, and endeavour to represent the pain and terror felt by the creature when its foot is caught by the sharp saw-like teeth of the trap.

Not far from the town of Henderson, (Kentucky), but on the opposite side of the Ohio river, in the State of Indiana, there is a pond nearly one mile in length, with a depth of water varying from twelve to fifteen feet. Its shores are thickly lined with cane, and on the edge of the water stand many large and lofty cypress trees. We often used to seat ourselves on a fallen trunk, and watch in this secluded spot the actions of the birds and animals which resorted to it, and here we several times observed Otters engaged in catching fishes and devouring them. When pursuing a fish, they dived expertly and occasionally remained for more than a minute below the surface. They generally held their prey when they came to the top of the water, by the head, and almost invariably swam with it to a half-sunken log, or to the margin of the pond, to eat the fish at their ease, having done which, they returned again to the deep water to obtain more.

One morning we observed that some of these animals resorted to the neighbourhood of the root of a large tree which stood on the side of the pond opposite to us, and with its overhanging branches shaded the water. After a fatiguing walk through the tangled cane-brake and thick underwood which bordered the sides of this lonely place, we reached the opposite side of the pond near the large tree, and moved cautiously through the mud and water

Plate LI

N°11

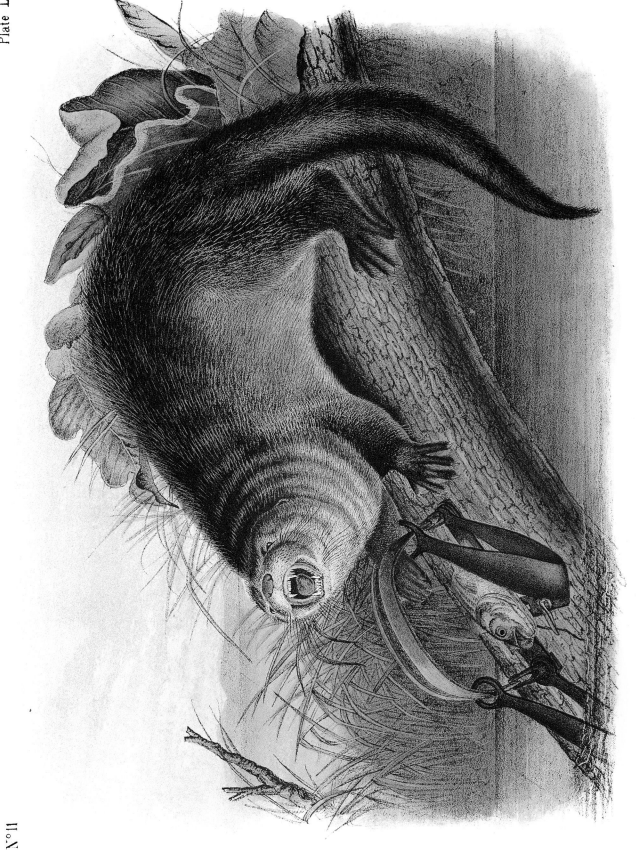

Drawn from Nature by J. J. Audubon. F R S F L S

Lith. Printed & Co.^d by J. T. Bowen, Phila.^a

Canada Otter

towards its roots: but the hearing or sight of the Otters was attracted to us, and we saw several of them hastily make off at our approach. On sounding the tree with the butt of our gun, we discovered that it was hollow, and then having placed a large stick in a slanting position against the trunk, we succeeded in reaching the lowest bough, and thence climbed up to a broken branch from which an aperture into the upper part of the hollow enabled us to examine the interior. At the bottom there was quite a large space or chamber to which the Otters retired, but whether for security or to sleep we could not decide.

Next morning we returned to the spot, accompanied by one of our neighbours, and having approached, and stopped up the entrance under water as noiselessly as possible, we cut a hole in the side of the tree four or five feet from the ground, and as soon as it was large enough to admit our heads, we peeped in and discovered three Otters on a sort of bed composed of the inner bark of trees and other soft substances, such as water grasses. We continued cutting the hole we had made, larger, and when sufficiently widened, took some green saplings, split them at the but-end, and managed to fix the head of each animal firmly to the ground by passing one of these split pieces over his neck, and then pressing the stick forcibly downwards. Our companion then crept into the hollow, and soon killed the Otters, with which we returned home.

The American Otter frequents running streams, large ponds, and more sparingly the shores of some of our great lakes. It prefers those waters which are clear, and makes a hole or burrow in the banks, the entrance to which is under water.

This species has a singular habit of sliding off the wet sloping banks into the water, and the trappers take advantage of this habit to catch the animal by placing a steel-trap near the bottom of their sliding places, so that the Otters occasionally put their foot into it as they are swiftly gliding toward the water.

In Carolina, a very common mode of capturing the Otter is by tying a pretty large fish on the pan of a steel-trap, which is sunk in the water where it is from five to ten feet deep. The Otter dives to the bottom to seize the fish, is caught either by the nose or foot, and is generally found drowned. At other times the trap is set under the water, without bait, on a log, one end of which projects into the water, whilst the other rests on the banks of a pond or river; the Otter, in endeavouring to mount the log, is caught in the trap.

Mr. GODMAN, in his account of these singular quadrupeds, states that "their favourite sport is sliding, and for this purpose in winter the highest ridge of snow is selected, to the top of which the Otters scramble, where, lying on the belly with the fore-feet bent backwards, they give themselves an impulse with their hind legs and swiftly glide head-foremost down the declivity, sometimes for the distance of twenty yards. This sport they continue apparently with the keenest enjoyment until fatigue or hunger induces them to desist."

This statement is confirmed by CARTWRIGHT, HEARNE, RICHARDSON, and more recent writers who have given the history of this species, and is in accordance with our own personal observations.

The Otters ascend the bank at a place suitable for their diversion, and sometimes where it is very steep, so that they are obliged to make quite an effort to gain the top; they slide down in rapid succession where there are many at a sliding place. On one occasion we were resting ourself on the bank of Canoe Creek, a small stream near Henderson, which empties into the Ohio, when a pair of Otters made their appearance, and not observing our proximity, began to enjoy their sliding pastime. They glided down the soap-like muddy surface of the slide with the rapidity of an arrow from a bow, and we counted each one making twenty-two slides before we disturbed their sportive occupation.

This habit of the Otter of sliding down from elevated places to the borders of streams, is not confined to cold countries, or to slides on the snow or ice, but is pursued in the Southern States, where the earth is seldom covered with snow, or the waters frozen over. Along the reserve-dams of the rice fields of Carolina and Georgia, these slides are very common. From the fact that this occurs in most cases during winter, about the period of the rutting season, we are inclined to the belief that this propensity may be traced to those instincts which lead the sexes to their periodical associations.

RICHARDSON says that this species has the habit of travelling to a great distance through the snow in search of some rapid that has resisted the severity of the winter frosts, and that if seen and pursued by hunters on these journeys, it will throw itself forward on its belly and slide through the snow for several yards, leaving a deep furrow behind it, which movement is repeated with so much rapidity, that even a swift runner on snow shoes has some difficulty in overtaking it. He also remarks that it doubles on its track with much cunning, and dives under the snow to elude its pursuers.

The Otter is a very expert swimmer, and can overtake almost any fish, and

as it is a voracious animal, it doubtless destroys a great number of fresh water fishes annually. We are not aware of its having a preference for any particular species, although it is highly probable that it has. About twenty-five years ago we went early one autumnal morning to study the habits of the Otter at Gordon and Spring's Ferry, on the Cooper River, six miles above Charleston, where they were represented as being quite abundant. They came down with the receding tide in groups or families of five or six together. In the space of two hours we counted forty-six. They soon separated, ascended the different creeks in the salt marshes, and engaged in capturing mullets (*Mugil*). In most cases they came to the bank with a fish in their mouth, despatching it in a minute, and then hastened again after more prey. They returned up the river to their more secure retreats with the rising tide. In the small lakes and ponds of the interior of Carolina, there is found a favourite fish with the Otter, called the fresh-water trout (*Grystes salmoides*).

Although the food of the Otter in general is fish, yet when hard pressed by hunger, it will not reject animal food of any kind. Those we had in confinement, when no fish could be obtained were fed on beef, which they always preferred boiled. During the last winter we ascertained that the skeleton and feathers of a wild duck were taken from an Otter's nest on the banks of a rice field reserve-dam. It was conjectured that the duck had either been killed or wounded by the hunters, and was in this state seized by the Otter. This species can be kept in confinement easily in a pond surrounded by a proper fence where a good supply of fish is procurable.

On throwing some lives fishes into a small pond in the Zoological Gardens in London, where an Otter was kept alive, it immediately plunged off the bank after them, and soon securing one, rose to the surface holding its prize in its teeth, and ascending the bank, rapidly ate it by large mouthfuls, and dived into the water again for another. This it repeated until it had caught and eaten all the fish which had been thrown into the water for its use. When thus engaged in devouring the luckless fishes the Otter bit through them, crushing the bones, which we could hear snapping under the pressure of its powerful jaws.

When an Otter is shot and killed in the water, it sinks from the weight of its skeleton, the bones being nearly solid and therefore heavy, and the hunter consequently is apt to lose the game if the water be deep; this animal is, however, usually caught in strong steel-traps placed and baited in its haunts; if caught by one of the fore-feet, it will sometimes gnaw the foot off, in order to make its escape.

Otters when caught young are easily tamed, and although their gait is ungainly, will follow their owner about, and at times are quite playful. We have on two occasions domesticated the Otter. The individuals had been captured when quite young, and in the space of two or three days became as tame and gentle as the young of the domestic dog. They preferred milk and boiled corn meal, and refused to eat fish or meat of any kind, until they were several months old. They became so attached to us, that at the moment of their entrance into our study they commenced crawling into our lap— mounting our table, romping among our books and writing materials, and not unfrequently upsetting our ink-stand and deranging our papers.

The American Otter has one litter annually, and the young, usually two and occasionally three in number, are brought forth about the middle of April, according to Dr. RICHARDSON, in high northern latitudes. In the Middle and Southern States they are about a month earlier, and probably litter in Texas and Mexico about the end of February.

The nest, in which the Otter spends a great portion of the day and in which the young are deposited, we have had opportunities of examining on several occasions. One we observed in an excavation three feet in diameter, in the bank of a rice field; one in the hollow of a fallen tree, and a third under the root of a cypress, on the banks of Cooper river, in South Carolina; the materials— sticks, grasses and leaves—were abundant; the nest was large, in all cases protected from the rains, and above and beyond the influence of high water or freshets.

J. W. AUDUBON procured a fine specimen of the Otter, near Lagrange in Texas, on the twenty-third of February, 1846. It was shot whilst playing or sporting in a piece of swampy and partially flooded ground, about sunset,— its dimensions we have already given.

Early writers have told us that the common Otter of Europe had long been taught to catch fish for its owners, and that in the houses of the great in Sweden, these animals were kept for that purpose, and would go out at a signal from the cook, catch fish and bring it into the kitchen in order to be dressed for dinner.

This, however improbable it may at first appear, is by no means unlikely, except that we doubt the fact of the animal's going by itself for the firsh.

BEWICK relates some anecdotes of Otters which captured salmon and other fish for their owners, for particulars of which we must refer our readers to his History of Quadrupeds.

Our late relative and friend, N. BERTHOUD, Esq., of St. Louis, told us some time since, that while travelling through the interior of the State of Ohio, he stopped at a house where the landlord had four Otters alive which were so gentle that they never failed to come when he whistled for them, and that when they approached their master they crawled along slowly and with much apparent humility towards him, and looked somewhat like enormous thick and short snakes.

Geographical Distribution.

The geographical range of this species includes almost the whole continent of North America, and possibly a portion of South America. It has, however, been nearly extirpated in our Atlantic States east of Maryland, and is no longer found abundantly in many parts of the country in which it formerly was numerously distributed.

It is now procured most readily, in the western portions of the United States and on the Eastern shore of Maryland. It is still abundant on the rivers and the reserve-dams of the rice fields of Carolina, and is not rare in Georgia, Louisiana and Texas.

A considerable number are also annually obtained in the British provinces. We did not capture any Otters during our journey up the Missouri to the Yellow Stone River, but observed traces of them in the small water courses in that direction.

General Remarks.

Much perplexity exists in regard to the number of species of American Otters, and consequently in determining their nomenclature. RAY, in 1693, described a specimen from Brazil under the name of *Braziliensis*. It was subsequently noticed by BRISSON, BLUMENBACH, D'AZARA, MARC-GRAVE, SCHREBER, SHAW, and others. We have not had an opportunity of comparing our North American species with any specimen obtained from Brazil. The loose and unscientific descriptions we have met with of the Brazilian Otter, do not agree in several particulars with any variety of the species found in North America; there is, however, a general resemblance in size and colour. Should it hereafter be ascertained by closer investigations that the species existing in these widely removed localities are mere varieties, then the previous name of *Braziliensis* (RAY) must be substituted for that of *L.*

Canadensis, FR. CUVIER.

In addition to the yet undecided species of RAY, FR. CUVIER has separated the Canada from the Carolina species, bestowing on the former the name of *L. Canadensis*, and on the latter that of *L. Lataxina*. GRAY has published a specimen from the more northern portions of North America under the name *Lataxina Mollis*; and a specimen which we obtained in Carolina, and presented to our friend Mr. WATERHOUSE of London, was, we believe, published by him under another name.

Notwithstanding these high authorities, we confess we have not been able to regard them in any other light than varieties, some more strongly marked than others, of the same species. The *L. Lataxina* of FR. CUVIER, and the specimen published by WATERHOUSE, do not present such distinctive characters as to justify us in separating the species from each other or from *L. Canadensis*. The specimen published by RICHARDSON under the name of *L. Canadensis*, (Fauna Boreali Americana,) was that of a large animal; and the *Mollis* of GRAY was, we think, a fine specimen of the Canada Otter, with fur of a particular softness. We have, after much deliberation, come to the conclusion that all these must be regarded as varieties of one species. In dentition, in general form, in markings and in habits, they are very similar. The specimen from Texas, on account of its lighter colour and somewhat coarser fur, differs most from the other varieties; but it does not on the whole present greater differences than are often seen in the common mink of the salt marshes of Carolina, when compared with specimens obtained from the streams and ponds in the interior of the Middle States. Indeed, in colour it much resembles the rusty brown of the Carolina mink. In the many specimens we have examined, we have discovered shades of difference in colour as well as in the pelage among individuals obtained from the South and North, in localities removed a thousand miles from each other, we could not discover that they were even varieties. In other cases these differences may be accounted for from the known effects of climate on other nearly allied species, as evidenced in the common mink. On the whole we may observe, that the Otters of the North are of a darker colour and have the fur longer and more dense than those of the South. As we proceed southward the hair gradually becomes a little lighter in colour and the fur less dense, shorter, and coarser. These changes, however, are not peculiar to the Otter. They are not only observed in the mink, but in the raccoon, the common American rabbit, the Virginian deer, and nearly all the species that exist both in the northern and southern portions of our continent.

We shall give a figure of *L. Mollis* of GRAY, in our third volume.

Vulpes Velox.—Say.

Swift Fox. Kit Fox.

Plate lii.—Male. Natural Size.

V. gracilis, supra cano fulvaque varices, infra albus; v. fulvo minor.

Characters.

Smaller than the American red fox, body slender, gray above, varied with fulvous; beneath, white.

Synonymes.

KIT FOX, or small burrowing fox of the plains. Lewis and Clark, vol. i., p. 400. Vol. iii., pp. 28. 29.
CANIS VELOX, Say. Long's Expedition, vol. ii., p. 339.
    "   "   Harlan's Fauna, 91.
    "   "   Godman's Nat. Hist., vol. i., p. 282.
CANIS CINEREO ARGENTATUS, Sabine, Franklin's Journey, p. 658.
    "   (vulpes) CINEREO ARGENTATUS, Richardson, Fa. B. Ame. p. 98.

Description.

This little species of Fox bears a great resemblance to our American red fox, in shape, but has a broader face and shorter nose than the latter species; in colour it approaches nearer to the gray fox. Its form is light and slender, and gives indication of a considerable capacity for speed; the tail is long, cylindrical, bushy, and tapering at the end.

The entire length from the insertion of the superior incisors to the tip of the occipital crest, is rather more than four inches and three-tenths: the least distance between the orbital cavities nine-tenths of an inch; between the insertion of the lateral muscles at the junction of the frontal and parietal bones, half an inch. The greatest breadth of this space on the parietal bones, thirteen-twentieths of an inch."—(SAY.) The hair is of two kinds, a soft dense and rather woolly fur beneath, intermixed with longer and stronger hairs.

Colour.

The fur on the back, when the hairs are separately examined, is from the roots, for three-fourths of its length, of a light brownish gray colour, then yellowish brown, then a narrow ring of black, then a larger ring of pure white, slightly tipped at the apical part with black. The upper part of the nose is pale yellowish brown, on each side of which there is a patch of brownish, giving it a hoary appearance in consequence of some of the hairs being tipped with white; moustaches black; upper lip margined by a stripe of white hairs. There is a narrow blackish brown line between the white of the posterior angle of the mouth, which is prolonged around the margin of the lower lip. The upper part of the head, the orbits of the eyes, the cheeks and superior surface of the neck, back, and hips, covered with intermixed hairs, tipped with brown, black, and white, giving those parts a grizzled colour. Towards the posterior parts of the back there are many long hairs interspersed, that are black from the roots to the tip. The sides of the neck, the chest, the shoulders and flanks, are of a dull reddish orange colour; the lower jaw is white, with a tinge of blackish brown on its margins; the throat, belly, inner surface of legs, and upper surface of feet, are white. The outside of the forelegs, and the posterior parts of the hindlegs, are brownish orange. The slight hairs between the callosities of the toes are brownish. The tail is on the under surface yellowish gray with a mixture of black, and a few white hairs; the under surface is brownish yellow and black at the end.

Dimensions.

	Feet.	Inches.
From point of nose to root of tail, ...	1	8
Tail, (vertebræ,)	0	$9\frac{3}{4}$
" to end of hair, ...	1	0
From tip of nose to end of head, ...	0	$2\frac{1}{8}$
Between the eyes, ...	0	$1\frac{1}{4}$
Breadth between the ears, ...	0	$2\frac{3}{8}$

Weight $8\frac{1}{2}$ lbs.

Measurement of a young animal killed at Fort Union.

	Feet	Inches
From point of nose to root of tail, ...	1	$0\frac{1}{4}$
Tail, (vertebræ,)	0	$4\frac{7}{8}$
" to end of hair, ...	0	$5\frac{3}{4}$
Width at the shoulders, ...	0	$7\frac{1}{4}$
Length of head, ...	0	$3\frac{1}{2}$
Between the eyes, ...	0	$0\frac{7}{8}$
Breadth between the ears, ...	0	$1\frac{1}{4}$

Habits.

The First Swift Fox we ever saw alive was at Fort Clark on the upper Missouri river, at which place we arrived on the 7th of June, 1843. It had been caught in a steel-trap by one of its fore-feet, and belonged to Mr. CHARDON, the principal at the Fort, who with great kindness and politeness presented it to us; assuring us that good care would be taken of it during our absence, (as we were then ascending the river to proceed to the base of the Rocky Mountains,) and that on our return to the Mandan village, we might easily take it with us to New-York.

Mr. CHARDON informed us that this Fox was a most expert rat catcher, and that it had been kept in a loft without any other food than the rats and mice that it caught there. It was a beautiful animal, and ran with great rapidity from one side of the loft to another, to avoid us. On our approaching, it showed its teeth and growled much like the common red fox.

Soon after we left Fort Clark, between the western shore of the Missouri river and the hills called the "Trois mamelles" by the Canadian and French trappers, on an open prairie, we saw the second Swift Fox we met with on this journey. Our party had been shooting several buffaloes, and our friend ED. HARRIS, Esq., and ourself, were approaching the hunters apace. We were on foot, and Mr. HARRIS was mounted on his buffalo horse, when a Swift Fox darted from a concealed hole in the prairie almost under the hoofs of my friend's steed. My gun was unfortunately loaded with ball, but the Fox was chased by Mr. HARRIS, who took aim at it several times but could not draw sight on the animal; and the cunning fellow doubled and turned about and around in such a dexterous manner, that it finally escaped in a neighbouring ravine, and we suppose gained its burrow, or sheltered itself in the cleft of a rock, as we did not see it start again. This slight adventure with this (so called) Swift Fox convinced us that the accounts of the wonderful speed of this animal are considerably exaggerated; and were we not disposed to retain its name as given by Mr. SAY, we should select that of Prairie Fox as being most appropriate for it. Mr. HARRIS, mounted on an Indian horse, had no difficulty in keeping up with it and overrunning it, which caused it to double as just mentioned. Had our guns been loaded with buck shot we should not doubt have killed it. It is necessary to say, perhaps, that all the authors who have written about this fox (most of whom appear to have copied Mr. SAY's account of it) assert that its extraordinary swiftness is one of the most remarkable characteristics of the animal. GODMAN observes that the fleetest antelope or deer, when running at full speed, is passed by this little Fox with the greatest ease, and such is the celerity of its motion, that it is compared by the celebrated travellers above quoted, LEWIS and CLARK and Mr. SAY, "to

the flight of a bird along the ground rather than the course of a quadruped."

There is nothing in the conformation of this species, anatomically viewed, indicating extraordinary speed. On the contrary, when we compare it with the red fox or even the gray, we find its body and legs shorter in proportion than in those species, and its large head and bushy tail give it rather a more heavy appearance than either of the foxes just named.

Dr. RICHARDSON informs us that the Saskachewan river is the most northern limit of the range of the Kit Fox. Its burrows he says are very deep and excavated in the open plains, at some distance from the woody country. LEWIS and CLARK describe it as being extremely vigilant, and say that it betakes itself on the slightest alarm to its burrow.

On our return to Fort Union after an excursion through a part of the adjacent country, we found at some distance from the stockade a young Swift Fox which we probably might easily have captured alive; but fearing that its burrow was near at hand, and that it would soon reach it an evade our pursuit, Mr. HARRIS shot it. This was the last specimen of this Fox that we were able to observe during our journey; we have given its measurement in a former part of this article. On our return voyage, we found on arriving at Fort Clark that the living Swift Fox given us by Mr. CHARDON was in excellent condition. It was placed in a strong wooden box lined in part with tin, and for greater security against its escape, had a chain fastened to a collar around its neck. During our homeward journey it was fed on birds, squirrels, and the flesh of other animals, and finally safely reached our residence, near New-York, where it was placed in a large cage box two-thirds sunk beneath the surface of the ground, completely tinned inside, and half filled with earth. When thus allowed a comparatively large space and plenty of earth to burrow in, the Fox immediately began to make his way into the loose ground, and soon had dug a hole large enough to conceal himself entirely. While in this commodious prison he fed regularly and ate any kind of fresh meat, growing fatter every day. He drank more water than foxes generally do, seemed anxious to play or wash in the cup which held his supply, and would frequently turn it over, spilling the water on the floor of the cage.

The cross fox which we described in our first volume does not appear to require water, during the winter months at least, when fed on fresh meat; as one that we have had in confinement during the past winter would not drink any, and was not supplied with it for two or three months. Probably in a wild state all predatory animals drink more than when in confinement, for they are compelled to take so smuch exercise in the pursuit of their prey, that the evaporation of fluids, by perspiration, must go on rapidly; besides which, they would probably often try to appease the cravings of hunger by drinking freely, when unable to procure sufficient food.

Geographical Distribution.

The Swift Fox appears to be found on the plains of the Columbia river valley, as well as the open country of the region in which it has generally been observed, the extensive prairies of the eastern side of the Rocky Mountains.

It does not appear to be an inhabitant of New Mexico, Texas or California, as far as our information on the subject extends.

General Remarks.

Our esteemed friend, Sir JOHN RICHARDSON, (Fauna Boreali Americana, p. 98,) has supposed that SCHREBER's description of *Canis cinereo argentatus*, applied to this species, and hence adopted his specific name, to the exclusion of SAY's name of *C. Velox*. In our first volume, (p. 172,) we explained our views on this subject. In the descriptions of *C. Virginianus* of SCHREBER, and *C. Argenteus*, ERX., they evidently described mere varieties of the gray fox, (*V. Virginianus*); we have consequently restored SAY's specific name, and awarded to him the credit of having been the first scientific describer of this animal.

Plate LII

Drawn from Nature by J.J. Audubon, F.R.S. F.L.S.

Drawn on Stone by Wm E. Hitchcock

Lith. Printed & Cold by J.T. Bowen, Philada

Swift Fox

Mephitis Mesoleuca.—Licht.

Texan Skunk.

Plate liii. Male.—Natural Size.

M. Vitta solitaria media antice (in vertice) rotundata, acqua lata ad basin caudae usque continuata, hac tota alba.

Characters.

The whole back, from the forehead to the tail, and the tail, white; nose not covered with hair.

Synonymes.

MEPHITIS MESOLEUCA, Lichtenstein. Darstellung neuer oder wenig bekannter Säugethiere. Berlin, 1827, 1834. Tab. 44, Fig. 2.
MEPHITIS NASUTA, Bennett. Proceedings of the Zoological Society, 1833, p. 39.
M. MESOLEUCA, Licht. Ueber die Gattung Mephitis. Berlin, 1838, p. 23.

Description.

In form, this species bears a considerable resemblance to the common American skunk, (*Mephitis chinga*.) Like all the other species of skunk, this animal has a broad and fleshy body; it is wider at the hips than at the shoulders, and when walking, the head is carried near the ground, whilst the back is obliquely raised six or seven inches higher; it stands low on its legs, and progresses rather slowly. Forehead, slightly rounded; eyes, small; ears, short and rounded; hair, coarse and long; under fur, sparse, woolly, and not very fine; tail, of moderate length and bushy; nose, for three-fourths of an inch above the snout, naked. This is a characteristic mark, by which it may always be distinguished from the common American skunk, the latter being covered with short hair to the snout. Palms naked.

Colour.

The whole of the long hair, including the under fur on the back, and the tail on both surfaces, is white. This broad stripe commences on the forehead about two inches from the point of the nose, running near the ears, and in a straight line along the sides and over the haunches, taking in the whole of the tail. The nails are white; the whole of the under surface of the body black, with here and there a white hair interspersed. On the forefeet around the palms and on the edges of the under surface, there are coarse whitish hairs.

The peculiarities in the colour of this species appear to be very uniform, as the specimens we examined in the Berlin Museum and in the collection of the Zoological Society in London, corresponded precisely with the specimen from which this description has been made.

Dimensions.

	Feet.	Inches.
From point of nose to root of tail, ...	1	$4\frac{1}{2}$
Tail (vertebræ), ...	0	7
Do. to end of hair, ...	0	11
Breadth of head between the ears, ...	0	3
Height of ear, ...	0	$0\frac{3}{10}$
Length of heel to longest claw, ...	0	$2\frac{1}{2}$
Breadth of white stripe on the middle of the back, ...	0	5

Weight, 5 lbs.

Habits.

This odoriferous animal is found in Texas and Mexico, and is very similar in its habits to the common skunk of the Eastern, Middle and South-western States. A specimen procured by J. W. AUDUBON, who travelled through a portion of the State of Texas in 1845 and 6, for the purpose of obtaining a knowledge of the quadrupeds of that country, was caught alive in the neighbourhood of the San Jacinto; it was secured to the pack saddle of one of his baggage mules, but managed in some way to escape during the day's march, and as the scent was still strong on the saddle, it was not missed until the party arrived at the rancho of Mr. McFADDEN, who kept a house of entertainment for man and beast, which by this time was greatly needed by the travellers.

The almost endless varieties of the *Mephitis chinga*, the common skunk, many of which have been described as distinct species by naturalists, have, from our knowledge of their curious yet not specific differences, led us to admit any new species with doubt; but from the peculiar characteristics of this animal, there can be no hesitation in awarding to Prof. LICHTENSTEIN the honour of having given to the world the first knowledge of this interesting quadruped.

The *Mephitis Mesoleuca* is found on the brown, broomy, sedgy plains, as well as in the woods, and the cultivated districts of Texas and Mexico. Its food consists in part of grubs, beetles, and other insects, and occasionally a small quadruped or bird, the eggs of birds, and in fact everything which this carnivorous but timid animal can appropriate to its sustenance.

The retreats of this Skunk are hollows in the roots of trees or fallen trunks, cavities under rocks, &c.; and it is, like the northern species, easily caught when seen, (if any one has the resolution to venture on the experiment,) as it will not endeavour to escape unless it be very near its hiding place, in which case it will avoid its pursuer by retreating into its burrow, and there remaining for some time motionless, if not annoyed by a dog, or by digging after it.

The stomach of the specimen from which our drawing was made, contained a number of worms, in some degree resembling the tape worm at times found in the human subject. Notwithstanding this circumstance, the individual appeared to be healthy and was fat. The rainy season having set in (or at least the weather being invariably stormy for some time) after it was killed, it became necessary to dry its skin in a chimney. When first taken, the white streak along the back was as pure and free from any stain or tinge of darkness or soiled colour as new fallen snow. The two glands containing the fetid matter, discharged from time to time by the animal for its defence, somewhat resembled in appearance a soft egg.

This species apparently takes the place of the common American skunk, (*Mephitis chinga*,) in the vicinity of the ranchos and planatations of the Mexicans, and is quite as destructive to poultry, eggs, &c., as its northern relative. We have not ascertained anything about its season of breeding, or the time the female goes with young; we have no doubt, however, that in these characteristics it resembles the other and closely allied species.

The long and beautiful tail of this Skunk makes it conspicuous among the thickets or in the musquit bushes of Texas, and it most frequently keeps this part elevated so that in high grass or weeds it is first seen by the hunters who may be looking for the animal in such places.

Geographical Distribution.

The Mephitis Mesoleuca is not met with in any portion of the United States eastward and northward of Texas. It is found in the latter State and in most parts of Mexico. We have, however, not seen any skunk from South America which corresponds with it.

General Remarks.

Naturalists have been somewhat at a loss to decide on the name by which this species should be designated, and to what author the credit is due of having been the first describer.

The specimens obtained by LICHTENSTEIN were procured by Mr. DEPPE, in the vicinity of Chico, in Mexico, in 1825, and deposited in the museum of Berlin. In occasional papers published by Dr. LICHTENSTEIN, from 1827 to 1834, this species with many others was first published. In 1833, BENNETT published in the proceedings of the Zoological Society, the same species under the name of *M. Nasuta*. The papers of LICHTENSTEIN, although printed and circulated at Berlin, were not reprinted and collected into a volume till 1834. Having seen the original papers as well as the specimens at Berlin, and being satisfied of their earlier publication, we have no hesitation in adopting the name of LICHTENSTEIN as the first describer and publisher.

Plate LIII.

Lith. Printed & Col.ᵈ by J.T.Bowen Phil.ᵃ

Texan Skunk.

Drawn from Nature by J J Audubon, F.R. S.F L.S.

Mus Decumanus.—Pall.

Brown Or Norway Rat.

Plate liv. Males, Female, And Young. Natural size.

Mus, cauda longissima squamata, corpore setoso griseo, subtus albido.

Characters.

Grayish-brown above, dull white beneath, tail nearly as long as the body, feet not webbed; of a dingy white colour.

Synonymes.

MUS DECUMANUS, Pallas, Glir., p. 91—40.
"　　　"　　　Schreber, Saugthiere, p. 645.
"　　　"　　　Linn., Syst. Nat. ed. Gmel., t. p. 127.
MUS AQUATICUS, Gesner's Quadr., p. 732.
MUS DECUMANUS, Shaw's Genl. Zool., ii., p. 50 t. 130.
SURMULAT, Buff., Hist. Nat. viii., p. 206 t. 27.
MUS DECUMANUS, Cuv., Regne Animal, 1, p. 197.
"　　　"　　　Godman, vol. ii., p. 78.
"　　　"　　　Dekay, p. 79.
MUS AMERICANUS, Dekay, American Black Rat, p. 81.

Description.

Body, robust; head, long; muzzle, long, but less acute than that of the black rat; eyes, large and prominent; moustaches, long, reaching to the ears; ears, rounded and nearly naked; tail, generally a little shorter than the body, (although occasionally a specimen may be found where it is of equal length,) slightly covered with short rigid hairs. There are four toes on each of the fore-feet, with a scarcely visible rudimental thumb, protected by a small blunt nail; five toes on each of the hind feet; the feet are clothed with short adpressed hairs. The fur seldom lies smooth, and the animal has a rough and not an inviting appearance.

Colour.

Outer surface of the incisors, reddish-brown; moustaches, white and black; the former colour preponderating; the few short scattered hairs along the outer edges of the ear, yellowish brown; eyes, black; hair on the back, from the roots, bluish-gray, then reddish-brown, broadly tipped with dark brown and black. On the under surface, the softer and shorter hair is from the roots ashy-gray broadly tipped with white.

Varieties.

1st. We have on several occasions, through the kindness of friends, received specimens of white rats which were supposed to be new species. They proved to be albinos of the present species. Their colour was white throughout, presenting the usual characteristics of the albino, with red eyes. One of this variety was preserved for many months in a cage with the brown rat, producing young, that in this instance all proved to be brown.

2d. We have at different times been able to procure specimens of a singular variety of this species that seems to have originated in this country. For the first specimen we were indebted to our friend Dr. SAMUEL WILSON of Charleston. Two others were sent to us from the interior of South Carolina. One was presented to us by a cat, and another was caught in a trap. In form, in size, and in dentition, they are precisely like the brown rat. The colour, however, is on both surfaces quite black. In some specimens there is under the chest and on the abdomen, a longitudinal white stripe similar to those of the mink. The specimens, after being preserved for a year or two, lose their intense black colour, which gradually assumes a more brownish hue. We examined a nest of the common brown rat containing 8 young, 5 of which were of the usual colour, and 3 black. The specimen obtained by Mr. BELL of New-York and published by Dr. DEKAY, New-York Fauna, p. 81, under the name of *Mus Americanus*, undoubtedly belonged to this variety, which appears to have of late years become more common in the Southern than in the Northern States. This is evidently not a hybrid produced between *Mus Decumanus* and *Mus Rattus*, as those we have seen present the shape and size of the former, only differing in colour.

Dimensions.

	Inches.
From point of nose to root of tail, ...	10
Tail, ...	9
From point of nose to ear, ...	$2\frac{1}{2}$
Height of ear, ...	$\frac{3}{8}$

Habits.

The brown rat is unfortunately but too well known almost in every portion of our country, and in fact throughout the world, to require an elaborate account of its habits, but we will give such particulars as may we hope be interesting. It is one of the most prolific and destructive little quadrupeds about the residences of man, and is as fierce as voracious. Some cases are on record where this rat has attacked a man when he was asleep, and we have seen both adults and children who, by their wanting a piece of the ear, or a bit of the end of the nose, bore painful testimony to its having attacked them while they were in bed; it has been known to nibble at an exposed toe or finger, and sometimes to have bitten even the remains of the shrouded dead who may have been exposed to its attacks.

The Norway Rat is very pugnacious, and several individuals may often be seen fighting together, squealing, biting, and inflicting severe wounds on each other. On one occasion, we saw two of these rats in furious combat, and so enraged were they, that one of them whose tail was turned towards us, allowed us to seize him, which we did, giving him at the same time such a swing against a gate post which was near, that the blow killed him instantly—his antagonist making his escape.

During the great floods or freshets which almost annually submerge the flat bottom-lands on the Ohio river at various places, the rats are driven out from their holes and seek shelter under the barns, stables, and houses in the vicinity, and as the increasing waters cover the low grounds, may be seen taking to pieces of drift wood and floating logs, &c., on which they sometimes remain driving along with the currents for some distance. They also at such times climb up into the lofts of barns, smokehouses, &c., or betake themselves to the trees in the orchards or gardens. We once, at Shippingport, near the foot of the falls of the Ohio river, whilst residing with our brother-in-law, the late N. BERTHOUD, went out in a skiff, during a freshet which had exceeded those of many previous years in its altitude, and after rowing about over the tops of fences that were secured from rising with the waters by being anchored by large cross-timbers placed when they were put up, under the ground, to which the posts were dove-tailed, and occasionally rowing through floating worm-fences which had broken away from their proper locations and were lying flat upon the surface of the flowing tide, we came to the orchard attached to the garden, and found the peach and apple trees full of rats, which seemed almost as active in running among the branches as squirrels. We had our gun with us and tried to shoot some of them, but the cunning rogues dived into the water whenever we approached, and swam off in various direction, some to one tree and some to another, so that we were puzzled which to follow. The rats swam and dived with equal facility and made rapid progress through the water. Many of them remained in the orchard until the freshet subsided, which was in the course of a few days. Whether they caught any fish or not during this time we cannot say, but most of them found food enough to keep them alive until they were able once more to occupy their customary holes and burrows. During these occasional floods on our western rivers, immense numbers of spiders and other insects take refuge in the upper stories of the houses, and the inhabitants find themselves much incommoded by them as well as by the turbulent waters around their dwellings. Such times are, however, quite holidays to the young folks, and skiffs and batteaux of every description are in requisition, while some go about on a couple of boards, or paddle from street to street on large square pine logs. When the flats are thus covered, there is generally but little current running on them, although the main channel of the river flows majestically onward, covered with floating logs and the fragments of sheds, haystacks, &c., which have left their quiet homes on the sides of the river many miles above, to float on a voyage of discovery down to the great Mississippi, unless stopped by the way by the exertions of some fortunate discoverer of their value, who rowing out among the drifting logs, roots and branches, ties a rope to the frail floating tenement, and tows it to the trunk of a tree, where he makes it fast, for the water to leave it ready for his service, when the river has again returned to its quiet and customary channel. Stray flat boats loaded with produce, flour, corn and tobacco, &c., are often thus taken up, and are generally found and claimed afterwards by their owners. The sight of the beautiful Ohio thus swelling

Plate LV

Nº 11.

On Stone by Wᵐ E. Hitchcock.

Drawn from Nature by J.J. Audubon, F.R.S. F.L.S.

Lith Printed & Col⁴ by J.T. Bowen, Phil.

Brown or Norway Rat

proudly along, and sometimes embracing the country with its watery margin extended for miles beyond its ordinary limits, is well worth a trip to the West in February or March. But these high freshets do not occur every year, and depend on the melting of the snows, which are generally dissolved so gradually that the channel of the river is sufficient to carry them off.

In a former work, (Ornithological Biography, vol. 1, p. 155,) we have given a more detailed account of one of the booming floods of the Ohio and Mississippi rivers, to which we beg now to refer such of our readers as have never witnessed one of those remarkable periodical inundations.

Mr. OGDEN HAMMOND, formerly of Throg's Neck, near New-York, furnished us with the following account of the mode in which the Norway Rat captures and feeds upon the small sand clams which abound on the sandy places along the East river below high water mark. He repaired to a wharf on his farm with one of his men at low water: in a few moments a rat was seen issuing from the lower part of the wharf, peeping cautiously around before he ventured from his hiding place. Presently one of the small clams buried in the soft mud and sand which they inhabit, threw up a thin jet of water about a foot above the surface of the ground, upon seeing which, the rat leaped quickly to the spot, and digging with its forepaws, in a few moments was seen bringing the clam towards his retreat, where he immediately devoured it.

When any of these clams lie too deep to be dug up by the rats, they continue on the watch and dig after the next which may make known its whereabouts by the customary jet of water. These clams are about $\frac{3}{4}$ of an inch long and not more than $\frac{5}{8}$ of an inch wide; their shells are slight, and they are sometimes used as bait by fishermen.

The Brown or Norway Rat was first introduced in the neighbourhood of Henderson, Kentucky, our old and happy residence for several years, within our recollection.

One day a barge arrived from New-Orleans (we think in 1811) loaded with sugar and other goods; some of the cargo belonged to us. During the landing of the packages we saw several of these rats make their escape from the vessel to the shore, and run off in different directions. In a year from this time they had become quite a nuisance; whether they had been reinforced by other importations, or had multiplied to an incredible extent, we know not. Shortly after this period we had our smokehouse floor taken up on account of their having burrowed under it in nearly every direction. We killed at that time a great many of them with the aid of our dogs, but they continued to annoy us, and the readers of our Ornithological Biography are aware, that ere we left Henderson some rats destroyed many of our valued drawings.

This species migrates either in troops or singly, and for this purpose takes passage in any conveyance that may offer, or it plods along on foot. It swims and dives well, as we have already remarked, so that rivers or water-courses do not obstruct its progress. We once knew a female to secrete herself in a wagon, loaded with bale rope, sent from Lexington, (Ky.) to Louisville, and on the wagon reaching its destination, when the coils of rope were turned out, it was discovered that the animal had a litter of several young ones: she darted into the warehouse through the iron bars which were placed like a grating in front of the cellar windows. Some of the young escaped also, but several of them were killed by the wagoner. How this rat was fed during the journey we do not know, but as the wagons stop every evening at some tavern, the probability is that she procured food for herself by getting out during the night and picking up corn, &c.

The Norway Rat frequently deserts a locality in which it has for some time remained and proved a great pest. When this is the case, the whole tribe journey to other quarters, keeping together and generally appearing in numbers in their new locality without any previous warning to the unlucky farmer or housekeeper to whose premises they have taken a fancy.

When we first moved to our retreat, nine miles above the city of New-York, we had no rats to annoy us, and we hoped it would be some time before they discovered the spot where we had located ourselves. But in the course of a few months a great many of them appeared, and we have occasionally had eggs, chickens and ducklings carried off by them to the number of six or more in a night. We have never been able to get rid of this colony of rats, and they have even made large burrows in the banks on the water side, where they can hardly be extirpated.

The Norway Rat is quite abundant in New-York and most other maritime cities, along the wharves and docks, and becomes very large. These animals are frequently destroyed in great numbers, while a ship is in port, after her cargo has been discharged, by smoking them; the fumes of sulphur and other suffocating materials, being confined to the hold by closing all parts, windows and hatches. After a thorough cleaning out, a large ship has been known to

have had many thousands on board. Our old friend, Capt. CUMINGS, who in early life made many voyages to the East Indies, relates to us, that one of his captains used to have rats caught, when on long voyages, and had them cooked and served up at his table as a luxury. He allowed his sailors a glass of grog for every rat they caught, and as the supply was generally ample, he used to invite his mates and passengers to partake of them with due hospitality. Our friend, who was a mate, had a great horror of the captain's invitations, for it was sometimes difficult to ascertain in what form the delicate animals would appear, and to avoid eating them. Not having ourselves eaten rats, (as far as we know,) we cannot say whether the old India captain's fondness for them was justified by their possessing a fine flavour, but we do think prejudices are entertained against many animals and reptiles that are, after all, pretty good eating.

In the account of the black rat in our first volume, (Mus rattus,) pp. 190, 191, and 192, we gave some details of the habits of the present species, and stated our opinion in regard to its destroying the black rat. Dr. GODMAN considered the Norway Rat so thorough an enemy of the black rat, that he says, (vol. 2, p. 83,) in speaking of the latter, that it is now found only in situations to which the Brown Rat has not extended its migrations. According to the same author, who quotes R. SMITH, Rat Catcher, p. 5, 1768, (see GODMAN, vol. 2, p. 77,) the Brown Rat was not known even in Europe prior to the year 1750. RICHARDSON says, (probably quoting from HARLAN, Fauna, p. 149,) that it was brought from Asia to Europe, according to the accounts of historians of the seventeenth century, and was unknown in England before 1730. PENNANT, writing in 1785, says he has no authority for considering it an inhabitant of the new continent (America). HARLAN states that the Norwegian rat did not, as he was credibly informed, make its appearance in the United States any length of time previous to the year 1775. HARLAN does not give the Brown Rat as an American species, giving only what he considered indigenous species.

The Brown Rat brings forth from 10 to 15 young at a litter, and breeds several times in a year. Fortunately for mankind, it has many enemies: weasels, skunks, owls, hawks, &c., as well as cats and dogs. We have never known the latter to eat them, but they may at times do so. Rats are also killed by each other, and the weak ones devoured by the stronger.

This species becomes very fat and clumsy when living a long time in mills or warehouses. We have often seen old ones so fat and inactive that they would fall back when attempting to ascend a staircase.

We will take our leave of this disagreeable pest, by saying, that it is omnivorous, devouring with equal voracity meat of all kinds, eggs, poultry, fish, reptiles, vegetables, &c. &c. It prefers eels to other kinds of fish, having been known to select an eel out of a large bucket of fresh fish, and drag it off to its hole. In vegetable gardens it devours melons, cucumbers, &c., and will eat into a melon, entering through a hole large enough to admit its body, consuming the tender sweet fruit, seeds and all, and leaving the rind almost perfect. Where rats have gained access to a field or vegetable garden, they generally dig holes near the fruits or vegetables, into which they can make an easy retreat at the approach of an enemy.

We have represented several of these rats in our plate about to devour muskmelons, for which they have a strong predilection.

Geographical Distribution.

The *Mus Decumanus* is found in all the temperate parts of the world where man has been able to carry it in ships. It has not as yet penetrated into the fur countries, to the Rocky Mountains and California. The *Neotoma Drummondi* would probably be able to destroy it, being quite as fierce and much larger, should its wanderings lead it into the territory occupied by the latter. The Brown or Norway Rat is met with almost every where from Nova Scotia to and beyond our southern range, except in the western and northern regions above mentioned, and there even it will soon be found in California, at the mouth of the Columbia river, and among the settlements in Oregon.

General Remarks.

We had assigned to LINNÆUS the credit of having been the first describer of the Brown Rat. On turning however to his 12th edition, we find no notice of this species. In a subsequent edition published by GMELIN in 1778, a description is added. It had however been previously described by PALLAS in 1767 under the name which it still retains. He is therefore entitled to the priority.

Sciurus Rubicaudatus.—Aud. and Bach.

Red-Tailed Squirrel.

Plate lv. Natural Size.

S. supra sub rufus cano mistus, subtus sordide flavus, magnitudine inter s. cinereum et s. migratorium; cauda auriculisque rufis.

Characters.

Intermediate in size between the cat squirrel (S. Cinereus) and the Northern gray squirrel (S. Migratorius); ears and tail, red; body, light-brown mixed with gray above, soiled buff beneath.

Description.

In form this species resembles the northern gray squirrel, possessing evidently all its activity; its proportions are more delicate, and it weighs less, than the cat squirrel. It is considerably smaller than the great-tailed squirrel of SAY, (S. Sayi). Although a little larger than the northern gray squirrel, its tail is shorter, and its fur a little coarser. The only specimen in which we were enabled to examine the dentition, had but twenty teeth; the small front molars which appear to be permanent in the northern gray squirrel, and deciduous in several other species, were here entirely wanting.

Colour.

The fur on the back is in half its length from the roots, plumbeous, succeeded by a narrow marking of light brown, then black, tipped with whitish, a few interspersed hairs are black at the apical portion; on the under surface the hairs are yellowish-white at the roots, and reddish-buff at the tips. The long hairs on the under surface of the tail are red through their whole extent. On the upper surface of the tail the hairs are reddish with three black annulations, tipped with red. Moustaches, black; ears, around the eye, sides of face, throat and neck, inner surface of legs, upper surface of feet and belly, dull buff; tail, rufous.

Dimensions.

	Inches.
Length, from point of nose to root of tail, ...	13
Do. vertebræ, ...	10
Do. to end of hair, ...	$12\frac{1}{2}$
Height of ear, ...	$\frac{1}{2}$
Heel to end of longest nail, ...	$2\frac{7}{8}$

Habits.

We have obtained no information in regard to the habits of this species, but have no doubt it possesses all the sprightliness and activity of other squirrels, particularly the Northern gray and cat squirrels, as well as the great tailed squirrel, to which in form and size it is allied.

Geographical Distribution.

The specimen from which our drawing was made, was procured in the State of Illinois. This squirrel is also found in the barrens of Kentucky: we possess a skin sent to us by our good friend Dr. CROGHAN, procured we believe near the celebrated Mammoth cave, of which he is proprietor.

Mr. CAROT, of Boston, likewise has one, as well as we can recollect, in his collection. We sought in vain, while on our journey in the wilds of the Upper Missouri country, for this species, which apparently does not extend its range west of the well-wooded districts lying to the east of the great prairies. It will probably be found abundant in Indiana, although it has been hitherto most frequently observed in Illinois. Of its northern and southern limits, we know nothing, and it may have a much more extended distribution than is at present supposed.

Genus Bison.—Pliny.

Dental Formula.

Incisive $\frac{0}{8}$; *Canine* $\frac{0-0}{0-0}$; *Molar* $\frac{6-6}{6-6}$ = 32.

Head, large and broad; forehead, slightly arched; horns, placed before the salient line of the frontal crest; tail, short; shoulders, elevated; hair, soft and woolly.

The generic name is derived from PLINY, who applied the word Bison, wild ox, to one of the species on the Eastern continent.

There are five species of Buffalo that may be conveniently arranged under this genus: one existing in the forests of Southern Russia in Asia, in the Circassian mountains, and the desert of Kobi; one in Ethiopia and the forests of India, one on the mountains of Central Asia, one in Ceylon, and one in America. In addition to this, the genus Bos, which formerly included the present, contains five well determined species, one inhabiting the country near the Cape of Good Hope, one in Central Africa, one in the Himalaya mountains and the Birman Empire, one in India, and one in the forests of Middle Europe.

Bison Americanus.—Gmel.

American Bison.—Buffalo.

Plate lvi. Male.

Plate lvii. Female, Male and Young.

B. capite magno, lato, fronte leviter arcuata; cornibus parvis, brevibus, teretibus, extrorsum dein sursum versis; cauda breve, cruribus gracilibus armis excelsis, villo molli, lanoso.

Characters.

Forehead, broad, slightly arched; horns, small, short, directed laterally and upwards; tail; short; legs, slender; shoulders, elevated · hair, soft and woolly.

Synonymes.

TAURUS MEXICANUS, Hernandez, Mex., p. 587, Fig. male, 1651.
TAUREAU SAUVAGE, Hennepin, Nouv. Discov., vol. i., p. 186, 1699.
THE BUFFALO, Lawson's Carolina, p. 115, Fig.
  "   "   Catesby's Carolina, p. 115, fig.
  "   "   Hearne's Journey, p. 412.
  "   "   Franklin's First Voy., p. 113.
  "   "   Pennant's Arctic Zool., vol. i., p. 1.
  "   "   Long's Expedition, vol. iii., p. 68.
  "   "   Warden's U. S., vol. i., p. 248.
BOS AMERICANUS, Linn., S. N., ed Gmel. I, p. 204.
  "   "   Cuv., Regne an 1, p. 270.
BOS AMERICANUS, Harlan, 268.
  "   "   Godman, vol. iii., 4.
  "   "   Richardson, Fa., p. 79.
BUFFALO, Hudson's Bay Traders, Le Boeuf, Canadian Voyagers.
AMERICAN Ox, Dobs, Hudson's Bay, 41.

Description.

Male, killed on the Yellow Stone river, July 16th, 1843.

The form bears a considerable resemblance to that of an overgrown domestic bull, the top of the hump on the shoulders being considerably higher than the rump, although the fore-legs are very short; horns, short, stout, curved upward and inward, one foot one inch and a half around the curve; ears, short and slightly triangular towards the point; nose, bare; nostrils, covered internally with hairs; eyes, rather small in proportion to the size of the animal, sunk into the prominent projection of the skull; neck, and forehead to near the nose, covered with a dense mass of shaggy hair fourteen inches long between the horns, which, as well as the eyes and ears, are thereby partially concealed; these hairs become gradually shorter and more woolly towards the muzzle. Under the chin and lower jaw there is an immense beard, a foot or upwards in length.

Neck, short; hairs along the shoulder and fore-legs about four inches long. The beard around the muzzle resembles that of the common bull. A mass of hair rises on the hind part of the fore-leg, considerably below the knee. A ridge of hairs commences on the back and runs to a point near the insertion of the tail. On the flanks, rump and fore-legs the hairs are very short and fine.

On the hind-legs there are straggling long hairs extending to the knee, and a few tufts extending six inches below the knee; hind-legs, and tail, covered with short hairs; within a few inches of the tip of the tail there is a tuft of hair nearly a foot in length. The pelage on the head has scarcely any of the soft woolly hair which covers other parts of the body, and approaches nearer to hair than to wool.

A winter killed specimen.

From the neck, around the shoulder and sides, the body is covered with a dense heavy coat of woolly hair, with much longer and coarser hairs inter-mixed. There is a fleshy membrane between the forelegs, like that in the common domestic bull, but not so pendulous.

Female.

In form and colour the female bears a strong resemblance to the male; she is, however, considerably smaller, and of a more delicate structure. Her horns are of the same length and shape as those of the male, but are thinner and more perfect, in consequence of the cows engaging less in combat than the bulls. The hump is less elevated; the hair on the forehead shorter and less bushy; the rings on the horns are more corrugated than on those of our domestic cattle.

Spinous processes rising from the back bone or vertebræ of the bull, and forming the hump: they are flat, with sharp edges both anteriorly and posteriorly; the two longest are eighteen and a quarter inches long, three inches at the end which is the widest, and two inches at the narrowest; the first, fifteen inches; second, (largest,) eighteen and a quarter inches in length; third, sixteen and a half; fourth, sixteen; the fifth, fifteen inches, and the rest gradually diminishing in size; the fifteenth spinous process being three and a half inches long; the remainder are wanting in our specimen. The whole of the processes are placed almost touching each other at the insertion and at the end, and their breadth is parallel to the course of the back-bone. In the centre or about half the distance from the insertion to the outer end of them, they are (the bone being narrower in that part) from a quarter to one inch apart. The ribs originate and incline outward backward and downward from between these upright spinous bones.

Colour.

A summer specimen.

Head, neck, throat, fore-legs, tail and beard, dark brownish-black; hoofs, brown; rump, flanks, line on the back, blackish brown; horns nearly black. Upper surface of body light-brown; the hairs uniform in colour from the roots, the whole under surface blackish-brown.

The colour of the female is similar to that of the male.

At the close of the summer when the new coat of hair has been obtained, the Buffalo is in colour between a dark umber, and liver-shining brown; as the hair lengthens during winter, the tips become paler.

Young male, twelve months old.

A uniform dingy brown colour, with a dark brown stripe of twisted woolly upright hairs, extending from the head over the neck shoulders and back to the insertion of the tail. The hairs on the forehead, which form the enormous mass on the head of the adult, are just beginning to be developed.

Under the throat and along the chest the hairs extend in a narrow line of about three inches in length; the bush at the end of the tail is tolerably well developed. Hairs on the whole body short and woolly.

A calf, six weeks old, presents the same general appearance, but is more woolly. The legs, especially near the hoofs, are of a lighter colour than the adult.

A calf taken from the body of a cow, in September, was covered with woolly hair; the uniform brownish, or dim yellow, strongly resembling the young of a domesticated cow.

Habits.

Whether we consider this noble animal as an object of the chase, or as an article of food for man, it is decidedly the most important of all our contemporary American quadrupeds; and as we can no longer see the gigantic mastodon passing over the broad savannas, or laving his enormous sides in the deep rivers of our wide-spread land, we will consider the Buffalo as a link, (perhaps sooner to be forever lost than is generally supposed,) which to a slight degree yet connects us with larger American animals, belonging to extinct creations.

But ere we endeavour to place before you the living and breathing herds of Buffaloes, you must journey with us in imagination to the vast western prairies, the secluded and almost inaccessible valleys of the Rocky Mountain chain, and the arid and nearly impassable deserts of the western table lands of our country; and here we may be allowed to express our deep, though unavailing regret, that the world now contains only few and imperfect remains of the lost races, of which we have our sole knowledge through the researches and profound deductions of geologists; and even though our knowledge of the osteology of the more recently exterminated species be sufficient to place them before our "mind's eye," we have no description and no figures of the once living and moving, but now departed possessors of these woods, plains, mountains and waters, in which, ages ago, they are supposed to have dwelt. Let us however hope, that our humble efforts may at least enable us to perpetuate a knowledge of such species as the Giver of all good has allowed to remain with us to the present day. And now we will endeavour to give a good account of the majestic Bison.

In the days of our boyhood and youth, Buffaloes roamed over the small and beautiful prairies of Indiana and Illinois, and herds of them stalked through the open woods of Kentucky and Tennessee; but they had dwindled down to a few stragglers, which resorted chiefly to the "Barrens," towards the years 1808 and 1809, and soon after entirely disappeared. Their range has since that period gradually tended westward, and now you must direct your steps "to the Indian country," and travel many hundred miles beyond the fair valleys of the Ohio, towards the great rocky chain of mountains which forms the backbone of North-America, before you can reach the Buffalo, and see him roving in his sturdy independence upon the vast elevated plains, which extend to the base of the Rocky Mountains.

His with us then to the West! let us quit the busy streets fo St. Louis, once considered the outpost of civilization, but now a flourishing city, in the midst of a fertile and rapidly growing country, with towns and villages scattered for hundreds of miles beyond it; let us leave the busy haunts of men, and on good horses take the course that will lead us into the Buffalo region, and when we have arrived at the sterile and extended plains which we desire to reach, we shall be recompensed for our toilsome and tedious journey: for there we may find thousands of these noble animals, and be enabled to study their habits, as they graze and ramble over the prairies, or migrate from one range of country to another, crossing on their route water-courses, or swimming rivers at places where they often plunge from the muddy bank into the stream, to gain a sand-bar or shoal, midway in the river, that affords them a resting place, from which, after a little time, they can direct their course to the opposite shore, when, having reached it, they must scramble up the bank, ere they can gain the open prairie beyond.

There we may also witness severe combats between the valiant bulls, in the rutting season, hear their angry bellowing, and observe their sagacity, as well as courage, when disturbed by the approach of man.

The American Bison is much addicted to wandering, and the various herds annually remove from the North, at the approach of winter, although many may be found, during that season, remaining in high latitudes, their thick woolly coats enabling them to resist a low temperature, without suffering greatly. During a severe winter, however, numbers of them perish, especially the old, and the very young ones. The breeding season is generally the months of June and July, and the calves are brought forth in April and May; although occasionally they are produced as early as March or as late as July. The Buffalo most frequently has but one calf at a time, but instances occur of their having two. The females usually retire from the herd either singly or several in company, select as solitary a spot as can be found, remote from the haunt of wolves, bears, or other enemies that would be most likely to molest them, and there produce their young.

Occasionally, however, they bring forth their offspring when the herd is migrating, and at such times they are left by the main body, which they rejoin as soon as possible. The young usually follow the mother until she is nearly ready to have a calf again. The Buffalo seldom produces young until the third year, but will continue breeding until very old. When a cow and her very young calf are attacked by wolves, the cow bellows and sometimes runs at the enemy, and not unfrequently frightens him away; this, however, is more generally the case when several cows are together, as the wolf, ever on the watch, is sometimes able to secure a calf when it is only protected by its mother.

The Buffalo begins to shed its hair as early as February. This falling of the winter coat shows first between the fore-legs and around the udder in the female on the inner surface of the thighs, &c. Next, the entire pelage of long hairs drop gradually but irregularly, leaving almost naked patches in some places, whilst other portions are covered with loosely hanging wool and hair.

Red-tailed Squirrel.

Drawn from Nature by J. J. Audubon, F.R.S.F.L.S.

At this period these animals have an extremely ragged and miserable appearance. The last part of the shedding process takes place on the hump. During the time of shedding, the Bison searches for trees, bushes, &c., against which to rub himself, and thereby facilitate the speedy falling off of his old hair. It is not until the end of September, or later, that he gains his new coat of hair. The skin of a Buffalo, killed in October, the hunters generally consider, makes a good Buffalo robe; and who is there, that has driven in an open sleigh or wagon, that will not be ready to admit this covering to be the cheapest and the best, as a protection from the cold, rain, sleet, and the drifting snows of winter? for it is not only a warm covering, but impervious to water.

The Bison bulls generally select a mate from among a herd of cows and do not leave their chosen one until she is about to calve.

When two or more males fancy the same female, furious battles ensue and the conqueror leads off the fair cause of the contest in triumph. Should the cow be alone, the defeated lovers follow the happy pair at such a respectful distance, as will ensure to them a chance to make their escape, if they should again become obnoxious to the victor, and at the same time enable them to take advantage of any accident that might happen in their favour. But should the fight have been caused by a female who is in a large herd of cows, the discomfited bull soon finds a substitute for his first passion. It frequently happens, that a bull leads off a cow, and remains with her separated during the season from all others, either male or female.

When the Buffalo bull is working himself up to a belligerent state, he paws the ground, bellows loudly, and goes through nearly all the actions we may see performed by the domesticated bull under similar circumstances, and finally rushes at his foe head foremost, with all his speed and strength. Notwithstanding the violent shock with which two bulls thus meet in mad career, these encounters have never been known to result fatally, probably owing to the strength of the spinous process commonly called the hump, the shortness of their horns, and the quantity of hair about all their fore-parts.

When congregated together in fair weather, calm or nearly so, the bellowing of a large herd (which sometimes contains a thousand) may be heard at the extraordinary distance of ten miles at least.

During the rutting season, or while fighting, (we are not sure which,) the bulls scrape or paw up the grass in a circle, sometimes ten feet in diameter, and these places being resorted to, from time to time, by other fighting bulls, become larger and deeper, and are easily recognised even after rains have filled them with water.

In winter, when the ice has become strong enough to bear the weight of many tons, Buffaloes are often drowned in great numbers, for they are in the habit of crossing rivers on the ice, and should any alarm occur, rush in a dense crowd to one place; the ice gives way beneath the pressure of hundreds of these huge animals, they are precipitated into the water, and if it is deep enough to reach over their backs, soon perish. Should the water, however, be shallow, they scuffle through the broken and breaking ice, in the greatest disorder, to the shore.

From time to time small herds, crossing rivers on the ice in the spring, are set adrift, in consequence of the sudden breaking of the ice after a rise in the river. They have been seen floating on such occasions in groups of three, four, and sometimes eight or ten together, although on separate cakes of ice. A few stragglers have been known to reach the shore in an almost exhausted state, but the majority perish from cold and want of food rather than trust themselves boldly to the turbulent waters.

Buffalo calves are often drowned, from being unable to ascend the steep banks of the rivers across which they have just swam, as the cows cannot help them, although they stand near the bank, and will not leave them to their fate unless something alarms them.

On one occasion Mr. KIPP, of the American Fur Company, caught eleven calves, their dams all the time standing near the top of the bank. Frequently, however, the cows leave the young to their fate, when most of them perish. In connection with this part of the subject, we may add, that we were informed when on the Upper Missouri river, that when the banks of that river were practicable for cows, and their calves could not follow them, they went down again, after having gained the top, and would remain by them until forced away by the cravings of hunger. When thus forced by the necessity of saving themselves to quit their young, they seldom, if ever, returned to them.

When a large herd of these wild animals are crossing a river, the calves or yearlings manage to get on the backs of the cows, and are thus conveyed safely over; but when the heavy animals, old and young, reach the shore, they sometimes find it muddy or even deeply miry; the strength of the old ones struggling in such cases to gain a solid footing, enables them to work their way out of danger in a wonderfully short time. Old bulls, indeed, have been known to extricate themselves when they had got into the mire so deep that but little more than their heads and backs could be seen. On one occasion we saw an unfortunate cow that had fallen into, or rather sank into a quicksand only seven or eight feet wide; she was quite dead, and we walked on her still fresh carcase safely across the ravine which had buried her in its treacherous and shifting sands.

The gaits of the Bison are walking, cantering, and galloping, and when at full speed, he can get over the ground nearly as fast as the best horses found in the Indian country. In lying down, this species bends the fore-legs first, and its movements are almost exactly the same as those of the common cow. It also rises with the same kind of action as cattle.

When surprised in a recumbent posture by the sudden approach of a hunter, who has succeeded in nearing it under the cover of a hill, clump of trees or other interposing object, the Bison springs from the ground and is in full race almost as quick as thought, and is so very alert, that one can scarcely perceive his manner of rising on such occasions.

The bulls never grow as fat as the cows, the latter having been occasionally killed with as much as two inches of fat on the boss or hump and along the back to the tail. The fat rarely exceeds half an inch on the sides or ribs, but is thicker on the belly. The males have only one inch of fat, and their flesh is never considered equal to that of the females in delicacy or flavour. In a herd of Buffaloes many are poor, and even at the best season it is not likely that all will be found in good condition; and we have occasionally known a hunting party, when Buffalo was scarce, compelled to feed on a straggling old bull as tough as leather. For ourselves, this was rather uncomfortable, as we had unfortunately lost our molars long ago.

The Bison is sometimes more abundant in particular districts one year than another, and is probably influenced in its wanderings by the mildness or severity of the weather, as well as by the choice it makes of the best pasturage and most quiet portions of the prairies. While we were at Fort Union, the hunters were during the month of June obliged to go out twenty-five or thirty miles to procure Buffalo meat, although at other times, the animal was quite abundant in sight of the fort. The tramping of a large herd, in wet weather, cuts up the soft clayey soil of the river bottoms, (we do not not mean the bottom of rivers,) into a complete mush. One day, when on our journey up the Missouri river, we landed on one of the narrow strips of land called bottoms, which formed the margin of the river and was backed by hills of considerable height at a short distance. At this spot the tracks of these animals were literally innumerable, as far as the eye could reach in every direction, the plain was covered with them; and in some places the soil had been so trampled as to resemble mud or clay, when prepared for making bricks. The trees in the vicinity were rubbed by these buffaloes, and their hair and wool were hanging on the rough bark or lying at their roots. We collected some of this wool, we think it might be usefully worked up into coarse cloth, and consider it worth attention. The roads that are made by these animals, so much resemble the tracks left by a large wagon-train, that the inexperienced traveller may occasionally imagine himself following the course of an ordinary wagon-road. These great tracks run for hundreds of miles across the prairies, and are usually found to lead to some salt-spring, or some river or creek, where the animals can allay their thirst.

The captain of the steamboat on which we ascended the Missouri, informed us, that on his last annual voyage up that river, he had caught several Buffaloes, that were swimming the river. The boat was run close upon them, they were lassoed by a Spaniard, who happened to be on board, and then hoisted on the deck, where they butchered secundum artem. One day we saw several that had taken to the water, and were coming towards our boat. We passed so near them, that we fired at them, but did not procure a single one. On another occasion, one was killed from the shore, and brought on board, when it was immediately divided among the men. We were greatly surprised to see some of the Indians, that were going up with us, ask for certain portions of the entrails, which they devoured with the greatest voracity. This gluttony excited our curiosity, and being always willing to ascertain the quality of any sort of meat, we tasted some of this sort of tripe, and found it very good, although at first its appearance was rather revolting.

The Indians sometimes eat the carcasses of Buffaloes that have been drowned, and some of those on board the Omega ond day asked the captain most earnestly to allow them to land and get at the bodies of three Buffaloes which we passed, that had lodged among the drift-logs and were probably half putrid. In this extraordinary request some of the squaws joined. That, when stimulated by the gnawings of hunger, Indians, or even Whites, should feed upon carrion, is not to be wondered at, since we have many instances of cannibalism and other horrors, when men are in a state of starvation, but these Indians were in the midst of plenty of wholesome food and we are inclined to think their hankering after this disgusting flesh must be attributed to a natural taste for it, probably acquired when young, as they are no doubt sometimes obliged in their wanderings over the prairies in winter, to devour

Plate LVI

N°. 12.

On Stone by Wm. E. Hitchcock.

American Bison or Buffalo

Drawn from Nature by J.J. Audubon. F.R.S. F.L.S

Lith. Printed & Cold by J.T. Bowen. Phil.

carrion and even bones and hides, to preserve their lives. In the height of the rutting-season, the flesh of the Buffalo bull is quite rank, and unfit to be eaten, except from necessity, and at this time the animal can be scented at a considerable distance.

When a herd of Bisons is chased, although the bulls run with great swiftness their speed cannot be compared with that of the cows and yearling calves. These, in a few moments leave the bulls behind them, but as they are greatly preferred by the hunter, he always (if well mounted) pursues them and allows the bulls to escape. During the winter of 1842 and 43, as we were told, Buffaloes were abundant around Fort Union, and during the night picked up straggling handfuls of hay that happened to be scattered about the place. An attempt was made to secure some of them alive, by strewing hay as a bait, from the interior of the old fort, which is about two hundred yards off, to some distance from the gateway, hoping the animals would feed along into the enclosure. They ate the hay to the very gate: but as the hogs and common cattle were regularly placed there, for security, during the night, the Buffaloes would not enter, probably on account of the various odours issuing from the interior. As the Buffaloes generally found some hay scattered around, they soon became accustomed to sleep in the vicinity of the fort, but went off every morning, and disappeared behind the hills, about a mile off.

One night they were fired at, from a four-pounder loaded with musket-balls. Three were killed, and several were wounded, but this disaster did not prevent them from returning frequently to the fort at night, and they were occasionally shot, during the whole winter, quite near the fort.

As various accounts of Buffalo-hunts have been already written, we will pass over our earliest adventures in that way, which occurred many years ago, and give you merely a sketch of the mode in which we killed them during our journey to the West, in 1843.

One morning in July, our party and several persons attached to Fort Union, (for we were then located there,) crossed the river, landed opposite the fort, and passing through the rich alluvial belt of woodland which margins the river, were early on our way to the adjacent prairie, beyond the hills. Our equipment consisted of an old Jersey wagon, to which we had two horses attached, tandem, driven by Mr. CULBERTSON, principal at the fort. This wagon carried Mr. HARRIS, BELL, and ourselves, and we were followed by two carts, which contained the rest of the party, while behind came the running horses or hunters, led carefully along. After crossing the lower prairie, we ascended between the steep banks of the rugged ravines, until we reached the high undulating plains above. On turning to take a retrospective view, we beheld the fort and a considerable expanse of broken and prairie-land behind us, and the course of the river was seen as it wound along, for some distance. Resuming our advance we soon saw a number of antelopes, some of which had young ones with them. After travelling about ten miles farther we approached the Fox river, and at this point one of the party espied a small herd of Bisons at a considerable distance off. Mr. CULBERTSON, after searching for them with the telescope, handed it to us and showed us where they were. They were all lying down and appeared perfectly unconscious of the existence of our party. Our vehicles and horses were now turned towards them and we travelled cautiously to within about a quarter of a mile of the herd, covered by a high ridge of land which concealed us from their view. The wind was favourable, (blowing towards us,) and now the hunters threw aside their coats, tied handkerchiefs around their heads, looked to their guns, mounted their steeds, and moved slowly and cautiously towards the game. The rest of the party crawled carefully to the top of the ridge to see the chase. At the word of command, given by Mr. CULBERTSON, the hunters dashed forward after the bulls, which already began to run off in a line nearly parallel with the ridge we were upon. The swift horses, urged on by their eager riders and their own impetuosity, soon began to overtake the affrighted animals; two of them separated from the others and were pursued by Mr. CULBERTSON and Mr. BELL; presently the former fired, and we could see that he had wounded one of the bulls. It stopped after going a little way and stood with its head hanging down and its nose near the ground. The blood appeared to be pouring from its mouth and nostrils, and its drooping tail showed the agony of the poor beast. Yet it stood firm, and its sturdy legs upheld its ponderous body as if nought had happened. We hastened toward it but ere we approached the spot, the wounded animal fell, rolled on its side, and expired. It was quite dead when we reached it. In the mean time. Mr. BELL had continued in hot haste after the other, and Mr. HARRIS and Mr. SQUIRE had each selected, and were following one of the main party. Mr. BELL shot, and his ball took effect in the buttocks of the animal. At this moment Mr. SQUIRE's horse threw him over his head fully ten feet: he fell on his powder-horn and was severely bruised; he called to some one to stop his horse and was soon on his legs, but felt sick for a few moments. Friend HARRIS, who was perfectly cool, neared his bull, shot it through the lungs, and it fell dead on the spot. Mr. BELL was still in

pursuit of his wounded animal and Mr. HARRIS and Mr. SQUIRE joined and followed the fourth, which, however, was soon out of sight. We saw Mr. BELL shoot two or three times, and heard guns fired, either by Mr. HARRIS or Mr. SQUIRE, but the weather was so hot that fearful of injuring their horses they were obliged to allow the bull they pursued to escape. The one shot by Mr. BELL, tumbled upon his knees, got up again, and rushed on one of the hunters, who shot it once more, when it paused, and almost immediately fell dead.

The flesh of the Buffaloes thus killed was sent to the fort in the cart, and we continued our route and passed the night on the prairie, at a spot about half way between the Yellow-Stone and the Missouri rivers. Here, just before sundown, seven more bulls were discovered by the hunters, and Mr. HARRIS, Mr. BELL and Mr. CULBERTSON each killed one. In this part of the prairie we observed several burrows made by the swift fox, but could not see any of those animals although we watched for some time in hopes of doing so. They probably scented our party and would not approach. The hunters on the prairies, either from hunger or because they have not a very delicate appetite, sometimes break in the skull of a buffalo and eat the brains raw. At sunrise we were all up, and soon had our coffee, after which a mulatto man called LAFLEUR, an excellent hunter attached to the American Fur-Company, accompanied Mr. HARRIS and Mr. BELL on a hunt for antelopes, as we wanted no more Buffaloes. After waiting the return of the party, who came back unsuccessful, we broke up our camp and turned our steps homeward.

The Buffalo bulls which have been with their fair ones are at this season wretchedly poor, but some of them, which appear not to have much fondness for the latter, or may have been driven off by their rivals, are in pretty good condition. The prairies are in some places whitened with the skulls of the Buffalo, dried and bleached by the summer's sun and the frosts and snows of those severe latitudes in winter. Thousands are killed merely for their tongues, and their large carcasses remain to feed the wolves and other rapacious prowlers on the grassy wastes.

A large Bison bull will generally weigh nearly two thousand pounds, and a fat cow, about twelve hundred. We weighed one of the bulls killed by our party and found it to reach seventeen hundred and twenty seven pounds, although it had already lost a good deal of blood. This was an old bull and was not fat; it had probably weighed more at some previous period. We were told that at this season a great many half-breed Indians were engaged in killing Buffaloes and curing their flesh for winter-use, on Moose river, about 200 miles north of us.

When these animals are shot at a distance of fifty or sixty yards, they rarely, if ever, charge on the hunters. Mr. CULBERTSON told us he had killed as many as nine bulls from the same spot, unseen by these terrible animals. There are times, however, when they have been known to gore both horse and rider, after being severely wounded, and have dropped down dead but a few minutes afterwards. There are indeed instances of bulls receiving many balls without being immediately killed, and we saw one which during one of our hunts was shot no less than twenty-four times before it dropped.

A bull that our party had wounded in the shoulder, and which was thought too badly hurt to do much harm to any one, was found rather dangerous when we approached him, as he would dart forward at the nearest of his foes, and but that his wound prevented him from wheeling and turning rapidly, he would certainly have done some mischief. We fired at him from our six-barrelled revolving pistol, which, however, seemed to have little other effect than to render him more savage and furious. His appearance was well calculated to appal the bravest, had we not felt assured that his strength was fast diminishing. We ourselves were a little too confident, and narrowly escaped being overtaken by him through our imprudence. We placed ourselves directly in his front, and as he advanced, fired at his head and ran back, not supposing that he could overtake us; but he soon got within a few feet of our rear, with head lowered, and every preparation made for giving us a hoist; the next instant, however, we had jumped aside, and the animal was unable to alter his headlong course quick enough to avenge himself on us. Mr. BELL now put a ball directly through his lungs, and with a gush of blood from the mouth and nostrils, he fell upon his knees and gave up the ghost, falling (as usual) on the side, quite dead.

On another occasion, when the same party were hunting near the end of the month of July, Mr. SQUIRE wounded a bull twice, but no blood flowing from the mouth, it was concluded the wounds were only in the flesh, and the animal was shot by Mr. CULBERTSON, OWEN McKENZIE, and Mr. SQUIRE, again. This renewed fire only seemed to enrage him the more, and he made a dash at the hunters so sudden and unexpected, that Mr. SQUIRE, attempting to escape, rode between the beast and a ravine which was near, when the bull turned upon him, his horse became frightened and leaped down the bank, the Buffalo following him so closely that he was nearly unhorsed; he lost his presence of mind and dropped his gun; he, however, fortunately hung on by the mane and recovered his seat. The horse was the fleetest, and saved his life. He told us subsequently that he had never been so terrified before. This bull was fired at several times after SQUIRE's adventure, and was found to have twelve balls lodged in him when he was killed. He was in very bad condition, and being in the rutting season we found the flesh too rank for our dainty palates and only took the tongue with us.

Soon afterwards we killed a cow in company with many bulls and were at first afraid that they would charge upon us, which in similar cases they frequently do, but our party was too large and they did not venture near, although their angry bellowings and their unwillingness to leave the spot showed their rage at parting with her. As the sun was now sinking fast towards the horizon on the extended prairie, we soon began to make our way toward the camping ground and passed within a moderate distance of a large herd of Buffaloes, which we did not stop to molest but increasing our speed reached our quarters for the night, just as the shadows of the western plain indicated that we should not behold the orb of day until the morrow.

Our camp was near three conical hills called the Mamelles, only about thirty miles from Fort Union, although we had travelled nearly fifty by the time we reached the spot. After unloading and unsaddling our tired beasts, all hands assisted in getting wood and bringing water, and we were soon quietly enjoying a cup of coffee. The time of refreshment to the weary hunter is always one of interest: the group of stalwart frames stretched in various attitudes around or near the blazing watch-fires, recalls to our minds the masterpieces of the great delineators of night scenes; and we have often at such times beheld living pictures, far surpassing any of those contained in the galleries of Europe.

There were signs of grizzly bears around us, and during the night we heard a number of wolves howling among the bushes in the vicinity. The service berry was abundant and we ate a good many of them, and after a hasty preparation in the morning, started again after the Buffaloes we had seen the previous evening. Having rode for some time, one of our party who was in advance as a scout, made the customary signal from the top of a high hill, that Buffaloes were in sight; this is done by walking the hunter's horse backward and forward several times. We hurried on and found our scout lying close to his horse's neck, as if asleep on the back of the animal. He pointed out where he had discovered the game, but they had gone out of sight, and (as he said) were travelling fast, the herd being composed of both bulls and cows. The hunters mounted at once, and galloped on in rapid pursuit, while we followed more leisurely over hills and plains and across ravines and broken ground, at the risk of our necks. Now and then we could see the hunters, and occasionally the Buffaloes, which had taken a direction toward the Fort. At last we reached an eminence from which we saw the hunters approaching the Buffaloes in order to begin the chase in earnest. It seems that there is no etiquette among Buffalo hunters, and this not being understood beforehand by our friend HARRIS, he was disappointed in his wish to kill a cow. The country was not as favourable to the hunters as it was to the flying herd. The females separated from the males, and the latter turned in our direction and passed within a few hundred yards of us without our being able to fire at them. Indeed we willingly suffered them to pass unmolested, as they are always very dangerous when they have been parted from the cows. Only one female was killed on this occasion. On our way homeward we made towards the coupee, an opening in the hills, where we expected to find water for our horses and mules, as our supply of Missouri water was only enough for ourselves.

The water found on these prairies is generally unfit to drink, (unless as a matter of necessity,) and we most frequently carried eight or ten gallons from the river, on our journey through the plains. We did not find water where we expected, and were obliged to proceed about two miles to the eastward, where we luckily found a puddle sufficient for the wants of our horses and mules. There was not a bush in sight at this place, and we collected Buffalo dung to make a fire to cook with. In the winter this prairie fuel is often too wet to burn, and the hunters and Indians have to eat their meat raw. It can however hardly be new to our readers to hear that they are often glad to get any thing, either raw or cooked, when in this desolate region.

Young Buffalo bulls are sometimes castrated by the Indians, as we were told, for the purpose of rendering them larger and fatter; and we were informed, that when full grown they have been shot, and found to be far superior to others in the herd, in size as well as flavour. During severe winters the Buffaloes become very poor, and when the snow has covered the ground for several months to the depth of two or three feet, they are wretched objects to behold. They frequently in this emaciated state lose their hair and become covered with scabs; and the magpies alight on their backs and pick the sores. The poor animals in these dreadful seasons die in great numbers.

A singular trait in the Buffalo when caught young, was related to us, as follows: When a calf is taken, if the person who captures it places one of his fingers in its mouth, it will follow him afterwards, whether on foot or on horseback, for several miles.

We now give a few notes from our journal kept at Fort Union, which may interest our readers.

August 7th, 1843, a Buffalo cow was killed and brought into the fort, and to the astonishment of all, was found to be near her time of calving. This was an extraordinary circumstance at that season of the year.

August 8th, The young Buffaloes have commenced shedding their first (or red) coat of hair, which drops off in patches about the size of the palm of a man's hand. The new hair is dark brownish black. We caught one of these calves with a lasso, and had several men to hold him, but on approaching to pull off some of the old hair, he kicked and bounced about in such a furious manner that we could not get near him. Mr. CULBERTSON had it however taken to the press post, and there it was drawn up and held so closely that we could handle it, and we tore off some pieces of its old pelage, which hung to the side with surprising tenacity.

The process of butchering or cutting up the carcass of the Buffalo is generally performed in a slovenly and disgusting manner by the hunters, and the choicest parts only are saved, unless food is scarce. The liver and brains are eagerly sought for, and the hump is excellent when broiled. The pieces of flesh from the sides are called by the French, fillets, or the depouille; the marrow bones are sometimes cut out, and the paunch is stripped of its covering of fat.

Some idea of the immense number of Bisons to be still seen on the wild prairies, may be formed from the following account, given to us by Mr. KIPP, one of the principals of the American Fur Company. "While he was travelling from Travers' Bay to the Mandan nation in the month of August, in a cart heavily laden, he passed through herds of Buffalo for six days in succession. At another time he saw the great prairie near Fort Clark on the Missouri river, almost blackened by these animals, which covered the plain to the hills that bounded the view in all directions, and probably extended farther."

When the Bisons first see a person, whether white or red, they trot or canter off forty or fifty yards, and then stop suddenly, turn their heads and gaze on their foe for a few moments, then take a course and go off at full speed until out of sight, and beyond the scent of man.

Although large, heavy, and comparatively clumsy, the Bison is at times brisk and frolicksome, and these huge animals often play and gambol about, kicking their heels in the air with surprising agility, and throwing their hinder parts to the right and left alternately, or from one side to the other, their heels the while flying about and their tails whisking in the air. They are very impatient in the fly and mosquito season, and are often seen kicking and running against the wind to rid themselves of these tormentors.

The different Indian tribes hunt the Buffalo in various ways: some pursue them on horseback and shoot them with arrows, which they point with old bits of iron, or old knife blades. They are rarely expert in loading or reloading guns, (even if they have them,) but in the closely contested race between their horse and the animal, they prefer the rifle to the bow and arrow. Other tribes follow them with patient perseverance on foot, until they come within shooting distance, or kill them by stratagem.

The Mandan Indians chase the Buffalo in parties of from twenty of fifty, and each man is provided with two horses, one of which he rides, and the other being trained expressly for the chase, is led to the place where the Buffaloes are started. The hunters are armed with bows and arrows, their quivers containing from thirty to fifty arrows according to the wealth of the owner. When they come in sight of their game, they quit the horses on which they have ridden, mount those led for them, ply the whip, soon gain the flank or even the centre of the herd, and shoot their arrows into the fattest, according to their fancy. When a Buffalo has been shot, if the blood flows from the nose or mouth, he is considered mortally wounded; if not, they shoot a second or a third arrow into the wounded animal.

The Buffalo, when first started by the hunters, carries his tail close down between the legs; but when wounded, he switches his tail about, especially if intending to fight his pursuer, and it behooves the hunter to watch these movements closely, as the horse will often shy, and without due care the rider may be thrown, which when in a herd of Buffalo is almost certain death. An arrow will kill a Buffalo instantly if it takes effect in the heart, but if it does not reach the right spot, a dozen arrows will not even arrest one in his course, and of the wounded, many run out of sight and are lost to the hunter.

At times the wounded Bison turns so quickly and makes such a sudden rush upon the hunter, that if the steed is not a good one and the rider perfectly cool, they are overtaken, the horse gored and knocked down, and the hunter thrown off and either gored or trampled to death. But if the horse is a fleet one, and the hunter expert, the Bison is easily outrun and they escape. At best it may be said that this mode of Buffalo hunting is dangerous sport, and one requires both skill and nerve to come off successfully.

The Gros Ventres, Blackfeet and Assinaboines often take the Buffalo in large pens, usually called parks, constructed in the following manner.

Two converging fences built of sticks logs and brushwood are made, leading to the mouth of a pen somewhat in the shape of a funnel. The pen itself is either square or round, according to the nature of the ground where it is to be placed, at the narrow end of the funnel, which is always on the verge of a sudden break or precipice in the prairie ten or fifteen feet deep, and is made as strong as possible. When this trap is completed, a young man very swift of foot starts at daylight, provided with a Bison's hide and head, to cover his body and head when he approaches the herd that is to be taken, on nearing which he bleats like a young Buffalo calf, and makes his way slowly towards the mouth of the converging fences leading to the pen. He repeats this cry at intervals, the Buffaloes follow the decoy, and a dozen or more of mounted Indians at some distance behind the herd gallop from one side to the other on both their flanks, urging them by this means to enter the funnel, which having done, a crowd of men women and children come and assist in frightening them, and as soon as they have fairly entered the road to the pen beneath the precipice, the disguised Indian, still bleating occasionally, runs to the edge of the precipice, quickly descends, and makes his escape, climbing over the barricade or fence of the pen beneath, while the herd follow on till the leader (probably an old bull) is forced to leap down into the pen, and is followed by the whole herd, which is thus ensnared, and easily destroyed even by the women and children, as there is no means of escape for them.

This method of capturing the Bison is especially resorted to in October and November, as the hide is at that season in good condition and saleable, and the meat can be preserved for the winter supply. When the Indians have thus driven a herd of Buffalo into a pen, the warriors all assemble by the side of the enclosure, the pipe is lighted, and the chiefs smoke to the honour of the Great Spirit, to the four points of the compass, and to the herd of Bisons. As soon as this ceremony has ended, the destruction commences, guns are fired and arrows shot from every direction at the devoted animals, and the whole herd is slaughtered before the Indians enter the space where the Buffaloes have become their victims. Even the children shoot tiny arrows at them when thus captured, and try the strength of their young arms upon them.

It sometimes happens, however, that the leader of the herd becomes alarmed and restless while driving to the precipice, and should the fence be weak, breaks through, and the whole drove follow and escape. It also sometimes occurs, that after the Bisons are in the pen, which is often so filled that they touch each other, the terrified crowd swaying to and fro, their weight against the fence breaks it down, and if the smallest gap is made, it is immediately widened, when they dash through and scamper off, leaving the Indians in dismay and disappointment. The side fences for the purpose of leading the Buffaloes to the pens extend at times nearly half a mile, and some of the pens cover two or three hundred yards of ground. It takes much time and labour to construct one of these great traps or snares, as the Indians sometimes have to bring timber from a considerable distance to make the fences and render them strong and efficient.

The Bison has several enemies: the worst is, of course, man; then comes the grizzly bear; and next, the wolf. The bear follows them and succeeds in destroying a good many; the wolf hunts them in packs, and commits great havoc among them, especially among the calves and the cows when calving. Many Buffaloes are killed when they are struggling in the mire on the shores of rivers where they sometimes stick fast, so that the wolves or bears can attack them to advantage; eating out their eyes and devouring the unresisting animals by piecemeal.

When we were ascending the Missouri river, the first Buffaloes were heard of near Fort Leavenworth, some having a short time before been killed within forty miles of that place. We did not, however, see any of these animals until we had passed Fort Croghan, but above this point we met with them almost daily, either floating dead on the river, or gazing at our steamboat from the shore.

Every part of the Bison is useful to the Indians, and their method of making boats, by stretching the raw hide over a sort of bowl-shaped frame work, is well known. These boats are generally made by the women, and we saw some of them at the Mandan village. The horns are made into drinking vessels, ladles, and spoons. The skins form a good bed, or admirable covering from the cold, and the flesh is excellent food, whether fresh or dried or made into pemmican; the fat is reduced and put up in bladders, and in some cases used for frying fish, &c.

The hide of the Buffalo is tanned or dressed altogether by the women, or squaws, and the children; the process is as follows: The skin is first hung on a post, and all the adhering flesh taken off with a bone, toothed somewhat like a saw; this is performed by scraping the skin downwards, and requires consider-

able labour. The hide is then stretched on the ground and fastened down with pegs; it is then allowed to remain till dry, which is usually the case in a day or two. After it is dry the flesh side is pared down with the blade of a knife fastened in a bone, called a grate, which renders the skin even and takes off about a quarter of its thickness. The hair is taken off with the same instrument and these operations being performed, and the skin reduced to a proper thickness, is covered over either with brains, liver or grease, and left for a night. The next day the skin is rubbed and scraped either in the sun or by a fire, until the greasy matter has been worked into it, and it is nearly dry; then a cord is fastened to two poles and over this the skin is thrown, and pulled, rubbed and worked until quite dry; after which it is sewed together around the edges excepting at one end; a smoke is made with rotten wood in a hole dug in the earth, and the skin is suspended over it, on sticks set up like a tripod, and thoroughly smoked, which completes the tanning and renders the skin able to bear wet without losing its softness or pliability afterwards.

Buffalo robes are dressed in the same manner, only that the hair is not removed and they are not smoked. They are generally divided into two parts: a strip is taken from each half on the back of the skin where the hump was, and the two halves, or sides, are sewed together after they are dressed, with thread made of the sinews of the animal; which process being finished, the robe is complete and ready for market.

The scrapings of the skins, we were informed, are sometimes boiled with berries, and make a kind of jelly which is considered good food in some cases by the Indians. The strips cut off from the skins are sewed together and make robes for the children, or caps, mittens, shoes, &c. The bones are pounded fine with a large stone and boiled, the grease which rises to the top is skimmed off and put into bladders. This is the favourite and famous marrow grease, which is equal to butter. The sinews are used for stringing their bows, and are a substitute for thread; the intestines are eaten, the shoulder-blades made into hoes, and in fact (as we have already stated) nothing is lost or wasted, but every portion of the animal, by the skill and industry of the Indians, is rendered useful.

Balls are found in the stomach of the Buffalo, as in our common domestic cattle.

Having heard frequent discussions respecting the breeding of the Bison in a domesticated state, and knowing that ROBERT WICKLIFFE, Esq., of Kentucky, had raised some of these animals, we requested his son, then on his way to Europe, to ask that gentleman to give us some account of their habits under his care, and shortly afterwards received a letter from him, dated Lexington Nov. 6th, 1843, in which he gives an interesting account of the Bison breeding with the common cow, and other particulars connected with this animal. After expressing his desire to comply with our request intimated to him by his son, he proceeds to give us the following information: "as far," he writes, "as his limited knowledge of natural history and his attention to these animals will permit him to do." He proceeds: "The herd of Buffalo I now possess have descended from one or two cows that I purchased from a man who brought them from the country called the Upper Missouri; I have had them for about thirty years, but from giving them away and the occasional killing of them by mischievous persons, as well as other causes, my whole stock at this time does not exceed ten or twelve. I have sometimes confined them in separate parks from other cattle, but generally they herd and feed with my stock of farm cattle. They graze in company with them as gently as the others. The Buffalo cows, I think, go with young about the same time the common cow does, and produce once a year; none of mine have ever had more than one at a birth. The approach of the sexes is similar to that of the common bull and cow under similar circumstances at all times when the cow is in heat, a period which seems, as with the common cow, confined neither to day, nor night, nor any particular season, and the cows bring forth their young of course at different times and seasons of the year, the same as our domesticated cattle. I do not find my Buffaloes more furious or wild than the common cattle of the same age that graze with them.

"Although the Buffalo, like the domestic cow, brings forth its young at different seasons of the year, this I attribute to the effect of domestication, as it is different with all animals in a state of nature. I have always heard their time for calving in our latitude was from March until July, and it is very obviously the season which nature assigns for the increase of both races, as most of my calves were from the Buffaloes and common cows at this season. On getting possession of the tame Buffalo, I endeavoured to cross them as much as I could with my common cows, to which experiment I found the tame or common bull unwilling to accede, and he was always shy of a Buffalo cow, but the Buffalo bull was willing to breed with the common cow.

"From the domestic cow I have several half breeds, one of which was a heifer; this I put with a domestic bull, and it produced a bull calf. This I castrated, and it made a very fine steer, and when killed produced very fine

Plate LVII.

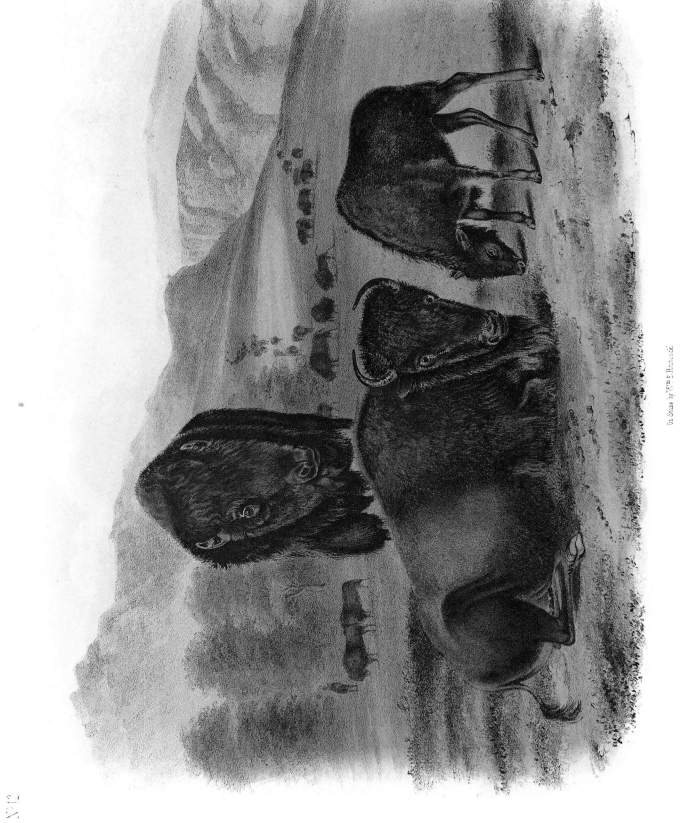

On Stone by W.m E. Hitchcock

American Bison or Buffalo

Drawn from nature by J. Audubon PR.S.F.L.S

beef. I bred from the same heifer several calves, and then, that the experiment might be perfect, I put one of them to the Buffalo bull, and she brought me a bull calf which I raised to be a very fine large animal, perhaps the only one to be met with in the world of his blood, viz., a three quarter, half quarter, and half quarter of the common blood. After making these experiments, I have left them to propagate their breed themselves, so that I have only had a few half breeds, and they always prove the same, even by a Buffalo bull. The full blood is not as large as the improved stock, but as large as the ordinary cattle of the country. The crossed or half blood are larger than either the Buffalo or common cow. The hump, brisket, ribs and tongue of the full and half blooded are preferable to those of the common beef, but the round and other parts are much inferior. The udder or bag of the Buffalo is smaller than that of the common cow, but I have allowed the calves of both to run with their dams upon the same pasture, and those of the Buffalo were always the fattest; and old hunters have told me, that when a young Buffalo calf is taken, it requires the milk of two common cows to raise it. Of this I have no doubt, having received the same information from hunters of the greatest veracity. The bag or udder of the half breed is larger than that of full blooded animals, and they would, I have no doubt, make good milkers.

"The wool of the wild Buffalo grows on their descendants when domesticated, but I think they have less of wool than their progenitors. The domesticated Buffalo still retains the grunt of the wild animal, and is incapable of making any other noise, and they still observe the habit of having select places within their feeding grounds to wallow in.

"The Buffalo has a much deeper shoulder than the tame ox, but is lighter behind. He walks more actively than the latter, and I think has more strength than a common ox of the same weight. I have broke them to the yoke, and found them capable of making excellent oxen; and for drawing wagons, carts, or other heavily laden vehicles on long journeys, they would, I think, be greatly preferable to the common ox. I have as yet had no opportunity of testing the longevity of the Buffalo, as all mine that have died, did so from accident or were killed because they became aged. I have some cows that are nearly twenty years old, that are healthy and vigorous, and one of them has now a sucking calf.

"The young Buffalo calf is of a sandy red or rufous colour, and commences changing to a dark brown at about six months old, which last colour it always retains. The mixed breeds are of various colours; I have had them striped with black, on a gray ground like the zebra, some of them brindled red, some pure red with white faces, and others red without any markings of white. The mixed bloods have not only produced in my stock from the tame and the Buffalo bull, but I have seen the half bloods reproducing; viz.: those that were the product of the common cow and wild Buffalo bull. I was informed that at the first settlement of the country, cows that were considered the best for milking, were from the half blood, down to the quarter, and even eighth of the Buffalo blood. But my experiments have not satisfied me that the half Buffalo bull will produce again. That the half breed heifer will be productive from either race, as I have before stated, I have tested beyond the possibility of a doubt.

"The domesticated Buffalo retains the same haughty bearing that distinguishes him in his natural state. He will, however, feed or fatten on whatever suits the tame cow, and requires about the same amount of food. I have never milked either the full blood or mixed breed, but have no doubt they might be made good milkers, although their bags or udders are less than those of the common cow; yet from the strength of the calf, the dam must yield as much or even more milk than the common cow."

Since reading the above letter, we recollect that the Buffalo calves that were kept at Fort Union, though well fed every day, were in the habit of sucking each other's ears for hours together.

There exists a singular variety of the Bison, which is however very scarce, and the skin of which is called by both the hunters and fur traders a "beaver robe." These are valued so highly that some have sold for more than three hundred dollars. Of this variety Mr. CULBERTSON had the goodness to present us with a superb specimen, which we had lined with cloth, and find a most excellent defence against the cold, whilst driving in our wagon during the severity of our northern winters.

Geographical Distribution.

The range of the Bison is still very extensive; but although it was once met with on the Atlantic coast, it has, like many others, receded and gone west and south, driven onward by the march of civilization and the advance of the axe and plough. His habits, as we have seen, are migratory, and the extreme northern and southern limits of the wandering herds not exactly defined. Authors state, that at the time of the first settlement of Canada it was not known in that country, and SAGARD THEODAT mentions having heard that bulls existed in the far west, but saw none himself. According to Dr. RICHARDSON, Great Slave Lake, latitude 60°, was at one time the northern boundary of their range; but of late years, according to the testimony of the natives, they have taken possession of the flat limestone district of Slave Point on the north side of that lake, and have wandered to the vicinity of Great Marten Lake, in latitude 63° or 64°. The Bison was not known formerly to the north of the Columbia river on the Pacific coast, and LEWIS and CLARK found Buffalo robes were an important article of traffic between the inhabitants of the east side and those west of the Rocky mountains.

The Bison is spoken of by HERNANDEZ as being found in New Spain or Mexico, and it probably extended farther south. LAWSON speaks of two Buffaloes that were killed in one season on Cape Fear river, in North Carolina. The Bison formerly existed in South Carolina on the seaboard, and we were informed that from the last herd seen in that State, two were killed in the vicinity of Columbia. It thus appears that at one period this animal ranged over nearly the whole of North America.

At the present time, the Buffalo is found in vast herds in some of the great prairies, and scattered more sparsely nearly over the whole length and breadth of the valleys east and west that adjoin the Rocky Mountain chain.

Putorius Erminea.—Linn.

White Weasel.—Stoat.

Plate lix. Male and Female in summer pelage. Natural size.

P. Hyeme alba; æstate supra rutila, infra alba caudae apice nigro.

Characters.

White, in winter; in summer, brown above, white beneath; tip of the tail, black.

Synonymes.

MUSTELA ERMINEA, Briss. Règne An., p. 243, 2.
     "   "   Linn., Syst. Nat., 12. i., p. 68. 7.
     "   "   Schreb., Säugth., p. 496, 11 t. 137.
     "   "   Erxleben Syst., p. 474, 13.
VIVERA ERMINEA, Shaw, Gen. Zool., i., 2 p. 426 t. 99.
     "   "   Pennant, Arctic Zoology, i., p. 75.
HERMINE, Buffon, C. C., p. 240, t.
MUSTELA ERMINEA, Parry's First Voyage, Sup. 135.
     "   "   Parry's Second Voy., App 294.
     "   "   Franklin's First Journey, p. 652.
     "   "   Godman, Ame. Nat. Hist., vol. i., p. 193, fig. 1.
     "   "   Harlan, p. 62.
PUTORIUS NOVEBORACENSIS, Dekay, Nat. Hist. New-York, p. 36.

Description.

Body, long and slender, with a convex nose and forehead; limbs, short, and rather stout; tail, long and cylindrical; moustaches, long, extending beyond the ears; ears, low, broad and round, do not entirely surround the auditory opening, sparingly covered with short hairs on both surfaces. There are five toes on each foot, the inner toe much the shortest; the toes are clothed with hairs, covering the nails; fur, soft and short; tail, hairy, and bushy at the end. There are two glands situated on each side of the under surface of the tail, which contain an offensive white musky fluid.

Colour.

In winter, in the latitude of Pennsylvania and New-York, all the hairs are snowy white from the roots, except those on the end of the tail, which for about one and three-fourth inches is black. We received specimens from Virginia obtained in January, in which the colours on the back had undergone no change, and remained brown; and from the upper and middle districts of South Carolina killed at the same period, when no change had taken place, and

Plate LIX.

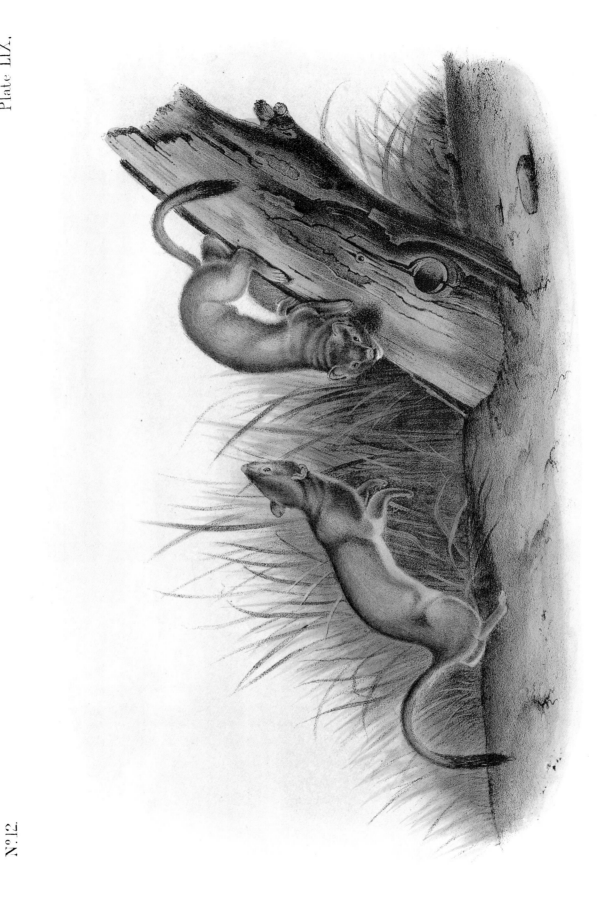

White Weasel; Ermine.

it was stated that this, the only species of Weasel found there, remained brown through the whole year. These specimens are now in our possession, and we have arrived at the conclusion that the farther South we advance, the less perfect is the change from brown to white. We have specimens from Long Island, obtained in winter, which retain shades of brown on the head and dorsal line. Those from the valleys of the Virginia mountains have broad stripes of brown on the back, and specimens from Abbeville and Lexington, S. Carolina, have not undergone the slightest change. We were informed by our friend Mr. BROMFIELD an eminent botanist of England, that in the Isle of Wight, the place of his residence, the Ermine underwent only a partial change in winter.

In summer, the upper surface of the body is of a chesnut-brown colour, a little darker on the dorsal line; under surface, the upper lips to the nose, chin, throat, inner surfaces of legs, and belly, white; the line separating the colour of the back from that on the under surface, is very distinct, but irregular, and in some specimens, the white on the belly extends further up along the sides than in others. Whiskers white and black; the former preponderating; end of tail, as in winter, black.

Dimensions.

Old male.

		Inches.
Nose to root of tail,	. . . .	$10\frac{1}{2}$
Tail (vertebræ),	. . . .	$5\frac{1}{2}$
" to end of hair,	. . . .	7
Breadth between the ears,	. . . .	$1\frac{1}{4}$
Length of head,	. . . .	2
Stretch of legs from end, to end of claws,	. . . .	14
Length of hind foot, to end of nails,	. . . .	$1\frac{3}{4}$
" fore-foot, to "	. . . .	$1\frac{1}{2}$
Black tip of tail,	. . . .	3

Habits.

The name of Ermine is associated with the pride of state and luxury, its fur having from time immemorial been the favourite ornament of the robes of princes, judges and prelates. From its snowy whiteness it is emblematic of the purity which they *ought* to possess.

To us the Ermine, in its winter dress, has always appeared strikingly beautiful. On a wintry day, when the earth was covered with a broad sheet of snow, our attention has sometimes been arrested by this little animal peering out from a log heap, or the crevices of a stone fence; its eyes in certain shades of light appearing like sapphires, its colour vieing in whiteness and brilliancy with the snowy mantle of the surrounding landscape.

Graceful in form, rapid in his movements, and of untiring industry, he is withal a brave and fearless little fellow; conscious of security within the windings of his retreat among the logs, or heap of stones, he permits us to approach him to within a few feet, then suddenly withdraws his head; we remain still for a moment, and he once more returns to his post of observation, watching curiously our every motion, seeming willing to claim association so long as we abstain from becoming his persecutor.

Yet with all these external attractions, this little Weasel is fierce and bloodthirsty, possessing an intuitive propensity to destroy every animal and bird within its reach, some of which, such as the American rabbit, the ruffed grouse, and domestic fowl, are ten times its own size. It is a notorious and hated depredator of the poultry house, and we have known forty well grown fowls to have been killed in one night by a single Ermine. Satiated with the blood of probably a single fowl, the rest, like the flock slaughtered by the wolf in the sheepfold, were destroyed in obedience to a law of nature, an instinctive propensity to kill. We have traced the footsteps of this bloodsucking little animal on the snow, pursuing the trail of the American rabbit, and although it could not overtake its prey by superior speed, yet the timid hare soon took refuge in the hollow of a tree, or in a hole dug by the marmot, or skunk. Thither it was pursued by the Ermine, and destroyed, the skin and other remains at the mouth of the burrow bearing evidence of the fact. We observed and Ermine, after having captured a hare of the above species, first behead it and then drag the body some twenty yards over the fresh fallen snow, beneath which it was concealed, and the snow tightly pressed over it; the little prowler displaying thereby a habit of which we became aware for the first time on that occasion. To avoid a dog that was in close pursuit it mounted a tree and laid itself flat on a limb about twenty feet from the ground, from which it was finally shot. We have ascertained by successful experiments, repeated more than a hundred times, that the Ermine can be employed, in the manner of the

ferret of Europe, in driving our American rabbit from the burrow into which it has retreated. In one instance, the Ermine employed had been captured only a few days before, and its canine teeth were filed in order to prevent its destroying the rabbit; a cord was placed around its neck to secure its return. It pursued the hare through all the windings of its burrow and forced it to the mouth, where it could be taken in a net, or by the hand. In winter, after a snow storm, the ruffed grouse has a habit of plunging into the loose snow, where it remains at times for one or two days. In this passive state the Ermine sometimes detects and destroys it. In an unsuccessful attempt at domesticating this grouse by fastening its feet to a board in the mode adopted with the stool pigeon, and placing it high on a shelf, an Ermine which we had kept as a pet, found its way by the curtains of the window and put an end to our experiment by eating off the head of our grouse.

Notwithstanding all these mischievous and destructive habits, it is doubtful whether the Ermine is not rather a benefactor than an enemy to the farmer, ridding his granaries and fields of many depredators on the product of his labour, that would devour ten times the value of the poultry and eggs which, at long and uncertain intervals, it occasionally destroys. A mission appears to have been assigned it by Providence to lessen the rapidly multiplying number of mice of various species and the smaller rodentia.

The white-footed mouse is destructive to the grains in the wheat fields and in the stacks, as well as the nurseries of fruit trees. LE CONTE'S pine-mouse is injurious to the Irish and sweet potato crops, causing more to rot by nibbling holes into them than it consumes, and WILSON's meadow-mouse lessens our annual product of hay by feeding on the grasses, and by its long and tortuous galleries among their roots.

Wherever an Ermine has taken up its residence, the mice in its vicinity for half a mile round have been found rapidly to diminish in number. Their active little enemy is able to force its thin vermiform body into the burrows, it follows them to the end of their galleries, and destroys whole families. We have on several occasions, after a light snow, followed the trail of this weasel through fields and meadows, and witnessed the immense destruction which it occasioned in a single night. It enters every hole under stumps, logs, stone heaps and fences, and evidences of its bloody deeds are seen in the mutilated remains of the mice scattered on the snow. The little chipping or ground squirrel, *Tamias Lysteri*, takes up its residence in the vicinity of the grain fields, and is known to carry off in its cheek pouches vast quantities of wheat and buckwheat, to serve as winter stores. The Ermine instinctively discovers these snug retreats, and in the space of a few minutes destroys a whole family of these beautiful little *Tamiæ*; without even resting awhile until it has consumed its now abundant food its appetite craving for more blood, as if impelled by an irresistible destiny it proceeds in search of other objects on which it may glut its insatiable vampire-like thirst. The Norway rat and the common house-mouse take possession of our barns, wheat stacks, and granaries, and destroy vast quantities of grain. In some instances the farmer is reluctantly compelled to pay even more than a tithe in contributions towards the support of these pests. Let however an Ermine find its way into these barns and granaries, and there take up its winter residence, and the havoc which is made among the rats and mice will soon be observable. The Ermine pursues them to their farthest retreats, and in a few weeks the premises are entirely free from their depredations. We once placed a half domesticated Ermine in an outhouse infested with rats, shutting up the holes on the outside to prevent their escape. The little animal soon commenced his work of destruction. The squeaking of the rats was heard throughout the day. In the evening, it came out licking its mouth, and seeming like a hound after a long chase, much fatigued. A board of the floor was raised to enable us to ascertain the result of our experiment, and an immense number of rats were observed, which, although they had been killed on different parts of the building, had been dragged together, forming a compact heap.

The Ermine is then of immense benefit to the farmer. We are of the opinion that it has been over-hated and too indiscriminately persecuted. If detected in the poultry house, there is some excuse for destroying it, as, like the dog that has once been caught in the sheepfold, it may return to commit farther depredations; but when it has taken up its residence under stone heaps and fences, in his fields, or his barns, the farmer would consult his interest by suffering it to remain, as by thus inviting it to a home, it will probably destroy more formidable enemies, relieve him from many petty annoyances, and save him many a bushel of grain.

Let us not too hastily condemn the little Ermine for its bloodthirsty propensities. It possesses well-developed canine teeth, and obeys an instinct of nature. Man, with organs not so decidedly carnivorous, and possessed of the restraining powers of reason and conscience, often commits a wanton havoc on the inferior animals, not so much from want of food, as from a mere love of sport. The buffalo and the elk he has driven across the Mississippi, and their haunts are now restricted to the prairies of the far West. Even now thousands are slaughtered for amusement, and their tongues only are used, whilst their carcasses are left to the wolves. He fills his game bag with more woodcock, partridges and snipe, than he requires; his fishing-rod does not remain idle even after he has provided a full meal for his whole family; and our youngsters are taught to shoot the little warbler and the sparrow as a preparatory training for the destruction of larger game.

The Ermine is far from being shy in its habits. It is not easily alarmed, and becomes tolerably tame when taken young, for we have on several occasions succeeded in our attempts at domesticating it, but it appeared to us that these pets were not quite as gentle as many ferrets that we have seen in Europe. When not kept in confinement, they were apt to stray off into the fields and woods, and finally became wild. The tracks of this species on the snow are peculiar, exhibiting only two footprints, placed near each other, the succeeding tracks being far removed, giving evidences of long leaps. We have frequently observed where it had made long galleries in the deep snow for twenty or thirty yards, and thus in going from one burrow to another, instead of travelling over the surface, it had constructed for itself a kind of tunnel beneath.

The Ermine is easily taken in any kind of trap. We have on several occasions, when observing one peeping at us from its secure hole in the wall, kept it gazing until a servant brought a box trap baited with a bird or piece of meat, which was placed within a few feet of its retreat. The Ermine, after eyeing the trap for a few moments, gradually approached it, then after two or three hasty springs backwards returned stealthily into the trap, seized the bait, and was caught. We find in our note-book the following memorandum: "On the 19th June, 1846, we baited a large wire trap with maize: on visiting the trap on the following day we found it had caught seven young rats and a Weasel; the throats of the former had all been cut by the Weasel, and their blood sucked; but what appeared strange to us, the Weasel itself was also dead. The rats had been attracted by the bait: the Weasel went into the trap and killed them; and whether it met its death by excessive gluttony, or from a wound inflicted by its host of enemies, we are unable to determine.

This species does not appear to be very abundant any where. We have seldom found more than two or three on any farm in the Northern or Eastern States. We have ascertained that the immense number of tracks often seen in the snow in particular localities were made by a single animal, as by capturing one, no signs of other individuals were afterwards seen. We have observed it most abundant in stony regions: in Dutchess and Ontario counties in New-York, on the hills of Connecticut and Vermont, and at the foot of the Alleghanies in Pennsylvania and Virginia. It is solitary in its habits, as we have seldom seen a pair together except in the rutting season. A family of young, however, are apt to remain in the same locality till autumn. In winter they separate, and we are inclined to think that they do not hunt in couples or in packs like the wolf, but that, like the bat and the mink, each individual pursues its prey without copartnership, and hunts for its own benefit.

The only note we have ever heard uttered by the Ermine is a shrill querulous cry: this was heard only when it was suddenly alarmed, or received a hurt, when its sharp scream was always attended with an emission of the offensive odour with which nature has furnished it as a means of defence. Although nocturnal in its habits, the Ermine is frequently met with at all hours of the day, and we have seen it in pursuit of the common rabbit under a bright shining sun at noon-day.

We doubt whether the Ermine ever digs its own burrows, and although when fastened to a chain in a state of confinement we observed it digging shallow holes in the ground, its attempts at burrowing were as awkward as those of the rat; the nests we have seen were placed under roots of trees, in stone heaps, or in the burrows of the ground squirrel, from which the original occupants had been expelled. The rutting season is in winter, from the middle of February to the beginning of March. The young, from four to seven, are born in May, in the latitude of New-York. We were informed by a close observer, that in the upper country of Carolina, the young had been seen as early as the 25th of March. The colour of the young when a week old, is pale yellow on the upper surface.

The Ermine avoids water, and if forcibly thrown into it, swims awkwardly like a cat. It does not, like the fisher and pine marten, pursue its prey on trees, and seems never to ascend them from choice; but from dire necessity, when closely pursued by its implacable enemy, the dog.

One of the most singular characteristics of this species, viz., its change of colour from brown in summer to pure white in winter, and from white in spring to its summer colour, remains to be considered. It is well known that about the middle of October the Ermine gradually loses its brown summer-coat and assumes its white winter-pelage, which about the middle of March is replaced by the usual summer colour.

As far as our observations have enabled us to form an opinion on this subject, we have arrived at the conclusion, that the animal sheds its coat twice a year, i.e., at the periods when these semi-annual changes take place. In autumn, the summer hair gradually and almost imperceptibly drops out, and is succeeded by a fresh coat of hair, which in the course of two or three weeks becomes pure white; while in the spring the animal undergoes its change from white to brown in consequence of shedding its winter coat, the new hairs then coming out brown. We have in our possession a specimen captured in November, in which the change of colour has considerably advanced, but is not completed. The whole of the under surface, the sides, neck and body to within half an inch of the back, together with the legs, are white, as well as the edges of the ears. On the upper surface, the nose, forehead, neck, and an irregular line on the back, together with a spot on the outer surface of the fore-leg, are brown, showing that these parts change colour last.

In reference to the change of pelage and colour as exhibited in spring, we add some notes made by the senior author of this work, in March, 1842, on a specimen sent to him alive by OGDEN HAMMOND, Esq.

The Weasel this evening, the 6th of March, began to show a change of colour; we were surprised to see that all around its nose, the white hair of its winter dress had changed suddenly to a silky black hue, and this extended to nearly between the ears. Here and there also were seen small spots of black about its rump, becoming more apparent toward the shoulders, and forming as it were a ridge along the back of the animal.

March 10th. By noon the change was wonderfully manifested. The whole upper surface of the head had become black to the eye, as well as the ridge of the back, the latter part having become quite clouded, and showing an indescribable motley mixture of closely-blended white, black, and blackish brown.

18th. This day the change of colour reached the root of the tail, where it formed a ring of about one inch, of the same reddish black colour. All other parts remained white, slightly tinged with pale lemon colour. It fed, as we perceived, more voraciously than ever since we have had it in our possession. No less than three of four mice were devoured to-day, and what is very strange, it left no remains of either hair, skull, feet, or any other part of these animals; and on this day, the 18th of March, it ate a very large piece of fresh beef, weighing nearly half a pound.

19th. Last night our Weasel made great progress, for this morning we found the coloured ridge on the back broader and less mottled. The posterior coloured part of the head had joined the ridge of the back. The posterior part of the hind legs had become brown, and we observed a small spot the size of a sixpence on each upper part of the thighs. At this juncture we think the animal is beautiful.

22d. This morning we found all the white hair on the outward ridge of the back had fallen, and portions of the thighs and shoulders had become broader; the coloured parts were of a rich brown to the very nose, and there existed indications of small dark spots coming from the sides of the belly, somewhat like so many beads strung on a thread, separated from the lower edge of the back ridge by a line of white of about half an inch. The weasel continues as lively as ever. When asleep, it curls its body around, and the tail encircles the whole animal, the end covering the nose. The eyes appear to be kept carefully uncovered. The general tints of the coloured parts of this Weasel were very much darker than in any other specimen which we have in our collection. When angry, it emitted a sharp shrill cry, and snapped with all its might at the objects presented to it. It was very cleanly in its habits, never rendering its sleeping apartment disagreeable.

28th. Our Weasel got out of its cage by pushing the wires apart, passing through an aperture not exceeding five-eighths of an inch, as we suppose by putting its head diagonally through the bars. The door and windows of our room were closed, however, and, when we entered, our little fellow looked at us as if well acquainted, but soon ran behind a box. It devoured last night at least half a pound of beef, kept in the room for its day's ration. We placed the cage, with the door open, on the floor, and by walking round the box that concealed it, the animal was induced to run towards the cage, and was again secured in it.

We have often observed this species whilst retreating; if near its place of concealment, it does so backwards, and we observed the same movement when it passed from one section of its cage to the other, dragging its food and concealing it among the straw. While we were sitting at a distance from its retreat, it proceeded by leaps very swiftly to within two or three feet of us, when it suddenly threw itself round and retreated backward, as mentioned before.

The purplish brown was now augmented on the thighs and shoulders to the knee joints, no white hairs remaining mixed with those that were coloured. Beneath the jaws, separate small brown spots appeared at equal distances, leaving an intermediate space of white, as was the case along the flanks. The root of the tail had acquired no farther change. Since last week our animal has diffused a very strong disagreeable odour, musky and fetid, which may be attributable to this being its breeding season; we observed that the smell was more disagreeable in the mornings and evenings, than at mid-day.

April.—On paying our accustomed visit to our Weasel this evening, we found it dead, which put a stop to any further observation of its habits. Its measurements are as follows:

	Inches.
From point of nose to end of tail, ...	10½
Tail (vertebræ), ...	5
Tail to end of hair, ...	6
Height of ear, ...	¾
Breadth of ear, ...	⅝
Fore claws and hind claws stretching out to the black hair of the tail, ...	14¼

Geographical Distribution

If, as we feel confident after having examined more than a hundred specimens from both continents, the American Ermine is identical with that of Europe, it will be found to have the widest range of any quadruped at present known. It exists in the colder portions of Asia, and in the temperate, as well as in all the Northern States of Europe. We have seen specimens from England and Scotland, from France, Germany, Switzerland, Denmark, Sweden, and Russia.

In America, its geographical range is also very extensive. Dr. DEKAY (see Fauna, N. Y., p. 37) supposes it to be a northern animal, found as far south as Pennsylvania. We agree with him in his supposition that it is a northern animal, as it is only found in the Southern States where the country is mountainous or considerably elevated. It exists in the polar regions of America as far north as FRANKLIN, PARRY, RICHARDSON, LYON and other explorers were able to penetrate. It is found in Nova Scotia and Canada, and in all the Eastern and Northern States. We observed it along the whole chain of mountains in Virginia and North Carolina. We obtained a specimen from Abbeville in South Carolina, from our friend Dr. BARRETT, a close observer and a good naturalist; and another from Mr. FISHER, from Orangeburg District. We have ascertained that it exists in the mountains of Georgia, where we are penning this article. We saw a specimen procured by TOWN-SEND in Oregon, and have heard of its existence in North California. It is, however, not found in the maritime districts of any of the Southern States, and in Carolina and Georgia does not approach within fifty miles of the seaboard;

and even when it exists on the most elevated portions of country, it is, like the ruffed grouse in similar localities, a rare species.

General Remarks.

Writers on Natural History, up to the time of HARLAN, GODMAN and RICHARDSON, without having instituted very close comparisons, considered the species existing in Asia, Europe and America, to be identical. At a somewhat later period, however, naturalists, discovering on patient and close investigation that nearly all our species of quadrupeds as well as birds differed from the closely allied species on the eastern continent, began to doubt the identity of the Ermine existing in Europe and America. We have been unable to ascertain whether these doubts originated from any difference in specimens from these countries, or from a belief that so small an animal could scarcely be found on both continents, and thus prove an exception to a general rule. We admit that were an animal restricted to the temperate climates on either continent, and not found in the polar regions, there would be a strong presumptive argument against the identity of closely allied species existing in Europe and America. The Ermine of the eastern continent is known to exist where the two continents nearly approach each other, perhaps occasionally have been united by a solid bridge of ice, and probably may be so again during some of the coldest seasons of the polar winters and being capable of travelling on the snow, and resisting the severest cold, this animal is fully able to cross from one continent to the other, like the white bear, or Arctic fox, species which are admitted as identical on both continents. Our species, moreover, is known to exist equally far north, and has been traced nearer to the poles than even the musk-ox.

We observed, in the Museum of the Zoological Society, that the specimen brought by RICHARDSON was regarded as a new species by C. L BONA-PARTE, Esq., (now Prince of Musignano.)

In the recent work of Dr. DEKAY, we perceive it has been described as a new species, under the name of *Putorius Noveboracensis*. In a spirit of great fairness and candour, however, he states: "I have never seen the true Ermine in its summer dress, and only know it from PENNANT's description: ears edged with white; head, back, sides and legs, pale tawny brown; under side of the body white; lower part of the tail brown, end black." The only point of difference, then, is in the ears edged with white. PENNANT's specimen unquestionably was obtained at the period of time when the animal had only partially changed colour, as in all these cases the specimens before us, both from Europe and America, have their ears edged with white. We have compared a great number of specimens from both continents, and have several of each lying before us; the edges of the ears in summer colour are all brown, and neither in size, dentition, nor colour, can we observe a shade of difference.

Sciurus Sub-Auratus.—Bach.

Orange-Bellied Squirrel.—Golden-Bellied Squirrel.

Plate lviii. Male and Female.—Natural Size.

S. Magnitudine, S. migratorium superæns, S. Carolinensi cedens; supra cinereus flavido-undutus, subtus saturate aureus, cauda corpore longiore.

Characters.

Size intermediate between the Northern gray and the little Carolina squirrel; tail longer than the body; colour, above, gray, with a wash of yellow; beneath, deep golden yellow.

Synonyme.

GOLDEN-BELLIED SQUIRREL, Sciurus Sub-auratus.—Bachman, Mon. Genus Sciurus, p. 12.

Description.

In the two specimens now before us, which are very similar in size and markings, there is no appearance of the small anterior upper molar found in several other species of this genus. We conclude, therefore, that it either does not exist at all, or drops out at a very early period; and accordingly set down this species as having only twenty teeth, viz.:

$$\text{Incisive } \tfrac{2}{2}; \text{ Canine } \tfrac{0-0}{0-0}; \text{ Molar } \tfrac{4-4}{4-4} = 20.$$

The upper incisors are of moderate size; their colour is deep orange brown; the lower incisors are a little paler; head, of medium size; ears short and pointed, clothed with hair on both surfaces. The body seems more formed for sprightliness and agility than that of the small Carolina Squirrel, and in this respect comes nearest to the northern gray squirrel. The tail is long, and nearly as broad as that of the last named species.

Colour.

The whole upper surface gray, with a distinct yellow wash. The hairs which give this outward appearance are grayish slate colour at their base, then broadly annulated with yellowish, then black, and near the tips annulated with yellowish-white; sides of the face and neck, the whole of the inner side of the limbs, feet, and the under parts, deep golden yellow; on the cheeks and sides of the neck, however, the hairs are obscurely annulated with black and whitish; the ears are well clothed on both surfaces with tolerably long hair of the same deep golden hue as the sides of the face; hairs of the feet mostly blackish at the root, some obscurely tipped with black; hairs of the tail, black at the root, and the remaining portion bright rusty yellow; each hair annulated with black three times; the under surface of the tail is chiefly bright rusty yellow; whiskers, longer than the head, black.

Dimensions.

	Inches.	Lines.
Length of head and body, ...	10	6

Orange-bellied Squirrel.

Drawn from Nature by J.J.Audubon, F.R.S.F.L.S.

"	of tail, (vertebræ,)	9	2
"	including fur,	12	0
"	of palm to end of middle fore-claw,	1	7
"	of heel to point of middle nail,	2	7
"	of fur on the back,	0	7
Height of ear posteriorly,		0	5
Breadth of tail with hair extended,		8	6

Weight 1¼ lbs.

Habits.

During the winter season the city of New-Orleans is thronged by natives of almost every land, and the Levee (which is an embankment extending along the margin of the river) presents a scene so unlike anything American, that as we walk along its smooth surface we may imagine ourselves in some twenty different countries, as our eyes fall upon many a strange costume, whose wearer has come from afar, and is, like ourselves, perchance, intent on seeing the curiosities of this Salmagundi city. Here a Spanish gentleman from Cuba, or a Mexican, next a pirate or thief, perhaps, from the same countries; all Europe is here represented, and the languages of many parts of the world can be heard whilst walking even half a mile; the descendants of Africa are here metamorphosed into French folks, and the gay bandanna that turbans the heads of the coloured women, is always adjusted with good taste, and is their favourite head-dress.

But the most interesting figures are the few straggling Choctaw and Chickasaw Indians, who bring a variety of game to the markets, and in their blankets, red flannel leggings, moccasins and bead finery, form a sort of dirty picturesque feature in the motley scene, and generally attract the artist's eye: many of these Indians have well formed legs and bodies, and their half-covered shoulders display a strength and symmetry indicating almost a perfect development of the manly form—their sinews and muscles being as large as is compatible with activity and grace. Whilst conversing with one of these remnants of a once numerous race, it was our good fortune to see for the first time the singular and beautiful little Orange-bellied Squirrel which the Indian hunter had brought with him along with other animals for sale, having procured it in the recesses of the forest on the borders of an extensive swamp.

Rarely indeed does the Orange-bellied Squirrel leave its solitary haunts and quit the cypress or sweet-gum shades, except to feed upon pecan-nuts, berries, persimmons, or other delicacies growing in the uplands; and it does not hoard up the small acorn from the swamp-oak until late in the autumn, knowing that the mild winters of Louisiana are seldom cold enough to prevent it from catching an unlucky beetle from time to time during the middle of the day, or interfere with searches for food among the dry leaves and decaying vegetable substances in the woods. Besides, early in the year the red-maple buds will afford a treat to which this little squirrel turns with as much eagerness as the horse that has been kept all winter upon hay and corn, dashes into a fine field of grass in the month of May.

The hole inhabited by the present species is generally in some tall tree growing in the swamp, and perhaps sixty or one hundred yards from the dry land, and the animal passes to it from tree to tree, or along some fallen monarch of the woods, over the shallow water, keeping his large eye bent upon the surrounding lands in fear of some enemy; and, in faith, he runs no little risk, for should the red-shouldered hawk, or the sharped-shinned, dart upon him, he is an easy prey; or, on a warm day, a snake, called the "water moccasin," curled up in his way, might swallow him, "tail and all." But good fun it must be to see the sportsman following in pursuit, splashing and floundering through the water, sometimes half-leg deep, and at others only up to the ankles, but stumbling occasionally, and making the "water fly;" so that when he *has* a chance to pull trigger, he is certain to snap *both barrels!*

Of the breeding of this species we know nothing, nor can we say more of its habits, which are yet to be farther investigated.

In our plate, by an accidental error, the present species is set down as *Sciurus sub-auratus,* AUD. AND BACH.—it should have been BACHMAN, as the species was originally described in the monograph of the genus sciurus by Dr. BACHMAN, from two specimens sent by J. J. AUDUBON from New Orleans, in 1837.

Geographical Distribution.

We have not heard of the occurrence of this species farther north than Louisiana, and think it probable its range will be found to extend west and south of that state into Texas, and perhaps Mexico.

Putorius Frenata.—Licht.

Bridled Weasel.

Plate lx.—Males. Natural Size.

P. magnitudine P. ermineæ, supra fulvus, infra ex flavicante albus; naso, dorso, majore capitis parte, auribusque nigris; macula inter aures et vitta frontali albis.

Characters.

Size of the ermine; nose, back part of the head, and ears, black; a white spot between the ears, and a band over the forehead, white; yellowish-brown above, yellowish-white beneath.

Synonyme.

MUSTELA FRENATA, Lichtenstein. Darstellung neuer oder wenig bekannter Säugethiere XLII., Tafel. Berlin, 1827–1834.

Description.

This species in form bears a considerable resemblance to the Ermine of the more northern parts of America. It is however rather stouter, the neck shorter, the ears narrower and higher, and the tail a little longer. In its dentition it is also similar to the common weasel, being a true *putorius*, with thirty-four teeth, having only four molars on each side of the upper jaw, and five beneath, whilst the genus *Mustela* is characterized by having thirty-eight teeth, five on each side of the upper jaw, and six beneath. The ears and tail are clothed with hair, the fur is a little shorter and slightly coarser than that of the Ermine.

Colour.

Moustaches, ears on both surfaces, nose, and around the eyes, black; a broad band of white rises in the forehead above the nose, extending around the head between the eyes and ears, reaching the neck and throat including the chin, the colours of which as well as the inner surfaces of the fore-legs are white; there is also a white spot on the back of the head between the ears. The colour is dark brownish black from the neck, reaching the white band on the forehead, where the lines of separation are distinctly but irregularly preserved. On the under surface from the chest to the tail including the inner surface of the thighs, a light fawn colour; tail, the colour of the back till within an inch of the tip, where it gradually darkens into black. The black at the end of the tail is not only shorter but less distinct than the corresponding parts on the ermine in summer colour.

The colour of the back and outer surfaces of the legs is light yellowish brown, gradually darkening on the neck till it reaches and blends with the dark brown colours on the hind head.

Dimensions.

	Inches.
From point of nose to root of tail,	11
Tail (vertebræ),	5
Do. to end of hair,	6
Height of ear,	0½
Breadth of skull,	1⅜
From heel to end of longest nail,	1⅛

Habits.

We have personally no knowledge of the habits of this rare and comparatively new species. The specimen from which Dr. LICHTENSTEIN made his description and figure, was obtained by F. DEPPE, Esq., in the vicinity of the city of Mexico, where the animal was indiscriminately called *Comadreja, Oronzito* and *Onzito.* He was unable to collect any information in regard to its habits. The specimen from which our description and figure were made, was captured by Mr. JOHN K. TOWNSEND. We conversed with an American officer, who informed us that he had occasionally seen it near Monterey in

Plate LX

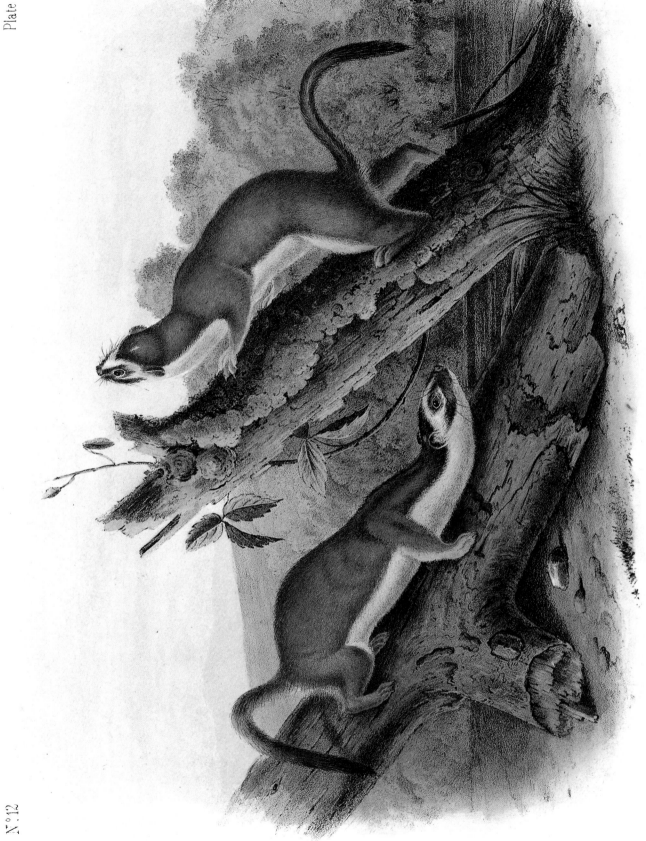

Drawn from Nature by J. Audubon. F.R.S.F.L.S

On Stone by Wᵐ E. Hitchcock

Lith. Printed & Col'd by J.T. Bowen Philad.

Bridled Weasel.

Mexico, that it there bore no better character than its congener the Ermine in the more northern parts of America; that it was destructive to poultry and eggs, and very commonly took up its residence in the outhouses on plantations, and under such circumstances was regarded as as great nuisance. Fortunately for them, the species was considered as quite rare in the northern parts of Mexico, as the Mexican who pointed out this animal to our officer stated, this was the first *Comadreja* he had seen in five years.

Geographical Distribution.

As we have not heard of the existence of our Ermine in Mexico, we are inclined to the belief that this species takes the place of the Ermine in the South, and that with similar roving and predacious habits it has a more extended geographical range than is at present known. The field of natural history in Texas, California, and Mexico, has been as yet very imperfectly explored. We have only heard of the Bridled Weasel as being found in four widely separated localities—in Texas between the Colorado and Rio Grande, in Mexico in the vicinity of the capital, and in the northern parts near Monterey, and in the valleys of the mountains south-west of that city.

General Remarks.

In comparing this singularly marked species with others from the Eastern and Western hemispheres, we have been struck with the uniformity existing on both continents in the nearly equal distribution of predacious animals, and in their close resemblance to each other, in size, form and habits. The badger in Europe (*Meles vulgaris*) is in America replaced by *M. Labradoria*. The European Otter (*Lutra vulgaris*) has its representative in America in our Canada otter (*Lutra Canadensis*). The European mink (*P. lutreola*) is replaced by our nearly similar (*P. vison*). The European ferret (*P. furo*) by our western black-footed ferret (*P. nigripes*). The ermine and common weasel of the north of Europe (*P. erminea*) and (*P. vulgaris*) by our ermine and brown weasel (*P. erminea*) and (*P. fusca*) in the Northern and Middle States of America, and the Java ferret (*P. nudipes*) has its representative near the tropics in America in our (*P. frenata*), nearly of the same size, and with similar habits. There is evidently great wisdom in this arrangement of Providence. Countries under similar latitudes producing large numbers of the smaller rodentia, require a certain number of carnivorous animals to prevent their too rapid multiplication, which in the absence of such a provision of nature would be destructive of the interests of the husbandman.

Genus Procyon.—Storr.

Dental Formula.

Incisive $\frac{6}{6}$; *Canine* $\frac{1-1}{1-1}$; *Molar* $\frac{6-6}{6-6}$ = 40.

Muzzle, pointed and projecting beyond the lower jaw; ears, short and oval; tail, bushy, and long. Feet, five toed, with strong nails not retractile; soles of feet, (posterior,) naked; the species rest on the heel, but walk on the toes. Mammæ, six ventral; there is a gland on each side of the anus which secretes a slightly offensive fluid.

The generic name is derived from the Greek πϱο, before, and χυων, a dog.

Two species only have been noticed: one in the northern, and the other in the southern parts of North America.

Procyon Lotor.—Linn.

Raccoon.

Plate lxi.—Male. Natural Size.

P. corpore supra canescente plus minus in nigrum vergente, infra, auriculis pedibusque albicantibus; facie albida, fascia sub oculari obliqua nigra, cauda rufescente annulis 4–5 nigris.

Characters.

Body above, grayish mixed with black; ears, and beneath, whitish; a black patch across the eye. Tail with 4 or 5 annulations of black and gray.

Synonymes.

ARECON, Smith's Voyages, xiii., p. 31.
URSUS LOTOR, Linn., 12th ed., p. 70.
    "   "   Erxleben, Syst., p. 165–4.
    "   "   Schreber Säugth., p. 521, 5 t. 143.
LE RATON, Buffon, vol. viii., p. 337, t. xliii.
RACCOON BEAR, Pennant's Arct. Zool., vol. i., p. 69.
PROCYON LOTOR, Cuv., Règne Animal, vol. i., p. 143.
    "   "   Sabine, Journal, p. 649.
    "   "   Harlan, p. 53.
    "   "   Godman, vol. i., p. 53.
    "   "   Dekay, New-York Fauna, p. 26.
PROCYON NIVEA, Gray, Magazine of Nat. Hist., vol. i., 1837, p. 580.

Description.

The body is rather stout, the legs of moderate length, and the appearance of the animal would indicate that although he is not intended for great speed, he is still by his compact and well organized structure, his strong and muscular limbs and short and stout claws, capable of a tolerably rapid race, and is able to climb, although not with the agility of the squirrel, still with greater alacrity than his near relative the bear.

Head, rather round; nose, tapering, sharp, and the snout moveable; point of the nose, naked; eyes, round, and of moderate size; moustaches, few, very rigid, resembling bristles, extending to the chin; ears, low, erect, elliptical, with their tips much rounded, clothed with hair on both sides; on the inner surface the hairs are longer and less dense; tail, of moderate length and bushy. In its feet the Raccoon is partially plantigrade, hence it was classed by LINNÆUS among the bears, under the genus *Ursus*; soles of feet, naked. When it sits, it often brings the whole hind sole to the ground, resting in the manner of the bear. The canine teeth are large and extend beyond the lips. The nails are strong, hooked and sharp, not covered with hair. The body is densely clothed with two kinds of hair; the outer and longer, long and coarse; the inner, softer and more like wool.

Colour.

Point of nose, and soles of feet, black; nails, dark brown; moustaches, nearly all white; ears, lips, above the snout and chin, dingy white; above the eyes, and around the forehead, light gray. A dark brown patch extends from each side of the neck and passes the eyes, over the nose, nearly reaching the snout, and gradually fading on the forehead into the colours of the back; eyes, black; the longer hairs on the back are dark brown at the roots, then yellowish-white for half their length, and are broadly tipped with black; the softer fur beneath, pale brown throughout the whole body; on the sides and belly, the longer hairs and dingy white from the roots; the tail has about six distinct black rings, and is tipped with black; these rings alternate with five light yellowish-brown annulations.

Dimensions.

Old male, received from Dr. JOHN WRIGHT.

	Inches.
Nose to anterior canthus,	$1\frac{3}{8}$
" " corner of mouth,	$2\frac{1}{4}$
" " root of ear,	$7\frac{3}{8}$
" " " of tail,	$26\frac{1}{2}$
Tail, (vertebræ),	8
" to end of hair,	$9\frac{1}{2}$
Length of head,	$7\frac{1}{2}$
Breadth of head,	$4\frac{1}{8}$

Weight, 22 lbs.

Habits.

The Raccoon is a cunning animal, is easily tamed, and makes a pleasant

On Stone by W. el. Hitchcock.

Raccoon.

Drawn from Nature by J. W. Audubon   Lith. Printed & Col.ᵈ by J.T. Bowen, Phil.

monkey-like pet. It is quite dexterous in the use of its fore-feet, and will amble after its master in the manner of a bear, and even follow him into the streets. It is fond of eggs, and devours them raw or cooked with avidity, but prefers them raw of course, and if it finds a nest will feast on them morning, noon and night without being satiated. It will adroitly pick its keeper's pockets of anything it likes to eat, and is always on the watch for dainties. The habits of the muscles (*unios*) that inhabit our fresh water rivers are better known to the Raccoon than to most conchologists, and their flavour is as highly relished by this animal as is that of the best bowl of clam soup by the epicure in that condiment.

Being an expert climber, the Raccoon ascends trees with facility and frequently invades the nest of the woodpecker, although it may be secure against ordinary thieves, by means of his fore-feet getting hold of the eggs or the young birds. He watches too the soft-shelled turtle when she is about to deposit her eggs, for which purpose she leaves the water and crawling on to the white sand-bar, digs a hole and places them underneath the heated surface. Quickly does the rogue dig up the elastic ova, although ever so carefully covered, and appropriate them to his own use, notwithstanding the efforts of the luckless turtle to conceal them.

Sometimes, by the margin of a pond, shrouded, or crouched among tall reeds and grasses, Grimalkin-like, the Raccoon lies still as death, waiting with patience for some ill-fated duck that may come within his reach. No negro on a plantation knows with more accuracy when the corn (maize) is juicy and ready for the connoisseur in roasting ears, and he does not require the aid of fire to improve its flavour, but attacks it more voraciously than the squirrel or the blackbird, and is the last to quit the cornfield.

The favourite resorts of the Raccoon are retired swampy lands well covered with lofty trees, and through which are small water-courses. In such places its tracks may be seen following the margins of the bayous and creeks, which it occasionally crosses in search of frogs and muscles which are found on their banks. It also follows the margins of rivers for the same purpose, and is dexterous in getting at the shell-fish, notwithstanding the hardness of the siliceous covering with which nature has provided them. In dry seasons, the receding waters sometimes leave the muscles exposed to the heat of the sun, which destroys their life and causes their shells to open, leaving them accessible to the first animal or bird that approaches.

In the dreary months of winter should you be encamped in any of the great Western forests, obliged by the pitiless storm to remain for some days, as we have been, you will not be unthankful if you have a fat Raccoon suspended on a tree above your camp, for when kept awhile, the flesh of this species is both tender and well-flavoured.

The Raccoon when full grown and in good condition we consider quite a handsome animal. We have often watched him with interest, cautiously moving from one trunk to another to escape his view. His bright eye, however, almost invariably detected us ere we could take aim at him, and he adroitly fled into a hollow tree and escaped from us.

We once met with one of these animals whilst we were travelling on horseback from Henderson to Vincennes, on the edge of a large prairie in a copse, and on approaching it ran up a small sapling from which we shook it off with ease; but as soon as it reached the ground it opened its mouth and made directly towards us, and looked so fierce, that drawing a pistol from our holsters, we shot it dead when it was only a few feet from us.

The young are at their birth quite small; (about the size of a half-grown rat;) some that we saw in Texas were not more than two days old and were kept in a barrel. They uttered a plaintive cry not unlike the wail of an infant.

The Raccoon usually produces from four to six young at a time, which are generally brought forth early in May, although the period of their littering varies in different latitudes.

When the Indian corn is ripening, the Raccoons invade the fields to feast on the rich milky grain, as we have just stated, and as the stalks are too weak to bear the weight of these marauders, they generally break them down with their fore-paws, tear off the husks from the ears, and then munch them at their leisure. During this inviting season, the Raccoon is not the only trespasser on the corn fields, but various animals are attracted thither to receive their portion, and even the merry school-boy shares the feast with them, at the risk of paying for his indulgence by incurring the necessity of a physician's prescription the next day. The havoc committed in the Western States by squirrels and other animals is almost incalculable, and no vigilance of the farmer can guard against the depredations of these hungry intruders, which extend from farm to farm, and even penetrate to those embosomed in the forests, where settlements are few and far between.

The Raccoon is not strictly a nocturnal animal; and although it generally visits the corn fields at night, sometimes feeds on the green corn during the day; we have seen it thus employed during the heat of summer, and it will occasionally enter a poultry house at mid-day, and destroy many of the feathered inhabitants, contenting itself with the head and blood of the fowls it kills.

The nest or lair of the Raccoon is usually made in the hollow of some broken branch of a tree. When tamed, these animals are seldom induced to lie or sleep on a layer of straw.

There exists a species of oyster in the Southern States of inferior quality which bears the name of Raccoon Oyster: it lies imbedded in masses in the shallow waters of the rivers. These oysters are covered by high tides, but are exposed at low water. On these the Raccoons are fond of feeding, and we have on several occasions seen them on the oyster banks. We have however never had an opportunity of ascertaining by personal observation the accuracy of a statement which we have frequently heard made with great confidence, viz., that the Raccoon at low tide in endeavouring to extricate these oysters from the shell, is occasionally caught by the foot in consequence of the closing of the valve of the shell fish, when numbers of these being clustered and imbedded together, the Raccoon cannot drag them from their bed, and the returning tide drowns him.

The naturalist has many difficulties to encounter when inquiring into facts connected with his pursuit: every one acquainted with the habits of even our common species must know, that the information gained from most of those who reside near their localities, from their want of particular observation, is generally very limited, and probably the most interesting knowledge gained by such queries, would be the result of a comparison of the accounts given at different places. From the Alleghany mountains, the swamps of Louisiana, and the marshes of Carolina, we have received nearly the same history of the cunning manœuvres and sly tricks of the Raccoon in procuring food.

We add the following notes on a Raccoon kept for a considerable time in a tame state or partially domesticated.

When it first came into our possession it was about one-third grown. By kind treatment it soon became very docile, but from its well known mischievous propensities we always kept it chained.

It was truly omnivorous: never refusing any thing eatable, vegetable or animal, cooked or uncooked, all was devoured with equal avidity. Of some articles however it seemed particularly fond: as sugar, honey, chestnuts, fish and poultry. The animal would become almost frantic when either of the two first was placed near it, but beyond its reach. No means would be left untried to obtain the dainty morsel. It would rush forward as far as the chain permitted, and stretch out a fore-paw toward the object of its wishes to its utmost extent, which failing to reach it, the other was extended; again disappointed, the hind limbs were tried in succession, by which there was a nearer approach to the food, on account of the animal being chained by the neck.

On being offered food when hungry, or roused up suddenly from any cause, or when in active play, the eye was of a lustrous green, changing apparently the whole countenance.

It had a strong propensity to roll food and other things under its paws; segars in particular, especially when lighted. We have observed a similar propensity in young bears.

On placing a pail of water within its reach, it ran to it, and after drinking would examine the contents to the bottom with the fore-paws, seemingly expecting to find some fish or frog. If any thing was found it was speedily brought to the surface and scrutinized. We have seen it throw chips, bits of china and pebbles, &c., into the pail, and then fish them out for amusement, but never saw it put a particle of its food in to soak, except in a few instances when it threw in hard corn, but we do not think it was for this purpose.

After playing for a short time in the water it would commonly urinate in it and then upset the pail.

We gave it a fish weighing two pounds. The Raccoon turned it in all directions in search of a convenient point of attack. The mouth, nose, fins, vent, &c., were tried. At length an opening was made at the vent, into which a paw was deeply inserted; the intestines were withdrawn and eaten with avidity. At the same time an attempt was made to insert the other paw into the mouth of the fish to meet its fellow. This disposition to use the paws in concert, was shown in almost every action, sometimes in a very ludicrous manner. On giving the animal a jug, one paw would be inserted in the aperture, and a hundred twists and turns would be made to join its fellow on the outside.

After devouring as much of the fish as it wished, it placed the paws on the remainder and lay down to doze, until hunger returned, watching the favourite food, and growling at any animal which happened to pass near it. By degrees this propensity to defend its food passed off, and it would allow the dog or fox to partake of it freely. We placed a half-grown fox within its reach: the Raccoon instantly grasped it with its legs and paws and commenced a close examination. It thrust its pointed nose in the ear of the fox to the very bottom, smelling and snuffing as if determined to find out the nature of the animal. During this time it showed no disposition to injure the fox.

The Raccoon can scent an object for some distance with accuracy. We suffered ours to go loose on one occasion, when it made directly for some small marmots confined in a cage in another room.

Our pet Raccoon whose habits we are relating evinced a singular propensity to listen to things at a distance, however many persons were around him, even though he might be at the moment eating a frog, of which food he was very fond. He would apparently hear some distant noise, then raise his head and continue listening, seeming every moment more absorbed; at last he would suddenly run and hide himself in his burrow. This seems to be connected with some instinct of the animal in his wild state, probably whilst sitting on a tree sunning himself, when he is in the habit of listening to hear the approach of an enemy, and then hurrying to his hole in the tree.

Enjoying the hospitality of a friend one night at his plantation, the conversation turned on the habits of animals: and in speaking of the Raccoon he mentioned that it fed on birds and rabbits generally, but in winter robbed the poultry houses. The negroes on his plantation he said kept good dogs, and relied on them for hunting the Raccoon.

Whenever a Raccoon was about to attack the poultry house, the dogs scenting him give a shrill cry, which is the signal for his owner to commence the hunt. He comes out armed with an axe, with a companion or two, resolved on a Raccoon hunt. The dog soon gives chase with such rapidity, that the Raccoon, hard pressed, takes to a tree. The dog, close at his heels, changes his whining cry while running to a shrill short sharp bark. If the tree is small or has limbs near the ground so that it can be easily ascended, the eager hunters climb up after the "coon." He perceives his danger, endeavours to avoid his pursuers by ascending to the farthest topmost branch, or the extremity of a limb; but all his efforts are in vain, his relentless pursuers shake the limb until he is compelled to let go his hold, and he comes toppling heavily to the ground, and is instantly seized by the dogs. It frequently happens however that the trees are tall and destitute of lower branches so that they cannot be climbed without the risk of life or limb. The negroes survey for a few moments in the bright moonlight the tall and formidable tree that shelters the coon, grumble a little at the beast for not having saved them trouble by mounting an easier tree, and then the ringing of their axes resounds through the still woods, awakening echoes of the solitude previously disturbed only by the hooting of the owl, or the impatient barking of the dogs. In half an hour the tree, is brought to the ground and with it the Raccoon, stunned by the fall: his foes give him no time to define his position, and after a short and bloody contest with the dogs, he is despatched, and the sable hunters remunerated,—for his skin they will sell to the hatters in the nearest town, and his flesh they will hang up in a tree to freeze and furnish them with many a savoury meal.

The greatest number of Raccoons, however, are killed by log-traps set with a figure of 4 trigger, and baited with a bird or squirrel, an ear of corn, or a fish: either the appetite or curiosity of these animals will entice them into a trap or entangle them in a snare.

Another mode of destroying this species is by fire-hunting, which requires good shooting, as the animal only shows one eye from behind the branch of a tree, which reflecting the light of the fire-hunter's torch, shines like a ball of phosphorus, and is generally knocked out at twenty-five or thirty yards by a good marksman.

The Raccoon, like the bear, hibernates for several months during winter in the latitude of New-York, and only occasionally and in a warm day leaves its retreat, which is found in the hollow of some large tree. We once however tracked in deep snow the footsteps of a pair of this species in the northern parts of New-York, and obtained them by having the tree in which they lay concealed cut down. They had made a circle in company of about a mile, and then returned to their winter domicil.

The specimen from which the representation on our plate was taken was a remarkably fine male, and was sent to us alive by our friend, the late Dr. JOHN WRIGHT of Troy, New-York.

Geographical Distribution.

The Raccoon has a very extensive geographical range. Captain Cook saw skins at Nootka Sound which were supposed to be those of the Raccoon. DIXON and PARLTOCK obtained Raccoon skins from the natives of Cook's River in latitude 60°. It is supposed by RICHARDSON that this animal extends farther north on the shores of the Pacific, than it does on the eastern side of the Rocky Mountains. He farther states, that the Hudson's Bay Company procured about one hundred skins from the southern parts of the fur districts as far north as Red River, latitude 50°. We have not been able to trace it on the Atlantic coast farther north than Newfoundland. It is found in the Eastern, Northern and Middle States, and seems to become more abundant as we proceed southwardly. In some of the older States its numbers have greatly diminished, in consequence of the clearing of the forests, and the incessant wars waged against it by the hunters. In South Carolina, Georgia, Alabama, Mississippi and Louisiana, it is still found in great numbers, is regarded as a nuisance to the corn fields, and is at particular seasons hunted at night by sportsmen and negroes. We have been informed by our friend DANIEL MORRISON, Esq., of Madison Springs in Georgia, that in his frequent visits to Arkansas between the Washita and Red Rivers, the Raccoons are very plentiful and are frequently seen travelling about in open day, and that many corn fields are nearly destroyed by the Raccoon and the bear.

It was seen by LEWIS and CLARK at the mouth of the Columbia river. We possess several specimens obtained in Texas, and were informed by a friend, that although he had not seen it in California, he had heard of its existence in the northern parts of that State.

General Remarks.

As might be expected, an occasional variety is found in this species.

We possess a specimen nearly black; another yellowish white, with the annulations in the tail faint and indistinct. A nest of young was found in Christ Church parish in South Carolina, two of which were of the usual colour, the other two were white; one of them was sent to us; it was an albino, with red eyes, and all the hairs were perfectly white with the exception of faint traces of rings on the tail. We have no doubt that a similar variety was described by GRAY, under the name of *Procyon nivea*.

We have accordingly added his name as a synonyme. Our friend Dr. SAMUEL GEORGE MORTON of Philadelphia kept one for some time alive which was of a yellowish cream colour, and was also and albino.

Genus Elaphus.—Griffith.

Dental Formula.

Incisive $\frac{0}{8}$; *Canine* $\frac{1-1}{0-0}$; *Molar* $\frac{6-6}{6-6} = 34$.

Horns, (existing only in the male,) round; very large; antlers terminating in a fork or in snags from a common centre, suborbital sinus; canine teeth in the male, in the upper jaw; a muzzle.

The generic name is derived from the Greek Ελαφος, a Stag, or Elk; the name was applied by PLINY, LINNÆUS, and other naturalists, to designate a particular species existing in Europe, *Cervus Elaphus*.

Three well-determined species may be arranged under this genus; one existing in Europe, one in Walhihii, (the Nepaul Stag,) and one in America.

Elaphus Canadensis.—Ray.

American Elk.—Wapite Deer.

Plate lxii. Male and Female. Natural size.

E. Cervus Virginianus robustior cornibus amplissimis ramosis teretibus, frontalibus amplis; cauda brevissima. Color rufescens, hieme fuscescens, uropygio flavicante stria nigra circumscripto.

Characters.

Larger than the Virginian deer. Horns, large, not palmated, with brow antlers; a naked space round the lachrymal opening. Tail, short. Colour, yellowish-brown above, a black mark extending from the angle of the mouth along the sides of the lower jaw. A broad pale yellowish spot on the buttocks.

Synonymes.

STAG, Pennant, Arctic Zool., vol. i., p. 27.
WEWASKISS, Hearne, Journal, p. 360.
RED DEER, Umfreville.
Do.   do.   Ray, Synops. Quad., p. 84.

C. STRONGYLOCEROS, Schreber, Säugethiere, vol. ii., p. 1074, pl. 247, F. q. G.
ALCES AMERICANUS, Jefferson's Notes on Virginia, p. 77.
THE ELK, Lewis and Clark, vol. ii., p. 167.
C. WAPTITE, Barton, Med. and Phys. Journal, vol. i., p. 36.
ELK, Smith, Med. Reports, vol. ii., p. 157, fig. Male, Female, and Young.
CERVUS (ELAPHUS) CANADENSIS, (The Wapite,) Synopsis of the Species of Mammalia. Griffith's Cuvier, p. 776.
C. CANADENSIS, Harlan, p. 236.
Do.   do.   Godman, vol. ii., p. 294, fig. Male.
CERVUS STRONGYLOCEROS, Richardson, (The Wapite.) p. 251.
ELAPHUS CANADENSIS, Dekay, New-York Fauna, p. 118, plate 28, fig. 2.

Description.

The Elk is of an elegant, stately and majestic form, and the whole animal is in admirable proportion. It bears so strong a resemblance to the red deer of Europe, that it was for a long time regarded as a mere variety of the same species. It is, however, much larger in size, and on closer examination differs from it in many particulars.

Head, of moderate size; muzzle, broad and long, rather small, not very prominent; ears, large; legs, rather stout, finely proportioned; hoofs, rather small.

From between the horns to the end of the frontal bone, beyond the nasal opening sixteen inches, length of horns following the curvature of the main branch four feet; with all the roots three and a quarter inches, by two and a quarter thick. There are six points on each horn, irregularly disposed, varying in length from nine to sixteen inches, excepting one which is two and a half inches only in length. At their points the horns curb backward and upward, and are about three feet five inches apart, at about half the distance from their roots to the extreme tip of the longest point or main branch. The horns at the insertion are three and three-quarter inches apart from the ring or crown at their roots.

In examining a number of elk horns we find a very remarkable variety, no two antlers being exactly alike on the same animal. We possess one pair which has a blunt prong extending downward on the right side of the face about nine inches, whilst the corresponding prong on the opposite side is turned upwards. The horns of this individual have five prongs on one horn and seven on the other. The horns are longitudinally channelled, most of the prongs inclining forward and upward, especially those nearest the roots of the main horn. All the horns are large and round, with brow antlers. The weight of the horns on full grown animals, as we have ascertained by weighing about a dozen of large size, is from thirty to forty-five pounds.

The three hindermost teeth in the upper jaw are double; the remainder single. There are in the upper jaw of the male two very small canine teeth inclining forward almost on a line with the jaw. There is a short rudimentary mane on the fore-shoulder, and under the throat during the winter there are long black hairs.

There is a space on the outer side of the hind legs covered by a tuft, which is of an irregular oval shape, of about one and a half inch in length, the hairs which cover it being an inch long, lying flat and backwards, with shorter hairs extending down the leg several inches below the space.

The hairs on the body generally are very coarse, rather short; longest on the back of the ham, where the whitish patch and the black line on the latter unite.

The tail, which in summer is not bushy, is thinly clothed with hair running to a point. A young male has its horns which are in velvet, nearly perpendicular, running but slightly backwards to the length of fourteen inches, where they divide into three short prongs.

Colour.

Male.

Muzzle, nostrils, and hoofs, black; head, dark brown; neck, rather darker, being nearly black; on each side of the under jaw there is a longitudinal white patch, between which there is a large black stripe extending along the lines of the under jaw, dividing about four inches from the mouth, and continuing downward to the throat, where it unites again and is diffused in the general black colour of the throat and neck, leaving in its course a white space between the bone of the lower jaw, nearly as large as a man's hand.

There is no light-coloured ring, or space, around the eyes as in the European red deer, but in the present species the space around the socket of the eye is scarcely a shade lighter than the surrounding parts of the head.

Under surface of the ear, yellowish white, with a hue of dark brown on the margin; on the outer surface of the ear, there is a white patch about four inches in length and nearly two inches wide, covering about a third of the ear, and running from near the root of the ear upwards at the lower edge.

In the younger males the head, face and back of the neck are not nearly as dark as in specimens of old animals; the under jaw and throat however as well as a space above the nostrils are black as in the latter. The upper and under surfaces of body and legs are light brownish gray, the legs being rather darker than the body.

On the rump there is a broad patch of light grayish white commencing nine inches above the root of the tail, spreading downward on each side to a point in the ham, ten inches below the tail. It is fourteen inches across opposite the root of the tail, (from one ham to the other,) and twenty-two inches in length from the back to the termination on the thigh or ham below the tail. This grayish white patch is bordered on the thighs by a strongly marked black space which also separates it all around, although less conspicuously from the general colour of the body. We have observed that in young specimens this pale mark on the rump is less conspicuous, and in one specimen is not even perceptible, and this peculiarity has most probably misled some of our authors in regard to the species.

In specimens of about two years old the light but scarcely perceptible markings on the rump gradually change to grayish brown between the hind legs. In a still younger specimen of a male about eighteen months old which has the horns three inches in height, (which are completely clothed with soft brownish hairs to their summits,) there is scarcely any black on the neck, and the white on the rump is not visible.

Female in summer colour.

We possess this animal in a state of confinement: she has like all the females of this species no horns. She bears a strong resemblance in form and colour to the male. Her neck is rather thinner and longer, and her legs and body more slender. Her eyes are mild, and she is in her disposition very gentle and docile. The hair in summer is like that of the male, uniform in colour from the roots to the surface.

Winter colour.

Both males and females in winter assume a very heavy coat of dark gray hair all over the body. These hairs are about two and a half inches to three long and are moderately coarse and strong.

When examined separately they have a wavy or crimped appearance. The white patch on the rump is strongly developed in contrast with the dark iron-gray colour of the winter coat. At this season the male has a remarkable growth of hairs on the throat as well as on the back of the neck, which increase considerably in length, so that the latter might easily be mistaken for the rudiment of a mane.

Dimensions.

Adult male (killed on the Upper Missouri River).

	Feet.	Inches.
From nose to root of tail,	7	8¾
Length of tail,	0	1¾
" of eye,	0	1¾
From tip of nose to root of ear,	1	8
Length of ear,	0	9¼
Height to shoulders,	4	10
Rump,	5	2
Girth back of fore-legs,	5	6½

The females we measured were rather smaller than the above: one killed on the Yellow Stone River measured seven feet six and a half inches from nose to root of tail, and four feet seven inches from top of shoulder to the ground.

Habits.

On our plate we have represented a pair of Elks in the foreground of a prairie scene, with a group of small figures in the distance; it gives but a faint idea of this animal in its wild and glorious prairie home: Observe the splendid buck, as he walks lightly, proudly, and gracefully along. It is the season of love: his head is raised above the willows bordering the large sand-bar on the shores of the Missouri, his spreading antlers have acquired their full growth, the velvet has been rubbed off, and they are hard and polished. His large amber-coloured eyes are brightened by the sun, his neck is arched, and every vein is distended. He looks around and snuffs the morning air with dilated nostrils: anon he

No. 13

Plate LXII

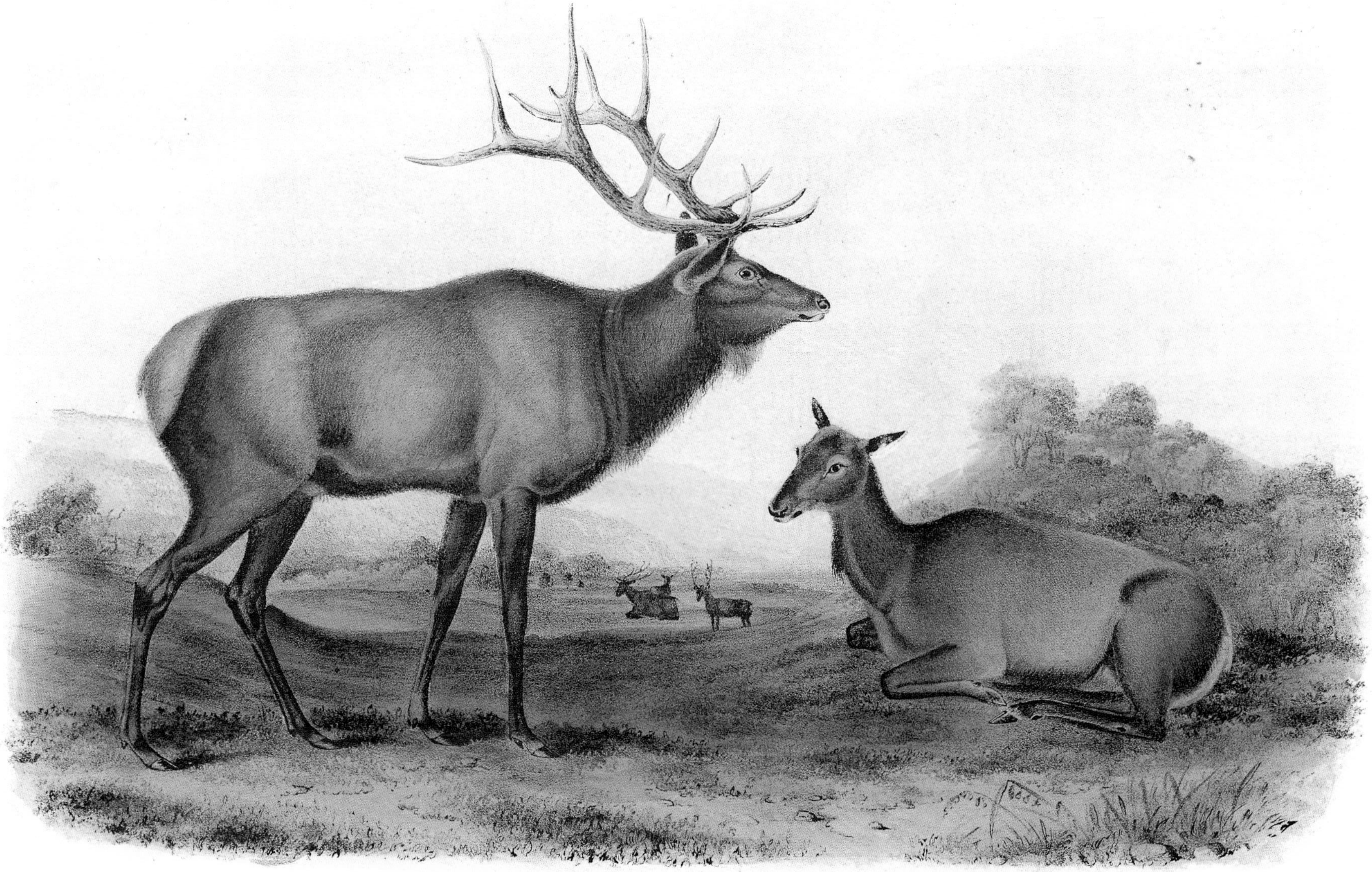

On Stone by W.E. Hitchcock

Drawn from Nature by J.J. Audubon, F.R.S.F.L.S.

American Elk_ Wapiti Deer

Lith. Printed & Col.d by J.T. Bowen Phil.

stamps the earth with his fore-feet and utters a shrill cry somewhat like the noise made by the loon. When he discovers a group of females he raises his head, inclines it backwards, and giving another trumpet-like whistle, dashes off to meet them, making the willows and other small trees yield and crack as he rushes by. He soon reaches the group, but probably finds as large and brave a buck as himself gallanting the fair objects of his pursuit, and now his eyes glow with rage and jealousy, his teeth are fiercely champed together making a loud harsh noise, his hair stands erect, and with the points of his immense horns lowered like the lance of a doughty knight in times of yore, he leaps towards his rival and immediately a desperate battle ensues. The furious combatants sway backwards and forwards, sideways or in circles, each struggling to get within the other's point, twisting their brawny necks, and writhing as they endeavour to throw their opponent off the ground. At length our valorous Elk triumphs and gores the other, so that he is worsted in the fight, and turns ingloriously and flies, leaving the field and the females in possession of the victor: for should there be any young Elks present during such a combat, they generally run off.

The victorious buck now ranges the tangled woods or leads the does to the sand-bars or the willow-covered points along the broad stream. After a certain period, however, he leaves them to other bucks, and towards the latter part of February his antlers drop off, his body is much emaciated, and he retires to some secluded spot, where he hopes no enemies will discover him, as he is no longer vigorous and bold, and would dread to encounter even a single wolf.

When we first settled (as it is termed) in the State of Kentucky, some of these animals were still to be met with; but at present we believe none are to be found within hundreds of miles of our then residence. During a journey we made through the lower part of the State, armed as usual with our double-barrelled gun, whilst passing through a heavy-timbered tract not far from Smithland at the mouth of the Cumberland River, we espied two Elks, a male and female, which started out of a thicket not more than forty or fifty yards from us. Our gun being loaded with balls, we fired successfully and brought down the buck. The tavern keeper at Smithland went after the animal with a wagon and brought him into the little village. The hunters in the neighbourhood said they had not seen or heard of Elks in that part of the State for several years, although some were to be found across the Ohio, in the state of Illinois.

At the time we are writing (1847) the Elk is not seen in any numbers until you ascend the Missouri River for a great distance. In that part of the country, where the points in the river are well covered with wood and under-brush, they are to be found to times in considerable numbers. These animals however do not confine themselves to the neighbourhood of the water-courses, but roam over the prairies in large herds. Unless disturbed or chased, they seldom leave a secluded retreat in a thickly-wooded dell, except to go to the river to drink, or sun themselves on the sand-bars. They are partial to the islands covered with willow, cotton wood, &c., and fringed with long grass, upon which they make a bed during the hot sultry hours of the day. They also form a bed occasionally in the top of a fallen tree.

During hot weather, when mosquitoes abound in the woods, they retire to ponds or proceed to the rivers and immerse their bodies and heads, leaving merely enough of their noses above the water to allow them to breathe.

Whilst ascending the Missouri river in the steamer Omega, we observed a fawn of this species one morning running along the shore under a high bank. It was covered with yellowish white spots, was as nimble and active as a kitten, and soon reached a place where it could ascend the bank, when it scampered off amid the tall grass. We had on board a servant of Mr. CHARDON named ALEXIS LABOMBARDE who was a most expert hunter. We soon saw another fawn, and ALEXIS went after it, the boat having stopped to wood. He climbed the bank and soon overtook the little animal, but having no rope or cord with him, was at a loss how to secure his captive. He took off his suspenders and with these and his pocket-handkerchief managed to fasten the fawn around the neck, but on attempting to drag it toward the boat the suspenders gave way and the fawn dropped into the stream, and swam a few yards lower down, where it again landed; one of our party witnessed from the steamboat the ineffectual efforts of LABOMBARDE and ran up to his assistance, but also without a rope or cord, and after much ado the animal again swam off and escaped.

The food of the Elk consists generally of the grass found in the woods, the wild pea-vines, the branches of willows, lichens, and the buds of roses, &c. During the winter they scrape the snow from the ground with their fore-feet, and eat the tender roots and bark of shrubs and small trees.

On our reaching Fort Pierre we were presented by Mr. PICOT with a most splendidly prepared skin of a superb male Elk, and a pair of horns. The latter measured four feet six and a half inches in length; breadth between the points twenty-seven and a half inches. The circumference of the skull or base ten inches, the knob twelve inches, between the knobs three inches. This animal,

one of the largest ever seen by Mr. PICOT, was killed in the month of November, 1832.

HEARNE says that the Elk is the most stupid of all the deer kind; but our experience has led us widely to differ from that traveller, as we have always found these animals as wary and cunning as any of the deer tribe with which we are acquainted. We strongly suspect HEARNE had reference to another species, the American reindeer.

We chanced one day to land on a sand-bar covered with the broad deep tracks of apparently some dozen Elks: all the hunters we had in our boat prepared to join in the chase, and we among the rest, with our old trusty double-barrelled gun, sallied forth, and while passing through a large patch of willows, came suddenly upon a very large buck; the noble animal was not more than a few steps from where we stood: our gun was levelled in an instant, and we pulled trigger, but the cap did not explode. The Elk was startled by the noise of the falling hammer, and wheeling round, throwing up the loose soil with his hoofs galloped off among the willows towards the river, making a clear path through the small trees and grass. We ran to intercept him, but were too late, and on reaching the bank the Elk was already far out in the stream, swimming rapidly with its shoulders and part of its back above water. On the opposite shore there was a narrow beach, and the moment the Elk touched the bottom, it sprang forward and in a bound or two was out of sight behind the fringing margin of trees on the shore. This, we are sorry to say, was the only Elk we had an opportunity of firing at whilst on our last western expedition.

The pair from which the figures on our plate were taken we purchased at Philadelphia: they had been caught when young in the western part of Pennsylvania; the male was supposed to be four or five years old, and the female also was full grown. These Elks were transported from Philadelphia to our place near New-York, and we had a capacious and high enclosure made for them. The male retained much of its savage habits when at liberty, but the female was quite gentle. When she was first put in the pen, where the buck was already pacing round seeking for a weak point in the enclosure, he rushed towards her, and so terrified her that she made violent exertions to escape, and ran at full speed with her head up and her nostrils distended, round and round, until we had the large box in which she had been brought up from Philadelphia placed in the enclosure, when she entered it as a place of refuge, and with her head towards the opening stood on her defence, on which the male gave up the pursuit, and this box was afterwards resorted to whenever she wished to be undisturbed.

We had some difficulty in taking the bridle off from the head of the buck, as he kicked and pranced furiously whenever any one approached for that purpose, and we were forced to secure his head by means of a lasso over his horns, and drawing him by main force to a strong post, when one of our men cut the leather with a knife.

While these two Elks were kept by us they were fed on green oats, hay, Indian corn, and all such food as generally is given to the cow, excepting turnips, which they would not touch.

We found that the pair daily ate as much food as would have sufficed for two horses. They often whistled (as the hunters call this remarkable noise, which in calm weather can be heard nearly a mile); this shrill sound appears to be produced by an almost spasmodic effort, during which the animal turns its head upwards and then backwards. While we were outlining the male, we often observed him to dilate the lachrymal spaces or openings adjoining the eyes, so that they were almost as wide as long. When we drew near he would incline his head sideways, curl back his upper lip, and show a portion of his tongue and fine teeth, which last he ground or grated together, turning his head the while from side to side, and eyeing us with a look of angry suspicion. His eyes enlarged, and his whole figure partook of the excitement he felt.

The process of rubbing off the velvet from the horns was soon accomplished by this animal; he began the moment he had been taken out of his box, to rub against the small dog-wood and other trees that stood within the enclosure. At a later period of the year we have observed the Elk rubbing his antlers against small trees, and acting as if engaged in fight; whether this manœuvre be performed for the purpose of loosening the horns, towards the period when they annually drop off, we, in parliamentary language, are not prepared to say.

Elks at times congregate from the number of fifty to several hundreds, and in these cases the whole herd follow the movements of their leader, which is generally the largest and the strongest male of the party. They all stop when he stops, and at times they will all turn about with as much order and with far greater celerity than a troop of horse, of which, when thus seen in array, they forcibly remind us.

From accident or otherwise great differences exist in the formation of the antlers of the Elk, although the horns of all the American *Cervii* are so specifically distinct as to enable the close observer to tell almost at a glance to what species any shown to him belonged. The ease with which these animals pass, encumbered with their ponderous and wide-spreading antlers, through the heavy-timbered lands of the West, is truly marvellous; and we can hardly help wondering that they are not oftener caught and entangled by their horns. Instances there doubtless are of their perishing from getting fastened between vines, or thick growing trees, but such cases are rare.

The male Elk drops his horns in February or March. The one we had dropped one on the ninth of March, and as the other horn held on for a day or two longer, the animal in this situation had quite an awkward appearance. After the horns fall, the head looks sore, and sometimes the places from which they have been detached are tinged with blood. As soon as the huge antlers drop off, the Elks lose their fierce and pugnacious character, and the females are no longer afraid of them; while on the other hand, the males show them no farther attentions whatever.

The young, sometimes one, but usually two in number, are brought forth in the latter end of May of June. It is stated by GODMAN, we know not on what authority, that when twins are produced they are generally male and female.

A friend of ours related to us some time ago the following anecdote. A gentleman in the interior of Pennsylvania who kept a pair of Elks in a large woodland pasture, was in the habit of taking pieces of bread or a few handfuls of corn with him when he walked in the enclosure, to feed these animals, calling them up for the amusement of his friends. Having occasion to pass through his park one day, and not having provided himself with bread or corn for his pets, he was followed by the buck, who expected his usual gratification: the gentleman, irritated by the pertinacity with which he was accompanied, turned round, and picking up a small stick, hit the animal a smart blow, upon which, to his astonishment and alarm, the buck, lowering his head, rushed at him and made a furious pass with his horns: luckily the gentleman stumbled as he attempted to fly, and fell over the prostrate trunk of a tree, near which lay another log, and being able to throw his body between the two trunks, the Elk was unable to injure him, although it butted at him repeatedly and kept him prisoner for more than an hour. Not relishing this proceeding, the gentleman, as soon as he escaped, gave orders to have the unruly animal destroyed.

The teeth of the Elk are much prized by the Indians to ornament their dresses; a "queen's robe" presented to us is decorated with the teeth of fifty-six Elks. This splendid garment, which is made of antelope skins, was valued at no less than thirty horses!

The droppings of the Elk resemble those of other deer, but are much larger.

The Elk, like other deer, lie down during the middle of the day, and feed principally at early morning, and late in the evening. They drink a good deal of water.

This species can be easily domesticated, as we have observed it in menageries and in parks both of Europe and America. The males, like those of the Virginian deer, as they advance in age, by their pugnacious habits are apt to become troublesome and dangerous. The Elk lives to a great age, one having been kept in the possession of the elder PEALE of Philadelphia for thirteen years; we observed one in the Park of a nobleman in Austria that had been received from America twenty-five years before.

Geographical Distribution.

We have every reason to believe, that the Elk once was found on nearly every portion of the temperate latitudes of North America. It has never advanced as far north as the moose deer, but it ranges much farther to the south. The earliest explorers of America nearly all speak of the existence of the stag, which they supposed was identical with the stag or red deer of Europe. It differs from the Virginian deer, which continues to range in the vicinity of settlements and is not driven from its favourite haunts by the cry of the hounds or the crack of the rifle. On the contrary the Elk, like the buffalo, takes up its line of march, crosses broad rivers and flies to the yet unexplored forests, as soon as it catches the scent and hears the report of the gun of the white man. At present there is only a narrow range on the Alleghany mountains where the

Elk still exists, in small and decreasing numbers, east of the Missouri, and these remnants probably of large herds would undoubtedly migrate elsewhere were they not restricted to their present wild mountainous and hardly accessible range, by the extensive settlements on the west and south.

Mr. PEALE of Philadelphia mentioned to us some fifteen years ago, that the only region in the Atlantic States where he could procure specimens of the Elk was the highest and most sterile mountains in the northwest of Pennsylvania, where he had on several occasions gone to hunt them.

Dr. DEKAY (New-York Fauna, p. 119) mentions, on the authority of BEACH and VAUGHAN, two hunters in whose statements confidence could be placed, that as late as 1826, Elks were seen and killed on the north branch of the Saranac. On a visit to Western Virginia in 1847, we heard of the existence of a small herd of Elk that had been known for many years to range along the high and sterile mountains about forty miles to the west of the Red Sulphur Springs. The herd was composed of eight males, whose number was ascertained by their tracks in the snow. One of these had been killed by a hunter, and the number was reduced to seven. Our informant, a friend in whom the highest confidence could be placed, supposed, as all the individuals in the herd had horns, the race would soon disappear from the mountains. As, however, the males at certain seasons keep in separate groups, we have no doubt there was a similar or large herd of females in the same range; but the number is doubtless annually lessening, and in all probability it will not be many years before the Elk will be entirely extirpated, to beyond several hundred miles west of the Mississippi.

This animal, according to RICHARDSON, does not extend its range farther to the north than the 56th or 57th parallel of latitude, nor is it found to the eastward of a line drawn from the south end of Lake Winnepeg to the Saskatchewan in the 103d degree of longitude, and from thence till it strikes the Elk river in the 111th degree. It is found on the western prairies, and ranges along the eastern sides of the mountains in Texas and New Mexico. It is also found in Oregon and California. Its most southern geographical range still remains undetermined.

General Remarks.

The family of Elks was by all our old authors placed in the same genus with the true deer, (Cervus,) to which they are very closely allied in their character and habits. As that genus however has been greatly enlarged in consequence of the discovery of new species, the deer have been conveniently divided into several sub-genera, of which our species is the largest and most interesting among the true Elks (Elaphus).

The American Elk, Wappite, or Stag, was for a long period considered identical with the European red deer, (C. Elaphus,) and was, we believe, first treated as a distinct species by RAY. It was subsequently noticed by JEFFERSON and described and figured in the Medical Repository. The difference between these two species is so great that they may be distinguished at a glance. Our Elk is fully a foot higher at the shoulders than the European red stag. The common stag or red deer is of a uniform blackish brown, whilst the Elk has all its upper parts and lower jaw yellowish brown. It has also a black mark on the angle of the mouth which is wanting in the other. In the European species the circle around the eye is white, in the American it is brown. There are other marks of difference which it is unnecessary to point out, as the species are now regarded by all naturalists as distinct.

Our esteemed friend Dr. RICHARDSON has applied to this species the name of Cervus strongyloceros of SCHREBER, because the figure of PERRAULT (Mem. sur les an. vol. 2, p. 45) did not exhibit the pale mark on the rump, and he thought it not improbable that PERRAULT's figure was that of the black-tailed deer (Cervus macrotis). We do not believe that the latter species ever reaches the latitude where PERRAULT's specimen was procured; but as we have already stated in this article, younger specimens of our Elk exhibit only faint traces of this pale mark on the rump, and in some they are entirely wanting. We have scarcely a doubt that RAY's description was intended to apply to our American Elk, and we have therefore adopted his specific name.

Lepus Callotis.—Wagler.

Black Tailed Hare.

Plate lxiii. Male.—Natural Size.

L. magnitudine, L. glacialem adæquans, supra flavescente fusco canoque varius, subtus albus; auribus pedibusque prælongis, cauda longa, nigra.

Characters.

Size of the polar hare; ears and legs, very long; tail, long and black; mottled with gray and yellowish-brown above, beneath, white.

Synonymes.

LEPUS CALLOTIS, Wagler, 1832.
    "   NIGRICAUDATUS, Bennett, Proceedings of the Zoological Society of London, 1833, p. 41, marked in the Catalogue of the Zoological Society, 582.
LEPUS NIGRICAUDATUS, Bachman, Journal of the Academy Nat. Sciences, Philadelphia, vol. viii., pt. 1, p. 84, an. 1839.

Description.

This interesting species is similar to others composing a certain group of hares found in America, characterized by being large, and having very long ears, and long and slender legs and bodies, the whole form indicating capacity for long leaps and rapid locomotion. In all these characteristics, *Lepus Callotis* approaches nearest to TOWNSEND's hare, (*Lepus Townsendii*,) which may be considered the type of this group.

Colour.

The whole of the upper surface, fawn colour, tipped with black; hairs on the back, silvery gray for one-third of their length, then pale fawn, then black, then fawn, tipped with black. Back of the neck, brownish black, slightly tipped with fawn. A number of hairs of unusual length (two and one-fourth inches,) and delicately interspersed along the sides; in the greatest abundance along the shoulders. These hairs are black from the base for two-thirds of their length, the remainder pale fawn; sides, and under parts of the neck, dingy pale fawn, gradually becoming white on the chest; haunches, legs and under surface white; the hairs on the rump annulated with black, and near the root of the tail almost entirely black; the whole of the tail on the upper surface to the extremity black; on the under surface the hairs are black from the roots, slightly tipped with grayish brown. Hairs on the under surface of the feet, in some specimens red, in others a soiled yellowish-brown. Ears, posteriorly for two-thirds of their breadth black at the roots, gradually blending into fawn, and on the inner third the longitudinal line of demarcation being very distinct; this fawn colour is mixed with black hairs, edged at the tip with black, the remainder of the edge fawn; the outer margin of the posterior surface to its apex pure white. Inner surface of the ears nearly naked, except at the outer edge, where they are clothed with short grizzled brown hairs. Whiskers white and black, the former predominating; chin and throat, white. The marginal line of demarcation between the colour of the back and that of the under surface, is somewhat abrupt across the upper portion of the thighs, and very distinctly marked.

Dimensions.

	Inches.
Length from point of nose to root of tail,	20
Tail (vertebræ),	$1\frac{1}{2}$
" including fur,	$2\frac{1}{2}$
From heel to longest nail,	$4\frac{3}{4}$
Head over the curve,	$4\frac{1}{2}$
From eye to nose,	$1\frac{1}{4}$
Ears posteriorly,	$4\frac{3}{4}$
Greatest breadth,	$2\frac{1}{3}$

Habits.

Our account of this species is principally derived from the journals of J. W. AUDUBON, kept during the journey through part of Texas, made for the purpose of procuring the animals of that State, and obtaining some knowledge of their habits for our present work, in 1845 and 1846, with an extract from which we now present our readers.

"One fine morning in January, 1845, at San Antonio de Bexar, as I mounted my faithful one-eyed chesnut horse, admiring his thin neck and bony legs, his delicate head and flowing flaxen tail and mane, I was saluted with a friendly good morning by Mr. CALAHAN, then holding the important office of mayor of the little village; and on his ascertaining that my purpose was to have a morning hunt on the prairies and through the chapparal, which I did day after day, he agreed to accompany me in search of the animals I was anxiously trying to obtain, and in quest of which I rode over miles of prairie with my bridle on the knobbed pummel of my Texan saddle, the most comfortable saddle I have ever tried, (being a sort of half Spanish, half English build,) my horse with his neck stretched out and his head about on a level with his shoulders, walking between four and five miles an hour, turning to the right or to the left agreeably to the slightest movement of my body, so well was he trained, leaving both hands and eyes free, so that I could search with the latter every twig, tussock or thicket, and part the thick branches of the chapparal of musquit, prickly holly, and other shrubs, which I am inclined to think quite equal to any East-Indian jungle in offering obstructions to the progress of either horse or man.

Mr. CALAHAN having mounted, we set out, and after about an hour's hard work, occupied in crossing one of the thickest covers near the town, gained the broad and nearly level prairie beyond, across which to the west we could see varied swelling undulations, gradually fading into the faint outline of a distant spur, perhaps of the rocky chain of mountains that in this latitude lie between the water courses flowing toward the Gulf of Mexico, and the streams that empty into the Gulf of California: so far away indeed seemed these faint blue peaks that it required but a little stretch of the imagination to fancy the plains of California but just at the other side. I was enchanted with the scene, scarcely knowing whether the brilliant fore-ground of cacti and tropical plants, the soft indefinite distance, or the clear summer blue sky, was most beautiful. My companion observing my enthusiasm, warmed into praises of his adopted country: he had, he said, fought hard for it, and exclaimed, it is a country worth fighting for; when my reply, of whatever nature it might have been, was prevented, and all ideas of blue mountains, vast rolling prairies, &c., were cut short by a jackass rabbit bounding from under our horses' feet; he was instantly followed by my worthy friend the mayor at full speed on his white pony, for otherwise he would have stopped in a hundred yards or so. Away they went, and as my friend's horse was a running nag, he doubtless expected to overtake the Hare, which had only gained about fifty yards start during our momentary surprise. The Hare, as I quickly observed, did not make much shorter leaps than the horse. I could see it at each bound appear like a jack-o'-lantern floating with the breeze over a swamp, but in less time than I have taken to write this, they had ran a mile, the Hare doubled and was a hundred yards in advance, but could not stop and look behind, for he had such a race that he knew well no time was to be lost in gaining some bed of cactus or chapparal. Now on came both Hare and hunter, and the race was of the swiftest when another double caused the rider to pull up with such force that his stirrup leather broke, and the space between the mayor and the object of his pursuit was widened to a quarter of a mile, and the chase ended; our friend dismounting to refit. We had not the good fortune to start another of these hares that day.

Some time afterwards while at Castroville, a little place of about a dozen huts and one house, this Hare was procured by a party of Indians and brought to J. W. AUDUBON, who writes: "I chanced to be visited by some of the Shawnee Indians who were in the neighbourhood on a hunting expedition. They were highly astonished and pleased with my drawings, which I exhibited to them while trying to explain what animals I wanted. I made a hasty sketch of a hare with immensely long ears, at which I pointed with an approving nod of the head, and then made another sketch smaller and with shorter ears, at which last I shook my head and made wry faces; the Indians laughed, and by their guttural eugh, haugh, li, gave me to understand that they comprehended me; and in a day or two, I had a beautiful specimen of the Black-tailed Hare brought to me, but with the head shot off by a rifle ball. The Indians were quite disappointed that it did not answer my purpose, and smoothed down the fur on the body, which is the only part of the skin they generally preserve, and what they thought I wanted.

The specimen I drew from was shot by POWEL, one of Colonel HAYS' rangers, from whom I received many attentions and who acted most kindly while with me on one of my excursions from San Antonio. This Hare is so rare in those parts of Texas that I visited, that I can say little of its habits. It appears to be solitary, or nearly so, fond of high open prairie with clumps of trees, or rather bushes and thickets about them, trusting to its speed for safety and only taking cover from hawks and eagles. Near San Petruchio, as I was

Plate LXIII

Drawn from Nature by J J Audubon, F R S F L S

On Stone by W. E. Hitchcock

Lith. Printed & Col.d by J T Bowen Philad.a

Black-tailed Hare.

informed, this Hare is more abundant than in this vicinity, and two or three of them can occasionally be started in a morning's ride."

The specimen from which Mr. BENNETT described and named this Hare (*Lepus nigricaudatus*, Bennett, Zoological Proceedings, 1833, p. 41), has a more definitely marked line of white along the sides and legs than the one I drew from; but this species varies so much in its markings, that one figure with the characters given is probably as like the majority as another.

The line of white and black near the tip of the ears extended longitudinally, is by many considered a good specific character, but it does not, I think, hold out in respect to this animal.

It is singular that this fine species of Hare should be so rare in the collections of Europe; I saw only two, and did not hear of the existence of any in the museums which I had not an opportunity of examining.

Since the Mexican war broke out, several have been sent home by our officers. We have the pleasure of acknowledging the receipt of a fine skin from Lieutenant ABERT, who also favoured us with some skins of quadrupeds from the vicinity of Santa Fe, which we shall have occasion to notice elsewhere, and for which we return him our best thanks.

This species is called the *Jackass* Rabbit in Texas, owing to the length of its ears.

Geographical Distribution.

This Hare is found as far north as Santa Fe, in the great prairies; it does not, however, occur near the shores of the lower Red River, nor near the Gulf of Mexico; indeed, until we get as far south as about latitude 30°, from which parallel to the southward it becomes more abundant, and may be said to be the common Hare of Mexico. Whether it is found beyond the limits of North America we are unable to say, but suppose not, as the museums of Europe have been better supplied with South American species than with those of our northern portion of the Western hemisphere, and as already observed, do not contain more than the two specimens mentioned above, one of which is stated to have been received from Mexico and the other from California.

General Remarks.

There is a specimen in the Berlin Museum, labelled Lepus Callotis, WAGLER, described by him in 1832. This specimen corresponds in all essential particulars with that which exists in the Zoological Museum of London, described by BENNETT. Hence we are obliged to adopt WAGLER'S name, he having the priority as the first scientific describer; although in our plate we adopted BENNETT's name, not supposing the two specimens alike until our subsequent visit to Berlin.

Putorius Pusillus. —Dekay.

The Small Weasel.

Plate lxiv.—Natural Size.

P. erminia tertia parti minore; caudâ breviuscula. Supra rufo-fuscus subtus albus.

Characters.

A third smaller than the Ermine; tail rather short; Colour, brown above white beneath.

Synonymes.

MUSTELA (PUTORIUS) VULGARIS, Bach., Fauna Bor. Am., vol. i., p. 45.
P. VULGARIS, Emmons, Mass. Report, 1840, p. 44.
MUSTELA PUSILLA, Dekay, Nat. Hist. N. Y., p. 34.

Description.

This is much the smallest of all our species of Weasel, if we are to judge from two specimens that are in our possession, which appear to be full grown. The tail is about one-fourth the length of the body, and is a little longer than that of the common Weasel (M. *Vulgaris*) of Europe. It is, however, a still smaller animal, and differs from it in several other particulars: its ears are less broad, its feet smaller, the colour on the back is a shade darker, the white on the under surface extends much farther along the sides, towards the back, and the dividing line between the colours on the upper and lower surface is more distinct. The head is small, neck slender, and the body vermiform. Whiskers the length of the head, ears very small, toes and nails slender, covered with hairs.

Colour.

We are inclined to believe that this species does not become white in winter. We kept a small weasel alive throughout a winter in our boyhood, but cannot now decide whether it was this species or another, (*P. Fuscus*,) which we will describe in our next volume. That species underwent no change in winter. It is more glossy than the ermine in summer pelage and a shade paler in colour. It is light yellowish brown on the head, neck, and the whole of the upper surface; this colour prevails on the outer portions of the fore-legs to near the feet, the outer surface of the hind-legs, the rump, and the whole of the tail, which is not tipped with black as in the ermine. The white on the under surface commences on the upper lips and extends along the neck, inner surface of the legs, rises high up along the sides, including the outer and inner surfaces of the feet. The moustaches are white and black, the former colour predominating.

Dimensions.

	Inches.
Length from point of nose to root of tail,	7
Head and neck,	3
Tail (vertebræ),	2
" including fur,	$2\frac{1}{8}$

Habits.

From the form and structure of this species, we might naturally presume that it possesses all the habits of the ermine. It feeds on insects, eggs of birds, and mice, but from its diminutive size we are led to suppose that it is not mischievous in the poultry house, and would scarcely venture to attack a full-grown Norway rat.

Geographical Distribution.

The specimens from which our descriptions were made, were obtained in the State of New-York, one at the Catskills, and the other at Long Island. If it should prove to be the species we once had in captivity, it exists also in the northern part of New-York, where we captured it. RICHARDSON asserts that it exists as far to the North as the Saskatchewan river, and Captain Bayfield obtained specimens at Lake Superior.

General Remarks.

Sir John RICHARDSON states that this species, like the ermine, becomes white in winter in the fur countries. We are disposed to believe that this is not the case in the latitude of New-York. This fact, however, is no evidence that the species in those widely separated localities are different. The ermine in the northern part of Virginia seldom undergoes a perfect change, and in Carolina remains brown throughout the whole year. Sir John RICHARDSON states (p. 45) that the specimens presented to the Zoological Society by Capt. BAYFIELD, agreed in all respects with the common weasel of Europe. We, however, examined these specimens and compared them with the European weasel, and found no difficulty in discovering characters by which the species are separated. We have an indistinct recollection that the prince of Musignano named the specimen in the Zoological Society; but as he did not, as far as we know, describe it, we have, according to our views on these subjects, assigned to Dr. DEKAY the credit of the specific name.

By an error, this species was marked on the plate, *Putorius fuscus*, which we request our readers to correct.

Plate LXIV

N.° 13

Drawn from Nature by J. W. Audubon.

On Stone by W. H. Hitchcock

Little American Brown Weasel.

Lith. Printed & Col.d by J. T. Bowen, Phil.

Mus Humilis.—Bachman.

Little Harvest Mouse.

Plate lxv. Males and Females.—Natural size.

M. corpore supra rutilo-cinereo, et quoad baccas et lineam in utrisque lateribus ferrugineo; subtus flavo-albente. M. musculus minor.

Characters.

Smaller than the house mouse; colour, reddish-gray above; cheeks and line along the side, light ferruginous; beneath, white with a yellowish tinge.

Synonymes.

MUS HUMILIS, Bach. Read before the Academy of Nat. Sciences, 1837. Journal Acad., vol. vii.
MUS HUMILIS, Bach., Acad. Nat. Sciences, Oct. 5th, 1841.

Description.

Incisors, small and short; head, much more rounded, nose, less pointed, and skull, proportionally broader than the corresponding portions in the common house-mouse; legs, rather short, and slender; there are four toes on the fore-feet, with a minute and almost imperceptible nail in the place of a thumb; on the hind-foot there are five toes; claws short, weak, sharp, and slightly hooked; nose, short and pointed; the moustaches are composed of a few hairs, not rigid, of the length of the head; the eyes are smaller and less prominent than those of the white-footed mouse, resembling those of the common house-mouse; the ears are of moderate size, broad at base, erect, ovate, clothed on both surfaces and around the edges with short adpressed hairs, extending a little beyond the fur; palms naked; upper surface of feet covered with hairs to the end of nails; the tail is round when the animal is in a living state, but after the specimens are dried, becomes square; it is thinly clothed with short hairs; the fur on the whole body is short, glossy, and very fine.

Colour.

Teeth, yellow; nails, white; eyes, black; moustaches, mostly white; a few near the nostrils black; nose, cheeks, ears on both surfaces, and a line extending from the sides of the neck running along the shoulder and separating the colours of the back and under surface, dark buff; on the back, the hairs are plumbeous at the roots, then yellowish fawn colour; upper lips, chin, and throat, white; neck and under surface of body white shaded with buff.

Dimensions.

	Inches.
From point of nose to root of tail, ...	$2\frac{3}{4}$
Tail, ...	2
Height of ear, ...	$\frac{3}{8}$

Habits.

By the casual observer, this diminutive little species, on being started from its retreat in the long grass, or under some fence or pile of brushwood, might be mistaken for the young of the white-footed mouse (*Mus leucopus*), or that of the jumping mouse (*Meriones Americanus*). It however differs widely from either, and bears but a general resemblance to any of our American species.

About twenty years ago, whilst we were endeavouring to make ourselves acquainted with the species of smaller rodentia existing in the Southern States, we discovered this little Mouse in the grass fields and along the fences of the plantations a few miles from Charleston, S. C. We procured it in the way in which field mice and other small quadrupeds in all countries can be most easily obtained, by having what are denominated figure of 4 traps, set along fences and ditches in the evening, baited with meat and seeds of various kinds. On the following morning we usually were rewarded with a number of several interesting species. We on two occasions preserved this Mouse in a domestic state, once for a year, during which time it produced two broods of young: the first consisting of four were born in May, the second of three in July. They reared all their young. We fed them at first on pea or ground nuts, (*Hypogea arachis*,) cornmeal, (maize,) the latter they preferred boiled, but after having tempted their appetites with the seeds of the Egyptian Millet, (*Pennisitum tiphoideum*,) we discovered that they relished it so well, we allowed it finally to become their exclusive food. They refused meat on all occasions. They were very gentle, allowed themselves to be taken into the hand, and made no attempt to bite, or scarcely any to escape. The young, when born, were naked and blind, but in a very few days became covered with hair, and at a week old were seen peeping out of their nests. We did not discover that the female dragged the young, attached to the teats, in the manner of the white-footed mouse. We placed a female in a cage with a male of the white-footed mouse: they lived on tolerably good terms for six months, but produced no young. We then placed the same female with the male of the common mouse. The latter immediately commenced fighting with our little pet, and in the morning she was found dead in the cage, bitten and mutilated in various places.

This to us is a rare species; after a search of twenty years we have obtained only a dozen specimens from the fields. The nests, which we have oftener seen than their occupants, were placed on the surface of the ground among the long grass, composed of soft withered grasses, and covered over in the manner of the nest of WILSON's meadow mouse. We have also seen the nests of this species under brush-heaps and beneath the rails of fences, similarly constructed.

We doubt whether this species is of much injury to the farmer. It consumes but little grain, is more fond of residing near grass fields, on the seeds of which it subsists, than among the wheat fields. We have observed in its nest small stores of grass seeds—the outer husks and other remains of the Broom grass (*Andropogon dissitiflorum*)—also that of the Crab grass (*Digitaria sanguinalis*,) and small heaps of the seeds of several species of *paspalum, poa* and *panicum*, especially those of *panicum Italicum*.

The specimen from which this description was taken was a little the largest of any we have seen. It was a female captured on the 10th December, and containing four young in its matrix; we presume therefore that this species, like the field mice in general, produce young several times during the summer.

Geographical Distribution.

We have met with this species sparingly in South Carolina along the seaboard, and received it from Dr. BARRATT, of Abbeville, S. C. We procured a specimen in Ebenezer, (Georgia,) where the inhabitants stated they had never before observed it. A specimen was sent to me by our friend Mr. RUFFIN, who obtained it in Virginia. If we have not inadvertently blended two species, this animal can be traced as far to the north-east as the State of New-York, several having been procured in traps on the farms in the vicinity of the city.

General Remarks.

By some mistake this animal was set down on our plate as *Mus minimus* (AUD. and BACH.) It should have been *Mus humilis* (*Bach.*), being the name assigned to it by its first describer. We sent a minute description of this species to the Academy of Natural Sciences in 1837, which was read by our friend Dr. MORTON; although informed that it was published in the transactions of the Society, we have not seen it in print. A second description was published in the transactions of the same Society, October, 1841. We have not ascertained that the species has been noticed by any other naturalist.

In examining the teeth of this species, we have found that the tuberculous summits on the molars were less distinct than in those which legitimately belong to the genus *Mus*, and that there are angular ridges on the enamel by which it approaches the genus *Arvicola*; it is in fact an intermediate species, but in the aggregate of its characteristics perhaps approaches nearest to *Mus*, where we for the present have concluded to leave it.

Plate LXV

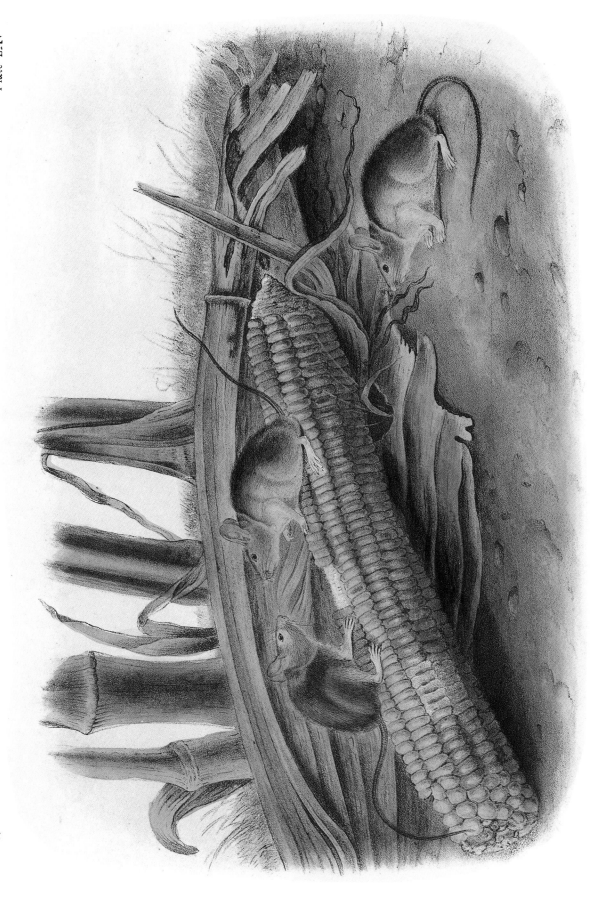

On Stone by W. E. Hitchcock

Little Harvest Mouse

Drawn from Nature by J. Audubon, F.R.S.F.L.S.

Lith Printed & Col.d by J.T. Bowen, Phil.

Genus Didelphis.—Linnæus.

Dental Formula.

$$Incisive \; \frac{10}{8}; \; Canine \; \frac{1-1}{1-1}; \; Molar \; \frac{7-7}{7-7} \; or \; \frac{6-6}{7-7} = 48 \; or \; 50.$$

Head, long and conical; muzzle, pointed; ears, large, membraneous, rounded, and almost naked; tongue, acculeated; internal toe of the hind foot, opposable to the fingers, and destitute of a nail, pendactylous; nails, curved; tail, long, scaly, and slightly covered with rigid hair; stomach, simple. Female, with a pouch.

The generic name is derived from the Greek, *dis*, twice or double, and *delphis*, a womb.

The interesting group of the Marsupialia has recently been arranged by OWEN into five tribes and families, and sixteen genera; these include about seventy known species, to which additions are continually making; the Virginian Opossum being, however, the only species known in America north of Mexico. Most of the other species of this genus (as at present restricted,) inhabit tropical America. It is composed of fifteen species, some of which are still doubtful.

Didelphis Virginiana.—Shaw.

Virginian Opossum.

Plate lxvi. Female, and Young Male seven months old. Natural size.

D. pilis laneis basi albis, apice fuscis; sericeis longis albis; facie, rostro colloque pure albis; auriculis nigris apice flavicantibus; caudâ corpore breviore basi pilosâ tota albicante.

Characters.

Hair soft and woolly, white near the roots, tipped with brown; the long hairs white and silky; face near the snout, pure white; ears, black; base and margin, whitish; tail, shorter than the body; base, covered with whitish hair.

Synonymes.

VIRGINIAN OPOSSUM, Pennant, Hist. Quad., vol. ii., p. 18, pl. 63.
    "   "   " Arctic Zoology, vol. i., p. 73.
SARIGUE DES ILLINOIS, Buff., sup. 6.
OPOSSUM AMERICANUS, D'Azara, Quad. du Paraguay.
DIDELPHIS VIRGINIANA, Shaw's Zool., vol. i., p. 73.
MARSUPIALL AMERICANUM, Tyson, in Phil. Trans., No. 239, p. 105.
COWPER, bid., No. 290, p. 1565.
OPOSSUM, Catesby's Carolina, p. 120, fig. e.
    " Barton's Facts, Observations and Conjectures relative to the generation of the Opossum of N. Am., London, 1809 and 1813.
POSSUM, Lawson's Carolina, p. 120, fig. e.
D. VIRGINIANUS, Harlan, Fauna, p. 119.
    "   " Godman, vol. ii., p. 7, fig.
VIRG. OPOSSUM, Griffith, vol. iii., p. 24.
    "   " Dekay, Nat. Hist. N. Y., p. 3, fig. 2, pl. 15.
OPOSSUM, Notes on the generation of the Virginian Opossum, (Didelphis Virginiana,) J. Bachman, D. D., Transactions of the Acad. of Nat. Sciences, April, 1848, p. 40.
    Letter from M. Michel, M. D., on the same subject, Trans. Acad. Nat. Sciences, April, 1848, p. 46.

Description.

Body, stout and clumsy; head, long and conical; snout, pointed: the nostrils at the extremity of the long muzzle open on the sides of protruberant naked and glandulous surface. Ears, large, thin, and membraneous; mouth, wide, and borders rounded; jaws, weak; eyes, placed high on the forehead, small, and without external lids, oblique; moustaches, on the sides of the face, and a few over the eye, strong and rigid. The tongue is covered with rough papillæ. Nails, of moderate length, curved; inner toe on the posterior extremities destitute of a nail and opposable to the other toes, thus forming a kind of hand. Tail, (which may be considered a useful appendage to the legs in aiding the motions of the animal), prehensile and very strong, but capable of involution only on the under side, long, round, and scaly, covered with a few coarse hairs for a few inches from the base, the remainder with here and there a hair scattered between. Soles of the hind feet, covered with large tubercles. The female is furnished with a pouch containing thirteen mammæ arranged in a circle, with one in the centre.

The fur is of two kinds, a soft woolly hair beneath, covered by much longer hairs, which are, however, not sufficiently dense to conceal the under coat. The woolly hair is of considerable length and fineness, especially in winter.

Colour.

The woolly hair on the upper surface of the body, when blown aside, is white at the base and black at the tips; the long interspersed hairs are mostly white; a few towards the points exhibit shades of dark brown and black; moustaches, white, and black; eyes, black; ears, black, at base, the borders edged with white to near the extremities, where they are broadly patched with white; snout and toes, flesh coloured; face, neck, and nails, yellowish white; a line of dark brown commences on the forehead, widens on the head, and extends to the shoulders—there is also a line of dark brown under the chest; the feet in most specimens are brownish black; we have seen an occasional one where they were reddish brown; tail, brown.

The young differ somewhat in colour from the old: they are uniformly lighter in colour, the head being quite white, with a very distinct black dorsal line commencing faintly on the hind head, and running down the back to near the rump.

Dimensions.

	Inches.
A well grown female:	
From point of nose to root of tail,	$15\frac{1}{2}$
Length of tail,	12
Height of ear,	$1\frac{7}{8}$
Breadth of ear,	$1\frac{1}{4}$
Orifice of the distended pouch in diameter,	$15\frac{1}{2}$
Teats measured immediately after the young had been withdrawn,	1

Weight, 12lbs.

Young, ten days old, nostrils open, ears pretty well developed:	
Length of head and body,	$1\frac{1}{2}$
Tail,	$\frac{1}{2}$

Weight, 22 grains.

Habits.

In our first volume (pp. 111, 112) we have spoken of the curiosity eagerly indulged, and the sensations excited, in the minds of the discoverers of our country, on seeing the strange animals that they met with. Travellers in unexplored regions are likely to find many unheard-of objects in nature that awaken in their minds feelings of wonder and admiration. We can imagine to ourselves the surprise with which the Opossum was regarded by Europeans when they first saw it. Scarcely any thing was known of the marsupial animals, as New Holland had not as yet opened its unrivalled stores of singularities to astonish the world. Here was a strange animal, with the head and ears of the pig, sometimes hanging on the limb of a tree, and occasionally swinging like the monkey by the tail! Around that prehensile appendage a dozen sharp-nosed, sleek-headed young, had entwined their own tails, and were sitting on the mother's back! The astonished traveller approaches this extraordinary compound of an animal and touches it cautiously with a stick. Instantly it seems to be struck with some mortal disease: its eyes close, it falls to the ground, ceases to move, and appears to be dead! He turns it on its back, and perceives on its stomach a strange apparently artificial opening. He puts his fingers into the extraordinary pocket, and lo! another brood of a dozen or more young, scarcely larger than a pea, are hanging in clusters on the teats. In pulling the creature about, in great amazement, he suddenly receives a gripe on the hand—the twinkling of the half-closed eye and the breathing of the creature, evince that it is not dead, and he adds a new term to the vocabulary of his language, that of "playing 'possum."

Like the great majority of predacious animals, the Opossum is nocturnal in its habits. It suits its nightly wanderings to the particular state of the weather. On a bright starlight or moonlight night, in autumn or winter, when the weather is warm and the air calm, the Opossum may every where be found in the Southern States, prowling around the outskirts of the plantation, in old

On Stone by Wᵐ E. Hitchcock

Virginian Opossum

Drawn from Nature by J.J. Audubon, F.R.S.F.L.S   Lith Printed & Colᵈ by J T Bowen, Phil.

deserted rice fields, along water courses, and on the edges of low grounds and swamps; but if the night should prove windy or very cold, the best nosed dog can scarcely strike a trail, and in such cases the hunt for that night is soon abandoned.

The gait of the Opossum is slow, rather heavy, and awkward; it is not a trot like that of the fox, but an amble or pace, moving the two legs on one side at a time. Its walk on the ground is plantigrade, resting the whole heel on the earth. When pursued, it by no means stops at once and feigns death, as has often been supposed, but goes forward at a rather slow speed, it is true, but as fast as it is able, never, that we are aware of, increasing it to a leap or canter, but striving to avoid its pursuers by sneaking off to some thicket or briar patch; when, however, it discovers that the dog is in close pursuit, it flies for safety to the nearest tree, usually a sapling, and unless molested does not ascend to the top, but seeks an easy resting place in some crotch not twenty feet from the ground, where it waits silently and immoveably, till the dog, finding that his master will not come to his aid, and becoming weary of barking at the foot of the tree, leaves the Opossum to follow the bent of his inclinations, and conclude his nightly round in search of food. Although a slow traveller, the Opossum, by keeping perseveringly on foot during the greater part of the night, hunts over much ground, and has been known to make a circle of a mile or two in one night. Its ranges, however, appear to be restricted or extended according to its necessities, as when it has taken up its residence near a corn field, or a clump of ripe persimmon trees, (*Diosperos Virginiana*,) the wants of nature are soon satisfied, and it early and slowly carries its fat and heavy body to its quiet home, to spend the remainder of the night and the succeeding day in the enjoyment of a quiet rest and sleep.

The whole structure of the Opossum is admirably adapted to the wants of a sluggish animal. It possesses strong powers of smell, which aid it in its search after food; its mouth is capacious, and its jaws possessing a greater number and variety of teeth than any other of our animals, evidencing its omnivorous habits; its fore-paws, although not armed with retractile claws, aid in seizing its prey and conveying it to the mouth. The construction of the hind-foot with its soft yielding tubercles on the palms and its long nailless opposing thumb, enable it to use these feet as hands, and the prehensile tail aids it in holding on to the limbs of trees whilst its body is swinging in the air; in this manner we have observed it gathering persimmons with its mouth and fore-paws, and devouring them whilst its head was downwards and its body suspended in the air, holding on sometimes with its hind-feet and tail, but often by the tail alone.

We have observed in this species a habit which is not uncommon among a few other species of quadrupeds, as we have seen it in the raccoon and occasionally in the common house dog—that of lying on its back for hours in the sun, being apparently dozing, and seeming to enjoy this position as a change. Its usual posture, however, when asleep, is either lying at full length on the side, or sitting doubled up with its head under its fore-legs, and its nose touching the stomach, in the manner of the raccoon.

The Opossum cannot be called a gregarious animal. During summer, a brood composing a large family may be found together, but when the young are well grown, they usually separate, and each individual shifts for himself; we have seldom found two together in the same retreat in autumn or winter.

Although not often seen abroad in very cold weather in winter, this animal is far from falling into that state of torpidity to which the marmots, jumping mice, and several other species of quadrupeds are subject. In the Southern States, there are not many clear nights of starlight or moonshine in which they may not be found roaming about; and although in their farthest northern range they are seldom seen when the ground is covered with snow, yet we recollect having come upon the track of one in snow a foot deep, in the month of March, in Pennsylvania; we pursued it, and captured the Opossum in its retreat—a hollow tree. It may be remarked, that animals like the Opossum, raccoon, skunk, &c., that become very fat in autumn require but little food to support them through the winter, particularly when the weather is cold.

The Opossum, although nocturnal in its general habits, is not unfrequently, particularly in spring and summer, found moving about by day. We have on several occasions met with it in the woods at mid-day, in places where it was seldom molested.

Nature has wisely provided this species with teeth and organs indicating its omnivorous character and its possessing an appetite for nearly all kinds of food; and in this particular it exhibits many of the propensities and tastes of the raccoon. It enters the corn fields (maize), crawls up the stalks, and sometimes breaks them down in the manner of the raccoon, to feed on the young and tender grains; it picks up chesnuts, acorns, chinquapins and beach nuts, and munches them in the manner of the bear. We have, on dissection, ascertained that it had devoured blackberries, whortleberries, and wild cherries, and its resort to the persimmon tree is proverbial. It is also insectivorous, and is seen scratching up the leaves in search of worms, and the larvæ of insects, of which it is very fond. In early spring it lays the vegetable kingdom under contribution for its support, and we have observed it digging up the roots of the small atamamasco lily, (*Zepherina atamasco*,) and the young and tender shoots of the China brier, (*Smilax rotundifolia*,) as they shoot out of the ground like asparagus. It is moreover decidedly carnivorous, eating young birds that it may detect on the ground, sucking the eggs in all the partridge, towheebunting and other nests, it can find in its persevering search. It destroys mice and other rodentia, and devours whole broods of young rabbits, scratching about the nest and scattering the hair and other materials of which it was composed. We have observed it squatting in the grass and brier thickets in Carolina, which are the common resort of the very abundant cotton rat, (*Sigmodon hispidum*,) and from patches of skin and other mutilated remains, we satisfied ourselves that the Opossum was one among many other species designed by Providence to keep in check the too rapid increase of these troublesome rats. We must admit that it sometimes makes a sly visit to the poultry house, killing a few of the hens and playing havoc among the eggs. The annoyances of the farmer, however, from this mischievous propensity, are not as great as those sustained from some of the other species, and cannot for a moment be compared with the destruction caused by the weasel, the mink, or the skunk.

The domicile of the Opossum in which it is concealed during the day, and where it brings forth its young, which we have often examined, is found in various localities. This animal is a tolerable digger, although far less expert in this quality than the Maryland marmot, its den is usually under the roots of trees or stumps, when the ground is so elevated as to secure it from rains and inundations. The hollow of a large fallen tree, or an opening at the roots of a standing one, also serve as a convenient place for its nest. The material which we have usually found composing this nest along the seaboard of Carolina is the long moss (*Tillandsia usnoides*); although we have sometimes found it composed of a bushel or more of oak and other leaves.

On firing into a squirrel's nest which was situated in the fork of a tree some forty feet from the ground, we brought down an Opossum, which had evidently expelled its legitimate occupant. The Florida rat is known to collect heaps of sticks and leaves, and construct nests sometimes a yard in diameter and two feet high: these are usually placed on the ground, but very frequently on the entangled vines of the grape, smilax, and supple jack, (*Ziziphus volubilis*.) In these nests an Opossum may occasionally be found, dozing as cozily as if he had a better right than that of mere possession.

Hunting the Opossum is a very favourite amusement among domestics and field labourers on our Southern plantations, of lads broke loose from school in the holidays, and even of gentlemen, who are sometimes more fond of this sport than of the less profitable and more dangerous and fatiguing one of hunting the gray fox by moonlight. Although we have never participated in an Opossum hunt, yet we have observed that it afforded much amusement to the sable group that in the majority of instances make up the hunting party, and we have on two or three occasions been the silent and gratified observers of the preparations that were going on, the anticipations indulged in, and the excitement apparent around us.

On a bright autumnal day, when the abundant rice crop has yielded to the sickle, and the maize has just been gathered in, when one or two slight white frosts have tinged the fields and woods with a yellowish hue, ripened the persimmon, and caused the acorns, chesnuts and chinquepins (*Castanea pumilla*) to rattle down from the trees and strewed them over the ground, we hear arrangements entered into for the hunt. The Opossums have been living on the delicacies of the season, and are now in fine order, and some are found excessively fat; a double enjoyment is anticipated, the fun of catching and the pleasure of eating this excellent substitute for roast pig.

"Come, men," says one, "be lively, let us finish our tasks by four o'clock, and after sundown we will have a 'possum hunt." "Done," says another, "and if an old coon comes in the way of my smart dog, Pincher, I be bound for it, he will shake de life out of him." The labourers work with increased alacrity, their faces are brightened with anticipated enjoyment, and ever and anon the old familiar song of "'Possum up the gum tree" is hummed, whilst the black driver can scarcely restrain the whole gang from breaking out into a loud chorus.

The paraphernalia belonging to this hunt are neither showy nor expensive. There are no horses caparisoned with elegant trappings—no costly guns imported to order—no pack of hounds answering to the echoing horn; two or three curs, half hound or terriers, each having his appropriate name, and each regarded by his owner as the best dog on the plantation, are whistled up. They obey the call with alacrity, and their looks and intelligent actions give evidence that they too are well aware of the pleasure that awaits them. One of these humble rustic sportsmen shoulders an axe and another a torch, and the whole arrangement for the hunt is completed. The glaring torch-light is soon seen dispersing the shadows of the forest, and like a jack o'lantern, gleaming along the skirts of the distant meadows and copses. Here are no old trails on which the cold-nosed hound tries his nose for half an hour to catch the scent. The tongues of the curs are by no means silent—ever and anon there is a sudden start and an uproarious outbreak: "A rabbit in a hollow, wait, boys, till I twist him out with a hickory." The rabbit is secured and tied with a string around the neck: another start, and the pack runs off for a quarter of a mile, at a rapid rate, then double around the cotton fields and among the ponds in the pine lands—"Call off your worthless dog, Jim, my Pincher has too much sense to bother after a fox." A loud scream and a whistle brings the pack to a halt, and presently they come panting to the call of the black huntsman. After some scolding and threatening, and resting a quarter of an hour to recover their breath and scent, they are once more hied forwards. Soon a trusty old dog, by an occasional shrill yelp, gives evidence that he has struck some trail in the swamp. The pack gradually make out the scent on the edges of the pond, and marshes of the rice fields, grown up with willows and myrtle bushes (*Myrica cerifera*). At length the mingled notes of shrill and discordant tongues give evidence that the game is up. The race, though rapid, is a long one, through the deep swamp, crossing the muddy branch into the pine lands, where the dogs come to a halt, unite in conclave, and set up an incessant barking at the foot of a pine. "A coon, a coon! din't I tell you," says Monday, "that if Pincher come across a coon, he would do he work?" An additional piece of split lightwood is added to the torch, and the coon is seen doubled up in the form of a hornet's nest in the very top of the long-leaved pine, (*P. palustris*). The tree is without a branch for forty feet or upwards, and it is at once decided that it must be cut down: the axe is soon at work, and the tree felled. The glorious battle that ensues, the prowess of the dogs, and the capture of the coon, follow as a matter of course. See our article on the raccoon, pp. 80, 81, where we have briefly described such a scene.

Another trail is soon struck, and the dogs all open upon it at once: in an instant they rush, pell mell, with a loud burst of mingled tongues, upon some animal along the edge of an old field destitute of trees. It proves to be an Opossum, detected in its nightly prowling expedition. At first, it feigns death, and, rolling itself into a ball, lies still on the ground; but the dogs are up to this " 'possum playing," and seize upon it at once. It now feels that they are in earnest, and are not to be deceived. It utters a low growl or two, shows no fight, opens wide its large mouth, and, with few struggles, surrenders itself to its fate. But our hunters are not yet satisfied, either with the sport or the meat: they have large families and a host of friends on the plantation, the game is abundant, and the labour in procuring it not fatiguing, so they once more hie on the dogs. The Opossum, by its slow gait and heavy tread, leaves its foot-prints and scent behind it on the soft mud and damp grass. Another is soon started, and hastens up the first small gum, oak, or persimmon tree, within its reach; it has clambered up to the highest limb, and sits crouching up with eyes closed to avoid the light. "Off jacket, Jim, and shake him down; show that you know more about 'possum than your good-for-nutten fox-dog." As the fellow ascends, the animal continues mounting higher to get beyond his reach; still he continues in pursuit, until the affrighted Opossum has reached the farthest twig on the extreme branches of the tree. The negro now commences shaking the tall pliant tree top; while with its hind hands rendered convenient and flexible by its opposing thumb, and with its prehensile tail, the Opossum holds on with great tenacity. But it cannot long resist the rapidly accumulating jerks and shocks: suddenly the feet slip from the smooth tiny limb, and it hangs suspended for a few moments only by its tail, in the meantime trying to regain its hold with its hind hands; but another sudden jerk breaks the twig, and down comes the poor animal, doubled up like a ball, into the opened jaws of eager and relentless canine foes; the poor creature drops, and yields to fate without a struggle.

In this manner half a dozen or more Opossums are sometimes captured before midnight. The subsequent boasts about the superior noses, speed and courage of the several dogs that composed this small motley pack—the fat feast that succeeded on the following evening, prolonged beyond the hour of midnight, the boisterous laugh and the merry song, we leave to be detailed by others, although we confess we have not been uninterested spectators of such scenes.

"Let not ambition mock their useful toil,
"Their homely joys and destiny obscure.
"Nor grandeur hear with a disdainful smile,
"The simple pleasures of the humble poor."

The habit of feigning death to deceive an enemy is common to several species of quadrupeds, and we on several occasions witnessed it in our common red fox (*V. Fulvus*). But it is more strikingly exhibited in the Opossum than in any other animal with which we are acquainted. When it is shaken from a tree and falls among grass and shubbery, or when detected in such situations, it doubles itself into a heap and feigns death so artfully, that we have known some schoolboys carrying home for a quarter of a mile an individual of this species, stating that when they first saw it, it was running on the ground, and they could not tell what had killed it. We would not, however, advise that the hand should on such occasions be suffered to come too familiarly in contact with the mouth, lest the too curious meddler should on a sudden be startled with an unexpected and unwelcome gripe.

This species has scarcely any note of recognition, and is remarkably silent; when molested, it utters a low growl; at other times its voice resembles the hissing of a cat. The Opossum displays no cunning in avoiding traps set to capture it, entering almost any kind of trap, very commonly being taken in a log trap called a dead fall.

From its very prolific nature it can afford to have many enemies. In addition to the incessant war waged against it by men and dogs, we have ascertained that its chief enemy among rapacious birds is the Virginian owl, (*Strix Virginiana*,) which flying abroad at the same hour in which the Opossum is on foot, pounces on it, and kills it with great ease. We have heard of an instance in which it was seen in the talons of the white-headed eagle, (*Habietus leucocephalus*,) and of two or three in which the great henhawk (*F. Borealis*) was observed feeding upon it. We recollect no instance of its having been killed by the wild cat or the fox. The wolf, it is said, seizes on every Opossum it can find, and we have heard of two instances where half-grown animals of this species were found to have been swallowed by the rattlesnake.

Although the dog hunts it so eagerly, yet we have never been able to ascertain that it ever feeds upon its flesh; indeed, we have witnessed the dog passing by the body of a fresh killed Opossum, and going off half a mile farther to feed on some offensive carcase.

The Opossum is easily domesticated when captured young. We have, in endeavouring to investigate one of the very extraordinary characteristics of this species, preserved a considerable number in confinement, and our experiments were continued through a succession of years. Their nocturnal habits were in a considerable degree relinquished, and they followed the servants about the premises, becoming troublesome by their familiarity and their mischievous habits. They associated familiarly with a dog on the premises, which seemed to regard them as necessary appendages of the motley group that constituted the family of brutes in the yard. They devoured all kinds of food: vegetables, boiled rice, hominy, meat both raw and boiled, and the scraps thrown from the kitchen; giving the preference to those that contained any fatty substance.

On one occasion a brood of young with their mother made their escape, concealed themselves under a stable, and became partially wild; they were in the habit of coming out at night, and eating scraps of food, but we never discovered that they committed any depredations on the poultry or pigeons. They appeared however to have effectually driven off the rats, as during the whole time they were occupants of the stable, we did not observe a single rat on the premises. It was ascertained that they were in the habit of clambering over fences and visiting the neighbouring lots and gardens, and we occasionally found that we had repurchased one of our own vagrant animals. They usually, however, returned towards daylight to their snug retreat, and we believe would have continued in the neighbourhood and multiplied the species had they not in their nightly prowlings been detected and destroyed by the neighbouring dogs.

A most interesting part of the history of this animal, which has led to the adoption of many vulgar errors, remains to be considered, viz., the generation of the Opossum.

Our investigations on this subject were commenced in early life, and resumed as time and opportunity were afforded, at irregular, and sometimes after long intervals, and were not satisfactorily concluded until within a month of the period of our writing this article, (June, 1849). The process by which we were enabled to obtain the facts and arrive at our conclusions is detailed in an article published in the Transactions of the Academy of Natural Sciences, April, 1848, p. 40. Subsequent investigations have enabled us to verify some of these facts, to remove some obscurities in which the subject was yet involved, and finally to be prepared to give a correct and detailed history of a peculiarity in the natural history of this quadruped, around which there has hitherto been thrown a cloud of mystery and doubt.

Our early authors—MARCGRAVE, PISON, VALENTINE, BEVERLY, the MARQUIS OF CHASTELLUX, PENNANT, and others, contended that "the pouch was the matrix of the young Opossum, and that the mammæ are, with regard to the young, what stalks are to their fruits." DE BLAINVILLE and Dr. BARTON speak of two sorts of gestation, one uterine and the other mammary. BLUMENBACH calls the young when they are first seen on the mammæ, abortions; and Dr. BARTON's views (we quote from GRIFFITH) are surprisingly inaccurate: "The Didelphes," he says, "put forth, not fœtuses but gelatinous bodies; they weigh at their first appearance generally about a grain, some a little more, and seven of them together weighed ten grains." In 1819, GEOFFROY St. HILLAIRE propounded to naturalists the following question: "Are the pouched animals born attached to the teats of the mother?" GODMAN, in his American Natural History, published in 1826, gave to the world a very interesting article on the Opossum, full of information in respect to the habits, &c., comprising all the knowledge that existed at that day in regard to this species. He was obliged, however, to admit, vol. 2, p. 7, "the peculiarities of its sexual intercourse, gestation, and parturition, are to this day involved in profound obscurity. Volumes of facts and conjectures have been written on the subject, in which the proportion of conjecture to fact has been as a thousand to one, and the difficulties still remain to be surmounted." And DEKAY, in the work on the Quadrupeds of the State of N. York, (Nat. Hist. of N. York, 1842, p. 4,) states: "The young are found in the external abdominal sac, firmly attached to the teat in the form of a small gelatinous body, not weighing more than a grain. It was along time believed that there existed a direct passage from the uterus to the teat, but this has been disproved by dissection. Another opinion is, that the embryo is excluded from the uterus in the usual manner and placed by the mother to the teat; and a third, that the embryo is formed where it is first found. Whether this transfer actually takes place, and if so, the physiological considerations connected with it, still remain involved in great obscurity."

The approaches to truth in these investigations have been very gradual, and the whole unusually slow. COWPER, TYSON, DE BLAINVILLE, HOME and others, by their examinations and descriptions of the organs of the Marsupialiæ, prepared the way for farther developments. A more judicious examination and scientific description by OWEN and others, of the corresponding organs in the kangaroo, the largest of all the species composing these genera, and the discovery of the fœtus in utero, enabled naturalists to conclude, that the similar structure in the Opossum would indicate a corresponding result. No one, however, was entitled to speak with positive certainty until the young were actually detected in the uterus, nor could an explanation of the peculiarity in the growth of the fœtus be made until it was examined in its original bed.

We have been so fortunate in five instances as to have procured specimens in which the young were observed in this position, and therefore feel prepared to speak with certainty. We are not aware that the young of the Virginian Opossum had been previously detected in the uterus.

All our investigations were made in South Carolina, where this is a very abundant species. For some years we attempted to arrive at the object of our researches by preserving these animals in a state of confinement. But they were subject to many accidents: they frequently made their escape from their cages, and some of them became overburdened with fat and proved sterile, so that we did not succeed in a single instance in obtaining young from females in a state of confinement. From this cause the naturalists of Europe, and especially those of France, who were desirous of making investigations in regard to our Opossum, have been so long unsuccessful. Their usual complaint has been, "Your Opossums do not breed in confinement." In this, Dr. BARTON and our young friend Dr. MICHEL were more fortunate, but in both cases the young were produced before they were enabled to detect them in their previous existing position. We varied our experiments by endeavouring to discern the precise period when young were usually produced. We ascertained, that about the close of the first week in March, a little earlier or later, according to the age of the individual, or warmth, or coldness, of the previous winter, was the time when in this latitude this event usually occurs. Here, however, another difficulty presented itself, which for several successive seasons, thwarted us in our investigations. In the third week of February 1847, by offering premiums to the servants on several neighbouring plantations we obtained in three nights thirty-five Opossums, but of that number there was not a single female. A week afterwards, however, when the young were contained in the pouch, we received more females than males. From this circumstance we came to the conclusion that during the short period of gestation, the females, like those of some other species of quadrupeds, particularly the American black bear, conceal themselves in their burrows and can seldom be found. We then changed our instructions for capturing them, by recommending that they should be searched for in the day time, in hollow logs and trees and places where they had been previously known to burrow. By this means we were enabled at different times to obtain a small number in the state in which we were desirous of examining them. We feel under great obligations to several gentlemen of Carolina for aiding us in our investigations by procuring specimens, especially our relative Colonel HASKELL, Mr. JOHNSON, and JAMES FISHER, Esq., a close observer and intelligent naturalist. The latter, by his persevering efforts, pursued for some years at Jordan's Mills, on the upper waters of the Edisto, obtained two females in May, 1849, in the particular state in which he knew we were anxious to procure them, and brought them to us without having been previously aware that we had published the facts a year before.

The Opossums we were enabled to examine were dissected on the 11th, 14th and 18th February, 1848, and on the 12th and 22d May, 1849. Some of these had advanced to near the time of parturition. The young of those brought us by Mr. FISHER each weighed $2\frac{1}{2}$ grains. Those of one, sent us by Col. HASKELL, weighed 3 grains; and the young of another which we obtained by a Cæsarian operation, at a moment when all the rest had been excluded, and this individual alone remained, weighed 4 grains.

We remarked, that this however was a little the largest of six that composed the family, five of which were already in the pouch and attached to the teats. The largest one weighed $3\frac{3}{4}$, and another $3\frac{1}{2}$ grains. The weight, then, of the young Opossum at the moment of birth, is between 3 and 4 grains, varying a little in different specimens as is the case in the young of all animals.

The degree of life and animation in young Opossums at the moment of birth has been greatly underrated. They are neither abortions, as BLUMENBACH represented them, nor as Dr. BARTON has described them—"not fœtuses, but gelatinous bodies, weighing about a grain more or less, seven of them together weighing 10 grains"—but little creatures that are nearly as well developed at birth as the young of the white-footed mouse and several other species of rodentia. They are covered by an integument, nourished by the mammæ, breathe through nostrils, perform the operations of nature, are capable of a progressive movement at the moment of their birth, and are remarkably tenacious of life. The individual which was dissected from the parent in the manner above detailed, moved several inches on the table by crawling and rolling, and survived two hours; the thermometer in the room was at the time standing at 66° Fahrenheit. The period of gestation is from fifteen to sixteen days. We received a female from a servant who informed us, that he had that morning seen it in intercourse with the male. We first saw the young on the morning of the 17th day. Our friend Dr. MIDDLETON MICHEL, a gentleman of high scientific attainments, and who had long been engaged in investigating the characters and habits of this species, in a communication made to us, (Trans. of the Acad. Nat. Sciences, April, 1848, p. 46,) assured us from his personal observation in which he was careful to note the hour of the day, the exact period is 15 days. As he possessed better opportunities of deciding in regard to the time, the animals being in a state of domestication, we are rather more disposed to yield to his observations than to our own; there is, however, only the difference of a day between us.

The young, when first born, are naked and flesh-coloured; the eyes, together with the ears, are covered by a thin integument through which these organs and the protuberances of the ears are distinctly visible. The mouth is closed, with the exception of a small orifice, sufficiently large to receive the teat, which is so thin and attenuated that it seems no larger than the body of a pin. Length of body, 7—12ths of an inch; of tail, 2—10ths. The nails, which can be seen with the naked eye, are very distinct when viewed with a microscope, and are of a dark brown colour, small and much hooked. The nostrils are open; the lungs filled with air, and when placed in water, the young float on the surface.

The number of young usually found in the pouch appear to be less than those that are born. The highest number we have found in the pouch was thirteen, the smallest six; whereas the preserved uterus brought to us by Mr. FISHER, contained fifteen. In all such cases, where a greater number of young are produced than there are teats, the last of the brood must inevitably perish, as those that are attached appear incapable of relinquishing their hold.

The manner in which the young at birth reach the pouch, and become attached to the teats, has been the subject of much speculation and inquiry. We had an opportunity of examining this process in part, without, however, having been aware at the time that it was going on. We intended to dissect a small female Opossum, which had been a few days in our possession, but ascertained in the morning at seven o'clock on the day our examination was to have been made, that she had three young in her pouch; supposing from her small size, that she would produce no additional number, we concluded to spare her life. She was confined in a box in our study; when we occasionally looked at her, we found her lying on one side, her shoulders elevated, her body drawn up in the shape of a ball; the pouch was occasionally distended with her paws—in this position the parts reached the edge of the pouch; she was busily employed with her nose and mouth licking, as we thought, her pouch, but in which we afterwards ascertained, were her young.

At six o'clock in the afternoon we were induced to examine her again, in consequence of having observed that she had for several hours appeared very restless, when we discovered that she had added four more to her previous number, making her young family now to consist of seven. With no inconsiderable labour and the exercise of much patience, we removed three of the young from the teats, one of which perished under the process, we replaced the two living ones in the pouch; at nine o'clock examined her again and found both the young once more attached. We came to the conclusion, that she shoved them into the pouch, and with her nose or tongue moved them to the vicinity of the teats, where by an instinct of nature, the teat was drawn into the small orifice of the mouth by suction. We observed subsequently, that a young one that had been extracted from its parent a few moments before the time when it would have been born, and which had been rolled up in warm cotton, was instinctively engaged in sucking at the fibres of the cotton, and had succeeded in drawing into its mouth a considerable length of thread. A nearly similar process was observed by our friend Dr. MICHEL. He states: "The female stood on her hind legs, and the body being much bent, the young appeared and were licked into the pouch."

There is a great difficulty in deciding the question, whether the mother aids the young in finding the teats, in consequence of the impossibility of the spectators being able to know what she is actually doing, whilst her nose is in the pouch. We believe the majority of naturalists who had an opportunity of witnessing our experiments came to the conclusion, that the mother, after shoving them into the pouch, left them to their own instinct, and they became attached without her assistance. We tried another experiment that suggested itself to us. Believing that the mother would not readily adopt the young of another, or afford them any assistance, we removed six out of ten that composed her brood, returned two of her own to the pouch, together with three others fully double the size, that had been obtained from another female. She was soon observed doubled up with her nose in the pouch, and continued so for an hour, when she was examined and one of her own small ones was found attached to the teat. Seven hours afterwards she was examined again, and both the small ones were attached, but the three larger ones still remained crawling about the pouch. On the following morning, it was ascertained that the mother had adopted the strangers, as the whole family of different sizes were deriving sustenance from her.

On another occasion, a female Opossum had been sent to us caught by a dog and much wounded, in consequence of which she died a few days afterwards, but first producing seven young which to every appearance had been still born. Yet they were in the pouch, and it appeared to us that the mother's uncontrollable attachment to her young, induced her to place her offspring in the pouch, even after they were dead.

An interesting inquiry remains to be answered: Is the Opossum a placental or non-placental animal? Until we were favoured with a recent opportunity of carefully examining a uterus, containing nine young on one side, and six on the other, kindly brought to us by our friend JAMES FISHER, we were unable fully to answer this question. Our dissections and examinations were witnessed by Professors MOULTRIE, HUME, Drs. HORLBECK, MICHEL, PORCHER and others.

The Opossum is, as far as we are able to judge from the specimens examined, a non-placental animal, inasmuch as there could not be detected the slightest adhesion between the exterior membrane of the fœtus and the internal surface of the mother. The membranes consisted of a vitelline sac, filled with ramifications of omphalo-mesenteric vessels, there was a slight appearance of an umbilical cord and umbilical vessels, constituting a true allantois, but no portions of them were attached to the uterus. There was no appearance of a placenta.

The growth of the young Opossum is suprisingly rapid. We weighed the largest young one at a week old and found it had increased from $3\frac{3}{4}$ grains to 30 grains. Length of head and body exclusive of tail, $1\frac{1}{4}$ inch; tail, $\frac{1}{2}$ inch. The young at this age were very tenacious of life, as on removing two, they remained alive on the floor without any covering through a cool night, in a room containing no fire, and still exhibited a slight motion at twelve o'clock on the following day. The teats of the mother after the young had been gently drawn off measured an inch in length, having been much distended, and appeared to have been drawn into the stomach of the young. The pouches of the young females were quite apparent; they used their prehensile tails, which could now be frequently seen entwined around the necks of others. At twelve days old the eyes were still closed, a few hairs had made their appearance on the moustache; the orifice of the ears were beginning to be developed, and the nails were quite visible and sharp.

When the young are four weeks old, they begin from time to time to relax their hold on the teats, and may now be seen with their heads occasionally out of the pouch. A week later, and they venture to steal occasionally from their snug retreat in the pouch, and are often seen on the mother's back securing themselves by entwining their tails around hers. In this situation she moves from place to place in search of food, carrying her whole family along with her, to which she is much attached, and in whose defence she exhibits a considerable degree of courage, growling at any intruder, and ready to use her teeth with great severity on man or dog. In travelling, it is amusing to see this large family moving about. Some of the young, nearly the size of rats, have their tails entwined around the legs of the mother, and some around her neck, thus they are dragged along. They have a mild and innocent look, and are sleek, and in fine condition, and this is the only age in which the word pretty can be applied to the Opossum. At this period, the mother, in giving sustenance to so large a family, becomes thin, and is reduced to one half of her previous weight. The whole family of young remain with her about two months, and continue in the vicinity till autumn. In the meantime, a second and often a third brood is produced, and thus two or more broods of different ages may be seen, sometimes with the mother, and at other times not far off.

The Opossum, with the exception of our gray rabbit, is one of the most prolific of our quadrupeds. We consider the early parts of the three months of March, May and July, as the periods in South Carolina when they successively bring forth; it is even probable that they breed still more frequently, as we have observed the young during all the spring and summer months. In the month of May, 1830, whilst searching for a rare species of coleoptera, in removing with our foot some sticks composing the nest of the Florida rat, we were startled on finding our boot unceremoniously and rudely seized by an animal which we soon ascertained was a female Opossum. She had in her pouch five very small young whilst, seven others, about the size of full grown rats were detected peeping from under the rubbish. The females produce young at a year old. The young born in July do not bring forth as early as those born in March, but have their young as soon as the middle of the succeeding May. There is, of course, in this as well as in other species, some degree of irregularity in the time of their producing, as well as in the number of their young. We have reason to believe, also, that this species is more prolific in the southern than in the Middle States.

Geographical Distribution.

The Hudson River may be regarded as the farthest eastern limit of the Opossum. We have no doubt but that it will in time be found existing to the east of the Hudson, in the southern counties of New-York as well as on Long-Island and the warmer parts of the Eastern States, as the living animals are constantly carried there, and we have little doubt that if it was considered important it could be encouraged to multiply there. It has been stated to us that in New-Jersey, within five or ten miles of New-York, as many as ten or fourteen of these animals have within a few years past been taken in an autumn by means of traps, but that their number is gradually diminishing. It is common in New-Jersey and Pennsylvania, becoming more abundant as we proceed southwardly through North Carolina, South Carolina, Georgia, Louisiana and Texas, to Mexico; inhabiting in great numbers the inter-tropical regions. To the west we have traced it in all the south-western states. It exists in Indiana, Mississippi, Missouri, and Arkansas, and extends to the Pacific; it is said to exist in California. It is somewhat singular, that in every part of America, as far as we have been able to observe, the geographical range of the Opossum is very nearly the same as that of the persimon tree, of whose fruit it is so fond. This we regard, however, as merely accidental, as this food is not essential to its support. The Opossum neither ceases to multiply or to thrive in seasons in which the persimon has failed.

General Remarks.

In our plate, we gave PENNANT as the originator of the scientific name of this species. We find, however, that he only calls it the Virginia Opossum, with a reference to the *Didelphys marsupialis*, LINNEUS. GMELIN subsequently arranged it under *Didelphys marsupialis*. As SHAW, in 1800, as far as we have been able to ascertain, seems to have been the first who applied the Latin specific name, *D. Virginiana*, we have, in accordance with the rules laid down by naturalists, given him the credit of the specific name.

Genus Canis.—Linnæus.

Dental Formula.

$$Incisive \ \frac{6}{6}; \ Canine \ \frac{1—1}{1—1}; \ Molar \ \frac{6—6}{6—6} = 40.$$

The three first in the upper jaw, and the four in the lower, trenchant but small, and called also false molars. The great carnivorous tooth above bi-cuspid, with a small tubercle on the inner side, that below with the posterior lobe altogether tubercular, and two tuberculous teeth behind each of the great carnivorous teeth. Muzzle, elongate; tongue, soft; ears, erect, (sometimes pendant in the domestic varieties.) Fore feet, pendactylous; hind feet, tetradactylous. Teats, both inguinal and vental.

Canis Lupus.—Linn.—(Var. Ater.)

Black American Wolf.

Plate lxvii. Male.

C. niger, magnitudine, formaque C. lupi.

Characters.

Size and shape of the Common American Wolf; Canis, lupus occidentalis; colour black.

Synonymes.

LOUP NOIR DE CANADA, Buffon, vol. ix., p. 364–41.
BLACK WOLF, Long's Expd., vol. i., p. 95.
"   Say, Frankl. Jour., vol. i., p. 172.
"   Griffith, Anim. King., vol. 2., p. 348.
"   Godman, Nat. Hist., vol. i., p. 267.
CANIS LYACON, Harlan's Fauna, p. 82.
VAR. E. LUPUS ATER, Black Amer. Wolf, Richardson, Fauna Boreali Amer., p. 70.

Description.

We regard this animal as a mere variety of the Common American Wolf, to be hereafter described and need only here observe, that all the Wolves we have examined, such as the *Canis nubilis* of SAY, the White Wolf, the Red Texan Wolf and Black Wolf, are of the same form, although in size the White Wolf is considerably the largest.

Colour.

Face, legs, point of tail and under jaw, black; body, irregularly and transversely barred with blackish brown and greyish; sides of the neck, greyish brown; behind the shoulders, under the belly and on the forehead, greyish brown. Some specimens are darker than others—we have examined several that were perfectly black on the whole surface of the body.

Dimensions.

	Feet.	Inches.
Length of head and body	3	2
Do. of tail vertebræ		11
Do. including fur	1	1
Height of ear		3

Habits.

Not an individual of the party saw a Black Wolf during our trip up the Missouri, on the prairies near Fort Union, or along the shores of that portion of the Yellow Stone River that we visited. Mr. SAY speaks of its being the most common variety on the banks of the Missouri, but, unfortunately, does not state precisely where.

Wolves of this colour were abundant near Henderson, Kentucky, when we removed to that place, and we saw them frequently during our rambles through the woods after birds.

We found a Black Wolf in one of our wild turkey pens, early one morning.

He observed us, as we approached, but instead of making his escape, squatted close down, like a dog which does not wish to be seen. We came up within a few yards of the pen, and shot him dead, through an opening between the logs. This Wolf had killed several fine turkeys, and was in the act of devouring one, which was, doubtless, the reason he did not attempt to make his escape when we approached him.

There is a strong feeling of hostility entertained by the settlers of the wild portions of the country, toward the Wolf, as his strength, agility, and cunning, (in which last qualification, he is scarcely inferior to his relative, the fox,) tend to render him the most destructive enemy of their pigs, sheep, or young calves, which range in the forest; therefore, in our country, he is not more mercifully dealt with than in any other part of the world. Traps and snares of various sorts are set for catching him in those districts in which he still abounds. Being more fleet and perhaps better winded than the fox, the Wolf is seldom pursued with hounds or any other dogs in open chase, unless wounded. Although Wolves are bold and savage, few instances occur in our temperate regions of their making an attack on man; and we have only had one such case come under our own notice. Two young negroes, who resided near the banks of the Ohio, in the lower part of the State of Kentucky, about thirty years ago, had sweethearts living on another plantation, four miles distant. After the labours of the day were over, they frequently visited the fair ladies of their choice, the nearest way to whose dwelling lay directly across a large cane brake. As to the lover every moment is precious, they usually took this route to save time. Winter had set in cold, dark and gloomy, and after sunset scarcely a glimpse of light or glow of warmth were to be found in that dreary swamp, except in the eyes and bosoms of the ardent youths who traversed these gloomy solitudes. One night, they set forth over a thin crust of snow. Prudent, to a certain degree, the lovers carried their axes on their shoulders, and walked as briskly as the narrow path would allow. Some transient glimpses of light now and then met their eyes in the more open spaces between the trees, or when the heavy drifting clouds parting at times allowed a star to peep forth on the desolate scene. Fearfully, a long and frightful howl burst upon them, and they were instantly aware that it proceeded from a troop of hungry and perhaps desperate wolves. They paused for a moment and a dismal silence succeeded. All was dark, save a few feet of the snow-covered ground immediately in front of them. They resumed their pace hastily, with their axes in their hands prepared for an attack. Suddenly, the foremost man was assailed by several wolves which seized on him, and inflicted terrible wounds with their fangs on his legs and arms, and as they were followed by many others as ravenous as themselves, several sprung at the breast of his companion, and dragged him to the ground. Both struggled manfully against their foes, but in a short time one of the negroes had ceased to move; and the other, reduced in strength and perhaps despairing of aiding his unfortunate comrade or even saving his own life, threw down his axe, sprang on to the branch of a tree, and speedily gained a place of safety amid the boughs. Here he passed a miserable night, and the next morning the bones of his friend lay scattered around on the snow, which was stained with his blood. Three dead wolves lay near, but the rest of the pack had disappeared; and Scipio sliding to the ground, recovered the axes and returned home to relate the terrible catastrophe.

About two years after this occurrence, as we were travelling between Henderson and Vincennes, we chanced to stop for the night at the house of a farmer, (for in those days hotels were scarce in that part of the good State of Indiana.) After putting up our horses and refreshing ourself, we entered into conversation with our worthy host, and were invited by him to visit the wolf pits which he had constructed about half a mile from the house. Glad of the opportunity, we accompanied him across the fields to the skirts of the adjoining forest, where he had three pits within a few hundred yards of each other. They were about eight feet deep, broadest at the bottom, so as to render it impossible for the most active animal to escape from them. The mouth of each pit was covered with a revolving platform of boughs and twigs, interlaced together and attached to a cross piece of timber, which served for an axle. On this light sort of platform, which was balanced by a heavy stick of wood fastened to the under side, a large piece of putrid venison was tied for bait. After examining all the pits, we returned to the house, our companion remarking that he was in the habit of visiting his pits daily, in order to see that all was right; that the wolves had been very bad that season; had destroyed nearly all his sheep, and had killed one of his colts. "But," added he, "I am now paying them off in full, and if I have any luck, you will see some fun in the morning." With this expectation we retired to rest, and were up at day-light. "I think," said our host, "that all is right; for I see the dogs are anxious to get away to the pits, and although they are nothing but curs, their noses are pretty keen for wolves." As he took up his gun and axe and a large knife, the dogs began to howl and bark, and whisked around us as if full of delight. When we reached the first pit, we found the bait had been disturbed and the platform was somewhat injured, but the animal was not in the pit. On

Plate LXVII

N° 14

On Stone by W.E. Hitchcock

Black American Wolf

Lith. Printed & Col^d by J.T. Bowen Phil^a

Drawn from Nature by J. W. Audubon

examining the second pit, we discovered three famous fellows safe enough in it, two black and one brindled, all of good size. They were lying flat on the earth, with their ears close down to their heads, their eyes indicating fear more than anger. To our astonishment, the farmer proposed descending into the pit to hamstring them, in order to haul them up, and then allow them to be killed by the dogs, which, he said, would sharpen his curs for an encounter with the wolves, should any come near his house in future. Being novices in this kind of business, we begged to be lookers on. "With all my heart," cried the farmer, "stand here, and look at me," whereupon he glided down, on a knobbed pole, taking his axe and knife with him, and leaving his rifle to our care. We were not a little surprised at the cowardice of the wolves. The woodman stretched out their hind legs, in succession, and with a stroke of the knife cut the principal tendon above the joint, exhibiting as little fear, as if he had been marking lambs. As soon as he had thus disabled the wolves, he got out, but had to return to the house for a rope, which he had not thought of. He returned quickly, and, whilst I secured the platform in a perpendicular position on its axis, he made a slip knot at one end of the rope, and threw it over the head of one of the wolves. We now hauled the terrified animal up; and motionless with fright, half choked, and disabled in its hind legs, the farmer slipped the rope from its neck, and left it to the mercy of the dogs, who set upon it with great fury and worried it to death. The second was dealt with in the same manner; but the third, which was probably oldest, showed some spirit the moment the dogs were set upon it, and scuffled along on its forelegs, at a surprising rate, snapping all the while furiously at the dogs, several of which it bit severely; and so well did the desperate animal defend itself, that the farmer, apprehensive of its killing some of his pack, ran up and knocked it on the head with his axe. This wolf was a female, and was blacker than the other dark-coloured one.

Once, when we were travelling on foot not far from the southern boundary of Kentucky, we fell in with a Black Wolf, following a man with a rifle on his shoulders. On speaking with him about this animal, he assured us that it was as tame and as gentle as any dog, and that he had never met with a dog that could trail a deer better. We were so much struck with this account and the noble appearance of the wolf, that we offered him one hundred dollars for it; but the owner would not part with it for any price.

Our plate was drawn from a fine specimen, although not so black a one as we have seen. We consider the Dusky Wolf and the Black Wolf as identically the same.

As we shall have occasion to refer to the characteristics of Wolves generally again, we shall not prolong this article; the Black, as already stated, being, in fact, only a variety. In our account of the Common Gray Wolf of the North, and the White Wolf of the Prairies, which last is very common, we shall give farther and more specific details of their breeding and other matters.

Geographical Distribution.

All packs of American Wolves usually consist of various shades of colour and varieties, nearly black, have occasionally been found in every part of the United States. The varieties, with more or less of black, continue to increase as we proceed farther to the south, and in Florida the prevailing colour of the wolves is black. We have seen two or three skins procured in N. Carolina. There is a specimen in the Museum of the Philosophical Society of Charleston, obtained at Goose Creek, a few years ago, that is several shades darker than the specimen from which our drawing was made; and in a gang of seventeen wolves, which existed in Colleton District, S. C., a few years ago (sixteen of which were killed by the hunters in eighteen months), we were informed that about one fifth were black and the others of every shade of colour—from black to dusky grey and yellowish white. We have heard of this variety in the southern part of Missoui, Louisiana, and the northern parts of Texas.

Sciurus Capistratus. —Bosc.

Fox Squirrel.

Plate lxviii

S. magnus, colorem variens; naso auriculisque albis; pilis crassis; cauda corpore longiore.

Characters.

Size, large; tail, longer than the body; hair, coarse; ears and nose, white; subject to great variety in colour.

Synonymes.

SCIURUS CAPISTRATUS; Bosc, Ann. du Mus., vol. i., p. 281.
"   VULPINUS? Linn. Ed. Gmel., 1788.
"   NIGER; Catesby.
BLACK SQUIRREL; Bartram's Travels in North America.
SCIURUS CAPISTRATUS; Desm. Mammalogie, p. 332.
"   VARIEGATUS; Desm. Mammalogie, p. 333.
"   CAPISTRATUS; Cuv., Regne Animal, vol. i., p. 139.
FOX SQUIRREL, Lawson's Carolina, p. 124.
SCIURUS CAPISTRATUS; Harlan.
SCIURUS VULPINUS; Godman.

Description.

This is the largest and most interesting species of the genus, found in the United States. Although it is subject to great varieties of colour, occasioning no little confusion by the creation of several nominal species, yet it possesses several striking and uniform markings by which it may, through all its varieties, be distinguished at a glance from any other.

The Fox Squirrel is furnished with the following teeth, viz:—

$$\text{Incisive } \frac{2}{2}; \text{ Canine } \frac{0-0}{0-0}; \text{ Molar } \frac{4-4}{4-4} = 20.$$

But although we have thus given to this species but four grinders in the upper jaw, which peculiarity applies to nearly all the specimens that may be examined,—yet, in a very young animal, obtained on the 5th of April, in South Carolina, and which had apparently left the nest but a day or two, we observed a very minute, round, deciduous, anterior grinder on each side. These teeth, however, must be shed at a very early period; as in two other specimens, obtained on the 20th of the same month, they were entirely wanting. The teeth of all our squirrels present so great a similarity, that it will be found impossible to designate the species from these alone, without referring to other peculiarities which the eye of the practical naturalist may detect. In young animals of this species, the tuberculous crowns on the molars are prominent and acute; these sharp points, however, are soon worn off, and the tubercles in the adult are round and blunt. The first molar in the upper jaw is the smallest, and is triangular in shape; the second and third one a little larger and square; and the posterior one, which is about the size of the third, is rounded on its posterior surface. The upper incisors, which are of a deep orange colour anteriorly, are strong and compressed, deep at their roots, flat on their sides; in some specimens there is a groove anteriorly running longitudinally through the middle, presenting the appearance of a double tooth; in others, this tooth is wanting. In the lower jaw, the anterior grinder is the smallest; the rest increase in size to the last, which is the largest.

Nose, obtuse; forehead, slightly arched; whiskers, a little longer than the head; ears, rounded, covered with short hairs on both surfaces; there is scarcely any projection of fur beyond the outer surface, as is the case in nearly all the other species; the hair is very coarse, appearing in some specimens geniculate; tail, broad and distichous; legs and feet, stout; and the whole body has more the appearance of strength than of agility.

Colour.

In the grey variety of this species, which is—as far as we have observed—the most common, the nose, extending to within four or five lines of the eyes, the ears, feet, and belly, are white; forehead and cheeks, brownish black; the hairs on the back are dark plumbeous near the roots, then a broad line of cinereous, then black, and broadly tipped with white, with an occasional black hair interspersed, especially on the neck and fore shoulder, giving the animal a light grey appearance; the hairs of the tail are, for three-fourths of their length, white from the roots, then a ring of black, with the tips white. This is the variety given by Bosc and other authors as *Sciurus capistratus.*

Second variety: the Black Fox Squirrel. Nose and ears, white; a few light-coloured hairs on the feet; the rest of the body and tail, black; there are, occasionally, a few white hairs in the tail. This is the original Black Squirrel of CATESBY and BARTRAM, (*Sci. Niger.*)

Third variety. Nose, mouth, under jaw and ears, white; head, thighs and

Fox Squirrel.

Drawn from Nature by J.J. Audubon F.R.S.F.L.S.

Lith Printed & Col.ᵈ by J.T. Bowen, Ph.

belly, black; back and tail, dark grey. This is the variety alluded to by DESMAREST, (Ency. Method, Mammalogie, 333.)

There is a fourth variety, which is very common in Alabama, and also occasionally seen in the upper districts of South Carolina and Georgia, which has on several occasions been sent to us as a distinct species. The ears and nose, as in all the other varieties, are white. This, indeed, is a permanent mark, running through all the varieties, by which this species may be easily distinguished. Head and neck, black; back, a rusty blackish brown; neck, thighs, and belly, bright rusty colour; tail, annulated with black and red. This is the variety erroneously considered by the author of the notes on McMUR-TRIE's "Translation of Cuvier," (see vol. i., Appendix, p. 433,) as *Sciurus rufiventer.*

The three first noted above are common in the lower and middle districts of South Carolina; and, although they are known to breed together, yet it is very rare to find any specimens indicating an intermediate variety. Where the parents are both black, the young are invariably of the same colour—the same may be said of the other varieties; where, on the other hand, there is one parent of each colour, an almost equal number are of the colour of the male, the other of the female. On three occasions, we had an opportunity of examining the young produced by progenitors of both colours. The first nest contained two black and two grey; and the third, three black and two grey. The colour of the young did not, in a majority of instances, correspond with that of the parent of the same sex: although the male parent was black, the young males were frequently grey, and *vice versa.*

Dimensions.

	Inches.	Lines.
Length of head and body	14	5
" tail vertebræ	12	4
" tail to tip	15	2
" palm and middle fore claw	1	9
" sole and middle hind claw	2	11
" fur on the back		8
Height of ear, posteriorly		7

Habits.

Although there is a general similarity of habit in all the species of *Sciurus,* yet the present has some peculiarities which we have not noticed in any other. The Fox Squirrel, instead of preferring rich low lands, thickly clothed with timber, as is the case with the Carolina Grey Squirrel, is seldom seen in such situations; but prefers elevated pine ridges, where the trees are not crowded near each other, and where there is an occasional oak and hickory interspersed. It is also frequently found in the vicinity of rich valleys, to which it resorts for nuts, acorns and chinquepins, (*castanea pumila,*) which such soils produce. In some aged and partially decayed oak, this Squirrel finds a safe retreat for itself and mate; a hollow tree of any kind is sufficient for its purpose if Nature has prepared a hole, it is occupied, if otherwise, the animal finds no difficulty in gnawing one or several, for its accommodation. The tree selected is in all cases hollow, and the Squirrel only gnaws through the outer shell in order to find a residence, which requires but little labour and skill to render it secure and comfortable. At other times, it takes possession of the deserted hole of the ivory-billed woodpecker, (*Picus principalis.*) The summer duck (*Anas sponsa*) too, is frequently a competitor for the same residence; contests for possession occasionally take place between these three species, and we have generally observed, that the tenant that has already deposited its eggs or young in such situations is seldom ejected. The male and female summer duck unite in chasing and beating with their wings any Squirrel that may approach their nests, nor are they idle with their bills and tongues, but continue biting, hissing and clapping their wings until the intruder is expelled. On the other hand, when the Squirrel has its young in the hole of a tree, and is intruded on, either by a woodpecker or a summer duck, it immediately rushes to its hole, and after having entered remains at the mouth of it, occasionally protruding its head, and with a low angry bark keeps possession, until the intruder, weary of the contest, leaves it unmolested. Thus Nature imparts to each species additional spirit and vigour in defence of its young; whilst at the same time, the intruder on the possessions of others, as if conscious of the injustice of his acts, evinces a degree of pusillanimity and cowardice.

In the vicinity of the permanent residence of the Fox Squirrel, several nests, composed of sticks, leaves and mosses, are usually seen on the pine trees. These are seldom placed on the summits, but in the forks, and more frequently where several branches unite and afford a secure basis for them. These nests may be called their summer home, for they seem to be occupied only in fine weather, and are deserted during wintry and stormy seasons.

In December and January, the season of sexual intercourse, the male chases the female for hours together on the same tree, running up one side and descending on the other, making at the same time a low gutteral noise, that scarcely bears any resemblance to the barking which they utter on other occasions. The young are produced from the beginning of March, and sometimes earlier, to April. The nests containing them, which we have had opportunities of examining, were always in hollow trees. They receive the nourishment of the mother for four or five weeks, when they are left to shift for themselves, but continue to reside in the vicinity of, and even to occupy the same nests with, their parents till autumn. It has been asserted by several planters of Carolina, that this species has two broods during the season.

The food of the Fox Squirrel is various; besides acorns, and different kinds of nuts, its principal subsistence for many weeks in autumn is the fruit extracted from the cones of the pine, especially the long-leaved pitch pine, (*Pinus palustris.*) Whilst the green corn is yet in its milky state, this Squirrel makes long journeys to visit the fields, and for the sake of convenience frequently builds a temporary summer-house in the vicinity, in order to share with the little Carolina squirrel and the crow a portion of the delicacies and treasures of the husbandman; where he is also exposed to the risks incurred by the thief and plunderer: for these fields are usually guarded by a gunner, and in this way thousands of squirrels are destroyed during the green corn season. The Fox Squirrel does not appear to lay up any winter stores—there appears to be no food in any of his nests, nor does he, like the red squirrel, (*Sciurus hudsonius,*) resort to any hoards which in the season of abundance were buried in the earth, or concealed under logs and leaves. During the winter season he leaves his retreat but seldom, and then only for a little while and in fine weather in the middle of the day. He has evidently the power, like the marmot and racoon, of being sustained for a considerable length of time without much suffering in the absence of food. When this animal makes his appearance in winter, he is seen searching among the leaves where the wild turkey has been busy at work, and gleaning the refuse acorns which have escaped its search; at such times, also, this squirrel does not reject worms and insects which he may detect beneath the bark of fallen or decayed trees. Towards spring, he feeds on the buds of hickory, oak, and various other trees, as well as on several kinds of roots, especially the wild potato. (*Apios tuberosa.*) As the spring advances farther, he is a constant visitor to the black mulberry tree, (*Morus rubra,*) where he finds a supply for several weeks. From this time till winter, the fruits of the field and forest enable him to revel in abundance.

Most other species of this genus when alarmed in the woods immediately betake themselves to the first convenient tree that presents itself,—not so with the Fox Squirrel. When he is aware of being discovered whilst on the ground, he pushes directly for a hollow tree, which is often a quarter of a mile distant, and it requires a good dog, a man on horseback, or a very swift runner, to induce him to alter his course, or compel him to ascend any other tree. When he is silently seated on a tree and imagines himself unperceived by the person approaching him, he suddenly spreads himself flatly on the limb, and gently moving to the opposite side, often by this stratagem escapes detection. When, however, he is on a small tree, and is made aware of being observed, he utters a few querulous barking notes, and immediately leaps to the ground, and hastens to a more secure retreat. If overtaken by a dog, he defends himself with great spirit, and is often an overmatch for the small terriers which are used for the purpose of treeing him.

He is very tenacious of life, and an ordinary shot gun, although it may wound him repeatedly, will seldom bring him down from the tops of the high pines to which he retreats when pursued, and in such situations the rifle is the only certain enemy he has to dread.

This Squirrel is seldom seen out of its retreat early in the morning and evening, as is the habit of other species. He seems to be a late riser, and usually makes his appearance at 10 or 11 o'clock, and retires to his domicile long before evening. He does not appear to indulge so frequently in the barking propensities of the genus as the other and smaller species. This note, when heard, is not very loud, but hoarse and gutteral. He is easily domesticated, and is occasionally seen in cages, but is less active and sprightly than the smaller species.

As an article of food, the Fox Squirrel is apparently equally good with any other species, although we have observed that the little Carolina squirrel is usually preferred, as being more tender and delicate. Where, however, squirrels are very abundant, men soon become surfeited with this kind of game, and in Carolina, even among the poorer class, it is not generally considered a great delicacy.

This species, like all the rest of the squirrels, is infested during the summer months with a troublesome larva (*Oestrus*), which fastening itself on the neck or shoulders, must be very annoying, as those most affected in this manner are usually poor and their fur appears thin and disordered. It is, however, less exposed to destruction from birds of prey and wild beasts than the other species. It leaves its retreat so late in the morning, and retires so early in the afternoon, that it is wholly exempt from the rapacity of owls, so destructive to the Carolina squirrel. We have seen it bid defiance to the attacks of the red-shouldered hawk (*Falco lineatus*), the only abundant species in the south; and it frequents high grounds and open woods, to which the fox and wild cat seldom resort, during the middle of the day, so that man is almost the only enemy it has to dread.

Geographical Distribution.

This species is said to exist sparingly in New Jersey. We have not observed it farther north than Virginia, nor could we find it in the mountainous districts of that state. In the pine forests of North Carolina, it becomes more common. In the middle and maritime districts of South Carolina it is almost daily met with, although it cannot be said to be a very abundant species anywhere. It exists in Georgia, Alabama, Mississippi, Florida and Louisiana.

General Remarks.

This Squirrel has been frequently described under different names. Bosc appears to be entitled to the credit of having bestowed on it the earliest specific name. GMELLIN, in 1788, named it *S. vulpinus*. The black squirrel of CATESBY is the black variety of the present species.

Genus Condylura.—Illiger.

Dental Formula.

Incisive $\frac{2}{4}$; *Canine* $\frac{1-1}{1-1}$; *Molar* $\frac{8-8}{7-7}$ = 40.

Muzzle, long, extremity ciliated; ears, none; external eyes, small; feet, pendactylous; nails before, formed for digging—those behind, weak and small.

The generic name *Condylura* was given by ILLIGER, founded on an accidental character. A figure of DELAFAILLE erroneously represents the tail as knobbed; hence the genus was formed from two Greek words—Χονδαδας (nodus) and οδϑη (cauda) "knobbed tail."

There is but one well determined species of this genus at present known.

Condylura Cristata.—Linn.

Common Star-Nosed Mole.

Plate lxix.—Natural size.

C. naribus carunculatus; caudâ corpore breviore; vellus obscure cinereo, nigricans, subtus dilutior.

Characters.

Nostrils, surrounded by a circle of membraneous processes; tail, shorter than the body; colour, brownish black above, a shade lighter beneath.

Synonymes.

SOREX CRISTATUS, Linn., Ed. 12, p. 73.
LONG-TAILED MOLE, Pennant's Hist. Quad., vol. ii., p. 232 to 90, f. 2.
    "   " Pennant's Arct. Zool., vol. i., p. 140.
TALPA LONGICAUDATA ERX. Syst., tom. i., p. 188.
LONG-TAILED MOLE, Condylura a lonquequeue, Desm. Mamm., f. i., p. 158.
    "   " Condylura cristata, Harlan, p. 36.
    "   " Godm. vol. i., p, 100.
    "   " C. macroura, Harlan, p. 39.
    "   " C. longicaudata, Richardson Fauna, p. 13; C. macroura, p. 234.
    "   " C. cristata, De Kay, N. Hist. N. Y., p. 12.

Description.

In the upper jaw there are two large incisive teeth hollowed in front in the shape of a spoon. The next tooth on each side is long, pointed, conical, with two tubercles, one before and the other behind at the base, resembling in all its characters a canine tooth: these are succeeded by five small molars on each side, the posterior one being the largest. There are three true molars on each side, with two acute tubercles on the inner side—the first or anterior of these molars is the largest, the second a little smaller, and the third or posterior one the smallest. In the lower jaw there are four large incisors, spoon shaped, and bearing a strong resemblance to those in the upper jaw. The next on each side are tolerably long sharp, conical teeth, corresponding with those above which we have set down as canine. The four succeeding teeth on each side, which may be regarded as false molars, are lobed and increase in size as they approach the true molars; the tree molars on each side resemble those above, having two folds of enamel forming a point.

In the shape of its body this species bears a considerable resemblance to the Common Mole of Europe (*Talpa Europea*) and to BREWER's Shrew Mole (*Scalops Brewerii*); in the indications on the nose, however, it differs widely from both. The body is cylindrical, about as stout as that of our Common Shrew Mole, and has the appearance of being attached to the head without any distinct neck. Muzzle, slender and elongated, terminated with a cartilaginous fringe which originated its English name—the Star-nosed Mole. This circular disk is composed of twenty cartilaginous fibres, two of which situated beneath the nostrils are shortest. The eyes are very small. Moustaches, few and short. There is an orifice in place of an external ear, which does not project beyond the skin. Fore feet, longer and narrower than those of the Common Shrew, feet longer and narrower than those of the Common Mole; palms, naked, covered with scales; claws, flattened, acute, channelled beneath; hind extremities longer than the fore ones, placed far back; feet nearly naked, scaly; tail, subcylindrical, sparingly covered with coarser hair. It is clothed with dense soft fur.

Colour.

Eyes, black; nose and feet, flesh colour; point of nails and end of cartilaginous fringe, roseate. The fur on the whole body, dark plumbeous at the roots, and without any annulations, deepening towards the apex into a brownish black. In some shades of light the Star Nose appears perfectly black throughout. On the under surface it is a shade lighter. In the colour of the feet we have seen some variations: a specimen before us, has dark brown feet, another pale ashy brown, and a third yellowish white; the majority of specimens, however, have their feet brownish white. One specimen is marked under the chin, throat and neck with light yellowish brown, the others are darker in those parts.

Dimensions.

	Inches.
From point of nose to root of tail	5
Tail	3
From heel to end of claw	$\frac{7}{8}$
Breadth of palm	$\frac{3}{8}$

Habits.

As far as we have been able to ascertain, the habits of this species do not differ very widely from those of our Common Shrew Mole. We doubt, however, whether its galleries ever run to so great a distance as those of the latter animal, nor does it appear to be in the habit of visiting high grounds. It burrows and forms galleries under ground, and appears to be able to make rapid progress in soft earth. Its food is of the same nature as that of the Common Mole, and it appears to prefer the vicinity of brooks or swampy places, doubtless because in such localities earth worms and the larvæ of various insects are generally abundant.

The proper use of the radiating process at the end of the nose has not been fully ascertained, but as the animal has the power of moving these tendrils in various directions, they may be useful in its search after worms or other prey, as is the moveable snout of the Shrew Mole. When confined in a box, or on the floor of a room, this Mole feeds on meat of almost any kind. It is not as strong as the Common Mole, nor as injurious to the farmer, since it avoids cultivated fields, and confines itself to meadows and low swampy places.

During the rutting season the tail of the Star-nosed Mole is greatly enlarged, which circumstance caused Dr. HARLAN to describe a specimen taken at that season as a new species, under the name *Condylura macroura*.

Dr. GODMAN's account of the abundance of this species does not coincide with our own experience on this subject. He says, "In many places it is scarcely possible to advance a step without breaking down their galleries, by which the surface is thrown into ridges and the surface of the green sward in no slight degree disfigured." We have sometimes supposed that he might have mistaken the galleries of the Common Shrew Mole for those made by the Star-Nose, as to us it has always appeared a rare species in every part of our Union.

In a few localities where we were in the habit, many years ago, of obtaining the Star-nosed Mole, it was always found on the banks of rich meadows near running streams. The galleries did not run so near the surface as those of the Common Shrew Mole. We caused one of the galleries to be dug out, and obtained a nest containing three young, apparently a week old. The radiations on the nose were so slightly developed that until we carefully examined them we supposed they were the young of the Common Shrew Mole. The nest was spacious, composed of withered grasses, and situated in a large excavation under a stump. The old ones had made their escape, and we endeavoured to preserve the young; but the want of proper nourishment caused their death in a couple of days.

The specimen of the Star-nosed Mole, from which our plate was drawn, was sent to us by our highly esteemed friend JAMES G. KING, Esq., having been captured on a moist piece of ground at his country seat in New Jersey, opposite the city of New-York.

Geographical Distribution.

This species is found sparingly in all the northern and eastern states. Dr. RICHARDSON supposes it to exist as far north as Lake Superior. We obtained a specimen five miles from the Falls of Niagara, on the Canada side, and have traced it in all the New-England States. We received specimens from Dr. BREWER, obtained near Boston, and from W. O. AYRES, Esq., from Long Island. We caught a few of these animals near New-York, and obtained others from various parts of the state. We saw a specimen at York, Pennsylvania, and found another at Frankfort, east of Philadelphia. We captured one in the valleys of the Virginia Mountains, near the Red Sulphur Springs, and received another from the valleys in the mountains of North Carolina, near the borders of South Carolina, and presume it may follow the valleys of the Alleghany ridge as far to the south as those latitudes. We have never found it in South Carolina or Georgia, but to the west we have traced it in Ohio and the northern parts of Tennessee.

General Remarks.

We have been induced to undertake a careful examination of the teeth of this species, which forms the type of the genus, in consequence of the wide differences existing among authors in regard to the characters of the teeth. DEMAREST gave six incisors above and four below in the under jaw, cheek-teeth fourteen above and sixteen beneath. In this arrangement he is followed by HARLAN, GODMAN, GRIFFITH, DE KAY and others. The description of the teeth, by DESMAREST, is very accurate, and so is the very recent one of Dr. DE KAY. F. CUVIER, on whose judgment, in regard to characters founded on dentition, we would sooner rely than on that of any other naturalist, has on the other hand, (*Des dents des Mammifères*, 1825, p. 56,) given descriptions and figures of these teeth, there being two incisive, two canine, and sixteen molar above, and two incisive, two canine, and fourteen molar below. Our recent examination of a series of skulls are in accordance with his views, and we have adopted his dental arrangement. The difference, however, between these authors is more in appearance than in reality. The incisors, canine, and false molars, in their character so nearly approach each other, that it is exceedingly difficult to assign to the several grades of teeth their true position in the dental system.

LINNÆUS described this species under the name of *Sorex cristatus*, in 1776, (12th edition, p. 73); PENNANT, in 1771, gave a description and poor figure of what he called the Long-tailed Mole; and in 1777, ERXLEBEN bestowed on the animal thus figured, the name of *S. longicaudata*. PENNANT's specimen was received from New-York, and although it was badly figured it was correctly characterized "Long tailed Mole, with a radiated nose," and in his "Arctic Zoology" he describes it as "the nose long, the end radiated with short tendrils." The whole mistake we conceive was made by DESMAREST, whose work we have found exceedingly inaccurate, misled, probably, by PENNANT's figure, without looking at his description. He gives one of the characters *"point des crâtes nasales,"* when PENNANT had stated quite the reverse. Hence the error of HARLAN, whose article on *Condylura longicaudata* is a translation of DESMAREST. We feel confident that this supposed species must be struck from the list of true species in our *Fauna*.

The *Condylura macroura* of HARLAN, (*Fauna Americana*, p. 30,) was regarded as a new species, in consequence of a specimen with the tail greatly enlarged. It was a second time published by RICHARDSON, who adopted HARLAN's name; GODMAN first suggested the idea that this might be traced to a peculiarity in the animal at a particular season. It is known that a similar enlargement takes place annually in the neck of the male deer during the rutting season. We have examined several specimens where the tail was only slightly enlarged, and the swelling was just commencing, and we possess one where one half of the tail from the root is of the usual large size of *C. macroura*, and the other half towards the end is abruptly diminished so as to leave one half of the tail to designate a new species and the other half forcing it back to its legitimate place in the system of nature.

The singular character (knotted tail) on which this Genus was erroneously founded should suggest to the naturalist the necessity of caution. The tails of quadrupeds in drying often assume a very different shape from that which they originally possessed. This is especially the case among the Shrews and mice, that are described from dried specimens, as square-tailed, angular or knobbed, whereas in nature their tails were round.

Genus Sorex.—Linn.

Dental Formula.

Incisive $\frac{2}{2}$; Lateral incisive or false Canine from $\frac{3\text{ to }5}{2-2}$; Molar from $\frac{4\text{ to }5}{3-3}$; from 26 to 34 teeth.

Incisive teeth in the upper jaw indented at their base; in the lower, proceeding horizontally from their aveoli and turned upwards towards their points where they are usually of a brown colour; lateral incisive or false canine, conical, small, shorter than the cheek-teeth.

Muzzle and nose, much elongated; snout, moveable. Ears and eyes, small; pendactylous; nails, hooked. A series of glands along the flanks, exuding a scented unctuous matter.

The generic name is derived from the Latin word *Sorex*, a Shrew, field rat.

Authors have described about twenty-three species of Shrews, twenty existing on the Eastern continent and thirteen in N. America. Many of these species are not as yet determined, we can scarcely doubt from past discoveries that this number will in time be greatly increased. They are, no doubt, susceptible of being arranged into different groups and genera.

We know no genus in which the American naturalist has a greater prospect of success in adding new species than that of Sorex.

Sorex Parvus.—Say.

Say's Least Shrew.

Plate lxx. Natural Size.

S. supra fuscenti-cinereus, infra cinereus; dentibus nigricaudatus; cauda brevi, sub-cylindrica.

Characters.

Body above brownish ash, cinereous beneath. Teeth black, tail short, sub-cylindrical.

Synonymes.

SOREX PARVUS, Say, Long's Exped., vol. i., p. 163.
"   "   Linsby, Am. Journal, vol. xxxix., p. 388.
"   "   Harlan, p. 28. Godman, vol. i., p. 78, pl., fig 2.
"   "   Dekay, Nat. Hist. N. Y., p. 19.

Plate LXIX

N° 14

Common Star - Nose Mole.

On Stone by N E Hitchcock

New ... Nature of H. Audubon. F.R.S.F.L.S.

Lith Printed & Col by J T Bowen P

Description.

Dental System.

Incisive $\frac{2}{2}$; *Lateral incisive* $\frac{4-4}{2-2}$; *Molar* $\frac{4-4}{4-4}$ = 32.

In the upper jaws the incisors are small, much hooked, and have a posterior lobe; the succeeding lateral incisors, are minute, conical, not lobed, the two anterior ones much the largest. The first grinder is smaller than the second and third, the fourth is the smallest. In the lower jaw the incisors are a little smaller than those in the upper. They are much more hooked and have each a large posterior lobe. The two lateral incisors are small not lobed—the grinders have each two sharp points rising above the enamel. The second tooth is largest and the third smallest. Nose slender and long, but less so than that of many other species, especially that of *S. longirostris* and *S. Richardsonii*. Muzzle, bi-lobate, naked; moustaches, numerous, long, reaching to the shoulders; body, slender; eyes, very small, ears, none; the auditory opening being covered by a round lobe, without any folds above; feet sparsely clothed with minute hairs, palms naked; tail thickly clothed with minute hairs, fur, short, close, soft, and silky.

Colour.

All the teeth are at their points intensely black; whiskers, white and black; point of nose, feet, and nails, whitish; the hair is, on the upper surface plumbeous, from the roots, and of an ashy-brown at the tips; a shade lighter on the under surface: under the chin it is of an ashy grey gradually blending with the colours on the back.

Dimensions.

	Inches.
From point of nose to root of tail, ...	$2\frac{7}{8}$
Tail, ...	$\frac{3}{4}$

Habits.

This little creature, to which the above name was attached by SAY, was first captured by Mr. TITIAN R. PEALE, during LONG's Expedition to the Rocky Mountains, at Engineer Cantonment on the Missouri, where it was found in a pit-fall excavated for catching wolves.

Look at the plate, reader, and imagine the astonishment of the hunter on examining the pit intended for the destruction of the savage prowlers of the prairies, when, instead of the game that he intended to entrap, he perceived this, the Least Shrew, timidly running across the bottom.

The family to which this Shrew belongs, is somewhat allied in form and habits to the mole, but many species are now probably extinct.

We have seen a fragment of a fossil remainder of the tooth of a Sorex, found by our young friend Dr. LECONTE, of New-York, in the mining region adjoining Lake Superior, from the size of which, the animal must have been at least a yard long, and no doubt was, with its carnivorous teeth, a formidable beast of prey; whether it had insects and worms of a corresponding size to feed upon, in its day and generation, is a matter of mere conjecture, as even the wonderful discoveries of geologists have thrown but little light on the modes of life of the inhabitants of the ancient world, although some whole skeletons are found from time to time by their researches.

The Least Shrew feeds upon insects and larvæ, worms and the flesh of any dead bird or beast that it may chance to discover.

It also eats seeds and grains of different kinds. It burrows in the earth, but seeks its food more upon the surface of the ground than the mole, and runs with ease around its burrow about fences and logs. Some birds of prey pounce upon the Shrew, whilst it is playing or seeking its food on the grass, but as it has a musky, disagreeable smell, it is commonly left after being killed, to rot on the ground, as we have picked up a good many of these little quadrupeds, which to all appearance had been killed by either cats, owls or hawks. This smell arises from a secretion exuded from glands which are placed on the sides of the animal (Geoffroy, Mem. Mus. Hist. Nat., Vol. i., 1815). This secretion, like that of most animals, varies according to the age, the season, &c., and prevails more in males than females.

Of the mode in which the Least Shrew passes the winter we have no very positive information. It is capable of sustaining a great degree of cold. We have never found one of these animals in a torpid state, when examining burrows, holes, or cavities in and under rocks or stones, &c., for the purpose of ascertaining, if possible, the manner in which they passed the winter. We have seen minute tracks on the surface of the snow where it was four feet in depth in the Northern parts of New-York, which we ascertained were the foot-prints of a Shrew which was afterwards captured, although we cannot be certain that it was this species. It had sought the dried stalks of the pig weed (*chenopodium album*) on which the ripened seeds were still hanging and upon which it had evidently been feeding.

We are unacquainted with any other habits of this minute species.

Geographical Distribution.

If authors have made no mistake in the designation of this species, as we strongly suspect, it has a wide geographical range: according to RICHARDSON, it is found as far to the north as Behring's Straits. The specimens from which our figures were taken, were obtained in the immediate vicinity of New-York. Dr. DEKAY, in his Nat. Hist. of New-York, p. 20, mentions that although he had been unsuccessful in obtaining it in New-York, a specimen was found in Connecticut, by Mr. LINSLEY. We have not ascertained its southern range, all we know of its existence in the west, is from SAY's short description of the only specimen obtained west of the Missouri.

General Remarks.

All our authors seem anxious to obtain SAY's Least Shrew, and we have seen dozens of specimens of young Shrews of several species, labeled in the cabinets "*Sorex Parvus.*"

Although there were few more accurate describers than SAY, yet his description of *S. parvus*, is too imperfect, to enable us to feel confident of the species. There was no examination of its dental system, and his description would easily apply to half a dozen other species. The characters by which we may separate the different Shrews are not easily detected, they very much resemble each other in form, colour and habits; they are minute nocturnal animals and not easily procured.

There exist but few specimens in our cabinets to enable us to institute comparisons, and a century will pass away before all our species are discovered. We have very little doubt, that when the species which was obtained in the far West and described by SAY, and that of RICHARDSON from the far north, and ours from the vicinity of New-York, are obtained and compared and their dental system carefully examined, it will be ascertained that they are three distinct species, and our successors will be surprised that the old authors gave to the Shrews so wide a geographical range.

SAY's description is subjoined for convenient comparison. "Body above brownish cinereous, beneath cinereous; head elongated, eyes and ears concealed; whiskers long, the longest nearly attaining the back of the head; nose naked emarginate; front teeth black, lateral ones piceous; feet whitish, five-toed; nails prominent, acute, white; tail short, sub-cylindrical, of moderate thickness, slightly thicker in the middle—whitish beneath. Length of head and body, two inches four lines, of tail, 0.75." RICHARDSON's animal was according to his description, dark brownish grey above, and grey beneath. Length of head and body two inches three lines, tail one inch.

Canis latrans.—Say.

Prairie Wolf,—Barking Wolf.

Plate lxxi.—Male. One-third Natural Size.

C. cano cinereus nigris et opace pulvo-cinnameo-variegatus; lateribus pallidioribus; fasciâ taise lâta brevinigrâ; cauda rectâ fusiformi cineraceo-cinnameoque variegata apice nigra.

Characters.

Hair cinereous grey, varied with black above and dull fulvous cinnamon; sides paler than the back, obsoletely fasciate, with black above the legs; tail straight, bushy, fusiform, varied with grey and cinnamon, tip black.

Synonymes.

SMALL WOLVES, Dr Praly, Louisiana, vol. ii., p. 54.

Plate LXX.

On Stone by Wᵐ E. Hitchcock.

Lith. Printed & Colᵈ by J T. Bowen, Philad.

Say's Least Shrew.

Drawn from Nature by J. J. Audubon, F.R.S.F.L.S.

PRAIRIE WOLF, Gass. Journal, p. 56.
PRAIRIE WOLF and BURROWING DOG, Lewis and Clark, vol. i., p.
              102, 13, 203, vol. iii., pp. 102, 136, 203.
    "   "   Schoolcraft's Travels, 285.
CANIS LATRANS, Say, Long's Exped. i., p. 168.
    "   "   Harlan, p. 33.
    "   "   God., 1 vol., 26.
    "   "   Richardson, F. B. Ar. 75.
LYCISCUS CAJOTTIS, Hamilton Smith, Nat. Lib., vol. iv., p. 164, p. 6.

Description.

The Barking or Prairie Wolf is intermediate in size, between the large American Wolf and the grey Fox (*V. virginianus.*) It is a more lively animal than the former, and possesses a cunning fox-like countenance. In seeing it on the prairies, and also in menageries, in a state of domestication, we have often been struck with its quick, restless manner, and with many traits of character that reminded us of sly reynard.

The nose is sharp and pointed; nostrils moderately dilated and naked—the upper surface to the forehead covered with compact short hairs; eyelids placed obliquely on the sides of the head. Eyes rather small—moustaches few, very rigid, extending to the eyes, four or five stiff hairs rising on the sides of the neck below the ears. Head rather broad; Ears, erect, broad at base, running to an obtuse point, clothed with compact soft fur in which but few of the longer hairs exist; body, tolerably stout; legs, of moderate length, shorter in proportion than those of the common Wolf; Tail, large and bushy, composed like the covering of the body of two kinds of hair, the inner soft and woolly, the outer longer and coarser and from two to three and a half inches in length. Soles of the feet naked, nails rather stout, shaped like those of the dog. The whole structure of the animal is indicative of speed, but from its compact shape and rather short legs we would be led to suppose that it was rather intended for a short race than a long heat.

Colour.

Nostrils, around the edges of the mouth, and moustaches, black; upper surface of nose, and around the eyes, reddish brown; upper lip, around the edges of the mouth, and throat, white; eye-lids, yellowish white; hairs on the forehead, at the roots reddish brown, then a line of yellowish white tipped with black, giving it a reddish grey appearance. Inner surface of the ears (which are thinly clothed with hair) white; outer surface, yellowish brown; the fore legs reddish brown, with a stripe of blackish extending from the fore shoulder in an irregular black line over the knee to near the pans. Outer surface of the hind legs, reddish brown, inner surface a little lighter.

On the back the soft under fur is dingy yellow; the longer hair from the roots to two-thirds of its length black, then a broad line of yellowish brown, broadly tippd with black. Neck, reddish brown; throat and all beneath, yellowish white, with bars under the throat and on the chest and belly of a reddish tinge. On the tail the softer hair is plumbeous, the longer hairs are like those on the back, except on the tip of the tail where they are black for nearly their whole length. The description here given is from a very fine specimen obtained at San Antonio in Texas. There is not however a uniformity of colour in these animals, although they vary less than the large wolves. The specimen which RICHARDSON described was obtained on the Saskatchewan. We examined it in the Zoological Museum of London; it differs in some shades of colours from ours—its ears are a little shorter, its nose less pointed, and the skull less in breadth—but it was evidently the same species, and could not even be regarded as a distinct variety. The many specimens we examined and compared, in various tints of colour differed considerably, some wanting the brown tints, being nearly grey, while many had black markings on the shin and forelegs which were absent in others. In all descriptions of wolves, colour is a very uncertain guide in the designation of species.

Dimensions.

	Feet.	Inches.
From point of nose to root of tail	2	10
Tail vertebræ,		11
Do. to end of hair,	1	3
Height of ear,		3
Breadth of do. at the base,		3
From heel to end of longest nail,		6
Point of nose to corner of eye,		$3\frac{1}{2}$
Breadth of skull,		4
Fore shoulder to end of longest nail,	1	1
Breadth across the forehead,		$2\frac{1}{8}$

Habits.

We saw a good number of these small wolves on our trip up the Missouri river, as well as during our excursions through those portions of the country which we visited bordering on the Yellow Stone.

This species is well known throughout the western parts of the States of Arkansas and Missouri, and is a familiar acquaintance of the "voyageurs" on the upper Missouri and Mississippi rivers. It is also found on the Saskatchewan. It has much the appearance of the common grey Wolf in colour, but differs from it in size and manners.

The Prairie Wolf hunts in packs, but is also often seen prowling singly over the plains in search of food. During one of our morning rambles near Fort Union, we happened to start one of these wolves suddenly. It made off at a very swift pace and we fired at it without any effect, our guns being loaded with small shot at the time; after running about one hundred yards it suddenly stopped and shook itself violently, by which we perceived that it had been touched; in a few moments it again started and soon disappeared beyond a high range of hills, galloping along like a hare or an antelope.

The bark or howl of this wolf greatly resembles that of the dog, and on one occasion the party travelling with us were impressed by the idea that Indians were in our vicinity, as a great many of these wolves were about us and barked during the night like Indian dogs. We were all on the alert, and our guns were loaded with ball in readiness for an attack.

In Texas the Prairie Wolves are perhaps more abundant than the other species; they hunt in packs of six or eight, which are seen to most advantage in the evening, in pursuit of deer. It is amusing to see them cut across the curves made by the latter when trying to escape, the hindmost Wolves thus saving some distance, and finally striking in ahead of the poor deer and surrounding it, when a single Wolf would fail in the attempt to capture it. By its predatory and destructive habits, this Wolf is a great annoyance to the settlers in the new territories of the west. Travellers and hunters on the prairies, dislike it for killing the deer, which supply these wanderers with their best meals, and furnish them with part of their clothing, the buck-skin breeches, the most durable garment, for the woods or plains. The bark or call-note of this Wolf, although a wild sound to the inhabitant of any settled and cultivated part of the country, is sometimes welcomed, as it often announces the near approach of daylight; and if the wanderer, aroused from his slumbers by the howling of this animal, raises his blanket and turns his head toward the east, from his camping-ground underneath the branches of some broad spreading live-oak, he can see the red glow, perchance, that fringes the misty morning vapours, giving the promise of a clear and calm sunrise in the mild climate of Texas, even in the depth of winter. Should day-light thus be at hand, the true hunter is at once a-foot, short space of time does he require for the duties of the toilet, and soon he has made a fire, boiled his coffee, and broiled a bit of venison or wild turkey.

This Wolf feeds on birds, small and large quadrupeds, and when hard pressed by hunger, even upon carrion or carcasses of buffaloes, &c. It is easily tamed when caught young, and makes a tolerable companion, though not gifted with the good qualities of the dog. We had one once, which was kept in a friend's store in the west, and we discovered it to be something of a rat catcher. This individual was very desirous of being on friendly terms with all the dogs about the premises, especially with a large French poddle that belonged to our friend, but the poodle would not permit our half-savage barking Wolf to play with him, and generally returned its attempted caresses with an angry snap, which put all further friendly demonstrations out of the question. One day we missed our pet from his accustomed place near the back part of the ware-house, and while we were wondering what had become of him, were attracted by an unusual uproar in the street. In a moment we perceived the noise was occasioned by a whole pack of curs of high and low degree, which were in full cry, and in pursuit of our Prairie Wolf. The creature thus hard beset, before we could interfere, had reached a point opposite a raised window, and to our surprise, made a sudden spring at it and jumped into the warehouse without touching the edges of the sills, in the most admirable manner, while his foes were completely baffled.

After this adventure the Wolf would no longer go out in the town and seemed to give up his wish to extend the circle of his acquaintance.

The Barking or Prairie Wolf digs its burrows upon the prairies on some slight elevation, to prevent them from being filled with water. These dens have several entrances, like those of the red fox. The young, from five to seven and occasionally more in number, are brought forth in March and April. They associate in greater numbers than the larger Wolves, hunt in packs, and are

Plate LXXI.

N°15.

Drawn from Nature by J.W. Audubon

On Stone by Wm E. Hitchcock

Lith. Printed & Col^d by J.T. Bowen, Philad

Prairie Wolf

said by RICHARDSON to be fleeter than the common Wolf. A gentleman, an experienced hunter on the Saskatchewan, informed him that the only animal on the plains which he could not overtake when mounted on a good horse, was the prong-horned antelope, and that the Prairie Wolf was next in speed.

All our travellers have informed us, that on the report of a gun on the prairies, numbers of these Wolves start from the earth, and warily approach the hunter, under an expectation of obtaining the offal of the animal he has killed.

The skins of the Prairie Wolves are of some value, the fur being soft and warm; they form a part of the Hudson Bay Company's exportations, to what extent we are not informed. RICHARDSON says they go under the name of cased-wolves skins, not split open like those of the large Wolf, but stripped off and inverted or cased, like the skin of a fox or rabbit.

Geographical Distribution.

According to RICHARDSON, the northern range of this species is about the fifty-fifth degree of latitude. It is found abundantly on the plains of the western prairies and sparingly on the plains adjoining the woody shores of the Columbia river. It exists in California, and is found in Texas and on the eastern side of the mountains in New Mexico. We have traced it to within the tropics, but are not aware that it reaches as far south as Panama. The western branches of the Missouri river appear to be its farthest eastern range.

General Remarks.

There has been but little difficulty in the nomenclature of this species. Hamilton Smith, we perceive, has given it a new name, from a specimen obtained in Mexico. The description of its habits, by LEWIS and CLARKE, is full and accurate and in accordance with our own observations.

Canis Lupus.—Linn.—(Var. Albus.)

White American Wolf.

Plate lxxii. Male. One-third natural size.

C. magnitudine formaque C. lupi; vellere flavido-albo; naso canescente.

Characters.

Size and shape of the grey wolf, fur over the whole body of a yellowish-white colour, with a slight tinge of grey on the nose.

Synonymes.

WHITE WOLF, Lewis and Clark, vol. i., p. 107, vol. iii., p. 263.
CANIS LUPUS, Albus, Sabine, Frank. Journ., p. 652.
WHITE Wolf, Frank. Journal, p. 312.
      "   " Lyon's Private Journal, p. 279.
LUPUS ALBUS VAR. B. WHITE WOLF, Richardson, F. B. A., p. 68.

Description.

In shape, this Wolf resembles all the other varieties of large North American Wolves. (The prairie or barking Wolf, a distinct and different species, excepted.) It is large, stout, and compactly built; the canine teeth are long; others stout, large, rather short. Eyes, small. Ears, short and triangular. Feet, stout. Nails, strong and trenchant. Tail, long and bushy. Hairs on the body, of two kinds; the under coat composed of short, soft and woolly hair, interspersed with longer coarse hair five inches in length. The hairs on the head and legs are short and smooth, having none of the woolly appearance of those on other portions of the body.

Colour.

The short fur beneath the long white coat, yellowish white, the whole outer surface white, there is a slight tinge of greyish on the nose. Nails black; teeth white.

Another Specimen.—Snow-white on every part of the body except the tail, which is slightly tipped with black.

Another.—Light grey on the sides legs and tail; a dark brown stripe on the back, through which many white hairs protrude, giving it the appearance of being spotted with brown and white. This variety resembles the young Wolf noticed by RICHARDSON, (p. 68) which he denominates the pied Wolf.

Dimensions.

	Feet.	Inches.
From point of nose to root of tail,	4	6
Do. tail, vertebræ,	1	2
Do. do. end of hair,	1	8
Height of ear,		3½

Habits.

The White Wolf is far the most common variety of the Wolf tribe to be met with around Fort Union, on the prairies, and on the plains bordering the Yellow Stone river. When we first reached Fort Union we found Wolves in great abundance, of several different colours, white, grey, and brindled. A good many were shot from the walls during our residence there, by EDWARD HARRIS, Esq., and Mr. J. G. BELL. We arrived at this post on the 12th of June, and although it might be supposed at that season the Wolves could procure food with ease, they seemed to be enticed to the vicinity of the Fort by the cravings of hunger. One day soon after our arrival, Mr. CULBERTSON told us that if a Wolf made its appearance on the prairie, near the Fort, he would give chase to it on horseback, and bring it to us alive or dead. Shortly after, a Wolf coming in view, he had his horse saddled and brought up, but in the meantime the Wolf became frightened and began to make off, and we thought Mr. CULBERTSON would never succeed in capturing him. We waited, however, with our companions on the platform inside the walls, with our heads only projecting above the pickets, to observe the result. In a few moments we saw Mr. CULBERTSON on his prancing steed as he rode out of the gate of the Fort with gun in hand, attired only in his shirt, breeches and boots. He put spurs to his horse and went off with the swiftness of a jockey bent upon winning a race. The Wolf trotted on and every now and then stopped to gaze at the horse and his rider, but soon finding that he could no longer indulge his curiosity with safety, he suddenly gallopped off with all his speed, but he was too late in taking the alarm, and the gallant steed soon began to gain on the poor cur, as we saw the horse rapidly shorten the distance between the Wolf and his enemy. Mr. CULBERTSON fired off his gun as a signal to us that he felt sure of bringing in the beast, and although the hills were gained by the fugitive, he had not time to make for the broken ground and deep ravines, which he would have reached in few minutes, when we heard the crack of the gun again, and Mr. CULBERTSON galloping along dexterously picked up the slain Wolf without dismounting from his horse, threw him across the pummel of his saddle, wheeled round and rode back to the Fort, as fast as he had gone forth, a hard shower of rain being an additional motive for quickening his pace, and triumphantly placed the trophy of his chase at our disposal. The time occupied, from the start of the hunter, until his return with his prize did not exceed twenty minutes. The jaws of the animal had become fixed, and it was quite dead. Its teeth had scarified one of Mr. CULBERTSON's fingers considerably, but we were assured that this was of no importance, and that such feats as the capture of this wolf were so very common, that no one considered it worthy of being called an exploit.

Immediately after this real wolf hunt, a sham Buffalo chase took place, a prize of a suit of clothes being provided for the rider who should load and shoot the greatest number of times in a given distance. The horses were mounted, and the riders started with their guns empty—loaded in a trice, while at speed, and fired first on one side and then on the other, as if after Buffaloes. Mr. CULBERTSON fired eleven times in less than half a mile's run, the others fired less rapidly, and one of them snapped several times, but as a snap never brings down a Buffalo, these mishaps did not count. We were all well pleased to see these feats performed with much ease and grace. None of the riders were thrown, although they suffered their bridles to drop on their horses necks, and plied the whip all the time. Mr. CULBERTSON's mare, which was of the full, black foot Indian breed, about five years old, was highly valued by that gentleman, and could not have been purchased of him for less than four hundred dollars.

Plate LXXII

On Stone by Wᵐ E. Hitchcock

Lith Printed & Colᵈ by J.T. Bowen, Phil

White American Wolf

Drawn from Nature by J W Audubon

To return to the wolves.—These animals were in the habit of coming at almost every hour of the night, to feed in the troughs where the offal from the Fort was deposited for the hogs. On one occasion, a wolf killed by our party was devoured during the night, probably by other prowlers of the same species.

The white wolves are generally fond of sitting on the tops of the eminences, or small hills in the prairies, from which points of vantage they can easily discover any passing object on the plain at a considerable distance.

We subjoin a few notes on wolves generally, taken from our journals, made during our voyage up the Missouri in 1843.

These animals are extremely abundant on the Missouri river, and in the adjacent country. On our way up that extraordinary stream, we first heard of wolves being troublesome to the farmers who own sheep, calves, young colts, or any other stock on which these ravenous beasts feed, at Jefferson city, the seat of government of the State of Missouri; but to our great surprise, while there not a black wolf was seen.

Wolves are said to feed at times, when very hard pressed by hunger, on certain roots which they dig out of the earth with their forepaws, scratching like a common dog in the ground. When they have killed a Buffalo or other large animal, they drag the remains of the carcass to a concealed spot if at hand, then scrape out the loose soil and bury it, and often lie down on the top of the grave they have thus made for their victim, until urged again by hunger, they exume the body and feast upon it. Along the banks of the river, where occasionally many Buffaloes perish, their weight and bulk preventing them from ascending where the shore is precipitous, wolves are to be seen in considerable numbers feeding upon the drowned Bisons.

Although extremely cunning in hiding themselves, at the report of a gun wolves soon come forth from different quarters, and when the alarm is over, you have only to conceal yourself, and you will soon see them advancing towards you, giving you a fair chance of shooting them, sometimes at not more than thirty yards distance. It is said that although they frequently pursue Buffalo, &c., to the river, they seldom if ever follow them after they take to the water. Their gait and movements are precisely the same as those of the common dog, and their mode of copulating, and the number of young brought forth at a litter is about the same. The diversity of their size and colour is quite remarkable, no two being quite alike.

Some days while ascending the river, we saw from twelve to twenty-five wolves; on one occasion we observed one apparently bent on crossing the river, it swam toward our boat and was fired at, upon which it wheeled round and soon made to the shore from which it had started.

At another time we saw a wolf attempting to climb a very steep and high bank of clay, when, after falling back thrice, it at last reached the top and disappeared at once. On the opposite shore another was seen lying down on a sand bar like a dog, and any one might have supposed it to be one of those attendants on man. Mr. BELL shot at it, but too low, and the fellow scampered off to the margin of the woods, there stopped to take a last lingering look, and then vanished.

In hot weather when wolves go to the river, they usually walk in up to their sides, and cool themselves while lapping the water, precisely in the manner of a dog. They do not cry out or howl when wounded or when suddenly surprised, but snarl, and snap their jaws together furiously. It is said when suffering for want of food, the strongest will fall upon the young or weak ones, and kill and eat them. Whilst prowling over the prairies (and we had many opportunities of seeing them at such times) they travel slowly, look around them cautiously, and will not disdain even a chance bone that may fall in their way; they bite so voraciously at the bones thus left by the hunter that in many cases their teeth are broken off short, and we have seen a number of specimens in which the jaws showed several teeth to have been fractured in this way.

After a hearty meal, the wolf always lies down when he supposes himself in a place of safety. We were told that occasionally when they had gorged themselves, they slept so soundly that they could be approached and knocked on the head.

The common wolf is not unfrequently met with in company with the Prairie wolf (Canis latrans.) On the afternoon of the 13th of July, as Mr. BELL and ourselves were returning to Fort Union, we counted eighteen wolves in one gang, which had been satiating themselves on the carcass of Buffalo on the river's bank, and were returning to the hills to spend the night. Some of them had their stomachs distended with food and appeared rather lazy.

We were assured at Fort Union that wolves had not been known to attack men or horses in that vicinity, but they will pursue and kill mules and colts even near a trading post, always selecting the fattest. The number of tracks or rather paths made by the wolves from among and around the hills to that station are almost beyond credibility, and it is curious to observe their sagacity in choosing the shortest course and the most favourable ground in travelling.

We saw hybrids, the offspring of the wolf and the cur dog, and also their mixed broods: some of which resemble the wolf, and others the dog. Many of the Assiniboin Indians who visited Fort Union during our stay there, had both wolves and their crosses with the common dog in their trains, and their dog carts (if they may be so called) were drawn alike by both.

The natural gait of the American wolf resembles that of the Newfoundland dog, as it ambles, moving two of its legs on the same side at a time. When there is any appearance of danger, the wolf trots off, and generally makes for unfrequented hilly grounds, and if pursued, gallops at a quick pace, almost equal to that of a good horse, as the reader will perceive from the following account. On the 16th of July 1843, whilst we were on a Buffalo hunt near the banks of the Yellow Stone river, and all eyes were bent upon the hills and the prairie, which is very broad, we saw a wolf about a quarter of a mile from our encampment, and Mr. OWEN McKENZIE was sent after it. The wolf however ran very swiftly and was not overtaken and shot until it had ran several miles. It dodged about in various directions, and at one time got out of sight behind the hills. This wolf was captured, and a piece of its flesh was boiled for supper; but as we had in the mean time caught about eighteen or twenty Cat-fish, we had an abundant meal and did not judge for ourselves whether the wolf was good eating or not, or if its flesh was like that of the Indian dogs, which we have had several opportunities of tasting.

Wolves are frequently deterred from feeding on animals shot by the hunters on the prairies, who, aware of the cautious and timid character of these rapacious beasts, attach to the game they are obliged to leave behind them a part of their clothing, a handkerchief, &c., or scatter gun powder around the carcass, which the cowardly animals dare not approach although they will watch it for hours at a time, and as soon as the hunter returns and takes out the entrails of the game he had left thus protected, and carries off the pieces he wishes, leaving the coarser parts for the benefit of these hungry animals, they come forward and enjoy the feast. The hunters who occasionally assisted us when we were at Fort Union, related numerous stratagems of this kind to which they had resorted to keep off the wolves when on a hunt.

The wolves of the prairies form burrows, wherein they bring forth their young, and which have more than one entrance; they produce from six to eleven at a birth, of which there are very seldom two alike in colour. The wolf lives to a great age and does not change its colour with increase of years.

Geographical Distribution.

This variety of wolf is found as far north in the Arctic regions of America as they have been traversed by man. The journals of HEARNE, FRANKLIN, SABINE RICHARDSON, and others, abound with accounts of their presence amid the snows of the polar regions. They exist in the colder parts of Canada, in the Russian possessions on the western coast of America, in Oregon, and along both sides of the Rocky Mountains, to California on the west side and Arkansas on the east. We examined a specimen of the White Wolf killed in Erie county, N. Y., about forty years ago; on the Atlantic coast they do not appear; although we have seen some specimens of a light grey colour they could not when compared with those of Missouri, be called white wolves.

General Remarks

Cold seems necessary to produce the Wolves of white variety. Alpine regions from their altitudes effect the same change. REGNARD informs us that in Lapland, Wolves are almost all of a whitish grey colour—there are some of them white. In Siberia, wolves assume the same colour. The Alps, on the other hand, by their elevation, may be compared to the regions around the Rocky Mountains of America. In both countries wolves become white. We devoted some hours to comparing the large American, European, and Asiatic Wolves, assisted by eminent British Naturalists, in the British Museum and the Museum of the Zoological Society. We found specimens from the Northern and Alpine regions of both continents bore a strong resemblance to each other in form and size, their shades of colour differed only in different specimens from either country, and we finally came to the conclusion that the naturalist who should be able to find distinctive characters to separate the wolves into different species, should have credit for more penetration than we possess.

Genus Ovis.—Linn., Briss., Erxleben, Cuv., Bodd., Geoff.

Dental Formula.

Incisive $\frac{0}{8}$; *Canine* $\frac{0—0}{0—0}$; *Molar* $\frac{6—6}{6—6}$ = 32.

Horns common to both sexes, sometimes wanting in the females, they are voluminous, more or less angular, transversely wrinkled, turned laterally in spiral directions, and enveloping an osseous arch, cellular in structure.

They have no lachrymal sinus, no true beard to the chin, the females have two mammæ; tail, rather short; ears, small, erect; legs, rather slender; hair, of two kinds, one hard and close, the other woolly; gregareous. Habit analogous to the goats. Inhabit the highest mountains of the four quarters of the globe.

The generic name is derived from the latin *Ovis*—a sheep.

There are four well determined species, one the Mouflon of BUFFON, Musmon (*Ovis Musmon*) is received as the parent of the domesticated races. It is found in Corsica, Sardinia, and the highest mountain chains of Europe. One inhabiting the mountains and steppes of northern Asia, Tartary, Siberia and the Kurile Islands, one the mountains of Egypt, and one America.

Ovis Montana.—Desm.

Rocky Mountain Sheep.

Plate lxxiii. Male and Female.

O. cornibus crassissimis spiralibus; corpore gracile; artubus elevatis; pilo brevi rigido rudi badio; clunibus albis o ariete major; rufo cinereus.

Characters.

Longer than the domestic sheep, horns of the male long, strong and triangular, those of the female compressed; colour deep rufous grey, a large white disk on the rump.

Synonymes.

ARGALI, COOK'S third voyage in 1778.
WILD SHEEP OF CALIFORNIA. Venegus.
    "   "   Clavigero.
WHITE BUFFALO, McKenzie voy. p. 76. An. 1789.
MOUNTAIN GOAT, Umfreville, Hudson's Bay. p. 164.
MOUNTAIN RAM, McGillivary, N. York. Med. Reposit. vol. 6. p. 238.
BIG HORN, Lewis and Clark. vol. 1. p. 144.
BELIER SAUVAGE d'AMERIQUE. Geoff, An. du. mus. t. 2. pl. 60.
ROCKY MOUNTAIN SHEEP. Warden. U. S. vol. 1. p. 217.
MOUFFLON d'AMERIQUE. Desm. Mamm. p. 487.
BIG HORNED SHEEP. (Ord.)
    "   "   Blainv. in Jour. de Physic. 1817.
OVIS AMMON. Harlan. Fauna. p. 259.
THE ARGALI, Godm. Nat. Hist. vol. 2. p. 329.
OVIS MONTANA. Richardson. F. B. Amer. p. 271.
OVIS PYGARJAS VAR OVIS AMMON. Griffith An. King. Spec. 873.

Description.

Male. This is a much larger animal than any variety of our largest sized sheep. It is also considerably larger than the Argali on the eastern continent.

The horns of the male are of immense size. They arise immediately above the eyes, and occupy nearly the whole head, they being only separated from each other by a space of three-fourths of an inch at the base. They form a regular curve, first backwards, then downwards and outward—the extremities being eighteen inches apart. They are flattened on the sides and deeply corrugated, the horns rising immediately behind.

The ears, are short and oval, clothed with hair on both surfaces. The general form of the animal is rather elegant, resembling the stag more than the Sheep. The tail is short.

The hair bears no resemblance to wool, but is similar to that of the American Elk and Reindeer. It is coarse, but soft to the touch, and slightly crimped throughout its whole length; the hairs on the back are about two inches in length, those on the sides one and a half inches. At the roots of these hairs, especially about the shoulders and sides of the neck, a small quantity of short soft fur is perceptible. The legs are covered with short compact hairs.

The female Rocky Mountain Sheep resembles some of the finest specimens of the common Ram. Its neck is a little longer, as are also the head and legs, and in consequence it stands much higher. Its horns resemble more those of the goat than of the Sheep, in fact, whilst the fine erect body of the male reminds us of a large deer with the head of a ram, the female looks like a fine specimen of the antelope. The horns bend backwards and a little outwards, and are corrugated from the roots to near the points. Tail very short and pointed, covered with short hairs. Mammæ two ventral.

Colour.

The whole upper surface of the body, outer surface of the thighs, legs, sides and under the throat, light greyish brown, forehead and ears a little lighter. Rump, under the belly and inner surface of hind legs, greyish white; the front legs, instead of being darker on the outside and lighter on the inside, are darker in front, the dark extending round to the inside of the legs, and covering nearly a third of the inner surface. Tail and hoofs black. A narrow dorsal line from the neck to near the rump, conspicuous in the male, but comparatively quite obscure in the female. RICHARDSON states that the old males are almost totally white in spring.

Dimensions.

	Feet.	Inches.
Male figure in our plate.		
Length	6	
Height at shoulder	3	5
Length of tail	0	5
Girth of body behind the shoulders	3	11
Height to rump	3	$10\frac{3}{4}$
Length of horn around the curve	2	$10\frac{1}{2}$
Do. of eye		$1\frac{1}{4}$
Weight 344 lbs. including horns.		
Female figure in our plate.		
Nose to root of tail	4	7
Tail	0	5
Height of rump	3	$4\frac{1}{2}$
Girth back of shoulders	3	$4\frac{1}{2}$
Horns—$44\frac{1}{2}$ lbs.		
Weight 240 lbs. (Killed July 3d, 1843.)		

Habits.

It was on the 12th of June, 1843, that we first saw this remarkable animal; we were near the confluence of the Yellow Stone river with the Missouri, when a group of them, numbering twenty-two in all, came in sight. This flock was composed of rams and ewes, with only one young one or lamb among them. They scampered up and down the hills much in the manner of common sheep, but notwithstanding all our anxious efforts to get within gun-shot, we were unable to do so, and were obliged to content ourselves with this first sight of the Rocky Mountain Ram.

The parts of the country usually chosen by these animals for their pastures, are the most extraordinary broken and precipitous clay hills or stony eminences that exist in the wild regions belonging to the Rocky Mountain chain. They never resort to the low lands or plains except when about to remove their quarters, or swim across rivers, which they do well and tolerably fast. Perhaps some idea of the country they inhabit (which is called by the French Canadians and hunters, "mauvaise terres") may be formed by imagining some hundreds of loaves of sugar of different sizes, irregularly broken and truncated at top, placed somewhat apart, and magnifying them into hills of considerable size. Over these hills and ravines the Rocky Mountain Sheep bound up and down among the sugar loaf shaped peaks, and you may estimate the difficulty of approaching them, and conceive the great activity and sure-footedness of this species, which, together with their extreme wildness and keen sense of smell, enable them to baffle the most vigorous and agile hunter.

They form paths around these irregular clay cones that are at times from six to eight hundred feet high, and in some situations are even fifteen hundred feet or more above the adjacent prairies, and along these they run at full speed, while to the eye of the spectator below, these tracks do not appear to be more than a few inches wide, although they are generally from a foot to eighteen inches in breadth. In many places columns or piles of clay, or hardened earth, are to be seen eight or ten feet above the adjacent surface, covered or coped with a slaty flat rock, thus resembling gigantic toad stools, and upon these singular places the big horns are frequently seen, gazing at the hunter who is winding about far below, looking like so many statues on their elevated pedestals. One cannot imagine how these animals reach these curious places, especially with their young along with them, which are sometimes brought forth on these inaccessible points, beyond the reach of their greatest enemies, the wolves, which prey upon them whenever they stray into the plains below.

The "mauvaise terres" are mostly formed of greyish white clay, very sparsely covered with small patches of thin grass, on which the Rocky Mountain Sheep feed. In wet weather it is almost impossible for any man to climb up one of these extraordinary conical hills, as they are slippery, greasy and treacherous. Often when a big horn is seen on the top of a hill, the hunter has to ramble round three or four miles before he can reach a position within gun-shot of the game, and if perceived by the animal, it is useless for him to pursue him any further that day.

The tops of some of the hills in the "mauvaise terres" are composed of a conglomerated mass of stones, sand, clay and various coloured earths, frequently of the appearance and colour of bricks. We also observed in these masses a quantity of pumice stone, and these hills, we are inclined to think are the result of volcanic action. Their bases often cover an area of twenty acres; there are regular horizontal strata running across the whole chain of these hills, composed of different coloured clay, coal and earth, more or less impregnated with salt and other minerals, and occasionally intermixed with lava, sulphur, oxide and sulphate of iron; and in the sandy parts at the top of the highest hills, we found shells, but so soft and crumbling as to fall to pieces when we attempted to pick them out. We found in the "mauvaise terres," also, globular shaped masses of heavy stone and pieces of petrified wood, from fragments two or three inches wide, to stumps of three or four feet thick, apparently cotton wood and cedar. On the sides of some of the hills at various heights, are shelf-like ledges or rock projecting from the surface in a level direction, from two to six and even ten feet, generally square or flat. These ledges are much resorted to by the big horns during the heat of the day. Between these hills there is sometimes a growth of stunted cedar trees, underneath which there is a fine sweet grass, and on the summits in some cases a short dry wiry grass is found, and quantities of that pest of the Upper Missouri country, the flat-broad-leaved Cactus, the spines of which often lame the hunter. Occasionally the hills in the "mauvaise terres" are separated by numerous ravines, often not more than ten or fifteen feet wide, but sometimes from ten to fifty feet deep, and now and then the hunter comes to the brink of one so deep and wide as to make his head giddy as he looks down into the abyss below. The edges of the cañons (as these sort of channels are called in Mexico) are overgrown with bushes, wild cherries, &c., and here and there the Bison will manage to cut paths to cross them, descending in an oblique and zigzag direction; these paths however are rarely found except where the ravine is of great length, and in general the only mode of crossing the ravine is to go along the margin of it until you come to the head, which is generally at the base of some hill, and thus get round.

These ravines exist between nearly every two neighbouring hills, although there are occasionally places where three or more hills form only one. All of them however run to meet each other and connect with the largest, the size of which bears its proportion to that of its tributaries and their number.

Where these ravines have no outlet into a spring or water course they have subterranean drains, and in some of the valleys and even on the tops of the hills, there are cavities called "sink holes;" the earth near these holes is occasionally undermined by the water running round in circles underneath, leaving a crust insufficient to bear the weight of a man, and when an unfortunate hunter treads on the deceitful surface it gives way, and he finds himself in an unpleasant and at times dangerous predicament. These holes sometimes gradually enlarge and run into ravines below them. It is almost impossible to traverse the "mauvaise terres" with a horse, unless with great care, and with a thorough knowledge of the country. The chase or hunt after the big horn, owing to the character of the country, (as we have described it,) is attended with much danger, as the least slip might precipitate one headlong into the ravine below, the sides of the hills being destitute of every thing to hold on by excepting a projecting stone or tuft of worm wood, scattered here and there, without which even the most daring hunter could not ascend them.

In some cases the water has washed out caves of different shapes and sizes, some of which present the most fantastic forms and are naked and barren to a great degree. The water that is found in the springs in these broken lands is mostly impregnated with salts, sulphur, magnesia, &c.; but unpleasant as it tastes, it is frequently the only beverage for the hunter, and luckily is often almost as cold as ice, which renders it less disagreeable. In general this water has the effect very soon of a cathartic and emetic. Venomous snakes of various kinds inhabit the "mauvaise terres," but we saw only one copper-head.

Conceiving that a more particular account of these countries may be interesting, we will here insert a notice of them given to us by Mr. DEWEY, the principal clerk at Fort Union. He begins as follows:

"This curious country is situated, or rather begins half way up White river, and runs from south east to north west for about sixty miles in length, and varying from fifteen to forty miles in width. It touches the head of the Teton river and branches of Chicune, and joins the Black Hills at the south fork of the latter river. The hills are in some places five or six hundred yards high and upwards. They are composed of clay of various colours, arranged in layers or strata running nearly horizontally, each layer being of a different colour, white, red, blue, green, black, yellow, and almost every other colour, appearing at exactly the same height on every hill.

"From the quantity of pumice stone and melted ores found throughout them, one might suppose that they had been reduced to this state by volcanic action. From the head of the Teton river, to cross these hills to White river is about fifteen miles; there is but one place to descend, and the road is not known; the only way to proceed is to go round the end of them on the banks of the White river, and following that stream ascend to the desired point. In four day's march a man will make about fifteen miles in crossing through the "mauvaise terres." At first sight these hills look like some ancient city in ruins, and but little imagination is necessary to give them the appearance of castles, walls, towers, steeples, &c. The descent is by a road about five feet broad, winding around and among the hills, made at first probably by the bisons and the big horn sheep, and now rendered practicable by the Indians and others who have occasion to use it. It is however too steep to travel down with a loaded horse or mule, say about one foot in three, for a mile or so, after which the bases of the hills are about level with each other, but the valleys between them are cut up by great ravines in almost every direction from five to twenty and even fifty feet deep."

"In going over this part of the country great precaution is necessary, for a slip of the foot would precipitate either man or horse into the gulf below. When I descended, the interpreter, B. Daumine, a half breed, (having his eyes bandaged) was led by the hand of an Indian." Something like copperas in taste and appearance is found in large quantities, as well as pumice stone, every where. This country is the principal residence of the big horn sheep, the panther and grizzly bear; big horns especially are numerous, being in bands of from twenty to thirty, and are frequently seen at the tops of the highest peaks, completely inaccessible to any other animal. There is but one step from the prairie to the barren clay, and this step marks the difference for nearly its whole length. These "mauvaise terres" have no connexion or affinity to the surrounding country, but are, as it were, set apart for the habitation of the big horns and bears. The sight of this barren country causes one to think that thousands of square miles of earth have been carried off, and nothing left behind but the ruins of what was once a beautiful range of mountains. The principal part of these hills is white clay, which when wet is soft and adhesive, but the coloured strata are quite hard and are never discoloured by the rain, at least not to any extent, for after a hard rain the streams of water are of a pure milk white colour, untinged by any other, and so thick that ten gallons when settled will only yield about two gallons of pure limpid water, which, however, although clear when allowed to stand awhile, is scarcely drinkable, being salt and sulphurous in taste. The sediment has all the appearance of the clay already mentioned, which is nearly as white as chalk. There is only one place where wood and pure sweet water can be found in the whole range, which is at a spring nearly in the centre of the tract, and one day's journey from the White river, towards the Chicune. This appears a little singular, for if it were not for this the voyageur would be obliged to take a circuitous route of from four to five days. This spring is surrounded by a grove of ash trees, about two hundred yards in circumference. It immediately loses itself in the clay at the edge of the timber, and near the spring the road descends about sixty feet and runs through a sort of avenue at least half a mile wide, on each side of which are walls of clay extending horizontally about fifteen miles, and eighty feet high, for nearly the whole distance. Between these walls are small sugar-loaf shaped hills, and deep ravines, such as I have already described. The colours of the strata are preserved throughout. The principal volcano is the "Côte de tonnerre," from the mouth of which smoke and fire are seen to issue nearly at all times. In the neighbourhood and all around, an immense quantity of pumice stone is deposited, and from the noises to be heard, no doubt whatever exists that eruptions may from time to time be expected. There is another smaller hill which I saw giving forth heated vapours and smoke, but in general if the weather is clear the summits of the Black hills are obscured by a mist, from which circumstance many superstitions of the Indians have arisen. The highest of the Black hills are fully as high as the Alleghany mountains, and their remarkable shapes and singular characters deserve the attention of our geologists, especially as it is chiefly

Plate LXXIII.

N.º 15

Rocky Mountain Sheep

among these hills that fossil petrefactions are abundantly met with.

The Rocky Mountain Sheep are gregarious, and the males fight fiercely with each other in the manner of common rams. Their horns are exceedingly heavy and strong, and some that we have seen have a battered appearance, showing that the animal to which they belonged must have butted against rocks or trees, or probably had fallen from some elevation on to the stony surface below. We have heard it said that the Rocky Mountain Sheep descend the steepest hills head foremost, and they may thus come in contact with projecting rocks, or fall from a height on their enormous horns.

As is the case with some animals of the deer tribe, the young rams of this species and the females herd together during the winter and spring, while the old rams form separate flocks, except during the rutting season in December.

In the months of June and July the ewes bring forth, usually one, and occasionally, but rarely, two.

Dr. RICHARDSON, on the authority of DRUMMOND, states that in the retired parts of the mountains where the hunters had seldom penetrated, he (DRUMMOND) found no difficulty in approaching the Rocky Mountain Sheep, which there exhibited the simplicity of character so remarkable in the domestic species; but that where they had been often fired at, they were exceedingly wild, alarmed their companions on the approach of danger by a hissing noise, and scaled the rocks with a speed and agility that baffled pursuit. He lost several that he had mortally wounded, by their retiring to die among the secluded precipices." They are, we are farther informed on the authority of DRUMMOND, in the habit of paying daily visits to certain caves in the mountains that are encrusted with saline efflorescence. The same gentleman mentions that the horns of the old rams attain a size so enormous, and curve so much forwards and downwards, that they effectually prevent the animal from feeding on the level ground.

All our travellers who have tasted the flesh of the Rocky Mountain Sheep, represent it as very delicious when in season, superior to that of any species of deer in the west, and even exceeding in flavour the finest mutton.

We have often been surprised that no living specimen of this very interesting animal has ever been carried to Europe, or any of our Atlantic cities, where it would be an object of great interest.

Geographical Distribution.

This animal is found, according to travellers, as far to the North as lat. 68, and inhabits the whole chain of the Rocky Mountains on their highest peaks down to California. It does not exist at Hudson's Bay, nor has it been found to the eastward of the Rocky Mountain chain.

General Remarks.

The history the early discovery of this species, of specimens transmitted to Europe from time to time, obtained in latitudes widely removed from each other, of its designation under various names, and of the figures, some of which were very unnatural, that have been given of it, are not only interesting but full of perplexity. It appears to have been known to Father PICOLO, the first Catholic missionary to California, as early as 1697, who represents it as large as a calf of one or two years old; its head much like that of a stag, and its horns, which are very large, are like those of a ram; its tail and hair are speckled and shorter than a stag's, but its hoof is large, round, and cleft as an ox's. I have eaten of these beasts; their flesh is very tender and delicious." The Californian Sheep is also mentioned by HERNANDEZ, CLAVIGERO, and other writers on California. VANEGAS has given an imperfect figure of it, which was for a long time regarded as the Siberian Argali. Mr. DAVID DOUGLASS, in the Zoological Journal, in April, 1829, describes a species under the name of *Ovis Californica*, which he supposed to be the sheep mentioned by PICOLO. COOK, in his third voyage evidently obtained the skin of the Rocky Mountain Sheep on the north west coast of America. Mr. McGILLIVERY, in 1823, presented to the New-York Museum a specimen of this animal, and published an account of it in the Medical Repository of New-York. This specimen being afterwards sent to France, a description and figure of it were published. LEWIS and CLARK, some years afterwards, brought male and female specimens to Philadelphia, which were figured by GRIFFITH and GODMAN.

Several eminent naturalists, and among the rest Baron CUVIER, considered it the same as *Ovis Ammon*, supposing it to have crossed Behring's Straits on the ice. We have never had an opportunity of comparing the two species, but have examined them separately. Our animal is considerably the largest, and differs widely in the curvature of its horns from those of the eastern continent. We have no doubt of its being a distinct species from *Ovis Ammon*.

We doubt moreover, whether *Ovis Californica* will be found distinct from *Ovis Montana*; the climate in those elevated regions is every where cold. There are no intermediate spaces where the northern species ceases to exist, and the southern to commence, and when we take into consideration the variations of colour in different individuals, as also in the same individual in summer and winter, we should pause before we admit *Ovis Californica* as a true species. We have therefore added this name as a synonyme of *Ovis Montana*.

Scalops Breweri.—Bach.

Brewer's Shrew Mole.

Plate lxxiv.

S. lanugine sericea, vellus obscure cinereo nigricans subtus fuscescens, palmæ anguste, cauda depressa, latus pilis hirsuta.

Characters.

Glossy cinereous black above, brownish beneath, palms narrow, tail flat, broad and hairy.

Description.

Teeth, Incisive $\frac{2}{4}$; false molars $\frac{12}{12}$; true molars $\frac{8}{6} = 44$.

The head of *Scalops Breweri* is narrower and more elongated than that of *Sc. Aquaticus*. The cerebral portion of the skull is less voluminous, the inter-orbital portion is narrower, each of the intermaxillary bones in *Sc. Aquaticus* throws out a process, which projects upwards and forms the upper boundary of the nasal cavity, and very slightey separated by the nasal bones, whilst in *Sc. Breweri* these processes are shorter and scarcely project upwards above the plane of the nasal bone. Thus when we view the snout of *Sc. Aquaticus*, laterally, it is distinctly recurved at the tip, whereas in *Sc. Breweri* the upper surface is almost plain. But the most striking difference between these skulls is exhibited in the dentition, inasmuch as, in our present species, there are altogether forty-four teeth, in *Sc. Aquaticus* there are but thirty-six. Thus in the number of teeth *Sc. Breweri* resembles *Sc. Townsendi*.

The body of Brewer's Shrew Mole is perhaps a little larger than that of *Sc. Aquaticus*. Its snout is less flattened and narrower; its nostrils, instead of being inserted in a kind of boutir, as in the European *Talpa*, and the swine, or on the upper surface of the muzzle, as in the common shrew mole, are placed on each side, near the extremities of the nose. This species is pentadactylous, like all the rest of the genus, claws longer, thinner and sharper than the common shrew mole. Palm much narrower. Its most striking peculiarity, however, is its tail, which, instead of being round and nearly naked, like that of *Sc. Aquaticus*, is flat and broad, resembling in some respects that of the Beaver, and is very thickly clothed, above and beneath, with long stiff hairs, which extend five lines beyond the vertebræ.

Colour.

The colour, above and beneath, is a glossy cinereous black, like velvet; precisely similar to that of the European mole (*Talpa Europea*) with which we compared it. Under the throat there is a slight tinge of brown, the tail is ashy brown above, light beneath. The ewe is about one-third longer than that of the common shrew mole.

Dimensions.

	Inches.	Lines.
Length of the head and body	5	11
Tail vertebræ	1	0
Do. including fur	1	5
Breadth of tail	0	4
Do. of palm	0	4
Length of do to end of middle claw	0	7

In the Museum of the Zoological Society of London there is a specimen obtained from the United States, which evidently is the same species. It is

Plate. LXXIV

Drawn from Nature by J. J. Audubon. FRSFLS

On Stone by W. E. Hitchcock

Lith. Printed & Col.d by J. T. Bowen, Phila.

Brewer's Shrew Mole.

marked in the printed catalogue No. 145, "*Sc. Breweri* Bachman's M. SS.*" It however differs in having the fur more compact, and shorter, the colour somewhat darker, and in fact almost black. The hairs of the tail, instead of being brownish ash colour, are black, and the hind feet, instead of being covered above with brownish white hairs, as in our specimens, are brownish black.

Dimensions Of The Skull Of The Above Three Species.

	LENGTH OF SKULLS.		WIDTH. LENGTH OF PALATE.	
	Inches.	Lines.	Lines.	Lines.
Sc. Aquaticus	1	4	8	7
S. Townsendi	1	$7\frac{1}{4}$	$9\frac{1}{2}$	$8\frac{1}{5}$
S. Breweri	1	3	$7\frac{1}{3}$	$6\frac{1}{2}$

Habits.

In a collection of the smaller rodentia procured for us in New England by our friend THOMAS M. BREWER, Esq. an intelligent naturalist, we were surprised and gratified at finding this new species of shrew mole; the specimen having been obtained by Dr. L. M. YALE, at Martha's Vineyard, an island on the coast of New England. In its habits it approaches much nearer the star-nosed mole (*Condylura cristata*) than any species of shrew mole. Its burrows are neither as extensive or so near the surface of the earth as those of the common shrew mole. We observed that the meadows in the valleys of Virginia, where this species is found, seldom exhibited any traces of their galleries, which are so conspicuous where the common species exists. We only possessed one opportunity of seeing this species alive. It ran across the public road near the red sulphur springs in Virginia; in its mode of progression it reminded us of the hurried, irregular and awkward manners of the common shrew mole. It had, as we ascertained, pursued its course under ground, at about five inches from the surface, until it reached the trodden and firm gravelly road, which it attempted to cross and was captured. It evidenced no disposition to bite. From the fact of our having seen three specimens, which were accidentally procured in a week, we were led to suppose that it was quite common in that vicinity. We have not found its nest, and regret that we have nothing farther to add in regard to its habits.

Geographical Distribution.

Our first specimen, as we have stated, was received from Martha's Vineyard. Our friend, the late Dr. WRIGHT, procured four specimens in the vicinity of Troy, N. Y. We obtained specimens in Western Virginia. It no doubt exists in all the intermediate country.

General Remarks.

We suspect that this species has hitherto been overlooked in consequence of its having been blended with the common shrew mole. We observed two specimens in the museum of the Zoological Society, London, originally marked "*Talpa Europea* from America." On examining them, however, we found them of this species.

Sorex Carolinensis. —Bach.

Carolina Shrew. Males and Females.

Plate lxxv.

S. carolinensis, corpore griseo—cinerascente; cauda brevis, depressa.

Characters.

Carolina Shrew, with a short flat tail; ears not visible; body of a nearly uniform iron grey colour.

Description.

Intermediary incisors $\frac{2}{2}$

Lateral incisors $\frac{5-5}{2-2}$; *Molars,* $\frac{5-5}{3-3}$ = 34.

The four front teeth are yellowish white, with their points deeply tinged with chestnut brown; all the rest are brown, a little lighter near the sockets. The upper intermediary incisors have each, as is the case in most other species of this genus, an obtuse lobe, which gives them the appearance of having a small tooth growing out from near the roots. The three lateral incisors are largest; the posterior ones very small; the first and fifth grinders are the smallest; the other three nearly equal. In the lower jaw the two first teeth are lobed; the lateral incisors are comparatively large, and crowded near the grinders. The molars are bristled with sharp points except the last, which is a tuberculous tooth.

The muzzle is moderately long and slender, and pointed with a naked deep lobed lip. The whiskers are composed of hairs apparently all white, a few of those situated in front of the eyes extending to the occiput, the rest rather short. There are no visible ears, even where the fur is removed; the auditory opening is an orifice situated far back on the sides of the head running obliquely. The orifice of the eye is so small that it can only be discovered by the aid of a good magnifying glass. The tail is flat, thickly covered with a coat of close hair, and terminated by a small pencil of hairs. The fore feet are rather broad for this genus, measuring a line and a half in breadth, resembling in some respects those of the shrew mole, (*Scalops canadensis*.) The toes are five, the inner a little shorter than the outer one; the third and fourth nearly equal. The nails are sharp, rather long, a little arched, but not hooked. The hind feet are more slender than the fore ones; naked beneath, and covered above, as are also the fore feet, by a thin coat of short adpressed hairs.

Colour.

The fur presents the beautiful velvety appearance common to most species of this genus. The colour of the whole body is nearly uniform, considerably lustrous on the upper surface, and in most lights dark iron gray, rather darker about the head; on the under surface the fur is of nearly the same general appearance, but is a shade lighter.

Dimensions.

	Inches.
Length of body	3
" of tail	$\frac{5}{8}$
" of head	1
" of palm to the end of nails	$\frac{5}{16}$
" of hind feet	$\frac{1}{2}$

Habits.

It is difficult to know much of the habits of the little quadrupeds composing this genus. Living beneath the surface of the earth, feeding principally on worms and the larvæ of insects, shunning the light, and restricted to a little world of their own, best suited to their habits and enjoyments, they almost present a barrier to the prying curiosity of man. They are occasionally turned up by the plough on the plantations of the south, when they utter a faint, squeaking cry, like young mice, and make awkward and scrambling attempts to escape, trying to conceal themselves in any tuft of grass, or under the first clod of earth that may present itself. On two occasions, their small but compact nests were brought to us. They were composed of fibres of roots and withered blades of various kinds of grasses. They had been ploughed up from about a foot beneath the surface of the earth, and contained in one nest five, and in the other six young. In digging ditches, and ploughing in moderately high grounds, small holes are frequently seen running in all directions, in a line nearly parallel with the surface, and extending to a great distance, evidently made by this species. We observed on the sides of one of these galleries, a small cavity containing a hoard of coleopterous insects, principally composed of a rare species (*Scarabæus tityus*), fully the size of the animal itself, some of them were nearly consumed, and the rest mutilated, although still living.

Geographical Distribution.

This quadruped is found in various localities, both in the upper and maritime districts of South Carolina. We recently received specimens from our

Drawn from Nature by J.J.Audubon, F.R.S.F.L.S.

On Stone by W.ᵐ E. Hitchcock

Lith. Printed & Col.ᵈ by J.T.Bowen, Phil.

Carolina Shrew

friend Dr. BARRETT, of Abbeville District; and we have been informed·by Dr. PICKERING, to whose inspection we submitted a specimen, and who

pronounced it undoubtedly an undescribed species, that it had been observed as far north as Philadelphia.

Cervus Alces.—Linn.

Moose Deer.

Plate lxxvi. Old Male and Young.

C. magnitudine Equi; capite permagno, labro auribusque elongatis; collo brevi, dense jubato, cornibus palmatis, cauda brevissima, vellere fusco cinereo, in nigrum vergente.

Characters.

Size of a horse. Head, very large; snout and ears, long; neck, short, with a thick mane. Horns spreading into a broad palm. Tail, short. Colour, blackish-gray.

Synonymes.

ELAN, STAG, or APTAPTOU. De Monts Nova Francia, p. 250. An. 1604.
ESLAN OU ORINAL. Sagard-Theodat, Canada, p. 749. An. 1636.
ORINAL. La Hontan, Voy., p. 72. An. 1703.
MOOSE DEER. Dudley, Phil. Trans. No. 368, p. 165. An. 1721.
ORINAL. Charlevoix. Nouv. France. Vol. v., p. 185. An. 1741.
    " Dupratz, Louis. Vol. i., p. 301.
MOOSE DEER. Pennant, Arct. Zool. Vol. i., p. 17, Fig. 1784.
MOOSE. Umfreville, Huds. Bay. An. 1790.
    " Herriot's Travels, 1807, Fig.
C. ALCES. Harlan. Fauna, p. 229.
    " Godman, Am. Nat. Hist., Vol. ii., p. 274.
THE ELK. Hamilton Smith.
    " Griffith's Cuv., Vol. v., p. 303.
AMERICAN BLACK ELK. Griffith's Cuv., Vol. iv., p. 72., plate of head.
ELK. In Nova Scotia, proceedings of the Zoological Society, 1849, p. 93.
CERVUS ALCES. De Kay, N. Hist. N. Y., p. 115.

Description.

This is the largest of any known species of deer. Major SMITH (Cuv. An. Kingdom, by Griffiths, Vol. iv., p. 73) says, "For us, who have the opportunity of receiving the animal in all the glory of his full grown horns, amid the scenery of his own wilderness, no animal could appear more majestic or more imposing." Having ourselves on one occasion been favoured with a similar opportunity, when we had the gratification of bringing one down with a rifle and of examining him in detail as he lay before us, we confess he appeared awkwad in his gait, clumsy and disproportioned in limbs, uncouth and inelegant in form, and possessing less symmetry and beauty than any other species of the deer family. His great size, enormous head, and face like a horse, and the thundering noise of the saplings bending and snapping around him as he rattled over the fallen logs, was to us the only imposing part of the spectacle. To do justice, however, to the description of the moose, by SMITH, who was a close observer and a naturalist of considerable attainments, we should quote his succeeding observations: "It is, however, the aggregate of his appearance which produces this effect; for when the proportions of its structure are considered in detail, they certainly will seem destitute of that harmony of parts which in the imagination produces the feeling of beauty."

The head forcibly reminds us of that of an enormous jackass; it is long narrow and clumsily shaped, by the swelling on the upper part of the nose and nostrils; the snout is long and almost prehensile—the muzzle extending four inches beyond the lower lip. The nostrils are narrow and long, five inches in length. The eye is deep-seated, and in proportion to the large head is small. The ears are long, 14 inches, heavy and asinine. The neck is very short, and is surmounted by a compact mane of moderate length composed of coarse rigid hairs. There is in both sexes a tuft of coarse hairs, resembling hog's bristles, beneath the throat, which is attached to a pendulous gland, more conspicuous in young than in old animals; this gland with the attached hair is ten inches long. The horns, which are found only on the males, are, when a year old, merely short knobs; they increase in size after each annual shedding, and after the fourth year become palmated, and may be termed full grown about the fifth year. They palms on the horns of the Moose are on the widest part on a moderate-sized male about 11 inches wide. The space between the roots, $6\frac{1}{2}$

inches; greatest breadth at the root, $6\frac{1}{2}$ inches; from the root to the extremity, measuring around the curve, 2 feet 10 inches. The first branch or prong on the inner side of the horn commences nine inches from the base. It here divides into two branches, one being ten and the other eleven inches in length, measuring in a curve from the root to the largest point 25 inches. These two prongs on each side incline forward, are almost round, and are pointed like those of elk horns. The palms on the main branches of the horns not only differ in different individuals, but do not often correspond on the head of the same animal. In the specimen from which we are describing, the lower and longest point on the palm is on one side 12 inches, and on the corresponding one on the opposite side only 4 inches; on the remainder of the palm there are on one side six points, on the other seven; the palm is about half an-inch in breadth at the centre, thickening towards the base to one inch.

The horns are irregularly and slightly channelled, and are covered with whitish marks on the front surface, somewhat resembling the channels and irregular windings of grubs or sawyers between the bark and wood in old decayed trunks of trees; on the posterior surface these marks in form bear considerable resemblance to veins in the leaves of ferns. The width across the horns measuring from the outer tips rises 3 feet 4 inches; weight of the horns, 42 pounds.

The nose, including the nostrils, is thickly clothed with short hair—a triangular spot on the nose bare. The hair on the mane is coarse and compact, 10 inches in length; both surfaces of the ears are covered with dense hairs.

The outer hair is throughout coarse and angular; it is longer on the neck and shoulders than on any other part of the body; under these long hairs there is a shorter, woolly, more dense and finer coat.

Colour.

The teeth are white; horns brownish yellow, the extremities of the prongs becoming yellowish white. The eyes are black; nose, forehead and upper lip, yellowish fawn; inner surface of ears, yellowish white; outer surface, grayish brown. Sides of head, yellowish brown. On the neck, dark grayish brown, composed of hairs that are white, black and yellow; under the chin, yellowish brown. Hairs on the appendage under the throat, black; lower lip and chin, dark gray, formed of a mixture of white and black hairs; the softer, shorter hairs on the body are ashy gray; the long hairs when examined separately are whitish at the base, then cinereous and tipped with black, giving it a brownish black appearance.

On the under surface of the body the colour is considerably lighter than on the back, having a tinge of yellowish white; under surface of the tail, ashy white. The young animals, for the first winter, are of a reddish brown colour; individuals even of the same age often differ in colour, some being darker than others, but there is always a striking difference between the summer and winter colours, the hairs in winter becoming darker; as the moose advances in age, the colour continues to deepen until it appears black; thence it was named by HAMILTON SMITH, not inappropriately as regards colour, "the American Black Elk."

Dimensions.

	Feet.	Inches.
From point of nose to root of tail,	6	11
Tail (vertebræ),		8
Tail to end of hair,		$9\frac{1}{2}$
From shoulder to point of hoof,	4	6
Height of ear,	1	2
From point of nose to interior canthus of eye,	1	10

Weight of horns, 56 pounds.
Weight of the whole animal, from 800 to 1200 pounds.

Dimensions of a Male procured in Ontario County, N. Y., in 1806.

	Feet.	Inches.
Length from point of nose to root of tail,	7	2
" of tail,		11
Height at shoulders,	5	00
Width of horns at tip,	2	3
Widest part,	3	1

Weight of horns, 69 pounds.

Plate LXXVI

On Stone by Wᵐ E Hitchcock

Lith. Printed & Colᵈ by J T Bowen.

Moose Deer.

Drawn from Nature by J W Audubon

Habits.

We have favoured by MR. KENDALL, of the Literary Society of Quebec, with the following account of the Moose Deer, with which we will begin our article on this noble quadruped.

"The Moose are abundant to the north of Quebec and in the norther parts of the state of Maine. In the neighbourhood of Moose River and the lakes in its vicinity, they are very abundant. In the summer they are fond of frequenting lakes and rivers, not only to escape the attacks of insects which then molest them, but also to avoid injuring their antlers, which during their growth are very soft and exquisitely sensitive, and besides, such situations afford them abundance of food.

"They there feed on the water-plants, or browse upon the trees fringing the shores. In the winter they retire to the dry mountain ridges, and generally 'yard', as it is termed, on the side facing the south, where there are abundance of maple and other hard-wood trees upon which to feed, either by browsing on the tender twigs or peeling the bark from the stems of such as are only three or four inches in diameter. Their long, pendulous upper lip is admirably adapted for grasping and pulling down the branches, which are held between the fore legs until all the twigs are eaten. They peel off the bark by placing the hard pad on the roof of the mouth against the tree, and scraping upwards with their sharp, gouge-like teeth, completely denuding the tree to the height of seven or eight feet from the surface of the snow. They remain near the same spot as long as any food can be obtained, seldom breaking fresh snow, but keeping to the same tracks as long as possible.

"The antlers begin to sprout in April, and at first appear like two black knobs. They complete their growth in July, when the skin which covers them peels off and leaves them perfectly white; exposure to the sun and air, however, soon renders them brown. When we consider the immense size to which some of them grow in such a short period of time, it seems almost incredible that two such enormous excrescences could be deposited from the circulating system alone; the daily growth is distinctly marked on the velvety covering by a light shade carried around them. The first year the antlers are only about one inch long; the second year, four or five inches, with perhaps the rudiment of a point; the third year about nine inches, when each divides into a fork still round in form; the fourth year they become palmated, with a brow antler and three or four points; the fifth season they have two crown antlers and perhaps five points; the points increasing in size each year, and one or two points being added annually, until the animal arrives at its greatest vigour; after which period they decrease in size and the points are not so fully thrown out. The longest pair I ever met with had eighteen points, (others have seen them with twenty-three points,) they expanded five feet nine inches to the outside of the tips; the breadth of palm, eleven inches without the points; circumference of shaft, clear of the burr, nine inches; weight, seventy pounds! The old and vigorous animals invariably shed them in December; some of four and five years old I have known to carry them as late as March, but this is not often the case.

"The rutting season commences in September; the males then become very furious, chasing away the younger and weaker ones. They run bellowing through the forest, and when two of equal strength meet, have dreadful conflicts, and do not separate until one or both are severely injured. I bought a pair of antlers from a Penobscot Indian, with one of the brow antlers and the adjoining prong broken short off. The parts were at least $1\frac{1}{2}$ inches in diameter, and nearly as hard as ivory. At that season they are constantly on the move, swimming large lakes and crossing rivers in pursuit of the female.

"The female brings forth in May. The first time she produces one fawn, but ever-afterwards two. It is supposed by hunters that these twins are always one a male and the other a female.

"In summer the hair of the Moose is short and glossy—in winter long and very coarse, attached to the skin by a very fine pelicle, and rendered warm by a thick coat of short, fine wool. The hair on the face grows upwards from the nose, gradually turning and ending in a thick, bushy tuft under the jaws. The young males have generally a long, pendulous gland, growing from the centre of this tuft, and covered with long hair, sometimes a foot long.

"Their flesh is very coarse, though some people prefer it to any other; it is apt to produce dysentery with persons unaccustomed to use it. The nose or *moufle*, as it is generally called, if properly cooked is a very delicious morsel. The tongue is also considered a delicacy; the last entrail (called by hunters the bum-gut) is covered with round lumps of suety fat, which they strip off and devour as it comes warm from the animal, without any cooking. Also the marrow warm from the shanks is spread upon bread, and eaten as butter. I must confess that the disgusting luxury was rather *too rich* to tempt me to partake of it. I have seen some officers of the Guards enjoy it well enough!

"The seasons for hunting the Moose are March and September. In March,

when the sun melts the snow on the surface and the nights are frosty, a *crust* is formed, which greatly impedes the animal's progress, as it has to lift its feet perpendicularly out of the snow or cut the skin from its shanks by coming in contact with the icy surface.

"It would be useless to follow them when the snow is soft, as their great strength enables them to wade through it without any difficulty. If you wish to see them previous to shooting them from their "yard," it is necessary to make your approach to leeward, as their sense of smelling and hearing is very acute: the crack of a breaking twig will start them, and they are seldom seen any more, until fatigue compels them to knock up, and thus ends the chase. Their pace is a long trot. It is necessary to have two or three small curs (the smaller the better), as they can run upon the snow without breaking through the crust; their principal use is to annoy the Moose by barking and snapping at their heels, without taking hold. A large dog that would take hold would be instantly trampled to death. The males generally stop, if pressed, and fight with the dogs; this enables the hunter to come up unobserved and dispatch them. Sometimes they are killed after a run of an hour, at other times you may run them all day, and have to camp at night without a morsel of provisions or a cloak, as everything is let go the moment the Moose starts, and you are too much fatigued to retrace your steps to procure them. Your only resource is to make a huge fire, and comfort yourself upon the prospect of plenty of Moose-meat next day. As soon as the animal finds he is no longer pursued, he lies down, and the next morning he will be too stiff to travel far. Generally, a male, female, and two fawns are found in a 'yard.'

"When obliged to run, the male goes first, breaking the way, the others treading exactly in his tracks, so that you would think only one has passed. Often they run through other 'yards,' when all join together, still going in Indian file. Sometimes, when meeting with an obstacle they cannot overcome, they are obliged to branch off for some distance and again unite; by connecting the different tracks at the place of separation you may judge pretty correctly of their number. I have seen twelve together, and killed seven of them.

A method of hunting this animal is as follows:

"In September, two persons in a bark canoe paddle by moonlight along the shore of the lake imitating the call of the male, which, jealous of the approach of a stranger, answers to the call and rushes down to the combat. The canoe is paddled by the man in the stern with the most deathlike silence, gliding along under the shade of the forest until within short shooting distance, as it is difficult to take a sure aim by moonlight; the man in the bow generally fires, when if the animal is only wounded, he makes immediately for shore, dashing the water about him into foam; he is tracked by his blood the next day to where he has lain down, and where he is generally found unable to proceed any further. Many are killed in this manner in the neighbourhood of Moose River every season.

Hunters sometimes find out the beaten tracks of the Moose (generally leading to the water), and bend down a sapling and attach to it a strong hempen noose hanging across the path, while the tree is confined by another cord and a sort of trigger. Should the animal's head pass through the dangling snare, he generally makes a struggle which disengages the trigger, and the tree springing upward to its perpendicular, lifts the beast off his legs, and he is strangled!"

Mr. JOHN MARTYN, of Quebec, favoured us with the following notes on the Moose deer: "This animal in the neighbourhood of this city (Quebec) is mostly found in the hard woods during the winter. At this season several associate together and form groups of two, three, or four, and make what is called 'a yard,' by beating down the snow; and whilst in such places they feed on all the branches they can reach, and indeed even strip the tree of their bark, after which they are forced to extend their 'yards,' or remove to some other place, but rather than leave the first, they will even break branches as large as a man's thigh. In skinning off the bark, the animal places its upper lip firmly against it, whether upward, downward or sideways, and with its teeth, which are all on its lower jaw, takes a firm hold and tears it away in strips more or less long and broad, according to the nature of the bark of the tree.

It is ascertained by the hunter whether a Moose has been lately or not in its yard, by removing the surface of the snow from around the foot of the trees already barked above, and if they have been barked below the surface of the snow, the animal has left the spot for sometime, and it is not worth while to follow any of its tracks. The contrary, of course, takes place with different observations. At this season the female is generally accompanied by two of her calves, one two years old and generally a bull, the other the calf of the preceding spring.

These animals vary much in their colour, some being grayish brown, and others nearly black. The grayish Moose is generally the largest, often reaching the height of seven or eight feet. The females receive the males in the month of October, and at this period the latter are excessively vicious and dangerous when approached, whilst the females evince the same fierceness at the time of having calves. In some instances during the rutting season, when two males accidentally meet, they fight prodigiously hard, tearing up the earth beneath for yards around, and leaving marks of blood sufficient to prove that their encounter has been of the severest nature.

Their usual mode of defence consists in striking at their enemies with their forefeet; but in fighting with each other the males use both feet and horns, and they have sometimes been killed with marks of old wounds about their head and other parts of the body. As an instance of the force with which the Moose strikes, the following anecdote may be related: a bull-terrier in attempting to seize one by the nose, was struck by the animal with its forefoot, and knocked off to a distance of twenty feet; the dog died next day.

The Moose deer frequently turn against the hunters, even before being shot at or in the least wounded. They walk, trot, and gallop, and can leap a great distance at a single bound; like other species of deer they bend their bodies very low at times, to pass beneath branches of fallen trees, not even half their height from the earth. When pursued, they enter the most tangled thickets, and pass through them as if not feeling the impediments, the brushwood, fallen logs, &c., opposed to the hunter's progress. The calves when born are about the size of a few days old colt, but are more slender, and look very awkward on account of their apparent disproportionate long and large legs. When caught at three months old, they eat leaves, &c.; but how long they are suckled by their dam we have not been able to ascertain.

"During the summer they frequently resort to the shores of rivers, creeks or lakes, on the margins of which their tracks are seen, like those of common cattle; they enter the water and immerse their bodies to save themselves from the bites of flies, &c.

In all probability, where wolves are yet abundant, these are their most dangerous enemies besides man; but at the present time, few of these rapacious animals are to be found in the neighbourhood of Quebec. The Moose deer are frequently killed while in the water, or on the shores of some pond, lake or river; but when their young are with them, they will run and chase the hunter, and it is sometimes difficult for him to escape, unless he is so fortunate as to shoot and bring them down.

"The flesh is considered very good, especially the *moufflon*, which forms the upper lip, and is very rich, juicy and gelatinous. This is cleaned and dressed in the same manner as 'calves' head.' The hunters salt their meat for winter use. The steaks are as good as beef steaks; but the Moose are not generally fat, although their flesh is juicy and at times tender. The young at the age of twelve months are never tough, and their flesh is preferable to that of the old beasts. The inside of the mouth above, or palate, is extremely hard, and lays in folds, giving this animal the power of gripping (seizing) the bark or the branches of trees, by which means it tears them off with ease. This pad is placed immediately beneath the extremity of the *moufflon*, and is about two inches long.

"These animals feed principally on the birch, the *moose-wood*, the aspen, and various kinds of leaves and grasses; in captivity they eat hay and other dry food, even hard ship-biscuit. The females are called 'cows,' the males 'bulls,' and the young 'calves.' Their droppings resemble those of the deer kind. Although the Moose swim well they are not known to dive, they swim with the head and part of the neck above water, like cattle. When pursued in boats they frequently attempt to upset them, and at times open their mouths and make a loud snorting noise, striking at the same time with their forefeet, and occasionally sink the canoes of the Indians or hunters. Upon one occasion, a young man going fishing, and having his fowling-piece along, on turning a point of a lake, saw a large Moose in the water and fired at it with shot, tickling it severely. The Moose at once made for the canoe; and whilst the alarmed fisherman was attempting to escape, his boat became entangled in the branches of a fallen tree, when he was forced to give up the canoe and get away as he best could; the animal on reaching the boat completely demolished it. Unfortunately, the females are sometimes killed when they are with calf. They do not generally make any noise in the woods, unless when provoked, but in captivity they utter a plaintive sound, much resembling that made by the black bear. They never are seen on the ice like the rein-deer; it would seem by the formation of their hoofs that they might walk well on the rocks, or on the ice, but they keep in the woods, and when walking over snow their feet usually sink into it until they reach the earth.

"A Mr. Bell, residing at Three Rivers, has a Moose which has been taught to draw water in a cart or in a sleigh during winter, but there is no possibility of working it during the rutting season. We have never heard of any attempt to ride on the Moose deer. Their horns, which are large, palmated, and heavy, are dropped in the months of December and January, begin to show again in the latter part of March, and in two months or thereabouts attain their full size. When covered over with 'velvet,' as it is called, they are very curious. A

pair of good Moose horns sells at the high price of twenty dollars! The velvet is scraped off against trees and bushes in the manner employed by our Virginian deer. Horns have been measured when reversed and standing on the ground four feet seven inches, and ordinary pairs often measure five feet and upwards.

"It is said that the Moose can smell at a very great distance, and that the moment they scent a man or other enemy they make off and are not easily overtaken. On the first glimpse of man, if they are lying down they rise to their feet and are off at once, and often before they are observed by the hunter. When closely pursued, they turn and make a dash at the enemy, scarcely giving him time to escape, and the hunter's best plan in such cases is to keep cool and shoot the animal as it rushes towards him, or if unprepared, he had best ascend a tree with all convenient dispatch. Sometimes the hunter is obliged to save himself by dodging around a tree, or by throwing down some part of his dress, upon which the Moose expends his fury, trampling on it until torn to tatters.

"Moose-hunting is followed by white or red skinned hunters in the same manner. He, however, who has been born in the woods, possesses many advantages over the 'civilized' man. The white hunters generally provide themselves, previous to their starting, amply with provisions and ammunition to last them about three weeks, and sometimes go in a sleigh. The guns used are mostly single-barrelled, of ordinary size, but suited for shooting balls as well as shot,—rifles are rarely used in Canada. After leaving the settlements, the first day's journey takes them ten or twelve miles, when they select a proper place in a snowy district, as near a stream as possible.

"It the weather is fine, they cut down trees and make a camp, some of the party provide water, and others light the fires and clear off the snow for yards around, whilst evergreen trees are stripped of their branches to make up a floor and covering for them in their temporary shelter. The hunters having made all snug, cook their meat and eat it before a fire that illuminates the woods around, and causes the party to appear like a set of goblins through the darkness of night. On many such occasions the *bedding* is singed, and per chance a whisker! The feet may be partially roasted, whilst the shoulders, the hands, and probably the nose, are suffering greatly from the severity of the weather, for the thermometer may be occasionally thirty degrees below zero! The march to this spot is frequently made on snow-shoes, which are taken off, however, whilst the party are forming the encampment, clearing away the snow, and making a path to the water, which being covered with snow and ice, requires to be got at by means of shovels and axes. Before daylight, the kettles are put on the fires, tea and coffee are made, breakfast swallowed in a few moments, and the party on foot, ready to march toward the hunting-ground. On the way, every one anxiously looks out for tracks of the game, and whether hares or grouse come in the way they are shot and hung up on the trees; but if game of any kind has been thus hung up by others, whether Indians or white hunters, the party leaves it sacredly untouched—for this is the etiquette of the chase throughout this portion of country. When they at last reach the ground, the party divide, and seek for the Moose in different directions. It is agreed that no one shall shoot after separating from the rest, unless it be at the proper game, and also that in case of meeting with Moose, or with fresh signs, they are to return, and make ready to proceed to the spot together next day. Sometimes, however, this rule is broken through by some one whose anxiety (excitement) at sight of a Moose makes him forget himself and his promise. As soon as a 'yard' has been discovered, all hands sally forth, and the hunt is looked upon as fairly begun. If on approaching the 'yard,' their dogs, which are generally mongrels of all descriptions, start a Moose, the hunters, guided by their barking and the tracks of the pack and the Moose through the snow, follow with all possible celerity. The dogs frequently take hold of the Moose by the hind legs, the animal turns, and stands at bay, and the hunters thus have an opportunity to come up with the chase.

"On approaching, when at the proper distance (about sixty to eighty yards) the nearest man takes a decided aim, as nearly as possible under the forearm and through the neck, and fires, or, if fronting the beast, in the centre of the breast.

"If wounded only, the second hunter fires also, and perhaps the third, and the animal succumbs at last, though it sometimes manages to run, stumble, and scramble, for miles. After skinning the Moose, the heart and liver, and the marrow-bones, are taken out, and a good large piece of the flesh is taken to 'camp,' and is speedily well cooked and placed smoking hot before the hungry hunters. After killing all the Moose of a 'yard' or that they can find near their camp, the party pack up their material, break up the camp, and return home."

It not unfrequently happens, that a wounded Moose, or even one that has not been wounded, will turn upon the hunter, who then has to run for his life, and many instances of such incidents are related, including some hair-breadth escapes. One of these I will relate: Two Indians being on a hunt and having met with the game, one of them shot, and missed; the Moose turned upon him, and he fled as fast as he could, but when about to reach a large tree, from behind which he could defy his opponent, his snow shoes hooked in some obstacle and threw him down. The Moose set upon him furiously and began trampling on him, but the Indian drew out a knife, and succeeded in cutting the sinews of the forelegs of the animal, and finally stabbed him so repeatedly in the belly that he fell dead, but unluckily fell on the prostrate hunter, who would have been unable to extricate himself, had not his companion come to his assistance. The poor man, however, had been so much injured that he never recovered entirely, and died about two years afterwards.

During some seasons the snows are so deep, and at times so soft, that the Moose cannot go *over* the snow, but have to make their way through it, giving a great advantage to the hunters, who, on broad snow-shoes can stand or run on the surface without much difficulty. On one occasion of this nature a Moose was seen, and at once followed. The poor animal was compelled to *plough* the snow, as it were, and the hunters came up to it with ease, and actually placed their hands on its back. They then endeavoured to drive it towards their camp and secure it alive. The Moose, however, would not go in the proper direction, and they finally threw it down, and attempted to fasten its legs together; but as they had no ropes, and could not procure any better substitute for them than withes, the beast got away, and after a long chase they, being very much fatigued, shot it dead. When the snow is thus soft, the Moose deer has been known to evade the hunters by pushing ahead through tangled thickets, more especially *hackmetack* and briary places which no man can go through for any length of time without extreme labour. The Indians, however, will follow the Moose in such cases day and night, provided the moon is shining, until the animal is so fatigued that it can be overtaken and killed with ease. Instances have been known where as many as five have been killed in one day by two Indians. The Moose is not unfrequently caught in the following manner: A rope is passed over a horizontal branch of a tree, with a large noose and slip-knot at one end, whilst a heavy log is attached to the other, hanging across the limb or branch, and touching the ground. The Moose, as it walks along, passes its head through the noose, and the farther it advances, the tighter it finds itself fastened, and whilst it plunges terrified onwards, the log is raised from the ground until it reaches the branch, when it sticks, so that no matter in what manner the Moose moves, the log keeps a continued strain, rising and falling, but not giving the animal the least chance to escape, and at last the poor creature dies miserably. They are also 'pitted' at times, but their legs are so long, that this method of *securing* them seldom succeeds, as they generally manage to get out."

The Moose is well known to travellers who have crossed the Rocky Mountains, where this animal is principally called by the French name, "L'Orinal."

Whilst at Quebec, in 1842, we procured the head and neck of a very large male, (handsomely mounted); which was shot in the state of Maine, where the Moose is still frequently found.

Moose deer are abundant in Labrador, and even near the coast their tracks, or rather paths, may be seen, as distinctly marked as the cow-paths about a large stock-farm. In this sterile country, where the trees are so dwarfish that they only deserve the name of shrubs, and where innumerable barren hills arise, with cold clear-water ponds between, the Moose feeds luxuriously on the scanty herbage and the rank summer grasses that are found on their sides; but in winter the scene is awfully desolate, after the snows have fallen to a great depth; the whistling winds, unimpeded by trees or forests, sweep over the country, carrying with them the light snow from the tops and windward sides of the hills in icy clouds, and soon forming tremendous drifts in the valleys. No man can face the storm-driven snows of this bleak, cold country; the congealed particles are almost solid, and so sharp and fine that they strike upon the face or hands like small shot; the tops of the hills are left quite bare

and the straggling Moose or rein deer seek a precarious supply of mosses along their sides. At this season the Moose sometimes crosses the Gulf of St. Lawrence, on the ice to Newfoundland, of follows the coast towards the shore opposite Nova Scotia, and there passes the Gulf and wanders into more woody and favoured regions for the winter.

The following is from our friend S. W. RODMAN, Esq., of Boston, an excellent sportsman, and a lover of nature, to whom we are indebted for many kindnesses.

"Our party was returning from lake Miramichi, about the middle of July, by the marshy brook, which connects it with the Miramichi river. The canoe men were poling slowly and silently, in order not to disturb the numerous ducks which breed in those uninhabited solitudes, as we were anxious to vary our constant fish diet; salmon either boiled or "skinned" being set before us morning, noon and night. We had not fired a gun to disturb the silence. My own and my brother's canoes were close together, when I saw an animal suddenly spring on to its feet from the long marshy grass about forty yards in advance of us. I said quickly "Cariboo," "Cariboo," "stoop low;" which we all did and continued moving on. It was about the size of a yearling heifer, but taller, of a bright, light, red colour, with long ears pricked forward, and a large soft eye; and stood perfectly still, looking at us. We had gone perhaps ten yards, when there appeared from the long grass by its side, first the ears, then the huge head and muffle of an old cow Moose, the first one being as I now knew her calf, of perhaps four or five months old. She gradually rose to her knees, then sat upon her haunches, and at last sprang to her feet, her eyes all the time intently fixed upon us. The calf in the meanwhile had moved slowly off. At this moment we both fired without any apparent effect, the shot being too light to penetrate the thick hide. She turned instantly, showing a large and apparently well filled udder, struck into the tremendous trot, for which the Moose is so celebrated, crossed the deep brook almost at a stride, then the narrow strip of meadow, and disappeared, crashing through the alders which intervened between the meadow and the dark evergreen forests beyond.

Our oldest woodsman, Porter, assured us that she was one of the largest of her kind, and that it was rare good fortune to approach so near to this noblest denizen of our northern forests. We were much gratified, but our regret as sportsmen was still greater, at not having been prepared to take advantage of such an opportunity as will probably never again occur to either of us. We constantly both before and afterwards saw the tracks of cariboo and Moose about our camps."

Geographical Distribution.

Capt. FRANKLIN, in his last expedition, states that several Moose were seen at the mouth of Mackenzie River, on the shores of the Arctic Sea, in latitude 69°. Farther to the eastward towards the Copper-mine River, we are informed by RICHARDSON, they are not found in a higher latitude than 65°. MACKENZIE saw them high up on the eastern declivity of the Rocky Mountains, near the sources of the Elk River; LEWIS and CLARK saw them at the mouth of the Oregon. To the east they abound in Labrador, Nova Scotia, New-Brunswick, and Lower Canada. In the United States they are found in very diminished numbers in the unsettled portions of Maine and at long intervals in New-Hampshire and Vermont. In the state of New-York, according to the observations, made by Dr. DEKAY, (Nat. Hist. N. Y., p. 117), which we believe strictly correct, they yet exist in Herkimer, Hamilton, Franklin, Lewis and Warren counties, and their southern limit along the Atlantic coast is 43° 30'.

General Remarks.

We have considerable doubts whether our Moose deer is identical with the Scandinavian elk (*Cervus alces*, of authors), and have therefore not quoted any of the synonymes of the latter, but having possessed no favourable opportunities of deciding this point, we have not ventured on the adoption of any of the specific names which have from time to time been proposed for the American Moose.

Genus Antilocapra.—Ord.

Dental Formula.

Incisive $\frac{0}{0}$; *Canine* $\frac{0—0}{0—0}$; *Molar* $\frac{6—6}{6—6}$ = 32.

Horns common to both sexes; small in the female; horns persistent, greatly compressed, rough, pearled, slightly striated, with an anterior process, and the point inclining backwards; eye large; no suborbital sinus; no inguinal pores; no muzzle; facial line, converse; no canines; no succentorial hoofs; tail very short; hair stiff, coarse, undulating, flattened; female, mammæ.

Habit, peaceable, gregarious, herbivorous, confined to North-America.
Only one well determined species belongs to this genus.

The generic name *Antilocapra*, is derived from the two genera *Antilope* and *Capra*, Goat Antelope.

Antilocapra Americana.—Ord.

Prong-Horned Antelope.

Plate lxxvii. Male and Female.

Cornibus pedalibus compressis, intus planis, antiæ granulatis striatisque propugnaculo compresso procurvo cum cornum parte posteriore retrorsum uncinata furcam constituiente; colore russo fuscescente, gutture, cluniumque disco albis: statura, Cervus Virginianus.

Plate LXXVII

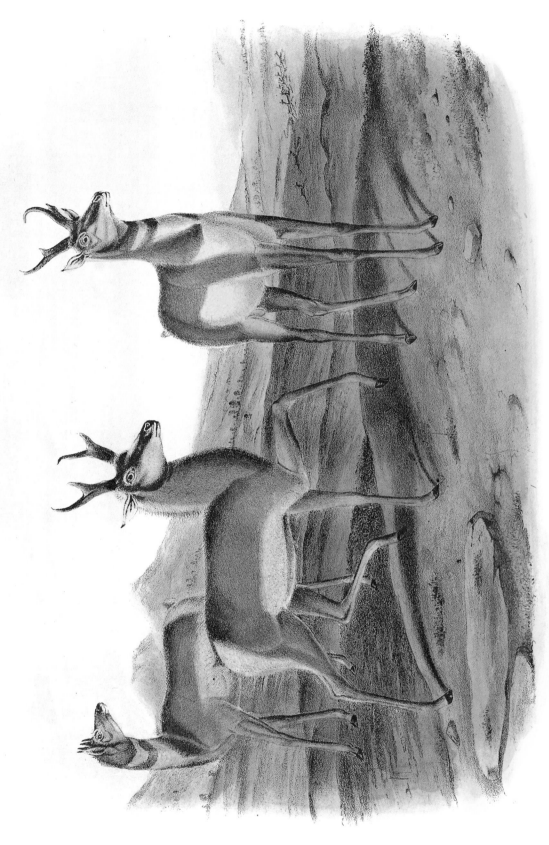

On Stone by Mᵐᵉ E. Hitchcock

Drawn from Nature by J. J. Audubon

Lith Printed & Col⁴ by J. T. Bowen Phil.

Prong-Horned Antelope.

Characters.

Horns compressea, flat on the inner side, pearled and striated, with a compressed snag to the front; colour, reddish dun; throat and disk on the buttocks, white. Size of the Virginia deer.

Synonymes.

TEUTHLAMACAMÆ. Hernandez, Nov.-Hispan, p. 324, fig. 324. An. 1651.
LE SQUENOTON. Hist. d'Amerique, p. 175. An. 1723.
SQUINATON. Dobb's, Hudson's Bay, p. 24. An. 1744.
ANTILOPE, CABRE OR GOAT. Gass Journal, pp. 49, 111.
ANTILOPE. Lewis and Clarke Journ., Vol. i., pp. 75, 208, 396; Vol. ii., p. 169.
ANTILOPE AMERICANA. Ord, Guthrie's Geography. 1815.
CERVUS HAMATUS. Blainville, Nouv-Ball. Society. 1816.
ANTILOCAPRA AMERICANA. Ord, Jour. de Phys., p. 80. 1818.
ANTILOPE FURCIFER. C. Hamilton Smith, Lin. Trans., Vol. xiii., plate 2. An. 1823.
ANTILOPE PALMATA. Smith, Griffith, Cuv., Vol. v., p. 323.
ANTILOPE AMERICANA. Harlan Fauna, p. 250.
"   Godman, Nat. Hist., Vol. ii., p. 321.
ANTILOPE FURCIFER. Richardson, F. B. A., p. 261, plate 21.

Description.

The Prong-horned Antelope possesses a stately and elegant form, and resembles more the antelope than the deer family. It is shorter and more compactly built than the Virginia deer; its head and neck are also shorter and the skull is broader at the base. The horns of the male are curved upwards and backwards with a short triangular prong about the centre, inclined inwards, not wrinkled. Immediately above the prong the horn diminishes to less than half the size, below the prong the horn is flat and very broad, extremity of the horn sharp and pointed, and of the prong blunt. There are irregular little points on the horns of the male, two or three on each side. One specimen has two on the inside of each horn and one on the outside irregularly disposed.

Nostrils large and open, placed rather far back, eyes large and prominent, ears of moderate size, acuminate in shape; on the back of the neck in winter specimens there is a narrow ridge of coarse hairs resembling a short mane. In summer there only remains of this mane a black stripe on the upper surface of the neck; eyelashes profuse; there is no under-fur. The hairs are of a singular texture, being thick, soft, wavy and slightly crimped beneath the surface: they are brittle, and when bent do not return to their original straight form, interiorly they are white, spongy and pithy; scrotum pendulous. There is not the slightest vestige of any secondary hoofs on either of its fore or hind legs, such as are seen in deer and other animals. The hoofs are strong and compact, small and diminishing suddenly to a point.

Colour.

The nose is yellowish brown, eye lashes black, the orbits with a blackish brown border, outer edge and points of the ears brownish black. There is a white band about two inches wide in front of and partly encircling the throat, narrowing to a point on each side of the neck; beneath this is a brown band about the same breath, underneath which is a grayish white spot of nearly a triangular shape; this is formed by a patch on each side of the throat of yellowish brown. The chest, belly, and sides to within five or six inches of the back are grayish white. A large light-coloured patch of nine inches in breadth exists on the rump, similar to that on the Rocky Mountain sheep and the elk. This whitish patch is separated by a brown-yellowish line, running along the vertebræ of the back to the tail. Legs, pale brownish yellow, approaching to dull buff colour, all the upper surface yellowish brown; under jaw and cheek, pale or grayish white; lips, whitish.

Female.—The female is a size smaller than the male. The neck is shorter. The form is similar, except that the markings are rather fainter; the brownish yellow which surrounds the different whitish or grayish white spots and bands being much paler than in the male. The horn is destitute of a prong; it is only three inches in length, nearly straight, and running to an acute point. The female possesses no mane.

Dimensions.

	Feet.	Inches.
From point of nose to root of tail,	4	2
Height, to shoulder from end of hoof,	3	1
Length of ear,		4
Length of prong,		6

Habits.

Reader, let us carry you with us to the boundless plains over which the prong-horn speeds. Hurra for the prairies and the swift antelopes, as they fleet by the hunter like flashes or meteors, seen but for an instant, for quickly do they pass out of sight in the undulating ground, covered with tall rank grass. Observe now a flock of these beautiful animals; they are not afraid of man—they pause in their rapid course to gaze on the hunter, and stand with head erect, their ears as well as eyes directed towards him, and make a loud noise by stamping with their forefeet on the hard earth; but suddenly they become aware that he is no friend of theirs, and away they bound like a flock of frightened sheep—but far more swiftly do the graceful antelopes gallop off, even the kids running with extraordinary speed by the side of their parents—and now they turn around a steep hill and disappear, then perhaps again come in view, and once more stand and gaze at the intruder. Sometimes, eager with curiosity and anxious to examine the novel object which astonishes as well as alarms them, the antelopes on seeing a hunter, advance toward him, stopping at intervals, and then again advancing, and should the hunter partly conceal himself, and wave his handkerchief or a white or red rag on the end of his ramrod, he may draw the wondering animals quite close to him and then quickly seizing his rifle send a ball through the fattest of the group, ere the timid creatures have time to fly from the fatal spot.

The Indians, we were told, sometimes bring the antelope to within arrow-shot (bow-shot), by throwing themselves on their backs and kicking up their heels with a bit of a rag fastened to them, on seeing which moving amid the grass the antelope draws near to satisfy his curiosity.

The atmosphere on the western prairies is so pure and clear that an antelope is easily seen when fully one mile off, and you can tell whether it is feeding quietly or is alarmed; but beautiful as the transparent thin air shews all distant objects, we have never found the great western prairies equal the *flowery* descriptions of travellers. They lack the pure streamlet wherein the hunter may assuage his thirst—the delicious copses of dark, leafy trees; and even the thousands of fragrant flowers, which they are poetically described as possessing, are generally of the smaller varieties; and the Indian who roams over them is far from the ideal being—all grace, strength and nobleness, in his savage freedom—that we from these descriptions conceive him. Reader, do not expect to find any of the vast prairies that border the Upper Missouri, or the Yellow-Stone rivers, and extend to the Salt Lakes amid the Californian range of the Rocky Mountains, verdant pastures ready for flocks and herds, and full of the soft perfume of the violet. No; you will find an immense waste of stony, gravelly, barren soil, stretched before you; you will be tormented with thirst, half eaten up by stinging flies, and lucky will you be if at night you find wood and water enough to supply your fire and make your cup of coffee; and should you meet a band of Indians, you will find them wrapped in old buffalo robes, their bodies filthy and covered with vermin, and by stealing or begging they will obtain from you perhaps more than you can spare from your scanty store of necessaries, and armed with bows and arrows or firearms, they are not unfrequently ready to murder, or at least rob you of all your personal property, including your ammunition, gun and butcher knife!

The Prong-horned Antelope brings forth its young about the same time as the common deer: from early in May to the middle of June; it has generally two fawns at a birth. We have heard of no case in which more than that number has been dropped at a time, and probably in some cases only one is fawned by the dam. The young are not spotted like the fawn of the common deer, but are of a uniform dun colour. The dam remains by her young for some days after they are born, feeding immediately around the spot, and afterwards gradually enlarging her range; when the young are a fortnight old they have gained strength and speed enough to escape with their fleet-footed mother from wolves or other four-footed foes. Sometimes, however, the wolves discover and attack the young when they are too feeble to escape, and the mother then displays the most devoted courage in their defence. She rushes on them, butting and striking with her short horns, and sometimes tosses a wolf heels over head, she also uses her forefeet, with which she deals severe blows, and if the wolves are not in strong force, or desperate with hunger, puts them to flight, and then seeks with her young a safer pasturage, or some almost inaccessible rocky hill side.

The rutting season of this species commences in September, the bucks run for about six weeks, and during this period fight with great courage and even a degree of ferocity. When a male sees another approaching, or accidentally comes upon one of his rivals, both parties run at each other with their heads lowered and their eyes flashing angrily, and while they strike with their horns they wheel and bound with prodigous activity and rapidity, giving and receiving severe wounds,—sometimes like fencers, getting within each others "points," and each hooking his antagonist with the recurved branches of his horns, which bend considerably inwards and downwards.

The Prong-horned Antelope usually inhabits the low prairies adjoining the covered woody bottoms during spring and autumn, but is also found on the high or upland prairies, or amid broken hills, and is to be seen along the margins of the rivers and streams: it swims very fast and well, and occasionally a herd when startled may be seen crossing a river in straggling files, but without disorder, and apparently with ease.

Sometimes a few of these animals, or even only one or two by themselves may be seen, whilst in other instances several hundreds are congregated in a herd. They are remarkably shy, are possessed of a fine sense of smell, and have large and beautiful eyes, which enable them to scan the surface of the undulating prairie and detect the lurking Indian or wolf, creep he ever so cautiouly through the grasses, unless some intervening elevation or copsewood conceal his approach. It is, therefore, necessary for the hunter to keep well to *leeward*, and to use extraordinary caution in "sneaking" after this species; and he must also exercise a great deal of patience and move very slowly and only at intervals, when the animals with heads to the ground or averted from him, are feeding or attracted by some other object. When they discover a man thus stealthily moving near them, at first sight they fly from him with great speed, and often retire to the broken grounds of the clay hills, from which they are not often tempted to stray a great distance at any time. As we have already mentioned, there are means, however, to excite the timid antelope to draw near the hunter, by arousing his curiosity and decoying him to his ruin. The antelopes of the Upper Missouri country are frequently shot by the Indians whilst crossing the river; and, as we were informed, preferred the northern side of the Missouri; which, no doubt, arises from the prevalence on that bank of the river of certain plants, trees or grasses, that they are most fond of. Males and females are found together at all seasons of the year. We have been told that probably a thousand or more of these animals have been seen in a single herd or flock at one time, in the spring.

It was supposed by the hunters at Fort Union, that the prong-horned antelope dropped its horns; but as no person had ever shot or killed one without these ornamental and useful appendages, we managed to prove the contrary to the men at the fort by knocking off the bony part of the horn, and showing the hard, spongy membrane beneath, well attached to the skull and perfectly immoveable.

The Prong-horned Antelope is never found on the Missouri river below *L'eau qui court*; but above that stream they are found along the great Missouri and its tributaries, in all the country east of the Rocky Mountains, and in many of the great valleys that are to be met with among these extraordinary "big hills." None of these antelopes are found on the shores of the Mississippi, although on the headwaters of the Saint Peter's river they have been tolerably abundant. Their walk is a slow and somewhat pompous gait, their trot elegant and graceful, and their gallop or "run" light and inconceivably swift; they pass along, up or down hills, or along the level plain with the same apparent ease, while so rapidly do their legs perform their graceful movements in propelling their bodies over the ground, that like the spokes of a fast turning wheel we can hardly see them, but instead, observe a gauzy or film-like appearance where they should be visible.

In autumn, this species is fatter than at any other period. Their liver is much prized as a delicacy, and we have heard that many of these animals are killed simply to procure this choice morsel. This antelope feeds on the short grass of the prairies, on mosses, buds, &c.; and suffers greatly during the hard winters experienced in the north-west; especially when the snow is several feet in depth. At such times they can be caught by hunters provided with snow shoes, and they are in this manner killed, even in sight of Fort Union, from time to time.

It is exceedingly difficult to rear the young of this species; and, although many attempts have been made at Fort Union, and even an old one caught and brought within an enclosure to keep the young company, they became furious, and ran and butted alternately against the picket-wall or fence, until they were too much bruised and exhausted to recover. WILLIAM SUBLETTE, Esq., of St. Louis, Missouri, however, brought with him to that city a female antelope, caught when quite young on the prairies of the far west, which grew to maturity, and was so very gentle, that it would go all over the house, mounting or descending the stairs, and occasionally going on to the roof of the building he lived in. This female was alive when we first reached St. Louis, but not being aware of its existence, we never saw it. It was killed before we left by a buck-elk, belonging to the same gentleman.

Whilst on our journey in the far west, in 1843, on one occasion, we had the gratification of seeing an old female, in a flock of eight or ten antelopes, suckling its young. The little beauty performed this operation precisely in the manner of our common lambs, almost kneeling down, bending its head upwards, its rump elevated, it thumped the bag of its mother, from time to time, and reminded us of far distant scenes, where peaceful flocks feed and repose under the safeguard of our race, and no prowling wolf or hungry Indian defeats the hopes of the good shepherd who nightly folds his stock of the Leicester or Bakewell breed. Our wild antelopes, however, as we approached them, scampered away; and we were delighted to see that first, and in the van of all, was the young one!

On the 21st July, 1843, whilst in company with our friend, EDWARD HARRIS, Esq., during one of our hunting excursions, we came in sight of an antelope gazing at us, and determined to stop and try if we could bring him toward us by the trick we have already mentioned, of throwing our legs up in the air and kicking them about, whilst lying on our back in the grass. We kicked away first one foot and then the other, and sure enough, the antelope walked slowly toward us, apparently with great caution and suspicion. In about twenty minutes he had advanced towards us some two or three hundred yards. He was a superb male, and we looked at him for several minutes when about sixty yards off. We could see his fine protruding eyes; and being loaded with buck-shot, we took aim and pulled trigger. Off he went, as if pursued by a whole Black-foot Indian hunting party. Friend HARRIS sent a ball at him, but was as unsuccessful as ourselves, for he only ran the faster for several hundred yards, when he stopped for a few minutes, looked again at us, and then went off, without pausing as long as he was in sight. We have been informed by LAFLEUR, a man employed by the Company, that antelopes will escape with great ease even when they have one limb broken, as they can run fast enough upon three legs to defy any pursuit. Whilst we were encamped at the "Three Mamelles," about sixty miles west of Fort Union, early one morning an antelope was heard *snorting*, and was seen by some of our party for a few minutes only. This snorting, as it is called, resembles a loud whistling, singing sound prolonged, and is very different from the loud and clear snorting of our common deer; but it has always appeared to us to be almost useless to attempt to describe it; and although at this moment we have the sound of the antelope's snort *in our ears*, we feel quite unable to give its equivalent in words or syllables.

The antelope has no lachrymal pits under the eyes, as have deer and elks, nor has it any gland on the hind leg, so curious a feature in many of those animals of the deer tribe which drop their horns annually, and only wanting (so far as our knowledge extends) in the *Cervus Richardsonii*, which we consider in consequence as approaching the genus *Antilope*, and in a small deer from Yucatan and Mexico, of which we had a living specimen for some time in our possession.

The prong-horned antelope often dies on the open prairies during severe winter weather, and the remains of shockingly poor, starved, miserable individuals of this species, in a state of the utmost emaciation, are now and then found dead in the winter, even near Fort Union and other trading posts.

The present species is caught in pens in the same manner nearly as the bison, (which we have already described at p. 97) but is generally despatched with clubs, principally by the women. In the winter of 1840, when the snow was deep in the ravines, having drifted, Mr. LAIDLAW, who was then at Fort Union, caught some of them by following them on horse-back and forcing them into these drifts, which in places were as much as ten to twelve feet deep. They were brought to the fort in a sleigh, and let loose about the rooms; they were to appearance so very gentle that the people suffered their children to handle them, although the animals were loose. They were placed in the carpenter's shop, one broke its neck by leaping over a turning-lathe, and the rest all died; for as soon as they had appeased the cravings of hunger, they began to fret for their accustomed liberty, and regained all their original wildness. They leaped, kicked and butted themselves against every obstacle, until to much exhausted to recover.—These individuals were all captured by placing nooses, fixed on the end of long poles, round their necks, whilst they were embedded in the soft and deep snow drifts, to which they had been driven by Mr. LAIDLAW.

There are some peculiarities in the gait of this species that we have not yet noticed. The moment they observe a man or other strange object producing an alarm, they bound off for some thirty or forty yards, raising all their legs at the same time, and *bouncing*, at it were, from two to three feet above the ground; after this they stretch their bodies out and gallop at an extraordinary speed. We have seen some which, when started, would move off and run a space of several miles, in what we thought did not exceed a greater number of minutes!

From what we have already said, it will be inferred that the wolf is one of the most formidable enemies of this species. We have, however, not yet mentioned that in some very cold and backward seasons the young, when first born at such times, are destroyed by these marauders in such numbers that the hunters perceive the deficiency and call them scarce for the next season. Antelopes are remarkably fond of saline water or salt, and know well where the *salt-licks* are found. They return to them daily, if near their grazing grounds, and lay down by them, after licking the salty earth or drinking the salt water. Here they will remain for hours at a time, in fact until hunger drives them to seek in other places the juicy and nourishing grasses of the prairie. This species is fond of taking its stand, when alone, on some knoll, from which it can watch the movements of all wanderers on the plains around, and from which a fair chance to run in any direction is secured, although the object of its fear may be concealed from view occasionally by a ravine, or by another projecting ridge like its own point of sight.

We had in our employ a hunter on the Yellow-Stone River, who killed two female antelopes and broke the leg of a third at one shot from an ordinary western rifle. The ball must have passed entirely through the two first of these animals.

We have represented on our plate two males and a female in the foreground, with a flock of these timid creatures running at full speed in the distance.

We subjoin the following account of the Antelopes seen by J. W. AUDUBON and his party on their overland journey through Northern Mexico and Sonora to California.

"Leaving Altar, Sonora, the country was flat and uninteresting, except that large patches of coarse grass, sometimes miles in length, took the place of the naked clay plains we had been riding through. The tall cactus, described by FREMONT and EMORY, in its eccentric forms was remarkable enough even by daylight, but at night, a very little superstition, with the curved and curiously distorted forms, produced in some cases by disease of the plant, or by the violent gales that periodically sweep those prairies, might make the traveller suppose this was a region in which beings supernatural stalked abroad. The shrill whistle of the Antelope, new to us all, added to the wild and unearthly character of the scene. The Maricapos Indians were said to be friendly, but we *did not know it*, and after our long watchings against Camanche, Apatche, Wako and Paramanii, who among us, as we knew how Indians sometimes personate the animals of the section they live in, but listened with intense interest to the slightest noise foreign to our previous knowledge. The short quick stampings of impatience or nervousness, continually repeated by the animals, were, however, soon distinguished in the stillness of our prairie camp at night, and feeling thus assured that only one of the deer tribe was the cause of our anxiety, blankets and tent soon covered us, and we left the beautiful and innocent creatures, now that we knew them, to their own reflections, if any they made, as to who and what we were, until morning.

At day light, RHOADES and VAN HORN, two hunters good as ever accompanied a train across the broad prairies ranged over by Buffalo, Elk, or Deer, looked out the trails, and reported Antelopes; but brought none to camp; not expecting to see any more of this herd, we started on our tramp towards the great Sonora Desert.

STEVENSON had a new horse, and as he had never been mounted without blindfolding him, after the Mexican fashion with young horses, being wild, his owner, by way of making him *more gentle*, commenced beating him with a stick that might have been selected to kill him; before I had time to know what was going on and interfere for the poor horse, he had looked to his own interests, pulled away, and with a bounding gallop went off, like an escaped prisoner, leading four of our best men and horses some ten miles ahead of the train, and when the runaway was at length overtaken, VAN HORN, PENNYPACKER, Mc. CUSKER, and myself were greatly in advance; the curve we had made from the road was slight, and on reaching it again, no trail told that the company had passed, so we had time to look about us, and loitered to rest our tired horses, when simultaneously we saw the back of a deer or Antelope; its head was hidden by the tall grass in which it was grazing on the soft juicy young shoots at the roots of the old tussocks: VAN HORN, with his unerring aim and Mississippi rifle, the eccentric twist of which, no doubt taken from WESSON's patent, renders these guns superior to all we have tried, was told to kill it. For a few seconds he was lost to our sight, though only a hundred yards from us, so low did he squat in the sparse tufts of dead grass and stinking wormwood. How curious it is to stand waiting the result of the skill and caution of the well tried hunter, at such a time; again and again we saw the back of the Antelope, as he passed one bunch of shrubbery after another, but never saw our hunter: at every moment we expected to see the wary animal with sense of smell so keen as nine times out of ten to save him from his enemies, bound away; but how different was his bound when he did leap, not forward, but straight upward. And now we saw VAN HORN, a quarter of a mile off, running to where the last leap was made by his prey, and

then came on the sluggish air, the crack of his rifle, almost after we had forgotten to listen for it, as a rifle cracks nowhere except on prairies, where neither woods, rocks or hills send back the sound. When I saw this beautiful creature, a most magnificent male, the first I had ever seen in the flesh, though the drawing for the 'Quadrupeds' had been long made and published, how I wished to redraw it! delicate even to the descriptions of the gazelle, muscular and sinewy as the best bred grey hound that Scotland even produced.

I anticipated a treat, as VAN HORN gave me a hind quarter for our men, which I tied doubly secure to my saddle. But when night came, after ten hours' ride, although we enjoyed our steaks, the deer of the Cordilleras was too fresh in our memories to permit us to say that this Antelope was the best meat we had eaten."

* * * "The eastern spurs of the coast range were just behind us; the black-tailed deer was scarcely past, for a few miles back, high up on one of the conical velvety hills of this range, we had seen three, looking at us from under one of the dwarf oaks that grow at a certain altitude, in forms peculiar to this country; above or below, either a different formation or total absence of shrubbery occurring. We were winding along the base of a moderate line of hills of the *Sierra Nevada*, when what we took for a flock of sheep, the trail of which we had been following for three days on the way to the mines from Los Angeles, was discovered, and we hoped for mutton, to say nothing of the company we anticipated; but our flock of sheep was like the 'Phantom Bark,' for it 'seemed never the nigher,' *au contraire*, turning a hill went out of sight, and we never got another view; we saw another flock some miles on, and at first, supposing it the same, wondered how they could travel so fast. This was probably another portion of the one we had trailed for so many days. We were gratified by the whole flock running near us, from which we argued we were in the chosen country of the Antelope, the broad Tule valley. The flock ran 'shearing' about, as the formation of the land compelled them to turn to the right or left, showing their sides alternately in light and shade. When they are on the mountain sides and discover a foe, or any object that frightens them, the whole flock rush headlong for the plains, whether the enemy is likely to intercept them or not, and they seem to fly with the single idea, that they are in a dangerous place, and must change it for some other, no matter what; at times a whole flock would run to within shot of our company, determined as it were to go through the line, and I believe in one or two instances would have done so, if they had not been shot at by our too impatient party. When on the plains, the same desire possesses them to get to the hills, and back they go a hundred or two in a flock, seldom slackening their speed, except for a few seconds to look again, and be more frightened than ever at what had first startled them. The rolling hills of the western line of the Sierra Nevada were their most favourite locality in this valley, as far as we saw, but LAYTON and myself met an accidental individual or two, nearly up to Sacramento city, as we travelled through the beautiful, park-like scenes of this portion of California to the diggings of the head waters of the "American Fork."

As to the shedding of the horns of this species, I never was able to ascertain it, but a fine buck we killed, late in November, had a soft space between the head and horn, over the bone, that looked as if it had grown that length in one season. A young Antelope is better eating than a deer, but an old one, is *decidedly goaty*.

Geographical Distribution.

The Prong-horned Antelope is an inhabitant of the western portions of North America, being at no time found to the east of the Mississippi river. Its most northerly range is, according to RICHARDSON, latitude 53° on the banks of the north branch of the Saskatchewan. They range southerly on the plains east of the Rocky Mountains into New Mexico. The precise latitude we have not been able to ascertain, but we have seen specimens that were said to have been obtained along the eastern ridge of the mountains within the tropics in Mexico. The account given by HERNANDEZ, as well as his bad figure of his *Teuthlamacame*, can apply to no other species; this was obtained in Mexico. LEWIS and CLARKE found it on the plains west of the Columbia River, and it is now known to be an inhabitant of California. It has, therefore, a very extensive geographical range.

General Remarks.

We have after much reflection and careful examination, concluded to adopt Mr. ORD'S genus *Antilocapra* for this species. It differs in so many particulars from the true Antelopes, that naturalists will be compelled either to enlarge the character of that genus, or place it under one already formed. Its horns are branched, of which no instance occurs among all the species of Antelope; it is destitute of crumens or lachrymal openings, and is entirely deficient in the posterior or accessory hoofs, there being only two on each foot.

Major HAMILTON SMITH, (Cuv. Animal Kingdom, Vol. v., p. 321,) formed a genus under the name of *Dicranocerus*, under which he placed a second species which he named *A palmata*. Although the generic name given by SMITH is in many respects preferable, as being more classically correct, still, if we were to be governed by the principle that we should reject a genus because the compound word from which it is derived is composed of two languages, or if it does not designate the precise character of the species, we would be compelled to abandon many familiar genera, established by LINNÆUS himself.

The specific name of ORD, we have also adopted in preference to the more characteristic one "*furcifer*" of SMITH, under a rule which we have laid down in this work not to alter a specific name that has been legitimately given.

We have added the *A palmata*, palmated Antelope of Major SMITH, as a synonyme. We have compared so many specimens differing from each other in shades of colour and size of horns, that we have scarcely a doubt of his having described a very old male of the Prong-horned Antelope.

Cervus Macrotis.—Say.

Mule Deer.

Plate lxxviii. Female—Summer Pelage.

C. cornibus sub-dichotomo-ramosis; auriculis longissimis; corpore supra pallide rufescente-fusco, caudâ pallide rufescente cincreâ, apice compresso subtus nudi-osculo nigro.

Characters.

Horns cylindrical, twice forked; ears very long; body above, brownish grey; tail short, above, pale reddish ash colour, except at the extremity on its upper surface, where it is black. Hair on the body coarse, like that of the Elk; very long glandular openings on the sides of hind legs.

Synonymes.

JUMPING DEER. Umfreville, Hudson's Bay, p. 164.
BLACK TAILED or MULE DEER. Gass Journ. p. 55.
BLACK TAILED DEER, MULE DEER. Lewis and Clarke. Vol. 1, pp. 91, 92, 106, 152, 239, 264, 328. Vol. 2, p. 152. Vol. 3, p. 27, 125.
MULE DEER. Warden's United States. Vol. 1, p. 245.
CERF MULET. Desmarest Mam., p. 43.
BLACK TAILED or MULE DEER. James Long's Exped. Vol. 2, p. 276.
CERVUS MACROTIS, Say. Long's Expedit. Vol. 2, p. 254.
" " Harlan Fauna, p. 243.
" " Sabine. Franklin's Journey, p. 667.
" " Godman's Nat. Hist. Vol. 2, p. 305.
GREAT EARED DEER. Griffith's An. King. Vol. 4, p. 133; Vol. 5, p. 794.

Description.

In size this species is intermediate between the Elk and the Virginian Deer, and a little larger than the Columbian Black Tailed Deer, to be noticed hereafter. It is a fine formed animal, bearing a considerable resemblance to the Elk, its long ears constitute its only apparent deformity.

Male.—Antlers slightly grooved, tuberculated at base, a small branch near the base, corresponding to the situation and direction of those of the *C. Virginianus*. The curvature of the anterior line of the antlers, is similar in direction but less in degree than in the Common Deer; near the middle of the entire length of the antlers they bifurcate equally and each of these processes again divides near the extremity, the anterior of these smaller prongs being somewhat longer than the posterior ones. The lateral teeth are larger in proportion to the intermediate teeth than those of the *Virginianus*. The ears are very long, extending to the principal bifurcation, about half the length of the whole antler. The lachrymal aperture is longer than in the Virginian Deer, the hair is coarser and is undulated or crimped like that of the Elk; the hoofs are shorter and wider than those of the common Deer, and more like those of the Elk, the tip of the trunk of the tail is somewhat compressed and almost destitute of hair.

Female.—Summer Pelage.—In the length and form of its ears, the animal from which we describe constantly reminds us of the mule, and in the particular may not have been inappropriately named the Mule Deer. The female is considerably larger than the largest male of the Virginian Deer we have ever examined. The head is much broader and longer from the eye to the point of the nose, the eye large and prominent, the legs stouter, and the tail shorter. The gland on the outer surface of the hind legs below the knee, covered by a tuft of hair, is of the unusual length of six inches, whilst in the common deer it is only one inch long. Around the throat, the hair is longer than in the corresponding parts of the Virginian Deer, and near the lower jaw under the throat, it has the appearance of a small tuft or beard. The tail of the summer-specimen is slightly tufted, indicating that in winter it might have a distinct tuft at the end. It is rounded and not broad and flat like that of the Virginian Deer.

The hair on the body is coarse, and lies less compact and smooth, that on the thighs near the buttocks, resembles white cotton threads cut off abruptly.

Colour.

Upper portion of nose and sides of face ashy grey; the forehead is dark brown, and commences a line running along the vertebræ of the back, growing darker till it becomes nearly black. Eyebrows and a few streaks on and along the neck dark brown. Neck, and sides of body, yellowish brown. Outer surface of legs a shade lighter than the sides of the body. Under the chin, inner surface of legs, and belly, greyish white. Belly between the forelegs brownish or yellowish-brown, a line of which colour runs up to the neck. It differs from the Virginian Deer in being destitute of the dark markings under the chin, and has them less conspicuous around the nose. From the root of the tail extending downwards on both buttocks there is a lightish patch seven inches in diameter, making an approach to the yellowish white spot on the buttocks, so characteristic in the elk, rocky mountain sheep, and pronged horned antelope. From the root of the tail to near the extremity the hairs are ashy white. Point of tail for two inches black.

There are no annulations on the hair, which is uniform in colour from the roots.

Dimensions.

Female.	Feet.	Inches.
Nose to anterior canthus of eye		6½
Length of eye		1¼
Nose to opening of ear	1	¼
" end " "	1	8¼
Breadth of ear		3½
Nose to point of shoulder	2	1
Nose to root of tail	4	10
Tail vertebræ		5½
End of hair		10
Tip of shoulder to elbow	1	5
" " " to bottom of feet	3	3
Height to rump	3	6¼
Girth back of shoulder	3	1¾
Round the neck	1	2¾
Nose to angle of mouth		3½
Between eyes at anterior canthus		4
Behind the eyes round the head	1	6

Weight, 132 lbs.

Dimensions of a Male, as given by Say.	Inches.
Length from base of antlers to origin of basal process,	2
From basal process to principal bifurcations	4½ to 5
Posterior branch	2½ to 3
From anterior base of antlers to tip of superior jaw	9¼
Of the ears	7½
Trunk of the tail	4
Hair at the tip of tail	3 to 4

Habits.

The first opportunity was afforded us of observing this magnificent animal, on the 12th of May as we were ascending the Missouri, about eleven hundred miles above Fort Leavenworth. On winding along the banks, bordering a long and wide prairie, intermingled with willows and other small brush wood, we suddenly came in sight of four Mule or black-tailed Deer, which after standing a moment on the bank and looking at us, trotted leisurely away, without appearing to be much alarmed. After they had retired a few hundred yards, the two largest, apparently males, elevated themselves on their hind legs and pawed each other in the manner of the horse. They occasionally stopped for a moment, then trotted off again, appearing and disappearing from time to time, when becoming suddenly alarmed, they bounded off at a swift pace, until out of sight. They did not trot or run as irregularly as our Virginian Deer, and they appeared at a distance darker in colour, as the common Deer at this season is red. On the 25th of the same month, we met with four others, which in the present instance did not stop to be examined; we saw them at a distance rapidly and gracefully hurrying out of sight. On the evening of the same day, one of our hunters brought to us a young Buck of this species, the horns of which, however, were yet too small to enable us to judge what would be their appearance in the adult animal. When on the Upper Missouri, near Fort Union, we obtained through the aid of our hunters, the female Black-tailed Deer, from which our figure, description and measurements have been made. We regret exceedingly that we were so unfortunate as not to have been able to procure a male, the delineation of which we must leave to our successors.

The habits of this animal approach more nearly those of the Elk, than of either the long-tailed or Virginian Deer. Like the former they remove far from the settlements, fly from the vicinity of the hunter's camp, and when once fairly started, run for a mile or two before they come to a pause.

The female produces one or two young, in the month of June.

We have figured a female in summer pelage, and have represented the animal in an exhausted state, wounded through the body, and about to drop down, whilst the hunter is seen approaching, through the tall grass, anticipating the moment when she will reel and fall in her tracks.

Geographical Distribution.

The Mule Deer range along the eastern sides of the Rocky Mountains, through a vast extent of country; and according to LEWIS and CLARKE are the only species on the mountains in the vicinity of the first falls of the Columbia River. Their highest northern range, according to RICHARDSON, is the banks of the Saskatchewan, in about latitude 54°; they do not come to the eastward of longitude 105 in that parallel. He represents them as numerous on the Guamash flats, which border on the Kooskooskie River. We found it a little to the east of Fort Union on the Missouri River. It ranges north and south along the eastern sides of the Rocky Mountains through many parallels of latitude until it reaches north-western Texas, where it has recently been killed.

General Remarks.

Since the days of LEWIS and CLARKE, an impression has existed among naturalists that there were two species of black-tailed Deer; the one existing to the east of the Rocky Mountains, and the other, bordering on the Pacific, and extending through upper California. Although the descriptions of those fearless and enterprising travellers are not scientific, yet their accounts of the various species of animals, existing on the line of their travels, have in nearly every case been found correct, and their description of habits very accurate. They state that "the black-tailed fallow Deer are peculiar to this coast (mouth of the Columbia,) and are a distinct species, partaking equally of the qualities of the Mule and the common Deer (C. Virginianus.) The receptacle of the eye more conspicuous, their legs shorter, their bodies thicker and larger. The tail is of the same length with that of the common Deer, the hair on the under side, white; and on its sides and top of a deep jetty black; the hams resembling in form and colour those of the Mule Deer, which it likewise resembles in its gait. The black-tailed Deer never runs at full speed, but bounds with every foot from the ground at the same time, like the Mule Deer. He sometimes inhabits the woodlands, but more often the prairies and open grounds. It may be generally said that he is of a size larger than the common Deer, and less than the Mule Deer. The flesh is seldom fat, and in flavour is far inferior to any other of the species! It will be seen from the above, that they regarded the Mule Deer of the plains of Western Missouri as a distinct species from the black-tailed Deer, which existed along the Pacific coast near the Columbia river.

SAY gave the first scientific description of the Mule Deer, which he named "Cervus Macrotis," which having the priority we have retained. RICHARD-SON, whilst at the Saskatchewan, sought to obtain specimens of this animal for description, but it being a season of scarcity, the appetites of the hunters proved superior to their love of gain, and they devoured the Deer they had shot, even to their skins. When after his return to Europe, in 1829, he published the animals obtained in the expedition, he very properly added such other species as had been collected by the labours of DOUGLASS, DRUM-MOND and other naturalists, who had explored the northern and western portions of America. Finding in the Zoological Museum a specimen of black-tailed Deer, procured on the western coast of America, by DOUGLASS, he concluded that it was the species described by SAY, C. macrotis; at the close of his article, he refers to the animal mentioned by LEWIS and CLARKE, as the black-tailed Deer of the western coast, of which he states, that he had seen no specimen, designating it (F. B. Am. p. 257) C. macrotis, var. Columbiana. We have, however, come to the conclusion that the animal described by RICHARDSON was the very western species to which LEWIS and CLARKE refer, and that whilst his description of the specimen was correct, he erred in the name, he having described not the Mule Deer of LEWIS and CLARK and SAY, but the Columbian black-tailed Deer, our drawing of which was made from the identical specimen described and figured by RICHARDSON. We have named it, after its first describer, Cervus Richardsonii.

The following characters will serve to designate the species.

C. Richardsonii, considerably smaller than C. macrotis, the male of the former species being smaller than the female of the latter. The hair of C. macrotis is very coarse and spongy, like that of the elk, that of C. Richardsonii is much finer and more resembles that of the Virginian Deer. The C. Richardsonii has no glandular opening on the outer surface of the hind leg below the knee joint, approaching in this particular the antelopes which are also without such openings, whilst the corresponding portion in C. macrotis is longer than that of any known species of Deer, being six inches in length. They differ in the shape of their horns, C. Richardsonii having the antlers more slender, much less knobbed, and less covered with sharp points than those of the latter. They are also destitute of the basal process, so conspicuous in C. macrotis. We regret exceedingly that from circumstances beyond our control, we have been enabled to give a figure of the female only of C. macrotis, and of the male only of C. Richardsonii. The former was figured from the specimen we obtained at Fort Union, and for the latter we are indebted to the directors of the Zool. Society of London, who very kindly permitted us to make a drawing from the specimen previously described and figured by RICHARDSON.

NOTE.—In connection with this subject, we are deeply pained to be compelled to notice the obstructions thrown in the way of our pursuits by the directors of the National Insitute at Washington, which city we visited shortly after the return of our exploring expedition, when we were kindly invited by Mr. PEALE to an examination of the valuable specimens of Natural History, collected by our adventurous country-men. We pointed out to him one or two skins of the black-tailed Deer from the Western coast, which we both agreed differed from the C. Macrotis of SAY. We proposed to him that he should give a short description of the species, and select the name, which we would afterwards adopt in our work—this is in accordance with the mode usually pursued, and would have only occupied an hour. After the lapse of several years, we made an application by letter to the directors of the Institution for the privilege of making a drawing of the specimen; this we were not only refused, but were even denied the privilege of looking at the specimen, which we were very anxious to see, in order to be enabled to point out in the most satisfactory manner the characteristics by which these two closely allied species of Deer inhabiting our country could be distinguished from each other.

We cannot but contrast the narrow-minded policy pursued towards us in our application at Washington, with the liberality and generosity which was at all times extended to us in Europe under similar circumstances. When we visited England in 1838, the Directors of the Zoological Society opened its museum and assigned to us a private room, of which they gave us the key, and which we occupied for nearly a month—the specimens were taken from the cases by their attendants and brought to us, and when we discovered in the collection undescribed species, we were encouraged and aided in describing them. The same facilities were afforded us in the British museum, and in those of Edinburgh, Paris, Berlin, Dresden, and Zurich. The British Government, as well as our own, gave us all the assistance which could be rendered by either, consistent with other public services, and we derived material advantages from the aid afforded us by the revenue service and the various military stations we have visited in our researches, in Labrador—in Florida—in the far West, and in Texas.

We know not who were the Directors of the National Institute when our reasonable request was so cavalierly rejected, nor have we inquired whether any changes in policy have since taken place in regard to the collection of animals at Washington, but we feel it our duty publicly to protest against a conduct so narrow, selfish, and inconsistent with the liberality of our free institutions and so little adapted to promote one of the objects sought to be gained by the exploring expedition—viz: the advancement of natural history.

Plate LXXVIII

Nº 16

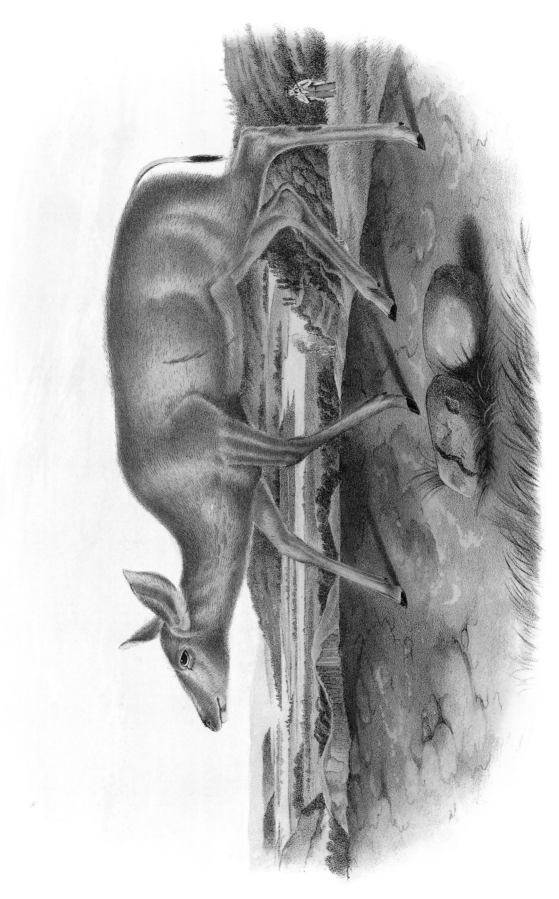

Drawn from Nature by J W Audubon

On Stone by Wm E. Hitchcock

Black-tailed Deer

Lith Printed & Cold by J T Bowen, Phil

When the Hudsons Bay Company received an intimation that we would be glad to obtain any specimens they could furnish us from their trading posts in the arctic regions, they immediately gave orders to their agents and we secured from them rare animals and skins, procured at considerable labour and expense, and sent to us without cost, knowing and believing that in benefitting the cause of natural science they would receive a sufficient reward.

Spermophilus Annulatus.—Aud. and Bach.

Plate lxxix.—Male.

S. Super cervinus, pilis nigris, interspersis, subtus albido. Caudâ corpore longiore, annulis, 17—20 nigris.

Characters.

Reddish-brown above, speckled with black beneath. Tail, which is longer than the body, annulated, with from seventeen to twenty black bands.

Synonyme.

SPERMOPHILUS ANNULATUS. Aud. & Bach. Transactions of the Academy of Natural Sciences, Oct. 5th, 1841.

Description.

In size, this species is scarcely larger than the Hudson's Bay Squirrel, (*S. Hudsonius.*) In the shape of the head it resembles *Spermophilus Parryi*. The ears are quite small, being scarcely visible above its short coat of rather coarse, adpressed hairs; they are thickly covered with hair on both surfaces. The nose is sharp; whiskers, (which are numerous,) the length of the head. Eyes of moderate size, situated on the sides of the head. The os-frontis is rounded between the orbits, as in *S. Franklinii*. The cheek pouches are pretty large, and open into the mouth immediately anterior to the grinders. The body is more slender than the spermophiles in general, and in this, and several other peculiarities which will be mentioned, this species approaches the genus *Sciurus*. On the fore-foot, a sharp, conical nail is inserted on the tubercle which represents the thumb. There are four toes, covered to the extremities with a close, smooth coat of hair. The first and the fourth toe are of equal length. The second and third, which are longest, are also uniform in length. The nails are short, crooked and sharp, like those of the Squirrels, and not like those of the Marmots and Spermophili in general, which are long and slender, and but slightly curved. The legs are long and slender. The hair on the back is rather short, and lies close and smooth. The short fur beneath this coarser hair is rather sparingly distributed. On the under surface, the hairs are longer, and so thinly and loosely scattered as to leave the skin visible in many places, especially on the abdomen, and inner surface of the thighs. The hind feet, which are thickly covered with short, smooth hairs, have five toes. The soles, as well as palms, are naked. The tail, by its great length and singular markings, presents a distinguishing peculiarity in this species; it is flattened, and the hairs admit of a distichous arrangement; but the tail is narrower, and less bushy than those of the Squirrels.

Colour.

The incisors are deep orange; nails, brown; whiskers, black; nose and sides of the face, chestnut-brown. There is a line of soiled white above and around the eyes. The hairs on the upper surface are yellowish-brown at the roots, barred about the middle with black; then another line of yellowish-brown and tipped with black, giving it a dark, greyish-brown, and in some lights a speckled appearance. The small spots are, however, no where well defined; upper surface of the feet and legs, yellowish-brown; the under parts, chin, throat, belly, and inner surface of the legs and thighs are white. The tail is annulated with about nineteen black, and the same number of cream-coloured bands, giving it a very conspicuous appearance. These annulations commence about three inches from the root of the tail, and continue to be well defined till near the extremity, where the colours become more blended, and the rings are scarcely visible. On the under surface, the tail is pale reddish-brown, irregularly, and not very distinctly barred with black.

Dimensions.

	Inches.	Lines.
Length from point of nose to root of tail,	8	2
" tail vertebræ,	8	0
" to end of hair,	9	4
From heel to end of middle hind claw,	1	10
Height of ear, posteriorly,	0	1½
Length of longest fore-claw,	0	2
length of longest hind claw,	0	2½

Habits.

We possess no knowledge of the habits of this species, but presume from its form, that it possesses the burrowing propensities of the genus. All the *Spermophili* avoid thickly wooded countries, and are either found in rocky localities, or burrowing in the prairies.

Geographical Distribution.

The specimen we have described above, was obtained on the Western Prairies, we believe on the east of the Mississippi river; the locality was not particularly stated. It was politely presented to us by Professor SPENCER F. BAIRD, of Carlisle, Pennsylvania, a young Naturalist of eminent attainments.

General Remarks.

In every department of Natural History, a species is occasionally found which forms the connecting link between two genera, rendering it doubtful under which genus it should properly be arranged. Under such circumstances, the Naturalist is obliged to ascertain, by careful examination, the various predominating characteristics, and finally, place it under the genus to which it bears the closest affinity in all its details. The Spermophili are intermediate in character between the Squirrels and Marmots. They have the lightness of form of the former, and burrow in the ground like the latter. By their cheek pouches, of which the true Squirrels and Marmots are destitute, they are distinguished from both. The second inner toe on the forefoot of the Spermophili is the longest, whilst in the Squirrels the third is longest. But in these closely-allied genera, there are species which approach those of another genus. Thus our Maryland Marmot, (*A Monax*,) has a rudimentary cheek-pouch, in which a pea might be inserted, yet in every other particular it is a true *Arctomys*. The downy Squirrel, (*Sciurus lanuginosus*, see Journal Acad. Nat. Science, Vol. 8th, part 1st, p. 67,) by its short ears, broad head, and not very distichous tail, approaches the Spermophili, yet by its being destitute of cheek-pouches, by its soft, downy fur, and its hooked, sharp claws, of which the third, as in the Squirrels, is longest, it is more allied to Sciurus. On the other hand, the species now under consideration has the long legs, slender form, and sharp, hooked claws of the Squirrel. The two middle toes of the fore-feet being of equal length, prove its affinity to both genera; but in the general shape of its body, its cheek pouches, its short ears, and smooth, rigid hair, it must be regarded as belonging to the genus Spermophilus. We consider this species and the downy Squirrel as connecting links between Sciurus and Spermophilus, as we regard *Sciurus Hudsonius* the connecting link between Tamias and Sciurus.

On Stone by W. E. Hitchcock.

Drawn from Nature by J. Audubon. FRS FL S

Lith Printed & Col.d by J T Bowen, Phil.

Annulated Marmot Squirrel.

Arvicola Pinetorum.—Leconte.

Leconte's Pine-Mouse.

Plate lxxx.—Male and Female.

A. Capite crasso; naso obtuso; vellere curto; molli bombycino, instar velleri Talpæ; supra fusco-canâ, subtus plumbeo.

Characters.

Head large, nose blunt; fur short, soft, silky and lustrous, like that of the mole. Colour, above, brown, beneath, plumbeous.

Synonymes.

PSAMMOMY'S PINETORUM, Le Conte, Annals of the Lyceum of Natural History of New-York, Vol. III. p. 3, p. 2.
ARVICOLA SCALOPSOIDES, Mole Arvicola. Aud. and Bach. Transactions Acad. Nat. Sciences, October, 1841.
ARVICOLA ONEIDA, De Kay, Nat. Hist., N. Y., p. 88.

Description.

This species bears some resemblance to WILSON's Meadow Mouse; it is, however, less in size, and its fur is shorter, more compact and glossy; body rather stout, short and cylindrical; head large and short; nose blunt, and hairy, except the nostrils, which are naked; incisors of moderate size; moustaches, fine, and nearly all short, a few reaching the ear; eyes very small; auditory openings large; ears very short, not visible beyond the fur, thin and membranous, with a few scattered hairs on the upper margin; neck short and thick; legs short and slender, covered with very short, adpressed hairs, not concealing the nails; palms naked. There are four toes on the fore foot, of which the second, on the inner side, is the longest, the first and third nearly equal, and the fourth shortest; in place of a thumb, there is a minute, straight, but not blunt, nail. The hind feet have five toes, the middle longest, the two next on each side being of equal length, and a little shorter than the middle one; the inner toe is considerably shorter, and the fourth, placed far back, is the shortest. The nails are weak, nearly straight sharp, but not hooked. The fur on the whole body is short. compact and soft, and on the back, glossy.

Colour

The eyes are black; nostrils flesh-colour; incisors light yellowish; moustaches nearly all white, with a few interspersed of a dark brown colour. Hair from the root plumbeous, tipped on the upper surface with glossy brown. These tips are so broad that they conceal the ashy-grey colours beneath; cheeks chestnut-brown, upper surface of tail, brown, feet, light-brown, nails, whitish. The hairs on the under surface are shorter than those on the back, and instead of being broadly tipped with brown, like those on the back, are very slightly tipped with very pale brown and whitish, giving the chin, throat, neck and inner surface of legs and whole under surface of body a pale ash colour. The line of demarcation between the colours of the back and under surface, is very distinct in most specimens, commencing on the edges of the mouth, running along the sides of the neck, thence along the shoulder, including the fore legs—along the sides, the two opposite lines meeting near the root of the tail. We have observed in this species a considerable difference in different specimens, both in size and colour, having met some which were but little more than three inches long, whilst others were five. In some, the colours on the back were of a much deeper brown than in others, whilst in others, the brown markings on the cheeks were altogether wanting. It should be observed that in this species, as well as in all our field mice, the colours are much lighter, and inclined to cinereous after the shedding of the hair in summer; the colours gradually deepen and become brighter toward autumn and winter, and are most conspicuously dark brown in spring.

Dimensions.

	Inches.
From point of nose to root of tail, ...	$3\frac{1}{4}$
Tail, ...	$\frac{1}{2}$
Another Specimen.	
Length of head and body, ...	$4\frac{1}{4}$
Tail, ...	$\frac{3}{4}$

Habits.

The manners of this species do not differ very widely from those exhibited by many other field mice. They however, avoid low grounds, so much the resort of the meadow mice, and prefer higher and drier soils.

This mouse is rather an inhabitant of cultivated fields than of woods, and is seldom found in the forest far removed from the vicinity of plantations, to which it resorts, not only to partake of the gleanings of the fields, but to lay its contributions on the products of the husbandman's labours, claiming a share before the crops are gathered. In the Northern states, it is found in potato fields and in vegetable gardens, gnawing holes into the sides of the potatoes, carrots, ruta-baga, and common turnips, following the rows where green peas and corn have been planted, bringing down threats of vengeance from the farmer on the poor ground mole, which, feeding only on worms, is made a kind of cat's-paw by this mischievous little field mouse, which does the injury in most cases, whilst the other is saddled with the blame. In the South it is, next to the Norway rat, the most troublesome visitant of the cellars and banks in which the sweet potato is stored, destroying more than it consumes, by gnawing holes into the tubers, and causing them to rot. Wherever a bed of Guinea corn, Egyptian millet, or Guinea grass is planted, there you will soon observe numerous holes and nests of this species. We have recently seen an instance where a large bed of kohlrabi was nearly destroyed by it; the bulbs appearing above the surface were gnawed into holes, which, in some instances, penetrated to the centre. Our friend, the owner, had, as usual, laid the mischief on the broad shoulders of the hated and persecuted ground mole, of whose galleries not a trace could be seen in the vicinity. A number of small holes at the root of a stump, in the garden, indicated the true author of these depredations, and on digging, about a dozen of LECONTE's field Mice were captured. This species is particularly fond of the pea or ground nut, (hypogea.) On examining the beds where this nut is cultivated, we have observed the rows on whole acres perforated in every direction by small holes, giving evidence that this troublesome little pest had been at work. In endeavouring to save and collect the seeds of the Gama grass, (*Tripsacum dactyloides,*) we generally found ourselves forestalled by this active and voracious little rat.

This species has young three or four times during the summer. One which we had in confinement, produced young three times, having three, seven, and four, in the different broods. The young were nearly all raised, but, when full-grown, became pugnacious and persecuted each other so much that we were obliged to separate them. They were almost exclusively fed on ground nuts, corn meal and sweet potatoes, but seemed to relish both boiled rice and bread. We have seen nine young taken from one nest.

The nest of this species is generally found under ground, at the distance of about a foot from the surface; it is small, and composed of light, loose materials, collected in the vicinity.

This prolific field rat possesses many enemies to diminish its numbers. The house cat not only watches for it about the fields and gardens, but is fond of devouring it, whilst the bodies of shrews and ground moles are not eaten. The very common Owl, (*Syrnium nebulosum,*) the Barn Owl (*Strix Americana,*) the Weasel, Ermine and Mink, all make this species a considerable part of their subsistence.

The only note we have ever heard from this mouse is a low squeak, only uttered when it is either struck suddenly or greatly alarmed. In a state of confinement it was remarkably silent, except when two were engaged in fighting.

Geographical Distribution.

LE CONTE's Field Mouse has an extensive geographical range. We have received specimens from our friend, Dr. BREWER, obtained in Massachusetts. It is found in Connecticut, is quite abundant on the farms in Rhode-Island, and in the immediate vicinity of New-York. We found it at Milestown, a few miles from Philadelphia. Mr. RUFFIN sent us several specimens from Virginia. We procured it in North Carolina, and received a specimen from Dr. BARRITT, Abbeville, South Carolina. It becomes more abundant as you approach the seaboard, in Carolina and Georgia; and we have specimens sent to us from Alabama, Mississippi and Florida. We have traced it no farther south, have not heard of it to the west of the Mississippi, and are informed that it does not exist in Texas.

General Remarks.

From the diminutive figure in WILSON's Ornithology, we might be led to the conjecture that he had this little species in view. The accurate description given by ORD, applies, however, only to the *Arvicola Pennsylvanica*. The first

Plate LXXX

N°. 16

Leconte's Pine Mouse.

scientific description that appears of this species was given by LE CONTE, (Annals of the Lyceum of Nat. Hist. N. Y., Vol. III., p. 3.) Finding that there were some variations in the dentition from the long established genus *Arvicola*, he formed for it a new genus, under the name of *Psamomys*. As this name, however, had been pre-occupied by RUPPEL for an Arabian species, the American translator, (Dr. McMURTRIE,) of CUVIER's Animal Kingdom, proposed changing the genus to *Pitymis*, Pine Mouse. The variations in the teeth, however, we have found by comparison, do not afford sufficient characters to warrant us in removing it from *Arvicola*, to which, from its shape and habits, it seems legitimately to belong.

We do not feel warranted in changing the specific name of LE CONTE, but that name is not expressive of one of its characteristics, as, although it may have been found in the pine woods, we have never, in a single instance, detected it in such localities. We have always found it either in the open fields, or along fences, in the vicinity of gardens and farms.

This species is subject to many changes in colour, and is so variable in size, that it is easy to mistake it; hence we have added as synonymes, our *A. Scalopsoides*, and the *A. Oneida* of Dr. DE KAY.

Cervus Virginianus. — Pennant.

Common American Deer.

Plate lxxxi. — Fawn. Natural Size.

Plate cxxxvi. — Male and Female. — Winter pelage.

C. cornibus mediocribus, ramosis, sub-complanatis, retrorsum valde inclinatis, dein antrorsum versis; ramo basali-interno retrorso; ramis plurimis posticis, retrorsum et sursum spectantibus, sinubus suborbitalibus plicam cutaneam formantibus; vellere aestate fulvo; hyeme canescentefusco.

Characters.

Horns middle sized, tending to flatten, strongly bent back and then forwards; a basal antler on the internal side, pointing backwards; several snags on the posterior edge, turned to the rear, and upwards; suborbital sinus making a fold; colour, fulvous in summer, gray-brown in winter.

Synonymes.

VIRGINIAN DEER. Penn. Syn., p. 51
" " Penn. Quadrupeds. Vol. 1, p. 104.
" " Shaw's General Zoology. Vol. 2, p. 284.
AMERIKANISCHER HIRSCH. Kalm Reise. Vol. 2, p. 326. 3d. p. 482.
VIRGINISCHER HIRSCH. Zimmerm. Geogr. Gesch. Vol. 2, p. 129.
CERF DE LA LOUISIANE. Cuv. Regn. An., 1ère p. 256.
CERVUS VIRGINIANUS. Gmel. Vol. 1, p. 179.
DAMA AMERICANUS. Erxl. Syst., p. 312.
C. VIRGINIANUS. Harlan. Fauna Am., p. 239.
" Godm. Am. Nat. Hist. Vol. 2. p. 306.
C. MEXICANUS ET CLAVATUS. Hamilton Smith, p. 315. Griff. Cuv. Vol. 4. p. 127. Vol. 5, p. 315.
C. VIRGINIANUS. Dekay's N. Y. Fauna, p. 113.

Description.

Muzzle sharp; head rather long; eyes large and lustrous; lachrymal pits covered by a fold of the skin. Tail moderately depressed. Legs slender. A glandular pouch surrounded by a thick tuft of rigid hairs inside of the hind legs.

Colour.

The Virginian Deer varies considerably in colour at different periods of the year. In the spring it is of a dusky reddish or fulvous colour above, extending over the whole head, back, upper surface of the tail and along the sides. In the autumn it is of a bluish or lead colour, and in winter the hairs on the upper surface are longer and more dense and of a brownish dark tint. Beneath the chin, throat, belly inner surface of legs, and under side of tail, white. There is no perceptible difference in colour between the sexes.

The fawns are at first, bright reddish-brown, spotted with irregular longitudinal rows of white. These spots become less visible as the animal grows older, and in the course of about four months the hairs are replaced by others, and it assumes the colour of the old ones.

Dimensions.

	Feet.	Inches.
Length from nose to root of tail,	5	4
" of tail, (vertebræ),		6
" including hairs,	1	1
" Height of ear,		5½

Habits.

Perhaps no species of wild animal inhabiting North-America, deserves to be regarded with more interest than the subject of our present article, the Common or Virginian Deer; its symmetrical form, graceful curving leap or bound, and its rushing speed, when flying before its pursuers, it passes like a meteor by the startled traveller in the forest, exciting admiration, though he be ever so dull an observer.

The tender, juicy, savoury, and above all, digestible qualities of its flesh are well known; and venison is held in highest esteem from the camp of the backwoodman to the luxurious tables of the opulent, and, when not kept too long (a common error in our large cities by the way) a fat haunch with jelly and chafing dishes is almost as much relished, as a "hunter's steak," cooked in the open air on a frosty evening far away in the west. The skin is of the greatest service to the wild man, and also useful to the dweller in towns; dressed and smoked by the squaw, until soft and pliable, it will not shrink with all the wettings to which it is exposed. In the form of mocasins, leggings, and hunting shirts, it is the most material part of the dress of many Indian tribes, and in the civilized world is used for breeches, gloves, gaiters, and various other purposes.

From the horns are made beautiful handles for various kinds of cutlery.

The timidity of the Deer is such, that it hurries away, even from the sight of a child, and it is but seldom that the hunter has any danger to apprehend, even from a wounded buck; it does but little injury to the fields of the planter, and is a universal favourite with old and young of both sexes in our Southern States.

The Virginian, or as we wish to designate it, the Common Deer, is the only large animal, if we except the bear, that is not driven from the vicinity of man by the report of the deer-driver's gun, or the crack of the hunter's rifle; the buffalo and the elk are now rarely seen east of the Mississippi. Hunted by hounds and shot at from day to day, the Deer may retreat from this persecution for a little while, but soon returns again to its original haunts. Although it scarcely ever occupies the same bed on successive nights, yet it is usually found in the same range, or drive as it is called, and often not fifty yards from the place, where it was started before. It is fond of lingering around fences and old fields, that are partially overspread with brush-wood, briar-patches and other cover, to screen it from observation. In the southern States the Deer, especially in summer when they are least disturbed, are fond of leaping the outer fences of plantations, lying through the day in some tangled thicket, overgrown with cane, vines and briars; and in such places you may be so fortunate as to start an old buck in August or September, and many an overgrown denizen of the forest has bowed his huge antlers and fallen a sacrifice to his temerity in seeking a resting-place too near some pea-patch, where his hoofs left traces for many weeks of his nightly depredations.

This habit of resting during the day in the near vicinity of their feeding ground, is however not universal. We during last summer were invited to visit a large cornfield in which a quantity of the Carolina cowpea had been planted among the corn. This had been the nightly resort of the Deer during the whole summer—their tracks of various sizes covered the ground, as if flocks of sheep had resorted to it, and scarcely a pod or even a leaf was remaining on the vines. The Deer, however, were not in the vicinity, where there were several favourable and extensive covers; they were trailed to some small islands, in a marsh nearly two miles off. We ascertained that the Deer inhabiting the swamps on the east side of the Edisto river, where there are but few cultivated farms, were in the nightly habit of swimming the Edisto and visiting the pea-fields in Barnwell, on the opposite side, returning before day-light to their customary haunts, some four or five miles distant.

The localities selected by Deer as places of rest and concealment during the day are various, such as the season of the year and the nature of the country and climate may suggest to the instincts of the animal. Although we have

Plate LXXXI

On Stone by Wᵐ E. Hitchcock

Drawn from Nature by J.W. Audubon

Common American Deer

Fawn

Lith Printed & Colᵈ by J.T.Bowen,Phil

occasionally in mountainous regions, especially in the higher mountains of Virginia and the Green Mountains of Vermont, detected a Deer lying without concealment on an elevated ledge of bare rock, like the ibex and chamois on the Alps, yet as a general habit, the animal may be said to seek concealment, either among clumps of myrtle or laurel bushes, (*Kalmia*), in large fallen tree-tops, briar-patches, clusters of alder bushes, (*alnus*), or in tall broom-grass, (*Andropogon dissitiflorus*). In cold weather it prefers seeking its repose in some sheltered dry situation, where it is protected from the wind, and warmed by the rays of the sun; and on these occasions it may be found in briar-patches which face the south, or in tufts of broom-grass in old uncultivated fields. In warm weather it retires during the day to shady swamps, and may often be started from a clump of alder or myrtle bushes near some rivulet or cool stream. To avoid the persecution of moschetoes and ticks, it occasionally, like the moose in Maine, resorts to some stream or pond and lies for a time immersed in the water, from which the nose and a part of the head only project. We recollect an occasion, when on sitting down to rest on the margin of the Santee river, we observed a pair of antlers on the surface of the water near an old tree, not ten steps from us. The half-closed eye of the buck was upon us; we were without a gun, and he was, therefore, safe from any injury we could inflict on him. Anxious to observe the cunning he would display, we turned our eyes another way, and commenced a careless whistle, as if for our own amusement, walking gradually towards him in a circuitous route, until we arrived within a few feet of him. He had now sunk so deep in the water that an inch only of his nose, and slight portions of his prongs were seen above the surface. We again sat down on the bank for some minutes, pretending to read a book. At length we suddenly directed our eyes towards him, and raised our hand, when he rushed to the shore, and dashed through the rattling canebrake, in rapid style.

The food of the common Deer varies at different periods of the year. In winter, it feeds on buds of several kinds of shrubs, such as the wild rose the hawthorn, various species of bramble, (*Rubus*,) the winter green (*Pyrola*,) the Partridge Berry, (*Mitchella repens*,) the Deer Leaf, (*Hopea tinctoria*,) the bush Honeysuckle, (*Azalea*,) and many others. In spring and summer it subsists on tender grasses, being very select in its choice and dainty in its taste. At these seasons it frequently leaps fences, and visits the fields of the planter, taking an occasional bite at his young wheat and oats, not overlooking the green corn, (*Maize*,) and giving a decided preference to a field planted with cow-peas, which it divests of its young pods and tender leaves; nor does it pass lightly by berries of all kinds, such as the Huckleberry, Blackberry and Sloe, (*Viburnum prunifolium*.) We are informed by a friend that in the vicinity of Nashville, (Tennessee,) there is an extensive park containing about three hundred Deer, the principal food of which is the luxuriant Kentucky blue-grass, (*Poa pratensis*.) In autumn it finds an abundance of very choice food in the chestnuts, chinquepins and beech-nuts strewn over the ground. The localities of the various oaks are resorted to, and we have seen its tracks most abundantly under the Live Oak, (*Quercus virens*,) the acorns of which it appears to prefer to all others. We once observed three deer feeding on these acorns, surrounded by a flock of wild turkeys, all eagerly engaged in claiming their share. The fruit of the Persimmon tree, after having been ripened by the frosts of winter, falls to the ground, and also becomes a favourite food of the Deer.

Possessing such a choice of food, we might suppose this animal would be always fat: this, however, is not the case, and except at certain seasons of the year, the Deer is rather poor. The bucks are always in fine order from the month of August to November, when we have seen some that were very fat. One which we killed weighed one hundred and seventy-five pounds. We have been informed that some have reached considerably over two hundred pounds. In November, and sometimes a little earlier, the rutting season commences in Carolina, when the neck of the buck begins to dilate to a large size. He is now constantly on foot, and nearly in a full run, in search of the does. On meeting with other males, tremendous battles ensue, when, in some rare instances, the weaker animal is gored to death; generally, however, he flies from the vanquisher, and follows him, crest fallen, at a respectful and convenient distance, ready to turn on his heels and scamper off at the first threat of his victorious rival. In these rencontres, the horns of the combatants sometimes become interlocked in such a manner that they cannot be separated, and the pugnacious bucks are consigned to a lingering and inevitable death by starvation. We have endeavoured to disengage these horns, but found them so completely entwined that no skill or strength of ours was successful. We have several times seen two, and on one occasion, three pairs of horns thus interlocked, and ascertained that the skulls and skeletons of the Deer had always been found attached. These battles only take place during the rutting season, when the horns are too firmly attached to be separated from the skull. Indeed, we have seen a horn shot off in the middle by a ball, whilst the stump still continued firmly seated on the skull. The rutting season continues about

two months, the largest and oldest does being earliest sought for, and those of eighteen months at a later period. About the month of January, the bucks drop their horns, when, as if conscious of having been shorn of their strength and honours, they seem humbled, and congregate peaceably with each other, seeking the concealment of the woods, until they can once more present their proud antlers to the admiring herd. Immediately after the rutting season, the bucks begin to grow lean. Their incessant travelling during the period of venery—their fierce battles with their rivals, and the exhaustion consequent on shedding and replacing their horns by a remarkably rapid growth, render them emaciated and feeble for several months. About three weeks after the old antlers have been shed, the elevated knobs of the young horns make their appearance. They are at first soft and tender, containing numerous blood-vessels, and the slightest injury causes them to bleed freely. They possess a considerable degree of heat, grow rapidly, branch off into several ramifications, and gradually harden. They are covered with a soft, downy skin, and are now in what is called "velet." When the horns are fully grown, which is usually in July or August, the buck shows a restless propensity to rid himself of the velet covering, which has now lost its heat, and become dry: hence he is constantly engaged in rubbing his horns against bushes and saplings, often destroying the trees by wounding and tearing the bark, and by twisting and breaking off the tops. The system of bony development now ceases altogether, and the horns become smooth, hard, and solid.

The does are fattest from November to January. They gradually get thinner as the season of parturition approaches, and grow lean whilst suckling their young.

The young are, in Carolina, produced in the month of April; young does, however, seldom yean till May or June. In the Northern States, they bring forth a little later, whilst in Florida and Texas the period is earlier. It is a remarkable, but well ascertained fact, that in Alabama and Florida, a majority of the fawns are produced in November. The doe conceals her young under a prostrate tree-top, or in a thick covert of grass, visiting them occasionally during the day, especially in the morning, evening, and at night. The young fawns, when only a few days old, are often found in so sound a sleep that we have, on several occasions, seen them taken up in the arms before they became conscious that they were captives. They are easily domesticated, and attach themselves to their keepers in a few hours. A friend possesses a young deer that, when captured, during the last summer, was placed with a she goat, which reared it, and the parties still live in habits of mutual attachment. We have seen others reared by a cow. A goat, however, becomes the best foster-mother. They breed in confinement, but we have found them trouble-some pets. A pair that we had for several years, were in the habit of leaping into our study through the open window, and when the sashes were down they still bounced through, carrying along with them the shattered glasses. They also seemed to have imbibed a vitiated and morbid taste, licked and gnawed the covers of our books, and created confusion among our papers. No shrub in the garden, however valuable to us, was sacred to them; they gnawed our carriage harness, and finally pounced upon our young ducks and chickens, biting off their heads and feet, leaving the body untouched.

The doe does not produce young until she is two years old, when she has one fawn. If in good order, she has two the following year. A very large and healthy doe often produces three, and we were present at Goose Creek when an immense one, killed by J. W. AUDUBON, was ascertained, on being opened, to contain four large and well formed fawns. The average number of fawns in Carolina is two, and the cases where three are produced are nearly as numerous as those in which young does produce only one at a birth.

The wild doe is attached to her young, and its bleat will soon bring her to its side, if she is within hearing. The Indians use a stratagem, by imitating the cry of the fawn, with a pipe made of a reed, to bring up the mother, which is easily killed by their arrows. We have twice observed the doe called up by this imitation of the voice of the young. She is, however, so timid that she makes no effort in defence of her captured offspring, and bounds off at the sight of man.

The common Deer is a gregarious animal, being found on our western prairies in immense scattered herds of several hundred. After the rutting season the males, as we have before stated, herd together and it is only during the season of intercourse that both sexes are found in company. The does, however, although congregating during a considerable portion of the year, are less gregarious than many species of African antelopes, the buffalo, or our domestic sheep; as they are found during the summer separated from the rest of the gang or troop, and are only accompanied by their young.

The Deer is one of the most silent of animals, and scarcely possesses any notes of recognition. The fawn has a gentle bleat that might be heard by the keen ears of its mother at the distance probably of a hundred yards. We have never heard the voice of the female beyond a mere murmur when calling her young, except when shot, when she often bleats loudly like a calf in pain. The buck when suddenly started sometimes utters a snort, and we have at night heard him *emitting* a shrill whistling sound, not unlike that of the chamois of the Alps, that could be heard at the distance of half a mile. The keen sense of smell the Deer possess enable them to follow each other's tracks. We have observed them smelling on the ground and thus following each other's trail for miles. We were on an autumnal morning seated on a log in the pine lands of Carolina when a doe came running past us. In the course of ten minutes we observed a buck in pursuit, with his nose near the ground, following in all the windings of her course. Half an hour afterwards came a second buck, and during another interval a third small buck pursued the same trail. The sense of sight appears imperfect—as we have often, when standing still, perceived the Deer passing within a few yards without observing us, but we have often noticed the affrighted start when we moved our position or when they scented us by the wind. On one occasion we had tied our horse for some time at a stand;—on his becoming restless we removed him to a distance—a Deer pursued by dogs ran near the spot where the horse had originally stood, caught the scent, started suddenly back, and passed within a few feet of the spot where we were standing, without having observed us. Their sense of hearing is as keen as that of smell. In crawling towards them in an open wood, against the wind, you may approach within gun shot, but if you unfortunately break a stick, or create a rustling among the leaves, they start away in an instant.

This animal cannot exist without water, being obliged nightly to visit some stream or spring for the purpose of drinking. During the present year (1850) a general drought prevailed throughout our southern country. On the Hunting Islands between Beaufort and Savannah, the Deer, we were informed, nearly all perished in consequence of the streams on these Islands having dried up. Deer are fond of salt, and like many other wild animals resort instinctively to salt-licks or saline springs. The hunters, aware of this habit, watch at these "licks," as they are called, and destroy vast numbers of them. We have visited some of these pools, and seen the Deer resorting to them in the mornings and evenings and by moon light. They did not appear to visit them for the mere purpose of drinking, but after walking around the sides, commenced licking the stones and the earth on the edges, preferring in this manner to obtain this agreeable condiment, to taking a sudden draught and then retiring. On the contrary they lingered for half an hour around the spring, and after having strayed away for some distance, they often returned a second and even a third time to scrape the sides of it, and renew the licking process. Our common Deer may be said to be nocturnal in its habits, yet on the prairies, or in situations where seldom disturbed, herds of Deer may be seen feeding late in the morning and early in the afternoon. Their time for rest, in such situations, is generally the middle of the day. In the Atlantic States, where constantly molested by the hunters, they are seldom seen after sunrise, and do not rise from their bed until the dusk of the evening. The Deer is more frequently seen feeding in the day time during spring and summer, than in winter; a rainy day, and snowy wintery weather, also invite it to leave its uncomfortable hiding place and indulge in its roaming habits. We have no doubt, that in localities where Deer have been constantly hunted, they, from a sense of fear, allow you to approach much nearer to their place of concealment than in situations where they are seldom disturbed. They continue lying still, not because they are asleep or unaware of your approach, but because they are afraid to expose themselves to view, and hope by close concealment to be passed without being observed. We have seen them lying with their hind legs drawn under them ready for a spring—their ears pressed flat on the sides of the neck, and their eyes keenly watching every movement of the intruder. Under these circumstances your only chance of success is to ride slowly around the animal as if he was not observed, and suddenly fire before he leaps from his bed. This effect to fear, on your near approach, is not confined to our Deer; it may be seen in the common partridge, the snipe, and other game birds. Before being hunted, they are restless—are unwilling to assume the crouching posture called setting, and rise at a distance from their pursuers; but after having been a few times disturbed and shot at, they, in the language of sportsmen, become tame, and permit themselves to be nearly trodden on before they can be induced to rise; this apparent tameness is in reality wildness, and their squatting and hiding the effect of terror to which they are prompted by an instinct of self-preservation.

The gait of this Deer is various. In walking it carries its head very low, and pursues its course cautiously and silently, occasionally moving its ears and whisking its tail; the largest animal is usually the leader of the herd, which travel in what is called Indian file, there seldom being two abreast. Walking is the ordinary pace of the Deer unless frightened, or in some state of excitement. When first started, without being much alarmed, it gives two or three springs, alighting with apparent awkwardness on three feet—and immediately afterwards resting on the opposite side, erecting its white tail and throwing

it from side to side. A few high bounds succeed, whilst the head is turned in every direction to enable it to detect the cause of alarm. The leaps and high boundings of the Deer are so graceful, that we have never witnessed them without excitement and admiration. When, however, the Deer observes you before it is routed from its bed, it bolts off with a rush, running low to the ground, with its head and tail on a line with the body , and for a few hundred yards rivalling the speed of a race horse. But this rattling pace cannot be kept up for any length of time—after the first burst its speed slackens, it foams at the mouth, and exhibits other evidences of fatigue. We have sometimes seen it overtaken and turned by an active rider in the open wood, and under other favourable circumstances, and on one occasion a fat buck was headed by a fearless driver, lashed with his whip, brought to bay, and finally knocked in the head and taken without having been shot. We have witnessed a few instances where a pack of hounds, after a four hours' chase, succeeded in running down a Deer. These cases are, however, rare, nor would we give any encouragement to this furious Sylvan race, in which the horse and his mad rider are momentarily exposed to the danger of a broken neck from the many holes in the pine lands. The Deer, after an attempt at bringing it to bay, frequently succeeds in escaping from the hunter and the hounds, by dashing into a swamp or crossing a river, and even should it be captured, after a long chase the venison is found to be insipid and of no value.

In riding through the woods at night in the vicinity of Deer, we have often heard them stamp their feet, the bucks on such occasions giving a loud snort, then bounding off for a few yards and again repeating the stamping and snorting, which appear to be nocturnal habits.

Deer take the water freely, and swim with considerable rapidity; their bodies are on such occasions submerged, their heads only being visible above the surface. We have witnessed them crossing broad rivers and swimming the distance of two miles. When thus under way, they cleave the water with such celerity that a boat can scarcely overtake them.

Along our southern sea-board the Deer, when fatigued by the hounds, plunge into the surf and swim off for a mile or two, floating or swimming back with the returning tide, when they ascend the beach near the same place where they entered the water.

As already remarked, the flesh of our common Deer is the best flavoured and most easy of digestion of all the species with which we are acquainted, except the black-tailed Deer; it is superior to the Elk or Moose of our country, or the red Deer or Roebuck of Europe. It is, however, only a delicacy when it is fat, which is generally the case from the beginning of August to the month of December. In Carolina, the haunch and loin only are served up on the tables of the planters, the shoulders and skin are the perquisites of the driver, or negro huntsman. The Indians eat every part of the Deer, not omitting the entrails and the contents of the stomach—the latter many of the tribes devour raw, without subjecting them to any cooking or roasting process. It is stated, even by white men, that the stomach, with all its half-digested ingredients, is very palatable. Hunger and hardships seldom fail to give a zest to the appetite. Vegetable food is scarce in the wilderness or on the prairies. The traveller who has long been obliged to sleep in a tent and make his toilet in the woods, soon becomes indifferent to the etiquette of civilized life, and does not inquire whether his dish has been prepared according to the recipe of the cookery-books. A Deer paunch contains a mixture of many ingredients, picked up from various shrubs, seeds, and grasses, and may become a substitute for vegetables where the kitchen-garden has not yet been introduced. According to a northern traveller (LYON's Narrative, p. 242), who referred, however, to another animal, the reindeer of our continent, it is "acid and rather pungent, resembling a mixture of sorrel and radish leaves," its smell like "fresh brewer's grains." As we have never been subjected to the necessity of testing the virtues of this primitive chowder, we are unable to pronounce it a delicacy, and must leave the decision to those who may be disposed to make the experiment.

The capture of the common Deer exercised the ingenuity and patience of the Indian, ages before the pale faces intruded on his hunting-grounds, with their rifles, their horses, and hounds. He combatted with the wolf and the cougar for their share of the prey, leaving on our minds a melancholy impression of the near approach of the condition of savage life to that of the brute creation. Different modes of hunting were suggested by the peculiar face of the localities of the country, and the degrees of intelligence or native cunning of the several tribes. The bow and arrow evidently must have been in common use throughout the whole length and breadth of our land, as the numerous arrow-heads still every where turned up by the plough abundantly attest.

The Rein Deer, inhabiting the extensive, cold, and inhospitable regions of the British possessions to the north of Quebec, were caught in snares manufactured from the hide, and sometimes of the sinews, of the animal. During the season of their annual migrations, rude fences of brush-wood were constructed, which were a mile or two apart at the entrance, narrowing down to nearly a point at the other end, in which the snares were placed, and at the termination of this "cul de sac" was erected a high fence or pound, secured by stakes, stones, and other strong materials, in which the Deer that escaped from the snares were finally enclosed and shot with arrows. The common Deer, however, is more suspicious and timid, and will seldom suffer itself to be circumvented in this manner.

The American Rein Deer is also brought near to the hunter lying in wait behind the concealment of a clump of bushes, or heap of stones, by the waving of a small flag of cloth, or a deer's tail, which, exciting its attention, it falls a sacrifice to its curiosity. This stratagem is also successfully practised on our western prong-horned Antelope.

The Common Deer is frequently brought within bow-shot by the Indians, who call up the does, as we have already mentioned, by imitating, with a pipe made of a reed, the bleating of the fawn, and also the bucks, by an imitation of the shrill, whistling sound which they emit during the rutting season. The wily savage often clothes himself in the hide of a Deer, with the horns and ears attached—imitating the walk and other actions of the animal, by which means he is enabled to approach and almost mingle with the herd, and kill several with his arrows before they take the alarm. Since the introduction of fire-arms, however, many tribes of Indians have laid aside the bow and arrow, and adopted the gun. The traders who visit them, usually supply them with an inferior article, and we have never seen any considerable number of Indians expert in the use of the rifle. The late Dr. LEITNER informed us that the Florida Indians seldom shot at a Deer beyond twenty-five or thirty yards, exercising great patience and caution before they ventured on firing; the result, however, under these favourable circumstances, was usually successful. We believe the Indians of North America never used poisoned arrows in the destruction of game, like the natives of Caffraria and other portions of Africa, or the aborigines of Brazil and the neighbouring regions of South America.

The white man conducts his hunting excursions in various modes suited to his tastes and adapted to the nature of the country in which he resides. In mountainous, rocky regions, where horses cannot be used with advantage, he goes on foot, armed with a rifle, carries no dog, and seeks for the Deer in such situations as his sagacity and experience suggest. He either espies him in his bed, or silently steals upon him behind the convert of the stem of a large tree whilst he is feeding, and leisurely takes a steady and fatal aim. On the contrary, in situations adapted to riding, where the woods are thickly clothed with underbrush, where here and there wide openings exist between briar-patches, and clumps of myrtlebushes, as in the Southern States, the Deer are almost universally chased with hounds, and instead of the rifle, double-barrelled deer-guns, of different sizes, carrying from twelve to twenty buck-shot, are alone made use of by the hunters.

It may not be uninteresting to our readers if we point out the different modes in which Deer hunts are conducted.

In the early settlement of our country, when men hunted for food, and before they accustomed themselves to study their ease and comfort even in the chase, "still hunting," as it is termed, was universally practised. The wolves and other depredating animals, by which the colonists were surrounded, as well as the proximity of hostile Indians, almost precluded them for many years from raising a sufficient supply of sheep, hogs, and poultry. The cultivation of a small field furnished them with bread, while for meat they were chiefly dependent on the gun. Hence a portion of their time was from a kind of necessity devoted to the chase. The passion for hunting seems however to be innate with many persons, and we have observed that it often runs in families and is transmitted to their posterity, as is known to be the case with the descendants of the hunters in the Alps. There are even now many persons in our country, who devote weeks and months to the precarious employment of Deer hunting, when half the industry and fatigue in regular labour would afford their families every necessary and comfort. Hunting is a pleasant recreation, but a very unprofitable trade; it often leads to idleness, intemperance, and poverty.

For success in still-hunting it is essential that the individual who engages in it, should be acquainted with the almost impenetrable depths of the forest, as well as the habits of the Deer. He must be expert in the use of the rifle, possess a large stock of patience, and be constitutionally adapted to endure great fatigue. Before the dawn of day, he treads the paths along which the animal strays in returning from its nightly rambles to the covert usually its resting-place for the day. He ascends an elevation, to ascertain whether he may not observe the object of his search feeding in the vallies. If the patience and perseverance of the morning are not attended with success, he seeks for the Deer in its bed—if it should be startled by his stealthy tread and spring up, it stops for a moment before bounding away, and thus affords him the chance of a shot; even if the animal should keep on its course without a pause, he frequently takes a running, or what is called a chance shot, and is often

successful.

There is another mode of deer hunting we saw practised many years ago in the Western parts of the State of New-York, which we regard as still more fatiguing to the hunter, and as an unfair advantage taken of the unfortunate animals. The parties sally out on a deep snow, covered by a crust, which sometimes succeeds a rain during winter. They use light snow-shoes and seek the Deer in situations where in the manner of the moose of Nova Scotia, they have trampled paths through the snow in the vicinity of the shrubs on which they feed. When started from these retreats they are forced to plunge into the deep snow; and breaking through the crust leave at every leap traces of blood from their wounded legs; they are soon overtaken, sometimes by dogs, at other times by the hunters, who advance faster on their snow-shoes than the exhausted Deer, which fall an easy prey either to the hunter's knife or his gun. In this manner thousands of Deer were formerly massacred in the Northern States.

We have ascertained that our common Deer may be easily taken by the grey-hound. A pair of the latter, introduced into Carolina by Col. CATTEL, frequently caught them after a run of a few hundred yards. The Deer were trailed and started by beagles—the grey-hounds generally kept in advance of them, making high leaps in order to get a glimpse of the Deer which were soon overtaken, seized by the throat, and thrown down. The nature of the country, however, from its swamps and thick covers often prevented the huntsmen from coming up to the captured animal before it was torn and mutilated by the hounds, and many Deer could not be found, as the pack becomes silent as soon as the Deer is taken. We predict, however, that this will become the favourite mode of taking Deer on the open western prairies, where there are no trees or other obstructions, and the whole scene may be enacted within view of the hunters.

Some hunters, who are engaged in supplying the salt and red Sulphur Springs of Virginia with venison during summer, practise a novel and an equally objectionable mode in capturing the Deer. A certain number of very large steel-traps made by a blacksmith in the vicinity, are set at night in the waters of different streams at the crossing-places of the Deer. The animal when thus captured instead of tearing off its leg by violent struggles is said to remain standing still, as passive as a wolf when similarly entrapped. Another and still more cruel mode is sometimes practiced in the South: The Deer have particular places where they leap the fences to visit the pea-fields; a sharpened stake is placed on the inside of the fence—the Deer in leaping over is perforated through the body by this treacherous spike, and is found either dead or dying on the following morning. It is also a frequent practice in the South for the hunter during clear nights to watch a pea-field frequented by Deer. To make sure of this game he mounts some tree, seats himself on a crotch or limb which is above the current that would convey the scent to the keen olfactories of the Deer, and from this elevation leisurely waits for an opportunity to make a sure shot.

In some parts of the Northern and Middle States the Deer are captured by the aid of boats. We observed this mode of hunting pursued at Saratoga and other lakes, and ascertained that it was frequently attended with success. The hounds are carried to the hills to trail, and start the Deer before day light. Some of the hunters are stationed at their favourite crossing places to shoot them should they approach within gun shot. After being chased for an hour or two the Deer pushes for the lake. Here on some point of land a party lie in wait with a light and swift boat; after the Deer has swam to a certain distance from the shore he is headed and approached by the rowers, a noose is thrown over the head, and the unfortunate animal drawn to the side of the boat, when the captors proceed to cut its throat in violation of all the rules of legitimate sporting.

Fire hunting is another destructive mode of obtaining Deer. In this case two persons are essential to success. A torch of resinous wood is carried by one of the party, the other keeps immediately in front with his gun. The astonished Deer instead of darting off seems dazzled by the light, and stands gazing at this newly kindled flame in the forest. The hunter sees his eyes shining like two tapers before him; he fires and is usually successful; sometimes there are several Deer in the gang, who start off for a few rods at the report of the gun, and again turn their eyes to the light. In this manner two or three are frequently killed within fifty yards of each other. This kind of hunting by firelight is often attended with danger to the cattle that may be feeding in the vicinity, and is prohibited by a law of Carolina, which is however frequently violated. The eyes of a cow are easily mistaken for those of a deer. We conversed with a gentleman who informed us that he had never indulged in more than one fire-hunt, and was then taught a lesson which cured him of his passion for this kind of amusement. He believed that he saw the eyes of a Deer and fired, the animal bounded off, as he was convinced, mortally wounded. In the immediate vicinity he detected another pair of eyes and fired again. On returning the next morning to look for his game, he found that he had slaughtered two favourite colts. Another related an anecdote of a shot fired at what was supposed to be the shining eyes of a Deer, and ascertained to his horror that it was a dog standing between the legs of a negro, who had endeavoured to keep him quiet. The dog was killed and the negro slightly wounded.

There is still another mode of Deer hunting which remains to be decribed. It is called "driving," and is the one in general practice, and the favourite pastime among the hospitable planters of the Southern States. We have at long intervals, occasionally joined in these hunts, and must admit that in the manner in which they were conducted, this method of Deer hunting proved an exciting and very agreeable recreation. Although we regret to state that it is pursued by some persons at all seasons of the year, even when the animals are lean and the venison of no value, yet the more thoughtful and judicious huntsmen are satisfied to permit the Deer to rest and multiply for a season, and practice a little self-denial, during summer when the oppressive heats which usually prevail—the danger of being caught in heavy showers—and the annoyance of gauzeflies, mosquitoes, and ticks, present serious drawbacks to its enjoyment. The most favourable season for this kind of amusement is from the beginning of October to January. The Deer are then in fine order; the heats of summer are over; the crops of rice gathered, and the value of the planter's crop can be calculated. The autumn of the Southern States possesses a peculiar charm; high winds seldom prevail, and the air is soft and mellow ; although many of the summer warblers have migrated farther to the south, yet they have been replaced by others: The blue-bird, cat-bird, and mocking-bird have not yet lost their song, and the swallows and night-hawks are skimming through the air in irregular and scattered groups on their way to the tropics. Vegetation has been checked, but not sufficiently destroyed to give a wintry aspect to the landscape. The *Gentians Gerardias* and other autumnal flowers are still disclosing a few lingering blossoms and emitting their fragrance. The forest trees present a peculiar and most striking appearance. A chemical process has been going on among the leaves, since the first cool nights have suspended the circulation, giving to those of the maple and sweet gum, a bright scarlet hue, which contrasted with the yellow of the hickory, and the glossy green of the magnolia grandiflora, besides every shade of colour that can be imagined, render an American forest, more striking and beautiful than that of any other country. It is the season of the year that invites to recreation and enjoyment. The planters have been separated during the summer; some have travelled from home—others have resided as their summer retreats;—they are now returning to their plantations, and the intercourse of the neighbourhood, that has been suspended for a season, is renewed. We recall with satisfaction some past scenes of pleasureable associations of this kind. The space already taken up by this article will preclude us from entering into minute detail, and restrict us to a few incidents which will present the general features of a Carolina Deer hunt. We comply with the oft-repeated invitation to make our annual visit to our early and long-tried friend Dr. DESEL at his hospitable residence some twenty miles from the city, which his friends have named Liberty Hall. The mind requires an occasional relaxation as well as the body. We have resolved to fly for a day or two, from the noise and turmoil of the city—to leave books and cares behind us—to break off the train of serious thought—to breathe the fresh country air, and mingle in the innocent sports of the field and the forest. Reader, you will go with us and enter into our feelings and enjoyments. As we approach the long avenue a mile from the residence of the companion of thirty-five years, we are espied by his domestics who welcome us with a shout, and inform us that their "Boss" is looking out for us. Our friend soon perceives us, and hurries to the gate. How pleasant are the greetings of friendship—the smiling look of welcome, the open hand, and the warm heart of hospitality.

The usual invitation is sent to a neighbour, to lunch, dine, and meet a friend. The evening is spent in social converse and closed with the family bible, and offerings of gratitude and praise to the Giver of all good. The sleep of him, who has escaped from the din of the city to the quiet of the country, is always refreshing. The dawn of day invites us to a substantial breakfast. The parties now load their double-barrelled guns, whilst the horses are being saddled. The horn is sounded, and the driver, full of glee, collects his impatient hounds. The party is unexpectedly augmented by several welcome guests. Our intelligent friend HARRIS, from New-Jersey, has come to Carolina, to be initiated into the mysteries of Deer hunting, as a preparation to farther exploits on the Western prairies, among the elk and the buffalo; with him comes AUDUBON, the Nestor of American ornithology, and his son, together with Dr. WILSON. After the first greetings are over, we hasten to saddle additional horses for those of our guests, who are disposed to join us. The old ornithologist, having no relish for such boyish sports, sallies to the swamps in search of some rare species of woodpecker. We proceed to the drives, as they are called, viz., certain woods, separated by old fields and various openings, in some parts of which the Deer have their usual run, where the parties take their stands. These drives are designated by particular names, and we are familiar with Crane pond, Gum thicket, the Pasture, the Oak swamp, and a number of bays, one of which we would be willing to forget, for there we missed a Deer, and the bay was named after us, to our mortification. The driver is mounted on a hardy, active, and sure-footed horse, that he may be enabled to turn the course of the Deer, if he attempts to run back, or to stop the dogs. We were carried round to our stands by our host, when a Deer bounced up before us; in an instant a loud report is heard waking the echoes of the forest—the animal leaps high into the air, and tumbles to the ground. Thus, our venison is secured, and we carry on our farther operations from the mere love of sport. Anxious to give our friend HARRIS an opportunity of killing his first Deer, we place him at the best stand. Our mutual wishes are soon gratified. He is stationed at the edge of a bay—a valley overgrown with bay-trees (*Magnolia glauca*)—which from that day received the cognomen of Harris' bay. The hounds after considerable trailing rouse two noble bucks, one of them bounds out near our friend. He is obliged to be ready in a moment, before the Deer comes in the line with another hunter. At the report of his gun we perceive that the buck is wounded. "Mind," cries out friend WILSON, "your shot have whistled past me." Friend H. grows pale at the thought of having endangered the life of another, but we comfort him by stating, that his shot had not reached within fifty yards of the nervous hunter, and moreover, that the old buck was wounded and would soon be his. We observed where he had laid down in the grass, and was started up again by the dogs. Now for a chase of a wounded buck. He takes through an old field once planted with cotton, now full of ruts and ditches, and grown up with tall broom-grass. We agree to let the boys have the pleasure of the chase whilst we are the silent spectators. They bound over ditches and old corn-fields, firing as they run. Suddenly the hounds become silent, and then the loud sounding of the horn is heard mingled with the whoops of the hunters, which inform us, that the game is secured; it proves to be a majestic buck. The successful hunter is now obliged to submit to the ordeal of all who have fleshed their maiden sword, and killed their first Deer. "I submit," he said good naturedly, "but spare my spectacles and whiskers." So his forehead and cheeks were crossed with the red blood of the buck, and the tail was stuck in his cap. The hunt proceeded merrily and successfully. Young AUDUBON, however, had not yet obtained a shot. At length a Deer was started near our host. He would not shoot it, but strove to drive it to his neighbour. He ran after it, and shouted, stumbled over a root, and in the fall threw off his spectacles; but as he was groping for them among the leaves, he ascertained that his generous efforts had been successful; the Deer had been turned to Mr. AUDUBON. One barrel snapped—then came a sharp report from the other—a loud whoop succeeded, and we soon ascertained that another Deer had fallen. We now conceived that we had our wishes for a successful hunt fully gratified; the dinner hour had arrived. Five noble Deer were strung upon the old pecannut tree in sight of our festive hall. The evening passed off in pleasant conversation—some of those present displayed their wit and poetical talents by giving the details of the hunt in an amusing ballad, which however has not yet found its way into print. Thus ended a Carolina Deer hunt.

We regret to be obliged to state, that the Deer are rapidly disappearing from causes that ought not to exist. There are at present not one-fifth of the number of Deer in Carolina that existed twenty years ago. In the Northern and Middle States, where the farms have been subdivided, and the forests necessarily cleared, the Deer have disappeared because there was no cover to shelter them. In the Southern States, however, where there are immense swamps subject to constant inundations and pine barrens too poor for cultivation, they would remain undiminished in numbers were it not for the idle and cruel practice of destroying them by firelight, and hunting them in the spring and summer seasons by overseers and idlers. There is a law of the State forbidding the killing of Deer during certain months in the year. It is, however, never enforced, and Deer are exposed for sale in the markets of Charleston and Savannah at all seasons. In some neighbourhoods, where they were formerly abundant, now none exist, and the planters have given up their hounds. In New-Jersey and Long Island, where the game laws are strictly enforced, Deer are said to be on the increase. In some parts of Carolina, where the woods are enclosed with fences, not sufficiently high to prevent the Deer from straying out, but sufficient to prevent the hunters from persecuting them in summer, they have greatly multiplied and stocked the surrounding neighbourhoods. If judicious laws were framed and strictly enforced the Deer could be preserved for ages in all our Southern States, and we cannot refrain from submitting this subject to the consideration of our southern legislators.

Geographical Distribution.

This animal is found in the State of Maine; north of this it is replaced by larger species, the moose and reindeer. It exists sparingly in Upper Canada. In all the Atlantic States it is still found, although in diminished numbers. Where care has been used to prevent its being hunted at unseasonable periods of the year, as in New-York and New-Jersey, it is said to be rather on the increase. In the mountainous portions of Virginia it is hunted with success. It is still rather common in North and South Carolina, Georgia and Florida, especially in barren or swampy regions, of which vast tracts remain uncultivated. In Mississippi, Missouri, Arkansas, and Texas, it supplies many of the less industrious inhabitants with a considerable portion of their food. It is very abundant in Texas and New Mexico, and is a common species in the northern parts of Mexico. We cannot say with confidence that it exists in Oregon, and in California it is replaced by the black tailed Deer.—*C. Richardsonii.*

General Remarks.

This species has been given under different names, and we might have added a long list of synonymes. The specimens we saw in Maine and at Niagara were nearly double the size of those on the hunting islands in South Carolina. The Deer that reside permanently in the swamps of Carolina are taller and longer legged than those in the higher grounds. The deer of the mountains are larger than those on the sea-board, yet these differences, the result of food or climate, will not warrant us in multiplying them into different species.

Canis Lupus.—Linn: Var. Rufus.

Red Texan Wolf.

Plate lxxxii.—Male.

C. Colore supra inter fulvum nigrum variante, subtus dilutior; cauda apice nigro.

Characters.

Varied with red and black above, lighter beneath. End of tail black.

Description.

In shape the Red Texan Wolf resembles the common gray variety. It is more slender and lighter than the white Wolf of the North West, and has a more cunning fox-like appearance. The hairs on the body are not woolly like those of the latter but lie smooth and flat. Its body and legs are long, nose pointed, and ears erect.

Colour.

The body above is reddish-brown mixed up with irregular patches of black; the shorter hairs being light yellowish-brown at the roots, deepening into reddish at the tips; many of the longer hairs interspersed are black from the roots through their whole extent. Nose, outer surface of ears, neck, and legs, chestnut-brown, a shade paler on the under surface. There is a brown stripe on the fore-legs extending from the shoulders to near the paws. Moustaches few and black; inner surfaces of ears soiled-white; nails black; along the upper lip, under the chin, and on the throat, grayish-white. Upper surface and end of tail, as well as a broad band across the middle portion, black.

Dimensions.

	Feet.	Inches.
From point of nose to root of tail, ...	2	11
Tail, ...	1	1

Habits.

This variety is by no means the only one found in Texas, where Wolves, black, white and gray, are to be met with from time to time. We do not think, however, that this Red Wolf is an inhabitant of the more northerly prairies, or even of the lower Mississippi bottoms, and have, therefore, called him the Red Texan Wolf.

The habits of this variety are nearly similar to those of the black and the white Wolf, which we have already described, differing somewhat, owing to local causes, but showing the same sneaking, cowardly, yet ferocious disposition.

It is said that when visiting battle-fields in Mexico, the Wolves preferred the slain Texans or Americans, to the Mexicans, and only ate the bodies of the latter from necessity, as owing to the quantity of pepper used by the Mexicans in their food, their flesh is impregnated with that powerful stimulant. Not vouching for this story, however, the fact is well known that these animals follow the movements of armies, or at least are always at hand to prey upon the slain before their comrades can give them a soldier's burial, or even after that mournful rite; and if anything could increase the horrors displayed by the gory ensanguined field, where man has slain his fellows by thousands, it would be the presence of packs of these ravenous beasts disputing for the carcasses of the brave, the young, and the patriotic, who have fallen for their country's honour!

No corpse of wounded straggler from his troop, or of unfortunate traveller, butchered by Camanches, is ever "neglected" by the prowling Wolf, and he quarrels in his fierce hunger in his turn over the victim of similar violent passions exhibited by man!

The Wolf is met on the prairies from time to time as the traveller slowly winds his way. We will here give an extract from the journal kept by J. W. AUDUBON while in Texas, which shows the audacity of this animal, and gives us a little bit of an adventure with a hungry one, related by POWELL, one of the gallant Texan Rangers.

"Like all travellers, the ranger rides over the wide prairie in long silences of either deep thought or listless musings, I have never been able to decide which; but when, riding by the side of WALKER or HAYS, who would like to say that a vacant mind was ever in the broad brow or behind the sparkling eye either of him with the gray, or of him with the brown? but at times when watching closely I have thought I could trace in the varying expression, castle after castle mounting higher and higher, till a creek 'to water at,' or a deer which had been sound asleep and to windward of us, started some 30 or 40 yards off our path to wake up the dreamers of our party. No one is certain that his queries will be welcome to the backwoodsman on a march through a strange country, any more than would be those of a passenger, put to the captain of a vessel as he leans over the weather-rail looking what the wind will be, or thinking of the disagreeable bustle he will have, when he gets into port, compared to his lazy luxury on shipboard: but as I rode by the side of POWELL we started no deer, nor came to a 'water hole,' but a Red Wolf jumped up some two or three hundred yards from us, and took to the lazy gallop so common to this species; 'Run you ——,' cried POWELL, and he sent a yell after him that would have done credit to red or white man for its shrill and startling effect, the Wolf's tail dropped lower than usual, and now it would have taken a racer to have overtaken him in a mile; a laugh from POWELL, and another yell, which as the sound reached the Wolf made him jump again, and POWELL turned to me with a chuckle, and said, 'I had the nicest trick played me by one of those rascals you ever heard of.' The simple, how was it, or let's have it, was all that he wanted, and he began at the beginning. 'I was out on a survey about 15 miles west of Austin, in a range that we didn't care about shooting in any more than we could help, for the Camanches were all over the country; and having killed a deer in the morning, I took the ribs off one side and wrapping them in a piece of the skin, tied it to my saddle and carried it all day, so as to have a supper at night without hunting for it; it was a dark, dismal day, and I was cold and hungry when I got to where I was to camp to wait for the rest of the party to come up next day; I made my fire, untied my precious parcel, for it was now dark, with two sticks put up my ribs to roast, and walked off to rub down and secure my horse, while they were cooking; but in the midst of my arrangements I heard a stick crack, and as that in an Indian country means something, I turned and saw, to my amazement, for I thought no animal would go near the fire, a large Red Wolf actually stealing 'my ribs' as they roasted; instinct made me draw a pistol and 'let drive' at him; the smoke came in my face and I saw nothing but that my whole supper was gone. So not in the most philosophical manner I lay down, supperless, on my blanket; at daylight I was up to look out for breakfast, and to my surprise, my half-cooked ribs lay within twenty feet of the fire, and the Wolf about twenty yards off, dead; my ball having been as well aimed as if in broad daylight.' "

We have represented a fine specimen of this Wolf, on a sand-bar, snuffing at the bone of a buffalo, which, alas! is the only fragment of "animal matter" he has in prospect for breakfast.

Plate LXXXII.

N°17

Drawn from Nature by J.W. Audubon

On stone by W.E. Hitchcock

Lith & Printed & Col.d by J T Bowen, Philad.a

Red Texan Wolf.

Geographical Distribution.

In all species of quadrupeds that are widely diffused over our continent, it has often appeared to us that toward the north they are more subject to become white—toward the east or Atlantic side gray—to the south black—and toward the west red. The gray squirrel, (*S. migratorius*), of the Northern and Eastern States presents many varieties of red as we proceed westwardly towards Ohio. In the south, the fox squirrel in the maritime districts is black as well as gray, but not red. On proceeding westwardly, however, through Georgia and Alabama, a great many are found of a rufous colour. In Louisiana, there are in the southern parts two species permanently black as well as the foxsquirrel, which in about half the specimens are found black, and the remainder reddish. The same may be said in regard to the Wolves. In the north there is a tendency towards white—hence great numbers are of that colour. Along the Atlantic coast, in the Middle and Northern States, the majority are gray. To the south,

in Florida, the prevailing colour is black, and in Texas and the southwest the colour is generally reddish. It is difficult to account, on any principles of science, for this remarkable peculiarity, which forms a subject of curious speculation.

This variety of Wolf is traced from the northern parts of the State of Arkansas, southerly through Texas into Mexico; we are not informed of its southern limits.

General Remarks.

The Wolves present so many shades of colour that we have not ventured to regard this as a distinct species; more especially as it breeds with those of other colours, gangs of Wolves being seen, in which this variety is mixed up with both the gray and black.

Genus Lagomys.—Geoff.

Dental Formula.

$$\textit{Incisive } \frac{2-2}{1-1}; \textit{ Canine } \frac{0-0}{0-0}; \textit{ Molar } \frac{5-5}{5-5} = 26.$$

Teeth and toes similar to those of the genus Lepus, upper incisors in pairs, two in front and two immediately behind them, the former large and the latter small.

Ears moderate; eyes, round; hind legs not much longer than fore legs; fur under the feet; no tail; mammæ four or six; clavicles nearly perfect.

Native of cold and Alpine regions. They lay up stores for winter provision which is never done by the true hares. They have a call-note resembling that of some species of *Tamiæ*.

The name of this sub-genus, *Lagomys*, is derived from the Greek woods λαγωζ, (*lagos*), a Hare, and μυζ, (*mus*), a Mouse.

Four species of this genus are described; one, the *Pika*, exists in the northern mountains of the Old World, one in Mongolian Tartary, one in the south eastern parts of Russia, and one in the Rocky Mountains of North America.

Lagomys Princeps.—Richardson.

Little-Chief Hare.

Plate lxxxiii.—Males.—Natural Size.

L. Ecaudatus, fuscus, latere pallidior, subtus griseus, capite brevi; auriculis rotundatis.

Characters.

Tailless; colour blackish brown, beneath gray; head short and thick; ears rounded.

Synonymes.

LEPUS (LAGOMYS PRINCEPS). Rich. Fauna B. Am. p. 227.
    "   "   "   Fischer's Mamalium. p. 503.

Description.

"One comparing the skull of this animal with that of a true Hare, there appears a larger cavity in proportion to its size, fot the reception of the brain. The breadth of the skull, too, behind, is increased by very large and spongy processes. The bone anterior to the orbit is not cribriform as in the Hares, although it is thin, and there is no depression of the frontal bone between the orbits.

The upper anterior incisors are marked with a deep furrow near their anterior margins, and have cutting edges which present conjointly three well marked points, the middle one of which is common to both teeth, and is shorter than the exterior one. These incisors are much thinner than the incisors of the Hare, and are scooped out like a gouge behind. The small round posterior or accessary upper incisors, have flat summits. The lower incisors are thinner than those of the Hares, and are chamfered away toward their summits, more in the form of a gouge than like the chisel-shaped-edge of the incisors of a Hare.

Grinders.—The upper grinders are not very dissimilar to those of the Hare, on the crowns, but the transverse plates of enamel are more distinct. They differ in each tooth having a very deep furrow on its inner side, which separates the folds of enamel. This furrow is nearly obsolete in the Hares, whilst in the *lagomys* it is as conspicuous as the separation betwixt the teeth. The small posterior grinder which exists in the upper jaw of the adult Hare is entirely wanting in the different specimens of the Little-Chief Hare which I have examined. The lower grinders, from the depths of their lateral grooves, have at first sight a greater resemblance to the grinders of some animal belonging to the genus *Arvicola* than those of a Hare; their crowns exhibit a single series of acute-triangles with hollow areas. The first grinder has three not very deep grooves on a side, and is not so unlike the corresponding tooth of a Hare as those which succeed it. The second, third, and fourth, have each a groove in both sides so deep as nearly to divide the tooth, and each of the crowns exhibits two triangular folds of enamel. The posterior grinder forms only one triangle."—(RICHARDSON).

In size this species is a little smaller than the alpine *pika* of Siberia. The body is thick; the head broad and short, and the forehead arched. The ears are ovate, and do not appear to have any incurvations on their inner margins. The eyes are small, resembling those of the *arvicolæ*; there is a marked prominent tubercle at the root of each claw.

Colour.

The Little-Chief Hare is, on the upper surface dark brown, varied with irregular bands of brownish-black running from the sides across the back. There are slight variations in different specimens, some having these blackish markings more distinct than others. The fur is, for three-fourths of its length, of a grayish-black colour, then partly yellowish-brown and white; on the sides of the head and fore shoulders this yellowish-brown colour prevails more than in other parts. The ears are bordered with white; the whole under surface is yellowish-gray, and the small protuberance, which represents the tail, light coloured.

Dimensions.

	Inches.
Length of head and body	$6\frac{1}{2}$
" from nose to eye	$\frac{3}{4}$
Breadth of ear	$\frac{3}{4}$
Fur on the back	$\frac{3}{4}$
Length of head	$2\frac{1}{4}$
Height of ear	1
Length of heel	$1\frac{1}{8}$

Habits.

Little is known with regard to the habits of this animal. The following extract is made from the Fauna Boreali Americana:

"Mr. DRUMMOND informs me, that the Little-Chief Hare frequents heaps of loose stones, through the interstices of which it makes its way with great facility. It is often seen at sunset, mounted on a stone, and calling to its mate by a peculiar shrill whistle. On the approach of man, it utters a feeble cry, like the squeak of a rabbit when hurt, and instantly disappears, to reappear in a minute or two, at the distance of twenty or thirty yards, if the object of its apprehension remains stationary. On the least movement of the

Plate LXXXIII

N° 17.

Drawn from Nature by J. Audubon. F.R.S. F.L.S.

On Stone by W. E. Hitchcock.

Little Chief Hare.

Lith. Printed & Cold. by J. T. Bowen, Phil.

intruder, it instantly conceals itself again, repeating its cry of fear; which, when there are several of the animals in the neighbourhood, is passed from one to the other. Mr. DRUMMOND describes their cry as very deceptive, and as appearing to come from an animal at a great distance, whilst in fact the little creature is close at hand; and if seated on a grey limestone rock, is so similar, that it can scarcely be discovered. These animals feed on vegetables. Mr. DRUMMOND never found their burrows, and he thinks they do not make any, but that they construct their nests among the stones. He does not know whether they store up hay for winter or not, but is certain, that they "do not come abroad during that season."

To the above account, it affords us pleasure to annex the extract of a letter, which we received from Mr. NUTTALL on the same subject.

Of this curious species of Lepus, (L. princeps of RICHARDSON), we were not fortunate enough to obtain any good specimens. I found its range to be in that latitude (42°) almost entirely alpine. I first discovered it by its peculiar cry, far up the mountain of the dividing ridge between the waters of the Columbia and Colorado, and the Missouri, hiding amongst loose piles of rocks, such as you generally see beneath broken cliffs. From this retreat I heard a slender, but very distinct bleat, so like that of a young kid or goat, that I at

first concluded it to be such a call; but in vain trying to discover any large animal around me, at length I may almost literally say, the mountain brought forth nothing much larger than a mouse, as I discovered that this little animal was the real author of this unexpected note."

Geographical Distribution.

Dr. RICHARDSON states, that this animal inhabits the Rocky Mountains from latitude 52° to 60°. The specimen of Mr. TOWNSEND was procured in latitude 42°, and therefore within the limits of the United States.

General Remarks.

Until recently it was not supposed, that we had in America any species of this genus. We have compared it with the Pika, (Lagomys alpinus), of the Eastern continent, described by PALLAS. Our animal is not only of smaller size, but differs from it in the formation of the skull and several other particulars.

Spermophilus Franklinii.—Sabine.

Franklin's Marmot Squirrel.

Plate lxxxiv.—Male and Female.—Natural Size.

S. corpore super cervino ferrugineave creberrimè nigro maculato subter albido, vultu ex nigro canescenti, caudâ elongata cylindricâ pilis albis nigro ter quatorve torquatis vestita.

Characters.

Cheek pouches, the upper surface of the body spotted thickly with black, on a yellowish-brown ground, under surface grayish-white; face black and white, intimately and equally mixed; tail long, cylindrical, and clothed with hairs which are ringed alternately with black and white.

Synonymes.

ARCTOMYS FRANKLINII. Sabine. Linnean Transactions, Vol. 13, p. 19.
"   "   Franklin's Journey, p. 662.
"   "   Harlan's Fauna, p. 167.
"   "   Godman, Nat. Hist. Vol. 2d p. 109.
"   "   Richardson, F. B. Am. p. 168. pl. 12.

Description.

Franklin's Marmot is about the size of the Carolina Gray Squirrel, and resembles it in form, its ears however are shorter, and its tail, which is narrower, presents a less distichous appearance. The ears have an erect rounded flap, and although not as large as those of S. Douglassii, are prominent, rising above the fur considerably more than those of S. Richardsonii or S. Annulatus. The body is rather slender for this genus; eyes large and rather prominent; cheek pouches small; moustaches few and short.

The legs are shorter than those of the squirrels, and stouter than those of S. Annulatus. The thumb has one joint, with a small nail; the second toe from the inside is the longest; the palms are naked. The soles of the hind feet are hairy for about two-thirds of their length from the heels. The claws are nearly straight being much less hooked than those of S. Annulatus.

The hair is rather coarse, and the under fur not very dense.

The tail is clothed with hair, but has on it no under fur. It is capable of a somewhat distichous arrangement, but as we are informed by Sir JOHN RICHARDSON, when this animal is pursued, the tail is cylindrical, the hairs standing out in every direction. The hind feet, when stretched out, reach to the middle of the tail.

Colour.

Incisors orange; eyes and whiskers, black; nails, dark-brown; the septum and naked margins of the nostrils, and margins of the lips are of a light flesh-colour; eyelids, white; below the nostrils, sides of face, chin, and throat, yellowish-white. Upper parts of the head to beyond the ears and neck, light

brindled-gray, composed of blackish hairs tipped with white, without any admixture of brown. The hairs on the back, are at the roots, plumbeous, then brown, succeeded by a line of black, and finally tipped with brown, giving it on the back a brownish-speckled appearance. On the chest and inner surfaces of legs white, with a slight brownish tinge. The hairs on the tail are barred with black and white; they are light-coloured at the roots, then twice barred with black and white, and broadly tipped with white. Towards the extremity of the tail there is a broader black bar, the apical portion being white. When the tail is distichously arranged it presents two indistinct longitudinal stripes of black.

Dimensions.

	Inches.
From point of nose to insertion of tail,	9¾
Tail (vertebræ),	4¾
To end of hair,	5¾
From heel to end of middle claw,	2
Height of ear,	¼

Habits.

We possess but little information of the habits of several of the Spermophili of America. None of the species are found in the settled portions of our country, where opportunities are afforded the naturalist to observe and note down their habits; every one has undoubtedly an interesting history attached to its life, which yet remains to be collected and written. RICHARDSON observes of this species, that it lives in burrows in the sandy soil amongst the little thickets of brushwood that skirt the plains. That it is about three weeks later in its appearance in the spring than the *Arctomys Richardsonii*, probably from the snow lying longer on the shady places it inhabits, than on the open plains frequented by the latter. It runs on the ground with considerable rapidity, but has not been seen to ascend trees. It has a louder and harsher voice than the *A. Richardsonii*, more resembling that of *Sciurus Hudsonius* when terrified. Its food consists principally of the seeds of liguminous plants, which it can procure in considerable quantity as soon as the snow melts and exposes the crop of the preceding year. Mr. TOWNSEND, who observed it in Oregon, does not refer particularly to any habit differing from the above.

Geographical Distribution.

This is a northern and western species; Dr. RICHARDSON having obtained it in the neighbourhood of Carlton House, and TOWNSEND near the Columbia River.

General Remarks.

Although several different Spermophiles bear a strong resemblance to each other, we have not observed that this species has as yet been mistaken for any other, and it has as far as we can ascertain retained its name without change in the works of all new describers.

Plate LXXXIV.

On stone by W E Hitchcock

Drawn from Nature by J.J.Audubon F.R.S.F.L.S.

Franklin's Marmot Squirrel.

Lith⁴ Printed & Col⁴ by J T Bowen: Philad⁴

Genus Meriones.—Illiger.

Dental Formula.

Incisive $\frac{2}{2}$; *Canine* $\frac{0-0}{0-0}$; *Molar* $\frac{3-3}{3-3}$ = 16.

Cheek-teeth tuberculous, the first with three, the second with two, and the third with one, tubercle.

Nose sharp, ears moderate; fore-feet short, with the rudiment of a thumb; hind legs long, terminated by five toes with nails, each with a distinct metatarsus. Tail, very long and slender; mammæ, from two to four pectoral, and from two to four abdominal.

Habits nocturnal, many hibernate.

There have been eleven species described as belonging to this genus, as it is now restricted; one well determined species has been discovered in North America, the rest are found in sandy and elevated regions, in parts of Asia and Africa.

The word Meriones is derived from the Gr. μηριον, (*mĕriŏn*), the thigh.

Meriones Hudsonicus.—Zimmerman.

Jumping Mouse.

Plate lxxxv.—Male and Female.—Natural Size.

M. Supra saturate fuscus, infra albus, lineâ laterali flava inter colorem fuscom albumque intermedia; caudâ corpore longiore.

Characters.

Dark reddish-brown above, with white underneath; sides yellow, separating the colours of the back from the white beneath; tail much longer than the body.

Synonymes.

DIPUS HUDSONICUS. Zimmerman. Geogr. Geschich., II. p.
    "   AMERICANUS. Barton, Am. Phil. Trans., 4. vol. p. 358—282. A. D. 1782.
    "   CANADENSIS. Davies' Linn. Trans., 4. 155.
GERBILLE DU CANADA. Desm. Mammal., p. 132.
    "   "   Fr. Cuvier in Dict. des Sc. Nat., 18. p. 464.
MERIONES LABRADORIUS. Sabine, Franklin's Journ., p. 155 and 157.
G. CANADENSIS ET LABRADORIUS. Harlan, Fauna, p. 155 and 157.
    "   "   Godman, vol. 2. p. 94 and 97.
MERIONES LABRADORIUS. Richardson, Fau. Bore. Am., p. 144.
    "   AMERICANUS. De Kay. Nat. Hist. N. Y., p. 71. pl. XXIV., fig. 2d.

Description.

Head, narrow and conical. Nose, tolerably sharp, with an obtuse tip projecting a little beyond the incisors. Nostrils small, facing sideways and protected anteriorly by a slight ventricose arching of their naked inner margins. The mouth is small and far back. Whiskers, long, extending to the shoulder; eyes, small; ears, semi-oval, rounded at the tips, clothed on both surfaces with short hair. Fore feet small, nail in place of a thumb; hind legs long and slender; there are five hind-toes, each with a long slender tarsal bone; the toes, when expanded, resembling those of some species of birds. The soles are naked to the heels; upper surface of hind-feet covered with short adpressed hairs; tail, long, scaly, has a velvety appearance, soft to the touch, is thinly covered with such soft short hairs, that without a close examination it would appear naked. The hair on the body is of moderate fineness, and lies smooth and compact.

Colour.

Upper surface of nose, forehead, neck, ears, and a broad line on the back, dark-brown; the hairs being plumbeous at their roots, tipped with yellowish-brown and black; under the nose, along the sides of the face, outer surface of the legs, and along the sides, yellowish; lips, chin, and all the under surface white; as is also the under surface of the tail in some specimens, though in others brownish-white. The colours between the back and sides, as well as between the sides and belly, are in most specimens separated by a distinct line of demarcation. This species is subject to considerable variations in colour. We have seen some young animals, in which the dark reddish-brown stripe along the back was wholly wanting; others where the line of demarcation between the colours was very indistinct; nearly all are pure white on the under surface; but we possess two specimens that are tinged on those parts with a yellowish hue.

Dimensions.

	Inches.
Length of head and body	$2\frac{3}{8}$
do of tail	$4\frac{3}{4}$
Height of ear posteriorly	$\frac{1}{4}$
From heel to longest nail	$1\frac{7}{8}$

Habits.

This species was familar to us in early life, and we possessed many opportunities of studying its peculiar and very interesting habits. We doubt whether there is any quadruped in the world of its size, that can make its way over the ground as rapidly, or one that can in an open space so quickly evade the grasp of its pursuers. The ploughman in the Northern and Middle States, sometimes turns up this species from under a clod of earth, when it immediately commences its long leaps. He drops his reins and hurries after it; whilst the little creature darts off with great agility, pursuing an irregular zig-zag direction, and it requires and active runner to keep pace with it, as it alternately rises and sinks like the flying-fish at sea, and ere the pursuer is aware, is out of sight, hidden probably behind some clod, or concealed under a tuft of grass. We have frequently seen these mice start from small stacks of wheat, where the bundles had been temporarily collected previous to their being removed to the barn. In such cases they usually effect their escape among the grass and stubble. A rapid movement seems natural to this animal, and is often exhibited when it is not under the influence of fear, and apparently for mere amusement. Our kind friend Maj. LE CONTE, now of New-York, informs us, that he has seen it in former times, near the northern end of the Island of New-York, springing from the ground and passing with the velocity of a bird, until its momentum being exhausted it disappeared in the tall grass, apparently with ease and grace, again springing forth in the same manner. It must not, however, from hence be believed that the Jumping Mouse walks on its hind feet only, and progresses at all times by leaps, without using its fore-feet. We have frequently seen it walking leisurely on all its feet, in the manner of the white-footed mouse. It is chiefly when alarmed, or on special occasions, that it makes these unusual leaps; the construction of the body proves that this species could not for any length of time be sustained on its tarsi. In its leaps we have always observed that it falls on all its four feet.

We experienced no difficulty in capturing this species in box-traps, and preserved a female in a cage from spring to autumn; she produced two young a few days after being caught; she reared both of them, and they had become nearly of full size before autumn, when by some accident our pets escaped. We placed a foot of earth at the bottom of the cage, in this they formed a burrow with two outlets. They used their feet and nails to advantage, as we observed them bury themselves in the earth, in a very short time. They were usually very silent, but when we placed a common mouse in the cage, squeaked with a loud chattering noise, like some young bird in pain. They skipped about the cage, were anxious to make their escape from the mouse, and convinced us that this species is very timid. They were in their habits strictly nocturnal, scarcely ever coming out of their holes during the day, but rattling about the wires of the cage throughout the night.

We observed that every thing that was put into their cage, however great might be the quantity, was stored away in their holes before the next morning. We fed them on wheat, maize, and buckwheat. They gave the preference to the latter, and we observed that when they had filled their store-house with a quart of buckwheat, they immediately formed a new burrow in which they deposited the surplus.

We are inclined to believe that this species produces several times during the summer, as we have seen the young on several occasions in May and August; they are from two to four; we have usually found three.

The fact of the females being frequently seen with the young attached to their teats, carrying them along in their flight when disturbed, is well ascertained. We have also observed this in several other species; in the white-footed mouse, the Florida rat, and even the common flying squirrel. We are not, however, to argue from this that the young immediately after birth become attached to the teats in the manner of the young opossums, and are incapable of relaxing their hold; on the contrary the female we had in

Plate LXXXV

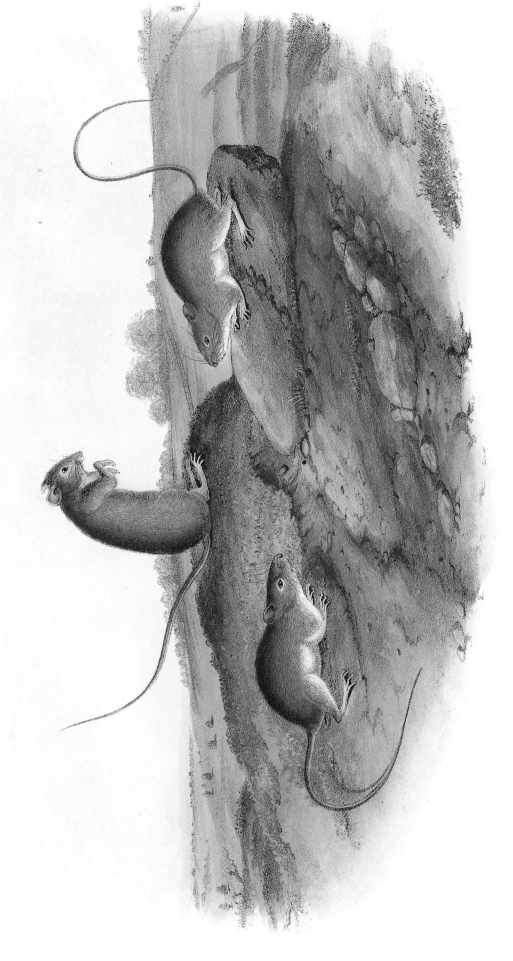

On Stone by Wm E Hitchcock

Jumping Mouse.

confinement, only dragged her young along with her, when she was suddenly disturbed, and when in the act of giving suck; but when she came out, of her own accord, we observed that she had relieved herself from this incumbrance. This was also the case with the other species referred to.

Dr. DEKAY, regards it as a matter of course that in its long leaps, it is aided by the tail. We doubt whether the tail is used in the manner of the kangaru; the under surface of it is never worn in the slightest manner, and exhibits no evidence of its having been used as a propeller. Its long heel and peculiarly long slender tarsal bones on each toe, seem in themselves sufficient to produce those very long leaps. We have often watched this species, and although it moves with such celerity as to render an examination very difficult, we have been able to decide, as we think, that the tail is not used by the animal in its surprising leaps and rapid movements.

The domicil of the Jumping Mouse in summer, in which her young are produced, we have always found near the surface, seldom more than six inches under ground, sometimes under fences and brushwood, but more generally under clods of earth, where the sward had been turned over in early spring, leaving hollow spaces beneath, convenient for the summer residence of the animal. The nest is composed of fine grass, mixed with which we have sometimes seen feathers, wool, and hair.

We are, however, under an impression that the Jumping Mouse in winter resorts to a burrow situated much deeper in the earth, and beyond the influence of severe frosts, as when fields were ploughed late in autumn, we could never obtain any of this species. It may be stated as a general observation, that this animal is a resident of fields and cultivated grounds; we have, however, witnessed two or three exceptions to this habit, having caught some in traps set at night in the woods, and once having found a nest under the roots of a tree in the forest, occupied by an old female of this species with three young two-thirds grown; this nest contained about a handful of chestnuts, which had fallen from the surrounding trees.

It is generally believed, that the Jumping Mouse, like the Hampster of Europe, (*Cricetus vulgaris*), and the Marmots, (*Arctomys*), hibernates, and passes the winter in a profound lethargy. Although we made some efforts many years ago, to place this matter beyond a doubt by personal observation, we regret that our residence, being in a region where this species does not exist, no favourable opportunity has since been afforded us.

Naturalists residing in the Northern and Middle States could easily solve the whole matter, by preserving the animal in confinement through the winter.

To us the Jumping Mouse has not been an abundant species in any part of our country. Being, however, a nocturnal animal, rarely seen during the day unless disturbed, it is in reality more numerous than is generally supposed. We have frequently caught it in traps at night in localities where its existence was scarcely known.

This species, feeding on small seeds, does very little injury to the farmer; it serves, like the sparrow, to lessen the superabundance of grass seeds, which are injurious to the growth of wheat and other grains; it is fond of the seeds of several species of *Amaranthus*, the pigweed, (*Ambrosia*), burr-marygold, beggar or sheep ticks, (*Bidens*), all of which are regarded as pests, he therefore should not grumble at the loss of a few grains of wheat or buckwheat. Its enemies are cats, owls, weasels, and foxes, which all devour it.

Geographical Distribution.

If there is no mistake in regarding all the varieties of Jumping Mice in the northern parts of America as one species, this little animal has a range nearly as extensive as that of the white-footed Mouse. It exists, according to RICHARDSON, as far to the North as great Slave Lake, Lat. 62°. It is found in Labrador and Nova Scotia, and in Upper and Lower Canada. We have seen it in the Eastern and Middle States, and obtained a specimen on the mountains of Virginia, but have not traced it farther to the South; although we are pretty sure that it may, like the *Sciurus Hudsonius* be found on the whole range of the Alleghanies. SAY observed it on the base of the Rocky Mountains, and Mr. TOWNSEND brought specimens from Oregon, near the mouth of the Columbia River. We can scarcely doubt, that it will yet be discovered on both sides of the mountains in California and New-Mexico.

General Remarks.

On looking at our synonymes our readers will discover that this species has been described under an endless variety of names. We have omitted a reference to RAFINESQUE, who indicated several new species in the American Monthly Magazine. We have concluded, that a writer exhibiting such a want of accuracy, who gives no characters by which the species can be known, and who has involved the science in great confusion, and given such infinite trouble to his successors, does not deserve to be quoted.

We had attached to our plate the specific name given by Dr. BARTON, (*M. Americanus*), this we would have preferred to either of the others, especially as it now seems probable, that this is the only species in North America. The names *Hudsonius, Labradorius,* and *Canadensis,* are all exceptionable, as it appears to be as abundant in the Northern and Eastern States, as it is in Hudson's Bay, Labrador, or Canada. There is an evident impropriety, although we confess when hard pressed for a name we have often committed the error ourselves, in naming species after localities where they have been found. The *Meles Labradoria* of SABINE, and the *Lepus Virginianus* of HARLAN, are both familiar examples. Having recently had an opportunity of consulting the original description of ZIMMERMAN, published between the years 1778 and 1783, we are convinced that he was the first scientific describer, and we have accordingly adopted his name. BARTON, at a little later period, published a good description with a figure. DAVIES shortly afterwards published it under the name of *Dipus Canadensis.* SABINE published a specimen with a mutilated tail, which he named *M. Labradorius,* and RICHARDSON a specimen from the North, which he referred to the northern species, under the name of *M. Labradorius,* supposing there was still another species, which had been described as *G. Canadensis.* We have compared many specimens from all the localities indicated by authors. There is a considerable variety in colour, young animals being paler and having the lines of demarcation between the colours less distinct. There is also a great difference between the colour of the coat of hair in the spring, before it is shed, and that of the young hair which replaces the winter pelage. The tail varies a little, but is always long in all the specimens. The ears, size, and habits of all are similar. We have thus far seen no specimen that would warrant us in admitting more than one species into our American Fauna.

Genus Felis.—Linn.

Incisive $\frac{6}{6}$; *Canine* $\frac{1-1}{1-1}$; *Molar* $\frac{4-4}{3-3}$ = 30.

There are two conical teeth, or false molars, in the upper jaw, which are wanting in the genus *Lynx*; a large carnivorous tooth with three lobes; the fourth cheek-tooth in the upper jaw nearly flat, and placed transversely; the two anterior cheek-teeth in the lower jaw false.

Head, round; ears, short and generally triangular, not tufted; in many species a white spot on their outer surfaces; no mane; tail, long; tongue roughened with prickles; anterior extremities with five toes, posterior, with four; nails curved, acute, and retractile.

Habit savage, feeding in a state of nature on living animals only, which they seize by surprise, and not by the chase, as is the habit of the dog wolf, &c.; leaping and climbing with facility; speed moderate; sense of sight good; that of smell imperfect.

There are 33 species of *Long-tailed Cats* described, inhabiting the four quarters of the world. Four species only are positively known to exist north of the tropics in America.

The generic name is derived from the latin word *Felis*—a cat.

Felis Pardalis.—Linn.

Ocelot, or Leopard-Cat.

Plate lxxxvi.—Male.—$\frac{1}{2}$ Natural Size. Winter Pelage.

F. Magnitudine. Lynx rufus. Cana. (*s. potius flava*), maculis ocellaribus magnis fulvis nigro-limbatis, in lateribus facias oblequas formantibus; fronte striis 2 lateribus nigricantibus caudâ corporis longitudine dimedia.

Characters.

Size of the Bay Lynx; general colour gray, marked with large fawn-coloured spots, bordered with black, forming oblique bands on the flanks; two black lines bordering the forehead laterally.

Synonymes.

FELIS PARDALIS. Linn., p. 62.
"   "   Harlan's Fauna, p. 96.

N° 18

Plate LXXXVI

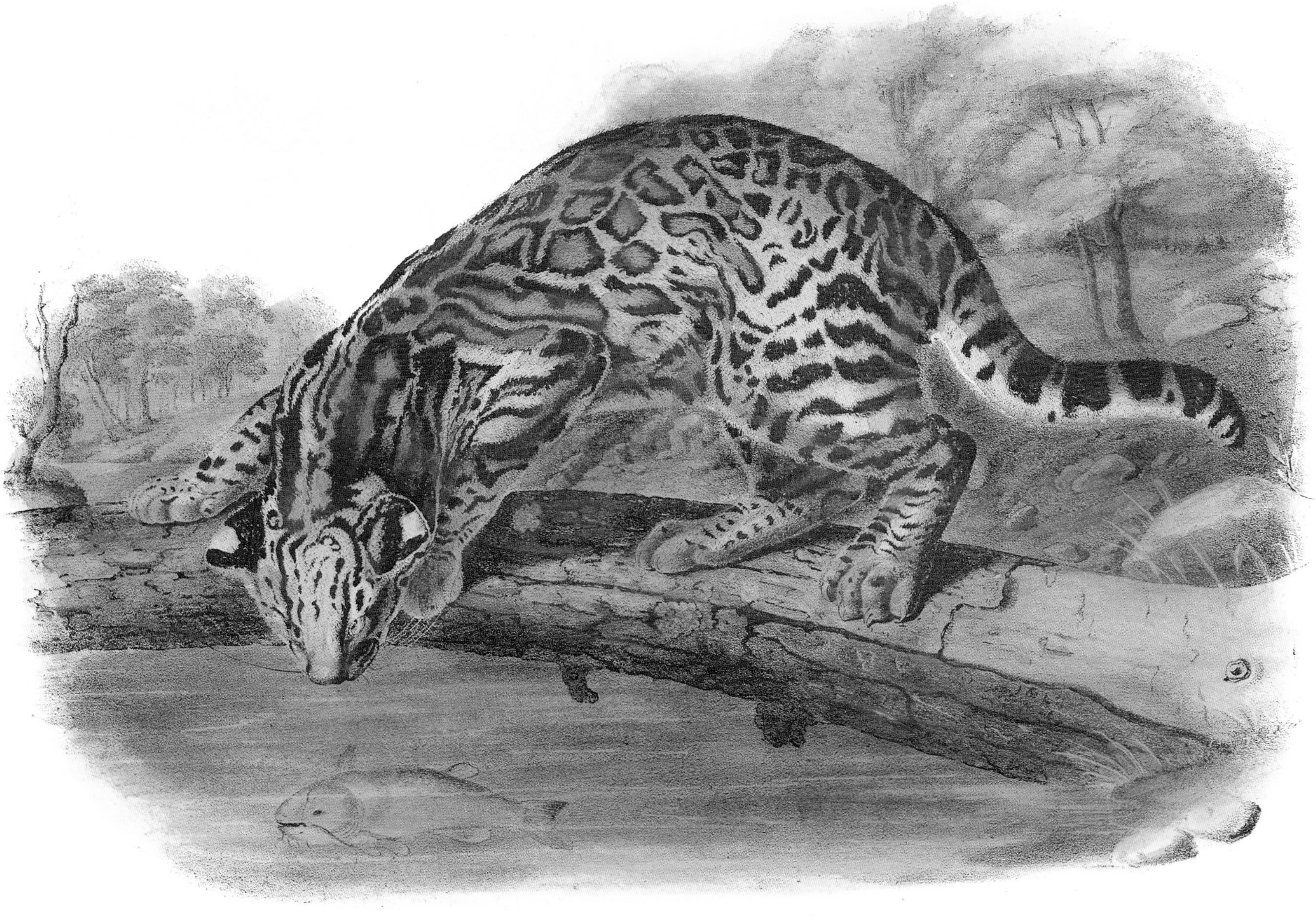

Drawn from Nature by J. W. Audubon

Ocelot or Leopard-Cat.

Lith. Printed & Col^d by J. T. Bowen, Phil^a

		Cuv. An. King., vol. 2, p. 476.
"	"	Griffith's An. King., vol. 5, p. 167.
"	"	Shaw's Zoology, vol. 2d, p. 356.

Description.

Head, short; neck, long and thin; body, long and slender, tail, rather thick, and of moderate size; hair, rather soft, and not very dense.

Colour.

The outer surface of the ear is black, with a white patch beneath; chin and throat white, with a black bar immediately beneath the chin, and another under the neck. On the chest and under surface, white, with irregular black patches. There are small black spots disposed on the head, surrounded by reddish-brown, a black line runs longitudinally on the sides of the head to the neck. The whole back is marked with oval figures, and in some specimens with longitudinal black stripes edged with fawn-colour. Upper surface of the tail irregularly barred with black and white, the extremity black.

Specimens vary much in their markings, and we have not found two precisely alike.

Dimensions.

Male, procured by Col. HARNEY in Texas, seven miles from San Antonio, December, 1845.

	Feet.	Inches.
From point of nose to root of tail, ...	2	11
Tail, ...	1	3
Height from nails to shoulder, ...	1	2
" of ear posteriorly, ...		$1\frac{3}{4}$

Female.

	Feet.	Inches.
Length of head and body	2	4
" tail	1	1
From nose to shoulder.	1	1

Habits.

Before describing the habits of this beautiful species, we must enter into the difficult task of separating it from several other spotted, leopard-like cats, that have been confounded with it. Of these, the most similar in appearance is perhaps the *Felis mitis*, which is found in the tropical portions of North America, and in the warmer parts of South America.

The *Felis mitis* has in fact been figured, and described by SHAW, Vol. 2, p. 356, (unless we deceive ourselves), as the Ocelot, (our present species) while his figure of the *Jaguar*, (opposite p. 354), is probably drawn from the Ocelot, although, so poor a figure as to be hardly recognisable. The descriptions and figures of the Ocelot, that we find in old works on natural history, are so confusing, and unsatisfactory, that we are obliged to throw aside all reference to them in establishing any one of the feline tribe as our animal, and leave the reader to decide whether BUFFON, speaking of the Ocelot, as two feet and a-half high and about four feet in length, meant the subject of our article, which is only two feet-six inches long from nose to root of tail, the *Felis mitis*, or the Jaguar; and whether PENNANT referred to the same animal, which he describes, when speaking of the Ocelot, "as about four times the size of a large cat," (about the size of our specimen of the Ocelot).

The description of this species in LINNÆUS is so short, that it is almost equally applicable to either the Jaguar, the Ocelot, or Felis mitis: "*Felis cauda elongata, corpore maculis superioribus virgatis, inferioribus orbiculatis.*" Sys. Nat. Gmel. p. 78. BRISSON is also very concise in giving the character of the Ocelot; *F. rufa, in ventre exalbo flavicans, maculis nigris in dorso longis, in ventre orbiculatis variegata.*" Quadr. 169. We are on the whole inclined to consider the species described by PENNANT as the Mexican Cat, the Ocelot or Leopard-Cat of the present article, and the larger animal described by other authors, as the *Felis mitis*, as young of the Jaguar, or perhaps females of this last named species, and we have not yet met with the *Felis mitis* within our range, although we have seen such an animal alive in New-York, one having been brought by sea from Yucatan.

Our animal is quite well known in Texas as the Leopard-Cat, and in Mexico is called the Tiger-Cat, it is in the habit of concealing itself in hollows in trees, and also by squatting upon the larger branches. It is rather noctunal, and preys upon the smaller quadrupeds, and on birds, eggs, &c., when they can be seized on the ground.

The activity and grace of the Leopard-Cat, are equal to the beauty of its fur, and it leaps with ease amid the branches of trees, or runs with swiftness on the ground. These Cats seldom stray far from woods, or thickets bordering on rivers, streams, or ponds, very rarely lying on the hill-sides, or out on the plains.

They run like foxes, or wild-cats, when chased by the hunters with hounds or other dogs, doubling frequently, and using all the stratagems of the gray fox, before they take a straight course, but when hard pressed and fatigued, they always ascend a tree, instead of running to earth.

Like all the cat tribe, the Ocelot is spiteful when confined in a cage, and snarls and spits at the spectator when he draws near; but we have never seen it strike through the bars like the leopard, which sometimes inflicts severe wounds on the incautious or fool-hardy person, who, to see it better, approaches too closely its prison.

According to our information, the Ocelot only has two young at a litter, but we have not had an opportunity of ascertaining this point ourselves.

The specimen from which our figure was drawn, was procured by Gen. HARNEY, who sent it fresh killed to J. W. AUDUBON, then at San Antonio on an expedition in search of the quadrupeds of Texas, for our work. We here give an extract from his journal.

"But for the kindness of Col. HARNEY, I might never have made the drawing of this most beautiful of all the North American feline race. Col. HARNEY sent for my trunks, and while I waited the return of the sergeant's guard, who went to fetch them, I saw him daily. He introduced me to Mrs. BRADLY, where he and Capt. MYERS, afterwards my friend, boarded, and the lady of the house made it a home to me.

I was invited out to the camp, and as I talked of the animals I was most anxious to procure, all seemed desirous to aid me. Col. HARNEY, fond of field sports, as active and industrious as he was tall and magnificent-looking, walked at day light the lone prairies and swamps with shouts of encouragement to his small pack of well-chosen dogs, till they in turn burst forth in full cry on the hot trail of a magnificent specimen of this most interesting species. I had just returned from an examination of all my steel-traps; some were sprung, yet nothing but fur was left, showing that a strong wolf or lynx had been caught, but had pulled away; thus preventing perhaps, the capture of some smaller animal that I wanted; and rats, mice, skunks, or other little quadrupeds, were eaten nightly whilst fast in the steel teeth, by these prowlers. I sat down, to think of spring guns, and long for means to prevent this robbery of my traps, when a sergeant came in, with the result of Col. HARNEY's morning's chase, the beautiful Ocelot, from which my drawing was made.

This was a new animal to me, as, though I knew of its existence, I had never seen one, so that my delight was only equalled by my desire to paint a good figure of it. Its beautiful skin makes a most favourite bullet pouch, and its variegated spots are only surpassed by the rich glossy coat and fur of the far famed 'black otter.'"

In his many long hunts. Col. HARNEY must have often and often past the lurking Wako and Camanche, who quailed at his soldierly bearing, while any other man would have had perchance a dozen arrows shot at him.

Geographical Distribution.

We have heard of an occasional specimen of this cat having been obtained in the southern parts of Louisiana. NUTTALL saw it in the State of Arkansas; our specimens were procured in Texas. It is common in Mexico; its southern range has not been accurately determined.

General Remarks.

Much confusion still exists among writers in reference to the spotted cats of Mexico and South America, which can only be removed by the careful observations of naturalists in the native regions of these closely allied species.

Vulpes Fulvus. —Desm

American Red Fox.

Plate lxxxvii. —Male.

V. Rufo-fulvoque varius; collo subtus ventreque imo albis; pectore cano; antibrachiis antice prodiisque nigris; digitis fulvis; caudâ apice albâ.

Characters.

Fur reddish or fulvous; beneath the neck and belly white; chest gray; front part of the fore legs and feet, black; toes fulvous; tip of the tail white.

Synonymes.

CANIS FULVUS. Desm. Mamm. p. 203.
   "   "   Fr. Cuvier, in Dict. des. Sc. Nat. VIII. p, 568.
RENARD DE VIRGINIE. Palesot de Beauvois Mem. Sur.
LE RENARD. Bullet, Soc. Phil.
RED FOX. Sabine, Franklin's Journ. p. 656.
CANIS FULVUS. Harlan, 89.
   "   "   Godman, vol. 1, p. 280.
VULPES FULVUS. Rich. Fauna, B. A. p. 91.
   "   "   De Kay, Nat. Hist. N. Y., p. 44, fig. 1, pl. 7.

Description.

This animal bears so strong a resemblance to the European Fox (*v. vulgaris*), that it was regarded as the same species by early naturalists. No one, however, who will compare specimens from both countries, can have a doubt of their being very distinct. Our Red Fox is a little the largest, its legs are less robust, its nose shorter and more pointed, the eyes nearer together, its feet and toes more thickly clothed with fur, its ears shorter, it has a finer and larger brush, and its fur is much softer, finer, and of a brighter colour.

It stands higher on its legs than the Gray Fox, and its muzzle is not so long and acute, as in that species. It is formed for lightness and speed, and is more perfect in its proportions than any other species in the genus with which we are acquainted.

The hair on the whole body is soft, silky, and lustrous; the ears are clothed with short hairs on both surfaces, and the feet and toes are so clothed with hair, that the nails are concealed. The body of this species has a strong musky smell, far less disagreeable, however, than that of either the skunk or mink. It becomes less offensive in a state of domestication.

Colour.

Point of nose, outer extremity of ears, and outer surfaces of legs below the knees, black; forehead, neck, flanks, and back, bright-reddish, and a little deeper tint on the back and fore-shoulders; around the nostrils, margins of the upper jaw, and chin, pure white; throat, breast and a narrow space on the under surface, dingy-white; extreme end of brush slightly tipped with white; inner surface of ears, and base of the outer surface, yellowish. The hair on the body is of two sorts: long hairs interspersed among a dense coat of softer, brighter, and more yellowish fur; on the tail the longer interspersed hairs are more numerous, and many of them are quite black, giving the tail a more dusky appearance than the rest of the body.

In addition to the distinct varieties of this species, the black and cross Fox, we have seen some shades of difference in colour in the red variety. In some the colours on the back are considerably darker than in others. We have seen several with the nose and chin nearly black, and in others the white tip at the tail is replaced with black. (*See* Addendum.)

Dimensions.

	Feet.	Inches.
From point of nose to root of tail, ...	2	6
Tail (vertebræ)	1	1
" to end of hair, ...	1	5
Height at shoulders, ...	1	1
" of ears posteriorly		$2\frac{3}{4}$

Habits.

This Fox, in times gone by, was comparatively rare in Virginia, and farther south was unknown. It is now seldom or never to be met with beyond Kentucky and Tennessee. Its early history is not ascertained, it was probably for a long time confounded with the Gray Fox, (which is in many parts of the country the most abundant species of the two,) and afterwards was supposed to have been imported from England, by some Fox-hunting governor of one of the "colonies." It was first distinguished from the Gray Fox and hunted, in Virginia; but now is known to exist in all the Northern States, and we are somewhat surprised that it should so long have been overlooked by our forefathers. No doubt, however, the cultivation and improvement of the whole country, is the chief reason why the Red Fox has become more numerous than it was before the Revolution, and it will probably be found going farther south and west, as the woods and forests give place to farms, with hens, chickens, tame turkeys, ducks, &c., in the barn-yards.

The Red Fox is far more active and enduring than the Gray, and generally runs in a more direct line, so that it always gives both dogs and hunters a good long chase, and where the hounds are not accustomed to follow, it will frequently beat-out the whole pack, and the horses and huntsmen to boot.

In some parts of the country, however, it is chased and killed with dogs, in fine style. The following account of the mode of taking the Red Fox, at the sea side in New-Jersey, near Cape May, is from an interesting letter written to us in December, 1845, by our friend EDWARD HARRIS, Esq., of Moorestown, in the neighbourhood of Philadelphia; it is quite different from the ordinary mode of hunting the Red Fox. He begins thus:

"On Saturday, a week ago, I went to Cape May Court-house, where I spent Monday and Tuesday among the quails, (*perdrix virginianus*), which I found exceedingly abundant, but the ground so bad for shooting, that in both days two of us shot but thirty-three birds. On Wednesday my friend Mr. HOLMES took me to BEASLEY's Point at the northern extremity of the county; here I was sorry to learn that young BEASLEY, who was to have returned from Philadelphia on the Saturday previous, had not yet made his appearance; his father, however, showed a great desire to forward my views in regard to "Monsieur Reynard." The next day it rained cats and dogs, and TOM BEASLEY did not arrive in the stage. In the afternoon it cleared off sufficiently to make a "a drive" in the point, where we started a noble specimen in beautiful pelage, but alas! he would not come near the standers.

The next morning, we drove the same ground, being the only place on the main land where there was any prospect of driving a Fox to standers without dogs, (of which there are none in the vicinity). This time we saw none. After dinner I took my pointer, and bagged eight brace and a half of quails, having this time found them on good ground. The next day, Saturday, with three drivers, and three standers, we drove the beach for five and a-half miles, without seeing a fox, and so ended this unsuccessful expedition. I had great hopes of this beach, (PECK's), as it had not been hunted since the winter before the last, although some of the gunners told me they had seen but few "signs" since that time.

The mode of driving, which requires no dogs, is for the drivers to be furnished with two boards, or shingles, which they strike together, or with what is better, a rattle, similar to a watchman's. The standers are sent ahead to a narrow part of the beach, where the creeks of the salt-marshes approach nearest to the sand-hills: when they are supposed to have reached their stands, the drivers enter, and walk abreast among the bushes, between the sand-hills and the marshes, making all the noise they can, with their lungs, as well as their boards or rattles; and these unusual noises are almost sure to drive the Foxes to the standers, where if they pass harmless, they have again to run the gauntlet to the end of the beach, at the inlet, where, Mr. BEASLEY assures me, he has known seven Red Foxes cornered, out of which four were killed, and three escaped from bad shooting. We made four drives in the five and a-half miles.

The Red Fox brings forth from four to six young at a litter, although not unfrequently as many as seven. The young are covered, for some time after they are born, with a soft woolly fur, quite unlike the coat of the grown animal, and generally of a pale rufous colour. Frequently, however, the cubs in a litter are mixed in colour, there being some red and some black-cross Foxes together: when this is the case it is difficult to tell which are the red and which the cross Foxes until they are somewhat grown. In these cases the parents were probably different in colour.

This animal feeds upon rats, rabbits, and other small quadrupeds, and catches birds, both by lying in wait for them, and by trailing them up in the manner of a pointer dog, until watching an opportunity he can pounce or spring upon them. In our article on the Gray Fox, (vol. 1., p. 164) we have described the manner in which this is done by that species, and the Red Fox hunts in the same way.

The Red Fox also eats eggs, and we have watched it catching crickets in an open field near an old stone wall. It is diverting to witness this—the animal leaps about and whirls round so quickly as to be able to put his foot on the insect, and then gets hold of it with his mouth; we did not see him snap at them; his movements reminded us of a kitten playing with a mouse.

We once knew a Red Fox that had been chased frequently, and always escaped at the same spot, by the hounds losing the track: the secret was at last found out, and proved to be a trick somewhat similar to the stratagem of the Gray Fox related in our first volume, p. 171; the Red Fox always took the same course, and being ahead of the dogs so far that they could not see him, leaped from a fallen log on to a very sloping tree, which he ascended until concealed by the branches, and as soon as the dogs passed he ran down and leaping on to his old track ran back in his former path. So dexterously was this "tour" performed that he was not suspected by the hunters, who once or twice actually whipped their dogs off the trail, thinking they were only following the "back track."

The Red Fox is in the habit of following the same path, which enables the fox hunters to shoot this species from "stands," even in a country where the animal has room enough to take any course he may choose to run. The "hunters" who go out from the city of New-York, are a mixed set, probably including Germans, Frenchmen, Englishmen, and Irishmen, and each one generally takes his own dog along, (on the speed and prowess of which he is ready to bet largely,) and the hunt is organized on the height beyond Weehawken in "the Jerseys," where a good many Red Foxes are to be found, as well as more Gray ones.

The men are all on foot, and station themselves along ridges, or in gaps in the rocky hilly country, now running to a point, to try and see a shot, now yelling to their dogs, and all excitement and hubbub. If the Fox doubles much, he is very apt to get shot by some one before he passes all the "standers," and the hunters then try to start another; but the Fox often gets away, as the underbrush is thick and a good deal of the ground swampy, and in that case he makes for a large rocky hill which stands in the Newark marshes, familiarly known as *Rattle-snake* hill. When running across the low level to this strong-hold the Fox is frequently seen by the whole company of hunters, and the chase is lengthened out to a run of many miles, as Reynard will turn again toward the high ridges nearer the Hudson River.

We will give an account of one of these hunts as related by some young friends, who having two fine harriers (to contribute their share of dogs to the pack,) were gladly hailed by the other gentlemen in the field.

"After some beating about among the thickets and ravines, we found the dogs had strayed away down the side of the hills nearly to the level of the marshes, and raising our horn to call them up, observed that they were running toward a cur-dog that appeared to have come from somewhere in them; we immediately gave a loud halloo, and urged all the hounds to the chase. The cur turned tail at once, the whole pack "opened" after him in full cry, and all the hunters came running forth from the woods to the brow of the hill, whence we had a view of the whole scene. The cur looked a good deal like a Fox, at a distance, and most of the hunters thought he was one "certain," he shewed good bottom, took several leaps over the stone walls and fences, and dodged about and round patches of briars and rocks with extraordinary agility, until he got fairly off towards his home, when he positively "streaked it," until, to the utter amazement of the hunters, he jumped on to a wall enclosing a small farm yard, and disappeared within, immediately setting up a loud bark of defiance, while some of the hunters who had expressed most confidence, were loudly laughed at by their comrades, who banteringly asked what they would take for their dogs, &c., and broke out in fresh roars of merriment."

The Red Fox is taken in traps, but is so very wary that it is necessary to set them with great nicety.

DR. RICHARDSON tells us that the best fox hunters in the fur countries use *assafœtida, castoreum,* and other strong smelling substances, with which they rub their traps and the small twigs set up in the neighbourhood, alleging that Foxes are fond of such perfumes.

The same author informs us that their flesh is ill tasted, and is eaten only through necessity.

Red Foxes have gradually migrated from the Northern to the Southern States. This change of habitation may possibly be owing to the more extensive cultivation to which we have alluded, (at p. 265, in this article,) as a reason for this species having become more numerous than it was before the Revolution. This idea, however, would seem to be overthrown by the continued abundance of Gray Foxes in the Eastern States. In the early history of our country the Red Fox was unknown south of Pennsylvania, that State being its Southern limit. In process of time it was found in the mountains of Virginia, where it has now become more abundant than the Gray Fox. A few years afterwards it appeared in the more elevated portions of North Carolina, then in the mountains of South Carolina, and finally in Georgia; where we have recently observed it.

This species was first seen in Lincoln County, Georgia, in the year 1840, since then it has spread over the less elevated parts of the country, and is not rare in the neighbourhood of Augusta. We are informed by Mr. BEILE, an intelligent observer of the habits of animals, that on one occasion near Augusta, as he was using a call for wild turkeys, a little before sunrise, in the vicinity of Augusta, two Red Foxes came to the call, supposing it to be that of a wild turkey, and were both killed by one discharge of his gun.

In order to ascertain whether the speed of the Red Fox was as great in the south as in the colder regions of the north, several gentlemen near Augusta, in the winter of 1844, resolved to test the question by a regular Fox chase. They congregated to the number of thirty, with one hundred hounds, many of them imported dogs, and all in fine running order. They started a Fox at two o'clock on a moonlight morning. He took to a pretty open country on the west bank of the Savannah river. A number of gentlemen were mounted on fleet horses. Mr. BEILE rode in succession three horses during the chase, two of which were good hunters. The persuit of the flying beast was kept up till three o'clock in the afternoon, having continued thirteen hours, when the horses and the whole pack of hounds were broken down, and the hunt was abandoned. This account does not accord with that given by RICHARDSON, who states (Fauna Boreali. Am. p. 93,) "The Red Fox does not possess the wind of its English congener. It runs for about a hundred yards with great swiftness, but its strength is exhausted in the first burst, and it is soon overtaken by a wolf or a mounted huntsman." It is quite evident that our estimable friend never had an opportunity of participating in the chase of the American Red Fox.

Whilst the Gray Fox seldom is known to dig a burrow, concealing its young usually beneath the ledges of rocks, under roots, or in the hollow of some fallen tree, the Red Fox on the contrary, digs an extensive burrow with two or three openings. To this retreat the Fox only flies after a hard chase and as a last resort. If, as often happens, the burrow is on level ground it is not very difficult by ascertaining the direction of the galleries and sinking a hole at intervals of seven or eight feet, to dig out and capture the animal. When thus taken he displays but little courage—sometimes, like the Opossum, closing his eyes and feigning death.

The young, from four to six at a birth, are born in February and March, they are blind when born, and are not seen at the mouth of the den for about six weeks.

It is at this period, when the snows in the Northern States are still on the ground, that the Fox, urged by hunger and instinct, goes out in search of prey. At a later period, both the parents hunt to provide food for their young. They are particularly fond of young lambs, which they carry off for miles to their burrows. They also kill geese, turkeys, ducks, and other poultry, and have a bad reputation with the farmer. They likewise feed on grouse and partridges, as well as on hares, squirrels, and field-rats of various species, as we have previously mentioned.

Geographical Distribution.

The Red Fox exists in the fur countries to the North, is found in Labrador to the East, and in the Russian settlements on the West of our continent. Its Southern limit at present is Abbeville, in South Carolina, and Augusta, in Georgia; a few individuals have been seen in those States, near the sea-board. It also appears in Tennessee, Kentucky, and Missouri. We have not heard of its existence in Florida, Louisiana, or Texas.

General Remarks.

It is now so generally admitted that the Red Fox of America is a distinct species from the European Fox; that a comparison seems unnecessary. We have seen no specimen in this country that can be referred to *Canis vulpes.*

Plate LXXXVII.

N° 18

On Stone by Wm E. Hitchcock

American Red Fox

Lith. Printed & Cold by J.T. Bowen, Philad.a

Drawn from Nature by J.J. Audubon, F.R.S. F.L.S.

Lepus Artemisia.—Bach.

Worm-wood Hare.

Plate lxxxviii.—Male and Female.—Natural Size.

L. Parvus, canescens, nucha et cruribus dilute ferugineis, cauda supra canescens, subtus alba, gula et ventre albis, vellere toto ad basin cano; auriculis longitudine capitis, tarsus dense vestitis.

Characters.

Small; of a gray colour, pale rufus on the back of the neck and legs; tail, above, the colour of the body; beneath, white; under parts of the neck, and lower surface of the body, white; alll the fur gray at the base; ears as long as the head; tarsus, well clothed.

Synonymes.

LEPUS ARTEMISIA. Bach, Worm-wood Hare. Journal Acad. Nat. Sciences, vol. 8, p. 1, p. 94.

Description.

This small Hare is a little less than our common gray Rabbit. the ears are longer and more conspicuous. The head is much arched, and the upper incisors deeply grooved.

Colour.

This species is grayish-black and brownish-white above; the fur is soft, pale-gray at the base, shaded into brownish externally, annulated with brownish-white near the apex, and black at the tips; under parts and inner sides of the limbs, white; the hairs pale-gray at the base; neck, with the hairs on the sides, and under parts gray, tipped with brownish-white, having a faint yellow hue; chin and throat grayish-white, the hairs being gray at their base, and white at their tips. The whole back of the neck and limbs exteriorly of a pale rusty-fawn colour; hairs on the neck uniform to the base; soles of the feet, very pale soiled yellowish-brown; tail, coloured above as the back, with an admixture of grayish-black hairs, beneath, white; ears, externally on the anterior part, coloured as the crown of the head; posteriorly, ashy white; at the apex margined with black; internally, nearly naked, excepting the posterior part, where they are grizzled with grayish black and white; in the apical portion they are chiefly white.

Dimensions.

	Inches.	Lines.
Length from nose to root of tail,	12	0
From heel to point of longest nail,	3	2
Height of ears externally,	2	8
From ear to point of nose,	2	7
Tail (vertebræ) about,	1	1
To end of fur,	1	9

Habits.

Mr. Townsend, who procured this species at Fort Walla-walla, remarks, "it is here abundant but very shy and retired, keeping constantly in the densest wormwood bushes, and leaping with singular speed from one to another when pursued. I have never seen it dart away and run to a great distance like other Hares. I found it very difficult to shoot this animal, for the reasons stated. I had been residing at Fort Walla-walla for two weeks, and had procured only two, when at the suggestion of Mr. PAMBRUN, I collected a party of a dozen Indians armed with bows and arrows, and sallied forth. We hunted through the wormwood within about a mile of the Fort, and in a few hours returned bringing eleven Hares. The keen eyes of the Indians discovered the little creatures squatting under the bushes, where to a white man they would have been totally invisible. This Hare, when wounded and taken, screams like our common species.

Geographical Distribution.

"This small Hare," we are informed by Mr. TOWNSEND, "inhabits the wormwood plains near the banks of the streams in the neighbourhood of Fort Walla-walla. I cannot define its range with any degree of certainty, but I have every reason to believe that it is very contracted, never having met with it many miles from this locality."

Sciurus Sayii.—Aud. and Bach.

Say's Squirrel.

Plate lxxxix.—Males.—Natural Size.

S. Sciurus cinereus magnitudine sub æquans. Corpore supra lateribusque cano-nigroque variis; capitis lateribus orbitis que pallide cano-ferrugineis; genis auriculusque saturate fuscis; caudâ supra ferrugineo-nigroque varia, infra splendide ferrugineâ.

Characters.

About the size of the cat-squirrel (S. cinereus); body above, and on the sides mixed with gray and black; sides of the head and orbits, pale ferruginous; cheek and under the eye; dusky; tail, above, mixed with ferruginous and black, beneath, bright ferruginous.

Synonymes.

SCIURUS MACROURUS. Say, Long's Exped. vol. 1., p. 115.
S. MAGNICAUDATUS. Harlan, Fauna, p. 178.
S. MACROUREUS. Godman's Nat. Hist. vol. 2, p. 134.

Description.

In size and form this species bears a considerable resemblance to the Cat-Squirrel (*S. cinereus*). It is a little longer in body, not quite as stout, and has shorter ears. In length and breadth of tail, they are about equal. The first molar tooth in the upper jaw, which in some of the species is deciduous and in others permanent, was wanting in the six specimens we examined; we presume, however, it exists in very young animals; mammæ, 8, placed equi-distant on the sides of the belly; palms, as is usual in this genus, naked, the rudimental thumb protected by a short blunt nail; the feet are covered with hair, which extends between the toes, half concealing the nails; hair on the body, of moderate length, not as coarse as that of the Fox-Squirrel, (*S. capistratus*), but neither as fine or woolly as that of *S. cinereus*. Our specimens were obtained in summer.—SAY has remarked:

"The fur of the back in the summer dress, is from three-fifths to seven-tenths of an inch long; but in the winter dress, the longest hairs of the middle of the back are from one inch to one and three-fourths in length. He also remarks that it is only in winter that the ears are fringed, which is the necessary consequence of the elongation of the hair; in our summer specimens, the ears are thinly clothed with hair, not rising above the margins.

Colour.

The fur on the back, is for one half its length from the base plumbeous, then pale cinnamon, then a narrow line of black, then cinereous, and broadly tipped with black, giving it what is usually termed an iron-gray colour; the hairs on the under surface are of a light-ash colour at base, and without any annulations brighten into ferruginous at apex, the paler colours beneath giving way to the broader markings on the extremities; the eyes and moustaches are black; nails, dark-brown; sides of face, around the eyes, both surfaces of ears, feet, chin, neck, inner surfaces of legs, and under surface of tail, bright ferruginous; the hairs on the tail, are at their roots reddish-yellow, with three black annulations, and are broadly tipped with reddish yellow.

Dimensions.

	Feet.	Inches.
From point of nose to root of tail	1	0
Tail (vertebræ)		10$\frac{1}{2}$
" to end of fur		13
Height of ear posteriorly		$\frac{5}{8}$

Plate LXXXVII.

N° 18.

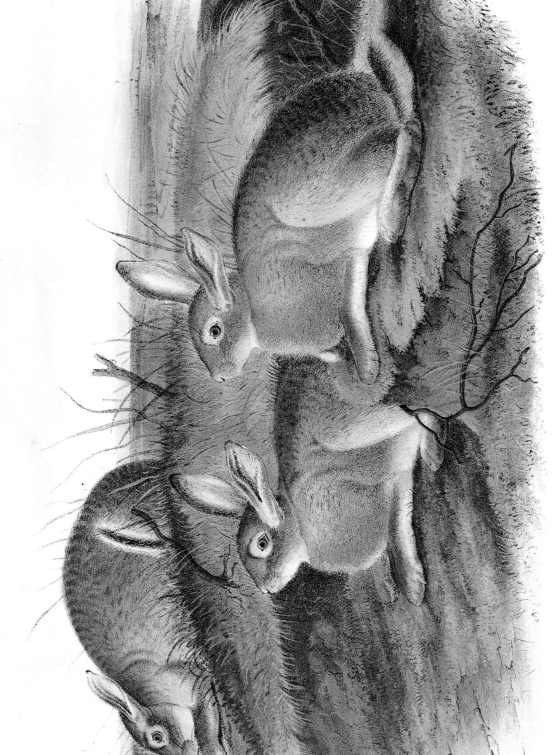

On Stone by W E Hitchcock

Drawn from Nature by J.J.Audubon, F.R.S.F.L.S

Worm-wood Hare.

Lith⁴ Printed & Col⁴ by J.T.Bowen, Philad⁴

Habits.

The habits of this Squirrel are not very different from those of the Cat Squirrel, to which it is most nearly allied. It does not run for so great a distance on the ground before taking a tree as the southern Fox Squirrel, nor does it leap quite as actively from tree to tree as the northern Gray Squirrel, (*S. migratorius*,) but appears to possess more activity, and agility than the Cat Squirrel.

The forests on the rich bottom lands of the Wabash, the Illinois, and the Missouri rivers are ornamented with the stately pecan-tree (*Carya?livæformis*), on the nuts of which these squirrels luxuriate; they also resort to the hickory and oak trees, in the vicinity of their residence, as well as to the hazel bushes, on the fruits of which they feed.

They are becoming troublesome in the corn-fields of the farmer, who has commenced planting his crops in the remote but rapidly improving states and territories west of the Ohio.

The flesh is represented by all travellers as delicate, and is said to be equal in flavour to that of any of the species.

Geographical Distribution.

This squirrel is found along the shores of the Missouri, and in the wooded portions of the country, lying east and north of that river; we have received several specimens, from Michigan, and it seems to be observed west and north of that State.

General Remarks.

This species was first discovered by Mr. THOMAS SAY, and by him described and named *Sciurus Macrourus*. This name, unfortunately, was preoccupied, the Ceylon Squirrel having been so designated: (vide PENNANT, Hist. Quad. ii. p. 140, No. 330.)

Dr. HARLAN and Dr. GODMAN in their respective works, seeing this, applied other names. The former calls it (*Sciurus magnicaudatus*,) the latter (*Sciurus macroureus*.) Authors copied Mr. SAY's description almost literally. Dr HARLAN gives SAY's name (*S. macrourus*,) as a synonyme, and Dr. GODMAN gives his name (*Sciurus macroureus*) as SAY's name: giving in a note intimation that he has taken the liberty of changing the name by the addition of a single letter, which he considers sufficient to render further change unnecessary. Neither of these gentlemen claimed the discovery of this species, gave original descriptions, or appear to have ever seen the animal; and, according to all rules which should govern naturalists, they had no right to name it. We, therefore, having procured a good many specimens, and having from them identified, and described this species, have used the grateful privilege of naming it in honour of its discoverer, Mr. SAY, and have given Dr. HARLAN's and Dr. GODMAN's names as synonymes.

Mus Musculus. —Linn.

Common Mouse.

Plate xc. —Male, Female, and Young. —Natural Size.

M. Corpore fusco; subtus ciner ascenti.

Characters.

Dusky gray above, cinereous beneath.

Synonymes.

MUS MUSCULUS. Linn., 12 Ed., p. 83.
MOUSE. Pennant, Arct. Zool. vol. 1, p. 131.
MUS MUSCULUS. Say, Long's Expedition, vol. 1, p. 262.
"   "   Harlan, p. 149.
"   "   Godman, vol. 2, p. 84.

Description.

The Common Mouse is more generally and familiarly known than any other species, and therefore requires no very minute description. It is small in size; head, elongated; nose, sharp; ears, large, erect, ovate, and nearly naked on both surfaces; legs, slender; nails, sharp, slightly hooked; tail, round, nearly as long as the body, scaly, and slightly covered with short hair.

Colour.

Eyes, black; incisors, yellowish; whiskers, mostly black; fur on the back, plumbeous at the roots, slightly tipped with brownish, giving it a dusky grayish colour; ears a shade lighter; under surface, and beneath the tail, obscure ash-colour.

There are some varieties:—very rarely one is found black, others spotted white and black; one variety is an albino, white with red eyes, breeds in confinement, and produces young with white colour, and the red eyes of the parents.

Dimensions.

	Inches.
Length of head and body	$3\frac{1}{4}$
" Tail	$3\frac{1}{8}$
Height of ear	$4\frac{1}{10}$

Habits.

We have attempted to shew a portion of a shelf in a pantry, on which stands a china jar, with its indigo-blue peaked mountains, its fantastic trees and its (take them altogether) rather remarkable landscapes, reminding us more of the sweetmeats it contains than of aught in the way of nature; and we have also portrayed a plate, with a piece of hard old cheese in it, on which a Mouse is standing in the act of listening, while another in the plate, and two more on the shelf, likewise appear a little startled, and are expecting to be disturbed ere they can make their intended meal; the little rascals have reason to fear, for the careful housekeeper has heard them of late, squealing in their squabblings with each other, has found the marks of their teeth on the bread and butter, and is determined to get rid of them instanter, if possible; she is calling now to her faithful pussy cat, and inquiring for the trap.

But although the thievish Mouse is often frightened, and may be said to eat his dinner with "a cat" over his head, although he is assailed with pokers, broomsticks, &c., whenever he unluckily runs across the floor, and in fact is killed as often as his death can be compassed by the ingenuity of man, or the cunning and quickness of his ally the cat, the Mouse will not retire from the house, and even where the supply of food for him is small, or in rooms that have long been shut up, he may be found; and would he let our drawings and books alone, we should willingly allow him the crumbs from our table; but he will sometimes gnaw into shreds valuable papers, to make a bed behind some bureau or old chest. He in his turn frightens man at times, and should the hard-hearted hoarding wretch who has made gold his God, while with aged, trembling hands, locked in his inmost chamber, he counts his money-bags, but hear a little Mouse; what a feeling of terror shoots through his frame; despair seems for an instant to be written on his face, and he clutches convulsively the metal to which he is a slave; another moment, and he recovers, but he is still agitated, and hastily secures with locks and bolts the treasure which is to him more precious than the endearments of a wife, the love of children, the delights of friendship and society, the blessings and prayers of the poor, or the common wants of humanity in his own person.

Many a young lady will scream at sight of a poor little Mouse, and many a brave young man might be startled in the stillness of the night by the noise made by this diminutive creature, especially if given to the reading of the "Mysteries of Udolpho" or the "Castle of Otranto," late in the hours of darkness, alone in a large old lumbering house.

The Common Mouse is a graceful, lively little animal—it is almost omnivorous, and is a great feeder, although able to live on but little food if the supply is scanty. This species has from four to ten young at a litter, and the female suckles her young with tender care. When first born, they are very small, almost naked, and of a pinkish colour. The Mouse has several litters every year. We kept a pair in confinement, which produced four times, having from four to nine in each litter. Dr. GODMAN quotes Aristotle, who says that "a pregnant female being shut up in a chest of grain; in a short time a hundred and twenty individuals were counted."

On examining our corn-crib in the spring, and cleaning it out; although it

Plate LXXXIX

N°.18

Drawn from Nature by J.J.Audubon, F.R.S. F.L.S.

Lith. by Wm F. Hitchcock.

Lith Printed & Cold by J.T.Bowen, Philada

Say's Squirrel

was constructed with a special view to keep off rats and vermin, being on posts, and the floor raised from the ground some three feet, with boards outside inclining downwards all round, we found and killed nearly fifty Mice. A basket in the crib, hanging by a rope from a cross-beam, in which we had put some choice corn for seed, had been entered by them, and every grain of corn in it devoured. We found in the basket nothing but husks, and the remains of a Mouse's nest. The animal must therefore have climbed up to the roof of the crib, and then descended the cord by which the basket of corn was suspended.

The activity, agility, and grace of the Mouse, have made it a favourite pet with the prisoner in his solitary cell, and it has been known to answer his call, and come out of its hiding places to play with the unfortunate captive, showing the greatest fondness for him, and eating out of his hand without fear.

Of late years, white Mice have been in request in London, where they are taught various tricks, and are exhibited by boys in the streets. It is stated that in order to increase the number of this variety, persons exclude them from the light, this they pretend causes a great many of them to be born albinos. We are however satisfied from personal experience that a pair of albinos, accidentally produced, would continue to propagate varieties of the same colour without the aid of darkness; as is the case in the albino variety of the English rabbit.

Geographical Distribution.

The Common Mouse is not a native of America, but exists in all countries where ships have landed cargo, and may be said to tread closely on the heels of commerce. It was brought to America in the vessels that conveyed to our shores the early emigrants.

Genus Ursus. —Linn.

Dental Formula.

$$Incisive \ \frac{6}{6}; \ Canine \ \frac{1-1}{1-1}; \ Molar \ \frac{6-6}{7-7} = 42.$$

Head, large; body, stout, and covered with a coat of thick hair; ears, large, slightly acuminated.

Legs, stout; five toes, furnished with strong curved claws, fitted for digging.

Tail, short; mammæ, six, two pectoral and four ventral; no glandular pouch under the tail.

Omnivorous, nocturnal, but frequently seen wandering about during the day.

The generic name is derived from the Latin *ursus*, a Bear.

Eight species of this genus have been described, three existing in Europe, one of which, the Polar Bear, is common also to America, one in the mountainous districts of India, one in Java, one in Thibet, and three in North America.

Ursus Maritimus. —Linn.

Polar Bear. —White Bear.

Plate xci. —Male.

U. Capite elongata; cranio applanato; collo longo; pilis longis mollibus, albis.

Characters.

Head, elongated; skull flat; neck, long; hair, long, soft, and white.

Synonymes.

WHITE BEAR. Marten's Spitz. Trans., p. 107. An. 1675.
URSUS MARITIMUS. Lin. Syst.
URSUS ALBUS. Brisson, Regne, an. p. 260.
L'OURS BLANC. Bufffon, vol. 15, p. 128. An. 1767.
URSUS MARINUS. Pallas, vol. 3, p. 69.
POLAR BEAR. Penn. Arct. Zool., p. 53.
URSUS MARITIMUS. Parry's 1st voyage, Supp., p. 183.
"   "   Franklin's 1st voyage, p. 648.
"   "   Parry's 2nd voyage, Appendix, p. 288.
"   "   Richardson, Fauna, p. 30.
"   "   Scoresby's Account of the Arctic Regions.

Description.

Head and muzzle narrow, prolonged on a straight line with the fore-head, which is flattened; snout, naked; ears, short; neck, long; body, long in proportion to its height; soles of the hind feet equal to one-sixth of the length of the body; hair, rigid compact and long on the body and limbs, is from two to three inches in length, with a small quantity of fine and woolly hair next the skin. The whole animal wears the appearance of great strength without much agility.

Colour.

The naked extremity of the snout, the tongue, margins of the eyelids, and the claws, are black; lips, purplish black; eye, dark-brown; interior of the mouth pale violet. The hairs on every part of the body are of a yellowish-white colour.

Dimensions.

Specimen in the Charleston Museum:—

	Feet.	Inches.
Head and body, ...	6	9
Tail, (vertebræ), ...		10
" to end of hair, ...	1	1
Height of ear, ...		$3\frac{3}{4}$
Height from shoulder, ...	3	3
Girth around the body, ...	6	7
" around the hind leg, ...	1	$1\frac{3}{8}$
Length of canine teeth, ...		$0\frac{3}{4}$
" of incisors, ...		

We append the following measurements taken from specimens in the flesh, by Capt. J. C. Ross, R.N., F.R.S., &c.:—

	MALE. Inches.	FEMALE. Inches.
Length from snout to end of tail, ...	94	78
Snout to shoulder, ...	33.5	26.3
Snout to occiput, ...	18.4	15.6
Circumference before the eyes, ...	20.4	15.8
At broadest part of the head, ...	32.2	28
At largest part of the abdomen, ...	65.2	57.6
Length of alimentary canal.	61	52
Weight, ...	900lbs.	700lbs.

The weight varies very much accoridng to the season and condition of the animal.

The largest measured 101.5 inches in length, and weighed 1028 lbs., although in poor condition.

Habits.

We have journeyed together, friend reader, through many a deep dell, and wild wood, through swamp and over mountain; we have stemmed the current of the Mississippi, sailed on our broad lakes, and on the extended sea coast, from Labrador to Mexico; we have coursed the huge buffalo over the wide prairies, hunted the timid deer, trapped the beaver, and caught the fox; we have, in short, already procured, figured, and described, many of our animals; and now, with your permission, we will send you with the adventurous navigators of the Polar Seas, in search of the White Bear, for we have not seen this remarkable inhabitant of the icy regions of our northern coast amid his native frozen deserts; and can therefore give you little more than such information as may be found in the works of previous writers on his habits. During our visit to Labrador in 1833, we coasted along to the north as fas as the Straits of Belleisle, but it being midsummer, we saw no

Plate XC

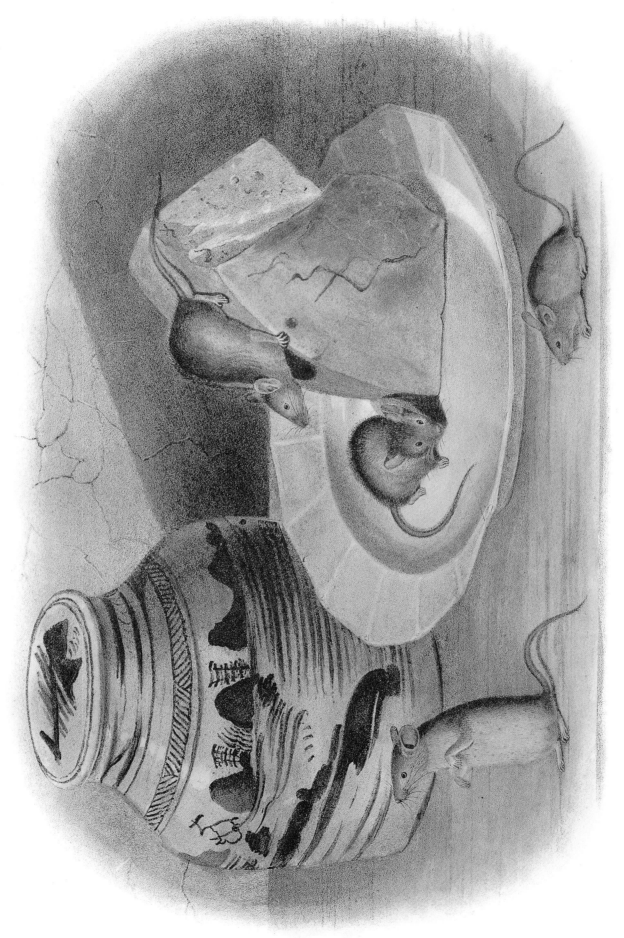

Common Mouse.

Polar Bears, although we heard from the settlers that these animals were sometimes seen there; (on one occasion, indeed, we thought we perceived three of them on an ice-berg, but the distance was too great for us to be certain), although the abundance of seals and fish of various kinds on the shores, would have afforded them a plentiful supply of their ordinary food. They are doubtless drifted far to the southward on ice-bergs from time to time, but in our voyages to and from Europe we never saw any, although we have been for days in the ice.

The Polar Bear is carnivorous, in fact omnivorous, and devours with equal voracity the carcases of whales, abandoned, and drifted ashore by the waves; seals, dead fish, vegetable substances, and all other eatable matters obtainable, whether putrid or fresh. Dr. RICHARDSON, in the Fauna Boreali Americana, has given a good compiled account of this animal, and we shall lay a portion of it before our readers. The Dr. says:—"I have met with no account of any Polar Bear, killed of late years, which exceeded nine feet in length, or four feet and a-half in height. It is possible that larger individuals may be occasionally found; but the greatness of the dimensions attributed to them by the older voyagers has, I doubt not, originated in the skin having been measured after being much stretched in the process of flaying."

The great power of the Polar Bear is portrayed in the account of a disastrous accident which befel the crew of BARENTZ's vessel on his second voyage to Waigat's Straits. "On the 6th of September, 1594, some sailors landed to search for a certain sort of stone, a species of diamond. During this search, two of the seamen lay down to sleep by one another, and a White Bear, very lean, approaching softly, seized one of them by the nape of the neck. The poor man, not knowing what it was, cried out "who has seized me thus behind?" on which his companion, raising his head, said, "Holloa, mate, it is a Bear," and immediately ran away. The Bear having dreadfully mangled the unfortunate man's head, sucked the blood. The rest of the persons who were on shore, to the number of twenty, immediately ran with their match-locks and pikes, and found the Bear devouring the body; on seeing them, he ran upon them, and carrying another man away, tore him to pieces. This second misadventure so terrified them that they all fled. They advanced again, however, with a reinforcement, and the two pilots having fired three times without hitting the animal, the purser approached a little nearer, and shot the Bear in the head, close by the eye. This did not cause him to quit his prey, for, holding the body, which he was devouring, always by the neck, he carried it away as yet quite entire. Nevertheless, they then perceived that he began himself to totter, and the purser and a Scotchman going towards him, they gave him several sabre wounds, and cut him to pieces, without his abandoning his prey.

In BARENTZ's third voyage, a story is told of two Bears coming to the carcase of a third one that had been shot, when one of them, taking it by the throat, carried it to a considerable distance, over the most rugged ice, where they both began to eat it. They were scared from their repast by the report of a musket, and a party of seamen going to the place, found that, in the little time they were about it, they had already devoured half the carcase, which was of such a size that four men had great difficulty in lifting the remainder. In a manuscript account of Hudson's Bay, written about the year 1786, by Mr. Andrew Graham, one of PENNANT's ablest correspondents, and preserved at the Hudson's Bay house, an anecdote of a different description occurs. "One of the Company's servants who was tenting abroad to procure rabbits, (*Lepus Americanus*), having occasion to come to the factory for a few necessaries, on his return to the tent passed through a narrow thicket of willows, and found himself close to a White Bear lying asleep. As he had nothing wherewith to defend himself, he took the bag off his shoulder and held it before his breast, between the Bear and him. The animal arose on seeing the man, stretched himself and rubbed his nose, and having satisfied his curiosity by smelling at the bag, which contained a loaf of bread and a rundlet of strong beer, walked quietly away, thereby relieving the man from his very disagreeable situation."

Dr. RICHARDSON says, "They swim and dive well, they hunt seals and other marine animals with great success. They are even said to wage war, though rather unequally, with the walrus. They feed likewise on land animals, birds, and eggs, nor do they disdain to prey on carrion, or, in the absence of this food, to seek the shore in quest of berries and roots. They scent their prey from a great distance, and are often attracted to the whale vessels by the smell of burning *kreng*, or the refuse of the whale blubber."

The Dr. quotes Captain LYONS, who thus describes the mode in which the Polar Bear surprises a seal:—"The Bear, on seeing his intended prey, gets quietly into the water, and swims to the leeward of him, from whence, by frequent short dives, he silently makes his approaches, and so arranges his distance, that, at the last dive, he comes to the spot where the seal is lying. If the poor animal attempts to escape by rolling into the water, he falls into the bear's clutches; if, on the contrary, he lies still, his destroyer makes a powerful spring, kills him on the ice, and devours him at leisure." Captain LYONS

describes the pace of the Polar Bear, at full speed, as "a kind of shuffle, as quick as the sharp gallop of a horse."

The Polar Bear is by no means confined to the land, on the contrary he is seldom if ever seen far inland, but frequents the fields of ice, and swims off to floating ice or to ice-bergs, and is often seen miles from shore.

It is said that these animals "are often carried from the coast of Greenland to Iceland, where they commit such ravages on the flocks that the inhabitants rise in a body to destroy them." Captain SABINE saw one about midway between the north and south shores of Barrow's Straits, which are forty miles apart, although there was no ice in sight to which he could resort to rest himself upon. The Polar Bear is said to be able to make long leaps or springs in the water.

This species is found farther to the north than any other quadruped, having been seen by Captain PARRY in his adventurous boat-voyage beyond 82 degrees of north latitude.

PENNANT, who collected from good authorities much information relative to their range, states that they are frequent on all the Asiatic coasts of the Frozen Ocean, from the mouth of the Obi eastward, and abound in Nova Zembla, Cherry Island, Spitzbergen, Greenland, Labrador, and the coasts of Baffin's and Hudson's Bays. Dr RICHARDSON says,—"They were seen by Captain PARRY within Barrow's Straits, as far as Melville Island; and the Esquimaux to the westward of Mackenzie river, told Captain FRANKLIN that they occasionally, though very rarely, visited that coast. The exact limit of their range to the westward is uncertain, but they are said not to be known on the islands in Behring's Straits, nor on the coast of Siberia to the eastward of Tchutskoinoss. They are not mentioned by LANGSDORFF and other visitors of the Northwest Coast of America; nor did Captain BEECHEY meet with any in his late voyage to Icy Cape. None were seen on the coast between the Mackenzie and Copper-Mine River; and PENNANT informs us, that they are unknown along the shores of the White Sea, which is an inlet of a similar character."

Dr. RICHARDSON does not think that the Polar Bear is under the same necessity for hibernating that exists in the case of the Black Bear, which feeds chiefly on vegetable matters, and supposes that although they may all retire occasionally to caverns in the snow, the pregnant females alone seclude themselves for the entire winter. In confirmation of this idea the Dr. mentions that "Polar Bears were seen in the course of the two winters that Capt. PARRY remained on the coast of Melville Peninsula; and the Esquimaux of that quarter derive a considerable portion of their subsistence, not only from the flesh of the female Bears, which they dig together with their cubs from under the snow, but also from the males, that they kill when roaming at large at all periods of the winter. To this statement is added HEARNE's account; he says:—"The males leave the land in the winter time and go out on the ice to the edge of the open water in search of seals, whilst the females burrow in deep snow-drifts from the end of December to the end of March, remaining without food, and bringing forth their young during that period; that when they leave their dens in March, their young, which are generally two in number, are not larger than rabbits, and make a foot-mark in the snow no bigger than a crown piece."

"In winter," says Mr. GRAHAM, "the White Bear sleeps like other species of the genus, but takes up its residence in a different situation, generally under the declivities of rocks, or at the foot of a bank, where the snow drifts over it, to a great depth; a small hole, for the admission of fresh air, is constantly observed in the dome of its den. This, however, has regard solely to the she Bear, which retires to her winter-quarters in November, where she lives without food, brings forth two young about Christmas, and leaves the den in the month of March, when the cubs are as large as a shepherd's dog. If, perchance, her offspring are tired, they ascend the back of the dam, where they ride secure either in water or ashore. Though they sometimes go nearly thirty miles from the sea in winter, they always come down to the shores in the spring with their cubs, where they subsist on seals and sea-weed. The he Bear wanders about the marshes and adjacent parts until November, and then goes out to the sea upon the ice, the preys upon seals."

The Esquimaux account of the hibernation of the Polar Bear is curious: it was related to Capt. LYONS by one of their most intelligent men, rejoicing in the euphonious name of (Mr.) Ooyarrakhioo! and is as follows:—"At the commencement of winter the pregnant bears are very fat, and always solitary. When a heavy fall of snow sets in, the animal seeks some hollow place in which she can lie down and remain quiet, while the snow covers her. Sometimes she will wait until a quantity of snow has fallen, and then digs herself a cave: at all events, it seems necessary that she should be covered by, and lie amongst, the snow. She now goes to sleep, and does not wake until the spring sun is pretty high, when she brings forth two cubs. The cave by this time has become much larger by the effect of the animal's warmth and breath,

Plate XCI.

N° 19

Drawn from Nature by J. N. Audubon.

On Stone by Wm E. Hitchcock.

Lith Printed & Col⁴ by J. T. Bowen, Phil.

Polar Bear

so that the cubs have room to move, and they acquire considerable strength by continually sucking. The dam at length becomes so thin and weak, that it is with great difficulty she extricates herself, when the sun is powerful enough to throw a strong glare through the snow which roofs the den." The Esquimaux affirm that during this long confinement the Bear has no evacuations, and is herself the means of preventing them by stopping all the natural passages with moss, grass, or earth. The natives find and kill the Bears during their confinement by means of dogs, which scent them through the snow, and begin scratching and howling very eagerly. As it would be unsafe to make a large opening, a long trench is cut of sufficient width to enable a man to look down and see where the bear's head lies, and he then selects a mortal part, into which he thrusts his spear. The old one being killed, the hole is broken open, and the young cubs may be taken out by the hand, as having tasted no blood, and never having been at liberty, they are then very harmless and quiet. Females, which are not pregnant, roam throughout the whole winter in the same manner as the males.

The Polar Bear is at certain seasons and under peculiar circumstances a dangerous animal. Like the Grizzly Bear it possesses both strength and activity enough to render it at all times formidable. Although, like all Bears, it appears clumsy, can run with great swiftness either on the ground or on the ice, and it can easily ascend the slippery sides of icebergs by the assistance of its claws, being in the habit of mounting on their ridges and pinnacles to look out for food or survey the surrounding fields of ice.

When in confinement, the great strength of this Bear is sometimes manifested to the terror of the spectators. One that was secured in a cage fronted with rods of inch iron, bolted into a horizontal flat plate of the same metal, several inches wide, near the bottom, and well fastened at top, in the stout oak boarding of which the cage was constructed, one day when we were present became enraged by the delay of his keeper in bringing his food, and seized two of the rods with such a furious grip that one of them bent and instantly came out, when the huge beast nearly made his escape, and was only prevented from succeeding by the promptness of the attendants, who instantly placed the wooden front, used when travelling, on the open part of the broken cage and closed it effectually. This Bear, like all others we have seen caged, was very restless, and would walk backwards and forwards in his prison-house for hours together, always turning his head toward the bars in front, at each end of this alternating movement, and occasionally tossing his head up and down as he walked to and fro.

Many anecdotes are related of accidents to the crews of boats detached from whaling vessels to kill the White Bear, and by all accounts it appears to be exceedingly dangerous to attack this animal on the ice. One of these accounts, with others of a different character, we will repeat here, although they have been published by several authors.

Dr. SCORESBY tells us, that "a few years ago, when one of the Davis's Strait whalers was closely beset among the ice at the 'South-west,' or on the coast of Labrador, a Bear that had been for sometime seen near the ship, at length became so bold as to approach alongside, probably tempted by the offal of the provision thrown overboard by the cook. At this time the people were all at dinner, no one being required to keep the deck in the then immovable condition of the ship. A hardy fellow, who first looked out, perceiving the Bear so near, imprudently jumped upon the ice, armed only with a handspike, with a view, it is supposed, of gaining all the honour of the exploit of securing so fierce a visitor by himself. But the bear, regardless of such weapons, and sharpened probably by hunger, disarmed his antagonist, and seizing him by the back with his powerful jaws, carried him off with such celerity, that on his dismayed comrades rising from their meal and looking abroad, he was so far beyond their reach as to defy pursuit."

An equally imprudent attack made on a Bear by a seaman employed in one of the Hull whalers, was attended with a ludicrous result. "The ship was moored to a piece of ice, on which, at a considerable distance, a large Bear was observed prowling about for prey. One of the ship's company, emboldened by an artificial courage derived from the free use of rum, which in his economy he had stored for special occasions, undertook to pursue and attack the Bear that was within view. Armed only with a whale-lance, he resolutely, and against all persuasion, set out on his adventurous exploit. A fatiguing journey of about a half a league, over a yielding surface of snow and rugged hummocks, brought him within a few yards of the enemy, which, to his surprise, undauntedly faced him, and seemed to invite him to the combat. His courage being by this time greatly subdued, partly by evaporation of the stimulus, and partly by the undismayed and even threatening aspect of the Bear, he levelled his lance, in an attitude suited either for offensive or defensive action, and stopped. The Bear also stood still; in vain the adventurer tried to rally courage to make the attack; his enemy was too formidable, and his appearance too imposing. In vain, also, he shouted, advanced his lance, and made feints of

attack; the enemy, either not understanding, or despising such unmanliness, obstinately stood his ground. Already the limbs of the sailor began to quiver; but the fear of ridicule from his messmates had its influence, and he yet scarcely dared to retreat. Bruin, however, possessing less reflection, or being regardless of consequences, began, with audacious boldness, to advance. His nigh approach and unshaken step subdued the spark of bravery, and that dread of ridicule that had hitherto upheld our adventurer; he turned and fled. But now was the time of danger; the sailor's flight encouraged the Bear in turn to pursue, and being better practised in snow travelling, and better provided for it, he rapidly gained upon the fugitive. The whale-lance, his only defence, encumbering him in his retreat, he threw it down, and kept on. This fortunately excited the Bear's attention; he stopped, pawed, bit it, and then renewed the chase. Again he was at the heels of the panting seaman, who, conscious of the favourable effects of the lance, dropped one of his mittens; the stratagem succeeded, and while Bruin again stopped to examine it, the fugitive improving the interval, made considerable progress ahead. Still the Bear resumed the pursuit with a most provoking perseverance, except when arrested by another mitten, and finally, by a hat, which he tore to shreds between his teeth and paws, and would, no doubt, soon have made the incautious adventurer his victim, who was now rapidly losing strength, but for the prompt and well-timed assistance of his shipmates—who, observing that the affair had assumed a dangerous aspect, sallied out to his rescue. The little phalanx opened him a passage, and then closed to receive the bold assailant. Though now beyond the reach of his adversary, the dismayed fugitive continued onwards, impelled by his fears, and never relaxed his exertions, until he fairly reached the shelter of his ship. The Bear once more came to a stand, and for a moment seemed to survey his enemies with all the consideration of an experienced general; when, finding them too numerous for a hope of success, he very wisely wheeled about, and succeeded in making a safe and honourable retreat."

Several authors speak of the liver of the Polar Bear as being poisonous. This is an anomaly for which no reason has yet been assigned; the fact seems, however, well ascertained. All the other parts of the animal are wholesome, and it forms a considerable article of food to the Indians of the maritime Arctic regions.

The skin of the Polar Bear is a valuable covering to these tribes, and is dressed by merely stretching it out on the snow, pinning it down, and leaving it to freeze, after which the fat is all scraped off. It is then generally hung up in the open air, and "when the frost is intense, it dries most perfectly; with a little more scraping it becomes entirely dry and supple, both skin and hair being beautifully white." "The time of the year at which the sexes seek each other is not positively known, but it is most probably in the month of July, or of August. HEARNE, who is an excellent authority, relates that he has seen them killed during this season, when the males exhibited an extreme degree of attachment to their companions. After a female was killed, the male placed his fore-paws over her, and allowed himself to be shot rather than relinquish her dead body."

"The pregnant females during winter seek shelter near the skirt of the woods, where they excavate dens in the deepest snow-drifts, and remain there in a state of torpid inaction, without food, from the latter part of December or early in January till about the end of March; they then relinquish their dens to seek food on the sea-shore, accompanied by their cubs."—GODMAN, Vol. I., pp. 152, 153.

The affection of the female Polar Bear for her young is exemplified by several stories in the Polar voyages. SCORESBY says, "a she Bear with her two cubs, were pursued on the ice by some of the men, and were so closely approached, as to alarm the mother for the safety of her offspring. Finding that they could not advance with the desired speed, she used various artifices to urge them forward, but without success. Determined to save them, if possible, she ran to one of the cubs, placed her nose under it, and threw it forward as far as possible; then going to the other, she performed the same action, and repeated it frequently, until she had thus conveyed them to a considerable distance. The yound Bears seemed perfectly conscious of their mother's intention, for as soon as they recovered their feet, after being thrown forward, they immediately ran on in the proper direction, and when the mother came up to renew the effort, the little rogues uniformly placed themselves across her path, that they might receive the full advantage of the force exerted for their safety."

The sagacity of the Polar Bear is said to be great, and it is very difficult to entrap this animal, as he scents the ground, and cautiously approaches even when the snare is concealed by the snow. SCORESBY relates an instance of a Bear which, having got his fore-foot in a noose, very deliberately loosened the slip-knot with the other paw, and leisurely walked off to enjoy the bait which he had abstracted.

Capt. J. C. Ross states in regard to this species:—"During our stay at Fury Beach many of these animals came about us, and several were killed. At that time we were fortunately in no want of provisions, but some of our party, tempted by the fine appearance of the meat, made a hearty meal off the first one that was shot. All that partook of it soon after complained of a violent headache, which with some continued two or three days, and was followed by the skin peeling off the face, hands, and arms; and in some who had probably partaken more largely, off the whole body. On a former occasion I witnessed a somewhat similar occurrence, when, on Sir Edward Parry's Polar journey, having lived for several days wholly on two Bears that were shot, the skin peeled off the face, legs, and arms of many of the party. It was then attributed rather to the quantity than the quality of the meat, and to our having been for sometime previous on very short allowance of provisions. The Esquimaux eat its flesh without experiencing any such inconvenience, but the liver is always given to the dogs, and that may possibly be the noxious part. The Esquimaux of Boothia Felix killed several during their stay in our neighbourhood in 1830, all males."

Geographical Distribution.

The Polar Bear inhabits the north of both continents, having been found in the highest latitudes ever reached by navigators. It was seen by Capt. Parry in latitude 82°. It exists on all the Asiatic coasts of the Frozen Ocean, from the mouth of the Obi, eastward, and abounds in Nova Zembla and Spitzbergen. In America it is found in Greenland, Labrador, and on the coasts of Baffin's and Hudson's Bays. They seem not to be found on the islands in Behring's Straits.

McKENSIE informs us that these animals are unknown in the White Sea, or on the coast of Siberia to the eastward of Tchutskoinoss. They have been seen on floating icebergs from fifty to a hundred miles at sea. Capt. Ross states that this species was found in greater numbers in the neighbourhood of Port Bowen and Batty Bay in Prince Regent's Inlet, than in any other part of the Polar Regions that were visited by the several expeditions of discovery. This he supposed was owing to the food they were enabled to procure in that vicinity, Lancaster Sound being but seldom covered by permanently fixed ice, and therefore affording them means of subsistence during the severity of an arctic winter, and also from its being remote from the haunts of the Esquimaux.

Lynx Rufus—Var. Maculatus.—Horsfield and Vigors.

Texan Lynx.

Plate xcii.—Female.—Winter pelage.

L. rufo-grisea, dorso saturatiore, corporis lateribus memberisque externe bruneo-maculatis, gulâ, corpore infra, membrisque internè albis, bruneo latius maculati auribus pencillatis.

Characters.

Brownish-gray on the upper surface, sides of body and outer surface of legs, with small brown spots; under surface of body and inner surface of legs, white, broadly spotted with brown; ears, pencilled.

Synonymes.

FELIS MACULATUS. Horsfield and Vigors.
" " Zoological Journal, vol. 4, p. 380.
" " Reichenbach, Regnum Animale, vol. 1, p. 6, pl. 37.

Description.

In size, in shape, in its naked soles—in the form of the skull—the disposition and character of its teeth, and in all its habits, this species is so much like the Bay Lynx, (*L. rufus*,) that were it not for the different shades of colour, and the peculiar markings of some parts of the body, no naturalist would have ventured to describe it as a new species. One of the characters given to this supposed species by its original describers is that of pencilled ears; this character, however, exists also in the Bay Lynx; in both cases these hairs drop out when the other hairs are shed in spring, and are not replaced till the following autumn. The same peculiarity exists in many of our American squirrels. There is, as in *L. rufus*, a short ruff under the throat of the male. The hair is of two kinds: the inner, fine, and the outer and longer, not very coarse, and the fur, although much shorter, is fully as fine as that of specimens of the Bay Lynx obtained in Pennsylvania and New-York.

Colour.

The hairs on the back are at their roots yellowish-white, gradually becoming light-yellow, which colour continues for three-fourths the length, when they are barred with brownish-black, then yellowish-brown, tipped with black; on the sides, the hairs are tipped with white; on the under surface, they are white throughout, with a shade of pale-yellow at the base. Where black spots exist on the body, the hairs are less annulated—are dark-brown at the roots, deepening into black; and in some spots on the sides, and the bands on the tail, the hairs are pure black from the roots.

Moustaches, white; around the nose, around the eye, and cheeks, pale fawn colour; lips white; forehead, obscurely and irregularly marked with longitudinal stripes of dark-brown on a light-yellowish ground-colour. There are two black lines commencing at a point on a line with the articulation of the lower jaw, where they form an acute angle, diverging from thence to the sides of the neck, and unite with the ruff, where it is an inch broad. The ears are yellowish-white on the inner surface, black on the outer, with a broad white patch in the middle, including nearly their whole breadth. The slight pencil of hairs at the extremity of the ear is black; on the back the colours are waved, and blended with obscure yellowish and brown spots—assuming on the dorsal line slight indications of narrow longitudinal stripes. The feet, on the upper surface are dotted with small brown spots; on the under surface the ground colour is whitish, with irregular patches of black. This is more especially the case on the inner surfaces of the thighs and fore legs, which present long stripes and patches of black, somewhat irregularly disposed. The tail is white on the under surface, barred above with rufous and black; towards the extremity there is first a bar of black about one-third of an inch wide, then brownish-gray, then an inch of black; the white on the under surface rises above the black, making the tip of the tail white.

Dimensions.

	Male.—Weight 25 lb.		Female.—Weight 20 lb.	
	Feet.	Inches.	Feet.	Inches.
End of nose to eye,		2		$1\frac{3}{4}$
" " to burr of ear,		$4\frac{3}{4}$		$3\frac{5}{8}$
Between ears,		$3\frac{1}{8}$		3
Nose to crown of head,		$5\frac{1}{2}$		$5\frac{1}{4}$
" to root of tail,	2	9	2	5
Tail (vertebræ)		7		6
" " to end of hair,		$7\frac{1}{2}$		$6\frac{1}{2}$
Hind legs (stretched) beyond tail,		$11\frac{1}{2}$		10
Fore " " beyond nose,		$6\frac{1}{2}$		6
Height of shoulder from ground,	1	$7\frac{1}{2}$	1	$5\frac{1}{2}$
Round body behind shoulder,	1	$4\frac{1}{2}$	1	$2\frac{1}{2}$
" " at the loin,	1	$4\frac{1}{2}$	1	0

Habits.

This variety of Lynx may be called the Common Wild-Cat of Texas, where it is occasionally found even on the prairies, although it generally confines itself to the neighbourhood of woods and chaparal.

The Texan Wild-Cat is, like the *Lynx rufus*, a wily and audacious depredator—he steals the fowls from the newly-established rancho, or petty farm; follows the hares, rats, and birds, and springs upon them in the tall rank grass, or thick underbrush, and will sometimes even rob the ranger of a fine turkey; for should the Wild-Cat be lurking in the dense thicket, when the crack of the rifle is heard, and the wild gobbler or hen falls slanting to the earth, he will, instead of flying with terror from the startling report of the gun, dart towards the falling bird, seize it as it touches the ground, and bear it off at full speed, even if in sight of the enraged and disappointed marksman who brought down the prize. In general, however, the Southern Lynx (as this species is sometimes called) will fly from man's presence, and will only come abroad during the day when very hard pressed by hunger, when it may be occasionally seen near little thickets, on the edges of the prairies, or in the open ground, prowling with the stealth sneaking gait observed in the domestic cat, when similarly employed. This species of Wild-Cat is better able to escape from an ordinary pack of dogs, than the Common Lynx, being accustomed to the great distances across the high dry prairies, which it must frequently cross at full speed. We have known one chased, from 11 o'clock in the morning till dark night, without being "treed." The animal, in fact, prefers running, to resorting to a tree at all times, and will not ascend one unless it be nearly exhausted, and hard pressed by the hounds.

Geographical Distribution.

This variety of the Bay Lynx is believed to exist throughout Mexico; we have seen specimens, obtained in that country, in several Museums of Europe, especially those of Berlin and Dresden; in the latter, the specimen described and figured by REICHENBACH is preserved. His figure, however, which we have compared with the original, is likely to mislead; the legs and tail being much too long. It exists in New Mexico, and we have heard that a Wild-Cat, supposed to be the present variety, is found in California. The specimen from which our drawing was made, was procured with several others by JOHN W. AUDUBON, in the vicinity of Castroville, on the head waters of the Medina, in Texas; we possess a specimen nearly of the same markings, procured by our deceased friend, the late lamented Dr. WURDEMANN.

General Remarks.

We have admitted this as a variety of the Bay Lynx with some doubt and hesitation, and not without misgivings that it might yet be proved to be a distinct species. The permanency of its colours, together with the smaller size of our specimens, and their softer fur, may afford sufficient characters to entitle it to the name of *Maculatus*, as given by HORSEFIELD and VIGORS. Aware, however, of the many varieties in the Bay Lynx, we have not felt authorised to regard it as positively distinct.

Putorius Nigripes.—Aud. and Bach.

Black-Footed Ferret.

Plate xciii.—Male.—Natural Size.

P. Magnitudine mustelam martem equans, fronte, caudæ, apice, pedibus-que nigris; supra e flavido fuscus infra albus.

Characters.

Size of the pine martin; forehead, feet, and extremity of tail, black; yellowish-brown above, white beneath.

Synonyme.

PUTORIUS NIGRIPES. Aud. and Bach, Quadrupeds of North America. vol. 2, pl. 93.

Description.

In its dentition this species possesses all the characteristics belonging to putorius and from the number and disposition of the teeth, cannot be placed in the genus, *mustela*. The canine teeth are stout and rather long, extending beyond the lips; they are slightly arched and somewhat blunt; the two outer incisors in the upper jaw are largest, the remainder are smaller, but regular and conspicuous. The first false molar is small but distinctly visible, it is without a lobe; the second is larger and has a slight lobe on each side. The great tuberculous tooth has two points and an external lobe; the last molar is rather small. In the lower jaw the incisors are small, and much crowded together. The three false molars on each side increase in size from the first, which is smallest and simple, to the third, which is largest and tuberculated. The great internal tooth has three lobes but no tubercle on the inner side, as is the case in the genus *mustela*; the last, or back tooth, is small but simple.

Body, very long; head, blunt; forehead, arched and broad; muzzle, short; eyes, of medium size; moustaches, few; ears, short, erect, broad at base, and triangular in shape, clothed on both surfaces with short hair; neck, long; legs, short and stout; toes, armed with sharp nails, very slightly arched; the feet on both surfaces covered with hair even to the soles, concealing the nails.

The pelage is of two kinds of hair, it is short soft and very fine, the outer and interspersed hairs are not so fine, but are not long and very coarse. The fur is finer than that of the mink or pine marten, and even shorter than that of the ermine. The hairs below the ears, under the forearms and belly are the coarsest; the tail is cylindrical, and less voluminous than that of the mink, containing more coarse hair, and less fine fur, than in that animal.

Colour.

The long hairs on the back are at the roots whitish, with a yellowish tinge, broadly tipped with reddish-brown; the soft under fur is white, with a yellowish tinge, giving the animal on the back a yellowish-brown appearance, in some parts approaching to rufous; on the sides and rump the colour is a little lighter, gradually fading into yellowish-white. Whiskers, white and black; nose, ears, sides of face, throat, under surface of neck, belly, and under surface of tail, white, a shade of brownish on the chest between the forelegs. There is a broad black patch commencing on the forehead, enclosing the eyes, and running down within a few lines of the point of the nose; outer and inner surfaces of the legs, to near the shoulders and hips, black, with a tinge of brownish; the tip fo the tail is black, for two inches from the extremity.

Dimensions.

	Feet.	Inches.
From point of nose to root of tail, ...	1	7
" " Tail, (vertebræ)		4
" head to end of hairs		$5\frac{1}{4}$
Height of ear posteriorly, ...		$\frac{1}{2}$
From shoulder to end of foreleg, ...		4

Habits.

It is with great pleasure that we introduce this handsome new species; it was procured by Mr. CULBERTSON on the lower waters of the Platte River, and inhabits the wooded parts of the country to the Rocky Mountains, and perhaps is found beyond that range, although not observed by any travellers, from LEWIS and CLARK to the present day. When we consider the very rapid manner in which every expedition that has crossed the Rocky Mountains, has been pushed forward, we cannot wonder that many species have been entirely overlooked, and should rather be surprised at the number noticed by LEWIS and CLARK, and by NUTALL, TOWNSEND, and others. There has never yet been a Government expedition properly organized, and sent forth to obtain *all* the details, which such a party, allowed *time* enough for thorough investigation, would undoubtedly bring back, concerning the natural history and natural resources of the regions of the far west. The nearest approach to such an expedition having been that so well conducted by LEWIS and CLARK. Nor do we think it at all probable that Government will attend to such matters for a long time to come. We must therefore hope that private enterprise will gradually unfold the zoological, botanical, and mineral wealth of the immense territories we own but do not yet occupy.

The habits of this species resemble, as far as we have learned, those of the ferret of Europe. It feeds on birds, small reptiles and animals, eggs, and various insects, and is a bold and cunning foe to the rabbits, hares, grouse, and other game of our western regions.

The specimen from which we made our drawing was received by us from Mr. J. G. BELL, to whom it was forwarded from the outskirts or outposts of the fur traders on the Platte river, by Mr. CULBERTSON. It was stuffed with the wormwood so abundant in parts of that country, and was rather a poor specimen, although in tolerable preservation. We shall have occasion in a future article to thank Mr. BELL for the use of other new specimens, this being only one of several instances of his kind services to us, and the zoology of our country, in this way manifested.

Geographical Distribution.

As before stated, the specimen which we have figured and described was obtained on the lower waters of the Platte river. We are not aware that another specimen exists in any cabinet.

Plate XCII

On Stone by Wm E Hitchcock

Texan Lynx.

Lepus Nuttallii.—Bachman.

Nuttall's Hare.

Plate xciv.—Males.—Natural Size.

L. parvus, supra fuscus cum aureo mistus subtus dilute flavo-canescens, auriculis amplis rotundatisque, cauda longiuscula, subtus albus.

Characters.

Small; tail of moderate length, general colour above, a mixture of light buff and dark brown, beneath, light yellowish grey; ears, broad and rounded; lower surface of the tail white.

Description.

The anterior upper incisors are more rounded than those of the American Hare, but in the deep longitudinal furrows, and in other particulars they bear a striking resemblance to those of that species; the accessory, upper incisors resemble those of the Hares in general. The lower incisors are rather thinner than those of the American Hare, and like the upper, more of an oval shape. The upper grinders are furrowed longitudinally, like those of other Hares, and have a slight furrow on the inner side, but not more apparent than in *Lepus aquaticus*; indeed, all the American Hares have this furrow, which differs considerably in individuals belonging to the same species.

This Hare bears some resemblance to the young of *Lepus sylvaticus*; the forehead is more arched, and there is no depression in the frontal bone, as in the American Hare; its fur is also much softer, and differs in colour; the whiskers are nearly the length of the head. The ears appeared rather short and shrivelled in the dried specimen, but when moistened for the purpose of having a drawing of them made became much distended; the incurvation on their outer margin was as distinct as in other Hares, bearing no resemblance to the funnel-shaped ears of the *pika*. The tail in the living animal must be conspicuous, although in the dried specimen it is concealed by the long fur of the posteriors. The feet are thickly clothed with soft hair, completely covering the nails. There are five toes on the fore and four on the hind feet.

Colour.

Teeth, yellowish white; whiskers, white and black; the former colour predominating; the whole of the upper surface of the body, a mixture of buff and dark brown; under surface light buff-grey. The fur on the back is, for three-fourths of its length from the roots, plumbeous, then light ash mixed with buff; and the long interspersed hairs are all tipped with black. The ears are pretty well clothed, internally and externally, with hairs of an ash colour, bordered with a line of black anteriorly, and edged with white. From behind the ears to the back, there is a very broad patch of buff, and the same colour, mixed with rufus, prevails on the outer surface of the legs, extending to the thighs and shoulders. The soles of the feet are yellowish brown. The claws, which are slightly arched, are light brown for three-fourths of their length, and are tipped with white; under surface of the tail, white.

Dimensions.

	Inches.
Length from point of nose to insertion of tail,	$6\frac{1}{4}$
" of Heel,	2
" Fur on the back,	$\frac{3}{4}$
" of Head,	$2\frac{1}{8}$
Height of ear,	$1\frac{1}{2}$
Tail vertebræ,	$\frac{3}{4}$
Including fur,	$1\frac{1}{4}$

Habits.

The only information which we have been able to obtain of the habits of this diminutive species is contained in the following note from Mr. NUTTALL, which accompanied the specimen.

"This little Hare we met with west of the Rocky Mountains, inhabiting thickets by the banks of several small streams which flow into the Shoshonee and Columbia rivers. It was frequently seen, in the evening, about our encampment, and appeared to possess all the habits of the *Lepus Sylvaticus*."

Geographical Distribution.

We have not heard of the existence of this Hare in any part of California, or New Mexico; and although it is doubtless found in other localities than those mentioned above, we cannot venture to assert that it is widely distributed.

General Remarks.

We described this species from the only specimen we have had an opportunity of examining. It would be satisfactory to be able to investigate further, as it needs more information than we have been able to obtain, to pronounce decidedly upon its characters, and give its true geographical distribution.

Mus (Calomys) Aureolus.—Aud. and Bach.

Orange-Coloured Mouse.

Plate xcv.—Male and Females.—Natural Size.

M. supra saturate luteus infra pallide flavus; auriculis longis, cauda corpore curtiore.

Characters.

Ears long; tail shorter than the body; bright orange-coloured above, light buff beneath.

Description.

This species bears a general resemblance in form to the white-footed Mouse, (*Muse leucopus*.) It is, however, a little larger, and its ears rather shorter. Head, long; nose, sharp; whiskers, extending beyond the ears. Fur, very soft and lustrous. The legs, feet, and heels, clothed with short, closely adpressed hairs, which extend beyond the nails; ears, thinly covered with hairs, which do not entirely conceal the colour of the skin; mammæ, four; situated far back.

Colour.

Head, ears, and whole upper surface, bright orange; the fur being for three-fourths of its length from the roots, dark plumbeous; whiskers, nearly black, with a few white hairs interspersed; tail, above and beneath, dark brown; throat, breast, and inner surface of the forelegs, white; belly, light buff. There are no very distinct lines of separation between these colours.

Dimensions.

	Inches.	Lines.
Length of head and body,	4	3
" Tail,	3	1
" Head,	1	3
" Ear posteriorly,	0	3
" Tarsus, including nail,	0	9

Habits.

In symmetry of form and brightness of colour, this is the prettiest species of *Mus* inhabiting our country. It is at the same time a great climber. We have only observed it in a state of nature in three instances in the oak forests of South Carolina; it ran up the tall trees with great agility, and on one occasion concealed itself in a hole (which apparently contained its nest,) at least thirty feet from the ground. The specimen we have described, was shot from the extreme branches of an oak, in the dusk of the evening, where it was busily engaged among the acorns. It is a rare species in Carolina, but appears to be more common in Georgia, as we received from Major LE CONTE, three specimens obtained in the latter State.

Plate XCIII

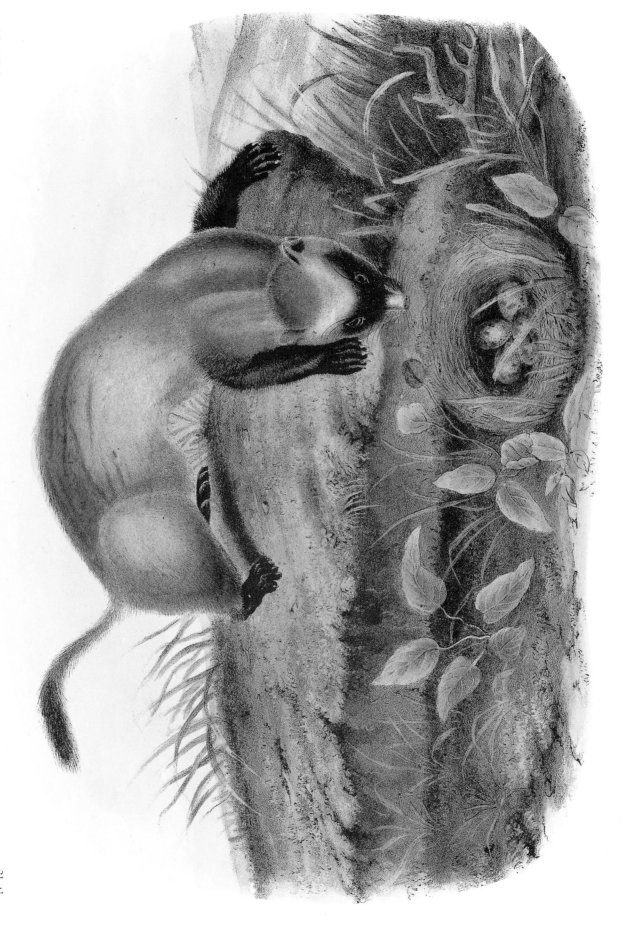

Black Footed Ferret

Geographical Distribution.

We found this species in Carolina, where it is rather rare; we also obtained specimens from Georgia; we have no doubt but further investigation will give it a more extensive geographical range.

General Remarks.

We have arranged this species under the sub-genus of Mr. WATER-HOUSE, proposed in the Zoological Society of London, Feb. 17th, 1837, (see their transactions.) It is thus characterized; "Sub-genus *Calomys*, (from Καλος beautiful and *mus*.) Fur, moderate, soft; tarsus almost entirely clothed beneath the hair. Front molar, with three indentations of enamel on the inner side, and two on the outer; and the last molar with one on each side. The type *mus* (*calomys*,) *bimaculatus*. Two other species have been described, from South America; *mus* (*calomys*) *elegans*, and *m. gracilipes*.

Felis Concolor. — Linn.

The Cougar. — Panther.

Plate xcvi. — Male: — Plate xcvii. — Female and young.

F. immaculata fulva; auriculis nigricantibus, cauda elongatâ, apice nigra neque floccosâ.

Characters.

Uniformly tawny-yellow; ears, blackish behind; tail, elongated, apex black, without a tuft.

Synonymes.

FELIS CONCOLOR, Linn. Syst. Nat., ed. Gmel., l. p. 79.
"   "   Schreb Saugth., p. 394.
"   "   Buffon, Hist. Nat., t. 9.
"   "   Gonazouara, D'Azara Anim. du Paraguay.
"   "   Desmarest in Nouv. Dict., p. 90, 2.
PUMA, Leo Americanus, Hernandez.
F. CONCOLOR, Cuv. Regne Animal, vol. 1, p. 161.
BROWN TIGER, Pennant's Syn. p. 179.
BLACK TIGER,   "   180.
F. CONCOLOR, Harlan, Fauna Am., p. 94.
"   "   Godman, vol. 1, p. 291.
"   "   Dekay's Nat. Hist. N. Y., p. 47.

Description.

Body, long and slender; head, small; neck, long; ears, rounded; legs, short and stout; tail, long, slender and cylindrical, sometimes trailing; fur, soft and short.

Colour.

Body and legs, of a uniform fulvous or tawny colour; under surface, reddish-white; around the eyes, grayish-yellow; hairs within the ears, yellowish-white; exterior of the ears, blackish; lips, at the moustache, black; throat, whitish; tail of the male, longer than that of the female, brown at tip, not tufted.

We have seen several specimens differing from the above in various shades of colour. These accidental variations, however, are not sufficient to warrant us in regarding these individuals as distinct species.

The young are beautifully spotted and barred with blackish-brown, and their hair is soft and downy.

Dimensions.

Male, shot by J. W. AUDUBON, at Castroville, Texas 28th January, 1846.

	Feet.	Inches.
From point of nose to root of tail	5	1
Tail	3	1
Height of ear posteriorly		3
Length of canine teeth, from gums		$1\frac{3}{4}$

Female, killed 26th January, 1846.

	Feet.	Inches.
Length of head and body	4	11
" Tail	2	8
" Height of ear		3
" of canine teeth		$1\frac{1}{2}$

Weight, 149 lbs.

Habits.

The Cougar is known all over the United States by the name of the panther or painter, and is another example of that ignorance or want of imagination, which was manifested by the "Colonists," who named nearly every quadruped, bird, and fish, which they found on our continent, after species belonging to the Old World, without regard to more than a most slight resemblance, and generally with a total disregard of propriety. This character of the "Colonists," is, we are sorry to say, kept up to a great extent by their descendants, to the present day, who in designating towns and villages throughout the land, have seized upon the names of Rome, Carthage, Palmyra, Cairo, Athens, Sparta, Troy, Babylon, Jericho, and many other ancient cities, as well as those of Boston, Portsmouth, Plymouth, Bristol, Paris, Manchester, Berlin, Geneva, Portland, &c., &c., from which probably some of the founders of our country towns may have emigrated. We sincerely hope this system of nomenclature will henceforth be discarded; and now let us go back to the Cougar, which is but little more like the true *panther* than an opossum is like the kangaroo! Before, however, entirely quitting this subject, we may mention that for a long time the Cougar was thought to be the lion; the supposition was that all the skins of the animal that were brought into the settlements by the Indians were skins of females; and the lioness, having something the same colour and but little mane, it occurred to the colonists that the skins they saw could belong to no other animal!

The Cougar is found sparsely distributed over the whole of North America up to about latitude 45°. In former times this animal was more abundant than at present, and one was even seen a few miles from the city of New-York within the recollection of Dr. DEKAY, who speaks of the consternation occasioned by its appearance in Westchester County, when he was a boy.

The Cougar is generally found in the very wildest parts of the country, in deep wooded swamps, or among the mountain cliffs and chasms of the Alleghany range. In Florida he inhabits the miry swamps and the watery everglades; in Texas, he is sometimes found on the open prairies, and his tracks may be seen at almost every cattle-crossing place on the sluggish bayous and creeks with their quick-sands and treacherous banks. At such places the Cougar sometimes finds an unfortunate calf, or perhaps a cow or bullock, that has become fast in the oozy, boggy earth, and from exhaustion has given up its strugglings, and been drowned or suffocated in the mire.

This species at times attacks young cattle, and the male from which our drawing was made, was shot in the act of feeding upon a black heifer which he had seized, killed, and dragged into the edge of a thicket close adjoining the spot. The Cougar, is however, generally compelled to subsist on small animals, young deer, skunks, raccoons, &c., or birds, and will even eat carrion when hard pressed by hunger. His courage is not great, and unless very hungry, or when wounded and at bay, he seldom attacks man.

J. W. AUDUBON was informed, when in Texas, that the Cougar would remain in the vicinity of the carcase of a dead horse or cow, retiring after gorging himself, to a patch of tall grasses, or brambles, close by, so as to keep off intruders, and from which lair he could return when his appetite again called him to his dainty food. In other cases he returns, after catching a pig or calf, or finding a dead animal large enough to satisfy his hungry stomach, to his accustomed haunts, frequently to the very place where he was whelped and suckled.

Dr. DEKAY mentions, that he was told of a Cougar in Warren County, in the State of New-York, that resorted to a barn, from whence he was repeatedly dislodged, and finally killed. "He shewed no fight whatever. His mouth was found to be filled with the spines of the Canada porcupine, which was probably the cause of his diminished wariness and ferocity, and would in all probability have finally caused his death."

The panther, or "painter," as the Cougar is called, is a noctural animal more by choice than necessity, as it can see well during the day time. It steals upon its intended prey in the darkness of night, with a silent, cautious step, and with great patience makes its noiseless way through the tangled thickets of the

Plate XCIV.

No.19.

On Stone by W.E. Hitchcock.

Lith Printed & Col.d by J.T. Bowen Phil.a

Drawn from Nature by J.W. Audubon.

Nuttall's Hare.

deepest forest. When the benighted traveller, or the wearied hunter may be slumbering in his rudely and hastily constructed bivouac at the foot of a huge tree, amid the lonely forest, his fire nearly out, and all around most dismal, dreary, and obscure, he may perchance be roused to a state of terror by the stealthy tread of the prowling Cougar; or his frightened horse, by its snortings and struggles to get loose, will awaken him in time to see the glistening eyes of the dangerous beast glaring upon him like two burning coals. Lucky is he then, if his coolness does not desert him, if his trusty rifle does not miss, through his agitation, or snap for want of better flint; or well off is he, if he can frighten away the savage beast by hurling at him a blazing brand from his nearly extinguished camp-fire. For, be sure the animal has not approached him without the gnawing hunger—the desire for blood, engendered by long fasting and gaunt famine. Some very rare but not well authenticated instances have been recorded in our public prints, where the Cougar at such times has sprang upon the sleeper. At other times the horses are thrown into such a fright, that they break all fastenings and fly in every direction. The late Mr. ROBERT BEST of Cincinnati, wrote to Dr. GODMAN, that one of these animals had surprised a party of travellers, sprung upon the horses, and so lacerated with its claws and teeth their flanks and buttocks, that they with the greatest difficulty succeeded in driving the poor creatures before them next morning, to a public house some miles off. This party, however, had no fire, and were unarmed.

A planter on the Yazoo river, some years ago, related the following anecdote of the Cougar to us. As he was riding home alone one night, through the woods, along what is called a "bridle-path" (i.e. a horse-track), one of these animals sprang at him from a fallen log, but owing to his horse making a sudden plunge forward, only struck the rump of the gallant steed with one paw, and could not maintain his hold. The gentleman was for a moment unable to account for the furious start his horse had made, but presently turning his head saw the Cougar behind, and putting spurs to his horse, galloped away. On examining the horse, wounds were observed on his rump corresponding with the claws of the Cougar's paw, and from their distance apart, the foot must have been spread widely when he struck the animal.

Another respectable gentleman of the State of Mississipi gave us the following account. A friend of his, a cotton planter, one evening, while at tea, was startled by a tremendous outcry among his dogs, and ran out to quiet them, thinking some person, perhaps a neighbour, had called to see him. The dogs could not be driven back, but rushed into the house; he seized his horsewhip, which hung inside the hall door, and whipped them all out, as he thought, except one, which ran under the table. He then took a candle and looking down, to his surprise and alarm discovered the supposed refractory dog to be a Cougar. He retreated instanter, the females and children of his family fled frightened half out of their senses. The Cougar sprang at him, he parried the blow with the candlestick, but the animal flew at him again, leaping forward perpendicularly, striking at his face with the fore-feet, and at his body with the hind-feet. These attacks he repelled by dealing the Cougar straight-forward blows on its belly with his fist, lightly turning aside and evading its claws, as he best could. The Cougar had nearly overpowered him, when luckily he backed toward the fire-place, and as the animal sprang again at him, dodged him, and the panther almost fell into the fire; at which he was so terrified that he endeavoured to escape, and darting out of the door was immediately attacked again by the dogs, and with their help and a club was killed.

Two raftsmen on the Yazoo river, one night encamped on the bank, under a small tent they carried with them, just large enough to cover two. They had a merry supper, and having made a large fire, retired, "turned in" and were soon fast asleep. The night waned, and by degrees a drizzling rain succeeded by a heavy shower pattering on the leaves and on their canvas roof, which sheltered them from its fury, half awakened one of them, when on a sudden the savage growl of a Cougar was heard, and in an instant the animal pounced upon the tent and overthrew it. Our raftsmen did not feel the full force of the blow, as the slight poles of the tent gave way, and the impetus of the spring carried the Panther over them; they started up and scuffled out of the tent without further notice "to quit," and by the dim light of their fire, which the rain had nearly extinguished, saw the animal facing them and ready for another leap; they hastily seized two of the burning sticks, and whirling them around their heads with loud whoops, scared away the midnight prowler. After this adventure they did not, however, try to sleep under their tent any more that night!

We have given these relations of others to show that at long intervals, and under peculiar circumstances, when perhaps pinched with hunger, or in defence of its young, the Cougar sometimes attacks men. These instances, however, are very rare, and the relations of an affrighted traveller must be received with some caution, making a due allowance for a natural disposition in man to indulge in the marvellous.

Our own experience in regard to the habits of this species is somewhat limited, but we are obliged to state that in the only three instances in which we observed it in its native forests, an impression was left on our minds that it was the most cowardly of any species of its size belonging to this genus. In our boyhood, whilst residing in the northern part of New-York, forty-eight years ago, on our way to school through a wood, a Cougar crossed the path not ten yards in front of us. We had never before seen this species, and it was, even at that early period, exceedingly rare in that vicinity. When the Cougar observed us he commenced a hurried retreat; a small terrier that accompanied us gave chase to the animal, which, after running about a hundred yards, mounted an oak and rested on one of its limbs about twenty feet from the ground. We approached and raised a loud whoop, when he sprang to the earth and soon made his escape. He was, a few days afterwards, hunted by the neighbours and shot. Another was treed at night, by a party on a raccoon hunt; supposing it to be a raccoon, one of the men climbed the tree, when the Cougar leaped to the ground, overturning one of the young hunters that happened to be in his way, and made his escape. A third was chased by cur-dogs in a valley in the vicinity of the Catskill mountains, and after half an hour's chase ascended a beech-tree. He placed himself in a crotch, and was fired at with duck-shot about a dozen times, when he was finally killed, and fell heavily to the ground. A Mr. RANDOLPH, of Virginia, related to us an amusing anecdote of a rencontre which he and a Kentuckian had in a valley of one of the Virginia mountains with a Cougar. This occurrence took place about thirty years ago. They had no guns, but meeting him near the road, they gave chase with their horses, and after a run of a few hundred yards he ascended a tree. RANDOLPH climbed the tree, and the Cougar sprang down, avoiding the Kentuckian, who stood ready to attack him with his club. The latter again followed, on his horse, when he treed him a second time. RANDOLPH again climbed after him, but found the animal was coming down, and disposed to fight his way to the ground. He stunned him with a blow, when the Cougar let go his hold, fell to the earth, and was killed by his comrade, who was waiting with his club below.

From all the conversations we have had with hunters who were in the habit of killing the Cougar, we have been brought to the conviction that a man of moderate courage, with a good rifle and a steady arm, accompanied by three or four active dogs, a mixture of either the fox-hound or grey-hound, might hunt the Cougar with great safety to himself, and with a tolerable prospect of success.

This animal, which has excited so much terror in the minds of the ignorant and timid, has been nearly exterminated in all our Atlantic States, and we do not recollect a single well authenticated instance where any hunter's life fell a sacrifice in a Cougar hunt.

Among the mountains of the head-waters of the Juniatta river, as we were informed, the Cougar is so abundant, that one man has killed for some years, from two to five, and one very hard winter, he killed seven. In this part of the country the Cougar is hunted with half-bred hounds, the full-blooded dogs lacking courage to attack so large and fierce looking an animal when they overtake it. The hunt is conducted much in the manner of a chase after the common wild-cat. The Cougar is "treed" after running about fifteen or twenty minutes, and generally shot, but sometimes it shews fight before it takes to a tree, and the hunters consider it great sport: we heard of an instance of one of these fights, in which the Cougar got hold of a dog, and was killing it, when the hunter in his anxiety to save his dog, rushed upon the Cougar, seized him by the tail and broke his back with a single blow of an axe.

According to the relations of old hunters, the Cougar has three or four young at a litter. We have heard of an instance of one being found, a very old female, in whose den there were five young, about as large as cats, we believe, however, that the usual number of young, is two.

The dens of this species are generally near the mouth of some cave in the rocks, where the animal's lair is just far enough inside to be out of the rain; and not in this respect like the dens of the bear, which are sometimes ten or twelve yards from the opening of a large crack or fissure in the rocks. In the Southern States, where there are no caves or rocks, the lair of the Cougar is generally in a very dense thicket, or in a cane-brake. It is a rude sort of bed of sticks, weeds, leaves, and grasses or mosses, and where the canes arch over it; as they are evergreen, their long pointed leaves turn the rain at all seasons of the year. We have never observed any bones or fragments of animals they had fed upon, at the lairs of the Cougar, and suppose they always feed on what they catch near the spot where they capture the prey.

The tales related of the cry of the Cougar in the forest in imitation of the call of a lost traveller, or the cry of a child, must be received with much caution, and may in many of their exaggerations be set down as vulgar errors. In a state of captivity, we have never heard the male uttering any other note than a low growl; the female, however, we have frequently heard uttering a kind of

Plate XCV.

Nº 19.

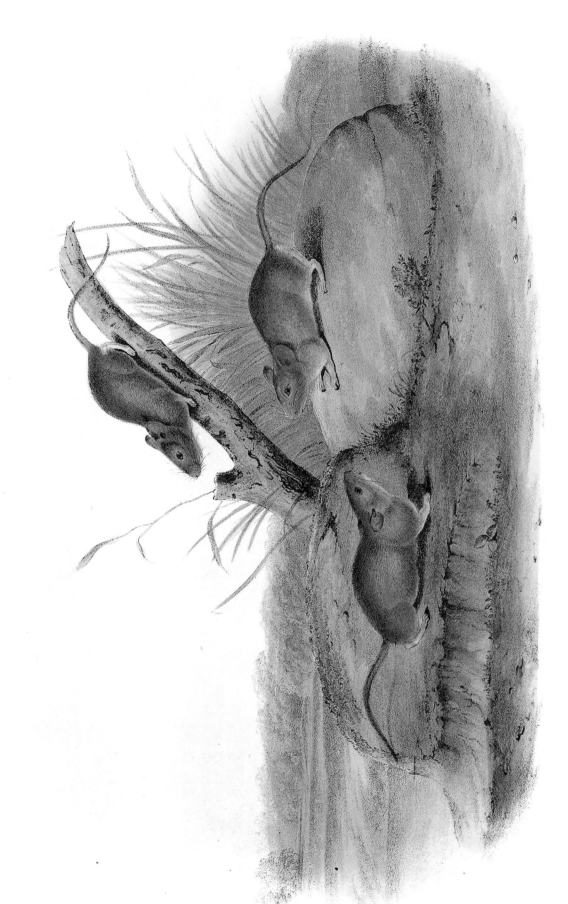

Drawn from Nature by J.W. Audubon

On Stone by Wᵐ E Hitchcock

Lith. Printed & Cold by J T Bowen Phila.

Orange Colored Mouse

mewing like that of a cat, but a more prolonged and louder note, that could be heard at the distance of about two hundred yards. All the males, however, of the cat kind, at the season when the sexes seek each other, emit remarkable and startling cries, as is evidenced by the common cat, in what is denominated caterwauling. We have observed the same habit in the leopard, the ocelot, and in our two species of lynx. It is not impossible, therefore, that the male Cougar, may at the rutting season have some peculiar and startling notes. The cries, however, to which persons have from time to time directed our attention, as belonging to the Cougar, we were well convinced were uttered by other animals. In one instance, we ascertained them to proceed from a red fox which was killed in the hunt, got up for the purpose of killing the Cougar. In other cases the screams of the great horned, the barred, or the screech owl are mistaken for the cries of this animal.

The female Cougar is a most affectionate mother, and will not leave her young cubs, unless occasionally to procure food to support her own strength; she therefore often becomes very lean and poor. The female we have figured, was in this condition; we procured one of her cubs and figured it, presenting its beautiful spots, seldom before noticed. The other made its escape.

The whelps are suckled by the dam until about half grown, and then hunt with the old ones (which generally go in pairs) until the mother is with young again, or the young ones find mates for themselves, and begin to breed.

The period of gestation of the Cougar is ninety-seven days, as has been ascertained at the Zoological Society of London, (Proceedings, 1832, p. 62.) In the Northern and Middle States, the young are produced in the spring. In the Southern States, however, where the animal is supplied with an abundance of food, and not much incommoded by the cold, the young have in some instances been discovered in autumn. J. W. AUDUBON found, in Texas, young Cougars nearly half grown in February.

Geographical Distribution.

This species has a wide geographical range. It was formerly found in all the Northern and Eastern States, and we have seen a specimen procured in Upper Canada. The climates of Lower Canada, New Foundland, and Labrador, appear to be too cold for its permanent residence. In all the Atlantic States it was formerly found, and a few still exist in the less cultivated portions. It is occasionally shot in the extensive swamps, along the river courses of Carolina, Georgia, Mississipi, and Louisiana; it is found sparingly on the whole range of the Alleghanies, running through a considerable portion of the United States. It has crossed the Rocky Mountains, and exists on the Pacific, in Oregon and California; it is quite abundant in Florida and Texas; is found within the tropics in Mexico, and Yucatan, and has penetrated through Panama into Guyana and South America, where it is sometimes called the Puma.

General Remarks.

The variations of size, to which this species is subject, have created much confusion among our books of Natural History, and added a considerable number of supposed new species. After having examined very carefully very many specimens, both in a prepared state, and alive in menageries, procured in most parts of North and South America, we have arrived at the conclusion that the Cougar of North America and the Puma of our Southern Continent are one and the same species, and cannot even be regarded as varieties.

Genus Bassaris. —Lichtenstein.

Dental Formula.

Incisive $\frac{6}{6}$; *Canine* $\frac{1-1}{1-1}$; *Molar* $\frac{6-6}{6-6}$ = 40.

Body, long and rather slender; head, round; snout, attenuated like that of a fox; eyes, rather large; eyelids, oblong, lateral; ears, conspicuous, of moderate size, their points rounded.

There are five toes on each foot; tail, nearly the length of the body.

Hairs on the body, short and dense, much longer on the tail.

The specific name is derived from the Greek, Βασσαρις, (*bassaris*), a little fox.

This is the only species in the genus.

Bassaris Astuta. —Licht.

Ring-tailed Bassaris.

Plate xcviii. —Male—Natural Size.

B. Supra gilvus nigro-variegatus, auriculis, macula supra oculari et ventre flavido-albis; cauda, annulis octo albis nigrisque alternantibus, picta.

Characters.

Dull yellow, mixed with black, above; a spot above the eye, ears, and under surface, yellowish-white; tail, eight times ringed with black and white.

Synonymes.

CACAMITZTLI, Hernandez.
TEPE-MAXTLATON, Hernandez.
BASSARIS ASTUTA, Lichtenstein, Darstellung neuer, oder wenig bekannter Säugethiere, Tafel 43, Berlin, 1827–1834.

Description.

The first impression made by this animal on the observer is, that he has met with a little fox; its erect sharp nose, and cunning look, are all fox-like. It however, by its long and moveable muzzle approaches the civets, (*viverra*,) the genets, (*gennetta*,) and the coatis (*ictides.*)

The head is small; skull, not much flattened; nose, long; muzzle, pointed, naked; moustaches, numerous, long and rigid; ears, long, erect, ovate, clothed with short hair on the outer surface; sparingly within; neck and body, long; legs, longer than those of the martens, but shorter than those of the fox; nails, sharp and much hooked; toes, covered with hairs concealing them; palms, naked; tail, with long coarse hairs, containing scarcely any under fur; the inner hair on the back, is of moderate fineness, interspersed with rather coarser and longer hairs. The longer hairs on the back are about an inch in length, those on the tail, two inches, and the under-fur, on the back, half an inch.

Colour.

The hair on the back is grayish, for three-fourths of its length from the roots, then pale yellowish-white, then yellowish-brown, deepening into black at the tips; the under-fur is first plumbeous, then yellowish-white; this disposition of colours gives it a brindled brownish-black appearance on the head and upper surface. Moustaches, black; point of nose, dark brown. There is a light grayish spot above the eye; ears, chin, throat, neck and belly, yellowish-white. The tail is regularly and conspicuously ringed with bars of white and black, alternately; the upper white one very indistinct; the next black-obscure and increasing in more conspicuous bands of white and black to the end, which is broadly tipped with black; on the upper surface of tail, the black colours predominate, and on the under surface, the white.

Dimensions.

	Feet.	Inches.
From point of nose to root of tail, ...	1	6
Tail, (vertebræ), ...	1	2
" to end of hair, ...	1	4
From point of nose to head, between the ears, ...		$3\frac{1}{8}$
Height of ear, posteriorly, ...		$1\frac{3}{8}$
Breadth of ear at base, ...		1
From shoulder to end of toes, ...		6
Length of longest moustache, ...		$3\frac{1}{4}$

Habits.

The greater portion of Texas is prairie-land, and it is chiefly along the water courses, that trees are found growing together in numbers sufficient to constitute a "wood." On certain level and clayey portions of the prairie, however, the land is swampy, and is covered with several kinds of oaks and a few other trees. The well-known musquit tree or bush is found generally

Plate XCVI.

Nº 20.

Drawn on Stone by Wᵐ E. Hitchcock

Lith Printed & Colᵈ by J T Bowen, Philadᵃ

Drawn from Nature by J W Audubon.

The Cougar

Male.

distributed in the western parts of the State. it resembles the acacia in leaf, and has a small white pea-shaped blossom; at a distance it looks something like an old peach tree. Its wood is similar to coarse mahogany in appearance, and burns well, in fact beautifully, as the coals keep in for a long time; and the wood gives out little or no smoke. The musquit bottoms are furnished with these trees, they are small, about the size of the alder, and grow much in the same way; the musquit has sharp thorns. The musquit *grass*, (*Holcus lanatus*), resembles what is called, *guinea* grass, it is broader, shorter, softer, and more curly.

The general features of the States of Texas, as it will be seen by the foregoing, do not indicate a country where many tree-climbing animals could be found, and the present beautiful species, which Professor LICHTENSTEIN most appropriately named Bassaris *astuta*, is by no means common. It is a lively, playful, and nimble creature, leaps about on the trees, and has very much the same actions as the squirrel, which it resembles in agility and grace, always having a hole in the tree upon which it resides, and betaking itself to that secure retreat at once if alarmed.

The Bassaris Astuta is shy and retired in its habits, and in the daytime often stays in its hole in some tree, so that we were only able to procure about half a-dozen of these animals during our stay in Texas; among which, to our regret, there was not a single female.

The food of this species is chiefly small animals, birds, and insects; they also eat nuts, as we were told, descending from their hiding place and travelling to the pecan and other trees, for the purpose of feeding on the nuts which, if true, is singular, as they are decidedly carnivorous in their dentition.

They are much attached to the tree on which they live, which is generally a post-oak, a live-oak, or other large tree, and they seldom quit the immediate vicinity of their hole, unless when driven out by thrusting a stick at them, when they ascend the trunk of the tree, and jump about among the higher branches so long as the pole is held close to their nest; as soon as this is withdrawn, they descend and at once re-enter their dwelling-place and hide themselves. These animals have a singular habit of eating or gnawing off the bark around the mouth of their holes, and where the bark does not appear freshly peeled off at their hole, you may be certain the animal is not at home, or has deserted the place. Their holes are generally the result of natural decay, and are situated on knobs, or at the ends of branches broken short off close to the main trunk.

They generally select a hole of this kind on the lower side of a leaning tree, probably for better protection from the rain; their holes vary in depth, but are seldom more than about a foot or eighteen inches to the bottom; they are usually furnished with moss or grass, for bedding. Sometimes pecan shells are found in these holes, which no doubt affords presumptive evidence that the Bassaris feeds upon this nut.

When scolding or barking at an intruder, the ring-tailed Raccoon, (as this animal is called by the Texans), holds the tail over its back, bending it squirrel fashion; this animal, however, does not stand upon his hind feet like a squirrel, and cannot jump or leap so far. We have not heard of their springing from one branch to another beyond the distance of about ten feet, and when frightened at the presence of a man, they will sometimes run along a branch even toward him, in order to get within jumping distance of another, evincing more timidity than a squirrel exhibits in springing among the boughs, although they run up the bark with ease, holding on with their claws.

Sometimes the Ring-tailed Bassaris may be seen squatted on the top of a branch, basking in the sun, and half rolled up, appearing almost asleep. On the slightest manifestation of danger, however, he darts into his hole, (which is always within a foot or two of his basking place), and he is seen no more. We have the impression that only one of these singular animals is to be found on a tree at a time—they, therefore, are not very social in their habits, and, as the live-oak and other trees are generally very much scattered, and many of them have no holes suitable for residences for the Bassaris, it is very difficult to procure one. At the foot of many of the trees whereon they dwell, the cactus, brush-wood, and chapperal generally are so thick and tangled, that a man would be pretty well scratched should he attempt to penetrate the thorny, prickly thicket which surrounds the dwelling-place of this solitary and singular animal.

Notwithstanding the shyness and retired habits of this species, it is easily tamed, and when it has been confined in a cage a sufficient length of time, is frequently let loose in the houses of the Mexicans, where it answers the purpose of a playful pet, and catches mice and rats. We have seen one that was thus domesticated, running about the streets of a little Mexican village, and we were informed that one was kept as a great pet in a Camanche camp, visited by the Indian who hunted for us during our explorations of the western part of Texas. As far as we could ascertain, the northern limit of the range of this species is somewhere in the neighbourhood of the southern branches of Red river. As you travel south they are more abundant, and probably are found throughout all Mexico; we were informed by our friend, the celebrated Col. HAYS, the Ranger, that he saw them more abundant in the mountainous region near the head-waters of the San Saba river than at any other place.

The Bassaris produces three or four young at a birth, as has been ascertained from the animal kept in confinement.

Geographical Distribution.

This animal exists in Mexico, and is common in the immediate vicinity of the capital of that name; our specimens were obtained in Texas, which appears to be its northern limit.

General Remarks.

This species is called by the Mexicans caco-mixtle. It is mentioned no less than four times by HERNANDEZ under the names of Cacamiztli and Tepe-Maxtlaton. The first specimens were sent to Berlin in 1826, by Mr. DEPPE, and the earliest scientific description was given by LICHTENSTEIN, who named it as above.

Spermophilus Ludovicianus. —Ord.

Prairie Marmot-Squirrel.—Wishtonwish.—Prairie Dog.

Plate xcix.—1. Male.   2. Female.   3. Young.—Natural Size.

S. super cervinus pilis nigris interspersis; subtus sordide albus, ungue pollicari conico majusculu, caudâ brevi apicem versus fusco torquatâ.

Characters.

Back, reddish brown, mixed with grey and black; belly, soiled white; tail, short, banded with brown near the tip; thumb-nail, rather large, and conical.

Synonymes.

PRAIRIE DOG, Lewis and Clark's Exp., 1st vol., p. 67.
WISHTONWISH, Pike's Expedition, &c., p. 156.
ARCTOMYS LUDOVICIANUS, Ord, in Guthrie, Geog., 2d, 302, 1815.
ARCTOMYS MISSOURIENSIS, Warden, Descr. des Etats Unis, vol. 5., p. 567.
ARCTOMYS LUDOVICIANUS, Say, Long's Exped., 1st vol., p. 451.
ARCT. LUDOVICIANUS, Harlan, p. 160.
      "   "   Godman, vol. 2, p. 114.

Description.

This animal in its external form has more the appearance of a marmot, than of a spermophile. It is short, thick, and clumsy, and is not possessed of the light, squirrel-like shape, which characterizes the *spermophili*. In its small cheek-pouches, however, being three-fourths of an inch in depth, and in the structure of its teeth, it approaches nearer the *spermophili*, and we have accordingly arranged it under that genus.

The head is broad and depressed; nose short and blunt, hairy to the nostrils. Incisors, large, protruding beyond the lips; eyes, large; ears, placed far backwards, short, and oblong, being a mere flap nearly covered by the short fur; neck, short and thick; legs, short and stout. This species is pendactylous; the rudimental thumb on the fore-feet protected by a sharp, conical nail; nails, of medium size, scarcely channelled beneath, nearly straight, and sharp, extending beyond the hair; tail, short and bushy; hair on the body, rather coarse; under-fur, of moderate fineness. The female has ten mammæ arranged along the sides of the belly.

Colour.

The hair on the back is, from the roots, for one-third of its length, bluish-black, then soiled-white—then light-brown; some of the hairs having yellowish-white, and others black, tips. The hairs on the under-surface, are at the roots bluish, and for nearly their whole length yellowish-white, giving the

Plate XCVII.

Drawn from Nature by J.W. Audubon.

Drawn on Stone by W.E. Hitchcock.

The Cougar.

Lith Printed & col.ᵈ by J.T. Bowen, Phil.

sides of face, cheeks, chin, and throat, legs, belly, and undersurface of tail a yellowish-white colour. Teeth, white; moustaches and eyes, black; nails, brown. The tail partakes of the colour of the back for three-fourths of its length, but is tipped with black, extending one inch from the end.

Dimensions.

	MALE.		FEMALE.	
Nose to root of tail, ...	13	inches.	$12\frac{5}{8}$	inches.
" to end of tail, ...	$16\frac{3}{4}$	do	$15\frac{3}{4}$	do
Tail, vertebræ, ...	$2\frac{5}{8}$	do	$2\frac{1}{4}$	do
" to end of hair, ...	$3\frac{1}{8}$	do		
Nose to anterior canthus, ...	$1\frac{1}{4}$	do	$1\frac{1}{8}$	do
Height of ear, ...	$\frac{7}{16}$	do	$\frac{7}{16}$	do
Width between eyes, ...	$1\frac{1}{2}$	do	$1\frac{5}{16}$	do
Length of fore-hand, ...	$1\frac{5}{16}$	do	$1\frac{1}{4}$	do
" of heel and hind-foot	$2\frac{1}{8}$	do	2	do
Depth of pouch, ...	$\frac{3}{5}$	do		
Diameter of ditto, ...	$\frac{5}{8}$	do		

Feet slightly webbed at base.

Habits.

The general impression of those persons who have never seen the "Prairie Dog" called by the French Canadians "*petit chien*," would be far from correct in respect to this little animal, should they incline to consider it as a small "dog." It was probably only owing to the sort of yelp, chip, chip, chip, uttered by these marmots, that they were called Prairie *Dogs*, for they do not resemble the genus *Canis* much more than does a common gray squirrel!

This noisy *spermophile*, or marmot, is found in numbers, sometimes hundreds of families together, living in burrows on the prairies; and their galleries are so extensive as to render riding among them quite unsafe in many places. Their habitations are generally called "dog-towns," or villages, by the Indians and trappers, and are described as being intersected by streets (pathways) for their accommodation, and a degree of neatness and cleanliness is preserved. These villages, or communities, are, however, sometimes infested with rattle-snakes and other reptiles, which feed upon the marmots. The burrowing owl, (*Surnia cunicularia,*) is also found among them, and probably devours a great number of the defenceless animals.

The first of these villages observed by our party, when we were ascending the Missouri river in 1843, was near the "Great bend" of that stream. The mounds were very low, the holes mostly open, and but few of the animals to be seen.

Our friend EDWARD HARRIS, Mr. BELL and MICHAUX, shot at them, but we could not procure any, and were obliged to proceed, being somewhat anxious to pitch our camp for the night, before dark. Near Fort George, (a little farther up the river,) we again found a village of these marmots, and saw great numbers of them. They do not *bark*, but utter a chip, chip, chip, loud and shrill enough, and at each cry jerk their tail, not erecting it, however, to a perpendicular.

Their holes are not straight down, but incline downwards, at an angle of about forty degrees for a little distance and then diverge sideways or upwards. We shot at two of these marmots which were not standing across their holes apparently, but in front of them, the first one we never saw after the shot; the second we found dying at the entrance of the burrow, but at our approach it worked itself backward—we drew our ramrod and put the screw in its mouth, it bit sharply at this, but notwithstanding our screwing, it kept working backward, and was soon out of sight at beyond the reach of our ramrod.

Mr. BELL saw two enter the same hole, and Mr. HARRIS observed three. Occasionally these marmots stood quite erect, and watched our movements, and then leaped into the air, all the time keeping an eye on us. We found that by lying down within twenty or thirty steps of their holes, and remaining silent, the animals re-appeared in fifteen or twenty minutes. Now and then one of them, after coming out of its hole, issued a long and somewhat whistling note, perhaps a call, or invitation to his neighbours, as several came out in a few moments. The cries of this species are probably uttered for their amusement, or as a means of recognition, and not, especially, at the appearance of danger. They are, as we think, more in the habit of feeding by night than in the day time; their droppings are scattered plentifully in the neighbourhood of their villages.

A few days after this visit to the Prairie Dogs, one of our hunters, who had been out a great part of the night, brought in three of them, but they had been killed with very coarse shot, and were so badly cut and torn by the charge, that they were of little use to us. We ascertained that these marmots are abundant

in this part of the country, their villages being found in almost every direction.

From the number of teats in the female, the species is no doubt very prolific.

On our return down the river, we killed two Prairie Dogs on the 23d of August, their notes resembled the noise made by the Arkansas flycatcher precisely.

We have received an interesting letter from Col. ABERT of the Topographical bureau at Washington City, giving us an account of the quadrupeds and birds observed by Lieut. ABERT, on an exploratory journey in the south-west, in New Mexico, &c. Lieut. ABERT observed the Prairie Dogs in that region of country, in the middle of winter; he says "our Prairie Dog (a marmot) does not hibernate, but is out all winter, as lively and as pert as on any summer day."

This is not in accordance with the accounts of authors, who have it that this animal does hibernate. We find it stated that it "closes accurately the mouth of the burrow, and constructs at the bottom of it a neat globular cell of fine dry grass, having an aperture at top sufficiently large to admit a finger, and so compactly put together that it might almost be rolled along the ground uninjured." We feel greatly obliged to Lieut. ABERT, for the information he gives us, which either explodes a long received error, or acquaints us with a fact of some importance in natural history—that changes of climate will produce so great an effect as to abrogate a provision of nature, bestowed upon some animals, to enable them to exist during the rigorous winters of the north; so that, by migrating to a warmer region, species that would, in high latitudes be compelled to sleep out half their lives, could enjoy the air and light, and luxuriate in the sense of "being alive" all the circling year! We have not been able to gather any information in relation to this subject since receiving the above-mentioned letter, but in our article on *Arctomys monax*, (vol. i., p. 20) some curious facts were related in respect to the effect of artificial heat, applied from time to time to that animal, when in a torpid state, which produced each time a temporary animation; thus shewing that a certain absence of caloric causes hibernation immediately, while its presence arouses the powers of life in a few minutes. The special construction of hibernating animals is not (as far as we have ascertained) yet explained by the researches of comparative anatomy.

Lewis and Clark give a very good description of the Prairie Dog, at page 67, vol. 1. They poured five barrels of water into one of their holes without filling it, but dislodged and caught the owner. They further say that after digging down another of the holes for six feet, they found on running a pole into it that they had not yet dug half-way to the bottom; they discovered two frogs in the hole, and near it killed a dark rattlesnake, which had swallowed one of the Prairie Dogs.

Our friend Dr., now Sir JOHN RICHARDSON, (in the Fauna Boreali Americana,) has well elucidated the notices of this and other species described in LEWIS and CLARK's "Expedition," but, appears not to be certain whether this animal has cheek-pouches or not, and is puzzled apparently by the following: "the jaw is furnished with a *pouch* to contain his food, but not so large as that of the common squirrel." The Dr. in a note says—"It is not easy to divine what the "common squirrel is which has ample cheek-pouches." We presume that this passage can be made plain by inserting the word *ground* so that "common *ground*-squirrel" be the reading. The "common ground-squirrel" was doubtless well known to LEWIS and CLARK, and has ample cheek-pouches (see our account of *Tamias Lysterii*, vol. 1, p. 65.) This explanation would not be volunteered by us but for our respect for the knowledge and accuracy of LEWIS and CLARK, both of whom we had the pleasure of personally knowing many years ago.

For an amusing account of a large village of these marmots, we extract the following from KENDALL's Narrative of the Texan Santa Fé Expedition, vol. 1, p. 189. "We had proceeded but a short distance, after reaching this beautiful prairie, before we came upon the outskirts of the commonwealth, a few scattering dogs were seen scampering in, their short, sharp yelps giving a general alarm to the whole community. The first brief cry of danger from the outskirts was soon taken up in the centre of the city, and now nothing was to be heard or seen in any direction but a barking, dashing, and scampering of the mercurial and excitable denizens of the place, each to his burrow.

Far as the eye could reach the city extended, and all over it the scene was the same. We rode leisurely along until we had reached the more thickly settled portion of the place. Here we halted, and after taking the bridles from our horses to allow them to graze, we prepared for a regular attack upon the inhabitants. The burrows were not more than ten or fifteen yards apart, with well trodden paths leading in different directions, and I even fancied I could discover something like regularity in the laying out of the streets.

We sat down upon a bank under the shade of a musquit, and leisurely

On Stone by Wⁿ E. Hitchcock

Ring Tailed Bassaris

Drawn from Nature by J.W. Audubon   Lith. Printed & Colᵈ J.T. Bowen Philᵃ

surveyed the scene before us. Our approach had driven every one to his home in our immediate vicinity, but at the distance of some hundred yards the small mound of earth in front of each burrow was occupied by a Dog, sitting erect on his hinder legs, and coolly looking about for the cause of the recent commotion. Every now and then some citizen, more adventurous than his neighbour, would leave his lodgings on a flying visit to a friend, apparently exchange a few words, and then scamper back as fast as his legs would carry him.

By-and-by, as we kept perfectly still, some of our near neighbours were seen cautiously poking their heads from out their holes, and looking craftily, and, at the same time, inquisitively about them. Gradually a citizen would emerge from the entrance of his domicil, come out upon his observatory, perk his head cunningly, and then commence yelping somewhat after the manner of a young puppy—a quick jerk of the tail accompanying each yelp. It is this short bark alone that has given them the name of Dogs, as they bear no more resemblance to that animal, either in appearance, action, or manner of living, than they do to the hyena.

We were armed, one with a double-barrelled shot-gun, and another with one of Colt's repeating-rifles of small bore, while I had my short heavy rifle, throwing a large ball, and acknowledged by all to be the best weapon in the command. It would drive a ball completely through a buffalo at the distance of a hundred and fifty-yards, and there was no jumping off or running away by a deer when struck in the right place; to use a common expression, "he would never know what had hurt him." Hit one of the Dogs where we would, with a small ball, he would almost invariably turn a peculiar somerset, and get into his hole, but by a ball, from my rifle, the entire head of the animal would be knocked off, and after this, there was no escape. With the shot-gun again, we could do nothing but waste ammunition. I fired it at one Dog not ten steps off, having in a good charge of buckshot, and thought I must cut him into fragments. I wounded him severely, but with perhaps three or four shot through him, he was still able to wriggle and tumble into his hole.

For three hours we remained in this commonwealth, watching the movements of the inhabitants and occasionally picking off one of the more unwary. No less than nine were got by the party; and one circumstance I would mention as singular in the extreme, and shewing the social relationship which exists among these animals, as well as the kind regard they have for one another. One of them had perched himself upon the pile of earth in front of his hole, sitting up and exposing a fair mark, while a companion's head was seen poking out of the entrance, too timid, perhaps, to trust himself farther. A well-directed ball from my rifle carried away the entire top of the former's head, and knocked him some two or three feet from his post perfectly dead. While reloading, the other boldly came out, seized his companion by one of his legs, and before we could reach the hole had drawn him completely out of sight. There was a touch of feeling in the little incident, a something human, which raised the animals in my estimation, and ever after I did not attempt to kill one of them, except when driven by extreme hunger."

Mr. KENDALL says, further on, of these animals:—"They are a wild, frolicsome, madcap set of fellows when undisturbed, uneasy and ever on the move, and appear to take especial delight in chattering away the time, and visiting from hole to hole to gossip and talk over each other's affairs—at least, so their actions would indicate. When they find a good location for a village, and there is no water in the immediate vicinity, old hunters say, they dig a well to supply the wants of the community. On several occasions I crept close to their villages, without being observed, to watch their movements. Directly in the centre of one of them I particularly noticed a very large Dog, sitting in front of the door or entrance to his burrow, and by his own actions and those of his neighbours, it really seemed as though he was the president, mayor, or

chief—at all events, he was the "big dog" of the place. For at least an hour I secretly watched the operations in this community. During that time the large Dog I have mentioned received at least a dozen visits from his fellow-dogs, which would stop and chat with him a few moments, and then run off to their domicils. All this while he never left his post for a moment, and I thought I could discover a gravity in his deportment not discernible in those by which he was surrounded. Far is it from me to say, that the visits he received were upon business, or had anything to do with the local government of the village; but it certainly appeared so. If any animal has a system of laws regulating the body politic, it is certainly the Prairie Dog."

This marmot tumbles, or rolls over, when he enters his hole, "with an eccentric bound and half-somerset, his hind-feet knocking together as he pitches headlong into the darkness below; and before the spectator has recovered from the half-laugh caused by the drollery of the movement, he will see the Dog slowly thrust his head from his burrow, and with a pert and impudent expression of countenance, peer cunningly about, as if to ascertain the effect his recent antic had caused."

Mr. KENDALL thinks that the burrowing owl, which he mentions as "a singular species of owl, invariably found residing in and about the dog towns," is on the best of terms with these marmots, and says, "as he is frequently seen entering and emerging from the same hole, this singular bird may be looked upon as a member of the same family, or at least, as a retainer whose services are in some way necessary to the comfort and well-being of the animal whose hospitality he shares." This idea is doubtless incorrect, and we would almost hazard the assertion that these owls prey upon the young, or even the adults, of these marmots; they also, probably, devour the bodies of those which die in their holes, and thus may stand toward the animals in the light of sexton and undertaker! Mr. KENDALL is entirely correct in what he says about the rattle-snakes, which dwell in the same lodges with the Dogs. "The snakes I look upon as loafers, not easily shaken off by the regular inhabitants, and they make use of the dwellings of the Dogs as more comfortable quarters than they can find elsewhere. We killed one a short distance from a burrow, which had made a meal of a half-grown Dog; and although I do not think they can master the larger animals, the latter are still compelled to let them pass in and out without molestation—a nuisance, like many in more elevated society, that cannot be got rid of."

Mr. KENDALL and his companions found the meat of this species "exceedingly sweet, tender, and juicy—resembling that of the squirrel, only that it was much fatter."

None of these animals were seen by J. W. AUDUBON in his journey through that part of Texas lying between Galveston and San Antonio, and he only heard of one village, to the northward and westward of Torrey's Lodge; they do not approach the coast apparently, being found only on the prairies beyond, or to the westward of the wooded portions of that State. A collector of animals and birds, who has passed the last three years in various parts of Mexico, and who showed us his whole collection, had none of these marmots, and we suppose their range does not extend as far south as the middle portions of that country.

Geographical Distribution.

This species is found on the banks of the Missouri and its tributaries. It also exists near the Platte river in great abundance. It was seen by J. W. AUDUBON in limited numbers in Sonora and on the sandy hills adjoining the Tulare Valley, and in other parts of California. We do not know whether it is an inhabitant of Oregon or not.

Plate XCIX

No20.

Drawn from Nature by J. Audubon, FRSF. S   On Stone by Wm E Hitchcock   Lith. Printed & Col.d by J T Bowen, Phil.

Prairie Dog — Prairie Marmot Squirrel.

Mus Missouriensis.—Aud. and Bach.

Missouri Mouse.

Plate C.—Females.—Natural Size.

M. capite amplo, cruribus robustis, auriculis sub albidis, cauda curta, corpore supra dilute fusca, infra alba.

Characters.

Head, broad; legs, stout; ears, whitish; tail, short, light fawn colour above, white beneath.

Synonyme.

MUS MISSOURIENSIS, Aud. and Bach., Quads. North America, vol. 2, plates, pl. 100.

Description.

At first sight we might be tempted to regard this animal, as one of the endless varieties of the white-footed mouse. It is, however, a very different species, and when examined in detail, it will be discovered that the colour is the only point of resemblance. The body is stouter, shorter, and has a more clumsy appearance. The nose is less pointed; ears, much shorter and more rounded; and the tail, not one-third of the length.

Head, short and blunt; nose, pointed; eyes, large; ears, short, broad at base and round, sparsely clothed with short hairs on both surfaces; moustaches, numerous, long, bending forwards and upwards; legs, stout; four toes on the fore-feet, with the rudiment of a thumb, protected by a conspicuous nail; nails, rather long, slightly bent, but not hooked. The hind-feet are pendactylous; the palms are naked; the other portions of the feet and toes, covered with short hairs, which do not, however, conceal the nails. The tail is short, round, stout at base, gradually diminishing to a point; it is densely covered with very short hair; the fur on both surfaces is short, soft and fine.

Colour.

Teeth, yellowish; whiskers, nearly all white, a few black hairs interspersed. The fur on the back is plumbeous at the roots of near the points, the hairs on the sides are broadly tipped with yellowish-fawn, and on the back, are first fawn, and then slightly tipped with black; on the under surface, the hairs are at the roots plumbeous, broadly tipped with white. The ears are nearly white, having a slight tinge of buff on the outer and inner surfaces, edged with pure white; on the sides of the cheeks, and an irregular and indistinct line along the sides, the colours are brighter than those on the flanks, and may be described as light yellowish-brown. The feet, on both surfaces, belly, and under surface of tail, white; from this admixture, this species is on the back, light fawn, with an indistinct line on the back, and upper surface of tail, of a shade darker colour.

Dimensions.

	Inches.
From point of nose to root of tail, ...	$4\frac{1}{2}$
" " tail, ...	$1\frac{1}{8}$
Height of ear, posteriorly, ...	$\frac{3}{8}$

Habits.

We close our second volume with this new species of mouse, of which we have given three figures. This pretty little animal was discovered for us by Mr DENIG, during our sojourn at, and in the neighbourhood of Fort Union in 1843. It was in full summer pelage, having been killed on the 14th of July. At that time being in quest of antelopes and large animals, we did not give it that close attention, which we should have done. A glance at our plate, or an examination of our description, will suffice to convince any one of its being entirely new. This species is much larger, and has a thicker and shorter tail than *mus leucopus*.

Expecting to get more of them we did not make any notes of the habits of those killed at that time, and which had doubtless been observed by the hunters, who procured them. The next day after they were brought in, we left the fort on an expedition to the Yellow-Stone river, from which we did not return for some time.

As a short description of our mode of travelling, &c., the first day's journal is here given. "July 15, Saturday, we were all up pretty early, making preparations for our trip to the Yellow-Stone river. After breakfast the party who were going, announced themselves as ready, and with a wagon, a cart, and two extra men from the fort, we crossed the Missouri, and at 7 o'clock, were fairly under way; HARRIS, BELL, CULBERTSON, and ourself in the wagon, SQUIRES, PROVOST, and OWEN on horseback, while the cart brought a skiff, to be launched on the Yellow-Stone when we should arrive at that river. We travelled rather slowly until we had crossed a point and headed the ponds on the prairie at the foot of the hills opposite the fort. We saw one sharp-tailed grouse, but although Mr. HARRIS searched for it diligently, it could not be started. Soon after this we got one of the wheels of our wagon fast in a crack or crevice in the ground, and wrenched it so badly that we were obliged to get out and walk, while the men set to work to repair the wheels which were all in a rickety condition; after the needful fixing-up had been done, the wagon overtook us, and we proceeded on. Saw some antelopes on the prairie, and many more on the tops of the hills bounding our view to the westward. We stopped to water the horses at a "saline," where we observed that buffaloes, antelopes, and other animals had been to drink, and had been lying down on the margin. The water was too hot for us to drink. After sitting for nearly an hour to allow the horses to get cool enough to take a bait, for it was very warm, we again proceeded on until we came to the bed of a stream, which during spring overflows its banks, but now exhibits only pools of water here and there. In one of these pools we soaked our dry wagon wheels, by way of tightening the "tires," and here we refreshed ourselves and quenched our thirst. SQUIRES, PROVOST, and OWEN, started on before us to reconnoitre, and we followed at a pretty good pace, as the prairie was hereabouts firm and tolerably smooth. Shot a red-winged black-bird. Heard the notes of NUTTALL's short-billed marsh-wren,—supposed by some of our party to be those of a new bird. Saw nothing else; reached our camping-place at about 6 o'clock. Unloaded the wagon and cart, hobbled the horses, and turned them out to grass. Two or three of the men went off to a point above our camp, in search of something for supper. We took the red-winged black-bird, and a fishing-line, and went to the bank of the famed Yellow-Stone river, (near the margin of which our tent was pitched,) and in this stream of the far west, running from the bases of the Rocky Mountains, we threw our line, and exercised our piscatory skill so successfully as to catch some cat fish. These fish we found would not bite at pieces of their own kind, with which we tried them; after expending our bird bait, we therefore gave up fishing. One of our men took a bath, while two others, having launched the skiff rowed across the river to seek for deer or other game on the opposite shore. Toward dark the hunting parties all returned to camp without success; and we found the cat-fish the principal portion of our supper, having no fresh meat at all.

Our supper over, all parties shortly disposed themselves to sleep as they best could. About 10 o'clock, we were all disturbed by a violent thunder storm, accompanied by torrents of rain and vivid flashes of lightning; the wind arose and blew a gale; all of us were a-foot in a few moments; and amid some confusion, our guns, loaded with ball, and our ammunition, were placed under the best covering we could provide, our beds huddled together under the tent along with them, and some of us crawled in on top of all, while others sought shelter under the shelving bank of the river. This storm benefitted us, however, by driving before the gale the mosquitoes, to keep off which we had in vain made a large fire, before we laid ourselves down for the night."

As there is little grain of any kind grown in this part of the country, the Missouri Mouse no doubt exists on the seeds and roots of wild plants entirely, of which it is able to lay up a store for the winter in holes in the ground. It may, however, possibly resort to the patches of corn planted by the squaws of some of the Indian tribes, at the time that grain is ripe. We brought with us from this country, when we returned home, some ears of a very small corn, (maize,) which ripens early, and bears its fruit near the ground. Having planted it on our place, we found that it was advanced enough to be eaten at table as a vegetable, several weeks before the ordinary kinds of corn known about New-York. We, therefore, distributed some of the seed among our farming neighbours, and likewise sent some to England to Lord DERBY and other friends, but this was unfortunately lost. We incline to believe that this corn would ripen well in the climate of England or Scotland. Unluckily, ours has become mixed by having been planted too near common corn, and is now depreciated or reduced to nearly the same thing as the latter.

Geographical Distribution.

This species was discovered in the State of Missouri.

Plate C

N° 20

Drawn from Nature by J W Audubon

Lith Printed & Col.ᵈ by J T Bowen, Phil

Missouri Mouse

General Remarks.

The Missouri Mouse bears some resemblance to the common and very widely distributed White-footed Mouse. Its comparatively heavy and clumsy form—-its large head and short tail have induced us to regard it as a distinct species. In the mice, shrews, and bats, we have no doubt several interesting species will yet be detected in our country.

Felis Onca.—Linn.

Jaguar.

Plate Ci.—Female.

F. Supra fulva, subtus albus; corpore ocellis annularibus nigris ornato, in series subparallelis per longitudinem dispositis; ocellis, punctis nigris subcentralibus, in signitis.

Characters.

Yellow, with a white belly; body marked with open black circle-like figures, each containing one or more nearly central black dots; these black, circle-like markings disposed in nearly longitudinal parallel lines.

Synonymes.

FELIS ONCA. Linn. Syst. Natur. vol. xii. p. 61; Gmel. vol. i. p. 77, pl. 4
    (4 ed.).
"   "   Schreber, Säugth. p. 388, pl. 6.
"   "   Erxleben Syst. p. 513, pl. 9.
"   "   Zimm. Geogr. Gesch. ii. pp. 162, 268.
"   "   Cuv. Ann. du Mus. xiv. p. 144. 4 T. 16.
"   "   "   Regne Animale, vol. i. p. 260. Ossements Fossiles,
    vol. iv. p. 417.
"   "   F. Cuv. Dict. Sci. Nat., vol. viii. p. 223.
"   "   Desm. in Nouv. Dict., vol. vi. p. 97, pl. 4.
"   "   "   Mammal., pp. 219, 338.
"   "   Desmoulins, Dict. Class 3d, p. 498.
"   "   Temm. Monog., p. 136.
"   PANTHERA. Schreber, t, 99.
"   GAUDA ELONGATA. Brown's Jamaica.
TIGRIS REGIA. Briss. Regne Animale, p. 269, fig. 7.
TLATLAUHQUI OCELOTL. TIGRIS MEXICANA. Hernandez, Mex., p.
    498, fig. c.
JAGUARA. Maregr. Brazil, p. 235, fig. c.
JAGUAR. Buff. Nat. Hist., tom. ix. p. 201.
YAGOUARÉTÉ. D'Azara, vol. i. p. 114.
BRAZILIAN PANTHER. Pennant's Synopsis, pp. 127, 176.
"   TIGER. Pennant's Quadrupeds, p. 286.
ONZA PINTADO. Lusitanis, in Bresil. Cumang Maconis.
FELIS JAGUAR. Hamilton Smith. Griffith's An. Kingdom, vol. v. p. 164.
"   ONCA. Harlan, Fauna, p. 95.

Description.

The Jaguar compares with the Asiatic tiger in size and in shape; its legs, however, are shorter than those of the royal tiger, although its body is perhaps as heavy.

Head, large; jaws, capable of great expansion; incisors, large, and slightly curved inwards; ears, rather small, rounded, clothed with short hairs on the inside. Body, rather inclining to be stout, and shorter and less elegant than the cougar: at the shoulders the Jaguar is not much more raised from the earth, but it stands higher from the ground near the rump.

Feet, clothed with hair covering the retractile nails; the pads of the feet, naked; a few hairs between the toes; tail, long, and generally half elevated when walking; whiskers, few, strong, and bristly.

Hair of two kinds; the longest (which is only from four to five eighths of an inch in length) is the coarser; the shortest is a softer and finer fur, and is not very thickly distributed.

Colour.

Where the black markings do not prevail, the hairs are light greyish-brown at the roots and on the surface rich straw-yellow, deepest near the shoulders and back, and paler on the sides and legs; nose to near the eye nearly a uniform lightish-brown; forehead spotted with black in somewhat curved lines, the spots becoming larger towards the back of the head; whiskers black at the roots, then white for two thirds of their length to the points; lips and chin, white; a black line on the sides of the mouth; around the eye, whitish-yellow; iris, light-yellow; a black stripe between the ears on the back part of the head. There is no white patch behind the ear, as in the cougar and the wild cat.

All the black spots on the body are composed of hairs which are black from their roots; outer edge of the ear, black for half an inch in width; a row of black spots running along the back to and beyond the root of the tail for about a foot along its upper surface; the sides of the body are marked with black rings of irregular and somewhat oval shapes, with yellow-brown centres having dots of pure black in them. These black rings are, on the edge of the back somewhat diamond shaped, with from one to three little black spots inside. Many of these circles or squares are not perfect: some are formed by several dots and curved black patches which turn inwards.

On the shoulders and the outer surfaces of the legs, these rings or squares are succeeded by black spots or patches lessening in size as they approach the claws. The hair on the under surface is dull-white from the roots, with large patches of black; belly, inner sides of legs, and throat, white, blotched or spotted with black. These patches are irregular in size, being from one eighth of an inch to two inches in extent. Tail, general colour spotted black on a yellow ground, like the outsides of the legs.

A living Jaguar from Mexico which we examined in its cage at Charleston, became very beautiful after shedding its hair in spring: the general colour of its body was bright-yellow, and the rings and spots were brilliant black.

There was another living specimen in the same collection, from Brazil, which resembled the one from Mexico in its general markings, but was larger, more clumsy, and had shorter and thicker legs. There were, however, no characters by which the species could be separated.

Dimensions.

	Feet.	Inches.
From point of nose to root of tail,	4	1
Length of tail,	2	1 (?)
Height of ear,		$2\frac{3}{4}$
Shoulder to end of claw,	2	
Length of largest claw,		2
Around the wrist,		$7\frac{1}{2}$
" " chest,	3	
" " head,	1	$9\frac{3}{4}$
Breadth between the eyes,		3

Habits.

Alike beautiful and ferocious, the Jaguar is of all American animals unquestionably the most to be dreaded, on account of its combined strength, activity, and courage, which not only give it a vast physical power over other wild creatures, but enable it frequently to destroy man.

Compared with this formidable beast, the cougar need hardly be dreaded more than the wild cat; and the grizzly bear, although often quite as ready to attack man, is inferior in swiftness and stealthy cunning. To the so much feared tiger of the East he is equal in fierceness; and it is owing, perhaps, to his being nocturnal in his habits to a great extent, that he seldom issues from the deep swamps or the almost impenetrable thickets or jungles of thorny shrubs, vines, and tangled vegetation which compose the chaparals of Texas and Mexico, or the dense and untracked forests of Central and Southern America, to attack man. From his haunts in such nearly unapproachable localities, the Jaguar roams forth towards the close of the day, and during the hours of darkness seizes on his prey. During the whole night he is abroad, but is most frequently met with in moonlight and fine nights, disliking dark and rainy weather, although at the promptings of hunger he will draw near the camp of the traveller, or seek the almost wild horses or cattle of the ranchero even during daylight, with the coolest audacity.

The Jaguar has the cunning to resort to salt-licks, or the watering-places of the mustangs and other wild animals, where, concealing himself behind a bush, or mounting on to a low or sloping tree, he lies in wait until a favorable opportunity presents itself for springing on his prey. Like the cougar and the

No. 21

Plate CI.

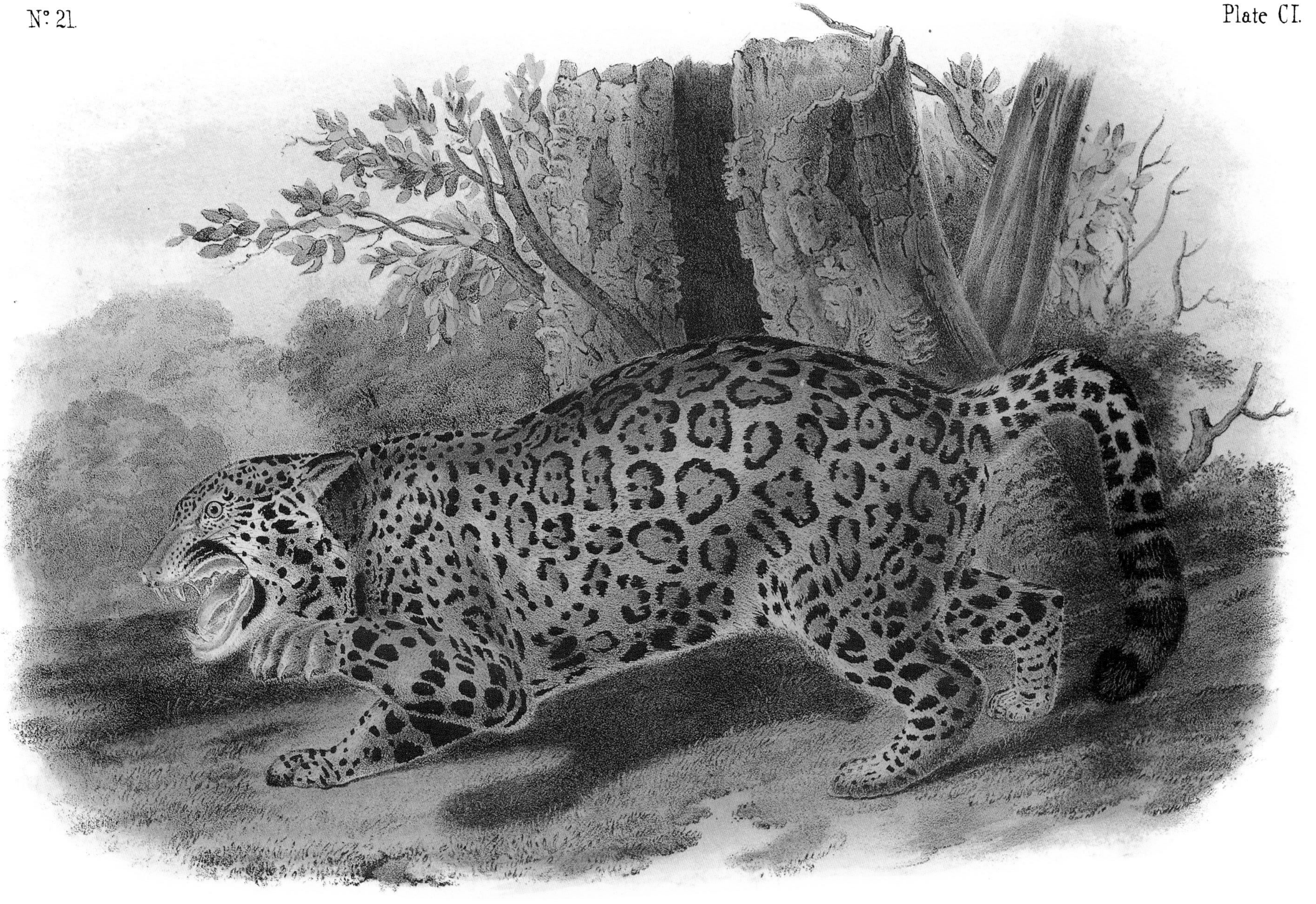

On Stone by W.E. Hitchcock.

Drawn from Nature by J.W. Audubon.

Lith.d Printed & Col.d by J.T. Bowen, Philad.a

The Jaguar.

wild cat, he seeks for the peccary, the skunk, opossum, and the smaller rodentia; but is fond of attacking the larger quadrupeds, giving the preference to mustangs or horses, mules, or cattle. The colts and calves especially afford him an easy prey, and form a most important item in the grand result of his predatory expeditions.

Like the lion and tiger, he accomplishes by stealth or stratagem what could not be effected by his swiftness of foot, and does not, like the untiring wolf, pursue his prey with indomitable perseverance at top speed for hours together, although he will sneak after a man or any other prey for half a day at a time, or hang on the skirts of a party for a considerable period, watching for an opportunity of springing upon some person or animal in the train.

Col. HAYS and several other officers of the Rangers, at the time J. W AUDUBON was at San Antonio de Bexar, in 1845, informed him that the Jaguar was most frequently found about the watering-places of the mustangs, or wild horses, and deer. It has been seen to spring upon the former, and from time to time kills one; but it is much more in the habit of attacking colts about six months old, which it masters with great ease. Col. HAYS had killed four Jaguars during his stay in Texas. These animals are known in that country by the Americans as the "Leopard," and by the Mexicans as the "Mexican tiger." When lying in wait at or near the watering-places of deer or horses, this savage beast exhibits great patience and perseverance, remaining for hours crouched down, with head depressed, and still as death. But when some luckless animal approaches, its eyes seem to dilate, its hair bristles up, its tail is gently waved backwards and forwards, and all its powerful limbs appear to quiver with excitement. The unsuspecting creature draws near the dangerous spot; suddenly, with a tremendous leap, the Jaguar pounces on him, and with the fury of an incarnate fiend fastens upon his neck with his terrible teeth, whilst his formidable claws are struck deep into his back and flanks. The poor victim writhes and plunges with fright and pain, and makes violent efforts to shake off the foe, but in a few moments is unable longer to struggle, and yields with a last despairing cry to his fate. The Jaguar begins to devour him while yet alive, and growls and roars over his prey until his hunger is appeased. When he has finished his meal, he sometimes covers the remains of the carcass with sticks, grass, weeds, or earth, if not disturbed, so as to conceal it from other predacious animals and vultures, until he is ready for another banquet. The Jaguar often lies down to guard his prey, after devouring as much as he can. On one occasion a small party of Rangers came across one while feeding upon a mustang. The animal was surrounded by eight or ten hungry wolves, which dared not interfere or approach too near "the presence." The Rangers gave chase to the Jaguar, on which the wolves set up a howl or cry like a pack of hounds, and joined in the hunt, which ended before they had gone many yards, the Jaguar being shot down as he ran, upon which the wolves went back to the carcass of the horse and finished him.

The Jaguar has been known to follow a man for a long time. Colonel HAYS, whilst alone on a scouting expedition, was followed by one of these animals for a considerable distance. The colonel, who was aware that his footsteps were scented by the animal, having observed him on his trail a little in his rear, had proceeded a good way, and thought that the Jaguar had left, when, having entered a thicker part of the wood, he heard a stick crack, and being in an Indian country, "whirled round," expecting to face a Wakoe; but instead of a red-skin, he saw the Jaguar, about half-crouched, looking "right in his eye," and gently waving his tail. The colonel, although he wished not to discharge his gun, being in the neighborhood of Indians who might hear the report, now thought it high time to shoot, so he fired, and killed him in his tracks. "The skin," as he informed us, "was to beautiful, it was a pleasure to look at it."

These skins are very highly prized by the Mexicans, and also by the Rangers; they are used for holster coverings and as saddle cloths, and form a superb addition to the caparison of a beautiful horse, the most important animal to the occupants of the prairies of Texas, and upon which they always show to the best advantage. ·

In a conversation with General HOUSTON at Washington city, he informed us that he had found the Jaguar east of the San Jacinto river, and abundantly on the head waters of some of the eastern tributaries of the Rio Grande, the Guadaloupe, &c.

These animals, said the general, are sometimes found associated to the number of two or more together, when they easily destroy horses and other large quadrupeds. On the head waters of the San Marco, one night, the general's people were aroused by the snorting of their horses, but on advancing into the space around could see nothing, owing to the great darkness. The horses having become quiet, the men returned to camp and lay down to rest as usual, but in the morning one of the horses was found to have been killed and eaten up entirely, except the skeleton. The horses on this occasion were hobbled and picketed; but the general thinks the Jaguar frequently catches

and destroys wild ones, as well as cattle. The celebrated BOWIE caught a splendid mustang horse, on the rump of which were two extensive scars made by the claws of a Jaguar or cougar. Such instances, indeed, are not very rare.

Capt, J. P. McCOWN, U. S. A., related the following anecdote to us: —At a camp near the Rio Grande, one night, in the thick, low, level musquit country, when on an expedition after Indians, the captain had killed a beef which was brought into camp from some distance. A fire was made, part of the beef hanging on a tree near it. The horses were picketed around, the men outside forming a circular guard. After some hours of the night had passed, the captain was aroused by the soldier next him saying, "Captain, may I shoot?" and raising himself on his arm, saw a Jaguar close to the fire, between him and the beef, and near it, with one fore-foot raised, as if disturbed; it turned its head towards the captain as he ordered the soldier not to fire, lest he should hurt some one on the other side of the camp, and then, seeming to know it was discovered, but without exhibiting any sign of fear, slowly, and with the stealthy, noiseless pace and attitude of a common cat, sneaked off.

The Jaguar, in its South American range, was long since noticed for its ferocity by HUMBOLDT and others. In some remarks on the American animals of the genus felis, which we find in the Memoirs of the Wernerian Nat. Hist. Society of Edinburgh, vol. iv., part 2, p. 470, it is stated that the Jaguar, like the royal tiger of Asia, does not fly from man when it is dared to close combat, when it is not alarmed by the great number of its assailants. The writer quotes an instance in which one of these animals had seized a horse belonging to a farm in the province of Cumana, and dragged it to a considerable distance. "The groans of the dying horse," says HUMBOLDT, "awoke the slaves of the farm, who went out armed with lances and cutlasses. The animal continued on its prey, awaited their approach with firmness, and fell only after a long and obstinate resistance." In the same article, the writer states that the Jaguar leaps into the water to attack the Indians in their canoes on the Oronoko. This animal called the Yagouareté in Paraguay if we are not mistaken, the foregoing article goes on to say, is described by gentlemen who have hunted it in that country, as a very courageous and powerful animal, of great activity, and highly dangerous when at bay. He also says: "Both this species and the puma are rendered more formidable by the facility with which they can ascend trees.

"A very beautiful Jaguar from Paraguay was some time ago carried alive to Liverpool. When the animal arrived, it was in full health, and though not fully grown was of a very formidable size and strength. The captain who brought it could venture to play with it, as it lay on one of the boats on deck, to which it was chained; but it had been familiarized to him from the time it was the size of a small dog."

In Griffith's Cuvier, vol. ii. p. 457, it is stated in a quotation from D'Azara, that the Jaguar is reported to "stand in the water out of the stream, and drop its saliva, which, floating on the surface, draws the fish after it within reach, when it seizes them with the paw, and throws them ashore fore food." At the same page, it is said, "The Jaguar is hunted with a number of dogs, which, although they have no chance of destroying it themselves, drive the animal into a tree, provided it can find one a little inclining, or else into some hole. In the first case the hunters kill it with fire-arms or lances; and in the second, some of the natives are occasionally found hardy enough to approach it with the left arm covered with a sheepskin, and to spear it with the other—a temerity which is frequently followed with fatal consequences to the hunter."

The Jaguars we examined in a menagerie at Charleston had periodical fits of bad temper: one of them severely bit his keeper, and was ready to give battle either to the Asiatic tiger or the liron, which were kept in separate cages.

We add some extracts, with which we hope our readers will be interested:

"In the province of Tucuman, the common mode of killing the Jaguar is to trace him to his lair by the wool left on the bushes, if he has carried off a sheep, or by means of a dog trained for the purpose. On finding the enemy, the gaucho puts himself into a position for receiving him on the point of a bayonet or spear at the first spring which he makes, and thus waits until the dogs drive him out—an exploit which he performs with such coolness and dexterity that there is scarcely an instance of failure. In a recent instance related by our capitaz, the business was not so quickly completed. The animal lay stretched at full length on the ground, like a gorged cat. Instead of showing anger and attacking his enemies with fury, he was playful, and disposed rather to parley with the dogs with good humour than to take their attack in sober earnestness. He was now fired upon, and a ball lodged in his shoulders, on which he sprang so quickly on his watching assailant that he not only buried the bayonet in his body, but tumbled over the capitaz who held it, and they floundered on the ground together, the man being completely in his clutches. 'I thought,' said the brave fellow, 'I was no longer a capitaz, while I held my arm up to protect my throat, which the animal seemed in the act of seizing; but when I expected to feel his fangs in my flesh, the green fire of his eyes which blazed upon me flashed out in a moment. He fell on me, and expired at the very instant I thought myself lost for ever.'"—*Captain Andrews's Travels in South America*, vol. i. p. 219.

"Two Indian children, a boy and girl eight or nine years of age, were sitting among the grass near the village of Atures, in the midst of a savannah. It was two in the afternoon when a Jaguar issued from the forest and approached the children, gambolling around them, sometimes concealing himself among the long grass, and again springing forward, with his back curved and his head lowered, as in usual with our cats. The little boy was unaware of the danger in which he was placed, and became sensible of it only when the Jaguar struck him on the head with one of his paws. The blows thus inflicted were at first slight, but gradually became ruder. The claws of the Jaguar wounded the child, and blood flowed with violence. The little girl then took up a branch of a tree, and struck the animal, which fled before her. The Indians, hearing the cries of the children, ran up and saw the Jaguar, which bounded off without showing any disposition to defend itself."—*Humboldt's Travels and Researches, &c.*, Edinburgh, 1833, p. 245.

HUMBOLDT speculates on this cat-like treatment of the children, and we think it very likely that occasionally the Jaguar plays in a similar manner with its prey, although we have not witnessed it, nor heard of any authentic case of the kind.

D'AZARA says (vol. i. p. 116) that the black Jaguar is so rare that in forty years only two had been killed on the head waters of the river Parana. The man who killed one of these assured him that it did not differ from the Jaguar (Yagouarété), except that it was black, marked with still blacker spots, like those of the common Jaguar.

The Jaguar generally goes singly, but is sometimes accompanied by his favourite female. The latter brings forth two young at a time, the hair of which is rougher and not so beautiful as in the adult. She guides them as soon as they are able to follow, and supplies and protects them, not hesitating to encounter any danger in their defence.

The Jaguar, according to D'AZARA, can easily drag away a horse or an ox; and should another be fastened or yoked to the one he kills, the powerful beast drags both off together, notwithstanding the resistance of the terrified living one. He does not conceal the residue of his prey after feeding: this may be because of the abundance of animals in his South American haunts. He hunts in the stealthy manner of a cat after a rat, and his leap upon his prey is a very sudden, quick spring: he does not move rapidly when retreating or running. It is said that if he finds a party of sleeping travellers at night, he advances into their midst, and first kills the dog, if there is one, next the negro, and then the Indian, only attacking the Spaniard after he had made this selection; but generally he seizes the dog and the meat, even when the latter is broiling on the fire, without injuring the men, unless he is attacked or is remarkably hungry, or unless he has been accustomed to eat human flesh, in which case he prefers it to every other kind. D'AZARA says very coolly, "Since I have been here the Yagouarétés (Jaguars) have eaten six men, two of whom were seized by them whilst warming themselves by a fire." If a small party of men or a herd of animals pass within gunshot of a Jaguar, the beast attacks the last one

of them with a loud roar.

During the night, and especially in the love season, he frequently roars, uttering in a continued manner, *pou, pou, pou*.

It is said that when the Spaniards settled the country from Montevideo to Santa-Fé de Vera Cruz, so many Jaguars were found that two thousand were killed annually, but their numbers have been greatly diminished (D'AZARA, vol. i. p. 124). We have no positive information as to the present average annually killed, but presume it not to exceed one tenth the above number.

Geographical Distribution.

This species is known to exist in Texas, and in a few localities is not very rare, although it is far from being abundant throughout the state. It is found on the head waters of the Rio Grande, and also on the Nueces. Towards the west and southwest it extends to the mountainous country beyond El Paso. HARLAN speaks of its being occasionally seen east of the Mississippi. This we think somewhat doubtful. It inhabits Mexico and is frequently met with in almost every part of Central America. HUMBOLDT mentions having heard its constant nightly screams on the banks of the Oronoco. It is known to inhabit Paraguay and the Brazils, and may be regarded as the tiger of all the warmer parts of America, producing nearly as much terror in the minds of the feeble natives as does its congener, the royal tiger, in the East. It is not found in Oregon, and we have not met with any account of it as existing in California.

General Remarks.

BUFFON, in describing the habits of the Jaguar, appears to have received his accounts of the timidity of this species from those who referred to the Ocelot, which is generally admitted to be a timid animal. He erroneously supposed that when full grown it did not exceed the size of an ordinary dog, in which he egregiously underrated its dimensions. It is certainly a third heavier than the Cougar, and is not only a more powerful, but a far more ferocious animal. This species exhibits some varieties, one of which, the black Jaguar, is so peculiar that it has been conjectured that it might be entitled to a distinct specific name. The exceeding rarity, however, of the animal, and the variations to which nearly all the species of this genus are subject, induce us to set it down as merely a variety. It must be observed that it is rare to find two specimens of uniform colour; indeed the markings on each side of the same animal are seldom alike. BUFFON (vol. v. p. 196. pl. 117–119) has given three figures of the Jaguar, the first and third of which we consider as the Ocelot, and the second as probably the Panther (*F. Pardus*) of the eastern continent. HAMILTON SMITH, in GRIFFITH'S CUVIER (vol. ii. pp. 455, 456), has given us two figures of this species, differing considerably in colour and markings: the former is very characteristic. He has named this species *Felis Jaguar*, which is inadmissible. There is some resemblance in this species to the panther (*F. Pardus*), as also to the leopard (*F. Leopardus*) of Africa, but they are now so well described as distinct species that it is scarcely necessary to point out the distinctive marks of each. BUFFON's panthère femelle, pl. 12, and SHAW's, Gen Zool., Part I., pl. 84, evidently are figures of our Jaguar.

Mephitis Macroura.—Licht.

Large-Tailed Skunk.

Plate cii.—Male.

M. magnitudine felis cati (domestica), fusco-niger, striis duaous albis dorsalibus, vitta alba frontali, cauda capite longiore.

Characters.

Size of the domestic cat; general colour, brownish-black; a white stripe on each side of the back, and on the forehead; tail longer than the head.

Synonymes.

MEPHITIS MACROURA. Licht., Darstellung neuer oder wenig bekannter Säugthiere, Berlin, 1827-34, Tafel xlvi.
" MEXICANUS GRAY. Loudon's Mag., p. 581, 1837.

Description.

Body, as in other species of this genus, stout; head, small; nose short, rather acute, and naked; ears short, rounded, clothed, with short hair on both surfaces; eyes, small; claws, slender and weak; soles of the feet naked.

The body is covered with two kinds of hair; the first long and glossy, the fur underneath soft and woolly; tail very long, rather bushy, covered with long hairs, and without any of the softer and shorter fur.

Colour.

There are slight variations in the markings of the specimens we examined in the museums of Berlin and London, and in those we possess. This species appears, however, to be less eccentric in colour and markings than the common skunk *M. chinga.*

In the specimen from which our figure was made, there is a rather broad longitudinal white stripe running from the nose to near the back of the head; upper surface of neck and back, white, with a narrow black dorsal stripe beginning on the middle of the back and running down on the upper surface of the tail; a spot of white under the shoulder, and another along the flanks; the hairs on the tail are irregularly mixed with white and black; under surface black.

Another skin from the same region has a narrower stripe on the forehead, the usual white stripes from the back of the head along the sides nearly meeting again at the root of the tail, leaving the dorsal black patch very much broader than in the specimen just described, and of an oval shape; the tail contains a greater number of black hairs, and towards the tip is altogether black; sides, legs, and whole under surface, black.

LICHTENSTEIN's figure resembles this specimen in form and markings, with the exceptions that it represents scarcely any black patch on the back, and that it exhibits a longitudinal white stripe running from the shoulder to the hip. LICHTENSTEIN has also described and figured the young of this species, which very closely resembles the adult.

Dimensions.

Male.—Killed January 28, 1846.

	Feet.	Inches.
From point of nose to root of tail, ...	1	4
Tail (vertebræ), ...	1	1
" to end of hair, ...	1	6
Between ears, ...		2¼
Girth around the body, behind fore-legs, ...		9
" " belly, ...	1	2½
Height from sole of fore-foot to top of shoulders, ...		8½

Weight 4½ lb.—specimen fat.

Habits.

In Texas, during the winter of 1845–6, specimens of this skunk were obtained by J. W. AUDUBON; the first he met with was seen on one of the high and dry prairies west of Houston, on the road to Lagrange; this was, however, only a young one. It was easily caught, as these animals never attempt to escape by flight, depending on the fetid discharges which they, like the common skunk, eject, to disgust their assailant and cause him to leave them in safety. By throwing sticks and clods of dirt at this young one, he was induced to display his powers in this way, and teased until he had emptied the glandular sacs which contain the detestable secretion. He was then comparatively disarmed, and by thrusting a forked stick over the back of his head, was pinned to the ground, then seized and thrust into a bag, the mouth of which being tied up, he was considered safely captured, and was slung to one of the pack-saddles of the baggage-mules. The fetor of this young skunk was not so horrid as that of the common species (*Mephitis chinga*).

On arriving at the camping ground for the night, the party found that their prisoner had escaped by gnawing a hole in the bag, being unobserved by any one.

This species is described as very common in some parts of Texas, and its superb tail is now and then used by the country folks by way of plume or feather in their hats. J. W. AUDUBON, in his Journal, remarks: "We were much amused at the disposition manifested by some of the privates in the corps of Rangers, to put on extra finery when opportunity offered. At one time a party returned from a chase after Indians whom they had overtaken and routed. Several of them had whole turkey-cocks' tails stuck on one side of their hats, and had long pendant trains of feathers hanging behind their backs, which they had taken from the 'braves' of the Wakoes. One young fellow, about eighteen years of age, had a superb head-dress and suit to match, which he had taken from an Indian, whom, to use his own expression, he had scared out of it; he had, to complete the triumphal decoration of his handsome person, painted his face all the colours of the rainbow, and looked fierce enough. In contrast with these freaks of some of the men, we noticed that their tried and chivalrous leaders, HAYS, WALKER, GILLESPIE, and CHEVALIER, were always dressed in the plainest costume the 'regulations' permitted."

The Large-Tailed Skunk feeds upon snakes, lizards, insects, birds' eggs, and small animals; and it is said that at the season when the pecan (*Carya olivaeformis*) ripens, they eat those nuts, as well as acorns. This is strange, considering their carnivorous formation. They burrow in winter, and live in hollows and under roots. They produce five or six young at a birth.

We are indebted to Col. GEO. A. McCALL, U. S. A., for the following interesting account of an adventure with one of these Skunks, which, besides being written in an entertaining and lively manner, sets forth in a strong light the dread the very idea of being defiled by these offensive brutes causes in every one who has ever been in those parts of the country they inhabit:—

"In New Mexico, in September last, returning from Los Vegas to Santa Fé, I halted for the night at Cottonwood creek. Here, I pitched my tent on the edge of a beautiful grove of the trees (*Populus angulatus*) which give name to the stream.

"Wishing to reach my destination at an early hour on the morrow, I directed the men to be up before day, in order that they might feed their horses, get their breakfast, and be ready to take the road as soon as it was fairly daylight. After a refreshing sleep, I awoke about an hour before day, and the familiar sound of my horse munching his corn by the side of my tent, where he was usually picketed, informed me that my men were already astir. At this hour, the moon, almost at the full, was low in the west, and flung its mellow light adown the mountain gorge, in rays that were nearly horizontal. And therefore, not finding it necessary to strike a light, I was on the point of rising, when I heard, as I thought, my servant opening the mess-basket, which stood near the foot of my bed. I spoke to him; but receiving no answer, I turned my eyes in that direction, and discovered on the front wall of my tent a little shadow playing fantastically over the canvas, upon which the moon's rays fell, after passing over my head. With a hunter's eye, I at once recognized in this shadow the outline of the uplifted tail of a *Mephitis Macroura*, vulgo Large-Tailed *Skunk*, whose body was concealed from my view behind the mess-basket. Into this, doubtless attracted by the scent of a cold boiled bacon-ham, he was evidently endeavouring to effect an entrance.

"Being well acquainted with his habits and character, I knew I must manage to get rid of my visitor without seriously alarming or provoking him, or I should in all probability be the sufferer. I therefore thought I would at first, merely in a quiet way, signify my presence; on discovering which, perhaps, he would take the hint, and his departure at the same time. So, 'I coughed and cried hem!' but my gentleman only raised his head above the top of the basket for a moment, and then renewed his efforts to lift the lid. I now took up one of my boots that lay by my bed, and struck the heel smartly against the tent-pole. Again the intruder raised his head, and regarded me for a moment; after which he left the basket and passed round the foot of my bed, which, I should mention, was spread upon the ground. At first, I thought he had, indeed, taken the hint, and was about to slope off. But I had, in fact, only excited his curiosity; and the next moment, to my horror, I saw him turn

On Stone by W.E.Hitchcock.

Large-Tailed Skunk.

Drawn from Nature by J.W.Audubon   Lith.ᵈ Printed & Col.ᵈ by J.T Bowen, Philad.ᵃ

up by the side of my bed, and come dancing along with a dainty, sidling motion, to examine into the cause of the noise. His broad white tail was elevated, and jauntily flirted from side to side as he approached. In fact, his approach was the sauciest and most provokingly deliberate thing conceivable. As every step brought him nearer to my face, the impulse I felt to bolt head-foremost through the opposite side of the tent, was almost irresistible; but I well knew that any sudden motion on my part, whilst in such close proximity to the rascal, would be very apt so to startle him as to bring upon me that which I was seeking to escape, and of which I was, in truth, in mortal dread; whilst, on the other hand, I was equally aware that my safety lay in keeping perfectly still, for it was quite probable that the animal, after having satisfied his curiosity, would, if uninterrupted, quietly take his departure. The trial was a severe one, for the next moment the upright white tail was passing within a foot of my very face. I did not flinch, but kept my eye upon it, although the cold sweat broke out upon my forehead in great globules. At length the fellow finding nothing to alarm him, turned about and with a sidelong motion danced back again to the mess-basket. Finding now that he had no thought of taking himself away, I exclaimed internally, 'Mortal man cannot bear a repetition of what I have just experienced!' and laid my hand upon my rifle, which stood at my head. I weighed the chances of killing the animal so instantly dead that no discharge of odour would take place; but just at this moment he succeeded in raising the top of the basket and I heard his descent among the spoons. 'Ha! ha! old fellow, I have you now!' I said to myself; and the next instant I was standing on the top of the mess-basket, whither I had got without the slightest noise, and where I now heard the rascal rummaging my things little suspecting that he was at the time a prisoner. I called my servant—a negro. George made his appearance, and as he opened the front of the tent paused in surprise at seeing me standing *en dishabille* on the top of the mess-basket. 'George,' said I, in a quiet tone, 'buckle the straps of this basket.' George looked still more surprised on receiving the order, but obeyed it in silence. I then stepped gently off, and said, 'Take this basket very carefully, and without shaking it, out yonder, in front, and set it down easily.' George looked still more bewildered; but, accustomed to obey without question, did as he was directed. After he had carried the basket off to a considerable distance, and placed it on the ground, he looked back at the door of the tent, where I still stood, for further orders. 'Unbuckle the straps,' said I; it was done. 'Raise the top of the basket:' he did so; while at the same time, elevating my voice, I continued, *'and let that d——d Skunk out!'* As the last words escaped from my lips the head and tail of the animal appeared in sight, and George, giving vent to a scream of surprise and fear, broke away like a quarter-horse, and did not stop until he had put a good fifty yards between himself and the mess-basket. Meanwhile, the Skunk, with the same deliberation that had marked his previous course (and which, by the way, is a

remarkable trait in the character of this animal), descended the side of the basket, and, with tail erect, danced off in a direction down the creek, and finally disappeared in the bushes. I then, having recovered from a good fit of laughter, called to George, who rather relunctantly made his appearance before me. He was still a little out of breath, and with some agitation, thus delivered himself, 'Bless God, massa, if I had known there was a Skunk in the mess-basket, I never would have touched it *in this world!*' 'I knew that well enough, George, and that was the reason I did not tell you of it.'

"It is only necessary further to say that the animal, having been neither alarmed nor provoked in any way, did not on this occasion emit the slightest odour; nor was any trace left in my tent or mess-basket, to remind me afterwards of the early morning visitor at my camp on Cottonwood creek."—Philadelphia, June 24th, 1851."

We have heard of some cases in which this Skunk, having penetrated into the tents of both officers and men, on our southwestern frontier, has been less skilfully managed, and the consequences were so bad as to compel the abandonment of even the tents, although soused into creeks and scrubbed with hopes of destroying the "hogo."

Geographical distribution.

This species exists on the western ranges of the mountains in Mexico. The specimen described by LICHTENSTEIN was obtained by Mr. DEPPE in the mountains to the northwest of the city of Mexico. The animal was seen by Col. G. A. McCALL in New Mexico, between Los Vegas and Santa Fé. The specimen figured by JOHN W. AUDUBON was obtained near San Antonio, and he describes it as common in the western parts of Texas. It is not found in Louisiana, nor near the sea-shore in Texas. It will, we think, be found to inhabit some portions of California, although we cannot state this with certainty.

General Remarks.

There are several species of this genus, which are found to vary so much in the distribution of their colours that many mere varieties were described as new species, without any other characters than those presented by the number of stripes on the back, or the predominance either of black or white spots on the different protions of the body. BUFFON described five species. Baron CUVIER, in his "Ossemens Fossiles," took much pains in endeavoring to clear up the difficulties on the subject of these animals yet, owing to his not possessing specimens, and his too great dependence on colour, he multiplied the number of some species which are now found to be mere varieties, and omitted others which are unquestionably true species.

Arctomys Pruinosus.—Pennant.

Hoary Marmot.—The Whistler.

Plate Ciii.—Males.

A. vellere cano longo, denso, maxime in thorace humorisque, in partibus posterioribus fulvo-flavescente, cauda comosa fusco nigriscente.

Characters.

Fur, long, dense, and hoary, particularly on the chest and shoulders; hinder parts dull yellowish-brown; tail bushy, blackish-brown.

Synonymes.

HOARY MARMOT. PENNANT, Hist. Quadr., vol. ii. p. 130.
"   "   "   Arctic Zool., vol. i. p. 112.
GROUND-HOG. Mackenzie's Voyage, p. 515.
WHISTLER. Harmon's Journal, p. 427.
ARCTOMYS (?) PRUINOSUS. Rich, Zool. Jour., No. 12, p. 518. Mar. 1828.
"   "   Rich, Fauna Boreali Americana, p. 150.
QUISQUIS-QUI-PO. Cree Indians.
DEH-IE. Cheppewyans.
SOUFFLEUR, or MOUNTAIN-BADGER. Fur-Traders.
ARCTOMYS PRUINOSA. Harlan, Fauna, p. 169.
"   CALLIGATA. Eschscholtz, Zoologischer Atlas, Berlin, 1829, pl. 6, part 2, p. 1.

Description.

In form, this animal (which we examined whilst it was alive at the Zoological Gardens in London) bears a considerable resemblance to the European Marmot (*Arotomys Marmota*). It also resembles the Maryland Marmot (*A. Monax*). Being, at the time we saw it, excessively fat, the body, when it lay down, spread out or flattened like that of the badger; it was so covered with dense and very long hair that it was difficult to recognize the true outline; it subsequently shed its hair, and our figure was taken in its new and shorter pelage. The animal is rather longer than the Maryland Marmot; head, of moderate size; eyes, rather small but conspicuous; ears, oval and covered with hair on both surfaces; feet short, robust, and clothed with hair; nails strong, slightly arched, free; tail, short, and thickly clothed with long and coarse hair to the extremity. The pelage is a soft and dense fur beneath, covered with longer and more rigid hairs.

Colour.

Fur on the back, dark at base, the outer portion white, with black points more or less extended; on the rump it is dull-brown at the roots, with black and yellow towards the extremities. The general appearance of the animal, owing to the admixture of these dark-brown and white hairs, of which the white predominate, is hoary-brown.

Upper surface of nose, ears, back part of the head, and nails, black; a black band runs backwards from behind the ears for about an inch and a half, and then descends nearly vertically on the neck, where it vanishes; sides of muzzle, and behind the nostrils above, as well as chin, pure white; cheeks, grizzled with rust-colour and black; moustaches, nearly all black, a few, light brown.

Plate CIII.

Nº 21.

Hoary Marmot. The Whistler.

There are a few white hairs on the middle toes of the fore-feet; tail black, varied with rusty-brown, and a few whitish hairs with black points; whole under parts pale rust colour, with a slight mixture of black on the belly; extremities of the ears slightly tipped with white; upper incisors, yellow; lower, nearly white.

Dimensions.

	Foot.	Inches.	Lines.
Length from point of nose to root of tail,	1	7	
" of tail (vertebræ),		5	6
" " including hair,		7	9
Point of nose to end of head,		3	4
Ear,			5½
Palm and nail,		2	9
Nail,			9
Tarsus,		3	8
Nail on hind foot,			8

Habits.

This Marmot was described by PENNANT, from a skin preserved in the Leverian Museum, which was for many years the only specimen in any known collection. It appears to have afterwards become a question whether there was such an animal, or whether it might not prove to be the Maryland Marmot, the original specimen, above mentioned, having been lost. HARLAN says of it, "This specimen was supposed to have come from the northern parts of North America." GODMAN does not mention it. Dr. RICHARDSON quotes PENNANT's description, and states that he did not himself obtain a specimen; but "if correct" in considering it as the same as the Whistler of HARMON, "we may soon hope to know more of it, for the traders who annually cross the Rocky Mountains from Hudson's Bay to the Columbia and New Caledonia are well acquainted with it." He also mentions that one, (HARMON's Whistler, we presume) which was procured for him by a gentleman, was so much injured that he did not think it fit to be sent." The Doctor then gives the following account of it, and appears to have been quite correct in supposing it identical with the animal referred to by HARMON: "The Whistler inhabits the Rocky Mountains from latitude 45° to 62°, and probably farther both ways: it is not found in the lower parts of the country. It burrows in sandy soil, generally on the sides of grassy hills, and may be frequently seen cutting hay in the autumn, but whether for the purpose of laying it up for food, or merely for lining its burrows, I did not learn. While a party of them are thus occupied, they have a sentinel on the lookout upon an eminence, who gives the alarm on the approach of an enemy, by a shrill whistle, which may be heard at a great distance. The signal of alarm is repeated from one to another as far as their habitations extend. According to Mr. HARMON, they feed on roots and herbs, produce two young at a time, and sit upon their hind-feet when they give their young suck. They do not come abroad in the winter."

"The Indians take the Whistler in traps set at the mouths of their holes, consider their flesh as delicious food, and, by sewing a number of their skins together, make good blankets."

Our drawing of this Marmot was made from the specimen now in the museum of the Zoological Society of London, which is, we believe, the only one, even at this day, to be found in Europe, with the exception of a "hunter's skin" (i. e., one without skull, teeth, or legs), which was presented to the British Museum by Dr. RICHARDSON, and was probably the one he refers to in the extract we have given above from the Fauna Boreali Americana. The specimen in the Zoological Museum is well preserved, the animal, which was alive when presented to the Society by B. KING Esq., having died in the Menagerie (Zoological Gardens) in Regent's Park.

The living animal, when we observed it, seemed to be dull and sleepy. Its cage was strewed with grass and herbs, on which it had been feeding.

Geographical Distribution.

The first specimen of this species was brought to England from Hudson's Bay. The specimen we have figured was obtained on Captain BACK's expedition. It inhabits the Rocky Mountains from 45° to 62°, and will probably be found both to the north and south of these latitudes.

General Remarks.

It is somewhat remarkable that an animal so large as the Hoary Marmot—so widely diffused throughout the fur countries, where it is seen by traders and hunters—should be so little known to naturalists. When the living animal was brought to the Zoological Gardens it excited much interest, as the existence of the species had for many years been doubted.

We spent an hour at the Museum of the Zoological Society in London with Dr. RICHARDSON and Mr. WATERHOUSE, examing the specimen to which ESCHSCHOLZ had given the name of A. Calligata; and we manimously came to the conclusion that it was the A. Pruinosus.

Sciurus Colliæi.—Rich.

Collie's Squirrel

Plate civ.—Males.

S. Supra e fresco-nigro flavoque varius subtus ex flavescente albidus; magnitudine S. migratorii.

Characters.

Size of Sciurus Migratorius; upper parts mottled brownish black and yellow; under surface cream white.

Synonymes.

SCIURUS COLLIÆI. Richardson, Append, to Beechey's Voyage.
"   "   Bachman, Proc. Zool. Soc. 1838 (Monog. of Genus Sciurus).

Description.

In size and form this species bears some resemblance to the migratory gray Squirrel of the middle or northern States; the tail, however, in the only specimen which exists in any collection, appears much smaller and less distichous, and the animal, when other specimens are examined, may prove to be intermediate in size between the Carolina gray Squirrel and S. Migratorius.

The fur is rather coarse, and the tail appears to be somewhat cylindrical; ears, of moderate size, ovate, clothed with short hairs on both surfaces, but not tufted.

Colour.

Above, grizzled with black and dull-yellow; sides of the muzzle, under parts of the body, and inner sides of limbs, dull-white; tail, moderate, the hairs grayish-white, three times annulated with black. Hairs of the body, both above and beneath, grey at the roots, those on the back having lengthened black tips broadly annulated with dull-yellow. The hairs of the head resemble those of the back, except on the front, where they are annulated with dull-white; top of the muzzle, brown; cheeks, greyish; insides of ears, yellowish, indistinctly freckled with brown; outsides, grizzled with black and yellow on the forepart, but posteriorly covered with long whitish hairs; hairs on the feet, black at the roots, white at the tips, the feet and legs being dirty cream-colour, pencilled with dusky; whiskers, long as the head, composed of bristly black hairs. The above description was taken by us from the specimen in the Zoological Society's Museum, London; the skin was not in very good condition, and a portion of the tail was wanting.

Dimensions.

	Inches.	Lines.
Length from nose to root of tail,	10	9
" of tail to end of hair,	9	6
Height of ear posteriorly,		6
Tarsus (including nail),	2	5
Nose to ear,	2	0

Habits.

Our figures of this Squirrel were made from the specimen presented to the Zoological Society of London by Captain BEECHEY; the original from which

Collies Squirrel.

Drawn from Nature by J.W.Audubon   Lith.Printed & Col.ᵈ by J.T.Bowen,Phil.

the species was described and named by our friend Dr. RICHARDSON.

All the information we have as to the habits of this animal is contained in the above-mentioned appendix (p. 8): "Mr. COLLIE observed this Squirrel, in considerable numbers, sporting on trees at San Blas in California (?), where its vernacular name signifies 'Little Fox-Squirrel.' It feeds on fruits of various kinds. Although unwilling to incur the risk of adding to the number of synonymes with which the history of this large genus is already overburdened, I do not feel justified in referring it to any of the species admitted into recent systematic works; and I have therefore described it as new, naming it in compliment to the able and indefatigable naturalist who procured the specimen."

Geographical Distribution.

This species was given by RICHARDSON, as appears by the above quota-
tion, as existing at San Blas, California; this place, however, if we have not mistaken the locality, is in the district of Xalisco in Mexico, and within the tropics; it is doubtful, therefore, whether the species will be found to inhabit any portion of California. J. W. AUDUBON did not observe it in his travels through Upper California.

General Remarks.

This species is very nearly allied to *Sciurus Aureogaster* of F. CUVIER, and it is yet possible that it may prove a variety of that very variable species, in which the under parts of the body are somtimes white, instead of the usual deep-red colour.

A specimen of *S. Aureogaster* in the Museum at Paris has the under parts of the body white, with small patches of red, and with a few scattered red hairs here and there mingled with the white ones.

Pseudostoma Douglasii. — Rich.

Columbia Pouched-Rat.

Plate cv. — Males.

P. Supra fusca, lateribus subrufis, ventre pedibusque pallidioribus, cauda and poris dimidio longiore.

Characters.

Above, dusky brown; reddish on the sides; paler beneath and on the feet; tar exceeding half the length of the body.

Synonyme.

GEOAYS DOUGLASII. Richardson, Columbia Sand-Rat, Fauna Boreali Americana, p. 200, pl. 18 B.

Description.

Head, large and depressed; ears, short, ovate, extending beyond the fur; nose, blunt; nostrils, small and round, separated by a line in the septum; they have a small naked margin. Mouth, of moderate size; lips, and space between the nose and upper incisors, covered with short hair; incisors strong, and slightly recurved; upper ones with a distinct furrow on the anterior surface, near their inner edge; cheek pouches, large, opening externally (like those of all the other species belonging to this genus), and lined on the inside with very short hairs.

The pouches extend from beneath the lower jaw along the neck to near the shoulders; whiskers, short; body cylindrical, resembling that of the mole, and covered with short, dense, velvety fur; the tail, which is round and tapering, although at first sight appearing naked, is covered with hair throughout its whole length, but most densely near the root; legs short, and moderately robust; fore-toes short, the three middle ones united at their base by a skin, the outer one smaller and farther back; thumb, very small and armed with a claw; claws, sharp-pointed, compressed, and slightly curved; palms naked, and on the posterior part filled by a large, rounded callosity. The palms in this species are much smaller than in *P. Bursarius*; the hind-feet are rather more slender than the fore-feet, and their claws are decidedly smaller; soles of hind-feet, entirely naked, and without any conspicuous tubercles; heel, naked, and narrow; feet and toes, thickly clothed with hair extending to the nails.

Colour.

Incisors, dull orange; whiskers, nearly all white; upper surface of body, top of the head, and along the sides of the pouches, dusky-brown; sides, reddish-brown; edges of pouches, dark-brown; under surface of body, feet, and tail, pale buff; nails, yellowish-white.

Dimensions.

	Inches	Lines
Length of head and body, ...	6	6
" head, ...	1	10
" tail (vertebræ), ...	2	10
From point of nose to eye, ...		11
" " " auditory opening, ...	1	8
Between the eyes, ...		7
From wrist joint to end of middle claw, ...	1	

Habits.

This species of Sand-Rat was first obtained by Mr. DAVID DOUGLAS, near the mouth of the Columbia river, since which, specimens have been sent to England by various collectors. According to Mr. DOUGLAS, the animal, "when in the act of emptying its pouches, sits on its hams like a Marmot or Squirrel, and squeezes its sacs against the breast with the chin and fore-paws."

"These little Sand-Rats are numerous in the neighbourhood of Fort Vancouver, where they inhabit the declivities of low hills, and burrow in the sandy soil. They feed on acorns, nuts (*Corylus rostrata*), and grasses, and commit great havoc in the potato-fields adjoining to the fort, not only by eating the potatoes on the spot, but by carrying off large quantities of them in their pouches."—*Fauna Boreali Americana*, p. 201.

Geographical Distribution.

This species inhabits the valleys to the west of the Rocky Mountains, and seems to have been most frequently observed in about the latitude of the mouth of the Columbia River. Its probable range may extend as far as California to the south, and the Russian Possessions in the opposite direction. We have seen some mutilated specimens, which appeared to be of this species, obtained by a party in the western portion of New Mexico, but so dilapidated were they, that it was impossible to decide positively as to their identity, and they may have been skins of another species, called by Dr. RICHARDSON *Geomys Umbrinus*, which he was informed came from the southwestern part of Louisiana.

General Remarks.

Mr. DOUGLAS informed Dr. RICHARDSON "that the outside of the pouches was cold to the touch, even when the animal was alive, and that on the inside they were lined with small, orbicular, indurated glands, more numerous near the opening into the mouth. When full, the pouches had an oblong form, and when empty they were corrugated or retracted to one third of their length."

We presume this information is correct, although the mistake made by supposing the "inverted" pouches of some species of Pseudostoma, to be in their natural position (see the genus *diplostoma* of RAFFINESQUE, adopted by RICHARDSON), leads us to look with caution on any accounts of the pouches of our Sand-Rats from this source.

Plate CV.

N°. 21

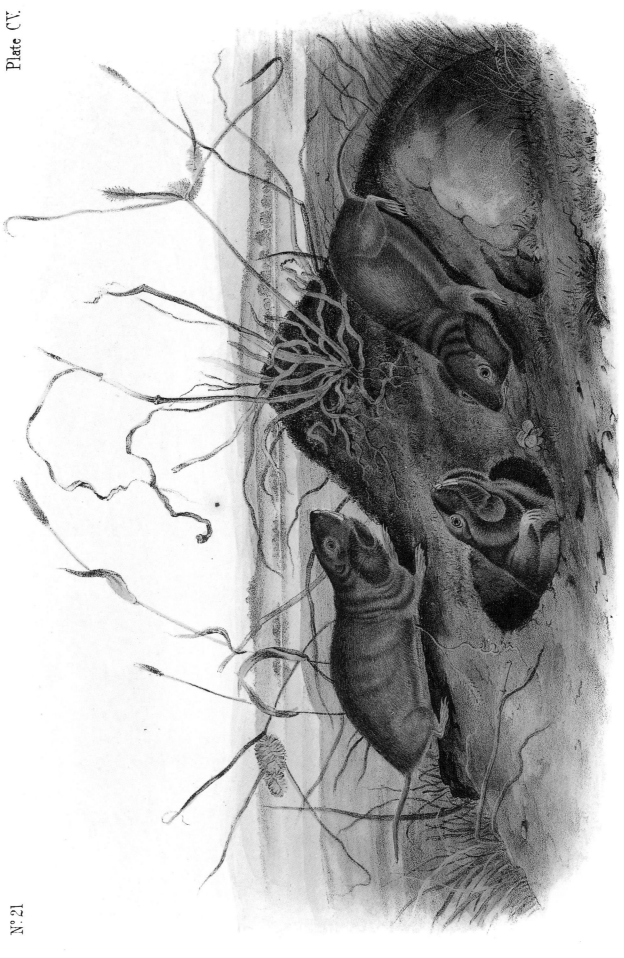

Drawn from Nature by J.W. Audubon.

On Stone by W.E. Hitchcock

Lith⁴ Printed & Col⁴ by J.T. Bowen, Philad⁴

Columbia Pouched Rat.

Cervus Richardsonii.—Aud. and Bach.

Columbian Black-Tailed Deer.

Plate cvi.—Males.

C. Supra subrufus, infra albus, auriculis mediocribus, angustioribus quam in C. macrotide, corpore minore, ungulis angustioribus et acutioribus quam in uto, macula albida in natibus nulla, cornilbus teretibus bis bifurcatis.

Characters.

Ears, moderate, narrower than in C. Macrotis; *size, less than* C. Macrotis; *hoofs, narrower and sharper; no light patch on the buttocks; colour, reddishbrown above, white beneath; horns, cylindrical, twice bifurcated.*

Synonymes.

CERVUS MACROTIS. Rich (non SAY) Black-tailed Deer, Fauna Boreali Americana, p. 254, pl. 20.
CALIFORNIA DEER, of gold diggers.

Description.

Male.—In size this animal a little exceeds the Virginian Deer, but it is less than the Mule Deer (*C. Macrotis*); in form it is shorter and stouter than *C. Virginianus*.

There is a tuft of long pendulous hairs hanging down from the umbilicus backward to between the thighs. The horns are nearly cylindrical, and are twice forked; the first bifurcation being ten inches from the base—about five to six inches longer to that fork than in *C. Macrotis*, as described by SAY. There is a knob, in the specimen from which we describe, on one horn, about four inches from the base; the horn continues in a single branch for about ten inches, where it divides into two branches, each of which has two points; and the antlers may be said to bear some resemblance to those of the Red Deer of Europe, much greater than do those of the Virginian Deer or Elk.

Ears, of moderate size; head, proportionately a little shorter than the head of the Virginian Deer and nose less pointed; hoofs, narrow and sharp, and longer and more pointed than those of the Mule Deer (*C. Macrotis*), which are round and flattened.

The lachrymal openings are large, and situated close beneath the eye; tail, rather short, stouter and more bushy than that of *C. Macrotis*.

Colour.

A brown mark originating between the nostrils is continued behind their naked margins, downwards, towards the lower jaw, uniting with a dark patch situated behind the chin; chin and throat, white; forehead, dark-brown; neck, back, sides, and hips, brownish-gray; hairs clothing those parts, brown from their roots to near their tips, where they exhibit a pale yellowish-brown ring surmounted by a black tip; on the back part of the neck there is a dark line down the middle of the back, becoming lighter as it recedes from the neck.

The chest is blackish-brown, running around the shoulder somewhat like the mark of a collar; a dark line extends from under the chest to the centre of the belly; the anterior of the belly is fawn-coloured, the posterior part white, as are likewise the insides of the thighs; the tail, at its junction with the back, is dark brown, and this colour increases in depth to the tip, which is black; the under side of the tail is clothed with long white hairs; the legs are mixed yellowish-brown and black anteriorly, and pale brownish-white posteriorly.

Dimensions.

	Feet.	Inches.
Length from tip of nose to brow (between the horns),	1	
" " " to root of tail,	5	4
" of tail (vertebræ),		6
" " (to end of hair),		9
Height at shoulder,	2	6
Width of horns between superior prongs,	1	8
" " " posterior pair of points,	1	3

Habits.

This beautiful Deer is found variously dispersed over the western portions of the North American continent, where it was first noticed by LEWIS and CLARK, near the mouth of the Columbia River; but not until the discovery of the golden treasures of California did it become generally known to white men. In that country, along the hill sides and in the woody dells and "gulches," the hardy miners have killed hundreds, nay thousands, of Black-tailed Deer; and it is from the accounts they have given that it is now known to replace, near the great Sierra Nevada, the common or Virginian Deer which is found east of the Rocky Mountains; all the hunters who have visited California, and whom we have seen, tell us that every Deer they shot there was the Black-tailed species.

J. W. AUDUBON killed a good many of these Deer, and describes them as tender and of good flavour; and during the time his party encamped on the Tuolome River, and in the "dry diggings" near Stockton, when he kept two of his men busy shooting for the support of the others, they generally had one or two Deer brought into camp every day. The mode of hunting them was more similar to what is called Deer-stalking in Scotland than to the methods used for killing Deer in the eastern part of the Union. Sometimes the hunters (who had no dogs) would start before day, and, gaining the hills, anxiously search for fresh tracks in the muddy soil (for it was then the rainy season, and the ground everywhere wet and soft), and, having found a trail, cautiously follow; always trying to keep the wind in such a direction as not to carry the scent to the animals. After discovering a fresh track, a search of a most tedious and toilsome nature awaited them, as the unsuspecting Deer might be very near, or miles off, they knew not which; at every hill-top they approached, they were obliged to lie down and crawl on the earth, pausing when they could command the view to the bottom of the valley which lay beyond the one they had just quitted; and after assuring themselves none were in sight, carefully following the zigzag trail, proceed to the bottom. Again another summit has been almost reached; now the hunters hope for a shot: eye and ear are strained to the utmost, and they move slowly forward; the ridge of the next hill breaks first upon their sight beyond a wide valley. The slope nearest them is still hidden from their view. On one side the mountains rise in steeper and more irregular shapes; pine-trees and oaks are thickly grown in the deepest and most grassy spot far below them. The track trends that way, and silently they proceed, looking around at almost every step, and yet uncertain where their game has wandered. Once the trail has been almost lost in the stony, broken ground they pass, but again they have it; now they approach and search in different directions the most likely places to find the Deer, but in vain; at last they gain the next summit: the object of their chase is at hand; suddenly they see him—a fine buck—he is yet on the declivity of the hill, and they cautiously observe his motions. Now they see some broken ground and rocky fragments scattering towards the left; they redouble their caution; locks are ready cocked; and, breathing rapidly, they gain the desired spot One instant—the deadly rifle has sent its leaden messenger and the buck lies struggling in his gore.

Short work is made of the return to camp if no more Deer signs are about; and a straight cut may bring the hunters home in less than an hour, even should they have been two or three in following their prize.

Sometimes the Deer start up suddenly, quite near, and are shot down on the instant; occasionally, after a long pursuit, the crack of a rifle from an unknown hunter deprives the others of their chance; and—must we admit it—sometimes they miss; and not unfrequently they see no game at all.

Mr. J. G. BELL informed us that while he was digging gold in a sequestered and wild cañon, in company with a young man with whom he was associated in the business, they used to lie down to rest during the heat of the day, and occasionally he shot a Black-tailed Deer, which unsuspectingly came within shooting distance down the little brook that flowed in the bottom of the ravine. He also used to rise very early in the mornings occasionally, and seek for the animals in the manner of still-hunting, as practised in the United States. One morning he killed three in this manner, before his breakfast-time, and sold them, after reserving some of the best parts for himself and companion, for eighty dollars apiece! He frequently sold Deer subsequently, as well as hares and squirrels, birds, &c., which he shot at different times, for enormous prices. Many of the miners, indeed, turned their attention to killing Deer, elk, bear, antelopes, geese, ducks, and all sorts of game and wild fowl, by which they realized considerable sums from selling them at San Francisco and other places. We have heard of one person who, after a luckless search for gold, went to killing Deer and other game, and in the course of about eighteen months had made five thousand dollars by selling to the miners at the diggings.

The gait of this species is not so graceful as that of the Virginian Deer, it

No 22.

Plate CVI.

Drawn from Nature by J.W. Audubon.

On Stone by W.P. Hitchcock

Lith. Printed & Col.d by J.T. Bowen, Phila.da

Columbian Black Tailed Deer.

bounds rather more like the roebuck of Europe than any other of our Deer except the Long-tailed Deer, and is reported to be very swift. The season of its breeding is earlier than that of the common Deer, and it no doubt brings forth the same number of young at a time.

Geographical Distribution.

This beautiful Deer was first met with by J. W. AUDUBON on the eastern spurs of the coast range of mountains after leaving Los Angeles and traversing a portion of the Tule valley in California. On entering the broad plain of the San Joaquin and river of the lakes, few Black-tailed Deer were met with, and the elk and antelope took their place. The party again found them abundant when they reached the hills near the Sierra Nevada, on their way towards the Chinese diggings, about eighty miles southeast of Stockton.

They may be said to inhabit most of the hilly and undulating lands of California, and as far as we can judge probably extend on the western side of the grand ridge of the Rocky Mountains nearly to the Russian Possessions.

We have not heard that they are met with east of the bases of that portion of the Cordilleras which lies in the parallel of San Francisco, or north or south of that latitude, although they may exist in the valleys of the Colorado of the west in a northeast direction from the mouth of that river, which have as yet not been much explored.

General Remarks.

According to our present information, there is only one specimen of this Deer in the collections of objects of natural history in Europe, and this is in the museum of the Zoological Society in London, where it was, when we saw it, (erroneously) labelled *C. Macrotis.*

At the Patent Office in Washington city there is a skin of a Deer (one of the specimens brought from the northwest coast of America by the Exploring Expedition), which has been named by Mr. PEALE *C. Lewisii.*

We have not positively ascertained whether it be distinct from our *C. Richardsonii,* but presume it will prove to be well separated from it, as well as from all our hitherto described Deer, and we shall endeavour to figure it, if a good species, and introduce it into our fauna under the name given it by Mr. PEALE.

We have detected an error in the description of the horns of *C. Macrotis* (see vol. ii. p. 206), where a portion of the description of those of *C. Richardsonii* seems to have been introduced by mistake.

Arctomys Lewisii.—Aud. and Bach.

Lewis's Marmot.

Plate cvii.—Males.

A. Rufo-fulvus, pedibus albo-virgatis, cauda apice albo; magnitudine leporis sylvatici, forma a monacis.

Characters.

Size of the grey rabbit; general shape of the head and body similar to that of A. monax; colour reddish-brown; feet barred with white; end of tail white.

Description.

Head, rather small; body, round and full; ears short, ovate, with somewhat acute points, clothed with short hairs on both sides; whiskers long, extending beyond the ears; nose blunt, naked; eyes, of moderate size; teeth, rather smaller than those of the Maryland marmot; feet, short; nails, rather long and arched, the nail on the thumb being large and nearly the size of the others; tail short, round, not distichous, thickly clothed with hair to the end; the hair is of two kinds—a short, dense fur beneath, with longer and rigid hairs interspersed.

Colour.

Nose, black; incisors, yellowish-white; nails, black; the whole upper surface and the ears, reddish-brown; this colour is produced by the softer fur underneath being light yellowish-brown, and the longer hairs, at their extremities, blackish-brown. On the haunches the hairs are interspersed with black and yellowish-brown; feet and belly, light salmon-red; tail, from the root for half its length, reddish-brown, the other half to the tip soiled white; above the nose, edges of ears and along the cheeks, pale reddish-buff.

There is a white band across the toes, and another irregular one behind them; and an irregularly defined dark-brown line around the lack of the head and lower part of the chin, marking the separation of the head from the throat and neck.

Dimensions.

	Feet.	Inches.
From point of nose to root of tail, ...	1	4
Tail, (vertebræ), ...		2
" (to end of hair), ...		3
Point of nose to ear, ...		2
" " to eye, ...		1
Heel to middle claw, ...		$2\frac{1}{2}$

Habits.

From the form of this animal we may readily be convinced that it possesses the characteristics of the true Marmots. These animals are destitute of cheek-pouches; they burrow in the earth; live on grasses and grains; seldom climb trees, and when driven to them by a dog do not mount high, but cling to the bark, and descend as soon as the danger is over. As far as we have been able to ascertain, all the spermophiles or burrowing squirrels are gregarious, and live in communities usually numbering several hundreds, and often thousands. On the contrary, the Marmots, although the young remain with the mother until autumn, are found to live solitarily, or at most in single pairs. It was not our good fortune ever to have met with this species in a living state, hence we regret that we are unable to offer anything in regard to its peculiar habits.

Geographical Distribution.

We have no doubt this species, like the other Marmots, has an extensive geographical range, but coming from so distant a part of our country as Oregon, which has been so little explored by naturalists, we are obliged to make use of the vague term "shores of the Columbia river" as its habitat.

General Remarks.

We have not felt at liberty to quote any authorities or add any synonymes for this species, inasmuch as we cannot find that any author has referred to it. The specimen from which our figure was made, and which we believe is the only one existing in any collection, was sent to the Zoological Society by the British fur-traders who are in the habit of annually carrying their peltry down the Columbia river to the Pacific. It is labelled in the museum of the Zoological Society, No. 461, page 48 Catalogue, *Arctomys branchyura?* HARLAN. The history of the supposed species of HARLAN is the following: LEWIS and CLARK (Expedition, vol. ii. p. 173) describe an animal from the plains of the Columbia under the name of burrowing squirrel. No specimen was brought. HARLAN and RAFINESQUE in quick succession applied their several names to the species, the former styling it *Arctomys brachyura* and the latter *Anisonyx brachyura.* When the present specimen was received at the Museum, the name of *A. brachyura* was given to it, with a doubt. On turning to LEWIS and CLARK's descriptions, the only guides which any naturalists possess in reference to the species, we find that they refer to an animal whose whole contour resembles that of the squirrel, the thumbs being remarkably short and equipped with blunt nails, and the hair of the tail thickly inserted on the sides only, which gives it a flat appearance, whereas the animal of this article does not resemble a squirrel in its whole contour; its thumbs, instead of being remarkably short and equipped with blunt nails, have long nails nearly the length of those on the other toes, and the tail, instead of being flat with the hairs inserted on the sides, is quite round. It differs also so widely in several other particulars that we deem it unneccessary to institute a more minute comparison. We have little doubt that LEWIS and CLARK, who, although not scientific naturalists, had a remarkably correct knowledge of animals, and described them with great accuracy, had, in their account of the burrowing squirrel, reference to some species of spermophile—probably *Spermophilus Townsendii,* described in this volume—which certainly answers the description referred to much nearer than the species of this article.

Plate CVII

N.º 22

Drawn on Stone by Wm E. Hitchcock

Lith Prtd & Cold by J.T. Bowen Ph.

Lewis' Marmot.

Lepus Bachmani. — Waterhouse.

Bachman's Hare.

Plate cviii. — Males.

L. Supra fascus, lateribus cinereo fuscis, ventre albo rufo-tincto; L. sylvatico aliquantulo minor, auriculis capite paullo longioribus.

Characters.

A little smaller than the gray rabbit; ears rather longer than the head; tarsi, short. Colour, brown above, gray-brown on the sides, belly white, tinged with rufous.

Synonymes.

LEPUS BACHMANI. Waterhouse, Proceedings Zool. Soc. 1838, p. 103.
"   "   Bachman's Hare, Bach. Jour. Acad. Nat. Sci. Phila, vol. viii. part 1, p. 96.
"   "   Waterhouse, Nat. Hist. Mamm., vol. ii. p. 124.

Description.

This Hare bears a general resemblance to the gray rabbit (*L. sylvaticus*), but is considerably smaller: the fur is softer and the ears shorter than in that species.

Upper incisors, much arched, and deeply grooved; claws, slender and pointed—the claw of the longest toe remarkably slender; ears longer than the head, sparingly furnished with hair quite fine and closely adpressed externally; tail, short; feet, thickly clothed with hair covering the nails.

Colour.

The fur on the back and sides is deep gray at the roots, annulated near the ends of the hairs with brownish-white, and black at the points. On the belly the hair is gray at the roots and white at the points, with a tinge of red; chest and fore parts of the neck, gray-brown, each hair being dusky at the tip; chin and throat, grayish-white; the hairs on the head are brownish rufous; on the flanks there is an indistinct pale longitudinal dash just above the haunches; under surface of tail white, edged with brownish black; general colour of the tarsus above, dull-rufous; sides of tarsus, brown; ears, on the fore part mottled with black and yellowish-white, on the hinder part greyish-white; internally the ears are dull orange, with a white margin all around their openings; their apical portion is obscurely margined with black.

Dimensions.

	Inches.	Lines.
Length from point of nose to root of tail, ...	10	
Tail (vertebræ), ...		9
" to end of fur, ...	1	3
Ear internally, ...	2	8
From heel to point of longest nail, ...	3	
Tip of nose to ear, ...	2	5

Habits.

The manners of this pretty Hare, as observed in Texas by J. W. AUDUBON, appear to assimilate to those of the common rabbit (*Lepus sylvaticus*), the animal seldom quitting a particular locality, and making its form in thick briar patches or tufts of rank grass, keeping near the edges of the woody places, and being seen in the evenings, especially for a short time after sunset, when it can be easily shot.

We have been favoured with the following particulars as to the habits of this Hare by our esteemed friend Captain J. P. McCOWN of the United States Army:

"This Hare is deficient in speed, and depends for its safety upon dodging among the thick and thorny chaparals or nopal clusters (*cacti*) which it inhabits, never venturing far from these coverts.

"Large numbers can be seen early in the morning or late in the evening, playing in the small openings or on the edges of the chaparals, or nibbling the tender leaves of the nopal, which seems to be the common prickly pear of our country, only much larger from congeniality of climate."

"The principal enemies of these Hares in Texas are the cat species, hawks, and snakes."

During the war with Mexico, some of the soldiers of our army who were stationed on the Mexican frontier had now and then a sort of battue, to kill all the game they could in their immediate vicinity; and by surrounding a space of tolerably open ground, especially if well covered with high grass or weeds, and approaching gradually to the centre, numbers of these Hares were knocked down with clubs as they attempted to make their escape, as well as occasionally other animals which happened to be secreted within the circle. We were told that a raw German recruit, who had once or twice before been made the butt of his comrades, having joined only a few days, was invited to partake of the sport, and as the excitement became quite agreeable to him, was amongst the foremost in knocking down the unfortunate Hares, as they dashed out or timidly squatted yet a moment, hoping not to be observed; when suddenly one of his companions pointed out to him a *skunk*, which, notwithstanding the din and uproar on all sides, was very quietly awaiting the course of events. The unlucky recruit darted forward:—we need say nothing more, except that during the remainder of the war the skunk was, by that detachment, known only as the "Dutchman's rabbit."

This Hare so much resembles the common rabbit, that it has been generally considered the same animal; and this is not singular, for the gray rabbit does not extend to those portions of our country in which BACHMAN'S Hare is found, and few, save persons of some observation, would perceive the differences between them, even if they had both species together so that they could compare them.

Geographical Distribution.

Lieut. ABERT, of the United States Army, procured specimens of this Hare in the neighbourhood of Santa Fé, which were the first that were made known to naturalists as existing east of California, as the animal was described from a specimen sent by DOUGLAS from the western shores of America. It now appears that it occupies a great portion of Texas, New Mexico, and California, probably extending south through great part of Mexico. Its northeastern limit may be about the head waters of the Red river or the Arkansas.

General Remarks.

From the small size of this Hare, it was at one time considered possible that it might prove to be only the young of some other species of *Lepus*, but its specific characters are now fully established, and it is, at present, known as more numerous in some localities than even the gray rabbit.

This species was discovered among a collection of skins in the museum of the Zoological Society by Dr. BACHMAN and Mr. WATERHOUSE, and the latter gentleman having desired the doctor to allow him to describe and name it, called it *L. Bachmani*, in compliment to him. Our figures were made from the specimen described by Mr. WATERHOUSE, which is yet in the museum of the Zoological Society at London. We have obtained many skins since, from Texas and the southwestern portions of New Mexico.

Plate CVIII

Nº 22

On Stone by W.E. Hitche

Drawn from Nature by J.W. Audubon

Bachman's Hare

Spermophilus Mexicanus. —Light.

Mexican Marmot Squirrel (Spermophile).

Plate cix. —Old Male, and Young.

S. magnitudine sciuri Hudsonici, auriculis brevibus, cauda longa, corpore supra rufo-fulvo, maculis vel strigio albis, subtus albo flavescente.

Characters.

Size of Sciurus Hudsonicus; *ears, short; tail, long; body, above, reddish-tawny, with white spots or bars; beneath, yellowish-white.*

Synonymes.

CITILUS MEXICANUS. Licht., Darstellung neurer oder wenig bekannter Säugthiere, Berlin, 1827–1834.
SPERMOPHILUS SPILOSOMA. Bennett, Proc. Zool. Soc., London, 1833, p. 40.

Description.

Form, very similar to the leopard spermophile (*S. tridecemlineatus*), although the present species is the larger of the two; ears, short, and clothed with short hairs; body, moderately thick; legs, rather short; toes and nails, long; tail, somewhat flat, distichous, and shorter than the body.

Colour.

Upper surface, rufous-brown, spotted with yellowish-white, the spots bordered posteriorly with black; under parts pale buff-white; this colour extends somewhat upwards on the sides of the animal; feet, pale-yellow; tarsi, hairy beneath, the hairs extending forwards to the naked fleshy pads at the base of the toes; claws, dusky horn colour, with pale points; the fur at the roots (both on the upper and under parts of the animal) is gray.

The eye is bordered with whitish-yellow; head and ears, rufous-brown; upper surface of tail, dark-brown, edged with a white fringe on the sides; towards the extremities the hairs are yellow, but they have a broad black band in the middle of their length; under surface of the tail of an almost uniform yellowish-hue, slightly inclining to rust colour.

Dimensions.

Adult male.

	Inches.	Lines.
From point of nose to root of tail, ...	10	
Tail (vertebræ), ...	4	
" including hair, ...	5	
Nose to end of head, ...	2	6
Length of ears, ...		4
From elbow of fore-leg to end of longest nail, ...	2	6
Tarsus (of hind leg), ...	1	9

Measurements of the specimen named *S. Spilosoma* by Mr. BENNETT:

Young.

	Inches.	Lines.
From point of nose to root of tail, ...	5	9
Tail (vertebræ), ...	2	9
" including hair, ...	3	6
Nose to ear, ...	1	3
Tarsus and nails, ...	1	3
Length of nail of middle toe, ...		$2\frac{1}{3}$
" fore foot and nails, ...		$9\frac{1}{2}$
" middle toe of fore foot to nail, ...		$2\frac{1}{2}$

Habits.

This Mexican Spermophile has all the activity and sprightliness of the squirrel family, and in its movements greatly reminds one of the little ground-squirrel (*Tamias Lysteri*) of the middle and northern States. It feeds standing on its hind feet and holding its food in the fore paws like a common squirrel, and is remarkable for the flexibility of its back and neck, which it twists sideways with a cunning expression of face while observing the looker on. When caught alive this pretty species makes a pet of no common attractions, having beautiful eyes and being very handsomely marked, while its disposition soon becomes affectionate, and it retains its gay and frolicsome habits. It will eat corn and various kinds of seeds, and is fond of bits of potatoe, apple, or any kind of fruit, as well as bread, pastry, cakes, &c.: grasses and clover it will also eat readily, and in fact it takes any kind of vegetable food. Even in the hottest summer weather this animal is fond of making a nest of tow and bits of carpet, and will sleep covered up by these warm materials as comfortably as if the temperature was at freezing point outside instead of 85°.

For some time we have had a fine living animal of this species in a cage, and he has been a source of great amusement to the little folks, who are fond of feeding him and pleased to see his antics. When threatened he shows fight, and approaches the bars of his cage gritting or chattering with his teeth like a little fury, and sometimes uttering a sharp squeak of defiance; but when offered any good thing to eat he at once resumes his usual playful manner, and will take it from the hand of any one. In eating corn this little animal picks out the soft part and leaves the shell and more compact portion of the grain untouched.

At times he will coil himself up, lying on one side, almost entirely concealed by the tow and shredded carpet; if then disturbed, he looks up out of one eye without changing his position, and will sometimes almost bear to be poked with a stick before moving. Like the human race he occasionally shows symptoms of laziness or fatigue, by yawning and stretching. When first placed in his cage he manifested some desire to get out, and attempted to gnaw the wires: he would now and then turn himself upside down, and with his fore paws holding on to the wires above his head bite vigorously at the horizontal wires for half a minute at a time, before changing this apparently uncomfortable position. This Spermophile is not in the habit of eating a very great deal at a time, but seems to prefer feeding at intervals, even when plenty of food lies within his reach, retiring to his snug nest and sleeping for a while after eating a sufficient portion. When thus sleeping we sometimes found him lying on his back, with his fore paws almost joined, held close by his nose, while his hind legs were slightly turned to one side so as to give his body the appearance of complete relaxation.

These animals are said to be tolerably abundant in Mexico and California, but only in the wooded districts. We were informed that they could easily be procured near Vera Cruz, Tuspan, Tampico, &c.

Geographical Distribution.

LICHTENSTEIN informs us that Mr. DEPPE procured this animal in 1826, in the neighbourhood of Toluca in Mexico, where it was called by the inhabitants by the general term *Urion*, which was also applied to other burrowing animals. Captain BEECHY states that his specimen was procured in California, and we are informed by Captain J. P. McCOWN that it exists along the Rio Grande and in other parts of Texas, where he has seen it as a pet in the Mexican ranchos.

General Remarks.

In our first edition (folio plates), we gave figures of the *young* of this species as *S. spilosoma* of BENNETT, but having since ascertained that his specimen was only the young of *S. Mexicanus*, a species which had been previously published, we have now set down *S. spilosoma* as a synonyme of the latter, and have placed the figures of both old and young on the same plate.

Drawn from Nature by J.W.Audubon

Drawn on Stone by Wᵐ E. Hitchcock

Lith Printed & Colᵈ by J.T.Bowen, Phil

Mexican Marmot-Squirrel.

Adult male and young

Pseudostoma Talpoides. — Rich.

Mole-Shaped Pouched Rat.

Plate cx. — Males.

P. Magnitudine muris ratti, corpore nigro cinerescente, capite pro protione parvo, mento albo, macula alba ad gulam, pedibus posticis quadridigitatis.

Characters.

Size of the black rat; head, small in proportion; body, grayish-black; chin, white; a white patch on the throat; only four perfect toes on the hind feet.

Synonymes.

CRICETUS (?) TALPOIDES. Rich, Zool. Jour. No. 12, p. 5, pl. 18.
? GEOMYS ? TALPOIDES.   "   F. B. A., p. 204.
OOTAW-CHEE-GOES-HEES. Cree Indians.

Discription.

Body, shaped like that of the mole; head, rather small; nose, obtuse and covered with short hairs; incisors, strong, with flat anterior surfaces; upper ones short and straight, and each marked with a single very fine groove close to their inner edge; lower incisors, long, curved inwards, and not grooved; whiskers, composed of fine hairs as long as the head; eyes, small; auditory opening, small and slightly margined; ears, scarcely visible beyond the fur.

The pouches have an opening on the sides of the mouth externally, and are of moderate size; extremities, very short; the fore foot has four toes and the rudiment of a thumb; the middle toe is longest and has the largest claw, the first and third are equal to each other in length, the outer one is shorter and placed far back, and the thumb, which is still farther back, consists merely of a short claw; the fore claws the long, compressed, slightly curved, and pointed; they are, however, less robust than those of some other species of the genus, especially *P. bursarius.* On the hind feet there are four short toes, armed with compressed claws much shorter than those on the fore feet, and the rudiment of a fifth toe, so small that it can be detected only after a minute inspection; tail, very slender, cylindrical, and rather short, covered with a smooth coat of short hairs.

The hair is nearly as fine as that of the common shrew mole, and is close and velvety.

Colour.

Whiskers, black; incisors, yellowish-white, approaching flesh colour; chin and throat, white; outer edges of the pouch, light gray; tail, grayish-brown; the body generally, grayish-black, with faint brownish tints in some lights.

Dimensions.

	Inches.	Lines.
Length of head and body,	7	4
Tail to end of hair,	2	5
From point of nose to eye,		9
From point of nose to auditory opening,	1	3
Height of back,	2	
Length of lower incisors,		5
" fur on the back,		6
" middle fore claw,		4
From heel to end of middle hind claw,		11

Habits.

Very little is known of the habits of this peculiar sand-rat. The manners, however, of all the species of the genus *Pseudostoma* are probably very similar: they live principally under ground, and leave their galleries, holes, or burrows, pretty much as we of the genus *Homo* quit our houses, for the purpose of procuring the necessaries of life, or pleasure, although they do find a portion of their food while making the excavations which serve them as places in which to shelter themselves and bring forth their young. They are generally nocturnal, and in the day time prefer coming abroad during cloudy weather.

They never make their appearance, nor do they work in their galleries or burrows during the winter in our northern latitudes, unless it be far beneath the hard frozen ground, which would not permit them to make new roads.

RICHARDSON says that as soon as the snow disappears in the spring, and whilst the ground is as yet only partially thawed, little heaps of earth newly thrown up attest the activity of this animal.

The specimen from which our figures were made was presented to the Zoological Society by Mr. LEADBEATER, who obtained it from Hudson's Bay. It also served Dr. RICHARDSON for his description: he was inclined to identify it with a small animal inhabiting the banks of the Saskatchewan, which throws up little mounds in the form of mole hills, but generally rather larger; he, however, could not procure any specimens.

As an evidence that this animal never feeds upon worms, he mentions the fact that none exist in high northern latitudes. A gentleman who had for forty years superintended the cultivation of considerable pieces of ground on the banks of the Saskatchewan, informed him that during the whole of that period he never saw an earthworm turned up. All the species of *Pseudostoma,* as far as our knowledge goes, feed on bulbs, roots, and grasses.

The pouches serve as sacks, in which after filling them with food they carry it to their nests in their subterranean retreats, where they deposit considerable quantities, which evidently serve them as supplies throughout the winter.

We are under the impression that none of the species of this genus become perfectly dormant in winter, as we have observed in Georgia a few fresh hillocks thrown up by the Southern pouched-rat after each warm day in that season.

Geographical distribution.

As before stated, this species was obtained at Hudson's Bay, and is supposed by RICHARDSON to exist on the Saskatchewan, thus giving it a considerable western range, should there not indeed prove to be a different species, which is, however, rather probable.

General Remarks.

Until very recently there has been much confusion among writers in regard to the organization of the family of pouched-rats, which appear to be exclusively confined to the American continent—some supposing that the natural position of the pouch was that of a sac hanging suspended on each side of the throat, with the opening *within* the mouth.

For the probable origin of this error we refer our readers to the first volume of this work, p. 338, where we gave some remarks on the *Pseudostoma bursarius,* and this genus generally.

Genus Ovibos. — Blainville.

Dental Formula.

Incisive $\frac{0}{8}$; *Canine* $\frac{0-0}{0-0}$; *Molar* $\frac{6-6}{6-6}$ = 32.

Body, low and compact; legs, short and covered with smooth short hairs; feet, hairy under the heel; forehead, broad and flat; no suborbital sinus; muzzle, blunt and covered with hair; horns, common to both sexes, in contact on the summit of the head, flat, broad, then tapering and bent down against the cheeks, with the points turned up; ears, short, and placed far back; eyes, small; tail, short.

Hair, very abundant, long, and woolly; size and form intermediate between the ox and the sheep; inhabits the northern or Arctic portions of North America.

The generic name is derived from two Latin words—*ovis,* sheep, and *bos,* ox.

There is only one known existing species of this genus, although *fossil* skulls have been found in Siberia, from which the name of *Ovibos pallentis* is given in systematic European works.

Ovibos Moschatus. — Gmel.

Musk-Ox.

Drawn from Nature by J W Audubon.

On Stone by W.E.Hitchcock.

Lith.Printed & Col.d by J T.Bowen.Philad.

Mole-shaped Pouched Rat

Plate cxi.—Males.

O. Fuscescente-niger, cornibus basi approximatis planis, latissimis, deorsum flexis, ad malas appressis apice extrorsum sursumque recurvis; mas magnitudine vaccæ biennis.

Characters.

Adult male, size of a small two year old cow; horns, united on the summit of the head, flat, broad, bent down against the cheeks, with the points turned up. Colour, brownish-black.

Synonymes.

LE BOEUF MUSQUÉ. M. Jeremie. Voyage au Nord, t. iii. p. 314.
   "   "   Charlevoix, Nouv, France, tom. v. p. 194.
MUSK-OX. Drage, Voyage, vol. ii. p. 260.
   "   Dobbs, Hudson's Bay, pp. 19, 25.
   "   Ellis, Voyage, p. 232.
   "   Pennant, Quadr., vol. i. p. 31.
   "   "   Arctic Zoology, vol. i. p. 9.
   "   Hearne's Journey, p. 137.
   "   Parry's First Voyage, p. 257, plate.
   "   "   Second Voyage, pp. 497, 503, 512 (specimen in British Museum).
BOS MOSCHATUS. Gmel. Syst.
   "   "   Capt, Sabine (Parry's First Voyage, Supplement, p. 189).
   "   "   Mr. Sabine, Franklin's Journey, p. 668.
   "   "   Richardson, Parry's Second Voyage, Appendix, p. 331.
OVIBOS MOSCHATUS. Richardson, Fauna Boreali Americana, p. 275.
MATAEH-MOOSTOOS (UGLY BISON). Cree Indians.
ADGIDDAH-YAWSEH (LITTLE BISON). Chipewyans and Copper Indians.
OONINGMAK. Esquimaux.
OVIBOS MOSCHATUS. Harlan. Fauna, p. 264.
BOS MOSCHATUS—The MUSK-OX. Godman, Nat. Hist. vol. iii. p. 29.

Description.

Horns, very broad at base, covering the brow and crown of the head, touching each other for their entire breadth from the occipital to the frontal region: as the horns rise from their flatly-convex bases they become round and tapering, like those of a common cow, and curve downwards between the eye and the ear to a little below the eye, where they turn upwards and outwards (in a segment of a circle), to a little above the angle of the eye, ending with tolerably sharp points. The horns for half their length are rough, with small longitudinal splinters of unequal length, beyond which they are smooth and rather glossy, like those of a common bull.

Head, large and broad; nose, very obtuse; nostrils, oblong openings inclining towards each other downwards from above; their inner margins naked; united at their base. There is no other vestige of a muzzle; the whole of the nose, and the lips, covered with a short coat of hairs; there is no furrow on the upper lip.

The head, neck, and shoulders are covered with long bushy hair; and there is a quantity of long straight hair on the margins of the mouth and the sides of the lower jaw.

Eyes, moderately large, and the hair immediately around them shorter than on other parts of the cheeks; ears, short, and scarcely visible through the surrounding long hair, which is more or less waved or crimped, and forms a sort of ruff back of the neck; legs, short and thick, clothed with short hair unmixed with wool; hoofs, flat, small in proportion to the size of the animal, and resembling those of the reindeer. The cow differs from the bull in having smaller horns (the bases of which, instead of touching each other, are separated by a hairy space), and in the hair on the throat and chest being shorter. The female is considerably smaller than the male.

Colour.

The general colour of the hair of the body is brown; on the neck and between the shoulders it is of a grizzled hue, being dull light-brown, fading on the tips into brownish-white; on the centre of the back it presents a soiled whitish colour, forming a mark which is aptly termed by Captain PARRY the saddle. The hips are dark-brown, and the sides, thighs, and belly, nearly black; the short soft hairs on the nose and lips are whitish, with a tinge of reddish-brown; legs, brownish-white; tips of horns, and hoofs, black; tail, dark brown.

Dimensions.

	Feet.	Inches.
Length from nose to root of tail, about	5	6

Habits.

For our description and account of the habits of this very peculiar animal we have resorted to other authors, never having ourselves had an opportunity of seeing it alive, and in fact knowing it only from the specimen in the British Museum, from which our figures were drawn, and which is the only one hitherto sent to Europe, so difficult is it to procure the animal and convey the skin, with the skull, leg bones, &c., in a tolerable state of preservation, from the barren lands of the northern portions of British America, and where an almost perpetual winter and consequent scarcity of food make it very difficult to prevent the Indians, or white hunters either, from eating (we should say devouring) everything that can by any possibility serve to fill their empty stomachs—even skins, hoofs, and the most refuse parts of any animal they kill.

To give a better idea of the effects of hunger on man, at times, in these wild and desert countries, we will relate a case that happened to Dr. RICHARDSON while upon an expedition. One of his men, a half-breed and a bad fellow, it was discovered, had killed a companion with whom he had been sent upon a short journey in the woods for intelligence, and had eaten a considerable portion of his miserable victim.

Dr. RICHARDSON, watching this monster from hour to hour, perceived that he was evidently preparing and awaiting an opportunity to kill him, possibly dreading the punishment he deserved for his horrible crime, and perhaps thinking the doctor's body would supply him with food till he could reach the settlements and escape:—anticipating his purpose, the doctor very properly shot him.

Sir JOHN relates an instance in which all his efforts to obtain a skin of the black-tailed deer were baffled by the appetites of his hunters, who ate up one they killed, hide and all. Even on the fertile prairies of more southern portions of our continent, starvation sometimes stares the hunter in the face. At one time a fine specimen of the mule deer (*Cervus macrotis*), shot for us on the prairies far up the Missouri river, was eaten by our men, who concealed the fact of their having killed the animal until some days afterwards.

Sir GEORGE SIMPSON, of the Hudson's Bay Fur Company, most kindly promised some years ago that he would if possible procure us a skin of the Musk-Ox, which he thought could be got within two years—taking one season to send the order for it to his men and another to get it and send the skin to England. We have not yet received this promised skin, and therefore feel sure that the hunters failed to obtain or to preserve one, for during the time that has elapsed we have received from the Hudson's Bay Company, through the kindness of Sir GEORGE, an Arctic fox, preserved in the flesh in rum, and a beautiful skin of the silver-gray fox, which were written for by Sir GEORGE at our request in 1845, at the same time that gentleman wrote for the skin of the Musk-Ox. We give an extract from Sir GEORGE's letter to us: "With reference to your application for skins of the Musk-Ox, I forwarded instructions on the subject to a gentleman stationed at the Hudson's Bay Company's post of Churchill, on Hudson's Bay, but the distance and difficulties of communication are so great that he will not receive my letter until next summer; and he cannot possibly procure the specimens you require before next winter, nor can these be received in England before the month of October, 1847, and it is doubtful that they will be received even then, as those animals are scarce, and so extremely timid that a year might be lost before obtaining one."

Sir GEORGE SIMPSON was pleased to close this letter with a highly complimentary expression of the pleasure it would afford him to assist us in the completion of our work; and among the difficulties and worrying accompaniments of such a publication as ours, it has been an unmixed gratification to have with us the sympathies and assistance of gentlemen like Sir GEORGE and many others, and of so powerful a corporation as the Hudson's Bay Fur Company.

Dr. RICHARDSON in a note explains a mistake made by PENNANT, who appears to have confounded the habitat of the Musk-Ox with that of the bison and states that our animal is found on the lands of the *Cris* or *Cristinaux* and *Assinibouls*, which are plains extending from the Red river of Lake Winnipeg to the Saskatchewan, on which tracts the buffalo is frequently found, but not the Musk-Ox.

Plate CXI

Drawn from Nature by J.W. Audubor

Drawn on Stone by Wᵐ E. Hitchcock

Musk Ox.

Lith. Printed & Cold by J.T. Bowen, Phil

The accounts of old writers, having reference to an animal found in New Mexico, which PENNANT refers to the Musk-Ox, may be based upon the existence of the Rocky Mountain sheep in that country, which having been imperfectly described, has led some authors to think the Musk-Ox was an inhabitant of so southern a locality.

"The country frequented by the Musk-Ox is mostly rocky, and destitute of wood except on the banks of the larger rivers, which are generally more or less thickly clothed with spruce trees. Their food is similar to that of the caribou—grass at one season and lichens at another; and the contents of their paunch are eaten by the natives with the same relish that they devour the 'nerrooks' of the reindeer. The droppings of the Musk-Ox take the form of round pellets, differing from those of the caribou only in their greater size.

"When this animal is fat, its flesh is well tasted, and resembles that of the caribou, but has a coarser grain. The flesh of the bulls is highly flavoured, and both bulls and cows, when lean, smell strongly of musk, their flesh at the same time being very dark and tough, and certainly far inferior to that of any other ruminating animal existing in North America.

"The carcase of a Musk-Ox weighs, exclusive of the offal, about three hundred weight, or nearly three times as much as a barren ground caribou, and twice as much as one of the woodland caribou.

"Notwithstanding the shortness of the legs of the Musk-Ox, it runs fast, and climbs hills or rocks with great ease. One, pursued on the banks of the Coppermine, scaled a lofty sand cliff, having so great an acclivity that we were obliged to crawl on hands and knees to follow it. Its foot-marks are very similar to those of the caribou, but are rather longer and narrower. These oxen assemble in herds of from twenty to thirty, rut about the end of August and beginning of September, and bring forth one calf about the latter end of May or beginning of June.

"HEARNE, from the circumstance of few bulls being seen, supposed that they kill each other in their contests for the cows. If the hunters keep themselves concealed when they fire upon a herd of Musk-Oxen, the poor animals mistake the noise for thunder, and, forming themselves into a group, crowd nearer and nearer together as their companions fall around them; but should they discover their enemies by sight or by their sense of smell, which is very acute, the whole herd seek for safety by instant flight. The bulls, however, are very irascible, and particularly when wounded will often attack the hunter and endanger his life, unless he possess both activity and presence of mind. The Esquimaux, who are well accustomed to the pursuit of this animal, sometimes turn its irritable disposition to good account; for an expert hunter having provoked a bull to attack him, wheels round it more quickly than it can turn, and by repeated stabs in the belly puts an end to its life. The wool of the Musk-Ox resembles that of the bison, but is perhaps finer, and would no doubt be highly useful in the arts if it could be procured in sufficient quantity."—*Richardson, F. B. A.*, p. 277.

"The Musk-Oxen killed on Melville Island during PARRY's visit, were very fat, and their flesh, especially the heart, although highly scented with musk, was considered very good food. When cut up it had all the appearance of beef for the market. HEARNE says that the flesh of the Musk-Ox does not at all resemble that of the bison, but is more like that of the moose, and the fat is of a clear white, tinged with light azure. The young cows and calves furnish a very palatable beef, but that of the old bulls is so intolerably musky as to be excessively disagreeable."—*Godman*, vol. iii. p. 35.

According to PARRY, this animal weighs about seven hundred pounds. The head and hide weigh about one hundred and thirty pounds. "The horns are employed for various purposes by the Indians and Esquimaux, especially for making cups and spoons. From the long hair growing on the neck and chest the Esquimaux make their musquito wigs, to defend their faces from those troublesome insects. The hide makes good soles for shoes and is much used for that purpose by the Indians."

Geographical Distribution.

The Musk-Ox resorts to the barren lands of America lying to the north of the 60th parallel of north latitude. HEARNE mentions that he once saw the tracks of one in the neighbourhood of Fort Churchill, lat. 59°; and in his first journey to the north he saw many in the latitude of 61°. At present, according to what is said, they do not reach the shores of Hudson's Bay; farther to the westward they are rarely seen in any number; lower than lat. 67°. RICHARDSON states that he had not heard of their being seen on the banks of Mackenzie's river to the southward of Great Bear lake. They range over the islands which lie to the north of the American continent as far as Melville Island, in latitude 75°, but they do not extend to Greenland, Lapland, or Spitzbergen. There is an extensive tract of barren country skirting the banks of the Mackenzie river, northwest of the Rocky Mountains, which also is inhabited by the Musk-Ox; it is not known in New Caledonia, on the banks of the Columbia, nor in any portion of the Rocky Mountains; nor does it cross over to the Asiatic shore: consequently it does not exist in any part of northern Asia or Siberia.

Captain PARRY noticed its appearance on Melville Island in the month of May; it must therefore be regarded as an animal the native home of which is within the Arctic Circle, the dwelling-place of the Esquimaux.

General Remarks.

The Musk-Ox is remarkable amongst the animals of America, for never having had more than one specific appellation, whilst other species of much less interest have been honoured with a long list of synonymes. JEREMIE appears to have given the first notice of it: he brought some of the wool to France, and had stockings made of it which were said to have been more beautiful than silk. The English voyagers of an early period gave some information respecting it, but PENNANT has the merit of being the first who systematically arranged and described it, from the skin of a specimen sent to England by HEARNE, the celebrated traveller. From its want of a naked muzzle and some other peculiarities, M. BLAINVILLE placed it in a genus intermediate (as its name denotes) between the sheep and the ox.

Lepus Californicus.—Gray.

Californian Hare.

Plate cxii.

L. magnitudine L. glacialis, formâ L. timide; supra flavescente-fuscus, subtus albus, flavo valdetinctus.

Characters.

Nearly the size of the polar hare; dark brown on the back, light brownish-red on the neck; lower parts deeply tinged with yellow.

Synonymes.

LEPUS CALIFORNICUS. Gray, Mag. Nat. Hist. 1837, vol. i., new series, p. 586.
"   RICHARDSONII. Bach. Jour. Acad. Nat. Sci., vol. viii. p. 88.
"   BENNETTII. Gray, Zoology of the Voyage of H. M. S. Sulphur, Mamm., p. 35, pl. 14, 1843.

Description.

Head, small, and not elongated; ears, very large, much longer than the head; eyes, very large; body, stout; limbs, long and slender; fur, of moderate length; tail, long and flat; feet, rather small; legs and feet, thickly clothed with short hairs nearly concealing the nails.

Colour.

The back, from the shoulder to the insertion of the tail, is strongly marked with black and rufous-brown, the hairs being pale plumbeous for two thirds of their length from the roots, then very pale brown, then black, then yellowish-brown, and tipped with black. Chest, sides of the body, and outer surface of limbs, more or less rufous. Abdomen, whitish tinged with buff; upper surface of the tail blackish-brown, lower surface yellowish-white; around the eye, pale buff; back of the neck, grayish cinnamon colour; legs and feet, cinnamon. The outer surface of the ears is longitudinally divided into two colours, the anterior portion or half being grizzled reddish-brown, becoming darker as it approaches the tip of the ear, the hairs being annulated with black and pale yellow; the posterior portion dingy yellowish-white, growing as it approaches the tip, until it blends with the black colour which terminates the upper half of the outside of the ear; the interior edge of the ear is pale yellow, each hair slightly tipped with black; one half of the inner surface of the ear is nearly naked, but covered with very delicate and short hairs, the other portion thinly

Plate CXII.

Lith⁴Printed&Col⁴by J T.Bowen,Philad⁴

Californian Hare.

Drawn from Nature by J.W.Audubon.

clothed with hair gradually thickening towards the outer edge, where it is grizzly-brown; edge of the ear for two thirds from the head, yellowish-white; the remainder to the tip, soft velvety black. This black colour extends in a large patch on to the outer surface of the ear at the tip.

Dimensions.

	Inches.	Lines.
Length from point of nose to root of tail,	22	
" eye to point of nose,	2	1
Height of ear, posteriorly,	5	10
Heel, to point of middle claw,	4	8
Tail, including hair,	3	3

Habits.

The habits of all hares are much the same; and this family is a general favourite for the beauty, timid gentleness, and fleetness its various species exhibit, although some of them are annoying to the gardener. In America, however, many species of Hare inhabit territories too far from cultivated fields or gardens for them to be able to nibble even at a cabbage plant.

Many pleasant evening hours have we passed, walking through forest-shaded roads in the last rays scattered here and there by the sinking sun, observing the playful "rabbits" leaping gracefully a few paces at a time, then stopping and looking about, ignorant of our proximity and unconscious of danger. But we are now to give the habits of the Californian Hare, for which take the following account of the animal as observed by J. W. AUDUBON:

"The Californian Hare appears to possess just brains enough to make him the greatest coward of all the tribe I have seen, for once startled he is quite as wild as a deer, and equally heedless as to the course he takes, so that as he has not the keen sense of smell of the deer to warn him of danger in any direction, he sometimes makes a great fool of himself in his haste, and I have had these Hares run to within three feet of me, before I was seen, even where there was no cover but a sparse prairie grass."

"It was after toiling night and day through the sands of the Colorado desert, and resting afterwards at Vallecito and San Felipe, while marching along the streams through the rich fields of Santa Maria, that I saw the first Californian Hare. I knew him at sight: he showed no *white tail* as he ran, and looked almost black amongst the yellow broom-sedge as he divided it in his swift course. His legs seemed always under his body, for so quick was the movement that I could not see them extended, as in other Hares, from one bound to another; he seemed to alight on his feet perpendicularly at each leap, with a low-squatting springy touch to the earth, and putting his enormously long ears forward, and then back on his neck, and stretching out his head, appeared to fly over the undulating ridges of the prairie as a swallow skims for insects the surface of a sluggish river in summer."

Very few of these Hares were seen by J. W. AUDUBON's party until they had travelled some distance further north, and it was only after they had left the plains of the San Joaquin for the mines that they became a common animal, and in fact often their sole resource for the day's meat.

J. W. AUDUBON says that a single Hare of this species, with a little fat pork to fry it with, often lasted himself and a companion, as food when travelling, for two days. Nearly every miner has eaten of this fine Hare, which is well known in all the hilly portions of Upper California.

The Californian Hare brings forth about five young at a time, which are generally littered in the latter part of April or beginning of May. J. W. AUDUBON says: "I shot a female only a few days before her young would have been born: she had five beautiful little ones, the hair and feet perfect, and a white spot on the forehead of each was prominent. I never shot another afterwards, and was sad at the havoc I had committed."

We do not know whether this species breeds more than once in the year or not, but it probably does, as Mr. PEALE says: "A female killed on the twenty-fourth of September was still suckling her young."

The Californian Hare is more frequently met with in uplands, on mountain sides, and in bushy places, than in other situations. During the rainy season it was not seen by J. W. AUDUBON in low and wet grounds, although it doubtless resorts to them during the dry weather of summer.

Mr. PEALE says, these Hares "when running, carry the ears erect, and make three short and one long leap; and that the Indians catch them by setting hedges of thorny brush, with openings at intervals, in which they set snares, so constructed as to catch the Hares when passing, without the use of springes; the noose is made of a substance like hemp, very strong and neatly twisted with cords."

Geographical Distribution.

This species was seen by J. W. AUDUBON during his journey from Texas to California; it was first met to the northward of the Colorado desert, and was quite abundant as the party approached the mining districts of California, where it was found as far north as the American fork; it was met with in the southern parts of Oregon by the United States Exploring Expedition. We are not informed whether it exists to the eastward of the Nevada range of mountains.

General Remarks.

This Hare was first obtained by Mr. DOUGLAS, and sent with other animals from California to England. It was described by Mr. GRAY, and being, from its large size and rich colouring, one of the most conspicuous among the North American Hares, we regret that that eminent naturalist should have also (by some mistake) given it the name of *L. Bennettii*, and for ourselves we must plead guilty to having erroneously named it *L. Richardsonii*. The identity of this beautiful animal has been also somewhat obscured by Mr. PEALE, who confounded it with a species from the Cape of Good Hope, which bears the name of *Longicaudatus*, and was described in London.

Canis Familiaris.—Linn. (Var. Borealis.—Desm.)

Esquimaux Dog.

Plate cxiii.—Males.

C. magnitudine C. Terræ Novæ, capite parvo, auribus erectis, cauda comosa, cruribus pedibusque robustioribus, colore cinereo, albo nigroque notato.

Characters.

About the size of the Newfoundland dog; head, small; ears, erect; tail, bushy; legs and feet, stout; general colour gray, varied with white and dark markings.

Synonymes.

CANIS FAMILIARIS, var. N. Borealis. Desm., Mamm., p. 194.
ESQUIMAUX DOG. Captain Lyons, Private Journal, pp. 244, 332.
"   "   Parry's Second Voyage, pp. 290, 358.
CANIS FAMILIARIS, var. A. Borealis—ESQUIMAUX DOG. F. B. A.,
            p. 75.

Description.

Head, rather small; ears, short and pointed; body, thick and well formed; eye, of moderate size; feet, clothed with thick short hair concealing the nails; tail, bushy, and longest at the end; hair, long, with thick wool beneath.

Colour.

Muzzle, black; inner portion of ears, blackish; top of nose, forehead, a space around the eyes, outer edges of ears, cheeks, belly, and legs, whitish; crown of the head, and back, nearly black; sides, thinly covered with long black, and some white, hairs; underneath there is a shorter dense coat of yellowish-gray woolly hair which is partly visible through these long hairs.

The tail, like the back, is clothed with black and white hairs, the latter greatly predominating, especially at the tip.

VOL. III.—8

Dimensions.

	Feet.	Inches.
Length from point of nose to root of tail,	4	3
" of tail (vertebræ),	1	2
" including hair,	1	5

Plate CXIII.

Drawn from Nature by J W Audubon

Drawn on Stone by Wm E. Hitchcock

Lith Printed & Cold by J.T Bowen, Phil

Esquimaux Dog.

Height of ear, inside, ...	3
Width between the eyes, ...	$2\frac{1}{4}$
" " ears, ...	$4\frac{1}{4}$

Habits.

So much has been written about the admirable qualities of the dog, that it would be quite useless for us to enter upon the subject; we shall also avoid the question of the origin of the various races, which in fact have been so intermixed that it would be an almost Quixotic task to endeavour to trace the genealogy of even the "noblest" of them. Those, however, that have, like the Esquimaux Dog, for centuries retained their general characters, and have not been exposed to any chance of "amalgamation" with other races, exhibit habits as well as forms and colours sufficiently permanent to warrant the naturalist in describing them, and in many cases their history is exceedingly interesting.

The Esquimaux Dogs are most useful animals to the savages of our Arctic regions, and when hitched to a sled many couples together, will travel with their master over the ice and snow at great speed for many miles without much fatigue, or draw heavy burthens to the huts of their owners. When on the coast of Labrador we had the following account of the mode in which these dogs subsist, from a man who had resided in that part of the world for upwards of ten years. During spring and summer they ramble along the shores, where they meet with abundance of dead fish, and in winter they eat the flesh of the seals with are killed and salted in the spring or late in the autumn when these animals return from the north. This man informed us also that when hard pushed he could relish the fare he thus provided for his Dogs just as much as they did themselves. We found several families inhabiting the coast of Labrador, all of whom depended entirely on their Dogs to convey them when visiting their neighbours, and some of whom had packs of at least forty of these animals. On some parts of the coast of Labrador the fish were so abundant during our visit that we could scoop them out of the edge of the water with a pocket-handkerchief: at such times the Esquimaux Dogs catch them, wading in and snapping at them with considerable dexterity as the surf retires; when caught they eat them at once while they are still alive.

We were informed that when these Dogs are on a journey in winter, should they be overtaken by a severe snow-storm, and thereby prevented from reaching a settlement within the calculated time, and if the provisions intended for them in consequence give out, in their ravenous hunger they devour the driver, and even prey upon one another. Such cases were related to us, as well as others in which, by severe whipping and loud cries the Dogs were forced into a gallop and kept on the full run until some house was reached and the sleigh driver saved.

These animals are taught to go in harness from the time they are quite young pups, being placed in a team along with well trained Dogs when only two or three months old, to gain experience and learn to obey their master, who wields a whip of twenty or thirty feet length of lash, with a short, heavy handle.

On a man approaching a house where they are kept, these Dogs sally forth with fierce barkings at the intruder, and it requires a bold heart to march up to them, as with their pointed ears and wiry hair they look like a pack of wild wolves. They are in fact very savage and ferocious at times, and require the strictest discipline to keep them in subjection.

Captain LYON gives an interesting account of the Esquimaux Dog, part of which we shall here lay before you: "A walrus is frequently drawn along by three or four of these Dogs, and seals are sometimes carried home in the same manner, though I have in some instances seen a Dog bring home the greater part of a seal in panniers placed across his back. The latter mode of conveyance is often used in summer, and the Dogs also carry skins or furniture overland to the sledges when their masters are going on any expedition. It might be supposed that in so cold a climate these animals had peculiar periods of gestation, like the wild creature; but on the contrary, they bear young at every season of the year, the pups seldom exceeding five at a litter. Cold has very little effect on them; for, although the dogs at the huts slept within the snow passages, mine at the ships had no shelter, but lay alongside, with the thermometer at 42° and 44° (below zero!) and with as little concern as if the weather had been mild. I found by several experiments, that three of my dogs could draw me on a sledge weighing 100 pounds at the rate of one mile in six minutes; and as a proof of the strength of a well-grown Dog, my leader drew 196 pounds singly, and to the same distance, in eight minutes. At another

time, seven of my Dogs ran a mile in four minutes, drawing a heavy sledge full of men. Afterwards, in carrying stores to the Fury, one mile distant, nine Dogs drew 1611 pounds in the space of nine minutes. My sledge was on runners neither shod nor iced; but had the runners been iced, at least 40 pounds might have been added for each Dog."

Captain LYON had eleven of these Dogs, which he says "were large and even majestic looking animals; and an old one, of peculiar sagacity, was placed at their head by having a longer trace, so as to lead them through the safest and driest places." "The leader was instant in obeying the voice of the driver, who never beat, but repeatedly called to him by name. When the Dogs slackened their pace, the sight of a seal or a bird was sufficient to put them instantly to their full speed; and even though none of these might be seen on the ice, the cry of 'a seal!'—'a bear!'—'a bird!' &c., was enough to give play to the legs and voices of the whole pack. It was a beautiful sight to observe the two sledges racing at full speed to the same object, the Dogs and men in full cry, and the vehicles splashing through the holes of water with the velocity and spirit of rival stage-coaches. There is something of the spirit of professed whips in these wild races; for the young men delight in passing each other's sledge, and jockeying the hinder one by crossing the path. In passing on different routes the right hand is yielded, and should an inexperienced driver endeavour to take the left, he would have some difficulty in persuading his team to do so. The only unpleasant circumstance attending these races is, that a poor dog is sometimes entangled and thrown down, when the sledge, with perhaps a heavy load, is unavoidably drawn over his body.

"The driver sits on the fore part of the vehicle, from whence he jumps, when requisite, to pull it clear of any impediments which may lie in the way; and he also guides it by pressing either foot on the ice. The voice and long whip answer all the purposes of reins, and the Dogs can be made to turn a corner as dexterously as horses, though not in such an orderly manner, since they are constantly fighting; and I do not recollect to have seen one receive a flogging without instantly wreaking his passion on the ears of his neighbours. The cries of the men are not more melodious than those of the animals; and their wild looks and gestures, when animated, give them an appearance of devils driving wolves before them. Our Dogs had eaten nothing for forty-eight hours, and could not have gone over less than seventy miles of ground; yet they returned to all appearance as fresh and active as when they first set out."

These Dogs curl the tail over the hip in the manner of house dogs generally.

Our drawing was made from a fine living Dog in the Zoological Garden at London. Some have since been brought to New York alive by the ships fitted out and sent to the polar seas in search of the unfortunate Sir JOHN FRANKLIN and his party by Mr. HENRY GRINNELL, of that city.

Geographical Distribution.

This animal, as the name imports, is the constant companion of the Esquimaux, but extends much beyond the range of that tribe of Indians, since it is found not only at Labrador, but among various tribes of northern Indians, and was observed by travellers in the Arctic regions to the extreme north; we are unacquainted with its western limits.

General Remarks.

We have been induced, in our account of American animals, to give figures and descriptions of this peculiar variety of Dog, inasmuch as it appears to have been a permanent variety for ages, and is one of the most useful animals to the Indians residing in the polar regions. Whether it be an original native Dog, or derive its origin from the wolf, is a subject which we will not here discuss, farther than to state, in opposition to the views of Dr. RICHARDSON, that our figures do not represent these animals as very closely allied to the wolf; on the contrary, their look of intelligence would indicate that they possess sagacity and aptitude for the service of man, equal at least to that of many favourite breeds of Dog. The fact also of their breeding at all seasons of the year, their manner of placing the tail in sport, and their general habits, give evidence of their being true Dogs and not wolves, the only difference between them and some other varieties consisting in their having erect pointed ears, which are peculiar to the Dogs of savage nations, and not altogether absent in some of our common breeds, as we have witnessed in the shepherd's Dog of Europe and some cur Dogs in America, erect ears of a similar character.

Spermophilus Lateralis. —Say.

Say's Marmot-Squirrei, or Spermophiles.

Plate cxiv.

S magnitudine Sciuri Hudsonici; stria laterali flavescente alba nigro marginata.

Characters.

Size of Sciurus Hudsonicus; *a yellowish-white stripe bordered with dark brownish-black on each flank.*

Synonymes.

SMALL GRAY SQUIRREL. Lewis and Clark, vol. iii. p. 35.
SCIURUS LATERALIS. Say, Long's Expedition, vol. ii. p. 46.
"   "   Harlan, Fauna Americana, p. 181.
ROCKY MOUNTAIN GROUND SQUIRREL. Godman, Nat. Hist., vol. ii. p. 144.
ARCTOMYS (SPERMOPHILUS) LATERALIS. Rich., Zool. Jour., vol. ii., No. 12, p. 519.
"   "   "   SAY's MARMOT. Rich., F.B.A., p. 174, pl. 13.

Description.

The body in form resembles the Spermophiles, with a slight approach to the Tamiæ; head, rather large; forehead, convex; nose, obtuse and covered with short hairs, except a naked space around the nostrils; incisors, flattened anteriorly; mouth placed pretty far back; whiskers, shorter that the head; a few long black hairs over the eye and posterior part of the cheeks; eyes, rather large; ears, oval and somewhat conspicuous, appearing like the ears of most animals of this genus, with the exception that they seem as if trimmed or cut short; they are thickly clothed on both surfaces with short hairs, and have a small doubling of the anterior margin to form a helix, which where it approaches the auditory canal is covered with longer hairs.

Legs, shorter and shouter than those of the squirrel family; feet, shaped like those of the *Spermophili;* claws, stronger, straighter, and better adapted for digging than those of the *Tamiæ;* the thumb tubercle is far back, and has a small obtuse nail; soles (of hind feet), naked to the heel, as are also the palms (of fore feet) and the under surface of the toes; upper surface of the feet, covered with short hairs which scarcely reach to the claws; tail depressed, slightly distichous, nearly linear, very slightly broadest towards the tip; there are no annulations in the hairs of the tail.

Colour.

Above, brownish-ash, intermixed with blackish, producing a hoary brownish-gray; there is no vestige of a dorsal line. A yellowish-white stripe appears on the neck, and running backwards along the sides, terminates at the hip; it is widest in the middle, being there three lines broad; and in some specimens it is faintly seen along the sides of the neck, reaching the ear; this white stripe is bounded above and below between the shoulder and the hip by a pretty broad border of brownish-black; top of the head and neck, tipped with ferruginous; the sides, all the ventral parts, inner surfaces of the legs, breast, and throat, yellowish-white, in parts tinged with brown.

Cheeks, and sides of the neck, chesnut-brown; ears, brown on their margins, paler near the base; a circle around the eye, upper lip, and chin, nearly white; nails, black; tail, black above, with an intermixture of brownish-white hairs, and bordered with white; the under surface is yellowish-brown, margined with black and brownish-white.

Dimensions.

	Inches.	Lines.
Length of head and body,	8	
" head,	2	2
" tail (vertebræ),	2	9
" " (including fur),	3	9
" middle fore claw,		4½
" palm and middle fore claw,		11
" sole and middle claw (of hind-foot),	1	6
Height of ear,		4
Breadth of base of external ear,		5

Habits.

This beautiful inhabitant of the wooded valleys of the Rocky Mountains was not seen by us on our journey up the Missouri river, although it is probably found within the district of country we traversed. We are therefore unable to give any personal information in regard to its habits, and we find but little in the works of others.

Mr. DRUMMOND obtained several specimens on the Rocky Mountains as far north as latitude 57°, and observed that it burrowed in the ground.

Mr. SAY did not give any account of its habits, and probably the specimen he described was brought into camp by the hunters attached to the expedition, without his ever having seen the animal alive.

All the Spermophiles that we have seen are lively, brisk, and playful, resembling the common ground-squirrels (*Tamias Lysteri*) in their general habits.

The Mexican women make pets of some of the species inhabiting that country, and they become very fond of their mistresses, running over their shoulders, and sometimes nestling in their bosoms, or the pockets of their gowns.

Geographical Distribution.

DRUMMOND obtained several specimens on the Rocky Mountains, in latitude 57°. LEWIS and CLARK state that it is common to every part of that range where wood abounds. We have not been able to determine the limits of its southern migrations, and have no information as to its existence in California.

General Remarks.

This species was first observed by LEWIS and CLARK, but was named and described by Mr. SAY, who placed it among the ground-squirrels. Dr. RICHARDSON subsequently gave a very accurate description of it, and transferred it through *Arctomys* to the subgenus *Spermophilus*, although considering it intermediate between the nearly allied subgenera *Spermophilus* and *Tamias*, with respect to its claws and teeth.

It is, however, in reality a *Spermophilus* and not a *Tamias*, as can earily be seen from the form of the body, the shortness of the legs, shape of the feet, and more especially its strong and nearly straight nails. On the other hand, the longitudinal lines on the back, and the shape of the tail, indicate a slight approach to the *Tamiæ*.

At the close of this article we embrace the opportunity of adding another species to this interesting genus, the habitat of which is, however, we regret to say, so much involved in obscurity that we cannot with certainty, at present, add it to the list of our North American mammalia.

Shortly after the return of the United States Exploring Expedition under the command of Captain WILKES, we happened to meet several of the naturalists who had been attached to the expedition. Some one—we cannot now recollect the gentleman—presented us with this specimen, stating that he could not tell where it had been obtained; the specimen has from that time remained in our collection without our having been able to gain any information in regard to its habitat, and without our learning that any other specimen has been procured, although we have anxiously sought to obtain farther intelligence on the subject.

This family is represented in the old world by few and peculiarly marked species, to none of which can we refer our animal, whilst on the other hand it bears in form, size, and markings, a strong connection with the American spermophiles, and will, as we are inclined to think, yet be found in some part of the western sea-coast regions of America.

We introduce it under the following name and description:

Spermophilus Pealei.—Aud. and Bach.

S. Tamiâ Lysteri paullulum major; striis albis quinque, cum quatuor fuscis alternantibus.

Characters.

A size larger than Tamias Lysteri; *five white and four brown stripes.*

Description.

Head, smaller and shorter, and ears considerably longer and less abruptly terminated than in SAY's *S. lateralis*: it is a little smaller than that species; legs more slender, and tail longer, broader, and more distichous than in *S. lateralis*; whiskers, long, a few of them extending beyond the ears.

On the fore feet there are four toes, without any vestige of a thumb or nail, the claws are short and small, and are covered with hair; palms, naked; there are five toes on each hind foot; the hair on the body is short and smooth, but is a little longer and also coarser on the under surface.

Colour.

A narrow white stripe rising on the back of the head runs along the centre of the back (or dorsal line) to the root of the tail; another white stripe on each side originates behind the ear and runs along the upper part of the side, narrowing on the hips till it reaches the sides of the root of the tail; a second white stripe on each side (lower than the last mentioned) runs from the shoulder to the hip, somewhat blended with a marked gray colour beneath it, which joins the colour of the under surface; between these white stripes are four much broader: the two nearest the central white dorsal line are speckled light grayish-yellow and brown between the ears, gradually darkening into reddish on the centre of the back, and to brown near the tail; the two outer brown stripes begin on the shoulder and run to the hips.

Forehead, speckled gray with a slight tinge of rufous towards the nose; ears, thinly clothed with hair of a light gray on the outer surface and dull white within; from the lower white stripe on each side, a grayish space extends between the shoulder and ham; under the belly, inner sides of legs, throat, and chin, white; the hams and shoulders are gray outside.

Whiskers, black; teeth, orange; nails, brown; on the tail the hairs are yellowish-white from the roots, then black, then have a broader annulation of yellowish-white, then another of black, and are broadly tipped with white.

VOL. III.—9

Dimensions.

From point of nose to root of tail, ...	$6\frac{1}{2}$	inches.
Tail (vertebræ), ...	$3\frac{1}{2}$	"
" (to end of fur), ...	$4\frac{1}{2}$	"
Point of nose to ear, ...	$1\frac{3}{4}$	"
Height of ear, ...	$\frac{5}{8}$	"
Palm to end of middle nail, ...	$\frac{3}{4}$	"
Tarsus to longest nail on hind foot, ...	$\frac{3}{4}$	"

Arvicola Xanthognatha.—Leach.

Yellow-Cheeked Meadow-Mouse.

Plate cxv.—Adult and Young.

A. Supra saturate fusca, subtus argenteo-cinereis, oculis circulo pallide luteo cinctis, genis flavis.

Characters.

Dark brown on the back; under parts, silvery grey; pale orange around the eyes; cheeks, yellow.

Synonymes.

ARVICOLA XANTHOGNATHA. Leach, Zool. Miss., vol. i. p. 60, t. 26.
      "   "   Harlan, Fauna, p. 136.
      "   "   Godman, Nat. Hist., vol. ii. p. 65.

CAMPAGNOL AUX JOUES FAUVES. Desm., Mamm., p. 282.
ARVICOLA XANTHOGNATHUS. Rich., Fauna Boreali Americana, p. 122.

Description.

Of the upper molars, the posterior one is the largest, and it has three grooves on its side; the two anterior have two grooves each, making in all ten ridges in the upper molar teeth on each side; of the lower molars, the anterior is the largest, and it has four grooves; the other two have each two.

Body, nearly cylindrical; legs, short; nose, obtuse; the lip is on a line with the incisors; ears, large, rounded, and hairy on both surfaces; whiskers, about the length of the head; tail, shorter than the head, well covered with hairs lying smoothly and coming to a point at the extremity; legs, rather stout, covered with short hair lying closely and smoothly; fore feet with naked palms; fore toes with a callosity protected by a very minute nail in place of a thumb; the first a little shorter than the third, second largest, and fourth shortest.

The toes are well covered with smooth hair above, and are naked below; the hair of the wrist projects a little over the palms; claws, small; hind feet with five toes, of which the three middle ones are nearly equal in length; the posterior part of the sole is covered with hair; soles of hind feet, narrower and longer than the palms of the fore feet; fur soft and fine, about four lines and a half long on the head, and nine on the posterior part of the back.

Colour.

The fur, from the roots to near the tips, is grayish-black; on the head and back the tips are yellowish-brown or black, the black pointed hairs being the longest; the colour resulting is a mixture of dark brown and black, without spots; sides, paler than the back; under parts, silvery bluish-gray.

Anterior to the shoulder, dark gray; there is a blackish-brown stripe on the centre of the nose; on each side of the nose a reddish-brown patch which extends to the orbit; around the eye, pale orange; whiskers, black; tail, brownish-black above, whitish beneath; feet, dark brown on the upper surface, whitish on the under.

Dimensions.

	Inches.	Lines.
Length from point of nose to root of tail, ...	8	
" of head, ...	1	10
" of tail, ...	1	6
Breadth of ear, ...		7
Hind foot, from heel to point of claw of middle toe, ...		10

Habits.

The descriptions of its habits given by the few writers who have referred with positive certainty to this species, are very meagre, but all the arvicolæ, with slight variations, are similar in habit; they live in low grounds, usually preferring meadows; burrow in the banks of ponds and near water-courses, feed on grasses and seeds, have a considerable number of young at a birth, are somewhat nocturnal, and make galleries of various lengths, which enable them to traverse the neighbourhood of their nestling places and procure the roots of grasses and plants.

This species, as is mentioned by RICHARDSON and other observers, makes its long galleries under the mossy turf, on the dry banks of lakes and rivers, and also in the woods; the specimens brought by us from Labrador were obtained from beneath large masses of moss growing on the rocks.

In some portions of the far north these hardy little animals are abundant: they are common in Labrador, and were easily captured by turning up some of the patches of moss, as just mentioned, when they were knocked over by the young men of our party.

We are told that this species has seven young at a time.

Geographical Distribution.

The original specimen described by LEACH, was obtained from Hudson's Bay: we procured several in Labrador.

Although supposed, by some writers, to exist within the limits of the United States, we have never been able to refer any species of Arvicola that has been discovered in our States or territories to this particular animal.

Plate CXIV.

N° 23

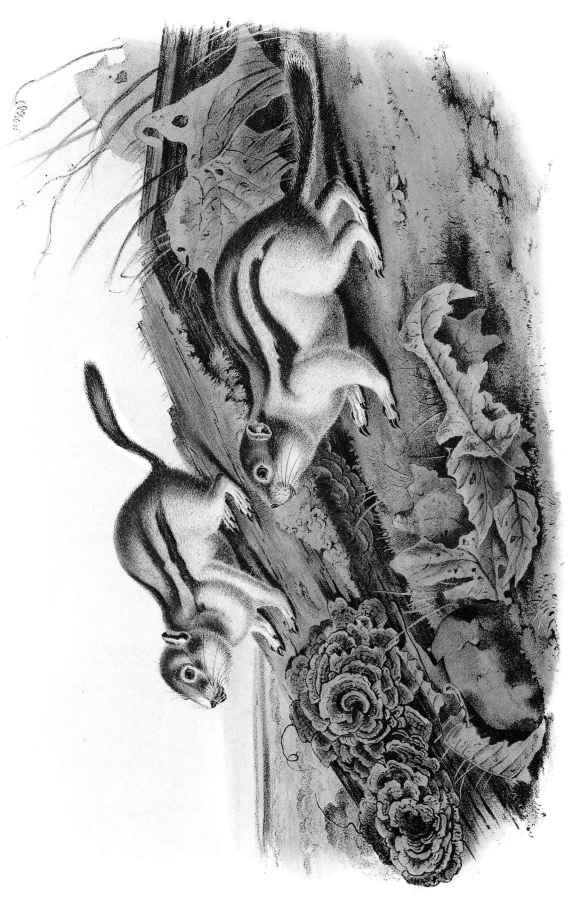

Drawn on stone by W.E. Hitchcock

Lith⁴ Printed & Col⁴ by J.T. Bowen, Philad⁴.

Drawn from Nature by J.W. Audubon

Say's Marmot Squirrel.

General Remarks.

As before stated, LEACH described this Arvicola, and he also gave a very poor figure of it; SAY supposed it to exist on the banks of the Ohio, but we think he had in view a different species; HARLAN appears not to have seen it, but gives the short description of LEACH, stating, however, that it exists in Pennsylvania and Ohio, which we presume was owing to his having mistaken for it some variety of WILSON's meadow-mouse (*A. Pennsylvanica*); GODMAN seems to have fallen into a similar mistake; and the *Arvicola xanth-* *ognatha* of SABINE is evidently the *A. Pennsylvanica* of Ord.

Dr. DeKAY says it is found in various parts of the State of New York, but we have not been able to procure it, although we have sought for it for years; and moreover we feel obliged to state that the description (which is a very unsatisfactory one), and the figure given in the "Zoology of the State of New York," refer to quite a different animal, probably one among the many varieties of *A. Pennsylvanica*.

We feel little hesitation in stating that this species does not exist in any part of the United States, but is exclusively a northern animal.

Vulpes Fulvus.—Desm.
(Var. Argentatus.—Rich.)

American Black or Silver Fox.

Plate cxvi.—Female.

V. magnitudine V. fulvi, argenteo niger, cauda ad apicem alba.

Characters.

Size of the red fox (vulpes fulvus); *body, silvery black; tip of the tail, white.*

Synonymes.

RENARD NOIR OU BAHYNHA. Sagard Theodat., Canada, p. 744.
EUROPEAN FOX—var. A, black. Pennant, Arct. Zool., vol. i., p. 46.
RENARD NOIR OU ARGENTÈ. Geoffroy, Collect. du Museum.
GRIZZLED FOX. Hutchins, MSS.
RENARD ARGENTÈ. F. Cuvier, Mamm. Lith., 5 livr.
CANIS ARGENTATUS. Desm., Mamm., p. 203.
   "   " Sabine, Franklin's Journey, p. 657.
   "   " Harlan, Fauna, p. 88.
   "   " THE BLACK OR SILVER FOX. Godman, Nat. Hist., i. 274, plate.
   " FULVUS, var. ARGENTATUS. Rich. BLACK OR SILVER FOX, F. B. A., p. 94.
BLACK FOX. DeKay, Nat. Hist. New York, p. 45.
TSCHERNOBURI. Russians.

Description.

Specimen from the Hon. Hudson's Bay Company.

Body, clothed with two kinds of hair; the longest, or outer hair, extends in some parts two inches beyond the under or shorter fur, especially on the neck, beneath the throat, behind the shoulders, along the flanks, and on the tail; this hair is soft, glossy, and finer than even that of the pine marten.

The under fur is unusually long and dense, measuring in some places two inches, and is exceedingly fine, feeling to the hands as soft as the finest sea-island cotton; this under fur surrounds the whole body even to the tail, on which it is a little coarser and has more the appearance of wool; it is shortest on the legs and forehead, and least dense on the belly; the hairs composing this fur, when viewed separately, exhibit a crimped or wavy appearance; on the ears and nose scarcely any long hairs are to be seen, these parts being thickly clothed with fur.

The soles of the feet are so thickly clothed with woolly hair that no callous spots are visible.

Colour.

The under fur is uniformly blackish-brown or chocolate; the long hairs are brown at their roots, then silver gray, and are broadly tipped with black; the hairs on the neck, and on a dorsal line extending to the root of the tail, are black, forming a broad black line at the neck, which narrows towards the tail.

Chin, throat, and whole under surface, brownish-black; a tuft of white hairs on the neck near the chest; another white tuft near the umbilicus; upper parts glossy silvery black; sides, sprinkled with many shining silvery white hairs, which produce a somewhat hoary appearance; tail, brownish-black to near the extremity, where it is broadly tipped with white.

Dimensions.

	Feet.	Inches.
Nose to root of tail,	2	5
Length of tail,	1	7
Height of ear,		$2\frac{3}{4}$
From nose to end of ear stretched back,		$8\frac{1}{2}$
" " eyes,		$3\frac{1}{8}$

Habits.

Our account of the habits of this beautiful Fox will be perhaps less interesting to many than our description of its skin; for, as is well known, the Silver-gray Fox supplies one of the most valuable furs in the world, not only for the luxurious nobles of Russia and other parts of Europe, but for the old-fashioned, never-go-ahead Chinese, and other Eastern nations.

In the richness and beauty of its splendid fur the Silver-gray Fox surpasses the beaver or the sea-otter, and the skins are indeed so highly esteemed that the finest command extraordinary prices, and are always in demand.

The Silver-gray Fox is by no means abundant, and presents considerable variations both in colour and size. Some skins are brilliant black (with the exception of the end of the tail, which is invariably white); other specimens are bluish-gray, and many are tinged with a cinereous colour on the sides: it perhaps is most commonly obtained with parts of its fur hoary, the shiny black coat being thickly interspersed with white or silvery-blue tipped hairs.

According to Sir JOHN RICHARDSON, a greater number than four or five of these Foxes is seldom taken in a season at any one post in the fur countries, though the hunters no sooner find out the haunts of one than they use every art to catch it. From what he observed, Sir JOHN does not think this Fox displays more cunning in avoiding a snare than the red one, but the rarity of the animal, and the eagerness of the hunters to take it, make them think it peculiarly shy.

This animal appears to be as scarce in northern Europe as in America; but we do not mean by this to be understood as considering the European Black Fox identical with ours.

The Black or Silver Fox is sometimes killed in Labrador, and on the Magdeleine Islands, and occasionally—very rarely—in the mountainous parts of Pennsylvania and the wilder portions of the northern counties of New York, where, however, PENNANT's marten is generally called the "Black Fox," by the hunters and farmers.

It gives us pleasure to render our thanks to the Hon. Hudson's Bay Company for a superb female Black or Silver-gray Fox which was procured for us, and sent to the Zoological Gardens in London alive, where J. W. AUDUBON was then making figures of some of the quadrupeds brought from the Arctic regions of our continent for this work. Having drawn this beautiful animal, which was at the time generously tendered us, but thinking it should remain in the Zoological Gardens, as we have no such establishment in America, J. W. AUDUBON declined the gift in favor of the Zoological Society, in whose interesting collection we hope it still exists. When shall we have a Zoological Garden in the United States?

This variety of the Fox does not differ in its propensities from the red Fox or the cross Fox, and its extraordinary cunning is often equalled by the tricks of these sly fellows.

The white tip at the end of the tail appears to be a characteristic of the Silver-gray Fox, and occurs in every specimen we have seen.

It is stated in MORTON's New England Canaan (p. 79), that the skin of the Black Fox was considered by the Indians, natives of that part of the colonies, as equivalent to forty beaver skins; and when offered and accepted by their kings, it was looked upon as a sacred pledge of reconciliation.

The present species has been seen "mousing" in the meadows, near Ipswich, Massachusetts, as we were informed by the late WILLIAM OAKES, who also wrote to us that "the common and cross Foxes were abundant about the White

Plate CXV

On Stone by W.E. Hitchcock

Drawn from Nature by J W Audubon

Lith Printed & Col.d by J T Bowen, Philad.a

Yellow-cheeked Meadow Mouse.

Mountains, and that they were most easily shot whilst scenting and following game, when their whole attention appears to be concentrated on that one object."

This Fox is occasionally seen in Nova Scotia, and a friend there informs us that some have been shot in his vicinity.

Geographical Distribution.

As this variety of the Red Fox chiefly occurs in the colder regions of our continent, we cannot set it down as a regular inhabitant of even the southern parts of the State of New York, nor any part of Pennsylvania or New Jersey.

The specimens which have been obtained in the two former States were killed at long intervals, and were, moreover, not of so fine a pelage or so beautiful a colour as those from more northern latitudes.

The skins sold to the American Fur Company are from the head waters of the Mississippi river, and the territories northwest of the Missouri, and are considered equal to the best.

General Remarks.

The production of peculiar and permanent varieties in species of animals in a wild or natural state, is a subject of remarkable interest, although it cannot be explained on any data with which we are at present acquainted.

It is singular that in several species of red Foxes, widely removed from each other in their geogrpahical ranges, the same peculiarities occur. The red Fox of Europe (*Canis vulpes*), a species differing from ours, produces no varieties in the southern and warmer parts of that continent, but is everywhere of the same reddish colour, yet in high northern latitudes, especially in mountainous regions, it exhibits not only the black, but the cross Fox varieties.

In the western portions of our continent the large red Fox of LEWIS and CLARK, which we described from a hunter's skin in our first volume (p. 54), and to which we have elsewhere given the name of *Vulpes Utah*, runs into similar varieties.

Sciurus Nigrescens.—Bennett.

Dusky Squirrel.

Plate cxvii.—Male.

S. Subniger, corpore griseo sparsim vario, lateribus flavo-fuscescentibus, cauda corpore multo longiore.

Characters.

Prevailing colour dusky, slightly grizzled on the body with gray; sides, dusky yellow; tail much longer than the body.

Synonymes.

SCIURUS NIGRESCENS. Bennett, Proceedings of the Zoological Society.
　　"　　　　"　　　　　Bachman, Monog. Genus Sciurus, read before the Zool. Soc., August 14, 1838.

Description.

In size this species is nearly equal to the cat-squirrel (*Sciurus cinereus*). Head, rather small; ears, of moderate size, not tufted; feet, robust; tail, very long, and less distichous than in other squirrels, it presenting in the stuffed specimen a nearly cylindrical shape; ears and feet, clothed with short hairs; hairs of the body, short and close; whiskers, about the length of the head.

Colour.

The prevailing colour on the back is grayish-black; crown of the head, and legs, grayish; sides of the neck, upper parts of the thighs, and rump, grizzled with pale yellow; cheek, chin, throat, neck, breast, and whole of the under surface, including the inside of the legs, dingy gray; fore parts, same colour as the back; hairs of hinder parts of thighs, black; hairs of the tail, black at the roots, then gray, then broadly banded with black, then broadly tipped with white; feet, black.

The hairs on the toes are grizzled with white points; whiskers, black; hairs on the back, plumbeous—black from the roots for two thirds of their length, then gray, then black, and at the tips whitish-gray; there are numerous strong black hairs interspersed over the body.

Dimensions.

	Inches.	Lines.
Length from point of nose to root of tail, ...	12	4
"　　of tail to end of hair, ...	15	4
"　　of tarsus (claws included), ...	2	7½
From tip of nose to ear, ...	2	2
Height of ear posteriorly, ...		8½

Habits.

The existence in North America of an unusual number of species of squirrels has been made known to our subscribers in the course of this publication. There are many closely allied, and many very beautiful species among them; all are graceful and agile, and possess very similar habits.

The great number of these nut-eating animals in North America would be a proof (were any such wanting) that nature has been more bountiful to our country in distributing nut-bearing trees over the whole extent of our continent than to other parts of the globe, and this in connexion with the fact that so great a proportion of wood-land cannot be found in any other part of the world of similar extent, marks America as intended for a very dense population hereafter. In Europe there is only one well determined species of squirrel known, at present at least, although at some remote period there may have been more.

In regard to the peculiar habits of the Dusky Squirrel, we have nothing to say. It is one of the species which, being shot or procured by collectors of objects of natural history, and sent to Europe, have there been described by naturalists who, having the advantages of museums which contain specimens from every part of the globe, and the largest libraries in the world also to which they can refer, may sometimes discover new species with much less difficulty, but also less certainty, than the student of nature must encounter while seeking for knowledge in the woods.

But the naturalist who learns from books only, and describes from dried skins, is at best liable to mistakes. We have in fact always found that where young animals, or accidental varieties, have been described as new species, this has been the result of study in the museum or cabinet, not in the fields.

Geographical Distribution.

This species, of which, so far as we know, only one specimen exists in any museum or collection, is stated to have been procured in California. We have not received any positive accounts of its occurrence there, but have no doubt it will be found, and its habits, as well as locality, determined ere long.

General Remarks.

This Squirrel was described by Dr. BACHMAN from the original specimen in the museum of the Zoological Society of London, in his Monograph of the Genus *Sciurus*, published in the Proceedings of the Zoological Society, and in the Magazine of Natural History, new series, 1839, p. 113; and our figure was drawn from the same skin by J. W. AUDUBON.

Plate CXVI.

N.º 24.

On Stone by W.E. Hitchcock.

Lith.ᵈ Printed & Col.ᵈ by J.T. Bowen Philad.ᵃ

Drawn from Nature by J.W. Audubon.

American Black or Silver Fox.

Cervus Leucurus.—Douglas.

Long-Tailed Deer.

Plate cxviii.—Male.

C. Cervo Virginiano minor, capite atque dorso fulvis nigro mistis, malis lateribusque dilutioribus, gastræo albo.

Characters.

Smaller than the Virginian deer; head and back, fawn-colour, mixed with black; sides and cheeks, paler, white beneath.

Synonymes.

ROEBUCK. Dobbs, Hudson's Bay, p. 41, Ann. 1744.
FALLOW, or VIRGINIAN DEER. Cook's Third Voyage, vol. ii. p. 292, Ann. 1778.
LONG-TAILED JUMPING DEER. Umfreville, Hudson's Bay, p. 190, Ann. 1790.
DEER WITH SMALL HORNS AND LONG TAIL (?) Gass, Journal, p. 55, Ann. 1808.
LONG-TAILED (?) RED DEER. Lewis and Clark, vol. ii. p. 41.
SMALL DEER OF THE PACIFIC. Idem, vol. ii. p. 342.
JUMPING DEER. Hudson's Bay traders.
CHEVREUIL. Canadian Voyagers.
MOWITCH. Indians west of the Rocky Mountains.

Description.

Form, elegant; lachrymal opening, apparently only a small fold in the skin close to the eye; limbs, slender; hoofs, small and pointed; tail, long in proportion to the size of the animal. Fur, dense and long; a pendulous tuft of hairs on the belly between the thighs; the glandular opening on the outside of the hind leg, small and oval in shape, the reversed hairs around it differing very little in colour from the rest of the leg. Hair, coarser than in the Virginian deer, and hoofs more delicate in shape.

Colour.

Head and back, rufous, mixed with black; sides and cheeks, paler; ears, above, dusky brown, inside edges, white; there is a small black spot between the nostrils, and a white ring around the eyes. Chin and throat, yellowish-white; tail, brownish-yellow above, inclining to rusty red near the tip, and cream white underneath and at the tip; neck, brownish-yellow from the throat downwards; under surface of the body, not so white as in the Virginian deer.

Dimensions.

Young male in the Academy of Natural Sciences, Philadelphia.

	Feet.	Inches.
From point of nose to root of tail,	4	2
Length of head,		$10\frac{1}{2}$
End of nose to eye,		$5\frac{1}{2}$
Tail to end of hair,	1	$1\frac{1}{2}$
Height of ear posteriorly,		5

Horns (two points about $\frac{3}{4}$ of an inch long, invisible without moving the surrounding hair).

Female presented by the Hudson's Bay Company to the museum of the Zoological Society.

	Feet.	Inches.
Length from point of nose to root of tail,	5	
" of head,		11
" of tail (including fur),	1	1

Habits.

In its general appearance this Deer greatly resembles the European roebuck, and seems to be formed for bounding along in the light and graceful manner of that animal. The species has been considered of doubtful authenticity, owing to the various lengths of tail exhibited by the common deer, many specimens of which we collected near the Rocky Mountains, not differing from *C. Virginianus* in any other particular, but with long tail, and for some time we did not feel inclined to give it a place in our work; from which we have excluded a great many false species, published by others from young animals or mere varieties, and compared by us with specimens exhibiting all the markings and forms set down as characters by the authors alluded to. At one time we examined the tails of some common deer in Fulton market, New York, and found that the longest exceeded nineteen inches, while the average length does not go beyond nine. The different form of the light, springy animal described by Mr. DOUGLAS will, however, at once separate it from *C. Virginianus* on comparison.

Sir JOHN RICHARDSON says: "This animal, from the general resemblance it has in size, form, and habits, to the *Cervus capreolus* of Europe, has obtained the name of *Chevreuil* from the French Canadians, and of Roebuck from the Scottish Highlanders employed by the Hudson's Bay Company. These names occur in the works of several authors who have written on the fur countries, and UMFREVILLE gives a brief, but, as far as it goes, a correct description of it." "This species does not, on the east side of the Rocky Mountains, range farther north than latitude 54°, nor is it found in that parallel to the eastward of the 105th degree of longitude."

Mr. DOUGLAS speaks of it as "the most common deer of any in the districts adjoining the river Columbia, more especially in the fertile prairies of the Cowalidske and Multnomah rivers, within one hundred miles of the Pacific Ocean. It is also occasionally met with near the base of the Rocky Mountains on the same side of that ridge. Its favourite haunts are the coppices, composed of *Corylus, Rubus, Rosa,* and *Amelanchir,* on the declivities of the low hills or dry undulating grounds. Its gait is two ambling steps and a bound exceeding double the distance of the steps, which mode it does not depart from even when closely pursued. In running, the tail is erect, wagging from side to side, and from its unusual length is the most remarkable feature about the animal. The voice of the male calling the female is like the sound produced by blowing in the muzzle of a gun or in a hollow cane. The voice of the female calling the young is *mœ, mœ,* pronounced shortly. This is well imitated by the native tribes, with a stem of *Heracleum lanatum,* cut at a joint, leaving six inches of a tube: with this, aided by a head and horns of a full grown buck, which the hunter carries with him as a decoy, and which he moves backwards and forwards among the long grass, alternately feigning the voice with the tube, the unsuspecting animal is attracted within a few yards in the hope of finding its partner, when instantly springing up, the hunter plants an arrow in his object. The flesh is excellent when in good order, and remarkably tender and well flavoured." "They go in herds from November to April and May, when the female secretes herself to bring forth. The young are spotted with white until the middle of the first winter, when they change to the same colour as the most aged."

LEWIS and CLARK considered it the same animal as the common deer, with the exception of the length of the tail. They found it inhabiting "the Rocky Mountains, in the neighbourhood of the Chopunnish, and about the Columbia, and down the river as low as where the tide-water commences." These travellers in another passage observe that "the common Fallow Deer with long tails (our present species), though very poor, are better than the black-tailed fallow deer of the coast, from which they differ materially."

We did not see any Deer of this species on our journey up the Missouri, nor do we think it is to be found east of the Rocky Mountains. The Virginian deer, on the contrary, disappears to the north and west, as RICHARDSON says he has not been able to discover the true *Cervus Virginianus* within the district to which the Fauna Boreali Americana refers.

Geographical Distribution.

On the east side of the Rocky Mountains this species does not range beyond lat. 54°, nor to the eastward of 105° longitude. DOUGLAS states that it is the most common Deer of any in the districts adjoining the Columbia River, more especially in the fertile prairies of the Cowalidske and Multnomah rivers within one hundred miles of the Pacific Ocean. It is also occasionally met with near the base of the Rocky Mountains on the same side of that chain.

General Remarks.

We have after some hesitation admitted this species, and as much has been said (although but little learned) of the western Long-tailed Deer since the days of LEWIS and CLARK, it is desirable that the species should be carefully investigated.

We overlooked the specimen of the Long-tailed Deer in the Zoological

On Stone by W.E.Hitchcock

Dusky Squirrel.

Drawn from Nature by J.W.Audubon   Lithᵈ Printed & Colᵈ by J.T.Bowen, Philadᵈ

Museum, from which the description of RICHARDSON was taken, and for a long time we had no other knowledge of the species than the somewhat loose description of it by DOUGLAS, who, although an enthusiastic collector of plants and something of a botanist, was possessed of a very imperfect knowledge of birds or quadrupeds, and probably had never seen the *Cervus Virginianus*, our Virginian Deer.

We have given what we consider an excellent figure by J. W. AUDUBON, from the original specimen, and there is now in the Academy of Sciences at Philadelphia a young male with was procured some years since by the late Mr. J. K. TOWNSEND on the Columbia River.

Genus Georychus.—Illiger.

Dental Formula.

Incisive $\frac{2}{2}$; *Canine* $\frac{0-0}{0-0}$; *Molar* $\frac{3-3}{3-3}$ = 16.

This subtenus in its dental formula is similar to *Arvicola*; eyes, very small; ears rising slightly above the auditory opening; thumb, conspicuous; nails on the fore feet fitted for digging; tail, very short.

Natives of cold climates, burrow in the earth, feed on seeds, roots, and grasses.

Ten species are admitted by naturalists, two of which are in Europe, four in Asia, and four in America.

The generic name Georychus was given by ILLIGER, from Γεωρζχος, digging the earth.

Georychus Hudsonius.—Forster.

Hudson's Bay Lemming.

Plate cxix.—Winter and Summer Pelage.

G. Auriculis nullis, maniculorum unguibus duobus intermediis, maximis, compressis, quasi duplicatis, per sulcum horizontalem divisis, colore in æstate rufo-fusco, in hyeme albo.

Characters.

Earless: the two middle claws of the fore feet unusually large, compressed, their blunt extremity being rendered double by a deep transverse notch. Colour reddish-brown in summer, white in winter.

Synonymes.

MUS HUDSONIUS. Forster, Phil. Trans., vol. lxii. p. 379.
   "   "   Pallas, Glires, p. 208.
   "   "   Linn. Gmel. 137.
HUDSON'S RAT. Pennant, Quadrupeds, vol. ii. p. 201.
   "   "   Arctic Zoology, vol. i. p. 132.
HARE-TAILED MOUSE. Hearne's Journey, p. 387.
LEMMUS HUDSONIUS. Captain Sabine, Parry's Supplement, First Voyage, p. 185.
   "   "   Mr. Sabine, Franklin's Journey, p. 661.
   "   "   Dict. de Sci. Naturelles, tom. viii. p. 566.
   "   "   Harlan, Fauna, p. 546.
ARVICOLA HUDSONIA. Rich., Parry's Second Voyage, Append., p. 308.
ARVICOLA (GEORYCHUS) HUDSONIUS—HUDSON'S BAY LEMMING. Rich., F.B.A., 132. Species 107, British Museum.
HUDSON'S BAY LEMMING. Godman, Nat. Hist., vol. ii. p. 73.

Description.

Size of a mole; body, thick and short; head, short and rounded; nose, very obtuse; eyes, small; no exterior ears; legs, short and stout; tail so short as to be only slightly visible beyond the fur of the hips; fur very fine and long; feet, clothed with long hairs; four toes on the fore feet, with the rudiment of a thumb not armed with a nail; the two middle toes are of equal length, and are each furnished with a disproportionately large claw, which is compressed, deep, very blunt at the extremity, and is there separated into two layers by a transverse furrow; the outer and inner toes have curved sharp-pointed claws; the upper layer is thinner, the lower one has a blunt rounded outline; the latter has been described as an enlargement of the callosity which exists beneath the roots of the claws of the Lemmings and meadow-mice. The hind feet have five toes armed with slender curved claws.

In the females and young the subjacent production of the claws is less conspicuous.

Colour.

Winter specimen.

Whiskers, black; the whole animal is white both on the upper and under surfaces, with black hairs interspersed along the line of the back and on the hips and sides, giving to those parts a grayish-brown tinge; tail, white.

Summer specimen.

Dark brown and black on the dorsal aspect; dark brown predominates on the crown of the head and dorsal line; towards the sides the colour is lighter; on the under parts of cheeks, the chest, and about the ears, bright nut colour prevails. The ventral aspect is grayish-white, more or less tinged with rust colour; the tail is brown in summer, and white in winter; although this species is distinctly white in winter, yet according to HEARNE the white colour never becomes so pure as that of the ermine.

Dimensions.

	Inches.	Lines.
Length of head and body, ...	5	4
" head, ...	1	4
" tail, ...		5
" middle fore claw, ...		$4\frac{1}{2}$

Habits.

Our only acquaintance with this species is through the works of the old writers and the Fauna Boreali Americana, we having failed to meet with it at Labrador. The first specimen we saw of it was in the museum of the Royal College of Surgeons at Edinburgh. Our drawing was made from specimens in the British Museum. Dr. RICHARDSON did not meet with this Lemming in the interior of America, and thinks it has hitherto been found only near the sea.

"Its habits are still imperfectly known. In summer, according to HEARNE, it burrows under stones in dry ridges, and Captain SABINE informs us that in winter it resides in a nest of moss on the surface of the ground, rarely going abroad."—*Fauna Boreali Americana*, p. 132.

HEARNE states that this little species is very inoffensive, and so easily tamed that if taken even when full grown it will in a day or two be perfectly reconciled, very fond of being handled, and will creep of its own accord into its master's neck or bosom.

Geographical Distribution.

This species inhabits Labrador, Hudson's straits, and the coast from Churchill to the extremity of Melville peninsula, as well as the islands of the Polar seas visited by Captain PARRY.

General Remarks.

This singular animal was originally described by FORSTER in the Philosophical Transactions. PALLAS received a number of skins from Labrador, one of which he sent to PENNANT, who described it in his History of the Quadrupeds and also in his Arctic Zoology. It was observed by both PARRY and FRANKLIN, and was described by RICHARDSON. A specimen was preserved in the Museum du Roi at Paris, and described in the Dict. des Sciences, and there is an excellent specimen in the British Museum.

Plate CXVIII

On Stone by W.E.Hitchcock.

Drawn from Nature by J W Audubon

Long-tailed Deer.

Lith.ᵈ Printed & Col.ᵈ by J T Bowen, Philad.ᵃ

Georychus Helvolus. — Rich.

Tawny Lemming.

Plate cxx. — Fig. 1.

G. Pollice instructus, naso obtuso albido, capite fulvo nigroque vario, corpore supra fulvo, infra pallidiore, magnitudine G. Norvegici.

Characters.

Size of the Lapland Lemming; nose, blunt and light coloured; head, tawny black; body, reddish-orange above, paler beneath; feet, furnished with thumbs.

Synonymes.

ARVICOLA (LEMMUS) HELVOLUS. Richardson, Zool. Jour., No. 12, p. 517, 1828.
"   (GEORYCHUS?) HELVOLUS. Rich., Fauna Boreali Americana,
          p. 128.

Description.

Body, stout; head, oval; nose, short, blunt, and nearly on a line with the incisors; eyes, small; ears, broad and not long—shorter than the fur, and clothed with hair near the edges; tail, very short, clothed with stiff hairs, which are longest near the extremity, and converge to a point; claws of both extremities much alike, greatly compressed, and sharp pointed; the claws have an oblong narrow groove underneath.

The thumbs on the fore feet consist almost entirely of a thick, flat, squarish nail, resembling that of the Norway Lemming, and have, as in that species, an obliquely truncated summit; in the Tawny Lemming, however, this summit presents two obscure points.

The fur on the body is about nine lines long; that on the nose and extremities, very short.

Colour.

Body, reddish-orange, interspersed on the back and sides with a number of hairs longer than the fur, which are tipped with black; on the upper parts of the head, around the eyes, and on the nape of the neck, the black hairs are more numerous, and the colour of those parts is mingled black and orange. Nose, grayish-brown; sides of the face, pale orange; margins of the upper lip, white; tail, coloured like the body; feet, brownish.

Dimensions.

	Inches.	Lines.
Length of head and body, ...	4	6
" tail, ...		7
" head, ...	1	6
Hind feet to end of claw, ...		8
Fore feet and claws, ...		4½

Habits.

Mr. DRUMMOND, who obtained this animal, procured no further information in regard to its habits than that it was found in Alpine swamps. It bears a strong resemblance to the Norway Lemming, and we may presume does not differ widely from that species in its habits, which it is said are migratory to a surprising extent, and about which some curious stories are related that we do not consider necessary to place in our work.

This Lemming is one of those animals we have never seen except the stuffed specimens. Our figure was drawn in London by J. W. AUDUBON from the original skin procured by Mr. DRUMMOND.

Geographical Distribution.

This animal was found in lat. 56°, in mountainous yet moist places, in the northwest. We have not heard of its existence in any other locality, but have no doubt it has a pretty extensive northern range.

General Remarks.

The Lemmings have been arranged by authors, CUVIER, ILLIGER, and others, under a distinct subgenus—*Georychus*.

They are characterized chiefly by the shortness of the ears and tail, and large strong claws, remarkably well fitted for digging; this subgenus, however, so nearly approaches the *Arvicolæ* in some of its species that it is difficult to decide in which genus they should really be placed.

Georychus Trimucronatus. — Rich.

Back's Lemming.

Plate cxx. — Figs. 2 and 3.

G. Auriculis vellere brevioribus, naso obtuso nigro, palmis tetradactylis, unguibus lanceolatis curvis, ungue pollicari lingulato, tricuspidato, corpore supra saturate castaneo, latere ferrugineo, subtus cinereo.

Characters.

Ears, somewhat shorter than the fur; nose, blunt and black; four claws on the fore feet of a lanceloate form, and a somewhat square thumb nail with three small points at the end; body, dark chesnut above, reddish-orange or rust colour on the sides, gray beneath.

Synonymes.

ARVICOLA TRIMUCRONATUS. Rich, Parry's Second Voyage, Append., p. 309.
"   (GEORYCHUS) TRIMUCRONATUS. Rich., Fauna Boreali Americana, p. 130.

Description.

In size a little inferior to the Hudson's Bay Lemming, or nearly equal to the Norwegian species; head, flat and covered by moderately long fur; ears, shorter than the fur, inclined backwards, and but thinly clothed with hair; eyes, small. Upper lip, deeply cleft; nose, obtuse, with a small naked but not pointed or projecting tip; whiskers, numerous; inside of the mouth, hairy, the hairs arising from projecting glandular folds; upper incisors, presenting a conspicuous but shallow groove with an obliquely notched cutting edge; there are three molar teeth on a side in each jaw. Fores legs, short; feet, moderately large, and turned outwards like those of a turnspit.

The tail projects a few lines beyond the fur, and is clothed with stiff hairs converging to a point; there are four toes on the fore feet, armed with moderate sized strong nails curved downwards and inclining outwards; they are of an oblong form, convex above, not compressed, excavated underneath more broadly than the nails of any of the other American Lemmings, and have sharp edges fitted for scraping away the earth; the thumb is almost entirely composed of a strong nail which has two slightly convex surfaces, a flat outline, and a truncated extremity from which three small points project; the palms are narrow; the posterior extremities are considerably longer than the fore legs and feet, the thighs and legs being tolerably distinct from the body; the sole is narrow, long, and somewhat oblique, having its inner edge turned a little forward; the toes are longer, and the claws as long but more slender than those of the fore feet, and they are much compressed.

In the Tawny Lemming the claws of both the fore and hind feet are compressed.

Colour.

Nose, deep black; whiskers, black at the roots, brownish or white at the tips, some entirely white; incisors, yellowish; head, back of the neck, and shoulders, mixed reddish-gray, formed from the mingling of yellowish and brown and black-tipped hairs; black, chesnut brown, with many of the long hairs tipped with black; sides, reddish-orange; belly, chin, and throat, gray,

Plate CLX.

Hudson's Bay Lemming

Drawn from Nature by J.W.Audubon

intermixed with many orange-coloured hairs.

The colouring of this animal very strongly resembles that of the Tawny Lemming, except that its nose is deep black, whilst that organ in the latter is pale.

Tail, dark brown above, grayish-white below; feet, dark yellowish-brown above, whiter beneath.

Dimensions.

Male, Killed at Fort Franklin.

	Inches.	Lines.
Length of head and body, ...	5	
" tail, ...		6
" head, ...	1	5
" ears, ...		4
" whiskers, ...	1	3
" fur on the back, ...		9
" palm and claw of middle toe, nearly		6
" claw of middle toe, ...		2
" sole and middle claw of hind foot, ...		9

Female 4¼ inches long.

Habits.

This Lemming was found in the spring season at Great Bear Lake, by Sir JOHN FRANKLIN, burrowing under the thick mosses which cover a large portion of the ground in high northern latitudes.

As soon as the surface of the ground had thawed, the little animal was observed at work making his progress beneath, and actively engaged in hunting for food.

In the winter it travels under the snow in semi-cylindrical furrows, very neatly cut to the depth of two inches and a half in the mossy turf; these hollow ways intersect each other at various angles, but occasionally run to a considerable distance in a straight direction; from their smoothness it was evident that they were not merely worn by the feet, but actually cut by the teeth; their width is sufficient to allow the animal to pass with facility.

The food of this Lemming seems to consist entirely of vegetable matters; it inhabits woody spots.

A female killed on Point Lake, June 26, 1821, contained six young, fully formed, but destitute of hair.

Geographical Distribution.

This animal was discovered by Captain BACK on the borders of Point Lake, in latitude 65°, on Sir JOHN FRANKLIN's first expedition. Mr. EDWARDS, the surgeon of the Fury, on Captain PARRY's second expedition, brought a specimen from Igloolik, in latitude $69\frac{10}{3}$°; and specimens were obtained on Sir JOHN FRANKLIN's second expedition, on the shores of Great Bear Lake.

General Remarks.

As we have been entirely unable to procure original information in regard to the habits of the two previously noticed and the present species of Lemming, we have largely quoted from the Fauna Boreali Americana, Sir JOHN RICHARDSON's valuable work, from which also our descriptions of these curious animals are chiefly taken, although we have transposed the paragraphs in order to suit the general arrangement which we adopted for this work.

No animals belonging to this genus were observed by us during our researches through the country bordering on the shores of the upper Missouri and Yellow Stone rivers in 1843, and the family is very probably restricted to the neighbourhood of the Arctic Circle.

Vulpes Lagopus.—Linn.

Arctic Fox.

Plate cxxi.—Winter and Summer Pelage.

V. Auriculis rotundatis brevibusque, margine inflexa; collari post genas; colore in æstate fusco, in hyeme albo.

Characters.

Ears, rounded, short, and folded at the edges; cheeks with a ruff; colour, in summer brown, in winter white.

Synonymes.

PIED FOXES. James's Voyage, Ann. 1633.
CANIS LAGOPUS. Linn., Syst., vol. i. p. 59.
"   "   Forster, Philos. Trans., lxii. p. 370.
ARCTIC FOX. Pennant's Arctic Zoology, vol. i. p. 42.
"   "   Hearne's Journey, p. 363.
GREENLAND DOG. Pennant's Hist. Quadr., vol. i. p. 257 (?) a young individual.
CANIS LAGOPUS. Captain Sabine, Parry's First Voyage, Supplement, 187.
"   "   Mr. Sabine, Franklin's Journal, p. 658.
"   "   Richardson, Parry's Second Voyage, Appendix, p. 299.
"   "   Harlan, Fauna Americana, p. 92.
ISATIS, or ARCTIC FOX. Godman's Nat. Hist., vol. i. p. 268.
CANIS (VULPES) LAGOPUS—ARCTIC FOX. Rich., Fauna Boreali Americana, p. 83.
STONE FOX. Auctorum.
TERREEANEE-ARIOO. Esquimaux of Melville Peninsula.
TERIENNIAK. Greenlanders.
WAPPEESKEESHEW-MAKKEESHEW. Cree Indians.
PESZI. Russians.

Description.

Male in winter pelage.

Head, not as much pointed as in other species of Fox; ears, rounded, and presenting somewhat the appearance of having been cropped; hairs on the ears, shorter than on the neighbouring parts.

The cheeks are ornamented by a projecting ruff which extends from behind the ears quite around the lower part of the face, to which it gives a pleasing appearance; legs, rather long than otherwise, and muscular, feet, armed with pretty strong, long, compressed, and slightly arched claws; soles of the feet, covered with dense woolly hair; body covered with two kinds of hair, the longer thinly distributed and fine, the shorter a remarkably fine straight wool or dense fur; on the tail and lower parts of the body the long hairs are similar to those on the body, and the wool or fur like that of the finest wool of the merino sheep. The tail is thick, round, and bushy, and shorter than that of the red Fox.

The shoulders and thighs are protected by long fur, but the anterior parts of the legs are covered with short hair, the hind legs having the shortest and smoothest coat.

Colour.

In winter every part of this animal is white, except the tip of the nose the nails and eyes. Eyes, hazle; tip of nose, black; nails, brownish. The hairs of the animal are all white from the roots to the tips.

We have, however, seen specimens in which the colour was not pure white, but rather a bluish or brownish-gray tint at the roots on the back shoulders and outside of the thighs, but particularly on the neck and tail. The proportion of the fur so coloured varies with the season of the year as well as with different individuals of the species. Sometimes it is confined to a small space at the roots of the hair, whilst in other cases the dingy colour is so widely spread as to tarnish the customary whiteness of the whole skin.

At almost all times the short hair clothing the posterior surface and margin of the ears, is dark brownish-gray for half its length from the roots, so as to give a bluish or brownish tinge to view when the hairs are blown apart.

Summer pelage.

In the month of May, when the snow begins to disappear, the long white hairs and fur fall off, and are replaced by shorter hair, which is more or less coloured. A specimen killed at York factory on Hudson's Bay, in August, is described by Mr. SABINE as follows: "The head and chin are brown, having some fine white hairs scattered through the fur; the ears externally are coloured like the head; within they are white; a similar brown colour extends along the back to the tail, and from the back is continued down the outside of all the legs; the whole of the under parts, and the insides of the legs, are dingy white.

Plate CXX

N°. 24

Drawn from Nature by J.W.Audubon.

Fig. 1   Tawny Lemming. – Fig.2 &3   Back's Lemming

The tail is brownish above, becoming whiter at the end, and is entirely white beneath."

Dimensions.

Specimen obtained on the northeastern portion of the American continent by Captain PETTIGRU, and presented by him to the museum of the Charleston College.

	Feet.	Inches.
From point of nose to root of tail,	2	4
Length of tail (vertebræ),		1
" " (including fur),	1	2
" head,		6
From point of nose to eye,		$2\frac{3}{4}$
Height of ear anteriorly,		2
From heel to point of middle claw,		$2\frac{1}{8}$
Longest nail on the fore foot,		$1\frac{1}{12}$
" " hind foot,		$\frac{3}{4}$

Average weight about eight pounds, varying, according to Captain LYON, from seven to nine and a half pounds when in good case.

Habits.

From our description of the Arctic Fox, it will have been observed that this animal is well adapted to endure the severest cold. In winter its feet are thickly clothed with hair, even on the soles, which its movements on the ice and snow do not wear away, as would be the case if it trod upon the naked earth. These softly and thickly haired soles serve the double purpose of preserving its feet from the effects of frost and enabling it to run briskly and without slipping over the smooth icy tracts it must traverse.

The Arctic Fox is a singular animal, presenting rather the appearance of a little stumpy, round-eared cur, than that of the sharp and cunning-looking Foxes of other species which are found in more temperate climes. The character (for all animals have a character) and habits of this species are in accordance with its appearance; it is comparatively unsuspicious and gentle, and is less snappish and spiteful, even when first captured, than any other Fox with which we are acquainted.

At times there is seen a variety of this Fox, which has been called the Sooty Fox, but which is in all probability only the young, or at any rate is not a permanent variety, and which does not turn white in winter, although the species generally becomes white at that season. It is said likewise that the white Arctic Foxes do not all assume a brown tint in the summer. RICHARD-SON says that only a majority of these animals acquire the pure white dress even in winter; many have a little duskiness on the nose, and others, probably young individuals, remain more or less coloured on the body all the year. On the other hand, a pure white Arctic Fox is occasionally met with in the middle of summer, and forms the variety named *Kakkortak* by the Greenlanders.

Mr. WILLIAM MORTON, ship's steward of the Advance, one of Mr. HENRY GRINNELL's vessels sent in search of Sir JOHN FRANKLIN and his party, although not a naturalist, has furnished us with some account of this species. He informs us that whilst the vessels (the Advance and Rescue) were in the ice, the men caught a good many Arctic Foxes in traps made of old empty barrels set with bait on the ice: they caught the same individuals in the same trap several times, their hunger or their want of caution leading them again into the barrel when only a short time released from captivity.

They were kept on board the vessels for some days, and afterwards let loose; they did not always appear very anxious to make their escape from the ships, and those that had not been caught sometimes approached the vessels on the ice, where first one would appear, and after a while another, showing that several were in the neighbourhood. They were occasionally observed on the rocks and snow on the land, but were not seen in packs like wolves; they do not take to the water or attempt to swim.

These Foxes when they see a man do not appear to be frightened: they run a little way, and then sit down on their haunches like a dog, and face the enemy before running off entirely. They are said to be good eating, the crews of the vessels having feasted on them, and are fat all the winter. They were occasionally seen following the polar bear to feed on his leavings, seals, flesh of any kind, or fish.

Those they captured were easily tamed, seldom attempting to bite even when first caught, and by wrapping a cloth around the hand some of them could be taken out of the barrel and held, not offering more resistance than a snap at the cloth.

Several beautiful skins of this animal were brought home by Dr. E. K. KANE, the accomplished surgeon of the expedition, and have since been presented by him to the Academy of Natural Sciences at Philadelphia.

Captain LYON, during two winters passed on Melville peninsula, studied with attention the manners of several of these animals. He says: "The Arctic Fox is an extremely cleanly animal, being very careful not to dirt those places in which he eats or sleeps. No unpleasant smell is to be perceived even in a male, which is a remarkable circumstance. To come unawares on one of these creatures is, in my opinion, impossible, for even when in an apparently sound sleep they open their eyes at the slightest noise which is made near them, although they pay no attention to sounds when at a short distance. The general time of rest is during the daylight, in which they appear listless and inactive; but the night no sooner sets in than all their faculties are awakened; they commence their gambols, and continue in unceasing and rapid motion until the morning. While hunting for food, they are mute, but when in captivity or irritated, they utter a short growl like that of a young puppy. It is a singular fact, that their bark is so undulated as to give an idea that the animal is at a distance, although at the very moment he lies at your feet.

"Although the rage of a newly caught Fox is quite ungovernable, yet it very rarely happened that on two being put together they quarrelled. A confinement of a few hours often sufficed to quiet these creatures; and some instances occurred of their being perfectly tame, although timid, from the first moment of their captivity. On the other hand, there were some which, after months of coaxing, never became more tractable. These we suppose were old ones.

"Their first impulse on receiving food is to hide it as soon as possible, even though suffering from hunger and having no fellow-prisoners of whose honesty they are doubtful. In this case snow is of great assistance, as being easily piled over their stores, and then forcibly pressed down by the nose. I frequently observed my Dog-Fox, when no snow was attainable, gather his chain into his mouth, and in that manner carefully coil it so as to hide the meat. On moving away, satisfied with his operations, he of course had drawn it after him again, and sometimes with great patience repeated his labours five or six times, until in a passion he has been constrained to eat his food without its having been rendered luscious by previous concealment. Snow is the substitute for water to these creatures, and on a large lump being given to them they break it in pieces with their feet and roll on it with great delight. When the snow was slightly scattered on the decks, they did not lick it up as dogs are accustomed to do, but by repeatedly pressing with their nose collected small lumps at its extremity, and then drew it into the mouth with the assistance of the tongue."

In another passage, Captain LYON, alluding to the above-mentioned Dog-Fox, says: "He was small and not perfectly white; but his tameness was so remarkable that I could not bear to kill him, but confined him on deck in a small hutch, with a scope of chain. The little animal astonished us very much by his extraordinary sagacity, for during the first day, finding himself much tormented by being drawn out repeatedly by his chain, he at length, whenever he retreated to his hut, took his carefully up in his mouth, and drew it so completely after him that no one who valued his fingers would endeavour to take hold of the end attached to the staple."

RICHARDSON says that notwithstanding the degree of intelligence which the anecdotes related by Captain LYON show them to possess, they are unlike the red Fox in being extremely unsuspicious; and instances are related of their standing by while the hunter is preparing the trap, and running headlong into it the moment he retires a few paces. Captain LYON received fifteen from a single trap in four hours. The voice of the Arctic Fox is a kind of yelp, and when a man approaches their breeding places they put their heads out of their burrows and bark at him, allowing him to come so near that they may easily be shot.

They appear to have the power of decoying other animals within their reach, by imitating their voices. "While tenting, we observed a Fox prowling on a hill side, and heard him for several hours afterwards in different places, imitating the cry of a brentgoose." They feed on eggs, young birds, blubber, and carrion of any kind; but their principal food seems to be lemmings of different species.

RICHARDSON thinks the "brown variety," as he calls it, the more common one in the neighbourhood of Behring's Straits. He states that they breed on the sea coast, and chiefly within the Arctic circle, forming burrows in sandy spots, not solitary like the red Fox, but in little villages, twenty or thirty burrows being constructed adjoining to each other. He saw one of these villages on Point Turnagain, in latitude $68\frac{1}{2}°$. Towards the middle of winter, continues our author, they retire to the southward, evidently in search of food, keeping as much as possible on the coast, and going much farther to the southward in districts where the coast line is in the direction of their march. Captain PARRY relates that the Arctic Foxes, which were previously numerous, began to retire from Melville peninsula in November, and that by January few remained. "Towards the centre of the continent, in latitude 65°, they are seen only in the winter, and then not in numbers; they are very scarce

Plate CXXI.

N° 25

Drawn on Stone by Wm E. Hitchcock

Lith. Printed & Col.d by J T Bowen Phil.

Arctic Fox.

Drawn from Nature by J W Audubon.

in latitude 61°, and at Carlton House, in latitude 53°, only two were seen in forty years. On the coast of Hudson's Bay, however, according to HEARNE, they arrive at Churchill, in latitude 59°, about the middle of October, and afterwards receive reinforcements from the northward, until their numbers almost exceed credibility. Many are captured there by the hunters, and the greater part of the survivors cross the Churchill river as soon as it is frozen over, and continue their journey along the coast to Nelson and Severn rivers. In like manner they extend their migrations along the whole Labrador coast to the gulf of St. Lawrence. Most of those which travel far to the southward are destroyed by rapacious animals; and the few which survive to the spring breed in their new quarters, instead of returning to the north. The colonies they found are however soon extirpated by their numerous enemies. A few breed at Churchill, and some young ones are occasionally seen in the vicinity of York factory. There are from three to five young ones in a litter."

The trap in which the Arctic Fox is taken by the Esquimaux, is described by authors as simple: it consists of a little hut built of stones, with a square opening on the top, over which some blades of whalebone are extended nearly across so as to form an apparently secure footing, although only fastened at one end, so that when the animal comes on to them to get the bait they bend downward and the Fox is precipitated into the hut below, which is deep enough to prevent his jumping out, the more especially because the whalebone immediately rises again to its position, and the bait being fastened thereto, several Foxes may be taken successively. Other traps are arranged so that a flat stone falls on the Fox when he by pulling at the bait disengages the trigger. These Foxes are also caught in traps made of ice (in which wolves are taken at times by the Esquimaux). These traps are thus described by Dr. RICHARDSON, and are certainly composed of the last material we, dwellers in more favoured lands, would think of for the purpose: "The Esquimaux wolf-trap is made of strong slabs of ice, long and narrow, so that a Fox can with difficulty turn himself in it, but a wolf must actually remain in the position in which he is taken. The door is a heavy portcullis of ice, sliding in two well-secured grooves of the same substance, and is kept up by a line, which, passing over the top of the trap, is carried through a hole at the farthest extremity; to the end of the line is fastened a small hoop of whalebone, and to this any kind of flesh-bait is attached. From the slab which terminates the trap, a projection of

ice or a peg of wood or bone points inwards near the bottom, and under this the hoop is slightly hooked; the slightest pull at the bait liberates it, the door falls in an instant, and the wolf (or Fox) is speared where he lies."

In speaking of the *Sooty Fox*, which is only a variety of the present species, Dr. RICHARDSON says: "On one occasion during our late coasting voyage round the northern extremity of America, after cooking our supper on a sandy beach, we had retired to repose in the boats, anchored near the shore, when two Sooty Foxes came to the spot where the fire had been made, and carrying off all the scraps of meat that were left there, buried them in the sand above high water mark. We observed that they hid every piece in a separate place, and that they carried the largest pieces farthest off."

Geographical Distribution.

Arctic Foxes have been as far north on the American continent as man has ever proceeded. They are numerous on the shores of Hudson's Bay, north of Churchill, and exist also in Bhering's straits; towards the centre of the continent in latitude 65°, they are seen only in the winter, and then not in numbers. They are very scarce in latitude 61°, and at Carlton house in latitude 53°, only two were seen in forty years. On the coast of Hudson's Bay, however, according to HEARNE, they arrive at Churchill, in latitude 59°, about the middle of October, and afterwards receive reinforcements from the northward. On the eastern coast of America they are found at Labrador, where they have been seen occasionally in considerable numbers; a few have been also observed in the northern parts of Newfoundland, about latitude 52°.

On the eastern continent they are found in Siberia, and in all the Arctic regions.

General Remarks.

We have had opportunities in the museums of London, Berlin, and more particularly at Dresden, of comparing specimens of this animal from both continents: we could not find the slightest difference, and have no hesitation in pronouncing them one and the same species.

Lutra Canadensis.—Sabine. Var.
(Lataxina Mollis.—Gray.)

Canada Otter.

Plate cxxii.—Male.

In our second volume (p. 12) we promised to give a figure of this variety of the Canada Otter, and in our remarks we noticed the publication of varieties of that animal as distinct species, by GRAY, F. CUVIER, and WATER-HOUSE.

Mr. GRAY, we presume, thought that a large and different species existed near Hudson's Bay, and named his specimen *Lataxina Mollis*, calling the animal the Great Northern Otter.

The figure now before you was published, notwithstanding our doubts as to the specific differences Mr. GRAY thinks are observable between the Otters of Hudson's Bay and those of Canada and the United States, for the purpose of giving a correct drawing of the identical specimen named and described by that gentleman, in order that it might be seen that it is only a large variety of

the common American Otter.

Besides giving a figure of Mr. GRAY's Otter, we have examined Otters from very distant localities, having compared some taken near Montreal with one shot on the Hackensack river, New Jersey, several killed in South Carolina, one trapped in Texas, and one from California, and we are of opinion that, although differing in size and colour, the Otters of all these different localities are the same species, viz. *L. Canadensis*, the Canada Otter.

Besides the variations observable in the colour of the Otter, the fur of the more northern species is finer than any of the others.

As already stated (vol. ii. p. 11) we have not had an opportunity of comparing specimens from Brazil with ours, and the description given by RAY of *Lutra Braziliensis* is so vague and unsatisfactory that we cannot state with confidence that his animal is identical with the North American species. We strongly suspect, however, that it is, in which case RAY's name, *L. Braziliensis*, should be susbstituted for *L. Canadensis*, to which we would add as synonymes *Lataxina Mollis* of GRAY, and another supposed species by the same author, *Lutra Californica*.

We have nothing to add to the account of the habits of this animal given in our second volume (see p. 5).

Genus Aplodontia.—Rich.

Dental Formula.

Incisive $\frac{2}{2}$; *Canine* $\frac{0-0}{0-0}$; *Molar* $\frac{5-5}{4-4}$ = 22.

Incisors, very strong, flatly convex anteriorly, without grooves, narrower behind. Molars, simple, remarkably even on the crowns. The first in the upper jaw, small, cylindrical, and pointed, is placed within the anterior corner of the second one, and exists in the adult. The rest of the molars are perfectly simple in their structure, without roots, and have slightly concave crowns, which are merely bordered with enamel, without any transverse ridges or eminences. On the exterior side of the four posterior pairs of upper molars, and the inner side

of all the lower ones, there is an acute vertical ridge extending the whole length of the tooth, formed by a sharp fold of enamel. When the molars are *in situ*, there is a wide semicircular furrow between each pair of ridges, formed by the two adjoining teeth; the side of each tooth opposite the ridge is convexly semicircular. The second grinder in the upper jaw, and the first in the lower one, are a little larger than the more posterior ones, and the former has a projection of enamel at its anterior corner, producing a second though smaller vertical ridge, within which the first small molar is situated leaning towards it. There is a slight furrow on the exterior sides of the lower molars, most conspicuous in the first one.

Palate, narrow, bounded by perfectly parallel and straight rows of molars.

Head, flat and broad; nose, a little arched, thick, and obtuse. Lower jaw, thick and strong, with a large triangular process, concave behind, projecting

Plate CXXII

No 25

On Stone by Wm E Hitchcock

Lith Printed & Col'd by J T Bowen Phil

Canada Otter

Drawn from Nature by J W Audubon

at its posterior inferior angle further out than the zygomatic arch. The transverse diameter of the articulating surface of the condyle is greater than the longitudinal one. The jaw is altogether stronger than is usual in the *Rodentia*.

Cheek-pouches, none; eyes, very small; ears, short and rounded, approaching in form to the human ear, and thickly clothed with fur like that of a muskrat, but not so long or fine. Limbs, robust, short; feet, moderately long, with naked soles; five toes on all the feet, rather short but well separated; the thumb of the fore feet is considerably shorter than the other toes; claws, particularly the fore ones, very long, strong, much compressed, and but little curved.

Tail, very short, concealed by the fur of the hips, mammæ six, the anterior pair situated between the fore legs.

Habits.—Form small societies, feeding on vegetable substances, and living in burrows.—*Richardson.*

There is only one species belonging to this genus known at present.

The name aplodontia is derived from απλοος, *aploos*, simple, and οδους, *odous*, a tooth.

Aplodontia Leporina.—Rich.

The Sewellel.

Plate cxxiii.—Male.

A. Fuscescens, magnitudine Leporis Sylvatici, corpore brevi robusto, capite magno, cauda brevissima.

Characters.

Size of the gray rabbit (Lepus Sylvaticus). *Body, short and thick; head, large; tail, very short. Colour, brownish.*

Synonymes.

SEWELLEL. Lewis and Clark, vol. iii. p. 39.
ARCTOMYS RUFA.   Harlan, Fauna, p. 308.
        "   "   Griffith, Cuv. Animal Kingdom, vol. v. p. 245, species 636.
APLODONTIA LEPORINA. Rich, Zool. Jour., No. 15, p. 335. January, 1829.
        "   "   —SEWELLEL. Rich, Fauna Boreali Americana, p. 211, pl. 18 c, figs. 7–14, cranium, &c.

Description.

Body, short, thick, and heavy, nearly reaching the ground; legs, short; head, large; nose, thick and blunt, densely covered with hair to the nostrils, which are small and separated by a narrow furrowed septum concealed by the hair.

Mouth, rather small; incisors, large and strong; lips, thick, and clothed with rigid hairs; a brush of white hair projects into the mouth from the upper lip near its union with the lower one; whiskers, strong, and longer than the head; a few stiff hairs over the eyes, on the cheeks, and on the outer sides of the fore-legs; the eye is very small; the external ear rises rather far back, and is short and rounded; it rises about four lines above the auditory opening, has a small fold of the anterior part of its base inwards, together with a narrow thick margin, representing a lobe. There are also folds and eminences in the cavity of the auricle; the ear is clothed on the outer surface with short and fine hairs, and on the inner, with hairs a little longer; tail, short, slender, and cylindrical, and almost concealed by the hair of the rump; legs, covered down to the wrists and heels with short fur; feet, shaped like those of the marmots; palms and under surfaces of the fore feet, naked; there are three small callous eminences at the roots of the toes, disposed as in the marmots, one of them being common to the two middle toes, one proper to the third toe, and the other to the little toe.

At the root of the thumb there is a large prominent callosity, and on the opposite side of the palm another one nearly the same size; the thumb is of sufficient length to be used in grasping, and is terminated by a smooth rounded nail; claws, large and very much compressed, slightly arched above, and nearly straight below; hind feet, more slender than the fore feet, and their claws one half smaller, rather more arched, and less compressed; soles, longer than the palms, and naked to the heel; they are furnished with four callous eminences situated at the roots of the toes, and two placed farther back, all more conspicuous than those on the hind feet of the spermophiles of America.

The hair is soft, and somewhat resembles the finer fur of the muskrat; the under fur is soft, tolerably dense, and about half an inch long; the longer hairs are not sufficiently numerous to conceal the under fur. The hair on the feet only reaches to the roots of the claws, which are naked.

A specimen of a young Sewellel brought by DOUGLAS and examined by RICHARDSON, in which the dentition was the same as in the adult, exhibited a new set of molar teeth, which had destroyed the greater part of the substance of the old teeth, leaving merely a long process before and another behind in each socket, resembling fangs.

Colour.

Incisors, yellow; claws, horn colour; general hue of the back, brownish, the long scattered hairs being tipped with black; belly, grayish, with many of the long hairs tipped with white; nose, nearly the colour of the back; lips, whitish; in some specimens there is a spot of pure white on the throat.

The hairs on the back, when blown aside, exhibit a grayish colour from the roots to the tips, which are brown.

Dimensions.

	Inches.	Lines.
Length of head and body, ...	14	
" tail, ...		6
Wrist joint to end of middle claw, ...	1	9
Middle claw, ...		6
Length of head, ...	3	4

Habits.

LEWIS and CLARK, who discovered this species during their journey across the Rocky Mountains to the Pacific, give us the following account of it:

"Sewellel is a name given by the natives to a small animal found in the timbered country on this coast. It is more abundant in the neighbourhood of the great falls and rapids of the Columbia than on the coast. The natives make great use of the skins of this animal in forming their robes, which they dress with the fur on, and attach them together with the sinews of the elk or deer. The skin when dressed is from fourteen to eighteen inches long, and from seven to nine in width: the tail is always separated from the skin by the natives when making their robes."

"This animal mounts a tree, and burrows in the ground, precisely like a squirrel. The ears are short, thin, and pointed, and covered with a fine short hair, of a uniform reddish-brown; the bottom or the base of the long hairs, which exceed the fur but little in length, as well as the fur itself, are of a dark colour next to the skin for two thirds of the length of this animal; the fur and hair are very fine, short, thickly set, and silky; the ends of the fur and tip of the hair are of a reddish-brown, and that colour predominates in the usual appearance of the animal. Captain LEWIS offered considerable rewards to the Indians, but was never able to procure one of these animals alive."

Mr. DOUGLAS gave Dr. RICHARDSON an Indian blanket or robe, formed by sewing the skins of the Sewellel together. This robe contained twenty-seven skins, selected when the fur was in fine order. They are described by Dr. RICHARDSON as all having the long hairs so numerous as to hide the wool or down at their roots, and their points have a very high lustre. The doctor appears to think there were skins of two species of Sewellel in this robe. We did not hear of this animal ever being found to the east of the Rocky Mountains. Our figure was drawn from a fine specimen in London.

We are inclined to think from the form of the Sewellel that it is a great digger; but LEWIS' account of its mounting a tree seems to us to require some modification; the Maryland marmot, to which it is somewhat allied in form and in the shape of its claws, when hard pressed will mount a tree for a little distance to avoid the pursuit of a dog, but is very awkward and soon descends; we presume the climbing properties of the Sewellel can scarcely be greater than those of the marmot.

From the number of mammæ exhibited in the female, we conclude that it produces five or six young at a time, and from the nature of the animal, these are probably brought forth, like those of the marmots, in nests within their

Plate CXXIII

On Stone by W.E.Hitchcock

The Sewellel

Drawn from Nature by J.W.Audubon

Lith.d Printed & Col.d by J.T.Bowen, Philad.a

burrows.

Geographical Distribution.

This singular species has been observed on the western slopes of the Rocky Mountains, in the valleys and plains of the Columbia, at Nisqually, and at Puget's sound, where it is said to be a common animal. It has also been procured in California.

General Remarks.

The history of this species, of which, however, little is known, is somewhat curious. LEWIS and CLARK appear to have been the only individuals who gave any notice of it until a very recent period, when DOUGLAS procured a specimen, and RICHARDSON gave a scientific account of the animal. The account LEWIS and CLARK gave dates back to 1804, and we have given the whole of their article above; these travellers, however, brought no specimens. After the journal of their adventurous expedition was published, RAFINES-

QUE ventured to give to the Sewellel the name of *Anysonix Rufa*, HARLAN named it *Arctomys Rufa*, and GRIFFITH introduced it into the animal kingdom under the same name; in 1829, RICHARDSON obtained a specimen, and the Sewellel was now for the first time examined by a naturalist. Believing that no one who had not seen or examined a species had a right to bestow a specific name, RICHARDSON rejected both the generic and specific names of previous writers, established for it a new genus, and gave it the name it now bears, and which it will doubtless preserve in our system of Zoology.

There are two specimens of this animal in the Patent Office at Washington city, which were procured by the Exploring Expedition under command of Captain WILKES. We were recently politely refused permission to take them out of the glass case (in which they have for some time past remained) to examine their fur and measure them. We will not take the trouble to make any further remarks on this subject, as we have in a note at page 211 of our second volume mentioned the obstructions thrown in our way by the directors of the National Institute at Washington, the officers in charge of the collection informing us that by high authority the specimens were "tabooed."

Putorius Nigrescens.—Aud. and Bach.

Mountain-Brook Mink.

Plate cxxiv.—Male.

P. Saturate fuscus, corpore minore quam in P. Visone, pedibus minus profunde palmatis, auriculis amplioribus et longioribus, vellere molliore et nitidiore quam in isto, dentibus longioribus in maxilla inferiore quam in superiore.

Characters.

Smaller than P. Vison; *teeth in the under jaw larger than the corresponding teeth in the upper jaw; feet, less deeply palmated than in* P. Vison; *ears, broader and longer; fur, softer and more glossy. Colour, dark brownish-black.*

Synonyme.

MOUNTAIN-MINK, of hunters.

Description.

In form, in dentition, and in the shape of the feet, this species bears a strong resemblance to a stout weasel; the head is broad and depressed, and shorter and more blunt than the head of *Putorius Vison*.

Ears, large, oval, and slightly acute, covered on both surfaces with short fur; legs, rather short and stout; feet, small, and less webbed than in *P. Vison*. The callosities under the toes are more prominent than in that species, and the palms scarcely half as long. Whiskers, very numerous, springing from the sides of the face near the nose; the body is covered with two kinds of hair, the under fur soft, and the long sparsely distributed hairs, coarse but smooth and glossy.

The toes are covered with short hairs almost concealing the nails, and the hairs between the toes leave only the tubercles or callosities on the under side of them visible.

Colour.

Fur, blackish-brown from the roots to the tips; whiskers and ears, blackish-brown; a patch on the chin, white; under surface of body, a shade lighter and redder than on the back; tail, blackish-brown, except towards the tip, where it is black.

Dimensions.

	Inches.	Lines.
Length of head and body,	11	
" tail (to end of hair),	7	
" " (vertebræ),	6	
" palms of fore feet,	1	2
From tarsus to end of nail on hind foot,	2	2
Height of ear externally,		6

For convenient comparison we add the measurements of three common minks (*P. Vison*) killed in Carolina. One was very old and his teeth were much worn; the other two were about eight months.

P. Vison, three specimens.

	Inches.	Inches.	Inches.
Lengths of body and head, respectively,	20	17	19
" tail, "	8	6	7
" palms of fore feet,	2		
" tarsus to longest nail,	3		

Habits.

We were familiar with the manners and ways of this smaller Mink in early life, and have frequently caught it in traps on the banks of a brook to which we resorted for the purpose of angling, and which in those days actually abounded with trout, as well as with suckers and perch. On this sparkling stream, where we passed many an hour, the little black Mink was the only species we observed. We found a nest of the animal under the roots of a large tree, where the young were brought forth, and we frequently noticed the old ones with fish in their mouths.

This species swim and dive swiftly and with apparent ease, but we most generally saw them on the ground, hunting as they stole along the winding banks of the stream, and following it high up into the hills towards its very source.

We remember seeing the young in the nest on two occasions; in each case the nest contained four.

In early spring we have traced this species of Mink into the meadows, where it had been busily engaged in capturing the common meadow-mouse (*A. Pennsylvanica*), whilst the snow was yet on the ground.

Having one day detected one of these little Minks in an outhouse, closing the door immediately we captured it without its making any attempt either to get away or to defend itself. The frightened little marauder was probably conscious that it was in a prison from which there was no possible chance of escape.

The large species (*P. Vison*) appears to be more plentiful than the Mountain-brook Mink, and is found about mill-ponds and large rivers quite as frequently as on the borders of small streams.

The Mountain-brook Mink is quite as destructive to young poultry and to all the tenants of the farm-yard, when it happens to approach the precincts in which they may be thought to be safely ranging, as the larger species, or even the weasel.

Geographical Distribution.

We have observed this species in the mountains of the State of Pennsylvania, as well as in the northern part of the State of New York, in Vermont, and in Canada, but have not met with nor heard of it in Virginia or any of the Southern States, and consequently are inclined to regard it as a northern species.

It was not seen by us on the Missouri river, although it probably exists some distance to the west, in the latitude of the great lakes.

Plate CXXIV

N° 25

Drawn from Nature by J W Audubon

On Stone by W^m E Hitchcock

Mountain Brook Mink

Lith. Printed & Col.^d by J T Bowen Phil.

General Remarks.

In our article on the common Mink (*Putorius Vison*, vol. i. p. 252) we referred to this smaller animal, but could not then find characters sufficient to separate the species.

Since that time, however, we have had abundant opportunities of comparing many specimens. We have seen some with their teeth much worn, and females which from the appearance of the teats had evidently suckled their young. They were all of the size and colour of the specimen above described, and we can no longer doubt that the latter is a distinct species from *P. Vison*.

The comparison in fact is not required to be made between these species, but between the present species and *P. lutreola* of Europe. We enjoyed opportunities of comparing *P. Vison* (the common and well known Mink) with the latter species in the museums of Berlin, Dresden, and London; but we had no opportunity of placing this little species by the side of the European.

We are inclined to believe, however, that the distinctive marks will be found in the small rounded feet and short tarsus of our present species, in its longer and rather more pointed ears, its shorter head, and longer lower incisors, together with a more general resemblance to our common weasel (*P. erminea*) in summer pelage.

Sorex Palustris. — Rich.

American Marsh Shrew.

Plate cxxv. — Males.

S. Mure musculo longior, cauda corporis fere longitudine, auriculis brevibus, pilosis, vellere absconditis, dorso canescente-nigro, ventro cinereo.

Characters.

Rather larger than the house mouse; tail, nearly as long as the body; short hairy ears, concealed by the fur; back, somewhat hoary black; belly, ash colour.

Synonymes.

SOREX PALUSTRIS. Rich., Zool. Jour., No. 12, April, 1828.
"   "   "   AMERICAN MARSH SHREW. F. B. A., p. 5.

Description.

Dental Formula. — Incisive $\frac{2}{2}$; Canine $\frac{4-4}{2-2}$; Molar $\frac{4-4}{3-3}$ = 30.

The two posterior lateral incisors are smaller than the two anterior ones on the same side, and the latter are a little longer than the posterior lobes of the intermediary incisors; all the lateral incisors have small lobes on their inner sides. Muzzle, tolerably long, and pointed; upper lip, bordered with rigid hairs; tips of posterior hairs reaching beyond the ears; the extremity of the muzzle, naked and bi-lobed; eyes, small but visible; ear, short and concealed by the fur, its margins folded in; a heart-shaped lobe covering the auditory opening, and a transverse fold above it. The upper margins of the ears are clothed with thick tufts of fur. Tail rounded, and covered with hair, terminated by a small pencil of hair at the tip; feet, clothed with rather short adpressed hairs, the hairs on the sides of the toes being arranged somewhat indistinctly in a parallel manner. The fur resembles that of the mole in softness, closeness, and lustre.

Colour.

The tips of the teeth have a shining chesnut-brown tint; the body is black above, with a slight hoary appearance when turned to the light; on the ventral aspect ash coloured; at the roots the hair is bluish-gray; the outside of the thighs and upper surface of the tail correspond in colour with the back; under surface of the tail, insides of thighs, and belly, greyish-white; feet, paler than the back.

Dimensions.

	Inches.	Lines.
Length from point of nose to root of tail,	3	6
" of tail,	2	7
" of head,	1	2
" from nose to eye,		7
Height of ear,		3
Length of hind foot from heel to end of nails,		9

Habits.

The habits of all Shrews (except those of the kind described by SHAKESPEARE) must necessarily be little known. These animals are so minute in the scale of quadrupeds that they will always be overlooked, unless sought after with great zeal, and even then it is often difficult to meet with or procure them. It may be said that it is only by chance that one is seen and taken now and then, even where they are known to exist. We have not seen more than five or six alive during several years, although dead ones have been found by us more frequently, and upon one occasion we found two that appeared to have recently died, lying close to each other. No wonder, then, that they may escape the observation of the most persevering student of nature, as their instinctive caution would, by causing them either to fly to some little hole or tuft of grass, or to remain still, when danger was near, render their discovery more than doubtful; or, if seen, it would be only for a moment. Not the least singluar circumstance connected with the family of Shrews is the fact that they can exist in extremely cold climates, and move about in winter, when the snow covers the ground. In his article on *Sorex palustris* Dr. RICHARDSON says it "most probably lives in the summer on similar food with the Water Shrew, but I am at a loss to imagine how it procures a subsistence during the six months of the year in which the countries it inhabits are covered with snow. It frequents borders of lakes, and HEARNE tells us that it often takes up its abode in beaver houses."

We might easily make some probable speculations as to the manners and customs of the present species, but prefer not doing so farther than to say that it very likely feeds on seeds, insects, and on the carcases of any small birds or other animals it finds dead in the fields, that in winter it has a store of provision laid by, only coming to the snow-covered surface on fine days for the purpose of getting a little fresh air, and that from the number of tracks sometimes seen at one place we consider it partly gregarious in its habits.

Our drawing was made from a specimen in the British Museum at London.

Geographical Distribution.

The American Marsh Shrew, according to the writers who have seen it exists in the northern parts of our continent from Hudson's Bay to the Coppermine river.

General Remarks.

We are not aware that any author has referred to this animal, except Dr. RICHARDSON; the specimen from which our drawing was made was the original one from which Dr. RICHARDSON described, and we believe this species has never been hitherto figured.

Nº 25

Plate CXXV

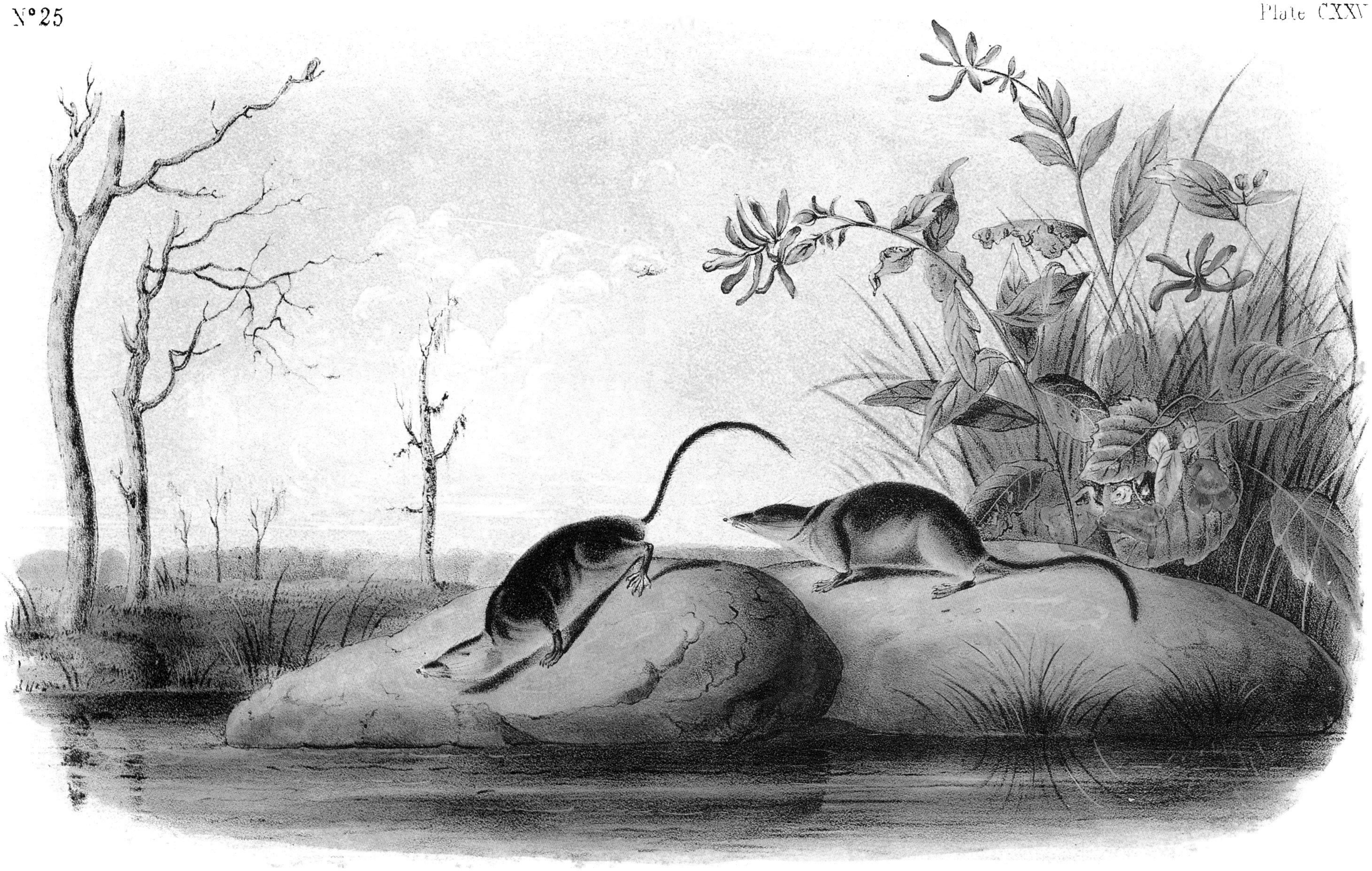

Drawn on Stone by Wm. E. Hitchcock

Drawn from Nature by J. W. Audubon

Lith. Printed & Colᵈ by J. T. Bowen Phil.

American Marsh Shrew

Genus Rangifer.—Hamilton Smith.

Dental Formula.

$$Incisive \ \tfrac{0}{8}; \ Canine \ \tfrac{1-1}{0-0}; \ Molar \ \tfrac{6-6}{6-6} = 34.$$

Horns in both sexes, irregularly palmated, bifurcated, and rather long; canine teeth in both sexes; muzzle, small.

According to our opinion, two species of this genus exist—one in the old world (*Rangifer tarandus*), commonly called the Lapland Reindeer, and the Caribou (*Rangifer caribou*) and its varieties, the Reindeer of the American continent. Should, however, the varieties of the Reindeer found in different parts of the Arctic circle on *both* continents form one species only, then there is but one species in the genus known at present.

Fossil remains of a Reindeer of small size have been found near Etampes in France.

The generic name, *Rangifer*, is not of Latin origin, but has been formed from the old French term *Rangier* or *Ranger*, a Reindeer, probably through the later *Rangifère*.

Rangifer Caribou.

Caribou or American Reindeer.

Plate cxxvi.—Males. Fig. 1.—Summer Pelage. Fig. 2.—Winter.

R. Magnitudine fere Elaphi Canadensis; in æstate saturate fuscus, in hyeme cinereus; vitta alba supra ungulas.

Characters.

Nearly the size of the American Elk (Elaphus Canadensis); *colour, deep brown in summer, grayish-ash in winter, a white fringe above the hoofs.*

Synonymes.

GENUS CERVUS. Linn., sectio Rangiferini.
CARIBOU, OU ASNE SAUVAGE. Sagard Theodat. Canada, p. 751, Ann.
    "   1636.
    "   La Hontan, t.i. p. 77, Ann. 1703.
    Charlevoix, Nouv. France, tom. v. p. 190.
REINDEER, or RAINDEER, Drage, Voy., vol. i. p. 25.
    "   Dobbs' Hudson's Bay, pp. 19, 22.
    "   Pennant's Arctic Zoology, vol. i. p. 22.
    "   Cartwright's Labrador, pp. 91, 112, 133.
    "   Franklin's First Voyage, pp. 240, 245.
CERVUS TARANDUS. Harlan, Fauna, p. 232.
    "   "   Godman, Nat. Hist., vol. ii. p. 283.
    "   "   —REINDEER or CARIBOU, Rich., F. B. A.,
        p. 238.
RANGIFER TARANDUS—REINDEER. DeKay, Nat. Hist. State of New
    York, p. 121.
ATTEHK. Cree Indians.
ETTHIN. Chippewyan Indians.
TOOKTOO. Esquimaux.
TUKTA. Greenlanders.
CARRÈ-BŒUF, or CARIBOU. French Canadians.

Description.

Young, about two years and a half old.

Larger and less graceful than the common American deer; body, stout and heavy; neck, short; hoofs, thin, flattened, broad and spreading, excavated or concave beneath; accessory hoofs, large but thin; legs, stout; no glandular opening and scarcely a perceptible inner tuft on the hind legs; nose, somewhat like that of a cow, but fully covered with soft hairs of moderate length; no beard, but on the under side of the neck a line of hairs about four inches in length which hang down in a longitudinal direction. Ears, small, short, and ovate, thickly clothed with hair on both surfaces; horns, one foot three and a half inches in height, slender (one with two, and the other with one, prong); prongs, about five inches long.

Hair, soft and woolly underneath, the longer hairs like those of the antelope, crimped or waved, and about one to one and a half inches long.

Colour.

At the roots the hairs are whitish, then become brownish-gray, and at the tips are light dun gray, whiter on the neck than elsewhere; nose, ears, outer surface of legs, and shoulder, brownish; a slight shade of the same tint behind the fore legs.

Hoofs, black; neck and throat, dull white; a faint whitish patch on the sides of the shoulders; forehead, brownish-white; belly, white; tail, white, with a slight shade of brown at the root and on the whole upper surface; outside of legs, brown; a band of white around all the legs adjoining the hoofs, and extending to the small secondary hoofs; horns, yellowish-brown, worn whiter in places.

There is a small patch of brown, faintly defined, around and behind the ears.

Description of the horns of another specimen.

The two main antlers are furnished with irregular and sharp points, and their extremity is pointed; some of these points are from six to eight inches long, but most of them are quite short; width between the horns on the skull, eight inches; width of horns at the root, two inches and three quarters; depth, one inch and three quarters; length of main horn, following the curve, three feet; there is a palmated brow antler with four points, on one side, inclining downwards and inwards; on the opposite horn there are two points, but the antler is not palmated; immediately above the brown antlers there is a branch or prong on each horn about fourteen inches in length, terminating in three points; these prongs incline forward and inward. About half the length of the horn from the skull there is another prong on each about two inches long; beyond these prongs each horn continues about the same thickness, spreading outwards slightly to within a few inches of its extremity, where one diverges into five points and the other into six. The horns are but slightly channelled; they are dark yellow. Between the tips, where they approach each other, the horns are two feet apart, and at their greatest width two feet eight inches.

The female Caribou has horns as well as the male, but they are smaller.

Dimensions.

Young—about two and a half years old.

	Feet.	Inches.
Length from nose to root of tail,	6	
" of tail (vertebræ),		4
" " (including hair),		6½
Height of shoulder,	3	6
Width between the eyes,		5½
From point of nose to lower canthus of eye,		9
" " to ear,	1	2
Height of ear posteriorly,		5

Habits.

The Caribou, or American Reindeer, is one of the most important animals of the northern parts of America, and is almost as graceful in form as the elk (*Elaphus Canadensis*), to which it is nearly equal in size; but it has never, we believe, been domesticated or trained to draw sledges in the manner of the Reindeer of the old world, although so nearly allied to that species that it has been by most authors considered identical with it.

Whilst separating the Caribou found in Maine and the States bordering on the St. Lawrence, and in Canada, Labrador, &c., from the Reindeer of Europe, we are inclined to think that the Reindeer found within the polar circle may be the European species, domiciled in that part of America, and that they sometimes migrate farther south than even Hudson's Bay. Sir JOHN RICHARDSON says the Reindeer or Caribou of North America "have indeed so great a general resemblance in appearance and manners to the Lapland Deer that they have always been considered to be the same species, without the fact having ever been completely established."—*Fauna Boreali Americana*, p. 238.

The greater size and weight of the Caribou found in Canada seem to have surprised Sir JOHN, but while he says in a note (p. 239), that "Mr. HENRY, when he mentions Caribou that weigh four hundred pounds, must have some other species of Deer in view," he has not done more than point out two varieties of Reindeer beside the one he considered identical with *Cervus tarandus* the European Reindeer, and to neither of these varieties can we with certainty refer the Caribou, our present animal. In the Fauna Boreali Americana (p. 241) one of these varieties—*C. tarandus, var. A. Arctica*, Barren-ground Caribou—is said to be so small that the bucks only weigh from ninety to one

Plate CXXVI.

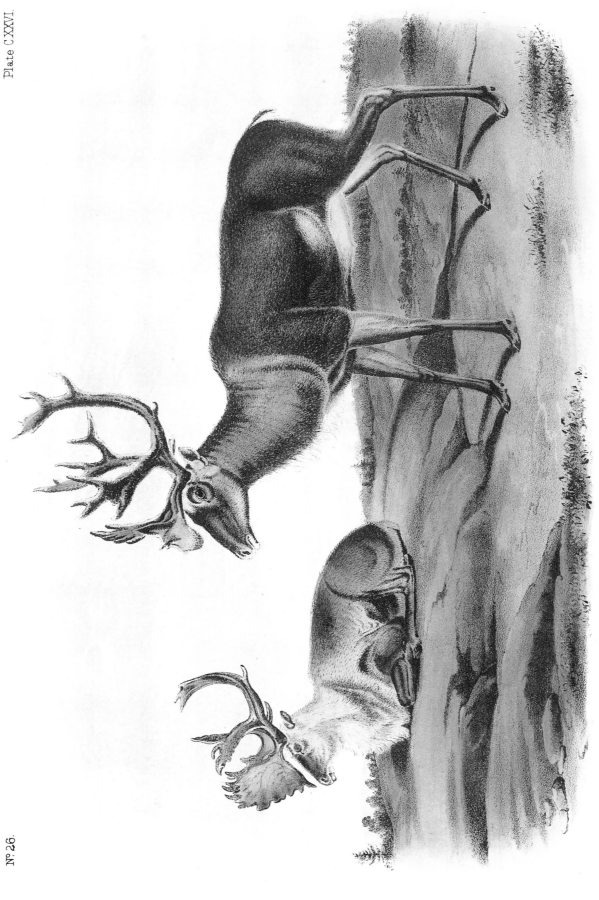

Caribou or American Rein Deer.

Drawn from Nature by J W Audubon.

hundred and thirty pounds, exclusive of the offal, when in good condition; the other variety—*C. tarandus, var. B. sylvestris,* Woodland Caribou (idem, p. 250)—is much larger than the Barren-ground Caribou, has smaller horns, and even when in good condition is vastly inferior as an article of food."

Leaving these supposed varieties where we found them—in doubt—we will proceed with an account of the habits of the Caribou detailed to us by Mr. JOHN MARTYN, Jr., of Quebec:

This species, that gentleman informed us, is not abundant near Quebec; it is mostly found in the swamps, wherever these are well supplied with moss-covered dead trees and bushes; the moss the animals prefer is a long and black species, and forms their chief subsistence during the winter months; but towards spring these animals remove to the sides of the hills or mountains, and even ascend to their summits occasionally, feeding on the newly swollen buds of different shrubs. Like the moose deer they shed their antlers about this period, and renew them in the summer months.

The Caribou is famous for its swiftness, and has various gaits, walking trotting or galloping alike gracefully and rapidly. By many people these animals are in fact thought to be much fleeter animals than the moose, and they are said to take most extraordinary leaps.

When pursued the Caribou immediately makes for a swamp and follows the margin, taking at times to the water and again footing it over the firm ground, and sometimes turning towards the nearest mountain crosses it to another morass. If hard pressed by the hunters (who now and then follow up the chase for four or five days) the animal ascends to the loftiest peaks of the mountains for greater security, and the pursuit becomes very fatiguing and uncertain. Upon one occasion two men followed several Caribou for a whole week, when, completely tired out they gave up the chase, which was then continued by two other hunters who at last succeeded in killing a couple of the animals at long shot. Sometimes, however, fresh tracks are found and the Caribou is surprised whilst lying down or browsing, and shot on the spot. When the snow is not deep and the lakes are covered with ice only, the animal if closely pushed makes for one of them and runs over the ice so fast that it is unable to stop if struck with alarm at any object presenting itself in front, and it then suddenly squats down on its haunches and slides along in that ludicrous position until, the impetus being exhausted, it rises again and makes off in some other direction. When the Caribou takes to the ice the hunters always give up the chase.

Sometimes when the mouth and throat of a fresh killed Reindeer are examined they are found to be filled with a blackish looking mucus, resembling thin mud, but which appears to be only a portion of the partially decomposed black mosses upon which it fed, probably forced into the throat and mouth of the animal in its dying agonies.

We were informed that two wood-choppers, whilst felling trees at a distance from any settlement, saw a Caribou fawn approaching them which was so gentle that it allowed them to catch it, and one of the men took it up in his arms; but suddenly the dam also made her appearance, and the men dropping the young one made after her in hopes of killing her with their axes. This object was of course soon abandoned, as a few bounds took the animal out of sight, and to their mortification they found that the fawn had escaped also during their short absence, and although they made diligent search for it, could not again be seen. At times, even the full grown Caribou appears to take but little heed of man.—A person descending a steep woody hill on a road towards a lake, saw several of them, which only turned aside far enough to let him pass, after which they came back to the road and proceeded at a slow pace up the hill. At another place a lad driving a cart was surprised to see five of these animals come into the road just before him, making a great noise through the woods. As soon as they got into the road they walked along quite leisurely, and on his cracking his whip only trotted a few paces and then resumed their walking.

When overtaken by dogs in chase, the Caribou stand at bay and show fight, and when thus brought to a stand will not pay much attention to the hunter, so that he can approach and shoot them with ease.

During our expeditions in Labrador we saw many trails of Reindeer through the deep and stiff moss; they are about as broad as a cowpath, and many times the fatigues of a long day's hunt over the sterile wilds of that country were lightened by following in these tracks or paths, instead of walking on the yielding moss.

We did not see any of these animals ourselves, but bought one from the Indians and enjoyed it very much, as we had had no fresh meat for nearly three months, except fishy ducks, a few curlews, and some willow-grouse.

We were informed that the Caribou are sometimes abundant on the island of Newfoundland, to which they cross on the ice from the mainland, and as the fishermen and French trappers at St. George's Bay told us, sometimes the herds stay so late in the spring that by the occasional early breaking up of the ice, they are prevented from leaving the island.

The horns of the Caribou run into various shapes, and are more or less palmated. The female of this species has also horns, which are not dropped until near the month of May. No two individuals of this species have the horns alike, nor do the horns of any grow into the same number of prongs, or resemble those of the last season. Notwithstanding this endless variety, there is always a specific character in the horns of this species (as well as in all our other deer), which will enable the close observer at once to recognise them.

"In the month of July," says Dr. RICHARDSON, "the Caribou sheds its winter covering, and acquires a short, smooth coat of hair, of a colour composed of clove brown, mingled with deep reddish and yellowish-browns, the under surface of the neck, the belly, and the inner sides of the extremities, remaining white in all seasons. The hair at first is fine and flexible, but as it lengthens it increases gradually in diameter at its roots, becoming at the same time white, soft, compressible, and brittle, like the hair of the moose deer. In the course of the winter the thickness of the hairs at their roots becomes so great that they are exceedingly close, and no longer lie down smoothly, but stand erect, and they are then so soft and tender below, that the flexible coloured points are easily rubbed off, and the fur appears white, especially on the flanks. This occurs in a smaller degree on the back; and on the under parts, the hair, although it acquires length, remains more flexible and slender at its roots, and is consequently not so subject to break. Towards the spring, when the Deer are tormented by the larvæ of the gad-fly making their way through the skin, they rub themselves against stones and rocks until all the coloured tops of the hair are worn off, and their fur appears to be entirely of a soiled white colour."

"The closeness of the hair of the Caribou, and the lightness of its skin, when properly dressed, render it the most appropriate article for winter clothing in the high latitudes. The skins of the young Deer make the best dresses, and they should be killed for that purpose in the month of August or September, as after the latter date the hair becomes too long and brittle. The prime parts of eight or ten Deer-skins make a complete suit of clothing for a grown person, which is so impervious to the cold that, with the addition of a blanket of the same material, any one so clothed may bivouack on the snow with safety, and even with comfort, in the most intense cold of an Arctic winter's night."

The same author gives the following habits of the variety he called "Arctica:" "The Barren-ground Caribou, which resort to the coast of the Arctic sea in summer, retire in winter to the woods lying between the sixty-third and the sixty-sixth degree of latitude, where they feed on the *usneæ, alectoriæ,* and other lichens, which hang from the trees, and on the long grass of the swamps. About the end of April, when the partial melting of the snow has softened the *cetrariæ, corniculariæ,* and *cevomyces,* which clothe the barren grounds like a carpet, they make short excursions from the woods, but return to them when the weather is frosty. In May the females proceed towards the sea-coast, and towards the end of June the males are in full march in the same direction. At that period the power of the sun has dried up the lichens on the barren grounds, and the Caribou frequent the moist pastures which cover the bottoms of the narrow valleys on the coasts and islands of the Arctic sea, where they graze on the sprouting carices and on the withered grass or hay of the preceding year, which is at that period still standing, and retaining part of its sap. Their spring journey is performed partly on the snow, and partly after the snow has disappeared, on the ice covering the rivers and lakes, which have in general a northerly direction. Soon after their arrival on the coast the females drop their young; they commence their return to the south in September, and reach the vicinity of the woods towards the end of October, where they are joined by the males. This journey takes place after the snow has fallen, and they scrape it away with their feet to procure the lichens, which are then tender and pulpy, being preserved moist and unfrozen by the heat still remaining in the earth. Except in the rutting season, the bulk of the males and females live separately: the former retire deeper into the woods in winter, whilst herds of the pregnant does stay on the skirts of the barren grounds, and proceed to the coast very early in spring. Captain PARRY saw Deer on Melville peninsula as late as the 23d or September, and the females, with their fawns, made their first appearance on the 22d of April. The males in general do not go so far north as the females. On the coast of Hudson's Bay the Barren-ground Caribou migrate farther south than those on the Coppermine or Mackenzie rivers; but none of them go to the southward of Churchill."

The Caribou becomes very fat at times, and is then an excellent article of food. As some particulars connected with its edible qualities are rather singular, we subjoin them from the same author: "When in condition there is a layer of fat deposited on the back and rump of the males to the depth of two or three inches or more, immediately under the skin, which is termed *depouillé* by the Canadian voyagers, and as an article of Indian trade, it is often of more value than all the remainder of the carcass. The *depouillé* is thickest at the commencement of the rutting season; it then becomes of a red colour, and acquires high flavour, and soon afterwards disappears. The females at that period are lean, but in the course of the winter they acquire a small *depouillé*, which is exhausted soon after they drop their young. The flesh of the Caribou is very tender, and its flavour when in season is, in my opinion, superior to that of the finest English venison, but when the animal is lean it is very insipid, the difference being greater between well fed and lean Caribou than any one can conceive who has not had an opportunity of judging. The lean meat fills the stomach but never satisfies the appetite, and scarcely serves to recruit the strength when exhausted by labour." "The Chepewyans, the Copper Indians, the Dog-Ribs and Hare Indians of Great Bear Lake, would be totally unable to inhabit their barren lands were it not for the immense herds of this Deer that exist there. Of the Caribou horns they form their fish-spears and hooks; and previous to the introduction of European iron, ice-chisels and various other utensils were likewise made of them." "The hunter breaks the leg-bones of a recently slaughtered Deer, and while the marrow is still warm devours it with much relish. The kidneys and part of the intestines, particularly the thin folds of the third stomach or manyplies, are likewise occasionally eaten when raw, and the summits of the antlers, as long as they are soft, are also delicacies in a raw state. The colon or large gut is inverted, so as to preserve its fatty appendages, and is, when either roasted or boiled, one of the richest and most savoury morsels the country affords, either to the native or white resident. The remainder of the intestines, after being cleaned, are hung in the smoke for a few days and then broiled. The stomach and its contents, termed by the Esquimaux *nerrooks*, and by the Greenlanders *nerrokak* or *nerriookak*, are also eaten, and it would appear that the lichens and other vegetable matters on which the Caribou feeds are more easily digested by the human stomach when they have been mixed with the salivary and gastric juices of a ruminating animal. Many of the Indians and Canadian voyagers prefer this savoury mixture after it has undergone a degree of fermentation, or lain to season, as they term it, for a few days. The blood, if mixed in proper proportion with a strong decoction of fat meat, forms, after some nicety in the cooking, a rich soup, which is very palatable and highly nutritious, but very difficult of digestion. When all the soft parts of the animal are consumed the bones are pounded small, and a large quantity of marrow is extracted from them by boiling. This is used in making the better kinds of the mixture of dried meat and fat, which is named *pemmican*, and it is also preserved by the young men and females for anointing the hair and greasing the face on dress occasions. The tongue roasted, when fresh or when half dried, is a delicious morsel. When it is necessary to preserve the Caribou meat for use at a future period, it is cut into thin slices and dried over the smoke of a slow fire, and then pounded betwixt two stones. This pounded meat is very dry and husky if eaten alone, but when a quantity of the back-fat or *depouillé* of the Deer is added to it, is one of the greatest treats that can be offered to a resident in the fur countries."

"The Caribou travel in herds, varying in number from eight or ten to two or three hundred, and their daily excursions are generally towards the quarter from whence the wind blows. The Indians kill them with the bow and arrow or gun, take them in snares, or spear them in crossing rivers or lakes. The Esquimaux also take them in traps ingeniously formed of ice or snow. Of all the Deer of North America they are the most easy of approach, and are slaughtered in the greatest numbers. A single family of Indians will sometimes destroy two or three hundred in a few weeks, and in many cases they are killed for the sake of their tongues alone."

Captain LYON's private journal contains some accounts of this species: "The Reindeer visits the polar regions at the latter end of May or the early part of June, and remains until late in September. On his first arrival he is thin and his flesh is tasteless, but the short summer is sufficient to fatten him to two or three inches on the haunches. When feeding on the level ground, an Esquimaux makes no attempt to approach him, but should a few rocks be near, the wary hunter feels secure of his prey. Behind one of these he cautiously creeps, and having laid himself very close, with his bow and arrow before him, imitates the bellow of the Deer when calling to each other. Sometimes, for more complete deception, the hunter wears his Deer-skin coat and hood so drawn over his head as to resemble, in a great measure, the unsuspecting animals he is enticing. Though the bellow proves a considerable attraction, yet if a man has great patience he may do without it, and may be equally certain that his prey will ultimately come to examine him, the reindeer being an inquisitive animal, and at the same time so silly that if he sees any suspicious object which is not actually chasing him, he will gradually and after many caperings, and forming repeated circles, approach nearer and nearer to it. The Esquimaux rarely shoot until the creature is within twelve paces, and I have frequently been told of their being killed at a much shorter distance. It is to be observed that the hunters never appear openly, but employ

stratagem for their purpose; thus, by patience and ingenuity, rendering their rudely formed bows and still worse arrows, as effective as the rifles of Europeans. When two men hunt in company they sometimes purposely show themselves to the Deer, and when his attention is fully engaged, walk slowly away from him, one before the other. The Deer follows, and when the hunters arrive near a stone, the foremost drops behind it and prepares his bow, while his companion continues walking steadily forward. This latter the Deer still follows unsuspectingly, and thus passes near the concealed man, who takes a deliberate aim and kills the animal. When the Deer assemble in herds there are particular passes which they invariably take, and on being driven to them are killed with arrows by the men, while the women with shouts drive them to the water. Here they swim with the ease and activity of water-dogs; the people in kayaks chasing and easily spearing them; the carcases float, and the hunter then presses forward and kills as many as he finds in his track. No springes or traps are used in the capture of these animals, as in practised to the southward, in consequence of the total absence of standing wood."

As presenting a striking illustration of the degree of cold prevailing in the Arctic regions, we may here mention that Dr. RICHARDSON describes a trap constructed by the Esquimaux to the southward of Chesterfield inlet, built of "compact snow." "The sides of the trap are built of slabs of that substance, cut as if for a snow house; an inclined plane of snow leads to the entrance of the pit, which is about five feet deep, and of sufficient dimensions to contain two or three large Deer. The pit is covered with a large thin slab of snow, which the animal is enticed to tread upon by a quantity of the lichens on which it feeds being placed conspicuously on an eminence beyond the opening. The exterior of the trap is banked up with snow so as to resemble a natural hillock, and care is taken to render it so steep on all sides but one, that the Deer must pass over the mouth of the trap before it can reach the bait. The slab is sufficiently strong to bear the weight of a Deer until it has passed its middle, when it revolves on two short axles of wood, precipitates the Deer into the trap, and returns to its place again in consequence of the lower end being heavier than the other. Throughout the whole line of coast frequented by the Esquimaux it is customary to see long lines of stones set on end, or of turfs piled up at intervals of about twenty yards, for the purposed of leading the Caribou to stations where they can be more easily approached. The natives find by experience that the animals in feeding imperceptibly take the line of direction of the objects thus placed before them, and the hunter can approach a herd that he sees from a distance, by gradually crawling from stone to stone, and remaining motionless when he sees any of the animals looking towards him. The whole of the barren grounds are intersected by Caribou paths, like sheep-tracks, which are of service to travellers at times in leading them to convenient crossing places of lakes or rivers."

The following account of a method of "impounding" Deer, resorted to by the Chepewyan Indians, is from HEARNE:

"When the Indians design to impound Deer, they look out for one of the paths in which a number of them have trod, and which is observed to be still frequented by them. When these paths cross a lake, a wide river, or a barren plain, they are found to be much the best for the purpose; and if the path run through a cluster of woods, capable of affording materials for building the pound, it adds considerably to the commodiousness of the situation. The pound is built by making a strong fence with brushy trees, without observing any degree of regularity, and the work is continued to any extent, according to the pleasure of the builders. I have seen some that were not less than a mile round, and am informed that there are others still more extensive. The door or entrance of the pound is not larger than a common gate, and the inside is so crowded with small counter-hedges as very much to resemble a maze, in every opening of which they set a snare, made with thongs of parchment Deer-skins well twisted together, which are amazingly strong. One end of the snare is usually made fast to a growing pole; but if no one of a sufficient size can be found near the place where the snare is set, a loose pole is substituted in its room, which is always of such size and length that a Deer cannot drag it far before it gets entangled among the other woods, which are all left standing, except what is found necessary for making the fence, hedges, &c. The pound being thus prepared, a row of small brush-wood is stuck up in the snow on each side of the door or entrance, and these hedge-rows are continued along the open part of the lake, river, or plain, where neither stick nor stump besides is to be seen, which makes them the more distinctly observed. These poles or brushwood are generally placed at the distance of fifteen or twenty yards from each other, and ranged in such a manner as to form two sides of a long acute angle, growing gradually wider in proportion to the distance they extend from the pound, which sometimes is not less than two or three miles, while the Deer's path is exactly along the middle, between the two rows of brushwood. Indians employed on this service always pitch their tents on or near to an eminence that affords a commanding prospect of the path leading to the pound, and when they see any Deer going that way, men, women, and children walk along the lake or river side under cover of the woods, till they get behind them, then step forth to open view, and proceed towards the pound in form of a crescent. The poor timorous Deer, finding themselves pursued, and at the same time taking the two rows of brushy poles to be two ranks of people stationed to prevent their passing on either side, run straight forward in the path till they get into the pound. The Indians then close in, and block up the entrance with some brushy trees that have been cut down and lie at hand for that purpose. The Deer being thus enclosed, the women and children walk round the pound to prevent them from jumping over or breaking through the fence, while the men are employed spearing such as are entangled in the snares, and shooting with bows and arrows those which remain loose in the pound. This method of hunting, if it deserve the name, is sometimes so successful that many families subsist by it without having occasion to move their tents above once or twice during the course of a whole winter; and when the spring advances, both the Deer and the Indians draw out to the eastward on the ground which is entirely barren, or at least which is called so in these parts, as it neither produces trees nor shrubs of any kind, so that moss and some little grass is all the herbage which is to be found on it."

With the following extract from the Fauna Boreali Americana, our readers may perhaps be amused: "The Dog-rib Indians have a mode of killing these animals, which, though simple, is very successful. It was thus described by Mr. WENTZEL, who resided long amongst that people: The hunters go in pairs, the foremost man carrying in one hand the horns and part of the skin of the head of a Deer, and in the other a small bundle of twigs, against which he, from time to time, rubs the horns, imitating the gestures peculiar to the animal. His comrade follows, treading exactly in his footsteps, and holding the guns of both in a horizontal position, so that the muzzles project under the arms of him who carries the head. Both hunters have a fillet of white skin round their foreheads, and the foremost has a strip of the same around his wrists. They approach the herd by degrees, raising their legs very slowly but setting them down somewhat suddenly after the manner of a Deer, and always taking care to lift their right or left feet simultaneously. If any of the herd leave off feeding to gaze upon this extraordinary phenomenon it instantly stops, and the head begins to play its part by licking its shoulders and performing other necessary movements. In this way the hunters attain the very centre of the herd without exciting suspicion, and have leisure to single out the fattest. The hindmost man then pushes forward his comrade's gun, the head is dropt, and they both fire nearly at the same instant. The Deer scamper off, the hunters trot after them; in a short time the poor animals halt to ascertain the cause of their terror, their foes stop at the same moment, and having loaded as they ran, greet the gazers with a second fatal discharge. The consternation of the Deer increases; they run to and from in the utmost confusion, and sometimes a great part of the herd is destroyed within the space of a few hundred yards."

We do not exactly comprehend how the acute sense of smell peculiar to the Reindeer should be useless in such cases, and should think the Deer could only be approached by keeping to the leeward of them, and that it would be a very difficult matter, even with the ingenious disguise adopted by the "Dog-Ribs," to get into the centre of a herd and leisurely single out the fattest.

Dr. RICHARDSON considers the variety he calls the woodland Caribou as much larger than the other, and says it has smaller horns, and is even when in good condition vastly inferior as an article of food. "The proper country of this Deer," he continues, " is a stripe of low primitive rocks, well clothed with wood, about one hundred miles wide, and extending at the distance of eighty or a hundred miles from the shores of Hudson's Bay, from Athapescow Lake to Lake Superior. Contrary to the practice of the barren-ground Caribou, the woodland variety travels to the southward in the spring. They cross the Nelson and Seven rivers in immense herds in the month of May, pass the summer on the low marshy shores of James' Bay, and return to the northward, and at the same time retire more inland in the month of September."

Geographical Distribution.

This species exists in Newfoundland and Labrador, extends westward across the American continent, and is mentioned both by PENNANT and LANGSDORFF as inhabiting the Fox or Aleutian Islands.

It is not found so far to the southward on the Pacific as on the Atlantic coast, and is not found on the Rocky Mountains, within the limits of the United States. According to PENNANT there are no Reindeer on the islands that lie between Asia and America. It is somewhat difficult to assign limits to the range of the Caribou: it is found, however, in some one or other of its supposed varieties, in every part of Arctic America, including the region from Hudson's Bay to far within the Arctic circle.

General Remarks.

The American Caribou or Reindeer has by most authors been regarded as identical with the Reindeer (*Rangifer tarandus*) of Europe, Greenland, and the Asiatic polar regions. The arguments in favour of this supposition are very plausible, and the varieties which the species exhibits in America, together with the fact that the antlers of the Reindeer assume an almost infinite variety of forms, that they differ not only in different specimens, but that the horns on each side of the head of the same animal often differ from each other, afford still stronger grounds for the supposition: notwithstanding all this, supposing that they are only varieties, they have become such permanently in our continent, and require separate descriptions, and as they must be known by particular names we have supposed we might venture on designating the American Reindeer as a distinct species, admitting at the same time that the subject requires closer comparisons than we have been able to institute, and further investigations.

We believe that several naturalists have bestowed new names on the American animal, but we are not aware that any one has described it, or pointed out those peculiarities which would separate the species. Among the rest, we were informed that our esteemed friend Professor AGASSIZ had designated it as *Tarandus furcifer*, and believing that he had described it we adopted his name on our plate; subsequently, however, we were informed that he had merely proposed for it the name of *Cervus hastatus*. He did not, however, describe it, and as the common name under which it has been known for ages past in Ameica will be most easily understood, and can by no possibility lead to any misapprehension as regards the species, we have named it *Rangifer Caribou*, and respectfully request our subscribers to alter the name on the plate accordingly.

Ursus Americanus.—Pallas.
(Var. Cinnamomum.—Aud. and Bach.)

Cinnamon Bear.

Plate cxxvii.—Male and Female.

U. Magnitudine formaque U. Americani; supra saturate cinnamomeus, naso et pilis ungues vestientibus flavis.

Characters.

Form and size of the common American black bear, of which it is a permanent variety. Colour, above dark cinnamon brown; nose and a fringe of hairs covering the claws, yellow.

Synonyme.

CINNAMON BEAR of the fur traders.

Description.

Form and size of the American Black Bear (*Ursus Americanus*). Hair, softer and more dense than that of the Black Bear, and under fur finer and longer.

Colour.

Nose, ochreous yellow; there is an angular yellow spot above each eye; margins of ears, and a narrow band of hairs around all the feet, concealing the claws, ochreous yellow; there is a line of brownish-yellow from the shoulder down and along the front leg; sides and hips, dark yellow; a line around the cheeks from the ear downwards, and a spot and streak between the ears, a little darker yellow; other parts of the body, cinnamon brown.

Dimensions.

	Feet.	Inches.
Length from point of nose to root of tail, ...	5	8
Height at shoulder, ...	3	1

Plate CXXVI.

Drawn from Nature by J. W. Audubon

On stone by W.E. Hitchcock

Lith.ᵈ Printed & Col.ᵈ by J.T.Bowen. Philad.ᵃ

Cinnamon Bear.

Length of tail, ... 1½

The Cinnamon Bear, like the common Black Bear, varies greatly in size. The dimensions above are unusually large.

Habits.

LEWIS and CLARK (Expedition, vol. ii. p. 303) mention that one of their men purchased a Bear-skin "of a uniform pale reddish-brown colour, which the Indians (Chopunnish) distinguished from every variety of the Grizzly Bear: this induced those travellers to inquire more particularly into the opinions held by the Indians as to the several species of Bears, and they exhibited all the Bear-skins they had killed in that neighbourhood, which the Indians immediately classed into two species—the Grizzly Bear, including all those with the extremities of the hair of a white or frosty colour, under the name of *hohhost*, and the black skins, those which were black with a number of entire white hairs intermixed, or white with a white breast, uniform bay, brown, and light reddish-brown, were ranged under the name the *Yackkah*. These we refer to the Cinnamon and other varieties of the Black Bear. LEWIS and CLARK, however, appear not to have considered these Bear-skins as belonging to the Black Bear, owing merely to the differences in colour, for they say the common Black Bear is "indeed unknown in that country." Their account of the fur of the brown Bears above mentioned corresponds, however, with the description of the Cinnamon Bear, they remarking that the skins of the Bears in that region differ from those of the Black Bears "in having much finer, thicker, and longer hair, with a greater proportion of fur mixed with it." LEWIS and CLARK considered that the Black Bear was always black, whereas it varies very considerably: they say nothing in regard to the sizes of the various coloured Bears above alluded to.

The Cinnamon Bear has long been known to trappers and fur traders, and its skin is much more valuable than that of the Black Bear. We have seen in the warehouse of Messrs. P. CHOUTEAU, JR., and Co., in New York, some beautiful skins of this animal, and find that those gentlemen receive some every year from their posts near the Rocky Mountains. Being a permanent variety, and having longer and finer hair than the common Black Bear, we might possibly have elevated it into a distinct species but that in every other particular it closely resembles the latter animal. By the Indians (according to Sir JOHN RICHARDSON) it is considered to be an accidental variety of the Black Bear.

The Cinnamon Bear, so far as we have been able to ascertain, is never found near the sea coast, nor even west of the Ohio valley until you approach the Rocky Mountain chain, and it is apparently quite a northern animal.

Of the habits of this variety we have no accounts, but we may suppose that they do not differ in any essential particulars from those of the Black Bear, which we shall shortly describe.

Our figures were made from living specimens in the gardens of the Zoological Society of London, which manifested all the restlessness usually exhibited by this genus when in a state of captivity.

We are inclined to consider Sir JOHN RICHARDSON's "Barren-ground Bear" a variety of the common black Bear,—perhaps our present animal; but not having seen any specimen of his *Ursus Arctos? Americanus*, we do not feel justified in expressing more than an opinion on this subject, which indeed is founded on the description of the colour of the Barren-ground Bear as given by RICHARDSON himself (see Fauna Boreali Americana, pp. 21, 22).

Geographical Distribution.

Sparingly found in the fur countries west and north of the Missouri, extending to the barren grounds of the northwest.

General Remarks.

We have given a figure of this permanent variety of Bear, not because we felt disposed to elevate it into a species, but because it is a variety so frequently found in the collections of skins made by our fur companies, and which is so often noticed by travellers in the northwest, that errors might be made by future naturalists were we to omit mentioning it and placing it where it should be. Whilst we are not disposed to figure an occasional variety in any species, and have throughout our work rather declined doing this, yet we conceive that figures of the permanent varieties may be useful to future observers in order to awaken inquiry and enable them to decide whether they are true species or mere varieties. We have done this in the case of some species of squirrel, the otter, and the wolves, as well as this variety of Bear. The yellow Bear of Carolina no doubt belongs to this variety, and probably the brown Barren-ground Bear of RICHARDSON may be referred to the same species, as all Bears vary very greatly in size.

Genus Capra.—Linn.

Dental Formula.

Incisive $\frac{0}{8}$; *Canine* $\frac{0—0}{0—0}$; *Molar* $\frac{6—6}{6—6}$ = 32.

Horns common to both sexes, or rarely wanting in the female; in domesticated races occasionally absent in both: they are directed upwards and curved backwards, and are more or less angular. No muzzle, no lachrymal sinus, nor unguinal pores; eyes, light coloured, pupil elongated; tail, short, flat, and naked at base; throat, bearded.

Mostly reside in the primitive and highest mountains of the ancient continent and America.

Habit, herbivorous; climbing rocks and precipices; producing two or three young at a time; gregarious.

There are six well determined species—one inhabiting the Alps, one in Abyssinia and Upper Egypt, one in the Caucasian mountains, one in the mountains of Persia, one in the Himalaya, and one in the Rocky Mountains of North America.

The generic name Capra is derived from the Latin *capra*, a goat.

Capra Americana.—Blainville.

Rocky Mountain Goat.

Plate cxxviii.—Male and Female.

C. Magnitudine ovem arietem adæquans, corpore robusto, cornibus parvis acutis lente recurvis, pilis albis, cornibus ungulisque nigris.

Characters.

Size of the domestic sheep; form of body, robust; horns, small and pointed, slightly curved backwards. Colour of hair, totally white.

Synonymes.

ANTILOPE AMERICANA ET RUPICAPRA AMERICANA. Blainville, Bulletin Socy. Phil, Ann. 1816, p. 80.
OVIS MONTANA. Ord, Jour. Acad. N. Sci. Phil., vol. i., part i., p. 8. Ann. 1817.
MAZAMA SERICEA. Raffinesque Smaltz, Am. Monthly Mag. 1817, p. 44.
ROCKY MOUNTAIN SHEEP. Jameson, Wernerian Trans., vol. iii. p. 306. Ann. 1821.
CAPRA MONTANA. Harlan, Fauna Americana, p. 253.
       "   "   Godman, Nat. Hist., vol. ii. p. 326.
ANTELOPE LANIGERA. Smith, Linnæan Trans., vol. xiii. p. 38, t. 4.
CAPRA AMERICANA. Rich., F. B. A., p. 268, plate 22.

Description.

Form of the body and neck, robust, like that of the common Goat; nose, nearly straight; ears, pointed, lined with long hair; the horns incline slightly backwards, tapering gradually and not suddenly, uncinated like those of the chamois, transversely wrinkled with slight rings for nearly half their length from the base, and sharp pointed; towards the tip they are smooth and polished. Tail short, and though clothed with long hair, almost concealed by the hairs which cover the rump; legs, thick and short; secondary hoofs, flat, grooved on the soles, and resembling those of the common Goat.

The coat is composed of two kinds of hair, the outer and longer considerably straighter than the wool of the sheep, but softer than that of the common Goat; this long hair is abundant on the shoulders, back, neck, and thighs; on the chin there is a thick tuft forming a beard like that of the latter animal;

Plate CXXVIII.

On Stone by Wm. E. Hitchcock.

Lith. Printed & Col.d by J.T. Bowen Phil.a

Drawn from Nature by J.J. Audubon

Rocky Mountain Goat

under the long hairs of the body there is a close coat of fine white silky wool, quite equal to that of the Cashmere Goat in fineness.

Colour.

Horns, and hoofs, black; the whole body, white.

Dimensions.

	Feet.	Inches.
Length of head and body, ...	3	4
" tail, ...		1
" head, ...		11
" horns, ...		5
Diameter of horns at base, ...		1

Habits.

Standing "at gaze," on a table-rock projecting high above the valley beyond, and with a lofty ridge of stony and precipitous mountains in the background, we have placed one of our figures of the Rocky Mountain Goat; and lying down, a little removed from the edge of the cliff, we have represented another.

In the vast ranges of wild and desolate heights, alternating with deep valleys and tremendous gorges, well named the Rocky mountains, over and through which the adventurous trapper makes his way in pursuit of the rich fur of the beaver or the hide of the bison, there are scenes which the soul must be dull indeed not to admire. In these majestic solitudes all is on a scale to awaken the sublimest emotions and fill the heart with a consciousness of the infinite Being "whose temple is all space, whose altar earth, sea, skies."

Nothing indeed can compare with the sensations induced by a view from some lofty peak of these great mountains, for there the imagination may wander unfettered, may go back without a check through ages of time to the period when an Almighty power upheaved the gigantic masses which lie on all sides far beneath and around the beholder, and find no spot upon which to arrest the eye as a place where once dwelt man! No—we only know the Indian as a wanderer, and we cannot say here stood the strong fortress, the busy city, or even the humble cot. Nature has here been undisturbed and unsubdued, and our eyes may wander all over the scene to the most distant faint blue line on the horizon which encircles us, and forget alike the noisy clamour of toiling cities and the sweet and smiling quiet of the well cultivated fields, where man has made a "home" and dwelleth in peace. But in these regions we may fine the savage grizzly bear, the huge bison, the elegant and fleet antelope, the large-horned sheep of the mountains, and the agile fearless climber of the steeps—the Rocky Mountain Goat.

This snow-white and beautiful animal appears to have been first described, from skins shown to LEWIS and CLARK, as "the Sheep," in their general description of the beasts, birds, and plants found by the party in their expedition. They say, "The Sheep is found in many places, but mostly in the timbered parts of the Rocky Mountains. They live in greater numbers on the chain of mountains forming the commencement of the woody country on the coast, and passing the Columbia between the falls and the rapids. We have only seen the skins of these animals, which the natives dress with the wool, and the blankets which they manufacture from the wool. The animal from this evidence appears to be of the size of our common sheep, of a white colour. The wool is fine on many parts of the body, but in length not equal to that of our domestic sheep. On the back, and particularly on the top of the head, this is intermixed with a considerable portion of long straight hairs. From the Indian account these animals have erect pointed horns."

The Rocky Mountain Goat wanders over the most precipitous rocks, and springs with great activity from crag to crag, feeding on the plants, grasses, and mosses of the mountain sides, and seldom or never descends to the luxuriant valleys, as the Big-Horn does. This Goat indeed resembles the wild Goat of Europe, or the chamois, in its habits, and is very difficult to procure. Now and then the hunter may observe one browsing on the extreme verge of some perpendicular rock almost directly above him, far beyond gun-shot, and entirely out of harm's way. At another time, after fatiguing and hazardous efforts, the hungry marksman may reach a spot from whence his rifle will send a ball into the unsuspecting Goat; then slowly he rises from his hands and knees, on which he has been creeping, and the muzzle of his heavy gun is "rested" on a loose stone, behind which he has kept his movements from being observed, and now he pulls the fatal trigger with deadly aim. The loud sharp crack of the rifle has hardly rung back in his ear from the surrounding cliffs when he sees the Goat in its expiring struggles reach the verge of the dizzy height: a moment of suspense and it rolls over, and swiftly falls, striking

perchance here and there a projecting point, and with the clatter of thousands of small stones set in motion by its rapid passage down the steep slopes which incline outward near the base of the cliff, disappears, enveloped in a cloud of dust in the deep ravine beneath; where a day's journey would hardly bring an active man to it, for far around must he go to accomplish a safe descent, and toilsome and dangerous must be his progress up the gorge within whose dark recesses his game is likely to become the food of the ever prowling wolf or the solitary raven. Indeed cases have been mentioned to us in which these Goats, when shot, fell on to a jutting ledge, and there lay fifty or a hundred feet below the hunter, in full view, but inaccessible from any point whatever.

Notwithstanding these difficulties, as portions of the mountains are not so precipitous, the Rocky Mountain Goat is shot and procured tolerably easily, it is said, by some of the Indian tribes, who make various articles of clothing out of its skin, and use its soft woolly hair for their rude fabrics.

According to Sir JOHN RICHARDSON, this animal has been known to the members of the Northwest and Hudson's Bay Companies from the first establishment of their trading posts on the banks of the Columbia River and in New Caledonia, and they have sent several specimens to Europe. The wool being examined by a competent judge, under the instructions of the Wernerian Society of Edinburgh, was reported to be of great fineness and fully an inch and a half long. "It is unlike the fleece of the common sheep, which contains a variety of different kinds of wool suitable to the fabrication of articles very dissimilar in their nature, and requires much care to distribute them in their proper order. The fleece under consideration is wholly fine. That on the fore part of the skin has all the apparent qualities of wool. On the back part it very much resembles cotton. The whole fleece is much mixed with hairs, and on those parts where the hairs are long and pendant, there is almost no wool."

"Mr. DRUMMOND saw no Goats on the eastern declivity of the mountains, near the sources of the Elk river, where the sheep are numerous, but he learned from the Indians that they frequent the steepest precipices, and are much more difficult to procure than the sheep. Their manners are said to greatly resemble those of the domestic Goat. The exact limits of the range of this animal have not been ascertained, but it probably extends from the fortieth to the sixty-fourth or sixty-fifth degree of latitude. It is common on the elevated part of the Rocky Mountain range that gives origin to four great tributaries to as many different seas, viz. the Mackenzie, the Columbia, the Nelson, and the Missouri rivers."—F. B. A., p. 269.

The flesh of this species is hard and dry, and is not so much relished as that of the Big-Horn, the Elk, &c., by the hunters or travellers who have journeyed towards the Pacific across the wild ranges of mountains inhabited by these animals.

Geographical Distribution.

The Rocky Mountain Goat inhabits the most elevated portions of the mountains from which it derives its name, where it dwells between the fortieth and sixtieth or sixty-fourth degree of north latitude. It is also found on the head waters of the Mackenzie, Columbia, and Missouri rivers. Mr. MACKENZIE informs us that the country near the sources of the Muddy river (Maria's river of LEWIS and CLARK), Saskatchewan, and Athabasca, is inhabited by these animals, but they are said to be scarcer on the eastern slopes of the Rocky Mountains than on the western.

General Remarks.

It is believed by some naturalists that Fathers PICCOLO and DE SALVA-TIERRA discovered this animal on the higher mountains of California. VANCOUVER brought home a mutilated skin he obtained on the northwest coast of America. LEWIS and CLARK (as we have already mentioned) obtained skins in 1804.

In 1816 M. DE BLAINVILLE published the first scientific account of it. Mr. ORD in 1817 described one of the skins brought home by LEWIS and CLARK, and Major CHARLES HAMILTON SMITH described a specimen in 1821, in the Linnæan Transactions for that year.

The resemblance of the animal to some of the antelopes, the chamois, the Goat, and the sheep, caused it to be placed by these authors under several genera. DE BLAINVILLE first made it an *antelope*, then named it *Rupicapra*— a subgenus of antelope to which the chamois belongs. ORD arranged it in the genus *Ovis*. SMITH called it *Antilope lanigera*. Besides these, RAFFINESQUE named it *Mazama sericea*. Dr. HARLAN and RICHARDSON were each correct, as we think, in placing it in the genus *Capra* (Goat). As in the Goat, the facial line in this species is nearly straight, while in the sheep and antelopes it is more or less arched. The sheep and the antelope are beardless, and the Goat is characterized by its beard, a conspicuous ornament in the present animal, which is moreover, in the form of its nose, the strength and

proportion of the limbs, and the peculiarities of the hoofs, allied closer to the Goats than to any other neighbouring genus.

Arvicola Borealis.—Rich.

Northern Meadow-Mouse.

Plate cxxix.—Male and Females.

A. ungue pollicari robusto præditus, auriculis vellere absconditis, cauda capitis fere longitudine, vellere longissima molli, dorso castaneo nigro mixto, ventre cano.

Characters.

Thumb nail, strong; ears, concealed in the fur; tail, about as long as the head; fur, very long and fine; on the back, chesnut colour mixed with black; on the belly, gray.

Synonymes.

MOUSE No. 15. Forster, Philos. Trans., vol. lxii. p. 380.
ARVICOLA BOREALIS. Rich., Zool. Jour., No. 12, April, 1828, p. 517.
" " " NORTHERN MEADOW-MOUSE. F. B. A., p. 127.
ARVINNAK. Dog-Rib Indians.

Description.

This species is a little less than WILSON's Meadow-Mouse (A. *Pennsylvanica*). It has the form and dentition of the other species of Arvicolæ. Head, rather large; forehead, convex; nose, short, and a little pointed; eyes, small; ears, low, rounded, and concealed by the surrounding fur; limbs, rather robust, clothed with short hairs, mixed on the toes and hind parts of the fore feet with longer hairs. Hind toes, more slender, and scarcely longer than the fore ones; fore claws, small, much compressed, arched, and acute, with a narrow elliptical excavation underneath; the hairs of the toes reach to the points of the nails, but cover them rather sparingly; the claws of the hind feet resemble those of the fore feet, but are not so strong; the thumb of the fore feet consists of a small squarish nail slightly convex on both sides, and having an obtuse point projecting from the middle of its extremity; the tail is round, well clothed with short stiff hairs running to a point, which do not permit the scales to be visible. There are considerable variations in the length of the tail, it being in one specimen a third longer than in others. The fur on the body is long in proportion to the size of the animal.

Colour.

Hair on the upper parts blackish-gray from the roots to the tips, some of which are yellowish or chesnut brown, and some black; the black tipped hairs are the longest, and are equally distributed amongst the others, giving the body a dark reddish-brown colour. There is a rufous patch under the ears. On the under part, and on the chin and lips, the colour is lead-gray, and the hairs are shorter than on the back and sides; tail, brown above and grayish beneath; hairs on the feet, ochreous yellow; claws, white.

Dimensions.

	Inches.	Lines.
Length of head and body,	4	6
" tail,	1	
" head,	1	3
Height of ear,		4
Breadth of ear,		3
Length of fore feet to end of middle claw,		$4\frac{1}{2}$
Hind feet, including heel and claw,		$7\frac{1}{2}$
Fur on the back,		10

Habits.

We have little to say in regard to the present species. RICHARDSON states that its habits are very similar to those of A. *xanthognatha*, and in our article on that species we have given an account of the general habits of the Arvicolæ (at p. 18 of the present volume), to which we refer our readers.

The northern Arvicolæ do not appear to become dormant from the effect of cold, but during the long Arctic winter dig galleries under the deep snows, in which they are enabled to search for seeds, grasses, or roots suited to their wants. We have ascertained by an examination of the bodies of several, more southern species of Arvicolæ, possessing similar habits, that so far from suffering in winter and becoming lean, they are usually in good case, and sometimes quite fat, during that season.

The length of the fur on the back of the present species (ten twelfths of an inch) is somewhat remarkable for so small an animal.

Geographical Distribution.

This species was found in numbers at Great Bear Lake, living in the vicinity of *Arvicola xanthognatha*. We have not been able to ascertain the extent of its range towards the south or west. We did not discover this Meadow-Mouse or hear of it on our expedition to the Yellow Stone and Upper Missouri rivers, nor has it been found, so far as we know, anywhere west of the Rocky Mountains.

General Remarks.

"The form of the thumb-nail allies this animal very closely to the Norway lemming, and to one or two species of American lemming, but its claws are smaller and more compressed, and apparently not so well calculated for scraping earth as the broader claws of the lemmings."—*Fauna Boreali Americana*, p. 127.

Thus far we agree with Dr. RICHARDSON; he, however, thinks that this species may be considered an intermediate link between the lemmings and the Meadow-Mice, and may without impropriety be ranked either as a true Meadow-Mouse or as a lemming.

After a careful examination of the original specimens, some years ago, we set it down as a true *Arvicola*, possessing more of the characteristics of that genus than of the genus *Georychus*.

Genus Dipodomys.—Gray.

Dental Formula.

Incisive $\frac{2}{2}$; *Canine* $\frac{0-0}{0-0}$; *Molar* $\frac{4-4}{4-4}$ = 20.

The incisors are of moderate length, rather weak, narrow, compressed, and curved inwards. In the upper jaw the first three molars are largest, the fourth a little smaller; in the lower jaw the molars are alike. The molars have rounded cutting edges.

Nose and head, of moderate size; sacs or pouches opening on the cheeks back of the mouth; fore feet, rather short, furnished with four toes and the rudiment of a thumb, covered by a blunt nail; hind legs very long, terminated by four toes on each foot; toes, each with a distinct metatarsus; tail, very long; *Mammæ*, four—two abdominal and two pectoral.

Habits, semi-nocturnal; food, seeds, roots, and grasses.

There is only one species belonging to this genus known. The generic name is derived from διπους, *dipous*, two footed, and μυς, *mus*, a mouse.

Dipodomys Phillippsii.—Gray.

Pouched Jerboa Mouse.

Plate cxxx.—Males.

D. Magnitudine prope Tamiæ Lysteri et formâ Dipodum; caudâ corpore et capite conjunctum multo longiore; sacculis buccalibus externis apertis; colore, supra fulvo, infra albo.

Characters.

Nearly the size of the common ground squirrel (Tamias Lysteri); *shaped like the jerboas; tail, much longer than the body; cheek pouches, opening externally; colour, light brown above, white beneath.*

Synonyme.

DIPODOMYS PHILLIPPSII. Gray, Ann. and Mag. Nat. Hist., vol. vii. p. 521. 1840.

Description.

Body, rather stout; head, of moderate size; nose, moderate, although the skull exhibits the proboscis extended five or six lines beyond the insertion of the incisors.

The whiskers (which proceed from the nose immediately above the upper edge of the orifices of the pouches) are numerous, rigid, and longer than the head; ears, of moderate size, ovate, and very thinly clothed with short hairs; the feet are thickly clothed with short hairs to the nails, which are free; short hairs also prevail on the soles and between the toes; fore feet, rather stout, but short; they have each four toes and the rudiment of a thumb, the latter covered by a conspicuous nail; nails, short, slender, and curved; second toe from the thumb longest, first and third nearly of equal length, and fourth shortest.

Hind legs, very long; the hind feet have each four toes, the two middle ones nearly of equal length, the first a little shorter, and the fourth, placed behind like a thumb, much the shortest; nails, nearly straight, sharp pointed, and grooved on the under surface; tail, rather stout—in the dried specimen it is round at base and much compressed, showing that its greatest diameter is vertical; it is thickly clothed with short hairs for two thirds of its extent, when the hairs gradually increase in length till they approach the extremity, at which they are so long as to present the appearance of a tuft-like brush. The fur is very soft and silky, like that of the flying-squirrel; the hairs of the tail are coarser. There are two abdominal and two pectoral mammæ.

In the upper jaw the incisors are rather small and weak; all the molars have simple crowns, which are more elevated on the interior than on the exterior edges; the anterior molar is nearly round, and almost of the same size as the two next molars, which are somewhat oval and are placed with their longest diameter transversely to the jaw; the fourth molar is the smallest and is nearly round.

In the lower jaw the three anterior molars are nearly of equal size, and are almost alike in shape; the fourth corresponding with the last molar on the upper jaw; there is a little depression in the centre of the crowns of the molars, and a slight ridge around the outer edges.

Colour.

Head, ears, back, and a stripe on the thigh from the root of the tail, light brown, the hairs on the back being plumbeous at the roots, then yellow slightly tipped with black. Whiskers, black, with a few white bristly hairs interspersed; upper and lower surfaces of tail, and a line on the under side of the tarsus, dark brown; sides, and tip of the tail, white; cheeks, white; there is a white stripe on the hips; the legs and under surface are white, as also a stripe from the shoulder to the ear. This white colour likewise extends high up on the flanks, where it gradually mingles with the brown of the back; nails, brownish.

Dimensions.

Male.—Specimen in the British Museum.

	Inches.	Lines.
Length of head and body,	5	
" tail,	6	6
" hind feet,	1	6

Female.—Procured by J. W. AUDUBON in California.

	Inches.	Lines.
Point of nose to root of tail,	4	6
Tail, including hair,	7	
Tarsus to end of longest nail,	1	6
Ear, inside, from auditory opening,		7
Longest hair of whiskers,	2	4

Habits.

The pretty colours and the liveliness of this little kangaroo-like animal, together with its fine eyes and its simplicity in venturing near man, of whom it does not seem afraid, would no doubt make it a favourite pet in confinement. It is able to exist in very arid and almost barren situations, where there is scarcely a blade of anything green except the gigantic and fantastic cacti that

Plate CXXIX

Northern Meadow Mouse

Lith. Printed & Col'd by J. T. Bowen.

grow in Sonora and various other parts of Western Mexico and California. As JOHN W. AUDUBON and his party travelled through these countries the *Dipodomys Phillippsii* was sometimes almost trampled on by the mules, and was so tame that they could have caught the animal by the hand without difficulty.

This species hop about, kangaroo fashion, and jump pretty far at a leap. When the men encamped towards evening, they sometimes came smelling and moving about the legs of the mules, as if old friends. One was observed by J. W. AUDUBON just before sunset; its beautiful large eyes seemed as if they might be dimmed by the bright rays which fell upon them as it emerged from a hole under a large boulder, but it frisked gaily about, and several times approached him so nearly, as he sat on a stone, that he could have seized it with his hands without any trouble, and without rising from his hard seat.

After a while, as the party had to take up the line of march again, he with some difficulty frightened it, when with a bound or two it reached its hole and disappeared underneath the large stone, but almost immediately came out again; and so great was its curiosity that as the party left the spot it seemed half inclined to follow them.

These animals appear to prefer the sides of stony hills which afford them secure places to hide in, and they can easily convey their food in their cheek-pouches to their nests.

The young when half grown exhibit the markings of the adults to a great extent. This species is crepuscular if not nocturnal, and was generally seen towards dusk, and occasionally in such barren deserts that it was difficult to imagine what it could get to feed on. A dead one was picked up one day while the party were traversing a portion of the great Colorado desert, where nothing could grow but clumps of cacti of different species, and not a drop of water could be found. The only living creatures appeared to be lizards of several kinds, and one or two snakes: the party felt surprised as they toiled on over the sun-baked clay, and still harder gravel, to find the little animal in such a locality.

Georgraphical Distribution.

Dr. J. L. LE CONTE found this species on the river Gila, and farther south, where he procured several specimens.

J. W. AUDUBON saw the *Dipodomys Phillippsii* in crossing the Cordilleras, in Sonora on the Gila, in the Tulare valley, and in various other parts of California. Its southern limits are undetermined, but it seems not to exist north of California.

General Remarks.

Mr. GRAY described this species, in the Annals and Magazine of Natural History, vol. vii. p. 521; he considered it the American representative of the African Jerboas, although, as he remarks, it differs from them in being provided with cheek pouches opening externally.

Our drawing was made from a beautiful specimen in the British Museum, which was the first one brought under the notice of naturalists, and the original of Mr. GRAY'S description of this singular animal; it was procured near Real del Monte, in Mexico.

Ursus Ferox.—Lewis and Clark.

Grizzly Bear.

Plate cxxxi.—Males.

M. Magnitudine U. Americanum longe superans, plantis et unguibus longioribus, auriculis brevioribus quam in isto; pilis saturate fuscis, apice griseis.

Characters.

Larger than the American Black Bear; soles of feet, and claws, longer, and ears shorter than in the Black Bear. Colour of the hair, dark brown, with paler tips.

Synonymes.

GRIZZLE BEAR. Umfreville, Hudson's Bay, p. 168. Ann. 1790.
GRISLY BEAR. Mackenzie's Voyage, p. 160. Ann. 1801.
WHITE, or BROWN-GREY BEAR. Gass' Journal of Lewis and Clark's Expedition, pp. 45, 116, 346. Ann. 1808.
GRIZZLY, BROWN, WHITE, AND VARIEGATED BEAR—URSUS FEROX. Lewis and Clark, Expedition, vol. i. pp. 284, 293, 343, 375; vol. iii. pp. 25, 268. Ann. 1814.
URSUS FEROX. De Witt Clinton, Trans. Philos. and Lit. Society New York, vol. i. p. 56. Ann. 1815.
GRIZZLY BEAR. Warden's United States, vol. i. p. 197. Ann. 1819.
GREY BEAR. Harmon's Journal, p. 417. Ann. 1820.
URSUS CINEREUS. Desm. Mamm. No. 253. Ann. 1820.
   "   HORRIBILLIS. Ord, Guthrie's Geography, vol. ii. p. 299.
   "   "   Say, Long's Expedition, vol. ii. p. 244, note 34. Ann. 1822.
   "   CANDESCENS. Hamilton Smith, Griffith An. Kingdom, vol. ii. p. 299; vol. v. No. 320. Ann. 1826.
   "   CINEREUS. Harlan, Fauna, p. 48.
GRIZZLY BEAR. Godman's Nat. Hist., vol. i. p. 131.
URSUS FEROX. Rich., Fauna Boreali Americana, p. 24, plate 1.

Description.

The Grizzly Bear in form resembles the Norwegian variety of *Ursus Arctos*, the Brown Bear of Europe; the facial line is rectilinear or slightly arched; head, short and round; nose, bare; ears, rather small, and more hairy than those of the Black Bear; legs, stout; body, large, but less fat and heavy in proportion, than that of the Black Bear.

Tail, short; paws and nails, very long, the latter extending from three to five inches beyond the hair on the toes; they are compressed and channelled. Hair, long and abundant, particularly about the head and neck, the longest hairs being in summer about three inches, and in winter five or six inches long. The jaws are strong, and the teeth very large.

The fore feet somewhat resemble the human hand, and are soft to the touch; they have larger claws than the hind feet. The animal treads on the whole palm and entire heel.

Colour.

The Grizzly Bear varies greatly in colour, so much so, indeed, that it is difficult to find two specimens alike: the young are in general blacker than the old ones. The hair however is commonly dark brown at the roots and for about three fourths of its length, then gradually fades into reddish-brown, and is broadly tipped with white intermixed with irregular patches of black or dull-brown, thus presenting a hoary or grizzly appearance on the surface, from which the vulgar specific name is derived.

A specimen procured by us presents the following colouring: Nose, to near the eyes, light brown; legs, forehead, and ears, black. An irregularly mixed dark grayish-brown prevails on the body, except on the neck, shoulders, upper portion of fore-legs, and sides adjoining the shoulders, which parts are barred or marked with light yellowish-gray, and the hairs in places tipped with yellowish or dingy white. Iris, dark brown.

Dimensions.

Male, killed by J. J. AUDUBON and party on the Missouri river, in 1843—not full grown.

	Feet.	Inches.
From point of nose to root of tail,	5	6
Tail (vertebræ),		3
" (including hair),		4
From point of nose to ear,	1	4
Width of ear,		3½
Length of eye,		1
Height at shoulder,	3	5
" rump,	4	7
Length of palm of fore foot,		8
Breadth of do.,		6
Length of sole of hind foot,		9½
Breadth of do.,		5½
Girth around the body, behind the shoulders,	4	1
Width between the ears on the skull,		7½

Plate CXXX

Nº 26

Painted Jerboa Mouse

Habits.

We have passed many hours of excitement, and some, perchance, of danger, in the wilder portions of our country; and at times memory recals adventures we can now hardly attempt to describe; nor can we ever again feel the enthusiasm such scenes produced in us. Our readers must therefore imagine, the startling sensations experienced on a sudden and quite unexpected face-to-face meeting with the savage Grizzly Bear—the huge shaggy monster disputing possession of the wilderness against all comers, and threatening immediate attack!

Whilst in a neighbourhood where the Grizzly Bear may possibly be hidden, the excited nerves will cause the heart's pulsations to quicken if but a startled ground-squirrel run past; the sharp click of the lock is heard, and the rifle hastily thrown to the shoulder, before a second of time has assured the hunter of the trifling cause of his emotion.

But although dreaded alike by white hunter and by red man, this animal is fortunately not very abundant to the eastward of the Rocky Mountains, and the chance of encountering him does not often occur. We saw only a few of these formidable beasts during our expedition up the Missouri river and in the country over which we hunted during our last journey to the west.

The Indians, as is well known, consider the slaughter of a Grizzly Bear a feat second only to scalping an enemy, and necklaces made of the claws of this beast are worn as trophies by even the bravest among them.

On the 22d of August, 1843, we killed one of these Bears, and as our journals are before us, and thinking it may be of interest, we will extract the account of the day's proceedings, although part of it has no connection with our present subject. We were descending the Upper Missouri river.

"The weather being fine we left our camp of the previous night early, but had made only about twelve miles when the wind arose and prevented our men from making any headway with the oars; we therefore landed under a high bank amongst a number of fallen trees and some drifted timber. All hands went in search of elks. Mr. CULBERTSON killed a deer, and with the help of Mr. SQUIRES brought the meat to the boat. We saw nothing during a long walk we took, but hearing three or four gunshots which we thought were fired by some of our party, we hastened in the direction from whence the reports came, running and hallooing, but could find no one. We then made the best of our way back to the boat and despatched three men, who discovered that the firing had been at an elk, which was however not obtained. Mr. BELL killed a female elk and brought a portion of its flesh to the boat. After resting ourselves a while and eating dinner, Mr. CULBERTSON, SQUIRES, and ourselves walked to the banks of the Little Missouri, distant about one mile, where we saw a buffalo bull drinking at the edge of a sand-bar. We shot him, and fording the stream, which was quite shallow, took away the 'nerf;' the animal was quite dead. We saw many ducks in this river. In the course of the afternoon we started in our boat, and rowed about half a mile below the Little Missouri. Mr. CULBERTSON and ourselves walked to the body of the bull again and knocked off his horns, after which Mr. CULBERTSON endeavoured to penetrate a large thicket in hopes of starting a Grizzly Bear, but found it so entangled with briars and vines that he was obliged to desist, and returned very soon. Mr. HARRIS, who had gone in the same direction and for the same purpose, did not return with him. As we were approaching the boat we met Mr. SPRAGUE, who informed us that he thought he had seen a Grizzly Bear walking along the upper bank of the river, and we went towards the spot as fast as possible. Meantime the Bear had gone down to the water, and was clumsily and slowly proceeding on its way. It was only a few paces from and below us, and was seen by our whole party at the same instant. We all fired, and the animal dropped dead without even the power of uttering a groan. Mr. CULBERTSON put a rifle ball through its neck, BELL placed two large balls in its side, and our bullet entered its belly. After shooting the Bear we proceeded to a village of 'prairie dogs' (*Spermophilus Ludovicianus*), and set traps in hopes of catching some of them. We were inclined to think they had all left, but Mr. BELL seeing two, shot them. There were thousands of their burrows in sight. Our 'patroon,' assisted by one of the men, skinned the Bear, which weighed, as we thought, about four hundred pounds. It appeared to be between four and five years old, and was a male. Its lard was rendered, and filled sundry bottles with 'real Bear's grease,' whilst we had the skin preserved by our accomplished taxidermist, Mr. BELL."

The following afternoon, as we were descending the stream, we saw another Grizzly Bear, somewhat smaller than the one mentioned above. It was swimming towards the carcase of a dead buffalo lodged in the prongs of a "sawyer" or "snag," but on seeing us it raised on its hind feet until quite erect, uttered a loud grunt or snort, made a leap from the water, gained the upper bank of the river, and disappeared in an instant amid the tangled briars and bushes thereabouts. Many wolves of different colours—black, white, red, or brindle—were also intent on going to the buffalo to gorge themselves on the carrion, but took fright at our approach, and we saw them sneaking away with their tails pretty close to their hind-legs."

The Grizzly Bear generally inhabits the swampy, well covered portions of the districts where it is found, keeping a good deal among the trees and bushes, and in these retreats it has its "beds" or lairs. Some of these we passed by, and our sensations were the reverse of pleasant whilst in such thick, tangled, and dangerous neighbourhoods; the Bear in his concealment having decidedly the advantage in case one should come upon him unawares. These animals ramble abroad both by day and night. In many places we found their great tracks along the banks of the rivers where they had been prowling in search of food. There are seasons during the latter part of summer, when the wild fruits that are eagerly sought after by the Bears are very abundant. These beasts then feed upon them, tearing down the branches as far as they can reach whilst standing in an upright posture. They in this manner get at wild plums, service berries, buffalo berries, and the seeds of a species of *cornus* or dog-wood which grows in the alluvial bottoms of the northwest. The Grizzly Bear is also in the habit of scratching the gravelly earth on the sides of hills where the vegetable called "pomme blanche" is known to grow, but the favourite food of these animals is the more savoury flesh of such beasts as are less powerful, fleet, or cunning than themselves. They have been known to seize a wounded buffalo, kill it, and partially bury it in the earth for future use, after having gorged themselves on the best parts of its flesh and lapped up the warm blood.

We have heard many adventures related, which occurred to hunters either when surprised by these Bears, or when approaching them with the intention of shooting them. A few of these accounts, which we believe are true, we will introduce: During a voyage (on board one of the steamers belonging to the American Fur Company) up the Missouri river, a large she-Bear with two young was observed from the deck, and several gentlemen proposed to go ashore, kill the dam, and secure her cubs. A small boat was lowered for their accommodation, and with guns and ammunition they pushed off to the bank and landed in the mud. The old Bear had observed them and removed her position to some distance, where she stood near the bank, which was there several feet above the bed of the river. One of the hunters having neared the animal, fired at her, inflicting a severe wound. Enraged with pain the Bear rushed with open jaws towards the sportsmen at a rapid rate, and with looks that assured them she was in a desperate fury. There was but a moment's time; the party, too much frightened to stand the charge, "ingloriously turned and fled," without even pulling another trigger, and darting to the margin of the river jumped into the stream, losing their guns, and floundering and bobbing under, while their hats floated away with the muddy current. After swimming a while they were picked up by the steamer, as terrified as if the Bear was even then among them, though the animal on seeing them all afloat had made off, followed by her young.

The following was related to us by one of the "engagés" at Fort Union. A fellow having killed an Indian woman, was forced to run away, and fearing he would be captured, started so suddenly that he took neither gun nor other weapon with him; he made his way to the Crow Indians, some three hundred miles up the Yellow Stone river, where he arrived in a miserable plight, having suffered from hunger and exposure. He escaped the men who were—first sent after him, by keeping in ravines and hiding closely; but others were despatched, who finally caught him. He said that one day he saw a dead buffalo lying near the river bank, and going towards it to get some of the meat, to his utter astonishment and horror a young Grizzly Bear which was feeding on the carcass, raised up from behind it and so suddenly attacked him that his face and hands were lacerated by its claws before he had time to think of defending himself. Not daunted, however, he gave the cub a tremendous jerk, which threw it down, and took to his heels, leaving the young savage in possession of the prize.

The audacity of these Bears in approaching the neighbourhood of Fort Union at times was remarkable. The waiter, "Jean Battiste," who had been in the employ of the company for upwards of twenty years, told us that while one day picking peas in the garden, as he advanced towards the end of one of the rows, he saw a large Grizzly Bear gathering that excellent vegetable also. At this unexpected and startling discovery, he dropped his bucket, peas and all, and fled at his fastest pace to the Fort. Immediately the hunters turned out on their best horses, and by riding in a circle, formed a line which enabled them to approach the Bear on all sides. They found the animal greedily feasting on the peas, and shot him without his apparently caring for their approach. We need hardly say the bucket was empty.

In GODMAN's Natural History there are several anecdotes connected with the Grizzly Bear. The first is as follows: A Mr. JOHN DOUGHERTY, a very experienced and respectable hunter belonging to Major LONG's expedition, relates that once, while hunting with another person on one of the upper

Plate CXXXI

No. 27.

Drawn from Nature by J.W. Audubon.

On stone by W.E. Hitchcock

Lith Printed & Col.d by J.T. Bowen, Philad.a

Grizzly Bear.

tributaries of the Missouri, he heard the report of his companion's rifle, and when he looked round, beheld him at a short distance endeavouring to escape from one of these beasts, which he had wounded as it was coming towards him. DOUGHERTY, forgetful of every thing but the preservation of his friend, hastened to call off the attention of the Bear, and arrived in rifle-shot distance just in time to effect his generous purpose. He discharged his ball at the animal, and was obliged in his turn to fly; his friend, relieved from immediate danger, prepared for another attack by charging his rifle, with which he again wounded the Bear, and saved Mr. DOUGHERTY from peril. Neither received any injury from this encounter, in which the Bear was at length killed.

On another occasion, several hunters were chased by a Grizzly Bear, which rapidly gained upon them. A boy of the party, who could not run so fast as his companions, perceiving the Bear very near him, fell with his face towards the ground. The animal reared up on his hind feet, stood for a moment, and then bounded over him, impatient to catch the more distant fugitives.

Mr. DOUGHERTY, the hunter before mentioned, relates the following instance of the great muscular strength of the Grizzly Bear: Having killed a bison, and left the carcass for the purpose of procuring assistance to skin and cut it up, he was very much surprised on his return to find that it had been dragged off whole, to a considerable distance by a Grizzly Bear, and was then placed in a pit which the animal had dug with his claws for its reception.

The following is taken from Sir JOHN RICHARDSON's Fauna Boreali Americana: "A party of voyagers, who had been employed all day in tracking a canoe up the Saskatchewan, had seated themselves in the bright light by a fire, and were busy in preparing their supper, when a large Grizzly Bear sprung over their canoe, that was placed behind them, and seizing one of the party by the shoulder, carried him off. The rest fled in terror, with the exception of a Metis, named BOURAPO, who grasping his gun, followed the Bear as it was retreating leisurely with its prey. He called to his unfortunate comrade that he was afraid of hitting him if he fired at the Bear, but the latter entreated him to fire immediately, without hesitation, as the Bear was squeezing him to death. On this he took a deliberate aim and discharged the contents of his piece into the body of the Bear, which instantly dropped its prey to pursue BOURAPO. He escaped with difficulty, and the Bear ultimately retired to a thicket, where it was supposed to have died; but the curiosity of the party not being a match for their fears, the fact of its decease was not ascertained. The man who was rescued had his arm fractured, and was otherwise severely bitten by the Bear, but finally recovered. I have seen BOURAPO, and can add that the account which he gives is fully credited by the traders resident in that part of the country, who are best qualified to judge of its truth from the knowledge of the parties. I have been told that there is a man now living in the neighbourhood of Edmonton-house who was attacked by a Grizzly Bear, which sprang out of a thicket, and with one stroke of its paw completely scalped him, laying bare the skull and bringing the skin of the forehead down over the eyes. Assistance coming up, the Bear made off without doing him further injury, but the scalp not being replaced, the poor man has lost his sight, although he thinks that his eyes are uninjured."

Mr. DRUMMOND, in his excursions over the Rocky Mountains, had frequent opportunities of observing the manners of the Grizzly Bear, and it often happened that in turning the point of a rock or sharp angle of a valley, he came suddenly upon one or more of them. On such occasions they reared on their hind legs and made a loud noise like a person breathing quick, but much harsher. He kept his ground without attempting to molest them, and they, on their part, after attentively regarding him for some time, generally wheeled round and galloped off, though, from their disposition, there is little doubt but he would have been torn in pieces had he lost his presence of mind and attempted to fly. When he discovered them from a distance, he generally frightened them away by beating on a large tin box, in which he carried his specimens of plants. He never saw more than four together, and two of these he supposes to have been cubs; he more often met them singly or in pairs. He was only once attacked, and then by a female, for the purpose of allowing her cubs time to escape. His gun on this occasion missed fire, but he kept her at bay with the stock of it, until some gentlemen of the Hudson's Bay Company, with whom he was travelling at the time, came up and drove her off. In the latter end of June, 1826, he observed a male caressing a female, and soon afterwards they both came towards him, but whether accidentally, or for the purpose of attacking him, he was uncertain. He ascended a tree, and as the female drew near, fired at and mortally wounded her. She uttered a few loud screams, which threw the male into a furious rage, and he reared up against the trunk of the tree in which Mr. DRUMMOND was seated, but never attempted to ascend it. The female, in the meantime, retired to a short distance, lay down, and as the male was proceeding to join her, Mr. DRUMMOND shot him also.

The young Grizzly Bears and gravid females hibernate, but the older males often come abroad in the winter in quest of food. MACKENZIE mentions the den or winter retreat of a Grizzly Bear, which was ten feet wide, five feet high, and six feet long.

This species varies very much in colour; we have skins in our possession collected on the Upper Missouri, some of which are nearly white, whilst others are as nearly of a rufous tint. The one that was killed by our party (of which we have also the skin) was a dark brown one.

The following is from notes of J. W. AUDUBON, made in California in 1849 and 1850: "High up on the waters of the San Joaquin, in California, many of these animals have been killed by the miners now overrunning all the country west of the Sierra Nevada. Greatly as the Grizzly Bear is dreaded, it is hunted with all the more enthusiasm by these fearless pioneers in the romantic hills, valleys, and wild mountains of the land of gold, as its flesh is highly prized by men who have been living for months on salt pork or dry and tasteless deer-meat. I have seen two dollars a pound paid for the leaf-fat around the kidneys. If there is time, and the animal is not in a starving condition, the Grizzly Bear always runs at the sight of man; but should the hunter come too suddenly on him, the fierce beast always commences the engagement.—And the first shot of the hunter is a matter of much importance, as, if unsuccessful, his next move must be to look for a sapling to climb for safety. It is rare to find a man who would willingly come into immediate contact with one of these powerful and vindictive brutes. Some were killed near 'Green Springs,' on the Stanislaus, in the winter of 1849–50, that were nearly eight hundred pounds weight. I saw many cubs at San Francisco, Sacramento city, and Stockton, and even those not larger than an ordinary sized dog, showed evidence of their future fierceness, as it required great patience to render them gentle enough to be handled with impunity as pets. In camping at night, my friend ROBERT LAYTON, and I too, often thought what sort of defence we could make should an old fellow come smelling round our solitary tent for supper; but as 'Old Riley,' our pack-mule, was always tied near, we used to quiet ourselves with the idea that while Riley was snorting and kicking, we might place a couple of well aimed balls from our old friend Miss Betsey (as the boys had christened my large gun), so that our revolvers, COLT's dragoon pistols, would give us the victory; but really a startling effect would be produced by the snout of a Grizzly Bear being thrust into your tent, and your awaking at the noise of the sniff he might take to induce his appetite.

"I was anxious to purchase a few of the beautiful skins of this species, but those who had killed 'an old Grizzly,' said they would take his skin home. It makes a first rate bed under the thin and worn blanket of the digger.

"The different colours of the pelage of this animal, but for the uniformity of its extraordinary claws, would puzzle any one not acquainted with its form, for it varies from jet black in the young of the first and second winter to the hoary gray of age, or of summer."

In TOWNSEND's "Narrative of a Journey across the Rocky Mountains to the Columbia River, &c." (Philadelphia, 1839), we find two adventures with the Grizzly Bear. The first is as follows: The party were on Black Foot river, a small stagnant stream which runs in a northwesterly direction down a valley covered with quagmires through which they had great difficulty in making their way. "As we approached our encampment, near a small grove of willows on the margin of the river, a tremendous Grizzly Bear rushed out upon us. Our horses ran wildly in every direction, snorting with terror, and became nearly unmanageable. Several balls were instantly fired into him, but they only seemed to increase his fury. After spending a moment in rending each wound (their invariable practice), he selected the person who happened to be nearest, and darted after him, but before he proceeded far he was sure to be stopped again by a ball from another quarter. In this way he was driven about amongst us for perhaps fifteen minutes, at times so near some of the horses that he received several severe kicks from them. One of the pack-horses was fastened upon by the brute, and in the terrified animal's efforts to escape the dreaded gripe, the pack and saddle were broken to pieces and disengaged. One of our mules also lent him a kick in the head, while pursuing it up an adjacent hill, which sent him rolling to the bottom. Here he was finally brought to a stand. The poor animal was so completely surrounded by enemies that he became bewildered. He raised himself upon his hind feet, standing almost erect, his mouth partly open, and from his protruding tongue the blood fell fast in drops. While in this position he received about six more balls, each of which made him reel. At last, as in complete desperation, he dashed into the water, and swam several yards with astonishing strength and agility, the guns cracking at him constantly. But he was not to proceed far. Just then, RICHARDSON, who had been absent, rode up, and fixing his deadly aim upon him, fired a ball into the back of his head, which killed him instantly. The strength of four men was required to drag the ferocious brute from the water, and upon examining his body he was found completely riddled; there did not appear to be four inches of his shaggy person, from the hips upward, that had not received a ball. There must have been at least thirty shots made at him, and probably few missed him, yet such was his tenacity of life that I have no doubt he would have succeeded in crossing the river, but for the last shot in the brain. He would probably weigh, at the least, six hundred pounds, and was about the height of an ordinary steer. The spread of the foot, laterally, was ten inches, and the claws measured seven inches in length. This animal was remarkably lean; when in good condition he would doubtless much exceed in weight the estimate I have given."

At p. 68, TOWNSEND says: "In the afternoon one of our men had a somewhat perilous adventure with a Grizzly Bear. He saw the animal crouching his huge frame in some willows which skirted the river, and approaching him on horseback to within twenty yards, fired upon him. The Bear was only slightly wounded by the shot, and with a fierce growl of angry malignity, rushed from his cover, and gave chase. The horse happened to be a slow one, and for the distance of half a mile the race was hard contested, the Bear frequently approaching so near the terrified animal as to snap at his heels, whilst the equally terrified rider, who had lost his hat at the start, used whip and spur with the most frantic diligence, frequently looking behind, from an influence which he could not resist, at his rugged and determined foe, and shrieking in an agony of fear, 'shoot him! shoot him!' The man, who was one of the greenhorns, happened to be about a mile behind the main body, either from the indolence of his horse or his own carelessness; but as he approached the party in his desperate flight, and his lugubrious cries reached the ears of the men in front, about a dozen of them rode to his assistance, and soon succeeded in diverting the attention of his pertinacious foe. After he had received the contents of all the guns, he fell, and was soon despatched. The man rode in among his fellows, pale and haggard from overwrought feelings, and was probably effectually cured of a propensity for meddling with Grizzly Bears."

Geographical Distribution.

The Grizzly Bear has been found as far north as about latitude 61°. It is an inhabitant of the western and northwestern portions of North America, is most frequently met with in hilly and woody districts, and (east of the Rocky Mountains) along the edges of the Upper Missouri and Upper Mississippi rivers, and their tributaries. On the west coast it is found rather numerously in California, generally keeping among the oaks and pines, on the acorns and cones of which it feeds with avidity.

The Grizzly Bear does not appear to have been seen in eastern Texas or the southern parts of New Mexico, and as far as we have heard has not been discovered in Lower California.

General Remarks.

To LEWIS and CLARK we are indebted for the first authentic account of the difference between this species and the Black Bear of America, although the Grizzly Bear was mentioned a long time previously by LA HONTAN and others.

DE WITT CLINTON, in a discourse before the New York Literary and Philosophical Society, was the next naturalist who clearly showed that this animal was specifically distinct from either the Polar or the common Bear.

LEWIS and CLARK's name, Grizzly, translated into *Ferox*, has been generally adopted by naturalists to designate this species, and we have admitted it in our nomenclature of this work. We believe that the name proposed for it by ORD (*Ursus horribilis*), and which SAY adopted, must, if we adhere to the rules by which naturalists should be guided in such matters, ultimately take the precedence.

The difference between the Grizzly Bear and the Black may be easily detected. The soles of the feet of the former are longer, and the heel broader; the claws are very long, whilst in the Black Bear they are quite short. The tail of the Grizzly Bear is shorter than that of the Black, and its body is larger, less clumsy and unwieldy, and its head flatter than the head of the latter.

The Grizzly Bear makes enormous long tracks, and differs widely from the Black Bear in its habits, being very ferocious, and fearlessly attacking man.

We think the average size and weight of this animal are much underrated. We have no hesitation in stating that the largest specimens would weigh considerably over one thousand pounds. We have seen a skin of the common Black Bear, shot in the State of New York, the original owner of which was said to have weighed twelve hundred and odd pounds when killed!

Canis Familiaris.—Linn. (Var. Lagopus.)

Hare-Indian Dog.

Plate cxxxii.—Male.

C. Magnitudine inter lupum et vulpem fulvum intermedius, auriculis erectis, cauda comosa, colore cinereo, albo nigroque notato.

Characters.

Intermediate in size between the wolf and red fox; ears, erect; tail, bushy; colour, gray, varied with white and dark markings.

Description.

The Hare-Indian Dog resembles the wolf rather more than the fox. Its head is small, muzzle slender, ears erect, eyes somewhat oblique, legs slender, feet broad and hairy, and its tail bushy and generally curled over its hip. The body is covered with long hair, particularly about the shoulders. At the roots of the hair, both on the body and tail, there is a thick wool. On the posterior parts of the cheeks the hair is long and directed backwards, giving the animal the appearance of having a ruff around the neck.

Colour.

Face, muzzle, belly, and legs, cream white; a white central line passes over the crown of the head to the occiput; the anterior surface of the ear is white, the posterior yellowish-gray or fawn colour; tip of nose, eye-lashes, roof of mouth, and part of the gums, black; there is a dark patch over the eye, and large patches of dark blackish-gray or lead colour, on the body mixed with fawn colour and white, not definite in form, but running into each other. The tail is white beneath, and is tipped with white.

Dimensions.

	Feet.	Inches.
Length of head and body, about	3	
Height at shoulder, about	1	2
Length of tail,	1	3

Habits.

This animal is more domestic than many of the wolf-like Dogs of the plains, and seems to have been entirely subjugated by the Indians north of the great lakes, who use it in hunting, but not as a beast for burthen or draught.

Sir JOHN RICHARDSON says (F. B. A., p. 79): "The Hare-Indian Dog is very playful, has an affectionate disposition, and is soon gained by kindness. It is not, however, very docile, and dislikes confinement of every kind. It is very fond of being caressed, rubs its back against the hand like a cat, and soon makes an acquaintance with a stranger. Like a wild animal it is very mindful of an injury, nor does it, like a spaniel, crouch under the lash; but if it is conscious of having deserved punishment, it will hover round the tent of its master the whole day, without coming within his reach, even if he calls it. Its howl, when hurt or afraid, is that of the wolf; but when it sees any unusual object it makes a singular attempt at barking, commencing by a kind of growl, which is not, however, unpleasant, and ending in a prolonged howl. Its voice is very much like that of the prairie wolf.

"The larger Dogs which we had for draught at Fort Franklin, and which were of the mongrel breed in common use at the fur posts, used to pursue the Hare-Indian Dogs for the purpose of devouring them; but the latter far outstripped them in speed, and easily made their escape. A young puppy, which I purchased from the Hare Indians, became greatly attached to me, and when about seven months old ran on the snow by the side of my sledge for nine hundred miles, without suffering from fatigue. During this march it frequently of its own accord carried a small twig or one of my mittens for a mile or two; but although very gentle in its manners it showed little aptitude in learning any of the arts which the Newfoundland Dogs so speedily acquire, of fetching and carrying when ordered. This Dog was killed and eaten by an Indian, on the Saskatchewan, who pretended that he mistook it for a fox."

The most extraordinary circumstance in this relation is the great endurance of the puppy, which certainly deserves special notice. Even the oldest and strongest Dogs are generally incapable of so long a journey as nine hundred miles (with probably but little food), without suffering from fatigue.

Geographical Distribution.

It is stated by Sir JOHN RICHARDSON that this species exists only among the different tribes of Indians that frequent the borders of Great Bear lake and the Mackenzie river.

General Remarks.

From the size of this animal it might be supposed by those who are desirous of tracing all the Dogs to some neighbouring wolf, hyena, jackal, or fox, that it had its origin either from the prairie wolf or the red fox, or a mixture of both.

The fact, however, that these wolves and foxes never associate with each other in the same vicinity, and never have produced an intermediate variety, or, that we are aware of, have ever produced a hybrid in their wild state, and more especially the fact that the prairie wolf, as stated by RICHARDSON, does not exist within hundreds of miles of the region where this Dog is bred, must lead us to look to some other source for its origin.

Its habits, the manner in which it carries its tail, its colour, and its bark, all differ widely from those of the prairie wolf.

We have never had an opportunity of seeing this animal and examining it, except in the stuffed specimen from which our drawing was made; we are therefore indebted to Sir JOHN RICHARDSON for all the information we possess in regard to its habits, and have in this article given the results of his investigations mostly in his own language.

Lepus Texianus.—Aud. and Bach.

Texan Hare—Vulgo Jackass Rabbit.

Plate cxxxiii.—Male.

L. Magnitudine, L. Californicum excedens, auriculis maximis, capite tertia parte longioribus, linea fusca supra in collo, striâ nigrâ a natibus usque ad caudæ apicem productâ, corpore supra luteo nigroque vario, subter, collo rufo gula atque ventre albis.

Characters.

Larger than the Californian Hare; ears, very large—more than one third longer than the head; a dark brown stripe on the top of the neck, and a black stripe from the rump, extending to the root of the tail and along its upper surface to the tip. Upper surface of body, mottled deep buff and black, throat and belly white, under side of neck dull rufous.

Description.

Crown of the head, depressed or flattened, forming an obtuse angle with the forehead and nose; ears, of immense size, being larger than in any other species of Hare known to us. Body, full, and rather stout; forelegs, of moderate length and size; thighs, stout and large; tarsus, of moderate length; nails, strong, deeply channelled beneath.

Colour.

Hairs on the upper surface of body, white from the roots for two thirds of their length, then brown, then dull buff, and tipped very narrowly with black. On the belly, throat, and insides of legs, the hairs are white from the roots to the tips.

One of our specimens has a black patch on the inner surface of the ear near its base; another has a brown patch in that place; anterior margin of the ears, buff; posterior portion of the ear for an inch and a half from the tip, whitish; a narrow line of dark brown runs from between the ears for an inch along the back of the neck; the anterior outer half of the ear, and the posterior inner half of the ear, are clothed with a mixture of particoloured gray and yellowish hairs; the posterior outside half of the ear is white, with the exception of the extreme point, which in one of our specimens has a slight margin of brown at the tip of the ear, while another specimen is more deeply tinged with brown for three fourths of its length.

Around the eye there is a light yellowish-gray ring; under surface of neck, rufous, faintly spotted or marked with brown; tail, black above, the same colour continuing on the rump and dorsal line in a stripe for about four inches from the root of the tail; eyes, orange hazel; nails, brown. The line of white on the belly and flanks is irregular in shape where it joins the dark colours of the upper surface, and in this respect differs from *Lepus callotis*, in which species the white extends higher up the sides and is continued in a tolerably straight line nearly to the tail.

Whiskers, white, a few of them black at the roots.

Dimensions.

		Feet.	Inches.	Lines.
From point of nose to root of tail,		1	9	
" " to ear,			4	1
Ear, externally,			6	5
Width of ear,			3	
Length of tarsus,			5	
" tail (including fur),			4	2
" longest whisker,			3	6

Habits.

This Hare received from the Texans, and from our troops in the Mexican war, the name of Jackass rabbit, in common with *Lepus callotis*, the Black-tailed Hare described in our second volume, p. 95. It is the largest of three nearly allied species of Hare which inhabit respectively New Mexico, Texas, Mexico, and California, viz. the present species, the Black-tailed, and the Californian Hare. It is quite as swift of foot as either of the others, and its habits resemble those of the Black-tailed Hare in almost every particular. The young have generally a white spot on the middle of the top of the head, and are remarkable for the rigidity of the fringe of hairs which margins the ears. The feet of this species do not exhibit the red and dense fur which prevails on the feet of the Black-tailed Hare (and from which it has sometimes been called the Red-footed Hare).

The Mexicans are very fond of the flesh of this animal, and as it is widely distributed, a great many are shot and snared by them. It is very good eating, and formed an important item in the provisions of JOHN W. AUDUBON's party whilst passing through Mexico, they at times killing so many that the men became tired of them.

Fabulous stories similar to those related of many other animals of which little was formerly known, have been told us of this Hare, which has been described as enormously large, and was many years ago mentioned to us as equal in size to a fox. Of course we were somewhat disappointed when we procured specimens, although it is a fine large species.

Among other old stories about the animals of Texas and Mexico, we have a rather curious one in CLAVIGHERO's notes or attempted elucidation of HERNANDEZ, which we give as translated by Capt. J. P. McCOWN from the Spanish. The *Ocotochtli*, according to Dr. HERNANDEZ, is a species of wild-cat. He says that "when it has killed any game it climbs a tree and utters a howl of invitation to other animals that come and eat and die, as the flesh was poisoned by its bite, when he descends and makes his meal from the store that his trick has put at his disposal."

Geographical Distribution.

This Hare appears to inhabit the southern parts of New Mexico, the western parts of Texas, and the elevated lands westward of the *tierras calientes* (low lands of the coast) of Mexico, and is found within a few miles of San Petruchio, forty miles from the coast: so J. W. AUDUBON was informed by some Rangers who accompanied a party sent from San Antonio in 1845, who having the use of "Col. HARNEY's" greyhounds, had many a chase, but never caught one! How near it approaches the sea coast we could not learn. It was not observed west of Ures in Sonora by J. W. AUDUBON, and seems to be replaced by the Californian Hare on the Pacific coast.

Its southern limit is unknown to us, but it probably extends some distance

N° 27

Plate CXXXII.

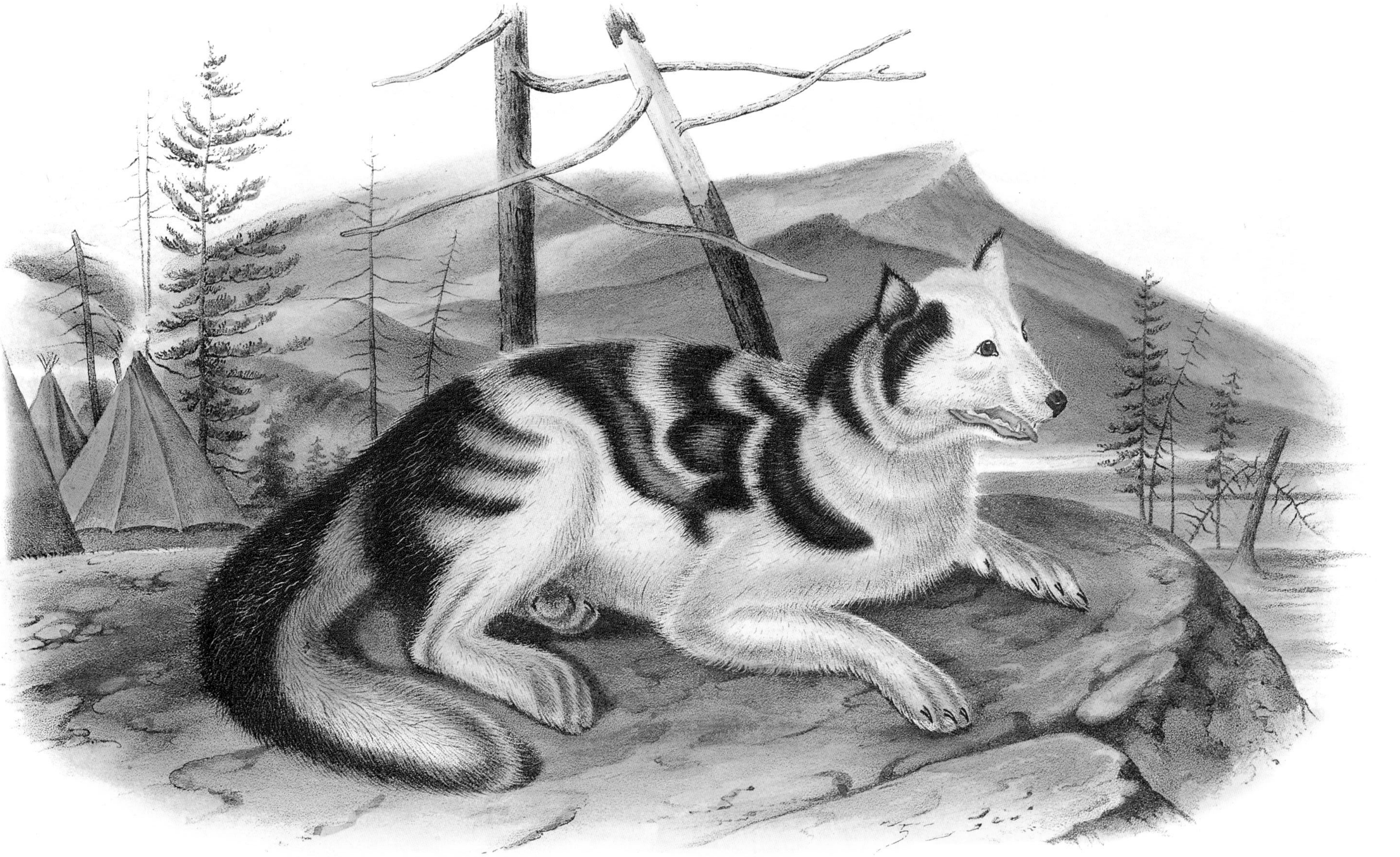

Drawn from Nature by J.W. Audubon

Hare-Indian Dog

Lith. Printed & Col^{d} by J.T. Bowen, Phil

beyond the city of Mexico.

General Remarks.

Since publishing our article on *Lepus Townsendii* we have received some accounts of the habits of a Hare which we presume may prove to be that animal; they are singular, and may interest our readers. Captain THOMAS G. RHETT, of the United States army, who was stationed at Fort Laramie for more than two years, observed the Hares of that neighbourhood to make burrows in the ground like rabbits. They ran into these holes when alarmed, and when chased by his greyhounds generally escaped by diving into them. The captain frequently saw them sitting at the mouths of their holes like prairie dogs, and shot them. Several that he thus killed had only their heads exposed outside of their burrow.

These holes or burrows are dug in a slanting direction, and not straight up and down like the badger holes. The females bring forth their young in them, and their habits must assimilate to those of the European rabbit. The captain states that they turn white in winter, but as he made no notes and brought no specimens, we cannot with certainty decide that they were the animal we named *L. Townsendii*. Should they prove to be the same, however, the name will have to be changed to *L. campestris*, a Hare of the plains which we had previously described, but subsequently thought was not that species, as it became white in winter, which we were told *L. Townsendii* did not. See our first volume, p. 30.

Arctomys Flaviventer.—Bach.

Yellow-Bellied Marmot.

Plate cxxxiv.—Male.

A. Supra flavido-albo nigroque griseus, capitis vertice nigro, subtus saturate flavus, nasi extremitate labiis, mentoque albis, pedibus fuscescente flavis, cauda subnigra.

Characters.

Upper parts, grizzled yellowish-white and black; crown of the head, chiefly black; under parts, deep yellow; point of nose, lips, and chin, white; feet, brownish-yellow; tail, blackish-brown.

Synonymes.

ARCTOMYS FLAVIVENTER. Bachman, Proc. Acad. Nat. Sci. Phila., October 5, 1841.
"   "   Catal. Zool. Soc. 1839, Specimen No. 459, Bachman's MSS.

Description.

In form this animal resembles the figures and descriptions of what was formerly considered the Canada Marmot (*Arctomys empetra*), which has since been ascertained to be the young of the Maryland Marmot (*A. monax*).

Head, rather small; ears, small and narrow; nails, short; tail, rounded, and rather long; the whole animal is thickly clothed with fur, somewhat softer than that of the Maryland Marmot.

The upper incisors have several indistinct longitudinal grooves.

Colour.

Fur on the back, grayish-black at base; on each hair a considerable space is occupied by dirty yellowish-white, which is gradually shaded towards the tips through brown into black, but the tips are yellowish-white.

Hairs on the under surface, grayish-black at base; hairs of the feet, chiefly black at base; cheeks, grizzled with white and dark brown, the latter colour prevailing; a rusty brown patch on the throat borders the white hairs on the chin; whiskers, mostly black; palms, entirely naked through their whole extent. There is an indistinct yellow elongated spot behind the nose, and also one behind or above the eye.

Dimensions.

	Inches.	Lines.
From point of nose to root of tail,	16	
Tail, to end of fur,	6	10
Heel, to point of nail,	2	6½
Height of ear posteriorly,		6⅓
From point of nose to ear,	3	

Habits.

The specimen from which our description of this Marmot was drawn up, was found by us among the skins sent to England by DRUMMOND and DOUGLAS, procured by those gentlemen in our northwestern territories, and placed in the museum of the Zoological Society of London. Since we described it, the skin has been stuffed and set up.

Not a line was written in regard to its habits or the place where it was killed; its form and claws, however, indicate that like the other species of Marmot found in America, it is a burrowing animal, and feeds on seeds, roots, and grasses. We may also presume it has four or five young at a birth.

Geographical Distribution.

As just stated, the exact locality in which this animal was captured has not been given, but judging from the route travelled over by DOUGLAS, we presume it was obtained in the mountainous districts that extend north and south between Western Texas and California, where it probably exists, but if seen has been supposed by the hunters and miners to be the common Marmot or woodchuck of the Atlantic States (*A. monax*).

General Remarks.

This species differs from the young of *Arctomys monax*, by some naturalists named *A. empetra*, as we ascertained by comparing it with several specimens of that so-called species, in the museum of the Zoological Society, its feet being yellow instead of black, as in those specimens, and the belly yellow, not deep rusty red. Besides, the hairs on the back are yellowish-white and black, in place of rusty brown, black, and white.

The head is narrower, the toes smaller, and the claws only half as long, as in the above specimens. The ears are also considerably smaller, narrower and more ovate than the ears of *A. monax*, which are round.

Arvicola Richardsonii.—Aud. and Bach.

Richardson's Meadow-Mouse.

Plate cxxxv.—Natural Size. Fig. 1.

A. fuscus nigro tinctus, subtus cinereus, cærulescente-canus, auriculis mediocribus vellere fere conditis, cauda capite paullulum longiore.

Characters.

Dull brown mixed with black, under parts bluish-gray; ears, of moderate size, nearly hidden by the fur; tail, a little longer than the head.

Synonyme.

ARVICOLA RIPARIUS? Ord. BANK MEADOW-MOUSE. Richardson, F. B. A., p. 120.

Description.

Head, rather large; incisors, large, much exposed, and projecting beyond the nose—upper, flattened anteriorly, marked with scarcely perceptible perpendicular grooves, and with a somewhat irregular and rather oblique

Plate CXXVII

Nº 27

Lith Printed & Col'd by J.T.Bowen, Phil.

Drawn from Nature by J.W. Audubon.

Texian Hare.

cutting edge—lower, twice as long as the upper, and narrower, slightly curved, and rounded anteriorly; nose, thick and obtuse; whiskers, few and rather short; eyes, rather small; ears, ovate, rounded at the tip, not easily distinguishable until the surrounding fur is blown or moved aside.

Body, more slender behind than at the shoulders, the hind-legs not being so far apart as the fore-legs; tail, rather short, tapering, and thinly covered with short hairs; fore-legs, short; feet, rather small, with four slender, well separated toes, and the rudiment of a thumb, which is armed with a minute nail; claws, small, compressed, and pointed; the third toe nearly equals the middle one, which is the longest.

The hair of the toes projects over the claws but does not conceal them; the toes of the hind-feet are longer than those of the fore-feet, and their claws are somewhat longer; the inner one is the shortest, the second longer than the third, and the third longer than the fourth; the first and fifth are considerably shorter than the others, and are placed farther back.

The fur on the back is about eight lines long, but not so soft and fine as in some other animals of the genus; it is nearly as long on the crown and cheeks, but is shorter and thinner on the chest and belly.

Colour.

Incisors, yellow; claws, white; whiskers, black; the whole dorsal aspect, including the shoulders and outsides of the thighs, is dull or dusky brown, proceeding from an intimate mixture of yellowish-brown and black, which colours are confined to the tips of the hairs and are so mingled as to produce a nearly uniform shade of colour without lustre.

From the roots to near the tips, the fur has a uniform shining blackish-gray colour; on the ventral aspect (lower parts) it is bluish-gray; the margin of the upper lip, the chin, and the feet, are dull white; tail, dark brown above, lighter beneath, the two colours meeting by an even line.

Dimensions.

Length of head and body, ...7 inches.
"   tail, ...2   "

Habits.

DRUMMOND, who procured this Meadow-Mouse, states that its habits are analogous to those of the common water-rat of Europe (*Arvicola amphibius*), with which it may be easily confounded, although the shortness of its tail may serve as a mark by which to distinguish it.

It frequents moist meadows amongst the Rocky Mountains, and swims and dives well, taking to the water at once when pursued. All Meadow-Mice indeed are capital swimmers. We some time since amused ourselves watching one that had fallen into a circular cistern partly built up with stone and partly excavated out of the solid rock by blasting, and which was plastered with cement on the inside to make it water-tight. This cistern had about four feet of water in it. On one side there was a projecting rounded knob of stone some five or six inches long and about two wide, which slanted out of the water so that the upper edge of it was dry. Upon this little resting-place there was a large *Arvicola Pennsylvanica* (Wilson's Meadow-Mouse) seated very quietly, having probably tumbled in the preceding night. When we approached the edge and looked down into the clear element we at first did not observe the Rat, but as soon as we espied him he saw us, immediately dived, and swam around underneath the surface quite rapidly; he soon arose, however, and regained his position on the ledge, and we determined to save him from what had been his impending fate—drowning or starving, or both. We procured a plank, and gently lowering one end of it towards the ledge, thought he would take advantage of the inclined plane thus afforded him, to come out; but in our awkwardness we suffered the plank to slip, and at the plash in the water the little fellow dived and swam around several times before he again returned to his resting place, where we now had the end of the board fixed, so that he could get upon it. As soon as he was on it, we began to raise the plank, but when we had him about three feet above the surface he dashed off into the water, making as pretty a dive as need be. He always looked quite dry, and not a hair of his coat was soiled or turned during these frequent immersions, and it was quite interesting to see the inquisitive looks he cast towards us, turning his head and appearing to have strong doubts whether we meant to help, or to make an end of him. We put down the plank again, and after two attempts, in both of which his timidity induced him to jump off it when he was nearly at the edge of the cistern, he at last reached the top, and in a moment disappeared amid the weeds and grasses around.

Geographical Distribution.

The only information we possess of the habitat of this animal is from DRUMMOND, who states that he captured it near the foot of the Rocky Mountains.

General Remarks.

This species possesses longer and stronger incisors than any other American Rat of this genus; its mouth presenting in fact a miniature resemblance to that of the musk-rat.

Although the *Arvicola xanthognatha* is a larger animal than the present, yet its incisors are not more than half as long as in this species.

We have named this Arvicola in honour of Sir JOHN RICHARDSON, who in describing it (Fauna Boreali Americana, p. 120), applied to it, with a doubt, the name of *Arvicola riparius*, ORD, from which it differs so much as to render a comparison here unnecessary.

Arvicola Drummondii.—Aud. and Bach.

Drummond's Meadow-Mouse.

Plate cxxxv. Figure with Short Tail.—Summer Pelage.

A. Corpore supra fusco, infra fusco-cinereo, ad latera rufo tińcto, robustiore et paulo majore quam in A. Pennsylvanicâ; auriculis vellere fere occultis; cauda brevi, capitis dimidium subequante.

Characters.

Body, above, dark brown; beneath, dull brownish-gray tinged with red. Stouter and rather larger than Wilson's Meadow-Mouse (A. Pennsylvanica); *ears, scarcely visible beyond the fur; tail, short, about half the length of the head.*

Synonymes.

ARVICOLA NOVEBORACENSIS—SHARP-NOSED MEADOW-MOUSE. Rich., F. B. A., p. 126.

Description.

Body, thick; head, of moderate size, tapering from the ears to the nose; nose, slender and more acute than in many other *Arvicolæ*, projecting a little beyond the incisors, which are rather large.

Ears, rounded, scarcely visible beyond the fur; tail, covered with short hairs, scarcely concealing the scales, converging to a point at the tip; legs, very short; feet, rather small; claws, weak and compressed; a very minute nail occupies the place of the thumb; the fur is a little coarser than that of A. Pennsylvanica.

The whiskers, which are not numerous, reach the cheeks.

Colour.

Hair on the back, and upper part of the head, grayish-black from the roots to near the tips, which are reddish-brown terminated with black; the resulting colour is an intimate mixture of brown and black, appearing in some lights dark reddish-brown, in others yellowish-brown mixed with blackish; around the eyes, yellowish-red; there is a lightish space behind the ears and along the sides; under surface, yellowish-gray, mingling on the sides with the colour of the back; upper surface of the tail, dark brown; under side, grayish-white; feet, dark gray, tinged with rufous.

Dimensions.

	Inches.	Lines.
Length of head and body, ...	4	3
" head, ...	1	4
" tail, ...	1	

Habits.

The specimen from which our drawing was made is one of those obtained by Mr. DRUMMOND, and was deposited by that gentleman in the museum of the Zoological Society at London, as well as many others to which we have

Plate CXXIV

N°.27.

Drawn from Nature by J.W.Audubon.

On stone by W.E.Hitchcock

Lith. Printed & Col.d by J.T.Bowen, Phila.da

Yellow bellied, Marmot.

already referred in our work. It was examined and described by Sir JOHN RICHARDSON, who mistook the animal for a supposed species found in the state of New York, and loosely described by RAFFINESQUE under the name of *Lemmus noveboracensis*, and which we refer to *A. Pennsylvanica*, with which we have compared the description.

DRUMMOND in regard to the habits of the present animal merely states that they are similar to those of *Arvicola xanthognatha*.

Geographical Distribution.

Valleys of the Rocky Mountains.

General Remarks.

As above mentioned, Sir JOHN RICHARDSON described this animal,

quoting from DESMAREST (Mamm., p. 286), RAFFINESQUE's description of the so-called *Lemmus noveboracensis*, which appears to apply to one of the varieties of WILSON's Meadow-Mouse (*Arvicola Pennsylvanica*), of which we possess specimens.

From an examination of many species, we have arrived at the conclusion that no *Arvicolæ* found on the Rocky Mountains are identical with any in the Atlantic States, and on a comparison of RICHARDSON's species with those referred to by RAFFINESQUE, we determined without much hesitation that the present is a new species under an old name, and we have consequently attached to it the name of its discoverer—DRUMMOND.

By some oversight this species was not named on our plate as distinct from *A. Richardsonii*, but is easily distinguished by its short tail—the two being on the same engraving.

Cervus Virginianus.—Pennant.

Common American Deer.

Plate cxxxvi.—Male and Female.

(Fawn.) Plate lxxxi.—Winter Pelage.

In our article on the Virginian Deer (vol. ii. p. 220), we gave descriptions of the characters and habits of this species; we now present figures of the adult male and female.

We have not much information to add to that already given: it may be of interest, however, to notice the annual changes which take place in the growth of the horns, from adolescence to maturity, and the decline which is the result of age.

At Hyde Park, on the estate of J. R. STUYVESANT, Esq., Dutchess county, New York, seven or eight Deer were kept for many years, and several raised annually. We had the opportunity at the hospitable mansion of Mr. STUYVESANT, of examining a series of horns, all taken from the same buck as they were annually shed, from the first spikes to the antlers that crowned his head when killed; and we now give a short memorandum showing the progress of their growth from year to year. In 1842, when this buck was one year old, his horns (spikes) had each one rudimentary prong—one about five eighths of an inch long, the other scarcely visible; in 1843 they had two prongs four to six inches long; in 1844, three prongs, and brow antlers, longest prong eight inches; in 1845, a littl larger in diameter, brow antlers longer and curved;

1846, rather less throughout in size; 1847, the two last prongs quite shortened. These last were somewhat broken by an accident, but evidently show that the animal had lost some degree of vigour. Age when killed, six years.

It should be observed that this animal was restricted to a park and was partially domesticated, being occasionally fed a little in the winter season; and being thus deprived of the wider range of the forest, the horns may not have exhibited all the peculiarities of the wild unrestrained buck.

We think however that the above will give a tolerably correct idea of the operations of nature in the annual production and conformation of the horns. They become longer and more branched for several years, until the animal has arrived at maturity, when either from age or disease they begin to decline.

In connection with this subject it may not be uninteresting to notice the effect of castration on the horns of the buck. When this operation has been performed during the season when the horns are fully grown, it is said they are not dropped, but continue on the head for many years; when the operation has been performed after they are dropped, there is no subsequent growth of horns, and the head appears ever afterwards like that of a doe.

We had an opportunity at the Blue Sulphur Springs in Virginia, of examining two tame bucks which had been castrated during the time that their horns were in velvet. Their horns continued to grow for several years; the antlers were of enormous length, and very irregularly branched, but the velvet was still retained on them; they presented a soft spongy appearance, and from slight scratches or injuries were continually bleeding; the neck had ceased to swell periodically as in the perfect bucks, they had become very large, seemed to be quite fat, and when first seen at a distance we supposed them to be elks.

Genus Enhydra.—Fleming.

Dental Formula.

$$\textit{Incisive } \frac{6}{4}; \textit{ Canine } \frac{4-4}{5-5}; \textit{ Molar } \frac{2-2}{3-3} = 38.$$

Head, small and globular; ears, short and conical, placed far back in the head.

Body, very long, covered with a dense glossy fur; tail, less than one fourth the length of the body, rather stout, depressed, covered with strong hairs on the sides.

Hind-feet, webbed.

LICHTENSTEIN says this genus has hind-feet like those of the common seals, ears resembling those of the seals of the genus *Otaria*, and a tail similar to that of the common Otter.

He places the Sea Otter (correctly, as we think) between the Otter and the seals that possess ears (*Otaria*).

Mammæ, two—ventral.

There is only one species in the genus.

Habit, living principally at sea and in bays and estuaries.

The generic name is derived from ενυδρος, *enudros*, aquatic; Gr. εν, *en*, in, and ύδωζ, *hudōr*, *water*.

Enhydra Marina.—Erxleben.

Sea Otter.

Plate cxxxvii.—Male.

E. perelongata, cauda depressa, corporis partem quartam æquante, pedibus posticis curtis, istis Phocarum similibus, colore castaneo vel nigro, vellere mollissimo; Lutrâ Canadensis duplo major.

Characters.

Body, very much elongated; tail, depressed and one fourth the length of the body; hind-feet, short, and resembling those of the seal; colour, chesnut brown or black; twice the size of the common Otter; fur, exceedingly fine.

Synonymes.

MUSTELA LUTRIS. Linn.
SEA BEAVER. Krascheninikoff, Hist. Kamsk. (Grieve's Trans.), p. 131. Ann. 1764.
MUSTELA LUTRIS. Schreber, Saügethiere, p. 465, fig. t. 128.
LUTRA MARINA. Erxleben, Syst. Ann. 1777.
    "   "   Steller, Nov. Com. Petrop., vol. ii. p. 267, t. 16.
SEA OTTER. Cook's Third Voyage, vol. ii. p. 295. Ann. 1784.
    "   "   Pennant's Arctic Zoology, vol. i. p. 88. Ann. 1784.

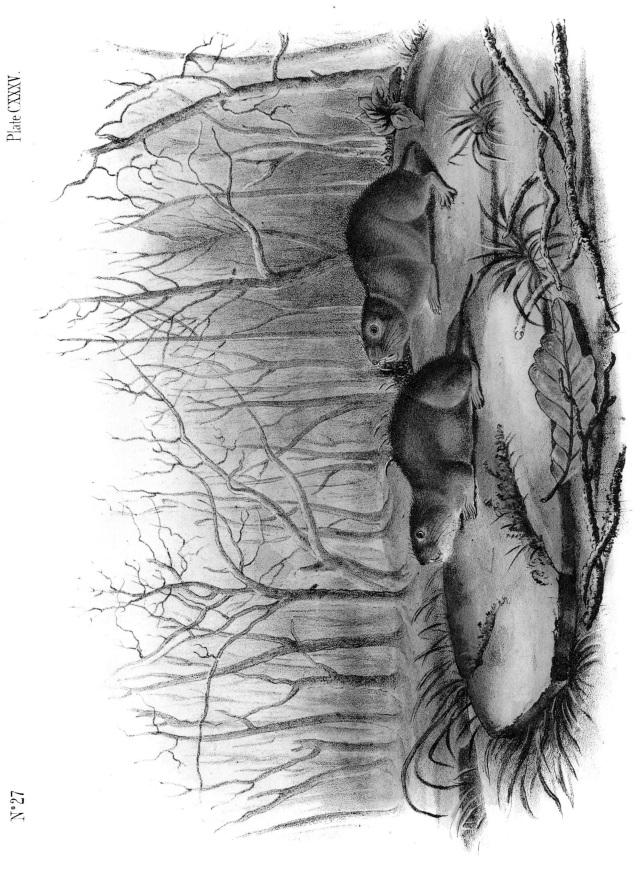

Drawn from Nature by J.W.Audubon

On stone by W.E.Hitchcock

Lith.d Printed & Col.d by J.T.Bowen, Philad.a

Richardsons Meadow Mouse.

LUTRA STELLERI. Lesson, Manual, pp. 156, 423.
SEA OTTER. Meares, Voyage, pp. 241, 260. Ann. 1790.
"   "   Menzies, Philos. Trans., p. 385. Ann. 1796.
ENHYDRA MARINA. Fleming, Phil. Zool., vol. ii. p. 187. Ann. 1822.
ENYDRIS STELLERI. Fischer, Synopsis, p. 228.
LUTRA MARINA. Harlan, Fauna, p. 72.
THE SEA OTTER. Godman's Nat. Hist., vol. i. p. 228.
ENYDRIS MARINA. Licht., Darstellung neuer oder wenig bekannter
     Saügethiere. Berlin, 1827–1834. Tafel xlix.
LUTRA (ENHYDRA) MARINA. Rich., Fauna Boreali Americana, p. 59.

Description.

Head, small in proportion to the size of the body; ears, short, conical, and covered with hair; eyes, rather large; lips, thick; mouth, wide, and furnished with strong and rather large teeth; fore-feet, webbed nearly to the nails, and much like those of the common Otter, five claws on each. Hind-legs and thighs, short, and better adapted for swimming than in other mammalia except the seals; hind-feet, flat and webbed, and toes being connected by a strong granulated membrane, with a skin skirting the outward toe; all the webs of the feet are thickly clothed with glossy hairs about a line in length.

One of the specimens referred to by Mr. MENZIES (the account of which is published in the Philosophical Transactions) measured eight inches across the hind-foot; the tongue was four inches long and rounded at the end, with a slight fissure, giving the tip a bifid appearance.

The tail is short, broad, depressed, and pointed at the end; the hair both on the body and tail is of two kinds—the longer hairs are silky, glossy, and not very numerous, the fur or shorter hair exceedingly soft and fine.

Colour.

The cheeks generally present a cast of grayish or silvery colour, which extends along the sides and under the throat; there is a lightish circle around the eye; top of the head, dark brown; the remainder of the body (above and beneath) is deep glossy brownish-black.

There is a considerable variety of shades in different specimens, some being much lighter than others. The longer hairs intermixed with the fur are in the best skins black and shining. In some individuals the fur about the ears, nose, and eyes is either brown or light coloured; the young are sometimes very light in colour, with white about the nose, eyes, and forehead.

The fur of the young is not equal in fineness to that of the adult.

Dimensions.

Adult.

	Feet.	Inches.
Length from point of nose to root of tail,	4	2
" of tail,		1

Young, about two years old.

	Feet.	Inches.
Length from end of nose to root of tail,	3	
" of tail,		7½
Width of head between the ears,		4
Height of ear,		¾
From elbow of fore-leg to end of nail,		4½
Length of hind-foot from heel to end of nail,		6¼
" fore toe,		¼
" inner hind-toe,		1
" outer hind-toe,		3
Circumference of the head, behind the ears,		10¼
" of body around the breast,	1	5
" " " loins,	1	10

Habits.

Next to the seals the Sea Otter may be ranked as an inhabitant of the great deep: it is at home in the salt waves of the ocean, frequently goes some distance from the "dull tame shore," and is sometimes hunted in sail-boats by the men who live by catching it, even out of sight of land.

But although capable of living almost at sea, this animal chiefly resorts to bays, the neighbourhood of islands near the coast, and tide-water rivers, where it can not only find plenty of food, but shelter or conceal itself as occasion requires.

It is a timid and shy creature, much disconcerted at the approach of danger, and when shot at, if missed, rarely allows the gunner a second chance to kill it.

Hunting the Sea Otter was formerly a favourite pursuit with the few sailors or stray Americans that lived on the shores of the Bay of San Francisco, but the more attractive search for gold drew them off to the mines when SUTTER's mill-race had revealed the glittering riches intermixed with its black sands. One of the shallops formerly used for catching the Sea Otter was observed by J. W. AUDUBON at Stockton, and is thus described by him: The boat was about twenty-eight feet long and eight feet broad, clinker built, and sharp at both ends like a whale-boat, which she may in fact have originally been, rigged with two lug sails, and looked like a fast craft. Whilst examining her the captain and owner came up to enquire whether he did not want to send some freight to Hawkins' Bar, but on finding that was not the object of his scrutiny, gave him the following account of the manner of hunting the Otter.

The boat was manned with four or five hands and a gunner, and sailed about all the bays, and to the islands even thirty or forty miles from the coast, and sometimes north or south three or four hundred miles in quest of these animals. On seeing an Otter the boat was steered quietly for it, sail being taken in to lessen her speed so as to approach gently and without alarming the game. When within short gun-shot, the marksman fires, the men spring to the oars, and the poor Otter is harpooned before it sinks by the bowsman. Occasionally the animals are sailed up to while they are basking on the banks, and they are sometimes caught in seines. The man who gave this information stated that he had known five Otters to be shot and captured in a day, and he had obtained forty dollars apiece for their skins. At the time J. W. AUDUBON was in California he was asked a hundred dollars for a Sea Otter skin, which high price he attributed to the gold discoveries.

Only one of these Otters was seen by J. W. AUDUBON whilst in California: it was in the San Joaquin river, where the bulrushes grew thickly on the banks all about. The party were almost startled at the sudden appearance of one, which climbed on to a drift log about a hundred yards above them. Three rifle balls were sent in an instant towards the unsuspecting creature, one of which striking near it, the alarmed animal slided into the water and sunk without leaving, so far as they could see, a single ripple. It remained below the surface for about a minute, and on coming up raised its head high above the water, and having seen nothing to frighten it, as they judged, began fishing. Its dives were made so gently that it was evidently as much at its ease in the water as a Grebe, and it frequently remained under the surface as long at least as the great northern diver or loon. They watched its movements some time, but could not see that it took a fish, although it dived eight or ten times. On firing another shot, the Otter appeared much frightened (possibly having been touched) and swimming rapidly, without diving, to the opposite shore, disappeared in the rushes, and they did not see it again.

In the accounts of this species given by various authors we find little respecting its habits, and it is much to be regretted that so remarkable an animal should be yet without a full "biography."

Sir JOHN RICHARDSON, who gives an excellent description of its fur from one who was engaged in the trade, says, "It seems to have more the manners of a seal than of the land Otter. It frequents rocks washed by the sea, and brings forth on land, but resides mostly in the water, and is occasionally seen very remote from the shore."

GODMAN states that "its food is various, but principally cuttle-fish, lobsters, and other fish. The Sea Otter, like most other animals which are plentifully supplied with food, is entirely harmless and inoffensive in its manners, and might be charged with stupidity, according to a common mode of judging animals, as it neither offers to defend itself nor to injure those who attack it. But as it runs very swiftly and swims with equal celerity it frequently escapes, and after having gone some distance turns back to look at its pursuers. In doing this it holds a fore-paw over its eyes, much in the manner we see done by persons who in a strong sunshine are desirous to observe a distant object accurately. It has been inferred that the sight of this animal is imperfect; its sense of smelling, however, is said to be very acute."

The latter part of the above paragraph at least, may be taken as a small specimen of the fabulous tales believed in olden times about animals of which little that was true had been learned.

Dr. GODMAN relates farther that the female Sea Otter brings forth on land after a pregnancy of eight or nine months, and but one at a birth, and states that the extreme tenderness and attachment she displays for her young are much celebrated. According to his account the flesh is eaten by the hunters, but while it is represented by some as being tender, juicy, and flavoured like young lamb, by others it is declared to be hard, insipid, and tough as leather. We advise such of our readers as may wish to decide which of these statements is correct, and who may be so fortunate as to possess the

Plate CXXXVI

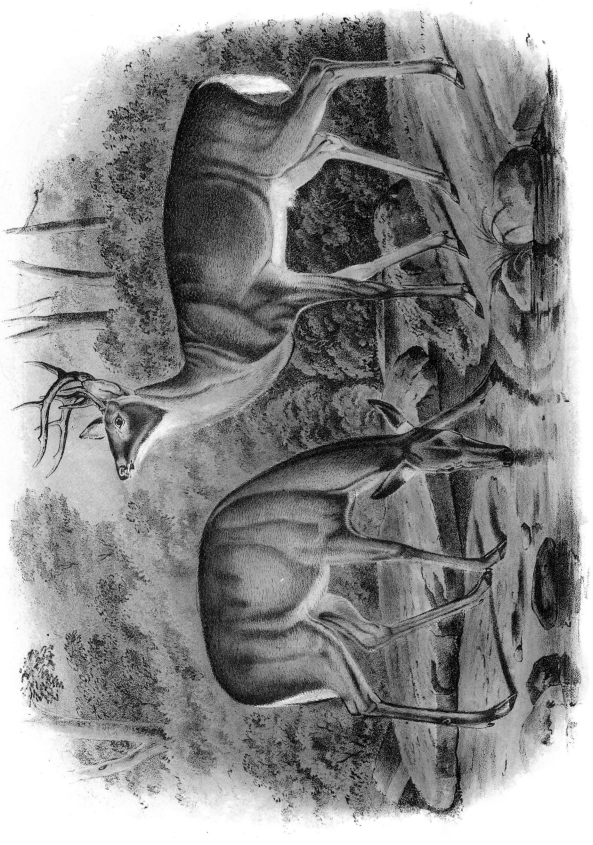

On Stone by J.T. Bowen.

Lith Printed & Colored by J. Bowen, Ph.

Drawn from Nature by J.W. Audubon.

Common or Virginian Deer.

means and leisure, to go to California and taste the animal—provided they can catch or kill one.

We will conclude our very meagre account of the habits of the Sea Otter by quoting the following most sensible remarks from Sir JOHN RICHARDSON, given in a note in the Fauna Boreali Americana, p. 60: "Not having been on the coasts where the Sea Otter is produced, I can add nothing to its history from my own observation, and I have preferred taking the description of the fur from one who was engaged in the trade, to extracting a scientific account of the animal from systematic works, which are in the hands of every naturalist."

Geographical Distribution.

The Sea Otter inhabits the waters which bound the northern parts of America and Asia, and separate those continents from each other, viz. the North Pacific Ocean and the various seas and bays which exist off either shore from Kamtschatka to the Yellow Sea on the Asiatic side, and from Allaska to California on the American.

General Remarks.

Although this animal has been known and hunted for more than a century, and innumerable skins of it have been carried to China (where they formerly brought a very high price), as well as to some parts of Europe, yet no good specimens, and but few perfect skulls of it, exist in any museum or private collection. The difference between the dentition of the young and the adult, being in consequence unknown, has misled many naturalists, and caused difficulties in the formation of the genus.

LINNÆUS, strangely enough, placed it among the martens (*Mustela*); ERXLEBEN, in the genus *Lutra*; FLEMING established for it a new genus (*Enhydra*); FISCHER in his synopsis endeavoured to bring this to the Greek (*Enydris*), which was also applied to it by LICHTENSTEIN.

The best generic descriptions of the Sea Otter that we have seen are those of the last named author, who has given two plates representing the skull and the teeth; the latter however were deficient in number, owing to the fact of his specimen being a young animal with its dentition incomplete. In the Philosophical Transactions (1796, No. 17) we have a description of the anatomy of this animal by EVERARD HOME and ARCHIBALD MENZIES, which gives a tolerable idea of its structure.

There are only two authors, so far as we are aware, who have given reliable accounts of the habits of the Sea Otter—STELLER and COOK. The information published by the former is contained in Nov. Com. Acad. Petropolit., vol. ii. p. 267, ann. 1751; the latter gives an account of the animal in his Third Voyage, vol. ii. p. 295.

Mustela Martes.—Linn.—Gmel.

Pine Marten.

Plate cxxxviii.—Male and Female.—Natural Size. Winter Pelage.

M. Magnitudine Putorio visone major, flavida, hic illic nigrescens, capite pallidiore, gulâ flavescente, cauda longa, floccosa, acuta.

Characters.

Larger than the mink; general colour, yellowish, blended with blackish in parts; head, lighter; throat yellow. Tail, long, bushy, and pointed.

Synonymes.

GENUS MUSTELA. Linn.
SUB-GENUS MUSTELA. Cuvier.
MUSTELA MARTES, Linn. Gmel., vol. i. p. 95.
PINE MARTEN. Pennant's Arctic Zoology, vol. i. p. 77.
MUSTELA MARTES. Sabine, Franklin's Journey, p. 651.
    "   Harlan, Fauna, p. 67.
    "   "   Godman, Nat. Hist., vol. i. p. 200.
    " ZIBELLINA (?). Godman, Nat. Hist., vol. i. p. 208.
    " MARTES. Rich., F. B. A., p. 51, summer specimen.
    " HURO. F. Cuv.
    " MARTES—AMERICAN SABLE. DeKay, Nat. Hist. State of New York, part i. p. 32, pl. 19, fig. 2, skull.

Description.

Head, long and pointed; ears, broad and obtusely pointed; legs rather long and tolerably stout; eyes, small and black; tail, bushy and cylindrical; toes, with long, slender, and compressed nails, nearly concealed by the hair. Hair, of two kinds—the outer long and rigid, the inner soft and somewhat woolly.

Colour.

This species varies a good deal in colour, so that it is difficult to find two specimens exactly alike; the under fur, however, does not differ as much in tint in different specimens as it does in fineness. Some individuals, particularly those captured in low latitudes, have much coarser fur than those from high northern regions or mountainous districts. The hair, which is about an inch and a quarter long, is of a pale dull grayish-brown from the roots outwards, dull yellowish-brown near the points, and is tipped with dark brown or black.

There is sometimes a considerable lustre in the fur of the Pine Marten; the hair on the tail is longer, coarser, and darker than that on the body, and the coat is darkest in winter; the yellowish-white markings on the throat vary in different individuals.

In the beginning of summer the dark-tipped hairs drop out, and the general colour of the fur is a pale orange brown, with little lustre; the tips of the ears, at all times lighter than the rest of the fur, become very pale in summer. The feet are generally darker coloured than the hair of the body. The tip of the nose is flesh coloured; eyes, black; nails, light brown.

Dimensions.

A winter-killed specimen, exceedingly poor.

		Foot.	Inches.
From point of nose to root of tail,	. . . .	1	5
Length of tail (vertebræ),	. . . .		7
" " (to end of hair),	. . . .		10
" fore-leg to end of longest nail,	. . . .		$5\frac{1}{4}$
" hind-foot from heel to end of claws,	. . . .		3
" ear on the outer surface,	. . . .		$1\frac{1}{4}$

We have measured larger specimens, 20, 21, and 22 inches from point of nose to root of tail.

Habits.

Let us take a share of the cunning and sneaking character of the fox, as much of the wide-awake and cautious habits of the weasel, a similar proportion of the voracity (and a little of the fetid odour) of the mink, and add thereto some of the climbing propensities of the raccoon, and we have a tolerable idea of the attributes of the little prowler of which we have just given the description and dimensions. The Pine Marten, as may be inferred from this compound, is shy, cruel, cunning, and active, and partakes of the habits of the predacious animals above mentioned, with the exception that it is not known to approach the residences of man like the fox, weasel, or mink, but rather keeps in dense woods where it can prey upon birds, their eggs and young, squirrels, the white-footed and other mice, shrews, wood-rats, &c., together with beetles and other insects, larvæ of different species, toads, frogs, lizards, water reptiles, and fish. It is also an eater of some kinds of berries and nuts (as we are informed), and is said to be fond of honey like the bear.

It has been supposed that the name Pine Marten was given to this animal because it inhabits the pine forests of the northern parts of this continent, and shows a preference for those trees, in the lofty tops of which it frequently resides. The Pine Marten, however, is often called the American Sable or the Sable, and in fact is more generally known to the country people of our northern States, and also to the furriers, by the latter name than by any other.

Sprightly and agile in its movements, the Pine Marten commonly procures abundance of food. It is prolific, bringing forth from six to eight young at a time, so that notwithstanding the value of its fur and the consequent pursuit of it during the proper season, it is still by no means a scarce animal. We have had several specimens sent to us by friends residing in the State of New York and in the wilder portions of our Canada frontier, which were procured among the woody hills of those districts.

Plate CXXXVII

N°. 28

Drawn from Nature by J W Audubon

Lith Printed & Col.d by J T Bowen. Philad

Sea Otter

According to Dr. DeKAY (New York Fauna, p. 33), this species is so active as to destroy great quantities of squirrels, the red squirrel (*Sciurus Hudsonius*) only escaping by its superior agility. Dr. GODMAN remarks that the "Pine Marten frequently has its den in the hollows of trees, but very commonly takes possession of the nest of some industrious squirrel, which it enlarges to suit its own convenience, after putting the builder to death."

Sir JOHN RICHARDSON says that "particular races of Martens, distinguished by the fineness and dark colour of their fur, appear to inhabit certain rocky districts." "A partridge's head, with the feathers, is the best bait for the log traps in which this animal is taken. It does not reject carrion, and often destroys the hoards of meat and fish laid up by the natives, when they have accidentally left a crevice by which it can enter. The Marten, when its retreat is cut off, shows its teeth, sets up its hair, arches its back, and makes a hissing noise like a cat. It will seize a dog by the nose and bite so hard, that unless the latter is accustomed to the combat, it suffers the little animal to escape."

The Indians sometimes eat the Pine Marten, but its flesh is rank and coarse. We have seen this species in confinement, when it appeared tolerably gentle, and had lost much of its snappish character.

The Pine Marten burrows in the ground at times, and the female brings forth her young in a fallen hollow log, a hole under rocks, or in a burrow, generally in April or May. These animals are chiefly caught with dead-falls baited with meat of any kind, birds, rabbits, squirrels, &c., and generally a hunter has many traps set, each of which he visits as often as once or twice a week. The Martens are sometimes devoured by larger animals after they have been caught. They are only trapped in the autumn and winter.

The fur of this species has been considered valuable, and when in fashion the skins were worth good prices. It is often palmed off on purchasers as fur of a more costly kind, and for this purpose is dyed any desired colour.

Geographical Distribution.

This species inhabits the wooded districts of the northern parts of America from the Atlantic to the Pacific in great numbers, and RICHARDSON remarks that it is particularly abundant where the trees have been killed by fire but are still standing. HEARNE observed that it is very rare in the district lying north of Churchill river, and east of Great Slave lake. PENNANT states that on the Asiatic side of Behring's straits, twenty-five degrees of longitude in breadth are equally unfrequented by the Marten, and for the same reason—the absence of trees.

The limit of its northern range in America is, like that of the woods, about the 68th degree of latitude. It is found in the hilly and wooded parts of the northern Atlantic States. We have seen specimens obtained from near Albany and from the Catskill Mountains, and it is also found in the northern parts of Pennsylvania. Its southern limit is about lat. 40°.

We have sought for it in vain in the mountains of Virginia, where notwithstanding, we think a straggler will occasionally make its appearance. On the eastern continent it inhabits all the north of Europe and Asia.

General Remarks.

Some American naturalists have expressed great doubts whether our American Marten is identical with that of the north of Europe, and have supposed that it might be designated under a separate specific name. We have not had an opportunity of comparing specimens from the two continents with each other, as we could find no museum in which specimens from both continents were contained. We have, however, examined and taken descriptions of them separately, and have been able to detect so little difference that we cannot regard them even as varieties.

It has been frequently asserted by hunters, that the true Sable exists in America; thus far, however, no specimen of that animal has been identified as coming from this country. Those that were shown to us under the name of Sables by furriers, we ascertained to be fine skins of a very dark colour of our common Pine Marten.

Spermophilus Macrourus.—Bennett.

Large-Tailed Spermophile.

Plate cxxxix.—Male.—Natural Size.

S. Magnitudine Sciurum cinereum adequans, vellere crassiusculo, in dorso lateribusque cinereo nigroque vario, cauda corporis longitudine, mediocriter comosa.

Characters.

Size of the cat-squirrel (Sciurus cinereus); *fur, rather coarse; body, mottled with black, and ashy white, forming irregular interrupted narrow transverse bars on the back and sides; tail, as long as the body, and moderately bushy.*

Synonymes

SPERMOPHILUS MACROURUS. Bennett, Proc. Zool. Soc., 1833, p. 41.
LONG-TAILED MARMOT. Zool. Soc. Catalogue, No. 456.
SCIURUS LUPTUS. Named in the Museum of the Jardin des Plantes, but not described.

Description.

This animal is shaped very much like a squirrel, although the ears are farther back in the head and the body is stouter than in that genus. Head, of moderate size, round, and elongated; nose, somewhat pointed; ears, large, broad, and ovate towards the points; feet, stout; nails, long, sharp, and considerably arched; tail, rounded, possessing none of the distichous arrangement of the tails of squirrels; tarsi, naked beneath; fur, moderately long, and rather coarse and harsh to the touch.

Colour.

Hairs of the back, blackish-gray at the base, annulated with white, or brownish-white, towards the tips, which are black; crown of the head, pure black; muzzle, rufous brown above, whitish on the sides; a narrow whitish space around the eyes; on the lower part of the cheeks and on the throat the hairs are brownish-white; cheeks, grizzled black and white; ears, internally covered with short hairs and partly coloured on the inner surface with dusky and soiled yellow; on the outside they are blackish-brown, becoming paler and grizzled towards the margins; feet, whitish, finely freckled with dusky markings, their general hue pale; tail, moderately bushy and sub-depressed; the hairs are long, varying from one and three quarters to two inches in length; they are of a brownish-white colour and are annulated by three broad black rings, the annulations nearest the apex of each hair considerably broader than the others. Upper and lower incisors, pale yellow; whiskers, black; claws, brown.

In the specimen here described the whole crown of the head is black, but we are informed by our friend WATERHOUSE that an imperfect skin of a second specimen which exists in the museum of the Zoological Society of London has the crown of the head gray.

Dimensions.

	Foot.	Inches.	Lines.
Length from point of nose to root of tail, ...	1	1	
" of tail (vertebræ), ...		7	9
" " (including hair), ...		10	
" from nose to ear, ...		2	5
Height of ear, ...			6
Heel to end of claws, ...		2	5
Length of nail of middle hind-toe, ...			$4\frac{1}{2}$
" fore-foot and nails, ...		1	6
" nail of middle toe of fore-foot, ...			$4\frac{1}{2}$

Habits.

Spermophilus Macrourus is an active and sprightly fellow, readily ascending trees on occasion, and feeding on nuts as well as seeds, roots and grasses.

This species is in some districts rather numerous, and when in the rainy season some of the low grounds are submerged, takes to the trees, and sometimes curious fights occur between it and the wood-peckers. Five or six of the latter will on observing the Spermophile, unite against him, and cutting about in the air, peck at him as they dart swiftly around the persecuted

Plate CXXXVIII

Drawn from Nature by J.W. Audubon

On Stone by W.E. Hitchcock

Lith. Printed & Col.d by J.T. Bowen, Phil.

Pine Marten

animal, which is lucky if a hollow into which he can retreat be near, and frequently indeed the wood-peckers' holes are entered by him, but the angry and noisy birds still keep up their cries and fly with fury at the hole, and although they can no longer peck the animal they keep him in a state of siege for a considerable time.

The origin of this anjmosity may be the fact of the Spermophile (as well as many kinds of squirrels) sometimes turning out the wood-peckers from their nests, an injury which unites them against the wrong-doer. By what process the birds are influenced to attack when the animal is not in their nests, nor even on a tree upon which they have built (or dug, we should say), we know not, but that the birds comprehend that union is strength is quite evident, and the Spermophile knows it too, for he always instantly tries to escape and conceal himself as soon as the vociferous cries of the first bird that observes him are heard, and before its neighbours called thereby to the fight can reach the spot.

We have not been able to ascertain how many young this Spermophile produces at a birth, nor at what season they are brought forth. It is seen on the plains and in localities where no trees grow, in which places it burrows or runs into holes in the rocks.

From our present information we are inclined to think that this species is sometimes in company with *S. Douglasii* in California, or at least inhabits the same districts.

Geographical Distribution.

This Spermophile exists in some portions of that part of Mexico which were traversed by J. W. AUDUBON on his way towards California, and is also found in the last named State.

General Remarks.

This species somewhat resembles *Spermophilus Douglasii*, but is a larger animal, the white patches over the shoulders moreover are wanting. The heel is hairy beneath, but the remaining part of the under surface of the foot is naked, whilst in *Spermophilus Douglasii* the whole foot is covered with hair beneath, up to the fleshy parts at the base of the toes.

Putorius Agilis.—Aud. and Bach.

Little Nimble Weasel.

Plate cxl.—Male and Female. Winter Pelage.

P. Magnitudine intermedius P. pusillum inter et P. fuscum; caudâ longâ, auriculis prominulis, æstate supra dilute fuscus, subtus albus, hyeme corpore toto caudaque niveis, cauda apice nigro.

Gharacters.

Intermediate in size between P. pusillus *and* P. fuscus; *tail, long; ears, prominent. Colour, in summer, light brown above, white beneath; in winter, body and tail, pure white, except the tip of the latter, which is broadly tipped with black.*

Description.

This hitherto undescribed species is light, slender, and graceful, with well proportioned limbs, giving evidence of activity and sprightliness; it may be termed a miniature of the ermine; it stands proportionately higher on its legs, and although the smaller animal of the two, has the most prominent ears; the hair is softer and shorter, both in summer and winter, than in either the ermine or Brown Weasel (*P. fuscus*); whiskers, numerous but rather short. Head, moderate; skull, broad; nose, short and rather pointed; feet, small; nails, partially concealed by the hair on the feet; tail, long, covered with fur to within one and three quarters of an inch of the end, where it terminates in long straight smooth hairs.

Colour.

In summer: Head, ears, neck, outer surface of thighs, all the upper portions of the back, and the tail on both surfaces to near the tip, light brown, which is the colour of the hair from the roots to the tips; end of the tail, black; chin, throat, chest, belly, and inner side of thighs, white; the brown colour extends far down on the sides and flanks, leaving a rather narrow stripe of white beneath, which is broadest on the neck; the line of demarcation between the upper and under colours on the sides is distinctly but somewhat irregularly drawn. All the feet are brown; whiskers and nails, dark brown; teeth, white.

In winter: Pure white on the whole body, and for about three inches on the tail; tip of the tail, black for an inch and three quarters; tip of nose, flesh colour; whiskers, mostly white, a few black.

Dimensions.

	Inches.
Point of nose to root of tail, ...	$8\frac{1}{2}$
Length of tail (vertebræ), ...	$3\frac{3}{4}$
" " (to end of hair), ...	$4\frac{3}{4}$
Point of nose to ear, ...	$1\frac{1}{4}$
Height of ear externally, ...	$\frac{1}{4}$

Habits.

We preserved a specimen of this little animal during several months in the winter, forty years ago, in the northern part of New York; it had been captured in a box trap, which was set near its hole in a pine forest, whither we had tracked it on the snow, believing from its small foot-prints that it was some unknown species of Rodentia. What was our surprise when on the following morning we discovered the eyes of this little marauder prying through the crevices of the trap. Supposing it to be a young ermine we preserved it through the winter, under the impression that it would become tame, and increasing in size, attain its full growth by the following spring; we were, however, disappointed in our expectations; it continued wild and cross, always printing on our gloves the form of the cutting edges of its teeth whenever we placed our hand within the box. It concealed itself in its nest, in a dark corner of the cage, during the whole day, and at night was constantly rattling and gnawing at the wires in the endeavour to effect its escape. We fed it on small birds, which it carried to its dark retreat and devoured greedily.

Having placed a common Weasel, twice the size of our animal, in the cage with it, the ermine immediately attacked our little fellow, which ensconced itself in a corner at the back of the cage, where with open mouth and angry eyes, uttering a hissing spitting or sputtering noise, he drew back his lips and showed his sharp teeth in defiance of his opponent.

To relieve him from a troublesome eompanion we removed the ermine. Towards spring we placed a Norway rat in his cage in order to test his courage. The rat and the Weasel retreated to opposite corners and eyed each other during the whole day; on the following morning we found the rat had been killed; but the Weasel was so much wounded that he died before evening.

We have no other information in regard to the habits of this Weasel. Its burrow, the entrance to which was very small, and without any hillock of earth at its borders, was situated in a high ridge of pine land.

We have no doubt that, like the ermine, in prowling about it finds its way into the retreats of the meadow-mouse, the little chipping squirrel, and other small animals, for although the rat above mentioned was too formidable an opponent, we are confident it could easily have mastered the little *Tamias Lysteri.*

Geographical Distribution.

We have only observed this Weasel in the northern part of the State of New York, but the specimens from which we drew our figures were procured by Mr. J. G. BELL in Rockland county in that State.

Plate CXXXIX

Nº 28

On Stone by W.E. Hitchcock

Drawn from Nature by J.W. Audubon

Lith Printed & Col.d by J.T. Bowen, Phil.

Large - tailed Spermophile

Ursus Americanus.—Pallas.

American Black Bear.

Plate cxli.—Male and Female.

U. Naso fere in eadem linea cum fronte, convexiore quam in U. feroce; plantis palmisque brevissimis, colore nigro vel fuscescente-nigro, lateribus rostri fulvis.

Characters.

Nose, nearly in a line with the forehead, more arched than in Ursus ferox; *palms and soles of the feet, very short; colour, black, or brownish-black; there is a yellowish patch on each side of the nose.*

Synonymes.

BLACK BEAR. Pennant, Arctic Zoology, p. 57, and Introduction, p. 120.
"   "   Pennant's History of Quadrupeds, vol. ii. p. 11.
"   "   Warden's United States, vol. i. p. 195.
URSUS AMERICANUS. Pallas, Spicil. Zool., vol. xiv. pp. 6–24.
"   "   Harlan, Fauna, p. 51.
"   "   Godman's Natural History, vol. i. p. 194.
"   "   Rich., Fauna Boreali Americana, p. 14.
"   "   DeKay, Nat. Hist. State of New York, p. 24, pl. 6, fig. 1.

Description.

The Black Bear is commonly smaller than the Grizzly Bear. Body and legs, thick and clumsy in appearance; head, short, and broad where it joins the neck; nose, slightly arched, and somewhat pointed; eyes, small, and close to each other; ears, high, oval, and rounded at the tips; palms and soles of the feet, short when compared with those of the Grizzly Bear; the hairs of the feet project slightly beyond the claws; tail, very short; claws, short, blunt, and somewhat incurved; fur, long, straight, shining, and rather soft.

Colour.

Cheeks, yellow, which colour extends from the tip of the nose on both sides of the mouth to near the eye; in some individuals there is a small spot of the same tint in front of the eye, and in others a white line commencing on the nose reaches to each side of the angle of the mouth; in a few specimens this white line continues over the cheek to a large white space mixed with a slight fawn colour, covering the whole of the throat, whence a narrow line of the fawn colour descends upon the breast. The hairs on the whole body are in most specimens glossy black; in some we examined they were brown, while a few of the skins we have seen were light brown or dingy yellow. From this last mentioned variety doubtless originated the names Cinnamon Bear, Yellow Bear of Carolina, &c. The outer edges of the ears are brownish-black; eyes and nails, black.

Dimensions.

A very large specimen.

	Feet.	Inches.
From nose to root of tail,	6	5
Height to top of shoulder,	3	1

A larger Bear than the above may sometimes be captured, but the general size is considerably less.

Habits.

The Black Bear, however clumsy in appearance, is active, vigilant, and persevering, possesses great strength, courage, and address, and undergoes with little injury the greatest fatigues and hardships in avoiding the pursuit of the hunter. Like the deer it changes its haunts with the seasons, and for the same reason, viz. the desire of obtaining suitable food, or of retiring to the more inaccessible parts, where it can pass the time in security, unobserved by man, the most dangerous of its enemies.

During the spring months it searches for food in the low rich alluvial lands that border the rivers, or by the margins of such inland lakes as, on account of their small size, are called by us ponds. There it procures abundance of succulent roots and tender juicy plants, upon which it chiefly feeds at that season. During the summer heat, it enters the gloomy swamps, passes much of its time in wallowing in the mud like a hog, and contents itself with crayfish, roots, and nettles, now and then seizing on a pig, or perhaps a sow, a calf, or even a full-grown cow. As soon as the different kinds of berries which grow on the mountains begin to ripen, the Bears betake themselves to the high grounds, followed by their cubs.

In retired parts of the country, where the plantations are large and the population sparse, it pays visits to the corn-fields, which it ravages for a while. After this, the various species of nuts, acorns, grapes, and other forest fruits, that form what in the western States in called *mast*, attract its attention. The Bear is then seen rambling singly through the woods to gather this harvest, not forgetting, meanwhile, to rob every *bee-tree* it meets with, Bears being expect at this operation.

The Black Bear is a capital climber, and now and then *houses* itself in the hollow trunk of some large tree for weeks together during the winter, when it is said to live by sucking its paws.

At one season, the Bear may be seen examining the lower part of the trunk of a tree for several minutes with much attention, at the same time looking around, and snuffing the air. It then rises on its hind-legs, approaches the trunk, embraces it with the fore-legs, and scratches the bark with its teeth and claws for several minutes in continuance. Its jaws clash against each other until a mass of foam runs down on both sides of the mouth. After this it continues its rambles.

The female Black Bear generally brings forth two cubs at a time, although, as we have heard, the number is sometimes three or four. The period of gestation is stated to be from six to seven weeks, but is mentioned as one hundred days by some authors. When born the young are exceedingly small, and if we may credit the accounts of hunters with whom we have conversed on the subject, are not larger than kittens. They are almost invariably brought forth in some well concealed den, or great hollow tree, and so cautions is the dam in selecting her place of accouchment, that it is extremely difficult to discover it, and consequently very rarely that either the female or her cubs are seen until the latter have obtained a much larger size than when born, are able to follow their dam, and can climb trees with facility.

Most writers on the habits of this animal have stated that the Black Bear does not eat animal food from choice, and never unless pressed by hunger. This we consider a great mistake, for in our experience we have found the reverse to be the case, and it is well known to our frontier farmers that this animal is a great destroyer of pigs, hogs, calves, and sheep, for the sake of which we have even known it to desert the pecan groves in Texas. At the same time, as will have been seen by our previous remarks, its principal food generally consists of berries, roots, and other vegetable substances. It is very fond also of fish, and during one of our expeditions to Maine and New Brunswick, we found the inhabitants residing near the coast unwilling to eat the flesh of the animal on account of its fishy taste. In our western forests, however, the Bear feeds on so many nuts and well tasted roots and berries, that its meat is considered a great delicacy, and in the city of New York we have generally found its market price three or four times more than the best beef per pound. The fore-paw of the Bear when cooked presents a striking resemblance to the hand of a child or young person, and we have known some individuals to be hoaxed by its being represented as such.

Perhaps the most acrid vegetable eaten by the Bear is the Indian turnip (*Arum triphyllum*), which is so pungent that we have seen people almost distracted by it, when they had inadvertently put a piece in their mouth.

The Black Bear is a remarkably swift runner when first alarmed, although it is generally "treed," that is, forced to ascend a tree, when pursued by dogs and hunters on horseback. We were, not very long since, when on an expedition in the mountains of Virginia, leisurely making our way along a road through the forest after a long hunt for deer and turkeys, with our gun thrown behind our shoulders and our arms resting on each end of it, when, although we had been assured there were no Bears in that neighbourhood, we suddenly perceived one above us on a little acclivity at one side of the road, where it was feeding, and nearly concealed by the bushes. The bank was only about fifteen feet high, and the Bear not more than twenty paces from us, so we instantly disengaged our gun, and cocking both barrels, expected to "fill our bag" at one shot, but at the instant and before we could fire, the Bear, with a celerity that astonished us, disappeared. We rushed up and bank and found the land on the top nearly level for a long distance before us, and neither very thickly wooded nor very bushy; but no Bear was to be seen, although our eye could penetrate the woods for at least two hundred yards. After the first disappointing glance around, we thought Bruin might have mounted a tree, but such was not the case, as on

Plate CXI

N°28

Drawn from Nature by J W Audubon

On stone by W E Hitchcock

Lith & Printed & Col⁴ by J T Bowen, Philad⁴

Little Nimble Weasel

looking everywhere nothing could be seen of his black body, and we were obliged to conclude that he had run out of sight in the brief space of time we occupied in ascending the little bank.

As we were once standing at the foot of a large sycamore tree on the borders of a long and deep pond, on the edge of which, in our rear, there was a thick and extensive "cane-brake," we heard a rushing roaring noise, as if some heavy animal was bearing down and passing rapidly through the canes, directly towards us. We were not kept long in suspense, for in an instant or two, a large Bear dashed out of the dense cane, and plunging into the pond without having even seen us, made off with considerable speed through the water towards the other shore. Having only bird-shot in our gun we did not think it worth while to call his attention to us by firing at him, but turned to the cane-brake, expecting to hear either dogs or men approaching shortly. No further noise could be heard, however, and the surrounding woods were as still as before this adventure. We supposed the Bear had been started at some distance, and that his pursuers, not being able to follow him through the almost impenetrable canes, had given up the hunt.

Being one night sleeping in the house of a friend who was a Planter in the State of Louisiana, we were awakened by a servant bearing a light, who gave us a note, which he said his master had just received. We found it to be a communication from a neighbour, requesting our host and ourself to join him as soon as possible, and assist in killing some Bears at that moment engaged in destroying his corn. We were not long in dressing, and on entering the parlour, found our friend equipped. The overseer's horn was heard calling up the negroes. Some were already saddling our horses, whilst others were gathering all the cur-dogs of the plantation. All was bustle. Before half an hour had elapsed, four stout negro men, armed with axes and knives, and mounted on strong nags, were following us at a round gallop through the woods, as we made directly for the neighbour's plantation.

The night was none of the most favourable, a drizzling rain rendering the atmosphere thick and rather sultry; but as we were well acquainted with the course, we soon reached the house, where the owner was waiting our arrival. There were now three of us armed with guns, half a dozen servants, and a good pack of dogs of all kinds. We jogged on towards the detached field in which the Bears were at work. The owner told us that for some days several of these animals had visited his corn, and that a negro who was sent every afternoon to see at what part of the enclosure they entered, had assured him there were at least five in the field that night. A plan of attack was formed: the bars at the usual entrance of the field were to be put down without noise; the men and dogs were to divide, and afterwards proceed so as to surround the Bears, when, at the sounding of our horns, every one was to charge towards the centre of the field, and shout as loudly as possible, which it was judged would so intimidate the animals as to induce them to seek refuge upon the deal trees with which the field was still partially covered.

The plan succeeded: the horns sounded, the horses galloped forward, the men shouted, the dogs barked and howled. The shrieks of the negroes were enough to frighten a legion of bears, and by the time we reached the middle of the field we found that several had mounted the trees, and having lighted fires, we now saw them crouched at the junction of the larger branches with the trunks. Two were immediately shot down. They were cubs of no great size, and being already half dead, were quickly dispatched by the dogs.

We were anxious to procure as much sport as possible, and having observed one of the Bears, which from its size we conjectured to be the mother of the two cubs just killed, we ordered the negroes to cut down the tree on which it was perched, when it was intended the dogs should have a tug with it, while we should support them, and assist in preventing the Bear from escaping, by wounding it in one of the hind-legs. The surrounding woods now echoed to the blows of the axemen. The tree was large and tough, having been girded more than two years, and the operation of felling it seemed extremely tedious. However, at length it began to vibrate at each stroke; a few inches along now supported it, and in a short time it came crashing to the ground.

The dogs rushed to the charge, and harassed the Bear on all sides, whilst we surrounded the poor animal. As its life depended upon its courage and strength, it exercised both in the most energetic manner. Now and then it seized a dog and killed him by a single stroke. At another time, a well administered blow of one of its fore-legs sent an assailant off, yelping so piteously that he might be looked upon as *hors du combat*. A cur had daringly ventured to seize the Bear by the snout, and was seen hanging to it, covered with blood, whilst several others scrambled over its back. Now and then the infuriated animal was seen to cast a revengeful glance at some of the party, and we had already determined to dispatch it, when, to our astonishment, it suddenly shook off all the dogs, and before we could fire, charged upon one of the negroes, who was mounted on a pied horse. The Bear seized the steed with teeth and claws, and clung to its breast. The terrified horse snorted and

plunged. The rider, an athletic young man and a capital horseman, kept his seat, although only saddled on a sheep-skin tightly girthed, and requested his master not to fire at the Bear. Notwithstanding his coolness and courage, our anxiety for his safety was raised to the highest pitch, especially when in a moment we saw rider and horse come to the ground together; but we were instantly relieved on witnessing the masterly manner in which SCIPIO dispatched his adversary, by laying open his skull with a single well directed blow of his axe, when a deep growl announced the death of the Bear.

In our country no animal, perhaps, has been more frequently the theme of adventure or anecdote than the Bear, and in some of our southwestern States it is not uncommon to while away the winter evenings with Bear stories that are not only interesting on account of the traits of the habits of the animal with which they are interspersed, but from the insight they afford the listener into the characteristics of the bold and hardy huntsmen of those parts.

In the State of Maine the lumbermen (wood-cutters) and the farmers set guns to kill this animal, which are arranged in this way: A funnel-shaped space about five feet long is formed by driving strong sticks into the ground in two converging lines, leaving both the ends open, the narrow end being wide enough to admit the muzzle of an old musket, and the other extremity so broad as to allow the head and shoulders of the Bear to enter. The gun is then loaded and fastened securely so as to deliver its charge facing the wide end of the enclosure. A round and smooth stick is now placed behind the stock of the gun, and a cord leading from the trigger passed around it, the other end of which, with a piece of meat or a bird tied to it (an owl is a favourite bait), is stretched in front of the gun, so far that the Bear can reach the bait with his paw. Upon his pulling the meat towards him, the string draws the trigger and the animal is instantly killed.

On the coast of Labrador we observed the Black Bear catching fish with great dexterity, and the food of these animals in that region consisted altogether of the fishes they seized in the edge of the water inside the surf. Like the Polar Bear, the present species swims with ease and rapidity, and it is a difficult matter to catch a full grown Bear with a skiff, and a dangerous adventure to attempt its capture in a canoe, which it could easily upset.

We were once enjoying a fine autumnal afternoon on the shores of the beautiful Ohio, with two acquaintances who had accompanied us in quest of some swallows that had built in a high sandy bank, when we observed three hunters about the middle of the river in a skiff, vigorously rowing, the steersman paddling too, with all his strength, in pursuit of a Bear which, about one hundred and fifty yards ahead of them, was cleaving the water and leaving a widening wake behind him on its unrippled surfaces as he made for the shore, directly opposite to us. We all rushed down to the water at this sight, and launching a skiff we then kept for fishing, hastily put off to intercept the animal, which we hoped to assist in capturing. Both boats were soon nearing the Bear, and we, standing in the bow of our skiff, commenced the attack by discharging a pistol at his head. At this he raised one paw, brushed it across his forehead, and then seemed to redouble his efforts. Repeated shots from both boats were now fired at him, and we ran alongside, thinking to haul his carcase triumphantly on board; but suddenly, to our dismay, he laid both paws on the gunwale of the skiff, and his great weight brought the side for an instant under water, so that we expected the boat would fill and sink. There was no time to be lost: we all threw our weight on to the other side, to counterpoise that of the animal, and commenced a pell-mell battery on him with the oars and a boat-hook; the men in the other boat also attacked him, and driving the bow of their skiff close to his head, one of them laid his skull open with an axe, which killed him instanter. We jointly hurraed, and tying a rope round his neck, towed him ashore behind our boats.

The Black Bear is very tenacious of life, and like its relative, the Grizzly Bear, is dangerous when irritated or wounded. It makes large beds of leaves and weeds or grasses, in the fissures of rocks, or sleeps in hollow logs, when no convenient den can be found in its neighbourhood; it also makes lairs in the thick cane-brakes and deep swamps, and covers itself with a heap of leaves and twigs, like a wild sow when about to litter.

The skin of the Black Bear is an excellent material for sleigh-robes, hammer-cloths, caps, &c., and makes a comfortable bed for the backwoodsman or Indian; and the grease procured from this species is invaluable to the hair-dresser, being equal if not superior to

"Thine incomparable oil Macassar!"

which we (albeit unacquainted with the mode of preparing it) presume to be a compound much less expensive to the manufacturer than would be the "genuine real Bear's grease"—not of the shops, but of the prairies and western woods.

N° 29

Plate CXLI

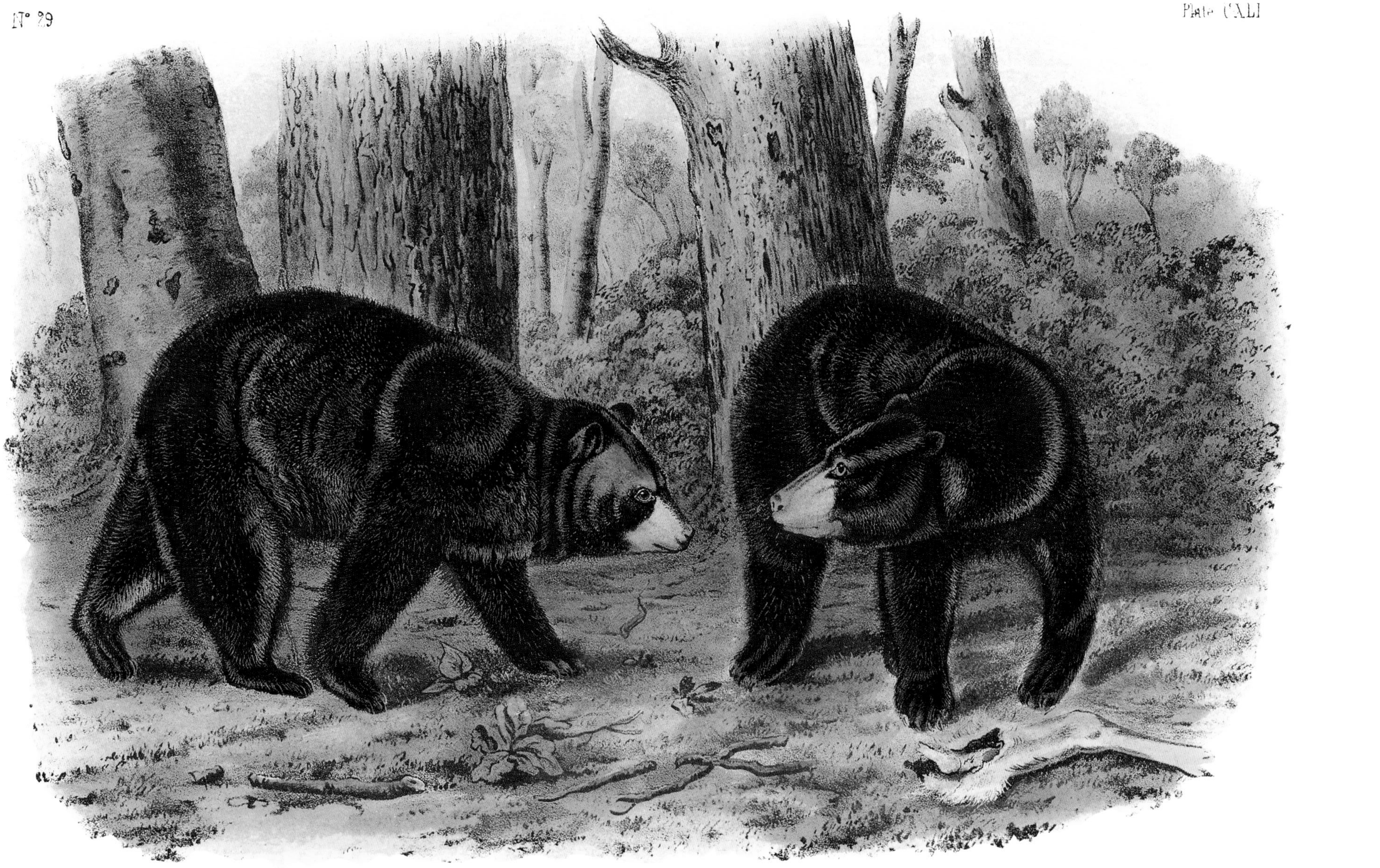

American Black Bear

The Black Bear is rather docile when in confinement, and a "pet" Bear is occasionally seen in various parts of the country. In our large cities, however, where civilization (?) is thought to have made the greatest advances, this animal is used to amuse the gentlemen of the fancy, by putting its strength and "pluck" to the test, in combat with bull-dogs or mastiffs. When the Bear has not been so closely imprisoned as to partially destroy his activity, these encounters generally end with the killing of one or more dogs; but occasionally the dogs overpower him, and he is rescued for the time by his friends, to "fight (again) some other day."

We are happy to say, however, that Bear-baiting and bull-baiting have not been as yet fully naturalized amongst us, and are only popular with those who, perhaps, in addition to the natural desire for excitement, have the hope and intention of winning money, to draw them to such cruel and useless exhibitions.

Among the many Bear stories that have been published in the newspapers, and which, whether true or invented, are generally interesting, the following is one of the latest, the substance of which we will give, as nearly as we can recollect it:

A young man in the State of Maine, whilst at work in a field, accompanied only by a small body, was attacked by a Bear which suddenly approached from the edge of the forest, and quite unexpectedly fell upon him with great fury. Almost at the first onset the brute overthrew the young farmer, who fell to the ground on his back, with the Bear clutching him, and biting his arm severely. Nothing but the utmost presence of mind could have saved the young man, as he was unarmed with the exception of a knife, which he could not get out of his pocket owing to the position in which he had fallen. Perceiving that his chance of escape was desperate, he rammed his hand and arm so far down the throat of the Bear as to produce the effect of partial strangulation, and whilst the beast became faint from consequent loss of breath, called to the boy to come and hand him the knife. The latter bravely came to the rescue, got the knife, opened it, and gave it to him, when he succeeded in cutting the Bear's throat, and with the exception of a few severe bites, and some lacerations from the claws of the animal, was not very much injured. The Bear was carried next day in triumph to a neighbouring village, and weighed over four hundred pounds.

Such assaults are, however, exceedingly rare, and it is seldom that even a wounded Bear attacks man.

Captain J. P. McCOWN has furnished us with the following remarks: "In the mountains of Tennessee the Bear lives principally upon mast and fruits. It is also fond of a bee-tree, and is often found seeking even a wasp's or yellow-jacket's nest. In the autumn the Bear is hunted when 'lopping' for chesnuts. Lopping consists in breaking off the branches by the Bear to procure the mast before it falls. When pursued by the dogs the Bear sometimes backs up against a tree, when it exhibits decided skill as a boxer, all the time looking exceedingly good-natured; but woe to the poor dog that ventures within its reach!

"The dogs generally employed for pursuing the Bear are curs and fice, as dogs of courage are usually killed or badly injured, while the cur will attack the Bear behind, and run when he turns upon him. No number of dogs can kill a Bear unless assisted by man.

"In 1841, the soldier of my regiment had a pet he-Bear (castrated) that was exceedingly gentle and playful with the men. It becoming necessary to sell or kill it, one of the soldiers led it down the streets of Buffalo and exposed it for sale. Of course it attracted a large crowd, and was bid for on all sides on account of its gentleness. But unfortunately Bruin was carried near a hogshead of sugar, and not disposed to lose so tempting a repast, quietly upset it, knocking out the head, and commenced helping himself in spite of the soldier's efforts to prevent the depredation. The owner of the sugar rushed out and kicked the Bear, which, not liking such treatment, gave in return for the assault made upon him, a blow that sent his assailant far into the street, to the terror of the crowd, which scattered, leaving him to satisfy his appetite for sugar unmolested."

The number of Black Bears is gradually decreasing in the more settled parts of the "back woods," but in some portions of Carolina and Georgia, where the vast swamps prevent any attempt to settle or cultivate the land, they have within a few years been on the increase, and have become destroyers of the young stock of the Planter (which generally range through the woods) to a considerable extent.

Sir JOHN RICHARDSON says that when resident in the fur countries this Bear almost invariably hibernates, and that about one thousand skins are annually procured by the Hudson's Bay Company from those that are destroyed in their winter retreats. "It generally selects a spot for its den under a fallen tree, and having scratched away a portion of the soil, retires to it at the commencement of a snow-storm, when the snow soon furnishes it with a close, warm covering. Its breath makes a small opening in the den, and the quantity of hoar-frost which occasionally gathers round the aperture serves to betray its retreat to the hunter."

The Black Bear is somewhat migratory, and in hard winters is found to move southwardly in considerable numbers, although not in company. They couple in September or October, after which the females retire to their dens before the setting in or very cold weather.

It is said that the males do not so soon resort to winter quarters as the females, and require some time after the love season to recover their lost fat. The females bring forth about the beginning of January.

The Indian tribes have many superstitions concerning the Bear, and it is with some of them necessary to go through divers ceremonies before proceeding to hunt the animal.

Geographical Distribution.

The Black Bear has been found throughout North America in every wooded district from the north through all the States to Mexico, but has not hitherto been discovered in California, where it appears to be replaced by the Grizzly Bear (*Ursus ferox*).

General Remarks.

This species was in the early stages of natural history regarded as identical with the Black Bear of Europe. PALLAS first described it as a distinct animal, since which its specific name has remained undisturbed; its varieties have however produced much speculation, and it has frequently been supposed, and not without some reason, that the Brown Bear of our western country was a species differing from the Black Bear.

In order to arrive at a correct conclusion on this subject we must be guided less by colour than by the form and structure of the animal and its length of heel and claws; it is evident that the size can afford us no clue whereby to designate the species, inasmuch as some individuals may be found that are nearly double the dimensions of others.

Pseudostoma Borealis. —Rich. MSS.

The Camas Rat.

Plate cxlii. Male, Female, and Young.—Natural Size.

P. Ex cinereo fulvus, cauda longa pilosa; P. bursario minor, et gracilior, dentibus unguibusque minoribus.

Characters.

Smaller and of more delicate form than Pseudostoma bursarius, *and teeth and claws much smaller. Tail, long, and clothed with hair. Colour, pale yellowish-gray.*

Synonymes.

GEOMYS BOREALIS. Rich., MSS.

PSEUDOSTOMA BOREALIS. Bach., Jour. Acad. Nat. Sciences Philadelphia, vol. viii. part 1, p. 103.
GEOMYS TOWNSENDII. Rich., MSS.

Description.

Head, of moderate size; ears, consisting of a small round opening margined by an elevated ridge, the highest portion of which is the posterior part, and is about one line in height. The ears not hidden by the fur, but distinctly visible. Body, moderately thick; claws of the fore-feet, slender and rather long; incisors, rather long (but not large for the genus); the upper ones have each a slight longitudinal groove situated close to the inner margin. Tip of nose, naked; feet, bare beneath; inner toe of fore-feet, rather short, outer next in length, middle longest, and the toes on either side of the central one about equal; there is a long brush of stiff white hairs on the inner side of the inner toe. On the hind-feet the central toe is longest, outer toes equal and short. Tail, hairy.

Plate CXLII

Drawn from Nature by J.W Audubon.

On Stone by Wm E. Hitchcock

Lith. Printed & Cold by J.T Bowen, Philada

The Camas Rat

Colour.

General colour, pale gray, the upper parts more or less washed with yellow; inside of pouches, under surface of body, feet, and tail, white. Hairs of the body, dark slate colour at the roots. There is a dusky spot behind the ears; incisors, yellow; claws, white; tail, above, grayish, tinged with yellow.

Dimensions.

	Inches.	Lines.
From nose to root of tail,	7	6
Tail,	2	
Tarsus and claws,	1	1½
Central claw of fore-foot,		5
Nose to ear,	1	6½

The above description was made from three specimens of this pouched Sand-rat, obtained by the late Mr. TOWNSEND, on the Columbia river, two of which appeared to be in summer pelage, and the third in its autumnal coat.

Description of another specimen sent by Mr. TOWNSEND, marked in RICHARDSON's MSS. as *Geomys Townsendii*:

Form and size of the animal, nearly the same as in the specimens just described, with the exception of the tail, which is considerably longer. General colour, very pale gray above, with a faint yellowish wash; end of nose, dusky gray; under parts, grayish-white; chin, pure white; tail and feet, white, the former grayish above. Hairs of the back, very pale gray at the roots, pale yellow near the tips, the extreme points cinereous. Teeth, yellowish-white; upper incisors, with a faint groove near the internal margin. Claws and fore-feet, moderate white.

Dimensions.

	Inches.	Lines.
From nose to tail,	7	6
Tail,	2	9
Tarsus,	1	3½
Central claw of fore-foot,		5
Nose to ear,	1	5

Habits.

The Camas Rat derives its name, according to RICHARDSON, from its fondness for the bulbous root of the quamash or camas plant (*Scilla esculenta*).

Like all the pouched Rats of America, it feeds upon nuts, roots, seeds, and grasses, and makes burrows, extending long distances, but not very far beneath the surface of the ground, throwing up mole-hills in places as it comes to the surface. These animals are generally found to be in a certain degree gregarious, or at least a good many of them inhabiting the same locality, and more or less associated together; and are said to be very common on the plains of the Multnomah river.

Mr. DOUGLAS informed Sir JOHN RICHARDSON that they may be easily snared in the summer.

We believe that some of the Indians of those parts of Oregon in which this burrowing Rat exists eat them, but have no information concerning the peculiarities they exhibit, the number of young they produce at a time, or the depredations they commit on the fields and gardens of the settlers.

In the Fauna Boreali Americana (p. 206), this pouched Rat (if we are not mistaken), is given as *Diplostoma bulbivorum*—Camas Rat—and under the impression that that name applies to our present animal, we have made the above remarks in relation to it.

Geographical Distribution.

Specimens were obtained both by DOUGLAS and DRUMMOND, about the same period of time, in the vicinity of the Columbia river in Oregon.

General Remarks.

On a visit to Europe we carried with us three specimens of pouched Sand-Rats, which we regarded as belonging to the same species, but being male, female, and young. Our object was to compare them with specimens taken from this country at the north and west by RICHARDSON, DOUGLAS, DRUMMOND, and other naturalists. RICHARDSON kindly showed us a specimen brought from the Columbia river by DOUGLAS, which, as we thought, appeared to be of the same species as our own. As he was then preparing a monograph of this perplexing genus, we requested him to describe the species, and add it to his monograph; he consequently gave it the above name. He however called another specimen which we had carried with us, *Geomys Townsendii*. We think his monograph was never published.

We have united what he considered two species—*Geomys Borealis* and *G. Townsendii*—into one, having added the latter as a synonyme; and we have rejected *Diplostoma* as a genus, not only because we conceive the characters on which it is founded to be the result of an unnatural disposition of the pouches in the dried skins, but for the reason mentioned above, viz., that we consider the so-called *Diplostoma bulbivorum* to be identical, with the animal we have just described as *Pseudostoma borealis*, although the description given by RICHARDSON has apparently no reference to the latter, but on the contrary describes his *Diplostoma* as having the true mouth *vertical* (?). He says: "The lips, which in fact are right and left, and not upper and under," &c. Besides, in the beginning of his article he mentions that the skull is wanting. We think we may therefore reasonably presume, that although the skin had been so twisted and disfigured by putting it into an unnatural form that the appellation which Mr. DOUGLAS gave it, as "the animal known on the banks of the Columbia by the name of the *Camas Rat*," did not seem to apply to it, we shall be right in rejecting both the generic and specific names given by our friend Sir JOHN RICHARDSON to so very imperfect a specimen, and in believing that the skin was in reality (although much injured and distorted) nothing but the Camas Rat, as DOUGLAS called it.

Pteromys Sabrinus.—Pennant.

Severn River Flying-Squirrel.

Plate cxliii.—Fig. 1.—Natural Size.

P. Magnitudine P. volucellum tertia parte excedens; caudâ corpore curtiore, patagio lumbari pone carpum in lobum rotundatum excurrente, colore flavescente-cano obscuriore inumbrato.

Characters.

One third larger than P. volucella; tail, shorter than the body; flying membrane having a small rounded projection behind the wrist. Colour, dull yellow gray, irregularly marked with darker.

Synonymes.

GREATER FLYING-SQUIRREL. Forster, Philos. Trans., vol. lxii. p. 379.
SEVERN RIVER FLYING-SQUIRREL. Pennant, Hist. Quad., vol. ii.
               p. 153.

"   "   " Arctic Zoology, vol. i.
               p. 122.
SCIURUS HUDSONIUS. Gmel., Syst., vol. i. p. 153.
"   SABRINUS. Shaw, Zool., vol. ii., part 1, p. 157.
PTEROMYS SABRINUS. Rich., Zool. Jour., No. 12, p. 519.
"   "   " F. B. A., p. 193.

Description.

Head, short and somewhat rounded; nose, short and obtuse; eyes, large; flying membrane, extending from the wrist to the middle of the hind-leg, nearly straight, having only a slight rounded projection close to the wrist; tail, depressed, slightly convex on its upper surface, but quite flat, or even somewhat concave, beneath; it is broadest about an inch from the body, and then tapers gradually but every slightly towards the extremity, which is rounded; the flattened form of the tail, and its distichous arrangement, is given to it in consequence of the fur on its sides being much longer than that on its upper surface; the extremities are small; the fore-legs connected with the flying membrane down to the wrist; the feet are hairy both above and below. There are four short toes on the fore-feet, and the claws are small, compressed, curved, and sharp pointed; under their roots there is a compressed callous

Fig. 1. *Severn River Flying Squirrel.*

Fig. 2. *Rocky Mountain Flying Squirrel.*

Drawn from Nature by J.W. Audubon   Lith, Printed & Colᵈ by J.T.Bowen, Philᵃ

space, projecting from the end of each toe, and there is a callosity in place of a thumb, armed with a very minute nail.

There are five hind toes; the claws resemble those of the fore feet, and are almost concealed by the hair of the toes; the soles are covered with a dense brush, like the feet of a rabbit or hare. The fur is soft, long, and silky on all parts.

Colour.

Incisors, deep orange; whiskers, black; a dark gray marking around the eye. The hairs on the upper surface of the head and body are of a deep blackish-gray colour from the roots to near the tips, which are pale reddish-brown, but distinctly presented only when the fur lies smoothly; on the flying membrane the colour is a shade darker in consequence of the under colour not being concealed by the lighter colour of the tips; the outer surfaces of the feet are pale bluish-gray; the margins of the mouth, sides of the nose, cheeks, and whole ventral aspect of the body, white, with a tinge of buff under the belly, and particularly under the flying membrane. Tail, nearly the colour of the back, with an intermixture however of black hairs; beneath, it is buff; hair on the soles, yellowish-white.

Dimensions.

	Inches.	Lines.
Length of head and body, ...	8	
Tail, including fur, ...	5	9
Height of ear, ...		5½
Heel to end of claw, ...	1	5½
Longest hind-toe and nail, ...		4¾
Fore-toe and nail, ...		5

Habits.

We found this interesting Flying-Squirrel in abundance at Quebec, and many of them were offered for sale in the markets of that city during our sojourn there. It appears indeed to take the place of the common small Flying-Squirrel of the United States (*P. volucella*) in Lower Canada, where we did not observe the latter east of Montreal.

We heard that one of these pretty animals was caught alive by a soldier who saw it on the plains of Abraham, and ran it down.

A brood of young of this species, along with the mother was kept in confinement by an acquaintance of ours, for about four months, and the little ones, five in number, were suckled in the following manner: the younglings stood on the ground floor of the cage, whilst the mother hung her body downwards, and secured herself from falling by clinging to the perch immediately above her head by her fore-feet. This was observed every day, and some days as frequently as eight or ten times.

This brood was procured as follows: a piece of partially cleared wood having been set on fire, the labourers saw the Flying-Squirrel start from a hollow stump with a young one in her mouth, and watched the place where she deposited it, an another stump at a little distance. The mother returned to her nest, and took away another and another in succession, until all were removed, when the wood-cutters went to the abode now occupied by the affectionate animal, and caught *her* already *singed* by the fire, and her five young unscathed.

After some time a pair of the young were given away to a friend. The three remaining ones, as well as the mother, were killed in the following manner:

The cage containing them was hung near the window, and one night during the darkness, a rat, or rats (*mus decumanus*), caught hold of the three young through the bars, and ate off all their flesh, leaving the skins almost entire, and the heads remaining inside the bars. The mother had had her thigh broken and her flesh eaten from the bone, and yet this good parent was so affectionately attached to her brood that when she was found in this pitiable condition in the morning, she was clinging to her offspring, and trying to nurse them as if they had still been alive.

This species is said to bear a considerable resemblance to the European Flying-Squirrel. It was first described by FORSTER, who not having distinguished it from the European animal, PENNANT stands as its discoverer.

We did not observe any of these Flying-Squirrels on the borders of the Yellow Stone or Upper Missouri, and have no further information as to their habits.

In our first volume (pp. 134, 135), we mentioned that Sir JOHN RICHARDSON speaks of a Flying-Squirrel which he considered a variety of *P. sabrinus*, and called *var. B. alpinus*. We then remarked that we hoped to be able to identify that variety when presenting an account of the habits of *P.*

sabrinus, and in our next article shall have the pleasure of doing so, having named it *P. alpinus*.

Geographical Distribution.

The northern range of this species is about latitude 52°; it has been captured on the shores of Lake Huron, and at the bottom of James Bay, at Moose Factory. We obtained specimens in the neighbourhood of Quebec, where in the autumn they were exceedingly abundant.

We have not a doubt it is found in the United States south of the river St. Lawrence, but at present have no evidence to that effect. It does not appear to exist on either slope of the Rocky Mountains, nor have we in fact been able to find any of our smaller Rodentia of the Atlantic States in those regions.

General Remarks.

As long as only two species of Flying-Squirrel were known in North America—the present species (*P. sabrinus*) and the little *P. volucella*—there was no difficulty in deciding on the species, but since others have been discovered in the far west, the task of separating and defining them has become very perplexing. We will however endeavour, in our next article, in which we shall describe *P. alpinus*, to point out those characters which may enable naturalists to distinguish the closely allied species.

The lower figure in the plate represents *P. sabrinus*, and should have been marked fig. 1. Our readers will please correct it accordingly.

Pteromys Alpinus.—Aud. and Bach.

Rocky Mountain Flying-Squirrel.

Plate cxliii.—Fig. 2.—Natural Size.

P. Magnitudine P. sabrino major, caudâ planâ, latâ, corpore longiore, patagio lumbari angusto, margine recta.

Characters.

Larger than Pteromys sabrinus; tail, flat and broad, longer than the body; flying membrane, short and with a straight border.

Synonyme.

PTEROMYS SABRINUS (VAR. ALPINUS). Rich., F. B. A., p. 195, pl. 18.

Description.

Head longer and body stouter than in *P. sabrinus*; the tail is also longer, much broader, more densely clothed with hair, and has a flatter and more elliptical form; the flying membrane is much smaller than in *P. sabrinus*, and the border is straight; the ears are thin and membranous, have a little fur at the base on the upper surface, and are thinly covered on both sides with short adpressed hairs; their form is semi-oval with rounded tips; the tail is flat, oblong, and oval in form; the extremities are rather stout, more especially the hind-feet; the soles, palms, and under surfaces of the toes are well covered with fur, except a small callous eminence at the end of each toe. There are five eminences on the palm, of which the two posterior ones are the largest; and four on the soles, situated at the root of the toes. There is a brush of soft fur near the outer edges of the soles; the fur is dense, very long, and has a woolly appearance; the longest hair on the back is fully an inch in length.

Colour.

Head, nose, and cheeks, light grayish, with a slight wash of yellow; surface of the fur on the back, yellowish-brown, without any tendency to the more red hue of the back in *P. sabrinus*.

The fur of the throat and belly is a grayish-white, without any tinge of buff colour; tail, blackish-brown above, a little paler beneath.

Dimensions.

	Inches.
From point of nose to root of tail, ...	8½
Tail (vertebræ), ...	5

" (including fur), ... $6\frac{1}{8}$

Heel to longest middle toe, ... $1\frac{1}{2}$

Height of ear posteriorly, ... $\frac{3}{8}$

Breadth between the outer edges of the flying membrane, ... $4\frac{3}{4}$

RICHARDSON states that there is a specimen in the Hudson's Bay Museum, which measures nine inches from the point of the nose to the root of the tail.

Habits.

We have learned little of the habits of this animal. DRUMMOND, who obtained it on the Rocky Mountains, states that it lives in pine forests, seldom venturing from its retreats except during the night.

From its heavy structure, and the shortness of the bony process that supports the flying membrane, we are led to infer that it is less capable of supporting itself in sailing from one tree to another, than the other species of this genus.

Geographical Distribution.

Both the specimens of DRUMMOND and TOWNSEND were obtained in crossing the Rocky Mountains on the usual route to the Columbia river. We have no doubt this species will be found on the western side of the Rocky Mountains, from the Russian settlements through Oregon to California.

General Remarks.

RICHARDSON regarded this species as a variety of *Pteromys sabrinus* (see our first volume, p. 134), and adopted for it the name *alpinus*, not to designate a species but a variety. We, on the other hand, consider it a true species, and have applied to it the name of *P. alpinus*, quoting RICHARDSON'S *var. alpinus* as a synonyme.

On comparing the specimen from which our drawing was made, with *P. sabrinus* from Quebec, the following appeared to be the points of difference: *alpinus* is considerably the larger animal, and although the legs appear somewhat shorter, they are stouter; the fur is more dense and longer, having quite a woolly appearance; the ears are shorter than in *P. sabrinus*, and are broader and more rounded. They may also be distinguished by the colour of their fur from each other, that of *alpinus* on the under surface being pure white from the roots, while the fur of *P. sabrinus* is tinged with yellowish. The most striking difference, however, is the extreme shortness of the bony process which supports the flying membrane at the fore-leg.

By some mistake of the engraver the numerals referring to the figures were misplaced—the upper and larger figure, marked figure 1, should have been figure 2, as it represents the present species (*P. alpinus*), and of course the lower figure, which is marked figure 2, should have been figure 1; it represents *P. sabrinus*. Our subscribers will please alter the figures on the plate accordingly.

Arvicola Townsendii.—Bach.

Townsend's Arvicola.

Plate cxliv. Fig. 1.—Male.—Natural Size.

A. Mure decumano duplo minor, auriculis erectis, vellere prominulis, colore in dorso plumbeo ad rufum vergente in capite colloque.

Characters.

Half the size of the Norway rat; ears, upright, and visible beyond the fur; Plumbeous on the back, inclining to rufous on the head and neck.

Synonyme.

ARVICOLA TOWNSENDII. Bachman, Jour. Acad. Nat. Sciences, vol. viii., part 1, p. 60.

Description.

Body, cylindrical; head, rather small; whiskers long, reaching beyond the ears; eyes, small; teeth, large; ears, large, broad, erect, extending considerably above the fur; feet, of moderate size; toes, like the rest of this genus; thumb, protected by a rather short acute nail; tail, scaly, sparingly covered with soft hair, a few hairs at its extremity; feet, clothed to the nails with short brown adpressed hairs; fur, on the back, about three lines long, much shorter beneath.

Colour.

Whiskers, white and black; teeth, yellow; fur on the upper part of the body, lead colour from the roots to near the tips, which present a mixture of white and black points, from which results a general plumbeous colour; under surface, grayish-ash; neck, sides of face, nose, and an obscure line above the eye, ashy-brown; tail, brownish, with a few white hairs at the tip; feet, yellowish-brown; claws, brown.

Dimensions.

	Inches.	Lines.
Length of head and body, ...	6	
Tail, ...	2	6
Fore-feet to point of nails, ...		9
Heel to point of nail, ...	1	
Breadth of ear, ...		5

Habits.

The late Mr. TOWNSEND, who captured this animal under an old log on the banks of the Columbia river, gave us no account of its habits. We should judge from its form, its conspicuous ears, and its general resemblance to the cotton rat of Carolina (*Sigmodon hispidum*), that it possesses many of its characteristics. It was found in the woods, but we imagine that it exists on the edges of the open country skirting the forests, feeding on roots, grasses, and seeds, nestling under logs and brushwood, and having, like the rest of the genus, four or five young at a birth.

Geographical Distribution.

The specimen here described was obtained on the 21st of July, 1835, by Mr. TOWNSEND, on the shores of the Columbia river. It no doubt is widely distributed on the western side of the Rocky Mountains, and replaces the Wilson's Meadow-Mouse of our northern Atlantic States.

General Remarks.

We find it exceedingly difficult to ascertain characters to designate the various species of Arvicolæ in our country; they resemble each other in many particulars, and especially in colour. We can however fine no description which answers to this species in RICHARDSON or any other author.

Arvicola Nasuta.—Aud. and Bach.

Sharp-Nosed Arvicola.

Plate cxliv. Fig. 2.—Male.—Natural Size.

A. A. Pennsylvanica longior, caudâ, capite, breviore; pedibus, tenuibus; calce brevissima; corpore supra, ferrugineo-fusco; subtus ex cinereo et flavo variegato.

Characters.

Larger than Arvicola Pennsylvanica; tail shorter than the head; legs small and slender; heel very short; body above, dark rusty brown, soiled yellowish-gray beneath.

Description.

The head of this species is rather longer and the nose sharper than in the Arvicolæ in general; the lower incisors are long and very much curved; the body is less cylindrical than that of Wilson's Meadow-Mouse; ears, circular, sparingly hairy within, and well covered with fur exteriorly; whiskers, shorter than the head; tail, thinly covered with hair.

The legs are rather slender, and are covered with short hairs; the fore-feet have naked palms; claws, small; tarsus, more than one third shorter than that of the much smaller *Arvicola Pennsylvanica*; the fur on the back is also shorter.

Colour.

Incisors, yellowish-white; fur on the back, from the roots to near the tips, grayish-black; the tips are yellowish-brown and black giving it a rusty brown appearance; the legs and tail are light brown; the chin, soiled white; the fur on the under surface of the body is dark cinereous from the roots to near the tips, where it is light coloured.

Dimensions.

	Inches.	Lines.
Length of head and body,	5	9
Head,	1	10
Tail,	1	6
Heel to point of nail,		6

For the sake of convenient comparison we give the dimensions of the largest of six specimens of Arvicola Pennsylvanica:

	Inches.	Lines.
Length of head and body,	4	2
Head,	1	4
Tail,	1	6
Heel to point of longest nail,		11

Habits.

We have found this species breeding in the vicinity of Wilson's Meadow-Mouse, although never nearer than a few hundred yards from the latter, and we have sometimes observed their nests in summer on large hillocks of sedge-grass (*carex*) growing in marshy localities, and surrounded by water; they do not occupy these exposed situations, however, in winter, but are found on more elevated knolls, under the roots of old trees or shrubs. They produce four or five young at a birth, and certainly breed twice, if not oftener, during the season.

Geographical Distribution.

The specimen which we have described was obtained by Dr. BREWER, near Boston. We received another from J. W. AUDUBON, who procured it at the falls of Niagara; we have also frequently found it in the northern parts of New York, where the *Arvicola Pennsylvanica* likewise exists; and we recently observed specimens near Detroit in Michigan. It appears, however, not to be found as far to the south as Wilson's Meadow-Mouse, as we have not succeeded in tracing it to the southern counties of Pennsylvania, where we have sought to obtain it.

General Remarks.

We are not certain that this species may not have been indicated, although not accurately, by RAFFINESQUE in the American Monthly Magazine, under the name of *Lemmus noveboracensis*. His descriptions, however, in every department of natural history, are so short, vague, and imperfect, that it is impossible to identify his species with any degree of certainty; they have created such confusion in the nomenclature that nearly all European and American naturalists have ceased to quote him as authority.

Sir JOHN RICHARDSON has described an Arvicola from the Rocky Mountains, which he refers to the above species (*A. noveboracensis*) of RAFFINESQUE, but which differs widely from the species here described.

Arvicola Oryzivora.—Bach.

Rice Meadow-Mouse.

Plate cxliv. Fig. 3 (Octavo Edition).

A. Pennsylvanicam equans, capite longo, rostro acuto, corpore gracili, auriculis prominulis, cauda longitudine trunci; supra ferruginea rufus, subtus subalbida.

Characters.

Size of Arvicola Pennsylvanica; *head, long; nose, sharp; body, slender; ears, prominent; tail, the length of the body, without including the head; colour, rusty brown above, beneath whitish.*

Description.

In form this species bears a distant resemblance to the cotton rat (*Sigmodon hispidum*); it is, however, a much smaller species. The ears, which are half the length of the head, are rounded, and are thickly clothed with hair on both surfaces; the feet are rather small; there is a short blunt nail in place of a thumb; under surface of palms, and tarsus, naked; toes on the hind-feet, long, the three middle ones of nearly an equal length; tail, rather long, thickly clothed on both surfaces with short hairs; whiskers, short, scarcely reaching the ears.

Colour.

The fur on the upper surface is slate colour, tipped with light brown and black, giving it on the dorsal aspect a dark grayish-brown tint, fading into lighter on the sides, and into whitish-gray on the belly and under surface; the ears are of the colour of the sides; feet, whitish; tail, brown on the upper surface, lighter beneath; whiskers, black and white.

Dimensions.

	Inches.	Lines.
Length of head and body,	5	2
" of tail,	4	
From end of heel to point of longest nail,	1	2
" point of nose to ear,	1	
Height of ear,		$5\frac{1}{2}$

Habits.

The Rice Meadow-Mouse, as its name implies, is found in particular localities in the banks of the rice-fields of Carolina and Georgia. It burrows in the dykes or dams a few inches above the line of the usual rise of the water. Its burrow is seldom much beyond a foot in depth. It has a compact nest at the extremity, where it produces its young in April. They are usually four or five. In spring this Mouse is in the habit of sitting on the dams near the water, and is so immoveable, and so much resembles the colour of the surrounding earth, that it is seldom noticed until it moves off to its retreat in the banks. We have observed it scratching up the rice when newly planted and before it had been overflowed by the water. When the rice is in its milky state this animal commences feeding on it, and continues during the autumn and winter, gleaning the fields of the scattered grains. We have also seen its burrows in old banks on deserted rice-fields, and observed that it had been feeding on the large seeds of the Gama grass (*Tripsicum dactyloides*), and on those of the wild rye (*Elymus Virginicus*). A singular part of the history of the Rice Mouse is the fact that in the extensive salt-marshes along the borders of Ashley and Cooper rivers, this species is frequently found a quarter of a mile from the dry ground. Its nest is suspended on a bunch of interlaced marsh grass. In this situation we observed one with five young. At certain seasons this little animal feeds on the seeds of the marsh grass (*Spartina glabra*). When these fail it sometimes retires to the shore for food, but has no disrelish to the small crustacea and mollusks that remain on the mud at the subsiding of the tide.

This species swims rapidly, and dives in the manner of the European water-rat (*Arvicola amphibia*), or of our *Arvicola Pennsylvanica*. In an attempt at capturing some alive, they swam so actively, and dived so far from us, that the majority escaped. Those we kept in captivity produced young in May and September; they were fed on grains of various kinds, but always gave the preference to small pieces of meat.

Geographical Distribution.

We obtained several specimens of this Mouse through the aid of our friend Dr. ALEXANDER MOULTRIE, who assisted us in capturing them on his rice plantation in St. John's parish, South Carolina. We procured a considerable number on the salt marshes near Charleston, saw several on the eastern banks of the Savannah river, and near Savannah; and the late Dr. LEITNER

Plate CXLIV

Fig. 1.

Fig 2

On Stone by Wm. E. Hitchcock

Fig 3

Fig 1.　Townsend's Arvicola.　　Fig 2.　Sharp-nosed Arvicola　　Fig 3.　Bank Rat

Drawn from Nature by J W Audubon

Lith Printed & Col.d by J T Bowen, Phil

brought us a specimen obtained in the Everglades of Florida. This Arvicola is said to exist as far to the north as New Jersey.

General Remarks.

We obtained specimens of *Arvicola Oryzivora* in the winter of 1816, but did not describe it until May 1836, when we designated it by the above name. Having occasion to send descriptions of several, then undescribed, species to the Academy of Natural Sciences of Philadelphia, we sent a specimen of this animal to Dr. PICKERING, requesting him and Dr. HARLAN to compare it with the *Arvicola riparia* of ORD, a species which we had not seen, stating our reasons why we regarded it as distinct. In searching in the Academy, a specimen of this species was found, and Dr. HARLAN, in opposition to the views of PICKERING, felt himself authorized to publish it in SILLIMAN'S American Journal (vol. xxxi.), bestowing on it the name of *Mus palustris*,

making use of the head of our specimen for an examination of the teeth.

The teeth and general appearance of this species, the form of its body, and especially its ears and tail being thickly clothed with hair, render it apparent that it does not belong to the genus Mus, but is more nearly allied to Arvicola. As the name "*Arvicola palustris*" is pre-occupied (HARLAN'S Fauna, p. 136), we are favoured with an opportunity of extricating it from the confusion of synonymes in which it would otherwise be involved, and of restoring it to its true genus under the name given by its legitimate describer.

In our large edition (plate 144) the third figure is lettered *Mus riparius*. We have since the publication of that plate ascertained that no such species as our so-called *Mus riparius* exists, and in consequence have stricken it out of the catalogue of North American mammalia, and have figured in place of it, in the octavo edition of our work (plate 144, fig. 3), *Arvicola oryzivora*, the subject of our present article.

Scalops Townsendii. — Bach.

Townsend's Shrew-Mole.

Plate cxlv. — Males. — Natural Size.

S. Magnitudine S. aquatico duplo major, supra rufo-fuscus. Dentibus xliv.

Characters.

Double the size of the common Shrew-Mole, with eight more teeth than that species; dark liver colour.

Synonymes.

COMMON MOLE. Mackenzie's Voyage to the Pacific, &c., p. 314.
MOLE. Lewis and Clark, Journey, vol. iii. p. 42.
SCALOPS CANADENSIS. Rich, Fauna Boreali Americana, p. 9.
" TOWNSENDII. Bach., Jour. Acad. Nat. Sci., vol. viii., part 1, p. 58.

Description.

Dental Formula. — Incisive $\frac{2}{4}$; Canine $\frac{6-6}{6-6}$; Molar $\frac{4-4}{3-3}$ = 44.

In the upper jaw the incisors are large, and a third higher than the canine teeth usually termed false molars, which immediately follow them; these are succeeded by three small teeth of a nearly conical shape, increasing in length from the first to the third; the fourth false molar on each side is the smallest; the fifth is a little larger in size, and slightly compressed; the sixth still larger, and has a considerable posterior projection; the four posterior ones; the first of these (which we have called a canine tooth) is rather small, and bilobed, with a small internal tubercle; the second and third are the largest and nearly resemble each other, exhibiting three distinct points, two external and posterior, and one anterior, the external ones being the longest, and the last molar being the smallest, and of a triangular form; in the lower jaw there are two very small incisors in front; next to these are two of a considerably larger size, which, although we have called them incisors, are nearly of the same shape and appearance as those which succeed them.

The canine or false molars, six on each side, are nearly the same size, and incline forwards; the three true molars, which succeed, are large, nearly uniform in size, and correspond with those in the upper jaw, although they are smaller.

Body, thick and cylindrical, shaped like the Shrew-Mole (*Scalops aquaticus*); the limbs are short, being concealed by the skin of the body nearly down to the wrist and ankle-joints.

Palms, naked, very broad, furnished with moderately long nails which are channelled beneath; tail, rather thick, tapering from the root to the tip, and nearly naked, being very sparingly clothed with short hairs; the vertebræ are equally four sided; fingers, very short, united to the roots of the nails; nails, slightly curved; hind-feet, more slender than the fore-feet, and distinctly webbed to the nails; the feet are thinly clothed above, with short hairs. The whole of the body, both upper and lower surface, presents a velvety appearance.

Colour.

The body is dark liver brown colour above, changing with the light in which it is viewed to silvery or black shades; the hair when blown aside exhibits a grayish-black colour to near the tips, which in some of the points are white, others brown black, producing the changeable colours above described. One of the specimens which we have seen—the one figured in our plate—has a whitish-yellow stripe about two lines wide, running in a somewhat irregular line along the under surface of the body to within an inch and a half of the insertion of the tail; there is also a white streak commencing on the forehead, spreading over the snout and around the edges of the mouth and lower jaws. The teeth are white; feet, point of nose, and tail, flesh colour; nails, light brown.

Dimensions.

	Inches.	Lines.
Length of head and body,	8	6
" tail,	1	6
Breadth of palm,		7

Habits.

We were informed by NUTTALL and TOWNSEND, who mistook this species for our common Shrew-Mole (*Scalops aquaticus*), that they dug and formed galleries, and threw up little mounds of earth precisely in the manner of that animal. They are well known to the farmers and settlers in the valleys of Oregon, as they traverse their fields and gardens, cutting up the ground in some places to an injurious extent.

Geographical Distribution.

This species is found in considerable abundance near the banks of the Columbia and other rivers in Oregon, where our specimens were obtained. We are unable to say what is the northern limit of this animal. It has not yet been found on the eastern side of the Rocky Mountains, and we have not been able to determine positively that it exists in California; but we have little doubt that it is the most common Shrew-Mole on the Pacific side of the North American continent, where our common species (*Scalops aquaticus*) does not appear to have been discovered.

General Remarks.

Sir JOHN RICHARDSON, who first described this animal from a specimen preserved in the museum of the Hon. Hudson's Bay Company, obtained by Mr. DAVID DOUGLAS, does not seem to have made a comparison between this Mole and our common Atlantic species. HARLAN had described the skull of the species which we have since described and figured as *Scalops Brewerii*, having forty-four teeth, and another which had thirty-six. RICHARDSON was thus induced to suppose that authors had varied in their descriptions of the *Scalops* from their having mentioned edentate spaces between the incisors and grinders, and had consequently described the young in those specimens which had only thirty-six teeth. The young, however, of our common *aquaticus* (or as CUVIER has called it, *Scalops Canadensis*) has only thirty teeth, the adult thirty-six, whilst the present species has forty-four.

On our pointing out to Sir JOHN RICHARDSON these particulars, he expressed himself gratified to have an opportunity of correcting the error into which he had inadvertently fallen.

Plate CXLV

N° 29

Drawn from Nature by J.W. Audubon

On Stone by Wm E. Hitchcock

Lith Printed & Col⁴ by J.T Bowen Phil

Townsend's Shrew Mole

Genus Dasypus.—Linn.

Dental Formula.

Incisive $\frac{0}{0}$ *or* $\frac{2}{4}$; *Canine* $\frac{0-0}{0-0}$; *Molars varying in the several species from 28 to 68; these teeth cylindrical, separate, and without enamel on the inner side.*

Head, long; mouth, small; tongue, partially extensible. Body, altogether covered with a shell, or plate armour. Four or five toes to the fore-feet, five toes to the hind-feet. Toes, armed with long nails for digging; mammæ, two or four. Tail, rather long, round.

Stomach, simple; intestines, without cæca.

Habit, living in woods, on ants, roots, and putrid animals; rolling themselves up for protection; confined to the warmer parts of America.

Nine species belonging to this genus have been described by authors.

The genus requires a revision, and the species will no doubt, from the rage which exists at present for making new genera, be greatly subdivided.

The generic appellation is derived from δασυς, *dasus*, rough, and πους, *pous*, a foot.

Dasypus Peba.—Desm.

Nine-Banded Armadillo.

Plate cxlvi.—Male.—Natural Size.

D. Dentibus primoribus laniariisque nullis, molaribus $\frac{8-8}{8-8}$ = 32, cauda tereti, cingulis circumdata, ad apicem solum nuda, testa zonis mobilibus, auriculis longissimis.

Characters.

No incisive or canine teeth; Molars $\frac{8-8}{8-8}$ = 32.
Tail, round, with rings nearly its whole length. Body, with mobile bands; ears, very long.

Synonymes.

DASYPUS PEBA. Desm., Mammal., p. 368.
" SEPTEM CINCTUS, D. OCTO CINCTUS, and D. NOVEM CINCTUS. Linn.
ARMADILLO BRAZILIANUS. Briss., Regne Animal, 40.
" MEXICANUS. " " 41.
" GUYANENSIS. " " 42.
CACHICAME. Buffon, Hist. Nat., x. p. 250.
TATOU NOIR. D'Azara, Paraguay, vol. ii. p. 175.
TATU PEPA. Marc., Brazil, 231.
NINE, EIGHT, OR SEVEN BANDED ARMADILLO. Pennant's Quadrupeds, Synopsis, pp. 324, 253.
PIG-HEADED ARMADILLO. Grew, Mus, p. 19, t. i.
SIX-BANDED ARMADILLO. Shaw's General Zoology, vol. i., part 1, p. 189.
GÜRTELTHIER MIT ACHTZEHN GÜRTELN. Schreb., pp. 227, 228.

Description.

This singular production of nature, it might be said, resembles a small pig saddled with the shell of a turtle; it is about the size of a large opossum; the head is small, and greatly elongated, and the neck can be retracted so far as to entirely withdraw the head under the shell. Muzzle, narrow and pointed; mouth, large; tongue, aculeated, and can be drawn out three inches beyond the nose.

The head and nose and covered with rather small plates irregularly shaped, most of them hexagonal. There are on the back nine transverse bands in the specimen from which we describe, although the number of bands is occasionally only seven or eight. The shoulders, hams, and rump are protected by two plates, covered with large scales regularly arranged in distinct rows following the direction of the movable transverse bands, and descending lower towards the ground than the bands, forming a sort of flap over the shoulders and over the hips like the skirt of a saddle. Thus the covering of the head may be compared to a helmet, and that of the shoulders and on the hind parts to breast-plates and thigh-pieces, the whole forming an almost impenetrable coat-of-mail.

The tail is protected by numerous rings, furnished with scales of the same substance, shape, and hardness, as those on other parts of the upper surface of the body. The texture of this shell-like covering of the Armadillo appears to be something between turtle-shell or horn, and very hard sole-leather. The eyes are small, and placed far back in the head, on a line with the corner of the mouth.

Legs, short and stout; nails, strong, sharp, very slightly hooked, and not channelled beneath; there are four toes on each fore-foot, the middle ones being much the longest, and the outer, shorter, and situated far behind; there are five toes on the hind-feet, the central being longest, the first and fifth shortest, and the two others nearly of an equal length. Ears, long, narrow, and pointed, destitute of hair, and the skin on their upper surface slightly granulated, but not protected by scales. The under surface of the body is only covered by a soft leathery skin, as also the legs; the front of each foot is protected by scales for about two inches above the toes.

A few scattered hairs can be observed on the under surface of the body, and here and there a single hair along the edges of the plates above; the animal may nevertheless be described as hairless. Mammæ, four.

Colour.

Entire surface of body, ochreous brownish-yellow; browner along the sides of the head and beneath the ears; feet and nails, yellowish-brown.

Dimensions.

	Foot.	Inches.
From point of nose to root of tail,	1	6
Tail,		8
Height of ear,		2
Point of nose to eye,		$2\frac{7}{8}$
Nose to ear,		$4\frac{1}{2}$
Longest nail on fore-foot,		1
" " on hind-foot,		$\frac{7}{8}$

Habits.

The Armadillo is not "a fighting character," but on the contrary is more peaceable than even the opossum, which will at times bite in a sly and treacherous manner, quite severely. Indeed nature, whilst giving to the Armadillo a covering of horn-plates or scales, which serve to protect it from many of its foes, has not supplied it, as she has other noncombating animals—the porcupine for instance—with sharp-pointed quills or spines, and its only means of aggression are its claws, which although large are better adapted for digging than aught else. The animal, however, sometimes has been known when caught by the tail, to kick rather hard with both fore and hind-legs, so that its captor was glad to let go, for it possesses great strength in the limbs. A friend of ours who formerly resided in South America had a pet Armadillo in his bed-chamber, where it generally remained quiet during the day, but in the dark hours was active and playful. One night after he had gone to bed, the Armadillo began dragging about the chairs and some boxes that were placed around the room, and continued so busily engaged at this occupation that our friend could not sleep. He at length arose and struck a light, when to his surprise he found boxes he had supposed greatly too heavy for such an animal to stir, had been moved and placed together so as to form a sort of den or hiding-place in a corner, into which the animal retreated with great apparent satisfaction, and from whence it could only be drawn out after a hard struggle, and the receipt of some severe strokes from its claws. But in general the Armadillo does not evince any disposition to resent an attack, and in fact one of them when teased by a pet parrot, struck out with its claws only till pressed by the bird, when it drew in its head and feet, and secure in its tough shell, yielded without seeming to care much about it, to its noisy and mischievous tormentor, until the parrot left it to seek some less apathetic and more vulnerable object to worry.

But when the Armadillo has a chance of escape by digging into the ground, it is no sluggard in its movements, and progresses towards the depths of the soil with surprising rapidity. This animal however on being much alarmed rolls itself up, and does not attempt to fly, and it is chiefly when it has been digging, and is at or near the mouth of a hole, that it tries to escape; preferring generally, to be kicked, tumbled about with a stick, or be bitten at by a dog, to making an effort to run.

We have heard it asserted that when it has the advantage of being on a hill or elevated spot, the Armadillo upon the approach of danger, forms a

Plate CXLVI.

Lith. Printed & Col.d by J.T. Bower, Phil

Nine-banded Armadillo

Drawn from Nature by J.W. Audubon

ball-shaped mass of its body, with the tail doubled under the belly, starts down the hill and rolls to the bottom.

The principal food of this genus consists of ants of various species, which are so abundant in some portions of Central and South America as to be great pests to the inhabitants of those parts of the world. A large species of this family, however (*Dasypus giganteus*), is described by D'AZARA as feeding on the carcases of dead animals; and it appears that in neighbourhoods where that Armadillo is found, the graves of the dead are protected by strong double boards, to prevent the animal from penetrating, and devouring the bodies. Armadillos are said to eat young birds, eggs, snakes, lizards, &c. It should perhaps here be remarked that the large Armadillo just mentioned, although covered with plates or scales like our present species (*D. peba*), and similar in form, is very different in its organization, and has indeed been characterized by F. CUVIER under the new genus *Priodontis*.

To return to our present species. The Nine-banded Armadillo is, as we were informed by Captain CHARLES H. BALDWIN, kept in Nicaragua, not only by the people of the ranchos, but by the inhabitants of some of the little towns, to free their houses from ants, which, as is said, it can follow by the smell. When searching for ants about a house, the animal puts out the tongue and scrapes the ants into the mouth from around the posts on which the houses are raised a little above the ground, and has been known to dig down under the floors, and remain absent for three or four weeks at a time.

When burrowing this species utters a slight squeak, quite faint however. They are said to dig down in a straight direction when they discover a subterranean colony of ants, without beginning at the mouth or entrance to the ant-hole. There are two favourite species of ant with the Armadillo in Nicaragua, one of which makes nests in the forks of trees in the forests. The tree ants are white, the others small and black. The Armadillos keep about the roots of the trees in order to feed upon the former, and as we have already said, dig for the latter. They also root up the ground with their pig-like snout, and do some damage to gardens. They are very persevering when in pursuit of ants, and whilst they turn up the light soil with the snout, keep the tongue busy taking in the insects.

It has been assured us that when a line of ants (which may sometimes extend some distance in the woods) are busily engaged in carrying provision to the general storehouse, they scatter in every direction at the instant the Armadillo begins to dig down towards their stronghold, evidently having some communication from head-quartes equivalent to "sauve qui peut."

The gait of these animals when not alarmed is like that of a tortoise, and about as fast. They have nails powerfully organized for digging, whilst their legs are only long enough to raise the body from the ground. The holes the Armadillo excavates in the earth for its own purposes, are generally dug at an angle of forty-five degrees, are winding, and from six to eight feet long.

The Armadillo is generally much darker in colour than the specimen we figured, which having been a pet, was washed and clean when we drew it. When in the woods these animals partake more or less of the colour of the soil in which they find their food, as some of the dirt sticks to their shell. Those that have been domesticated prefer sleeping above ground, but this animal when wild lives in burrows, holes in the roots of trees, or under rocks.

From our esteemed friend Capt. J. P. McCOWN, U. S. A., we have the following: "The Armadillo is to be found in the chaparals on the Rio Grande. I have seen their shells or coat-of mail on the prairies; whether carried there by larger animals, or birds, or whether they inhabit the prairies, I cannot say. I have seen many that were kept as pets and appeared quite tame. I am inclined to the opinion that there are two species—the larger living on the low and wet lands and in the canebrakes, the smaller occupying the rocky hills and cliffs."

This animal is said to produce three or four young at a time. Its flesh is eaten by the Spaniards and natives. It has been described to us by Americans who ate of it during the Mexican war, to be about equal to the meat of the opossum; we have heard, however, from South Americans, that it is considered quite a delicacy, being white, juicy, and tender; it is cooked by roasting it in the shell.

The South American negroes catch the Armadillo at night. When they are in the woods their dogs scent the animal and run it to its hole (if it be near enough to its retreat to reach it). It is then dug out by the blacks, although sometimes known to excavate its burrow to a considerable depth below its usual place of rest, whilst the diggers are at work after it. Two or three of these animals generally keep together, or near each other, and the negroes always expect to kill more, when they have captured one. They are said to run pretty fast when trying to reach their holes, but the manner of their gait at such times is not known to us. Their holes are often dug in the sides of steep banks or hills, and in thick and dense parts of the woods.

We have heard that in some parts of Nicaragua the Armadillos are so common that they can be purchased for a *medio*—six and a quarter cent piece.

Geographical Distribution.

This animal is described as existing in Brazil in South America; it is found in Guiana and Central America, is common in Mexico, and is found in the southern portions of Texas. It is not very uncommon near the lower shores of the Rio Grande.

General Remarks.

It is stated that another species of Armadillo inhabits the northern part of Mexico and penetrates also into Texas. Thus far, however, we have been unable to detect any other species than the present as having been seen within the geographical limits to which this work has been restricted.

It is now ascertained that the number of bands on the Armadillo forms no safe guide in designating the species, inasmuch as the bands vary in different individuals of the same species, and D'AZARA, moreover, has shown that there are individuals of different species which have the same number of bands.

Spermophilus Townsendii.—Bach.

American Souslik.

Plate cxlvii. Fig. 1.—Male.—Natural Size.

S. Magnitudine Sciuri Hudsonii, capite parvo, corpore gracilior, auribus caudaque brevibus, colore supra rufo-fusco griseo sparsim vario, infra pallidiore.

Characters.

Size of Sciurus Hudsonius (red squirrel); head, small; body, rather slender; ears and tail, short; colour, upper surface speckled with white and brown; beneath, yellowish-gray.

Synonymes.

ARCTOMYS (SPERMOPHILUS) GUTTATUS ?—AMERICAN SOUSLIK. Rich., F. B. A., p. 162.
SPERMOPHILUS TOWNSENDII—TOWNSEND'S MARMOT. Aud. and Bach., Jour. Acad. Nat. Sci. Phil., vol. viii., part 1, p. 61.

Description.

This animal has a convex and obtuse nose, with the frontal bone depressed; the body is rather long and slender; head, short; ears, slightly visible above the fur; cheek pouches, small; nails, slender, compressed, and slightly arched; the thumb protected by an acute and prominent nail; the second toe of the fore-foot, as in all the species of the genus, is longest, and not the third, as in the squirrels. The first toe is a little shorter than the second, and the third intermediate in length between the first and second. The tail appears (in the dried specimen) much flattened; it is clothed with hairs which are longest on the sides.

The fur is throughout remarkably soft, smooth, and lustrous.

Colour.

There is a line of white around the eye. The fur on the whole upper surface is, for one fourth of its length from the roots, dark bluish, or nearly black, then (a broad line of) silver gray, then (a narrow line of) dark brown edged with yellowish-white, giving it a brownish-gray appearance, speckled with white all over the back; these spots are longest near the dorsal line, becoming smaller half way down the sides. An indistinct line of separation between the colours of the upper the under surfaces appears high up along the hips and sides; on the under surface, the hairs are nearly black at the roots, and are cinereous at the tips; on the forehead, nose, and sides of the neck, there is a

Plate CXLVII

N° 30'

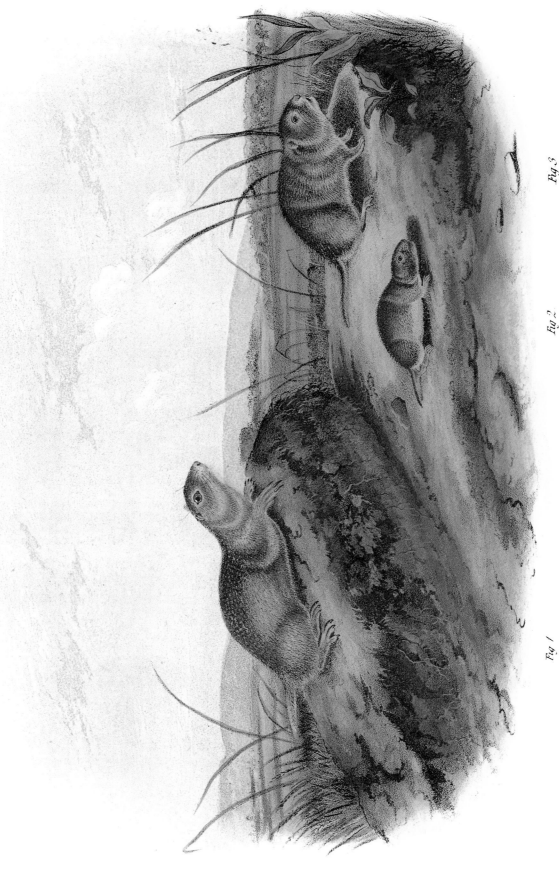

Fig 1   American Tawny Sousslik.   Fig 2   Oregon Meadow Mouse.   Fig 3   Texan Meadow Mouse.

Drawn from Nature by J W Audubon.

On Stone by W⁽ᵐ⁾ E Hitchcock

Fig 1   Fig 2   Fig 3

Lith Printed & Col⁽ᵈ⁾ by J T Bowen, Phil⁽ᵃ⁾.

slight tinge of light yellowish-brown. Tail, on the upper surface, light yellowish-brown edged with whitish; beneath, whitish, with a slight tinge of brown; teeth, white; nails, black.

Dimensions.

	Inches.	Lines.
From point of nose to root of tail, ...	8	9
Head, ...	1	10
Tail (vertebræ), ...	1	
" (to end of fur), ...	1	6
Length of heel to end of middle claw, ...	1	4

Habits.

In a letter addressed to us by the late Mr. TOWNSEND he states that this handsome Spermophile, in summer inhabits the prairies near the Wallawalla, where it is rather common; it becomes excessively fat, and is eaten by the Indians. It disappears in August and re-appears early in spring in a very emaciated state. We have heard from other sources that it lives in small families, like the Spermophiles, generally burrowing in holes, and that it is seen either sitting on the side of them or with the head partially protruded, but disappears in its underground retreat, on the approach of man or any other animal.

Geographical Distribution.

This species exists on the western sides of the Rocky Mountains in Oregon, where the few specimens we have seen have been obtained.

General Remarks.

RICHARDSON described this species under the name of *A. guttatus*, an animal described by PALLAS (Glir. tab. 6 B) existing on the Wolga in Russia; but BUFFON mentions of that species, that the name of Souslik is intended to express the great avidity that animal has for salt, which induces it to go on board vessels laden with that commodity, when it is often taken. We should judge that its American relative has less opportunity of indulging in such a propensity. We carried a specimen with us to Europe, and had an opportunity at the Berlin Museum of comparing it with specimens from Siberia; there is a general resemblance between the animals of the two countries, but they are scarcely more alike than the red squirrel of Europe (*Sciurus vulgaris*) and the red squirrel of America (*Sciurus Hudsonius*). They may be distinguished from each other at a glance by the large rounded spots on the back of the Russian animal, compared with the white and irregular specks in the American species.

As the name *guttatus* was pre-occupied, we have named this animal anew, and in doing so, called it after the gentleman who furnished us the specimen.

Arvicola Texiana.—Aud. and Bach.

Texan Meadow-Mouse.

Plate cxlvii. Fig. 2.—Male.—Natural Size.

A Sigmodon hispidum minore, supra rufo-fuscus nigro sparsim notato, striis nigris lateralis, lateribus fuscus, infra albido.

Characters.

Smaller than the cotton rat (Sigmodon hispidum); *back, brownish-yellow, spotted with irregular small blotches of black, a faint obscure stripe of black on each side. Sides, reddish-brown; belly, whitish-gray.*

Description.

This new species bears a general resemblance to the cotton rat of South Carolina and Georgia. Head, of moderate size; body, rather slender, and thin in the flanks; hair, soft; under fur, woolly; ears, large, ovate in shape, extending beyond the fur, and nearly naked behind, with, on the margins, a few scattered hairs. Whiskers, numerous, and about as long as the head; four toes on the fore-feet, with a small and almost imperceptible nail in place of thumb. Five toes on the hind-feet, the outer and inner of nearly equal length, the other three longer, and each of about the same length; legs, slender; feet, covered by short hairs, and with a few hairs between the toes, not however

concealing the nails; heel, narrow, and naked, as is also the under surface of the fore-feet.

Tail, rather long and slender, tapering to the point, and thinly covered with hairs.

Colour.

Fur, dark slate colour on the back at the roots, with reddish-yellow tips. The longer hairs, which are and soft, are irregularly marked with dark and yellowish-white at the base, and tipped with dark brown to where they mingle with the under fur. When the hair is laid smooth there is an obscure black stripe on the sides of the back, running from behind the shoulders towards the rump and converging across the buttocks to a point at the insertion of the tail; the remainder of the back between these stripes is somewhat irregularly, and very slightly, waved or barred as it were, with dark brown spots on a yellowish ground; head, yellowish-brown; sides of the neck, and along the flanks to the hip, brownish-yellow. A narrow line of yellowish-white extends under the chin and on the belly; tail, brown above, grayish-white beneath; ears, brownish yellow; whiskers, white, with a few brown hairs interspersed.

Dimensions.

	Inches.	Lines.
From point of nose to root of tail, ...	4	7
" " to ear, ...	1	3
" " to eye, ...		6
Length of tail, ...	4	
From heel to point of longest claw, ...	1	3

Habits.

This is an active and rather pugnacious little rat. It is sometimes to be seen near the edges of the chaparals, in which it makes its nest. it mostly feeds on seeds of wild grains and grasses, although it has recently shown a disposition to frequent the farm-yards of our enterprising Texan settlers. Like the Arvicolæ generally, this animal is a good swimmer, and takes the water when the rains flood the flat plains, which it has pleased the Texans to denominate "hog-wallow prairies." In the spring season this rat devours a good many eggs of such small birds as make their nests on the ground or in the rank grass and weeds, and it does no hesitate to eat any dead bird or small animal it may find.

Not being very numerous, it is difficult to procure it, and as setting traps for small animals, baited with meat, in the chaparal, has been found almost useless owing to larger quadrupeds than those intended to be caught seizing the flesh, and breaking the trap to pieces, or (as is often the case) devouring the small ones that may have been already entrapped, there is no probability that this or other small species which inhabit Texas and the neighbouring countries will become familiar objects in our collections of mammalia for some time to come. We have therefore placed our specimens of this rat in the museum of the Charleston College at Charleston, South Carolina, where may also be found the skins of some other animals first described in our work, and of which specimens, so far as we have heard, have not been procured by others.

Geographical Distribution.

This species was first discovered on the river Brasos, and afterwards seen in the country along the Nueces and Rio Grande, where chapparal thickets afford it shelter.

General Remaks.

Although this Meadow-Mouse approaches nearer to our cotton rat than any other Arvicola with which we are acquainted, it presents very striking differences; its form is lighter and more slender, its heel narrower, tail proportionably longer, and fur much softer. The cotton rat is of a uniform colour on the back, except the ends of the long hairs being tipped with white, but the Texan species presents a somewhat indistinct appearance of specks or spots of blackish on a yellow ground.

Arvicola Oregoni.—Bach.

Oregon Meadow-Mouse.

Plate cxlvii. Fig. 3.—Male.—Natural Size.

A. M. musculus magnitudine, gracilior, auribus brevibus vellere absconditis; colore supra cinereo fusco, subtus cinereo.

Characters.

Size of the house mouse; slender form; ears, short, nearly naked, and concealed by the fur; colour, ashy brown on the back, cinereous beneath.

Synonyme.

ARVICOLA OREGONI—OREGON MEADOW-MOUSE. Bachman, Jour. Acad. Nat. Sci., vol. viii., part i., p. 60.

Description.

Head, of moderate size; body, slender, eyes, small; ears, concealed by the fur and nearly naked, being clothed with but a few short and scattered hairs; feet, small; whiskers, as long as the head; a very minute blunt nail on the fore-foot; tail, and feet, clothed with short hairs.

Colour.

The fur, on the upper surface, is bluish from the roots to near the tips, where most of the points of the hairs are black, a shade of brownish appearing beneath; under surface, ashy white; above the eye, and immediately in front of the shoulders there is a line of light brown; whiskers, white and black, the latter predominating; feet, flesh coloured; incisors, yellow; tail, dark brown above, yellowish-white beneath, with the extreme end black. In TOWNSEND's Notes it is stated that the specimen we have described above, was an old male, captured on the 2d of November, 1836.

Dimensions.

	Inches.	Lines.
Length of head and body, ...	3	0
" of tail, ...	1	2

Habits.

We are unacquainted with the habits of this species, but should judge from its form resembling that of LE CONTE's pine mouse (*A. pinetorum*) that instead of having galleries on the surface of the earth, as is the general habit of the Meadow-Mice, this species lives principally under ground, and only comes to the surface at night, to seek its food; it evidently feeds more on roots than on seeds.

Geographical Distribution.

The Arvicola was captured in Oregon, near the Columbia river.

General Remarks.

Although its head is rather smaller in proportion than that of LECONTE's pine mouse (*Arvicola pinetorum*), and its body differing from that animal in colour, this species is nevertheless very similar to it in form, more especially in the almost naked lobe of the ear; and seems to be the representative of that Atlantic species in Oregon.

Putorius Fuscus.—Aud. and Bach.

Tawny Weasel.

Plate cxlviii. Male.—Natural Size.

P. Corpore inter putorius erminius et P. vulgaris intermedio; caudâ illius breviore, sed hujus longiore; apice nigro; vellere supra fusco; subtus albo.

Characters.

Intermediate in size between the ermine and the common weasel of Europe; tail, shorter than in the former, but longer than in the latter, with the extremity black; body, brown above, white beneath.

Synonymes.

MUSTELA FUSCA. Aud. and Bach., Jour. Acad. Nat. Sci. Phil., October 5, 1841, p. 94.
DeKay, Nat. Hist. State of New York, p. 35.

Description.

Body and neck, rather short in proportion to others of this genus, and far more robust than the common European Weasel. The feet especially appear a third larger, and are more thickly clothed with fur, which covers the palms and toes, and conceals the nails completely; ears, a little longer and more pointed than those of either the ermine or common Weasel.

In writing this description we have several specimens of the European common Weasel (*P. vulgaris*) before us, and the ends of the tails in that species are uniformly brown, with here and there a black hair interspersed. Although the hair of the present species is black at the extremity of the tail, like that of the ermine, yet these hairs are short and soft, and more like long fur, and do not present the long and coarse appearance of those of the latter species, but lie closer along the vertebræ, and form a sharp point at the extremity.

Claws, short and stout; incisors equally large with those of the ermine, but shorter; ears, large, obtusely pointed at tip, and thinly clothed with short adpressed hairs; tail, cylindrical, and narrowed down to a point of fine hairs, the tip somewhat resembling a large water-colour pencil or brush. Whiskers, as long as the head, and rather numerous. The hairs on the body are of two kinds: the longer hairs are a little more rigid, and far more numerous, than on the ermine, and the under fur is a little longer, coarser, and less woolly than fur of the latter animal.

Colour.

The whole upper surface, sides, outside of legs, feet, ears, and tail to within an inch of the extremity, uniform tawny brown, except on the centre of the back and top of the tail, where the colouring darkens. Thus the body of the animal is a shade darker than the summer colour of the ermine, while the colour of the tail is, for about an inch, nearly as black as in that species. The white on the lower surface is not mixed with brown hairs as in *Putorius vulgaris*, and not only occupies a broader space on the belly, but extends along the inner surface of the thighs as low as the tarsus, whilst in *P. vulgaris* the white scarcely reaches the thighs. The whole of the under surface is pure white; this colour does not commence on the upper lip, as is generally the case in the ermine, but on the chin, extending around the edges of the mouth, and by a well defined line along the neck, inner parts of the fore-legs, and inner parts of the thighs, tapering off to a point nearly opposite the heel on the hind-legs.

Whiskers, dark-brown, with a few white ones interspersed. The specimen from which our figure was drawn, was captured on Long Island in May 1834, and is therefore in summer pelage.

Dimensions.

For the sake of convenient comparison we will also here give the dimensions of the two species of Weasel to which our animal is most nearly allied, taken from specimens now before us.

	P. fuscus.		*P. erminea.*		*P. vulgaris.*	
	Inches.	Lines.	Inches.	Lines.	Inches.	Lines.
Length of head and body,	9	0	11	7	7	0
" tail (vertebræ),	2	9	4	6	1	9
" " (including fur), ...	3	2	6	2	2	1
Height of ear posteriorly,		3		2½		2

Habits.

We find from our notes, that in the State of New York in the winter of 1808, we kept a Weasel, which we suppose may have been this species, in confinement, together with several young ermines. The latter all became white in winter, but the former underwent no change in colour, remaining brown. On another occasion a specimen of a brown Weasel was brought to us in the month of December. At that season the ermines are invariably white. We cannot after the lapse of so many years say with certainty whether these specimens of Weasels that were brown in winter were those of the smaller, *Putorius pusillus*, or the present species; although we believe from our recollection of the size they were the latter. We therefore feel almost warranted in saying that this species does not change colour in winter.

We were in the habit of substituting our American Weasels for the European ferrets, in driving out the gray rabbit (*Lepus sylvaticus*) from the holes to which that species usually resorts in the northern States, when pursued by dogs (see vol. i. p. 59). Whilst the ermines seemed to relish this amusement vastly, the brown Weasel refused to enter the holes, and we concluded that the latter was the least courageous animal.

On one occasion we saw six or seven young Weasels dug out by dogs from under the roots of a tree in a swamp, which we believe to have been of this species.

Geographical Distribution.

The specimens which we have seen of this animal all came from different parts of the State of New York. We have however heard of the existence of a Weasel which is brown in winter in the States of Ohio and Michigan, which we have reason to believe is the present species.

General Remarks.

Our early writers on natural history were under the impression that we had but one, or at farthest two species of Weasel in our country.

GODMAN supposed that there was but one Weasel in North America, and that it was the common Weasel in summer, but was the ermine in summer pelage, turning white in winter. HARLAN gave DESMAREST's description of the European *Mustela vulgaris*, supposing that animal to exist in our country.

RICHARDSON gave two species as belonging to North America, one of which he supposed to be identical with the common Weasel of Europe. It is now ascertained that we have at least five species in the United States, four of which are found in the State of New York.

Sciurus Frémonti. —Townsend.

Frémont's Squirrel.

Plate cxlix. —Fig. 1. —Natural Size.

Magnitudine Sciuri Hudsonii; caudâ corpore breviore; auribus cristatis; colore supra albido, infra cinereo.

Characters.

Size of Sciurus Hudsonius; *tail, shorter than the body; ears, tufted. Colour, light gray above, ashy white beneath.*

Description.

Upper incisors, larger than those of *S. Richardsonii* or *S. lanuginosus*; lower incisors, longer and more curved than those of *S. Hudsonius*. The first or deciduous tooth wanting.

Body, short and stout, presenting less appearance of lightness and agility than that of the Hudson's Bay Squirrel; head, short and broad; forehead, but slightly arched; ears, rather short, broad, rounded, and much tufted; whiskers, long, reaching to the shoulders; legs, short and stout; the third toe on the fore-foot, slightly the longest; nails, compressed, and shorter, blunter, and less hooked than those of *S. Hudsonius*. Tail, a little shorter than the body, of tolerable breadth, and capable of a distichous arrangement.

The whole body is clothed with a dense coat of rather long and soft fur.

Colour.

Fur on the back, dark plumbeous from the roots; on the sides, tipped with light gray. There is a narrow dark reddish line along the centre of the back, caused by the hairs on the dorsal line being tipped with reddish-brown and black. On the under surface the fur is plumbeous at the roots, and tipped with ashy white. The tufts on the ears are black; whiskers, black; a line of dark brown runs from the end of the nose, blending gradually with the lighter tint of the forehead; there is a light circle around the eye; sides of the nose, and lips, yellowish-white; upper surface of feet, gray.

There is a slight and almost imperceptible black stripe about a line wide and three inches long, separating the colour of the sides from the ashy white tint of the under surface. Th annulations in the hairs of the tail are somewhat indistinct: from the roots for nearly half their length they are grayish-white, are then black, and are broadly tipped with white.

Dimensions.

	Inches.
Length of head and body,	7
" tail (vertebræ),	$4\frac{3}{4}$
" " (including fur),	$6\frac{1}{4}$
Height of ear posteriorly,	$\frac{3}{8}$
" " (including tufts),	$\frac{7}{8}$
Palm and middle fore-claw,	$1\frac{1}{8}$
Sole and middle hind-claw,	2

Habits.

We possess no information in regard to this animal farther than that it was obtained on the Rocky Mountains.

It no doubt, like all the other small species of Squirrels which are closely allied with it (*Richardsonii, Hudsonius, lanuginosus, &c.*), feeds on the seeds of pines, and other coniferæ.

All these squirrels inhabit elevated regions of country, and in addition to their habit of climbing, have burrows in the ground, wherein they make their dormitories, and dwell in winter; whilst in summer they select the hollow of a tree, in which they construct their nests.

Their note is peculiar, like *chicharee chicharee* repeated in quick succession, and differing from the *qua qua quah* note of the larger squirrels.

By their habit of burrowing or living in holes in the ground, these small squirrels make an approach to the genus *Tamias*, or ground squirrels.

Geographical Distribution.

The only specimen we have seen was obtained by Colonel FRÉMONT; it was procured on the Rocky Mountains, on his route by the south pass to California.

General Remarks.

The tufts on the ears of this species are considerably larger than in any other known species of squirrel in our country, except *Sciurus dorsalis*, a beautiful new squirrel discovered in California by Mr. WOODHOUSE, and recently described by that gentleman, and in this respect bear a resemblance to those on the ears of the common Squirrel of Europe (*Sciurus vulgaris*); the tufts, however, of the latter are twice the length of those of *S. Frémonti*, being an inch long, whilst in the latter they are half an inch in length.

These tufts, in the specimen, originate on the outer surface of the ear, near the base, and the edges of the ear are only covered with short hairs, whilst in the European species not only the posterior portions, but also the upper edges, or rims of the ear, are thickly haired, producing so large and thick a tuft that the animal at first sight appears to have an ear more than an inch long.

Plate CXLVIII

N°. 30

Drawn from Nature by J.W. Audubon.

Lith Printed & Col^d by J.T. Bowen, Phil

Tawny Weasel.

Sciurus Fuliginosus.—Bach.

Sooty Squirrel.

Plate cxlix. Fig. 2.—Natural Size.

Sciuro Hudsonio paullo major; caudâ nonnihil planâ, et corpore multo breviore; colore plerumque supra nigro, subfusco-flavo variegato; infra subfusco.

Characters.

A little larger than the Hudson's Bay Squirrel (S. Hudsonius); *tail, flattish, and much shorter than the body; general colour, black above, grizzled with brownish-yellow; beneath, brownish.*

Synonyme.

SCIURUS FULIGINOSUS. Bach., Monograph of the genus Sciurus, Trans. Zool. Soc., London, August, 1838.

Description.

Head, short, and broad; nose, very obtuse; ears, short, and rounded, slightly clothed with hair; feet and claws, rather short and strong; tail, short, and flattened, but not broad, resembling that of *Sciurus Hudsonius*; the form of the body is like that of the Carolina gray Squirrel.

Colour.

The limbs externally, and feet, are black, obscurely grizzled with brownish-yellow; on the under parts, with the exception of the chin and throat, which are grayish, the hairs are annulated with brownish-orange and black; at the roots, they are grayish-white; the prevailing colour of the tail is black above, the hairs being brown at the base, some of them obscurely annulated with brown, and at the apex pale brown; on the under side of the tail, the hairs exhibit pale yellowish-brown annulations.

Dimensions.

	Inches.	Lines.
Length of head and body,	10	
" tail (vertebræ),	6	9
" tail (including fur),	8	6
" palm to point of middle fore-claw,	1	8
" heel, to point of longest nail,	2	1
Height of ear posteriorly,		4
Length of fur on the back,		7

Habits.

This dusky looking species is found in low swampy situations, and is said to be very abundant in favourable localities.

During high freshets, when the swamps are overflowed to the height of several feet, they are very active among the trees, leaping from branch to branch, indifferent about the waters beneath. They feed chiefly on pecan nuts, and are deemed by the French inhabitants of Louisiana to be the most savoury of all the Squirrels.

Geographical Distribution.

We have heard of this species as existing only in Louisiana and Mississippi, and as being chiefly confined to the swamps.

General Remarks.

We are under the impression that this Squirrel is subject to considerable variations in colour. We obtained, through the kindness of Col. WADE HAMPTON, a number of specimens of the different Squirrels existing along the shores of the Mississippi, and among them we found several examples of this species. Some of them were of much lighter colours than the one which we described. In Louisiana, they are often so dark in colour, as to be called by the French inhabitants *le petit noir*.

The specimen from which our original description was made, was procured near New Orleans, on the 24th of March, 1837. It agrees in many particulars with a skin deposited in the late museum of Mr. PEALE at Philadelphia, which, with other specimens in that collection, is now probably lost for ever. Dr. HARLAN referred to it as *S. rufiventer*, but it did not agree with DESMAREST's description of that species, as we ascertained by comparing it. On examining the description Dr. HARLAN gave of the specimen to which he referred, we ascertained that instead of describing it himself, he had, with slight variations, translated DESMAREST's description.

Pseudostoma Floridana.—Aud. and Bach.

Southern Pouched Rat.

Plate cl. Fig. 1.—Old Male.—Natural Size.

Unica per longitudinem stria in dentibus qui secant superioribus; corpore P. bursario paullo exiguiore et minus robur prodente; sacculis genarum minoribus; palmis multo angustioribus; caudâ longiore; pilis crassioribus. Colore, supra subrufo-fusco, infra cinereo.

Characters.

A single longitudinal groove in the upper incisors; body, rather smaller and less stout in form that P. bursarius; *cheek-pouches, smaller; palms, much narrower; tail, longer; hair, coarser. Colour, above, brownish-yellow, beneath, gray.*

Description.

The body of this species is a little smaller and more slender and elongated than that of *P. bursarius*; head, small; nose, long, and not so blunt as in that animal. The fore-foot (or hand) has the palm narrow, and less tuberculated beneath than in *P. bursarius*; nails, narrower, a little longer, and much less arched than in that species; and the cheek-pouches are smaller. Tail, long (double the length of tail of *P. bursarius*), and has a little tuft of hair around the base; the rest of it, however, is naked. Feet, naked, instead of clothed with hair as in that animal.

In the upper jaw the incisors are of moderate size, narrow, with a single groove in the centre, and no groove on the inner edges, as in *P. bursarius*.

Septum, naked, with the nostrils entering in at the sides, immediately at the roots of the incisors; whiskers, rising from the sides of the nose, short, thin, and sparse; eyes, small, placed near each other in the head; the ears exhibit a slight margin around the auditory opening; they are placed far back, and not distant from each other; toes, five on each foot; on the fore-feet the middle toe with the nail is much the longest; the inner posterior toe is the smallest; there are a few short rigid hairs on the inner edge of the palm, but the foot may be described as naked; on the hind-foot, the claws, which are a little longer than those of *P. bursarius*, are hooked and channelled beneath; the hind-feet, to above the tarsus, are naked.

The hairs on the body are short, the coat not being half the length of the hairs of *P. bursarius*, and feeling much coarser and more rigid than in that species, especially on the under surface; the cheek-pouches are somewhat differently situated from those of *P. bursarius*: whilst in the latter species the upper edge is more than half an inch below the base of the superior incisors, the cheek-pouches in the present species open immediately into the mouth, the upper edge reaching them, so that while in *P. bursarius* the food has to be taken from the pouches and conveyed round to the mouth, the present species is able, by the peculiar form and situation of the opening of its pouch, to shove the food from the pouch immediately into the mouth. The pouches are, internally, sparsely covered with short hairs.

Colour.

Hair on the back, plumbeous from the roots for three fourths of its length, then yellowish, tipped with black; on the belly, the hairs are cinereous at base, and dirty yellow at the tips; under the throat, they are of a uniform ashy

Fig. 1

Fig. 2

On Stone by Wᵐ E. Hitchcock.

Fig. 1 Fremont's Squirrel. Fig. 2 Sooty Squirrel

Drawn from Nature by J W Audubon

Lith Printed & Colᵈ by J T. Bowen Philadᵃ

white. Whiskers, white, with a few (shorter ones) dark brown; teeth, pale orange; claws, light yellow, those on the hind-feet dark brown at the points; feet and tail, flesh colour. The result of the colouring of the hairs just mentioned is—back, brownish-yellow; nose and forehead, brown; under surface from the chest to the thighs, bluish-gray; throat, ashy white.

Dimensions.

	Inches.
From point of nose to root of tail, ...	$8\frac{3}{4}$
Tail, ...	4
Longest middle claw, ...	$\frac{3}{4}$
Palm, including claw, ...	$1\frac{5}{8}$
Breadth of head between the eyes, ...	$\frac{5}{8}$
" between ears, ...	$1\frac{1}{3}$

Habits.

The Southern Pouched Rat is very similar to the Canada Pouched Rat in its habits and manner of living, the chief differences in these respects between the former and the *Pseudostoma bursaria* being the natural result of different climate and situation.

This species is very remarkable for the apparently definite line of country it occupies, for, as far as we have been able to ascertain, although found in many places up to the southwestern bank of the Savannah river in Georgia, not one has ever been seen in South Carolina, or east of that river. This is the more singular as the wide range of the other species of this genus would lead us to suppose it not at all likely to be restricted by any fresh-water river, and indeed we can conceive no reason why it should not reach even to North Carolina and portions of Virginia, where sandy soils and dry pine lands similar to those it most frequents in Georgia, Florida, Alabama, and Mississippi, are widely extended.

Strangely enough, the common name applied to this animal where it is found is "Salamander."

The Southern Pouched Rat does not, like the *Pseudostoma bursarius*, remain under ground during the winter months, in a most probably dormant state, but continues its diggings throughout the year, and devours quantities of roots and grasses. It has hitherto been more frequently found living in the woods than near cultivated fields and plantations, but as the country becomes more settled will doubtless prove as great a pest in the gardens as its more northern relative, for an account of which see our first volume, pp. 332–339.

Geographical Distribution.

This species is found in the high pine barren regions, from the middle of Georgia and Alabama to the southern point of Florida, as far as the elevated portions of that State extend south.

We received two specimens from Major LOGAN in Dallas county, Alabama, several from Ebenezer, about twenty-five miles above Savannah in Georgia, and a number from the vicinity of Saint Augustine in East Florida.

We have not been able satisfactorily to ascertain its western range. We believe, however, it is not found west of the Mississippi. It is somewhat singular that this species is found on the very banks of the Savannah river, on the western side, and that notwithstanding, no traces of it have ever been seen east of that river, nor indeed in any portion of South Carolina, although there are extensive regions of high pine lands in that State which appear to be well suited to its habits.

General Remarks.

It is highly probable that this is the species referred to by RAFFINESQUE and others as the Georgia Hamster; inasmuch, however, as it was probably never seen by RAFFINESQUE, and he most likely formed his new genus *Geomys* from figures representing the cheek-pouches as rising within the mouth, and hanging like sacs under the throat, we have thought it as well to decline adopting his genus thus founded in error, and to omit quoting him in any part of our work as an authority.

Sorex Dekayi.—Bach.

DeKay's Shrew.

Plate cl. Fig. 2.—Young Male.—Natural Size.

Magnitudine Arvicolæ Pennsylvanicæ; colore supra ferrugineo, ex cinereo et flavo variegato, infra cinereo; caudâ brevi atque cylindraceâ.

Characters.

Size of Arvicola Pennsylvanica; rusty yellow gray colour above, cinereous beneath; tail, short and cylindrical.

Synonymes.

SOREX DEKAYI. Bachman, Jour. Acad. Nat. Sci., vol. vii., part 2, p. 377, pl. 23, fig. 4.
"   "   DeKay, Nat. Hist. of New York, p. 17, pl. 5, fig. 2.

Description.

Dental Formula.—Incisive $\frac{2}{2}$; Canine $\frac{5-5}{2-2}$; Molar $\frac{4-4}{3-3}$ = 32.

The two upper incisors are much curved, and pointed at tips; the lateral incisors are each crowned with two tubercles except the fifth, which is smooth; each grinder, on the upper surface, is furnished with four sharp points; in the lower jaw the incisors are also much curved; the first canine tooth is smaller than the second, and the molars are similar to those of the upper jaw. The body bears a resemblance to that of the shrew mole in shape. Head, rather short; nose, distinctly bilobate; nostrils, on the sides; the eye is a mere speck; there are no external ears; whiskers, the length of the head; the feet are more robust than those of any American Shrew we have examined, and are haired on the soles; feet, clothed with short fine hairs; the tail in the dry specimen is square, examined in the flesh is rounded, slightly dilated in the middle, and covered with short hair; hind-foot, three middle nails nearly equal, outer toe a little longer than the inner, which latter is the shortest.

Colour.

Nose, feet, and nails, reddish-brown; upper surface of body, rusty yellow gray; a shade lighter on the under surface; whiskers, for half the length from their roots cinereous, whitish at the tips; incisors, black.

Dimensions.

Female, captured in the garden at Minniesland near New York.

	Inches.
From point of nose to root of tail, ...	$4\frac{1}{2}$
Tail (vertebræ), ...	1
" (to end of hair), ...	$1\frac{1}{10}$
From heel to point of longest nail, ...	$\frac{5}{8}$
Breadth of fore-foot, ...	$\frac{1}{4}$

Male, one eighth of an inch longer than the female.

Habits.

We have always found it difficult to obtain satisfactory information as to the habits of the smaller quadrupeds, from the fact that many of our farmers and their men are unacquainted with the generic and even specific names, and consequently often mistake the habits of some genus or species for those of a very distinct one. The various species belonging to the genera *Scalops, Condylura,* and *Sorex,* are in most cases called (and considered to be) "ground moles," and thus are represented as all possessing the same habits. The gardener who caught for us the two specimens above described, said they were ground moles. On showing him that they were smaller, and had very different feet from those of any animal belonging to the genus *Scalops,* he said "they were only young ones, that their feet would become large by next year." On asking him about their nests, he said they were not old enough as yet to have young. When we requested him to show us their holes he first directed us to the ridges made in the soil by the ground mole.

After a careful examination, however, we ascertained that DEKAY's Shrew burrows deeper in the earth than *Scalops aquaticus*. The galleries of *S. DeKayi* run along at the depth of about a foot from the surface, and have apertures leading up to the open air at short distances from each other, by which the animals have ingress or egress. Ground moles seek worms and insects in the earth, whereas the Shrews come abroad on the surface, and run over the ground at night in quest of food, a habit in which the mole does not appear to indulge.

N° 30

Plate CL

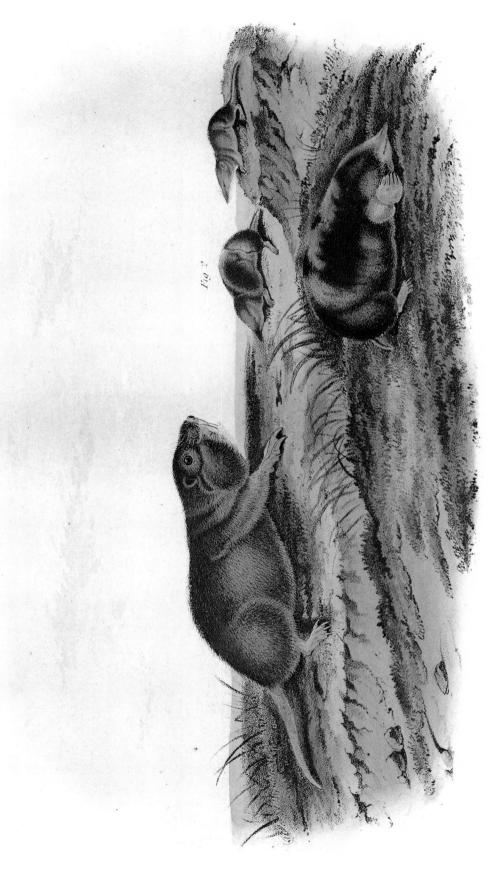

Fig 1 — Fig 2 — Fig 3 — Fig 4

On Stone by Wm E. Hitchcock

Fig 1. Southern Pouched Rat. Fig 2 Dekay's Shrew. Fig 3 Long-Nosed Shrew. Fig 4 Silvery Shrew Mole.

Drawn from Nature by J. J. Audubon

Lith. Printed & Col^d by J. T. Bowen, Phil

Geographical Distribution.

We received specimens of this small animal from Mr. COOPER, who obtained them in New Jersey; also one from Albany. We were present when two were captured near New York, and have neard of its existence in New England, Maryland, and Virginia.

General Remarks.

We have seen specimens of DEKAY's Shrew which exhibited a dark slaty gray appearance on the back and sides, and differed materially in colour from those from which we described.

This we attributed to the dark gray ones having been killed in the autumn or towards the approach of winter. Dr. DEKAY seems to have described a specimen with this slaty coloured fur; he gives its colour as "dark bluish throughout."

Sorex Longirostris. — Bach.

Long-nosed Shrew.

Plate cl. Fig. 3. — Male.

S. Castaneus, rostro longo, caudâ longâ, auriculis amplis, vellere non occultis.

Characters.

Nose, long; ears, large, and prominent; tail, long; general colour, chesnut.

Synonymes.

SOREX LONGIROSTRIS—LONG-NOSED SHREW. Bach., Jour. Acad. Nat. Sci., vol. vii., part 2, p. 370. Anno 1837.
OTISOREX PLATYRHINUS. DeKay, Nat. Hist. State of New York, p. 22, pl. 5, fig. 1. 1842.

Description.

Dental Formula.—Incisive $\frac{3}{3}$; Canine $\frac{5-5}{5-5}$; Molar $\frac{4-4}{3-3}$ = 32.

Nose, very long; whole upper jaw bordered with whiskers, extending to the middle of the ear; lower jaw, sparsely covered with the same kind of hair, but shorter; extremity of the muzzle, naked, deeply indented and bilobed; the eyes are distinctly visible, and larger than in most species of this genus; the ear extends considerably beyond the fur, is comparatively large and thickly clothed within and without, with short soft hairs; the auditory opening is covered with a large oblong lobe on which are sprinkled a few stiff long hairs; tail, nearly round, but in the dried specimen becoming square; it is clothed with short hair above and beneath, as also the feet and palms to the extremities of the nails; toes, five; the whole body is slender, and the feet small and weak. The fur is close, very fine, and glossy.

Colour.

Above, uniform chesnut; beneath, a shade lighter; points of the teeth, dark brown; nails, horn colour, tipped with black.

VOL. III.—32

Dimensions.

	Inches.
Length from the nose to the origin of the tail, ...	$1\frac{7}{8}$
" of tail, ...	1
" of head, ...	$\frac{7}{8}$
Height of ear, ...	$\frac{1}{4}$
Length of hind-foot from heel to end of nails, ...	$\frac{3}{8}$

We have since measured a specimen procured at Tulula falls in Georgia, the dimensions of which were as follows:

	Inches.	Lines.
Length from nose to origin of tail, ...	2	2
" of tail, ...	1	3

Habits.

We possess very little knowledge in regard to the habits of this little Shrew. The first specimen we saw was obtained in the swamps that border the Santee River, by Dr. ALEXANDER HUME; his labourers found it whilst digging a ditch through grounds nearly overflowed with water. Another was obtained in a singular manner. Whilst we were at the house of Major LEE in Colleton district, his huntsman brought in some wild ducks, and among the rest a hooded merganser (*Mergus cucullatus*). There was a protuberance on the throat of this bird, appearing as if it had not fully swallowed some article of food at the time it was shot. On opening the throat, it was found to contain this little Shrew, which was fresh, and not in the least mutilated.

We saw two or three Shrews in the same vicinity which we think were of this species, coming out of a bank on the edge of a rice field and swimming in the canal at the dusk of the evening. From the above circumstances we are induced to think that this quadruped prefers low swampy situations, and is to a certain extent aquatic in its habits. We more recently obtained a specimen from Col. W. E. HASKELL, of St. Paul's parish, South Carolina, which was a shade lighter, and a little larger, than others in our possession, but presented no specific differences.

Geographical Distribution.

The Long-nosed Shrew (although apparently very sparingly) is found in South Carolina. We saw a specimen in the possession of the keeper of the public house at the Tulula falls in the mountains of Georgia. It evidently extends throughout the middle States, and has been taken in New York and New England.

General Remarks.

The American Shrews may be easily arranged into three natural groups; first, those with short ears and tail, of which *Sorex DeKayi* would form the type; second, those with large palms, broadly fringed, such as *S. fimbripes*; and third, those with long ears and tail, of which the present species would be the type.

We perceive that Dr. DeKay has formed the present species into a new genus, *Otisorex*; but as the European naturalists has previously proposed a number of genera, one of which would include the present species, we prefer for the present leaving our American Shrews in the genus *Sorex*. We have no hesitation in sayin that Dr. DeKay's species *platyrhinus*, on which his genus was founded, is identical with *S. longirostris*, the subject of our present article.

Scalops Argentatus. — Aud. and Bach.

Silvery Shrew-Mole.

Plate cl. Fig. 4. — Female.

S. Pilis tota longitudine albo, plumboque annulatis; fronte, mentique albido flavescente.

Characters.

Hairs, from the roots regularly annulated with white and plumbeous; forehead and chin, yellowish-white. Colour of the body, shining silver gray.

Synonyme.

SCALOPS ARGENTATUS—SILVERY SHREW-MOLE. Aud. and Bach., Jour. Acad. Nat. Sci., October 5, 1841.

Description.

In form this species is cylindrical, like the common Shrew-Mole (*S. aquaticus*), to which it bears a strong resemblance. Muzzle, naked; and the nostrils inserted, not on the sides, as is the case in *Scalops Breweri*, but in the upper surface, near the point of the nose, as in *S. aquaticus*. Eyes, not visible, and appear covered by an integument; the lips are fringed with rather coarse hairs; this species is pendactylous, with naked palms and tail; the teeth are larger, shorter, and broader than those of the common Shrew-Mole; the fur is long and lustrous on the back, but much shorter and more compact on the under surface.

Colour.

Teeth, and nails, white; palms, hind-feet, and tail, flesh coloured; nose, forehead, lips, and chin, yellowish-white; the fur on the back is from the roots marked with alternate narrow bars of dark blue and white to near the extremities, where it is broadly barred with ashy white, and so slightly tipped with brown that the lighter colour beneath is still visible on the surface, giving it a beautiful silvery appearance, which presents a variety of changes, on being exposed to different rays of light. On the lower surface the hair is plumbeous from the roots to near the tips, where it is barred with whitish; it is tipped with light brown. There is a spot of white on the centre of the abdomen, which is apparently accidental, as we have occasionally observed it in other species of this genus, as well as in the true mole (*Talpa*) of Europe.

Dimensions.

	Inches.	Lines.
Length of head and body, ...	7	1
" tail, ...	1	
Breadth of palm, ...		10
From tarsus to point of longest nail, ...		7

Habits.

Dr. GEO. C. LEIB, who discovered this animal in the prairies of Michigan, gave us no account of its habits, which we presume are similar to those of the common Shrew-Mole.

Geographical Distribution.

We have not heard of this beautifully furred Mole in any other locality than that where our specimen was procured, which is the only one we have ever seen, and the one from which our figure and description have been made.

General Remarks.

Of the several species of Shrew-Mole that inhabit North America, this in point of colour is the most brilliant that has yet been brought to the notice of naturalists. Although it bears a general resemblance to the common Shrew-Mole, yet the characters it presents have induced us after some hesitation and doubt, to designate it as a new species. It is nearly double the size of the common Shrew-Mole; the fur is much longer and softer, and differs strikingly in colour and lustre. Our specimen was evidently a young animal, although the dentition was similar to that of *Sc. aquaticus*. Some of the small thread-like teeth that are placed behind the incisors in the upper jaw were wanting on one side, and were only barely visible on the other. The young of *Scalops aquaticus* have but thirty teeth until they are more than a year old; when they have arrived at their full vigour they are furnished permanently with thirty-six. The skulls of *Scalops Townsendii* and *S. Brewerii* each contain forty-four teeth.

Before we taken leave of the Shrew-Moles of our country, we have to add that RICHARDSON (F. B. A. p. 12), in noticing the assertion of BARTRAM that a true mole, *Talpa*, existed in America (in which he was supposed by later writers to be mistaken), asserts that there are several true moles in the museum of the Zoological Society of London, which were brought from America, and which differ from the ordinary European species (*Talpa Europea*), in being of a smaller size and having a shorter and thicker snout, their fur being brownish-black. DeKAY, in the Natural History of New York (p. 16), refers to the above statement. We however examined these specimens in the Zoological Museum, and found they consisted of only two species—our common *Scalops aquaticus*, which RICHARDSON strangely mistook for another species, and *Scalops Breweri*, to which he particularly referred. Thus far therefor no true specimen of the genus *Talpa* has been discovered in America, and we have no doubt that the species referred to by BARTRAM as the black mole was BREWER's Shrew-Mole, which in certain lights appears quite black.

Vulpes Utah.—Aud. and Bach.

Jackall Fox.

Plate cli.

V. corpore grandiore, pilis velleris longioribus nec non gracilioribus quam in V. fulvo, cauda magna cylindracea.

Characters

Larger than Vulpes fulvus; fur longer and finer than in that species; tail large and cylindrical.

Synonymes.

VULPES UTAH.—Aud. and Bach., Proc. Acad. Nat. Sci., Phil., 1852, p. 114.
VULPES MACROURUS, Baird, Stansbury's Report.

Description.

Claws slightly arched, compressed, channelled beneath, horn color; hair, of two kinds, first a coarse and long hair covering the fur beneath it; second, a dense and very soft fine fur, composed of hairs that are straight, but crimped and wavy, as in the silver grey fox. Fur plumbeous at the roots, gradually becoming dark brown towards the tips in those parts of the body which are dark colored on the surface; in those parts which are white, the fur is white from the roots, and on no part of the animal does it present any annulations.

The long hairs are dark-brown from the roots, yellowish-white near the middle of their length, and are tipped with black.

On the under surface the hairs are principally white their whole extent, with a few black ones intermixed; the fur on the tail is rather less fine and more woolly than on the body.

Feet covered with soft hair reaching beyond the toes; on the forehead the hair is rather coarse and short, with fine fur beneath.

Colour.

Greyish-white on the head, dark brown on the neck, greyish-brown on the dorsal line and on the sides; the throat, under surface of the body, insides of legs, and feet black.

The tail is irregularly banded with dark brown and dull white, the tip white for about three inches.

Another Specimen.—Nose, both surfaces of the legs, and behind the ears, dark, reddish-brown; whiskers black; under side of neck, and a line on the belly, liver brown. Fur on the back very fine, and dark ashy-grey from the roots: the longer hairs on the back are black at the roots, and are broadly tipped with white; fur on the sides, cinereous at the roots, and yellowish-white from thence to the end.

There is a reddish tinge on the neck, extending to the shoulders; sides of the face grizzly-brown; the hair on the tail is irregularly clouded with brown and dull white, and is lightest on the under surface.

Dimensions.

	Feet.	Inches.
From point of nose to root of tail, ...	2	8
Tail, (vertebræ,)	1	4
" (to end of hair,)	1	8
Circumference of tail, (broadest Part,)	1	8
From shoulder to fore-feet, ...	1	5
From rump to hind-feet, ...	1	6
Height of ears, (posteriorly,)		4
From point of nose to eye, ...		$3\frac{1}{8}$
Longest hairs on the brush, ...		5
" on the body, ...		3

Habits.

This animal was first noticed, by LEWIS and CLARK, as the large Red Fox of the plains, (vol. 2, p. 168,) and was referred to by us in the first volume of the Quadrupeds of North America, p. 54, where we described it from a hunter's skin.

Having obtained a beautiful specimen from Captain RHETT, of the United

States Army, we gave it the name of *Vulpes Utah*, as it is, so far as our information extends, chiefly found in the Utah territory, although it probably ranges considerably north of the Great Salt Lake.

The habits of this beautiful Fox are similar to those of the Red Fox, and it runs into many varieties of color.

Captain RHETT informed us that he killed the specimen, kindly presented to us by him, near Fort Laramie.

Several specimens of *Vulpes Utah* have been received at the Smithsonian Institution, and it will probably soon be well known.

Geographical Distribution.

This Fox, as we have ascertained since writing the above, is procured throughout the Rocky Mountain regions, although by no means abundantly, as far north as the traders of the fur companies push their outposts. It is found also in Oregon.

General Remarks.

The exploring expedition sent by the United States, (1838 to 1842) did not procure any specimens of this Fox, although we find by Mr. PEALE's Catalogue, they obtained the Vulpes Virginianus, in both Oregon and California.

Sciurus Mustelinus.—Aud. and Bach.

Weasel-Like Squirrel.

Plate clii.—Male. Fig. 1.

S. Cervice longissima; caudâ corpore longiore; pilis curtis, rigidis, compressis, teretibus; omni corporis parte nigerrima.

Characters.

Neck, very long; tail, longer than the body; hair, short, rigid, adpressed, and glossy; the whole body, jet black.

Synonyme.

SCIURUS MUSTELINUS—WEASEL SQUIRREL. Aud. and Bach., Proc. Acad. Nat. Sci. Phil., Oct. 5, 1841, p. 32.

Description.

The unusually long neck of this species, together with its long slender body, and smooth lustrous hair, give it somewhat the appearance of a weasel, and suggested to us the specific name.

Ears, of moderate size, and nearly naked, there being only a few hairs on the borders; feet, covered with very short hairs, which only reach to the roots of the nails; tail, long, not bushy, moderately distichous.

Colour.

The hairs, in every part of the body, are deep black from the roots to the tips, and the surface is glossy.

Dimensions.

	Inches.	Lines.
Length of head and body	10	
" tail, ...	13	
From shoulder to point of nose, ...	3	10
Tarsus, ...	2	5
Height of ear posteriorly, ...		6

Habits.

The Weasel-like Squirrel feeds in the woody portions of California, on acorns, the seeds of the pines and other trees, and makes its nest in the oaks or nut-bearing pines of that country, which, from their broad spreading branches and dense leafy boughs, afford it security against the hunter, as with equal cunning and agility it hides itself, when alarmed, amid the evergreen foliage, and except when surprised on the ground or near the earth, and shot instantly, can seldom be killed. There is no more tantalizing game, in fact, and as the branches interlock at a moderate elevation from the ground, the animal easily goes from one tree to another, and so swiftly that it is not often to be traced in its course of flight along the boughs.

We are unacquainted with the time of this animal's breeding, but presume it brings forth about four or five young at a birth. The young of all species of squirrels with which we are familiar, are born blind, and remain without sight from four to six weeks. This is an admirable provision of nature for their safety, as were they able to use their eyes at an earlier period, they would doubtless be tempted to quit the security of the nest and venture on to the branches, before they had gained strength enough to preserve their footing, and would thus probably fall to the earth and be killed.

Geographical Distribution.

The specimen from which our figure and description were made was procured in California. We have no authority for stating its northern or southern range, but consider it a western species—by which we mean that it is not found east of the Rocky Mountain chain.

General Remarks.

From its thin covering of hair, being nearly destitute of the soft fur usually clothing the squirrels, this species may be considered as belonging to a moderate or warm climate. It differs widely from all the other species of Black Squirrel (as well as all black varieties of Squirrel), in our country. It has shorter and coarser hair than *S. capistratus,* and is destitute of the white nose and ears of that species, with none of the white tufts invariably found in *S. niger*; and has a smaller body, although a much longer tail than *S. Auduboni,* without the white, yellow, and brown annulations in the hair which characterize that species.

Sciurus Auduboni.—Bach.

Large Louisiana Black Squirrel.

Plate clii. Fig. 2.—Male.

Paulo minor quam Sciurus Niger; aures breviores; dentes qui cibum secant latiores; cauda longitudine corpori par; capilli valde crassi, tactuque asperi, sed nihilominus nitidi. Color, supra niger; infra subfuscus.

Characters.

A little less than Sciurus niger; ears, shorter; incisors, broader; tail, as long as the body; fur, very coarse and harsh to the touch, but glossy; colour, above, black, beneath, brownish.

Synonymes.

LARGE LOUSIANA BLACK SQUIRREL—SCIURUS AUDUBONI. Bach., Monog. of the Genus Sciurus, p. 33. 1839.

Description.

Dental Formula.—Incisive $\frac{2}{2}$; Canine $\frac{0—0}{0—0}$; Molar $\frac{4—4}{4—4}$ = 20.

Our specimen has the above number of teeth. If the small anterior molar in the upper jaw exists in the young, which we suspect to be the case in all American species, it is deciduous; and we are warranted in arranging this species among those which have permanently but twenty teeth. In the upper jaw the anterior molar is triangular in shape, and crowned with three blunt tubercles; the other molars are quadrangular, with concave crowns.

Head, narrower, and body, thinner than in *S. niger;* ears, short and conical, covered on both surfaces with short adpressed hairs, presenting no tufts;

Plate CLI

Drawn from Nature by J.W. Audubon

On Stone by W.E. Hitchcock

Lith Printed & Col.d by J. T. Bowen Phila.

Fuckall Fox.

whiskers, longer than the head, extending to the shoulders. Fur on the back, very coarse.

Colour.

Incisors, deep orange; whiskers, black; back, upper parts, outsides of limbs, and feet, black, with a faint tinge of brown. Many of the hairs are however obscurely annulated with yellowish-white. The whole under surface, and the inner sides of the legs, are brownish. Most of the hairs on the under surface are grayish-white at the base, some are annulated with black and yellow, and others are brown.

Chin, black, with the extreme tip whitish; end of nose, brownish; tail, black; when viewed beneath, the hairs exhibit deep yellow annulations; most of the hairs are brownish towards the tip.

Dimensions.

	Inches.	Lines.
Length of head and body,	11	6
" tail (vertebræ),	8	9
" " (to end of hair),	11	6
" · palm to end of middle fore-claw,	1	6
Heel to point of longest nail,	2	6

Height of ear posteriorly,	3
Length of fur on the back,	6

Habits.

This southern Black Squirrel was first described by Dr. BACHMAN, from a specimen obtained by J. W. AUDUBON in Louisiana, and was named by him after its discoverer. It frequents high grounds, and has all the active, restless, and playful habits of the genus.

Geographical Distribution.

The Louisiana Black Squirrel has been seen west of the Mississippi, and as we think is occasionally found in Texas. It is sometimes offered for sale in the New Orleans markets, being shot in the neightbourhood of that city.

General Remarks.

We have been informed by some officers of the United States army that a Squirrel similar to the present species is found in Texas and in parts of New Mexico, but from there being no specimens we could not positively identify the Black Squirrels these gentlemen had observed with *S. Audubom*.

Sciurus Aberti.—Woodhouse.

Col. Abert's Squirrel.

Plate cliii.—Fig. 1.

S. Auribus magnis latisque, cristatis longis subnigris cinereisque crinibus; rubra in dorso striga.

Characters.

Ears large and broad, tufted with long blackish grey hairs; a reddish stripe on the back.

Synonymes.

SCIURUS DORSALIS.—Woodhouse, Proc. Acad. Nat. Sci., Phil., June, 1852, p. 110.
SCIURUS ABERTI.—Woodhouse, Proc. Acad. Nat. Sci. Phil., Dec., 1852, p. 220.

Description.

Ears large and broad, with very long tufts; tail very large; fur long, compact, and soft; claws long, very strong, and much curved; whiskers very long.

Colour.

General colour above dark grey, with the exception of the dorsal line and a band extending along the external base or hind part of the ear, which is of a rich ferruginous brown colour; beneath, white, with the exception of the perineum, which is grey; cheeks greyish white; tail grey above with a broad white margin, and white beneath; claws of a black colour with the exception of their points, which are light and almost transparent; whiskers black; iris dark brown.

Dimensions.

Dried Skin.	Inches.
Length from nose to root of tail, about,	13
From heel to point of longest nail,	$2\frac{8}{10}$
Height of ears, externally,	$1\frac{3}{10}$
" " to end of tufts,	$2\frac{8}{10}$
Breadth " _____	1
From ear to point of nose, about	$1\frac{7}{10}$
Tail (vertebræ), about	8
" to end of fur,	11

Habits.

Dr. WOODHOUSE, from whose description we have extracted above, makes the followings remarks: "This beautiful squirrel I procured whilst attached to the expedition under command of Capt. L. SITGREAVES, Topographical Engineer U. S. Army, exploring the Zuni and the great and little Colorado rivers of the west, in the month of October, 1851, in the San Francisco Mountain, New Mexico, where I found it quite abundant, after leaving which, I did not see it again."

Geographical Distribution.

So far as shown by the foregoing account, and according to our knowledge, this squirrel has not been seen except in the San Francisco Mountain, New Mexico. It is, however, most likely that it inhabits a considerable district of elevated and wooded country in that part of our Continent, and may hereafter be found in California or even Oregon.

General Remarks.

We have not been able to procure any further information regarding this species, which was first named *Sciurus dorsalis* by its discoverer, but a subsequent examination having satisfied him that this name had "already been applied by J. E. GRAY, to one of the same genus," he proposed "to call it *Sciurus Aberti*, after Col. J. J. ABERT, chief of the corps of Topographical Engineers, U. S. Army, to whose exertions science is much indebted."—(Proceed. Acad. Nat. Sci., Phil., Dec. 1852, p. 220.)

It gives us great pleasure to welcome this beautiful new animal under the name of Col. ABERT's Squirrel.

Sciurus Fossor.—Peale.

California Grey Squirrel.

Plate cliii. Fig. 2.

S. Supra e nigro alboque intermixtis griseus, subtus albus, auribus magnis, breviter pilosis, naso nigro, cauda disticha, albo-marginata, corpore longiore.

Characters.

Above, grey; beneath, white; ears not tufted, but clothed within and without with short hairs; nose black; tail distichous, tipped with white; body long and rather slender.

Synonymes.

SCIRUS FOSSOR.—Peale, Mam., &c., of the U. S. Exp. Exped., 1838–42. Phila. 1848.

Fig.1
Fig.2

Fig.1 *Weasel like Squirrel.*

Fig.2 *Large Louisiana Black Squirrel.*

Drawn from Nature by J.W. Audubon

SCIURUS HEERMANNI.—Dr. Le Conte, Proceed. Acad. Nat. Sci., Phil., Sept., 1852, p. 149.

Description.

Whiskers shorter than the head; ears large, subtriangular, rounded at the tip, and covered both within and without with short hair, which does not in any way form a fringe at the margin; tail long and distichous, with long hairs which are grey at the roots, black above and tipped with white; body long and rather slender; hair on the body long and not fine.

Colour.

Body above light grey, produced by an intermixture of black and white points; the hairs are grey at base, then black, and have a pure white annulation about the middle; intermixed with them are a few longer pure black hairs. A small spot towards the tip of the nose, and an indistinct line above the eyes are black; whiskers black. Beneath, the body is pure white, except the perineum, which is grey; tail grey, blackish towards the edges, and broadly margined with white; rather lighter in colour beneath.

Dimensions.

	Inches.	Lines.
From tip of nose to root of tail,	12	5
Head,	3	2
Length of ear,		9
Breadth of ear,		7
Fore foot to end of longest claw,	2	1
Hind foot to end of longest claw,	3	2
Tail, to end of vertebræ,	9	8
" hair,	13	

Habits.

This beautiful squirrel has been often killed by Mr. J. E. CLEMENTS, in the pine woods of California, near Murphy's "diggings." It is exceedingly swift on the ground, and will not readily take to a tree, or, if it does, ascends only a few feet, and then jumping down to the ground runs off with its tail held up but curved downwards towards the tip like that of a fox when in flight.

By the aid of a fast cur dog, it may, however, be put up a tree. In this case it hides if a hole offers in which to conceal itself; and unlike some others of its genus, seldom leaps from one tree to another over the higher boughs in the endeavour to make its escape.

It appears to make its nest generally in the decayed part of an oak tree, and in the desire to reach its secure retreat, is doubtless led to attempt to run to this tree on the ground, rather than by ascending the nearest trunk and jumping from branch to branch.

A large part of its food consists of nuts, which are stuck in hollows or holes bored in the pine trees by a species of woodpecker called by the Californians "Sapsuckers." These nuts are placed in holes in the bark, which are only so deep as to admit the nuts (which are placed small end foremost in them), leaving the large end visible and about flush with the bark—they thus present the appearance of pins or pegs of wood stuck into the trees, and are very curious objects to the eye of the stranger.

The California grey squirrel is a roving animal. One may sometimes see from one to a dozen in a morning's hunt in the pines, and again not meet any. They very seldom leave the pines, but are occasionally seen in the dry season following the beds of the then almost empty water courses, which afford them, in common with other animals and birds, water and such roots and grasses as they cannot find on the uplands at that period of the year.

They bark somewhat in the same tones as the grey squirrel of the Atlantic States, but immediately cease when they perceive they are observed by man. Sometimes they seem to be excited to the utterance of their cries by the whistling of the California partridges, which, near the hills, approach the edges of the pine woods.

Most of those shot by Mr. CLEMENTS were killed when running on the ground.

Geographical Distribution.

This species is found in California in the wooded districts on the sides of the hills, and extends to Oregon, as, in Mr. PEALE's work, we have accounts of its having been observed there.

It is also almost a sure conclusion that it is found on the ridges of the mountains, as far south as the nut-bearing trees invite it, and it may thus reach quite a low latitude.

General Remarks.

The pine nuts referred to in the account of the habits of this squirrel, as a favourite article of food for it, are placed on the cones of the *Sugar Pine*, (*Pinus Lambertii*, Douglas), so called from the gum which exudes from it, where the bark has been wounded, becomes hard and white, and is quite sweet to the taste.

The nuts are formed on the cones, sometimes twenty or thirty on one cone. The Indians pound and crack them. They are very good eating, and taste not unlike a hickory nut. The shell is thin, but hard, the nut covered with a skin like the peach kernel, &c.

We hesitated somewhat as to adopting the name (*Sciurus Fossor*) given to this species by Mr. TITIAN R. PEALE, as his volume on the "Mammalia and Ornithology" of the United States Exploring Expedition, &c., has been suppressed; but as about one hundred copies, it appears, were circulated, we think it is only justice to Mr. PEALE to quote his work, which, as it was printed in 1848, gives his name the priority over *Sciurus Heermanni*, under which this species was described by our friend Dr. LECONTE, September, 1852.

Its flesh is good eating, and it is sufficiently abundant in some parts of California to make it worth the hunting for market.

Spermophilus Harrisii.—Aud.and Bach.

Harris's Spermophile, or Marmot Squirrel.

Plate cliv.—Fig. 1.

S. Magnitudine *Tamiæ Lysteri;* strigis duobus albis dorsalibus ab humeris ad femora; fronte rufo-canescente, colle et ventre cinereis-albis, dorso fulvo-cinereo; cauda disticha.

Characters.

Size of Tamias Lysteri; a narrow white stripe on each side of the back, from the shoulder to the thighs; forehead reddish-grey; neck ashy-white running into yellowish iron-grey on the back; under surface ashy white; tail distichous.

Description.

Head small and delicate; neck, rather long; body slender; legs rather long, a few long hairs growing out and fringing the hind parts of the fore legs; the cheek pouches appear rather small in the dried specimen; ears thinly clothed on both surfaces with short adpressed hairs; short, somewhat triangular, and rather acute at the tips; tail of moderate length, depressed at base, with the hairs growing from the side, giving it a decidedly distichous appearance; the teeth resemble those of *T. Lysteri;* are rather small, and the lower incisors are slightly curved.

Whiskers not numerous, reaching the ear; hairs on the back very short, somewhat coarse, but lying very smoothly, giving the animal a glossy appearance; on the under surface they are coarse and rigid. There are five toes on each foot; on the fore-feet a small tubercle in place of a thumb, with a blunt nail; second nail from the thumb longest, as in the rest of the spermophili; on the hind feet the middle toes are longest, the two on each side being of nearly equal length, the outer considerably shorter, and the inner shortest; claws slightly compressed, and a little curved; feet clothed with short hairs, but which do not conceal the nails; the eyes are of moderate size, and are placed midway between the point of the nose and the root of the ear; soles of feet tuberculated and naked, except a few hairs between the toes.

Colour.

Incisors dingy yellow; whiskers and nails black; back and sides minutely speckled with white, on a yellowish-brown ground; the hairs are dark-brown

Plate CLIII

N.º 31

Fig.1 Col: Abert's Squirrel. _ Fig. 2. California Grey Squirrel.

Drawn from Nature by J W Audubon.

at the roots, then white, then black, and the tips brownish-white, with a tinge of yellow; on the nose and forehead, the speckled appearance of the back is superseded by a rufous tint; between the ears, on the neck, and a little downwards, towards the legs, greyish-white is the prevailing color; a narrow white stripe, rising from behind the shoulder, and running along the side of the back to the middle of the hips, there loses itself in the general colour of the body; around the eye, throat, chin, inner surface of legs, and whole under surface of body, whitish, with a few black hairs interspersed; a tinge of brownish-red on the outer surface of the fore legs is more strongly red on the thighs; feet and outer surface of legs yellowish white.

The hairs of the tail are whitish at the roots, twice annulated with black, and tipped with white.

There is a line of whitish yellow on the flanks, separating the colour of the back and sides from the under surface distinctly, and extending along beneath the reddish brown tint on the thighs, where it becomes a deeper yellow.

Dimensions.

	Inches.
Length of head and body	$5\frac{3}{4}$
" tail (vertebræ)	$3\frac{1}{4}$
" " to end of hair	$4\frac{1}{2}$
From tarsus to end of longest claw	$1\frac{1}{2}$
Length of fore leg from the shoulder	2
" hind leg from the thighs	$2\frac{1}{2}$
Breadth of tail, when distichously arranged	$1\frac{3}{4}$
Height of ear (posteriorly)	$\frac{1}{8}$
Longest claw on the fore foot	$\frac{1}{8}$

Habits.

There is nothing to be said by us about the habits of this species, as it has not been observed, so far as we know, since our specimen was procured, and we have not even a knowledge of the precise locality in which it was obtained by Mr. J. K. TOWNSEND, who gave the specimen to our esteemed friend, EDWARD HARRIS, Esq., from whom we received it some time since, and with whose name we have honoured this pretty little animal.

Geographical Distribution.

Probably west of the Rocky Mountains, on the route followed by Messrs, NUTTALL and TOWNSEND, in their journey to Oregon overland.

General Remarks.

This species bears a very slight resemblance to *Spermophilus lateralis* of SAY, but differs so widely from it that it is unnecessary to institute a close comparison. It is a smaller animal, the head and ears being diminutive compared with the latter; it has a single stripe of white on the sides of the back, whilst in *Lateralis* a broad white stripe is margined on each side by a stripe of black, giving it the appearance of having four black stripes on the back, while *S. Harrisii* has no black about the back or sides at all.

Arvicola Edax.—Le Conte.

California Meadow Mouse.

Plate cliv.—Fig. 2.

A. Brevis et robustus, supra spadiceo et nigro permixtus. Auribus extra pilos extantibus. Cauda mediocri, supra nigra, subtus cinerea.

Characters.

Body short and thick; above, brown mixed with black; ears not concealed by the hair; tail moderate length, black above, beneath grey.

Synonyme.

ARVICOLA EDAX.—Le Conte, Proc. Acad. Nat. Sci., Phil., Oct. 1853, p. 405.

Description.

Head short and blunt; ears round, not entirely concealed under the fur, hairy within and without, antitragus large and semicircular; feet covered with short, shining grey hair; thumb tubercle, with a short, very blunt nail; tail of moderate length, hairy above.

Colour.

Hair plumbeous black above and on the sides, tipped with shining brown mixed with black; beneath tipped with grey; feet grey; tail dusky above, grey beneath, with a slight brownish tinge.

Dimensions.

	Inches.
Length (including the tail)	5.5
" of head	1.4
" " ears	.5
" " fore leg	1.3
" " hind leg	1.5
" " tail	1.5

Habits.

This new Arvicola from California has doubtless the habits of the genus to which it belongs. Our friend Major LE CONTE does not, however, say anything in relation to its peculiarities, and as all our information of the existence even of the animal is derived from that gentleman, we have nothing to say further. We present our thanks to Major LE CONTE for the loan of the skin from which our figure was made.

Geographical Distribution.

California is named as the habitat of this Meadow Mouse; but we are not informed whether it is widely diffused there, or is confined to certain localities.

General Remarks.

The description and dimensions of the California Meadow Mouse above given are quoted with slight alterations from Major LE CONTE's paper cited above.

Plate CLIV

Fig 1

Fig.²

Fig.²

Drawn from Nature by J. W. Audubon.

Fig 1 Harris' Marmot Squirrel.   Fig 2 California Meadow Mouse.

Procyon Cancrivorus. —Cuv.

Crab-Eating Raccoon.

Plate clv.

P. Supra canescens plus minus in nigrum vergens, subtus flavo-albente, pedibus fuscescentibus, facie albidâ, fascia oculum circumcingente et cum oppositâ confluente nigra; caudâ rufescente, annulis nigris.

Characters.

Body, above greyish, more or less shaded with black; beneath, light yellow; feet brownish yellow; face whitish; a black band surrounding the eye uniting with the opposite one; tail reddish, annulated with black.

Synonymes.

URSUS CANCRIVORUS. —Cuv. Regne An., i., p. 138.
RATON CRABIER. —Buff. His. Nat., Suppl. vi., p. 236, t. 32.
AGUARA-POPÉ. —D'Azara, Essai i., p. 327.
PROCYON CANCRIVORUS. —Desm. in Nouv. Dict. xxxix., p. 93. 2.
    "   "   Briggins, Paraguay, p. 213.
    "   "   Prince Max. Wied, Beitrage ii., p. 301.
    "   "   Griffith An. Kingd., Synopsis, Species
                        325, p. 114.
    "   "   Weigmann, Arch. iii., p. 371.
    "   "   Rengger, Paraguay, p. 113.

Description.

Body longer and more slender than that of the common Raccoon (*P. lotor*), legs longer, ears shorter, less rounded, and more pointed, and tail thinner than in the latter species. The tail diminishes towards the end. Hairs coarse; nails prominent; feet closely haired; under; fur short and sparse.

Colour.

Point of nose black; whiskers white and black, a blackish band around the eyes, extending nearly to the ears; sides of the face, and above the eyes, and a spot on the forehead, whitish; extremities of ears yellowish white, their bases dark brown; nails black; tail barred with black and white; cheeks, jaws, under-part of the neck, breast, and belly, white, with a tinge of yellowish brown. Upper surface of body ash-brown.

Dimensions.

	Inches.
From point of nose to root of tail, ...	22
Tail (vertebræ), ...	9
Point of nose to ear, ...	$4\frac{1}{2}$
Fore leg to point of longest nail, ...	8
Thigh to point of longest nail, ...	8
Breadth of skull, ...	$3\frac{1}{2}$

Habits.

This Raccoon, as observed (in California) by Mr. J. E. CLEMENTS, generally conceals itself during the day in the oak trees which, from decay, afford holes into which it can retreat. It climbs with great agility up the rough bark of these until it reaches some decayed branch in which a cavity sufficiently large to hide in is found. There is a singular fact in this connexion, which is that most part of the rotted holes or places in these California oaks are found in the branches, not in the trunk. We are informed that many trees cut down for the purpose of making fencerails, &c., are quite sound in the main stem, but the reverse in the branches, and that occasionally a large lateral branch will break down and fall to the ground—perchance startling the hunter who may be listening in hopes of hearing the sound of an approaching animal.

The food of this species consists of acorns, grapes, berries, eggs, birds, &c., and of late it has been known to attack chickens on the farms of the isolated settlers, sometimes endeavouring to take them off the trees adjoining the houses.

The flesh of these animals, when boiled first, and afterwards roasted, is very palatable, and not much unlike fresh pork. They are, however, generally lean, and by no means as fat as the Raccoon of our Atlantic States.

This species has been seen by Mr. CLEMENTS on more than one occasion, apparently keeping company with the black-tailed deer (*C. Richardsonii*), being on the mountains, following the same route, among several of these animals.

Two of those killed by Mr. CLEMENTS had been put up a tree by a dog during the night, and were discovered by the barking of the latter in the morning. They were only about half a mile from the house, and when approached, did not offer to come down, or otherwise attempt to escape. They had not ascended the tree more than some twenty feet from the ground.

During the night these Raccoons appear to wander about, in quest of food, perhaps, to an extent that is almost surprising, so that their tracks can be seen in great numbers in various places, as, even in the dry season, the peculiar tenacity of the soil retains the impression made by their feet, almost as if it were the moulding-sand of the founder.

They are, however, very often observed near the water-courses, are fond of frogs, fish, &c., and their tracks are most likely to be seen in the neighbourhood of streams, even when they are partially dried up, and present only a water-hole here and there.

We have no further knowledge of the habits of this species than the information given in the works of BUFFON, SCHOMBURG, D'AZARA, RENGGER, WAGNER, and the Prince of NEUWIED. In Guiana it is found on the sea-coast; in Brazil and Paraguay, in the bushes and forests, near the rivers and lakes. Besides crabs, it eats birds, eggs, fruits, and is especially fond of sugar-cane. In two individuals that had been tamed, RENGGER did not observe the peculiarity that they dipped their food in the water. SCHOMBURG (Ann. Nat. Hist., iv. 434), however, mentions this habit of others which he saw.

In giving this account of the Crab-Eating Raccoon, we are not entirely without some doubts as to whether the animal found in Brazil and other parts of South America, may not be different from the one in Mexico, Texas, and California. We have, however, inclined to the conclusion that they are the same species, and this the more readily, as the Common Raccoon (*P. lotor*) has a range from Texas to quite a high norhtern latitude.

Geographical Distribution.

From South America, beyond the tropic, to the shores of the Gulf of Mexico, and on the west as far as California, this species is distributed, but is probably most abundant within the tropics. WAGNER states that it is found from the Caribbean Sea to the 26th parallel of south latitude; BUFFON and SCHOMBURG inform us it exists in Guiana, and we learn from Prince NEUWIED that it inhabits Brazil; while RENGGER and D'AZARA mention its occurrence in Paraguay.

General Remarks.

The figure of the Crab-Eating Raccoon, given in our plate, was made by J. W. AUDUBON in the British Museum, from a specimen procured in Mexico or California.

Our description was taken from another specimen in the Charleston. College Museum. This may account for any slight differences between the figure and description.

We have not possessed opportunities of instituting a careful comparison between this animal and *Procyon Lotor*; they appear, however, to be specifically distinct.

[Thus far we have endeavoured to describe the forms and give the habits of the quadrupeds figured in our work; we will now append some descriptions, and a list of those species we have not been able to portray, but which deserve to be noticed, as belonging to the "Quadrupeds of North America," and necessary to complete the list.]

Plate CLV

Nº 31

On Stone by Wm E. Hitchcock

Drawn from Nature by J. W. Audubon

Crab eating Raccoon

Lith Printed & Col⁴ by J. T. Bowen, Phila

Mephitis Zorilla.—Gmel.

Californian Skunk.

(Not figured.)

M. Fronte macula ovali alba insignita; maculâ albâ ad tempus utrumque, strigis quatuor albis, interrruptis in dorso et lateribus, caudæ apice albo.

Characters.

An oval spot of white on the forehead, and a large spot on each temple; four interrupted white stripes on the sides and back; tail broadly tipped with white.

Synonymes.

MEPHITIS ZORILLA.—Licht; Darstellung neue, oder wenig bekannter saügethiere, 1827–1834. Berlin, tafel xlviii., fig. 2.
LE ZORILLE.—Buffon, Hist. Nat., t. xiii., p. 302, table 41.
MEPHITIS BI-COLOR.—Loudon's Mag., vol.i., p. 581.
 "   ZORILLA.—Illiger.

Description.

In form, this species may be said to be a small image of the Common Skunk (*M. Chinga*).

Head, short in proportion; ears broad, rounded, clothed with hair on both surfaces; palms naked; nails short, grooved beneath, and slightly hooked; whiskers short and scattering; fur soft, like that of the domestic cat, and composed of two kinds of hair, the under hairs being soft and woolly, the others longer, interspersed among them. On the tail the hair is very coarse, and, toward the extremity, rigid.

Colour.

There ia a white patch on the forehead, and also between the eye and ear, extending beneath the ear to the middle of the body; another white stripe rises behind the ear, and runs parallel with the foregoing. These stripes are not quite uniform on each side; the body is spotted with white, forming three nearly uniform bars across the back. There are two white spots near the insertion of the tail, on the sides and rump. The white markings are set off by the colour of the remaining portions of the body, being blackish brown, very dark on the head and ears, a little lighter near the flanks.

Tail brownish black, tip (for about three inches) white.

Dimensions.

		Inches.
From point of nose to root of tail,	.....	$11\frac{1}{2}$
Tail (vertebræ),	.....	6
" (to end of hair),	.....	10
Shoulder to point of longest nail of fore-foot,	.....	5
Height of ear (posteriorly),	.....	$\frac{4}{10}$

Habits.

The habits of the present animal are only partially known; it is said to retreat to holes in the earth, or live under roots of trees, in the crevices of rocks, &c. It feeds upon insects, birds, and the smaller quadrupeds.

This Skunk, as we are moreover informed, is able to make itself so offensive that few persons are disposed to approach or capture it, rather keeping aloof, as from the Common Skunk of our Atlantic states, so well known for its "perfume."

Geographical Distribution.

This species was found to be rather abundant, by J. W. AUDUBON and J. G. BELL, in California; it was also found in Texas by the former. DEPPE had discovered it previously in California, in 1820, or thereabouts.

General Remarks.

The Zorilla was described by BUFFON (hist. Nat., tom. xiii., p. 302) as a species existing in South America; his figure, however, bore considerable resemblance to an African species (*Viverra Striata* of SHAW). Subsequently Baron CUVIER bestowed great attention on this genus, and came to the conclusion that all the American Skunks were mere varieties of each other.

As far as the endless varieties of our Atlantic Species (*M. Chinga*) are concerned, he was correct; but he was greatly in error in regarding the South American, Mexican, and Californian Skunks as being all of one species, for they differ greatly, not only in size, form, and internal organization, but also in colour.

Besides, many species of *Mephitis* present scarcely any variations in colour. The *Mephitis Chinga* seems to be like *Lepus callotis*, the Mexican hare, and *Lynx Rufus,* the bay lynx, a species that may be regarded as an exception rather than a type of the characteristic of the species.

CUVIER came to the conclusion, whilst pursuing his investigations, that BUFFON, in his Zorilla, had described the above named African species, but it now appears that BUFFON was correct, that his specimen came from America, and that the species is found within our limits, on the western coast: therefore we restore his specific name of Zorilla (Le Zorille) as a synonyme.

Canis (Lupus) Griseus.—Rich.

American Grey Wolf.

(Not figured.)

L. magnitudine canis lupi, cranio lato, gula caudaque villosis, pedibus latis, colore cinereo nigroque notato.

Characters.

About the size of the black and white wolves; skull broad; neck and tail covered with bushy hairs; feet broad; colour dark brindle grey.

Synonymes.

GREY WOLF.—Cook's Third Voyage, vol. ii., p. 293.
 "   Lewis and Clarke, vol. i., pp. 206, 283.
COMMON GREY WOLF.—Schoolcraft's Travels, p. 285.
CANIS (LUPUS) GRISEUS.—Sabine, Franklin's Voy., p. 654.
 "   LUPUS.—Parry, First, Second, and Third Voyages.
 "   "   Harlan, Fauna Americana, p. 81.
 "   "   Godman, American Nat. Hist., vol. i., p. 255, fig. 1.
 "   (LUPUS) OCCIDENTALIS.—(Var. α.) LUPUS GRISEUS, Rich. Fauna Borealis Americana, p. 66.

 "   OCCIDENTALIS, Common American Wolf.—De Kay, Nat. Hist. of N. Y., p. 42, plate 27, fig. 2.
CANIS LUPUS.—Emory, Mass. Report, 1838, p. 26; 1840, p. 28.
LUPUS GIGAS.—Townsend, Proc. Acad. Nat. Sci., Phila.
GIANT WOLF.—Col. G. A. McCall, U.S.A. (letter to Rev. John Bachman, see *infra*).
LOBO or LOVO.—Mexicans and Texans.

Description.

The American Grey Wolf bears a very striking resemblance to the European Wolf. There are, however, some differences which appear to be permanent, and which occur in all the varieties of American Wolves; the body is generally more robust; the legs shorter, and the muzzle thicker and more obtuse in the latter.

We have examined a number of European Wolves (see vol. ii., p. 162, White American Wolf), and although there were great differences between various specimens, we were not able to satisfy ourselves that the American Wolf is the largest, as is supposed by RICHARDSON. We regard them as generally about the same size, and as exhibiting only *varieties,* not specific differences. The body of the American Grey Wolf is long, and rather gaunt; muzzle elongated, and somewhat thicker than that of the Pyrenean Wolf; head thick; nose long; ears erect and conical; eyes oblique—as is the case in all the true wolves—pupil of the eye circular; tail straight, and bushy. The animal does not curl it over the back, like a dog.

Behind the cheek there is a bunch of hairs, which look like a collar. The hairs are of two kinds, the longer coarse and rather rigid, the under fur soft and woolly; whiskers very few, and coarse and rigid; nails long, slightly arched, and, in the specimen from which we describe, considerably worn, as are also the teeth.

Colour.

The long hairs, from their, roots, for one third of their length, are yellowish white, then a broad band of dark brown follows, succeeded by yellowish brown, and the tips are black. The under fur is ashy brown. On the under surface the long hairs are white nearly to the roots.

The general appearance of the upper surface is dark brindled grey, with an indistinct dorsal line a little darker than the colour of the sides.

The under parts are dull white.

Nostrils black; from the nose towards the eyes, reddish yellow. The outer surface of the ears, and outsides of hind legs, from the hip to the knee joint, are also reddish yellow. The whiskers are black.

Dimensions.

	Feet.	Inches.
Length from point of nose to root of tail, ...	4	
" of tail (vertebræ)	1	1
" " to end of hair, ...	1	5
Height of ear, ...		4
Breadth "		3
From point of nose to end of skull, ...		11½
" eye to point of nose, ...		5
" shoulder to longest nail, ...	2	4
Longest upper canine tooth, ...		1½
Length of the hair on the back, 3 to 4 inches.		

The above description and measurements were taken from a specimen in the possession of our distinguished friend, Prof. KIRTLAND, of Cleveland, Ohio. The animal was killed in February, and was, of course, in full winter pelage.

Habits.

We have given the general habits of the wolves in our second volume (see pp. 126, 156, 240), and now will favour our readers with the following letter from Col. GEO. A. McCALL, U.S.A., which will be found very interesting. It will be perceived that the Colonel thinks the Giant Wolf, or Lobo, a distinct species. We have, however, thought it best to give Mr. TOWN-SEND's name (*L. Gigas*) as a synonyme; and we have also appended to our list of names for the grey wolf, the common one of *Lobo*, or *Lovo*, used by the Mexicans and Texans, although it has been thought by some naturalists that the *Lobo* was a distinct species from any other wolf, and by the Mexican Rancheros it is described as tawny, and with a head like that of a lion.

"The Rev. JOHN BACHMAN, D. D.:

"Dear Sir,—On meeting you in Philadelphia, a few days ago—at which time I passed a most agreeable evening, in company with yourself and other distinguished naturalists, whom your arrival had brought together—you related to us in glowing language a variety of anecdotes, illustrative of the character and habits of different families of our Fauna; and, in the course of conversation, you inquired whether I had met, in the west, the *Giant Wolf* of N. America. I then mentioned some incidents, which occurred at Fort Gibson several years ago, exemplifying the greater fleetness, power of endurance, and courage of this species, when compared with the common wolf. As you were pleased to pronounce the 'long yarn' worth re-spinning, I, herewith, agreeably to your request, give you my reminiscence of the facts.

"The position of Fort Gibson is, as you are probably aware, near the junction of the Neosho with the Arkansas river; here, in the angle thus formed, is a prairie of some extent, which used to furnish, for the amusement of those who were fond of the *course* with greyhounds, at any time, a *start* of a prairie wolf (*L. Latrans*), not unfrequently a common wolf (*L. Occidentalis*), and, now and then, the giant wolf himself (*L. Gigas*). The last was easily recognised, even at a distance, by his shyness and his fleetness; and, as he was generally upon the lookout, it seemed impossible for two or three horsemen, with half a dozen greyhounds, to approach within half a mile of him before he showed a straight tail; and then his great speed always enabled him to reach cover before the dogs, notwithstanding that two or three of them were of high blood and great fleetness, could overcome the gap which, at the start,

separated them from the chase; and thus the sportsmen, after several killing rides, had always found themselves foiled by the watchfulness and the superior speed and bottom of this wolf.

"After a hard and unsuccessful race of this kind, several officers were one day returning home, when in passing the farm of a Cherokee Indian, they were told by him that a wolf of this description was in the habit of frequenting the grounds about his house, almost nightly; that he had committed numerous depredations, but that such was his cunning that he had eluded all efforts to kill or capture him. Being assured that a fresh trail might be struck at this point, any morning at daylight, the officers determined to try the fellow's bottom with the fox-hounds. Accordingly, a few nights afterwards—the moon having risen about one o'clock—a party was in the saddle, as soon as they could see upon the prairie, and on their way to the Cherkee's house, which was about seven miles from the Fort. They proceeded leisurely, and reached their destination about three o'clock, purposing to let their horses and dogs rest until daylight, before entering on the chase: the pack, I should mention, consisting of half a dozen fox-hounds, and two or three half-curs, the latter being fleeter and more courageous than the former. It so happened, however, that the dogs, not being coupled, struck the trail close to the house, just as they arrived; and away they went with a cry, and at a pace which showed that the giant was right before them. For some time the wolf kept within the narrow strip of covert which borders the Bayou Menard, and thus the horsemen were enabled, by a good moonlight, to keep parallel with him on the open plain. But the wolf finding at length that the cover afforded him no security from his pursuers, and trusting to the lightness of his heels, dashed boldly into the prairie, and made a straight course for the hills on the opposite side, at the distance of about three miles. Here he again took cover; but he was not allowed much time for repose, as the dogs were soon upon him, and the covert which here bordered the Neosho, being like that of the Bayou, narrow, he was soon forced to leave it and the hills, and again take to the plain. In this way the wolf made several bold dashes, running from one cover to another in a straight course of from one to three miles over the plain; and it was not until half past eight o'clock, A.M., that he was brought to bay. The *denouement* was brought about in this way: the wolf was at last drawing near to cover after one of the open dashes I have mentioned—his speed, to be sure, much abated, and the hounds and horsemen within sight, behind him—when he entered a large field that lay between him and the thicket he wished to gain. The field he soon crossed; and a good cover, with running water, was within a few yards of him. He knew the grounds well; but he did not calculate accurately the amount of strength necessary to clear the fence, which here was much higher than on the side were he had entered. Without pause, therefore, he boldly dashed at the obstacle which now alone separated him from all he stood so much in need of; but as he made the leap his head struck the topmost rail, and he rolled backwards, heavily, upon the ground. Here a shout of triumph from the hunters, who were within view and had witnessed his fall, broke upon his ear; and now he aroused all his remaining energies for one prodigious effort to effect his escape; nature, however, was too nearly exhausted to meet the call, and he fell prostrate upon the ground. Horses and hounds were the next moment closing around him, he gained the fence corner, and then turned upon his pursuers.

"A desperate fight ensured—one or two large and powerful half-hound half-cur dogs, in quick succession, rolled away before him, as he dashed against them with his heavy chest and shoulders. Time after time they returned to the charge, for the dogs had their mettle well aroused and were confident of victory, although each moment seemed to diminish the chances in their favour. With each successive round, dog after dog recoiled more or less injured by a quick and violent snap of the giant's jaws—here, on the right, sat a poor, inoffensive looking hound, whose excitement had led him into the depth of a contest for which nature had never intended him, now writhing in agony, and howling most piteously, his long twisted ears drooping lower than ever, while he cast a furtive glance at his lacerated back and shoulders, just released from the jaws of the giant wolf—there, on the left, lay sprawling, another, whose case seemed even more hopeless than the first.

"During the *melée* several pistols had been drawn, to despatch the wolf and save the dogs; but such was the intricacy of the affair, such the incessant change of position of the combatants, constantly interlocked, that the chances of killing the dogs by a shot were greater than of saving them; and this continued until dogs and wolf, both, were exhausted, when the latter was knocked on the head with a heavy club. And thus fell the giant wolf, after a run of five hours and a half.

"In this description I have gone much into detail; but my only desire was to illustrate that I fully believe to be the fact, viz. that the strength, fleetness, and endurance of this wolf are much greater than those of the common wolf, which was never known, in that country, to make anything like such a run as did this fellow. Indeed, it is only necessary to look at the large leg bone, the strong back, the deep shoulder, and broad chest of this wolf, to be satisfied of his superiority to the other, in the qualities I have enumerated. I am also inclined to think that he is more resolute, and not so easily cowed as the other species; and in support of this opinion, I proceed to the adventure that occurred to Lieut. HOSKINS, with one of this species.

"A few weeks after this, Lieutenant CHAS. HOSKINS, of the 4th Regt. of Infantry, who, being a bold rider and an ardent hunter, was one of the chief actors in the scene I have just described, had a severe encounter with a giant wolf, which I will endeavour to relate as he described it to me.

"He had mounted his horse just before sunset, one day in June, to breathe for an hour, the fresher air of the prairie, and had ridden at a leisurely pace about three quarters of a mile from the fort—his dogs, four or five greyhounds, were following listlessly at his heels, dreaming as little as himself of seeing a wolf—when on a sudden, from a small clump of shumach bushes, immediately at his side, there sprang an enormous giant wolf. By one of those instinctive impulses which it is difficult to describe, horse and dogs were launched upon him before an eye could twinkle. The wolf had but a few yards the start; and under such circumstances, although the fleetest of his congeners, he stood no chance of escaping from his still fleeter enemies; in fact, before he had run fifty yards he was caught by the flanks and stopped. Here a most furious fight commenced: it is a well known fact that the greyhound is sometimes a severe fighter, owing to his great activity and his quick, slashing snap, and HOSKINS's dogs were, in addition, in the habit of coursing the prairie-wolf during the fall and winter months, on which occasions the affair was very generally, after a short chase, terminated in about one minute, by the victim having his throat and bowels torn into ribands. This, however, was a different affair; they had encountered an ugly customer, and the battle was long and of varied aspect. Sometimes the wolf would break entirely clear from the dogs, leaving several of them floored; again, however, within a few yards he would be checked, and the battle be resumed; so that during a long struggle there was little change of ground.

"The fight was continued in this way, the prospect of victory or of defeat frequently changing, until both parties were quite exhausted.

"And now, here lay the wolf in the centre, with his tongue hanging from his jaws; and at the distance of a few feet, the dogs around him, bleeding and panting for breath. At this juncture, HOSKINS, who had not even a penknife in his pocket, was unable to terminate the affair; he sat upon his horse, a slient and admiring spectator of the strange scene. At length, when he thought his dogs had somewhat recovered their breath, he called on them to return to the charge. Old *Cleon*, a black dog of great strength and courage, was the only one who obeyed the summons—he sprang fiercely at the wolf's throat; the latter, however, who had risen to his feet, by a well timed snap, seized Cleon by the neck and hind head, and retaining his hold, was grinding away on the poor fellow's skull with his immense jaws. This was too much for any hunter to witness—a favourite dog held helpless, in a grip that threatened very speedily to end his days. HOSKINS was an experienced hunter, and a very cool and determined man—poor fellow, he afterwards fell, fighting most gallantly, at the battle of Monterey, Mexico: on this occasion he sprang from his horse and seized the wolf by the hind leg, and by a violent jerk caused him to release the dog, but only to find, in less than an instant, the jaws of the monster clamped upon his own leg. He told me, the following day, that he plainly felt the jar as the wolf's large canine teeth clashed against each other in the calf of his leg, so powerful was the snap of his jaws.

"The wolf, however, made no effort to shake or lacerate the wound; at the same time it occurred to the hunter that this would be the only effect of any exertion on his own part to extricate his limb; and therefore, with the wolf's jaws, he stood perfectly quiet, while poor Cleon, whose head was covered with blood, lay before him, apparently more dead than alive.

"In a moment, however, Cleon recovered and raised his head; and then his master spoke to him again. Promptly the old fellow obeyed the call, and this time he made good his hold upon the wolf's throat; whereupon our hunter's leg was at once released. The outer dogs now, having pretty well recovered their breath, also re-attacked the wolf; and this round so disabled him that the affair might be considered as decided. The dogs, however, had all been severely handled, and were again so completely blown that they were unable to make an end of the combat by killing him outright. At this juncture a Cherokee boy, who was on his way across the plain, came up; but neither had he a knife nor any other weapon. HOSKINS then, as his only resource, unbuckled the reins of his bridle (his horse, well used to such scenes, was quietly feeding, close by), and making of these a slip-noose, he, with the assistance of the boy, got this over the wolf's head, when pulling on the opposite ends, they succeeded in strangling the already exhausted animal. After resting with his dogs a little while HOSKINS was enabled to mount his horse and return home, with all of them except poor Cleon, who was so much exhausted as to be unable to keep his legs. A light wagon was immediately sent out for him, and the old dog was received at the fort in triumph, together with the body of his vanquished adversary. He was, nevertheless, laid up in hospital for several days, as was his master, whose leg became inflamed, and prevented his mounting his horse again for a fortnight.

"The next morning I saw the wolf hanging by the heels, at the front of the piazza of HOSKINS's quarters; and he was, beyond all comparison, the largest wolf that I ever laid eyes upon. His dimensions were taken at the time; but I have no memoranda, and I will not venture to speak from memory.

"The colour and general appearance, however, of these two specimens (the skins of which were preserved) were, I very well recollect, alike; viz. a mixture of rusty black and grey about the head, back, and flanks, interspersed with a yellowish rusty brown. But the striking marks of distinction were the large size and the breadth of the head, and the smallness of the tail, when compared with other species; the tail was decidedly short and scant of hair: the head was very remarkable—I speak of it as I saw it in the flesh—the front view, taking in what would be included within a line, drawn between the ears, and two others from those to the point of the nose, presented very nearly an equilateral triangle; the head of the common wolf being much more ovate. Had the skull been stripped of its integuments, I doubt not it would have shown, to a certain degree, a corresponding enlargement in the occipital region.

"I feel no hesitation in asserting that these wolves were of the species recently described by Mr. TOWNSEND as *L. Gigas;* for I did not at the time, nor have I at any time since, entertained in my own mind a doubt of this wolf being a distinct species.

"Without instituting any strict inquiry, from personal examination, as to species or varieties, I have seen a good deal of the wolves of the west during some years past, and from a difference I have observed in the manners or character of those I have met with in the field, I incline to the belief that an additional species, between *L. Occidentalis* and *L. Latrans* will yet be satisfactorily established.

"G. A. M."

PHILADELPHIA, *July*, 1851.

Arvicola Dekayi.—Aud. and Bach.

Glossy Arvicola.

(Not figured.)

A. Corpore longo ac tenui: naso acuto; auriculis et pedibus longis; vellere tereti ac nitente; supra fusca, subtus cano-fusco.

Characters.

Body long and slender; nose sharp; ears and legs long; fur smooth and lustrous; dark brown above, hoary brown beneath.

Synonymes.

ARVICOLA FULVA, Glossy Arvicola.—Aud. and Bach., Jour. Acad. Nat.

Sciences, Oct. 5, 1841.
ARVICOLA ONEIDA, Oneida Meadow Mouse.—De Kay, Nat. Hist. State of New York, 1842, pt. i. p. 88, plate 25, fig. 1.
"   "   Le Conte, Proc. Acad. Nat. Sciences, Phil., Oct. 25, 1853, p. 406.

Description.

This species presents more distinctive markings than any other of the American Arvicolæ; its body is less cylindrical, and its nose less obtuse than any of our other species; its ears are prominent, rising two lines above its smooth, compact fur; its lower incisors are very long, and much exposed, considerably curved; tail longer than the head, thinly covered with short hairs; legs long and slender, giving the animal that appearance of lightness and agility observable in the mouse.

Colour.

Incisors yellowish white; the hairs, which are very short, like those on the pine mouse of LE CONTE, are at the roots, on the upper surface, plumbeous, broadly tipped with brown, giving it a bright chestnut colour; the hairs on the legs and toes are a little lighter, on the under surface the colour is cinereous.

Dimensions.

	Inches.	Lines.
Length of head and body, ...	3	9
" tail, ...	1	4
Height of ear (posteriorly), ...		2½
Length of tarsus.		7

Habits.

We have obtained no information in regard to the habits of this species. DE KAY, who obtained a specimen in the neighbourhood of Oneida Lake, in the state of New York, says that it prefers moist places.

Geographical Distribution.

This Arvicola, according to DE KAY, exists in the western part of the state of New York. Our specimen was received from Mr. FOTHERGILL, who procured most of his specimens, we believe, from St. Lawrence county, New York.

We, however, understood that this individual came from Illinois.

General Remarks.

It will be perceived, from the dates of our several publications, that we described this species a year previous to DE KAY; the name we gave it, however (*Arvicola fulva*), is pre-occupied by *Lemmus fulvus*, Geoff, which is an arvicola found in France.

As DE KAY described the same animal, without a knowledge of our previous publication of it, we have named it after that naturalist, and have given his name (*A. Oneida*) as a synonyme.

Arvicola Apella.—Le Conte.

Woodhouse's Arvicola.

(Not figured.)

A. Auribus brevissimis sub pilis occultis, intus et extus pilosis. Pedibus gracilibus, brevibus. Cauda brevi, supra obscurè badia, subtus cinereo-plumbea.

Characters.

Ears very short, concealed beneath the fur, clothed with hair on both surfaces; feet slender and short; tail short, brown above, greyish beneath.

Synonyme.

ARVICOLA APELLA.—Le Conte, Proc. Acad. Nat. Sci., Phil., Oct. 25, 1853, p. 405.

Description.

Head short and blunt; ears rounded, very short, slightly hairy, both within and without entirely concealed under the fur, antitragus short, semi-circular. Legs very short; feet covered with short, shining hairs; thumb tubercle furnished with a short, blunt nail; tail very short.

Colour.

Hair dark lead-colour, above tipped with brown, redder on the sides; beneath grey, inclining to brownish on the chin and throat; feet pale brownish; tail brown above, greyish beneath.

Dimensions.

		Inches.	Lines.
Length (including the tail), ...		4	7
" of head, ...		1	
" " ears, ...			2
" " fore leg, ...			5
" " hind "		1	1
" " tail, ...			7

Habits.

This animal was procured in Pennsylvania by Dr. WOODHOUSE, in the cultivated portions of that state, and probably has the same propensities and instincts as the other Arvicolæ of North America.

As Major LE CONTE gave it no common name, we have taken the liberty of calling it WOODHOUSE's Arvicola, after the gentleman who procured it.

Arvicola Austerus.—Le Conte.

Baird's Arvicola.

(Not figured.)

A. Supra fusco et nigro permixtus, subtus obscurè *schistosus*. Auribus extra pilos extantibus, extus pilosis. Cauda gracili, densè pilosa.

Characters.

Colour, above mixed brown and black, beneath dark slate-colour, mixed with brown; ears longer than the fur, hairy on the outside; tail slender, thickly clothed with hair.

Synonyme.

ARVICOLA AUSTERUS.—Le Conte, Proc. Acad. Nat. Sci., Phila. Oct. 25, 1853, p. 405.

Description.

Head large and blunt; ears rounded, longer than the fur, outwardly hairy, inwardly only so on the upper margin; antitragus large, semi-circular; whiskers shorter than the head; feet covered with shining hair; thumb tubercle with a compressed, sharp, hooked nail.

Tail slender, covered with short hairs.

Colour.

Hair, above dark plumbeous, tipped with brown and black, beneath dark slate-coloured, mixed with brown, particularly on the breast, the upper and under surfaces of the body being nearly alike; whiskers black and grey; feet grey; tail mixed brown and black above, brownish grey beneath.

Dimensions.

		Inches.	Lines.
Length, ...		5	5
" of head, ...		1	3
" " ears, ...			8
" " fore leg, ...		1	1
" " hind		1	5
" " tail, ...		1	4

Habits.

Of the habits and manners of this species we have no account. Like the foregoing, it has had no common name bestowed on it by Major LE CONTE. We therefore have called it BAIRD's Arvicola, as it was found or obtained by Prof. BAIRD. It inhabits Wisconsin.

Arvicola Californica.—Peale

Californian Arvicola.

A. Subvariegatus rufescenti-fusco et nigro. Corpore brevi et robusto, pilis speciem hirsutici habentibus revera tamen mollibus et levibus. Auribus sub-magnis, pene sub pilis occultis. Cauda supra fusca, subtus fusco-cinerea.

Characters.

Body short and thick; hair long and shining, at the roots plumbeous black, above and on the sides tipped with reddish brown and black; ears rather large, nearly concealed by the fur; tail brown above, brownish grey beneath.

Synonymes.

ARVICOLA CALIFORNICA.—Peale, Zool. Explo. Exped., Mammalia, 46.
"   CALIFORNICUS.—Le Conte, Proc. Acad. Nat. Sciences,
Phila., Oct., 1853, p. 408.

Description.

Body short and thick; hair rather long, and shining: head blunt; ears large but almost concealed in the fur, hairy on both surfaces; feet clothed with short, glossy hair; tubercle of the thumb furnished with a compressed, blunt nail. Tail round; whiskers numerous, but slender.

Colour.

Hair of the body plumbeous black at the roots, above and on the sides tipped with reddish brown and black, in such a manner as to give it a hirsute appearance; feet greyish brown; whiskers black and white.

Dimensions.

	Inches.	Lines.
Length,	5	7
" of head,	1	3
" " fore leg,	2	
" " hind "	1	5
" " tail,	2	

Arvicola Occidentalis.—Peale.

Western Arvicola.

A. Pilis mollissimis et tenuissimis, extremitatibus superioribus rufis sine ulla nigri admistione, auribus sub-pilis occultis. Cauda, sub-compressa, supra et subtus concolore rufa.

Characters.

Hair very soft and fine; ears concealed under the fur, hairy only on the outside. Tail slightly compressed, reddish coloured above and beneath.

Synonymes.

ARVICOLA OCCIDENTALIS—Peale, Zool. Expl. Exped., i. c. 45.
"   "   Le Conte, Proc. Acad. Nat. Sciences, Oct.
25, 1853, p. 408.

Description.

Ears round, entirely concealed under the fur, hairy only on the outside, antitragus rather short; head blunt; feet covered with short, lustrous hair; thumb tubercle with a compressed, sharp nail. Tail slightly compressed.

Colour.

Hair dark plumbeous, above tipped with bright rufous without any admixture of black: beneath grey, hair on the feet rufous. Tail rufous, both above and below. Incisors pale yellow.

Dimensions.

	Inches.
Length of head and body,	$4\frac{3}{10}$
" tail,	$2\frac{1}{10}$
" hair beyond tail vertebræ,	$\frac{2}{10}$
" hind foot,	$\frac{5}{10}$
" fore " (from wrist to end of toes),	$\frac{5}{10}$
" head,	$1\frac{2}{10}$

Obtained at Puget's Sound, Oregon, by the United States Exploring Expedition.

Arvicola (Hesperomys) Campestris.—Le Conte.

New Jersey Field Mouse.

A. Supra fuscus, subtus cinereo-fuscus. Capite magno, auribus magnis, ovalibus, obtusis, pilis brevibus sparse vestitis.

Characters.

Above brown, beneath greyish. Head large; ears large oval, and thinly covered with hair.

Synonyme.

HESPEROMYS CAMPESTRIS.—Le Conte, Proc. Acad. Nat. Sci., Phila.,
Oct., 1853. p. 413.

Description.

Hair plumbeous black, above tipped with brown, beneath with cinereous brown, darker about the mouth. Head large; ears large, oval, blunt, thinly covered, both within and without, with very short, closely adpressed hair. Legs and feet brown. Tail well clothed with tolerably long hair.

Dimensions.

	Inches.	Lines.
Length,	3	4
" of head,	1	2
" " tail,	2	7

Habits.

"This species was found in the collection of the Academy of Natural Sciences, Philadephia, and labelled *Mus Campestris,* from New Jersey. The specimens were preserved in alcohol, and therefore scarcely fit to be described; there was, however, enough to show that they were different from any hitherto described animal." (LE CONTE.)

Arvicola (Hesperomys) Sonoriensis. — Le Conte.

Sonora Field Mouse.

A. Supra saturate cinereus fuscescente-cano leviter intermixtus, subtus albescens. Capite elongato, auribus magnis. Cauda modica.

Characters.

Above, dark grey slightly mixed with brownish; breast whitish. Head long and pointed; legs large; tail moderate.

Synonyme.

HESPEROMYS SONORIENSIS. — Le Conte, Proc. Acad. Nat. Sci., Phila., Oct., 1853, p. 413.

Description.

Hair above dark cinereous or slate-colour, slightly mixed with brownish grey, more thickly on the head, nose, and behind the ears, and with grey on the sides; beneath whitish, except on the throat, which is mixed slate-colour and whitish. Head elongated, pointed; ears large, oval, hairy both within and without, and with a distinct, narrow grey margin. Feet covered with short, whitish brown hair. Tail moderate, above dark brown, beneath paler.

Dimensions.

		Inches.	Lines.
Length,	....	3	3
" of head,	....	1	2
" ears,	....		4
" fore leg,	....	1	
" hind "	....	1	8
" tail,	....	1	9

"Resembles in some degree the *H. Leucopus.* Collected by the Boundary Commission, under Major GRAHAM." (LE CONTE.)

Arvicola Rubricatus. — Rich.

Red-Sided Meadow Mouse.

A. Supra obscurè plumbeus; subtus pallidè cinereus, lateribus miniatis, caudâ breviusculâ, pollice minimo.

Characters.

Back slate-coloured, belly ash-coloured, sides nearly scarlet, tail rather short. Thumb of fore foot rudimentary. Size a little greater than that of the common domestic mouse.

Synonyme.

ARVICOLA RUBRICATUS. — Rich. Zool. Beechey's Voy., Mammalia, p. 7.

The above are the characters of a meadow mouse, which burrows in the turfy soil on the shores of Behring's Straits, drawn up from Mr. COLLIE's notes. In the colours of its fur, and dimensions, it most resembles the *Arvicola æconomus* (PALL. glir. n. 125., pl. 14, A.), and appears to be quite distinct from any American meadow mouse hitherto described. There is no specimen in the collection. (RICHARDSON.)

Perognathus Penicillatus. — Woodhouse.

Tuft-tailed Pouched Rat.

Characters.

Above yellowish brown, beneath white; tail longer than the head and body, penicillate, with bright brown hair.

Synonyme.

PEROGNATHUS PENICILLATUS. — Woodhouse, Proc. Acad. Nat. Sciences, Phil., Dec., 1852, p. 200.

Description.

Head of moderate size, not easily distinguished from the neck; incisors small and partially exposed, upper ones sulcate in the middle. Nose small and rather pointed, extending some distance beyond the incisors; whiskers light brown, irregularly mixed with black; eyes dark brown, and of moderate size; ears nearly round and moderate, almost naked anteriorly, and covered posteriorly with fine brown fur; the tragus and antitragus are quite prominent. The external meatus is protected by a tuft of short, black bristles extending across the ear. Tail about one inch and a quarter longer than the head and body, round, gradually tapering, and covered with hair; on the superior and middle portion commences a row of long, silky hairs, which gradually increase in width until they form a tuft at the end. Fore legs short, feet small, with four well developed toes and a short thumb, which is armed with a nail; palms naked. Hind legs and feet long, having five toes, terminated by nails. Feet and toes covered with fine short fur; soles naked. The fur longer on the back than on the belly; it is thick, soft, and silky.

Colour.

Incisors yellow, top of head and back dark yellowish brown, lighter on the sides; fur at base light ash colour. Throat, belly, vent, fore legs, and inner portions of thighs white. The white commences at the nostrils, and forms a well marked line to the thighs, and extending down to the heel, leaving the front of thigh white, the remainder and outer portion light yellowish brown; feet white. Under portion of tail white, above dark brown; the long hair of the tail is a rich brown.

Dimensions.

		Inches.
Length from tip of nose to root of tail,	....	3.5
" of tail, (vertebræ),	....	3.7
" " ear anterior,	....	.3
" " whiskers,	....	1.7
" " os calcis, middle toe nail,	....	1.
Distance from anterior angle of orbit to tip of nose,	....	.6½

Geographical Distribution.

New Mexico, west of Rio Grande.

General Remarks.

Of the habits of this animal I know but little. The specimen in my possession is a male, and was procured in the San Francisco Mountain, New Mexico. (WOODHOUSE.)

Pseudostoma (Geomys) Fulvus—Woodhouse.

Reddish Pouched Rat.

Characters.

Light reddish brown above, beneath whitish. Ears small, round, and covered with thick, short, black fur. Tail long in proportion when compared with others of this genus.

Synonyme.

GEOMYS FULVUS.—Woodhouse, Proc. Acad. Nat. Sci., Phila., 1852, p. 201.

Description.

Head large, nose broad, covered with short, thick fur, with the exception of a small space at tip and the margins of the nostrils, which are naked. The nose extends a short distance beyond the plane of the incisors. The incisors are exserted, with three convex smooth sides, the exterior broadest, and of a yellowish colour; their cutting edges are even. The upper incisors extend downwards and inwards; the under ones are one-third longer than the upper, and slightly narrower. Ears small and round, covered with short, thick, black fur externally. Eyes larger than is common in this genus. Tail round, thick at base, and gradually tapering. The fore claws are long, compressed, slightly curved, and pointed. The claw on the middle toe is the longest, the fifth is the shortest, and that of the thumb resembles much the claw of the fourth toe of the hind foot, both as regards size and shape. The toes on the hind feet are a little longer and more slender than those of the fore feet; the nails short, somewhat conical and excavated underneath.

Colour.

Head, cheeks, back, and sides bright reddish brown, being darker on the top of the head and back. The breast, vent, feet, inner portion of legs and thighs white, slightly inclining to ash; abdomen very light reddish brown; fur at base dark ash colour above, beneath light ash. Edges of cheek pouches encircled with rufous; the long hair of the back extends about one-third the length of the tail. The tail is covered with short, white, silky hairs, terminating in small tuft. The fore feet above are covered with short, white hair; the toes on their inner side have a row of long white hairs; palms naked. Claws are opaque, white for half their extent, the other half transparent; there is a small, oblong, reddish brown spot in the centre of each. The hind feet are covered above with white hairs, soles naked. The lips, on their inner side, are covered with short, fine white hair, with a band of short, fine, black fur encircling the mouth. Whiskers silvery white.

Dimensions.

		Inches.
Length from tip of nose to root of tail,	. . . .	5.
" of tail (vertebræ),	. . . .	1.3
" from anterior angle of eye to tip of nose,	. . . .	.7
" " tip of nose to auditory opening,	. . . .	$1.1\frac{1}{2}$
" of os calcis, including middle toe and claw,	. . . .	1.1
" from elbow to end of middle hind claw,	. . . .	1.8
" of middle fore claw,	. . . .	.4
" " hind claw,	. . . .	$.2\frac{1}{2}$
" " fur on back,	. . . .	$.2\frac{1}{2}$
" " whiskers, about	. . . .	1.

Geographical Distribution.

New Mexico, west of Rio Grande.

General Remarks.

The specimen in my collection was procured near the San Franciano Mountain, New Mexico, where they were quite abundant.

These Pouched Rats of the genus Perognathus and Geomys I procured whilst attached as Surgeon and Naturalist to the party under command of Capt. SITGREAVES, U. S. Army, exploring the Zuñi, and Little and Great Colorado Rivers of the west. (WOODHOUSE.)

Arvicola Montana.—Peale.

Peale's Meadow Mouse.

A. Formâ rotundatâ; capite magno; auribus mediocribus et vellere pœne vestitis; dentibus flavis; oculis parvis, nigris; pilis subtilibus sericisque, in dorso brunneis nigrisque intermixtis; infrà plumbeis. Cauda pedibusque brevi nitente pilo indutis. Mystacibus albis nigrisque: mammis octo, quatuor in abdomine, in pectore totidem.

Characters.

Form rounded; the head large, ears moderate and nearly covered with fur; teeth yellow; eyes small, black; hair fine and silky; that of the back brown and black, intermixed; beneath lead-coloured; tail and feet covered with short, glossy hairs; whiskers white and black; teats eight in number, four pectoral, and four abdominal.

Synonyme.

ARVICOLA MONTANA.—Peale, Mammalia and Ornithology United States Exploring Expedition, vol. viii., p. 44.

Dimensions.

Total length $6\frac{1}{8}$ inches, including the tail, which is $1\frac{1}{2}$ inches long.

General Remarks.

Our specimen was obtained on the 4th of October, near the head waters of the Sacramento River, in California. (PEALE.)

In relation to *Arvicola Riparia* of ORD, we have concluded that it is identically the same as *A. Pennsylvanica* of that naturalist. We have given an account of this animal at p. 341, Vol. I. We merely mention that it is so much better known as *A. Pennsylvanica* than as *Riparia,* that we would, setting aside the dates of description by Mr. ORD, prefer to let the name of *Pennsylvanica* remain, and for the future consider *riparius* as a synonyme only.

We may further remark, that had we had an opportunity of examining a specimen of the so called *"Arvicola riparius,"* from the locality in which Mr. ORD procured his original, before our article on *A. Pennsylvanica* was published, we should have given either the one or the other name as a synonyme. We have lately had a fine specimen of this Arvicola from the locality from whence Mr. ORD obtained his original specimen.

Pseudostoma Castanops.—Baird.

Chestnut-cheeked Pouched Rat.

(In Stansbury's Report of the Expedition to the Great Salt Lake, p. 313.)

Description.

General colour pale yellowish brown. There is an ample patch of light chestnut on the side of the head and face, deepest above. The dorsal line is not darker than the rest of the fur. Size intermediate between *P. borealis* and *P. bursarius.*

Colour.

The colour of the fur above is slightly grizzled, and much lighter than in *P. bursarius;* beneath paler; throat, space between the fore legs and arms pale rusty. The chestnut marking on the side of the head is very strongly defined, occupying on each side a nearly circular space of about one and three quarter inches in diameter, with the ear as the centre. These chestnut spaces do not quite meet on the crown and occiput, but leave a rectilinear interval, coloured like the rest of the back, of about one-eighth of an inch in width. On the muzzle, however, from above the eyes the colour of the opposite sides is confluent. The hind feet and toes are thinly covered with whitish hairs, which on the fore feet appear more ferruginous.

The claws are white, but sufficiently transparent to allow the coagulated blood to show through them.

Dimensions.

	Inches.
Length to base of tail (approximate), ...	8

"	of tail, ...	$2\frac{5}{8}$
"	" hand (along the palm), ...	$1\frac{1}{4}$
"	" middle anterior claw, ...	$\frac{1}{4}$
"	" hind feet (along sole) from heel, ...	$1\frac{5}{8}$

Habits.

This beautiful species was collected by Lieutenant ABERT, on the prairie road to BENT's fork.

The above description and remark we have taken from Prof. BAIRD, with scarcely any alteration.

We have added an English name to the animal.

Pseudostoma (Geomys) Hispidum.—Le Conte.

P. Pilis concoloribus rufo-fuscis minus subtilibus tectus, cauda brevinuda, auribus obsoletis.

Synonyme.

GEOMYS HISPIDUM.—Dr. Le Conte, Proc. Acad. Nat. Sci., Phila., 1852, p. 158.

Description.

One specimen, Mexico, Mr. PEASE's collection. This species differs from all the others in having the fur very coarse and harsh, and entirely of a reddish brown colour. Beneath it is slightly greyish, but the difference in colour is by no means obvious. The ears are not at all prominent, being merely openings in the skin. The whiskers are as long as the head. The upper incisors are broken off, but enough remains to show that they were deeply grooved near the middle of the anterior surface; it is impossible to determine if there is a second submarginal groove. The tail is completely naked except at the root. The feet are precisely as in the other species of this division of the genus. (Dr. LE CONTE.)

Dimensions.

	Inches.
Length from nose to root of tail, ...	11.5
Tail, ...	3
Anterior foot to end of claw of third toe, ...	1.7
Posterior foot to end of claw of third toe, ...	1.9

Pseudostoma Umbrinus.—Rich.

Leadbeater's Sand Rat.

G. Super umbrinus, subter griseus, gulâ pedibusque albidis caudâ grisea vestitâ longitudine capitis.

Characters.

Umber brown on the dorsal aspect, grey below, with white feet and throat, and a grey hairy tail as long as the head.

Synonymes.

GEOMYS UMBRINUS.—Rich, Fauna Boreali Americana, p. 202.
" " Dr. Le Conte, Proc. Acad. Nat. Sci., Phila., 1852, p. 162.

Description.

Head large, nose wide and obtuse, and with the exception of the nostrils, covered with fur similar in colour and quality to that on the crown of the head. The nostrils are small round openings, half a line apart, with a furrowed septum, and having their superior margins naked and vaulted; a narrow, hairy, upper lip, not exceeding a line in width, separates the nostrils from the upper incisors. The whiskers are white, and are shorter than the head. The incisors are much exserted, and are without grooves on their anterior surfaces, which are slightly convex, and of a deep yellow colour. The lips unite behind the upper incisors, so as to form a naked furrow leading towards the mouth, which is rendered more complete by the stiffness of the hairs on each side of it. The cheek pouches are of a soiled buff colour, and are clothed throughout their exterior surface wtih very short, soft, whitish hairs, which do not lie so close as entirely to conceal the skin. The middle of the pouch is opposite to the ear, and its anterior margin extends forwards to between the eye and the angle of the mouth; its tip is rounded.

The body, in shape, resembles that of a mole. It is covered with a smooth coat of fur, of the length and quality of that of a meadow mouse; but possessing more nearly the lustre and appearance of the fur of a musk rat. For the greater part of its length from the roots upwards, it has a blackish grey colour. On the upper and lateral parts of the head, and over the whole of the back, the tips of the fur are of a nearly pure umber-brown color, deepest on the head, and slightly intermixed with chestnut brown on the flanks. The belly, and fore and hind legs, are pale grey, with, in some parts, a tinge of brown.

The sides of the mouth are dark-brown, with a few white hairs intermixed. The chin, throat, feet, and claws, are white. The tail is round and tapering, and is well covered with short greyish white hairs; the hairs on the sides of the fore-feet are rather stiff, and curve a little over the naked palms; those on the hind-feet are shorter; the posterior extremities are situated far forward.

Dimensions.

	Inches.	Lines.
Length of head and body, ...	7	
" of head, ...	1	8
" " tail, ...	1	9
Distance from the end of the nose to the anterior angle of the orbit, ...		9

Habits.

"Although this animal is not an inhabitant of the fur countries, the above description has been inserted with the view of rendering the account of the genus more complete." (RICHARDSON.)

RICHARDSON received no information respecting its manners or food. The specimen came from the south-western part of Louisiana.

Pseudostoma (Geomys) Mexicanus.—Le Conte.

P. Mexicanus, mollipilosus, saturate cinereus, supra nigro-tinctus, naso brunneo, cauda mediocri, pilosa, versus apicem subnuda, auribus brevibus, primoribus superioribus medio profunde sulcatis.

Synonymes.

ASCOMYS MEXICANUS.—Lichtenstein, Abhandl. Berl. Akad. 1827, 113.
    "   "   Brantz, Muiz. 27.
    "   "   Wagner, Schreb. Saügth. Suppl. 3, 384.
    "   "   Schinz, Syn. Mam. 2, 133.
SACCOPHORUS MEXICANUS.—Fischer, Richardson, Rep. Brit. Ass. 6, 156.
    "   "   Syn. Mam. 305.
    "   "   Eydoux, Voy. Favorite, 23, tab. 8.

Description.

One specimen, Mexico, Mr. J. SPEAKMAN. Fur very fine, shining, very dark cinereous, above tipped with black, beneath entirely cinereous; nose and whiskers brownish; breast and fore-legs slightly tinted with brown. Ears short. Upper incisors with a very deep groove on the middle of the anterior surface. Feet thinly clothed with brownish hair. Tail covered with hair, which is very dense and long at the base, gradually becoming shorter and more scanty, leaving the tip almost naked. (Dr. LE CONTE.)

Dimensions.

	Inches.
Length from nose to root of tail,	11
" tail,	5
Fore-foot to end of middle claw,	1.7
Hind-foot to end of middle claw,	1.7

Sorex Forsteri.—Richardson.

Forster's Shrew Mouse.

(Not figured.)

S. Caudâ tetragonâ longitudine corporis, auriculis brevibus vestitis, dorso xerampelino, ventre murino.

Characters.

Tail as long as the body and square; ears short and furry; back brown, belly pale yellowish brown.

Synonymes.

SHREW, No. 20.—Forster, Phil. Trans., vol. lxii., p. 381.
SOREX FORSTERI.—Richardson, Zool. Jour., No. 12, April, 1828.
    "   "   Bachman, Jour. Acad. Nat. Sci., Philadelphia. vol. vii., part ii., p. 386.

Description.

Nose, long, somewhat divided at the tip; ears, hairy, not much shorter than the fur, but still concealed; body slender; feet small; tail long, four-sided; hair short, fine, and smooth.

Colour.

The fur is for two thirds of its length dark cinereous above, tipped with brown; beneath it is cinereous.
Feet flesh coloured; nails white.

Dimensions.

	Inches.
Length of head and body,	$2\frac{3}{8}$
" of head,	$\frac{3}{4}$
Height of ear,	$\frac{1}{8}$
Length of tail,	$1\frac{1}{2}$
From point of nose to eye,	$\frac{3}{8}$

Sorex Cooperi.—Bach.

Cooper's Shrew.

(Not figured.)

Characters.

Body very small; nose long; no external ears; tail as long as the body; colour, dark brown.

Synonyme.

SOREX COOPERI.—Bachman, Jour. Acad. Nat. Sci., Philadelphia, vol. vii., part ii., 1837, p. 388.

Description.

Body very slender, head rather long, and nose thin and pointed; legs slender and long, especially the hind legs. They are covered with fine adpressed hairs to the extremities of the nails. Tail large and thick for the size of the animal; flattened on the sides and beneath, rounded above, clothed with fine hair and tipped with a pencil of hairs. They eye is small, but is visible through the fur, and apparently not covered by an integument.

The point of the nose is slightly divided; there is no external ear, and the transverse auditory opening is completely concealed by the fur.

Colour.

Hair cinereous for two thirds of its length above, and tipped with shining chestnut brown; beneath tipped with ash color; feet grey; tail brown above, silver grey beneath.

Dimensions.

	Inches.
From point of nose to tail,	$1\frac{7}{8}$
Length of tail,	$1\frac{7}{8}$
From eye to point of nose,	$\frac{3}{8}$
Length of head,	$\frac{3}{4}$
From heel to middle claw,	$\frac{7}{16}$

Sorex Fimbripes.—Bach.

Fringe-Footed Shrew.

Characters.

No external ears; tail a little shorter than the body; feet broad, fringed at the edges; body dark brown.

Synonyme.

SOREX FIMBRIPES.—Bach, Jour. Acad. Nat. Sciences, Philadelphia, vol. vii., part ii., p. 391.

Description.

Nose long and movable, with the tip slightly lobed; head large and flat. The eye is a mere speck, covered by the common integument, and is found with great difficulty. Whiskers, long, extending considerably beyond the head; no external ears, and the transverse auditory opening very small; fore-feet broad, and clothed with short fine hairs extending to the extremities of the nails, the edges on the lower surface considerably fringed beneath the palms with long brownish hairs. Tail of moderate size, square, and gradually tapering to the point.

The fur is considerably longer than in any other of our species of shrew of the same size.

Colour.

Teeth yellowish; whiskers white; there is a lightish edge around the upper lip; feet dingy yellow.

The fur on the upper surface is for two thirds of its length, bluish ash, and is tipped with brown, which gives it a changeable brown appearance. Throat and beneath dark fawn colour. Under side of tail buff; point of tail nearly black.

Dimensions.

	Inches.
From point of nose to root of tail,	$2\frac{1}{8}$
Length of tail,	$1\frac{1}{4}$
From orifice of ear to point of nose,	$\frac{4}{5}$
" eye to point of nose,	$\frac{5}{8}$
" heel to end of middle claw,	$\frac{1}{2}$
Breadth of fore-feet,	$\frac{5}{16}$
Length of whiskers,	1

Sorex Personatus.—St. Hillaire.

Synonymes.

SOREX PERSONATUS.—St. Hillaire, Guerin's Mag. de Zoologie pour 1833, pl. 14.
"   "   Bachman, Monogr. N. American species of Sorex, Jour. Acad. Nat. Sci., Phila., vol. vii., part ii., p. 398.

Description.

Hair reddish brown above, light ash coloured beneath, end of the nose blackish brown above, ears small and concealed in the fur; tail rather square, one third of the total length of the the animal.

Dimensions.

	Inches.
Length to root of tail,	2
" of tail,	1

Habits.

We have never seen this shrew. The specimen from which the description was taken by ST. HILLAIRE (translated above) was sent from America by MILBERT (1827).

Georychus Gœnlandicus.—Rich.

Greenland Lemming.

A. Exauriculatus, rostro acuto, palmis tetradactylis hirsutis; unguibus apice cylindrico producto, lineâ dorsali nigrâ.

Characters.

Earless; with a sharp nose; fore-feet hairy beneath, with four toes, armed with claws, having sharp cylindrical points; a dark stripe along the middle of the back.

Synonymes.

ARVICOLA (GEORYCHUS) GRŒNLANDICUS, Greenland Lemming.—Rich, Fauna Boreali Americana, p. 134.
MOUSE, Sp. 15.—Foster, Phila. Trans. lxii., p. 379?
HARE-TAILED RAT?—Pennant, Arct. Zool., vol. i., p. 133?
MUS GRŒNLANDICUS.—Richardson, Parry's Second Voy., App. p. 304.
OWINYAK—Esquimaux.

Description.

Size—rather less than a rat: head rounded, narrower than the body, tapering slightly from the auditory opening to the eyes; nose acute. There are no external ears, but the site of the auditory opening is denoted by an obscure transverse brownish streak in the fur. The eyes are near each other and small. The fur on the cheeks is a little puffed up. The upper lip is deeply divided; lower incisors twice the length of the upper ones; whiskers long; body thickly covered with long and soft fur. Tail very short; the *fore extremities* project very little beyond the fur; the palms incline slightly inwards, are small, and the toes very short; both are covered thickly above and below, with strong hairs curving downwards, and extending beyond the claws. The only naked parts on the foot are a minute, flat, unarmed callus, in place of a thumb, and a rounded smooth callus at the extremity of each toe. These callosities do not project forward under the claws, and have no resemblance to the large, compressed horny, under portions of the claws of the Hudson's Bay Lemming.

The claws are long, strong, curved moderately downwards, and inclining inwards. Soles of the hind-feet hairy, and the hairs project beyond the claws. The hind-feet have five toes, of which the three middle ones are nearly of a length. The hind-claws are slightly arched, narrow, but not sharp at the points; they are thin, hollowed out underneath, and calculated to throw back the earth which has been loosened by the fore-claws.

Colour.

The general colour of the upper parts of the body and of the head is dark greyish brown, arising from an intimate mixture of hairs tipped with yellowish-grey and black; the black tips are the longest, and, predominating down the centre of the back, produce a distinct stripe. The ventral aspect of the throat, neck, and body, exclusive of some rusty markings before the shoulders, is of an unmixed yellowish-grey colour, which unites with the darker colour of the back by an even line running on a level with the tail and inferior part of the cheek. The fur both on the back and underneath presents, when blown aside, a deep blackish-grey colour from the tips to the roots. The tail is of the same colour as the body at the root, but the part which projects beyond the fur of the rump is only a pencil of stiff white hairs.

The above is copied, with some alterations, from RICHARDSON's description, which was drawn up from a male, killed August 22, in Repulse bay.

Dimensions.

	Inches.	Lines.
Length of head and body, ...	6	3
" " tail, ...		9
" " fore-leg from palm to the axilla, ...	1	1
" " longest fore-claw, ...		4
" " palm of middle-claw, ...		6

" " whiskers, ...	1	4

Habits.

We refer our readers to the Fauna Boreali Americana for some interesting general remarks on the Lemmings, comparing those of the American continent with European speciess. We know nothing of the habits of this one.

Dipodomys Ordii.—Woodhouse

Ord's Pouched Mouse.

Characters.

Light reddish brown above, beneath white; tail short, and penicillate at the end.

Synonyme.

DIPODOMYS ORDII.—Woodhouse, Proc. Acad. Nat. Sci., Phila., 1853, p. 235.

Description.

A little smaller than *D. Philipsii,* Gray; head and tail shorter, nose long and pointed, extending some distance beyond the incisors; ears somewhat round, the anterior poriton almsot naked, posteriorly covered with short fine hair.

Colour.

Dark reddish brown above; sides light reddish brown; fur ash colour at base; side of the nose, half of the cheek, spot behind the ear, band across the thigh and beneath, pure white; a black spot at the base of the long whiskers; a superciliary ridge of white on either side; the penicillated portion of the tail is formed of long white hairs, with bright brown tips.

Dimensions.

	Inches.
Total length from tip of nose to root of tail, ...	5
" " of vertebræ of tail, ...	$4\frac{3}{10}$
" " of tail, including hair at tip, ...	$5\frac{5}{10}$
" " of os calcis, including middle toe and nail, ...	$1\frac{5}{10}$
" " of ear, ...	.45

Geographical Distribution.

Western Texas.

General Remarks.

This animal I procured at El Paso on the Rio Grande, on my way to Santa Fé, whilst attached to party under the commond of Captain L. SITGREAVES, United States Army. I have named it in honour of Mr. ORD, President of this Society. (WOODHOUSE.)

Arvicola (Hesperomys) Texana.—Woodhouse.

Characters.

Smaller than Mus leucopus, head shorter and more blunt, ears smaller and more round, brown above, and white, inclining to yellowish, beneath.

Synonyme.

HESPEROMYS TEXANA.—Woodhouse, Proc. Acad. Nat. Sci., Phila., 1853, p. 242.

Description.

Head large, blunt. Eyes prominent, and dark brown. Ears large, erect, roundish, oval, blunt, sparsely covered outwardly with short adpressed brown hairs, inwardly with grey. Thumb of fore-feet a tubercle, furnished with a long blunt nail, two middle toes the longest subequal. Hind-feet furred, with the exception of the sole. Whiskers long.

Colour.

Hair dark cinereous above, tipped with pale brown, and dusky, so as to have rather a mottled appearance; beneath white inclining to yellowish; the two colours, that is to say above and beneath, tolerably distinctly separated from each other in a straight line. Tail above brown, beneath white; nose mixed brown and grey, or pale brown. Whiskers black and grey; legs white on their inner surface only, feet white, the hairs projecting over the nails.

Dimensions.

	Inches.
Total length from tip of nose to root of tail, ...	$2\frac{1}{10}$
" " of tail, ...	$2\frac{1}{10}$
" " of head, ...	$1\frac{1}{10}$
Height of ear, ...	$\frac{4}{10}$
Breadth of ear, ...	$\frac{5}{10}$
Fore-legs, ...	1
Hind-legs, ...	$1\frac{6}{10}$

Geographical Distribution.

Western Texas.

General Remarks.

I procured this little animal on the Rio Grande near El Paso, whilst attached to the party under the command of Captain L. SITGREAVES, U. S. Topographical Engineers, on our way to explore the Zuni and Colorado rivers. Of its habits I know nothing. My attention was called to this animal by Major LE CONTE, who has been for some time engaged in the study of the mice of our country. (WOODHOUSE.)

Scalops Æneus.—Cassin.

Black-clawed Shrew Mole.

Synoyme.

SCALOPS ÆNEUS.—Cassin, Proc. Acad. Nat. Sci., 1853, p. 299.

Description.

Upper jaw, after the two incisors, having on each side seven false molars, which are pointed and nearly equal, except the last, which is double the size of either of the others, and has a small exterior basal lobe. Molars three; the first with four external lobes, the anterior being very small, the second large and pointed, the third short, blunt, and deeply emarginate, the fourth lobe also blunt and short; besides these the first molar has one interior and one posterior lobe, second molar with three short external lobes, the intermediate one emarginate; also two interior large and pointed, and one posterior similar to the interior lobe; third molar with two short external lobes; the posterior one emarginate, and two interior lobes and one posterior lobe.

Lower jaw with two incisors on each side, the anterior of which is the shorter; these are followed by six false molars, which are pointed and nearly equal in size, except the last, which is much larger and furnished with a minute posterior lobe at the base. Molars three, each deeply sulcate on the external surface and composed of two large external lobes and three smaller and shorter internal lobes.

First and fifth toes of fore-feet equal, second shorter, first and fifth toes of the hind-feet equal, other three nearly so.

Colour.

Entirely shining, brassy brown, very glossy, and in some lights appearing to be almost metallic; darker on the top of the head, and lighter and more obscure on the chin and throat; nose dusky; feet brownish; nails and first joint of the toes black; palms dusky; soles of the hind-feet dark brown; tail light brown, thinly furnished with scattering bristles.

Dimensions.

	Inches.
Total length (of specimen in spirits), about	5
" " of head,	2
" " of fore-feet,	1.15
" " of hind-feet,	1.40
" " of tail,	1.25

General Remarks.

This is the most beautiful species of mole yet discovered in America, and exhibits almost the brilliancy of colour which distinguishes the remarkable South African animals which form the genus Chrysochloris, of this family.

A single specimen, apparently fully adult, is in the collection of the Exploring Expedition, labelled as having been obtained in Oregon. In its dentition and otherwise it is a strict congener of *Scalops Townsendii,* but is much smaller and of a different color. Its black claws are especially remarkable, and distinguish it from all other species of the genus.

(CASSIN.)

Scalops Latimanus.—Bach.

Texan Shrew Mole.

Synoyme.

SCALOPS LATIMANUS.—Bach, Boston Jour. Nat. History, vol. i., p. 41.

Description.

Larger than the common shrew-mole, intermediate in size between *S. Townsendi* and *S. Breweri.* Hair longer and thinner than in either of the other species, and slightly curled. Palms larger than in any other known species. Tail naked.

Colour.

Colour nearly black.

Dimensions.

	Inches.	Lines.
Length to root of the tail,	7	7
" of the tail,		10
Breadth of the palm,		10
" of the tarsus,		7

Geographical Distribution.

Mexico and Texas.

Mus Le Contii.—Bach.

Le Conte's Mouse.

M. Supra rufo-fuscus, subtus albo-flavus; cauda corpore breviore.

Characters.

Tail shorter than body, reddish brown above, light fawn beneath.

Synonymes.

MUS LE CONTEI.—Aud. and Bach, Jour. Acad. Nat. Sci., Phila., vol. viii., pt. ii., P. 306.
REITHRODON LE CONTEI.—Le Conte, Proc. Acad. Nat. Sci., Phila., Oct. 1853, p. 413.

Description.

About half the size of a full grown mouse. Its body is covered by a very thick coat of soft fur and coarser hairs intermixed. The upper fore-teeth are deeply grooved. The head is of a moderate size; the fore-head so much arched as to present nearly a semicircle. Nose rather sharp, with a caruncle beneath each nostril pointing downwards. Whiskers shorter than the head. Ears round, moderate in size, and slightly protruding beyond the long fur, nearly naked; a few hairs are sprinkled along the inner margins. The legs are short and rather stout; feet covered with short adpressed hairs; nails long and but slightly hooked; adapted to digging. The rudimentary thumb is armed with a blunt nail. The tail, which is round, is sparsely clothed with hair.

Colour.

Teeth yellow; eyes black; nails light brown; whiskers white and black. The fur on the back and chest is plumbeous at base, tipped with a mixture of reddish brown, and dusky, giving it a dark reddish-brown appearance. The lips, chin, and feet are a soiled white. On the throat, belly, and under surface of the tail, the fur is cinereous; at the roots tipped with fawn colour. Upper surface of tail brown.

Dimensions.

	Inches.	Lines.
Length of head and body,	2	6
" of tail,	2	
Height of ear,		1½
length of tarsus,		5

General Remarks.

The specimen from which the above description was taken was procured in Georgia by Major LE CONTE.

Mus Michiganensis.

Michigan Mouse.

M. Buccis falvis, corpore supra fusco-canescente, subtus albido.

Characters.

Cheeks yellow, body light greyish-brown above, whitish beneath.

Synonyme.

MUS MICHIGANENSIS.—Aud. and Bach, Jour. Acad. Nat. Sci., Phila.,
vol. viii., pt. ii., p. 304.

Description.

The head is of moderate size at base, gradually tapering to a sharp-pointed nose. The eyes, which appear to be rather smaller than those of the white-footed mouse, are placed farther forward. Whiskers the length of the head. The ears on both surfaces are so sparingly clothed with short hairs as, without close examination, to appear naked. Legs short and slender, covered with hair to the extremities of the toes. Soles naked. On each fore-foot there are four toes, with a rudimental thumb, protected by short but rather sharp nails. The hind-feet are pendactylous. The tail, which is round, is clothed with rather short hairs. Mammæ, six pectoral and four abdominal. The fur on the whole body is very short and smooth.

Colour.

The incisors, which are small, are yellow. The whiskers are nearly all white; a few immediately below and above the eyes being black. On the cheeks there is a line of yellowish fawn colour running along the sides to the neck. The feet, nails, ears, and tail are light brown. The hairs on the upper surface are light plumbeous at the roots, and tipped with light brown and black. On the throat, inner surface of the thighs, and on the abdomen, they are yellowish white. There is no distinct line of demarcation between the colours of the back and under surface, nor does the white extend along the sides, as in the white-footed mouse.

Dimensions.

	Inches.	Lines.
Length of head and body, ...	4	
" of tail, ...	2	6
" of tarsus, ...		5
Height of ear, ...		4

General Remarks.

This species beans some resemblance in size and colour, both to the common house mouse (*M. musculus*) and the white-footed mouse (*M. leucopus*). The colour on the back resembles the former, and on the under surface the latter. Its tail is considerably shorter than either, and its ears less naked and much smaller than those of *M. leucopus*. Neither has it the white feet so characteristic of that species.

Perognathus (Cricetodipus) Parvus.—Peale.

P. Capite ovato: rostro elongato, acuminato piloso, exceptis naribus parvis convolutisque; labiis magnis, tumidis, et pilis brevibus consitis: mystacibus plurimis, albis: flocco alborum pilorum seu setarum in mento: genarum ventriculis amplis, disruptis extrinsecè ori, ex supremo labio ad guttur usque protentis; cavitate retrorsum ad aures pertingente pilosâ: oculis mediocribus: auribus parvis, rotundis, pilose fimbriatis: anterioribus cruribus parvis: pede mediocri, setosis marginato pilis: unguibus brevibus, uncinis, excepto polliculari in orbem figurato vel ad instar humani: posticis cruribus longis; pedibus magnis validisque, digitis quinque instructis, medio cæteris aliquantulò longiore; intimo digito brevissimo, attingente tantum metatarsa cæterorum ossa: unguibus omnibus brevibus, acuminatis modicè incurvis: caudâ longâ, attenuatâ, pilis brevibus sericis coopertâ; colore suprà sepiaco-brunneo, infrà albo; obscurâ lineâ transcurrente genas sub oculis.

Synonymes.

CRICETODIPUS PARVUS.—Peale, Mamm. of U. S. Exploring Expedition,
p. 53.
PEROGNATHUS PARVUS.—Dr. Le Conte, Proc. Acad. Nat. Sci., Phila.

Description.

Head ovate; the snout elongate, pointed, and covered with hair, excepting the nostrils, which are small and convolute; lips large, tumid, and covered with short hairs; whiskers numerous, white; a tuft of white hairs or bristles on the chin; cheek-pouches spacious, opening outside of the mouth, and reaching from the upper lip to the throat; the cavity extending backwards to the ears, and lined with hair; eyes medium size; ears small, round, and fringed with hairs; fore-legs small, the feet moderate, margined with bristly hairs; the nails short, curved, excepting that of the thumb, which is orbicular, or resembling the human thumb nail; hind-legs long; the feet large and strong, five-toed; the middle one slightly longer than the rest; inner toe shortest, reaching only to the end of the metatarsal bones of the others; all the nails short, pointed, and slightly curved; tail long, tapering, and clothed with silky hairs. Colour above sepia-brown; beneath white; a dark line crosses the cheeks beneath the eyes.

Dimensions.

	Inches.
Length of the head and body, ...	$1\frac{9}{10}$
" of head, from the nose to the occiput, ...	$\frac{9}{10}$
" of ears, ...	$\frac{3}{20}$
" of tail, ...	$2\frac{3}{10}$
" of fore-leg from the elbow, ...	$\frac{9}{20}$
" of fore-foot, ...	$\frac{3}{10}$
" of tibia, ...	$\frac{7}{10}$
" of hind-foot, ...	$\frac{8}{10}$
" of metatarsus, ...	$\frac{5}{10}$

General Remarks.

A single specimen of this singular animal was obtained in Oregon, but no notes were furnished by the person who obtained it. The formation of its hind-legs leaves but little room to doubt that its habits are similar to the jumping mice, *Meriones Labradorius* (RICHARDSON), which are inhabitants of the same region. Its singularly large head, which equals its body in bulk, its ample cheek-pouches, long hind-legs, and long tail, present a general form which is peculiar and altogether very remarkable. On dissection, the stomach was found to contain a pulpy matter, which appeared to be the remains of a bulbous root; the liver is very large, and consists of five foliaceous lobes; we were not able to detect any gall bladder.

The specimen is a female, and presents the rudiments of a fourth molar tooth in each side of the lower jaw, which would eventually have replaced the front ones, already much worn. (PEALE.)

Didelphis Breviceps.—Bennett

Synonyme.

DIDELPHIS BREVICEPS.—Bennett, Zool. Proc. for 1833, p. 40.

Description.

Allied to *D. Virginianus;* much smaller size and darker colour; ordinary woolly hairs of the body white at base, the apical half, brownish black. Beyond this woolly hair there is an abundance of immensely long bristly white hairs on the upper parts and sides of the body. Head, throat, and under parts of body brownish, the hairs being white, with the tips brown. Lips white; a broad white dash under the eye, joining the white lips; a longitudinal brownish stripe extending from the eye towards the tip of the muzzle; brownish black hairs also surround the eye. On the crown of the head there are long white hairs, interspersed like those of the body, but shorter. Ears black, naked, the apex whitish; limbs and feet brown-black; tail with minute bristly hairs, springing from between the scales; the basal half of the tail apparently blackish, and the apical half whitish.

Dimensions.

	Inches.	Lines.
From point of nose to insertion of tail,	12	6
Tail,	11	
Tarsus to end of longest claw,	2	
Ear to point of nose,	3	
Height of ear posteriorly,	1	1
Longest bristly hairs on the back,	3	

Geographical Distribution.

California. (BENNETT.)

Didelphis Californica.—Bennett.

Synonyme.

DIDELPHIS CALIFORNICA.—Bennett, Zool. Proc. for 1833, p. 40.

Description.

Body above brownish black, intermediate in size between *Didelphis Virginianus* and *D. Breviceps,* head much longer than that of *D. Breviceps,* ears and legs longer, the inner toe on the hind-foot much the longest.

Dimensions.

	Inches.	Lines.
From nose to root of tail,	14	
Tail,	13	9
From ear to point of nose,	3	11
Tarsus,	2	2
Hieght of ear posteriorly,	1	9

General Remarks.

The description given of the colours of *D. Breviceps* will, in most respects, apply to the present. The long white hairs interspersed throughout the fur, the black line running through the eye, and the black feet and legs, would lead to the supposition that the species were identical.

But there are, notwithstanding, many striking marks of difference. The inner toe of the present species is much larger and far separated from the second, which at first sight seems to be united by a web.

The animal is also more lightly coloured.

Brought by DOUGLAS from that portion of California nearest to Mexico. (BENNETT.)

Mus Carolinensis.

Carolina Mouse.

M. Dilute plumbeus, auribus longis et pilosis, cauda corpore longiore.

Characters.

Tail longer than the body; ears long and hairy. Color light plumbeous.

Synonymes.

MUS CAROLINENSIS.—Aud. and Bach, Jour. Acad. Nat. Sci., Phila., vol. viii., part ii., p. 306.
"   "   Le Conte, Proc. Acad. Nat. Sci., Phila., p. —, 1853.

Description.

In size this is smaller than the house mouse. The upper fore-teeth are slightly grooved. The head is short, the forehead arched, and the nose rather blunt. Eyes small, but prominent; whiskers longer than the head. The ears are rather long, and have a very conspicuous incurvation of their anterior margins, which are fringed with hairs; they are thickly clothed on both surfaces with very short hairs. The legs and feet are small and slender, hairy to the nails. The thumb is almost entirely composed of a short convex nail. The tail is long, clothed with short hairs, rounded in the living animal, but square when in a dried state. The fur, which is of moderate length, is thin, soft, and silky.

Colour.

The incisors are light yellow, tipped with black; eyes black; point of the nose, lips, chin, fore-feet, and nails, white. Whiskers dark brown. There is a narrow fawn-coloured ring around the eyes. Ears, legs, and tail light ashy brown. The fur on the back and sides is from the roots of an uniform light plumbeous colour; the under surface is scarcely a shade lighter.

Dimensions.

	Inches.	Lines.
Length of head and body,	2	4
" of tail,	2	9
Height of ear,		4
Length of tarsus,		$6\frac{1}{2}$

General Remarks.

This species exists very sparingly in the maritime districts of South Carolina, and is usually found in low grounds partially inundated. It readily takes to the water, and swims with great facility.

Sorex Richardsonii.—Bach.

Richardson's Shrew.

Synonymes.

SOREX PARVUS.—Rich (non Say), Fauna Boreali Americana, p. 8.
SOREX RICHARDSONII.—Bachman, Jour. Acad. Nat. Sci., Phila., vol.
vii., part ii., p. 383.

Description.

Ears short, about half the length of the fur, covered by short fine hairs; muzzle long and slender, the tip slightly lobed; the whole upper lip bordered with whiskers, reaching to the ears; the tail square, pointed at tip; body longer and thicker than that of *S. Forsteri;* feet slender, partaking, in this respect, of the character of most of the species of this genus; nails short and slightly hooked.

Colour.

The fur, from its roots to near the tip, has a dark bluish grey colour; from its closeness, however, this colour is not seen till the fur is removed; the whole upper surface is of a rusty brown colour; beneath cinereous; the feet and nails are light brown.

Dimensions.

		Inches.
Length of head and body,	....	$2\frac{3}{4}$
" of tail,	....	$1\frac{5}{8}$
" of head,	....	$\frac{7}{8}$
" from upper incisors to nostrils,	....	$\frac{1}{8}$
" from eye to point of nose,	....	$\frac{7}{16}$

Sorex Brevicaudus.—Say.

Short-tailed Shrew.

Characters.

Blackish plumbeous above, a little lighter beneath; smaller than S. Dekayi, tail a little longer.

Synonymes.

SOREX BREVICAUDUS.—Say, Long's Expedition, vol. i., p. 164.
"   "   Godman, vol. i., p. 79, plate 3, fig. 1.
"   "   Harlan, Fauna, p. 29.
"   "   Bachman, Jour. Acad. Nat. Sci., Phila., vol.
vii., part ii., p. 331.

Description.

The form of this species is more slender than that of DeKay's shrew, and it appears about one fifth less; the feet are a little longer and rather large for the size of the animal; the fur on the back long, nearly double the length of the other species; the fore-feet are naked; the hind ones sparsely covered with hair; the nose is distinctly lobed; the orifice to the internal ear is large, with two distinct half-divisions; the tail in the dried specimen appears to be square, sparsely clothed with hair which extends beyond the tip.

Colour.

The nose and tail are dark brown; feet and nails white; the whole upper surface of a blackish plumbeous colour; the under surface a little lighter.

Domensions.

		Inches.
Length from tip of the nose to root of tail,	....	$3\frac{1}{2}$
" of heel to end of tail,	....	$\frac{5}{8}$
" of tail,	....	1
" of head,	....	$\frac{3}{4}$
Breadth across the head,	....	$\frac{1}{2}$

General Remarks.

The teeth of this shrew are white, brightly tinged with chestnut brown on the points, except the third and fourth lateral incisors in the upper jaw, which have merely a brown speak at the tips, and the fifth, which is white; the posterior upper molar is small, though larger than that of *S. Dekayi;* the incisors are less curved than those of the latter species; there is also a striking difference in the head, that of the present species being considerably shorter, the skull more depressed and much narrower, appearing about one fourth less than that of DeKay's shrew.

From the number and appearance of its teeth, the specimen was evidently an old animal.

Pseudostoma Bulbivorum.—Rich.

Synonymes.

DIPLOSTOMA? BULBIVORUM.—Rich, Fauna Boreali Americana, p. 206.
DIPLOSTOMA (GEOMYS) BULBIVORUS.—Rich, Zoology of Beechey's
Voyage, p. 13.
GEOMYS BULBIVORUS.—Dr. Le Conte, Proc. Acad. Nat. Sci., Phila.,
1852, p. 162.

Description.

Body like that of a great mole; furnished with cheek-pouches, each pouch has a semi-cup-shaped cavity when distened; whiskers very short, eyes small. The *auditory openings* are moderately large, but there are no external ears. Tail short, round, and tapering, with an obtuse tip, and thinly clothed with hair. The legs are short, and are covered down to the wrist and ankle joints with fur similar to that of the body; there are five toes on each foot; the hind nails are short, conical, obtuse, and more or less excavated underneath. The nail of the fourth toe is more spoonshaped than the others.

Colour.

Incisors yellowish; on the dorsal aspect the fur has a colour intermediate between chestnut and yellowish brown, darker on the crown of the head than elsewhere; on the belly the brown is mixed with a considerable portion of grey. The lips, the lower jaw, the lining of the pouches, and a narrow space around the arms, are covered with white fur.

Close to the upper part of each side of the mouth there is a rhomboidal mark, which is clothed with hair of a liver brown colour.

The *hind-feet* are covered above with whitish hairs.

Dimensions.

		Inches.	Lines.
Length of head and body,	....	11	
" of head,	....	3	
Breadth of head behind the eyes, when the pouches are distended,	....	3	6
Length of tail,	....	2	6
" of upper incisors (the exposed portion),	....		6
" of lower incisors,	....		9

General Remarks.

We have altered in arrangement, and abridged, Sir JOHN RICHARDSON's description of this pouched rat, which, in some particulars, has so very great a resemblance to *P. bursarius,* as to have made us hesitate to place it in our work.

Dipodomys Agilis.—Gambel.

Characters.

Tail brownish, with an indistinct whitish vitta on each side; outer third to tip nearly uniform pale brown.

Synonymes.

DIPODOMYS AGILIS.—Gambel, Proc. Acad. Nat. Sci., Phila., vol. iv., p. 77.
   "   "   Dr. Le Conte,   "   " vol. vi., p. 224.

Description.

In the upper jaw the incisors are divided by a longitudinal furrow; head elongated, tapering from the ears to a sharp point; ears nearly round, sparsely hairy; eyes large; a large pouch on each side of the head opening externally on the cheeks. Both hind and fore-feet with four toes and a rudiment of a fifth. Hind-legs very long; tail strong, very slender, covered with hair, and ending in a penicillated tuft.

Two incisors and eight molars in both upper and lower jaws.

Colour.

Above, yellowish brown mixed with dusky; beneath, pure white, extending half way up the sides; eyes dark brown.

Dimensions.

	Inches.
Total length, including the tail,	$10\frac{1}{2}$
Length of tail,	$6\frac{1}{2}$

Habits.

This beautiful Jerboa-like animal is abundant in the vineyards and cultivated fields of the Pueblo de los Angeles, Upper California. Like the other pouched animals it forms extensive burrows, traversing the fields in different directions, and is only to be dislodged during the process of irrigation. It leaps with surprising agility, sometimes the distance of ten feet or more at a spring, and is difficult to capture. (GAMBEL.)

Dipodomys Heermanni.—Le Conte.

Synonyme.

DIPODOMYS HEERMANNI.—Le Conte, Proc. Acad. Nat. Sci., Phila., vol. vi., p. 224.

Description.

Tail shorter than the body; hairs on the outer third very long; ears moderately small; antitragus obsolete.

Colour.

Tail brown, becoming black towards the extremity, with a broad white vitta on each side; tip pure black.

General Remarks.

This species was procured in the Sierra Nevada, by Dr. HEERMANN. The specimen was not quite full grown. The above description, &c., we take from Dr. LE CONTE's remarks in the Proc. Acad. Nat. Sciences, Philadelphia, cited above.

Perognathus Fasciatus.—Wied.

P. Supra e flavescente cinereus, subtus albus, strigâ laterali pallide flavus.

Synonymes.

PEROGNATHUS FASCIATUS.—Wied, Nova Act., Leopold Car. Acad., 19, 369, tab. 34.
   "   "   Wagner, Schreber's Saügthiere, Suppl. 3, 612.
                                 Schintz, Syn. Mam., 2, 259.

Description.

The upper surface is brownish-grey; the hairs at the roots olive-grey, at the tip yellowish and blackish, whence the animal appears speckled with blackish and fulvous, or is somewhat striped.

The sides of the head, the region round the eyes, and upper margin of the ears, are of a more dull reddish-yellow. The under surface is pure white, which is separated from the colour of the back by a yellowish-red, or rust-red stripe extending from the nose along the whole side to the hind-legs, and down to the heel. The nose and lips appear flesh coloured through the whitish hair; the same is the case with the legs below the tibiæ. The tail is reddish-grey; more greyish above, and more whitish beneath.

Dimensions.

	Inches.	Lines.
Entire length,	4	$4\frac{1}{4}$
Length of tail (including hair),	2	1
" of fore-foot,		$3\frac{1}{2}$
" of hind-foot,		8

Geographical Distribution.

This species was procured in the territories west of the State of Missouri.

Sciurus Clarkii.—Smith.

Clark's Squirrel.

Synonyme.

SCIURUS CLARKII, Clark's Squirrel.—Griffiths, Cuvier, vol. iii., p. 189.

Description.

Back, upper parts of the head and neck, cheeks and tail, of a delicate silver grey colour; the shoulders, flanks, belly, and posterior extremities, both within and without, are white with a slight ochreous tint; on the sides of the nose and the fore-legs this tint deepens in intensity; the head is rather flattened and thick, the ears small and round; eyes black, and situated on the sides of the head very far distant from each other, leaving a wide expanse of forehead. The nostrils are semilunar in shape; the upper lip is cleft, and there is a black spot on the chin.

The tail, which is flat and spreading, is very beautiful, not so full near its interior as towards the middle, and again diminishing in breadth until it terminates in a point.

General Remarks.

We are greatly inclined to consider this squirrel as identical with *Sciurus Fossor*, of PEALE, which we have figured and described. Should other specimens of this species not be found and more postively determined, it would perhaps be better to retain the name of SCIURUS CLARKII, and give

S. Fossor as a synonyme.

Sciurus Annulatus.—Smith.

Lewis's Squirrel.

Synonyme.

SCIURUS ANNULATUS, Lewis's Squirrel.—Griffiths, Cuvier, vol. iii., p. 190.

Description.

Has the upper part of the head, neck, shoulders, fore arms, to the articulation of the arm, back, flank, the posterior moiety of the thighs and a band round the belly, of ochrey-grey colour; all the under parts, the inside of the limbs, and the paws are pure ochrey; the ears are small, round, and far back; the eyes are black, and surrounded with the same colour as the back; the nostrils open at the extremity of the muzzle, forming a denuded black snout; the upper lip is white and the whiskers very long. The tail is very beautiful, extremely thick and bushy, cylindrical, and annulated with seven black and six white bands, with the termination black.

"This appears to be the *S. Annulatus* described by DESMAREST, Encyclop. Method., article Mammalogie. His specific characters are: Fur of a bright greenish grey above, with lateral white bands, white underneath, tail longer than the body, round, annulated black and white." (LE CONTE.)

General Remarks.

This animal was, as well as *Sciurus Clarkii*, brought from the north-west by LEWIS and CLARK, on their return from their celebrated journey across our continent.

The specimens were deposited in PEALE's Museum, in Philadelphia, and were, it is supposed, burnt up when the remains of that collection were destroyed by fire.

Unless the peculiar *annulated* tail was the result of twisting that member when the animal was skinned, it is difficult to suppose this to have been a true squirrel. We do not know, however, any spermophile that will agree with the description of it.

We have above given descriptions of some quadrupeds which we have not ourselves had an opportunity of examining—the result of the observations of other zoologists— but are not at present able to state positively that *all* of them are founded on good species.

We add some names of animals that have been given by authors as belonging to our Fauna, but which we have not been willing to introduce as such into our work, and which may, we think, be safely omitted in future lists.

Sorex Cinereus.—Bach. Young of *S. Carolinensis*.
Ursus Arctos.—Rich. A doubtful species.
Sciurus Texianus.—Bach. Grey variety of *S. Capistratus,* without white ears.
   "   *Occidentalis.*—Bach. Variety of *S. Auduboni*.
Arvicola Nuttalli.—Harlan. Young *Mus leucopus*.
Mus Virginicus.—Gmel. Probably an albino of *Mus leucopus*.
Lepus Campestris.—Bach. This appears to be identical with *S. Townsendii,* and we should have given the latter name as the synonyme.
Lipuria Hudsonica.—This is supposed to have been a distorted or mutilated skin. There is no animal to correspond with the description of it.
Lepus Longicaudatus.—This is an African species from the Cape of Good Hope.
Felis Occidentalis.—Probably *Lynx rufus*.
   "   *Fasciata.*   "
Lutra Californica.—Grey, supposed to be *L. Canadensis*.
Felis Discolor.—*Felis Concolor*.
Condylura Macroura.—*C. Cristata*.
Mus Agrarius.—Godman. *Mus leucopus*.
Spermophilus Beecheyi.—Rich. *S. Douglassii*.
Sorex Talpoides.—Gapper. Probably *S. Carolinensis*.
Ixalus Probaton.—A Hybrid.—Not American.
Cervus Arctica.—Rich. Requires further examination.
Lepus Mexicanus.—*L. Nigricaudatus*.
Sciurus Aurogaster.—*S. Ferruginiventer*.
   "   *Californicus.*—*S. Nigrescens*.
Sorex Canadensis.—*Scalops Aquaticus*.
Saccomys Anthopilus.—South American.
Spermophilus Pealei.—Not American.

Addendum
Vulpes Fulvus.

The facts in regard to the history of the Red Fox on the Jersey coast that I have been able to collect, are few; such as they are I will give them to you.

Certain it is that they frequent the beaches in great numbers, and so far as I can learn, the Gray Fox is not found in the same places, nor is the raccoon, which we know to be so abundant on the sea islands and beaches of our southern coast. They pass to the beaches on the ice, in the winter season, when the "sounds" are frozen, and have frequently been seen in the day time, making their passage, though doubtless it is more frequently performed in the night. Their means of subsistence there are ample, consisting of wild fowl of various kinds, up which they spring while they are asleep upon the ponds and creeks, but more particularly upon the wounded fowl which escape from the numerous gunners, also crabs and fish, which are thrown up dead by the surf, and rabbits and wading birds, in the summer. A marvellous story is told of their sagacity in selecting the food they like best, which is vouched for by Mr. BEASLEY, and all the gunners along shore, but which I think requires confirmation, at least so far as to have the fish in question, seen by some naturalist in the state, described by the narrators, in order to ascertain its name, or describe it, if new, before its publication is ventured on. The story is, that a certain fish, called the cramp-fish, from its supposed power of paralizing the hand which touches it while living, is thrown ashore dead, by the surf in the winter season, that every one of these fishes contains a bird, such as the coot, (either *fusca* or *perspicillata*), or a gull, which appears to have destroyed the fish, by its proving rather hard to digest, without having been plucked. Mr. Fox finds the fish that has come to this deplorable end, and either in the vain hope of restoring animation to the unfortunate defunct, or for the gratification of a less noble impulse, he makes a longitudinal incision into the peritonæum of the subject, and extracts the bird, of which he makes a meal; but, mind you, Mr. Fox has profited by the awful example before him—he picks the bird before he eats it. Moral—never swallow what you cannot digest. But, to be serious, I do not mean to ridicule the fact, which I cannot but believe with the testimony which accompanies it, but if it be new, which I cannot answer for, it might in its plain, unvarnished form, without being announced in pedantic Latin, afford too tempting a morceau for the snarling critic. The fish are said to reach sometimes the length of four-feet, with a mouth twenty-two inches wide, they are scaled, and are said to resemble, somewhat, the sea cat-fish, with which I am not acquainted. The Fox on the beach when hunted by hounds, resorts to his usual trick of taking the water, to throw the dogs off the scent, by following the retreating surf, so that its return may efface his trail, then lying down among the sand hills to rest, while the dogs are at fault. In the woods on the main land both Red and Gray Foxes are abundant, the latter rather predominating. The Foxes are abundant on some of the beaches, and generally may be procured. Mr. SPENCER, of Mount Holly, has been on a party when five were killed, but I do not know where, nor whether it was this season or before."

We have not been able to procure the fish which is alluded to in the foregoing, but have no doubt of the correctness of the account. The Red Fox will eat fish as well as birds, and when hard pressed does not refuse even carrion. It is, therefore, probable that the discovery of the bird within the dead fish, may be the result of accident rather than of instinct, reason, or keenness of smell on the part of the Fox; for when he begins to devour a fish he must soon find the more savoury bird in its stomach, and being fonder of fowl than of fish, he would of course eat the bird and leave the latter. A Fox after having in this way discovered coots, gulls, or any other bird, would undoubtedly examine any dead fish that he came across, in hopes of similar good luck. Hence the foxes on the beaches have, we suppose, acquired the habit of extracting birds from the stomachs of such fish as have swallowed them, and are cast ashore dead by the storms on the coast; and they also at times get a plentiful meal from the dead birds that float ashore. We received a beautiful specimen of the Red Fox, in the flesh, from our friend Mr. HARRIS, not long after the foregoing letter, and our figure was drawn from it. We represented the animal just caught in a steel-trap.

INDEX OF COMMON NAMES

INDEX OF LATIN NAMES